Guide to Photocopied Historical

Materials in the United States

and Canada

This work was produced by Cornell University Press from copy that had been prepared for the American Historical Association by Dr. Richard W. Hale, Jr., and staff under the supervision of an advisory committee of which Professor Robert B. Eckles was Chairman.

Guide to Photocopied

Historical Materials

in the United States and Canada

EDITED BY

Richard W. Hale, Jr.

PUBLISHED FOR THE

American Historical Association

Cornell University Press

ITHACA, NEW YORK

CORNELL UNIVERSITY PRESS

First published 1961

Library of Congress Catalog Card Number: 61–17269

PRINTED IN THE UNITED STATES OF AMERICA

PREFACE

THE function of the Committee on Documentary Reproduction of the American Historical Association is to provide historians with research material and with bibliographical tools for this material. Five years ago the Committee discussed the need for a guide to manuscripts in photocopy and made plans for a first publication.

For the preparation of a basic volume, the Council on Library Resources, Inc., in October 1957 granted the necessary funds to the American Historical Association. Work began immediately. The editor of the volume, Dr. Richard W. Hale, Jr., with his staff compiled, collected, and edited material supplied by depositories. To make expert advice available to Dr. Hale, an advisory committee of historians, librarians, and archivists was appointed. The members of this committee were Lester K. Born and John W. Cronin of the Library of Congress, Edgar L. Erickson of the University of Illinois, W. Kaye Lamb of the Public Archives of Canada, Albert H. Leisinger of the National Archives, Loren C. MacKinney of the University of North Carolina, and the two historians who sign this preface.

The *Guide to Photocopied Historical Materials in the United States and Canada* is designed to supply basic bibliographical information on the photocopied manuscripts of interest to historians which are available in depositories in the United States and Canada. The *Guide*, upon which Dr. Hale zealously labored for two and a half years from his headquarters in Boston, does not purport to be all-inclusive. It contains all those bibliographical items he has been able to obtain with the co-operation of the depositories during the short period of the project. We hope that the *Guide*, a pioneer work, will be a useful tool for historians and other scholars in their search for primary source materials and that ways will shortly be found to continue the publication of bibliographical information on manuscripts in photocopy.

Robert B. Eckles, *Chairman*
The Committee on Documentary Reproduction
of the American Historical Association

Boyd C. Shafer, *Executive Secretary*
The American Historical Association

ACKNOWLEDGMENTS

ONE of the great pleasures of being the editor of the *Guide to Photocopied Historical Materials* has been the personal and institutional relationships that have come with the editorship. Looking at the list of reporting institutions brings to mind countless memories of unusual kindnesses done by those connected with those institutions, for those who co-operated with the *Guide* did so with great cordiality. To them I wish to express my heartfelt though inadequate thanks, along with my regret that there is not space in which to name them all.

Certain persons and groups that gave special assistance must be listed.

When the project was first proposed, the Archives Section of the Canadian Historical Association sponsored a pilot project that made it possible to work out the problems of setting up the *Guide* and thus facilitated the organization and the final submission of the proposal to the Council on Library Resources.

The Philadelphia Bibliographical Center, which has pioneered in the reporting of microfilm holdings through its *Union List of Microfilms,* agreed to exchange information and to make available not only its published holdings but also reports gathered since its 1957 *Supplement.* This saved duplication of effort and in many cases made it possible to go beyond reports previously made to the *Union List.*

First Boston University and then the Old South Association provided rent-free working quarters.

The Society of American Archivists, the Association for State and Local History, and the National Microfilm Association gave helpful counsel and aided the *Guide's* efforts.

The late Dr. Arthur Adams, of the New England Historic Genealogical Society, helped work out methods of abbreviating reports of local government records while preserving as much completeness as possible.

Mr. T. Harold Jacobsen and Miss Thelma Hill, of the Genealogical Society of the Church of Jesus Christ of Latter-Day Saints, aided in planning the reporting of the Society's storehouse of photoreproduced documents.

Thanks to the intercession of Professor Edgar L. Erickson, the British Museum provided valuable auxiliary information, as did the National Library of Australia.

Professors David Dowd of the University of Florida and Abraham P. Nasatir of San Diego State College helped greatly in the collection of material.

The staff which worked on the *Guide* — the two secretaries, first Miss Helen Hirschberg and then her successor, Mrs. Thomas Bristoll, and the others who came in to help finish the project, Miss Caroline Hollingsworth, Miss Joan Kerry, Mrs. C. Duncan, Mrs. B. Wyatt, Mr. David Wilmarth, and Mr. Donald Hall — were untiring in their efforts and made a very happy "office family."

Finally, I should like to express my very warm thanks to the Council on Library Resources and to the Advisory Committee for the many forms of help which they gave. I am especially indebted to Professor Robert B. Eckles, the Chairman of the Committee on Documentary Reproduction, and to Dr. Boyd C. Shafer, the Executive Secretary of the American Historical Association, for their untiring support and assistance.

RICHARD W. HALE, JR., *Editor*

CONTENTS

Preface, v

Acknowledgments, vii

Introduction, xvii

Bibliography, xxi

Location Symbols and Abbreviations, xxvii

UNION LISTING OF BODIES OF MSS IN PHOTOCOPY

INTRODUCTION

PHOTOCOPIED historical materials fall into two types, reproductions of publications and reproductions of manuscripts, which require different forms of treatment in this volume. Since reproductions of publications are well covered by bibliographies and other finding aids, the *Guide to Photocopied Historical Materials* simply lists those finding aids and refers the scholar to them. Such a list is the bibliography found on pages xxi-xxv. But since reproductions of manuscripts are not generally covered by finding aids, a union listing of holdings of bodies of historical manuscripts in photocopy has been made. That listing forms the major portion of this volume.

A standard method of describing such bodies of photoreproduced manuscripts has been adopted. An explanation of that method and of the reasons for its adoption follows. When photocopied materials are described for the benefit of scholars, the method of description must bring out those values which photocopy has for scholarship. Of these values two are primary. The first is exactness of textual reproduction, for a photocopy is free from human errors in transcription and may be trusted to be identical in text with the original from which it is made. From this fact follows the consequence, not always realized, that as far as text goes a photocopy must be described in exactly the same terms as the original from which it was made. This is why the *Guide* describes the textual contents of photocopied materials according to a standard method, which differs only in minor ways from that used by the National Catalog of Manuscript Collections. Because photocopies of transcripts do not give the same guarantee of faithfulness to the original, such photocopies are listed in the *Guide* only when they appear to have special value for the historian.

The second primary value of photocopy for the scholar lies in the fact that from some forms of photocopy additional photocopies can be made without going back to the original text. Such forms of photocopy combine in themselves the qualities of the printing press and the book. The great significance of the possibilities inherent in this power of regeneration is not as fully realized as it should be. If the original text, for example, has been copied on negative microfilm, from that negative microfilm may be made not only positive film but also enlargements and, if the quality of the film is good enough, micro-opaques. Each of these forms of "second generation" photocopy has its special advantages. Use of a positive film for reading in a machine allows preservation of the negative film as a "master negative," free from the ever-present danger that damage through careless handling in the reader or elsewhere may destroy its precious reproductive potential. Recent developments in the use of diazo and plastic films offer alternative rapid methods of making positives and thus encourage the careful preservation of master negatives. Furthermore, new techniques are bringing in possibilities of adaptation to special uses. By cutting positive film into strips or even into single frames and putting it into transparent jackets, which can themselves be inserted in many readers, it is possible to analyze a body of material and file it away for easy reference and retrieval. This sort of handling is particularly effective when sheet film or microfiches are used, as described in *National Micronews* (July, 1960). Similarly, single frames or short strips of positive — or even, if needed, negative — film may be inserted into aperture cards and so filed as to be quickly retrievable by mechanical or manual sorting devices. This method is used increasingly for the filing of maps and plans, for from the film so inserted in an aperture card can be made an enlargement to any size desired by the engineer or cartographer, and this enlargement will be trustworthy as to scale.

When enlargements are made, two possibilities occur. A scholar may have individual sheets to lay on his desk, so that he has before him, enlarged to the most suitable size, a text identical with the original, which he might have had to go a long distance to consult or which he might have had to consult under restrictions. If it is a question of a book that is out of print or otherwise difficult of access, it is now possible for the scholar to have that book textually reproduced, folded, and bound as a book.

Often negative microfilm can be used to make micro-opaques. Micro-opaques are opaque cards holding micro-images that can be brought out on the screen of a reader. There are several types of micro-opaques: Microprint, Microcard, and Microlex (all trade-mark names) were the earliest in order of coming into use. Micro-opaques have three advantages. They are easy to file and retrieve, since they can be stored in trays and files. They save space. The economics of their production is such that they form a good method for the cheap publication of extensive material of which, roughly, ten to two hundred copies may be desired. The classic example of such photopublication is the British *House of Commons Sessional Papers*, in Microprint, edited by Professor Edgar L. Erickson. This publication has used the power of microphotographic reproduction to bring together materials that in their original form are widely scattered and the economy of micropublication to make them available at marked savings. Thus the Microprint edition is both the most complete and the most available set of British parliamentary papers.

These examples of the regenerative power of some forms of photocopy show why the *Guide to Photocopied Historical Materials* takes care to report not only the fact of photocopying but the form and to draw a distinction between photocopies that have this regenerative power and those that do not.

There is no need to go into further detail as to the types of photocopy, especially as the progress of invention is rapidly putting existing information out of date. Those who wish to know more may refer to the following works:

For specifications of equipment: Ballou, Hubbard W., editor, *Guide to Microreproduction Equipment* (Annapolis, National Microfilm Association, 1959), with supplementary information regularly appearing in *National Micronews*.

For suggestions on methods of reproduction: Lewis, Chester M., and Offenhauser, William H., Jr., *Microrecording, Industrial and Library Applications* (New York, Interscience Publishers, 1956), and Herrman, Irvin A., *Manual of Office Reproduction* (New York, Office Publications Co., 1958).

For explanation of technical terms: Ten Eyck, Hendrix, *Glossary of Terms Used in Microreproduction* (Annapolis, National Microfilm Association, 1953). (In the present *Guide* "photocopy" is used to cover all documentary reproduction — a wider meaning than is given in the *Glossary* — but this had the approval of Mr. Ten Eyck.)

Standards by which to judge equipment, film, and the like are promulgated by the American Standards Association. The Association of Research Libraries, acting on the suggestion of the Committee on Documentary Reproduction of the American Historical Association, will shortly present a study of the best methods of bibliographical control of microforms, and the American Library Association Committee on Library Standards of Microfilm is reformulating its standards, bringing them up to date and including standards for bibliographical control. The Microfilm Advisory Committee of the Society of American Archivists is also at work on the problem of the proper management of microfilm.

Since these forthcoming instructions on the proper cataloguing of microforms are not yet in print, comments on the principles of such cataloguing are in order here, for many of the readers of the *Guide* will be concerned not only with the use of microfilm and other forms of photocopy but also with the procuring of new materials in photoform. The first step toward an adequate bibliographical control of photoforms is to make a correct and full description of the original material an integral part of the photoform, by including it in the material that is to be photoreproduced. Such a description is easily obtainable at the time of photoreproduction, for either it is at hand or it can be made by inspection of the material. The act of photoreproduction will then make this description a permanent part of the resultant photocopy. The scholar who orders a photocopy should feel it his duty to see that a proper description of the contents is made an integral part of the photocopy and should not leave this task to the technician. It is not fair to the technician to ask him to be a librarian or an archivist. Indeed, institutions which order photocopies should make the provision of a proper description a part of the order, and foundations which make grants for microfilming should make the provision of such a description a condition of the grant. This requirement is not an onerous one if it is satisfied at the time of photocopying. In many cases all that needs to be done is to put a catalogue card, or an accurate copy of it, into position for microfilming or otherwise photocopying. If photocopies contain accurate descriptions of their contents as integral parts, there will never be any fear of having to recatalogue at great expense or of finding that a second cataloguing has created a description varying from that of the original material. Furthermore, when the photocopy is regenerative, any second generation photocopies made from it will automatically contain correct descriptions.

The foregoing should explain the reasons that underlay the choice of a standardized method of describing bodies of manuscript in photocopy. The two examples below will show this method in use.

MATTHEWS, STANLEY, 1824–1889
  Civil War letters, 1861–1865, 95 items   OCHP
  N: OFH 1 reel
  P: OCHP   4542

BORDEAUX. BIBLIOTHÈQUE MUNICIPALE
  Recueil de pièces, lettres, mémoires re:
  Acadiens, 1766–1774, 611 p. Ibid.
  N: CaNBSjU   2220

The reader will note that the first part of the entry gives the name of the author, compiler, collector, or holder of the original material, frequently with dates and often with designations; the second part of the entry gives the title of the material, adds characterization or description when necessary, and then goes on to give dates, amount of original material, and location of the original material. The conclusion of the entry describes the type of photocopy made, locates it, and shows what "generations" are available. In general, descriptions of material are those of the *Cataloguing Rules for Author and Title Entries of the American Library Association* and the *Rules for Descriptive Cataloguing in the Library of Congress: Manuscripts.* Location symbols are those of the Library of Congress, the National Library of Canada, and the British Library Association. Information as to the form of photocopy follows the procedure of

Newspapers on Microfilm, with additions to meet special needs. The descriptions given to the material reported are intended to be self-explanatory, but a few comments on them may be helpful, as well as a few words on the extent of coverage in the reporting done to the *Guide* and on the organization of the material in the *Guide* by subject matter.

It should be noted that when any of the information mentioned above is not to be found in an entry it was not accessible.

The parts of the entries that refer to the original material are intended to conform as closely as possible, except for punctuation, to the descriptions which might be expected to be found on cards of the National Union Catalog of Manuscript Collections. In this Mr. Robert B. Slocum gave most helpful editorial checking. Entries were generally kept as short as possible. To this there has been one exception. When much material had the same author or holder, the description of it was combined into a single entry. To have done otherwise would have brought the *Guide* to inordinate length, as will be seen by inspection of some of the entries for Swedish records and those of the Church of Jesus Christ of Latter-Day Saints. Author entries follow standard library practice, except in some cases, where library practice so differs from that of standard bibliographies, standard footnoting, or customary archival nomenclature as to make the last three better precedents. Title entries follow the exact title in the few cases where a manuscript or body of manuscripts either has a title or has been given one in standard bibliographies. When, as in most cases, a title has had to be ascribed to a manuscript or body of manuscripts, that title has been couched in the language of *Rules for Descriptive Cataloguing in the Library of Congress: Manuscripts.* Here, however, words and phrases from the records of the holding institution have been directly quoted when that seemed necessary to identify material. This will explain why certain variations in style were unavoidable.

The parts of the entries referring to the photocopy follow the sequence of the photographic process. Original precedes first generation photocopy; first generation photocopy precedes second generation. Types of photocopy which do not have regenerative qualities are indicated by abbreviations beginning with the letter D; those that do have such qualities are indicated by abbreviations containing the letters N or P. Positive microfilms are listed only when they are complete copies of the negatives, and the fact that an institution is listed as holding a negative does not preclude its also holding a positive.

When material is held under specific restrictions, that fact is noted; details of such restrictions should be obtained from holding institutions.

Location symbols apply to holders both of photocopies and of originals. Symbols for institutions outside the United States are preceded by an international prefix, e.g., Ca for Canada, UK for Great Britain. Two British Library Association symbols have been lengthened, UKL for the British Museum to UKLBM and UKLRO for the Public Record Office to UKLPRO, since BM and PRO are the abbreviations customary among North American scholars for these two institutions. A few symbols of the Library of Congress list may now have been superseded since the amended list of 1959 did not reach the *Guide* until too late to be used.

Because one purpose of giving locations of photocopies was to facilitate the borrowing and copying of them, whenever loans and reproduction were permitted, a questionnaire was sent out to reporting institutions to determine what their policies were. This brought out the fact that most North American institutions follow a standard policy in regard to microfilms and other photocopies. They give access to all qualified persons, except in the case of specially restricted materials. They permit copies to be made, at the cost of those making the request for copies. They lend *positive* films through interlibrary loans. (Negatives are usually not lent, since damage to them would require refilming the original material.) It may be assumed that an institution follows this policy unless a paragraph mark, which signifies that loans are not permitted, appears beside its address in the list of Holders of Photocopies.

The coverage which the reader may expect from this union listing of holdings of bodies of manuscripts in photocopy may be summed up in this way: The *Guide* lists those bodies of historical and archival manuscripts which have been reported to it as being under institutional control at its assigned cut-off date of January 1, 1959. This brief statement should be expanded by defining each of the terms used in it. The *Guide* lists bodies of manuscripts, not individual pieces, except when such pieces form separate units. The term "archival" is used to indicate that government records are listed as well as personal papers. Current administrative records on microfilm are not, however, listed, as such listing would be an endless and fruitless task. As is pointed out above, photocopies of transcripts are not reported unless the transcripts in question seem to have real value. Only materials under institutional control are reported; private holdings are not given.

The institutions which were asked to report to the *Guide* were (1) those that had been in contact with the Committee on Documentary Reproduction in the past; (2) those listed in the *American Library Directory* as having "microfacilities"; (3) those listed by the Society of American Archivists as archives with microfilm holdings; (4) those suggested as possible holders of film; and (5) those reported to be either holders of negatives from which positives had been made or purchasers of film from the National Archives. Announcements in learned journals and at scholarly conventions brought in unsolicited reports. The editor also visited many institutions at the start of the project. On the advice of the Advisory Committee, no further reports were solicited after December 31, 1958, though some arrived in delayed response to previous inquiries or as the result of the search for master negatives from which positives had been made. A list of reporting institutions, accompanied by their addresses and location symbols, is covered in the section Location Symbols (see pp. xxvii-xxxiv).

Accuracy of information was sought by using photographic duplication of the records of reporting institutions whenever possible. The method varied from institution to institution. Catalogue cards might be duplicated by office copy machines; trays of catalogue cards might be put through a rotary microfilm camera as if they were bank checks or laid out on a flat-bed camera as if they were pages of a book. When the editor visited an institution, he sometimes microfilmed records with a portable camera. Whatever the method, the purpose was the same — to secure an exact copy of existing records, thus saving staff time and avoiding transcription error.

The information here presented about holdings of manuscripts in photocopy is organized in the same all-over sequence as that in the recently published *American Historical Association's Guide to Historical Literature,* that is, by accepted fields of history. For ease in organization subfields have been used wherever the nature of the material showed them, in fact, to exist. An index will be found on pages 221–241. It refers to the register number following each item. For obvious reasons self-indexing local government records are not indexed, but will be found in alphabetical sequence in the appropriate places.

For a list of abbreviations, see p. xxxiv.

BIBLIOGRAPHY

There are five types of finding aids to photocopied materials which can be of use to historians. These are:

1. Union lists of various kinds.
2. Descriptions of specific collections.
3. Sales lists of material available in microfilm and micro-opaque reproduction.
4. Lists of manuscript holdings, which contain descriptions of photocopies along with originals.
5. House organs of micro-publishers.

Finding aids in these five categories are listed below, with comments when appropriate.

The historian should be aware that in the future there will be a sixth type of finding aid, namely, lists of government and business records filmed for administrative reasons and later made available to scholars. At present this type of film is so vast in amount, so diverse in character, so recent in scope, and so unprovided with finding aids as to be out of the purview of the *Guide*. But the time will come when historians will want to use it, and they should be made aware of its existence.

UNION LISTS

Canadian Library Association, Ottawa
Newspaper microfilming project catalogue, 1951 —
(Title varies)
This both lists and locates holdings of the microfilms of this project. The current edition is in loose-leaf form and gives far fuller information as to each newspaper filmed than do earlier editions.

Eastman Kodak Company, Rochester, N.Y.
What's available on microprint cards. Rochester, N.Y., 1957

Horn, Andrew H.
Southern California union list of microtext editions.

Los Angeles, 1959

Philadelphia Bibliographical Center and Union Library Catalogue
Union list of microfilms. [Eleanor Este Campion, editor.] Ann Arbor, J. W. Edwards, 1951
With Supplements, 1949–1952 and 1952–1959, and a forthcoming Supplement, cumulative from 1949 to 1959.
This is the pioneer publication in this field. It now no longer includes newspapers, documents, or serials.

U.S. Library of Congress. Union Catalog Division
Newspapers on microfilm, Washington, 1951–
This locates master negatives and positive holdings of microfilmed newspapers, both in the United States and Canada. New editions come out regularly, the latest being 1959.

SELECTED LISTS, GUIDES, INDEXES OF SPECIAL COLLECTIONS OF PHOTOCOPIED MATERIALS

The American Historical Association. Committee for the Study of War Documents
A catalogue of films and microfilms of the German Foreign Ministry Archives, 1867–1920.
Prepared under the direction of Professor Howard Ehrmann. [Oxford, Oxford Univ. Press] 1959 [1958]

American Studies Association. Committee on Microform Bibliography
Bibliography of American culture, 1493–1875.
Compiled and edited by David R. Weimer. Ann Arbor, Mich., 1957

Anthropos–Institut, Posieux (Fribourg), Switzerland
Micro-bibliotheca Anthropos. (*Anthropos*, internationale Zeitschrift für Völker- und Sprachenkunde, vol. 48, 1953, p. 260–262)

Brown University. Library
List of Latin American imprints before 1800, selected from bibliographies of José Toribio Medina, micro-

filmed by Brown University. Providence, 1952

California. University. Bancroft Library
Preliminary guide to the microfilm collection in the Bancroft Library, by Mary Ann Fisher. Berkeley, University of California, 1955

California. University. Library
An index of German Foreign Ministry Archives, 1867–1920, microfilmed at Whaddon Hall for the General Library, University of California, Berkeley. Berkeley, 1957

Canada. Department of Labour. Library
Canadian labour papers available on microfilm. Ottawa, 1958

Canada. National Library
A microfilm copy of books and pamphlets described in Marie Tremaine's Bibliography of Canadian Imprints, 1751–1800. (*Report of the National Library*, 1957, p. 10)

Catholic University of America, Washington. Library
Microfilm reproductions of Catholic periodicals. [Washington, 1955]

Catholic University of America, Washington. Library
Serials on microfilm. [Washington, 1955]

Lists serials other than newspapers, and newspapers and Catholic University of America doctoral dissertations published in series.

Fonds National de la Recherche Scientifique, Brussels
Inventaire des microfilms des cartulaires de Flandres, d'Audenarde, de Liège et de Malines, de Gand, de la Dame de Cassel, de Hainaut, de Valenciennes, de Cambrai, de Namur, des empereurs, d'Artois, des registres aux chartres, des fiefs, terriers et mortesmains de Hainaut et d'un compte d'une aide de Luxembourg, Moyen Age et temps modernes, conservés à Lille, aux Archives départementales du Nord, série B, no. B 1561 à B 17349. [Bruxelles, 1952?]

Fonds National de la Recherche Scientifique, Brussels
Vienne III. Inventaire des microfilms des liasses et des registres suivants du fonds DD, section B: Verzeichnisse, Faszikel blau, Abschriften, varia, index et inventaires ... et du fonds Grosse Korrespondenz ... conservés à Vienne à l' "Oesterreichisches Staatsarchiv." [Bruxelles, 1952?]

France. Archives Nationales
Répertoire des microfilms de complément conservés aux archives nationales et communicables au public. Paris, Imprimerie Nationale, 1951.

France. Institut de Recherche et d'Histoire des Textes
Liste des manuscrits dont la photographie intégrale se trouve à l'Institut. (In its *Bulletin d'Information*. Paris, Centre Nationale de la Recherche Scientifique, no. 1, 1952, p. 39–48; no. 2, 1953, p. 88–94)

Free Europe Committee
Index to unpublished studies prepared for Free Europe Committee, Inc. Studies 1–378. New York, 1958

Hebrew Union College – Jewish Institute of Religion. American Jewish Periodical Center
Jewish newspapers and periodicals on microfilm. Cincinnati, 1957

Hungarian Academy of Sciences. Library
Catalogue of the rare Hebrew codices and manuscripts and ancient prints in the Kaufman Collection reproduced on microcards. Budapest, 1959

Kassel. Deutches Musikgeschichliches Archiv
Katalog der Filmsammlung, 1955– Kassel, Bärenreiter

Michigan. University. Library
A catalogue of German Foreign Ministry Archives, 1867–1920, microfilmed at Whaddon Hall for the University of Michigan under the direction of Howard M. Ehrmann. Ann Arbor, 1957

Modern Language Association of America
Reproductions of manuscripts and rare printed books (List complete to January 1, 1950). (PMLA, vol. 65, no. 3, April 1950, p. 289–338)

Royal Society of Medicine, London
Catalogue of British and American medical journals held on microfilm by the Photographic Unit of the Royal Society of Medicine. London, 1950

St. Louis University. Library
A checklist of the Vatican manuscript codices ... at the Knights of Columbus Vatican Film Library. (In *Manuscripta*, vol. I ff.)

St. Louis University. Library
Catalogues in the Knights of Columbus Vatican Film Library [by Charles J. Ermatinger]. (In *Manuscripta*, vol. I, 1957, p. 5–16, 89–101)

Tennessee. Archives
List of microfilms, 1958.
Supplement, 1959. [Nashville]

U.S. Historical American Buildings Survey
Catalog of the measured drawings and photographs of the Survey in the Library of Congress, March 1, 1941. Washington, 1941

U.S. Library of Congress
Checklist of archives in the Japanese Ministry of Foreign Affairs, Tokyo, Japan, 1868–1945; microfilmed for the Library of Congress, 1949–1951. Compiled by Cecil H. Uyehara under the direction of Edwin G. Beal. Washington, 1954

U.S. Library of Congress
Checklist of manuscripts in the libraries of the Greek and Armenian Patriarchates in Jerusalem, microfilmed for the Library of Congress, 1949–1950, prepared under the direction of Kenneth W. Clark, director and general editor for the Jerusalem Expedition. Washington, 1953

U.S. Library of Congress
Checklist of manuscripts in St. Catherine's monastery, Mount Sinai, microfilmed for the Library of Congress, 1950, prepared under the direction of Kenneth W.

Clark, general editor of the Mount Sinai Expedition, 1949–1950. Washington, 1952

U.S. Library of Congress
A descriptive checklist of selected manuscripts in the monasteries of Mount Athos microfilmed for the Library of Congress and the International Greek New Testament Project, 1952–1953, together with listings of photoreproductions of other manuscripts in monasteries of Mount Athos. . . . Compiled under the general direction of Ernest W. Saunders. Washington, 1957

U.S. Library of Congress
A guide to the microfilm collection of early state records, prepared by the Library of Congress in association with the University of North Carolina. Collected and compiled under the direction of William Sumner Jenkins; edited by Lillian A. Hamrick. Washington, 1950. Supplement, 1951

Professor Jenkins is steadily collecting more material; inquiries should be addressed to him at the Bureau of Public Records and Research, the University of North Carolina.

U.S. Library of Congress. Processing Department
British manuscripts project: a checklist of the microfilms prepared in England and Wales for the American Council of Learned Societies, 1941–1945. Compiled by Lester K. Born. Washington, 1953

U.S. National Archives
Guides to German records microfilmed at Alexandria, Virginia, by the American Historical Association. Washington, 1958–

Of these over thirty have been issued. To 1959 they included: 1, Reich Ministry of Economics; 2, Reich Commissioner for the Strengthening of Germandom; 3, National Socialist German Labor Party; 4, Organization Todt; 5 and 8, Miscellaneous German records; 6, Nazi cultural and research institutions and records re Axis relations and interests in the Far East; 7, Headquarters, German Armed Forces; 9, Private papers; 10, Reich Ministry for Armaments and War Production; 11, Fragmentary records of miscellaneous Reich Ministries and Offices; 12, German Army High Command; 13, Reich Air Ministry; 14, German Field Commands, Armies, part I; 15, Former German and Japanese Embassies and Consulates, 1890–1945.

Virginia Colonial Records Project, Virginia State Library, Richmond, Va.
Progress reports, 1955–

These carefully prepared descriptions of material it is proposed to microfilm are also intended to serve as a description of the films that are now being made.

Warsaw. Biblioteka Narodowa. Stacja Mikrofilmowa
Katalog mikrofilmow. r. 1– (zesz. 1–) 1951– Warszawa

White, H. L., compiler
Source material for Australian studies, in *Historical Studies*, vol. 7, no. 28, May, 1957, p. 1–14

Contains "original material of Australian interest up to 1860 in the Public Record Office in London, microfilmed by the Commonwealth National Library and the Public Library of New South Wales," p. 9–14.

SOME SALES LISTS

The American Antiquarian Society, Worcester, Mass.
Early American newspapers, 1704–1820. Worcester, 1960

These, edited by Ebenezer Gay, are on micro-opaque cards.

American Documentation Institute
Catalog of auxiliary publications in microfilms and photoprints. Washington, 1946

Canner (J. S.) and Company, Boston
Microcard reprints . . . catalog of publications available. Issued irregularly

Centrala Filmarkivet A.–B., Solna, Sweden
Sammandrag av tidningar, vilka ha arkivfotograferats (eller skola arkivfotograferas). [Solna, 1952]

Diaz, Albert James, editor
Guide to Microforms in print. Microcard Editions, Inc. Washington, D.C., 1961

This lists *publications* in microfilm, Microcard, Microlex, and Microprint and gives prices.

Godfrey Memorial Library, Middletown, Conn.
Corporation annual reports of all corporations listed on the New York Stock Exchange (1951–1956) and all corporations listed on the American Stock Exchange (1953–1956). Middletown, 195–

Historical Commission. Southern Baptist Convention
Microfilm catalogue. Basic Baptist materials, Nashville, Tenn., 1959

International Documentation Center, Stockholm-Vällingby, Sweden
Micro Library, vol. 1, no. 1–, April, 1958– Stockholm-Vällingby, Sweden

This publication performs for European micropublication the same useful service as the *Union List of Microfilms* has done, in the past, for microfilms in the United States.

Kentucky University. Press
Kentucky microcards, sponsored by the South Atlantic Modern Language Association. Modern Language Series. Lexington, Ky., University of Kentucky Press, 1958

Lost Cause Press, Louisville, Ky.
[List] published irregularly

Lists have various titles, such as Civil War History on Microcards; History of Science; 19th Century American Literature on Microcards; Kentucky Culture Series; British Culture; Somer's Tracts; Travels in the Confederate States; Travels in the Old South.

Lost Cause Press, Louisville, Ky.
Microcard reproductions of the books listed in Ellis

Morton Coulter's Travels in the Confederate States, a bibliography. Louisville, 195–

Lost Cause Press, Louisville, Ky.
Microcard reproductions of the books listed in Thomas Dionysius Clark's Travels in the Old South, a bibliography. Louisville, 195–

Louisville, Ky. Free Public Library
Selected titles of Thomas Jefferson's library on microcards. Louisville, 195–

Maxwell (I. R.) & Company, Ltd., London
A catalog of microfilms, microcards. London, 1956
A sales list based on the card file of serials in microcopy maintained in the Microfilming Clearing House in the Library of Congress.

Micro-Methods Ltd., East Ardsley, Wakefield, Yorkshire, England
Catalogue of published material available on microfilm, microfiche and microcard. [East Ardsley, 1959–]
Among the material issued are manuscripts, such as some from the Earl of Leicester's collection at Holkham Hall. Catalogues appear irregularly and include entries for a number of items microcopied originally by other firms.

Micro Photo Inc., Cleveland, Ohio
Newspapers on microfilm, 1953–. Cleveland, Ohio

Microcan, Inc., Boston
Catalogue of periodical sets in microcard reprint, 1957–1958. [Boston, 1958]

Microcard Foundation, Madison, Wis.
Catalog of Microcard publications. No. 1–, July, 1959–. Madison, Wis.

Microcard Foundation, Madison, Wis.
Microcard bulletin. No. 1–, June, 1948–. Madison, Wis.
Now supplanted by the Catalog of Microcard publications.

Microcard Foundation, Madison, Wis.
Unclassified Atomic Energy Commission reports, 1955–. Madison, Wis.

Microfilm Service & Sales Co., Dallas, Texas
Newspaper film-catalog. Dallas [1956?]

Microlex, Rochester, N.Y.
Law publications available in Microlex editions, Jan. 1, 1956–. [Rochester, N.Y.]

Microtext Publishing Corp. (formerly Technical Microcard Publishing Corp.). New York City
Microcards; publications, service, equipment. [New York, 195?]

Microtext Publishing Corp., New York City
Microtext. New York [195?]

Microthèque
Édition sur microfiche format 75x12 mm. de tous documents, pour archives-documentation (Livres-revues éditions rares ou épuisées). Paris, Les Appareils Controleurs [1958]

Minerva Mikrofilm A/S, Copenhagen
Minerva Mikrofilm A/S fortaeller lidt om mikrofilm, deres anvendelse, behandling og opbevaring. [Kobenhavn, 1958]
Lists Danish newspapers microfilmed to Oct. 1, 1957.

Oregon University. School of Public Health and Physical Education
Health and physical education Microcard bulletin. January 1, 1954–. Eugene, Ore., School of Public Health and Physical Education, University of Oregon

Readex Microprint Corporation, New York
The British House of Commons Sessional Papers, 1801–1900, edited by Edgar L. Erickson. New York, 1953

Readex Microprint Corporation, New York
The collected scientific and technical papers on Nuclear Science. New York [1956]

Readex Microprint Corporation, New York
Early American imprints, 1639–1800, based on Evans' American bibliography. Supplemented by titles not covered in Evans. New York, 195–

Readex Microprint Corporation, New York
Readex Microprint publications. New York [1956]

Readex Microprint Corporation, New York
The United Nations documents and official records. New York [1956]

Rekolid, Helsingfors
Catalogue containing microfilmed Finnish newspapers. Helsingfors, 1958

Rochester. University Press
Microcard publications in music, medicine, library science, Canadian studies, historical manuscripts. Autumn 1954–. Rochester, N.Y.

St. Louis University. Library
Microfilms of rare and out-of-print books, v.d.
Published at intervals, available from *Manuscripta*.

Smith (Peter), publisher, Gloucester, Mass.
List of scarce and desirable books on Microcards, 1957–. Gloucester, Mass.

South Carolina. Archives Department
List of publications of the South Carolina Archives Department, Columbia, 1957

State Historical Society of Wisconsin
Labor papers on microfilm; a combined list. Revised July 1, 1956. Madison, Wis., 1956. Supplement covering additional films prepared, July 1, 1956–June 30, 1957

U.S. National Archives
Federal population censuses, 1840–1880; a price list of microfilm copies of the original schedules. Washington, 1955
Earlier censuses than these have been filmed and are available from the National Archives. These are listed in the *Guide*, together with the M and T numbers helpful in ordering them, and in the list below.

U.S. National Archives
  List of National Archives microfilm publications [Compiled by the Exhibits and Publications Branch] Washington, 1961
  Supersedes previous lists of 1947, 1950, and 1953. The *Guide* lists some National Archives material not in this list but is not as up to date in listing publications proper.

Universal Microfilming Corporation, Salt Lake City, Utah
  A list of newspapers and periodicals available on microfilm. Salt Lake City, 1958

University Microfilms, Ann Arbor, Mich.
  American periodical series 1800–1850. 1st yr.— 1947–. Ann Arbor, Mich.

University Microfilms, Ann Arbor, Mich.
  Catalogue. No. 1–9. Ann Arbor, Mich.
  Last issue, no. 9, 1958.

University Microfilms, Ann Arbor, Mich.
  English books, 1475–1640. The first five years. Ann Arbor, 1956

University Microfilms, Ann Arbor, Mich.
  English books, 1475–1640. Consolidated cross index by S.T.C. numbers. Years 1–19. Ann Arbor, Mich., 1956

University Microfilms, Ann Arbor, Mich.
  English books on microfilm based on Donald Wing's A short-title catalog of books printed in England, Ireland, Scotland, Wales and British America, 1641–1700. Ann Arbor, Mich., 194–

University Microfilms, Ann Arbor, Mich.
  English books on microfilm based on Pollard and Redgrave's A short title catalogue of books printed in English or in England, Ireland, Scotland and Wales, 1475–1640. Ann Arbor, Mich., [194–]

University Microfilms, Ann Arbor, Mich.
  Microfilm abstracts, a collection of abstracts of doctoral dissertations which are available in complete form on microfilm. Vol. 1, no. 1–, 1938–. Ann Arbor, Mich.

University Microfilms, Ann Arbor, Mich.
  O–P Books, cumulative list as of January, 1960. Ann Arbor, Mich., [1960]
  This lists the xerographic enlargements from microfilm which may be procured from University Microfilms.

University Microfilms, Ann Arbor, Mich.
  Partial list of microfilms of S.T.C. books and a cross index by S.T.C. number. 1st yr. 1938–. Ann Arbor, Mich.

LISTS OF MANUSCRIPTS THAT CONTAIN DESCRIPTIONS OF PHOTOCOPIES

Canada. Public Archives
  Inventories, 1951–
  The inventories bound in blue deal with Record Groups (Fonds Officiels), in red with Manuscript Groups (Fonds des Manuscrits), and in green with holdings of historical societies. For reports of photocopies of especial value see: 1–5, Archives des Colonies, Archives Nationales, Ministère de la Guerre Ministere des Affaires Étrangères; 18, Documents anterieurs à la Cession; 19, Fur Trade and Indians; 23, Late Eighteenth Century papers; 26, Prime Ministers' papers; 27, Political figures, and the Collections of the Brome County, Norfolk, and Lennox and Addington Historical Societies.

Ewing, William S., compiler
  Guide to the manuscript collections in the William L. Clements Library. 2nd ed. Ann Arbor, 1953

Kane, Lucille M., and Johnson, Kathryn A.
  Manuscripts collections of the Minnesota Historical Society. St. Paul, 1955

Pennsylvania. Historical and Museum Commission
  Preliminary guide to the research materials of the Pennsylvania Historical and Museum Commission, Harrisburg, 1959

Shetler, Charles, compiler
  Guide to manuscripts and archives in the West Virginia collection, West Virginia University. Morgantown, West Va., 1958

HOUSE ORGANS

Micro Photo Inc., Cleveland, Ohio
  The micro photo reader; national newsletter of microfilming for libraries. Vol. 1–, 1959– Cleveland, Ohio

University Microfilms, Ann Arbor, Mich.
  Microcosm. Vol. 1–, 1955– Ann Arbor, Mich.

LOCATION SYMBOLS

Holders of Photocopies

A-Ar Alabama State Department of Archives and History, Washington Street, between Bainbridge and Union, Montgomery, Alabama ¶
Owing to legal restrictions the Alabama Archives cannot lend film and in many cases cannot provide copies of material which it holds for other institutions.

AB Birmingham Public Library, Birmingham, Alabama ¶

AkHi Alaska Historical Library and Museum, P.O. Box 2051, Juneau, Alaska ¶

AkU University of Alaska Library, College, Alaska

ArAO Ouachita Baptist College Library, Arkadelphia, Arkansas ¶

ArHi History Commission, Old State House, Little Rock, Arkansas

ArU University of Arkansas Library, Fayetteville, Arkansas

Az-Ar Department of Library and Archives, Phoenix, Arizona

AzFM Museum of Northern Arizona Library, P.O. Box 402, Fort Valley Road, Flagstaff, Arizona ¶

AzU University of Arizona Library, Tucson, Arizona

C California State Library, Library and Courts Building, Sacramento 9, California

C-S California State Library, Sutro Branch, Public Library Building, Civic Center, San Francisco 2, California

CBPac Pacific School of Religion Library, 1798 Scenic Avenue, Berkeley 9, California

CBSK Starr King School for the Ministry Library, 2441 Le Conte Avenue, Berkeley 9, California

CLCL Los Angeles County Law Library, 301 West First Street, Los Angeles 12, California

CLO Occidental College Library, 1600 Campus Road, Los Angeles 41, California

CLSU University of Southern California Library, University Park, Los Angeles 7, California

CLU University of California at Los Angeles Library, 405 Hilgard Avenue, Los Angeles 24, California

CSaT San Francisco Theological Seminary Library, Geneva Hall, San Anselmo, California

CSdS San Diego State College Library, 5402 College Avenue, San Diego 15, California

CSf San Francisco Public Library, Civic Center, San Francisco 2, California

CSfU University of San Francisco Library, 2130 Fulton Street, San Francisco 17, California ¶

CSmH Henry E. Huntington Library and Art Gallery, San Marino 9, California ¶

CSt Stanford University Libraries, Palo Alto, California

CSt-H The Hoover Institution on War, Revolution, and Peace, Stanford University, Stanford, California

CStBS University of California, Santa Barbara College Library, Goleta, California

CU University of California, General Library, Berkeley 4, California

CU-B Bancroft Library, University of California, Berkeley 4, California

CaACG Glenbow Foundation, 1202 Sixth Street, S.W., Calgary, Alberta, Canada

CaBVaU University of British Columbia Library, Vancouver 8, Canada

CaBViPA Provincial Archives, Victoria, British Columbia, Canada

CaMWP Public Archives of Manitoba, Provincial Library, 257 Legislative Building, Winnipeg 1, Manitoba, Canada

CaMWU   University of Manitoba Library, Winnipeg, Manitoba, Canada

CaNBFU   University of New Brunswick Library, Fredericton, New Brunswick, Canada

CaNBSM   New Brunswick Museum Library, Douglas Avenue, St. John, New Brunswick, Canada

CaNBSjU Saint Joseph's University Library, Moncton, New Brunswick, Canada

CaNfSM   Memorial University of Newfoundland Library, St. John's, Newfoundland, Canada

CaOKQ   Douglas Library, Queen's University, Kingston, Ontario, Canada

CaOOA   Public Archives of Canada, 330 Sussex Drive, Ottawa 2, Ontario, Canada

CaOOSJ   Scolasticat Saint-Joseph Library, Avenue des Oblats, Ottawa, Ontario, Canada

CaOTA   Department of Public Records and Archives, 14 Queen's Park Crescent West, Toronto 5, Ontario, Canada

CaOTPI   Pontifical Institute of Mediaeval Studies, 59 Queen's Park Crescent, Toronto 5, Ontario, Canada

CaOTV   Victoria University Library, Toronto, Ontario, Canada

CaQQA   Archives de la Province, Musée Provinciale, Québec, Québec, Canada

CaQQCRH Cercle des Recherches Historiques Musée Provinciale, Québec, Québec, Canada

CaSRA   Saskatchewan Archives Board, Regina, Saskatchewan, Canada

CaSSA   Saskatchewan Archives Office, University of Saskatchewan, Saskatoon, Saskatchewan

CoD   Denver Public Library, 1357 Broadway, Denver 3, Colorado

CoDU   University of Denver Libraries, Colorado Seminary, Denver 10, Colorado

CoHi   Colorado State Historical Society Library, State Museum Building, 14th and Sherman Streets, Denver 2, Colorado

CoU   University of Colorado Libraries, Boulder, Colorado

Ct   Connecticut State Library, Capitol Avenue, Hartford 15, Connecticut

CtHC   Hartford Seminary Foundation, Case Memorial Library, 55 Elizabeth Street, Hartford 5, Connecticut

CtN1CG   U.S. Coast Guard Academy Library, Mohegan Avenue, New London, Connecticut

CtSoP   Pequot Library, P.O. Southport, Connecticut

CtY   Yale University Library, New Haven, Connecticut

DCU   The Catholic University of America Library, Washington 25, District of Columbia

DDO   Dumbarton Oaks Research Library, 1703 32nd Street, N.W., Washington 7, District of Columbia

DFo   Folger Shakespeare Library, 201 East Capitol Street, Washington 3, District of Columbia

DGU   Georgetown University Libraries, 37th and O Streets, Washington 7, District of Columbia

DGW   George Washington University Library, 2023 G Street, N.W., Washington 6, District of Columbia

DHU   Howard University Library, Washington 1, District of Columbia

DLC   The Library of Congress, Washington 25, District of Columbia

DNA   National Archives, Pennsylvania Avenue at Eighth Street, N.W., Washington 25, District of Columbia ¶

DUSC   Library, Supreme Court of the United States, Washington 25, District of Columbia

De   Public Archives Commission, Hall of Records, Dover, Delaware

DeHi   Historical Society of Delaware, Old Town Hall, Sixth and Market Streets, Wilmington, Delaware ¶

DeU   University of Delaware, Memorial Library, Newark, Delaware

FSaHi   St. Augustine Historical Society Library, Webb Memorial Building, St. Francis Street, St. Augustine, Florida

FU   University of Florida Libraries, P.O. Box 3556, University Station, Gainesville, Florida

G-Ar   Georgia State Department of Archives and History, 1516 Peachtree Road, N.W., Atlanta, Georgia

GAHi   Atlanta Historical Society, 1753 Peachtree Street, N.E., Atlanta 9, Georgia

GEU   Emory University Library, Emory University P.O., Atlanta, Georgia

GHi   Georgia Historical Society, 501 Whitaker Street, Savannah, Georgia

GU   University of Georgia Libraries, Athens, Georgia

Hi-Ar   Board of Commissioners of Public Archives, Honolulu, Hawaii

HiU   University of Hawaii, 1801 University Avenue, Honolulu 14, Hawaii

I   Illinois State Historical Library, Centennial Building, Springfield, Illinois

I-Ar   Illinois State Archives, Archives Building, Springfield, Illinois

IAurC   Aurora College Library, Aurora, Illinois

IC   Chicago Public Library, 78 East Washington Street, Chicago 2, Illinois

ICA	Art Institute of Chicago, Michigan Boulevard at Adams Street, Chicago 3, Illinois
ICHi	Chicago Historical Society, North Avenue and Clark Street, Chicago 14, Illinois
ICL	Loyola University Library, 6525 North Sheridan Road, Chicago 26, Illinois
ICN	Newberry Library, 60 West Walton Street, Chicago 10, Illinois
ICP	McCormick Theological Seminary Library, 2330 North Halsted Street, Chicago 14, Illinois
ICU	University of Chicago Library, Chicago 37, Illinois
ICarbS	Southern Illinois University Library, Carbondale, Illinois
IKON	Olivet Nazarene College Library, Kankakee, Illinois
INS	Illinois State Normal University Library, Normal, Illinois
IP	Peoria Public Library, 111 North East Monroe Street, Peoria 3, Illinois
IRA	Augustana College Library, 35th and Seventh Avenue, Rock Island, Illinois
IU	University of Illinois Library, Urbana, Illinois
IU-H	Illinois Historical Survey, University of Illinois, 418 Lincoln Hall, Urbana, Illinois
IaU	State University of Iowa Library, Iowa City, Iowa
IdHi	Idaho Historical Society, 610 Parkway Drive, Boise, Idaho
IdPI	Idaho State College, Pocatello, Idaho
In	Indiana State Library, 140 North Senate Avenue, Indianapolis 4, Indiana ¶
InGrD	DePauw University, Greencastle, Indiana
InLPU	Purdue University Libraries, Lafayette, Indiana
InNd	University of Notre Dame, The University Library, P.O. Notre Dame, South Bend, Indiana
InNhW	Working Men's Institute Library, New Harmony, Indiana ¶
InRE	Earlham College Library, Richmond, Indiana
InU	Indiana University Library, Bloomington, Indiana
InValU	Valparaiso University Library, Valparaiso, Indiana
KAS	St. Benedict's College, The Abbey Library, Atchison, Kansas
KHi	Kansas State Historical Society, Memorial Building, Topeka, Kansas
KNM	Bethel College Historical Library, North Newton, Kansas
KU	University of Kansas Library, Lawrence, Kansas
KyBgW	Kentucky Library, Western Kentucky State College, Bowling Green, Kentucky ¶
KyHi	Kentucky Historical Society, Old Capitol Building, Frankfort, Kentucky ¶
KyLoCj	Courier-Journal and Louisville Times Library, 525 West Broadway, Louisville 8, Kentucky
KyLoU	University of Louisville Library, Belknap Campus, Louisville 8, Kentucky
KyU	University of Kentucky Libraries, Lexington, Kentucky
L-M	Louisiana State Museum Library, 616 Pirates Alley, New Orleans, Louisiana
LLafS	Southwestern Louisiana Institute, Stephens Memorial Library, Lafayette, Louisiana
LM	Ouachita Parish Public Library, 418 Jackson Street, Monroe, Louisiana ¶
LN	New Orleans Public Library, 1031 St. Charles Avenue, New Orleans 13, Louisiana ¶
LNBT	New Orleans Baptist Theological Seminary Library, 3939 Gentilly Boulevard, New Orleans 22, Louisiana
LNHT	Tulane University of Louisiana, Howard-Tilton Memorial Library, Audubon Place at Freret Street, New Orleans 18, Louisiana
LNaN	Northwestern State College of Louisiana, Russell Library, Natchitoches, Louisiana
LU	Department of Archives, Louisiana State University, University Station, Baton Rouge, Louisiana
M-Ar	Massachusetts Archives, Office of the Secretary, State House, Boston 33, Massachusetts ¶
MAnP	Phillips Academy Library, Andover, Massachusetts
MB	Boston Public Library, Copley Square, Boston 17, Massachusetts
MBD	The Diocesan Library, 1 Joy Street, Boston, Massachusetts
MBNeHg	New England Historic Genealogical Society, 9 Ashburton Place, Boston 8, Massachusetts ¶
MBU	Boston University, Chenery Library, Charles River Campus, 725 Commonwealth Avenue, Boston 15, Massachusetts
MCo	Concord Free Public Library, Concord, Massachusetts
MH	Harvard College Library, Harvard College, Cambridge 38, Massachusetts
MH-BA	Baker Library, Harvard University, Graduate School of Business Administration, Soldiers Field, Boston 63, Massachusetts
MHi	Massachusetts Historical Society, 1154 Boylston Street, Boston 15, Massachusetts
MNF	Forbes Library, West Street, Northampton, Massachusetts

MNtCA	Andover Newton Theological School, Hills Library, 169 Herrick Road, Newton Centre, Massachusetts
MSCV	Connecticut Valley Historical Society, William Pyncheon Memorial Building, Springfield, Massachusetts
MSaP	Peabody Museum of Salem, East India Marine Hall, 161 Essex Street, Salem, Massachusetts
MWA	American Antiquarian Society Library, corner Salisbury Street and Park Avenue, Worcester 9, Massachusetts
MWC	Clark University Library, 1 Downing Street, Worcester 10, Massachusetts
MdAA	Hall of Records Commission, Hall of Records, Annapolis, Maryland
MdAN	United States Naval Academy Library, Annapolis, Maryland
MdBE	Enoch Pratt Free Library, 400 Cathedral Street, Baltimore 1, Maryland
MdBJ	Johns Hopkins University Library, Charles and 34th Streets, Baltimore 18, Maryland
MeBa	Bangor Public Library, 145 Harlow Street, Bangor, Maine
MeWC	Colby College Library, Waterville, Maine
MiD-B	Burton Historical Collection, Detroit Public Library, 5201 Woodward Avenue, Detroit 2, Michigan
MiDA-A	Detroit Institute of Arts, Research Library and Archives of American Art, 5200 Woodward Avenue, Detroit 2, Michigan
MiFli	Flint Public Library, East Kearsley and Clifford Streets, Flint 2, Michigan
MiSs	Carnegie Public Library, Sault Ste. Marie, Michigan
MiU	University of Michigan Library, Ann Arbor, Michigan
MiU-C	William L. Clements Library, University of Michigan, Ann Arbor, Michigan
MiU-L	University of Michigan Law Library, University of Michigan, Ann Arbor, Michigan
MnCS	St. John's University Library, Collegeville, Minnesota ¶
MnHi	Minnesota Historical Society Library, Cedar and Central Streets, St. Paul 1, Minnesota
MnU	University of Minnesota Library, Minneapolis 14, Minnesota
MoHi	The State Historical Society of Missouri, Columbia, Missouri ¶
MoIT	Harry S. Truman Library, Independence, Missouri
MoS	St. Louis Public Library, Olive, 13th, and 14th Streets, St. Louis 3, Missouri
MoSC	Concordia Historical Institute, St. Louis 5, Missouri
MoSFR	Foundation for Reformation Research, 801 DeMun Avenue, St. Louis (Clayton) 5, Missouri
MoSHi	Missouri Historical Society, Lindell at DeBaliviere, St. Louis 12, Missouri
MoSU	St. Louis University Library, 21 North Grand Boulevard, St. Louis 3, Missouri
MoSW	Washington University Libraries, St. Louis 5, Missouri
MoU	University of Missouri Library, Columbia, Missouri
Ms-Ar	Mississippi Department of Archives and History Library, War Memorial Building, Jackson 5, Mississippi
MtBC	Montana State College Library, Bozeman, Montana
MtU	Montana State University Library, Missoula, Montana
N	New York State Library, Albany, New York
NB	Brooklyn Public Library, Ingersoll Building, Grand Army Plaza, Brooklyn 38, New York
NBLiHi	Long Island Historical Society Library, 128 Pierrepont Street, Brooklyn 1, New York
NBmA	The Adirondack Museum, Blue Mountain Lake, New York
NFt	Fort Ticonderoga Museum, Fort Ticonderoga, New York
NHi	The New-York Historical Society, 170 Central Park West, New York 24, New York
NIC	Cornell University Library, Ithaca, New York
NIC-I	New York State School of Industrial and Labor Relations Library, Cornell University, Ithaca, New York
NN	The New York Public Library, Fifth Avenue and 42nd Street, New York 18, New York ¶
NNC	Columbia University Libraries, 535 West 114th Street, New York 27, New York
NNCoCi	City College of New York Library, 135th Street and Convent Avenue, New York 31, New York
NNF	Fordham University Library, New York 58, New York
NNHol	Holland Society of New York, 15 William Street, New York 5, New York
NNJ	Jewish Theological Seminary of America Library, 3080 Broadway, New York 27, New York
NNNAM	New York Academy of Medicine Library, 2 East 103rd Street, New York 29, New York
NNNG	New York Genealogical and Biographical Society Library, 122–126 East 58th Street, New York 22, New York

NNP	Pierpont Morgan Library, 29 East 36th Street, New York 16, New York	NmU	University of New Mexico Library, Albuquerque, New Mexico
NNPr	Presbyterian Mission Library, 156 Fifth Avenue, New York 10, New York	Nv	Nevada State Library, Carson City, Nevada
NNQC	Queen's College Library, Flushing, New York	NvU	University of Nevada Library, Reno, Nevada
NNU	New York University Libraries, Washington Square, New York, New York	O	Ohio State Library, State Office Building, Columbus 15, Ohio
NNUT	Union Theological Seminary Library, Broadway at 120th Street, New York 27, New York	OAU	Ohio University Library, Athens, Ohio
		OCHP	Historical and Philosophical Society of Ohio, University of Cincinnati Library Building, Cincinnati 21, Ohio
NNWML	Wagner College Library, Grymes Hill, Staten Island 1, New York	OCl	Cleveland Public Library, 325 Superior Avenue, Cleveland 14, Ohio
NNYi	Yivo Institute for Jewish Research, Library and Archives, 1048 Fifth Avenue, New York 28, New York	OClWHi	Western Reserve Historical Society Libraries, 10825–10915 East Boulevard, Cleveland 6, Ohio
NPV	Vassar College Library, Poughkeepsie, New York	ODa	Dayton Public Library and Museum and Montgomery County Library, 215 East Third Street, Dayton 2, Ohio
NRU	The University of Rochester Library, Rochester 20, New York	OFH	Rutherford B. Hayes Library, 1337 Hayes Avenue, Fremont, Ohio
NSiHi	Staten Island Historical Society, Court and Center Streets, Richmond, Staten Island 6, New York	OHi	Ohio Historical Society Library, 15th and North High Streets, Columbus 10, Ohio
NStC	St. Bonaventure University, Friedsam Memorial Library, St. Bonaventure, New York	OLeWHi	Warren County Historical Society, P.O. Box 66, Lebanon, Ohio ¶
		OU	Ohio State University Libraries, Columbus 10, Ohio
NSyU	Syracuse University Libraries, Syracuse 10, New York	OWoC	College of Wooster Library, Wooster, Ohio
NbHi	Nebraska State Historical Society Library, 1500 R Street, Lincoln 8, Nebraska	OYesA	Antioch College Library, Yellow Springs, Ohio
Nc-Ar	North Carolina Department of Archives and History, Raleigh, North Carolina ¶	Ok	The Oklahoma State Library, 109 State Capitol, Oklahoma City 5, Oklahoma
NcD	Duke University Library, Durham, North Carolina	OkHi	Oklahoma Historical Society Library, North Lincoln Boulevard and 20th Street, Oklahoma City 5, Oklahoma
NcLjHi	Association of Methodist Historical Societies, Lake Junaluska, North Carolina	OkTG	Thomas Gilcrease Institute of American History and Art, P.O. Box 2419, Tulsa, Oklahoma
NcU	University of North Carolina Libraries, Chapel Hill, North Carolina	
Nh	New Hampshire State Library, Concord, New Hampshire ¶	OkTU	University of Tulsa Library, Tulsa 4, Oklahoma
NhD	Dartmouth College, Baker Library, Hanover, New Hampshire	OkU	The University of Oklahoma Library, Norman, Oklahoma
NhHi	New Hampshire Historical Society, Concord, New Hampshire	Or-Ar	Oregon State Archives, Oregon State Building, Salem, Oregon
Nj	New Jersey State Library, State House Annex, Trenton 25, New Jersey	OrHi	Oregon Historical Society, Portland 1, Oregon
NjMD	Drew University, Rose Memorial Library, Madison, New Jersey	OrP	Library Association of Portland, 801 South West Tenth Avenue, Portland 5, Oregon
NjP	Princeton University Library, Princeton, New Jersey	OrU	University of Oregon Library, Eugene, Oregon
NjPT	Princeton Theological Seminary Library, P.O. Box 111, Princeton, New Jersey	PBL	Lehigh University Library, Bethlehem, Pennsylvania
NjR	Rutgers University Library, New Brunswick, New Jersey ¶	PCarD	Dickinson College Library, Carlisle, Pennsylvania
NmSM	Museum of New Mexico Library, P.O. Box 1727, Santa Fe, New Mexico ¶	PDoHi	The Bucks County Historical Society, Doylestown, Pennsylvania ¶

PHC	Haverford College Library, Haverford, Pennsylvania
PHarH	Pennsylvania Historical and Museum Commission, State Museum Building, Harrisburg, Pennsylvania
PHi	Historical Society of Pennsylvania, 1300 Locust Street, Philadelphia 7, Pennsylvania
PP	Free Library of Philadelphia, Logan Square, Philadelphia 3, Pennsylvania
PPAmP	American Philosophical Society Library, 127 South Fifth Street, Philadelphia 6, Pennsylvania
PPBC	Philadelphia Bibliographical Center and Union Library Catalogue, 219 Logan Hall, University of Pennsylvania, Philadelphia 4, Pennsylvania
PPPrHi	Presbyterian Historical Society, Witherspoon Building, Philadelphia 4, Pennsylvania
PPT-L	Temple University School of Law, Law Library, 1715 North Broad Street, Philadelphia 22, Pennsylvania
PPY	Department of Records, Yearly Meeting of Friends, Philadelphia, Pennsylvania
PPiU	University of Pittsburgh Library, Pittsburgh 13, Pennsylvania
PSC	Swarthmore College Library, Swarthmore, Pennsylvania
PSC-F	Friends Historical Library of Swarthmore College, Swarthmore, Pennsylvania
PSt	Pennsylvania State University Library, University Park, Pennsylvania
PU	University of Pennsylvania Library, Central Building, 34th Street below Woodland Avenue, Philadelphia 4, Pennsylvania
PU-F	H. H. Furness Memorial Library, University of Pennsylvania, Philadelphia, Pennsylvania
PV	Villanova University Library, Villanova, Pennsylvania
PYHi	The Historical Society of York County, 225 Market Street, York, Pennsylvania
RHi	Rhode Island Historical Society, 52 Power Street, Providence, Rhode Island
RPB	Brown University Library, Providence 12, Rhode Island
RPJCB	John Carter Brown Library, Brown University, Providence, Rhode Island
Sc-Ar	South Carolina Archives Department, World War Memorial, Columbia 1, South Carolina
ScC	Charleston Library Society, Charleston, South Carolina
ScCC	College of Charleston Library, Charleston 10, South Carolina
ScHi	The South Carolina Historical Society, Fireproof Building, Charleston, South Carolina
ScU	University of South Carolina, McKissick Memorial Library, Columbia 1, South Carolina
SdHi	South Dakota State Historical Society, Pierre, South Dakota
SdU	State University of South Dakota Libraries, Vermillion, South Dakota
T	Tennessee State Library and Archives, Nashville 3, Tennessee
TC	Chattanooga Public Library, Chattanooga 3, Tennessee ¶
TM	Memphis Public Library, 33 South Front Street, Memphis 3, Tennessee ¶
TNF	Fisk University Library, Nashville 8, Tennessee
TNJ	Joint University Libraries, Nashville 5, Tennessee
TNSB	Southern Baptist Convention Historical Commission, Nashville, Tennessee
TSewU	University of the South Library, Sewanee, Tennessee
TxAbH	Hardin-Simmons University Library, Abilene, Texas
TxD	Dallas Public Library, Dallas, Texas
TxDHi	Dallas Historical Society, Hall of State, Dallas, Texas
TxH	Houston Public Library, Houston, Texas ¶
TxHR	Rice Institute, Fondren Library, P.O. Box 1892, Houston, Texas
TxU	University of Texas, Mirabeau B. Lamar Library, Austin 12, Texas
TxWB	Baylor University Library, Box 307, Baylor University Station, Waco, Texas
UHi	Utah State Historical Society Library, 603 East South Temple Street, Salt Lake City 2, Utah
UPB	Brigham Young University, Heber J. Grant Library, Provo, Utah
USlC	Office of the Church Historian of the Church of Jesus Christ of Latter-Day Saints, 47 East South Temple Street, Salt Lake City 1, Utah ¶
USlGS	Genealogical Society of the Church of Jesus Christ of Latter-Day Saints, 80 North Main Street, P.O. Box 749, Salt Lake City 11, Utah ¶
Vi	Virginia State Library, Capitol Street, Richmond 19, Virginia
ViSWC	Sweet Briar College, Mary Helen Cochran Library, Sweet Briar, Virginia
ViU	University of Virginia, Alderman Library, Charlottesville, Virginia
ViW	College of William and Mary Library, Williamsburg, Virginia
ViWC	Colonial Williamsburg, Williamsburg, Virginia

ViWi	The Institute of Early American History and Culture, Box 1298, Williamsburg, Virginia	FiHU	University of Helsinki, Helsinki, Finland
Vt-PR	Public Records Commission, Montpelier, Vermont ¶	FiHV	Valtionsarkisto, Helsinki, Finland
		FiHaM	Maakunta-Arkisto, Häme (Dept.), Hämeenlinna, Finland
VtHi	Vermont Historical Society, Montpelier, Vermont	FiOM	Maakunta-Arkisto, Oulu (Dept.), Oulu, Finland
WHi	State Historical Society of Wisconsin, 816 State Street, Madison, Wisconsin	FiTM	Maakunta-Arkisto, Turku-Pori (Dept.), Turku-Pori, Finland
WU	University of Wisconsin Libraries, Madison, Wisconsin	FiVM	Maakunta-Arkisto, Vaasa (Dept.), Vaasa, Finland
WaPS	State College of Washington Library, Pullman, Washington	FrAN	Archives Nationales, Paris, France
		FrB	Bibliothèque Municipale, Bordeaux, France
WaU	University of Washington Library, Seattle 5, Washington	FrBN	Bibliothèque Nationale, Paris, France
		FrC	Bibliothèque Municipale, Chartres, France
WaWW	Whitman College Library, Walla Walla, Washington ¶	FrD	Bibliothèque Municipale, Douai, France
		FrPM	Bibliothèque Mazarine, Paris, France
Wv-Ar	West Virginia Department of Archives and History, Charleston 5, West Virginia	GeMSA	Staatsarchiv, Marburg, Germany
		IcRN	National Record Office, Reykjavik, Iceland
WvU	West Virginia University Library, Morgantown, West Virginia	IiCU	Calcutta University, Calcutta, India
		ImDRO	Record Office, Douglas, Isle of Man
WyHi	Wyoming State Archives and Historical Department, State Office Building, Cheyenne, Wyoming ¶	IrDPRO	Public Record Office, Dublin, Ireland
		IrDSF	Society of Friends, Dublin, Ireland
		IrDT	Trinity College, Dublin, Ireland
WyU	University of Wyoming Library, Laramie, Wyoming	IrNL	National Library of Ireland, Dublin, Ireland
		IsJJH	Jewish Historical General Archives, Jerusalem, Israel

Holders of Original Materials

AsVN	National Bibliothek, Vienna, Austria	ItFA	Archivio di Stato, Florence, Italy
BeBr	Bibliothèque Royale de Belgique, Brussels, Belgium	ItFBN	Bibliotheca Nazionale Centrale, Florence, Italy
CaQMU	Université de Montréal, Montréal, Québec, Canada	ItMA	Archivio di Stato, Milan, Italy
		ItNA	Archivio di Stato, Naples, Italy
CmAHN	Archivo Histórico Nacional, Bogotá, Colombia	ItPadU	Padua Universitá, Padua, Italy
		ItTA	Archivio di Stato, Turin, Italy
DAL	Office of the Adjutant General, Washington 25, District of Columbia	ItVA	Archivio di Stato, Venice, Italy
		ItVat	Vatican Library, Vatican City
DBC	Bureau of the Census Library, Washington 25, District of Columbia	MnStJosS	College of St. Benedict, St. Joseph, Minnesota
DJ	Department of Justice Library, Tenth Street and Pennsylvania Avenue, Washington 25, District of Columbia	MxAGN	Archivo General de la Nación, Mexico City, Mexico
		MxBN	Biblioteca Nacional, Mexico City, Mexico
DS	Department of State Library, 401 23rd Street, N.W., Washington 25, District of Columbia	MxMC	Catedral, Mexico City, Mexico
		NeAU	Amsterdam Universiteit, Amsterdam, The Netherlands
DSI	Smithsonian Institution, Constitution Avenue at Tenth Street, N.W., Washington 25, District of Columbia	NeHAR	Algemeenes Riksarchivet, The Hague, The Netherlands
DaAL	Landsarkivet, Aabenraa, Denmark	NeLU	Leyden Universiteit, Leyden, The Netherlands
DaKH	Heerens Arkivet, Copenhagen, Denmark		
DaKL	Landsarkivet, Copenhagen, Denmark	NeR	Rotterdam Bibliotheek, Rotterdam, The Netherlands
DaKR	Rigsarkivet, Copenhagen, Denmark		
DaKU	Copenhagen Universitet, Copenhagen, Denmark	NoOR	Riksarkivet, Oslo, Norway
		NzDOU	Otago University, Dunedin, New Zealand
DaOL	Landsarkivet, Odense, Denmark	OrPL	Lewis and Clark College Library, Portland, Oregon
DaVL	Landsarkivet, Viborg, Denmark		

PLF	Franklin and Marshall College, Fackenthal Library, Lancaster, Pennsylvania	UKENRH	National Register House, Edinburgh, Scotland
SpAGI	Archivo General de Indias, Seville, Spain	UKGrP	Gloucester Public Library, Gloucester, England
SpEsc	El Escorial, Spain		
SvGL	Landsarkivet, Göteborg, Sweden	UKGwNM	National Maritime Museum, Greenwich, England
SvHL	Landsarkivet, Härnösand, Sweden	UKHfP	Hereford Public Library, Hereford, England
SvLL	Landsarkivet, Lund, Sweden	UKLBM	British Museum, London, England
SvNS	Stadsarkivet, Norrköping, Sweden	UKLFS	Friends Library, London, England
SvOL	Landsarkivet, Östersund, Sweden	UKLGU	Guildhall Library, London, England
SvSK	Kunglika Biblioteket, Stockholm, Sweden	UKLIT	Inner Temple Library, London, England
SvSR	Riksarkivet, Stockholm, Sweden	UKLLam	Lambeth Palace Library, London, England
SvUL	Landsarkivet, Uppsala, Sweden	UKLPRO	Public Record Office, London, England
SvUU	Uppsala Universitet, Uppsala, Sweden	UKLSmH	Somerset House, London, England
SvVL	Landsarkivet, Visby, Sweden	UKLU	London University, London, England
SvVaL	Landsarkivet, Vadstena, Sweden	UKLVA	Victoria and Albert Museum, London, England
SzGS	Archive, Geneva, Switzerland		
SzL	Archive, Liestal, Switzerland	UKLWi	Doctor Williams' Library, London, England
SzLa	Archive, Lausanne, Switzerland	UKLiC	Lincoln Cathedral, Lincoln, England
UKAbN	National Library of Wales, Aberystwyth, Wales	UKMP	Manchester Public Library, Manchester, England
UKBP	Birmingham Public Library, Birmingham, England	UKNU	Nottingham University, Nottingham, England
UKBeRO	Public Record Office, Belfast, Northern Ireland	UKO	Bodleian Library, Oxford, England
		UKOAS	All Souls College, Oxford, England
UKC	Cambridge University Library, Cambridge, England	UKOCC	Corpus Christi College, Oxford, England
		UKOME	Merton College, Oxford, England
UKCCC	Corpus Christi College, Cambridge, England	UKOOC	Oriel College, Oxford, England
UKCPE	Peterhouse, Cambridge, England	UKPlI	The Institute Library, Plymouth, England
UKCSR	Scott Institute for Polar Research, Cambridge, England	UKPrRO	Lancashire Record Office, Preston, Lancashire, England
UKCT	Trinity College, Cambridge, England	UKSuP	Sutherland Public Library, Sutherland, England
UKCdRO	Essex Record Office, Chelmsford, Essex, England		
		UKWar	Warwick Public Library, Warwick, England
UKE	National Library of Scotland, Edinburgh, Scotland	UKWrRO	Worcestershire Public Record Office, Worcester, England

ABBREVIATIONS

C. H.	courthouse in the city listed	N:	negative microfilm (35mm. unless otherwise stated)
DC:	direct or contact copy		
DCO	an arbitrary symbol, used by agreement with the Photostat Corporation, to avoid the trademark Photostat, which indicates copies, usually of the same size as the original, made by a machine manufactured by the corporation. This machine employs a lens and does not operate by direct contact.	P:	positive microfilm
		Ph:	photograph
		PP:	photoprint or enlargement from microfilm
		priv.	privately held material
dest.	destroyed	RN	reading negative, i. e., second- or third-generation film that is white on black like a master negative to make it easier to read
Ibid.	located at the holding institution given in the first line of the entry		

Union Listing of Bodies of MSS in Photocopy

GENERAL COLLECTIONS

AMERICAN COUNCIL OF LEARNED SOCIETIES
British Manuscripts Project: selections from
Bath (Longleat); Bedford; British Museum;
Cambridge; Downshire; Eton; Holkham;
Lincoln Cathedral; Northumberland (Alnwick
Castle); Oxford; Penshurst (De l'Isle and
Dudley); Sackville; and National Library of
Wales manuscripts
N: DLC   1

Described in U. S. Library of Congress.
British manuscripts project; a checklist

MODERN LANGUAGE ASSOCIATION OF AMERICA
Reproductions of manuscripts and rare printed
books, v.d.   v.p.
N: DLC   2
P: NNC

A list, complete to January, 1950, has been
published in PMLA, v. 65, p. 289-338

VATICAN. BIBLIOTECA VATICANA
Selected codices: Vaticani Latini; Barberiniani
Latini; Palatini Latini; Urbinates Latini; Regin-
enses Latini; Capponiani; Ottoboniani Latini;
Burghesiani; Rossiani; Chisiani; Ferrajoli;
Archivio di San Pietro; Graechi   Ibid.
N: MoSU   3

Listed by manuscript number in Manuscripta,
February 1957 ff.

BIBLIOGRAPHY—GENERAL

BRITISH MUSEUM
Catalogues (manuscript)   UKLBM
N: UKLBM 64 reels   4
P: CaOOA

RELIGION—GENERAL

ARMINIUS, JACOBUS, 1560-1609
Unpublished manuscripts and related
materials   NeAU NeLU NeR UKLBM
N: IKON 3 reels*   5

ATHOS (MONASTERIES)
Manuscripts (selections)   Ibid.
N: DLC   6

Described in A Descriptive Checklist of
Selected Manuscripts in the Monasteries
of Mount Athos

CAMBRIDGE. UNIVERSITY. LIBRARY
Taylor-Schechter collection: selections,
TSF (Rabbinics) 1, 2, 7, 12, 13   UKC
N: NNJ   7
P: NNJ

CAMBRIDGE. UNIVERSITY. LIBRARY
Taylor-Schechter collection: selections,
TS A (Bible), 1-22, 24-26, 28-32, 34-39;
Arabic, 1-18, 22-54   UKC
N: UKC   8
P: NNJ

ESCORIAL. BIBLIOTECA
Hebrew manuscripts, G I, 1-16; G II, 1-19;
G III, 1-22; G IV, 1-17   Ibid.
N: NNJ   9

FOUNDATION FOR REFORMATION RESEARCH,
St. Louis, Mo.
Manuscripts, 1535-1541, 6 items   v.p.
N: MoSFR   10

Described in Materials Microfilmed, October,
1958

ISIDORUS PELUSIOTA, Saint, ca. 370-ca. 450
Epistolae in Greek, 18th cent. ms., 74 p.
ms. 1121 National Library of Athens
ms. 342 Vatopedi Monastery, Mount Athos
N: RPB 32 frames   11

JERUSALEM (PATRIARCHATES, ARMENIAN and
ORTHODOX)
Manuscripts, v.d.   Ibid.
N: DLC   12

Described in Checklist of Manuscripts in the
Libraries of the Greek and Armenian
Patriarchates in Jerusalem

OXFORD. UNIVERSITY. BODLEIAN LIBRARY
Hebrew manuscripts, listed in Neubauer
Catalogue, ms. 1-84   UKO
N: UKO   P: NNJ   13

SINAI. SAINT CATHERINE (Basilian monastery)
Selected manuscripts   Ibid.
N: DLC   14

Described in Checklist of Manuscripts in
St. Catherine's Monastery, Mount Sinai,
microfilmed for the Library of Congress

ANCIENT WORLD

ASSYRIA

BRITISH MUSEUM. DEPT. OF EGYPTIAN AND
ASSYRIAN ANTIQUITIES
Cuneiform inscriptions (transcripts made by
T. G. Pinches, 1895-1899)   UKLBM
N: RPB 4 reels   15

STRASSMAIER, JOHANN NEPOMUK, 1846-1920
Copies of cuneiform tablets at British Museum
priv.
N: RPB 1 reel   16

PALESTINE

JOSEPHUS, FLAVIUS
Antiquitates judaicae, 219 l.   Codex Vaticanus
latinus 1998   ItVat
N: MoSW   17

GREECE

THEON, of Alexandria, 4th cent.
Commentarius in expeditos canones Ptolemaie,
13th-14th cent., 16th cent.   Par. Gr. 2399,
2493   FrBN
N: RPB   18

MIDDLE AGES

Bibliography

COSENZA, MARIO EMILO, compiler
Biographical and bibliographical dictionary
of the Italian humanists and of the world of
classical scholarship in Italy, 1300-1800
[card file] Renaissance Society of America
N: Ibid. 28 reels   19

FLORENCE. BIBLIOTECA MEDICEO-
LAURENZIANA
Index manuscriptorum Bibliothecae F:F:
Ordinis praedicatorum Florentiae ad
Sanctum Marcum, 1768   Ibid.
N: ICU 1 reel   20

HARVARD UNIVERSITY. LIBRARY
Check list of [photocopies of] manuscripts...
collected by Professor Charles H. Haskins,
1934 (typescript), 49 p.   MH
N: NNC   21

VIENNA. NATIONALBIBLIOTHEK
Die Handschriften des Stiftens Altenburg (Son-
derkatalog)   Ibid.
N: Ibid. 1 reel   P: DLC   22

WILSON, WILLIAM JEROME
Catalogue of Latin and vernacular alchemical
manuscripts in America, n.d.   priv.
N: DLC 1 reel   23

Government Records

MILAN (Duchy)
Documenti diplomatici, France, Feb. - July,
1461   Archivio di Stato, Milan
N: Ibid. 1 reel   P: OAU   24

MILAN. ARCHIVIO DI STATO
Documents prior to 1100   Ibid.
N: CtY 2 reels   25

VENICE
Archivi misti, 14th - 15th cent.   ItVA
N: PU 8 reels*   26

Business Papers

GENOA.   ARCHIVIO DI STATO
Pandects of the notaries, 1154-1313   Ibid.
N: WU 61 reels   27
P: CtY DLC

GOLASECCA, MAROLO, 1369-1392
Notarial chartulary   ItMA
N: CtY 2 reels   28

Collections

HASKINS, CHARLES HOMER, 1870-1937, collector
Manuscripts from European Libraries and
Archives on Medieval science and culture,
v.d.   v.p.
DCO: MH ca. 300 items   29

JOHNSON, ROSELLE PARKER, collector
The Roselle Johnson Memorial Collection of
medieval manuscripts on Alchemy   priv.
N: priv. 106 reels   30
P: NcU

LOWE, ELIAS AVERY, 1879- , collector
Medieval manuscripts, v.d.   v.p.
DCO: DLC 9 file drawers, 2 boxes, 2 bundles,
1 v.   31

MASSACHUSETTS MEDICAL LIBRARY
Collectanea chymica, 1464-1468, 237 ff.
De Ricci 18   Ibid.
N: DLC   32

NORTH CAROLINA. UNIVERSITY. LIBRARY.
Medieval bestiaries, v.d.   BeBR FrBN FrT
FrV SvUU UKC UKLBM UKO
N: NcU 8 reels   33

TORONTO. UNIVERSITY. ST. MICHAEL'S
COLLEGE. PONTIFICAL INSTITUTE OF
MEDIAEVAL STUDIES
Selected Mediaeval manuscripts, v.d.   v.p.
N: CaOTPI   34

Listed by holding institution and described in
Mediaeval Studies, v. 4 (1942), p. 126-128,
and by author, v. 5 (1943), p. 51-74

WISCONSIN. UNIVERSITY. LIBRARY
History of science materials on Mathematics
and Physics, 14th - 15th cents.   v.p.
N: WU 60 reels   35

Manuscripts by Author

ALBERTUS DE SAXONIA, d. 1390
De proportionibus, 26 p.   FrBN
N: WU   36

ALBIZZI, PEPO d'ANTONIO di LANDO degli
Secret ledger and memorial book, 14th cent.,
31 p.   ICN
N: ICN   37

ALFONSO X, el Sabio, king of Castile and
León, 1221-1284
Tabulae astronomicae, 48 p., ms. 2352
AsVN
N: RPB   38

Algorismus nouus de integris compendiose sine
figurarum...   NNC
N: MiU 1 reel   39

ANGRIANI, MICHAEL, d. 1405
Tabula super Moralia beati Gregorii super Job
FrPM
N: ?   40
P: MiU

APICIUS
De re culinaria, 9th cent., lib. i-ix, 58 ll.
NNNAM
N: NNNAM   41

APOLLINARIS CREMONENSIS
Apollinaris doctoris Tractatus super primo et
ultimo instanti Petri Mantuani, 1473, 25 p.
ItFR
N: NNC   42

AUGUSTINUS, AURELIUS, Saint, Bp. of Hippo,
354-430
Exposito in Psalmos, Pars I   ICN
N: ICN   43

AUGUSTINUS, AURELIUS, Saint, Bp. of Hippo,
354-430
Works, 12th cent. ms.   ICN
N: ICN 1 reel   44

BARTHOLOMAEUS, ANGLICUS, fl. 13th cent.
De proprietatibus rerum, 15th cent., 201 ll.
NNNAM
N: NNNAM   45

BERTHOLD DE MAISBERCH, 15th cent.
Commentarius super Proclo Diadocho
ms. Lat. 2192 ItVat
N: NNC   46

BERTHOLD DE MAISBERCH, 15th cent.
Expositio fratris Berthold de Maisberch, 343 p.
UKO
N: NNC   47

BOETHIUS, ANICIUS MANLIUS SEVERINUS,
480?-?524
De consolatione philosophiae   ms. 562 ItVat
N; CtY   48

BOETHIUS, ANICIUS MANLIUS SEVERINUS,
480?-?524
De consolatione philosophiae, 10th cent.   ICN
N: ICN 1 reel   49

BOETHIUS, ANICIUS MANLIUS SEVERINUS,
480?-?524
[Incipit] Domino Patri Symnacho Boethius
Indandis accipiendiso...   FrBN
N: RPB   50

BRUNI, LEONARDO, ARETINO, 1369-1444
De bello Punico, 15th cent. ms.   ICN
N: ICN 1 reel   51

CATTANI DA DIACCETO, FRANCESCO, 1466-
1522
Tractatus de pulchre, 154 p.   Lat. ms. 8696
FrBN
N: NNC   52

DATINI, FRANCESCO DI MARCO, ca. 1335-1410
Archive materials Datini Arch., Prato, Italy
N: IU   53

Deprecationes adversus infideles et contra
omnia labantis vite descrimina pie decantanda,
40 ff.   ICN
N: ICN   54

DUCAS, fl. 1455
Michaelis Ducae historia [in Greek]   FrBN
N: ?
P: MiU   55

ELIAS, fl. 6th cent.
Codex chartaceus, olim Colbertinus, 90 p.
ms. Lat. 6508 FrBN
N: NNC   56

FROISSART, JEAN, 1338?-1410
Chroniques, 15th cent., 529 p.   ICN
N: ICN   57

GALFRIDUS ANGLICUS, Dominican friar, fl. 1440
Medulla grammatice, 1468   UKCSJ
N: ?
P: ICU   58

GREGORIUS I, the Great, Saint, Pope, 540-604
On Job, Codex 711
N: CtY 5 strips on one reel   59

GREGORIUS, Saint, Bp. of Nyssa
Works, Greek ms., 11th-16th cent.   FrBN
N: ? 2 reels
P: MiU   60

GUILELMUS, Abp. of Tyre, ca. 1130 - ca. 1190
Historia rerum in partibus transmarinus
gestarum, 1095-1184 ItVat
N: MnU   61

HIERONYMUS, Saint
Epistola ad Eustochium de virginitate
sevanda ICN
N: ICN 1 reel   62

INNOCENTIUS III, Pope, 1161-1216
Liber miserie conditionis humanae, 14th cent.
Lewis European ms. 84   PP
N: PP   63

JOSEPH OF EXETER, fl. 1190
De bello Troiano ms. Lat. 15015 FrBN
N: NjP 1 reel   64

JULIANUS, Saint, Bishop of Toledo, d. 690
De origine mortis humanae, etc., 9th cent.,
72 ft.   ICN
N: ICN   65

LELAND, JOHN, 1506?-1552
Selectiora quaedam Epigrammata sive Encon-
miae, n.p., n.d.   Tanner ms. 464, v. 4
UKO
N: RPB 1 reel   66

ORESME, NICOLAS, Bp., d. 1382
Algorismus, 4 p.   UKOSj
N: WU   67

ORESME, NICOLAS, Bp., d. 1382
Algorismus proportionum, 26 p.   FrBN
N: WU   68

ORESME, NICOLAS, Bp., d. 1382
De latitudinibus formarum   Bayerisches
Staatsbibliothek, Munich
N: WU   69

PLÊTHÔN, GEÔRGIOS GEMISTOS, 15th cent.,
et al.
De generatione deorum, etc., 15th cent., 348 p.
ICN
N: ICN   70

POLO, MARCO, 1254-1323?
De mirabilibus orientalium regionum
Garrett ms. 157 NjP
N: NjP 1 reel   71

ROBERT DE COURCON, d. 1218
Summa magistri Roberti de Curcun De moral-
ibus questionibus Theologicis UKLBM
N: ?
P: MiU   72

SERAPION, the Younger, 12th cent. ?
De medicinis simplicibus, 1365, 111 ll.   NNNAM
N: NNNAM   73

THIERRY DE CHARTRES
Theodoric Carnotensis bibliotheca septem
artium liberalium, 12th cent. ms. 497 and 498
FrCh
DCO: CaOTPI
N: ICU   74

THOMAS OF CAPUA, Cardinal, d. 1243
Summa artis dictaminis ms. K.4.1   UKCCl
N: ?
P: MiU   75

TRIVET, NICHOLAS, 1258?-1328
Anglo-Norman Chronicle Arundel 56 UKLBM
Magd. Coll. 45 UKO
N: MH 2 reels   76

TRIVET, NICHOLAS, 1258?-1328
Commentum in Boethium, De consolatione
philosophiae CSmH
N: CtY   77

VILLANI, GIOVANNI, ca. 1275-1348
De origine civitatis Florentia, et de eiusdem
civibus, 1396 ms. Barb Lat. 2601 ItVat
N: NcU   78

VILLANI, GIOVANNI, ca. 1275-1348
De origine civitatis Florentiae et eiusdem
famosos civibus ms. Ashburnham 942 ItFML
N: Ibid. 1 reel   79
P: NcU

VINCENT DE BEAUVAIS, d. 1264
De morlai principis institutione UKCT UKCCC
UKOME
N: InNd   80

WILLIAM OF WHEATLEY, fl. 1310
In Boethi de consolatione philosophae ms. 28
UKOE
N: InNd   81

Manuscripts by Institutional Holder

AKADEMIIA NAUK, S.S.S.R. (formerly
IMPERIAL ACADEMY OF SCIENCES)
Old Slavonic manuscripts: Kniga Glimaia
Tropni Papa Innokentii; Kniga Glagolemaia
Papa Innokentii; Kniga Glagolemaia
Legidaries Ibid.
N: KU 6 reels   82

ARRAS, France. BIBLIOTHÈQUE MUNICIPALE
Manuscript no. 397 Ibid.
N: CaOTPI   83

AUXERRE, France. BIBLIOTHÈQUE
MUNICIPALE
Manuscript no. 43 Ibid.
N: CaOTPI   84

AVIGNON. MUSÉE CALVET. BIBLIOTHÈQUE
Manuscripts nos. 615, 1091 Ibid.
N: CaOTPI   85

AVRANCHES, France. BIBLIOTHÈQUE
MUNICIPALE
Manuscripts nos. 86, 124, 230 Ibid.
N: CaOTPI   86

BAMBERG, Germany. BAYERISCHES STAATS-
ARCHIV
Manuscripts: Can. 36, Patr. 47 Ibid.
N: CaOTPI   87

BASEL. UNIVERSITÄT
Fakultatsmatrikel, 1460-1525 Ibid.
N: InNd   88

BASEL. UNIVERSITÄT
[Incipit] Ab Jove principium magno deduxit
araciis carmina atnobis gennor tu maximus
auctor ..., n.d.   Ms. A.N. iv. 18 Ibid.
N: RPB 1 reel   89

BASEL. UNIVERSITÄT
Manuscripts nos. B.III.13, B.IV.4, B.V.30,
B.VII.30, F.II.25, O.II.24 Ibid.
N: CaOTPI   90

BOLOGNA. BIBLIOTECA COMMUNALE
Manuscripts nos. A.714, A.913, A.1029
[Pts. I-V], A. 1036 Ibid.
N: CaOTPI   91

BOLOGNA. UNIVERSITÀ. BIBLIOTECA
Codex 2216 Ibid.
N: NjP 1 reel   92

BOLOGNA. UNIVERSITÀ. BIBLIOTECA
Manuscripts nos. 753, 755, 861, 1180, 2635
Ibid.
N: CaOTPI   93

BORDEAUX. BIBLIOTHÈQUE MUNICIPALE
Manuscripts nos. 131, 140, 147, 163, 167, 421,
426 Ibid.
N: CaOTPI   94

BRITISH MUSEUM
Manuscripts: Add. 28873, Add. 35179,
Arundel, 325, 367, Cotton, Cleo. C.10,
Dom. A. viii, Dom. xi, Vesp. D. 10;
Harley, 106, 3082, 3530, 3596, 5431;
Royal 9. E.xiv, 10. C. vi, 11. B. iii,
12.D.xiv, 12.F.i, 13.A. xii, 15.B. iv,
20.D. 11, Sloane 2542 UKLBM
N: CaOTPI   95

BRUGES. BIBLIOTHÈQUE MUNICIPALE
Manuscripts nos. 78, 80, 98, 109, 133, 172,
175, 176, 177, 178, 180, 181, 185, 186, 187,
189, 191, 192, 208, 220, 228, 234, 247, 297,
303, 424, 463, 464, 478, 480, 482, 491, 497,
498, 500, 502, 503, 510, 513, 515, 516 Ibid.
N: CaOTPI   96

BRUSSELS. BIBLIOTHÈQUE ROYALE
DE BELGIQUE
Manuscripts nos. 1138, 1424, 1542, 1552,
1555, 1573, 1610, 1655, 2893, 2898, 2906,
2960, 10295-10304 Ibid.
N: CaOTPI   97

BUDAPEST. MAGYAR NEMZETI MŰZEUM
Tracatus de jure canonico; Tractatus for the
school of Esztergom Ibid.
N: InNd   98

CAMBRAI, France. BIBLIOTHÈQUE
MUNICIPALE
Manuscripts nos. 169, 176, 259, 486 Ibid.
N: CaOTPI   99
DCO: CaOTPI no. 169

CAMBRIDGE. UNIVERSITY. CORPUS CHRISTI
COLLEGE
Manuscripts nos. 35, 62, 206 Ibid.
N: CaOTPI   100

CAMBRIDGE. UNIVERSITY. FITZWILLIAM
MUSEUM
Manuscripts nos. McLean 154, 156 UKCF
N: CaOTPI   101

CAMBRIDGE. UNIVERSITY. GONVILLE AND
CAIUS COLLEGE
Manuscripts nos. 101/53, 281/674, 285/678,
325/525, 331/722, 341, 367/589, 459/718,
464/571, 504, 593, 668 Ibid.
N: CaOTPI   102

CAMBRIDGE. UNIVERSITY. LIBRARY
Manuscripts: Dd. vii. 16; Ff. iii. 27; Ii. ii. 10;
Ii. iv. 26; Ii. iv. 27 UKC
N: CaOTPI   103

CAMBRIDGE. UNIVERSITY. PEMBROKE
COLLEGE
Boethius, De disciplina scholiarum, with
commentary by William Whetely Ibid.
N: InNd   104

CAMBRIDGE. UNIVERSITY. PEMBROKE
COLLEGE
Manuscripts nos. 27, 72, 238 Ibid.
N: CaOTPI   105

CAMBRIDGE. UNIVERSITY. PETERHOUSE
Manuscripts nos. 102, 128, 152, 192, 204 pt. II,
205, 241   UKCPE
N: CaOTPI   106

CAMBRIDGE. UNIVERSITY. TRINITY COLLEGE
Manuscripts nos. 370, 373, 378 UKCT
N: CaOTPI   107

CAMBRIDGE. UNIVERSITY. TRINITY HALL
Boethius, De consolatione and Disciplina
scholiarum [in French] Ibid.
N: InNd   108

CARPENTRAS, France. BIBLIOTHÈQUE
MUNICIPALE
Manuscripts nos. 106, 292 Ibid.
N: CaOTPI   109

CHANTILLY, France. MUSÉE CONDAT
Manuscript no. 280 Ibid.
N: CaOTPI   110

CHARLEVILLE, France. BIBLIOTHÈQUE
MUNICIPALE
Breviarium Praemonstratense ms. 50 Ibid.
N: InNd   111

CLERMONT-FERRAND, France. BIBLIOTHÈQUE
MUNICIPALE
Manuscript no. 168 Ibid.
N: CaOTPI   112

DOLE, France. BIBLIOTHÈQUE
MUNICIPALE
Manuscript no. 79 Ibid.
N: CaOTPI   113

DOUAI, France. BIBLIOTHÈQUE MUNICIPALE
Manuscripts nos. 434, 454, 797 Ibid.
N: CaOTPI   114

DURHAM CATHEDRAL
Manuscript no. C. III. 15 Ibid.
N: CaOTPI   115

ERFURT, Germany. STADTBÜCHEREI
Manuscripts nos. CA F. 5, CA F. 133, CA F.
301, CA F. 393, CA Q. 18, CA Q. 220, CA Q.
257, CA Q. 268, CA Q. 270, CA O. 7, 58-60
Ibid.
N: CaOTPI   116

FLORENCE. BIBLIOTECA NAZIONALE
CENTRALE
Codices Magliabechiana XIX 166, 167 ItFBN
N: NjP 2 reels   117

GRENOBLE, France. BIBLIOTHÈQUE
MUNICIPALE
Manuscript no. 290 Ibid.
N: CaOTPI   118

GRENOBLE, France. BIBLIOTHÈQUE
MUNICIPALE
Manuscript no. 627 (391) Ibid.
N: DLC 1 reel   119

HEIDELBERG. UNIVERSITÄT
Manuscript no. 359.8 Ibid.
N: CaOTPI   120

INNSBRUCK, Austria. STADTBIBLIOTHEK
Manuscript no. 495 Ibid.
N: CaOTPI   121

LAON, France. BIBLIOTHÈQUE
MUNICIPALE
Manuscript no. 431 Ibid.
N: CaOTPI   122

LE MANS, France. BIBLIOTHÈQUE
MUNICIPALE
Manuscript no. 231 Ibid.
N: CaOTPI   123

LENINGRAD. PUBLICHNAIA BIBLIOTEKA
Hebrew manuscripts: Firkowicz 268, Melita
de Sahbi; Antonin 236 Ibid.
N: NNJ   124
P: NNJ

LEYDEN. RIJKSUNIVERSITEIT. BIBLIOTHEEK
Palestinian Talmud Ibid.
N: ?   125
P: NNJ

LINCOLN CATHEDRAL
Defensorium super redelaciones beate
Birgitte Ibid.
N: CtY   126

LINCOLN CATHEDRAL
Manuscripts nos. 15, 23, 24, 25, 26, 27, 159
Ibid.
N: CaOTPI   127

LOIRET, France (Dept.). ARCHIVES
Material re: University of Orleans, 1306-1583
Ibid.
N: InNd   128

MADRID. BIBLIOTECA NACIONAL
Manuscript no. 65 SpBN
N: CaOTPI   129

MODENA. BIBLIOTECA ESTENSE
Manuscript: Lat. 568, 51 p. Ibid.
N: priv.   130
P: ICN

MONTE CASSINO (Benedictine monastery)
Codex 871, 96 p. Ibid.
N: priv.   131
P: NIC

MOSCOW. PUBLICHNAIA BIBLIOTEKA (Lenin
Library)
Hebrew codices from Baron David Guenzberg
Collection, 289, 476, 512, 554, 594, 652, 705
778, 1332 Ibid.
N: ?   132
P: NNJ

MUNICH. BAYERISCHE STAATSBIBLIOTHEK
Codex Hebr. 216 Ibid.
N: NNJ   133

MUNICH. BAYERISCHE STAATSBIBLIOTHEK
Manuscripts nos. 54, 83, 478, CLM 317, CLM
518, CLM 761, CLM 817, CLM 2580, CLM
5304, CLM 5354, CLM 7335, CLM 8001, CLM
9559, CLM 14185, CLM 15824, CLM 17741,
CLM 18170, CLM 18478, CLM 19551, CLM
24801 Ibid.
N: CaOTPI   134

MUNICH. BAYERISCHE STAATSBIBLIOTHEK
Manuscripts nos. 12612, 14268, 19602, 19551
Ibid.
DCO: CaOTPI   135

MUNICH. BAYERISCHE STAATSBIBLIOTHEK
Manuscripts nos. CLM 444, CLM 6211, CLM

8482, CLM 15331, CLM 17272, CLM 22363 b
Ibid.
N: InND   136

MUNICH. UNIVERSITÄT
Ramon Lull material 10548, 10549 Ibid.
N: InNd   137

NEWBERRY LIBRARY, Chicago
Miscellaneous codex containing a number of
medieval texts of literary importance, among
them St. Brandan and St. Isodorus, 11th -12th
cents. ICN
N: ICN 1 reel   138

ORLEANS, France. BIBLIOTHÈQUE
MUNICIPALE
Manuscript no. 221 Ibid.
N: CaOTPI   139

ORTHODOX EASTERN CHURCH. LITURGY
AND RITUAL
Menaion Goislin Gr. 152 FrBN
N: NcD 1 reel   140

ORTHODOX EASTERN CHURCH. LITURGY AND
RITUAL
Menologion MdBWA
N: DDO   141

OXFORD. UNIVERSITY. ALL SOULS COLLEGE
Manuscript no. 72 UKOAS
N: CaOTPI   142

OXFORD. UNIVERSITY. BALLIOL COLLEGE
Manuscripts nos. 65, 112, 173 A, 207, 212,
214, 232 A, 232 B, 245, 246, 287, 299 Ibid.
N: CaOTPI   143

OXFORD. UNIVERSITY. BODLEIAN LIBRARY
Manuscript Laud misc. 686 UKO
N: InU   144

OXFORD. UNIVERSITY. BODLEIAN LIBRARY
Manuscripts: Add. C. 271, Can. Class. Lat.
291, Can. misc. 43, Can. misc. 562, Digby 55,
Digby 207, Digby 220, Laud misc. 146,
Lyell 49 UKO
N: CaOTPI   145

OXFORD. UNIVERSITY. CORPUS CHRISTI
COLLEGE
Manuscripts nos. 225, 280 UKOCC
N: CaOTPI   146

OXFORD. UNIVERSITY. MERTON COLLEGE
Manuscripts nos. 100, 106, 113, 135, 138,
280, 289, 292, 295 UKOME
N: CaOTPI   147

OXFORD. UNIVERSITY. ORIEL COLLEGE
Manuscript no. 15 UKOOC
N: CaOTPI   148

PADUA. UNIVERSITÀ
Matricula theologorum, med. et philos.
Germanorum   Ms. 466 Ibid.
N: DLC 1 reel   149

PARIS. BIBLIOTHÈQUE DE L'ARSENAL
Manuscripts nos. 263, 265, 379, 379 B, 386,
526, 561, 767, 769, 1117 Ibid.
N: CaOTPI   150

PARIS. BIBLIOTHÈQUE DE L'ARSENAL
Manuscript no. 2889, ca. 13th cent. Ibid.
N: DLC 1 reel   151

PARIS. BIBLIOTHÈQUE DE L'ARSENAL
Material re: Sorbonne and University of Paris
Ibid.
N: InNd   152

PARIS. BIBLIOTHÈQUE MAZARINE
Manuscripts nos. 180, 656, 657, 709, 787,
795, 873, 889, 894, 915, 962, 991, 3456, 3458,
3459, 3460, 3461, 3472, 3473, 3477, 3481,
3498, 3516, 3521, 3816 Ibid.
N: CaOTPI   153

PARIS. BIBLIOTHÈQUE NATIONALE
Manuscripts: Français, 241, 423, 565, 572, 1051,
1082, 1083, 1166, 1169, 1534, 1543, 1728, 2146,
2147, 2240, 3892, 12440, 12594, 20330, 23114,
24274, 24278, 24313; Français, Nouvelles Acqui-

MUSLIM WORLD

TIBET

Collections

CHINA

Government Records

Church Records

Personal Papers

Collections

College Records

WEST CHINA UNION UNIVERSITY, Chengtu,
Szechwan
Archives, minutes, reports
N: MH 2 reels   198

MONGOLIA

Institutions

MONGOLSKAIA NARODNO-REVOLIUTSIONNAIA
PARTIIA (Mongolian People's Party)
Protocols of 1st Assembly and 3rd Congress,
1924 (typescript translation) CSt-H
N: CSt-H 2 reels   199

JAPAN

Government Records

JAPAN. ARMY AND NAVY
Archives, 1868-1945 [unk.]
N: DLC reels 1-93, 101-141, 201-229
P: DLC   200

JAPAN. MINISTRY OF FOREIGN AFFAIRS
Records, 1867-1945 Ibid.
N: DLC 2116 reels   201

Described in Checklist of Archives in the
Japanese Ministry of Foreign Affairs

SUPREME COMMANDER FOR THE ALLIED
POWERS
Miscellaneous papers on Japan before and
during World War II, 1945-1948, 1 v. Ibid.
N: CU   202

U. S. DEPT. OF STATE. OFFICE OF INTELLI-
GENCE RESEARCH
The place of foreign trade in the Japanese
economy, 1946 Ibid.
N: CU 1 reel   203

U. S. NATIONAL ARCHIVES
List of captured Japanese records transferred
from the Department of the Army to the National Archives, 1868-1945, 1 v. DNA
N: CU 1 reel   204

Church Records

CHURCH OF JESUS CHRIST OF LATTER-DAY
SAINTS. JAPANESE MISSION
Records, 1902-1951 USlC
N: USlGS 1 reel   205

Personal Papers

MURRAY, DAVID, 1830-1905
Papers (on education in Japan), 1873-1879 DLC
N: CU 2 reels   206

SPROSTON, JOHN GLENDY, 1828-1862
Perry's visit to Japan; a journal, 1854, 105 p.
DLC
N: NNC   207

VERBECK, GUIDO HERMAN FRIDOLIN,
1830-1898
Letters from Japan, 1860-1898, 800 p. Board
of Foreign Missions of the Reformed Church
of America
N: CU   208

Business Papers

DE-SHIMA, Japan. FACTORIJ VAN DE
OOSTINDISCHE COMPAGNIE
Daily register, 1853-1860; despatches and
instructions, 1850-1854 NeHAR
N: DLC 5 reels   209

MALAYA

Church Records

MALACCA. ENGLISH EPISCOPAL CHURCH
Vital records, 1642-1888 NeHAR
N: USlGS 1 reel   210

THE PHILIPPINES

Government Records

MEXICO. ARCHIVO GENERAL DE LA NACIÓN
Ramo civil. Documentos de Filipinas MxAGN
N: ICN 31 reels   211

SPAIN. ARCHIVO GENERAL DE INDIAS, Seville
Audiencias. Filipinas. Selections from v. 1, 6,
12, 21, 74, 76, 77, 79, 80, 84, 85 SpAGI
N: ICN 5 reels   212

SPAIN. ARCHIVO GENERAL DE INDIAS, Seville
Audiencias. Filipinas. Two letters of Melchor
de Avilos, 1583; manuscript, 1597; documents
re: tributes, late 16th cent. SpAGI
N: DLC 5 feet   213
PP: DLC
N: ? 17 feet
P: DLC
PP: DLC
DCO: DLC 10 sheets

U. S. WAR DEPT.
Philippine Insurgent records, 1895-1901;
associated records of the War Department,
1900-1906 DNA
N: DNA 89 reels [M-254]   214

Personal Papers

LEROY, JAMES A.
Travelog of Philippines trip with Taft, 1905,
13 folders MiU
N: NcD 1 reel   215

Collections

SPAIN. ARCHIVO HISTÓRICO NACIONAL,
Madrid
Expulsum temporalites: selections re: Jesuits
in the Philippines Ibid.
N: ICN 1 reel   216

INDIA

Indian Material

Indian material has been made a separate section
since reports show that such material is used in
ways different from European language material.

BRAHMANAS. SATAPATHABRAHMANA
Satapathabrahmana, books 1-14 Universitäts-
bibliothek, Tübingen
N: MoSW 2 reels   217

KAVI SEKHARA
Gopala-vijaya, 99 p. IiCU
N: MH   218

PURANĀS. PADMAPURĀNA
Padma-purana or Manasa mangala. Bengali
version of Dvija Bamsidasa, 229 ll. ms. 27
of Bangiya Sahitya Parisat
N: MH   219

SIDDHANTA SARASVATI
Brhat-narodya-purana, 148 p. Asiatic Society
of Bengal
N: MH   220

UDDAVA-DASA
Braja-mangala (Life of Locana-dasa), 20 p.
IiCU
N: MH   221

Government Records

GREAT BRITAIN. INDIA OFFICE. RECORD
BRANCH
Manuscript records of British shipping, mainly
from the East Indies, 17th and 18th cents.
UKLBM
N: ICU 2 reels   222

Church Records

CHURCH OF JESUS CHRIST OF LATTER-DAY
SAINTS. INDIA
Records: East Indian Mission, 1852-1855;
Karachi Branch, 1903-1909 USlC
N: USlGS 1 reel   223

TRANQUEBAR, India. JERUSALEMS KIRKAN
Vital records, 1707-1818 DaKL
N: USlGS 1 reel   224

TRANQUEBAR, India. ZIONS KIRKE
Vital records, 3 v. DaKL
N: USlGS 1 reel   225

Business Papers

DAENDELS, HERMAN WILLEM, 1762-1818,
Governor General of the East Indies
In letters on commercial relations, 1807-1810
NeHAR
N: DLC 1 reel   226

EAST INDIA COMPANY (English), 1601-1857
Abstracts of letters received, selections,
1754-1775 Commonwealth Relations Office,
London
N: DLC 3 reels   227
P: DLC

EAST INDIA COMPANY (English), 1601-1857
Records, 1703-1750 London, India Office
Library
N: priv. 15 reels   228
P: ICU

Collections

GOA. ARQUIVO HISTÓRICO
Livros das monções do reino. Libro 14-20,
1630-1635 Ibid.
N: ICN 10 reels   229

LAMBETH PALACE. LIBRARY
Account of occurrences in the East Indies, Fort
St. George, India, May 12, 1693 UKLLam
N: CtY 1 reel   230

Ships' Logs

With ships' logs are included journals, diaries,
and other records of voyages.

MASSACHUSETTS (Ship)
Journal: from Calcutta to Simon's Bay-Batavia-
Nagasaki, Japan, 1799-1800, 76 p. MSaP
N: NNC   231

TURKEY

Government Records

GREAT BRITAIN. PUBLIC RECORD OFFICE
State papers foreign (Turkey), 1621-1626
UKLPRO
N: CtY 8 reels   232

Church Records

CHURCH OF JESUS CHRIST OF LATTER-DAY
SAINTS. TURKISH MISSION
Records, early to 1919 USlC
N: USlGS 1 reel   233

Collections

PRINCETON UNIVERSITY. LIBRARY
Testament de Amyra Sulthan Nichhemedy,
empereur des Turcs (translation from
Italian into French of a news letter of
Sept. 12, 1481) Garret 168 NjP
N: NjP 1 reel   234

PALESTINE

Church Records

CHURCH OF JESUS CHRIST OF LATTER-DAY
SAINTS. PALESTINE
Records of Turkish, Syrian, Armenian,
Palestine-Syrian, and Near East Missions,
1886-1951
N: USlGS 11 reels   235

GREAT BRITAIN

Bibliography

LONDON. FRIENDS LIBRARY
Card catalog of printed matter, manuscripts,
pictorial matter, and maps, 85,000 items,
through 1941 UKLFS
N: UKLFS 19 reels   236
P: PHC

LONDON. ROYAL COLLEGE OF MUSIC
Catalogue of manuscripts, 1931, 784 p.
(typewritten) Ibid.
N: CU   237

OXFORD. UNIVERSITY. ALL SOULS COLLEGE
"Key to the arrangement of the [Charles
Richard] Vaughan papers" UKOAS
N: DLC 1 reel   238
P: DLC

WINDSOR CASTLE. LIBRARY
18th century map catalog Ibid.
N: DLC   239

Census

GREAT BRITAIN. CENSUS, 1851
Census returns: no. 10, Northern Division;
no. 8, Northwestern Division; no. 6, West
Midland Division; no. 9, Yorkshire Division;
no. 3, South Midland Division UKLPRO
N: USlGS 213 reels   240

Government Records

GREAT BRITAIN (Commonwealth)
List of suspected persons, 1655-1657, 5 v.
Add. ms. 34011-34015 UKLBM
N: CSmH 1 reel   241

GREAT BRITAIN. ASSIZES (Northamptonshire)
Placita Itineris Northampton, 1329 Add. ms.
5924 UKLBM
N: DLC 1 reel   242

GREAT BRITAIN. BOARD OF TRADE
Archive of Companies Registration Office,
Edinburgh, 1856-1951 Ibid.
N: CU-B 120 reels   243
P: CU-B

GREAT BRITAIN. BOARD OF TRADE
Archive of Companies Registration Office,
London, 1844-1951 Ibid.
N: CU-B 542 reels   244
P: CU-B

GREAT BRITAIN. BOARD OF TRADE. B.T. 148
Dissolved companies'files (B.T. 31) UKLPRO
N: CU-B 34 reels   245

GREAT BRITAIN. COUNCIL OF STATE
Journal of Richard Cromwell's Council
Longleat
N: CSmH 1 reel   246

GREAT BRITAIN. COURT OF CHANCERY
Chancery depositions (selections): 17 James I-
21 James I, 1619-1624   C 24 bundles 460-505
UKLPRO
N: CtY 50 reels   247

GREAT BRITAIN. COURT OF STAR CHAMBER
Book of accounts of the Lords' diet in Star
Chamber   Exchequer accounts 407/51-55
UKLPRO
N: CtY 5 reels *   248

GREAT BRITAIN. COURT OF STAR CHAMBER
Book of writs UKLPRO
N: CtY 33 reels*   249

GREAT BRITAIN. COURT OF STAR CHAMBER
Divers precedents and decisions,
transcribed in 1636 Landsdowne 639 UKLBM
N: CtY 1 reel*   250

GREAT BRITAIN. COURT OF STAR CHAMBER
Proceedings, ca. 1608-1609, case numbers
St. Ch. 8/161/1, 8/19/10 and calendar,
St. Ch. 8 UKLPRO
N: CtY 3 reels   251

GREAT BRITAIN. COURT OF STAR CHAMBER
Register of certificates by judges and law-
officers, 1593-1595 Add. ms. 37045 UKLBM
N: CtY 1 reel*   252

GREAT BRITAIN. COURT OF STAR CHAMBER
Report of trials, 1598-1616 Harleian 1330
UKLBM
N: CtY 1 reel   253

GREAT BRITAIN. EXCHEQUER
Bedfordshire subsidy rolls 56 Eliz. I
UKLPRO
N: CtY   254

GREAT BRITAIN. EXCHEQUER
Lay subsidy rolls, 1421-1471 UKLPRO
N: ICU 6 reels   255

GREAT BRITAIN. EXCHEQUER
Lists of taxpayers in levies, 14th and 15th
cents. UKLPRO
N: ICU 10 reels   256

GREAT BRITAIN. EXCHEQUER
Pipe rolls, E372/50-E372/53 UKLPRO
N: CtY   257

GREAT BRITAIN. EXCHEQUER. KING'S
REMEMBRANCER
Memoranda rolls 16217 Edward I
UKLPRO
N: CtY 88 frames   258

GREAT BRITAIN. EXCHEQUER. KING'S
REMEMBRANCER
Port books, London, 1600-1625 UKLPRO
N: CtY 2 reels   259

GREAT BRITAIN. EXCHEQUER. KING'S
REMEMBRANCER. E 190
Port books, London, 1693-1697, 1717 ff.
UKLPRO
N: OWoC*   260

GREAT BRITAIN. LORD HIGH CHANCELLOR
Libri Pacis, 1559, 1561, 1573/4, 1582, 1583/4,
1584/5, 1604 Landsdowne 1218, Egerton 2345,
Lansdowne 35, Harleian 474, Lansdowne 737,
Harleian 6822. 28 UKLBM
N: CSmH 3 reels   261

GREAT BRITAIN. LORD HIGH CHANCELLOR
Libri Pacis, 1573/4, 1575 (2), 1577, 1579/80,
1596 S.P.D.93, 104, 106, 121, 145, Elizabeth
Case F#11, S.P.D.33, C.93/13 UKLPRO
N: CSmH 2 reels   262

GREAT BRITAIN. LORD HIGH CHANCELLOR
Libri Pacis, 1632-1685 S.P.D. bk. 1, 405,
C 193/12 UKLPRO
N: CCH 1 reel   263

GREAT BRITAIN. LORD HIGH CHANCELLOR
Liber Pacis, 1653 D-8-1 UKC
N: CCH 30 feet   264

GREAT BRITAIN. MINISTRY OF INFORMATION
Official press releases, Jan.,1945-Apr.,1946
priv.
N: ICU 16 reels   265
P: NNC

GREAT BRITAIN. OFFICE OF THE REVELS
Losely manuscripts, ca. 1540-1580 UKLPRO
N: CaOKQ 2 reels   266

GREAT BRITAIN. PRIVY COUNCIL
Proceedings of the Lords of the Council
from the withdrawing of James II UKO
N: CSmH 32 frames   267

GREAT BRITAIN. PRIVY COUNCIL
Register, 1660-1667 UKLPRO
N: CSmH 2 reels 1821 frames   268

GREAT BRITAIN. PUBLIC RECORD OFFICE
Calendars of state papers, foreign, v.77, 80,
81, 94 UKLPRO
N: CtY 5 reels*   269

GREAT BRITAIN. PUBLIC RECORD OFFICE
Inquisitions post mortem for Henry and Robert
Bures, 16th cent. UKLPRO
N: ICU 1 reel   270

GREAT BRITAIN. PUBLIC RECORD OFFICE
State papers, domestic (selections), 1566-1584
UKLPRO
N: NNC 1 reel   271

GREAT BRITAIN. PUBLIC RECORD OFFICE
State papers, domestic (selections),
1619-1625 UKLPRO
N: CtY 13 reels   272

GREAT BRITAIN. PUBLIC RECORD OFFICE
State papers, domestic, Charles I, 1625-1649
UKLPRO
N: CtY 160 reels   273

Parliamentary Records

Both formal and informal journals of Parliament
are listed together, in chronological sequence.

BOWYER, ROBERT, d. 1622
Parliamentary diary, Jan. 21 - Mar. 24, 1606,
May 15 - July 3, 1607, 1 v.   priv.
DCO: MnU   274

BARRINGTON, Sir THOMAS
Notes of proceedings in the House of Commons,
1621 Hatfield Broad Oak Church, Essex, Eng.
DCO: DLC   275

GREAT BRITAIN. PARLIAMENT, 1621. HOUSE
OF COMMONS
Notes of proceedings, March 14-16, 1621, by
Edward Nicholas, 9 p.   UKPRO
DCO: MnU   276

RICHARDSON, THOMAS, Speaker of the House
of Commons
Collections on the procedure and privileges of
the House of Commons, 1621 (copied 1710)
Add. ms. 36856 UKLBM
N: CtY 1 reel   277

GREAT BRITAIN. PARLIAMENT, 1624-1625.
HOUSE OF COMMONS
Proceedings, Apr.,1624-Apr., 1625
N: CtY   278

PYM, JOHN, 1584-1643
Diary for Parliament of 1624 (typescript)
N: CtY   279

GREAT BRITAIN. PARLIAMENT, 1628
Notes on the Parliament of 1628, probably
made by Denzil Holles, 2 v.   Harleian 5324,
2313 UKLBM
DCO: MnU   280

GREAT BRITAIN. PARLIAMENT, 1628. HOUSE
OF COMMONS
Notes of debates, by Edward Nicholas,
March 21 - June 11, 1628, 91 ll. (partly in
shorthand) UKLPRO
DCO: MnU   281

GREAT BRITAIN. PARLIAMENT, 1628. HOUSE
OF COMMONS
Notes on the Parliament of 1628 by Sir Richard
Grosvenor, 4 v.   IrDT
DCO: MnU   282

GREAT BRITAIN. PARLIAMENT, 1628. HOUSE
OF COMMONS.
Proceedings, Mar. 17 - June 26, 1628

[Stationer's accounts of speeches.] MHi UKLIT
UKO
DCO: MnU 2 v. 283

GREAT BRITAIN. PARLIAMENT, 1629. HOUSE
OF COMMONS
Journal, ms. Jan. 20-Mar. 2, 1629, 43 p. Ibid.
DCO: MnU 284

GREAT BRITAIN. PARLIAMENT, 1629. HOUSE
OF COMMONS
Notes... by Sir Richard Grosvenor, 211 p.
IrDT
DCO: MnU 285

GREAT BRITAIN. PARLIAMENT, 1629. HOUSE
OF COMMONS
Notes of proceedings, taken by Edward Nicholas,
70 p. (partly in shorthand) UKLPRO
DCO: MnU 286

GREAT BRITAIN. PARLIAMENT, 1640-1648.
HOUSE OF COMMONS
Diary of proceedings...Oct. 8, 1642-July 8,
1647...by Laurence Whitacre, 1 v. Add. ms
31116 UKLBM
DCO: MnU
N: CtY 2 reels 287
P: MH

GREAT BRITAIN. PARLIAMENT. HOUSE OF
COMMONS. COMMITTEE ON PRIVILEGES
Corrected draft of proceedings, Feb. 26-
June 17, 1646 Add. ms. 28, 716 UKLBM
N: CtY 1 reel 288

GREAT BRITAIN. PARLIAMENT
Journal, 1652-1658
N: CtY 289

BRICKDALE, MATTHEW
Notes of proceedings in the House of Commons,
Nov., 1770 - May, 1774 (American selections)
priv.
N: DLC
PP: DLC 290

Borough and City Records

ABINGDON, Berks., Eng.
Borough records, 1650-1839 C.H. Reading
N: USIGS 4 reels 291

BREAGE, Cornwall, Eng.
Index to Chancery proceedings, plaintiffs, 1758-
1800 Ibid.
N: USIGS 4 reels 292

BREAGE, Cornwall, Eng.
List of deforciants taken from the Feet of Fines
Calendar, 1635 Ibid.
N: USIGS 1 reel 293

EXETER, Eng.
City archives, 1500-1640 Ibid.
N: ? 69 reels
P: MH 294

HEREFORD, Eng.
Freemen's list, 1709-1837; miscellaneous
records, 1605-1825 UKHfP
N: USIGS 2 reels 295

LONDON. CORPORATION
Journals and Repertories, 1640-1660 Ibid.
N: Ibid. 11 reels 296
P: CSmH

LONDON. CORPORATION
Letter book of the City of London, v. QQ,
1640-1647 UKLGU
N: IaU 9 film strips 297

MAIDENHEAD, see 455, under GREAT BRITAIN,
Parish Records

MELCOMBE REGIS, Dorsets., Eng.
Borough account and order book, 1568-1570
MH
N: DFo 1 reel 298

STRATFORD-UPON-AVON, Warwicks., Eng.
Borough records, 1553-1706 Ibid.
N: DFo 18 reels 299

WOKINGHAM, see 562, under GREAT BRITAIN,
Parish Records

Manorial Records

ASHBURY MANOR, Berks., Eng.
Court rolls, 1572-1841 C.H. Reading
N: USIGS 1 reel 300

ASHRIDGE MANOR, Berks., Eng.
Court books, 1621-1754 C.H. Reading
N: USIGS 1 reel 301

BENHAM VALENCE CUM WESTBROOK IN
SPEEN MANOR, Berks., Eng.
Court rolls, 1562-1838; account rolls, 1444-
1446, 1453 C.H. Reading
N: USIGS 1 reel 302

BIRLINGHAM MANOR, Birlingham, Eng.
Court rolls, 1626, 1635, 1639, n.d. Ibid.
PH
Ph: PSC-F 303

BLEWBURY MANOR, Berks., Eng.
Court books, 1710-1938 C.H. Reading
N: USIGS 3 reels 304

BLEWBURY (Prebendal) MANOR, Berks., Eng.
Court books, 1665-1938 C.H. Reading
N: USIGS 1 reel 305

BRIMPTON MANOR (formerly SHALFORD), Berks.,
Eng.
Manor rolls, 1347-1786 C.H. Reading
N: USIGS 2 reels 306

BRITISH MUSEUM
Charters and rolls relating chiefly to
Norfolk and Suffolk, 14th - 17th cents.
UKLBM
N: ICU 1 reel 307

BRITISH MUSEUM
Charters relating chiefly to the eastern
counties: Thornage, 1562-1653; Redgrave,
1561-1703 UKLBM
N: ICU 2 reels 308

COOKHAM MANOR, Berks., Eng.
Court rolls, 1759-1838 C.H. Reading
N: USIGS 6 reels 309

EAST AND WEST ENBORNE MANOR, Berks.
Eng.
Court rolls, 1663, 1720-1811, 1837-1841
C.H. Reading
N: USIGS 1 reel 310

ELLESMERE MANOR, Salop, Eng.
Wills, 1630-1857 UKAbN
N: USIGS 2 reels 311

GOODRICH MANOR, Herefs., Eng.
Court rolls, 1507-1544; records, 1689-1789
UKHfP
N: USIGS 2 reels 312

GREAT FARINGDON MANOR, Berks., Eng.
Court books, 1737-1859 C.H. Reading
N: USIGS 4 reels 313

HAMPSTEAD MARSHALL MANOR, Berks., Eng.
Court rolls, 1668-1840 C.H. Reading
N: USIGS 1 reel 314

HURST MANOR, Berks., Eng.
Court books, 1600-1930 C.H. Reading
N: USIGS 2 reels 315

INKPEN MANOR, Berks., Eng.
Court rolls, 1307-1840; account rolls, 1300-
1473; other records, 1408, 1579, 1740-1757
C.H. Reading
N: USIGS 1 reel 316

KINTBURY EATON MANOR (formerly HOLT),
Berks., Eng.
Court rolls, 1663-1811, 1837-1840
C.H. Reading
N: USIGS 1 reel 317

ORLETON MANOR, Herefs., Eng.
Court records, ca. 1623-1849 UKHfP
N: USIGS 2 reels 318

SHAW MANOR, Berks., Eng.
Account rolls, 1405-1529 C.H. Reading
N: USIGS 1 reel 319

SHRIVENHAM HUNDRED AND MANOR, Berks.,
Eng.
Court books, 1523-1862 C.H. Reading
N: USIGS 12 reels 320

UFFINGTON MANOR, Berks., Eng.
Court book, 1720-1811 C.H. Reading
N: USIGS 1 reel 321

County Records

BERKSHIRE, Eng.
Court order books, 1703-1749, 1771-1853;
court records, 1737-1749, 1752, 1766, 1772-
1773; Parliamentary electors, 1839-1851; oaths
of allegiance, 1732-1868; militia records, 1715,
1758, 1892; vital records [Poor Law Unions],
1835-1943 C.H. Reading
N: USIGS 26 reels 322

CUMBERLAND Co., Eng.
Militia rolls, 1813-1831 C.H. Carlisle
N: USIGS 3 reels 323

DEVONSHIRE, Eng. QUARTER SESSIONS
Records, 1592-1633 C.H. Exeter
N: CtY 11 reels 324

DURHAM Co., Eng.
Poll books for Shire, 1820-1892; also Durham
burgesses, 1842-1877 UKSuP
N: USIGS 8 reels 325

ESSEX Co., Eng. RECORD OFFICE
Calendar of Essex Quarter Sessions Rolls,
1556-1714 UKCdRO
N: CSmH 15 reels 326
P: MH

ESSEX Co., Eng. RECORD OFFICE
Manorial surveys and deeds, 1100-1850
UKCdRO
N: USIGS 9 reels 327

ESSEX Co., Eng. RECORD OFFICE
Records of Essex overseers of the poor,
1779-1835; Essex militia returns, 1809-
1813 UKCdRO
N: USIGS 7 reels 328

HEREFORDSHIRE, Eng. QUARTER SESSIONS
Records, 1655-1888 C.H. Hereford
N: USIGS 66 reels 329

LANCASHIRE, Eng.
Jury lists of hundreds, 1778-1810 UKPrRO
N: USIGS 12 reels 330

LANCASHIRE, Eng. QUARTER SESSIONS
Order books, 1626-1888 UKPrRO
N: USIGS 66 reels 331

WESTMORELAND Co., Eng.
Land tax assessments, 1773-1832; poll books,
1820-1835; jury lists, 1775-1805, 1838, 1844
C.H. Kendal
N: USIGS 7 reels 332

WORCESTERSHIRE. RECORD OFFICE
Inventory of records, 5 v. UKWrRO
N: USIGS 3 reels 333

Parish Records

Since English parishes are both civil and religious
bodies, with intermingled records, two general
descriptive terms are used: parish registers and
the all-inclusive title, parish records. Only when
a single type of records has been filmed is the name
of that type of record used in place of parish records.

AINSWORTH, Lancs., Eng.
Parish registers, 1727-1948 Ibid.
N: USIGS 2 reels 334

ALDERMASTON, Berks., Eng.
Parish registers, 1558-1882; parish records,
1719-1918 C.H. Reading
N: USIGS 4 reels 335

ALDWORTH, Berks., Eng.
Parish registers, 1556-1910; parish records,
1707-1900 C.H. Reading
N: USIGS 1 reel   336

ALL SAINTS PARISH, Childwell, Lancs., Eng.
Parish registers, 1557-1753, 877 p. Ibid.
N: USIGS 1 reel   337

APPLEFORD, Berks., Eng.
Overseers' accounts, 1749-1780 C.H. Reading
N: USIGS 1 reel   338

APPLETON WITH EATON, Berks., Eng.
Parish registers, 1569-1848 C.H. Reading
N: USIGS 1 reel   339

ARBORFIELD, Berks., Eng.
Parish registers, 1705-1817; churchwardens'
accounts, 1740-1874 C.H. Reading
N: USIGS 1 reel   340

ARDINGTON, Berks., Eng.
Parish registers, 1674-1815; parish records,
1778-1889 C.H. Reading
N: USIGS 3 reels   341

ASHBURY, Berks., Eng.
Parish registers, 1704-1812; parish records,
1721-1862 C.H. Reading
N: USIGS 4 reels   342

ASTON INGHAM, Herefs., Eng.
Parish registers, 1739-1881 Dymock
N: USIGS 1 reel   343

ASTON TIRROLD, Berks., Eng.
Parish registers, 1726-1812; parish records,
1705-1936 C.H. Reading
N: USIGS 1 reel   344

ASTON UPTHORPE, Berks., Eng.
Churchwardens' accounts, 1801-1860; glebe and
tithe accounts, 1795-1839 C.H. Reading
N: USIGS 1 reel   345

BARNBY, Suffolk, Eng.
Parish registers, 1554-1949 Ibid.
N: USIGS 1 reel   346

BASILDON, Berks., Eng.
Parish registers, 1538-1813; parish records,
1775-1879 C.H. Reading
N: USIGS 1 reel   347

BEECH HILL, Berks., Eng.
Parish records, 1767-1896 C.H. Reading
N: USIGS 3 reels   348

BEENHAM, Berks., Eng.
Parish registers, 1573-1812; parish records,
1772, 1822, 1835 C.H. Reading
N: USIGS 1 reel   349

BENSINGTON, Oxon., Eng.
Parish registers, 1565-1812; parish accounts,
1707-1778; charity accounts book, 1813-1911
C.H. Reading
N: USIGS 1 reel   350

BESSELSLEIGH, Berks., Eng.
Tithe award, 1841-1842 C.H. Reading
N: USIGS 1 reel   351

BILLINGHAM, Durham, Eng.
Parish registers, 1570-1948 Ibid.
N: USIGS 1 reel   352

BINFIELD, Berks., Eng.
Parish registers, 1538-1812; parish records,
1648-1923 C.H. Reading
N: USIGS 3 reels   353

BLACKBURN, Lancs., Eng.
Poor law documents, 1695-1825 UKPrRO
N: USIGS 2 reels   354

BLAISDON, Gloucs., Eng.
Parish registers, 1635-1863 Dymock
N: USIGS 1 reel   355

BLEWBURY, Berks., Eng.
Parish registers, 1588-1674, 1720-1906;
parish records, 1665-1925 C.H. Reading
N: USIGS 3 reels   356

BOLTON-LE-SANDS, Lancs., Eng.
Parish accounts, 1750-1839 Kendal
N: USIGS 1 reel   357

BOXFORD, Berks., Eng.
Church rate, 1645; poor rate, 1708
C.H. Reading
N: USIGS 1 reel   358

BRADFIELD, Berks., Eng.
Parish registers, 1539-1835; parish records,
1751-1872 C.H. Reading
N: USIGS 4 reels   359

BRAY, Berks., Eng.
Parish registers, 1653-1812; parish records,
1602-1851 C.H. Reading
N: USIGS 6 reels   360

BRIGHTWALTON, Berks., Eng.
Parish registers, 1641-1826; parish records,
1700-1821 C.H. Reading
N: USIGS 1 reel   361

BRIGHTWELL, Berks., Eng.
Parish records, 1666-1836, 1861-1895; tithe
award, 1839-1841 C.H. Reading
N: USIGS 1 reel   362

BRINDLE, Lancs., Eng.
Parish registers, 1714-1948; parish records,
1775-1895 UKPrRO
N: USIGS 2 reels   363

BRITISH MUSEUM
Old charters and manuscripts re: Dymock,
Gloucs. Add. ms. 15668 UKLBM
N: 364

BUCKLAND, Berks., Eng.
Parish registers, 1691-1855; parish records,
1660-1666, 1693-1890 C.H. Reading
N: USIGS 4 reels   365

BUCKLEBURY, Berks., Eng.
Settlement papers, 1772-1841 C.H. Reading
N: USIGS 1 reel   366

BULLEY, Gloucs., Eng.
Parish registers, 1673-1876 Dymock
N: USIGS 1 reel   367

BURGHFIELD, Berks., Eng.
Parish registers, 1559-1643, 1662-1921;
parish records, 1661-1695, 1706-1871
C.H. Reading
N: USIGS 7 reels   368

BUSCOT, Berks., Eng.
Parish registers, 1676-1812; parish records,
1749-1899 C.H. Reading
N: USIGS 1 reel   369

CHADDLEWORTH, Berks., Eng.
Parish records, 1801-1869 C.H. Reading
N: USIGS 1 reel   370

CHARNEY BASSETT, Berks., Eng.
Marriages, 1754-1811 C.H. Reading
N: USIGS 1 reel   371

CHILDREY, Berks., Eng.
Parish registers, 1558-1812; churchwardens'
accounts, 1558-1688 C.H. Reading
N: USIGS 1 reel   372

CHURCH, Lancs., Eng.
Parish registers, 1746-1948 UKPrRO
N: USIGS 8 reels   373

CHURCHAM, Gloucs., Eng.
Parish registers, 1541-1856 Dymock
N: USIGS 1 reel   374

CLEWER, Berks., Eng.
Parish registers, 1653-1814; parish records,
1820-1841 C.H. Reading
N: USIGS 2 reels   375

COCKERHAM, Lancs., Eng.
Parish registers, 1659-1893; churchwardens'
accounts, 1738-1907 UKPrRO
N: USIGS 2 reels   376

COLESHILL, Berks., Eng.
Parish registers, 1559-1812; glebe and tithe,
1752-1799; churchwardens' accounts, 1656-
1677; parish records, 1693-1856 C.H. Reading
N: USIGS 1 reel   377

COMPTON, Berks., Eng.
Parish registers, 1553-1812 C.H. Reading
N: USIGS 1 reel   378

COMPTON BEAUCHAMP, Berks., Eng.
Parish registers, 1551-1812 C.H. Reading
N: USIGS 1 reel   379

COOKHAM, Berks., Eng.
Parish registers, 1563-1812 (transcript);
parish records, 1730-1739, 1774-1778, 1800-
1863 C.H. Reading
N: USIGS 4 reels   380

CROSTON, Lancs., Eng.
Parish registers, 1728-1948; parish records,
1681-1855 UKPrRO
N: USIGS 5 reels   381

CROWMARSH GIFFORD, Oxon., Eng.
Parish registers, 1575-1919; settlement
records, 1715-1755 C.H. Reading
N: USIGS 1 reel   382

CROXTON, Cambs., Eng.
Parish registers, 1538-1949 Ibid.
N: USIGS 1 reel   383

CUMNOR, Berks., Eng.
Parish records, 1654-1778, 1796-1846
C.H. Reading
N: USIGS 2 reels   384

DENCHWORTH, Berks., Eng.
Parish registers, 1538-1812; parish records,
1764-1893 C.H. Reading
N: USIGS 1 reel   385

DENT, Yorks., Eng.
Parish register, 1611-1837 Ibid.
N: USIGS 1 reel   386

DINGLEY, Northants, Eng.
Parish register, 1580-1812 UKHfP
N: USIGS 1 reel   387

DONNINGTON, Gloucs., Eng.
Parish registers, 1755-1900 Dymock
N: USIGS 1 reel   388

DRAYTON, Berks., Eng.
Parish records, 1658-1858 C.H. Reading
N: USIGS 2 reels   389

DYMOCK, Gloucs., Eng.
Parish registers, 1538-1901; parish records,
1592-1870 Dymock
N: USIGS 8 reels   390

EAST CHALLOW, Berks., Eng.
Parish registers, 1711-1812 C.H. Reading
N: USIGS 1 reel   391

EAST GARSTON, Berks., Eng.
Parish registers, 1554-1812 C.H. Reading
N: USIGS 1 reel   392

EAST HENDRED, Berks., Eng.
Parish registers, 1538-1837; parish records,
1785-1884 C.H. Reading
N: USIGS 2 reels   393

EAST LOCKINGE, Berks., Eng.
Parish registers, 1546-1812; charity accounts,
1692-1882 C.H. Reading
N: USIGS 1 reel   394

EASTHAMPSTEAD, Berks., Eng.
Parish registers, 1558-1900; parish records,
1699-1858 C.H. Reading
N: USIGS 1 reel   395

EATON HASTINGS, Berks., Eng.
Parish registers, 1574-1812; parish records,
1709-1930 C.H. Reading
N: USIGS 1 reel   396

ECCLESTON, Lancs., Eng.
Parish registers, 1701-1938 UKPrRO
N: USIGS 3 reels   397

ELTISLEY, Cambs., Eng.
Parish registers, 1653-1949 Ibid.
N: USIGS 1 reel   398

ENBORNE, Berks., Eng.
Parish register, 1666-1832; vestry minutes,
1850-1905 C.H. Reading
N: USIGS 1 reel   399

ENGLEFIELD, Berks., Eng.
Parish registers, 1559-1846; parish records,

1663-1854   C.H. Reading
N: USIGS 3 reels   400

EUXTON, Lancs., Eng.
Parish registers, 1774-1947 Ibid.
N: USIGS 2 reels   401

FARINGDON, Berks., Eng.
Parish registers, 1653-1812   C.H. Reading
N: USIGS 1 reel   402

FARNBOROUGH, Berks., Eng.
Parish register, 1739-1812   C.H. Reading
N: USIGS 1 reel   403

FINCHAMPSTEAD, Berks., Eng.
Parish registers, 1653-1838; parish records,
1705-1868   C.H. Reading
N: USIGS 2 reels   404

FLAUNDEN, Herts., Eng.
Parish register, 1729-1947 Ibid.
N: USIGS 1 reel   405

FLAXLEY, Gloucs., Eng.
Parish registers, 1564-1860   Dymock
N: USIGS 1 reel   406

FRAMPTON, Lincs., Eng.
Parish registers, 1558-1949 Ibid.
N: USIGS 2 reels   407

FRESSINGFIELD, Suffolk, Eng.
Parish registers, 1554-1949; tithes and
accounts, 1634-1812   Ibid.
N: USIGS 3 reels   408

FRIESTHORPE, Lincs., Eng.
Parish registers, 12th cent., 1620-1821
Ibid.
N: priv. 1 reel   409
P: USIGS

FRILSHAM, Berks., Eng.
Parish registers, 1711-1837; churchwardens'
accounts, 1769-1847   C.H. Reading
N: USIGS 1 reel   410

GARFORD, Berks., Eng.
Parish registers, 1733-1812; parish records,
1703-1897   C.H. Reading
N: USIGS 1 reel   411

GOOSNARGH, Lancs., Eng.
Parish registers, 1730-1948; churchwardens'
accounts, 1779-1939 UKPrRO
N: USIGS 2 reels   412

GREAT COXWELL, Berks., Eng.
Parish registers, 1558-1892; parish records,
1772-1936   C.H. Reading
N: USIGS 1 reel   413

GREAT HARWOOD, Lancs., Eng.
Parish registers, 1813-1948 UKPrRO
N: USIGS 6 reels   414

GREAT SOMERFORD, Wilts., Eng.
Parish registers, 1707-1947 Ibid.
N: USIGS 1 reel   415

GREATFORD WITH WILSTHORPE, Lincs., Eng.
Parish registers, 1755-1812 Ibid.
N: priv. 1 reel   416
P: USIGS

GREENHAM, Berks., Eng.
Parish registers, 1706-1812 C.H. Reading
N: USIGS 1 reel   417

GRINGLEY ON THE HILL, Notts., Eng.
Parish register, 1650-1949 Ibid.
N: USIGS 1 reel   418

HAGBOURNE, Berks., Eng.
Parish registers, 1661-1837; parish records,
1688-1769, 1823-1848   C.H. Reading
N: USIGS 1 reel   419

HALTWHISTLE, Northumberland, Eng.
Parish registers, 1691-1733   UKENRH
N: USIGS 1 reel   420

HAMPSTEAD MARSHALL, Berks., Eng.
Parish registers, 1675-1812   C.H. Reading
N: USIGS 1 reel   421

HAMPSTEAD NORRIS, Berks., Eng.
Parish registers, 1538-1892; churchwardens'
accounts, 1636-1939   C.H. Reading
N: USIGS 2 reels   422

HATLEY ST. GEORGE, Cambs., Eng.
Parish registers, 1580-1837 (includes East
Hatley) Ibid.
N: USIGS 1 reel   423

HIGHNAM, Gloucs., Eng.
Marriages, 1852-1860   Dymock
N: USIGS 1 reel   424

HINDLEY, Lancs., Eng.
Parish registers, 1698-1948 Ibid.
N: USIGS 8 reels   425

HINTON WALDRIST, Berks., Eng.
Parish registers, 1559-1812; parish records,
1641-1826   C.H. Reading
N: USIGS 1 reel   426

HOLY TRINITY MINORIES, London, Eng.
Parish registers, 1563-1898 Ibid.
N: USIGS 3 reels   427

HORSLEY, Gloucs., Eng.
Parish registers, 1587-1881 Ibid.
N: USIGS 2 reels   428

HULL, Yorks., Eng. DAGGER-LANE CHURCH
Parish registers and records, 1746-1831 Ibid.
N: USIGS 1 reel   429

HUNGERFORD, Berks., Eng.
Parish registers, 1559-1813; parish records,
1582-1856; borough records, 1582-1877
C.H. Reading
N: USIGS 20 reels   430

HURLEY, Berks., Eng.
Parish registers, 1560-1915; parish records,
1698-1901   C.H. Reading
N: USIGS 1 reel   431

HURST, Berks., Eng.
Parish registers, 1585-1812; parish records,
1603, 1676-1875   C.H. Reading
N: USIGS 2 reels   432

INKPEN, Berks., Eng.
Parish registers, 1633-1812 C.H. Reading
N: USIGS 1 reel   433

KEMPLEY, Gloucs., Eng.
Parish register, 1677-1861 Dymock
N: USIGS 1 reel   434

KENDAL, Westmoreland, Eng.
Papist estates, 1717; workhouse deaths, 1636-
1844; Friends' burials, 1865-1870; Parkside
cemetery burials, 1855-1953 Ibid.
N: USIGS 5 reels   435

KINGSTON LISLE AND FAWLER, Berks., Eng.
Parish registers, 1559-1888; parish records,
1704-1908   C.H. Reading
N: USIGS 3 reels   436

KIRTON, Lincs., Eng.
Parish registers, 1561-1949 Ibid.
N: USIGS 2 reels   437

LASSINGTON, Gloucs., Eng.
Parish registers, 1655-1883 Dymock
N: USIGS 1 reel   438

LATIMER, Bucks., Eng.
Parish register, 1756-1949, 370 p. Ibid.
N: USIGS 1 reel   439

LEA, Gloucs., Eng.
Parish registers, 1581-1895 Dymock
N: USIGS 1 reel   440

LETCOMBE REGIS, Berks., Eng.
Vestry minutes, 1883-1945 C.H. Reading
N: USIGS 1 reel   441

LEYLAND, Lancs., Eng.
Parish registers, 1736-1947; parish records,
1736-1872 Ibid.
N: USIGS 9 reels   442

LITTLE COXWELL, Berks., Eng.
Parish registers, 1582-1812; parish records,
1786-1879   C.H. Reading
N: USIGS 1 reel   443

LITTLE DEAN, Gloucs., Eng.
Parish register, 1684-1947 Ibid.
N: USIGS 1 reel   444

LITTLE SOMERFORD, Wilts., Eng.
Parish register, 1708-1947 Ibid.
N: USIGS 1 reel   445

LITTLE WITTENHAM, Berks., Eng.
Parish registers, 1538-1836; parish records,
1704-1745, 1769-1836   C.H. Reading
N: USIGS 1 reel   446

LIVERPOOL, Eng.
Parish registers: All Souls, 1853-1923; St.
Albans, 1846-1941; St. Bartholomew, 1841-
1928; St. George, 1734-1897; St. John's,
1785-1898; St. Martin-in-the-Fields, 1896-
1946; St. Mathias, 1534-1944; St. Matthew's,
1891-1915; St. Nicholas, 1659-1948; St. Paul's,
1769-1901; St. Peter's, 1704-1919; St. Titus,
1865-1917 Ibid.
N: USIGS   447

LIVERPOOL, Eng.
Records: Free Cemetery, 1806-1905; Rice Lane
Cemetery, 1861-1907; St. James Cemetery,
1829-1936 Ibid.
N: USIGS 24 reels   448

LONCOT, Berks., Eng.
Parish registers, 1664-1812   C.H. Reading
N: USIGS 1 reel   449

LONG WITTENHAM, Berks., Eng.
Parish registers, 1561-1629, 1737-1884; parish
records, 1690-1733, 1835-1875   C.H. Reading
N: USIGS 1 reel   450

LONGHAM, Norfolk, Eng.
Parish registers, 1558-1948 Ibid.
N: USIGS 2 reels   451

LONGWORTH, Berks., Eng.
Parish registers, 1559-1812; vestry minutes,
1818-1891   C.H. Reading
N: USIGS 1 reel   452

LOWDHAM, Notts., Eng.
Parish register, 1559-1942 Ibid.
N: USIGS 2 reels   453

LYFORD, Berks., Eng.
Clothing club records, 1857-1875
C.H. Reading
N: USIGS 1 reel   454

MAIDENHEAD, Berks., Eng.
Parish registers, 1795-1823; register of Free-
men, 1755-1834; borough records, 1633-1835
C.H. Reading
N: USIGS 3 reels   455

MANCHESTER, Eng.
Apprentice indentures, 1800-1830, 600 p.
UKMP
N: USIGS 3 reels   456

MANCHESTER, Eng. COLLEGIATE CHURCH
Parish register, 1654-1661 Ibid.
DCO: UKMP   457
N: USIGS

MANCHESTER, Eng. ST. JOHN AND ST. PETER'S
CHURCH
Parish registers, 1769-1928 Ibid.
N: USIGS 8 reels   458

MANCHESTER, Eng. WORKHOUSE
Religious creed register, 1881-1914 UKMP
N: USIGS 2 reels   459

MARCHAM, Berks., Eng.
Parish registers, 1658-1815   C.H. Reading
N: USIGS 1 reel   460

MARLBOROUGH, Wilts., Eng.
Parish registers: St. Mary, 1602-1894; St.
Peter and St. Paul, 1611-1909 Ibid.
N: USIGS 4 reels   461

MEDMENHAM, Bucks., Eng.
Poor rates, 1837-1843 C.H. Reading
N: USIGS 1 reel   462

MIDGHAM, Berks., Eng.
Parish records, 1717-1897 C.H. Reading
N: USIGS 2 reels   463

MILTON, Berks., Eng.
Parish registers, 1654-1814; parish records, 1742-1844 C.H. Reading
N: USIGS 1 reel   464

MINSTERWORTH, Gloucs., Eng.
Parish registers, 1633-1856 Dymock
N: USIGS 1 reel   465

MITCHELDEAN, Gloucs., Eng.
Parish registers, 1680-1877 Dymock
N: USIGS 1 reel   466

MOULSFORD, Berks., Eng.
Parish registers, 1754-1837 C.H. Reading
N: USIGS 1 reel   467

NEWBURY, Berks., Eng.
Borough records, 1676-1877 C.H. Reading
N: USIGS 10 reels   468

NEWENT, Gloucs., Eng.
Parish registers, 1672-1895 Dymock
N: USIGS 2 reels   469

NEWNHAM MURREN, Oxon., Eng.
Parish registers, 1678-1837; churchwardens' accounts, 1751-1893 C.H. Reading
N: USIGS 1 reel   470

NORTH COVE, Suffolk, Eng.
Parish registers, 1696-1948 Ibid.
N: USIGS 1 reel   471

NORTH ELHAM, Norfolk, Eng.
Parish register, 1538-1934 Ibid.
N: USIGS 2 reels   472

NORTH MORETON, Berks., Eng.
Parish registers, 1558-1812; overseers' accounts, 1713-1730 C.H. Reading
N: USIGS 1 reel   473

NORTON, Durham, Eng.
Parish registers, 1574-1948; parish records, 1755-1928 Ibid.
N: USIGS 5 reels   474

OGBOURNE ST. GEORGE, Wilts., Eng.
Parish registers, 1664-1947, 10 v. Ibid.
N: USIGS 1 reel   475

OLD HUTTON, Westmoreland, Eng.
Parish registers, 1813-1857 C.H. Kendal
N: USIGS 1 reel   476

OLD WINDSOR, Berks., Eng.
Parish registers, 1772-1813 C.H. Reading
N: USIGS 1 reel   477

OVER KELLET, Lancs., Eng.
Parish registers, 1813-1948; parish accounts, 1809-1838 UKPrRO
N: USIGS 2 reels   478

OXENHALL, Gloucs., Eng.
Parish registers, 1665-1950 Dymock
N: USIGS 1 reel   479

PADWORTH, Berks., Eng.
Parish registers, 1693-1812; parish records, 1828-1922 C.H. Reading
N: USIGS 1 reel   480

PANGBOURNE, Berks., Eng.
Parish records, 1801-1896 C.H. Reading
N: USIGS 2 reels   481

PASSENHAM, Northants, Eng.
Parish records, 1500-1930 Deanshanger School, Deanshanger
N: USIGS 4 reels   482

PAUNTLEY, Gloucs., Eng.
Parish registers, 1538-1856 Dymock
N: USIGS 1 reel   483

PEASEMORE, Berks., Eng.
Parish registers, 1538-1804; parish records, 1697-1777, 1783, 1786-1884 C.H. Reading
N: USIGS 2 reels   484

PRESHUTE, Wilts., Eng.
Parish registers, 1607-1947 Ibid.
N: USIGS 2 reels   485

PRESTON, Gloucs., Eng.
Parish registers, 1665-1866 Dymock
N: USIGS 1 reel   486

PRESTON RICHARD, Westmoreland, Eng.
Court book, 1678-1747; list of freeholders, 1818-1825 C.H. Kendal
N: USIGS 1 reel   487

PURLEY, Berks., Eng.
Parish registers, 1662-1908; parish records, 1825-1914 C.H. Reading
N: USIGS 1 reel   488

RADLEY, Berks., Eng.
Churchwardens' accounts, 1740-1763 C.H. Reading
N: USIGS 1 reel   489

RIBCHESTER, Lancs., Eng.
Parish registers, 1695-1931; parish records, 1650-1941 UKPrRO
N: USIGS 3 reels   490

RUDFORD, Gloucs., Eng.
Parish registers, 1729-1856 Dymock
N: USIGS 1 reel   491

ST. BARTHOLEMEW PARISH, Ripponden, Yorks., Eng.
Parish register, 1684-1949 Ibid.
N: USIGS 1 reel   492

ST. BOTOLPH'S ALDGATE, London, Eng.
Parish registers, 1558-1932; parish records, 1548-1678 Ibid.
N: USIGS 21 reels   493

ST. CHAD PARISH, Kirkby, Lancs., Eng.
Parish registers, 1678-1949 Ibid.
N: USIGS 3 reels   494

ST. GILES PARISH, Reading, Berks., Eng.
Parish registers, 1564-1892; poor rates, 1745-1869; parish records, 1518-1594 C.H. Reading
N: USIGS 26 reels   495

ST. JAMES' PARISH, Notts., Eng.
Parish registers, 1880-1935 Ibid.
N: USIGS 1 reel   496

ST. LAWRENCE HILMARTON, Wilts., Eng.
Parish register, 1645-1947 Ibid.
N: USIGS 1 reel   497

ST. LAWRENCE PARISH, Chorley, Lancs., Eng.
Parish registers, 1653-1947 Ibid.
N: USIGS 7 reels   498

ST. MARY PARISH, Great Sankey, Lancs., Eng.
Parish registers, 1728-1948 UKPrRO
N: USIGS 3 reels   499

ST. MARY PARISH, Kirkdale, Lancs., Eng.
Burial records, 1837-1898 Ibid.
N: USIGS 3 reels   500

ST. MARY THE VIRGIN (Church), West Derby, Lancs., Eng.
Parish registers, 1736-1947 Ibid.
N: USIGS 4 reels   501

ST. MARY THE VIRGIN PARISH, Bury, Lancs., Eng.
Parish registers, 1590-1947; parish accounts, 1692-1832 Ibid.
N: USIGS 16 reels   502

ST. MARY WHITECHAPEL, London, Eng.
Parish registers, 1558-1923 Ibid.
N: USIGS 26 reels   503

ST. MARY'S PARISH, Hemel Hempstead, Herts., Eng.
Parish register, 1558-1947; rate book, 1758-1771 Ibid.
N: USIGS 4 reels   504

ST. MARY'S PARISH, Reading, Berks., Eng.
Parish records, 1590-1907 C.H. Reading
N: USIGS 17 reels   505

ST. MICHAEL-ON-WYRE, Lancs., Eng.
Parish registers, 1707-1948; churchwardens' accounts, 1729-1839 UKPrRO
N: USIGS 2 reels   506

ST. PETER'S PARISH, Notts., Eng.
Parish registers and land records, 1400-1949 Ibid.
N: USIGS 6 reels   507

SANDHURST, Berks., Eng.
Parish registers, 1603-1695, 1754-1813; parish records, 1671-1696, 1751-1809 C.H. Reading
N: USIGS 2 reels   508

SEDGEFIELD, Durham, Eng.
Parish registers, 1813-1948 Ibid.
N: USIGS 3 reels   509

SELSIDE, Westmoreland, Eng.
Parish registers, 1813-1858 C.H. Kendal
N: USIGS 1 reel   510

SELSTON, Notts., Eng.
Parish registers, 1557-1936 Ibid.
N: USIGS 3 reels   511

SHELBOURNE, Wilts., Eng.
Parish registers, 1672-1812; churchwardens' accounts, 1787-1840 C.H. Reading
N: USIGS 1 reel   512

SHELLINGFORD, Berks., Eng.
Parish registers, 1678-1853; parish records, 1669-1899 C.H. Reading
N: USIGS 2 reels   513

SHINFIELD, Berks., Eng.
Parish registers, 1649-1840; parish records, 1654-1864 C.H. Reading
N: USIGS 9 reels   514

SHOTTESBROOK, Berks., Eng.
Churchwardens' records, 1854-1887 C.H. Reading
N: USIGS 1 reel   515

SHRIVENHAM, Berks., Eng.
Parish registers, 1575-1781, 1810 C.H. Reading
N: USIGS 1 reel   516

SONNING, Berks., Eng.
Parish records, 1630-1897 C.H. Reading
N: USIGS 6 reels   517

SOTWELL, Berks., Eng.
Parish records, 1727-1879 C.H. Reading
N: USIGS 1 reel   518

SOUTH MORETON, Berks., Eng.
Parish registers, 1599-1813 C.H. Reading
N: USIGS 1 reel   519

SPARSHOLT, Berks., Eng.
Parish registers, 1558-1812; parish records, 1674-1710, 1800-1832, 1845-1867 C.H. Reading
N: USIGS 2 reels   520

STANFORD-IN-THE-VALE, Berks., Eng.
Parish registers, 1558-1812; parish records, 1552-1705, 1733-1906 C.H. Reading
N: USIGS 2 reels   521

STAVELY, Westmoreland, Eng.
Parish registers, 1813-1858 C.H. Kendal
N: USIGS 1 reel   522

STEVENTON, Berks., Eng.
Parish registers, 1558-1812; parish records, 1726-1892 C.H. Reading
N: USIGS 1 reel   523

STOKE, Kent, Eng.
Parish registers, 1666-1891 Ibid.
N: USIGS 1 reel   524

STREATLEY, Berks., Eng.
Parish registers, 1720-1810; overseers' accounts, 1782-1810 C.H. Reading
N: USIGS 1 reel   525

STRETFORD, Lancs., Eng.
Parish registers, 1598-1855; parish accounts, 1694-1776 UKPrRO
N: USIGS 1 reel   526

SULHAMPSTEAD ABBOTS, Berks., Eng.
Parish registers, 1602-1812; parish records, 1694-1831 C.H. Reading
N: USIGS 2 reels   527

SULHAMPSTEAD BANNISTER, Berks., Eng.
Parish registers, 1654-1812; parish records, 1670-1744, 1796-1831 C.H. Reading
N: USIGS 1 reel   528

SUNNINGHILL, Berks., Eng.
Parish registers, 1561-1641, 1653-1837;
parish records, 1662-1912   C.H. Reading
N: USlGS 3 reels   529

SUNNINGWELL, Berks., Eng.
Parish registers 1565-1812   C.H. Reading
N: USlGS 1 reel   530

SUTTERTON, Lincs., Eng.
Parish registers, 1538-1949; churchwardens'
accounts, 1754-1949 Ibid.
N: USlGS 2 reels   531

SWINTON, Lancs., Eng.
Orphan children sent to Swinton School, and
emigrated to Canada, 1846-1948 UKMP
N: USlGS 1 reel   532

SWITHLAND, Leics., Eng.
Parish records, 1764-1814 Ibid.
N: USlGS 1 reel   533

TANFIELD, Durham, Eng.
Parish registers, 1710-1948 Ibid.
N: USlGS 5 reels   534

TAYNTON, Gloucs., Eng.
Parish registers, 1538-1856 Dymock
N: USlGS 1 reel   535

THATCHAM, Berks., Eng.
Parish registers, 1773-1805; parish records,
1654-1859 C.H. Reading
N: USlGS 6 reels   536

TIBBERTON, Gloucs., Eng.
Parish registers, 1659-1856 Dymock
N: USlGS 1 reel   537

TIDMARSH, Berks., Eng.
Parish registers, 1730-1812 C.H. Reading
N: USlGS 1 reel   538

TILEHURST, Berks., Eng.
Parish registers, 1559-1812; parish records,
1720-1872 C.H. Reading
N: USlGS 6 reels   539

TRING, Herts., Eng.
Parish registers, 1566-1947 Ibid.
N: USlGS 4 reels   540

UFTON NERVET, Berks., Eng.
Parish registers, 1636-1812; parish records,
1765-1876   C.H. Reading
N: USlGS 2 reels   541

UNDERBARROW, Westmoreland, Eng.
Parish registers, 1813-1853 C.H. Kendal
N: USlGS 1 reel   542

UPLEADON, Gloucs., Eng.
Parish registers, 1538-1856 Dymock
N: USlGS 1 reel   543

UPTON, Berks., Eng.
Parish register, 1588-1742 C.H. Reading
N: USlGS 1 reel   544

WADDESDON, Bucks., Eng.
Parish register, 1538-1734, 200 p. [unk.]
N: USlGS   545

WALLINGFORD, Berks., Eng.
Parish records: St. Mary le More, 1774-1780,
1824-1830; St. Peter's, 1720-1881; borough
records, 1227-1320, 1507-1852 C.H. Reading
N: USlGS 13 reels   546

WALTHAM ST. LAWRENCE, Berks., Eng.
Parish registers, 1559-1812; parish records,
1651-1810 C.H. Reading
N: USlGS 1 reel   547

WALTON-LE-WOLD, Leics., Eng.
Parish registers, 1566-1948 Ibid.
N: USlGS 1 reel   548

WANTAGE, Berks., Eng.
Parish registers, 1538-1812; parish records,
1657-1800 C.H. Reading
N: USlGS 4 reels   549

WARFIELD, Berks., Eng.
Parish registers, 1594-1598, 1685-1904;

parish records, 1580-1886 C.H. Reading
N: USlGS 4 reels   550

WASING, Berks., Eng.
Parish registers, 1730-1812; parish records,
1703-1841   C.H. Reading
N: USlGS 1 reel   551

WELFORD, Berks., Eng.
Parish registers, 1559-1812 C.H. Reading
N: USlGS 1 reel   552

WEST CHALLOW, Berks., Eng.
Parish registers, 1653-1812 C.H. Reading
N: USlGS 1 reel   553

WEST HANNEY, Berks., Eng.
Parish registers, 1565-1823; churchwardens'
accounts, 1760-1942   C.H. Reading
N: USlGS 1 reel   554

WEST ILSLEY, Berks., Eng.
Parish registers, 1558-1821; churchwardens'
accounts, 1824-1919 C.H. Reading
N: USlGS 1 reel   555

WEST WOODHAY, Berks., Eng.
Parish registers, 1725-1744, 1756-1812
C.H. Reading
N: USlGS 1 reel   556

WESTBURY-ON-SEVERN, Gloucs., Eng.
Parish registers, 1538-1883 Dymock
N: USlGS 2 reels   557

WHITE WALTHAM, Berks., Eng.
Parish registers, 1801-1815; parish records,
1811-1881   C.H. Reading
N: USlGS 1 reel   558

WICKHAM, Berks., Eng.
Parish registers, 1649-1812 C.H. Reading
N: USlGS 1 reel   559

WIGAN, Lancs., Eng.
Parish registers, 1581-1852 Ibid.
N: USlGS 11 reels   560

WINSTER, Westmoreland, Eng.
Parish registers, 1813-1835 C.H. Kendal
N: USlGS 1 reel   561

WOKINGHAM, Berks., Eng.
Parish registers, 1674-1812; parish records,
1762-1836; borough records, 1630-1869
C.H. Reading
N: USlGS 5 reels   562

WYBERTON, Lincs., Eng.
Parish registers, 1538-1949 Ibid.
N: USlGS 1 reel   563

YATTENDON, Berks., Eng.
Parish registers, 1558-1914 C.H. Reading
N: USlGS 1 reel   564

Probate Records

BEDFORDSHIRE (Archdeaconry)
Wills, 1484-1857 Ibid.
N: USlGS 77 reels   565

BEDFORDSHIRE (Archdeaconry). PECULIAR
OF BIGGLESWADE
Wills, 1540-1559, 1713-1858 Ibid.
N: USlGS 2 reels   566

BEDFORDSHIRE (Archdeaconry). PECULIAR
OF LEIGHTON BUZZARD
Wills, 1537-1554, 1736-1846 Ibid.
N: USlGS 1 reel   567

BRIDGNORTH (Peculiar), Salop, Eng.
Wills and administrations, 1635-1858 UKAbN
N: USlGS 6 reels   568

BUCKINGHAM (Archdeaconry)
Wills and administrations, 1483-1858 Ibid.
N: USlGS 102 reels   569

CANTERBURY (Archdiocese)
Wills and administrations from various Courts
and Peculiars, 1384-1858 UKLSmH
N: USlGS 407 reels   570

CHESTER (Diocese)
"Supra" wills, 1815-1858; act books, 1596-
1858; act books, "infra" wills, 1660-1858;
Consistory court wills, 1557-1838 UKAbN
N: USlGS 37 reels   571

CORNWALL (Archdeaconry)
Wills and administrations, 1600-1859 Bodmin
N: USlGS 90 reels   572

GREAT BRITAIN. DISTRICT PROBATE
REGISTRY, BIRMINGHAM
Staffordshire wills and administrations trans-
ferred from Lichfield Consistory Court and
other ecclesiastical jurisdictions, 1492-1860
Ibid.
N: USlGS 688 reels   573

GREAT BRITAIN. DISTRICT PROBATE
REGISTRY, BRISTOL
Wills and administrations from Bristol and
Gloucester Consistory Courts and various
Peculiars, 1541-1858 Ibid.
N: USlGS 109 reels   574

GREAT BRITAIN. DISTRICT PROBATE
REGISTRY, CARLISLE
Wills and administrations, manors of
Ravenstonedale and Temple Sowerby, 1575-
1854 Ibid.
N: USlGS 6 reels   575

GREAT BRITAIN. DISTRICT PROBATE
REGISTRY, CARLISLE
Wills from the Cumberland Consistory Court,
1561-1858 Ibid.
N: USlGS 264 reels   576

GREAT BRITAIN. DISTRICT PROBATE
REGISTRY, DURHAM
Wills and administrations from the Durham
Consistory Court and Peculiar Courts, 1540-
1858 Ibid.
N: USlGS 277 reels   577

GREAT BRITAIN. DISTRICT PROBATE
REGISTRY, LEWES
Wills and administrations of the Archdeaconry
of Lewes and the Deaneries of South Malling
and Battle, 1541-1858 Ibid.
N: USlGS 86 reels   578

GREAT BRITAIN. PRINCIPAL PROBATE
REGISTRY, i.e. Somerset House
Berkshire wills and administrations from the
Archdeaconry of Berkshire and Prerogative
courts, 1480-1857 Ibid.
N: USlGS 51 reels   579

GREAT BRITAIN. PRINCIPAL PROBATE
REGISTRY, i.e. Somerset House
Hertfordshire wills and administrations from
the Archdeaconries of St. Albans and of
Huntingdon, 1415-1858 UKLSmH
N: USlGS 26 reels   580

GREAT BRITAIN. PRINCIPAL PROBATE
REGISTRY, i.e. Somerset House
Probate records of Yorkshire deaneries,
courts, etc., 1502-1858 Ibid.
N: USlGS 131 reels   581

GREAT BRITAIN. PRINCIPAL PROBATE
REGISTRY, i.e. Somerset House
Surrey wills from the Archdeaconry of Surrey
and other ecclesiastical jurisdictions, 1534-
1858 UKLSmH
N: USlGS 74 reels   582

GREAT BRITAIN. PRINCIPAL PROBATE
REGISTRY, i.e. Somerset House
Wills and administrations from the
Archdeaconries of Essex and Colchester, and
of various Peculiars, 1420-1858 UKLSmH
N: USlGS 95 reels   583

GREAT BRITAIN. PRINCIPAL PROBATE
REGISTRY, i.e. Somerset House
Wills and administrations from the Archdeaconry
of Middlesex and the Archdeaconry of Middlesex,
Essex, and Hertfordshire, 1538-1838 UKLSmH
N: USlGS 65 reels   584

HEREFORD (Diocese). CONSISTORY COURTS
AND PECULIARS
Wills and administrations, 1442-1858 UKAbN
N: USlGS 140 reels   585

LANCASHIRE. RECORD OFFICE
Lancashire wills from the Chester Consistory
Court, 1700-1823 UKPrRO
N: USIGS 596 reels   586

LONDON (Archdeaconry)
Wills, 1368-1807; commissary court, 1374-
1857; consistory court, 1514-1857; commissary
court for Essex and Herts., 1431-1858; Royal
Peculiar of the Dean and Chapel of Westminster,
1504-1667; Royal Peculiar of St. Katherines
by the Tower, 1698-1803; Probate records,
1564-1858 UKLSmH
N: USIGS 443 reels   587

LONDON (Diocese)
Wills and administrations of Archdeaconry,
Consistory Court, Commissary Court for
Essex and Hertfordshire, and Peculiars, 1368-
1858 UKLSmH
N: USIGS 443 reels   588

NORTHAMPTON (Archdeaconry)
Wills, 1467-1858; probate records, 1663-1685
Birmingham District Probate Registry
N: USIGS 3 reels   589

OXFORDSHIRE (Archdeaconry)
Wills and administrations (including those
of Peculiars), 1528-1857 UKLSmH
N: USIGS 64 reels   590

RICHMOND (Archdeaconry)
Marriage bonds and affidavits, 1746-1799
UKPrRO
N: USIGS 48 reels   591

SALISBURY (Diocese)
Wills and administrations of Consistory Court,
Archdeaconries, Peculiars, and Prebends,
1543-1799 UKLSmH
N: USIGS 409 reels   592

SURREY (Archdeaconry)
Wills and administrations, 1484-1857 UKLSmH
N: USIGS 72 reels   593

WALES. NATIONAL LIBRARY, Aberystwyth
Shropshire wills of Prees, 16th and 17th cent.;
Shrewsbury, 1661-1857; Wombridge, 1787-1854
UKAbN
N: USIGS 4 reels   594

WALES. NATIONAL LIBRARY, Aberystwyth
Wills and administrations of Bullinghope or
Upper Bullingham and Moreton-on-Lugg,
Herefordshire, 1658-1854 UKAbN
N: USIGS 1 reel   595

WORCESTER (Diocese)
Wills and administrations of Consistory
Court, Dean and Chapter, and Prebends,
1451-1857 Birmingham District Probate
Registry
N: USIGS 632 reels   596

YORKSHIRE (Archdiocese)
Wills and administrations of Archdeaconries,
Prerogative courts, etc., 1389-1857 UKLSmH
N: USIGS 1393 reels   597

Church Records

CALKIN, ASA STARKWEATH, 1809-1873
Diary, of Utah and British Mission,
L. D. S. Church, 1850-1858 priv.
N: UPB 1 reel   598
P: UPB

CANTERBURY CATHEDRAL. LIBRARY
Canterbury records, 13th-16th centuries Ibid.
N: ICU 5 reels   599

CHURCH OF JESUS CHRIST OF LATTER-DAY
SAINTS. BRITISH MISSION
Annual genealogical reports of the British
Mission, 1907-1951 USIC
N: USIGS 12 reels   600

CHURCH OF JESUS CHRIST OF LATTER-DAY
SAINTS. BRITISH MISSION
Record of members of the British Mission,
early to 1948 USIC
N: USIGS 68 reels   601

FARRELL, GEORGE D.
Genealogy book and journal, mission to England,
1874-1876, 3 v. priv.
N: UPB   602
P: UPB

FRIENDS, SOCIETY OF
Records of the Society of Friends   Caton
manuscript, v. III, containing correspond-
ence of William Dewsbury (d. 1688) UKLFS
N: USIGS 1 reel   603
P: PHC

FRIENDS, SOCIETY OF
Swarthmore manuscripts, v. 1-4, and
Barclay manuscripts, v. 1-2 UKLFS
N: PHC 11 reels   604
P: MH

FRIENDS, SOCIETY OF. BEDFORDSHIRE AND
HERTFORDSHIRE [ENG.] QUARTERLY
MEETING
Abstracts of: births, 1643-1725; deaths,
1656-1725; marriages, 1658-1725 PHi
N: PSC-F   605

FRIENDS, SOCIETY OF. BERKSHIRE AND
OXFORDSHIRE [ENG.] QUARTERLY
MEETING
Abstracts of: births, 1612-1725; deaths,
1655-1725; marriages, 1648-1725 PHi
N: PSC-F   606

FRIENDS, SOCIETY OF. BRISTOL [ENG.]
MONTHLY MEETING
Abstracts of: supplement
N: PSC-F*   607

FRIENDS, SOCIETY OF. BRISTOL AND SOMER-
SETSHIRE [ENG.] QUARTERLY MEETING
Abstracts of: births, 1644-1725; deaths, 1650-
1725; marriages, 1657-1725 PHi
N: PSC-F   608

FRIENDS, SOCIETY OF. BUCKINGHAMSHIRE
[ENG.] QUARTERLY MEETING
Abstracts of: births, 1645-1725; deaths, 1656-
1725; marriages, 1658-1725 PHi
N: PSC-F   609

FRIENDS, SOCIETY OF. CAMBRIDGE AND
HUNTINGDONSHIRE [ENG.] QUARTERLY
MEETING
Births, 1631-1725; deaths, 1661-1725;
marriages, 1657-1725 Ibid.
N: PSC-F   610

FRIENDS, SOCIETY OF. CHESHIRE AND STAF-
FORDSHIRE [ENG.] QUARTERLY MEETING
Births, 1647-1725; deaths, 1655-1725;
marriages, 1655-1725 PPGen
N: PSC-F   611

FRIENDS, SOCIETY OF. COLCHESTER [ENG.]
MONTHLY MEETING
Steven Crisp collection of Quaker letters,
1655-1691 Ibid.
N: ? 1 reel   612
P: PHC

FRIENDS, SOCIETY OF. CORNWALL [ENG.]
QUARTERLY MEETING
Abstracts of: births, 1609-1725; deaths, 1656-
1725; marriages, 1657-1725 PHi
N: PSC-F   613

FRIENDS, SOCIETY OF. CUMBERLAND AND
NORTHUMBERLAND [ENG.] QUARTERLY
MEETING
Abstracts of: births, 1651-1725; deaths, 1656-
1725; marriages, 1650-1725 PHi
N: PSC-F   614

FRIENDS, SOCIETY OF. DERBYSHIRE AND
NOTTINGHAM [ENG.] QUARTERLY
MEETING
Births, 1632-1725; deaths, 1657-1725;
marriages, 1659-1725 Ibid.
N: PSC-F   615

FRIENDS, SOCIETY OF. DORSETSHIRE AND
HAMPSHIRE [ENG.] QUARTERLY MEETING
Abstracts of: births, 1649-1725; deaths, 1661-
1725; marriages, 1658-1725 PHi
N: PSC-F   616

FRIENDS, SOCIETY OF. DURHAM [ENG.]
MONTHLY MEETING

Abstracts of: supplement
N: PSC-F*   617

FRIENDS, SOCIETY OF. DURHAM [ENG.]
QUARTERLY MEETING.
Abstracts of: births, 1613-1725; deaths, 1655-
1725; marriages, 1644-1725 PHi
N: PSC-F   618

FRIENDS, SOCIETY OF. ENGLAND
Women petitioners against times (over
7,000 signatures)
N: PSC-F   619

FRIENDS, SOCIETY OF. ESSEX [ENG.]
QUARTERLY MEETING
Abstracts of: births, 1613-1725; deaths,
1655-1725; marriages, 1659-1725 PHi
N: PSC-F   620

FRIENDS, SOCIETY OF. GLOUCESTER AND
WILTSHIRE [ENG.] QUARTERLY MEETING.
Abstracts of: births, 1642-1735; deaths, 1655-
1725; marriages, 1656-1725 PHi
N: PSC-F   621

FRIENDS, SOCIETY OF. HEREFORD, WORCES-
TERSHIRE, AND WALES [ENG.] GENERAL
MEETING
Abstract of: births, 1635-1725; deaths, 1657-
1725; marriages, 1657-1725 PHi
N: PSC-F   622

FRIENDS, SOCIETY OF. KENT [ENG.] QUAR-
TERLY MEETING.
Abstracts of: births, 1646-1725; deaths, 1658-
1725; marriages, 1656-1725 PHi
N: PSC-F   623

FRIENDS, SOCIETY OF. LANCASHIRE [ENG.]
QUARTERLY MEETING.
Abstracts of: births, 1649-1725; deaths, 1657-
1725; marriages, 1649-1725 PHi
N: PSC-F   624

FRIENDS, SOCIETY OF. LINCOLNSHIRE [ENG.]
QUARTERLY MEETING.
Abstracts of: births, 1640-1725; deaths, 1657-
1725; marriages, 1657-1725 PHi
N: PSC-F   625

FRIENDS, SOCIETY OF. LONDON
YEARLY MEETING
Epistles received, v. 1-4, 1685-1829 UKLFS
N: PHC 2 reels   626

FRIENDS, SOCIETY OF. LONDON
YEARLY MEETING
Epistles sent, v. 1-4, 1683-1818 UKLFS
N: PHC 2 reels   627

FRIENDS, SOCIETY OF. LONDON
YEARLY MEETING
Meetings for sufferings. Letters which
passed between the Meeting for sufferings in
London and the Meeting for sufferings in
Philadelphia, 1757-1815. Also letters to and
from the governors of the different provinces
in America UKLFS
N: ? 1 reel   628
P: PHC

FRIENDS, SOCIETY OF. LONDON YEARLY
MEETING
Meeting for sufferings minutes, 1675-1860
UKLFS
N: ?   629
P: PSC-F

FRIENDS, SOCIETY OF. LONDON YEARLY
MEETING
Minutes, 1688-1860 UKLFS
N: ? 13 reels   630
P: PHC

FRIENDS, SOCIETY OF. LONDON
YEARLY MEETING
Morning meeting records, 1673-1726 UKLFS
N: USIGS   631
P: PHC

FRIENDS, SOCIETY OF. LONDON AND
MIDDLESEX [ENG.] QUARTERLY MEETING
Abstracts of: births, 1644-1719; deaths,
1670-1719; marriages, 1657-1719 PPGen
N: PSC-F   632

FRIENDS, SOCIETY OF. NORFOLK AND
NORWICH [ENG.] MONTHLY MEETINGS
Abstracts of: births, marriages, and burials,
1650-1729
N: PSC-F*   633

FRIENDS, SOCIETY OF. NORTHAMPTONSHIRE
[ENG.] MONTHLY MEETING
Abstracts of: births, marriages, and burials,
1647-1729
N: PSC-F*   634

FRIENDS, SOCIETY OF. SUFFOLK [ENG.]
MONTHLY MEETING
Abstracts of: marriages, births, and burials,
1653-1729
N: PSC-F*   635

FRIENDS, SOCIETY OF. SURREY AND SUSSEX
[ENG.] MONTHLY MEETING
Abstracts of: births, marriages, and burials,
1645-1729
N: PSC-F*   636

FRIENDS, SOCIETY OF. WARWICKSHIRE,
LEICESTERSHIRE AND RUTLAND [ENG.]
Abstracts of: births, marriages, and burials,
1623-1729
N: PSC-F*   637

FRIENDS, SOCIETY OF. WESTMORELAND
[ENG.] QUARTERLY MEETING
Abstracts of births, 1635-1729; deaths, 1657-
1729; marriages, 1635-1729 PPGen
N: PSC-F   638

FRIENDS, SOCIETY OF. YORKSHIRE [ENG.]
MONTHLY MEETING
Abstracts of: births, marriages, and burials,
1628-1729, 6 v.
N: PSC-F*   639

FRIENDS, SOCIETY OF. YORKSHIRE [ENG.]
MONTHLY MEETING
Abstracts of: supplement, burials
N: PSC-F*   640

HEREFORD CATHEDRAL, Hereford, Eng.
Manuscripts of the 8th to 15th cents. Ibid.
N: NjP 1 reel   641

HULL, Eng. PRESBYTERIAN CHURCH (now
ST. NINIAN'S CHURCH)
First minute book, 1643
N: ?   642
P: PPPrHi

KIMBALL, ABRAHAM A.
Diaries of British Mission, L.D.S. Church,
1878-1881, 1884-1887 priv.
N: UPB 1 reel   643
P: UPB

LONDON. FRIENDS' HOUSE
Swarthmore manuscript, v. 1-7 UKLFS
N: UKLFS 7 reels   644
P: PHC

LONDON. UNITED SYNAGOGUE
Vital records: Ashkenazi Jews of the Great
Synagogue, 1791-1885; German Jews of the
Hamburg Synagogue, 1770-1905; Ashkenazi
Jews of the New Synagogue, 1774-1896 Ibid.
N: USIGS 12 reels   645

NUTTALL, GEOFFREY FILLINGHAM, 1911- ,
transcriber
Early Quaker letters to 1660, Swarthmore ms.
UKLFS, 411 p. (typescript) CtY
N: ICN   646

PHIPPS, HENRY CLEMENT
Diary of Mormon mission to England, 1916
priv.
N: CaACG 1 reel   647
P: CaACG

PRESBYTERIAN CHURCH IN ENGLAND
Registers, various localities of England,
Malaya, India, Singapore, 1726-1953 UKLPr
N: USIGS 46 reels   648

ST. PAUL'S CATHEDRAL, London
Correspondence of Swiss Reformers with

English clergy, ca. 1559-1580 Ibid.
N: priv. 1 reel   649
P: DFo

SANSON, CHARLES, 1926-
Journals (British Mission, L.D.S. Church),
3 v. priv.
N: UPB 1 reel   650
P: UPB

SMART, ROBERT, compiler
Several letters, petitions, etc. of the old
Puritans, ca. 1570-ca. 1604 Sloane 271
UKLBM
N: DFo 1 reel   651

WESLYAN METHODIST MISSIONARY SOCIETY,
London
Outgoing correspondence, Conference minutes,
and Committee minutes, 1814-1867 Ibid.
N: CaOOA 4 reels   652
P: CaOTV

WESTMINSTER ASSEMBLY OF DIVINES
Minutes, 1643-1652, 3 v. UKLWi
N: UKLWi 2 reels   653
P: DFo ICU NjPT NNUT

WESTMINSTER ASSEMBLY OF DIVINES
Minutes, 1643-1652, 3 v. (transcript for Church
of Scotland Library)
N: DFo 3 reels   654
P: NNUT

YORK (Archdiocese)
Archbishop Drummond's visitations, returns,
1764; Bishopsthorpe manuscripts (selections)
Ibid.
N: CtY 24 reels   655

Personal Papers

ALCOCK, JOHN, 1430-1500
Registrum, 1486 Ely 6 UKC
N: NNF 1 reel   656
P: NNF

ALLEN, JOHN, of Plymouth, Eng.
Diary, 1664-1683 UKPlI
N: CtY 1 reel   657

ALLEN, WILLIAM, of Plymouth, England
Diary, 1671 UKPlI
N: CtY 1 reel   658

ANGLESEY, ARTHUR ANNESLEY, 1st EARL of,
1614-1684
Diaries, 1667-1684 Add. ms. 18730, 40860
UKLBM
N: MoSW 1 reel   659

ARNOLD, MATTHEW, 1822-1888
Correspondence with William Knight, 42 letters
NNP
N: ?   660
P: InLPU

AUCKLAND, WILLIAM EDEN,
1st BARON, 1744-1814
Correspondence and papers, 1600-1785, 8v.
Auckland Papers UKLBM
N: MiU 8 reels   661

BACON, Sir NATHANIEL, bart., 1547-1622
Correspondence and papers, 15th-18th
centuries Townsend papers, 2nd series, Add.
ms. 41139-41152 UKLBM
N: ICU 1 reel   662

BACON, Sir NICHOLAS, 1509-1579
Register of deeds relating to property in
Norfolk, Suffolk, Kent, and the City of London,
1562-1578 UKLBM
N: ICU 1 reel   663

BACON, Sir NICHOLAS, 1509-1579
Speeches in Parliament, 1557-1571
N: CtY   664

BARRINGTON FAMILY, of Barrington Hall,
Essex, Eng.
Correspondence and papers, 1490-1820
Egerton 2642-2651 UKLBM
N: CtY 12 reels   665

BARTON, BERNARD
Manuscripts UKLFS
N: PSC-F   666
P: PSC-F

BAYNES, Capt. ADAM, M.P.
Correspondence, 1645-1689 Add. ms. 21417-
426 UKLBM
N: CSmH 6 reels   667

BEACONSFIELD, BENJAMIN DISRAELI,
1st EARL of, 1804-1881
Disraeli-Austen correspondence, 189 items
Add. ms. 45908 UKLBM
N: OU   668

BEAKE, ROBERT, Mayor of Coventry, Eng.
Diary, 1655-1666
N: CtY 1 reel   669

BENTHAM, JEREMY, 1748-1832
Correspondence, 1817-1827 UKLUC
N: NNC 1 reel   670

BINYON, EDWARD
Diaries, 1769-1772
N: CtY 2 reels   671

BOND, PHINEAS
Letters, 1794-1811 UKLPRO
N: PHi 3 reels   672

BRAGG, JOHN, London shoemaker
Hadwen-Bragg family letters, 1774-1788
priv.
N: DLC 1 reel   673
PP: DLC

BURKE, EDMUND, 1729-1797
Letters and papers, 176?-1797
Wentworth-Fitzwilliam ms. UKSP
N: NNF 6 reels*   674
P: NNF

BURKE, EDMUND, 1729-1797
Letters to Charles O'Hara, 115 items priv.
N: NNF 1 reel *   675
P: NNF

BURKE, EDMUND, 1729-1797
Papers, 1744-1796 UKSP
N: KyU 11 reels*   676

BURKE, EDMUND, 1729-1797
Three letters UKSP
DCO: KyU   677

BUTTS, THOMAS, of Great Ryburgh, Norfolk, Eng.
Commonplace book, ca. 1570
N: CtY   678

CAESAR, Sir JULIUS, 1580-1625
Letters and papers re: Court of Requests,
1580-1604; proceedings in High Commissioners'
Court, 1611 Lansdowne 161 UKLBM
N: CtY 1 reel   679

CAESAR, Sir JULIUS, 1580-1625
Projects for increasing the royal revenue,
temp. Jas. I, 70 items Add. ms. 10038
UKLBM
N: CtY 1 reel   680

CALVERLEY, Sir WALTER, 1669-1722
Diary and memorandum book, 1660-1745
N: CtY 1 reel   681

CAMDEN, WILLIAM, 1551-1623
Papers, 17th cent. UKO
N: ICU 8 reels   682

CARLYLE, THOMAS, 1795-1881
Letters to John Forster UKLVA
N: ICU 1 reel   683

COLLINSON, PETER
Papers Linnean Society, London
N: PPAmP   684

CORNWALLIS, Sir CHARLES, d. 1629
Letterbook, 1605-1610 UKLBM
N: WaU 4 reels   685

CORNWALLIS, CHARLES CORNWALLIS,
2nd Earl and 1st Marquis, 1738-1805
Papers UKLPRO
N: DLC 80 reels   686

COTTON, BARTHOLOMEW
Historia Anglicana   UKLBM
N: PU-F   687

CRABBE, GEORGE, 1754-1832
Unpublished sermons, 1782-1832 ICU
N: CU 1 reel   688

CRUWYS, JOHN
Account book and diary, 1682-1685
N: CtY 1 reel   689

CUDWORTH, RALPH, 1617-1688
Manuscripts Add. ms. 4978-4987 UKLBM
N: NNC 4 reels   690

CUDWORTH, RALPH, 1617-1688
Papers (unpublished) UKLBM
N: NcD 1 reel   691

DARWIN, CHARLES ROBERT, 1809-1882
Correspondence... Down House, Kent, England
(British Association for Advancement of Science)
N: PPAmP 582 frames   692

DARWIN, CHARLES ROBERT, 1809-1882
Papers, 1825-1882 UKC
N: CSt 5 reels   693

DEFOE, DANIEL, 1661-1731
Papers UKLBM
N: ?   694
P: MiU

Devotional tracts, ca. 1491 ms. 221 UKCP
N: ICU 1 reel   695

DIGBY, Sir KENELM, 1603-1665
Letters, 1633-1635, 45 items (transcript)
priv.
DCO: NN   696

DILLWYN, WILLIAM
Diary, 1774-1789
N: CtY 1 reel   697

DOWDESWELL, WILLIAM, 1721-1775
Letters, 1765-1774, 53 items MiU-C
DCO: NNF *   698
N: NNF 1 reel

EDWARDS, THOMAS, 1699-1757
Correspondence, 1738-1756 UKO
N: ?   699
P: MiU

EFFINGHAM, FRANCIS HOWARD, 5th BARON of,
1643-1695
Papers, 1684-1688 DLC*
N: DLC 2 reels   700

EGREMONT, CHARLES WYNDHAM, 2nd
EARL of, 1710-1763
Papers, selections when Secretary of State
for the Southern Department, 1761-1763
UKLPRO
N: DLC 1 reel   701

ERLE, Sir WALTER
Parliamentary diary for 1624 (typescript)
N: CtY 2 reels   702

FAIRFAX FAMILY
Correspondence, musters, military commissions
UKLBM
N: CSmH 3 reels   703

FANE, Sir FRANCIS, d. 1689?
Commonplace book, 1672 Trustees and Guardians of Shakespeare's birthplace, Stratford-
upon-Avon
N: OU   704

FELL, MARGARET
Letters, 1652/3-1656, 3 items v.p.
DCO: PSC-F   705

FINCH FAMILY (Earls of Nottingham and
Winchelsea)
Papers, 1657-1744 priv.
N: CtY 8 reels   706

FORD, WILLIAM, of Branormlie, Devon, Eng.
Diary, 1782-1791
N: CtY 1 reel   707

FOX, CHARLES JAMES, 1749-1806
Correspondence, 1781-1783, 175 items priv.
DCO: MiU-C   708

FOX, GEORGE, 1624-1691
Letters and addresses   The John Tapper
Manuscript UKLFS
N: CU 1 reel   709

FOX, GEORGE, 1624-1691
Papers, 1659-1690/1, 10 items v.p.
DCO: PSC-F   710

FOX, GEORGE, 1624-1691
Swarthmore manuscripts, 2 v. UKLFS
N: CU 2 reels   711

FRANKLIN, JANE (GRIFFIN), Lady, 1792-1875
Letters and papers, 1861-1870, 1 v. HiU
N: HiU   712

FYFFE, Sir WILLIAM
Letter to John Fyffe, 1761   OkTG
N: OkTG 1 reel   713

GAWDY FAMILY, of Norfolk, Eng.
Correspondence and papers, 1509-1791
Egerton 2713-2722 UKLBM
N: CtY 22 reels   714

GIBSON, EDMUND, Bp., 1667-1784
Lambeth manuscripts 929-942 UKLLam
N: CSmH 8 reels   715

GODOLPHIN, SIDNEY, GODOLPHIN, 1st EARL
of, 1645-1712
Correspondence, 1701-1712, 441 p. Add. ms.
28055 UKLBM
N: NIC   716

GORDON, HARRY, d. 1766
Journal, 1766   Great Britain, Colonial Office
N: PPiU 1 reel   717

GRAHAM, Sir JAMES ROBERT GEORGE, Bart.,
1792-1861
Papers, ca. 1820-1860 priv.
N: ? 44 reels   718
P: ICN

HALDIMAND, Sir FREDERICK, 1718-1791
Haldimand papers, 1783-1784 UKLBM
N: WaPS 1 reel   719

HALE FAMILY, of King's Walden, Herts.,
Eng.
Correspondence and papers, 1526-1660,
379 p. Add. ms. 33572 UKLBM
N: OU   720

HAWKINS, EDWARD, 1789-1882
Correspondence, 1829-1863 UKOOC
N: CtY 1 reel   721

HERBERT, Sir THOMAS, 1606-1682
Carolina Threnodia (manuscript describing
last days of Charles I), 175 p.
N: CtY   722

HERVEY, JOHN HERVEY, BARON, 1696-1743
"True materials towards memoirs of the reign
of King George the Second," 4 v., ms.
Ickworth
N: CoU 2 reels   723

HORDERN, JOSEPH, attributed author
Diary of a Gentleman Farmer, of Caredon,
Staffs., Aug.-Dec., 1783, June,1804-Nov.,1806
N: CtY   724

HUME, DAVID, 1711-1776
"Memoranda and notes for my history of
England," 1749 CSmH
N: ICU 1 reel   725

HUNT, RICHARD, husbandman
Memorandum and letter book, 1626   UKBP
N: CtY 1 reel*   726

HUNTER, JOSEPH, 1783-1861
Virorum notabilium memoranda, 379 p. Add.
ms. 24482 UKLBM
N: DGU   727

HUXLEY, THOMAS HENRY, 1825-1895
Letters to Sir Charles Lyell, 1853-1873,

21 items   PPAmP
N: CSt   728

JEFFRIES, JOYCE
Diary, 1636-1647
N: CtY   729

JENKINS, JOHN JAMES
Records and recollections, 1761-1821 UKLFS
N: CtY 2 reels*   730

JOANNES DE GARLANDIA, ca.1195 - ca. 1272
Works in Latin, including those of Alexander
Neckham   ms. 132 UKLiC
N: ?   731
P: MiU

JONES, ERNEST, 1819-1868
Diary and newspaper clippings
N: Kodak London 1 reel   732
P: NNC

KELSALL, JOHN
Diaries, 1683-1743, and autobiography
N: CtY 3 reels   733

KING, GREGORY, 1648-1712
Autobiography, 1694 Rawlinson Ms. C 514
UKO
DCO: MdBJ   734

KING, GREGORY, 1648-1712
Natural and political observations and conclu-
sions upon the state and condition of England,
9 p.   Harleian 1898 UKLBM
DCO: MdBJ   735

KING, GREGORY, 1648-1712
Of the naval trade of England, 1697, 11 p.
Rawlinson D. 919 UKO
DCO: MdBJ   736

LEE, C.J.
Briefs of King's Bench causes, notes on King's
Bench causes and Privy Council hearings [unk.]
N: NNC 1 reel   737

MacDONALD, JAMES
Letters, 1761-1763, 7 items   UKLBM CSmH
DCO: MiU-C   738

MARCHANT, THOMAS
Diary, 1714-1728
N: CtY 2 reels   739

MIDDLESEX, LIONEL CRANFIELD, 1st EARL
of, 1575-1645
Letter to Secretary Conway re: land grants,
pension, his son's knighthood, and Irish
revenues, March 7, 1622/3, 3 p.   UKLPRO
DCO: MnU   740

MILDMAY, Sir HUMPHREY
Diary, 1631-1652   Harleian 454 UKLBM
N: CtY 11 reels*   741

MONCK, GEORGE, 1st DUKE of ALBEMARLE,
1608-1670
Order book, 1658-1660 UKO
N: CSmH 1 reel   742

MORE, HENRY, 1614-1687
Letters to Edward, Viscount Conway, and Anne,
his wife, 1650-1679 Add. ms. 23216 UKLBM
N: NNC 1 reel   743

MUDDIMAN, HENRY, 1629-1692
News-letters (manuscript), 1667-1679
Longleat
N: priv.   744
P: DFo 1 reel

MUNDEFORD, Sir EDMUND, of Feltwell,
Norfolk, Eng.
Family correspondence, 1600-1650; accounts,
1582-1639 Add. ms. 27399-27400 UKLBM
N: CtY 1 reel   745

NEWCASTLE, THOMAS PELHAM-HOLLES, 1st
DUKE OF, 1693-1768
Correspondence re: Deaconry of Chichester,
1733-1760 UKLBM
N: CtY   746

DGU card

NEWCASTLE, THOMAS PELHAM-HOLLES, 1st
DUKE OF, 1693-1768
Official correspondence (selections)
UKLBM
N: CtY 5 reels   747

NEWMAN, JOHN HENRY, Cardinal, 1801-1890
Correspondence, 1833-1890, 13 items priv.
N: CSmH   748

NEWMAN, JOHN HENRY, Cardinal, 1801-1890
Letters, 1811-1889 priv.
N: ? 1 reel   749
P: CU ICU MH NjP

NEWMAN, JOHN HENRY, Cardinal, 1801-1890
Letters, 1819-1865 UKO; 1828-1890 UKOOC
N: CtY 2 reels   750

NEWMAN, JOHN HENRY, Cardinal, 1801-1890
Papers (selections), 1804-1890 Oratory of
St. Philip Neri, Birmingham, Eng.
N: CtY   751

NICHOLSON, Sir FRANCIS, 1655-1728
Papers, ca. 1680-1720 ViWC
N: ViWC 100 feet   752
P: ViWC

POLE, REGINALD, Cardinal, 1500-1558
Registrarum expeditionum in Anglia,
1554-1557, 6 v. FrD
N: CtY 4 reels   753
P: CtY

PORTLAND, WILLIAM HENRY CAVENDISH
BENTINCK, 3rd DUKE of, 1738-1809
Letters, 1763-1785 UKNU
N: Rekordak 3 reels   754
P: NNF

POWNALL, THOMAS, 1722-1805
Miscellaneous letters, 1754-1764 UKLPRO
N: PPiU 1 reel   755

POWYS, CAROLINE, 1737-1808
Travel diaries Add. ms. 42163 UKLBM
N: CtY 1 reel*   756

PRICHARD, H. A.
Letters, 1925-1947 UKO
N: NcD 1 reel   757

PRIESTLEY, JOSEPH, 1733-1804
Correspondence with John Wilkinson, 1789-
1802, 68 items UKWar
DCO: DLC   758

PRYNNE, WILLIAM, 1600-1669
Mr. Prynne's reading on the petition of right
made in Parliament, March 17, 1627 Inner
Temple Library, London
N: DFo 1 reel   759

RIDER, Sir DUDLEY
Court book, May 6, 1754-May 8, 1756 priv.
N: priv.
P: PHi   760

RUGG, THOMAS
Diary, 1659-1672 UKLBM
N: CtY 2 reels   761

SENIOR, NASSAU WILLIAM, 1790-1864
Diary re: the Poor Law Amendment act, 1834,
270 p. UKLU
N: NNC   762

SHELBURNE, WILLIAM PETTY, 2nd EARL OF,
later 1st MARQUIS OF LANSDOWNE, 1737-1805
Papers, 1663-1797 MiU-C
DCO: DLC 10 boxes*   763

SLOANE, Sir HANS, Bart., 1660-1753
Correspondence, 17th and 18th cents. Sloane
4036-4069 UKL
N: ? 21 reels   764
P: MnU

SOPHIE CHARLOTTE, Queen of England,
1744-1818
Briefe an ihrem Bruder, 1775-1785
Hauptarchiv, Neustrelitz, Germany
N: DLC 1 reel   765
P: DLC

STEPHEN, JAMES, 1758-1832
Memoirs UKLBM
N: NcD 1 reel   766

STEVENSON, Rev. SETH E., East Retford,
Notts., Eng.
Diary, 1760-1775
N: CtY   767

STROTHERS
Journal, 1784-1785
N: CtY   768

THORNTON, Mrs. ALICE
Journal, 1625-
N: CtY   769

TOWNSHEND, GEORGE TOWNSHEND, 4th
VISCOUNT and 1st MARQUIS, 1724-1807
Papers, 1767-1807 MiU-C
DCO: DLC 2 boxes*   770

TWYSDEN, Sir ROGER, Bart., 1597-1672
Letters, notebooks and family papers,
16th-19th cents. UKLBM
N: ICU   771

VANE, Sir HENRY, 1613-1662
A letter to Sir Arthur Haselrig, Feb. 23, 1659
UKLBM
N: NNUT 1 reel   772

VAUGHAN, BENJAMIN, 1751-1835
Papers, 1776-1828 priv.
DCO: MiU-C 1 foot   773

WALPOLE, HORACE, 4th EARL of ORFORD,
1717-1797
Book of materials, 1759, 1771, 1786; letters,
1765-1796, 7 items priv.
N: DFo   774

WHARTON, GOODWIN
Autobiography, 1686-1704 UKLBM
N: CSmH 274 frames   775

WHARTON, HENRY, 1664-1695
Vita Johannis Fabricii, militis Angli,
1685, 25 p. UKLLam
N: NN   776

WHITEWAY, WILLIAM, of Dorchester, Eng.
Diary, 1618-1634 Egerton 784 UKLBM
N: CtY   777

WILKES, JOHN, 1727-1797
Collection re: John Wilkes MH
N: MoU 1 reel*   778

WODEHOUSE FAMILY
Papers re: families of Buttes, Bacon, and
Wodehouse and their estates in Norfolk and
Suffolk, 13th-19th cents. UKLBM
N: ICU 4 reels   779

YONGE, Dr. JAMES
A journal of all the memorable occurrences
of my life, 1667
N: CtY 1 reel   780

Business Papers

DAIMLER-HIRE LTD. IMPERIAL AIRWAYS
LTD.
Accounts and reports, 1922-1925 priv.
N: MH-BA 1 reel   781

LONDON. UNIVERSITY.
Trade Union minutes and reports, v.d. UKLU
N: NNC 1 reel   782

LONDON. VINTNERS COMPANY
Court book, 1608-1638 Ibid.
N: CtY 3 reels*   783

MANCHESTER, BOLTON AND BURY CANAL
PROPRIETORS
Minutes of meetings, 1790-1831 British
Transport Commission
N: PPiU 2 reels   784

OXFORD. UNIVERSITY. BODLEIAN LIBRARY
Manuscript records of British shipping from
the East Indies and China, 17th and 18th cents.

Rawlinson mss. A 189, 245, 289, 302, 303, 324,
334; C 869, 970; D 391, 592, 747, 813 UKO
N: ICU 2 reels   785

SHREWSBURY, Eng. FAIR
Records of horse and cattle sales, 1596-
1597
N: CtY 2 reels   786

SMITH, ADAM, 1723-1790
Wealth of Nations, early ms. draft, 1763
priv.
N: MH-BA 1 reel*   787

SMYTH, JOHN, the elder, of Nibley, d. 1641
Accounts, 1599-1641; papers, 1584-1647
UKGrP
N: CtY 15 reels   788

WEBB, BENEDICT, of Kingswood
Papers re: making oil for cloth making,
1621-1629 UKGrP
N: CtY 1 reel   789

Collections

BATH, MARQUISES OF. LIBRARY (Longleat)
Coventry manuscripts. Catalog and index.
Ibid.
N: DLC 18 reels   790

BRITISH MUSEUM
Collectanea theologica Harleian 211 UKLBM
N: ?   791
P: MiU

BRITISH MUSEUM
Satyrs and lampoons, ca. 1660 Harleian
7316-7319 UKLBM
N: CtY   792

CECIL FAMILY
Papers and other archival material, 1442-
1603 Hatfield House
N: DFo 128 reels   793
P: DFo UKLBM

COTTON, ISAAC, compiler
The methodical prosec[ution] of causes in the
High Court of Star Chamber, 1622, 150 ff.
Stowe 418 UKLBM
N: CtY 1 reel*   794

CRISP, STEPHEN, collector
Quaker letters and papers, 1665-1691, 2 v.
Colchester Meeting, Colchester, Eng.
N: PSC-F 1 reel   795

DULWICH COLLEGE, London, Eng.
Dulwich papers: manuscripts and muniments,
1323-1662 Ibid.
N: CtY 7 reels   796
P: CtY

GRAEFF, ARTHUR D., collector
Material re: Palatine exiles in England and
America, 1696-1760 UKLLam UKLPRO
N: USlGS 3 reels   797

HALLIWELL-PHILLIPS, JAMES ORCHARD,
collector
Shakespeare material, including Shottery
Meadow tenant roll, H. Neville estates
computers' roll, Stratford lease, 1573 on   C-S
N: DFo 1 reel   798
P: C-S

HENRY E. HUNTINGTON LIBRARY AND
ART GALLERY, San Marino, Calif.
Poems and pieces dealing with Winchester
College, 1615-1637 CSmH
N: NjP 1 reel   799

HEREFORD PUBLIC LIBRARY, Hereford, Eng.
Feet of fines of divers counties, 1509-1521,
94 p.; calendar of Chancery depositions before
1714, 158 p.; abstracts of Chancery proceedings relating to the family of Desborough, 24 p.
UKHfP
N: USlGS 1 reel   800

HUNTER, JOSEPH, 1783-1861
Collections re: John Milton Add. ms. 24,501
UKLBM
N: IU   801

LINNEAN SOCIETY OF LONDON
Books and manuscripts, 1580-1784 Ibid.
N: ? 51 reels   802
P: DSI MH
RN: CU

LONDON. FRIENDS LIBRARY
Barclay manuscripts UKLFS
N: UKLFS 2 reels   803
P: PHC

LONDON. FRIENDS LIBRARY
Letters from Fell family, 1660-1729 (Spence
manuscript, v. III only) UKLFS
N: ? 1 reel   804
P: PHC

NORTHUMBERLAND, DUKES OF. LIBRARY
(Syon House)
Manuscripts: D. XI. 1; D. III. 27; D. I. 1 a;
K. III. 1; K. II. 1 b-z; K. II. 1-3; K. II. 1. 4; K. II.
1. 5; K. II. 1 A-D; K. II. 1 S. 5 Ibid.
N: DLC 15 reels   805

Institutions

ABORIGINES PROTECTION SOCIETY, London
Minute books, 1848-1881, 1890-1909
Denison House
DCO: DLC   806

ASSOCIATES OF DOCTOR THOMAS BRAY FOR
FOUNDING CLERICAL LIBRARIES AND
SUPPORTING NEGRO SCHOOLS
Accounts and correspondence, 1753-1817
Society for the Propagation of the Gospel,
London
N: ViU   807
P: DLC ViU

BRITISH AND FOREIGN ANTI-SLAVERY
SOCIETY, London
Minute books, 1839-1911, 7 v.   Denison House
DCO: DLC   808

BRITISH AND FOREIGN ANTI-SLAVERY
SOCIETY, London
Minute books of Committee on Slavery, 1823-
1840; rough minutes, 1826-1835 Denison
House
DCO: DLC   809

BURY ST. EDMUNDS ABBEY
Registrum dimissionum terrarum ac
tenementorum (Anglice leases), 1517-1540
Harleian 308 UKLBM
N: ICU   810

BURY ST. EDMUNDS ABBEY
Rentals, customaries, and charters of lands,
1279-1312, 1433 Add. ms. 14,850 UKLBM
N: ICU   811

LONDON. COVENT GARDEN THEATRE
Account books, 1735-1800 UKLBM
N: DFo 5 reels   812

REDGRAVE HALL, Suffolk, Eng.
Redgrave Hall papers re: properties acquired
by Sir Nicholas Bacon from Bury St. Edmunds
Abbey, 13th-17th cents., 11 v.   UKLBM
N: ICU 2 reels   813

SOCIETY FOR THE PROPAGATION OF THE
GOSPEL IN FOREIGN PARTS
Correspondence and records, 1868-1874 Ibid.
N: CaOOA 100 feet   814
P: CaSSA

SOCIETY FOR THE PROPAGATION OF THE
GOSPEL IN FOREIGN PARTS
Journals of the Society and its committees,
1700-1787; miscellaneous manuscripts, 1776-
1857 Ibid.
N: DLC v. I-VIII   815
PP: DLC v. I-VIII
DCO: DLC v. IX-XXIV
P: TxU 90 reels

SOCIETY FOR THE PROPAGATION OF THE
GOSPEL IN FOREIGN PARTS
London records, 1680-1901 Ibid.
N: CLU 180 reels   816

SYON ABBEY, Middlesex Co., Eng.
Orders and constitutions and other papers
Arundel 146, Harleian 419, 2321 UKLBM
N: CtY 3 reels   817

Military Papers

ALLANSON, Col. CECIL
Transcript of hearing by Dardanelles Com-
mission, Jan., 1917   priv.
N: ViU   818

SYMS, JOHN
Diary of the Civil War in the West, 1642-1649
N: CtY   819

A treatise on the duties of a High Marshall in
the field, ca. 1550 MiU
N: DFo   820

TROUGHTON, CHRISTOPHER
A short relation of the service at the Isle of
Reez under... the Duke of Buckingham, 1627
26 l., Rawlinson D. 117 UKO
N: ?   821
P: NN

WALES

Bibliography

WALES. NATIONAL LIBRARY, Aberystwyth
Schedules of deeds and documents deposited in
the National Library of Wales UKAbN
N: USIGS 10 reels   822

Census

GREAT BRITAIN. CENSUS
Census returns (Welsh division), 1851
UKLPRO
N: USIGS 119 reels   823

Local Records

WALES. NATIONAL LIBRARY, Aberystwyth
Welsh marriage bonds and allegations, Bangor,
St. Asaph's, Llandaff, St. David's dioceses,
1615-1900 UKAbN
N: USIGS 104 reels   824

WALES. NATIONAL LIBRARY, Aberystwyth
Welsh wills: St. David's, St. Asaph's, Bangor,
Swansea, Brecon and Llandaff Dioceses, 1557-
1858 UKAbN
N: USIGS 265 reels   825

Church Records

CHURCH OF JESUS CHRIST OF LATTER-DAY
SAINTS. WALES
Mission and branch records, early to 1947
USlC
N: USIGS 7 reels   826

SCOTLAND

Bibliography

SCOTLAND. NATIONAL LIBRARY, Edinburgh
Catalogues of manuscripts in library UKE
N: CSmH 8 reels   827

Census

SCOTLAND. CENSUS
Census returns, 1841, 1851, 1861, 1871
UKENRH
N: USIGS 646 reels   828

Government Records

SCOTLAND. GENERAL REGISTER HOUSE
General index to births, 1855-1949; deaths,
1855-1941; marriages, 1855-1949 UKENRH
N: USIGS 380 reels   829

Church Records

FRIENDS, SOCIETY OF. SCOTLAND
MONTHLY MEETING
Abstracts of: births, marriages, and burials,
1647-1725
N: PSC-F*   830

SCOTLAND. GENERAL REGISTER HOUSE
Parochial registers of Scotland UKENRH
N: USIGS 1302 reels   831

Personal Papers

LAUDERDALE, JOHN MAITLAND, DUKE of,
1616-1682
Papers, 1641-1697 UKE
N: UKE 3 reels   832
P: CSmH

LOCKHART, JOHN GIBSON, 1794-1854
Correspondence Abbotsford Collection UKE
N: CU   833

IRELAND

Census

ELPHIN (Diocese), Ireland
Census, 1749 IrDPRO
N: USIGS 1 reel   834

IRELAND. CENSUS, 1821
Census returns: Cavan, Fermanagh, Galway,
Meath and Offaly Cos.   IrDPRO
N: USIGS 9 reels   835

IRELAND. CENSUS, 1831
Census returns: Londonderry Co. IrDPRO
N: USIGS 6 reels   836

IRELAND. CENSUS, 1841
Census returns: Killeshandra Parish, Cavan
IrDPRO
N: USIGS 8 reels   837

IRELAND. CENSUS, 1851
Census returns: Antrim and Fermanagh (incom-
plete) IrDPRO
N: USIGS 20 reels   838

IRELAND. CENSUSES, 1821, 1834, 1841, 1851
Families on the Crownlands of Pobble Ofiefe,
Co. Cork IrDPRO
N: USIGS 1 reel   839

Government Records

GREAT BRITAIN. ARMY
Records of Irish personnel, 1883-1931; Irish
death returns, 1914-1920 Customs House,
Dublin
N: USIGS 12 reels   840

IRELAND
Vital records: births, 1864-1870; marriages,
1845-1870; deaths, 1864-1870 Customs
House, Dublin
N: USIGS 675 reels   841

IRELAND. GENEALOGICAL OFFICE OF ARMS
Selected manuscripts Ibid.
N: USIGS 147 reels   842

IRELAND. GENERAL VALUATION AND
BOUNDARY SURVEY
General valuation of ratable property in
Ireland, 1849-1852 IrDPRO
N: USIGS 5 reels   843

IRELAND (Eire)
Vital records, 1922-1949 Customs House, Dublin
N: USIGS 29 reels   844

IRELAND (Eire). PUBLIC RECORD OFFICE
Dublin insurance papers, 1771; electors of Co. Longford, 1790; Catholic qualification rolls, 1778-1800; Catholic convert rolls, 1703-1800 IrDPRO
N: USIGS 3 reels   845

IRELAND (Eire). PUBLIC RECORD OFFICE
Prerogative wills, 1644-1834; will register books, 1828-1839; will books of the Principal Registry and District Registries, 1858-1901; prerogative and diocesan wills, 1859-1900; wills from private sources IrDPRO
N: USIGS 64 reels   846

IRELAND(Eire). REGISTRY OF DEEDS
Indexes (surnames and land) to deeds of Ireland, 1708-1904 Ibid.
N: USIGS 552 reels   847

Local Records

DUBLIN, Ireland
Marriage bonds, 1749-1813 IrDPRO
N: USIGS 1 reel   848

Church Records

CHURCH OF JESUS CHRIST OF LATTER-DAY SAINTS. IRELAND
Records: Dublin and Belfast Conference, 1850-1873; Barrow, 1868; Belfast, early to 1947; Lurgan and Gilford, 1861, branches USlC
N: USIGS 1 reel   849

FRIENDS, SOCIETY OF. BALLEYHAGEN [Ireland] MONTHLY MEETING
Marriage certificates, 1692-1789; minutes, 1705-1734 IrDSF
N: PSC-F 2 reels*
P: PSC-F   850

FRIENDS, SOCIETY OF. CARLOW [Ireland] MONTHLY MEETING
Births, ca. 1621-1859; deaths, ca. 1658-1859; marriages, ca. 1649-1859 Ibid.
N: Ibid.
P: PSC-F   851

FRIENDS, SOCIETY OF. CORK [Ireland] MONTHLY MEETING
Births, ca. 1625-1859; deaths, ca. 1661-1859; marriages, ca. 1660-1860 Ibid.
N: Ibid.
P: PSC-F   852

FRIENDS, SOCIETY OF. DUBLIN [Ireland] MONTHLY MEETING
Births, ca. 1631-1859; deaths, ca. 1647-1859; marriages, ca. 1631-1859 Ibid.
N: Ibid.
P: PSC-F   853

FRIENDS, SOCIETY OF. EDENDERRY [Ireland] MONTHLY MEETING
Births, ca. 1656-1859; deaths, ca. 1680-1859; marriages, ca. 1652-1810 Ibid.
N: Ibid.
P: PSC-F   854

FRIENDS, SOCIETY OF. GRANGE [Ireland] MONTHLY MEETING
Births, ca. 1653-1859; deaths, ca.1730-1859; marriages, ca.1678-1858 Ibid.
N: Ibid.
P: PSC-F   855

FRIENDS, SOCIETY OF. GRANGE [Ireland] MONTHLY MEETING
Minutes, 1726-1779 IrDSF
N: PSC-F 2 reels*
P: PSC-F   856

FRIENDS, SOCIETY OF. IRELAND
National register of: births, 1859-1949; deaths, 1859-1949; marriages, 1859-1949 Ibid.
N: Ibid.
P: PSC-F   857

FRIENDS, SOCIETY OF. LIMERICK [Ireland] MONTHLY MEETING
Births, ca. 1653-1859; deaths, ca.1660-1861; marriages, ca. 1652-ca.1863 Ibid.
N: Ibid.
P: PSC-F   858

FRIENDS, SOCIETY OF. LISBURN [Ireland] MONTHLY MEETING
Births, ca. 1725-1859; deaths, ca. 1733-1859; marriages, ca. 1717-ca.1859 Ibid.
N: Ibid.
P: PSC-F   859

FRIENDS, SOCIETY OF. LISBURN [Ireland] MONTHLY MEETING
Minutes of sufferings, 1675-1782
N: PSC-F*
P: PSC-F   860

FRIENDS, SOCIETY OF. LURGAN [Ireland] MONTHLY MEETING
Births, ca. 1607-1859; deaths, ca.1658-1859; marriages, ca.1634-1861 Ibid.
N: Ibid.
P: PSC-F   861

FRIENDS, SOCIETY OF. LURGAN [Ireland] MONTHLY MEETING
Marriages, births, deaths, 1655-1750; marriage certificates, 1715-1811; minutes, 1675-1779 IrDSF
N: PSC-F 6 reels*
P: PSC-F   862

FRIENDS, SOCIETY OF. MOATE [Ireland] MONTHLY MEETING
Births, ca. 1616-1859; deaths, ca.1655-1859; marriages, ca.1635-1854 Ibid.
N: Ibid.
P: PSC-F   863

FRIENDS, SOCIETY OF. MOUNTMELLICK [Ireland] MONTHLY MEETING
Births, ca. 1627-ca.1860; deaths, ca.1648-ca. 1849; marriages, ca. 1650-ca.1862 Ibid.
N: Ibid.
P: PSC-F   864

FRIENDS, SOCIETY OF. RICHHILL [Ireland] MONTHLY MEETING
Births, ca. 1662-1862; deaths, ca. 1681-1859; marriages, ca. 1680-1859 Ibid.
N: Ibid.
P: PSC-F   865

FRIENDS, SOCIETY OF. TIPPERARY [Ireland] MONTHLY MEETING
Births, ca. 1616-1859; deaths, ca.1670-1859; marriages, ca. 1636-1859 Ibid.
N: Ibid.
P: PSC-F   866

FRIENDS, SOCIETY OF. ULSTER [Ireland] QUARTERLY MEETING
Marriage certificates, 1731-1786; minutes, 1673-1770; wills and inventories, 1697-1731 IrDSF
N: PSC-F 6 reels*
P: PSC-F   867

FRIENDS, SOCIETY OF. WATERFORD [Ireland] MONTHLY MEETING
Births, ca. 1624-1859; deaths, ca. 1654-1859; marriages, ca. 1649-1859 Ibid.
N: Ibid.
P: PSC-F   868

FRIENDS, SOCIETY OF. WEXFORD [Ireland] MONTHLY MEETING
Births, ca. 1641-1859; deaths, ca.1653-1859; marriages, ca.1640-1859 Ibid.
N: Ibid.
P: PSC-F   869

FRIENDS, SOCIETY OF. WICKLOW [Ireland] MONTHLY MEETING
Births, ca. 1627-ca.1817; deaths, ca.1663-ca. 1806; marriages, ca.1637-ca.1799 Ibid.
N: Ibid.
P: PSC-F   870

FRIENDS, SOCIETY OF. YOUGHAL [Ireland] MONTHLY MEETING
Births, ca. 1661-1859; deaths, ca.1675-1859; marriages, ca. 1652-1859 Ibid.
N: Ibid.
P: PSC-F   871

Personal Papers

ARTHUR, THOMAS, M.D.
Miscellaneous entry book for Limerick, 1619-1630, and Dublin, 1631-1666
Add. ms. 31885 UKLBM
N: CtY 2 reels*   872

BERKELEY, GEORGE, Bp., 1685-1753
Commonplace book, 1734-1753, 179 p.
Add. ms. 39305 UKLBM
N: CU   873

CASEMENT, Sir ROGER, 1864-1916
A page of my diary, March 17 - April 8, 1916 priv.
DCO: PV*   874

CASEMENT, Sir ROGER, 1864-1916
Papers, 1914-1916 NN
N: ? 3 reels
P: CSt-H   875

CONOLLY, Lady LOUISA AUGUSTA, 1743-1821
Letters to the Duchess of Leinster, 1759-1776 [The Fitzgerald Correspondence], 2 v. ms. 618-619 IrNL
N: ICU 1 reel   876

KING, WILLIAM, Abp. of Dublin
Correspondence, 1699-1729 IrNL
N: ?
P: InU, NjP 5 reels   877

NAPIER, Lady SARAH, 1745-1826
Letters to the Duchess of Leinster, 1760-1794 [The Fitzgerald Correspondence], 2 v. ms. 618-619 IrNL
N: ICU 1 reel   878

UPPER OSSORY, JOHN FITZPATRICK, 2nd EARL of, 1745-1818
In-letters, 1760-1818 IrNL
N: IrNL 1 reel
P: NNF   879

WHATELEY, RICHARD, Abp., 1787-1863
Letters, 1821-1844 UKOO
N: CtY 1 reel   880

Business Papers

KENMARE, VISCOUNTS AND EARLS OF
Estate rental ledgers (Kerry, Limrick, and Bantry), 1740-1859 Customs House, Dublin
N: USIGS 8 reels   881

Collections

BALLEYTONE PAPERS
Domestic letters of an Anglo-Irish family, 1742-1792 priv.
N: IrNL 1 reel
P: NNF   882

IRELAND. NATIONAL LIBRARY
Gaelic manuscripts, v. d. v. p.
N: IrNL
P: MH   883

U. S. LIBRARY OF CONGRESS
Irish Rebellion Papers, 1866, 1909, 1915, 1916, priv.
Ph: DLC 41 items   884

ISLE OF MAN

Census

MAN, ISLE OF. CENSUS
Transcripts of returns, 1821-1871 ImDRO
N: USIGS 16 reels   885

Government Records

MAN, ISLE OF
Liber Assedationis [Manorial rolls] of the court

at Peel, 1515-1881 ImDRO
N: USIGS 10 reels   886

MAN, ISLE OF
Liber Assedationis [Manorial rolls] of the
court at Rushen, 1507-1870 ImDRO
N: USIGS 10 reels   887

MAN, ISLE OF
Liber Electorum [Register of Electors], 1867,
1874, 1875-1876, 1877-1878 ImDRO
N: USIGS 1 reel   888

MAN, ISLE OF
Liber Plitor [Book of Pleas], 1496-1831
ImDRO
N: USIGS 49 reels   889

MAN, ISLE OF
Libri Scaccarii [Books of the Court of Ex-
chequer], 1580-1793 ImDRO
N: USIGS 17 reels   890

MAN, ISLE OF
Liber Vastarum [Yearly courts held at Rushen],
1511-1880 ImDRO
N: USIGS 23 reels   891

MAN, ISLE OF
Military records: Manx Fencibles, 1793-1802;
Isle of Man Volunteers, 1864-1916 ImDRO
N: USIGS 1 reel   892

MAN, ISLE OF
Poll books, 1866-1905 ImDRO
N: USIGS 2 reels   893

MAN, ISLE OF
Tithe composition book, 1841 ImDRO
N: USIGS 1 reel   894

MAN, ISLE OF
Valuation of land taken under Asylum Act,
1864, 1870, 2 v.   ImDRO
N: USIGS 1 reel   895

MAN, ISLE OF (Archdeaconry)
Wills of Archdeacon's Court, 1627-1861
ImDRO
N: USIGS 72 reels   896

MAN, ISLE OF. ENQUEST COURT
Records, 1687-1852 ImDRO
N: USIGS 40 reels   897

Parish Registers

ANDREAS (Kirk), Isle of Man
Parish registers, 1649-1849 Ibid.
N: USIGS 1 reel   898

ARBORY (Kirk), Isle of Man
Parish registers, 1652-1849 Ibid.
N: USIGS 1 reel   899

BALDWIN, Isle of Man. ST. LUKE'S PARISH
Parish registers, 1826-1849 Ibid.
N: USIGS 1 reel   900

BALLAUGH, Isle of Man
Parish registers, 1598-1849 Ibid.
N: USIGS 1 reel   901

BRADDON (Kirk), Isle of Man
Parish registers, 1624-1849 Ibid.
N: USIGS 1 reel   902

BRIDE (Kirk), Isle of Man
Parish registers, 1693-1849 Ibid.
N: USIGS 1 reel   903

CASTLETOWN (Kirk), Isle of Man
Parish registers, 1826-1859 Ibid.
N: USIGS 1 reel   904

CONCHAN, Isle of Man
Parish registers, 1627-1851 Ibid.
N: USIGS 1 reel   905

DOUGLAS, Isle of Man
Vital records from parish registers and for
Catholics of the Isle of Man, 1705-1892 Ibid.
N: USIGS 5 reels   906

GERMAN (Kirk), Isle of Man
Parish registers, 1665-1858 Ibid.
N: USIGS 3 reels   907

JURBY, Isle of Man
Parish registers, 1606-1874 Ibid.
N: USIGS 2 reels   908

LEZAYRE (Kirk), Isle of Man
Parish registers, 1696-1849 Ibid.
N: USIGS 1 reel   909

LONAN (Kirk), Isle of Man
Parish registers, 1718-1868 Ibid.
N: USIGS 1 reel   910

MALEW, Isle of Man
Parish registers, 1649-1848 Ibid.
N: USIGS 4 reels   911

MALEW, Isle of Man. ST. MARK PARISH
Registers, 1712-1849 Ibid.
N: USIGS 2 reels   912

MAN, ISLE OF
Parish register transcripts, 1847-1883 ImDRO
N: USIGS 19 reels   913

MAROWN, Isle of Man
Parish registers, 1622-1849 Ibid.
N: USIGS 1 reel   914

MAUGHOLD (Kirk), Isle of Man
Parish registers, 1647-1849 Ibid.
N: USIGS 2 reels   915

MICHAEL (Kirk), Isle of Man
Parish registers, 1611-1849 Ibid.
N: USIGS 1 reel   916

PATRICK (Kirk), Isle of Man
Parish registers, 1714-1849 Ibid.
N: USIGS 2 reels   917

RAMSEY, Isle of Man
Parish registers, 1761-1849 Ibid.
N: USIGS 1 reel   918

RUSHEN (Kirk), Isle of Man
Parish registers, 1708-1849 Ibid.
N: USIGS 2 reels   919

ST. JUDE'S, Isle of Man
Parish registers, 1846-1859 Ibid.
N: USIGS 1 reel   920

SANTON (Kirk) [SAINT ANNE], Isle of Man
Parish registers, 1690-1916 Ibid.
N: USIGS 1 reel   921

SULBY, Isle of Man. ST. STEPHEN'S CHURCH
Parish registers, 1841-1877 Ibid.
N: USIGS 1 reel   922

Business Papers

KEWLEY, ELIZABETH, of Ballafreer, Marown,
Isle of Man
Household account book, 1818-1851 priv.
N: USIGS 1 reel   923

CHANNEL ISLANDS

Church Records

CHURCH OF JESUS CHRIST OF LATTER-DAY
SAINTS. CHANNEL ISLANDS
Record of members: early to 1876, 1900-1901;
also Gibraltar Branch, 1853-1855 USlC
N: USIGS 1 reel   924

SCANDINAVIA

Government Records

GREAT BRITAIN. PUBLIC RECORD OFFICE
State Papers, Foreign, selections re:
17th century northern European diplomatic

relations UKLPRO
N: DLC   925

Church Records

CHURCH OF JESUS CHRIST OF LATTER-DAY
SAINTS. SCANDINAVIAN MISSION
Records of deceased members (Denmark,
Norway, and Sweden), 1852-1896 USlC
N: USIGS 1 reel   926

DENMARK

Census

AABENRAA, Denm. LANDSARKIVET
Census returns: Aabenraa-Sønderborg,
Haderslev, and Tónder, 1769-1860 DaAL
N: USIGS 12 reels   927

DENMARK. CENSUS, 1726-1860
Census returns, of clerical districts in
Aarhus and various other cities and parishes
DaKL
N: USIGS 6 reels   928

DENMARK. CENSUS, 1771
Census returns: heads of families, various
counties DaKR
N: USIGS 4 reels   929

DENMARK. CENSUS, 1787
Census returns: counties and cities of
Denmark, bks. 1-61 DaKR
N: USIGS 43 reels   930

DENMARK. CENSUS, 1801
Census returns: counties and cities of
Denmark, bks. 1-77 DaKR
N: USIGS 38 reels   931

DENMARK. CENSUS, 1803
Census returns: Slesvig Holsten, Denmark,
and Schleswig-Holstein, Prussia, bks. 1-6
DaKR
N: USIGS 3 reels   932

DENMARK. CENSUS, 1834
Census returns: counties and cities of
Denmark, and of Tranquebar, Madras
Presidency, India
N: USIGS 40 reels   933

DENMARK. CENSUS, 1835
Census returns: Slesvig-Holsten, Prussia,
bks. 1-21 DaKR
N: USIGS 26 reels   934

DENMARK. CENSUS, 1840
Census returns: counties and cities of
Denmark and of Schleswig-Holstein, Prussia,
bks. 1-73 DaKR
N: USIGS 78 reels   935

DENMARK. CENSUS, 1845
Census returns: counties and localities of
Denmark, including Schleswig-Holstein,
Prussia   DaKR
N: USIGS 98 reels   936

DENMARK. CENSUS, 1850
Census returns: counties and localities of
Denmark and Virgin Islands (St. Croix,
St. John, St. Thomas) DaKR
N: USIGS 61 reels   937

DENMARK. CENSUS, 1855
Census returns: counties, etc., Denmark,
Virgin Islands (St. Croix, St. John, St. Thomas),
and Schleswig-Holstein, Prussia DaKR
N: USIGS 127 reels   938

DENMARK. CENSUS, 1860
Census returns: counties, etc., Denmark,
Virgin Islands (St. Croix, St. John, St. Thomas),
and Schleswig-Holstein, Prussia DaKR
N: USIGS 114 reels   939

Government Records

DENMARK. RIGSARKIVET
Ausländisches- und Geheim-Registratur, 1662-1690 DaKR
N: CLU 28 reels* 940

DENMARK. RIGSARKIVET
Danish diplomatic despatches from Nymwegen Congress, 1677-1679 DaKR
N: CLU 4 reels* 941

DENMARK. RIGSARKIVET
Danish trade, shipping, privateering, blockades, etc., 1778-1859 DaKR
N: CLU 10 reels* 942

DENMARK. RIGSARKIVET
" Geheim " protocols on foreign relations, 1736-1753 DaKR
N: CLU 6 reels* 943

Military Records

AABENRAA, Denm. LANDSARKIVET
Military levying rolls, various districts and localities, Aabenraa-Sønderborg, 1742-1865; Haderslev, 1782-1861; Tønder, 1737-1865 DaAL
N: USIGS 51 reels 944

DENMARK. HAEREN
Military levying rolls, various districts, 1789-1851 DaKR
N: USIGS 1253 reels 945

DENMARK. HAEREN
Vital records, while stationed in Slesvig, Denmark, Schleswig-Holstein, Prussia,and Oldenburg, Germany, 1758-1874 DaKL
N: USIGS 2 reels 946

DENMARK. HAEREN. ARKIVET
Army service records, 1739-1910; medal awards given to Army personnel, various counties, 1848-1850, 1864; records of Royal Frederick (Christian's) Soldier Home in Copenhagen, 1765-1854; Coastal fortifications of Copenhagen, 1870-1890 DaKH
N: USIGS 760 reels 947

DENMARK. HAEREN. ARKIVET
Berliens collections: officerer og Mellem-stabspersoner [card index of Army officers and personnel], ca. 1658-1841 DaKH
N: USIGS 3 reels 948

DENMARK. HAEREN. ARKIVET
Card index of non-commissioned Army officers, ca. 1757-1860; Feilberg and Dittman's collections: index of military personnel, ca. 1612-1888; military lists, Danish and Norwegian officers, 1648-1814 DaKH
N: USIGS 20 reels 949

DENMARK. MARINE
Military rolls, Navy quarters, schools, etc. of Copenhagen (Divisionsbøger I-II; Mand-talsbøger I-IV; Husbøger I-VIII; Praesenta-tionsbog), 1669-1888 DaKR
N: USIGS 115 reels 950

DENMARK. MARINE
Vital records, various ships, 1811-1813, 1840-1847 DaKL
N: USIGS 1 reel 951

DENMARK. RIGSARKIVET
Probate records of the military court [Generalanditøren], København, 1719-1863 DaKR
N: USIGS 5 reels 952

VIBORG, Denm. LANDSARKIVET
Military levying rolls (Army and Navy) of Jylland (Jutland), 1583-1893 DaKL
N: USIGS 87 reels 953

Local Records

COPENHAGEN. STADSARKIVET
Kopulationspengeprotokoll [records of marriage fees], 1720-1863; Borgerskabsprotokoll [records and lists of citizens], 1683-1865; Naeringsbevillinger [business licenses], 1779-1857; Vartov Hospital records, 1677-1804; Faesteprotokoll [magistrates records], 1687-1918; miscellaneous records Ibid.
N: USIGS 44 reels 954

Church Records

AABENRAA, Denm. LANDSARKIVET
Church records: various localities in Aabenraa-Sønderborg, 1573-1927; Haderslev, 1574-1941; Tønder, 1590-1944 DaAL
N: USIGS 246 reels 955

CHURCH OF JESUS CHRIST OF LATTER-DAY SAINTS. DENMARK
Branch records: Denmark, 1860-1934; Copenhagen, 1850-1854; immigration records of members, Denmark to U.S.A., 1872-1894; records of Danish Mission and branches (Scandinavian Mission to 1920), 1907-1954 USIC
N: USIGS 26 reels 956

COPENHAGEN. LANDSARKIVET
Church records, various localities: Bornholm, 1687-1895; Frederiksborg, 1637-1895; Holbaek, 1633-1892; København, 1617-1903; Maribo, 1632-1893; church records and parish registers, various localities in Sorø, 1628-1897; parish registers, various localities in Praestø, 1639-1897; parish register extracts of Slesvig, and Schleswig-Holstein, Prussia (Louis Bobe's excerpts), ca. 1628-1835 DaKL
N: USIGS 2835 reels 957

COPENHAGEN. LANDSARKIVET
Excerpts from parish registers: Julianehaab, 1778-1861; Egedesminde, 1769-1841; Godhavn, 1778-1833; Upernivik, 1779-1789; and other localities in Grønland (Greenland), 1742-1850; Syd-Strømø, Faroe Islands, 1757-1816; British Church in Elsinore (Helsingør), Denm., 1833-1843 DaKL
N: USIGS 1 reel 958

ODENSE, Denm. LANDSARKIVET
Church records, various localities in Odense, 1640-1893, and Svendborg, 1622-1894 DaOL
N: USIGS 393 reels 959

SJAELLAND, Denm. MOSAIC CONGREGATION
Vital records, 1815-1914 DaKL
N: USIGS 3 reels 960

VIBORG, Denm. LANDSARKIVET
Church records, various localities: Aalborg, 1564-1910; Aarhus, 1619-1895; Hjørring, 1646-1891; Randers, 1631-1892; Ribe, 1523-1904; Ringkøbing, 1633-1901; Skanderborg, 1659-1896; Thisted, 1641-1926; Vejle, 1635-1946; Viborg, 1659-1900 DaVL
N: USIGS 2198 reels 961

VIBORG, Denm. LANDSARKIVET
Parish register extracts (Lengnick's excerpts), various districts of Denmark, 17th-19th cents. DaVL
N: USIGS 29 reels 962

Probate Records

AABENRAA, Denm. LANDSARKIVET
Probate records of judicial districts, city administrations, etc. in Tønder, 1653-1866 DaAL
N: USIGS 21 reels 963

AABENRAA, Denm. LANDSARKIVET
Probate records, various districts, city administrations and private estates in Aabenraa-Sønderborg, 1640-1867 DaAL
N: USIGS 48 reels 964

AABENRAA, Denm. LANDSARKIVET
Probate records, various judicial districts, etc. in Haderslev, 1696-1867 DaAL
N: USIGS 27 reels 965

COPENHAGEN. LANDSARKIVET
Probate records, various districts, city and county administrations, deaneries, and judicial districts: Bornholm, 1681-1878; Frederiksborg, 1571-1867; Holbaek, 1641-1874; Hofretten [Royal Court], Underadmiralitets-retten [Naval Court], in Copenhagen, 1670-1868; Maribo, 1598-1865; Sorø, 1647-1892 DaKL
N: USIGS 4065 reels 966

COPENHAGEN. LANDSARKIVET
Skifte, Registreringsprotokoller [Probate records], various districts and towns in Praestø, 1570-1879 DaKL
N: USIGS 103 reels 967

COPENHAGEN. LANDSARKIVET
Skifteprotokoller for Amter, Amtstuer samt Godser og Institutioner [probate records, various private estates and institutions of Sjaelland], ca. 1571-1908 DaKL
N: USIGS 352 reels 968

DENMARK. FRIJSENBORG GODS
Probate records (skifteprotokoller, etc.) of Estates, now in Viborg, Aarhus, Randers, Vejle, and Skanderborg, 1719-1860 DaKL
N: USIGS 9 reels 969

ODENSE, Denm. LANDSARKIVET
Probate records, various judicial districts, city administrations, deaneries, etc. in Odense, 1602-1919, and Svendborg, 1624-1908 DaOL
N: USIGS 395 reels 970

ODENSE, Denm. LANDSARKIVET
Skifteprotokoller for Amter og Godser [probate records of various private estates and institutions]of Fyen (Odense and Svendborg), 1683-1880 DaOL
N: USIGS 184 reels 971

VIBORG, Denm. LANDSARKIVET
Probate records, various districts, city administrations, deaneries, diocesan archives, judicial districts: Aalborg, 1629-1886; Aarhus, 1669-1891; Hjørring, 1696-1881; Randers, 1676-1894; Ringkøbing, 1646-1883; Ribe, 1562-1883; Skanderborg, 1683-1869; Thisted, 1699-1877; Vejle, 1625-1882; Viborg, 1690-1874 DaVL
N: USIGS 1587 reels 972

VIBORG, Denm. LANDSARKIVET
Probate records of estates in Randers, 1710-1841 DaVL
N: USIGS 8 reels 973

VIBORG, Denm. LANDSARKIVET
Skifteprotokoll [probate records], various private estates and institutions in Jylland (Jutland), ca. 1603-1874 DaVL
N: USIGS 433 reels 974

VIBORG, Denm. LANDSARKIVET
Stiftamt; Skifteprotokol [Ecclesiastical jurisdiction in Ribe; probate records], 1707-1846 DaVL
N: USIGS 15 reels 975

Personal Papers

GJOE, MARCUS
London correspondence, 1669-1678 DaKR
N: CLU 12 reels* 976

HÖG, JUST
Correspondence from the Netherlands, 1671-1677 DaKR
N: CLU 5 reels* 977

Collections

COPENHAGEN. UNIVERSITET. BIBLIOTEK
Arnamagnaeanske hs. samling [Collection of Icelandic and Old Norse texts] DaKU
N: ICU 11 reels 978

FINLAND

Bibliography

FINLAND. VALTIONARKISTO
Kaupunkituomioistuimet (Lagmansratten);
Luettelo (Stadsdomstolar-Katalog)
[inventories of city and provincial archives
including Leningrad District, Russia and
Narva and environs, Estonia and to part of
the Court records of "Old Collection of
Accounts"], ca. 1550-1814 FiHV
N: USIGS 1 reel   979

FINLAND. VALTIONARKISTO
Suomen vanhemmen tilikirjakokoelman
luettelo [catalog of the " Old Collection of
Accounts"], 1530-1634, books 1-6807
FiHV
N: USIGS 1 reel   980

Census

FINLAND. VALTIONARKISTO
Henkikirjat - Mantalslängder [census returns]:
Häme; Kuopio (including parts of Viipuri
and Mikkeli); Mikkeli; Oulu (including parts of
Lappi); Turku-Pori; Uusimaa (including parts
of Turku-Pori); Vaasa; Viipuri (including
parts of Kymi), 1810-1860   FiHV
N: USIGS 73 reels   981

Government Records

FINLAND
Boskaps- m. fl. längder [earliest tax lists of
livestock and seed, etc.] of various districts
and counties of Finland, 1620, 1622, 1624,
1629-1630, 1632-1633, 1635-1637; of
Ahvenanmaa (Aland), 1621, 1629, 1635-1636
SvSR
N: USIGS 1 reel   982

Military Records

FINLAND. VALTIONARKISTO
Sotilasasiakirjoja, Pääkatselmusluettelo,
Militara Handlingar, Generalmönsterrullar
[military records of Finland: general muster
rolls, etc.], ca. 1600-1809 FiHV
N: USIGS 156 reels   983

Local Records

FINLAND. VALTIONARKISTO
Circuit court records, various judicial
districts of Mikkeli, 1747-1819; special
court records (copy), St. Michel, Mikkeli,
1749-1806; special court records (copy),
Rantasalmi, Mikkeli, 1787-1788, 1791-1792,
1797, 1803-1806 FiHV
N: USIGS 57 reels   984

FINLAND. VALTIONARKISTO
Circuit court records (copy) of judicial
districts in Northwest-, and Central Häme,
1623-1749 FiHV
N: USIGS 40 reels   985

FINLAND. VALTIONARKISTO
Circuit court records (copy), various
judicial districts in Turku- Pori, 1584-1750
FiHV
N: USIGS 141 reels   986

FINLAND. VALTIONARKISTO
Circuit court records, various judicial
districts in Viipuri, 1623-1821 FiHV
N: USIGS 132 reels   987

FINLAND. VALTIONARKISTO
City court records: Käkisalmi, Viipuri,
1646-1702; Sortavala, Viipuri, 1673-1697,
1700-1706; Viipuri, Viipuri, 1622-1708
FiHV
N: USIGS 25 reels   988

FINLAND. VALTIONARKISTO
Court records, 1789-1808; circuit court
records, 1798-1808, of judicial districts
now in Lappi, Finland, including parts in
Västerbotten, Sweden; special court records
(copy), 1748-1807, and Court of Appeal
records, 1798-1808, of Tornio (Tornea),
Lappi FiHV
N: USIGS 12 reels   989

FINLAND. VALTIONARKISTO
Court records and special court records of
Loviisa, Uusimaa, 1748-1810 FiHV
N: USIGS 55 reels   990

FINLAND. VALTIONARKISTO
Court records (copy) of judicial districts in
Southwest Finland (Raasepori, Pikkiö and
Halikko, Sääksmäki and Hollola Districts),
1603-1749 FiHV
N: USIGS 9 reels   991

FINLAND. VALTIONARKISTO
Court and city records of Helsinki, 1623-1884;
court records: Porvoo (Borgå), 1622-1805;
Tammisaari (Ekenäs), 1650-1809 FiHV
N: USIGS 38 reels   992

FINLAND. VALTIONARKISTO
Erikoistuomioistuimet - Specialdomstolar
[special court records (copy)of Oulu]: Kajaani
(Kajana), 1748-1807; Oulu, 1772-1806 FiHV
N: USIGS 4 reels   993

FINLAND. VALTIONARKISTO
Kaupunkituomioistuimet - Stadsdomstolar [city
administration records, mortgage records,
lower court proceedings, etc.]: Kajaani
(Kajana), 1659-1810; Oulu (Uleaborg), 1640-
1814; Raahe (Brahestad), 1659-1810 FiHV
N: USIGS 82 reels   994

FINLAND. VALTIONARKISTO
Kaupunkituomioistuimet - Stadsdomstolar
[court records]: City administration records,
lower court proceedings, etc. of
Hämeenlinna, Häme, 1666-1809 FiHV
N: USIGS 12 reels   995

FINLAND. VALTIONARKISTO
Kaupunkituomioistuimet- Stadsdomstolar;
Erikoistuomioistuimet - Specialdomstolar
[court records: special court records] of
Naantali (Nådental), Pori (Björneborg),
Rauma (Raumo), Turku (Abo), Uusikaupunki
(Nystad), Turku-Pori, Finland, 1622-1809
FiHV
N: USIGS 276 reels   996

FINLAND. VALTIONARKISTO
Kihlakunnanoikeus - Häradsrätt [circuit
court records (copy)] of Hollola Judicial
District, 1610-1749; Janakkala (Hauho)
Judicial District, Häme, 1749 FiHV
N: USIGS 13 reels   997

FINLAND. VALTIONARKISTO
Kihlakunnanoikeus - Häradsrätt [circuit
court records (copy)] of Kajaani Baronical
District, 1651-1659, 1674-1680 FiHV
N: USIGS 1 reel   998

FINLAND. VALTIONARKISTO
Kihlakunnanoikeus-Häradsrätt [circuit court
records (copy)]of various judicial districts
in Uusimaa, including parts of other
provinces, 1620-1749 FiHV
N: USIGS 96 reels   999

FINLAND. VALTIONARKISTO
Special court records of Old Finland, now
Viipuri, Kymi and Southeast Mikkeli, 1736-
1810 FiHV
N: USIGS 132 reels   1000

HÄME, Finland (Dept.). MAAKUNTA-ARKISTO,
Hämeenlinna
Circuit court records, various judicial dis-
tricts in Mikkeli, 1810-1870 FiHaM
N: USIGS 74 reels   1001

HÄME, Finland (Dept.). MAAKUNTA-ARKISTO,
Hämeenlinna
Circuit court records, various judicial
districts in Uusimaa, 1804-1873 FiHaM
N: USIGS 128 reel   1002

HÄME, Finland (Dept.). MAAKUNTA-ARKISTO,
Hämeenlinna
Tuomiokunta - domsaga [circuit court records],
various judicial districts in Häme, 1810-1867
FiHaM
N: USIGS 191 reels   1003

OULU, Finland (Dept.). MAAKUNTA-ARKISTO,
Oulu
Circuit court records, various judicial districts
in Lappi, 1810-1870; city court records of Tor-
nio (Tornea), Lappi, 1666-1878 FiOM
N: USIGS 97 reels   1004

OULU, Finland (Dept.). MAAKUNTA-ARKISTO,
Oulu
Circuit court records, various judicial
districts in Oulu, 1737-1884 FiOM
N: USIGS 137 reels   1005

OULU, Finland (Dept.). MAAKUNTA-ARKISTO,
Oulu
Ilmoitusasiain ptk., Perunkirjoitukset [city
court records: mortgage records, private
inventories]: Kajaani (Kajana), 1737-1882;
Oulu (Uleaborg), 1729-1860; Raahe (Brahestad),
1808-1861; and miscellaneous city records of
Oulu, 1778-1913 FiOM
N: USIGS 41 reels   1006

TORNIO, Lappi, Finland. RADHUSRÄTT,
KÄMNÄRSRÄTT
Renoverade Dombböcker [city and lower court
records (copy)], 1698-1801 SvSR
N: USIGS 1 reel   1007

TURKU-PORI, Finland (Dept.). MAAKUNTA-
ARKISTO, Turku
Circuit court records of judicial districts of
Ahvenanmaa (Aland), 1747-1861 FiTM
N: USIGS 154 reels   1008

TURKU-PORI, Finland (Dept.). MAAKUNTA-
ARKISTO, Turku
Circuit court records (copy), various judicial
districts in Häme (and parts of other pro-
vinces), 1793-1809; tax list extracts of
Hollola Judicial District, Häme, 1564-1641,
and court record extracts from the von Gerdte
Collection, 1564-1587 FiTM
N: USIGS 112 reels   1009

TURKU-PORI, Finland (Dept.). MAAKUNTA-
ARKISTO, Turku
Circuit court records, various judicial
districts in Turku-Pori, 1702-1874 FiTM
N: USIGS 834 reels   1010

TURKU-PORI, Finland (Dept.). MAAKUNTA-
ARKISTO, Turku
Circuit court records, various judicial
districts in Uusimaa, 1750-1809 FiTM
N: USIGS 224 reels   1011

TURKU-PORI, Finland (Dept.). MAAKUNTA-
ARKISTO, Turku
Court of Appeal records, chancery records,
and tax records of Turku-Pori, 1713-1899
FiTM
N: USIGS 380 reels   1012

TURKU-PORI, Finland (Dept.). MAAKUNTA-
ARKISTO, Turku
Court records (copy) of judicial districts in
Southwest and Southeast Finland, 1750-1776
FiTM
N: USIGS 31 reels   1013

TURKU-PORI, Finland (Dept.). MAAKUNTA-
ARKISTO, Turku
Court records (copy) of judicial districts now
in Western Finland, 1767, 1771-1773 FiTM
N: USIGS 2 reels   1014

TURKU-PORI, Finland (Dept.). MAAKUNTA-
ARKISTO, Turku
Raastuvanoikeus - Radstuvurättan [court
records], various localities in Turku-Pori,
1715-1892 FiTM
N: USIGS 88 reels   1015

TURKU-PORI, Finland (Dept.). MAAKUNTA-
ARKISTO, Turku
Records of various cities in Turku-Pori:
Pori, 1796-1827; Rauma (Raumo), 1630-
1861; Turku, 1625-1910; Uusikaupunki (Nystad),
1799-1874 FiTM
N: USIGS 244 reels   1016

TURKU-PORI, Finland (Dept.). MAAKUNTA-
ARKISTO, Turku
Tuomiokirja [court records] of judicial
districts in Western Uusimaa, including
assize divisions in Häme and Turku-Pori,
1776-1809 FiTM
N: USlGS 30 reels   1017

VAASA, Finland (Dept.). MAAKUNTA-ARKISTO,
Vaasa
Circuit court records (copy), Kemi Judicial
District, Lappi, 1776-1810; probate records,
1777-1810 FiVM
N: USlGS 47 reels   1018

VAASA, Finland (Dept.). MAAKUNTA-ARKISTO,
Vaasa
Circuit court records, various judicial districts
in Mikkeli, 1639-1862; city court records of
Savonlinna, Mikkeli, 1822-1860 FiVM
N: USlGS 196 reels   1019

VASSA, Finland (Dept.). MAAKUNTA-ARKISTO,
Vaasa
Circuit court records (copy) of judicial districts
in Northwest Finland (now Oulu), Vaasa and
parts of Lappi, 1626-1658 FiVM
N: USlGS 4 reels   1020

VAASA, Finland (Dept.). MAAKUNTA-ARKISTO,
Vaasa
Circuit court records, various judicial districts
in Oulu (and parts of Vaasa and Loppi), 1739,
1750-1812 FiVM
N: USlGS 215 reels   1021

VAASA, Finland (Dept.). MAAKUNTA-ARKISTO,
Vaasa
Circuit court records, various localities in
Vaasa, including parts of other districts,
1659-1878 FiVM
N: USlGS 624 reels   1022

VAASA, Finland (Dept.). MAAKUNTA-ARKISTO,
Vaasa
Circuit court records and Court of Appeal
records, various judicial districts in Viipuri,
including parts of other districts, 1812-1868
FiVM
N: USlGS 89 reels   1023

VAASA, Finland (Dept.). MAAKUNTA-ARKISTO,
Vaasa
City court records (copy: probate records) of
Oulu: Kajani (Kajana), 1750-1820; Oulu
(Uleaborg), 1750-1809; Raahe (Brahestad),
1750-1815 FiVM
N: USlGS 12 reels   1024

VAASA, Finland (Dept.). MAAKUNTA-ARKISTO,
Vaasa
City records: Käkisalmi, Viipuri, 1824-1892;
Viipuri, Viipuri, 1726-1895 FiVM
N: USlGS 15 reels   1025

VAASA, Finland (Dept.). MAAKUNTA-ARKISTO,
Vaasa
Court records and miscellaneous records,
various cities in Vaasa, ca. 1440-1885 FiVM
N: USlGS 217 reels   1026

VAASA, Finland (Dept.). MAAKUNTA-ARKISTO,
Vaasa
Lower court records of Eastern Finland,
1840-1867 FiVM
N: USlGS 1 reel   1027

VAASA, Finland (Dept.). MAAKUNTA-ARKISTO,
Vaasa
Tuomiokirja [court records] of judicial districts
now in Western Finland, 1750-1775 FiVM
N: USlGS 7 reels   1028

Church Records

CHURCH OF JESUS CHRIST OF LATTER-DAY
SAINTS. FINLAND
Records of the Finnish Mission [Scandinavian
Mission to 1920, Swedish Mission, 1920-1947]
early to 1952; Finnish Branch records, 1876-
1900 USlC
N: USlGS 1 reel   1029

FINLAND. VALTIONARKISTO
Army church records, 1742-1898 FiHV
N: USlGS 1 reel   1030

FINLAND. VALTIONARKISTO
Church records of the Finnish Guard (Army)
stationed in Uusimaa, 1761-1913; church
records of the Finnish Navy personnel of
Uusimaa, 1823-1881 FiHV
N: USlGS 29 reels   1031

FINLAND. VALTIONARKISTO
Church records, various localities in
Uusimaa, 1637-1949 FiHV
N: USlGS 464 reels   1032

HÄME, Finland (Dept.). MAAKUNTA-ARKISTO,
Hämeenlinna
Church records, various localities in Häme
(including Consistorial records of Tampere
Diocese, 1722-1860), 1458-1949 FiHaM
N: USlGS 817 reels   1033

HÄME, Finland (Dept.). MAAKUNTA-ARKISTO
Hämeenlinna
Church records, various localities in Kuopio,
1664-1950 FiHaM
N: USlGS 537 reels   1034

HÄME, Finland (Dept.). MAAKUNTA-ARKISTO,
Hämeenlinna
Church records, various localities in Mikkeli,
1664-1945 FiHaM
N: USlGS 307 reels   1035

HÄME, Finland (Dept.). MAAKUNTA-ARKISTO,
Hämeenlinna
Church records of Mikkeli: Heinävesi, 1750-
1911; Kerimäki, 1729-1878 FiHaM
N: USlGS 24 reels   1036

HÄME, Finland (Dept.). MAAKUNTA-ARKISTO,
Hämeenlinna
Church records of Punkalaidum (Pungalaitio),
Turku-Pori, 1690-1945 FiHaM
N: USlGS 12 reels   1037

HÄME, Finland (Dept.). MAAKUNTA-ARKISTO,
Hämeenlinna
Church records, various localities in Uusimaa,
1604-1949 FiHaM
N: USlGS 240 reels   1038

OULU, Finland (Dept.). MAAKUNTA-ARKISTO,
Oulu
Church records, various localities in Lappi,
Finland, 1577-1947 FiOM
N: USlGS 114 reels   1039

OULU, Finland (Dept.). MAAKUNTA-ARKISTO,
Oulu
Church records, various localities in Oulu,
1558-1948 FiOM
N: USlGS 360 reels   1040

TURKU-PORI, Finland (Dept.). MAAKUNTA-
ARKISTO, Turku
Church records of various localities in
Ahvenanmaa, 1613-1948 FiTM
N: USlGS 92 reels   1041

TURKU-PORI, Finland (Dept.). MAAKUNTA-
ARKISTO, Turku
Church records of various localities in
Turku-Pori, 1329-1949 FiTM
N: USlGS 1430 reels   1042

VAASA, Finland (Dept.). MAAKUNTA-ARKISTO,
Vaasa
Church records, various localities in Kuopio,
1723-1888 FiVM
N: USlGS 36 reels   1043

VAASA, Finland (Dept.). MAAKUNTA-ARKISTO,
Vaasa
Church records of Mikkeli: Heinävesi, 1744-
1888; Rantasalmi, 1700-1897; Viidennen
Suomen Ruotukoisen tarkk' ampuja pataljoona
[5th Finnish Sharpshooter Regiment], 1855-
1869 FiVM
N: USlGS 41 reels   1044

VAASA, Finland (Dept.). MAAKUNTA-ARKISTO,
Vaasa
Church and parish records, various localities
in Viipuri, 1681-1933 FiVM
N: USlGS 350 reels   1045

VAASA, Finland (Dept.). MAAKUNTA-ARKISTO,
Vaasa
Greek Catholic church records: Helsinki
(Helsingfors), Uusimaa, 1783-1877; Petsamo
(Pechenga, formerly in N.E. Oulu, later
Lappi, Finland, now part of Murmansk region,
Russia), 1855-1860; Turku (Abo), Turku-Pori,
1845-1867 FiVM
N: USlGS 10 reels   1046

VAASA, Finland (Dept.). MAAKUNTA-ARKISTO,
Vaasa
Parish and church records, various
localities in Vaasa, 1516-1949 FiVM
N: USlGS 724 reels   1047

Personal Papers

TURTIO, IDA
In-letters from Finland, 1939-1940, 11 items
priv.
N: CtY   1048

Collections

FINLAND. VALTIONARKISTO
Vanhempi tilikirjokoelma; äldre
räkenskapssamlingen ["Old Collection of
Accounts"], 1530-1634 FiHV
N: USlGS 569 reels   1049

FINLAND. VALTIONARKISTO
Yleisiä asiskirjoja - Allmänna handlingar
["New Collection of Accounts"], 1635-1809
FiHV
N: USlGS 461 reels   1050

HELSINGFORS. UNIVERSITET. BIBLIOTEK
Cyrillic catalog, 1954 FiHU
N: CSt-H 18 reels   1051

WASASTJERNA, OSCAR
[Suomalaisia Venajan sotapalveluksessa-
Finska medborgare i rysk militartjanst]
Finnish officers and citizens in Russian
military service, ca. 1819-1859, 1888-1901
FiHV
N: USlGS 1 reel   1052

ICELAND

Census

ICELAND. CENSUS, 1649-1901
Manntal, by county IcRN
N: USlGS 77 reels   1053

Government Records

ICELAND. NATIONAL RECORD OFFICE
Þ(th)ingbok [Provincial Court records], 1619-
1810; Skiptabók [probate records], 1743-1910;
Vedmálabók [mortgage records], 1799-1907;
Yfirfjarrad(d)abok [orphans' records], 1808-
1916; Manntalsbok [sheriffs' tax registers],
1702-1805; Dóma og (th)ingbók [Provincial
Court records] of Hunavatns and Eyjafjardar
counties, 1694-1796; Fermingarskýslur [con-
firmation records], 1831-1951 IcRN
N: USlGS 196 reels   1054

Church Records

CHURCH OF JESUS CHRIST OF LATTER-DAY
SAINTS. ICELANDIC MISSION
Records, 1873-1914 USlC
N: USlGS 1 reel   1055

ICELAND. NATIONAL RECORD OFFICE
Church records, various deaneries, 1649-1952
IcRN
N: USlGS 586 reels   1056

Personal Papers

BANKS, Sir JOSEPH, 1743-1820
  Voyage to Iceland, 1772, 94 p.   CaQMM
  N: CaQMM   1057

NORWAY

Bibliography

BERGEN, Norway. STATSARKIVET
  Catalogue of parish registers, kept at the
  State Archive of Bergen (including those of
  Rogaland, Sogn og Fjordane, Hordaland,
  and Bergen counties) Ibid.
  N: USIGS 1 reel   1058

NORWAY. RIKSARKIVET
  A card index to parish extracts, ca. 1664-1891
  NoOR
  N: USIGS 1 reel   1059

NORWAY. RIKSARKIVET
  Oslo: general index to mortgage records, 1694-
  1894; probate card index, 1656-1809 NoOR
  N: USIGS 40 reels   1060

OSLO. STATSARKIVET
  Inventory of all court records in Oslo, Hamar,
  and Kristiansand Archives (of judicial districts
  in Akershus, Aust-Agder, Hedmark,
  Opland, Oslo, Østfeld, Telemark, Vest-Agder,
  and Vestfold counties), ca. 1650-1900 Ibid.
  N: USIGS 1 reel   1061

TRONDHEIM. STATSARKIVET
  Liste over kirkebøkene [catalogue of parish
  registers kept at the State Archive at Trondheim (including Møre, Sør-Trøndelag, Nord-
  Trøndelag, Nordland, Troms, Finnmark, etc.
  counties)], 1664-1941 Ibid.
  N: USIGS 1 reel   1062

Census

BERGEN, Norway. STATSARKIVET
  Extra census of (Eldre) Ryfylke judicial
  district and Vikedal, Rogaland, 1762-1763
  Bk 41 Ibid.
  N: USIGS 1 reel   1063

NORWAY. CENSUS, 1663-1666
  Census returns of counties and localities:
  clerical districts and parishes [Prostier,
  Prestegjeld, and Sogn] NoOR
  N: USIGS 11 reels   1064

NORWAY. CENSUS, 1663-1666
  Census returns of counties and localities:
  judicial districts [Fogderier, Sorenskriverier,
  and Herreder] NoOR
  N: USIGS 13 reels   1065

NORWAY. CENSUS, 1701
  Census returns of counties and localities:
  judicial and clerical districts and parishes
  [Fogderier, Sorenskriverier, Herreder,
  Prestegjeld, and Sogn] NoOR
  N: USIGS 4 reels   1066

NORWAY. CENSUS, 1801
  Census returns of counties, districts, and
  localities: present and former names of
  counties NoOR
  N: USIGS 26 reels   1067

NORWAY. CENSUS, 1865
  Census returns of counties and localities:
  school and clerical districts with present
  and former names of counties NoOR
  N: USIGS 181 reels   1068

Court Records

BERGEN, Norway. STATSARKIVET
  Bergen church and civil records, 1663-1900
  Ibid.
  N: USIGS 135 reels   1069

BERGEN, Norway. STATSARKIVET
  Hordaland: court records, 1642-1701; probate
  records, 1668-1881; clerical probate records,
  various deaneries [Prosti], 1690-1810;
  mortgage records, 1733-1878; general index
  to mortgage records, 1735-1932; civil death
  records, 1830-1910 Ibid.
  N: USIGS 205 reels   1070

BERGEN, Norway. STATSARKIVET
  Rogaland: mortgage records (some extracts),
  1682-1872; general index to mortgage records,
  1760-1912; probate records, 1666-1883; probate
  card index, 1666-1788; civil death records,
  1862-1901 Ibid.
  N: USIGS 158 reels   1071

BERGEN, Norway. STATSARKIVET
  Sogn og Fjordane: court records, ca. 1648-
  1897; mortgage records, 1711-1887; general
  index to mortgage records, 1757-1909; probate
  records, 1666-1882; clerical probate records,
  various deaneries [Prosti], 1766-1846 Ibid.
  N: USIGS 185 reels   1072

HAMAR, Norway. STATSARKIVET
  Hedmark: court records, 1633-1701; probate
  records, 1662-1860; probate card index, 1663-
  1853; mortgage records, 1700-1857; general
  index to mortgage records, 1713-1895 Ibid.
  N: USIGS 159 reels   1073

HAMAR, Norway. STATSARKIVET
  Opland: court records, 1651-1701; mortgage
  records, 1689-1869; general index to mortgage records, ca. 1720-1870; probate records,
  1657-1887; probate card index, 1657-1903 Ibid.
  N: USIGS 126 reels   1074

KRISTIANSAND, Norway. STATSARKIVET
  Aust-Agder: court records, 1677-1701; probate
  records, 1692-1884; probate card index, 1640-
  1858; mortgage records, 1692-1886; general
  index to mortgage records, 1711-1907 Ibid.
  N: USIGS 225 reels   1075

KRISTIANSAND, Norway. STATSARKIVET
  Vest-Agder: court records, 1657-1701; mortgage records, 1688-1933; general index to
  mortgage records, 1695-1921; probate records,
  1666-1889; probate card index, ca. 1666-1760
  Ibid.
  N: USIGS 224 reels   1076

NORWAY. RIKSARKIVET
  Akershus: mortgage records and indexes, 1688-
  1881; probate card index, ca. 1680-1844; Buskerud: mortgage records, 1690-1864; general
  index to mortgage records, 1609-1867; probate
  card index, 1676-1824; Østfold: general index
  to mortgage records, 1689-1890; probate card
  index, ca. 1667-1802; Telemark: general index
  to mortgage records, 1692-1898; Vestfold:
  mortgage records, 1729-1807; general index
  to mortgage records, ca. 1750-1901 NoOR
  N: USIGS 230 reels   1077

OSLO. STATSARKIVET
  Akershus: court records, various judicial
  districts, 1651-1899 Ibid.
  N: USIGS 95 reels   1078

OSLO. STATSARKIVET
  Buskerud: court records, 1650-1705; mortgage
  records, 1688-1876; probate records, 1671-1885
  Ibid.
  N: USIGS 183 reels   1079

OSLO. STATSARKIVET
  Oslo: court records, 1652-1700; probate
  records, 1656-1901; mortgage records,
  1690-1875; civil death records, 1882-1890
  Ibid.
  N: USIGS 100 reels   1080

OSLO. STATSARKIVET
  Østfold: court records, 1650-1701; mortgage
  records, 1689-1873; probate records, 1667-
  1882; death records, 1836-1869 Ibid.
  N: USIGS 149 reels   1081

OSLO. STATSARKIVET
  Rogaland: court records, 1613-1701 Ibid.
  N: USIGS 22 reels   1082

OSLO. STATSARKIVET
  Telemark: court records, 1652-1704; mortgage
  records, ca. 1689-1839; probate records, 1665-
  1880; probate card index, ca. 1665-1784 Ibid.
  N: USIGS 97 reels   1083

OSLO. STATSARKIVET
  Vestfold: court records, 1665-1705; mortgage
  records, 1688-1852; probate records, 1666-
  1851 Ibid.
  N: USIGS 112 reels   1084

TRONDHEIM. STATSARKIVET
  Clerical probate records, Dalane Deanery
  [Prosti], Rogaland, 1741-1812 Ibid.
  N: USIGS 4 reels   1085

TRONDHEIM. STATSARKIVET
  Finnmark: court records, 1620-1701; probate
  records, 1686-1891; mortgage records, 1776-
  1887 Ibid.
  N: USIGS 40 reels   1086

TRONDHEIM. STATSARKIVET
  Møre: court records, 1648-1705; mortgage
  records, 1692-1877; general index to mortgage
  records, 1692-1935; probate records, 1668-
  1889; clerical probate records, various
  deaneries [Prosti], 1697-1812 Ibid.
  N: USIGS 174 reels   1087

TRONDHEIM. STATSARKIVET
  Nordland: court records, 1690-1709; mortgage
  records, 1700-1878; general index to mortgage
  records, 1710-1900; probate records, 1673-
  1879; clerical probate records, various
  deaneries [Prosti], 1701-1832 Ibid.
  N: USIGS 130 reels   1088

TRONDHEIM. STATSARKIVET
  Nord-Trøndelag: court records, 1654-1712;
  mortgage records, 1726-1877; general index
  to mortgage records, 1726-1893; probate records, 1656-1871; clerical probate records,
  various deaneries [Prosti], 1691-1815 Ibid.
  N: USIGS 119 reels   1089

TRONDHEIM. STATSARKIVET
  Sør-Trøndelag: court records, 1676-1880;
  mortgage records, 1670-1876; general index
  to mortgage records, 1726-1916; probate
  records, 1678-1901; clerical probate records,
  1691-1814 Ibid.
  N: USIGS 166 reels   1090

TRONDHEIM. STATSARKIVET
  Troms: mortgage records, 1739-1855; general
  index to mortgage records, ca. 1745-1889;
  probate records, 1706-1877; clerical probate
  records, Senja and Troms Deanery [Prosti],
  1697-1824 Ibid.
  N: USIGS 36 reels   1091

Church Records

BERGEN, Norway. STATSARKIVET
  Church records, various clerical districts:
  Hordaland, 1669-1926; Rogaland, 1664-1921;
  Sogn og Fjordane, 1689-1921 Ibid.
  N: USIGS 267 reels   1092

CHURCH OF JESUS CHRIST OF LATTER-DAY
SAINTS. NORWAY
  Records, early to 1952, Norwegian Mission and
  branches (Scandinavian Mission to 1920) USIC
  N: USIGS 7 reels   1093

HAMAR, Norway. STATSARKIVET
  Church records, various clerical districts:
  Hedmark, 1663-1901; Opland, 1691-1900 Ibid.
  N: USIGS 133 reels   1094

KRISTIANSAND, Norway. STATSARKIVET
  Church records, various clerical districts:
  Aust-Agder, 1683-1896; Vest-Agder, 1692-
  1900 Ibid.
  N: USIGS 151 reels   1095

NORWAY. RIKSARKIVET
Church records, various clerical districts,
parishes and institutions: Akershus, 1689-1914;
Buskerud, 1634-1903; Oslo, 1648-1893; Østfold,
1654-1894; Vestfold, 1623-1908 NoOR
N: USIGS 306 reels   1096

OSLO. STATSARKIVET
Church records, various clerical districts:
Telemark, 1649-1905 Ibid.
N: USIGS 58 reels   1097

TRONDHEIM. STATSARKIVET
Church records, various clerical districts:
Finnmark, 1705-1886; Møre, 1645-1927;
Nordland, 1669-1900; Nord-Trøndelag, 1689-
1902; Sør-Trøndelag, 1667-1908; Troms, 1706-
1896 Ibid.
N: USIGS 450 reels   1098

Personal Papers

KLOSTAR, ASBJÖRN, of Stavanger, Norway
In-letters priv.
N: DLC 20 feet   1099

SWEDEN

Bibliography

SWEDEN
Renoverade dombÖcker lappkatalog [Inventory
of court record extracts], 1602-1865 SvSR
N: USIGS 2 reels   1100
P: USIGS

Census

SWEDEN. CENSUS
Mantals- och boskapslängder [census returns
and livestock tax lists] of Northern Sweden,
1623-1750 SvSR
N: USIGS 56 reels   1101

Government Records

SWEDEN
Älvsborgs lösen [Älvsborgs ransom records],
ca. 1614-1619 SvSR
N: USIGS 40 reels   1102

SWEDEN
Boskapshjälpen, Kvarntullen och Räkenskaper
[livestock, seed, mill and accounts taxes],
1620-1641 SvSR
N: USIGS 6 reels   1103

SWEDEN
Emigrantlistor [emigration lists], 1851-1940
SvSSC
N: USIGS 168 reels   1104

SWEDEN
Lagmansrätterna Renoverade DombÖcker
[Court records, lower court of appeal of
Eastern and Northern Sweden], 1591-1700
SvSR
N: USIGS 10 reels   1105
P: USIGS

SWEDEN
Livgedinget [grants and incomes of royal widows
from livestock, seed, and mill taxes], 1620-
1625 SvSR
N: USIGS 2 reels   1106

SWEDEN
Livgedinget med Karl Gustafs underhållsländer,
JordebÖcker [land tax records re: support of
royal widows and Karl Gustaf], 1634-1718
SvSR
N: USIGS 17 reels   1107
P: USIGS

SWEDEN
Livgedinget med Karl Gustafs underhällsländer-
mantalslängder [tax census records re: support

of royal widows and Karl Gustaf], 1651-1718
SvSR
N: USIGS 11 reels   1108
P: USIGS

SWEDEN
Rådhusrätt, Kämnärsrättstäderna lappkatalog
[Inventory of city and lower court record
extracts], 1630-1847 SvSR
N: USIGS 1 reel   1109
P: USIGS

SWEDEN
Records of Royal Palace Court, 1688-1760
SvSR
N: USIGS 101 reels   1110

SWEDEN. ARMÉN. GARNISONS LIVGARDE
Vital statistics of the Royal Body Guards,
1706-1887 SvSS
N: USIGS 20 reels   1111

SWEDEN. GENERAL TULLSTYRELSEN
Lanttullen - Personella berättelser [Merit
lists and register of custom and excise tax
officials and personnel], 1748-1823   SvSR
N: USIGS 14 reels   1112

SWEDEN. GENERAL TULLSTYRELSEN
Sjötullen - Personella berättelser [Merit lists
and register of custom officials and personnel],
1765-1823 SvSR
N: USIGS 22 reels   1113

SWEDEN. RIKSARKIVET
Correspondence re: Island of St. Bartholomew,
W. I., between Sweden and Italy, 1869, Sweden
and France, 1876-1877 [in French] SvSR
N: ICU   1114

SWEDEN. RIKSARKIVET
JordebÖcker [land records] of Northern Sweden,
1631-1749 SvSR
N: USIGS 24 reels   1115

SWEDEN. RIKSARKIVET
Negotiations between Sweden and U.S., 1783-
1813; despatches from Swedish Minister in
Washington, 1812-1878; consular despatches,
1784-1818; draft despatches to Swedish Minister in Washington, 1812-1859; selections from
archives of Swedish Legation in Washington,
1860-1865 SvSR
N: DLC 15 reels, 1833 feet   1116
P: DLC
PP: DLC

Provincial Records

ÄLVSBORG, Sweden
JordebÖcker [land records], 1630-1750 SvSR
N: USIGS 56 reels   1117

ÄLVSBORG, Sweden
Mantals- och boskapslängder [census and tax
lists], 1620-1750 SvSR
N: USIGS 32 reels   1118

BLEKINGE, Sweden
JordebÖcker [land records], 1671-1750   SvSR
N: USIGS 9 reels   1119

BLEKINGE, Sweden
Mantalslängder [census returns], 1688-1742
SvSR
N: USIGS 5 reels   1120

GÄVLEBORG, Sweden
DombÖcker [court records of judicial districts],
1581-1840 SvHL
N: USIGS 163 reels   1121

GÄVLEBORG, Sweden
Gästriklands Domsaga [court records of judicial
districts], 1639-1849 SvHL
N: USIGS 67 reels   1122

GÄVLEBORG, Sweden
Hälsinglands Domsaga [court records of judicial
districts], 1639-1790 SvHL
N: USIGS 87 reels   1123

GÄVLEBORG, Sweden. HÄRADSRÄTT
Renoverade DombÖcker [court records (copy)],
1601-1821 SvSR
N: USIGS 56 reels   1124

GÄVLEBORG, Sweden. LAGMANSRÄTT
Dombok, Bouppteckningar, Småprotokoll,
Extra FÖrrättningar [court records, estate
inventories, probate records, special
proceedings], 1741-1850 SvHL
N: USIGS 314 reels   1125

GÖTEBORG OCH BOHUS, Sweden
Mantalslängder [census returns], 1669-1742;
Jordebok [land records], 1574-1750 SvSR
N: USIGS 45 reels   1126

GÖTEBORG OCH BOHUS, Sweden. LAGMANS-
RÄTT
Dombok [court records, various judicial
districts], 1593-1887 SvGL
N: USIGS 428 reels   1127

GOTLAND, Sweden
Dombok [court records, various judicial
districts], 1661-1878; Ägodelningsrätts
dombok [land division records], 1738-1874;
Bouppteckningar [estate inventories],
1644-1862 SvVL
N: USIGS 427 reels   1128

GOTLAND, Sweden
Jordebok [land records], 1646-1748 SvSR
N: USIGS 11 reels   1129

GOTLAND, Sweden
Jorderevisionsbok [land revision records],
various parishes, 1653-1654 SvVL
N: USIGS 1 reel   1130

GOTLAND, Sweden
Mantals-, Bakugns-, och Bevillningslängder
[census returns and tax lists], 1658-1750
SvSR
N: USIGS 7 reels   1131

GOTLAND, Sweden. HÄRADSRÄTT
Renoverade DombÖcker [court records (copy)],
1649-1821 SvSR
N: USIGS 9 reels   1132

GOTLAND, Sweden. LAGMANSRÄTT
Dombok [court records], 1690-1849   SvVL
N: USIGS 13 reels   1133

HALLAND, Sweden
Brandskattepenningar, Längder på Konungs-
skatten [state tax records and levy payments
on a ransom], 1645-1661; Mantalslängder
[census returns], 1662-1750; Jordebok [land
records], 1645-1750 SvSR
N: USIGS 45 reels   1134

JÄMTLAND, Sweden
Births, various parishes, 1688-1799 SvOL
N: USIGS 22 reels   1135

JÄMTLAND, Sweden
Dombok [court records]; Småprotokoll
[probate records]; Bouppteckningar [estate
inventories]; Extra FÖrrättningar [special
proceedings], 1717-1908 SvOL
N: USIGS 425 reels   1136

JÄMTLAND, Sweden. HÄRADSRÄTT
Dombok [circuit court records], 1621-1741
SvOL
N: USIGS 56 reels   1137

JÄMTLAND, Sweden. HÄRADSRÄTT
Renoverade DombÖcker [court records
(copy)], 1690-1838 SvOL
N: USIGS 7 reels   1138

JÖNKÖPING, Sweden
Boskaps-m.fl. längder [earliest tax lists of
livestock and seed], Smaland (now Jönköping,
Kalmar and Kronoberg), 1620-1635; Mantalslängder [census returns], 1643-1748; Jordebok
[land records], 1630-1748 SvSR
N: USIGS 81 reels   1139

JÖNKÖPING, Sweden. HÄRADSRÄTT
Dombok, Bouppteckningar, Småprotokoll, Urtima ting, Extra FÖrrättningar [court records,
private inventories, probate records, minutes
of special court sessions, special proceedings],
various judicial districts, ca. 1565-1862 SvVaL
N: USIGS 490 reels   1140

KALMAR, Sweden
Mantalslängder [census returns], 1633-1747;
Jordebok [land records], 1633-1750; Mickel
Siffridssons (Sigfridsson) [court records],
1567-1605 SvVaL
N: USIGS 65 reels   1141

KALMAR, Sweden. HÄRADSRÄTT
Dombok, Bouppteckningar, Lagfartsprotokoll,
Inteckningsprotokoll, Förmyndarskapsprotokoll,
etc. [court records, estate inventories, mortgage records, mortgage recordings, guardian
accounts, etc.], ca. 1548-1869 SvVaL
N: USIGS 1624 reels   1142

KOPPARBERG, Sweden
Mantals- och boskapslängder [census returns
and tax lists on livestock and seed, etc.],
1633-1750; Jordebok [land records], 1632-1748
SvSR
N: USIGS 43 reels   1143

KOPPARBERG, Sweden. HÄRADSRÄTT
Renoverade Domböcker [court records (copy)],
1602-1824 SvSR
N: USIGS 77 reels   1144

KRISTIANSTAD, Sweden
Mantalslängder [census returns], 1659, 1661,
1719, 1728, 1733, 1743; Jordebok [land records],
1658-1750 SvSR
N: USIGS 22 reels   1145

KRONOBERG, Sweden
Consistory court records: Domkapitels
arkiv - Skrifte-, och Prosteböcker
[cathedral chapter and diocesan court
archive; lists of inhabitants, esp. young
persons, etc.], 1691-1720 SvVaL
N: USIGS 4 reels   1146

KRONOBERG, Sweden
Mantals-och boskapslängder [census returns
and tax lists of livestock, etc.], 1640-1749;
Jordebok [land records], 1631-1748 SvSR
N: USIGS 44 reels   1147

KRONOBERG, Sweden. HÄRADSRÄTT
Dombok, Småprotokoll, Bouppteckningar,
Inteckningsprotokoll [court records, probate
records, estate inventories, mortgage record-
ings], 1603-1877 SvVaL
N: USIGS 843 reels   1148

MALMÖHUS, Sweden
Mantalslängder [census returns], 1658-1748;
Jordebok [land records], 1629-1750 SvSR
N: USIGS 64 reels   1149

MALMÖHUS, Sweden. HÄRADSRÄTT
Dombok, Förrättningar, Småprotokoll, Bouppteckningar, Urtima ting och Syner [court
records, special proceedings, probate records,
estate inventories, etc.], 1651-1861 SvLL
N: USIGS 1517 reels   1150

NORRBOTTEN, Sweden
Dombok, Småprotokoll, Bouppteckningar[court
records, probate records, estate inventories,
etc., various judicial districts], 1681-1878 SvHL
N: USIGS 524 reels   1151

NORRBOTTEN, Sweden
Härad - Katekismilängder [catechistic student
lists, various districts], 1683, 1687, 1689,
1699, 1713, 1739, 1741 SvLL
N: USIGS 3 reels   1152

NORRBOTTEN, Sweden. HÄRADSRÄTT
Renoverade Domböcker [court records (copy)],
1698-1829 SvSR
N: USIGS 67 reels   1153

NORRLAND, Sweden
Boskapslängder [tax lists of livestock and
seed], 1620-1636 SvSR
N: USIGS 6 reels   1154

ÖREBRO, Sweden
Härads m. fl. Rätters renoverada Domböcker
[old circuit and city court records (copy)],
1603-1822; Boskaps m. fl. längder [earliest tax
lists of livestock and seed, etc.], 1622-1636;
Mantalslängder [census returns of Örebro and
Värmland counties], 1642-1750; Jordeböcker
[land records of Örebro and Värmland
counties], 1630-1749 SvSR
N: USIGS 233 reels   1155

ÖSTERGÖTLAND, Sweden
Boskap- m. fl. längder [earliest tax lists of
livestock and seed, etc.], 1620-1633; Mantalslängder [census returns], 1631-1749; Jordebok
[land records], 1635-1749 SvSR
N: USIGS 86 reels   1156

ÖSTERGÖTLAND, Sweden
General court records, 1585-1595, 1598-1605,
1637-1638, 1642, 1645-1646, 1648, 1704;
Domkapitels arkiv - Katekisationslängder,
Protokoll [consistory court records -
Confirmation records and minutes of the
Cathedral Chapter and Diocesan Court
Archive at Linköping], 1600-1860 SvVaL
N: USIGS 55 reels   1157

ÖSTERGÖTLAND, Sweden. HÄRADSRÄTT
Dombok [court records], Småprotokoll [probate
records], Syneprotokoll [investigations], Boup-
pteckningar [private inventories], 1590-1907
SvVaL
N: USIGS 2151 reels   1158

SKARABORG, Sweden
Boskaps- m.fl. längder [earliest tax lists of
livestock and seed, etc. of Vastergotland (now
Skaraborg, etc.)], 1620-1640; Mantalslängder,
[census returns], 1621-1744; Jordebok [land
records], 1632-1750 SvSR
N: USIGS 91 reels   1159

SÖDERMANLAND, Sweden
Boskaps- m.fl. längder [earliest tax lists of
livestock and seed, etc.], 1623-1635; Jordebok
[land records], 1636-1754; Mantalslängder [cen-
sus returns], 1642-1748 SvSR
N: USIGS 49 reels   1160

SÖDERMANLAND, Sweden. HÄRADSRÄTT
Dombok [court records]; Småprotokoll [probate
records]; Urtima ting, Extra Förrättningar
[minutes of special court sessions]; Bouppteckningar [estate inventories], 1625-1894 SvUL
N: USIGS 266 reels   1161

SÖDERMANLAND, Sweden. HÄRADSRÄTT
Renoverade Domböcker [copy of court
records], 1591-1813 SvSR
N: USIGS 87 reels   1162

STOCKHOLM, Sweden
Jordebok [land records], 1636-1753;
Mantalslängder [census returns], 1653-1750
SvSR
N: USIGS 38 reels   1163

STOCKHOLM, Sweden. HÄRADSRÄTT
Dombok [court records]; Småprotokoll [probate
records]; Bouppteckningar [estate inventories]
Urtima ting, Extra Förrättningar [minutes of
special court sessions, proceedings and
investigations], 1594-1882 SvUL
N: USIGS 944 reels   1164

UPPSALA, Sweden
Boskaps- m. fl. längder [earliest tax lists of
livestock and seed], 1620-1639; Härads m. fl.
Rätters renoverade Domböcker [old circuit and
city court records (copy) of Uppland (now Uppsala and Stockholm counties), Jordebok [land
records], 1640-1742; Mantals-
och Boskapslängder [census returns and tax lists
of livestock], 1640-1742; Reduktionsjordebok
[land records and retractions], 1686 SvSR
N: USIGS 205 reels   1165

UPPSALA, Sweden. HÄRADSRÄTT
Dombok [court records]; Småprotokoll [probate
records]; Extra Förrättningar, Ägodelnings-
rättsprotokoll, Urtima ting [minutes of special
court sessions, proceedings and investigations];
Bouppteckningar [estate inventories] SvUL
N: USIGS 847 reels   1166

VÄRMLAND, Sweden
Jordebok [land records], 1630-1652; Mantals-
längder [census returns], 1639-1653 SvSR
N: USIGS 8 reels   1167

VÄSTERBOTTEN, Sweden
Domböcker [court records]; Småprotokoll
[probate records]; Bouppteckningar [estate
inventories], 1729-1881 SvHL
N: USIGS 401 reels   1168

VÄSTERBOTTEN, Sweden
Mantalslängder [census returns, agricultural

tax accounts, some land records], 1642-1749;
Jordeböcker [land tax records], 1630-1750
SvSR
N: USIGS 18 reels   1169

VÄSTERBOTTEN, Sweden. HÄRADSRÄTT
Renoverade Domböcker [court records (copy)],
1691-1809 SvSR
N: USIGS 23 reels   1170

VÄSTERNORRLAND, Sweden
Dombok [court records] (Angermanlands och
Södra Angermanlands Domsager) SvHL
N: USIGS 93 reels   1171

VÄSTERNORRLAND, Sweden
Dombok [court records]; Småprotokoll [probate
records]; Bouppteckningar [estate inventories];
various judicial districts, 1609-1882 SvHL
N: USIGS 436 reels   1172

VÄSTERNORRLAND, Sweden
Konsistori protokoll [consistory court records],
Domkapitel [Cathedral chapter minutes],
1660-1861 SvHL
N: USIGS 24 reels   1173

VÄSTERNORRLAND, Sweden. HÄRADSRÄTT
Renoverade Domböcker [court records (copy)],
1681-1845 SvSR
N: USIGS 124 reels   1174

VÄSTMANLAND, Sweden
Boskaps m.fl. längder [earliest tax lists of
livestock and seed], 1620-1633; Mantals- och
Boskapslängder [census returns and tax lists on
livestock, etc], 1625-1750; Jordeböcker [land
records], 1631-1748 SvSR
N: USIGS 53 reels   1175

VÄSTMANLAND, Sweden. HÄRADSRÄTT
Dombok [court records]; Småprotokoll [probate
records]; Urtima ting [minutes of special court
sessions]; Extra Förrättningar [special proceedings and investigations]; Bouppteckningar
[estate inventories], 1584-1893 SvUL
N: USIGS 804 reels   1176

VÄSTMANLAND, Sweden. HÄRADSRÄTT
Renoverade Domböcker [court records (copy)],
1593-1825 SvSR
N: USIGS 127 reels   1177

VISBY, Gotland, Sweden. DOMKAPITEL
Consistory court records of Gotland,
1586-1861 SvVL
N: USIGS 10 reels   1178

City Records

ARBOGA, Västmanland, Sweden. RÅDHUSRÄTT,
KÄMNÄRSRÄTT
Renoverade Domböcker [city and lower court
records (copy)], 1692-1701 SvSR
N: USIGS 2 reels   1179

ASKERSUND, Örebro, Sweden. RÅDHUSRÄTT,
KÄMNÄRSRÄTT
Renoverade Domböcker [city and lower court
records (copy)], 1699-1830 SvSR
N: USIGS 5 reels   1180

ENKÖPING, Uppsala, Sweden. RÅDHUSRÄTT,
KÄMNÄRSRÄTT
Renoverade Domböcker [city and lower court
records (copy)], 1714, Book 1 SvSR
N: USIGS 1 reel   1181

ESKILSTUNA, Södermanland, Sweden.
RÅDHUSRÄTT, KÄMNÄRSRÄTT
Renoverade Domböcker [city and lower
court records (copy)], 1697-1799 SvSR
N: USIGS 2 reels   1182

FALUN, Kopparberg, Sweden
Rådhusrätt, Kämnärsrätt: Renoverade Domböcker [city and lower court records (copy)],
1648-1701 SvSR
N: USIGS 2 reels   1183

GÄVLE, Gävleborg, Sweden. KÄMNERSRÄTT
Dombok [lower city court records], 1746-1849
SvHL
N: USIGS 49 reels   1184

GÄVLE, Gävleborg, Sweden. RÅDHUSRÄTT,
KÄMNÄRSRÄTT
Renoverade Domböcker [city and lower court

records (copy)], 1698-1764 SvSR
N: USIGS 10 reels   1185

GÄVLE, Gävleborg, Sweden. RÅDHUSRÄTT OCH
MAGISTRAT
Dombok [court records], 1573-1850; Brevkon-
cept [letters of administration], 1678-1852;
Inkomna skrivelser [official correspondences],
1670-1850; Konkursäkter [foreclosures], 1728-
1850 SvHL
N: USIGS 315 reels   1186

HÄRNÖSAND, Västernorrland, Sweden. RÅDHUS-
RÄTT OCH MAGISTRAT
Dombok [city court and administration records],
1681-1850; Småprotokoll, Bouppteckningar,
Protokoll [probate records, estate inventories,
minutes], 1709-1860 SvHL
N: USIGS 88 reels   1187

HÄRNÖSAND, Västernorrland, Sweden. RÅDHUS-
RÄTT, KÄMNÄRSRÄTT
Renoverade Domböcker [city and lower court
records (copy)], 1698-1699, Book 1 SvSR
N: USIGS 1 reel   1188

HEDEMORA, Kopparberg, Sweden
Rådhusrätt, Kämnärsrätt: Renoverade Domböcker [city and lower court records (copy)],
1614-1736 SvSR
N: USIGS 4 reels   1189

HUDIKSVALL, Gävleborg, Sweden. MAGISTRATEN
Protokoll [minute books], 1726-1834 SvHL
N: USIGS 7 reels   1190

HUDIKSVALL, Gävleborg, Sweden. RÅDHUSRÄTT
Dombok [court records], 1717-1840; Småprotokoll [probate records], 1725-1847; Bouppteckningar [estate inventories], 1709-1848 SvHL
N: USIGS 23 reels   1191

HUDIKSVALL, Gävleborg, Sweden. RÅDHUSRÄTT,
KÄMNÄRARÄTT
Renoverade Domböcker [court records (copy)],
1698-1725 SvSR
N: USIGS 2 reels   1192

KALMAR, Kalmar, Sweden
Dombok [city court records], ca. 1381-1830;
Justitieprotokoll [justiciary court records],
1723-1738; Politieprotokoll [city administration,
political minutes], 1759-1819; Småprotokoll
[probate records of the city court], 1758-1830;
Magistratsprotokoll [city administration min-
utes], 1764-1830; Kämnärsrätt-Protokoll och
Handlingar [city court, lower; minutes and tran-
sactions], 1672-1830; Accisrättsprotokoll [ex-
cise tax office minutes], 1647-1752; Syne och
Värderingsprotokoll [city administration inspec-
tions and appraisements], 1713-1825; Hallrätt-
Protokoll och Handlingar [manufacturer's inspection and license office, minutes and transac-
tions], ca. 1770-1826; Krigsrätt-Protokoll och
Handlingar [military court, minutes and transac-
tions], 1666-1779; Slottsrätt-Protokoll och
Handlingar [Royal castle court, minutes and
proceedings], 1744-1777; Borgarelängder [lists
of citizens], ca. 1657-1887; Bouppteckningar
[estate inventories], 1643-1860; Räkenskaper
[various accounts], 1614-1652 SvVaL
N: USIGS 238 reels   1193

KALMAR, Kalmar, Sweden
Förteckning, Kortregister [inventory of
archives and of court records], ca. 1524-1944
SvVaL
N: USIGS 1 reel   1194

KÖPING, Västmanland, Sweden. RÅDHUSRÄTT,
KÄMNÄRSRÄTT
Renoverade Domböcker [city and lower court
records (copy)], 1760-1783 SvSR
N: USIGS 4 reels   1195

LINDESBERG, Örebro, Sweden. RÅDHUSRÄTT,
KÄMNÄRSRÄTT
Renoverade Domböcker [city and lower court
records (copy)], 1697-1777 SvSR
N: USIGS 3 reels   1196

LINKÖPING, Östergötland, Sweden.
Köpebrev och lagfartshandlingar [contracts
and mortgage transactions], 1516-1800;
Mantals-, Taxerings-, Uppbords och
Restlängder [census and tax records], 1613-1847
Rådhusrätten och Magistratens Förteckning
[special inventory of city archives and of
court records], ca. 1546-1900; Hallrätt -
Protokoll och Handlingar [manufacturer's
inspection and license office minutes and
transactions], 1761-1811 SvVaL
N: USIGS 7 reels   1197

LINKÖPING, Östergötland, Sweden.
KÄMNÄRSRÄTT
Dombok [lower city court records], 1806-1848
SvVaL
N: USIGS 26 reels   1198

LINKÖPING, Östergötland, Sweden.
RÅDHUSRÄTT
Domböcker [city court records], 1609-1830;
Småprotokoll, Extraförrättningar [probate
records, special proceedings], 1696-1836;
Rådhusrättens och Magistratens koncept [city
court and administration records, first
outline], ca. 1600-1869; Bouppteckningar
[estate inventories], 1622-1852 SvVaL
N: USIGS 138 reels   1199

LINKÖPING, Östergötland, Sweden.
RÅDHUSRÄTT OCH MAGISTRAT
Koncept [city and administration records, first
outline], ca. 1600-1860; Förteckning [special
inventory of city archives and court records],
ca. 1546-1900 SvVaL
N: USIGS 38 reels   1200

LULEÅ, Norrbotten, Sweden. RÅDHUSRÄTT,
KÄMNÄRSRÄTT
Renoverade Domböcker [city and lower court
records (copy)], 1698-1807 SvSR
N: USIGS 3 reels   1201

LULEÅ, Norrbotten, Sweden. RÅDHUSRÄTT OCH
MAGISTRAT
Protokoll, Småprotokoll [minutes, probate re-
cords], 1737-1840; Bouppteckningar [estate
inventories], 1698-1838 SvHL
N: USIGS 19 reels   1202

MARIEFRED, Södermanland, Sweden
RÅDHUSRÄTT, KÄMNÄRSRÄTT
Renoverade Domböcker [city and lower
court records], ca. 1699-1809 SvSR
N: USIGS 3 reels   1203

NORA, Örebro, Sweden. RÅDHUSRÄTT, KÄM-
NÄRSRÄTT
Renoverade Domböcker, [city and lower court
records (copy)], 1697-1729 SvSR
N: USIGS 6 reels   1204

NORRKÖPING, Östergötland, Sweden
Arkivförteckning [inventory of archive], ca.
1384-1935 SvNS
N: USIGS 1 reel   1205

NORRKÖPING, Östergötland, Sweden.
KÄMNÄRSRÄTT
Dombok [lower city court records], 1721-1849
SvNS
N: USIGS 93 reels   1206

NORRKÖPING, Östergötland, Sweden. MAGISTRAT
Justitieprotokoll [justiciary minutes], 1789-1860;
Pleni-, Politie-, Ekonomi-, Ståthållarämbetets
Protokoller [minutes of the City Commission,
Finance Department, and Office of the City Governor, etc.], 1743-1860; Tomtöresrulla [register
of private land grants], 1720-1832; Handels-
kollegiums-, Hall-, och Manufakturrättens Protokoll och Dombok [transactions, minutes, and court
records of business and manufacturers' inspection
and license office], 1694-1859; Auktionsprotokoll
[minutes of auctions], 1722-1830; Inneliggande
handlingar till Magistratens justitieprotokoll
[supplementary transactions and minutes of the
city administration], 1790-1801 SvNS
N: USIGS 87 reels   1207

NORRKÖPING, Östergötland, Sweden. RÅDHUS-
RÄTT
Domar [court decisions], 1709-1799; Dombok
[court records], 1735-1858; Dombok i tvistemål
[civil lawsuits and decisions, etc.], 1850-1860;
Dombok i brottmål [criminal cases and deci-
sions], 1720-1860; Bouppteckningar [private
inventories], 1709-1877; Brottmålsprotokoll
[criminal court minutes], 1778-1849; Notarius
Publicus Protokoll [notary public records],
1725-1860; Konkursäkter [court proceedings of
bankruptcy cases], 1750-1830; Inneliggande
handlingar [supplementary court proceedings],
1720-1800; Stamningsrotel i civilmål [court
summons, civil cases], 1831-1959; Fastighets-

bok [register of real estate], 1813-1860 SvNS
N: USIGS 282 reels   1208

NORRKÖPING, Östergötland, Sweden.
RÅDHUSRÄTT OCH MAGISTRAT
City court and administration records, mis-
cellaneous minutes of civil and criminal cases,
etc., 1714-1772 SvNS
N: USIGS 35 reels   1209

NORRKÖPING, Östergötland, Sweden.
SJÖTULLSRÄTT
Protokoll [minutes of maritime customs office],
1725-1831 SvNS
N: USIGS 9 reels   1210

NORRTÄLJE, Stockholm, Sweden RÅDHUSRÄTT,
KÄMNÄRSRÄTT
Renoverade Domböcker [city and lower court
records (copy)], 1704-1718 SvSR
N: USIGS 1 reel   1211

NYKÖPING, Södermanland, Sweden.
RÅDHUSRÄTT, KÄMNÄRSRÄTT
Renoverade Domböcker [city and lower
court records (copy)], 1641-1701 SvSR
N: USIGS 2 reels   1212

ÖREBRO, Örebro, Sweden. RÅDHUSRÄTT, KÄM-
NÄRSRÄTT
Renoverade Domböcker [city and lower court
records (copy)], 1697-1704, 1710 SvSR
N: USIGS 2 reels   1213

ÖSTERSUND, Jämtland, Sweden
Justitiarits arkiv- Dombok, Småprotokoll
och Bouppteckning [city court and
administration; chief judicial administration
minutes, proceedings, mortgage records,
estate inventories, etc.], 1830-1836;
Rådhusrättens arkiv- Dombok [city court
records], 1858-1860; Magistratens Dombok
[city court administration records],
1858-1860; Småprotokoll [city court probate
records], 1858-1860 SvOL
N: USIGS 5 reels   1214

PITEÅ, Norrbotten, Sweden. RÅDHUSRÄTT,
KÄMNÄRSRÄTT
Renoverade Domböcker [city and lower court
records (copy)], 1698-1826 SvSR
N: USIGS 4 reels   1215

PITEÅ, Norrbotten, Sweden. RÅDHUSRÄTT OCH
MAGISTRAT
Dombok [city court and administration records],
1656-1850; Protokoll, Småprotokoll, Bouppteckningar [minutes, probate records, estate
inventories], 1745-1847 SvHL
N: USIGS 46 reels   1216

SALA, Västmanland, Sweden. RÅDHUSRÄTT,
KÄMNÄRSRÄTT
Renoverade Domböcker [city and lower court
records (copy)], 1697-1799 SvUL
N: USIGS 14 reels   1217

SÄTER, Kopparberg, Sweden
Rådhusrätt, Kämnärsrätt: Renoverade Domböcker [city and lower court records (copy)]
ca. 1644-1801 SvSR
N: USIGS 2 reels   1218

SIGTUNA, Stockholm, Sweden. RÅDHUSRÄTT,
KÄMNÄRSRÄTT
Renoverade Domböcker [city and lower court
records (copy)], 1701-1815 SvSR
N: USIGS 4 reels   1219

SKÄNNINGE, Östergötland, Sweden
Foredragningslistor [agenda cases lists],
1817-1878; Syneprotokoll [inspection minutes,
contracts, accounts, resolutions,
appraisements, etc.], 1694-1876; Burska-
protokoll [freeman guild minutes], 1673-1870;
Auktionsprotokoll [minutes of auctions],
1713-1855; Accis- och Hallrättsprotokoller
[excise tax , manufacturer's inspection and
license offices], 1716-1856; Konceptprotokoll
[first outline minutes], 1618-1847;
Bouppteckningar [probate records], 1742-1888;
Förteckning, Kortregister [inventory of
archive, court records], ca. 1606-1952
SvVaL
N: USIGS 16 reels   1220

SKÄNNINGE, Östergötland, Sweden. MAGISTRAT
Protokoll [minutes of city administration],
1762-1866 SvVaL
N: USIGS 9 reels   1221

SKANNINGE, Östergötland, Sweden.
RÅDHUSRÄTT
Dombok [city court records], 1609-1860;
Småprotokoll [probate records], 1693-1866;
SvVaL
N: USlGS 44 reels   1222

SÖDERHAMN, Gävleborg, Sweden.
RÅDHUSRÄTT OCH KÄMNÄRSRÄTT
Renoverade Domböcker [court records (copy)],
1698-1764   SvSR
N: USlGS 2 reels   1223

SÖDERHAMN, Gävleborg, Sweden. RÅDHUSRÄTT
OCH MAGISTRAT
Dombok [court and administration records],
1721-1840; Småprotokoll [probate records],
1740-1849; Bouppteckningar [estate inventories],
1718-1839   SvHL
N: USlGS 37 reels   1224

SÖDERKÖPING, Östergötland, Sweden
Tänkeböcker - Dombok [city administration
and court records], 1571-1675; Dombok och
Magistratsprotokoll, 1676-1860; Allmanna
Magistratensprotokoll [general administration
minutes], 1827-1859; [miscellaneous minutes,
tax lists], 1612-1874; Bouppteckningar [estate
inventories], 1614-1859; Förteckning [inventory
of city archive], ca. 1571-1946   SvVaL
N: USlGS 76 reels   1225

SODERKÖPING, Östergötland, Sweden.
RÅDHUSRATT
Småprotokoll [probate records], 1720-1869
SvVaL
N: USlGS 5 reels   1226

SÖDERTÄLJE, Stockholm, Sweden. RÅDHUSRÄTT
KÄMNÄRSRÄTT
Renoverade Domböcker [city and lower court
records (copy)], 1696-1793   SvSR
N: USlGS 5 reels   1227

STOCKHOLM, Stockholm, Sweden
Domar i civimal [lower court records (civil)],
1700-1720; Kriminalprotokoll [criminal court
records], 1661-1720; Domar i kriminalmal
[criminal court order books], 1668-1719;
Protokoll i enskilda arenden [minutes of city
magistrates and court officials], 1637-1679;
Justitie-kollegiate och formyndarekammarens
protokoll [judiciary court and orphans court
records], 1637-1750; Civilakter [common
pleas court records], 1660-1730   SvSS
N: USlGS 321 reels   1228

STOCKHOLM, Stockholm, Sweden
Mantalslängder [census returns], 1652-1860;
Taxeringslängd [tax lists], 1725-1825; Bouppteckningar [inventory lists, etc.], 1598-1855;
Fattigbevis [inventories and administrations],
1756-1860; Dödslistor [records of deaths], 1712-
1860; Borgmästere och rads arkivs förteckningar
och Tänkeböcker [records kept by mayors, councillors, etc.], 1592-1674; Ambetsbok [records],
1545-1659; Fraktböker [shipping accounts],
1551-1590; Tänkeböcker [municipal records],

[North suburban district], 1614-1635; Civil-
protokoll [civil administration], 1661-1720;
Handelskollegietsprotokoll [chamber of commerce minutes and accounts, etc.], 1635-1736;
Stadskonsistoriums protokoll [city commission
records and ordinances], 1595-1720   SvSS
N: USlGS 1041 reels   1229

STOCKHOLM, Sweden. CENTRALPRISON
NORRMALM
Vital statistics, 1827-1863   SvSS
N: USlGS 154 frames   1230

STOCKHOLM, Sweden. HÄRADSRÄTT
Renoverade Domböcker [court records (copy)]
1633-1811   SvSR
N: USlGS 130 reels   1231

STRANGNAS, Södermanland, Sweden. RÅDHUS-
RÄTT, KÄMNÄRSRÄTT
Renoverade Domböcker [city and lower court
records (copy)], 1697-1756   SvSR
N: USlGS 3 reels   1232

SUNDSVALL, Västernorrland, Sweden. RÅDHUS-
RÄTT , KÄMNÄRSRÄTT
Renoverade Domböcker [city and lower court
records (copy)], 1698-1850   SvSR
N: USlGS 29 reels   1233

TROSA, Södermanland, Sweden.
RÅDHUSRÄTT, KÄMNÄRSRÄTT
Renoverade Domböcker [city and lower court
records], 1695, 1698-1759   SvSP
N: USlGS 2 reels   1234

UMEA, Västerbotten, Sweden. RÅDHUSRÄTT,
KÄMNÄRSRÄTT
Renoverade Domböcker [city and lower court
records(copy)], 1698-1833   SvSR
N: USlGS 12 reels   1235

UPPSALA, Uppsala, Sweden. RÅDHUSRÄTT,
KÄMNÄRSRÄTT
Renoverade Domböcker [city and lower court
records (copy)], 1663-1726   SvSR
N: USlGS 4 reels   1236

VADSTENA, Östergötland, Sweden
Förteckning, Kortregister [inventory of
archive and of court records], ca. 1618-1937
SvVaL
N: USlGS 1 reel   1237

VADSTENA, Östergötland, Sweden. MAGISTRAT
Protokoll [city administration minutes],
1755-1876   SvVaL
N: USlGS 11 reels   1238

VADSTENA, Östergötland, Sweden. RÅDHUSRÄTT
Dombok [city court records], 1577-1860;
Småprotokoll [probate records], 1738-1886;
Bouppteckningar [estate inventories], 1651-
1870   SvVaL
N: USlGS 77 reels   1239

VADSTENA, Östergötland, Sweden.
RÅDHUSRÄTT OCH MAGISTRAT
Miscellaneous minute books, 1656-1885
SvVaL
N: USlGS 5 reels   1240

VÄSTERAS, Västmanland, Sweden. RÅDHUSRÄTT,
KÄMNÄRSRÄTT
Renoverade Domböcker [city and lower court
records(copy)], 1613-1701   SvSR
N: USlGS 13 reels   1241

VASTERVIK, Kalmar, Sweden
Förteckning, Kortregister [inventory of
archive and of court records], ca. 1619-1940
SvVaL
N: USlGS 1 reel   1242

VASTERVIK, Kalmar, Sweden
Rådhusrätt: Dombok [city court records],
1635-1860; Småprotokoll [probate records],
1736-1860; Inteckningsprotokoll [mortgage
recordings], 1805-1841; Förmyndarskaps-,
och Aktenskapsförords- Protokoll [guardian
accounts and marriage settlements], 1758-
1843; Magistratsprotokoll [city administration minutes], 1822-1860; Notarius Publicus
Protokoll och Handlingar [office of notary
public, minutes and transactions], 1711-1864;
Kämnärsrätt - Protokoll och Handlingar
[lower city court, minutes and transactions],
1654-1845; Accisrättens Protokoll och
Handlingar [excise tax office, minutes and
transactions], 1689-1810; Hallrättens
Protokoll [manufacturer's inspection and
license offices minutes], 1741-1847; Rådhusrättens och Magistrats Konceptprotokoll
[city court and administration, first outline],
1693-1870; Rådhusrättens och Magistratens
Arkiv [includes all other city records], 1651-
1896; Sjömanshus-Handlingar, Protokoll
[mercantile marine shipping office, minutes
and transactions], ca. 1722-1826   SvVaL
N: USlGS 155 reels   1243

VÄSTRA GASTRIKLAND, Gävleborg, Sweden
Domsaga-, Lagfarts-, Ägodelnings-, Småproto-
koller, etc. [probate records], 1801-1844   SvHL
N: USlGS 9 reels   1244

VAXHOLM, Stockholm, Sweden. RÅDHUSRÄTT,
KÄMNÄRSRÄTT
Renoverade Domböcker [city and lower court
records (copy)], 1697-1801   SvSR
N: USlGS 5 reels   1245

VAXJO, Kroneberg, Sweden. RÅDHUSRÄTT
Dombok [city court records], 1605-1849;
Småprotokoll [probate records], 1751-1849;
Intecknings och Accisrättens protokoller
[mortgage recordings, etc.], 1800-1846;

Bouppteckningar [estate inventories],
1725-1857;   SvVaL
N: USlGS 80 reels   1246

VIMMERBY, Kalmar, Sweden
Rådhusrätt - Domböcker [city court records],
1761-1859; Småprotokoll [probate records],
1785-1825; Inteckningsprotokoll [mortgage re-
cordings], 1793-1825; Förmyndareprotokoll
[Guardian accounts], 1798, 1800-1825; Särskil-
darådhusrättens-, Syne-, Accisrättens [Investi-
gations, minutes of the excise tax office, mortgage recordings, register of citizens], 1683-
1798; Bouppteckningar [estate inventories],
1759-1873; Magistratsprotokoll [city administration minutes], 1800-1839   SvVaL
N: USlGS 33 reels   1247

VISBY, Gotland, Sweden. ACCISRÄTT
Dombok [court records, excise tax office],
1731-1760, 1781-1802, 1810   SvVL
N: USlGS 1 reel   1248

VISBY, Gotland, Sweden. HALLRÄTT
Dombok [court records], manufacturer's
inspection and license office, 1741-1840
SvVL
N: USlGS 1 reel   1249

VISBY, Gotland, Sweden. KÄMNÄRSRÄTT
Dombok [court records], 1654-1849   SvVL
N: USlGS 50 reels   1250

VISBY, Gotland, Sweden. RÅDHUSRÄTT OCH
KÄMNÄRSRÄTT
Renoverade Domböcker [court records
(copy)], 1649-1700   SvSR
N: USlGS 3 reels   1251

VISBY, Gotland, Sweden. RÅDHUSRÄTT OCH
MAGISTRAT
Dombok [court records], 1624-1860; Lagfartsprotokoll och Fästebreve [mortgage records
and certificates], 1722-1862; minutes of
administration, 1842-1860; Bouppteckningar
[estate inventories], 1647-1870   SvVL
N: USlGS 58 reels   1252

VISBY, Gotland, Sweden. SJÖMANSHUS
Mercantile marine shipping office records,
1753-1908; personnel records of Visby City,
1799-1870; personnel records of southern
districts (Södra hårad), 1799-1870; personnel
records of northern districts (Norra hårad),
1753-1870   SvVL
N: USlGS 14 reels   1253

VISBY, Gotland, Sweden. SJÖTULLSRÄTT
Domböcker [court records, customs office],
1706-1831   SvVL
N: USlGS 5 reels   1254

Church Records

CHURCH OF JESUS CHRIST OF LATTER-DAY
SAINTS. SWEDEN
Records, Swedish Mission and branches, early
to 1951 (Scandinavian Mission to 1905)   USlC
N: USlGS 13 reels   1255

CHURCH OF JESUS CHRIST OF LATTER-DAY
SAINTS. SWEDISH MISSION
Emigration records, 1905-1932   USlC
N: USlGS   1256

GOTLAND, Sweden. LANDSARKIVET
Catalog of church records, ca. 1667-1940
SvVL
N: USlGS 1 reel   1257

OLSEN, CHARLES LUDWIG, 1856-1923
Autobiography (Swedish mission, L. D. S.
Church)   priv.
N: UPB 1 reel
P: UPB   1258

STOCKHOLM, Stockholm, Sweden
Church records, various parishes, etc.,
1581-1934   SvSS
N: USlGS 502 reels   1259

SVENSKA STATSKYRKAN. ÄLVSBORG
Church records, various localities, 1645-1865
SvGL
N: USlGS 117 reels   1260

SVENSKA STATSKYRKAN. BLEKINGE
Church records, various localities, 1612-1916
SvLL
N: USIGS 276 reels   1261

SVENSKA STATSKYRKAN. GÄVLEBORG
Church records, various localities, 1600-1908
SvHL
N: USIGS 428 reels   1262

SVENSKA STATSKYRKAN. GÖTEBORG OCH
BOHUS
Church records, various localities, 1577-1895
SvGL
N: USIGS 56 reels   1263

SVENSKA STATSKYRKAN. GOTLAND
Church records, various localities, 1582-1940
SvVL
N: USIGS 316 reels   1264

SVENSKA STATSKYRKAN. JÄMTLAND
Church records, various localities, 1482-1918
Ibid.
N: USIGS 150 reels   1265

SVENSKA STATSKYRKAN. JÖNKÖPING
Church records, various localities, 1580-1885
Ibid.
N: USIGS 605 reels   1266

SVENSKA STATSKYRKAN. KALMAR
Church records, various localities, 1577-1916
SvVaL
N: USIGS 512 reels   1267

SVENSKA STATSKYRKAN. KOPPARBERG
Church records, various localities, 1630-1894
SvUL
N: USIGS 253 reels   1268

SVENSKA STATSKYRKAN. KRISTIANSTAD
Church records, various localities, 1588-1910
SvLL
N: USIGS 713 reels   1269

SVENSKA STATSKYRKAN. KRONOBERG
Church records, various localities, 1612-1885
SvVaL
N: USIGS 377 reels   1270

SVENSKA STATSKYRKAN. MALMÖHUS
Church records, various localities, 1558-1917
SvLL
N: USIGS 1283 reels   1271

SVENSKA STATSKYRKAN. NORRBOTTEN
Church records, various localities, 1629-1914
SvHL
N: USIGS 132 reels   1272

SVENSKA STATSKYRAN. ÖREBRO
Church records, various localities, 1615-1865
SvUL
N: USIGS 889 reels   1273

SVENSKA STATSKYRKAN. ÖSTERGÖTLAND
Church records, various localities, 1555-1908
SvVaL
N: USIGS 754 reels   1274

SVENSKA STATSKYRKAN. SKARABORG
Church records, various localities, 1612-1884
SvGL
N: USIGS 83 reels   1275

SVENSKA STATSKYRKAN. SÖDERMANLAND
Church records, various localities, 1602-1888
SvUL
N: USIGS 390 reels   1276

SVENSKA STATSKYRKAN. STOCKHOLM
Church records, various localities, 1580-1881
SvUL
N: USIGS 430 reels   1277

SVENSKA STATSKYRKAN. UPPSALA
Church records, various localities, 1580-1894
SvUL
N: USIGS 371 reels   1278

SVENSKA STATSKYRKAN. VÄRMLAND
Church records, various localities, 1621-1900
SvGL
N: USIGS 267 reels   1279

SVENSKA STATSKYRKAN. VÄSTERBOTTEN
Church records, various localities, 1630-1894
SvHL
N: USIGS 165 reels   1280

SVENSKA STATSKYRKAN. VÄSTERNORRLAND
Church records, various localities, 1501-1936
SvHL
N: USIGS   1281

SVENSKA STATSKYRKAN. VÄSTMANLAND
Church records, various localities, 1581-1889
SvUL
N: USIGS 334 reels   1282

Personal Papers

APPELBOOM, HARALD
Reports and correspondence from The Hague,
1645-1674 SvSR
N: CLU 42 reels*   1283

Collections

STOCKHOLM. KUNGLIGA BIBLIOTEKET
Collection of Icelandic and Old Norse texts:
Vilmundar rímur vidutan, mss. 220-221,
259-261; Vilmundar saga vidutan slutet, ms.
261:4; Jóns saga leikara, ms. 274: II, 2
SvSK
N: ICU   1284

VISBY, Gotland, Sweden. DOMKYRKAN
Brevsamling [collection of old original letters
and extracts of letters], 1229-1885 SvVL
N: USIGS 1441 frames   1285

BALTIC COUNTRIES

Church Records

KURLÄNDISCHE RITTERSCHAFT. ARCHIV
Church record extracts: Latvia, Lithunia and
other Baltic states and neighboring provinces,
1636-1932 Zonales Archivlager, Goslar
N: USIGS 4 reels   1286

Guild Records

KURLÄNDISCHE RITTERSCHAFT. ARCHIV
Guild records, Latvia and Lithuania, ca. 1653-
1850 Zonales Archivlager, Goslar
N: USIGS 1 reel   1287

ESTONIA

Local Records

NARVA, Viru, Estonia
City administration records, 1684-1700; lower
court proceedings, 1687-1700 FiHV
N: USIGS 9 reels   1288

NARVA, Viru, Estonia
Kihlakunnanoikeus - Häradsrätt [circuit court
records, copy] of various judicial districts,
1684-1702 FiHV
N: USIGS 3 reels   1289

REVAL [TALLINN, HARJU], Estonia
City administration records, ca. 1000-1834;
tax records, ca. 1287-1834; list of citizens
[Bürgerlisten], etc., ca. 1380-1809; inventory
of vital records of churches, ca. 1777-1786,
1800; list of various craftsmen and apprentices,
ca. 1784-1786; accounts and property tax
reports of guilds, 1626-1750, 1788-1795;
clerical reports, etc., 1596-1599 [unk.]
N: USIGS 20 reels   1290

Guild Records

REVAL [TALLINN, HARJU], Estonia. CANUTE
GUILD
Records, 1562-1932 [unk.]
N: USIGS 15 reels   1291

REVAL [TALLINN, HARJU], Estonia. DOME
GUILD
Records, 1647-1920 [unk.]
N: USIGS 3 reels   1292

REVAL [TALLINN, HARJU], Estonia. GRAND
GUILD
Records, ca. 1509-1603, 1703, 1865-1918 [unk.]
N: USIGS 1 reel   1293

REVAL [TALLINN, HARJU], Estonia.
SCHWARZHAEUPTER GUILD
Records, 1550-1939 [unk.]
N: USIGS 7 reels   1294

Church Records

FINLAND. VALTIONARKISTO
Records of the German Congregation of
Narva (copy), 1644-1833; records of the
Swedish and Finnish Congregations of Narva,
1740-1752, 1762-1776 FiHV
N: USIGS 1 reel   1295

FRANCE

Bibliography

AIX, France. BIBLIOTHÈQUE MÉJANE
Table des lettres royaux, 1488-1613 Ibid.
N: DLC 11 reels   1296

AIX, France. BIBLIOTHÈQUE MÉJANE
Table des registres des lettres royaux du
Parlement [de Provence], ms. 933-1022
Ibid.
N: ? 1 reel   1297
P: DLC

DUNKERQUE, France. BIBLIOTHÈQUE
MUNICIPALE
Catalogue générale Ibid.
N: DLC 1 reel   1298

FRANCE. ARCHIVES NATIONALES
Inventaires: 47, 55, 64, 65, 66, 75, 84, 89,
91-94, 104-106, 108, 110, 112-114, 116, 118,
121, 134, 147-148, 167-169, 171, 174, 203,
205, 213, 216, 223, 225, 234, 237-238, 308,
310, 312, 314, 316-317, 319, 321, 323-325,
327-328, 331, 332, 335-339, 341, 387, 393,
409, 422 FrAN
N: DLC 199 reels   1299

NORD (Dept.), France. ARCHIVES
Inventaires, Nos. 72, 73, 88, 158 Ibid.
N: DLC 6 reels   1300

Government Records

FRANCE. ADMINISTRATION GÉNÉRALE
Selections, 1789-1800 FrAN
N: FU 23 reels   1301

FRANCE. ARCHIVES NATIONALES
Collection Dubois, 1789-1814, selections
FrAN
N: FU 4 reels   1302

FRANCE. ARCHIVES NATIONALES
Material on Revolutionary Clubs and the
Revolution of 1848 FrAN
N: DLC   1303

FRANCE. ARCHIVES NATIONALES
Musée des archives, 1792, 1794 A. E., Nos.
1381, 1418 FrAN
N: FU 2 reels   1304

FRANCE. ARCHIVES NATIONALES. MINUTIER
CENTRAL
Étude CVIII (Montaud), 1826 FrAN
N: FU 2 reels   1305

FRANCE. ASSEMBLÉE NATIONALE
Selections, 1789-1795 FrAN
N: FU 9 reels   1306

FRANCE. COMMISSION MILITAIRE ÉTABLIE
EN VENDEMAIRE, AN IV
Affaire du camp de Grenelle, 1795-1797 FrAN
N: FU 1 reel   1307

FRANCE. CONSULAT, NICE
Selections, 1844-1848
Archives départementales des Alpes-Maritimes,
Nice
N: FU 5 reels   1308

FRANCE. CONVENTION NATIONALE, 1792-1795.
COMITÉ DE SALUT PUBLIC
Registres, 1793-1794 AF II* 220-224, 226-227
FrAN
N: FU 8 reels   1309

FRANCE. CONVENTION NATIONALE, 1792-1795.
COMITÉ DE SALUT PUBLIC
Selections, 1793-1794 FrAN
N: FU 4 reels   1310

FRANCE. CONVENTION NATIONALE, 1792-1795.
COMITÉ DE SÛRETÉ GÉNÉRALE
Commission des vingt-et-un, 1794-1795 FrAN
N: FU 5 reels   1311

FRANCE. CONVENTION NATIONALE, 1792-1795.
COMITÉ DE SÛRETÉ GÉNÉRALE
Compatibilité, 1793-1794; passeports, Nov. 4,
1793-Apr. 18, 1794; D-XLIII, pièces 1-127
FrAN
N: FU 8 reels   1312

FRANCE. CONVENTION NATIONALE, 1792-1795.
COMITÉ DE SÛRETÉ GÉNÉRALE
Dossiers, série alphabétique (selections) FrAN
N: FU 45 reels   1313

FRANCE. CONVENTION NATIONALE, 1792-1795.
COMITÉ DE SÛRETÉ GÉNÉRALE
Enregistrement de correspondance à l'arrivée,
1792-1795 FrAN
N: FU 43 reels   1314

FRANCE. CONVENTION NATIONALE, 1792-1795.
COMITÉ DE SÛRETÉ GÉNÉRALE
Liste générale des émigrés FrAN
N: FU 2 reels   1315

FRANCE. CONVENTION NATIONALE, 1792-1795.
COMITÉ DE SÛRETÉ GÉNÉRALE
Registres, 1792-1795 AF II 254-301 FrAN
N: FU 49 reels   1316

FRANCE. CONVENTION NATIONALE, 1792-1795.
COMITÉ DE SÛRETÉ GÉNÉRALE
Registres des détenus, 1793-1794
F 7* 89-98 FrAN
N: FU 10 reels   1317

FRANCE. CONVENTION NATIONALE, 1792-1795.
COMITÉ DE SÛRETÉ GÉNÉRALE
Selections, 1789-1795 FrAN
N: FU 20 reels   1318

FRANCE. DIRECTION GÉNÉRALE DES DOMAINES.
DISTRICT DE MELUN
Ventes de biens nationaux, 1791 Q 19 M 5-7
Archives départementales de Seine-et-Marne,
Melun
N: FU 1 reel   1319

FRANCE. DIRECTOIRE EXÉCUTIF.
SECRÉTAIRERIE GÉNÉRALE
Registres d'enregistrement de demandes,
1796-1797, AF III* 66, 89, 105; rapports
ministériels, AF III 94 FrAN
N: FU 4 reels   1320

FRANCE. HAUTE COUR DE JUSTICE DE
VENDÔME ÉTABLIE LE 20 THERMIDOR,
AN IV
Affaire de Babeuf, 1796-1797 FrAN
N: FU 2 reels   1321

FRANCE. MINISTÈRE DE LA JUSTICE
Selections, 1793, 1795-1799 FrAN
N: FU 6 reels   1322

FRANCE. MINISTÈRE DE LA MAISON DU
ROI (ET DE L'EMPEREUR)
Selections, 1781, 1789, 1807-1813, 1815-1830

FrAN
N: FU 4 reels   1323

FRANCE. MINISTÈRE DE L'INTÉRIEUR.
DIVISION DE LA POLICE GÉNÉRALE
Selections re: émigrés and Babeuf, 1789-
1830 FrAN
N: FU 20 reels   1324

FRANCE. MINISTÈRE DES AFFAIRES
ÉTRANGÈRES
Correspondance des Consuls, Commerciale,
1837-1879, 14 v. FrAN
N: CU-B*
P: CU-B   1325

FRANCE. MINISTÈRE DES AFFAIRES ÉTRAN-
GÈRES
Poussin et al. Despatches from Copenhagen,
1702-1739 Ibid.
N: CLU 4 reels*   1326

FRANCE. PARLEMENT. PARIS
Débats du Parlement pendant la minorité de
Louis XIV FrAN
N: MnU   1327

FRANCE. PARLEMENT. PROVENCE
Délibérations, 1536-1590, 1629-1630, 1711-
1790 Archives départementales, Aix-en-
Provence
N: DLC 21 reels
P: DLC   1328

FRANCE. TRIBUNAL RÉVOLUTIONNAIRE,
1792-1794
Fonds du Parquet: Affaire du 9 thermidor
[an II] FrAN
N: FU 2 reels   1329

FRANCE. TRIBUNAL RÉVOLUTIONNAIRE
DU 10 MARS, 1793
Dossiers, 1793-1794 (selections) FrAN
N: FU 16 reels   1330

FRANCE. TRIBUNAL RÉVOLUTIONNAIRE
DU 8 PLUVIÔSE, AN III
Affaire Fouquier-Tinville et autres FrAN
N: FU 1 reel   1331

FRANCE. TRIBUNAL RÉVOLUTIONNAIRE DU
24 THERMIDOR, AN II
Dossiers (selections), 1794 FrAN
N: FU 4 reels   1332

City Records

AVEYRON (Dept.),France. ARCHIVES
Fonds du Bureau des Finances de Montauban,
328 p. Ibid. ms. copy FrBN
N: NNC of copy at FrBN   1333

BOSSEY and NEYDENS, Haute Savoie, France
Vital records, 1601-1779 SzGA
N: USIGS 1 reel   1334

LOCMARIAQUER, Belle-Île-en-Mer, France
Registre, 38 p. Archives départementales du
Morbihan, Vannes
N: CaNBSjU
P: CaNBSjU   1335

PARIS. PRÉFECTURE DE POLICE
Documents relatifs à la Loterie des Lingots
d'Or, 1850-1853 Ibid.
N: CU-B 10 reels*
P: CU-B   1336

SEINE (Dept.), France. ADMINISTRATION
GÉNÉRALE DE L'ASSISTANCE PUBLIQUE
Fonds Gabriel Bouquier, 1771-1782, 7 cahiers
Ibid.
N: FU 6 reels   1337

Church Records

CHURCH OF JESUS CHRIST OF LATTER-DAY
SAINTS. ALSACE-LORRAINE
Records of the Mulhouse Branch, early to
1948 USIC
N: USIGS 1 reel   1338

CHURCH OF JESUS CHRIST OF LATTER-DAY
SAINTS. FRENCH MISSION
Records, 1851-1953: French Mission, German
and Swiss-German Mission and West-German
Mission USIC
N: USIGS 3 reels   1339

DEUTSCHES ZENTRALARCHIV FÜR GENEALOGIE
Huguenot records for various districts of
France, 1600-1800 Ibid.
N: Ibid.
P: USIGS 98 reels   1340

Protestant churches in Ain, France (Dept.);
church records: Cessy, Segny, Sauverny,
Collonges, Farges, Gex, Lyon, 1609-1685
SzGA
N: USIGS 1 reel   1341

Jewish Community Records

BORDEAUX, France. JEWS
Malesherbes's diary of the Bordeaux Community
Députation [in Hebrew], 1788, 1790; Registre de
la Société de Bienfaisance, 1803-1909; Registre
de copie de lettres, 1809-1822 IsJJH
N: IsJJH 4 reels   1342

NANCY, France. JEWS
Consistoire Israélite de la Circumscription,
1820-1834; Registre des séances de la
Commission Administrative de la Synagogue,
1822-1823; Consistoire Israélite, 1832-1835
IsJJH 3 reels
N: IsJJH 3 reels
P: NNYi   1343

YIVO INSTITUTE FOR JEWISH RESEARCH,
New York
Documents and sundry papers on Jews in
France during German occupation, 1940-1945
NNYi
N: NNYi 1 reel   1344

Personal Papers

BARÈRE, BERTRAND, 1755-1841
Fonds B. Barère, 1817- ca.1830
Archives Départementales des Hautes-
Pyrénées (Tarbes)
N: FU 1 reel   1345

BARLOW, JOEL, 1754-1812
Notes for a projected history of the French
Revolution, ca. 1796 MH
N: MoU 1 reel*   1346

BEAUMARCHAIS, PIERRE AUGUSTIN CARON
DE, 1732-1799
Documents and letters, v.d. FrAN
N: MiU 7 reels   1347

CABET, ÉTIENNE, 1788-1856
Abrégé de l'histoire universelle à l'usage du
peuple et abrégé d'histoire d'Angleterre,
1840, 1093 p. FrBN
N: IaU 3 reels   1348

CABET, ÉTIENNE, 1788-1856
Letters, 1849-1851, 3 items FrBN
N: IaU   1349

CALONNE, CHARLES ALEXANDRE DE, 1734-1802
Papers (selections) [PC 1/123-125] UKLPRO
N: WyU 34 reels   1350

COCK, HENRIQUE
Letter to Furio Ceriol, 1584 FrBN
N: OU   1351

COLBERT DE MAULEVRIER, ÉDOUARD C. V.
Journal, 1798 priv.
N: PPAmP 250 frames   1352

CROMOT DuBOURG, MARIE FRANÇOIS JOSEPH
MAXIME, Baron, 1756-1836
Military journal, Mar.-Nov.,1781 PHi
N: RPB 1 reel   1353

DALADIER, ÉDOUARD, b. 1884- , defendant
[Stenographic report of the trial of Daladier, et al., before the Supreme Court of Justice at Riom, Feb. 19 - Apr. 2, 1942] (typescript)
N: DLC 1 reel   1354
P: DLC

DAVID, J. L. JULES, 1748-1825
Souvenirs et documents inédits, 1746-1800 FrBN Mss. Fr. Nouv. Acq. 6604-6606
N: FU 3 reels   1355

DESBORDES-VALMORE, MARCELINE F.J., 1786-1859
Letters, 1817-1854 FrD
N: IU 95 feet   1356

DESMAIZEAUX, PIERRE, 1673-1745
Correspondence
N: RPB 3 reels   1357

GRANVILLE, CHARLES BECARD DE, ca. 1666-1698
Les Partes des Indes, ca. 1695 OkTG
N: OkTG 1 reel   1358

LOUVOIS, FRANÇOIS MICHEL LE TELLIER, MARQUIS de, 1639-1691
Correspondence, 1681-1688 FrAN
N: NcU 6 reels   1359

Mémoires pour faire l'histoire des seigneurs de Coucy ms. Fr. 18616 FrBN
N: NjP 1 reel   1360

MONTESQUIEU, CHARLES LOUIS DE SECONDAT, BARON DE LA BRÈDE ET DE, 1689-1755
Réflexions et pensées, mss., v. 1   FrB
N: MiU 1 reel   1361

NAPOLÉON I, 1769-1821
Correspondence, 1795-1814, 25 items   priv.
DCO: NNQC   1362

NAPOLÉON I, 1769-1821
Papers, 1759-1814, 32 items
Heineman Foundation, New York
DCO: NcU   1363

PÉTAIN, HENRI PHILIPPE, 1856-1951, defendant
Compte rendu du procès devant la Haute Cour de Justice, 1945 Ibid.
N: DLC 1 reel   1364

RASER, WILLIAM
Notes on Paris and trip to Bordeaux, 1817-1818   priv.
DCO: NN 50 ll.   1365

SCALIGER FAMILY
Mémoire sur la généalogie des Scaligers, 1791 PPAmP
N: NhD   1366

STAËL-HOLSTEIN, ANNE LOUISE GERMAINE BARONNE DE, née NECKER, 1766-1817
Lettres à Fourcault de Pavant, 1804-1812 FrAN
N: MiU 1/2 reel   1367

VICQ-d'AZYR, FELIX, 1748-1794
Lettre au d'Ormeson, 15 Sept. 1783 FrAN
N: NcD   1368

VOLTAIRE, FRANÇOIS MARIE AROUET DE, 1694-1778
Letters, 1757-1774 PP
N: PHi 1 reel   1369

Business Papers

POUILLY, DE, FAMILY
Business records, including statements of marriage, 1739-1788, 3 v.   priv.
N: ICU 1 reel   1370

Collections

CAMBRAI, France. BIBLIOTHÈQUE MUNICIPALE
Manuscript no. 124, dated 1542, 4 v.   Ibid.
N: NjP 8 reels   1371

HARVARD UNIVERSITY. LIBRARY
Alchemical manuscripts: Paracelsus, Philosophia Paracelsi, n.d., 316 p.; Remedies for illnesses and wounds, alchemist's recipes [in French], 17th cent., 709 p.; Experimenta chemica [in Italian, Latin, German], 1654, 101 p.; Traité de la pratique hermetique, 1748, 2 v.; unidentified manuscript   MH
N: DLC 5 reels   1372

Institutions

CHATEAU FLEURY, Fleury en Bier, France
Estate documents, 1410-1703, 9 items   priv.
N: DLC 1 reel   1373

PARTI SOCIALISTE
Congresses, 1880-1882, 1890 Musée Social, Paris
N: WU 3 reels   1374

BELGIUM

Government Records

BELGIUM. MINISTÈRE DES AFFAIRES ÉTRANGÈRES
Records re: North America, 1834-1899 Ibid.
N: DNA 9 reels [T-125]   1375

Church Records

CHURCH OF JESUS CHRIST OF LATTER-DAY SAINTS. BELGIUM
Records, Belgium Mission and Branches (Netherlands Mission to 1923 and French Mission from 1923), to 1951 USlC
N: USlGS 2 reels   1376

Collections

BRUSSELS. BIBLIOTHÈQUE ROYALE DE BELGIQUE
Manuscript no. 9126 BeBR
N: NjP 1 reel   1377

NETHERLANDS

Bibliography

BOER, LOUIS P. DE, compiler
Inventory of records of Protestant churches in the Netherlands, prior to 1664 (typescript) NNNG
N: USlGS 1 reel   1378

NETHERLANDS. ALGEMEEN RIJKSARCHIEF
Catalogue of church and civil records of the Archives of Overijssel, Neth: inventory of vital records NeHAR
N: USlGS 1 reel   1379

NETHERLANDS. ALGEMEEN RIJKSARCHIEF
Catalogue of 10-yearly index, 1811-1842, and index of vital records, 1811-1842, of South Holland NeHAR
N: USlGS 1 reel   1380

NETHERLANDS. ALGEMEEN RIJKSARCHIEF
Inventaris van de Registers van de Burgerlijke Stand van Noord-Holland [Inventory of vital records], 1811-1842 (typescript) NeHAR
N: USlGS 1 reel   1381

NETHERLANDS. ALGEMEEN RIJKSARCHIEF
Inventory of church records, etc., of various provinces of the Netherlands, ca. 500 p. NeHAR
N: USlGS 1 reel   1382

NETHERLANDS. ALGEMEEN RIJKSARCHIEF
Marriage index, various localities in South

Holland, 1756-1811, with lists of communities, compiled by Joh. Jac. Bink from church and civil records NeHAR
N: USlGS 5 reels   1383

NETHERLANDS. ALGEMEEN RIJKSARCHIEF
Ten-yearly index to vital records of various communities, 1811-1842 NeHAR
N: USlGS 21 reels   1384

NETHERLANDS. RIJKSARCHIEF IN NOORDHOLLAND, Haarlem
Inventaris der Doop-, Trouw-, Begraaf- & Successie-Registers [inventory of registers of baptisms, marriages, burials, and inheritance tax records], ca. 1590-1828 Ibid.
N: USlGS 1 reel   1385

'S HERTOGENBOSCH, Neth. (Diocese, Catholic). ARCHIEF
Inventory of church records, ca. 1597-1914 Ibid.
N: USlGS 1 reel   1386

Census

NETHERLANDS. ALGEMEEN RIJKSARCHIEF
Census lists of the population of Limburg, Netherlands, and Limbourg, Belgium, 1796, 1800, 1806-1811, and records of changed surnames of Jewish persons NeHAR
N: USlGS 11 reels   1387

Government Records

AMSTERDAM. GEMEENTE-ARCHIEF
Civil and church records (Nederlandsche Hervormde Kerk, Catholic, Waalsche Gemeenten, Doopsgezinde Gemeenten, Joodsche Synagoge, English Presbyterian, Old Evangelical Lutheran, Hersteld Evangelical Lutheran, Old Flemish, Remonstrant Reformed, Greek Catholic, New Lutheran, Portugese Jewish, etc.) of North Holland, 1523-1942 Ibid.
N: USlGS 740 reels   1388

GOUDA, South Holland, Neth.
Tax records, various localities, 1604, 1680, 1713-1811; register of national militia of Bloemendaal, 1816 Ibid.
N: USlGS 2 reels   1389

HAGUE. GAARDERSARCHIEF
Impost [tax] on burials and marriages and vital records, various localities, South Holland, 1695-1872 Ibid.
N: USlGS 107 reels   1390

MAASTRICHT. STADSARCHIEF EN BIBLIOTHEEK
Court records of judicial districts in Limburg, Neth., Brabant and Luik (Liége), Belgium (Hooggerecht Brabant); city records of Maastricht (Burgerboeck), 1436-1795 Ibid.
N: USlGS 4 reels   1391

NETHERLANDS (United Provinces, 1581-1795)
Garrison in Aire and Rijsel, vital records, 1708-1735 NeHAR
N: USlGS 1 reel   1392

NETHERLANDS (United Provinces, 1581-1795) ADMIRALITEITSCOLLEGES
Records, 1586-1792 NeHAR
N: CU-B 34 reels   1393

NETHERLANDS. ALGEMEEN RIJKSARCHIEF
Civil and church records (Nederlandsche Hervormde Kerk, Catholic, Evangelisch-Lutherse Kerk, Doopsgezinde Gemeenten, Joodsche Synagoge) of Friesland, 1578-1906 NeHAR
N: USlGS 900 reels   1394

NETHERLANDS. ALGEMEEN RIJKSARCHIEF
Civil and church records (Nederlandsche Hervormde Kerk, Catholic, Joodsche Synagoge, Evangelisch-Lutherse Kerk, Waalsche Gemeenten, Doopsgezinde Gemeenten) of Gelderland, 1435-1947 NeHAR
N: USlGS 194 reels   1395

NETHERLANDS. ALGEMEEN RIJKSARCHIEF
Civil and church records (Nederlandsche Her-
vormde Kerk, Catholic, Joodsche Synagoge,
Evangelisch-Lutherse Kerk, etc.) of Groningen,
1544-1907 NeHAR
N: USIGS 957 reels   1396

NETHERLANDS. ALGEMEEN RIJKSARCHIEF
Civil and church records (Nederlandsche Her-
vormde Kerk, Waalsche Gemeenten, Lutherse
Kerk, etc.) of Limberg, 1562-1846 NeHAR
N: USIGS 579 reels   1397

NETHERLANDS. ALGEMEEN RIJKSARCHIEF
Civil and church records (Nederlandsche
Hervormde Kerk, Catholic, Waalsche Gemeen-
ten, Evangelisch-Lutherse Kerk, etc.) of
North Brabant, 1473-1946 NeHAR
N: USIGS 2076 reels   1398

NETHERLANDS. ALGEMEEN RIJKSARCHIEF
Civil and church records (Nederlandsche Her-
vormde Kerk, Catholic, Lutherse Kerk,
Waalsche Gemeenten, Doopsgezinde Gemeenten,
Joodsche Synagoge, etc.) of North Holland,
1540-1949 NeHAR
N: USIGS 2680 reels   1399

NETHERLANDS. ALGEMEEN RIJKSARCHIEF
Civil and church records (Nederlandsche Hervormde Kerk, Catholic, Waalsche Gemeenten, Joodsche Synagoge, Waalsche Gemeenten,
Lutherse Kerk, Mennonite) of Overijssel, 1423-
1888 NeHAR
N: USIGS 819 reels   1400

NETHERLANDS. ALGEMEEN RIJKSARCHIEF
Civil and church records (Nederlandsche Her-
vormde Kerk, Catholic, Evangelisch-Lutherse
Kerk, Waalsche Gemeenten, Joodsche Synagoge,
Lutherse Kerk, Doopsgezinde Gemeenten Rem-
onstrant, etc.) of South Holland, 1574-1955
NeHAR
N: USIGS 2047 reels   1401

NETHERLANDS. ALGEMEEN RIJKSARCHIEF
Civil and church records (Nederlandsche Hervormde Kerk, Catholic, Waalsche Gemeente,
Evangelisch-Lutherse Kerk, Doopsgezinde Gemeenten, Joodsche Synagoge, Remonstrant Reformed, etc.) of Utrecht, 1579-1952 NeHAR
N: USIGS 814 reels   1402

NETHERLANDS. ALGEMEEN RIJKSARCHIEF
Civil and church records (Nederlandsche Her-
vormde Kerk, Catholic) of Zeeland, 1578-1884
NeHAR
N: USIGS 44 reels   1403

NETHERLANDS. ALGEMEEN RIJKSARCHIEF
Material re: treaty of Breda: Legatie Arkiv 50
NeHAR
N: CCH 1 reel   1404

NETHERLANDS. ALGEMEEN RIJKSARCHIEF
Registers re: relations with the Hansa and
Scandinavia, 1449-1565, 54 v. NeHAR
N: DLC   1405

NETHERLANDS. ALGEMEEN RIJKSARCHIEF
Schepenen [administration records], various
localities of South Holland, 1619-1811 NeHAR
N: USIGS 4 reels   1406

NETHERLANDS. ALGEMEEN RIJKSARCHIEF
Secrete brieven, legatie, despatches from
Denmark, Sweden, England, the Netherlands
(Nymwege), and Russia NeHAR
N: CLU 18 reels*   1407

NETHERLANDS. ALGEMEEN RIJKSARCHIEF
Vital records, various localities in Drenthe,
1644, 1811-1842 NeHAR
N: USIGS 260 reels   1408

RIJNLAND, Netherlands. HOOGHEEMRAAD-
SCHAP
Records Ibid.
Microfiches: CU 3 trays   1409

ROTTERDAM, South Holland, Netherlands
Civil records, Charlois and Katendrecht,
1660-1811 Ibid.
N: USIGS 2 reels   1410

Church Records

AMSTERDAM. JOODSCHE SYNAGOGE
Records of the Jewish Congregation, 1856-
1941 [unk.]
N: USIGS 8 reels   1411

CHURCH OF JESUS CHRIST OF LATTER-DAY
SAINTS. NETHERLANDS MISSION
Records, early to 1948 USlC
N: USIGS 9 reels   1412

CHURCH OF JESUS CHRIST OF LATTER-DAY
SAINTS. WEST GERMAN MISSION
Military church records, Mecklenburg regiment
and grenadier battalion stationed in the
Netherlands, 1788-1795 [unk.]
N: USIGS 1 reel   1413

NETHERLANDS. ALGEMEEN RIJKSARCHIEF
Dutch Reformed Church and Baptist Church
records, various localities of Friesland, ca.
1617-1909 NeHAR
N: USIGS 4 reels   1414

NEDERLANDSCHE HERVORMDE KERK. DRENTHE
Records, various localities, 1626-1926 NeHAR
N: USIGS 29 reels   1415

Collections

AMSTERDAM. UNIVERSITEIT. BIBLIOTHEEK
Petitions, letters and pamphlets addressed to
the National Assembly by the Organization
Felix Libertade, 1795-1796 Ibid.
N: NNYi 1 reel   1416

BRITISH MUSEUM
Documents on British-Dutch relations, 1576-
1764 Add. ms. 17,677 A-DDDD UKLBM
N: CU-B 54 reels   1417

LEYDEN. BIBLIOTHÈQUE WALLONNE
Walloon Archive records, ca. 1093-1926
NeHAR
N: USIGS 19 reels   1418

SPAIN

Bibliography

CLARK, CHARLES UPSON, 1875-
Notebooks re: Spanish Archives, 1929-1939
DSI
N: CU-B 2 reels   1419

Government Records

GREAT BRITAIN. FOREIGN OFFICE F. O. 72
Consular Despatches from Spain, 1808-1825,
255 v. UKLPRO
N: CU-B   1420
P: CU-B

SPAIN. ARCHIVO GENERAL DE SIMANCAS
Estado: selections from Negociación de
Inglaterra, 1563-1583, 1603-1678, 1766-
1778; Embajada de Inglaterra, 1817-1819,
1822; Negociación de Francia, 1761-1763,
1775-1783; Negociación de Holanda, 1776-
1782 Ibid.
N: DLC 2236 feet   1421
PP: DLC

SPAIN. ARCHIVO GENERAL DE SIMANCAS
Guerra moderna, 1781-1805 Ibid.
N: CU-B 7 reels*   1422
P: CU-B

SPAIN. SERVICIO HISTÓRICO MILITAR. BIBLIO-
TECA CENTRAL MILITAR
Archives re: Loyalist activities during the
Spanish Civil War, 1936-1939 DLC
N: DLC 1 reel*   1423

Church Records

INQUISITION. SPAIN
Documents for Barcelona and Zaragossa, Oct.-
Nov., 1518, 1579 priv.
N: DLC 1 reel   1424
P: DLC

Personal Papers

LASTARRIA, MIGUEL DE
Papers, 1790-1798 UKLBM
N: NcD 1 reel   1425

MONTANO, VINCENTE
Arcano de príncipe, 1681 ms. 20586 SpBN
N: NcD 1 reel   1426

OVIEDO Y VALDEZ, GONZALO F., 1478-1557
Respuesta de la Epistola moral del Amirante,
1524; Catálogo de los Reyes de Castilla, 1535;
Batallas y quinquagenes, 1550 (6 versions,
varying titles) ms. 7075, Escorial R-1-7,
2217-2219, 3134, 3135, 11651 SpBN
N: TxU 2404 frames*   1427

PICO, PIO
Narración Histórica CU-B
N: CU-B 1 reel   1428

VAIL, AARON
Diary, while chargé d'affaires at Madrid,
July 15, 1840-July 23, 1842 N
N: NNC NHi   1429

ITALY

Bibliography

BERGAMO. BIBLIOTECA PUBBLICA COMUNALE
Catalogo generale Ibid.
N: DLC 1 reel   1430

BERGAMO. S. ALESSANDRO IN COLONNA
(Church). BIBLIOTECA
Catalogo dei manoscritti Ibid.
N: DLC 1 reel   1431

BRESCIA. BIBLIOTECA CIVICA QUERINIANA
Inventario del Archivio Storica Comunale; catalogo dei manoscritti (a libro); catalogo dei
manoscritti (a schede) Ibid.
N: DLC 2 reels   1432

CAVACEPPI, BARTOLOMEO, 1716-1799,
compiler
Catalogo delli monumenti esistenti, 1802
Biblioteca dalla storia dell'arte, Rome
N: ICU   1433

LUCCA. BIBLIOTECA GOVERNATIVA
Manuscript catalogs Ibid.
N: DLC 3 reels   1434

MANTUA. MUSEO CIVICO. BIBLIOTECA
Catalogo dei manoscritti Ibid.
N: DLC 1 reel   1435

MARUCELLI, FRANCESCO, 1625-1713
De bibliothecis et bibliopolis
Biblioteca Marucelliana, Florence
N: ICN   1436

PADUA. MUSEO CIVICO. BIBLIOTECA
Catalog dei manoscritti e incunaboli, vol. C
Ibid.
N: DLC 1 reel   1437

PADUA. SEMINARIO VESCOVILE. BIBLIOTECA
Catalog of manuscripts, with supplement and
index of names Ibid.
N: DLC 3 reels   1438

PADUA. UNIVERSITÀ. BIBLIOTECA
Catalogo dei manoscritti, catalogo alfabetico dei
manoscritti; catalogo dei manoscritti al numero
provvisorio Ibid.
N: DLC 3 reels   1439
P: DLC

VENICE. BIBLIOTECA NAZIONALE MARCIANA
Appendice, Codici Veneti; appendice, Codici
Francesi e Stranieri; appendice, Codici Italiani;
Class 7, Istoria Ecclesiastica, E Civil Ibid.
N: DLC 3 reels   1440

VENICE. BIBLIOTECA NAZIONALE MARCIANA
Elenco dei codici manoscritti Latini Italiani.
Riservati Ibid.
N: DLC 1 reel   1441

VENICE. BIBLIOTECA QUERINI STAMPALIA
Catalogo dei manoscritti Class 1-4 Ibid.
N: DLC 1 reel   1442

VENICE. MUSEO CIVICO E RACCOLTA
CORRER. BIBLIOTECA
Catalogue of Donna della Rose manuscripts
Ibid.
N: DLC 1 reel   1443

VENICE. MUSEO CIVICO E RACCOLTA
CORRER. BIBLIOTECA
Catalogo codici cicogna, 7 v. Ibid.
N: DLC 13 reels   1444

VENICE. MUSEO CIVICO E RACCOLTA
CORRER. BIBLIOTECA
Catalogs Ibid.
N: DLC 2 reels   1445

VENICE. MUSEO CIVICO E RACCOLTA
CORRER. BIBLIOTECA
Codici Gradenigo, Catalogo ed Indice: Elenco
Manoscritti Lasciati al Museo Civico Correr
dal Cav. Michiele Ibid.
N: DLC 2 reels   1446

VENICE. SEMINARIO PATRIARCALE.
BIBLIOTECA
Catalogo Codici Ibid.
N: DLC 1 reel   1447

VERONA. BIBLIOTECA CIVICA
Inventario manoscritti dei Codici Ibid.
N: DLC 1 reel   1448

Church Records

CHURCH OF JESUS CHRIST OF LATTER-DAY
SAINTS. ITALY
Mission and branch records, 1851-1868 [Italian
to 1854, Swiss-Italian 1854-1861, German 1861-
1868 and Swiss-German Mission 1868] USlC
N: USlGS 1 reel   1449

Parish records of Italian Protestant churches
in Piedmont, Italy: Angrogna, 1691-1948;
Bobbio, 1705-1947; LaTour (Torre Pellice),
1692-1932; Massel (Macella), 1830-1948;
Perrier (Perrero), 1719-1948; Pinerola (Pig-
nerol), 1856-1948; Pomaret (Pomaretto), 1715-
1890; Praly (Prali), 1838-1865; Pramol (Pra-
mollo), 1708-1903; Prarustin, 1639-1890; Rod-
oret (Rodaretto), 1838-1948; Rora, 1694-1948;
St. Germain (San Germano), 1752-1948; St.
Jean (San Giovanni), 1707-1946; Villa Seche
(Villasecca), 1730-1948; Villar (Villaro Pellice),
1555-1947 Torre Pellice, Italy
N: USlGS 66 reels   1450

Jewish Community Records

FLORENCE. COMUNITÀ ISRAELITICA
Due Regolamenti dell' Università, 1571, 1601;
Documenti riguardanti le case dei Catecumeni,
1610-1797; Pareri Rabbinici, 1614-1868; Atti
legali, 1623-1890; Supplice a Magistrati, 1630-
1808; Deliberazione del Tribunale dei Massari,
1630-1808; Lettere all' U. I. F. in genere d'affari
e questione legali, 1636-1695, 1730-1747; De-
creti governativi per gli Ebrei, 1639-1890; Deliberazione dei Magistrati riguardanti gli Ebrei,
1641; Censimento dell' anno 1642; Lettere dell'
'Università' Israelitica, 1648-1889; Relazioni
al Consiglio, 1657-1857; Proved. riguardanti
la proibizione del bacco, 1674-1794; Giurisdizioni
et competenze del Tribunale dei Massari, 1677-
1790; Copia et Appunti di deliberazioni, 1689-
1850; Proibizione di vari libri Ebraici, 1730;

Deliberazioni e verbali del Tribunale Massari,
1742-1789; Doti beneficenza, 1760-1851; Accad-
emia dei Faticanti esclusione degli Ebrei e re-
clamo dei Medesimi, 1779; Regolamenti vari
della Comunità e sue Institutioni, 1787-1899;
Tumulti contro gli Ebrei a Firenze e Livorno,
1790; Ferdinand I II, Feste dell' U. I. F. incopo-
nazione, nascita, figli, etc., 1791-1814; Reazi-
one et tumulto antisemitico in Toscana, 1799;
Sinedrio Napoleonico, 1804-1806; Instituzione
e deliberazione del Consistoro Dipartamentale,
1809-1814; Permesso di tenere le Botteghe
aperte nelle Feste Cattoliche, 1819-1830; Avvisi della Comunità, 1824-1901; Revoca dell'
Emancipazione, 1852; Avvisi di Istitutzione
Ebraiche, 1863-1910; Regulamenti della
Comunità, ca. 1850 -   Ibid.
N: IsJJH 29 reels   1451
P: NNYi

FLORENCE. COMUNITÀ ISRAELITICA.
ARCHIVIO
Ancona - Regolamento della Comunità, 1807;
Ferrara - Regolamenti della Comunità, 1772,
1777, 1829, 1850; Genova - Regolamento della
Comunità, 1824; Modena, Regolamenti della
Comunità, 1746; Pitigliano, Rovigo, Livorno,
Padova, Verona, Torino: Regolamenti della
Comuniti, 1812-1863 Ibid.
N: IsJJH 1 reel   1452
P: NNYi

LEGHORN. COMUNITÀ ISRAELITICA
Bolli, letteri, patenti, etc., 1552; Escamot et
Statutos, 1600; Testamenti, 1629-1713;
Elezioni e Uffizi, 1642-1785; Repertorio
antico, 1670-1710; Capitoli della 'Università'
di Livorno, 18th cent.; Servizio militare,
1833-1843 Ibid.
N: IsJJH 8 reels   1453
P: NNYi

PISA. COMUNITÀ ISRAELITICA
Decrete di sopressione e sua revoca, 1828
Ibid.
N: IsJJH   1454
P: NNYi

PISA. COMUNITÀ ISRAELITICA
Libro dei Registri dei nati, ketbod e testamonto,
1691-1749; Copie di benigni rescritti lettere et
altro, 1749-1782; Copia di letteri, 1773-1779,
1790-1804, 1811-1832; Registro di carte dotali
della nazione Ebrea di Pisa, 1774-1815; Minuta
di deliberizioni, 1817-1847 Ibid.
N: IsJJH 9 reels   1455
P: NNYi

Personal Papers

ACHILLINI, ALLESSANDRE, 1463-1512
Expositio Alexandri Achilini super Avicene
pulchra, 1509, 60 p. ItBoU
N: NNC   1456

ANDREANI, PAOLO
Journals, 1784-1791 priv.
N: PPAmP   1457

GANDOLFI, MAURO
Viaggio agli Stati Uniti, 1816 (copied in 1834)
ItBA
N: DLC 1 reel   1458
P: DLC

MARANA, GIOVANNI PAOLO, 1642-1693
Letter to Pidon de St. Olon [in Italian]
ms. 6829 FrPA
N: WU   1459

MARTINI, FRANCESCO DI GIORGIO, 1439-1502
Trattato di architettura civile e militare, 1491 ?
(2 versions) ItFBN ItS
N: MH   1460

ORETTI, MARCELLO
Manuscripts re: Italian artists, 18th cent. ItB
N: ICU 15 reels   1461

PROVENZALE, FRANCESCO (Francesco della
Torre), 1630-1704
Il schiavo di sua moglie, 1671 St. Cecilia
Library, Rome
N: NjP 1 reel   1462

PROVENZALE, FRANCESCO (Francesco della
Torre), 1630-1704
Stalladaura vendicate, 1678 St. Cecilia
Library, Rome
N: NjP 1 reel   1463

Collections

VENICE. ARCHIVIO DI STATO
Miscellanea Gregolin Ibid
N: DLC 1 reel   1464

College Records

PADUA. UNIVERSITÀ
Matricula Germanorum juridicae facultatis
Patavii ms. 459, 460 Ibid.
N: DLC 2 reels   1465

MALTA

Church Records

CHURCH OF JESUS CHRIST OF LATTER-DAY
SAINTS. MALTA
Mission records, 1852-1854 USlC
N: USlGS 1 reel   1466

GERMANY

Bibliography

BERLIN. PREUSSISCHE STAATSBIBLIOTHEK
Inventory of Greek manuscripts Ibid.
N: DLC 1 reel   1467

HEIDLEBERG. UNIVERSITÄT. BIBLIOTHEK
Nichtgedruckte Handschriftenkataloge Ibid.
N: NN 1 reel   1468

Census

MECKLENBURG-SCHWERIN, Germany. CENSUS,
ca. 1677-1689
Amtsverzeichnis, Volkszählungslisten [census
returns] [unk.]
N: USlGS 1 reel   1469

MECKLENBURG-SCHWERIN, Germany. CENSUS,
1819
Volkzählungslisten und Ortsverzeichnisse der
Domanial-, Ritter, und Kloster Ämter [census
returns] [unk.]
N: USlGS 60 reels   1470

Government Records

GERMANY
German records filmed at Alexandria, v.d.
v. p.
N: DNA   1471

For full details of this valuable collection, see
the finding aids still coming out from the National Archives, covering the 2600 or so reels of
which it consists.

GERMANY. AUSWÄRTIGES AMT
Records received by the National Archives
from the U.S. Dept. of State, ca. 1917-1945
DNA
N: DS 892 reels [T-120; T 136-141; T246, 249,
264]   1472

GERMANY. REICHSFÜHRER S.S. UND CHEF
DER DEUTSCHEN POLIZEI
[Himmler files, to complement files in Manu-
scripts Division, Library of Congress]
DCO: CSt-H 18 boxes   1473

GERMANY (Territory under Allied Occupation, 1945- U. S. Zone). MILITARY GOVERNOR
Monthly report, v. 1-3, 1945 DLC
N: DLC 1 reel   1474

City Records

ALT FIETZ, West Prussia, Germany
Official registration of inhabitants, 1918-1932 [unk.]
N: USIGS 1 reel   1475

CHURCH OF JESUS CHRIST OF LATTER-DAY SAINTS. EAST GERMAN MISSION
Vital records, Saxony: Annaberg, Chemnitz, 1498-1550; Arnoldsgrün (Kr. Zwickau), 1692-1788; Leutewitz bei Riesa, Dresden (Kr. Grossenhain), 1653-1839 [unk.]
N: USIGS 3 reels   1476

CHURCH OF JESUS CHRIST OF LATTER-DAY SAINTS. WEST GERMAN MISSION
Civil administration records, cities of Anhalt, Germany, ca. 1367-1733 [unk.]
N: USIGS 13 reels   1477

HORB (KR. SCHWARZWALD), Württemberg, Germany
Urbar und Einwohnerverzeichnis [land and tax records], 1697 [unk.]
N: USIGS 1 reel   1478

KÖNIGSBERG, Germany. PREUSSISCHE STAATSARCHIV
Folianten, Findbücher, Stadtesachen, Grund-buchindex, Kataster, Grundsteuerrole, 1198-1897 [unk.]
N: USIGS 179 reels   1479

PRENZLAU, Brandenburg, Prussia
Tax lists and accounts, ca. 1542-1840; enrollment lists and accounts, city militia and reserves, 1735-1850; Bürgerbuch [register of citizens], 1586, 1623-1918 [unk.]
N: USIGS 16 reels   1480

REUTLINGEN (KR. SCHWARZWALD), Württemberg, Germany
Baptisms, 1599-1631 [unk.]
N: USIGS 1 reel   1481

Church Records

BÜTZOW, Germany. ÉGLISE REFORMÉE DE FRANCE
Church records, 1698 - ca. 1774 [unk.]
N: USIGS*   1482

BÜTZOW, Germany. EVANGELISCH-REFORM-IERTE LANDESKIRCHE IN MECKLENBURG-SCHWERIN
Records, 1750-1875 [unk.]
N: USIGS *   1483

CHURCH OF JESUS CHRIST OF LATTER-DAY SAINTS. EAST GERMAN MISSION
Card index of persons of Königsberg, East Prussia: marriages, 1790-1874 [unk.]
N: USIGS 24 reels   1484

CHURCH OF JESUS CHRIST OF LATTER-DAY SAINTS. EAST GERMAN MISSION
Church records, various cities in Thuringia, 1551-1886 [unk.]
N: USIGS 83 reels   1485

CHURCH OF JESUS CHRIST OF LATTER-DAY SAINTS. EAST GERMAN MISSION
Church records, with some civil records [Standesamt], various cities in Prussia, 1405-1945 [unk.]
N: USIGS 2950 reels   1486

CHURCH OF JESUS CHRIST OF LATTER-DAY SAINTS. EAST GERMAN MISSION
Military church records, Anhalt: Bernburg, Eisleben, Dessau, Zerbst, Blankenburg, Saxe, Prussia, 1772-1941 [unk.]
N: USIGS 3 reels   1487

CHURCH OF JESUS CHRIST OF LATTER-DAY SAINTS. EAST GERMAN MISSION
Military church records and casualty lists of various German regiments, 1815-1873 [unk.]
N: USIGS 34 reels   1488

CHURCH OF JESUS CHRIST OF LATTER-DAY SAINTS. GERMANY
Records of German Mission and branches (German, Swiss-German, German-Austrian, East and West German Missions), 1851-1953 USIC
N: USIGS 39 reels   1489

EVANGELISCH-LUTHERISCHE LANDESKIRCHE IN MECKLENBURG - STRELITZ
Church records, various cities, 1611-1934 [unk.]
N: USIGS 155 reels   1490

GÜSTROW, Mecklenburg-Schwerin, Germany
Cathedral church records, 1634-1876 [unk.]
N: USIGS 3 reels   1491

GÜSTROW, Mecklenburg-Schwerin, Germany
Parish church (Pfarrkirche) records, 1677-1915 [unk]
N: USIGS 10 reels   1492

LUDWIGSLUST, Germany. BETHLEHEM CONGREGATION
Vital records, 1866-1934 [unk.]
N: USIGS 1 reel   1493

Jewish Community Records

ADELEBSEN, Prussia, Germany. JEWS
Protokollbuch, 1865-1889, 228 ll. IsJJH
N: IsJJH   1494
P: NNYi

ALTENKUNSTADT, Germany. JEWS
Sitzung-protokollbuch der Gemeinde, 1841-1868, 183 ll. IsJJH
N: IsJJH   1495
P: NNYi

ALTONA, Germany. JEWS
Communal register, 1738-1795 [in Hebrew]; Geburts- und Sterberegister, 1848-1853 IsJJH
N: IsJJH 2 reels   1496
P: NNYi

ALZENAU-WASSERLOS, Germany. JEWS
Protokollbuch der Kultusgemeinde, 1898-1937, 101 ll. IsJJH
N: IsJJH   1497
P: NNYi

BAMBERG, Germany. JEWS
Register of income and expenditures, 1705-1720 [in Hebrew]; Protokollbuch der Gemeindeverwal-tung, 1826-1834, 1904-1914, 1932-1933; Gemeinde Chronik, 1931-1938, 654 p. IsJJH
N: IsJJH   1498
P: NNYi

BEESKOW, Germany. JEWS
Protokollbuch, 1870-1925 IsJJH
N: IsJJH   1499
P: NNYi

BERLIN, Germany. JEWS
Tabelle der Jüdisches Hauseigentümer, 1744; Schulangelegenheiten der Jüdische Gemeinde, 1808-1833; Entwurf eines Panes zur Errichtung einer Jüdischen Gemeindeschule, 1825 IsJJH
N: IsJJH 3 reels   1500
P: NNYi

BEUTHEN, Germany. JEWS
Petition an die Schlessischen Provinzial-stände, 1847; Beschlüsse der Repräsentanten, 1857, 1866-1870, 362 ll. IsJJH
N: IsJJH   1501
P: NNYi

BEUTHEN, Germany. JEWS
Protokolle und Briefwechsel, 1867-1871, 154 ll. IsJJH
N: IsJJH   1502
P: NNYi

BEVERUNGEN, Germany. JEWS
Synagogen- und Gebetsordnung, 1809-1812, 24 ll. IsJJH
N: IsJJH   1503
P: NNYi

BOIZENBURG AN DEM ELBE, Germany. JEWS
Protokolle und bescheide, 1794-1833, 51 p. IsJJH
N: IsJJH   1504
P: NNYi

BOREK, Germany. JEWS
Protokolle der Repräsentanten, 1848-1890, 211 ll. IsJJH
N: IsJJH   1505
P: NNYi

CHURCH OF JESUS CHRIST OF LATTER-DAY SAINTS. EAST GERMAN MISSION
Card index of Jewish persons of Königsberg, East Prussia: vital records, 1826-1874 [unk.]
N: USIGS 29 reels   1506

Concentration camp inmates: Personal recollections (questionnaires), 1939-1945
Yad Vashem, Jerusalem
N: Ibid. 3000 feet   1507
P: NNYi

CRAILSHEIM, Germany. JEWS
Protokolle, 1811-1817 IsJJH
N: IsJJH 1 reel   1508
P: NNY

DARMSTADT, Germany. JEWS
Register of the Hessen-Darmstadt Obergraft-schaft, 1723 [in Yiddish]; Pinkas of debts, 1731-1739, 1741 [in Hebrew]; Register of Community debts, 1746, 1748, 1760 [in Hebrew]; Protokolle der israelitische Religionsgemeinde, 1876-1887, 773 ll. , 124 p. IsJJH
N: IsJJH   1509
P: NNYi

DITTLOFSRODA, Germany. JEWS
Protokollbuch der Kultusgemeinde, 1871-1935, 253 ll. IsJJH
N: IsJJH 127 frames   1510
P: NNYi

DORMITZ, Germany. JEWS
Gemeindebuch, 1850-1911 IsJJH
N: IsJJH   1511
P: NNYi

ELBING, Germany. JEWS
Protokollbuch, 1848-1911, 278 ll. IsJJH
N: IsJJH   1512
P: NNYi

EMMENDINGEN, Germany. JEWS
Communal register, 109 p. IsJJH
N: IsJJH   1513
P: NNYi

EMMENDINGEN, Germany. JEWS
Protokolle des Synagogenraths, 1851-1889, 1913-1928 IsJJH
N: IsJJH 2 reels   1514
P: NNYi

FORTH, Germany. JEWS
Protokolle der israelitischen Kultusgemeinde, 1847-1914, 93 ll. IsJJH
N: IsJJH   1515
P: NNYi

FRANKFURT AN DER ODER, Germany. JEWS
Protokollbuch, 1812-1815, 46 p. IsJJH
N: IsJJH   1516
P: NNYi

FRAUSTADT, Germany. JEWS
Protokollbuch für die Verwaltung, 1841-1859, 92 ll. IsJJH
N: IsJJH   1517
P: NNYi

FREIENWALDE, Germany. JEWS
Protokollbuch, 1864-1879, 229 p. IsJJH
N: IsJJH   1518
P: NNYi

FRIEDBERG, Germany. JEWS
Beerdigungsgesellschaft, 1814-1841;
Protokoll des Vorstands, 1855-1910 IsJJH
N: IsJJH 2 reels   1519
P: NNYi

FRIEDRICHSTADT, Germany. JEWS
Communal register, 1802-1860, 229 ll. IsJJH
N: IsJJH   1520
P: NNYi

GEISA, Germany. JEWS
Protokollbuch, 1872-1891, 230 ll. IsJJH
N: IsJJH   1521
P: NNYi

GIEBELSTADT, Germany. JEWS
Altes Protokollbuch, 1740-1799; Abrechnung,
1790, 58 ll. IsJJH
N: IsJJH   1522
P: NNYi

GÖTTINGEN, Germany. STADTARCHIV
Kaiserliche Privilegien der Juden, 1544;
Varia, die Juden betragend, 1569-1737;
Aufenthalt und Gewerbe der Juden, 1608;
Deduction und Gerechtsame der Juden
betragend, 18th cent.; die Onera der Juden
betragend, 1748-1781; Classification der
hiesiegen Schutz und Handels Juden, 1778-1799;
verschiedene Judenangelegenheiten, 1831-1838;
die Zahl der hierwohnenden Juden, 1842 IsJJH
N: IsJJH 9 reels   1523
P: NNYi

GRÜNBERG, Germany. JEWS
Protokollbuch für die Repräsentanten, 1855-
1909, 238 ll. IsJJH
N: IsJJH   1524
P: NNYi

HAMBURG, Germany. STADTBIBLIOTHEK
Germany-Minhagim customs, 16th-17th cent.
Ibid.
N: NNYi 1 reel   1525

HAMMELBURG, Germany. JEWS
Pinkas Hasheich Leshatz Vekabran [in
Hebrew], 1812-1829; die Wahl des Kultus-
vorstands, 1830-1885; Verhandlungen des
Vorstands der Kultusgemeinde, 1832-1833;
Protokollbuch des Kultusgemeinde Versamm-
lung, 1864-1935; Beerdigungsbuch, 1867;
Protokollbuch des Vorstandes der Kultus-
gemeinde, 1878-1936, 256 ll., 921 p. IsJJH
N: IsJJH   1526
P: NNYi

HANAU, Germany. JEWS
General-Protokoll, 1825-1922, 145 ll. IsJJH
N: IsJJH   1527
P: NNYi

HESSEN-DARMSTADT, Germany. JEWS
Land Judenschaftkommision Protokollen
Speciale, 1814-1817; Protokollen der israeli-
tischen Religionsgemeinde, 1852, 1854-1866,
187 ll. IsJJH
N: IsJJH   1528
P: NNYi

HOCHBERG, Germany. JEWS
Pinkas [Communal register], 1748-1802
[in Hebrew] IsJJH
N: IsJJH   1529
P: NNYi

JASTROW, Germany. JEWS
Protokollbuch der Repräsentanten, 1854,
362 p. IsJJH
N: IsJJH   1530
P: NNYi

JEWISH CONGREGATION, Beerfelden (Kr.
Erbach), Starkenburg, Hesse
Records, 1810-1875 [unk.]
N: USIGS 1 reel   1531

JEWISH CONGREGATION, Mecklenburg-Schwerin,
Germany
Records, 1787-1935 [unk.]
N: USIGS 2 reels   1532

KAUKENHEIM, Germany. JEWS
Verhältnisse der Juden, 1880-1905 IsJJH
N: IsJJH   1533
P: NNYi

KÖNIGSBERG, Germany. JEWS
Protokollbuch der Vorstands, 1896-1907,
150 ll. IsJJH
N: IsJJH   1534
P: NNYi

KÖNIGSBERG, Germany. PREUSSISCHE
STAATSARCHIV
Königsberg. Juden zur Sittengschichte, 1543;
Abschied, 1544; Judensachen, 1567-1722; Land-
tag Beschluss dass Juden in Preussen nich
geduldet werden, 1577; Conversi aus dem
Judentum, 1605; Juden-steuer in Preussen,
1701-1714; Bitte von den aus Grodno und Lit-
auen einresen zu dürfen, 1705; 70 Berichte
aus den Ämtern und Städten wegen der Juden
auf das Ausschreiben, 1717, 1720; Berichte
aus den Samländischen und Litauischen Ämtern,
1720; Berichte aus den Natangischen und Pol-
nischen Ämtern, 1720; Varia betragend Juden,
1722; Bestellung des Rabbi, 1744-1745; die
Jährliche Angabe der Judenschaft, 1745, etc;
Vergleitete und unvergleitete Juden, 1748;
General-Tabelle der Schutzjuden im Königreich Preussen, 1748; Barttracht der Juden,
1748; Edict betragend Pacht und Halten von
Wollspinnereien, 1752; Unterricht in Christ-
licher Religion für Juden, 1744-1792; der
Polnische Jude Hirsch, 1775; Bei Wegschaff-
ung verdächtiger Juden, 1775; Meyer Salomon
Jonas, 1778, 1779; Betragend Generalprivile-
gium für Juden Königsberg, 1787; Hoffaktor
Raphael Abraham zu Glogau, 1787; Acta general betragend Juden, 1791-1794; Historiche
Nachrichten von Langecona und Neuschottland,
1792; Städte und Ländereien Litauisches Dept.,
1792; Anglegung eines Lombards in Königsberg,
1792; Bankier Daniel Itzig Berlin, 1792; Im-
matrikulation fremder Juden, 1793; Nathan
Salomon Lewin, 1794; Generalprivilegien in
Königsberg, 1796; Verschiedene Judensachen,
1797, etc.;Bialystok, 1797-1807; Handelsverkehr
mit fremden Juden, 1811; Generalverzeichnis
der Juden, 1812; Staatsbürgerliche Rechte der
Juden, 1818-1844; Tilsit, Etablierung der
Juden, 1831-1841; Niederlassung der Juden,
Olenko, 1831-1851; Niederlassung der Juden,
Pillkallen, 1833; Gumbinen, Judenangelegen-
heiten, 1833-1845; Niederlassung der Juden,
Insterburg, 1843-1863; Verhältnisse der Juden,
Kreis Stallupoenen, 1847-1861, 1868-1890;
Kries Oletzko, 1848-1892; Kreis Tilsit,
1865, 1878-1889; Eydkuhnen, 1878-1889;
Kirchliche Verhältnisse der Juden, 1872;
Verhältnisse der Juden, Eydkuhnen, 1872-
1889; Kreis Ragnit, 1881-1889 IsJJH
N: IsJJH 50 reels   1535
P: NNYi

KURNIK, Germany. JEWS
Protokolle und Rechnungsbuch, 1781-1824,
84 ll. IsJJH
N: IsJJH   1536
P: NNYi

LAAGE, Germany. JEWS
Protokollbuch in den Versammlungen der
Gemeindeglieder, 1842-1896, 63 p. IsJJH
N: IsJJH   1537
P: NNYi

MAINZ, Germany. JEWS
Communal register [in Hebrew], 1751-1756;
Memorbuch [in Hebrew], 1834-1837, 293 ll.
IsJJH
N: IsJJH   1538
P: NNYi

MARIENBURG, Germany. JEWS
Protokollbuch des Vorstands der israelit-
ischen Gemeinde, 132 p. IsJJH
N: IsJJH   1539
P: NNYi

MARKSTEFT, Germany. JEWS
Pinkas Hakehila [Communal register], 1812-
1853, 81 ll. [in Hebrew] IsJJH
N: IsJJH   1540
P: NNYi

MITWITZ, Germany. JEWS
Gemeindebuch (Protokollbuch) der
Kultusgemeinde, 1843-1877, 56 ll. IsJJH
N: IsJJH   1541
P: NNYi

MÜHLHAUSEN IN THÜRINGEN, Germany. JEWS
Protokollbuch der Kultusgemeinde, 1880-1938,
218 ll. IsJJH
N: IsJJH   1542
P: NNYi

MÜNDEN, Prussia, Germany. JEWS
Protokollbuch, 1860-1876, 112 ll. IsJJH
N: IsJJH   1543
P: NNYi

NEUSTETTIN, Germany. JEWS
Protokollbuch, 1863-1935, 193 ll. IsJJH
N: IsJJH   1544
P: NNYi

NORDHAUSEN, Germany. JEWS
Protokollbuch, 1868-1872, 140 ll. IsJJH
N: IsJJH   1545
P: NNYi

NÜRNBERG, Germany. STADTARCHIV
Akten aus den Jahren 1463, 1504, 1519, 1530,
6 items Ibid.
N: IsJJH   1546

ORANIENBURG, Germany. JEWS
Protokollbuch der Gemeinde, 1861-1882, 45ll.
IsJJH
N: IsJJH   1547
P: NNYi

OTTENSOOS, Germany. JEWS
Communal and congregational minute book,
1853- , 119 ll. [in Hebrew] IsJJH
N: IsJJH   1548
P: NNYi

PASSWALK, Germany. JEWS
Protokollbuch der Synagogengemeinde,
1851-1915, 318 ll. IsJJH
N: IsJJH   1549
P: NNYi

PRUSSIA. JEWS
Judenwesen im Königreich Preussen, 1712
IsJJH
N: IsJJH   1550
P: NNYi

PYRITZ, Germany. JEWS
Sitzungsprotokoll der Vorstands, 1849-1854,
67 ll. IsJJH
N: IsJJH   1551
P: NNYi

RENDSBURG, Germany. JEWS
Gründungsurkunden der israelitischen Gemeinde,
1695, 1732; Community registers: 1793-1827
[in Yiddish], 1870 [in Hebrew], 1893-1936 [in
German]; Copia-Buch der israelitische Gemeinde,
1835-1852 IsJJH
N: IsJJH 4 reels   1552
P: NNYi

ROSONBERG, Germany. JEWS
Pinkas Hakohol [Communal register], 1687-
1867, 134 p. [in Hebrew] IsJJH
N: IsJJH   1553
P: NNYi

SCHWERIN, Germany. STAATSARCHIV
Jewish material: Boitzenburg, Sterbelisten,
Kassabuch, 1813-1920; Bruel, Geburtslisten,
Copulationen, 1787-1898; Bützow, Geburten,
Copulationen, Sterbelisten, 1813-1903;
Goldberg, Copulationen, Geburten, Sterbelisten,
1813-1916 IsJJH
N: IsJJH 8 reels   1554
P: NNYi

STADTLENGFELD (LENGFELD), Germany.
JEWS
Protokollbuch, 1912-1938, 43 ll. IsJJH
N: IsJJH   1555
P: NNYi

STETTIN, Germany. JEWS
Synagogengemeinde: Beschlüsse der Repräsen-
tanten, 1842, 1844, 1848, 1853-1869; General-
versammlungen, 1842-1843; Reorganization der
Hebra Kadisha, 1845-1875; Beschlüsse der
Aktiv-Vorstands Protokolle, 1849-1850 IsJJH
N: IsJJH 6 reels   1556
P: NNYi

STUTTGART, Germany. LANDESBIBLIOTHEK
　　Prescriptions, 1474-1509 [in Yiddish]　Ibid.
　　N: NNYi   1557

STUTTGART, Germany. LANDESBIBLIOTHEK
　　Prescriptions, 1690 [in Yiddish]　Ibid.
　　N: NNYi 1 reel   1558

VOEHL, Germany. JEWS
　　Pinkas Hakhila [Communal register], 1829-
　　1912, 91 ll. [in Hebrew]　IsJJH
　　N: IsJJH   1559
　　P: NNYi

WALLDORF, Germany. JEWS
　　Protokollbuch des Synagogen und Schulvorstands,
　　1845-1865, 221 ll.　IsJJH
　　N: IsJJH   1560
　　P: NNYi

WEISSENBURG, Germany. LANDRATSAMT.
　　ARCHIV
　　Akten-Juden, 1816-1936; Statuten der israeli-
　　tischen Kultusgemeinde in Ellingen, Treucht-
　　lingen, Pappenheim, 1867-1891　Ibid.
　　N: NNYi 2 reels   1561

WEISSENBURG, Germany. STADTARCHIV
　　Shuldschein eines Juden, 1592; Acta Comis.
　　des Königlichen Landgerichts Weissenburg,
　　1831; Synagogenordnung für die Israeli-
　　tischen Kultusgemeinden Mittelfranken, 1838;
　　Religions und Kirchenverhältnisse der Juden,
　　1862-1911; Handhabung der Synagogenordnung
　　in Treuchtlingen, 1863　IsJJH
　　N: IsJJH 5 reels   1562
　　P: NNYi

WORMS, Germany. JEWS
　　Kopialbuch, 1348-1640, 99 ll.　IsJJH
　　N: IsJJH   1563
　　P: NNYi

WRONKE, Germany. JEWS
　　Protokollbuch des Vorstands der Israelitischen
　　Gemeinde, 1834-1843　IsJJH
　　N: IsJJH 1 reel   1564
　　P: NNYi

ZERKOW, Germany. JEWS
　　Pinkas shel Hebra Beth Hamedrash, 1834
　　IsJJH
　　N: IsJJH   1565
　　P: NNYi

ZIRKE, Germany. JEWS
　　Protokollbuch der Repräsentanten der
　　Synagoge, 1848-1919, 160 ll.　IsJJH
　　N: IsJJH   1566
　　P: NNYi

Personal Papers

FREILIGRATH, FERDINAND, 1810-1876
　　Letters to Karl Heinzen, 1845-1858, 23 items
　　MiU
　　N: KyU 20 feet   1567

GOEBBELS, JOSEPH, 1897-1945
　　Diaries, 1942-1943　CSt-H
　　N: CSt-H 6 reels   1568
　　P: CtY DLC OU WU

GOEBBELS, JOSEPH, 1897-1845
　　Diary, 1925-1926 [in German]　CSt-H
　　N: CSt-H 1 reel   1569
　　P: CSt-H

HIMMLER, HEINRICH, 1900-1945
　　Diary, 1914-1922, Feb. 1924 [in German]
　　CSt-H
　　N: CSt-H 1 reel   1570
　　P: CSt-H

HUMBOLDT, ALEXANDER, Freiherr VON,
　　1769-1859
　　Selected letters   Westdeutsche Bibliothek,
　　Marburg Lahn
　　N: NN 2 reels   1571

KUPFER, EDGAR
　　Die letzten Jahre von Dachau, 1943-1945　priv
　　N: ICU 1 reel   1572

LEIBNITZ, Baron GOTTFRIED WILHELM VON,
　　1646-1716
　　Papers   Landsbibliotek, Hanover
　　N: PU 32 reels*   1573
　　P: CLU

L'OHE, WILHELM, 1808-1872
　　Letters to Johann Friedrich Wucherer, 1840-
　　1860　MnHi
　　N: ICU 1 reel   1574

LUTHER, MARTIN, 1483-1546
　　Letters to Ursula Schneidewein, June 4 and
　　July 10, 1539　MoSC
　　DCO: MoSC   1575

REGER, MAX, 1873-1916
　　Correspondence, 1902-1914　Reger Archiv,
　　Meiningen
　　N: DLC 6 reels   1576

SCHLEGEL, FRIEDRICH VON, 1772-1829
　　Notebooks, 1796-1823, 21 v.　Westdeutche
　　Bibliothek, Marburg, Philosophisches Seminar,
　　University of Munich
　　N: MoSW   1577

STINTZIUS, JACOBUS
　　Official Jena University obituary, April 6, 1609
　　1 p.　MoSC
　　DCO: MoSC   1578

STRESEMANN, GUSTAV, 1878-1929
　　Papers, 1887-1930　Germany. Auswärtiges
　　Amt
　　N: DNA 88 reels [part of T-120]   1579
　　P: NjP

Collections

Die Tätigkeit der Kommunisten in Deutchland
und in den von Deutschland besetzten Gebieten
nach Beginn des Krieges mit der Sowjetunion
(typescript)　CSt-H
　　N: CSt-H 1 reel   1580

Institutions

KÖNIGSBERG, Germany. PREUSSISCHE
　　STAATSARCHIV
　　Guild records of East Prussian cities
　　(formerly at the State Archive of Königsberg),
　　1597-1924 [unk.]
　　N: USIGS 17 reels   1581

SOZIALDEMOKRATISCHE PARTEI DEUTSCH-
　　LANDS. ZENTRALKOMITEE
　　Minutes, June, 1917　CSt-H
　　N: DLC 1 reel   1582

AUSTRIA

Bibliography

GOTTWEIG, Austria. STIFTSBIBLIOTHEK
　　Handschriften Katalog, 1844　Ibid.
　　N: PPAmP 4 reels   1583
　　P: DLC*

INNSBRUCK, Austria. LEOPOLD-FRANZENS
　　UNIVERSITÄT. BIBLIOTHEK
　　Handschriften Zettlekatalog; Handschriften
　　Bandkatalog　Ibid.
　　N: PPAmP 2 reels   1584
　　P: DLC

MELK, AUSTRIA. STIFTSBIBLIOTHEK
　　Handschriften Katalog　Ibid.
　　N: PPAmP 4 reels   1585
　　P: DLC*

Government Records

U.S. DEPT. OF STATE
　　Instructions to U.S. visitors to Vienna, 1875-
　　1877, v. 2　DNA
　　N: DNA 1 reel   1586
　　P: CLO

Church Records

CHURCH OF JESUS CHRIST OF LATTER-DAY
　　SAINTS. AUSTRIA
　　Records of Austrian Mission and branches
　　(Swiss-German, German Austrian, West-
　　German and Swiss-Austrian Missions), early
　　to 1953　USlC
　　N: USlGS 2 reels   1587

Jewish Community Records

VIENNA, Austria. JEWS
　　Vertreter-Collegium, darin: Sitzungsprotokolle,
　　1898-1899, 1901-1902, 1926-1929, Gemeindebuch,
　　1908-1937; Protokolle der Plenarsitzungen des
　　Kulturvorstandes, 1909, 1912-1925, 1928-1929,
　　1933-1934　IsJJH
　　N: IsJJH 6 reels   P: NNYi   1588

Personal Papers

CZERNY, CARL, 1791-1857
　　Erinnerungen aus meinem Leben, 1842, 30 p.
　　AsVGM
　　N: NNC   1589

WHITE, HENRY, 1850-1927
　　Papers re: Austrian Peace Treaty Conference
　　(typescript)　DLC
　　N: CSt-H 1 reel   1590

SWITZERLAND

City Records

AGIEZ, Vaud, Switz.
　　General index to records (mostly vital
　　records), including Agiez, Arnex (sur Orbe),
　　1631-1821　Sz La
　　N: USlGS 1 reel   1591

AIRE-LA-VILLE, Geneva, Switz.
　　Vital records, 1726-1829　SzGS
　　N: USlGS 1 reel   1592

APPLES, Vaud, Switz.
　　General index to records (mostly vital
　　records), including Bussy, Reverolle,
　　1627-1875　Sz La
　　N: USlGS 1 reel   1593

ARZIER, Vaud, Switz.
　　Vital records, communions and confirmations
　　(also Le Muids), 1710-1874　Sz La
　　N: USlGS 1 reel   1594

AVULLY, Geneva, Switz.
　　Vital records, 1798-1829　SzGS
　　N: USlGS 1 reel   1595

AVUSY, Geneva, Switz.
　　Vital records, 1759-1829　SzGS
　　N: USlGS 2 reels   1596

BEGNINS, Vaud, Switz.
　　General index to vital records (also Luins),
　　1627-1857　Sz La
　　N: USlGS 1 reel   1597

BERNEX, Geneva, Switz.
　　Vital records (also Onex, Confignon),
　　1617-1829　SzGS
　　N: USlGS 3 reels   1598

GENEVA, Geneva, Switz.
　　Register of deaths, ca. 1545-1798; death rec-
　　ords (volum[e]s feuille[s] minutes), 1744-1799;
　　vital records, 1798-1829　SzGS
　　N: USlGS 19 reels   1599

HERMANCE, Geneva, Switz.
　　Vital records, 1795-1829　SzGS
　　N: USlGS 1 reel   1600

LIESTAL, Basel, Switz.
Civil records (also Seltisberg), 1826-1883
Sz L
N: USIGS 6 reels 1601

TROINEX, Geneva, Switz.
Vital records, 1794-1829 SzGS
N: USIGS 1 reel 1602

Church Records

AIGLE, Vaud, Switz.
Church records, 1629-1821 Sz La
N: USIGS 3 reels 1603

AIRE-LA-VILLE, Geneva, Switz. CATHOLIC
CHURCH
Vital records, 1793-1877 SzGS
N: USIGS 1 reel 1604

ARISDORF, Basel, Switz.
Church records (also Giebenach and Hersberg),
1558-1875 Sz L
N: USIGS 2 reels 1605

ASSENS, Geneva, Switz. CATHOLIC CHURCH
Records (also Etagnières, Bioley), 1646-1893
SzLa
N: USIGS 1 reel 1606

AUBONNE, Vaud, Switz.
Church records (also Lavigny), 1629-1830
Sz La
N: USIGS 5 reels 1607

AVENCHES, Vaud, Switz.
Church records, 1569-1821 Sz La
N: USIGS 2 reels 1608

BALLAIGUES, Vaud, Switz.
General index to vital records, 1725-1886 Sz La
N: USIGS 1 reel 1609

BASEL, Basel, Switz.
Protestant church records, 1529-1897 Sz L
N: USIGS 33 reels 1610

BAULMES, Vaud, Switz.
Church records, 1636-1859 Sz La
N: USIGS 1 reel 1611

BELMONT SUR LAUSANNE, Vaud, Switz.
Church records (also Lutry), 1766-1866 Sz La
N: USIGS 1 reel 1612

BENKEN, Basel, Switz.
Vital records, 1535-1874, 5 v. Sz L
N: USIGS 1 reel 1613

BENNWILL, Basel, Switz.
Church records (also Hölstein), 1567-1865
Sz L
N: USIGS 2 reels 1614

BERCHER, Vaud, Switz.
Church records (also Fey, Rueyres), 1606-
1875 Sz La
N: USIGS 1 reel 1615

BERNEX, Geneva, Switz. CATHOLIC CHURCH
Vital records, 1803-1875 SzGS
N: USIGS 1 reel 1616

BEX, Vaud, Switz.
Church records, 1566-1821 Sz La
N: USIGS 5 reels 1617

BIÈRE, Vaud, Switz.
Church records (also Ballens, Mollens, Berolle)
1568-1821 Sz La
N: USIGS 2 reels 1618

BINNINGEN, Basel, Switz.
Church records (also Bottmingen and St. Mar-
grethen), 1597-1886 Sz L
N: USIGS 3 reels 1619
P: USIGS

BLONAY, Vaud, Switz.
Church records, 1624-1875 Sz La
N: USIGS 2 reels 1620

BOTTENS, Vaud, Switz. CATHOLIC CHURCH
Records (also Poliez-Le-Grand, Poliez-Pittet),
1627-1821 SzLa
N: USIGS 1 reel 1621

BRETZWIL, Basel, Switz.
Church records, 1607-1878 (also Lauwil and
Reigoldswil) Sz L
N: USIGS 2 reels 1622
P: USIGS

BUBENDORF, Switz.
Church records, 1529-1870 (also Ziefen, Ar-
boldswil, Lupsingen,and Ramlinsburg) Sz L
N: USIGS 2 reels 1623
P: USIGS

BULLET, Vaud, Switz.
Church records, 1782-1821 Sz La
N: USIGS 1 reel 1624

BURSINS, Vaud, Switz.
Church records (also Gilly, Vinzel), 1629-
1821 Sz La
N: USIGS 1 reel 1625

BURTIGNY, Vaud, Switz.
Church records (also Bassins), 1656-1821
Sz La
N: USIGS 1 reel 1626

BUUS, Basel, Switz.
Church records, 1559-1875 (also Maisprach
and Hemmiken) Sz L
N: USIGS 2 reels 1627
P: USIGS

CAROUGE, Geneva, Switz.
Church and civil records, 1746-1836 SzGS
N: USIGS 10 reels 1628

CAROUGE, Geneva, Switz. CATHOLIC CHURCH
Records, 1794-1873 SzGS
N: USIGS 2 reels 1629

CARTIGNY, Geneva, Switz.
Church and civil records (also Avully, Onex),
1617-1829 SzGS
N: USIGS 3 reels 1630

CÉLIGNY, Geneva, Switz.
Church and civil records, 1571-1829 SzGS
N: USIGS 2 reels 1631

CHAMPVENT, Vaud, Switz.
Church records, 1640-1862 Sz La
N: USIGS 1 reel 1632

CHANCY, Geneva, Switz.
Church and civil records (also Vallery, now
Chancy), 1598-1829 SzGS
N: USIGS 2 reels 1633

CHÂTEAUX D'OEX, Vaud, Switz.
Church records, 1551-1821 Sz La
N: USIGS 3 reels 1634

CHAVORNAY, Vaud, Switz.
Church records (also Bavoie, Corcelles),
1620-1875 Sz La
N: USIGS 2 reels 1635

CHÊNE-BOUGERIES, Geneva, Switz.
Church and civil records, 1664-1829 SzGS
N: USIGS 3 reels 1636

CHÊNE-BOURG, Geneva, Switz.
Church and civil records (also Thônex),
1601-1829 SzGS
N: USIGS 4 reels 1637

CHÊNE-BOURG, Geneva, Switz. CATHOLIC
CHURCH
Records, 1797-1875 SzGS
N: USIGS 1 reel 1638

CHESEAUX SUR LAUSANNE, Vaud, Switz.
Church records (also Bullens, Bournens,
Boussens), 1573-1821 Sz La
N: USIGS 2 reels 1639

CHEVROUX, Vaud, Switz.
Church records, 1734-1875 Sz La
N: USIGS 1 reel 1640

CHEXBRES, Vaud, Switz.
Church records, 1691-1821 Sz La
N: USIGS 1 reel 1641

CHOULEX, Geneva, Switz.
Church and civil records (also Meinier),
1632-1829 SzGS
N: USIGS 2 reels 1642

CHOULEX, Geneva, Switz. CATHOLIC CHURCH
Records, 1803-1876 SzGS
N: USIGS 1 reel 1643

CHURCH OF JESUS CHRIST OF LATTER-DAY
SAINTS. SWITZERLAND
Records of the Swiss missions and branches
(Swiss-Italian, Swiss-German, Swiss-
Austrian and French Missions), 1851-1953
USIC
N: USIGS 11 reels 1644

COLLEX-BOSSY, Geneva, Switz.
Church and civil records (also Bellevue),
1685-1829 SzGS
N: USIGS 4 reels 1645

COLLEX-BOSSY, Geneva, Switz. CATHOLIC
CHURCH
Records, 1820-1874 SzGS
N: USIGS 1 reel 1646

COLLONGE-BELLERIVE, Geneva, Switz.
Church and civil records, 1617-1829 SzGS
N: USIGS 2 reels 1647

COLLONGE-BELLERIVE, Geneva, Switz.
CATHOLIC CHURCH
Records, 1794-1892 SzGS
N: USIGS 1 reel 1648

COLOGNY, Geneva, Switz.
Church and civil records (also Vandoeuvres),
1724-1829 SzGS
N: USIGS 2 reels 1649

COLOMBIER, Vaud, Switz.
Church records, 1727-1856 Sz La
N: USIGS 1 reel 1650

COMBREMONT-LE-GRAND, Vaud, Switz.
Church records, 1622-1865 Sz La
N: USIGS 1 reel 1651

COMMUGNY, Vaud, Switz.
Church records, 1566-1821 Sz La
N: USIGS 2 reels 1652

COMPESIÈRES, Geneva, Switz.
Church and civil records (also Perly,
Certoux), 1777-1829 SzGS
N: USIGS 3 reels 1653

COMPESIÈRES, Geneva, Switz. CATHOLIC
CHURCH
Records, 1793-1877 SzGS
N: USIGS 1 reel 1654

CONCISE, Vaud, Switz.
Church records, 1582-1882 Sz La
N: USIGS 3 reels 1655

CONSTANTINE, Vaud, Switz.
Church records, 1680-1876 Sz La
N: USIGS 1 reel 1656

CORCELLES (près de PAYERNE), Vaud, Switz.
Church records, 1666-1821 SzLa
N: USIGS 1 reel 1657

CORSIER, Geneva, Switz.
Church and civil records (also Anières),
1634-1829 SzGS
N: USIGS 2 reels 1658

CORSIER SUR VEVEY, Vaud, Switz.
Church records (also Chardonne), 1581-1846
Sz La
N: USIGS 3 reels 1659

COSSONAY, Vaud, Switz.
Church records (also La Chaux), 1636-1821
Sz La
N: USIGS 2 reels 1660

COTTERD (BELLERIVE), Vaud, Switz.
Church records, 1568-1853   Sz La
N: USIGS 1 reel   1661

CRASSIER, Vaud, Switz.
Church records (also Crans), 1572-1821   Sz La
N: USIGS 2 reels   1662

CRISSIER, Vaud, Switz.
Church records (also Bussigny), 1570-1875
Sz La
N: USIGS 2 reels   1663

CRONAY, Vaud, Switz.
Church records (also Orzens and environs),
1687-1835   Sz La
N: USIGS 1 reel   1664

CUARNENS, Vaud, Switz.
Church records (also (L'Isle)-Mont la Ville),
1658-1821   Sz La
N: USIGS 1 reel   1665

CULLY, Vaud, Switz.
Church records, 1630-1821   Sz La
N: USIGS 1 reel   1666

CURTILLES, Vaud, Switz.
Church records (also Lucens), 1639-1875   Sz La
N: USIGS 2 reels   1667

DAILLENS, Vaud, Switz.
Church records (also Penthalaz, Bettens),
1586-1858   Sz La
N: USIGS 2 reels   1668

DARDAGNY, Geneva, Switz.
Church and civil records (also Malval, Russin),
1716-1829   SzGS
N: USIGS 2 reels   1669

DENEZY, Vaud, Switz.
Church records, 1709-1875   Sz La
N: USIGS 1 reel   1670

DIEGTEN, Basel, Switz.
Church records (also Eptingen), 1564-1910
Sz L
N: USIGS 3 reels   1671

DOMMARTIN, Vaud, Switz.
Church records (also Sugnenes, Poliez-Pittet),
1611-1821   Sz La
N: USIGS 1 reel   1672

DOMPIERRE, Vaud, Switz.
Church records, 1644-1875   Sz La
N: USIGS 1 reel   1673

DONATYRE, Vaud, Switz.
Church records, 1682-1837   Sz La
N: USIGS 1 reel   1674

DONNELOYE, Vaud, Switz.
Church records (also Bioley-Magnoux, Mézery,
Oppens), 1679-1836   Sz La
N: USIGS 1 reel   1675

EAUX-VIVES, Geneva, Switz.
Church and civil records, 1798-1829   SzGS
N: USIGS 3 reels   1676

ECHALLENS, Vaud, Switz.
Church records (also Villars-le-Terroir, Pen-
théréaz), 1674-1875   Sz La
N: USIGS 1 reel   1677

ECHALLENS, Vaud, Switz. CATHOLIC CHURCH
Records (also Villars-le-Terroir, Penthéréaz),
1639-1822   Sz La
N: USIGS 1 reel   1678

ECUBLENS, Vaud, Switz.
Church records (also Chavannes, St. Sulpice),
1598-1821   Sz La
N: USIGS 2 reels   1679

EPENDES, Vaud, Switz.
Church records (also Suchy and Essert), 1570-
1821   Sz La
N: USIGS 1 reel   1680

ETOY, Vaud, Switz.
Church records (also St. Prex and Buchillon),

1598-1821   Sz La
N: USIGS 2 reels   1681

FAOUG, Vaud, Switz.
Church records, 1582-1875   Sz La
N: USIGS 1 reel   1682

FIEZ, Vaud, Switz.
Church records (also Vugelles), 1613-1875
Sz La
N: USIGS 2 reels   1683

FRANKENDORF, Basel, Switz.
Church records (also Füllinsdorf), 1542-1876
Sz L
N: USIGS 4 reels   1684

GELTERKINDEN, Basel, Switz.
Church records (also Tecknau, Ormalingen,
Rickenbach), 1595-1871   Sz L
N: USLGS 3 reels   1685

GENEVA (Canton), Switz.
General index to church and civil records,
1542-1900   SzGS
N: USIGS 25 reels   1686

GENEVA (Canton), Switz.
Protestant church records: Jussy, Gy, Cologny,
Chéne, Vandoeuvres, Satigny, Dardagny, Gen-
thod, Sacconex, Céligny, Cartigny, Chancy,
Onex, Vallery (now Chancy), and Bossey, Ney-
dens, Haute Savoie, France, 1701-1715, 1791-
1836   SzGS
N: USIGS 1 reel   1687

GENEVA. CHAPELLE DE LA RÉSIDENCE DE
LA FRANCE ET DE SAVOIE
Vital records, 1687-1792   SzGA
N: USIGS 1 reel   1688

GENEVA (City), Switz.
Church records, 1546-1875   SzGS
N: USIGS 53 reels   1689

GENEVA (City), Switz.
General index to church and civil records,
1549-1798   SzGS
N: USIGS 17 reels   1690

GENEVA, Geneva, Switz. CATHOLIC CHURCH
Records, 1798-1873   SzGS
N: USIGS 3 reels   1691

GENTHOD, Geneva, Switz.
Church and civil records (also Malagny and
environs), 1565-1829   SzGS
N: USIGS 2 reels   1692

GIEZ, Vaud, Switz.
Church records (also Orges), 1728-1845   Sz La
N: USIGS 1 reel   1693

GIMEL, Vaud, Switz.
Church records (also Essertines and St.
Oyens), 1570-1865   Sz La
N: USIGS 2 reels   1694

GINGINS, Vaud, Switz.
Church records (also Chéserex, Trélex, Grens),
1597-1855   Sz La
N: USIGS 1 reel   1695

GOUMOENS-LA-VILLE, Vaud, Switz.
Church records (also Penthéréaz and
Eclagnens), 1678-1821   Sz La
N: USIGS 1 reel   1696

GRANCY, Vaud, Switz.
Church records (also Gollion), 1571-1864
Sz La
N: USIGS 1 reel   1697

GRANDSON, Vaud, Switz.
Church records (also Orges and Giez),
1576-1875   Sz La
N: USIGS 1 reel   1698

GRANDVAUX, Vaud, Switz.
Church records (also Villette [Lavaux]),
1627-1821   Sz La
N: USIGS 2 reels   1699

GRANGES (près de MARNAND), Vaud, Switz.

Church records (also Trey), 1564-1872   Sz La
N: USIGS 2 reels   1700

GRESSY, Vaud, Switz.
Church records (also Ursins, Belmont,
Valeyres, and Epauteyres), 1638-1875   Sz La
N: USIGS 1 reel   1701

GRYON, Vaud, Switz.
Church records, 1591-1875   Sz La
N: USIGS 1 reel   1702

JUSSY, Geneva, Switz.
Church and civil records (also Gy), 1550-1829
SzGS
N: USIGS 3 reels   1703

KILCHBERG, Basel, Switz.
Church records (also Zeglingen, Rünenberg),
1559-1889   Sz L
N: USIGS 3 reels   1704

L'ABBAYE, Vaud, Switz.
Church records, 1640-1821   Sz La
N: USIGS 3 reels   1705

LANCY, Geneva, Switz.
Church and civil records, 1704-1829   SzGS
N: USIGS 2 reels   1706

LANCY, Geneva, Switz. CATHOLIC CHURCH
Records, 1796-1873; Protestant registers,
1816-1817   SzGS
N: USIGS 1 reel   1707

LANGENBRUCK, Basel, Switz.
Church records, 1564-1912   Sz L
N: USIGS 3 reels   1708

LA SARRAZ, Vaud, Switz.
Church records (also Eclépens, Orny),
1641-1821   Sz La
N: USIGS 2 reels   1709

LA TOUR DE PEILZ, Vaud, Switz.
Church records, 1615-1821   Sz La
N: USIGS 2 reels   1710

LAUFELFINGEN, Basel, Switz.
Church records, 1566-1856   Sz L
N: USIGS 1 reel   1711

LAUSANNE, Vaud, Switz.
Church records, 1572-1821   Sz La
N: USIGS 12 reels   1712

LAUSANNE, Vaud, Switz. GERMAN CONGRE-
GATION
Church records, 1691-1829   Sz La
N: USIGS 2 reels   1713

LAUSEN, Basel, Switz.
Church records, 1542-1857   Sz L
N: USIGS 1 reel   1714

(LE) GRAND-SACONNEX, Geneva, Switz.
Church and civil records, 1672-1829   SzGS
N: USIGS 3 reels   1715

(LE) GRAND-SACONNEX, Geneva, Switz.
CATHOLIC CHURCH
Records, 1803-1876   SzGS
N: USIGS 3 reels   1716

LE LIEU, Vaud, Switz.
Church records, 1640-1821   Sz La
N: USIGS 2 reels   1717

LE MONT-SUR-LAUSANNE, Vaud, Switz.
Church records (also Romanel), 1719-1828
Sz La
N: USIGS 1 reel   1718

LES CROISETTES (REFORM SCHOOL), Vaud,
Switz.
General index, vital records, 1686-1821   Sz La
N: USIGS 1 reel   1719

LE SENTIER, Vaud, Switz.
Church records, 1688-1821   Sz La
N: USIGS 3 reels   1720

L'ETIVAZ, Vaud, Switz.
Church records, 1664-1821   Sz La

N: USIGS 1 reel 1721

LEYSIN, Vaud, Switz.
Church records, 1702-1821 Sz La
N: USIGS 1 reel 1722

LIESTAL, Basel, Switz.
Church records (also Seltisberg), 1542-1897
Sz L
N: USLGS 7 reels 1723

LIGNEROLLE, Vaud, Switz.
Church records (also Les Clées), 1647-1821
Sz La
N: USIGS 1 reel 1724

L'ISLE, Vaud, Switz.
Church records (also Montricher, Villars-
Bozon, La Coudre [L'Isle]), 1595-1821
Sz La
N: USIGS 2 reels 1725

LONAY, Vaud, Switz.
Church records, 1648-1875 Sz La
N: USIGS 1 reel 1726

LONGIROD, Vaud, Switz.
Church records (also Marchissy, St. Georges),
1676-1832 Sz La
N: USIGS 1 reel 1727

LUSSY, Vaud, Switz.
Church records (also Villars-sous-Yens,
Lully), 1705-1821 Sz La
N: USIGS 1 reel 1728

LUTRY, Vaud, Switz.
Church records, 1607-1856 Sz La
N: USIGS 2 reels 1729

MEINIER, Geneva, Switz.
Church and civil reocrds (also Choulex),
1644-1829 SzGS
N: USIGS 2 reels 1730

MEYRIN, Geneva, Switz.
Church and civil records, 1676-1829 SzGS
N: USIGS 4 reels 1731

MEYRIN, Geneva, Switz. CATHOLIC CHURCH
Records, 1805-1877 SzGS
N: USIGS 2 reels 1732

MÉZIÈRES, Vaud, Switz.
Church records, 1575-1875 Sz La
N: USIGS 3 reels 1733

MONTAGNY (près d'IVERDON), Vaud, Switz.
Church records (also Giez, Orges), 1608-
1875 Sz La
N: USIGS 1 reel 1734

MONTCHERAND, Vaud, Switz.
Church records, 1679-1844 Sz La
N: USIGS 1 reel 1735

MONTET, Vaud, Switz.
Church records (also Cudrefin), 1569-1875
Sz La
N: USIGS 1 reel 1736

MONTPREVEYRES, Vaud, Switz.
Church records (also Corcelles-le-Jorat),
1627-1891 Sz La
N: USIGS 1 reel 1737

MONTREUX, Vaud, Switz.
Church records, 1590-1856 Sz La
N: USIGS 3 reels 1738

MORGES, Vaud, Switz.
Church records (also Monnaz, Echichens,
Vaux, Tolochenaz), 1577-1821 Sz La
N: USIGS 3 reels 1739

MORRENS, Vaud, Switz.
Church records (also Montheron), 1643-1875
Sz La
N: USIGS 2 reels 1740

MOUDON, Vaud, Switz.
Church records, 1568-1867 Sz La
N: USIGS 6 reels 1741

MUNCHENSTEIN, Basel, Switz.
Protestant church records, 1669-1874 Sz L
N: USIGS 1 reel 1742

MUTTENZ, Basel, Switz.
Church records, 1530-1903 Sz L
N: USIGS 3 reels 1743

NOVILLE, Vaud, Switz.
Church records (also Chessel, Rennaz, Roche),
1615-1875 Sz La
N: USIGS 2 reels 1744

NYON, Vaud, Switz.
Church records, 1590-1875 Sz La
N: USIGS 5 reels 1745

OLLON, Vaud, Switz.
Church records, 1602-1821 Sz La
N: USIGS 3 reels 1746

OLTINGEN, Basel, Switz.
Protestant church records (also Anwil,
Wenslingen), 1543-1833 Sz L
N: USIGS 1 reel 1747

ONNENS, Vaud, Switz.
Church records (also Bonvillars), 1650-1846
Sz La
N: USIGS 1 reel 1748

ORBE, Vaud, Switz.
Church records, 1595-1834 Sz La
N: USIGS 3 reels 1749

ORMALINGEN, Basel, Switz.
Church records (also Hemmiken), 1741-1897
Sz L
N: USIGS 3 reels 1750

ORMONT-DESSOUS, Vaud, Switz.
Church records, 1577-1821 Sz La
N: USIGS 1 reel 1751

ORMONT-DESSUS, Vaud, Switz.
Church records, 1605-1862 Sz La
N: USIGS 2 reels 1752

ORON-LA-VILLE, Vaud, Switz.
Church records, 1618-1875 Sz La
N: USIGS 2 reels 1753

OULONS (ECHALLENS), Vaud, Switz.
Church records (also St. Barthélemy),
1630-1875 Sz La
N: USIGS 1 reel 1754

PAILLY, Vaud, Switz.
Church records (also Rueyres), 1725-1845
Sz La
N: USIGS 1 reel 1755

PALÉZIEUX-VILLAGE, Vaud, Switz.
Church records, 1617-1875 Sz La
N: USIGS 2 reels 1756

PAMPIGNY, Vaud, Switz.
Church records (also Sévery, Cottens,
Mauraz), 1595-1821 Sz La
N: USIGS 1 reel 1757

PAQUIER, Vaud, Switz.
Church records (also Démoret [St. Martin]),
1697-1867 Sz La
N: USIGS 1 reel 1758

PAYERNE, Vaud, Switz.
Church records, 1579-1874 Sz La
N: USIGS 4 reels 1759

PENEY-LE-JORAT, Vaud, Switz.
Church records (also Villars-Tiercelin),
1794-1875 Sz La
N: USIGS 1 reel 1760

PENTHAZ, Vaud, Switz.
Church records (also Vufflens-la-Ville, Max),
1656-1864 Sz La
N: USIGS 1 reel 1761

PERLY, Geneva, Switz.
Church and civil records (also Certoux and
St. Julien, Haute-Savoie, France), 1608-1829
SzGS
N: USIGS 2 reels 1762

PERROY, Vaud, Switz.
Church records (also Mont [-sur-Rolle],
Bougy-Villars, Allaman), 1607-1875 Sz La
N: USIGS 1 reel 1763

PETIT-SACONNEX, Geneva, Switz.
Church and civil records, 1621-1831 SzGS
N: USIGS 5 reels 1764

PLAINPALAIS (now GENEVA), Geneva, Switz.
Church and civil records, 1798-1833 SzGS
N: USIGS 4 reels 1765

POLIEZ-LE-GRAND, Vaud, Switz.
Protestant Church records (also Poliez-Pittet),
1630-1866 Sz La
N: USIGS 1 reel 1766

POMY, Vaud, Switz.
Church records (also Cuarny), 1684-1895
Sz La
N: USIGS 1 reel 1767

PRANGINS, Vaud, Switz.
Church records (also Duillier, Genolier),
1672-1850 Sz La
N: USIGS 1 reel 1768

PRATTELN, Basel, Switz.
Church records (also Augst), 1625-1879 Sz L
N: USIGS 4 reels 1769

PREGNY, Geneva, Switz.
Church and civil records, 1684-1829 SzGS
N: USIGS 3 reels 1770

PRESINGE, Geneva, Switz.
Church and civil records, 1742-1829 SzGS
N: USIGS 2 reels 1771

PRILLY, Vaud, Switz.
Church records (also Renens), 1589-1844
Sz La
N: USIGS 1 reel 1772

PROVENCE, Vaud, Switz.
Church records, 1670-1849 Sz La
N: USIGS 1 reel 1773

PULLY, Vaud, Switz.
Church records (also Belmont
[-sur-Lausanne]), 1582-1821 Sz La
N: USIGS 2 reels 1774

PUPLINGE, Geneva, Switz.
Church and civil records (also of
Ville-la-Grand, Haute-Savoie, France),
1636-1813 SzGS
N: USIGS 2 reels 1775

RANCES, Vaud, Switz.
Church records (also Valeyres [-sous-
Rances], Montcherand), 1616-1821 Sz La
N: USIGS 2 reels 1776

REIGOLDSWIL, Basel, Switz.
Church records (also Titterten), 1700-1875
Sz L
N: USIGS 2 reels 1777

RESSUDENS, Vaud, Switz.
Church records (also Grancour, Missy,
Chevroux), 1608-1821 Sz La
N: USIGS 2 reels 1778

ROLLE, Vaud, Switz.
Church records (also Bursinel, Dullit [now
Dully], Mont), 1607-1859 Sz La
N: USIGS 2 reels 1779

ROMAINMÔTIER, Vaud, Switz.
Church records (also Bretonnieres),
1628-1851 Sz La
N: USIGS 2 reels 1780

ROSSINIÈRE, Vaud, Switz.
Church records, 1564-1821 Sz La
N: USIGS 2 reels 1781

ROTHENFLUH, Basel, Switz.
Church records, 1559-1857 Sz L
N: USIGS 2 reels 1782

ROUGEMONT, Vaud, Switz.
  Church records, 1582-1821 Sz La
  N: USIGS 3 reels   1783

RUMLINGEN, Basel, Switz.
  Church records (also Buckten, Häfelfingen,
  Känerkinden, Wittinsburg), 1566-1868 Sz L
  N: USIGS 2 reels   1784

RUSSIN, Geneva, Switz.
  Catholic church and civil records, 1790-1829
  SzGS
  N: USIGS 2 reels   1785

SAINT BARTHÉLEMY, Vaud, Switz.
  Church records (also Bretigny
  [St. Barthélemy]), 1802-1823 Sz La
  N: USIGS 1 reel   1786

SAINT CERGUE SUR NYON, Vaud, Switz.
  Church records, 1597-1875 Sz La
  N: USIGS 1 reel   1787

SAINT CIERGES SUR MOUDON, Vaud, Switz.
  Church records (also Chapelle, Boulens,
  Sottens, Martherenges, Villars-Mendraz),
  1610-1821 Sz La
  N: USIGS 2 reels   1788

SAINTE CROIX, Vaud, Switz.
  Church records, 1702-1821 Sz La
  N: USIGS 2 reels   1789

SAINT LIVRES, Vaud, Switz.
  Church records (also Yens [sur Morges]),
  1599-1821 Sz La
  N: USIGS 2 reels   1790

SAINT MAURICE, Vaud, Switz.
  Church records, 1634-1875 Sz La
  N: USIGS 1 reel   1791

SAINT SAPHORIN [LAVAUX], Vaud, Switz.
  Church records (also Chexbres, Puidoux,
  Rivas [Lavaux]), 1581-1875 Sz La
  N: USIGS 2 reels   1792

SATIGNY, Geneva, Switz.
  Church and civil records, 1542-1829 SzGS
  N: USIGS 4 reels   1793

SAVIGNY SUR LAUSANNE, Vaud, Switz.
  Church records, 1644-1821 Sz La
  N: USIGS 2 reels   1794

SISSACH, Basel, Switz.
  Church records (also Böckten, Diepflingen,
  Itingen), 1548-1885 Sz L
  N: USIGS 4 reels   1795

SORAL, Geneva, Switz.
  Vital records (also Laconnex and Thairy,
  Haute-Savoie, France), 1599-1788, 1794-
  1813 SzGS
  N: USIGS 1 reel   1796

SORAL and LACONNEX, Geneva, Switz.
  CATHOLIC CHURCH
  Records (also Thônex, Vernier), 1801-1877
  SzGS
  N: USIGS 1 reel   1797

SUCHY, Vaud, Switz.
  Church records, 1719-1821 Sz La
  N: USIGS 1 reel   1798

SYENS, Vaud, Switz.
  Church records, 1594-1850 Sz La
  N: USIGS 1 reel   1799

TENNIKEN, Basel, Switz.
  Church records (also Zunzgen), 1578-1910
  Sz L
  N: USIGS 3 reels   1800

THIERRENS, Vaud, Switz.
  Church records (also Ogens, Neyruz,
  Correvon, Villars-le-Comte), 1592-1875
  Sz La
  N: USIGS 2 reels   1801

VALLORBE, Vaud, Switz.
  Church records, 1569-1866 Sz La
  N: USIGS 1 reel   1802

VANDOEUVRES, Geneva, Switz.
  Church and civil records (also Cologny),
  1621-1830 SzGS
  N: USIGS 2 reels   1803

VAULION, Vaud, Switz.
  Church records, 1629-1821 Sz La
  N: USIGS 1 reel   1804

VERNIER, Geneva, Switz.
  Church and civil records, 1688-1829 SzGS
  N: USIGS 3 reels   1805

VERSOIX, Geneva, Switz.
  Church and civil records, 1674-1831 SzGS
  N: USIGS 3 reels   1806

VERSOIX, Geneva, Switz. CATHOLIC CHURCH
  Records, 1795-1814 SzGS
  N: USIGS 1 reel (part)   1807

VEVEY, Vaud, Switz.
  Church records, 1613-1821 Sz La
  N: USIGS 5 reels   1808

VEYRIER, Geneva, Switz.
  Church and civil records, 1619-1838 SzGS
  N: USIGS 2 reels   1809

VEYRIER, Geneva, Switz. CATHOLIC CHURCH
  Records, 1793-1874 SzGS
  N: USIGS 1 reel part   1810

VICH, Vaud, Switz.
  Church records (also Genolier), 1674-1821
  Sz La
  N: USIGS 1 reel   1811

VILLARS-LE-GRAND, Vaud, Switz.
  Church records, 1695-1821 Sz La
  N: USIGS 1 reel   1812

VILLARZEL, Vaud, Switz.
  Church records, 1622-1821 Sz La
  N: USIGS 1 reel   1813

VILLENEUVE, Vaud, Switz.
  Church records, 1572-1881 Sz La
  N: USIGS 1 reel   1814

VUARRENS, Vaud, Switz.
  Church records (also Pailly, Vuarrengel,
  Essertines-sur-Yverdon, La Robellaz),
  1672-1875 Sz La
  N: USIGS 2 reels   1815

VUFFLENS-LA-VILLE, Vaud, Switz.
  Church records (also Mex), 1711-1821 Sz La
  N: USIGS 1 reel   1816

VUFFLENS-LE-CHÂTEAU, Vaud, Switz.
  Church records (also Denens, Chigny),
  1587-1875 Sz La
  N: USIGS 1 reel   1817

VULLIERENS-SUR-MORGES, Vaud, Switz.
  Church records, 1682-1849 Sz La
  N: USIGS 1 reel   1818

WALDENBURG, Switz. SANKT PETER KIRCHE
  Records, 1606-1889 Sz L
  N: USIGS 4 reels   1819

WINTERSINGEN, Basel, Switz.
  Church records (also Nusshof), 1563-1920
  Sz L
  N: USIGS 2 reels   1820

YVERDON, Vaud, Switz.
  Church records, 1602-1844 Sz La
  N: USIGS 6 reels   1821

YVONAND, Vaud, Switz.
  Church records (also Rovray), 1618-1821
  Sz La
  N: USIGS 1 reel   1822

ZIEFEN, Basel, Switz.
  Church records (also Arbotdswil, Lupsingen),
  1750-1876 Sz L
  N: USIGS 2 reels   1823

Personal Papers

KINLOCH, FRANCIS
  Correspondence, ca. 1780-1818 Bibliothéque
  Nationale Suisse, Geneva
  N: PPAmP 72 frames   1824

KINLOCH, FRANCIS
  Letters to Johannes von Müller, ca. 1776-1809
  Stadtbibliothek, Schaffhausen, Switz.
  N: PPAmP 344 frames   1825

SEGESSER VON BRUNNEG, PHILIPP
  Letters, ca. 1708-1761 Familienarchiv
  Segesser von Brunneg, Lucerne
  N: CU-B 1 reel*   1826

EASTERN EUROPE

Institutions

DEMOCRATIC MID-EUROPEAN UNION
  Minutes of meetings held in Washington and
  Philadelphia, Oct. 3-Nov. 26, 1918 (typescript)
  OO
  N: CSt-H 1 reel   1827

POLAND

Military Records

POLAND. ARMIA. KOSCIUSZKO SQUADRON
  Log, Oct., 1919-May, 1921, 2 v. DLC
  N: DLC 1 reel   1828

Local Records

KOKANIN, Kalisz, Poland
  Vital records, 1899-1939 [unk.]
  N: USIGS 1 reel   1829

RYCHNOW, Kalisz, Poland
  Vital records, 1907-1940 [unk.]
  N: USIGS 1 reel   1830

ZAGOROW, Kalisz, Poland
  Vital records, 1843-1940 [unk.]
  N: USIGS 18 reels   1831

Church Records

BLASZKI, Kalisz, Poland
  Catholic church records, 1807, 1826 [unk.]
  N: USIGS 1 reel   1832

BLASZKI, Kalisz, Poland
  Church records, 1875-1940 [unk.]
  N: USIGS 14 reels   1833

BORKOW, Kalisz, Poland
  Church records, 1885-1940 [unk.]
  N: USIGS 4 reels   1834

CATHOLIC CHURCH. POLAND
  Records: Ksieja, 1774-1811; Opolny, 1762-
  1807; Przasnyshiej, 1799-1811; Przasnysz,
  1866-1878; Przewodowo, 1799-1820; Prze-
  wodowshiej, 1777-1828; Sobowo, 1753-1789;
  Smogorzewo, 1810-1841; Smoperzno, 1768-
  1832; S(z)olec, 1746-1787 [unk.]
  N: USIGS 2 reels   1835

JOZEFOW, Kalisz, Poland
  Church records [Evang. Augsburgisch
  Gemeinde], 1907-1940 [unk.]
  N: USIGS 2 reels   1836

PAMIECIN, Kalisz, Poland
  Church records, 1893-1937 [unk.]
  N: USIGS 2 reels   1837

RYCHWAL, Kalisz, Poland
  Church records, 1822-1940 [unk.]
  N: USIGS 4 reels   1838

TYKADLOW, Kalisz, Poland
Church records, 1880-1940 [unk.]
N: USlGS 2 reels 1839

TYKOCIN, Lomza, Poland
Military church records, 1790-1803 [unk.]
N: USlGS 1 reel 1840

Jewish Community Records

BLASZKI, Kalisz, Poland. JEWISH
CONGREGATION
Records, 1871-1939 [unk.]
N: USlGS 4 reels 1841

DOBRZYCA, Poland. JEWS
Protokollbuch, 1809-1834, 90 ll. IsJJH
N: IsJJH 1842
P: NNYi

KATTOWITZ [KATOWICE], Poland. JEWS
Repräsentanten Versammlung, 1865-1875;
Synagogengemeinde, Protokollbuch des
Vorstandes, 1892-1900; Synagogen-Gemeinde
Journal, 1898-1911; Protokolle des
Gemeindevorstands, 1294 ll. IsJJH
N: IsJJH 1843
P: NNYi

KOBYLIN, Poland. JEWS
Przywilej Kahalu Zydow Skiego, 1778-1789,
5 p. IsJJH
N: IsJJH 1844
P: NNYi

LODZ, Poland. JEWS
Documents, papers, photographs, and notes
pertaining to the Jewish Ghetto, 1939-1944
NNYi 1845
N: NNYi

OLKUZ, Poland. JEWS
Pinkas shel Haherba Kadisha (Register of
the Burial Society), 1829-1903, 111 p.
IsJJH
N: IsJJH 1846
P: NNYi

WADOWICE, Krakow, Poland
Marriages of Jewish persons, 1877-1928 [unk.]
N: USlGS 1 reel 1847

Institutions

PRAGA BURIAL SOCIETY, Warsaw-Praga,
Poland
Register of the Praga Burial Society,
1785-1870, 246 p. IsJJH
N: IsJJH 1848
P: NNYi

CZECHOSLOVAKIA

Church Records

CHURCH OF JESUS CHRIST OF LATTER-DAY
SAINTS. CZECHOSLOVAKIA
Records of the Czechoslovakian Mission and
Prague District (German Mission to 1930),
1922-1950 USlC
N: USlGS 2 reels 1849

RUMANIA

Personal Papers

MARIA, Queen of Rumania, 1875-1938
Correspondence with Lavinia A. Small, 1929-
1938; will, 1938 priv.
N: ICU 3 reels 1850

HUNGARY

Church Records

CHURCH OF JESUS CHRIST OF LATTER-DAY
SAINTS. EAST GERMAN MISSION
Evangelical Lutheran Church records of
various localities in Bessarabia and Bukovina,
1778-1940 [unk.]
N: USlGS 80 reels 1851

CHURCH OF JESUS CHRIST OF LATTER-DAY
SAINTS. HUNGARY
Records, Hungarian Mission (Swiss-German
Mission), 1903-1914 USlC
N: USlGS 1 reel 1852

LUTHERAN CHURCH. HUNGARY
Records, various localities in Bukovina,
1778-1940 [unk.]
N: USlGS 27 reels 1853

RUSSIA

Local Records

FINLAND. VALTIONARKISTO
Court records (copy) of Inkeri Judicial District
(a former Swedish province, covering Leningrad
District in Russia, Narva, and Viru), 1667-
1668, 1684-1686, 1688-1689, 1691-1697 FiHV
N: USlGS 1 reel 1854

KOPORE, Leningrad, Russia
Kihlakunnanoikeus - Häradsrätt [Circuit court
records (copy)], 1684-1703 FiHV
N: USlGS 7 reels 1855

LENINGRAD (formerly ST. PETERSBURG),
Russia
Court records; Kaupunkituomioistuimet-
Stadsdomstolar [city administration records,
lower court proceedings, etc.] of Nevanlinna,
now part of Leningrad, 1684-1699 FiHV
N: USlGS 5 reels 1856

LENINGRAD (formerly ST. PETERSBURG).
KATARINA PARISH
Records, 1726-1900 SvSS
N: USlGS 52 reels 1857

LENINGRAD (formerly ST. PETERSBURG).
ST. MARIEN PARISH
Records, 1733-1899 FiHV
N: USlGS 49 reels 1858

PETROKREPOST, Leningrad, Russia
Circuit court records (copy) of Pänkinälinna
Judicial District (now Petrokrepost), 1684-1701
FiHV
N: USlGS 4 reels 1859

Personal Papers

CURTIN, JEREMIAH, 1835-1906
Correspondence as Secretary of Embassy
in Russia, 1861-1869 DS
N: WHi 1 reel 1860
P: WHi

DENIKIN, ANTON IVANOVICH, 1872-1947
Naviet na bieloe dvizhenie, 194- (typescript)
NNC
N: CSt-H 1 reel 1861

DMOWSKI, ROMAN
Central and Eastern Europe, 1917 (typescript)
CSt-H
N: CSt-H 1 reel 1862

FRANCIS, DAVID ROWLAND, 1850-1927
Papers re: Russian Revolution, 1917 MoHi
N: CSt-H 2 reels 1863

GIERS, NIKOLAI KARLOVICH DE, 1820-1895
Family papers, 1859-1895 priv.
N: CU 7 reels 1864

HARRIS, ERNEST LLOYD
The allies in Siberia, 1921 (typescript) DNA
N: CSt-H 1 reel 1865

KOLOBOV, M.
Borba s bol'shevikami na Dal'nam Vostokie.
(Khorvat. Kolchak. Semenov. Merkulovy.
Diterikhs) Vospominaniia uchastnika., 192?.
N: CSt-H 1 reel 1866

Ocherki revoliutsionnogo dvizheniia v Srednei
Azii; sbornik statei Feizuly Khodzhaeva [i dr.],
1923? (typescript)
N: CSt-H 1 reel 1867

PERSHIN, D. P.
Baron Ungern, Urga i Altan Bulak [Baron
Ungern, Urga and Altan Bulak, an eye witness
account of the troubled times in Outer (Khalka)
Mongolia, 193-] CSt-H
N: CSt-H 1 reel 1868

RIABUKHIN, N. M.
The story of Baron Ungern-Sternberg told by his
staff physician, 192- (typescript translation
from the Russian) CSt-H
N: CSt-H 1 reel 1869

SEMENOV, GRIGORII MIKHAILOVICH, 1890-1945
Ataman Semenov, 1937 (typescript) CSt-H
N: CSt-H 1 reel 1870

SEMENOV, GRIGORII MIKHAILOVICH, 1890-1945
Istoriia moei borby s bolshevikami, 1937
CSt-H
N: CSt-H 1 reel 1871

VOLOGODSKII, PETR VASIL'EVICH
Dnevnik, 1918-1925 CSt-H
N: CSt-H 1 reel 1872

WESTPHALEN, GEORG VON, 1639-1720
Despatches from Russia DaKR
N: CLU 5 reels* 1873

Collections

GOTLAND. LANDSARKIVET, Visby
Husförhörslangd [clerical survey] of the
Swedish Congregation of Gammalsvenskby
[Starosjvedskaja], Kherson, Russia, 1795,
1821, 1831, 1856, 1878 SvVL
N: USlGS 1 reel 1874

EXPLORATIONS

Personal Papers

BERNALDEZ, ANDRÉ, ca. 1450-1515
Memorial re: Ferdinand and Isabella (contains
account of voyages of Columbus), 1508-1511
OkTG
N: OkTG 2 reels 1875

CASAS, BARTOLOMÉ DE LAS, 1474-1566
Letter to Chancellor of Charles V, ca. 1519;
memorial to Philip II, 1555 OkTG
N: OkTG 1 reel 1876

CHAMPLAIN, SAMUEL DE, 1567?-1635
"Brief discours des choses plus Remarquables
..." [so-called "Champlain Manuscript"], ca.
1601, 46 ll. RPJCB
DCO: RPJCB 1877

COLUMBUS, CHRISTOPHER, 1451-1506
Abstract of journal of first voyage made by
Bartholomé de Las Casas [in Spanish] SpBN
DCO: MiU-C NN 151 p. 1878

COLUMBUS, CHRISTOPHER, 1451-1506
Documents collected by Col. John Bigelow in
1925, with memorandum relating to them
SpAGI
DCO: NN 34 p. 1879

CORONADO, FRANCISCO VÁSQUEZ DE,
1510-1554
El Alarde que se hizo de la Gente que el Virrey
enbio a Cíbola, 1540, 21 p.   SpAGI
DCO: MiU-C   1880

DE SOTO, HERNANDO, 1500-1542
Papers pertaining to de Soto, 1544-1791   v. p.
DCO: DLC 10 items   1881

THEVET, ANDRÉ, 1502-1590
Le grand insulaire et pilotage, 1586, 2 v.   FrBN
N: CU-B*
P: CU-B   1882

VERRAZANNO, GIOVANNI DA, 1485?-?1528
Letter to Francis I of France re: voyages
to North America, July 8, 1524, 22 p.
Cèllere Codex NNP
DCO: NN   1883

VERRAZZANO, GIOVANNI DA, 1485?-?1528
Viaggio fatto nell 1524 all' America (notes by
Verrazzano), 21 p.   NNP
N: NNP*   1884

Collections

FRANCE. ARCHIVES DE LA MARINE.
Série 3-JJ
Journals, reports, memoirs, and memoranda
re: exploration of North America, 1679-1833
FrAN
N: CaOOA Selections 4 reels   1885

WALES. NATIONAL LIBRARY, Aberystwyth
Material re: Madog   UKAbN
DCO: DLC   1886

SPANISH AMERICA

Government Records

SPAIN. ARCHIVO GENERAL DE INDIAS, Seville
Audiencias. Indiferente de Nueva Espana. Bull
re: establishment of bishopric of Tlascala, 1518-
1525; papers of Pedro de Peralta, 1654; docu-
ments re: "encomiendas," 1669-1750   SpAGI
N: ? 66 feet   1887
P: DLC
PP: DLC
DCO: DLC 19 sheets

SPAIN. ARCHIVO GENERAL DE INDIAS, Seville
Contración, 1st Sec. Patents re: despatch of
the Armadas, 1527-1621; letters to House of
Trade from Pedro Menéndez Marques, Francisco
de Bay, and the Duke of Medina Sidonia, 1571,
1586-1587   SpAGI
DCO: DLC 292 sheets   1888

SPAIN. ARCHIVO GENERAL DE INDIAS, Seville
Contraduría 1st Sec. Council of the Indies: Royal
orders re: friars going to Yucatan, 1601-1747,
and Fr. Luis Cancer to Florida, 1549; accounts
re: Yucatan, ca. 1691; "encomienda" formerly
held by Francisco de Montejo, 1614-1617   SpAGI
N: ? 36 feet   1889
P: DLC
PP: DLC
DCO: DLC 220 sheets

SPAIN. ARCHIVO GENERAL DE INDIAS, Seville
Justicia. Selected lawsuits, 1530-1580   SpAGI
N: ? 576 feet   1890
P: DLC
PP: DLC
DCO: DLC 1849 sheets

SPAIN. ARCHIVO GENERAL DE INDIAS, Seville
Justicia. Selections, 1515-1575 [miscellan-
eous suits, 1515-1575; Residencias: Hernán
Cortés, 1528-1533; Francisco de Montejo,
1544-1552; Luis de Céspedes y Oviedo, 1564-
1571]   SpAGI
N: DLC 40 reels   1891
P: DLC

SPAIN. ARCHIVO GENERAL DE INDIAS, Seville
Papeles de Estado: América en General,
1700-1836   SpAGI
DCO: DLC 12444 sheets   1892

SPAIN. ARCHIVO GENERAL DE INDIAS, Seville
Patronato, 1st Sec. Papal bulls and briefs,
1518-1700   SpAGI
DCO: DLC 84 sheets   1893

SPAIN. ARCHIVO GENERAL DE INDIAS, Seville
Patronato, 2nd Sec. Discoveries, descriptions,
and settlements, 1515-1595 [Columbus' lawsuits,
1515-1564; Cortes, 1518-1570; Florida, 1571-
1598; explorations north and south from Mexico,
1520-1627; exploration of New Mexico, 1568-
1602]   SpAGI
N: DLC 5 reels and 450 feet   1894
PP: DLC of 450 feet
DCO: DLC 503 sheets

SPAIN. ARCHIVO GENERAL DE INDIAS, Seville
Patronato, 3rd Sec. Relations of the merits
and services of the early conquerors and
discoverers, 1540-1624   SpAGI
N: DLC 26 reels   1895
N: ? 144 feet
P: DLC of 144 feet
PP: DLC of 144 feet
DCO: DLC 133 sheets

SPAIN. ARCHIVO GENERAL DE INDIAS, Seville
Patronato, 4th Sec. Papers re: the Avila-
Cortes conspiracy, 1566-1568   SpAGI
N: DLC 31 reels   1896
P: DLC

SPAIN. ARCHIVO GENERAL DE INDIAS, Seville
Patronato, 4th Sec. Papers re: the good
government of the Indies, 1480-1648 [General
papers, 1480-1616; Hispaniola, 1503-1586;
Puerto Rico, 1510-1599; Jamaica and other
islands, 1538-1597; New Spain, 1519-1648]
SpAGI
N: ?   1897
P: DLC 1 reel and 1 foot
DCO: DLC 2429 sheets

SPAIN. ARCHIVO GENERAL DE INDIAS, Seville
Patronato I, 7th Sec. Royal Armada: papers re:
English and French pirates, 1528-1596; Moorish
and Dutch pirates, 1528-1641; Hispaniola, and
treaty between Spain, France, and Portugal,
1544-1696; Maranhao, 1615; reconquest of Curaçao, 1639-1641   SpAGI
N: DLC 9 reels   1898
P: DLC

SPAIN. ARCHIVO GENERAL DE INDIAS, Seville
Patronato, 7th Sec. Royal Armada: papers re:
fleets to and from the West Indies, 1571-1597
SpAGI
DCO: DLC 127 sheets   1899

Collections

ENCINAS, DIEGO DE, collector
Provisiones [16th cent. manuscripts re: govern-
ment of the Spanish Indies], 1596   SpAGI
N: ? 226 feet   1900
P: DLC

MADRID. BIBLIOTECA DEL PALACIO
Juan des Vascones: Petición de derecho; select-
ions on Indian administration; Las Casas tract;
Zurita: Laws and royal ordinances of the Indies;
Tavari, Bulas, Tomo I; Fray Domingo de Sala-
zar: Tratado re: tributes in the Philippines   Ibid.
N: ? 170 feet   1901
P: DLC
PP: DLC

MADRID. BIBLIOTECA NACIONAL
Short selections re: Spanish America   SpBN
N: ? 315 feet   1902
P: DLC
PP: DLC

SEVILLE. BIBLIOTECA COLOMBINA
Opinions by Juan Ramírez, Oct. 10, 20, 1595
Ibid.
N: DLC 1 foot   1903
PP: DLC

SPAIN. ARCHIVO HISTÓRICO NACIONAL, Madrid
Ayala dictionary, selections: Cartas de Indias,
Letters to the King, selected items, 16th cent.
Ibid.
DCO: DLC 79 sheets   1904
N: ? 141 feet   P: DLC   PP: DLC

TOLEDO, Spain. BIBLIOTECA PÚBLICA
Malferit, De bello inferendo y conferendis
legibus hominibus novi orbis; Relación
historica dyscreptiva ... provinces of
Verapaz and Guatemala, 1635   Ibid.
N: ? 70 feet   1905
P: DLC

MEXICO

Bibliography

AUSTRIA. HAUS-, HOF-, UND STAATSARCHIV
Archiv Kaiser Maximilians von Mexiko:
Guides; Records, selections, 1861-1864
Ibid.
DCO: DLC 15007 sheets   1906

TEXAS. UNIVERSITY
Calendar of the Matamoros Archives   TxU
N: DLC 1 reel   1907
P: DLC

Government Records

FRANCE. MINISTÈRE DE LA GUERRE
Documents re: French intervention in Mexico,
1862-1869   Ibid.
N: DLC 33 reels   1908

FRANCE. MINISTÈRE DES AFFAIRES
ÉTRANGÈRES
Correspondance Politique, Mexique,
1848-1857, 12 v.   FrAN
N: CU-B*
P: CU-B   1909

GERMANY. AUSWÄRTIGES AMT
Documents re: Mexico and Central America,
1869-1920   Ibid.
N: CU-B 30 reels
P: CU-B   1910

GREAT BRITAIN. FOREIGN OFFICE. F.O. 50
Consular despatches from Mexico, 1822-1902,
531 v.   UKLPRO
N: CU-B
P: CU-B   1911

GREAT BRITAIN. FOREIGN OFFICE. F.O. 203
Embassy and Consular Archives, Mexico -
Correspondence, Ser. I, 1823-1902,
145 v.   UKLPRO
N: CU-B
P: CU-B   1912

GREAT BRITAIN. FOREIGN OFFICE. F.O. 204
Embassy and Consular Archives, Mexico -
Correspondence, Ser. II, 7 v.   UKLPRO
N: CU-B
P: CU-B   1913

GREAT BRITAIN. FOREIGN OFFICE. F.O. 205
Embassy and Consular Archives,
Mexico - Letterbooks, 1826-1899, 49 v.
UKLPRO
N: CU-B
P: CU-B   1914

MEXICO
Protomedicato, 1726-1815   MxAGN
N: NcD 5 reels   1915

MEXICO. ARCHIVO GENERAL DE LA NACION
Archivo del Hospital de Jesús, 1528-1800
Mx AGN
N: CU-B 71 reels   1916
P: CU-B

MEXICO. ARCHIVO GENERAL DE LA NACIÓN
Archivo Histórico de Hacienda, 1707-1819
MxAGN
N: CU-B 27 reels   1917
P: CU-B

MEXICO. ARCHIVO GENERAL DE LA NACION
Archivo Obregon-Calles   MxAGN
N: CU-B 21 reels   1918
P: CU-B MiEM

MEXICO. ARCHIVO GENERAL DE LA NACIÓN

Bandos, 1571-1819, 29 v.   MxAGN
N: CU-B
P: CU-B   1919

MEXICO. ARCHIVO GENERAL DE LA NACIÓN
Californias, 1664-1795, 82 v. MxAGN
N: CU-B   1920
P: CU-B

MEXICO. ARCHIVO GENERAL DE LA NACIÓN
Capellanías [chaplain's records], ca. 1740-1800
(genealogical part only) MxAGN
N: USIGS 4 reels   1921

MEXICO. ARCHIVO GENERAL DE LA NACIÓN
Civil, 1531-1790 MxAGN
N: CU-B 26 reels   1922
P: CU-B

MEXICO. ARCHIVO GENERAL DE LA NACIÓN
Civil [records of civil cases before the Real
Audiencia], selections, 1548-1599, 1605,
1755-1787 MxAGN
N: ? 360 feet   1923
P: DLC

MEXICO. ARCHIVO GENERAL DE LA NACIÓN
Compañía de Jesús, 1679-1752 MxAGN
N: CU-B 12 reels   1924
P: CU-B

MEXICO. ARCHIVO GENERAL DE LA NACIÓN
Correspondencia de los Virreyes, Series I,
1755-1821, 288 v. MxAGN
N: CU-B   1925
P: CU-B

MEXICO. ARCHIVO GENERAL DE LA NACIÓN
Correspondencia de los Virreyes, Series II,
1755-1808, 61 v. MxAGN
N: CU-B   1926
P: CU-B

MEXICO. ARCHIVO GENERAL DE LA NACIÓN
Criminal: Selections, 1702-1820 MxAGN
PP: CU-B 13 v.   1927

MEXICO. ARCHIVO GENERAL DE LA NACIÓN
Descripciones geográficas: Coahuayana, 1806;
Coalcomán, 1786-1810; Apatzingan, 1798-
1809; Colima, 1771-1772; Motines, 1684
MxAGN
N: TxU 90 feet*   1928

MEXICO. ARCHIVO GENERAL DE LA NACIÓN
General de Parte, 1570-1580,
2 v. MxAGN
N: CU-B   1929
P: CU-B

MEXICO. ARCHIVO GENERAL DE LA NACIÓN
Guerra Correspondencia: papers re: San
Miguel de Pensacola, 1760-1763 MxAGN
DCO: DLC 483 sheets   1930

MEXICO. ARCHIVO GENERAL DE LA NACIÓN
Historia, 1554-1825, 577 v. MxAGN
N: CU-B   1931
P: CU-B

MEXICO. ARCHIVO GENERAL DE LA NACIÓN
Historia: Operaciones de Guerra:
Correspondence with the Viceroy, Benito
Arminan, 1813-1817; Armejo, 1815-1819
MxAGN
DCO: DLC 642 sheets   1932

MEXICO. ARCHIVO GENERAL DE LA NACIÓN
Indios, 1574-1775 MxAGN
N: CU-B 11 reels   1933
P: CU-B

MEXICO. ARCHIVO GENERAL DE LA NACIÓN
Inquisición, ca. 1530- MxAGN
N: USIGS 145 reels   1934

MEXICO. ARCHIVO GENERAL DE LA NACIÓN
Inquisición, 1536-1701 MxAGN
N: CU-B 18 reels   1935
P: CU-B

MEXICO. ARCHIVO GENERAL DE LA NACIÓN
Inquisición : selections, 1560, 1570, 1571, 1580
MxAGN
N: ? 79 feet   1936
P: DLC

MEXICO. ARCHIVO GENERAL DE LA NACIÓN
Inquisición, ca. 1600-1800 (genealogical
part only) MxAGN
N: USIGS 168 reels   1937

MEXICO. ARCHIVO GENERAL DE LA NACIÓN
Intendencias, 1786-1821 82 v. MxAGN
N: CU-B   1938

MEXICO. ARCHIVO GENERAL DE LA NACIÓN
Islas. Indiferente. Documents re: San Miguel
de Pensacola, 1736-1737 MxAGN
DCO: DLC 79 sheets   1939

MEXICO. ARCHIVO GENERAL DE LA NACIÓN
Justicia, 1835-1840 MxAGN
N: CU-B 27 reels   1940
P: CU-B

MEXICO. ARCHIVO GENERAL DE LA NACIÓN
Marina, 1774-1805 MxAGN
N: CU-B 3 reels   1941

MEXICO. ARCHIVO GENERAL DE LA NACIÓN
Marriage documents, ca. 1625-1780 (genealogi-
cal parts only) MxAGN
N: USIGS 21 reels   1942

MEXICO. ARCHIVO GENERAL DE LA NACIÓN
Mercedes, 1542-1619, 35 v. MxAGN
N: CU-B   1943
P: CU-B

MEXICO. ARCHIVO GENERAL DE LA NACIÓN
Misiones, 1622-1835, 27 v. MxAGN
N: CU-B   1944

MEXICO. ARCHIVO GENERAL DE LA NACIÓN
Oficio de Soria, 1578-1819 MxAGN
N: CU-B 3 reels   1945

MEXICO. ARCHIVO GENERAL DE LA NACIÓN
Ordenanzas, 1580-1786, 20 v. MxAGN
N: CU-B   1946
P: CU-B

MEXICO. ARCHIVO GENERAL DE LA NACIÓN
Presidios, 1645-1820, 20 v. MxAGN
N: CU-B   1947

MEXICO. ARCHIVO GENERAL DE LA NACIÓN
Provincias Internas, 1689-1830, 265 v. MxAGN
N: CU-B   1948
P: CU-B

MEXICO. ARCHIVO GENERAL DE LA NACIÓN
Provincias Internas, selections, 1774-1776,
1793-1810, 1816, 1821-1822 MxAGN
DCO: DLC 1742 sheets   1949

MEXICO. ARCHIVO GENERAL DE LA NACIÓN
Reales Cédulas, 1609-1800, 238 v. MxAGN
N: CU-B   1950

MEXICO. ARCHIVO GENERAL DE LA NACIÓN
Reales Cédulas, Duplicados, 1530?-1804
188 v. MxAGN
N: CU-B   1951

MEXICO. ARCHIVO GENERAL DE LA NACIÓN
Reales Cédulas y Órdenes; documents re:
Flota and Montejo, 1550 MxAGN
N: ? 1 foot   1952
P: DLC
PP: DLC

MEXICO. ARCHIVO GENERAL DE LA NACIÓN
Tierras, 1566-1820 MxAGN
N: CU-B 24 reels   1953

MEXICO. ARCHIVO GENERAL DE LA NACIÓN
Tierras: lawsuits over land, 1549, 1559, 1561,
1583, 1680-1724, 1775 (selections) MxAGN
N: ? 263 feet   1954
P: DLC

MEXICO. ARCHIVO GENERAL DE LA NACIÓN
Tierras: Suit of Estaban Ximénez and Dona
Leonor de Henríquez against Diego Alvarado,
1722 MxAGN
N: DLC 57 feet   1955
P: DLC

MEXICO. ARCHIVO GENERAL DE LA NACIÓN
Vínculos [entailed estates]: 1686, 1687, 1797
(selections) MxAGN
DCO: DLC 69 sheets   1956

MEXICO. ARCHIVO GENERAL DE LA NACIÓN
Vínculos [entailed estates], ca. 1700-1800
MxAGN
N: USIGS 184 reels   1957

MEXICO. SECRETARÍA DE JUSTICIA
Report by Chico, Jefe Político, Alta Cali-
fornia, 1836 MxAGN
N: CSmH 1 reel   1958

MEXICO. SECRETARÍA DE LA DEFENSA
NACIONAL. ARCHIVO
Selections, 1808-1860 Ibid.
N: CU-B 93 reels* 16 mm.   1959
P: CU-B

MEXICO. SECRETARÍA DE RELACIONES
EXTERIORES
Selections: Asuntos administrativos,
Asuntos de Estado internacionales, Re-
laciones políticas de Estado, Asuntos de
Estado interiores, Comercio e industria
Ibid.
DCO: DLC 22627 sheets   1960

MORELIA, Mexico. AYUNTAMIENTO. ARCHIVO
Reales Cédulas, 15th-17th cents.; Libro de
Cabildos, 1654-1719, 1735-1741; Libro...
Capitulares, 1742-1811; Actas, 1809-1826
Ibid.
N: DLC 8 reels   1961

SPAIN. ARCHIVO GENERAL DE INDIAS, Seville
Audiencias. Guadalajara. Selections,
1608-1776 [documents re: conquest of New
Mexico, 1639-1754] SpAGI
N: ? 1526 feet   1962
P: DLC
PP: DLC

SPAIN. ARCHIVO GENERAL DE INDIAS, Seville
Audiencias. Mexico. Selections, 1525-1763
SpAGI
N: DLC 66 reels   1963
P: DLC
DCO: DLC 1145 sheets

SPAIN. ARCHIVO GENERAL DE INDIAS, Seville
Escribanía de Cámara, selections, 1565-1750
[Bishop Francisco de Toral of Yucatan vs. Fray
Diego de Landa, 1565; proceedings of the Fiscal
against Francisco de Montejo; revolt in pueblo
of Tekax, Yucatan, 1610; residencias of Govern-
ors, 1666-1750] SpAGI
N: DLC 15 reels   1964
P: DLC

SPAIN. ARCHIVO GENERAL DE INDIAS, Seville
Patronato I, 6th Sec. Special matters: papers
re: Juan de Palafox y Mendoza, former bishop
of Puebla de Los Angeles, 1642-1650 SpAGI
N: DLC 28 feet   1965
PP: DLC

U.S. DEPT. OF STATE
Selected documents re: U.S.- Mexican
affairs, 1913-1920 DNA
N: Mi 23 reels   1966
P: CU-B

City Records

GUADALAJARA, Jalisco, Mexico
Ramo Civil, 16th cent. -1844; Ramo Criminal,
1800-1818; Asuntos Eclesiásticos, 1676-1775;
Libros de Gobierno, 1692-1752; Tierras y
Aguas, 1584-1695 Ibid.
N: DLC 65 reels   1967

GUANAJUATO (City), Mexico. UNIVERSIDAD
Miscellaneous documents, 1611-1845 Ibid.
N: DLC 44 reels   1968

MÉRIDA, Yucatán, Mexico. DIOCESE (Catholic)
Royal cedulas, Indians Ibid.
N: ? 20 feet   1969
P: DLC

MICHOACÁN, Mexico. ARCHIVO GENERAL
DE NOTARIAS
Epoca Colonial Ibid.
N: DLC 27 reels   1970

OAXACA, Mexico. ARCHIVO DEL JUZGADO
Miscelánea histórica, 1710-1829 Ibid.
N: DLC 8 reels   1971

PÁTZCUARO, Michoacán, Mexico. ARCHIVO
MUNICIPAL
Miscellaneous documents, 16th and 17th cents.
Ibid.
N: DLC 11 reels   1972

TLAXCALA, Mexico
Miscellaneous documents, 1554-1820; Proto-
colos de Notarios, 1572-1615; Pueblo de
Huaquechula, 1599 Ibid.
N: DLC 35 reels   1973

Church Records

CHURCH OF JESUS CHRIST OF LATTER-DAY
SAINTS. MEXICO
Mission, ward and branch records: Chihuahua
Mission, 1919-1921; Chuichupa Ward, 1900-
1948; Diaz Ward, 1886-1912; Dublan Ward, to
1918; Dublan Branch, 1917-1948; Garcia Ward,
to 1942; Juarez Wards, 1887-1948; Morelos
Ward, 1900-1911; Oaxaca Ward, 1904-1911;
San Jose Ward, 1911-1912 USIC
N: USIGS 1 reel   1974

CHURCH OF JESUS CHRIST OF LATTER-DAY
SAINTS. MEXICO
Records of members and annual genealogical
reports of the Mexican Mission, early to 1951
USIC
N: USIGS 5 reels   1975

LA CONCEPCION TEQUIPEHUCA PARISH, D.F.,
Mexico
Records, 1895-1955 Ibid.
N: USIGS 122 reels   1976

LA VIRGEN DE LOS DOLORES DEL CAMPO
FLORIDO PARISH, D.F., Mexico
Records, 1902-1954 Ibid.
N: USIGS 110 reels   1977

MEXICO (City). CATEDRAL
Account book, mostly abstracted wills
[Testamentos], 1660-1859 MxMC
N: USIGS 2 reels   1978

MEXICO (City). CATEDRAL
Amonestaciones, matrimonios, información
matrimonial, actas matrimoniales, 1575-1954
MxMC
N: USIGS 498 reels   1979

MEXICO (City). CATEDRAL
Bautismo de castas, Españoles, legitimos y
naturales, expósitos, adultos y regimiento de
infantería, 1536-1953 MxMC
N: USIGS 119 reels   1980

MEXICO (City). CATEDRAL
Confirmaciones, 1611-1953 MxMC
N: USIGS 34 reels   1981

MEXICO (City). CATEDRAL
Defunciones de Españoles y castas, defunciones
de Indios, defunciones de fiebre viruela MxMC
N: USIGS 25 reels   1982

MEXICO (City). CATEDRAL
Padrón de la parroquia [membership list],
1670-1824, 1921 MxMC
N: USIGS 16 reels   1983

OAXACA, Mexico. CATEDRAL
Clavería. Libros de Recaudación y
Repartimiento, ca. 1700-1815;
Colecturía de Tlaxiaco, 1794-1837;
miscellaneous material, 1562-1832
Ibid.
N: DLC 15 reels   1984

PÁTZCUARO, Michoacán, Mexico. ARCHIVO
PARROQUIAL
Miscellaneous documents, 15th-17th cents.
Ibid.
N: DLC 2 reels   1985

REGINA COELI PARISH, D.F., Mexico
Records, 1772-1954 Ibid.
N: USIGS 132 reels   1986

SAGRADO CORAZÓN...VALLE GOMEZ PARISH,
D.F., Mexico
Records, 1946-1955 Ibid.
N: USIGS 22 reels   1987

SAN ANTONIO TOMATLÁN PARISH, D.F.,
Mexico
Records, 1902-1954 Ibid.
N: USIGS 59 reels   1988

SAN COSME PARISH, D.F., Mexico
Records, 1598-1954 Ibid.
N: USIGS 44 reels   1989

SANTA CATARINA PARISH, D.F., Mexico
Records, 1568-1953 Ibid.
N: USIGS 165 reels   1990

SANTA MARÍA DE GUADALUPE PARISH, D.F.,
Mexico
Records, 1596-1955 Ibid.
N: USIGS 220 reels   1991

SANTA MARÍA LA REDONDA PARISH, D.F.,
Mexico
Records, 1609-1954 Ibid.
N: USIGS 117 reels   1992

SANTA MARÍA TOLUCA, Mexico
Council House, ca. 1535 [in Aztec] NN
N: NN 1 reel*   1993
P: NN

SANTA TERESITA PARISH, D.F., Mexico
Records, 1938-1954 Ibid.
N: USIGS 45 reels   1994

SANTA VERACRUZ PARISH, D.F., Mexico
Records, including will abstracts
[Testamentos] and daily account book [diario
del Cuadrante], 1560-1953 Ibid.
N: USIGS 168 reels   1995

SANTO DOMINGO PARISH, D.F., Mexico
Baptisms of Indians, 1709-1753 Ibid.
N: USIGS 1 reel   1996

Personal Papers

ANDRES DE SAN MIGUEL, fray, 1577-1644
Obras, 16th cent. TxU
N: TxU 40 feet   1997

ANZA, JUAN BAUTISTA DE, 1735-1788
Diario de la ruta ... a la California septentrio-
nal por los ríos Gila y Colorado, Jan. 8-May
27, 1774, 60 p.
DCO: MxAGN   1998
P: Az-Ar

BUSTAMANTE, C. M.
Diary, 1822-1841 Zacatecas State Library,
Zacatecas
N: ViU   1999

CASAS, BARTOLOMÉ DE LAS, 1474-1566
Manuscript holograph re: dispute with Juan
Gines de Sepulveda
N: DLC   2000

CIUDAD REAL, ANTONIO DE, Father
Motul Maya dictionary, ca. 1610,
1338 p. RPJCB
DCO: RPJCB   2001

CORTÉS, JOSÉ, fl. 1799
Memorias sobre las Provincias del Norte
de Nueva España, 1799, 174 p. DLC
N: AzU   2002

GARCÉS, FRANCISCO TOMÁS HERMENEGILDO,
1738-1781
Diario ... a las márgenes del Colorado y Gila,
Oct. 21, 1775-May 31, 1776, 75 p.
DCO: MxAN
N: Az-Ar   2003

HEREYRA, PEDRO
Del regimiento entrada de Don Fernan Cortez
cuando entro eng su tierra de Indias, 1520,
30 p. TxU
DCO: NN   2004

HIDALGO Y COSTILLO, defendant
Military trial proceedings, 1810-1811
Bibliotheca Nacional de Arqueología, Mexico
City
DCO: DLC 155 sheets   2005

JUÁREZ, BENITO, 1806-1872
Archivo, 1849-1872 MxBN
N: TxU 46 reels *   2006

LERDO DE TEJADA, SEBASTIÁN, 1820-1889
Papers, 1857-1872 Archivo de la Secretaría
Pública de México priv.
N: TxU 100 feet   2007

LERDO DE TEJADA, SEBASTIÁN, 1820-1889
Su expediente personal, 1856-1872
Mexico, Ministerio de Relaciones Exteriores
N: TxU 100 feet*   2008

LOPEZ DE COGOLLUDO, DIEGO, 17th cent.
Historia de Yucathan, Madrid, 1688 priv.
N: ICN   2009

MADERO, FRANCISCO, 1873-1913
Archivo, 1911 MxBN
N: TxU 2 reels *   2010

MANGE, JUAN MATEO
Luz de tierra incognita en la América
septentrional, 1720 MxBN
N: CU-B 1 reel   2011

ROMERO, MATIAS, 1837-1898
Correspondencia, 1850-1899 Banco de Mexico
N: Ibid. 72 reels*   2012
P: CU-B DLC TxU

SEDELMAYR, JACOBO, 1703-1779
Diary, Oct.-Nov. 1749, 5p. SpAN
DCO: MxAN
N: Az-Ar   2013

Collections

ACADEMIA DE LA HISTORIA, Madrid, Spain
Treatise on legality and justice of war against
natives of West Indies, by Fray Vincente
Paletino de Corçula, 1559; Relación de las
Casas de Yucatán, by Fray Diego de Landa,
1565 Ibid.
N: ? 23 feet   2014
P: DLC

ASOCIACIÓN HISTÓRICA AMERICANISTA, Mexico
Selected material, 1737-1835 Ibid.
N: CU-B 1 reel   2015

CODICE AZCAPOTZALCO
Maguey manuscript, 17th cent., 30 p.
[in Nahuatl] ICN
N: CU 1 reel   2016

MEXICO. BIBLIOTECA NACIONAL
Selections, 1651-1806 MxBN
N: CU-B 7 reels   2017

PARIS. BIBLIOTHÈQUE NATIONALE
Selections from Fonds Mexicain, 1683-1777
FrBN
N: CU-B 1 reel*   2018

U.S. LIBRARY OF CONGRESS
Colonial Mexican church music, largely from
Puebla, 13 v. v.p.
N: DLC 3 reels   2019

U.S. LIBRARY OF CONGRESS
Harkness collection: Mexican manuscripts,
Peruvian manuscripts, 1531-1651 DLC
N: DLC 9 reels   2020

Institutions

MEXICO. MUSEO NACIONAL
Instituto de Antropología e Historia. Selections,
1697-1801 Ibid.
N: CU-B 4 reels   2021

CENTRAL AMERICA

CANAL ZONE

Church Records

CHURCH OF JESUS CHRIST OF LATTER-DAY
SAINTS. CANAL ZONE
Annual genealogical reports, in the Mexican
Mission, 1947-1951; branch records of the
Canal Zone Branch, Balboa, Panama, 1942-
1944 USlC
N: USlGS 2 reels   2022

COSTA RICA

Government Records

GREAT BRITAIN. FOREIGN OFFICE. F.O. 21
Consular despatches from Costa Rica,
1848-1902, 66 v. UKLPRO
N: CU-B   2023
P: CU-B

EL SALVADOR

Government Records

GREAT BRITAIN. FOREIGN OFFICE. F.O. 66
Consular despatches from El Salvador, 1856-
1902, 49 v. UKLPRO
N: CU-B   2024
P: CU-B

GUATEMALA

Government Records

GREAT BRITAIN. FOREIGN OFFICE. F.O. 15
Consular despatches from Guatemala, 1825-
1902, 352 v. UKLPRO
N: CU-B   2025
P: CU-B CtY

GUATEMALA
First constitutional convention
N: NcD   2026

SPAIN. ARCHIVO GENERAL DE INDIAS, Seville
Audiencias. Guatemala. Selections, 1526-1700
[Letters of Governors of Honduras and Costa
Rica, 1526-1699; of Bishops of Valladolid de
Comayagua, 1541-1700] SpAGI
N: ? 171 feet   2027
P: DLC
PP: DLC
DCO: DLC 411 sheets

Church Records

CHURCH OF JESUS CHRIST OF LATTER-DAY
SAINTS. GUATEMALA
Annual genealogical reports, in the Mexican
Mission, 1949-1951 USlC
N: USlGS 1 reel   2028

HONDURAS

Government Records

GREAT BRITAIN. FOREIGN OFFICE. F.O. 39
Consular despatches from Honduras, 1857-1902,
71 v. UKLPRO
N: CU-B   2029
P: CU-B

MOSQUITO COAST

Government Records

GREAT BRITAIN. FOREIGN OFFICE. F.O. 53
Consular despatches from the Mosquito Coast,
1844-1895, 77 v.   UKLPRO
N: CU-B   2030
P: CU-B

GREAT BRITAIN. FOREIGN OFFICE. F.O. 53
Mosquito Coast, correspondence re: land
grants, 1849-1865 UKLPRO
DCO: DLC   2031

NICARAGUA

Government Records

GREAT BRITAIN. FOREIGN OFFICE. F.O. 56
Consular despatches from Nicaragua, 1848-1902,
60 v. UKLPRO
N: CU-B   2032
P: CU-B

SOUTH AMERICA

Privateering Records

GREAT BRITAIN. HIGH COURT OF ADMIRALTY.
ADMIRALTY 13
Examination of ships captured by English
privateers in Spanish America or Brazil, 1555-
1605 UKLPRO
N: CU-B 15 reels   2033

Slave Trade Records

GREAT BRITAIN. FOREIGN OFFICE. F.O. 84
Consular despatches concerning slave trade
in Latin America, 1833-1862, 38 v. UKLPRO
N: CU-B   2034
P: CU-B

ARGENTINA

Church Records

CHURCH OF JESUS CHRIST OF LATTER-DAY
SAINTS. ARGENTINA
Record of members and annual genealogical
reports, South American Mission, 1925-1935;
Argentina Mission, 1935-1951 USlC
N: USlGS 2 reels   2035

CHILE

Government Records

GREAT BRITAIN. FOREIGN OFFICE. F.O. 16
Consular despatches from Chile, 1823-1902,
356 v. UKLPRO
N: CU-B   2036
P: CU-B

SPAIN. ARCHIVO GENERAL DE INDIAS, Seville
Audiencias. Chile. Legajo 16, selections SpAGI
DCO: DLC 55 sheets   2037

COLOMBIA

Government Records

FRANCE. MINISTÈRE DES AFFAIRES
ÉTRANGÈRES
Correspondance Politique, Colombie,
1842-1853, 3 v. FrAN
N: CU-B*   2038
P: CU-B

Personal Papers

PEDROSA Y GUERRERO, ANTONIO DE LA
Administrative papers CmAHN
N: ICN 1 reel   2039

PERU

Government Records

CUZCO, Peru
"Hordenanças fechas per el Sr. Don Francisco
de Toledo y otras cosas de republica;" original
register of foundation of the city, 1534-1537
NNP
N: DLC 1 reel   2040

CUZCO, Peru
Official records, 1529-1740 (manuscript and
transcript), 200 ff. NNP
N: NNP*   2041
P: NNP

GREAT BRITAIN. FOREIGN OFFICE. F.O. 61
Consular despatches from Peru, 1823-1851,
129 v. UKLPRO
N: CU-B   2042

SPAIN. ARCHIVO GENERAL DE INDIAS, Seville
Audiencias. Charcas. Ordinance, 1622 SpAGI
N: ? 4 feet   2043
P: DLC

SPAIN. ARCHIVO GENERAL DE INDIAS, Seville
Audiencias. Lima. Selections SpAGI
N: DLC 1 reel   2044
P: DLC
DCO: DLC 27 sheets

Personal Papers

MORALES DE ARAMBURU Y MONTERO, JOSEPH
Quaderno duplicado en que se da Peru
Noticia del verdadero ventajoso estado
politico de el Peru vajo la Governacion
de el Excelentissimo Senor Don Manuel
de Amat y Junient ... [Enero 25 de 1770]
72 ff. National Library of Peru
N: DLC   2045

URUGUAY

Church Records

CHURCH OF JESUS CHRIST OF LATTER-DAY
SAINTS. URUGUAY
Annual genealogical reports and record,
Argentine and Uruguay Missions, 1946-1952
USIC
N: USIC 2 reels   2046

VENEZUELA

Collections

BRITISH MUSEUM
Venezuela papers, 1530-1834, 15 v.
Add. ms. 35314-36353 UKLBM
N: CU-B   2047

NEWBERRY LIBRARY, Chicago. EDWARD E.
AYER COLLECTION
Administrative papers, Venezuela: selections,
1718-1798 (transcripts) VeAN Archivo del
Ayuntamiento, Caracas
N: ICN 1 reel   2048

SPANISH WEST INDIES

CUBA

Bibliography

HAVANA. HOSPITAL RÉAL
Inventory of Archives, 1804 Ibid.
DCO: LNHT 2 items   2049

U.S. DEPT. OF THE INTERIOR
Index to official published documents relating
to Cuba and the insular possessions of the
U.S., 1876-1906 DNA
N: DNA 3 reels [M-24]   2050

Government Records

SPAIN. ARCHIVO GENERAL DE INDIAS, Seville
Papelas Procedentes de Cuba, selections SpAGI
N: DLC 34 reels, 14932 feet   2051
P: DLC 34 reels
PP: DLC of the 14932 feet

DOMINICAN REPUBLIC

Government Records

U.S. NATIONAL ARCHIVES
Dominican Republic. Maps, topographical sur-
veys and field notes, made by the Geological
Survey, 1919-1920; maps and topographical
surveys made by the Marine Corps, 1921-1923
DNA
N: DNA 12 reels [T-182]   2052

HAITI

Personal Papers

TOUSSAINT L'OUVERTURE, PIERRE
DOMINIQUE, 1743-1803
In-letters re: political affairs in Haiti, 1788-
1802
DCO: NN 52 ll.   2053

PUERTO RICO

Government Records

PUERTO RICO
Convención constituyente. Diario de sessiones,
1951-1952 CU
N: DLC 1 reel   2054

PORTUGUESE AMERICA

BRAZIL

Church Records

AMSTERDAM, Neth. GEMEENTE-ARCHIEF
Baptisms of Pernambuco (or Recife), Brazil,
1633-1653 Ibid.
N: USIGS 1 reel part   2055

CHURCH OF JESUS CHRIST OF LATTER-DAY
SAINTS. BRAZIL
Records of members and annual genealogical
reports of the Brazilian Mission and branches
(South American Mission, 1925-1934), early
to 1951 USIC
N: USIGS 2 reels   2056

Personal Papers

KEYES, JULIA L.
Reminiscences of life in Brazil, 1867-1870
(typescript), 102 p.   priv.
N: NcU 112 frames   2057

FRENCH AMERICA

MARTINIQUE

Government Records

FRANCE. ARCHIVES DES COLONIES.
Série C-8-A
Correspondance générale, Martinique,
selections, v. 26 FrAN
N: DLC 1 reel   2058
P: DLC

BRITISH AMERICA

CANADA

Bibliography

CARTWRIGHT, Sir RICHARD JOHN, 1835-1912
Calendar of Cartwright Papers, 1793-1913
CaOTA
N: CaOOA 25 feet   2059

GREAT BRITAIN. PUBLIC RECORD OFFICE
Indexes and registers for series of Canadian
interest; comprehensive lists of Colonial
Office records UKLPRO
N: CaOOA 44 reels   2060

LENOX, JAMES, 1800-1880
Letters to Thomas O'Callaghan re: purchase
and reprinting of the Jesuit Relations, 1852-
1860, 195 items DLC
N: NN 1 reel   2061

Census

CANADA. DEPT. OF AGRICULTURE
Nominal census, 1871 CaOOA
N: CaOOS 119 reels   2062
P: CaOOA

Government Records

CANADA (United Province, 1841-1867).
EXECUTIVE COUNCIL
Land books, 1841-1867, 9 v. CaOOA
N: CaOOA 4 reels   2063
P: CaOOA

CANADA. CABINET
Papers re: Sioux Indians who have taken refuge
in Canada, 1875-1879 (Confidential Print) CaOOA
N: NN 15 feet   2064
P: CaOOA

CANADA. DEPT. OF INDIAN AFFAIRS
Records of: Commission for Indian Affairs,
1722-1748; Superintendent General, 1755-1790;
supplementary documents, 1717-1855 R.G.
10 CaOOA
N: CaOOA 4 reels   2065

CANADA. DEPT. OF NORTHERN AFFAIRS AND
NATIONAL RESOURCES
Forest surveys, inventories, and strength
tests, 1912-1956 CaOOA
N: CaOOA 22 reels 16 mm.*   2066

CANADA. GOVERNOR GENERAL
Despatches from the Colonial Office, 1784-1909,
436 v. CaOOA
N: CaOOA 107 reels   2067
P: CaOOA

CANADA. MILITIA
Militia lists, 1829-1896 CaOOA CaOOP
N: CaOOA 3 reels   2068

CANADA. PUBLIC ARCHIVES
Despatches and reports re: Fenian submarine
at New York, 1880-1881
Adm. 1; F.O. 5; F.O. 115 UKLPRO
N: CaOOA 1 reel   2069

CANADA. ROYAL COMMISSION ON DOMINION-
PROVINCIAL RELATIONS
Exhibits: 63, 93, 240, 259, 292, 308, 328, 329,
336, 341A, 358, 360, 362, 370-374, 376, 405,
411, 414-420, 420A, 422, 1935-1938 CaOOA
N: DLC 1 reel   2070

CHARENTE-MARITIME (Dept.), France.
ARCHIVES
Amirauté de Louisbourg: Records, 1718-
1763; Intendance de la Marine à Rochefort:
Records, 1690-1724; Notarial records,
selections, 1616-1680; dossier Le Gardeur
de Courtemanche, 1729-1786 Ibid.
N: CaOOA 45 reels   2071

FRANCE. ARCHIVES DE LA MARINE.
Série B-1
Décisions, selections, v. 9, 19-21, 29-30,
41-43, 50-52, 55, 85-87, 89-94, 96-102
FrAN
DCO: DLC 2775 sheets   2072

FRANCE. ARCHIVES DE LA MARINE. Série B-2
Ordres et dépêches, selections, v. 141, 142,
152, 154, 155, 167, 168, 170, 175, 413-415,

417, 420, 422, 424, 426, 427, 429, 431, 432
FrAN
N: DLC 8 feet   2073
DCO: DLC

FRANCE. ARCHIVES DE LA MARINE. Série B-4
Campagnes, selections, v. 10, 12, 14, 18-21,
23, 25, 37, 43-45, 50, 61, 62, 67, 68, 73, 76,
80, 91, 98, 106, 111, 115, 128, 130, 132, 134-
264, 266-268 FrAN
N: DLC 8145 feet   2074
PP: DLC
DCO: DLC 6468 sheets

FRANCE. ARCHIVES DE LA MARINE. SERVICE
HYDROGRAPHIQUE
Archives, selections FrAN
DCO: DLC 2861 sheets   2075

FRANCE. ARCHIVES DES COLONIES
Correspondance générale: côte B222 ancien,
v. 29 FrAN
N: DLC 1 reel   2076
P: DLC

FRANCE. ARCHIVES DES COLONIES. Série A
Actes du pouvoir souverain, selections,
v. 8, 9, 12 FrAN
N: DLC 2 reels   2077
P: DLC

FRANCE. ARCHIVES DES COLONIES. Série B
Lettres envoyées, 1663-1774, 194 v. FrAN
N: CaOOA 194 reels   2078

FRANCE. ARCHIVES DES COLONIES. Série B
Lettres envoyées, selections, v. 27, 36-41,
55, 56, 58, 60, 62, 64, 65, 67, 69-71, 73, 75,
77, 79, 82, 84, 86, 88, 90, 92, 94, 96, 98,
100, 102, 104, 106, 108, 110, 116, 120, 122,
125, 127, 131, 149, 158 FrAN
N: DLC 36 reels   2079
P: DLC

FRANCE. ARCHIVES DES COLONIES. Série C-2
Correspondance générale, selections, v. 23, 25
FrAN
N: DLC 2 reels   2080
P: DLC

FRANCE. ARCHIVES DES COLONIES. Série
C-11-A
Correspondance générale, Canada, 1540-1784,
126 v. FrAN
N: CaOOA 131 reels   2081
DCO: DLC 80,774 sheets

FRANCE. ARCHIVES DES COLONIES. Série
C-11-E
Des Limites et Postes, 1685-1787, 16 v.
FrAN
N: CaOOA 16 reels   2082
DCO: DLC 5,880 sheets

FRANCE. ARCHIVES DES COLONIES.
Série C-11-G
Correspondance Raudot-Pontchartrain. Corres-
pondance générale du Domaine d'Occident et de
l'Isle Royale, 1663-1758, 12 v. FrAN
N: CaOOA 12 reels   2083

FRANCE. ARCHIVES DES COLONIES.
Série F-2-B
Correspondance générale, commerce aux
colonies, v. 8, 9 FrAN
DCO DLC 2373 sheets   2084

FRANCE. ARCHIVES DES COLONIES. Série F-3
Collection Moreau de Saint-Méry, selections,
1492-1792 FrAN
N: CaOOA 19 reels   2085

FRANCE. ARCHIVES DES COLONIES.
Série F-3
Collection Moreau de Saint-Méry, selections
FrAN
N: DLC 3 reels v. 241-243   2086
P: DLC
DCO: DLC 3815 sheets v. 13-16, 84, 156,
285

FRANCE. ARCHIVES DES COLONIES.
Série F-5-A
Missions et cultes religieux, 1658-1784, 3 v.
FrAN
N: CaOOA 3 reels   2087
DCO: DLC 915 sheets

FRANCE. ARCHIVES DES COLONIES.
Série F-5A-3 COMMUNAUTÉS ET ÉGLISE
DU CANADA
État présent des Curés et Missions du Canada
en 1688, 1 v. FrAN
N: CaQQCRH 1 reel   2088

FRANCE. ARMÉE. AMÉRIQUE DU NORD
Montcalm-Lévis papers (headquarters papers),
1754-1778 CaOOA
N: CaOOA 4 reels   2089

FRANCE. MINISTÈRE DE LA GUERRE
Selections, 1681-1799: Correspondance;
Correspondance, suppléments A 4, B 9;
mémoires historiques; reconnaissances;
papiers du comte de Guibert; Donation Perret;
Fonds Préval; Travail du Roi; Régiments
FrAN
DCO: DLC 27293 sheets   2090

GREAT BRITAIN. ADMIRALTY. Adm. 1
Admiral's despatches, 1745-1830 UKLPRO
N: CaOOA 29 reels   2091

GREAT BRITAIN. AUDIT OFFICE. A.O. 3
Compensation to American Loyalists and
other refugees, 1788-1837, v. 276 UKLPRO
N: CaOOA 1 reel   2092

GREAT BRITAIN. COLONIAL OFFICE
Selections re: Indians CaOOA UKLPRO
DCO: MnHi 1 box   2093

GREAT BRITAIN. COLONIAL OFFICE. C.O. 5
Board of Trade. Original correspondence,
1754-1757 (Canadian selections) UKLPRO
N: CaOOA 95 feet   2094

GREAT BRITAIN. COLONIAL OFFICE. C.O. 42
Canada. Original correspondence, 1763
UKLPRO; (Ottawa Transcripts) CaOOA
N: CaQQLa Selections 2 reels   2095

GREAT BRITAIN. COLONIAL OFFICE.C.O. 42
Canada. Original correspondence, 1763-1902,
891 v. UKLPRO
N: CaOOA 581 reels   2096

GREAT BRITAIN. COLONIAL OFFICE. C.O. 42
Canada. Original correspondence, 1787-1814
(selections) UKLPRO
DCO: DLC   2097

GREAT BRITAIN. COLONIAL OFFICE. C.O. 43
Entry books, 1763-1873 UKLPRO
N: CaOOA 32 reels   2098

GREAT BRITAIN. COLONIAL OFFICE. C.O. 44
Canada. Acts, 1764-1925, 219 v. UKLPRO
N: CaOOA 29 reels   2099

GREAT BRITAIN. COLONIAL OFFICE. C.O. 47
Canada. Miscellanea, selections, 1764-1925
UKLPRO
N: CaOOA 27 reels   2100

GREAT BRITAIN. COLONIAL OFFICE. C.O. 323
Colonies, general. Original correspondence,
Canadian selections, 1795-1859 UKLPRO
N: CaOOA 31 reels   2101

GREAT BRITAIN. COLONIAL OFFICE. C.O. 325
Colonies, general. Miscellanea, Canadian
selections, 1790-1831 UKLPRO
N: CaOOA 3 reels   2102

GREAT BRITAIN. COLONIAL OFFICE. C.O. 383
Register of Acts, 1782-1892, 93 v. UKLPRO
N: CaOOA Canadian material, 1782-1887
6 reels   2103

GREAT BRITAIN. COLONIAL OFFICE. C.O. 384
Emigration. North America, Canadian selec-
tions, 1817-1851 UKLPRO
N: CaOOA 48 reels   2104

GREAT BRITAIN. COLONIAL OFFICE. C.O. 385
Emigration. Entry books, Canadian selections,
1832-1836 UKLPRO
N: CaOOA 1 reel   2105

GREAT BRITAIN. COLONIAL OFFICE. C.O.807
Confidential prints. North America, 1871-1891,
84 v. UKLPRO
N: CaOOA 5 reels   2106

GREAT BRITAIN. FOREIGN OFFICE. F.O. 5
United States of America. General corres-
pondence, series II. UKLPRO
N: CaOOA Canadian selections 81 reels 2107

GREAT BRITAIN. FOREIGN OFFICE.F.O.27
France. General correspondence, calendars
UKLPRO
N: CaOOA 1 reel   2108

GREAT BRITAIN. FOREIGN OFFICE, F.O. 97
Supplements to the general correspondence,
Canadian selections, 1780-1905 UKLPRO
N: CaOOA 21 reels   2109

GREAT BRITIAN. NAVY BOARD
In-letters from Canada, 1814-1932; in-letters
from Halifax, 1790-1832 UKLPRO
N: CaOOA 10 reels   2110

GREAT BRITAIN. PUBLIC RECORD OFFICE
Admiralty List XVIII and supplement UKLPRO
N: CaOOA 90 feet   2111

GREAT BRITAIN. WAR OFFICE. W.O. 1
In-letters, 1732-1922 UKLPRO
N: CaOOA Canadian selections, 1792-1800,
1849-1855 8 reels   2112

GREAT BRITAIN. WAR OFFICE. W.O. 12
Muster books and pay lists, general,
1732-1878 , 13,305 v. UKLPRO
N: CaOOA De Meuron and De Watteville
regiments, 1795-1816, 1801-1816
10 reels   2113

GREAT BRITAIN. WAR OFFICE. W.O. 17
Monthly returns, 1759-1865, 2810 v.
UKLPRO
N: CaOOA Canadian items 46 reels   2114

GREAT BRITAIN. WAR OFFICE. W.O. 44
Ordnance office. In-letters, 1682-1873 UKLPRO
N: CaOOA Canadian selections, 1812-1855
84 reels   2115

GREAT BRITAIN. WAR OFFICE. W.O. 55
Ordnance office. Miscellanea, 1586-1890,
2267 v. UKLPRO
N: CaOOA Canadian material, 1757-1863
2 reels   2116

GREAT BRITAIN. WAR OFFICE. W.O. 73
Monthly returns: Distribution of the Army,
1859-1912, 92 v. UKLPRO
N: CaOOA Canadian extracts, 1859-1906
21 reels   2117

U.S. DEPT. OF STATE
Correspondence relating to the American-
Canadian-British treaty inaugurating free
trade, 1848-1854 DNA
N: CaNfSM 1 reel   2118

U.S. OFFICE OF NAVAL RESEARCH
Encyclopedia arctica, ed. Vilhjalmur
Stefansson, 1950-1951, 16 v. (typescript)
NhD-A
N: NhD 15 reels   2119

Church Records

CHURCH OF JESUS CHRIST OF LATTER-DAY
SAINTS. CANADA
Records: Canadian Missions, 1907-1951;
British Columbia, Canadian, Columbia,
Hamilton, Kitchener, Lake, London, Mani-
toba, Montreal, New Brunswick, North
Saskatchewan, Nova Scotia, Ottawa, Toronto,
Saskatchewan and South Saskatchewan Dis-
tricts; Bracebridge, Brantford, London,
Oshawa, Ottawa, Regina, Thunder Bay,
Toronto, Vancouver and Winnipeg Branches
USIC
N: USIGS 12 reels   2120

COLONIAL AND CONTINENTAL CHURCH
SOCIETY, 1823-
Minute books, annual report, and occasional
papers, 1824-1872 CaQMM Ibid.
N: CaOOA 10 reels   2121
P: CaOOA

COMPAGNIE DE ST. SULPICE, 1641-1792, 1802-
Correspondence and papers re: Canada,
1663-1708　FrPSS
N: CaOOA　2 reels　　　　　　　　　　2122

METHODIST CHURCH. SYNODS. ASSOCIATE
SYNOD OF NORTH AMERICA
Extracts from minutes re: work in Canada,
1826-1858　Ibid.
N: CaOTV　1/4 reel　　　　　　　　　2123

PRESBYTERIAN CHURCH IN CANADA
Ecclesiastical and missionary record,
1844-1861　Ibid.
N: CaOTV　2 reels　　　　　　　　　　2124
P: CaOTV

Personal Papers

ABERDEEN, ISHBEL, COUNTESS and later
MARCHIONESS of, 1857-1939
Journals, 1890-1899　CaOOA
N: CaOOA　4 reels　　　　　　　　　　2125

BERNOU, CLAUDE, abbé
Letters to Abbé Eusèbe Renaudot re: explora-
tion of New France　N. A. 7497　FrBN
N: CaOOA　1 reel　　　　　　　　　　2126

BLAKE, EDWARD, 1833-1912
Papers, 1867-1910　CaOTA
N: CaOTU　34 reels　　　　　　　　　2127
P: CaOOA

BORDEN, Sir ROBERT LAIRD, 1854-1937
Papers, 1893-1937　CaOOA
N: CaOOA　130 reels　　　　　　　　　2128

BOURLEMAQUE, FRANÇOIS CHARLES DE,
1716-1764
Papers, 1759-1764　CaOOA
N: CaOOA　2 reels　　　　　　　　　　2129

BROCK, Sir ISAAC, 1769-1812
Orderly book, 1805　MiD-B
N: MiD-B　1 reel　　　　　　　　　　2130
P: CaOOA

BUCKINGHAM AND CHANDOS, RICHARD
GRENVILLE, 3rd DUKE of, 1823-1889
Letters re: Fenians in Canada and the United
States, 1867-1868, 208 p.　Add. ms. 41860,
43742　UKLBM
N: CaOOA　1 reel　　　　　　　　　　2131

BUISSEAUX, SAMUEL SPIFAME, Sieur de,
Letters re: English activities in North America,
1613-1614　FrBN
N: CaOOA　25 feet　　　　　　　　　　2132

CABART DE VILLERMONT, ESPRIT, fl. 1652-
1707
Correspondence re: New France, 1668-1692
Fonds Français 22799-22802　FrBN
N: CaOOA　1 reel　　　　　　　　　　2133

CAMPBELL, Sir ALEXANDER, 1822-1892
In-letters, 1855-1892　CaOTA
N: CaOOA　8 reels　　　　　　　　　　2134

CARDWELL, EDWARD CARDWELL, VISCOUNT,
1813-1886
Papers re: Canada, 1864-1874
P. R. O. 30/48　UKLPRO
N: CaOOA　90 feet　　　　　　　　　　2135

CARNAVON, HENRY HOWARD MOLYNEUX
HERBERT, 4th EARL of, 1831-1890
Papers as Colonial Secretary re: Canada,
1874-1878　P. R. O. 30/6　UKLPRO
N: CaOOA　6 reels　　　　　　　　　　2136

CASGRAIN, HENRI RAYMOND, abbé, 1831-1904
Correspondence with Francis Parkman, 1866-
1891　MH
N: CaQQL-Ar　1 reel　　　　　　　　　2137

CASGRAIN, HENRI RAYMOND, abbé, 1831-1904
Correspondence with Pascal Poirier and
Placide Gaudet　priv.
N: CaNBSjU　　　　　　　　　　　　2138

DAFOE, JOHN WESLEY, 1866-1944
Correspondence with Sir Clifford Sifton, 1901-
1925　CaOOA
N: CaOOA　2 reels*　　　　　　　　　2139
P: CaMWU

DAFOE, JOHN WESLEY, 1866-1944
Papers, 1896-1943　CaMWU
N: CaOOA　11 reels　　　　　　　　　2140
P: CaMWU　CaOOA

DENYS DE BONAVENTURE FAMILY
Papiers, 1655-1787　priv.
N: CaOOA　45 feet　　　　　　　　　　2141

DERBY, EDWARD GEOFFREY STANLEY,
14th EARL of, 1799-1869
Papers, Canadian selections, 1822-1852　priv.
N: CaOOA　3 reels *　　　　　　　　　2142

DERBY, EDWARD HENRY STANLEY,
15th EARL of, 1826-1893
Papers, Canadian selections, 1879-1891　priv.
N: CaOOA　1 reel　　　　　　　　　　2143

DES BARRES, JOSEPH FREDERICK WALLET,
1721-1824
Papers, 1784-1829　CaOOA　UKLPRO　UKLBM
N: CaOOA　1 reel　　　　　　　　　　2144

ELGIN AND KINCARDINE, JAMES BRUCE,
8th EARL of, 1811-1863
Selected correspondence, 1846-1855　priv.
N: CaOOA　6 reels　　　　　　　　　　2145

ELLICE FAMILY
Papers, 1761-1880　UKE
N: CaOOA　19 reels　　　　　　　　　2146
P: CaOOA　CU

ELLICE FAMILY
Papers, 1820-1875　UKE
N: CLU　19 reels　　　　　　　　　　2147

ENYS, JOHN
Journals in U.S. and Canada, 1776-1788　priv.
N: NjP　　　　　　　　　　　　　　2148

ENYS, JOHN
Papers, Canadian selections, 1784-1787　priv.
N: CaOOA　2 reels　　　　　　　　　　2149

EYRE, Sir WILLIAM, 1805-1859
Papers, 1841-1859 (P.R.O.30/46)　UKLPRO
N: CaOOA　4 reels　　　　　　　　　　2150

GRANVILLE, GRANVILLE GEORGE LEVESON-
GOWER, 2nd EARL of, 1815-1891
Papers re: Canada, 1839-1887　UKLPRO
N: CaOOA　3 reels　　　　　　　　　　2151

GREY, ALBERT HENRY GEORGE GREY,
4th EARL of, 1851-1917
Correspondence, 1904-1911　CaOOA
N: CaOOA　7 reels　　　　　　　　　　2152

GREY, ALBERT HENRY GEORGE GREY,
4th EARL of, 1851-1917
Supplementary correspondence, 1902-1916
UKDrU
DCO: CaOOA　　　　　　　　　　　　2153

GRIFFIN, MARTIN J., 1847-1921
Diaries, 1905-1916　priv.
N: CaOOA　1 reel, extracts　　　　　　2154

HEAD, Sir EDMUND, 1805-1868
Letters to Sir George Cornewall Lewis, 1840,
1849-1861, 190 p.　UKAbN
N: CaOOA　　　　　　　　　　　　　2155

HUTTON, Sir EDWARD
Papers re: Canada, 1898-1920　UKLPRO;
(transcript) CaOOA
N: CaOOA　2 reels　transcripts　　　　2156

INNIS, HAROLD ADAMS, 1894-1952
A history of communications　(manuscript)
priv.
N: priv.　　　　　　　　　　　　　2157
P: NNC

JOHNSTON, ALEXANDER, 1867-1951
Papers, 1900-1947
N: CaOOA　5 reels *　　　　　　　　　2158

JOSEPH, ABRAHAM, ca. 1815-1886
Diaries, 1837-1849　priv.
N: CaOOA　3 reels　　　　　　　　　　2159
P: CaOOA

KEPPEL, AUGUSTUS KEPPEL, 1st VISCOUNT,
1725-1786
Order books, Dec., 1754- Apr., 1755
KEP/1　UKGwNM
N: CaOOA　15 feet　　　　　　　　　　2160

KIMBERLEY, JOHN WODEHOUSE, 1st EARL of,
1826-1902
Papers re: Canada, 1865-1883　priv.
N: CaOOA　5 reels　　　　　　　　　　2161

LAURIER, Sir WILFRED, 1841-1919
Papers, 1854-1919　CaOOA
N: CaOOA　210 reels　　　　　　　　　2162
P: CaOKQ

LESCARBOT, MARC
Contrat de mariage　FrAN
DCO: CaNBSjU　4 p.　　　　　　　　　2163

LEVISCONTE, HENRY, d. 1857
Diary, Mar.- July, 1834, Aug.- Oct., 1835　priv.
N: CaOTA　25 feet　　　　　　　　　　2164
P: CaOOA

M'CLINTOCK, Sir FRANCIS LEOPOLD, 1819-1907
Journal kept on H. M. S. Intrepid and Fox; other
papers, 1852-1854　IrNL
N: CaOOA　　　　　　　　　　　　　2165
P: NhD

MacDONALD, Sir JOHN ALEXANDER, 1815-1891
Letter books, 1-28 A, 1855-1891　CaOOA
N: CaOOA　18 reels　　　　　　　　　2166
P: CaOOA

MACKENZIE, ALEXANDER, 1822-1892
Correspondence, 1852-1892　CaOKQ
N: CaOOA　3 reels　　　　　　　　　　2167

MACKENZIE, WILLIAM LYON, 1795-1861
Correspondence, 1818-1861　MiD-B
N: ?　1 reel　　　　　　　　　　　　2168
P: CaOOA

MACKENZIE, WILLIAM LYON, 1795-1861
Letters from patriots in Canada and the U.S.,
1824-1840　MiD
N: MiD-B　　　　　　　　　　　　　2169

MacNAB, Sir ALLAN NAPIER, 1798-1862
Papers, 1815-1862　priv.
N: CaOOA　2 reels　　　　　　　　　　2170

MacNAB, Sir ALLAN NAPIER, 1798-1862
Papers, 1815-1862, 9 bundles　Albemarle
ms.　UKLPRO
N: CaOOA　45 feet　　　　　　　　　　2171

MEREDITH, EDMUND ALLEN, 1817-1898
Diaries, 1844-1898　priv.
N: CaOOA　5 reels　　　　　　　　　　2172
P: CaOOA

MILES, ROBERT SEABORN, 1795-1870
Journals of journey to Athabaska District at
Fort Wedderburn, 1818-1819, 160 p.　priv.
N: CaOOA　　　　　　　　　　　　　2173

MILNES, ROBERT SHORE, 1746-1837
Entry book, 1799-1805　CaOOA
N: CaOOA　40 feet　　　　　　　　　　2174

MINTO, G.J.M.K. ELLIOT, 4th EARL of,
1845-1914
Papers re: Canada, 1884-1907　priv.
N: CaOOA　4 reels　　　　　　　　　　2175
P: CaOOA

MONKTON, ROBERT
Papers, 1742-1779　CaOOA
N: CaOOA　5 reels　　　　　　　　　　2176

MURRAY, JAMES, 1721-1794
Letters, 1759-1760 (Ottawa Transcripts)
CaOOA
N: CaQQLa　1 reel　　　　　　　　　　2177

NARES, Sir GEORGE STRONG, 1831-1915
Papers re: Arctic Expedition, 1875-1885
priv.
N: CaOOA　2 reels　　　　　　　　　　2178

PEEL, Sir ROBERT, Bart., 1788-1850
Correspondence re: Canada, 1841-1845
Add. ms. 40429, 49467, 40468, 49489, 49490,
40510, 40513, 40522, 40526, 40444 UKLBM
N: CaOOA 65 feet   2179

POTIER, PIERRE, S. J., 1708-1781
Itineraries, 1743-1754; Huron-French vocabu-
lary, 1754-1755, 47 p. CaQMBM CaQMSM
DCO: PHarH   2180

RICHARD, Mgr. MARCEL
Correspondance avec Mgr. Rogers, 1868-1916
priv.
N: CaNBSjU   2181

RICHMOND AND LENNOX, CHARLES LENNOX,
4th DUKE of, 1764-1819
Accounts of his death from bite of a rabid fox,
1819, 55 p.   priv.
N: CaOOA   2182

RUSSELL, Lord JOHN RUSSELL, 1st EARL,
1792-1878
Papers re: Canada, 1838-1855
P.R.O. 30/22 UKLPRO
N: CaOOA 90 feet   2183

SAVAGE, HUGH
Suggestions for a Canadian National Flag, 1926,
79 p. (typescript) priv.
N: CaOOA 1 reel   2184

SCHOMBERG, ALEXANDER
Journal re: Quebec expedition, with notes by
Wolfe, 1759, 63 p.   priv.
DCO: CaNBSM   2185

TUPPER, Sir CHARLES HIBBERT, 1855-1927
Papers, 1878-1926 CaBVaU
N: CaOOA 4 reels   2186

VEYSEY, JOHN, pilot
Records re: St. Lawrence River, 1760-1806
UKLPRO
N: CaOOA 20 feet   2187

WATSON, Sir DAVID, 1871-1922
War Diaries, 1914-1918 priv.
N: CaOOA 45 feet   2188

WOLFE, JAMES, 1727-1759
Diary, May 10-Aug. 7, 1759, 22 ll. CaQMM
DCO: DLC NN   2189

WOLFE, JAMES, 1727-1759
Journals of Quebec expedition, May-Aug.,
1759; June-Aug., 1759 CaQMM CaQQCi
N: CaOOA 19 frames   2190

Collections

BRITISH MUSEUM
Manuscripts re: Canada   Add. ms. 21661,
21662, 21666, 21670, 21678, 21690 UKLBM
N: CaQQLa 4 reels   2191

CLAIRAMBAULT, PIERRE, 1651-1740, collector
Papers re: La Salle, 1676-1702
Clairambault 1016 FrBN
N: CaOOA 1 reel   2192

CONTRECOEUR, CLAUDE PIERRE PÉCAUDY,
Sieur de, 1706-1775
Papiers Contrecoeur, 1686-1767 CaQQA
Fonds Viger-Verreau, cartons 1-5, 11, 17,
Fonds Verreau, ms. 084   CaQQLaS
N: PHarH 4 reels*   2193
P: CaOOA

GIPSON, LAWRENCE HENRY, collector
Material re: British North America, 1748-1775
UKLPRO v.p.
N: PBL   2194
DCO: PBL

MARGRY, PIERRE, 1818-1894, collector
Margry transcriptions (translation), 6 v.
MiD-B
N: ? 3 reels   2195
P: ICU

MARGRY, PIERRE, 1818-1894, collector
Papers re: Canada, 1605-1860
Margry 9273, 9283, 9281 FrBN
N: CaOOA 3 reels   2196

SPAIN. ARCHIVO GENERAL DE INDIAS, Seville
Documents re: Cartier and Roberval, ca. 1541-
ca. 1573 SpSAGI
N: CaOOA 30 feet   2197

Institutions

COMPANY FOR THE PROPAGATION OF THE
GOSPEL IN NEW ENGLAND AND THE PARTS
ADJACENT IN AMERICA, London
Records of Canadian interest, 1661-1913
UKLGU
N: CaOOA 12 reels   2198

SOCIETY FOR THE PROPAGATION OF THE
GOSPEL IN FOREIGN PARTS
Records of Canadian mission, 1701-1889 Ibid.
N: CaOOA 102 reels   2199

WESLEYAN METHODIST MISSIONARY SOCIETY,
London
In-letters from Canadian missionaries, 1800-
1867, 1877-1893; minutes re: Canadian mission
Ibid.
N: CaOTV 25 reels   2200
P: CaOOA

Ships' Logs

With ships' logs are included journals, diaries,
and other records of voyages.

LA CAPRICIEUSE (Ship)
Journal, Mission to Canada, 1855, 105 p.
(typescript) CaOOA
N: CaOOA 1 reel   2201

GREAT BRITAIN. ADMIRALTY. Adm. 51-53
Selected logs: Confiance, 1815-1817; Newash,
1816-1817; Surprise, 1815-1818
UKLPRO
N: CaOOA 60 feet   2202

MARITIME PROVINCES,
also ACADIA

Government records

FRANCE. ARCHIVES DES COLONIES
Dépôt des fortifications des colonies, cartons
1 à 4, pièces, 24 à 253 choix de pièces et cartes
concernant l'Acadie et Louisbourg
FrAN
N: CaNBSjU   2203

FRANCE. ARCHIVES DES COLONIES
Instructions à l'intendant De Meulles, 10 mai,
1682, 13 p.   FrAN
N: CaNBSjU   2204

FRANCE. ARCHIVES DES COLONIES. Série
C-11-C
Correspondance générale, Terre Neuve, Île
Royale, Louisbourg, Île St. Jean, Îles de la
Madeleine, Île Madame, et Gaspé, 1661-1856,
16 v. FrAN
N: CaOOA 17 reels   2205

FRANCE. ARCHIVES DES COLONIES.
Série C-11-D
Correspondance générale, Acadie, 1603-1714,
10 v. FrAN
N: CaOOA 9 reels   2206

FRANCE. ARCHIVES DES COLONIES.
Série C-11-D
Correspondance générale, Acadie, v. 2, 10
FrAN
N: DLC 2 reels   2207
P: DLC MeBh-Ar

FRANCE. ARCHIVES DES COLONIES.
Série C-11-F
Documents communiqués à la Commission des
Pêcheries en 1876. 1698-1814, 5 v. FrAN
N: CaOOA 5 reels   2208

FRANCE. ARCHIVES DES COLONIES.
Série C-12
Adresse des Acadiens du Fort Cumberland,
23 avril, 1763; lettre de Dangeau, 19 oct. 1765,
concernant les Acadiens à Miquelon FrAN
N: CaNBSjU   2209

FRANCE. ARCHIVES DES COLONIES.
Série G-1
Recensements d'Acadie, 1671-1686 FrAN
N: CaNBSjU   2210

FRANCE. ARCHIVES DES COLONIES. Série G-1
Recensement de Plaisance, T.N., Île Saint-
Jean, Île Royale FrAN; (transcript) CaOOA
N: CaNBSjU transcript   2211

FRANCE. ARCHIVES DES COLONIES. Série G-1
Registres d'état civil, recensements, et divers
documents: Louisbourg, 1754-1758; Île Royale,
1715-1756 FrAN; (transcript) CaOOA
N: CaOOA transcript 1 reel   2212

FRANCE. ARCHIVES DES COLONIES. Série G-13
Notariat d'Acadie, étude Loppinot, 1687-1710
FrAN
N: CaNBSjU   2213

Personal Papers

CLARKSON, JOHN
Mission to move Negroes from Nova Scotia and
New Brunswick to Sierra Leone, Aug.,1791-
Mar.,1792 DHU
N: DHU 1 reel   2214

DEFRANEY, commissaire des classes
Correspondence re: Acadiens à Cherbourg,
1763-1768, 48 p. Cherbourg, Archives de
la Marine
N: CaNBSjU   2215

DE MEULLES, intendant
Journal en Acadie, 1685-1686 CaNSHD
N: CaNBSjU   2216

GAULIN, ANTOINE, abbé
Relation de la mission...dans le pays des
Mikmaks et en Acadie, vers 1720, 23 p. FrAN
N: CaNBSjU   2217

LEMOYNE, inspecteur
Rapport sur les Acadiens en France Archives
départementales de la Vienne, Poitiers
N: CaNBSjU   2218

SOUTHACK, CYPRIAN, of Boston, Mass.
Memorial re: fishing trade of Quebec and
Nova Scotia, 1713 C.O. 194 UKLPRO
DCO: DLC   2219

Collections

BORDEAUX. BIBLIOTHÈQUE MUNICIPALE
Recueil de pièces, lettres, mémoires re:
Acadiens, 1766-1774, 611 p. Ibid.
N: CaNBSjU   2220

ILLE ET VILAINE (Dept.), France. ARCHIVES
Certificats des missionaires concernant les
registres acadiens, 16 p. Ibid.
N: CaNBSjU   2221

MASSACHUSETTS. ARCHIVES
Papers re: Acadians deported to Massachusetts,
1755-1769 "Massachusetts Archives" v. 23-24
M-Ar
N: M-Ar 2 reels   2222
P: CaOOA

PARIS. BIBLIOTHÈQUE NATIONALE
Pièces concernant Franquelin; mémoire sur la
seigneurie de Richard Denys; lettre de Fronte-
nac Clairambault 819 FrBN
N: CaNBSjU   2223

Institutions

COMPAGNIE DE L'ÉVANGELINE
Minutes des assemblées, 1910-1928, 2 v. Ibid.
N: CaNBSjU   2224

NEWFOUNDLAND

Government Records

GREAT BRITAIN. ADMIRALTY. Adm. 1
In-letters re: Newfoundland   UKLPRO
N: CaOOA 8 reels
P: CaNfSM   2225

GREAT BRITAIN. COLONIAL OFFICE. C.O. 194
Newfoundland, correspondence, 1696-1922,
250 v.   UKLPRO
N: CaOOA 170 reels
P: CaNfSM   2226

GREAT BRITAIN. COLONIAL OFFICE. C.O. 195
Newfoundland. Entry books, 1623-1872,
23 v.   UKLPRO
N: CaOOA 7 reels   2227

GREAT BRITAIN. COLONIAL OFFICE. C.O. 197
Newfoundland. Sessional papers, 1825-1925,
194 v.   UKLPRO
N: CaOOA Executive Council minutes only,
1833-1855, 1860-1901 9 reels   2228

GREAT BRITAIN. COLONIAL OFFICE. C.O. 199
Newfoundland. Miscellanea, selections, 1677-
1855 UKLPRO
N: CaOOA 18 reels   2229

GREAT BRITAIN. ORDNANCE WORKS,
ST. JOHN'S, Newfoundland
Issues and receipts, 1790-1791, 58 items
MiU-C
N: CaNfSM   2230

Local Records

NEWFOUNDLAND
Port records from Twillingate and Fogo,
1833-1899, and Greenspond, 1839-1897
R.G. 16 CaOOA
N: CaOOA 2 reels   2231

Church Records

WESLYAN METHODIST MISSIONARY SOCIETY,
London
Conference minutes, Newfoundland, 1824-1855
Ibid.
N: CaOOA 1 reel
P: CaOTV   2232

Personal Papers

AMHERST, Sir WILLIAM, 1732-1781
Journals, 1758-1762 Amherst Papers, CaOOA
N: CaNfSM 1 reel   2233

BANKS, Sir JOSEPH, 1743-1820
Journal of a voyage to Newfoundland and
Labrador, 1766 Royal Geographical
Institute of Australia, South Australian
Branch, Adelaide
N: CaOOA 25 feet
P: CaNfSM   2234

BANKS, Sir JOSEPH, 1743-1820
Papers, selections re: Newfoundland,   C-S
N: CaNfSM 1 reel   2235

BORDEN, Sir ROBERT LAIRD
Papers re: Newfoundland, 1911-1920 CaOOA
N: CaNfSM   2236

BOWELL, Sir MACKENZIE, 1823-1917
Papers re: Newfoundland, 1891-1893 CaOOA
N: CaNfSM   2237

CALVERT FAMILY
Avalon items, 1621-1756
Calvert papers MdHi
N: CaNfSM 1 reel   2238

CAMPBELL, Sir ALEXANDER, 1822-1892
Newfoundland Bait bill correspondence, 1887
CaOTA
N: CaNfSM 1 reel   2239

COCHRANE, Sir THOMAS JOHN, 1789-1872
Papers re: Newfoundland, 1804-1843 UKE
N: CaOOA 8 reels   2240

CURTIS, R.
Narrative of a voyage to St. John's,
Newfoundland, 1775 CaOOA
N: CaNfSM   2241

DOUGLAS, Sir HOWARD, 1776-1861
Letter books, 1824-1839 CaOOA
N: CaNBSM 1 reel   2242

DUCKWORTH, Sir JOHN THOMAS, 1st Bart.,
1748-1817
Letterbooks re: Newfoundland,
1810-1813 CtY
N: CaNfSM 1 reel   2243

DUFF, ROBERT, d. 1827
Papers re: Newfoundland, 1775-1784 UKGwNM
N: CaOOA 20 feet   2244

EDWARDS, RICHARD, 1715-1795
Letter books while governor of Newfoundland,
1779-1782 CaOT
N: CaNfSM 2 reels   2245

FOSTER, Sir GEORGE
Papers re: Labrador boundary, 1908-1912
CaOOA
N: CaNfSM   2246

GRAVES, THOMAS GRAVES, 1st BARON, 1725-
1802
Papers re: Newfoundland, 1761-1767 GRV/103-
107 UKGwNM
N: CaOOA 25 feet   2247

IBERVILLE, PIERRE LE MOYNE, Sieur d',
1661-1706
Letter re: Newfoundland, 1697, 14 p. CaQQA;
(transcript) CaOOA
N: CaNfSM transcript   2248

LAURIER, Sir WILFRED, 1841-1919
Papers re: Newfoundland, 1896-1911 CaOOA
N: CaNfSM   2249

LITTLE, PHILIP FRANCIS, 1824-1897
Papers, 1840-1890 priv.
N: CaNfSM 1 reel   2250

LITTLE, PHILIP FRANCIS, 1824-1897
Papers, 1840-1858 CaNfSM
N: CaOOA 35 feet   2251

POLE, Sir CHARLES MORICE, 1757-1830
Papers re: Newfoundland, 1795-1807
UKGwNM
N: CaOOA 90 feet   2252

REEVES, JOHN, 1752-1829
Manuscript history of Newfoundland   priv.
N: CaOOA
P: CaNfSM   2253

RICHARDSON, WILLIAM
Journal of a visit to Labrador, 1771 CaOOA
N: CaNfSM   2254

SHELBURNE, WILLIAM PETTY FITZMAURICE,
2nd EARL of, 1737-1805 (later 1st MARQUIS
of LANSDOWNE)
Papers re: Newfoundland, 1715/6-1783 MiU-C
N: CaNfSM 1 reel*   2255

STRACHAN, JOHN, Bp., 1778-1867
Papers re: Newfoundland, 4 items CaOTA
N: CaNfSM   2256

THOMPSON, Sir JOHN SPARROW DAVID,
1844-1894
Papers re: Newfoundland, 1888-1893 CaOOA
N: CaNfSM   2257

Business Papers

BIRD, JOSEPH, trader
Correspondence and papers re: Newfoundland

and Labrador trade, 1824-1844, Chancery 108,
v. 69-71 UKLPRO
N: CaOOA 3 reels   2258

JOB BROS. AND CO., St. John's, Newfoundland
Notebook on cod fishing, 1855-1882 CaNfSM
N: CaOOA 1 reel   2259

NEWMAN, HUNT AND COMPANY, London, and
predecessor organizations, 1774-
Business books and papers, 1774-1899 Ibid.
N: CaOOA 40 reels   2260

Collections

HERRNHUT, Germany. UNITÄT-VORSTEHER
COLLEGIUM. ARCHIV
Reise-journal des englischen Capitain Goss,
1753; Brief von Johann Beck in Deutsch,
Englisch und Grönländischer Sprache, 1758;
Correspondenz, 1752-1773; Protokolle des
Hausconferenz zu Nain, 1774-1781; zu Okak,
1776-1781; Wetterbeobachtungen in Labrador,
1771-1781 Ibid.
DCO: DLC 2411 sheets   2261

MASSACHUSETTS. ARCHIVES
Material re: Newfoundland, 1653-1771
M-Ar
N: CaNfSM   2262

NEW YORK HISTORICAL SOCIETY
Newfoundland material: stores expended at
Placentia, 1727; agreement between Governor
Edwards and American mariners, 1781 NHi
N: CaNfSM   2263

REEVES, JOHN, 1752-1829, collector
Five representations by the Board of Trade
re: Newfoundland fisheries, 1718-1790 Add.
ms. 38396 Liverpool papers, v. 207 UKLBM
N: CaOOA 20 feet   2264

Ships' Logs

VIPER (H. M. Ship)
Log, 1783 UKGwNM
N: CaNfSM   2265

NOVA SCOTIA

Government Records

FRANCE. ARCHIVES DES COLONIES. Série
C-11-B
Correspondance générale, Île Royale, 1712-
1762, 38 v. FrAN
N: CaOOA 39 reels
P: CaOOA   2266

FRANCE. ARCHIVES DES COLONIES. Série G-3
Records of notaries of Île-Royale, 1728-1758
FrAN
N: CaOOA 14 reels   2267

GREAT BRITAIN. COLONIAL OFFICE. C.O. 217
Nova Scotia and Cape Breton. Correspondence,
1702-1867, 242 v. UKLPRO
N: CaOOA 89 reels   2268

GREAT BRITAIN. COLONIAL OFFICE. C.O. 217
Nova Scotia, original correspondence,
selections, re: fisheries and boundaries,
1718, 1719, 1798 UKLPRO
DCO: DLC   2269

GREAT BRITAIN. COLONIAL OFFICE. C.O. 218
Nova Scotia and Cape Breton. Entry books,
1710-1867, 37 v. UKLPRO
N: CaOOA 8 reels   2270

GREAT BRITAIN. COLONIAL OFFICE. C.O. 219
Nova Scotia. Acts, 1749-1899; Cape Breton.
Acts, 1785-1809, 81 v. UKLPRO
N: CaOOA 7 reels Nova Scotia only to 1819
                                                      2271

GREAT BRITAIN. COLONIAL OFFICE. C.O. 221
Nova Scotia and Cape Breton. Miscellanea:

Memorials of Commissioners on the Boundaries
of Acadia, "Blue Books" UKLPRO
N: CaOOA 10 reels   2272

HALIFAX, N.S. DOCKYARD
Correspondence with Commander in Chief and
Navy Board, 1783-1848 CaOOA UKGwNM
N: CaOOA 16 reels   2273

Town Records

ANNAPOLIS ROYAL, N.S.
Township books,1790-1853 (also Wilmot, 1749-
1894; Winsor, 1799-1845) CaOOA
N: CaOOA 1 reel   2274
P: CaNS-Ar

Church Records

ANNAPOLIS ROYAL, N.S. ST. JEAN BAPTISTE
PAROISSE
Registre de baptèmes, mariages, et sépultures,
1727-1755 (transcript) CaOOA
N: CaOOA 1 reel   2275

BEAUBASSIN, N.S.
Parish register, 1712-1723, 1732-1735, 1740-
1748 (transcript by the Public Archives of
Canada from the original in Bureau de l'État-
Civil, Mairie de La Rochelle, La Rochelle,
France, 1956)
N: CaOOA   2276

CATHOLIC CHURCH. NOVA SCOTIA
Registre des actes de baptême, mariage, et
sépulture fait en la Nouvelle Écosse ou Acadie,
1768-1796 Ibid.
DCO: CaNBSjU 186 p.   2277

FRIENDS, SOCIETY OF. NOVA SCOTIA
MEETING
Men's minutes, 1787-1798
N: PSC-F   2278
P: PSC-F

GRAND PRÉ, N.S. ST. CHARLES DES MINES
Parish register, 1727-1755 (transcript) CaOOA
N: CaOOA 1 reel   2279

LUNENBERG, N.S. ZION LUTHERAN CHURCH
Records, 1817-1831 [in German] PPLT
N: USIGS 1 reel   2280

WESLYAN METHODIST MISSIONARY SOCIETY,
London
Conference minutes, Nova Scotia, 1823-1856
Ibid.
N: CaOOA 1 reel   2281
P: CaOTV

Personal Papers

NEWTON, HIBBERT, Collector of Customs for
Nova Scotia
Journal, 1722 MH
N: MHi   2282

PERKINS, SIMEON, 1735-1812
Diary, 1777-1812 Town Archives, Liverpool,
N.S.
N: CaOOA 2 reels   2283
P: CaOOA

PICHON, THOMAS
Papiers CaNSHP Bibliothèque de Vire, France
N: CaNBSjU   2284

NEW BRUNSWICK

Census

NEW BRUNSWICK
Census, 1851, 1861 CaOOA
N: CaOOA 14 reels   2285

Government Records

GREAT BRITAIN. ARMY. KING'S NEW
BRUNSWICK REGIMENT
Returns, 1793-1801 [unk.]
DCO: CaNBSM 75 p.   2286

GREAT BRITAIN. ARMY. 104th REGIMENT
Pay lists, 1812-1814 UKLPRO
N: CaNBSM 4 reels   2287
DCO: CaNBSM 66 p.

GREAT BRITAIN. COLONIAL OFFICE
Material re: St. John's river surveys, 1762,
1765 UKLPRO
N: CaNBSjU   2288

GREAT BRITAIN. COLONIAL OFFICE. C.O.188
New Brunswick. Original correspondence, 1784-
1869, 147 v. UKLPRO
N: CaOOA 67 reels   2289
P: CaNBSM

GREAT BRITAIN. COLONIAL OFFICE. C.O.188
New Brunswick. Original correspondence,
selections re: St. Croix boundary, 1798
UKLPRO
DCO: DLC   2290

GREAT BRITAIN. COLONIAL OFFICE. C.O.190
New Brunswick. Acts, 1786-1897, 18 v.
UKLPRO
N: CaOOA 16 reels   2291

GREAT BRITAIN. COLONIAL OFFICE. C.O.192
New Brunswick. Government gazettes, 1842-
1923, 26 v. UKLPRO
N: CaOOA 1848-1868, v. 1-10, 10 reels   2292

GREAT BRITAIN. COLONIAL OFFICE. C.O. 193
New Brunswick. Miscellanea, selections, 1786-
1867 UKLPRO
N: CaOOA 10 reels   2293

NEW BRUNSWICK
Shipping registers of Saint John, Chatham,
Dorchester, Moncton, Richibucto, Sackville,
St. Andrews, Miramichi, 1826-1925 CaOOA
N: CaOOA 24 reels   2294
P: CaNBSM

NEW BRUNSWICK. LIEUTENANT GOVERNOR
Despatches received from the Secretary of
State and other persons, 1784-1865 Ibid.
N: CaOOA 25 reels   2295
P: CaNBFU

NEW BRUNSWICK. LIEUTENANT GOVERNOR
Despatches sent, 1754-1854 CaOOA
N: CaOOA 12 reels   2296
P: CaNBFU

County Records

YORK Co., N.B.
Records, 1855-1868 CaNBFU
N: Photogrammetry Branch, Dept. of Lands
and Mines, N.B.   2297
P: CaNBFU

City Records

ST. JOHN, N.B.
Council minutes, 1790-1839 Ibid.
N: CaNBSM 58 filmstrips   2298

Church Records

ST. ANDREWS, N.B. PRESBYTERIAN CHURCH
Record book, 1834-1951 Ibid.
N: CaOOA 1 reel   2299

STE. ANNE DE RISTIGOUCHE ET CARLETON, N.B.
PAROISSE (Catholique)
Ancien registre, 1759-1795 Ibid.
DCO: CaNBSjU 160 p.   2300

WESLYAN METHODIST MISSIONARY SOCIETY,
London
Conference minutes, New Brunswick, 1826-
1855 Ibid.
N: CaOOA 1 reel   2301
P: CaOTV

Personal Papers

BROWN, JAMES, school inspector
Journal, 1844-1870, 1315 p.   priv.
DCO: CaNBSM   2302

CHIPMAN, WARD, 1754-1824
Letter book, 1811-1817 InU
N: CaNBSM 1 reel   2303

CHIPMAN FAMILY
Papers, 1767-1840 CaNBSM CaOOA
N: CaOOA 12 reels   2304
P: CaNBSM 5 reels

OWEN, WILLIAM, of Campobello, N.B.
Narrative of travels, 1761-1771, 246 p. NN
DCO: NN   2305

PERLEY, M.H., immigration agent,
of St. John, N.B.
Letter book, 1846 priv.
N: CaNBSM 1 reel   2306

ROBICHAUD, DOMITIEN
Lettres adressées à [lui] par divers personnages,
28 p. priv.
N: CaNBSjU   2307

WINSLOW, EDWARD, ca. 1746-1815
Papers, 1775-1815 CaNBSM
N: CaOOA 7 reels   2308

WINSLOW FAMILY
Papers CaNBFU
N: CaNBSM 8 reels   2309
P: CaOOA

Collections

MICHIGAN. UNIVERSITY. WILLIAM L.
CLEMENTS LIBRARY
New Brunswick material MiU-C
N: CaNBSM 2 reels*   2310

PRINCE EDWARD ISLAND

Census

FRANCE. ARCHIVES DES COLONIES. Série G 1
Recensements de l'Isle Saint Jean, 1728-1758,
sauf 1734 FrAN
N: CaNBSjU   2311

Government Records

GREAT BRITAIN. COLONIAL OFFICE. C.O. 226
Prince Edward Island, correspondence, 1769-
1872, 12 v. UKLPRO
N: CaOOA 3 reels   2312

GREAT BRITAIN. COLONIAL OFFICE. C.O. 227
Prince Edward Island. Entry books, 1769-1872,
12 v. UKLPRO
N: CaOOA 3 reels   2313

GREAT BRITAIN. COLONIAL OFFICE. C.O. 228
Prince Edward Island. Acts, 1770-1888, 31 v.
UKLPRO
N: CaOOA 7 reels (1770-1864)   2314

GREAT BRITAIN. COLONIAL OFFICE. C.O. 229
Prince Edward Island. Sessional Papers,
1770-1858 UKLPRO
N: CaOOA 8 reels   2315

GREAT BRITAIN. COLONIAL OFFICE. C.O.230
Prince Edward Island. Government gazettes,
1832-1925, 20 v. UKLPRO

N: CaOOA 1832-1875 v. 1-9 9 reels   2316

GREAT BRITAIN. COLONIAL OFFICE. C.O. 231
Prince Edward Island. Miscellanea, 1807-1871,
54 v. UKLPRO
N: CaOOA 11 reels   2317

Church Records

SAINT ANTOINE DE CASCUMPEQUE, P.E.I.
Parish register, 1839-1868 Ibid.
N: CaOOA 25 feet   2318

TIGNISH PARISH (Catholic), Tignish, P.E.I.
Marriage register, 1844-1869 Ibid.
N: CaOOA 25 feet   2319

QUEBEC

Census

CANADA (United Province, 1841-1867)
Canada East. Census, 1842, 1851, 1861
CaOOA
N: CaOOA 156 reels   2320
P: CaOOA

LOWER CANADA (1791-1841)
Census, 1825, 1831 CaOOA
N: CaOOA 8 reels   2321
P: CaOOA

Government Records

LOWER CANADA (1791-1841). EXECUTIVE
COUNCIL. LAND COMMITTEE
Minute books, 1787-1835, 9 v. CaOOA
DCO: CaQQA 8 v.   2322

LOWER CANADA (1791-1841). SURVEYOR
GENERAL
Book of reference for Seigneuries and
Townships, 1794 CaOOA
DCO: CaQQA   2323

QUEBEC (Province, 1763-1791). EXECUTIVE
COUNCIL
Minutes, 1776-1791 CaOOA
N: CaOOA 5 reels   2324

QUEBEC (Province, 1763-1791). GOVERNOR
GENERAL
Warrants and land grants, 1761-1767, 1 v.
CaOOA
DCO: CaQQA   2325

QUEBEC (Province, 1763-1791). LEGISLATIVE
COUNCIL
Minutes, 1764-1791 CaOOA
N: CaOOA 2 reels   2326

Church Records

HULL, Quebec. ST. JAMES CHURCH
Register, 1831-1853 Ibid.
N: CaOOA 1 reel   2327

MONTREAL (Archdiocese)
Selections, avec papiers de Mgr. de Mazainod
Ibid.
N: CaOOSJ   2328

QUEBEC (Diocese, Catholic)
Lettres des missionaires de l'I.P.E.
à l'évêque de Québec CaQQA
N: CaNBSjU   2329

QUEBEC (Diocese, Catholic). BISHOPS
Mandements, 1762-1833 CaQQLa
N: CaOOA 1 reel   2330

Personal Papers

BELCOURT, GEORGES ANTOINE, 1803-1874

Papers, 1832-1857 Archepiscopal Archives,
Quebec
N: MnHi 2 reels   2331

CHADWICK, JOSEPH
Journal...survey...Penobscot to Quebec,
1764, 17 p. UKLPRO
DCO: MiU-C   2332

CULL, HENRY, 1753-1833
Papers re: Eastern Townships, 1796-1824
CaOOA
N: CaOOA 50 feet   2333

FROBISHER, JOHN, 1740-1810
Letters, 1787-1788, 19 p. CaQMM
DCO: MnHi   2334

LE LACHEUR, WILLIAM, sea captain, Quebec
Letter book, 1786-1792 (typescript) priv.
N: CaOOA 15 feet   2335

MacDONALD, JOHN, of Garth
Autobiography, 1791-1816 CaQMM
N: CaQMM 1 reel   2336

MacDONELL, JOHN, 1768-1850
Journal, 1793-1795 CaQMM
N: CaQMM 1 reel   2337
DCO: MnHi 1 box

McLEOD, ARCHIBALD NORMAN
Diary, 1800-1801 CaQMM
DCO: MnHi 1 box   2338

POTIER, PIERRE, S. J., 1708-1781
Diary and "gazette," 1743-1750 CaQMSM
N: CaOOA 10 feet   2339

SMITH, WILLIAM, 1728-1793
Diary, 1784-1787 CaQQA
N: CaOOA 40 feet   2340

Business Papers

ANGUS, R. B.
Letter books as Manager of the Bank of Montreal, 1875-1879; as Director of the C.P.R.,
1881-1902 priv.
N: CaOOA 3 reels*   2341

BANK OF BRITISH NORTH AMERICA, 1836-1918
Minute books, 1836-1916 Bank of Montreal
N: Bank of Montreal 14 reels*   2342
P: CaOOA

BANK OF MONTREAL
Resolve books, 1817-1925; minute books,
1836-1916; letter books, 1869-1891 Ibid.
N: Ibid. 16 reels *   2343
P: CaOOA

[A GATINEAU RIVER LUMBERMAN]
Diary and notebook, 1859-1860, 2 v., 415 p.
priv.
N: CaOOA 20 feet   2344
P: CaOOA

McGILL (J. and A.) AND COMPANY, Montreal
Letter book, 1805-1807 CaQMM
DCO: MnHi 1 box   2345

MERCHANTS BANK OF CANADA
Minute books, 1864-1924 Bank of Montreal
N: Bank of Montreal 4 reels *   2346
P: CaOOA

MOLSONS BANK, 1855-1925
Minute books, 1869-1924 Bank of Montreal
N: Bank of Montreal   2347
P: CaOOA 4 reels *

Collections

BROME COUNTY HISTORICAL SOCIETY,
Knowlton, Quebec
Collections, 1774-1903 Ibid.
N: CaOOA   2348
P: Ibid.

VIGER, JACQUES, 1787-1858, collector
Mon Saberdache [my haversack, material of

historical interest], 1839-1858 CaQQLaA
N: CaQQLaA 8 reels   2349
P: CaNBFU CaOOA CaQMM CaQQA

Institutions

BEAVER CLUB, Montreal
Minutes, 1807-1827 CaQMM
DCO: MnHi 1 box   2350

ROYAL INSTITUTION FOR THE ADVANCEMENT
OF LEARNING, Montreal
Letter books and miscellaneous documents,
1820-1855 CaQMM
N: CaQMM 8 reels   2351
P: CaOOA CaQQA

SEMINAIRE DE QUÉBEC
Archives, chapitres 1-60, 1688-   CaQQLa-Ar
N: CaQQLa-Ar 1 reel   2352

SEMINAIRE DE QUÉBEC
Fonds Verreau, cartons 1-21 CaQQLa-Ar
N: CaQQLa-Ar 8 reels   2353
P: CaQQLa-Ar

SEMINAIRE DE QUÉBEC
Letters from Intendants, M-Z, 1685-
CaQQLa-Ar
N: CaQQLa 17 reels plus   2354

SEMINAIRE DE QUÉBEC
Livre de comptes, 1674-1768 CaQQLa-Ar
N: CaQQLa 3 reels   2355
P: CaQQLa

SOEURS GRISES, Montréal
Selections Ibid.
N: CaOOSJ   2356

ONTARIO

Census

CANADA (United Province, 1841-1867)
Canada West. Census, 1842, 1851, 1861
CaOOA
N: CaOOA 152 reels   2357
P: CaOOA

Provincial Records

GREAT BRITAIN. COLONIAL OFFICE
Despatches to the Lieutenant Governors of
Upper Canada, 1784-1868 CaOOA
N: CaOOA 35 reels   2358
P: CaOTA

ONTARIO. PROVINCIAL SECRETARY'S DEPT.
Index to land patents, 1790-1850, arranged
by townships CaOTA
N: CaOTA 4 reels   2359
P: CaOTA

UPPER CANADA (1791-1841)
State Papers, 1792-1840
N: CaOOA 17 reels   2360
P: CaOTA

UPPER CANADA (1791-1841). EXECUTIVE
COUNCIL
Minutes (state papers and land records),
1792-1867 CaOOA
N: CaOOA 28 reels   2361
P: CaOTA

UPPER CANADA (1791-1841). GENERAL BOARD
OF EDUCATION
Minutes, 1823-1833 CaOTU
DCO: CaOTA 169 p.   2362

District and County Records

BRANT Co., Ont.
General registers, 1866-1893; land grants, 1830-
1867; index to wills, 1830-1917 Ibid.
N: USIGS 3 reels   2363
P: CaOTA

BRUCE Co., Ont.
General registers, 1842-1880; wills, 1855-1884
Ibid.
N: USIGS 3 reels 2364
P: CaOTA

CAMDEN GORE DISTRICT, Ont.
Deeds, 1847-1860 Ibid.
N: USIGS 1 reel 2365
P: CaOTA

CHATHAM GORE DISTRICT, Ont.
Deeds, 1847-1860 Ibid.
N: USIGS 2 reels 2366
P: CaOTA

ELGIN Co., Ont.
Deeds, 1801-1852; index of surveys, 1876;
patent returns, 1900; wills and assignments,
1866-1879 Ibid.
N: USIGS 11 reels 2367
P: CaOTA

ESSEX Co., Ont.
Deeds, 1796-1861; deed index, 1796-1880;
patent returns, 1797-1867; registrations index,
from 1882; wills, 1864-1877 Ibid.
N: USIGS 12 reels 2368
P: CaOTA

GREY Co., Ont.
General registers, powers of attorney,
indentures, n.d. (North Riding); general
registers, 1862-1889 (South Riding); wills,
1862-1885 Ibid.
N: USIGS 4 reels 2369
P: CaOTA

HALDIMAND Co., Ont.
Deeds, 1840-1846; general register, 1800-
1883 Ibid.
N: USIGS 2 reels 2370
P: CaOTA

HALTON Co., Ont.
Deeds, 1803-1847; general registers, 1866-
1881; wills, n.d. Ibid.
N: USIGS 15 reels 2371
P: CaOTA

HURON Co., Ont.
Abstract index of surveys, 1857-1958; copies
of wills, 1854-1862; deeds, 1835-1847, 1855-
1866; wills and general registers, 1854-1881
Ibid.
N: USIGS 14 reels 2372
P: CaOTA

LINCOLN Co., Ont.
Commissioners' books, v. 1-2, deeds and
conveyances, 1817-1828; deeds, v. F (Lincoln
and Welland Cos.), 1846-1856; deeds: (Lincoln
and Haldimand), 1796-1807, 1815-1840, (Lincoln),
1840-1846; wills, 1866-1882, index only, ca.
1829-1917 Ibid.
N: USIGS 24 reels 2373
P: CaOTA

MIDDLESEX Co., Ont.
Court records, 1858-1861; deeds, 1801-1848,
(Western Part), 1801-1846; Oath of Allegiance,
ministers, 1847-1856; procedure book, 4th Division Ct., 1881-1885; surveys of townships, ca.
1855-1890; will registers, 1863-1900, early to
1904 Ibid.
N: USIGS 33 reels 2374
P: CaOTA

NEWCASTLE DISTRICT, Upper Canada
(now Ontario)
Assessment rolls, arranged by townships,
covering Northumberland, Durham, and
Peterborough counties, 1820-1870 CaOTA
N: CaOTA 18 reels 2375

NORFOLK Co., Ont.
Deeds, 1797-1840; patents granted before 1876;
wills, v. 1, 1865-1883 Ibid.
N: USIGS 6 reels 2376
P: CaOTA

OXFORD Co., Ont.
Deeds, 1800-1847; vital records, 1869-1873;
wills, 1866-1875 Ibid.
N: USIGS 17 reels 2377
P: CaOTA

SIMCOE Co., Ont.
Deeds, 1827-1847; index of surveys, 1957
Ibid.
N: USIGS 11 reels 2378
P: CaOTA

WATERLOO Co., Ont.
Deeds, 1798-1841, 1840-1853; general register,
wills, 1859-1876; guardianship grants, 1859-1920;
marriage returns, 1859-1869; naturalization of
aliens, 1853-1872 Ibid.
N: USIGS 14 reels 2379
P: CaOTA

WELLINGTON Co., Ont.
Deeds, 1840-1847; patent grants before 1875;
wills, powers of attorney, indentures, 1862-1879
(North); wills, powers of attorney, indentures,
1866-1876 (South) Ibid.
N: USIGS 9 reels 2380
P: CaOTA

WENTWORTH Co., Ont.
Index of surveys, 1797-1815; index to general
registers, wills (transcripts); patent grants,
1796-1847; wills, 1866-1881 Ibid.
N: USIGS 6 reels 2381
P: CaOTA

YORK Co., Ont.
Deeds, 1797-1847; wills, power of attorney,
1818-1889, 1847-1879 Ibid.
N: USIGS 7 reels 2382
P: CaOTA

Local Records

ACTON, Ont.
Deeds, 1874-1881 Ibid.
N: USIGS 2 reels 2383
P: CaOTA

ADELAIDE TOWNSHIP, Ont.
Assessment rolls, 1862-1863; council minutes,
1850-1911; deeds, 1847-1900; school census,
1896-1897 Ibid.
N: USIGS 22 reels 2384
P: CaOTA

ADJALA TOWNSHIP, Ont.
Deeds, 1847-1877 Ibid.
N: USIGS 8 reels 2385
P: CaOTA

ALDBOROUGH TOWNSHIP, Ont.
Assessment and collector rolls, 1859-1899;
council minutes, 1850-1900; deeds, 1847-1875
Ibid.
N: USIGS 17 reels 2386
P: CaOTA

AILSA CRAIG, Ont.
Deeds, 1861-1867, 1875-1906 Ibid.
N: USIGS 5 reels 2387
P: CaOTA

ALBEMARLE TOWNSHIP, Ont.
Deeds, 1859-1881 Ibid.
N: USIGS 3 reels 2388
P: CaOTA

ALBION TOWNSHIP, Ont.
Deeds, 1821-1876 Ibid.
N: USIGS 9 reels 2389
P: CaOTA

ALLANBURGH, Ont.
Abstract index of surveys, 1797-1957 Ibid.
N: USIGS 1 reel 2390
P: CaOTA

ALLISTON, Ont.
Deeds, 1875-1881 Ibid.
N: USIGS 5 reels 2391
P: CaOTA

ALVINSTON, Ont.
Council minutes, 1881-1899 Ibid.
N: USIGS 1 reel 2392
P: CaOTA

AMABEL TOWNSHIP, Ont.
Deeds, 1857-1877 Ibid.
N: USIGS 3 reels 2393
P: CaOTA

AMARANTH TOWNSHIP, Ont.
Deeds, 1847-1876 Ibid.
N: USIGS 7 reels 2394
P: CaOTA

AMHERSTBURG, Ont.
Assessment rolls, 1870-1883; assessment and
collector rolls, 1853-1856, 1860-1899; council
minutes, 1878-1900; deeds, 1853-1878; deed
index, from 1882 Ibid.
N: USIGS 14 reels 2395
P: CaOTA

ANCASTER TOWNSHIP, Ont.
Assessment and collector rolls, 1867-1899;
deeds, 1816-1829, 1847-1876 Ibid.
N: USIGS 14 reels 2396
P: CaOTA

ANDERDON TOWNSHIP, Ont.
Assessment rolls, 1870-1899; collector rolls,
1883-1890; council minutes, 1894-1899; deeds,
1847-1876 Ibid.
N: USIGS 8 reels 2397
P: CaOTA

ARKONA, Ont.
Deeds, 1855-1888 Ibid.
N: USIGS 2 reels 2398
P: CaOTA

ARRAN TOWNSHIP, Ont.
Deeds, 1855-1877 Ibid.
N: USIGS 5 reels 2399
P: CaOTA

ARTEMESIA TOWNSHIP, Ont.
Deeds, 1852-1875 Ibid.
N: USIGS 7 reels 2400
P: CaOTA

ARTHUR, Ont.
Deeds, 1872-1876 Ibid.
N: USIGS 1 reel 2401
P: CaOTA

ARTHUR TOWNSHIP, Ont.
Deeds, 1847-1876 Ibid.
N: USIGS 11 reels 2402
P: CaOTA

ASHFIELD TOWNSHIP, Ont.
Deeds, 1847-1876 Ibid.
N: USIGS 8 reels 2403
P: CaOTA

AURORA, Ont.
Deeds, 1863-1877 Ibid.
N: USIGS 4 reels 2404
P: CaOTA

AYLMER, Ont.
Assessment and collector rolls, 1872-1899;
council minutes, 1879-1900; deeds, 1872-1877
Ibid.
N: USIGS 9 reels 2405
P: CaOTA

BALAKLAVA, Ont.
Index of surveys, 1868-1957 Ibid.
N: USIGS 1 reel 2406
P: CaOTA

BARRIE, Ont.
Deeds, 1854-1876 Ibid.
N: USIGS 15 reels 2407
P: CaOTA

BARTON TOWNSHIP, Ont.
Deeds, 1816-1829, 1847-1877 Ibid.
N: USIGS 13 reels 2408
P: CaOTA

BAYFIELD, Ont.
Deeds, 1851-1883 Ibid.
N: USIGS 3 reels 2409
P: CaOTA

BAYHAM TOWNSHIP, Ont.
Council minutes, 1850-1901; deeds, 1847-1876
Ibid.
N: USIGS 17 reels 2410
P: CaOTA

BEAMSVILLE, Ont.
Council minutes, 1879-1890; deeds, 1855-1865
Ibid.
N: USIGS 2 reels　　　　　　　　　2411
P: CaOTA

BELLE RIVER, Ont.
Assessment rolls, 1876-1899; council minutes,
1876-1899　Ibid.
N: USIGS 3 reels　　　　　　　　　2412
P: CaOTA

BENTINCK, Ont.
Deeds, 1850-1876　Ibid.
N: USIGS 9 reels　　　　　　　　　2413
P: CaOTA

BERTIE TOWNSHIP, Ont.
Deeds, 1796-1876　Ibid.
N: USIGS 13 reels　　　　　　　　2414
P: CaOTA

BERVIE, Ont.
Index to surveys, 1862-1958　Ibid.
N: USIGS 1 reel　　　　　　　　　2415
P: CaOTA

BEVERLY TOWNSHIP, Ont.
Assessment rolls, 1816-1899; council minutes,
1850-1899; deeds, 1816-1876　Ibid.
N: USIGS 23 reels　　　　　　　　2416
P: CaOTA

BIDDULPH TOWNSHIP, Ont.
Assessment rolls, 1862-1899; deeds, 1847-1900
Ibid.
N: USIGS 22 reels　　　　　　　　2417
P: CaOTA

BINBROOK, Ont.
Deeds, 1847-1879　Ibid.
N: USIGS 5 reels　　　　　　　　　2418
P: CaOTA

BLANDFORD TOWNSHIP, Ont.
Deeds, 1832-1956　Ibid.
N: USIGS 6 reels　　　　　　　　　2419
P: CaOTA

BLANSHARD TOWNSHIP, Ont.
Assessment and collector rolls, 1851-1899;
council minutes, 1851-1903; deeds, 1839-1877;
vital records, 1895-1900　Ibid.
N: USIGS 15 reels　　　　　　　　2420
P: CaOTA

BLENHEIM, Ont.
Council minutes, 1897-1904; deeds, 1852-1875
Ibid.
N: USIGS 5 reels　　　　　　　　　2421
P: CaOTA

BLENHEIM TOWNSHIP, Ont.
Deeds, 1802-1957　Ibid.
N: USIGS 13 reels　　　　　　　　2422
P: CaOTA

BLYTH, Ont.
Deeds, 1856-1878　Ibid.
N: USIGS 3 reels　　　　　　　　　2423
P: CaOTA

BOLTON, Ont.
Deeds, 1855-1886　Ibid.
N: USIGS 1 reel　　　　　　　　　2424
P: CaOTA

BOSANQUET TOWNSHIP, Ont.
Assessment rolls, 1851-1899; council minutes,
1850-1899; deeds, 1835-1908　Ibid.
N: USIGS 14 reels　　　　　　　　2425
P: CaOTA

BOTHWELL, Ont.
Account books, 1876-1905; council minutes, 1883-
1904; deeds, 1856-1876; records, 1872-1900 Ibid.
N: USIGS 8 reels　　　　　　　　　2426
P: CaOTA

BRAMPTON, Ont.
Deeds, 1851-1877　Ibid.
N: USIGS 8 reels　　　　　　　　　2427
P: CaOTA

BRANT TOWNSHIP, Ont.
Deeds, 1853-1876　Ibid.
N: USIGS 7 reels　　　　　　　　　2428
P: CaOTA

BRANTFORD, Ont.
Assessment rolls, 1851-1899; council minutes,
1847-1903; deeds, 1833-1876　Ibid.
N: USIGS 47 reels　　　　　　　　2429
P: CaOTA

BRANTFORD TOWNSHIP, Ont.
Council minutes, 1858-1909; deeds, 1834-1876;
Freeholders' and householders' minutes, 1852-
1902　Ibid.
N: USIGS 24 reels　　　　　　　　2430
P: CaOTA

BROCK TOWNSHIP, Ont.
Deeds, 1819-1876　Ibid.
N: USIGS 10 reels　　　　　　　　2431
P: CaOTA

BRONTE, Ont.
Index of surveys, 1840-1958　Ibid.
N: USIGS 1 reel　　　　　　　　　2432
P: CaOTA

BROOKE, Ont.
Deeds, 1858-1868　Ibid.
N: USIGS 1 reel　　　　　　　　　2433
P: CaOTA

BROOKE TOWNSHIP, Ont.
Council minutes, 1868-1900; deeds, 1847-1875
Ibid.
N: USIGS 7 reels　　　　　　　　　2434
P: CaOTA

BROOKLIN, Ont.
Deeds, 1851-1867　Ibid.
N: USIGS 1 reel　　　　　　　　　2435
P: CaOTA

BRUCE TOWNSHIP, Ont.
Deeds, 1856-1876　Ibid.
N: USIGS 4 reels　　　　　　　　　2436
P: CaOTA

BRUSSELS, Ont.
Deeds, 1873-1876　Ibid.
N: USIGS 3 reels　　　　　　　　　2437
P: CaOTA

BURFORD TOWNSHIP, Ont.
Deeds, 1800-1876　Ibid.
N: USIGS 16 reels　　　　　　　　2438
P: CaOTA

BURLINGTON, Ont.
Deeds, 1874-1880　Ibid.
N: USIGS 3 reels　　　　　　　　　2439
P: CaOTA

BYNG, Ont.
Index of surveys, 1842-1957　Ibid.
N: USIGS 1 reel　　　　　　　　　2440
P: CaOTA

CAISTOR TOWNSHIP, Ont.
Assessment rolls, 1863-1899; council minutes,
1843-1899; deeds, 1847-1876　Ibid.
N: USIGS 10 reels　　　　　　　　2441
P: CaOTA

CAISTORVILLE, Ont.
Deeds, 1855-1865　Ibid.
N: USIGS 1 reel　　　　　　　　　2442
P: CaOTA

CALEDON TOWNSHIP, Ont.
Deeds, 1821-1877　Ibid.
N: USIGS 11 reels　　　　　　　　2443
P: CaOTA

CALEDONIA, Ont.
Deeds, 1852-1878; patent grants, 1845-1867
Ibid.
N: USIGS 5 reels　　　　　　　　　2444
P: CaOTA

CAMDEN TOWNSHIP, Ont.
Deeds, 1847-1876　Ibid.
N: USIGS 7 reels　　　　　　　　　2445
P: CaOTA

CANBORO, Ont.
Index of surveys, 1872-1956　Ibid.
N: USIGS 1 reel　　　　　　　　　2446
P: CaOTA

CANBOROUGH TOWNSHIP, Ont.
Deeds, 1817-1840, 1847-1877; patent grants,
1798-1836　Ibid.
N: USIGS 7 reels　　　　　　　　　2447
P: CaOTA

CANNINGTON, Ont.
Deeds, 1853-1885　Ibid.
N: USIGS 1 reel　　　　　　　　　2448
P: CaOTA

CARADOC TOWNSHIP, Ont.
Crown patents, 1821-1865; council minutes,
1853-1907; deeds, 1847-1899; non-resident
rolls and by-laws, 1853-1876　Ibid.
N: USIGS 31 reels　　　　　　　　2449
P: CaOTA

CARRICK TOWNSHIP, Ont.
Deeds, 1857-1876　Ibid.
N: USIGS 6 reels　　　　　　　　　2450
P: CaOTA

CAYUGA, Ont.
Deeds, 1838-1839, 1852-1886; patent grants,
1833-1866　Ibid.
N: USIGS 5 reels　　　　　　　　　2451
P: CaOTA

CAYUGA TOWNSHIP, Ont.
Patent grants, 1836-1861　Ibid.
N: USIGS 1 reel　　　　　　　　　2452
P: CaOTA

CHARLOTTEVILLE TOWNSHIP, Ont.
Council minutes, 1836-1899; deeds, 1840-1876
Ibid.
N: USIGS 12 reels　　　　　　　　2453
P: CaOTA

CHATHAM, Ont.
Assessment and collectors' rolls, 1862-1899;
council minutes, 1855-1901; deeds, 1850-1875;
voters on assessment roll, 1890-1899　Ibid.
N: USIGS 42 reels　　　　　　　　2454
P: CaOTA

CHATHAM TOWNSHIP, Ont.
Assessment and collector rolls, 1869-1899;
council minutes, 1862-1904; deeds, 1847-1876;
souvenir book, 1850-1953　Ibid.
N: USIGS 19 reels　　　　　　　　2455
P: CaOTA

CHATSWORTH, Ont.
Index of surveys, 1848-1957　Ibid.
N: USIGS 1 reel　　　　　　　　　2456
P: CaOTA

CHEAPSIDE, Ont.
Index of surveys, 1869-1955　Ibid.
N: USIGS 1 reel　　　　　　　　　2457
P: CaOTA

CHINGUACOUSY TOWNSHIP, Ont.
Deeds, 1820-1877　Ibid.
N: USIGS 14 reels　　　　　　　　2458
P: CaOTA

CHIPPAWA, Ont.
Deeds, 1853-1879　Ibid.
N: USIGS 2 reels　　　　　　　　　2459
P: CaOTA

CITY OF FALLS, Ont.
Deeds, 1853-1872　Ibid.
N: USIGS 2 reels　　　　　　　　　2460
P: CaOTA

CLIFFORD, Ont.
Deeds, 1874-1881　Ibid.
N: USIGS 1 reel　　　　　　　　　2461
P: CaOTA

CLINTON, Ont.
Deeds, 1851-1876　Ibid.
N: USIGS 6 reels　　　　　　　　　2462
P: CaOTA

CLINTON TOWNSHIP, Ont.
Assessment and collector rolls, 1863-1868;

council minutes, 1850-1904; deeds, 1847-1876
Ibid.
N: USIGS 14 reels 2463
P: CaOTA

COLBORNE TOWNSHIP, Ont.
Deeds, 1847-1877 Ibid.
N: USIGS 6 reels 2464
P: CaOTA

COLCHESTER NORTH TOWNSHIP, Ont.
Assessment rolls, collector rolls, 1881-1899;
council minutes, 1880-1899 Ibid.
N: USIGS 4 reels 2465
P: CaOTA

COLCHESTER SOUTH TOWNSHIP, Ont.
Assessment rolls, 1880-1885; collector rolls,
1883-1897; council minutes, 1859-1899 Ibid.
N: USIGS 5 reels 2466
P: CaOTA

COLCHESTER TOWNSHIP, Ont.
Assessment rolls, 1844-1878; deeds, 1847-
1876 Ibid.
N: USIGS 10 reels 2467
P: CaOTA

COLLINGWOOD, Ont.
Deeds, 1856-1877 Ibid.
N: USIGS 18 reels 2468
P: CaOTA

COLLINGWOOD TOWNSHIP, Ont.
Deeds, 1847-1876 Ibid.
N: USIGS 11 reels 2469
P: CaOTA

CORBETTON, Ont.
Index of surveys, 1883-1957 Ibid.
N: USIGS 1 reel 2470
P: CaOTA

CORUNNA, Ont.
Deeds, 1858-1868 Ibid.
N: USIGS 1 reel 2471
P: CaOTA

CROWLAND TOWNSHIP, Ont.
Deeds, 1798-1875 Ibid.
N: USIGS 6 reels 2472
P: CaOTA

CULROSS TOWNSHIP, Ont.
Deeds, 1857-1876 Ibid.
N: USIGS 5 reels 2473
P: CaOTA

DARLING ROAD, Ont.
Index of surveys, 1875-1953 Ibid.
N: USIGS 1 reel 2474
P: CaOTA

DAWN TOWNSHIP, Ont.
Assessment and collector rolls, 1860-1899;
council minutes, 1890-1900; deeds, 1847-1875
Ibid.
N: USIGS 11 reels 2475
P: CaOTA

DELAWARE TOWNSHIP, Ont.
Council minutes, 1859-1881; crown patents,
1797-1870; deeds, 1847-1905; vital records,
1874-1899 Ibid.
N: USIGS 16 reels 2476
P: CaOTA

DELHI, Ont.
Council minutes, 1894-1899; deeds, 1854-1904
Ibid.
N: USIGS 3 reels 2477
P: CaOTA

DERBY TOWNSHIP, Ont.
Deeds, 1847-1877 Ibid.
N: USIGS 4 reels 2478
P: CaOTA

DEREHAM TOWNSHIP, Ont.
Deeds, 1847-1875 Ibid.
N: USIGS 10 reels 2479
P: CaOTA

DOVER TOWNSHIP, Ont.
Assessment roll, 1851-1899; council minutes,
1848-1902; voters' list, 1886 Ibid.
N: USIGS 11 reels 2480
P: CaOTA

DOWNIE TOWNSHIP, Ont.
Deeds, 1847-1875 Ibid.
N: USIGS 8 reels 2481
P: CaOTA

DRAYTON, Ont.
Deeds, 1875-1882 Ibid.
N: USIGS 2 reels 2482
P: CaOTA

DRESDEN, Ont.
Assessment rolls, 1892-1899; council minutes
and by-laws, 1882-1899; deeds, 1851-1875;
vital records, 1895-1908; voters'list, 1882-1898
Ibid.
N: USIGS 12 reels 2483
P: CaOTA

DUBLIN, Ont.
Deeds, 1858-1885 Ibid.
N: USIGS 2 reels 2484
P: CaOTA

DUFFERIN Co., Ont.
General registers, 1831-1877 Ibid.
N: USIGS 4 reel 2485
P: CaOTA

DUNDAS, Ont.
Assessment and collector rolls, 1853-1899;
council minutes, 1848-1899; deeds, 1852-1877
Ibid.
N: USIGS 22 reels 2486
P: CaOTA

DUNN TOWNSHIP, Ont.
Deeds, 1836-1840, 1847-1876; patent grants,
1835-1862 Ibid.
N: USIGS 5 reels 2487
P: CaOTA

DUNNVILLE, Ont.
Deeds, 1832-1840, 1857-1880 Ibid.
N: USIGS 4 reels 2488
P: CaOTA

DUNWICH TOWNSHIP, Ont.
Assessment rolls, 1861-1899; council minutes,
1850-1900; deeds, 1847-1876 Ibid.
N: USIGS 16 reels 2489
P: CaOTA

DURHAM, Ont.
Deeds, 1859-1868, 1873-1880 Ibid.
N: USIGS 3 reels 2490
P: CaOTA

DUTTON, Ont.
Assessment rolls, 1891-1899; council minutes,
1890-1899 Ibid.
N: USIGS 2 reels 2491
P: CaOTA

EAST DOVER TOWNSHIP, Ont.
Deeds, 1847-1876 Ibid.
N: USIGS 9 reels 2492
P: CaOTA

EAST FLAMBOROUGH TOWNSHIP, Ont.
Assessment and collector rolls, 1841-1893;
census records, 1840-1841; council minutes,
1850-1873; deeds, 1816-1876 Ibid.
N: USIGS 15 reels 2493
P: CaOTA

EAST GARAFRAXA TOWNSHIP, Ont.
Deeds, 1823-1877 Ibid.
N: USIGS 6 reels 2494
P: CaOTA

EAST GWILLIMBURY TOWNSHIP, Ont.
Deeds, 1803-1877 Ibid.
N: USIGS 13 reels 2495
P: CaOTA

EAST LUTHER TOWNSHIP, Ont.
Deeds, 1841-1877 Ibid.
N: USIGS 3 reels 2496
P: CaOTA

EAST NISSOURI TOWNSHIP, Ont.
Deeds, 1846-1876 Ibid.
N: USIGS 8 reels 2497
P: CaOTA

EAST OXFORD TOWNSHIP, Ont.
Deeds, 1847-1875 Ibid.
N: USIGS 9 reels 2498
P: CaOTA

EAST TILBURY TOWNSHIP, Ont.
Deeds, 1847-1877 Ibid.
N: USIGS 5 reels 2499
P: CaOTA

EAST WHITBY TOWNSHIP, Ont.
Deeds, 1864-1876 Ibid.
N: USIGS 5 reels 2500
P: CaOTA

EAST WILLIAMS TOWNSHIP, Ont.
Assessment rolls, 1834-1899; deeds, 1835-
1906; voters' list, 1868-1871 Ibid.
N: USIGS 18 reels 2501
P: CaOTA

EAST ZORRA TOWNSHIP, Ont.
Deeds, 1847-1875 Ibid.
N: USIGS 8 reels 2502
P: CaOTA

EASTNOR TOWNSHIP, Ont.
Deeds, 1865-1885 Ibid.
N: USIGS 3 reels 2503
P: CaOTA

EGREMONT TOWNSHIP, Ont.
Deeds, 1848-1877 Ibid.
N: USIGS 6 reels 2504
P: CaOTA

EKFRID TOWNSHIP, Ont.
Assessment rolls, 1879-1891; deeds, 1847-
1902; land drainage records, 1883-1932 Ibid.
N: USIGS 21 reels 2505
P: CaOTA

ELDERSLIE TOWNSHIP, Ont.
Deeds, 1855-1877 Ibid.
N: USIGS 5 reels 2506
P: CaOTA

ELLICE TOWNSHIP, Ont.
Assessment rolls, 1852-1899; council minutes,
1842-1885; deeds, 1847-1875 Ibid.
N: USIGS 11 reels 2507
P: CaOTA

ELMA TOWNSHIP, Ont.
Assessment and collector rolls, 1854-1856;
council minutes, 1879-1900; deeds, 1856-1876;
vital records, 1896-1902 Ibid.
N: USIGS 11 reels 2508
P: CaOTA

ELORA, Ont.
Deeds, 1860-1877 Ibid.
N: USIGS 5 reels 2509
P: CaOTA

EMBRO, Ont.
Deeds, 1866-1880 Ibid.
N: USIGS 2 reels 2510
P: CaOTA

ENNISKILLEN TOWNSHIP, Ont.
Assessment and collector rolls, 1852-1899;
council minutes, 1867-1899; deeds, 1847-1876
Ibid.
N: USIGS 23 reels 2511
P: CaOTA

ERAMOSA TOWNSHIP, Ont.
Deeds, 1820-1840 Ibid.
N: USIGS 9 reels 2512
P: CaOTA

ERIN TOWNSHIP, Ont.
Deeds, 1822-1876 Ibid.
N: USIGS 14 reels 2513
P: CaOTA

ERROL, Ont.
Deeds, 1854-1868 Ibid.
N: USIGS 1 reel 2514
P: CaOTA

ESQUESING TOWNSHIP, Ont.
Deeds, 1847-1876 Ibid.
N: USIGS 12 reels 2515
P: CaOTA

ESSA TOWNSHIP, Ont.
Deeds, 1847-1876; patent grants, 1820-1865
Ibid.
N: USIGS 12 reels 2516
P: CaOTA

ESSEX, Ont.
Assessment rolls, 1885-1899; council minutes, 1884-1900; index to deeds, n.d. Ibid.
N: USIGS 4 reels
P: CaOTA
2517

ETOBICOKE TOWNSHIP, Ont.
Deeds, 1847-1878 Ibid.
N: USIGS 9 reels
P: CaOTA
2518

EUPHEMIA TOWNSHIP, Ont.
Assessment rolls, 1850-1898; council minutes, 1879-1889; deeds, 1847-1876 Ibid.
N: USIGS 11 reels
P: CaOTA
2519

EUPHRASIA TOWNSHIP, Ont.
Deeds, 1847-1876 Ibid.
N: USIGS 6 reels
P: CaOTA
2520

EXETER, Ont.
Deeds, 1855-1865, 1873-1875 Ibid.
N: USIGS 2 reels
P: CaOTA
2521

FENWICK, Ont.
Index of surveys, 1798-1958 Ibid.
N: USIGS 1 reel
P: CaOTA
2522

FERGUS, Ont.
Deeds, 1860-1876 Ibid.
N: USIGS 5 reels
P: CaOTA
2523

FINGAL, Ont.
Abstract index of surveys, 1876 Ibid.
N: USIGS 1 reel
P: CaOTA
2524

FLOS TOWNSHIP, Ont.
Deeds, 1847-1875; patent grants, 1821-1865 Ibid.
N: USIGS 8 reels
P: CaOTA
2525

FONTHILL, Ont.
Deeds, 1852-1872 Ibid.
N: USIGS 2 reels
P: CaOTA
2526

FORD CITY, Ont.
Deed index, memorials, n.d. Ibid.
N: USIGS 1 reel
P: CaOTA
2527

FOREST, Ont.
Assessment rolls, 1875-1899; council minutes, 1884-1899; deeds, 1860-1877 Ibid.
N: USIGS 6 reels
P: CaOTA
2528

FORT ERIE, Ont.
Deeds, 1854-1879 Ibid.
N: USIGS 4 reels
P: CaOTA
2529

FROOMFIELD, Ont.
Deeds, 1857-1867 Ibid.
N: USIGS 1 reel
P: CaOTA
2530

FULLARTON TOWNSHIP, Ont.
Deeds, 1847-1877 Ibid.
N: USIGS 6 reels
P: CaOTA
2531

GAINSBOROUGH TOWNSHIP, Ont.
Assessment rolls, 1864-1899; council minutes, 1888-1899; deeds, 1847-1876 Ibid.
N: USIGS 11 reels
P: CaOTA
2532

GALT, Ont.
Deeds, 1816-1875 Ibid.
N: USIGS 7 reels
P: CaOTA
2533

GARAFRAXA TOWNSHIP, Ont.
Minute book, 1869-1899 Ibid.
N: USIGS 1 reel
P: CaOTA
2534

GEORGETOWN, Ont.
Deeds, 1865-1878 Ibid.
N: USIGS 5 reels
P: CaOTA
2535

GEORGINA TOWNSHIP, Ont.
Deeds, 1821-1878 Ibid.
N: USIGS 6 reels
P: CaOTA
2536

GLANFORD TOWNSHIP, Ont.
Assessment rolls, 1846-1899; deeds, 1816-1829, 1847-1878 Ibid.
N: USIGS 9 reels
P: CaOTA
2537

GLENCOE, Ont.
By-laws, 1875-1922; deeds, 1875-1902 Ibid.
N: USIGS 8 reels
P: CaOTA
2538

GLENELG TOWNSHIP, Ont.
Deeds, 1849-1876 Ibid.
N: USIGS 7 reels
P: CaOTA
2539

GODERICH, Ont.
Deeds, 1850-1875 Ibid.
N: USIGS 12 reels
P: CaOTA
2540

GODERICH TOWNSHIP, Ont.
Deeds, 1847-1876 Ibid.
N: USIGS 9 reels
P: CaOTA
2541

GOSFIELD NORTH TOWNSHIP, Ont.
Assessment and collector rolls, 1857-1899; council minutes, 1850-1861, 1874-1887 Ibid.
N: USIGS 5 reels
P: CaOTA
2542

GOSFIELD SOUTH TOWNSHIP, Ont.
Assessment rolls, 1887-1899; council minutes, 1888-1899 Ibid.
N: USIGS 3 reels
P: CaOTA
2543

GOSFIELD TOWNSHIP, Ont.
Assessment rolls, 1850-1871; deeds, 1847-1876 Ibid.
N: USIGS 9 reels
P: CaOTA
2544

GRAND VALLEY, Ont.
Abstract index of surveys, 1836-1958 Ibid.
N: USIGS 1 reel
P: CaOTA
2545

GRANTHAM TOWNSHIP, Ont.
Assessment rolls, 1890-1899; council minutes, 1850-1900; deeds, 1847-1877 Ibid.
N: USIGS 13 reels
P: CaOTA
2546

GREENOCK TOWNSHIP, Ont.
Deeds, 1853-1876 Ibid.
N: USIGS 5 reels
P: CaOTA
2547

GREY TOWNSHIP, Ont.
Deeds, 1855-1876 Ibid.
N: USIGS 6 reels
P: CaOTA
2548

GRIMSBY, Ont.
Assessment rolls, 1877-1899; council minutes, 1876-1899 Ibid.
N: USIGS 2 reels
P: CaOTA
2549

GRIMSBY TOWNSHIP, Ont.
Deeds, 1847-1877 Ibid.
N: USIGS 8 reels
P: CaOTA
2550

GUELPH, Ont.
Deeds, 1830-1875 Ibid.
N: USIGS 23 reels
P: CaOTA
2551

GUELPH TOWNSHIP, Ont.
Deeds, 1862-1877 Ibid.
N: USIGS 6 reels
P: CaOTA
2552

HAGERSVILLE, Ont.
Assessment roll, 1899; council minutes, 1887-1899; index of surveys, 1874-1909; sexton's register, 1895-1910 Ibid.
N: USIGS 5 reels
P: CaOTA
2553

HAMILTON, Ont.
Abstract of deeds, 1875; assessment rolls, 1847-1899; council minutes, 1847-1901; deeds (with index),1796-1820, 1847-1876; applications United Empire Loyalists' Association of Canada Ibid.
N: USIGS 128 reels
P: CaOTA
2554

HANOVER, Ont.
Deeds, 1856-1891 Ibid.
N: USIGS 3 reels
P: CaOTA
2555

HARRISBURGH, Ont.
Deeds, 1856-1865 Ibid.
N: USIGS 1 reel
P: CaOTA
2556

HARRISTON, Ont.
Deeds, 1873-1876 Ibid.
N: USIGS 1 reel
P: CaOTA
2557

HARWICH TOWNSHIP, Ont.
Assessment roll, 1854-1899; council minutes, 1850-1902; deeds, 1847-1876 Ibid.
N: USIGS 26 reels
P: CaOTA
2558

HAY TOWNSHIP, Ont.
Deeds, 1848-1876 Ibid.
N: USIGS 6 reels
P: CaOTA
2559

HESPELER, Ont.
Deeds, 1859-1875 Ibid.
N: USIGS 2 reels
P: CaOTA
2560

HIBBERT, Ont.
Council minutes, 1854-1900; vital records, 1896-1903 Ibid.
N: USIGS 2 reels
P: CaOTA
2561

HIBBERT TOWNSHIP, Ont.
Assessment rolls, 1891-1899; deeds, 1847-1878 Ibid.
N: USIGS 8 reels
P: CaOTA
2562

HOLLAND LANDING, Ont.
Deeds, 1863-1897 Ibid.
N: USIGS 3 reels
P: CaOTA
2563

HOLLAND TOWNSHIP, Ont.
Deeds, 1849-1875 Ibid.
N: USIGS 6 reels
P: CaOTA
2564

HOMEDALE, Ont.
Deeds, 1856-1861 Ibid.
N: USIGS 1 reel
P: CaOTA
2565

HOUGHTON TOWNSHIP, Ont.
Council minutes, 1850-1899; deeds, 1840-1877 Ibid.
N: USIGS 7 reels
P: CaOTA
2566

HOWARD TOWNSHIP, Ont.
Assessment roll, 1850-1899; council minutes, 1843-1900; deeds, 1847-1876 Ibid.
N: USIGS 20 reels
P: CaOTA
2567

HOWICK TOWNSHIP, Ont.
Deeds, 1856-1876 Ibid.
N: USIGS 8 reels
P: CaOTA
2568

HULLETT TOWNSHIP, Ont.
Deeds, 1847-1876 Ibid.
N: USIGS 8 reels
P: CaOTA
2569

HULLSVILLE, Ont.
Index of surveys, 1854-1957 Ibid.
N: USIGS 1 reel
P: CaOTA
2570

HUMBERSTONE TOWNSHIP, Ont.
Deeds, 1798-1876 Ibid.
N: USIGS 10 reels
P: CaOTA
2571

HURON TOWNSHIP, Ont.
Deeds, 1857-1876 Ibid.
N: USIGS 4 reels
P: CaOTA
2572

INDIANA, Ont.
Index of surveys, ca. 1851-1956 Ibid.
N: USIGS 1 reel
P: CaOTA
2573

INGERSOLL, Ont.
Deeds, 1866-1876 Ibid.
N: USIGS 8 reels
P: CaOTA
2574

INNISFIL TOWNSHIP, Ont.
Deeds, 1847-1875; patent grants, 1820-1865
Ibid.
N: USIGS 15 reels
P: CaOTA
2575

INVERHURON, Ont.
Index of surveys, ca. 1858-1958 Ibid.
N: USIGS 1 reel
P: CaOTA
2576

IONA, Ont.
Index of surveys, before 1876 Ibid.
N: USIGS 1 reel
P: CaOTA
2577

JARVIS, Ont.
Abstract index surveys, 1846-1957 Ibid.
N: USIGS 1 reel
P: CaOTA
2578

JORDAN, Ont.
Deeds, 1855-1865 Ibid.
N: USIGS 1 reel
P: CaOTA
2579

JORDAN STATION, Ont.
Deeds, 1859-1865 Ibid.
N: USIGS 1 reel
P: CaOTA
2580

KEPPEL TOWNSHIP, Ont.
Deeds, 1859-1877 Ibid.
N: USIGS 4 reels
P: CaOTA
2581

KESWICK, Ont.
Deeds, 1853-1868 Ibid.
N: USIGS 1 reel
P: CaOTA
2582

KILBRIDE, Ont.
Abstract index of surveys, ca. 1855-1958 Ibid.
N: USIGS 1 reel
P: CaOTA
2583

KINCARDINE, Ont.
Abstract index of surveys, ca. 1860-1958;
deeds, 1853-1876 Ibid.
N: USIGS 7 reels
P: CaOTA
2584

KINCARDINE TOWNSHIP, Ont.
Deeds, 1853-1876 Ibid.
N: USIGS 6 reels
P: CaOTA
2585

KING TOWNSHIP, Ont.
Deeds, 1798-1876 Ibid.
N: USIGS 16 reels
P: CaOTA
2586

KINGSTON, Ont.
Council minutes, 1847-1880, 1871-1900; deeds,
1789-1851; patent returns for land grants, before
1902; procedure book for Sixth Division court,
1879-1900; Sixth Division court roll of jurors,
1849-1916; wills, 1854-1883 Ibid.
N: USIGS 26 reels
P: CaOTA
2587

KINGSVILLE, Ont.
Assessment rolls and collector rolls, 1886-
1899; council minutes, 1878-1899; deeds, 1851-
1885 Ibid.
N: USIGS 5 reels
P: CaOTA
2588

KINLOSS TOWNSHIP, Ont.
Deeds, 1855-1877 Ibid.
N: USIGS 5 reels
P: CaOTA
2589

KITCHENER, Ont.
Deeds, 1853-1876 Ibid.
N: USIGS 10 reels
P: CaOTA
2590

LAMBTON Co., Ont.
Deeds, 1821-1850; wills, deeds, judgments,
decrees in chancery, 1851-1886 Ibid.
N: USIGS 6 reels
P: CaOTA
2591

LEAMINGTON, Ont.
Assessment rolls, 1876-1899; council minutes,
1876-1899 Ibid.
N: USIGS 5 reels
P: CaOTA
2592

LISTOWEL, Ont.
Council minutes, 1878-1901; deeds, 1857-
1877 Ibid.
N: USIGS 8 reels
P: CaOTA
2593

LIVERPOOL, Ont.
Deeds (Borelia), 1852-1867; (Fairport), 1851-
1868; (Gouldville), 1851-1856; (Liverpool),
1854-1867 Ibid.
N: USIGS 1 reel
P: CaOTA
2594

LOBO TOWNSHIP, Ont.
Assessment rolls, 1848-1899; council minutes,
1885-1899; deeds, 1847-1903; voters' lists,
1876, 1883-1884 Ibid.
N: USIGS 20 reels
P: CaOTA
2595

LOGAN TOWNSHIP, Ont.
Council minutes, 1864-1892; deeds, 1848-1876;
vital records, 1895-1903 Ibid.
N: USIGS 9 reels
P: CaOTA
2596

LONDON TOWNSHIP, Ont.
Assessment and collector rolls, 1852-1899;
council minutes (township), 1819-1909, (city),
1844-1890; deeds, 1831-1902; finance committee records, 1869-1888; Gore cemetery
records, n.d.; wills, 1866-1902 Ibid.
N: USIGS 134 reels
P: CaOTA
2597

LOUISVILLE, Ont.
Abstract index of surveys, 1837-1956 Ibid.
N: USIGS 1 reel
P: CaOTA
2598

LOUTH TOWNSHIP, Ont.
Assessment rolls, 1884-1899; council minutes,
1793-1850, 1855-1899; deeds, 1847-1879 Ibid.
N: USIGS 7 reels
P: CaOTA
2599

LUCAN, Ont.
Deeds, 1855-1867, 1872-1907 Ibid.
N: USIGS 4 reels
P: CaOTA
2600

LUCKNOW, Ont.
Deeds, 1860-1878 Ibid.
N: USIGS 3 reels
P: CaOTA
2601

McGILLIVRAY TOWNSHIP, Ont.
Council minutes, 1843-1908; deeds, 1837-1900;
treasurers' records, 1875-1904 Ibid.
N: USIGS 21 reels
P: CaOTA
2602

McKILLOP TOWNSHIP, Ont.
Deeds, 1847-1876 Ibid.
N: USIGS 5 reels
P: CaOTA
2603

MAIDSTONE TOWNSHIP, Ont.
Assessment rolls, 1871-1899 (transcripts);
council minutes, 1854-1899; deeds, 1847-1876
Ibid.
N: USIGS 14 reels
P: CaOTA
2604

MALAHIDE TOWNSHIP, Ont.
Deeds, 1847-1876 Ibid.
N: USIGS 16 reels
P: CaOTA
2605

MALDEN TOWNSHIP, Ont.
Assessment rolls, 1843, 1848, 1870-1873, 1883-
1898; council minutes, 1887-1899; deeds, 1847-
1876; voters' list, 1890-1899 Ibid.
N: USIGS 8 reels
P: CaOTA
2606

MALTA, Ont.
Abstract index surveys, ca. 1857-1940 Ibid.
N: USIGS 1 reel
P: CaOTA
2607

MARA TOWNSHIP, Ont.
Deeds, 1843-1876 Ibid.
N: USIGS 6 reels
P: CaOTA
2608

MARKHAM, Ont.
Deeds, 1872-1882 Ibid.
N: USIGS 2 reels
P: CaOTA
2609

MARKHAM TOWNSHIP, Ont.
Deeds, 1847-1876 Ibid.
N: USIGS 12 reels
P: CaOTA
2610

MARSHVILLE, Ont.
Abstract index of surveys, 1828-1958 Ibid.
N: USIGS 1 reel
P: CaOTA
2611

MARYBOROUGH TOWNSHIP, Ont.
Assessment roll, 1879-1897; deeds, 1853-
1875; minute book, 1851-1899 Ibid.
N: USIGS 12 reels
P: CaOTA
2612

MATCHEDASH TOWNSHIP, Ont.
Deeds, 1849-1886; patent grants, 1820-1865 Ibid.
N: USIGS 3 reels
P: CaOTA
2613

MEAFORD, Ont.
Deeds, 1862-1868, 1875-1877 Ibid.
N: USIGS 3 reels
P: CaOTA
2614

MEDONTE TOWNSHIP, Ont.
Deeds, 1847-1875; patent grants, 1820-1865 Ibid.
N: USIGS 9 reels
P: CaOTA
2615

MELANCTHON TOWNSHIP, Ont.
Deeds, 1847-1876 Ibid.
N: USIGS 7 reels
P: CaOTA
2616

MERRITTON, Ont.
Assessment rolls, 1876-1899; council minutes,
1874-1899; deeds, 1874-1881 Ibid.
N: USIGS 6 reels
P: CaOTA
2617

MERSEA TOWNSHIP, Ont.
Assessment rolls, 1870-1898; collector rolls,
1863-1885; council minutes, 1850-1899; deeds,
1847-1875 Ibid.
N: USIGS 19 reels
P: CaOTA
2618

METCALFE TOWNSHIP, Ont.
Deeds, 1847-1906 Ibid.
N: USIGS 14 reels
P: CaOTA
2619

MIDDLETON TOWNSHIP, Ont.
Council minutes, 1850-1899; deeds, 1840-1876
Ibid.
N: USIGS 10 reels
P: CaOTA
2620

MILLBANK, Ont.
Deeds, 1858-1900 Ibid.
N: USIGS 3 reels
P: CaOTA
2621

MILTON, Ont.
Deeds, 1858-1877   Ibid.
N: USIGS 4 reels   2622
P: CaOTA

MILVERTON, Ont.
Vital records, 1895-1903   Ibid.
N: USIGS 1 reel   2623
P: CaOTA

MINTO TOWNSHIP, Ont.
Deeds, 1856-1876   Ibid.
N: USIGS 10 reels   2624
P: CaOTA

MITCHELL, Ont.
Assessment rolls, 1870-1899; council minutes,
1857-1902; deeds, 1851-1876   Ibid.
N: USIGS 12 reels   2625
P: CaOTA

MONO TOWNSHIP, Ont.
Deeds, 1821-1876   Ibid.
N: USIGS 11 reels   2626
P: CaOTA

MOORE TOWNSHIP, Ont.
Deeds, 1847-1876   Ibid.
N: USIGS 11 reels   2627
P: CaOTA

MOORETOWN, Ont.
Deeds, 1854-1868   Ibid.
N: USIGS 1 reel   2628
P: CaOTA

MORNINGTON TOWNSHIP, Ont.
Assessment and collector rolls, 1855-1898
(with missing years); council minutes, 1854-
1900; deeds, 1855-1877; vital records, 1896-
1900   Ibid.
N: USIGS 9 reels   2629
P: CaOTA

MORPETH, Ont.
Abstract index of surveys, 1862-1955   Ibid.
N: USIGS 1 reel   2630
P: CaOTA

MORRIS TOWNSHIP, Ont.
Deeds, 1856-1876   Ibid.
N: USIGS 7 reels   2631
P: CaOTA

MOSA TOWNSHIP, Ont.
Deeds, 1847-1901   Ibid.
N: USIGS 19 reels   2632
P: CaOTA

MOULTON TOWNSHIP, Ont.
Deeds, 1821-1840, 1847-1879; patent grants, ca.
1798-1839   Ibid.
N: USIGS 7 reels   2633
P: CaOTA

MOUNT FOREST, Ont.
Deeds, 1858-1877   Ibid.
N: USIGS 4 reels   2634
P: CaOTA

MULMUR TOWNSHIP, Ont.
Deeds, 1847-1876   Ibid.
N: USIGS 10 reels   2635
P: CaOTA

NANTICOKE, Ont.
Abstract index surveys, ca. 1842-1957   Ibid.
N: USIGS 1 reel   2636
P: CaOTA

NASSAGAWEYA TOWNSHIP, Ont.
Deeds, 1847-1876   Ibid.
N: USIGS 7 reels   2637
P: CaOTA

NELSON TOWNSHIP, Ont.
Deeds, 1847-1877   Ibid.
N: USIGS 11 reels   2638
P: CaOTA

NEW HAMBURG, Ont.
Deeds, 1858-1880   Ibid.
N: USIGS 3 reels   2639
P: CaOTA

NEWBURY, Ont.
Assessment roll, 1891-1892; council minutes,
1882-1906; deeds, 1873-1911   Ibid.
N: USIGS 6 reels   2640
P: CaOTA

NEWMARKET, Ont.
Deeds, 1850-1876   Ibid.
N: USIGS 7 reels   2641
P: CaOTA

NIAGARA FALLS, Ont.
Deeds, 1856-1871 (Drummondville); 1854-1876
(Elgin and Clifton)   Ibid.
N: USIGS 9 reels   2642
P: CaOTA

NIAGARA ON THE LAKE, Ont.
Assessment rolls, 1852-1899; council minutes,
1856-1899; deeds, 1847-1875   Ibid.
N: USIGS 8 reels   2643
P: CaOTA

NIAGARA TOWNSHIP, Ont.
Assessment rolls, 1847-1899; council minutes,
1863-1899; deeds, 1847-1879   Ibid.
N: USIGS 11 reels   2644
P: CaOTA

NICHOL TOWNSHIP, Ont.
Deeds, 1822-1878   Ibid.
N: USIGS 10 reels   2645
P: CaOTA

NITHBURG, Ont.
Abstract index surveys, 1836-1957   Ibid.
N: USIGS 1 reel   2646
P: CaOTA

NORMANBY TOWNSHIP, Ont.
Deeds, 1849-1876   Ibid.
N: USIGS 6 reels   2647
P: CaOTA

NORTH CAYUGA TOWNSHIP, Ont.
Deeds, 1823-1840, 1847-1875; patent grants,
1836-1866   Ibid.
N: USIGS 7 reels   2648
P: CaOTA

NORTH DORCHESTER TOWNSHIP, Ont.
By-laws of township, 1850-1910; council minutes,
1868-1905; deeds, 1847-1902   Ibid.
N: USIGS 24 reels   2649
P: CaOTA

NORTH DUMFRIES TOWNSHIP, Ont.
Deeds: 1852-1874, 1818-1843 (Halton Co.),
1847-1851 (formerly in Halton Co.)   Ibid.
N: USIGS 12 reels   2650
P: CaOTA

NORTH EASTHOPE TOWNSHIP, Ont.
Assessment rolls, 1865-1899; council minutes,
1843-1875, 1886-1916; deeds, 1847-1875 Ibid.
N: USIGS 12 reels   2651
P: CaOTA

NORTH GRIMSBY TOWNSHIP, Ont.
Council minutes, 1850-1857, 1883-1899 Ibid.
N: USIGS 1 reel   2652
P: CaOTA

NORTH GWILLIMBURY TOWNSHIP, Ont.
Deeds, 1803-1877   Ibid.
N: USIGS 7 reels   2653
P: CaOTA

NORTH NORWICH, Ont.
Deeds, 1859-1875   Ibid.
N: USIGS 5 reels   2654
P: CaOTA

NORTH OXFORD TOWNSHIP, Ont.
Deeds, 1816-1879   Ibid.
N: USIGS 8 reels   2655
P: CaOTA

NORTH WALSINGHAM TOWNSHIP, Ont.
Council minutes, 1884-1899   Ibid.
N: USIGS 1 reel   2656
P: CaOTA

NORVAL, Ont.
Abstract index surveys, ca. 1828-1958   Ibid.
N: USIGS 1 reel   2657
P: CaOTA

NORWICH, Ont.
Abstract index surveys, 1866-1952 Ibid.
N: USIGS 2 reels   2658
P: CaOTA

NOTTAWASAGA TOWNSHIP, Ont.
Deeds, 1847-1876; patent grants, 1833-1866
Ibid.
N: USIGS 17 reels   2659
P: CaOTA

OAKLAND TOWNSHIP, Ont.
Assessment rolls, 1857, 1863-1872, 1880-1890;
council minutes, 1850-1899; deeds, 1803-1876
Ibid.
N: USIGS 7 reels   2660
P: CaOTA

OAKVILLE, Ont.
Deeds, 1850-1876   Ibid.
N: USIGS 6 reels   2661
P: CaOTA

OIL SPRINGS, Ont.
Deeds, 1867-1883   Ibid.
N: USIGS 1 reel   2662
P: CaOTA

ONEIDA TOWNSHIP, Ont.
Deeds, 1849-1879; patent grants, 1836-1866
Ibid.
N: USIGS 7 reels   2663
P: CaOTA

ONONDAGA TOWNSHIP, Ont.
Assessment roll, 1879; council minutes, 1866-
1899; deeds, 1848-1878   Ibid.
N: USIGS 7 reels   2664
P: CaOTA

ORANGEVILLE, Ont.
Deeds, 1825-1877   Ibid.
N: USIGS 8 reels   2665
P: CaOTA

ORFORD TOWNSHIP, Ont.
Council minutes, 1850-1907; deeds, 1847-
1876   Ibid.
N: USIGS 9 reels   2666
P: CaOTA

ORILLIA TOWNSHIP, Ont.
Deeds, 1847-1877; patent grants, 1821-1865
Ibid.
N: USIGS 19 reels   2667
P: CaOTA

ORO TOWNSHIP, Ont.
Deeds, 1847-1877; patent grants, 1820-1865
Ibid.
N: USIGS 12 reels   2668
P: CaOTA

OSHAWA, Ont.
Deeds, 1855-1876; wills, 1854-1878   Ibid.
N: USIGS 8 reels   2669
P: CaOTA

OSPREY TOWNSHIP, Ont.
Deeds, 1854-1876   Ibid.
N: USIGS 5 reels   2670
P: CaOTA

OWEN SOUND, Ont.
Deeds, 1857-1875   Ibid.
N: USIGS 9 reels   2671
P: CaOTA

PAISLEY, Ont.
Deeds, 1874-1878   Ibid.
N: USIGS 4 reels   2672
P: CaOTA

PALMERSTON, Ont.
Deeds, 1875-1877   Ibid.
N: USIGS 1 reel   2673
P: CaOTA

PARIS, Ont.
Council minutes, 1850-1899; deeds, 1853-1877
Ibid.
N: USIGS 13 reels   2674
P: CaOTA

PARKHILL, Ont.
Assessment and collector rolls, 1872-1899;

council minutes, 1892-1914; deeds, 1872-1900
Ibid.
N: USIGS 11 reels
P: CaOTA
2675

PEEL TOWNSHIP, Ont.
Deeds, 1855-1876 Ibid.
N: USIGS 9 reels
P: CaOTA
2676

PELEE TOWNSHIP, Ont.
Assessment and collector rolls, 1868-1899;
council minutes, 1868-1900; deeds, 1868-1888,
index, from 1882; voters' lists, 1890-1897 Ibid.
N: USIGS 6 reels
P: CaOTA
2677

PELHAM TOWNSHIP, Ont.
Deeds, 1798-1875 Ibid.
N: USIGS 10 reels
P: CaOTA
2678

PENETANGUISHENE, Ont.
Deeds, 1857-1868 Ibid.
N: USIGS 3 reels
P: CaOTA
2679

PETERSBURGH, Ont.
Deeds, 1853-1873 Ibid.
N: USIGS 2 reels
P: CaOTA
2680

PETROLIA, Ont.
Assessment rolls, 1890-1899; council minutes,
1874-1902; deeds, 1867-1876; voters' lists, 1874-
1899 Ibid.
N: USIGS 12 reels
P: CaOTA
2681

PICKERING TOWNSHIP, Ont.
Deeds, 1798-1876 Ibid.
N: USIGS 12 reels
P: CaOTA
2682

PILKINGTON TOWNSHIP, Ont.
Assessment roll, 1858; deeds, 1852-1878;
minute book, 1852-1875 Ibid.
N: USIGS 7 reels
P: CaOTA
2683

PLYMPTON TOWNSHIP, Ont.
Assessment rolls, 1871-1899; council minutes,
1852-1900; deeds, 1847-1876 Ibid.
N: USIGS 16 reels
P: CaOTA
2684

POINT EDWARD, Ont.
Deeds, 1865-1887 Ibid.
N: USIGS 1 reel
P: CaOTA
2685

POOLE, Ont.
Deeds, 1854-1952; wills, 1859-1885 Ibid.
N: USIGS 6 reels
P: CaOTA
2686

PORT BRUCE, Ont.
Abstract index surveys, 1858-1863 Ibid.
N: USIGS 1 reel
P: CaOTA
2687

PORT BURWELL, Ont.
Abstract index surveys, before 1876 Ibid.
N: USIGS 1 reel
P: CaOTA
2688

PORT COLBORNE, Ont.
Deeds, 1853-1876 Ibid.
N: USIGS 3 reels
P: CaOTA
2689

PORT CREDIT, Ont.
Deeds, 1851-1901; wills, 1863-1885 Ibid.
N: USIGS 2 reels
P: CaOTA
2690

PORT DALHOUSIE, Ont.
Council minutes, 1863-1884; deeds, 1852-1877
Ibid.
N: USIGS 3 reels
P: CaOTA
2691

PORT DOVER, Ont.
Council minutes, 1879-1899; deeds, 1850-1880
Ibid.
N: USIGS 4 reels
P: CaOTA
2692

PORT ELGIN, Ont.
Deeds, 1874-1879 Ibid.
N: USIGS 2 reels
P: CaOTA
2693

PORT NELSON, Ont.
Abstract index surveys, ca. 1840-1958 Ibid.
N: USIGS 1 reel
P: CaOTA
2694

PORT PERRY, Ont.
Deeds, 1853-1877 Ibid.
N: USIGS 4 reels
P: CaOTA
2695

PORT ROBINSON, Ont.
Abstract index surveys, 1798-1957 Ibid.
N: USIGS 1 reel
P: CaOTA
2696

PORT ROWAN, Ont.
Abstract index of surveys, v. A, n.d. Ibid.
N: USIGS 1 reel
P: CaOTA
2697

PORT STANLEY, Ont.
Council minutes, 1879-1892; deeds, 1872-1888
Ibid.
N: USIGS 4 reels
P: CaOTA
2698

PRESTON TOWNSHIP, Ont.
Deeds, 1858-1878 Ibid.
N: USIGS 3 reels
P: CaOTA
2699

PROTON TOWNSHIP, Ont.
Deeds, 1854-1877 Ibid.
N: USIGS 4 reels
P: CaOTA
2700

PUSLINCH TOWNSHIP, Ont.
Deeds, 1833-1877 Ibid.
N: USIGS 9 reels
P: CaOTA
2701

RAINHAM TOWNSHIP, Ont.
Deeds, 1800-1876; patent grants, 1796-1864
Ibid.
N: USIGS 8 reels
P: CaOTA
2702

RALEIGH TOWNSHIP, Ont.
Deeds, 1847-1875 Ibid.
N: USIGS 12 reels
P: CaOTA
2703

RAMA TOWNSHIP, Ont.
Deeds, 1843-1878 Ibid.
N: USIGS 3 reels
P: CaOTA
2704

REACH TOWNSHIP, Ont.
Deeds, 1811-1876 Ibid.
N: USIGS 13 reels
P: CaOTA
2705

RICHMOND HILL, Ont.
Deeds, 1872-1885 Ibid.
N: USIGS 3 reels
P: CaOTA
2706

RIDGETOWN, Ont.
Deeds, 1836-1877 Ibid.
N: USIGS 2 reels
P: CaOTA
2707

RIDGEVILLE, Ont.
Abstract index surveys, ca. 1797-1958 Ibid.
N: USIGS 1 reel
P: CaOTA
2708

RIDGEWAY, Ont.
Abstract index surveys, ca. 1798-1950 Ibid.
N: USIGS 1 reel
P: CaOTA
2709

RIVERSDALE, Ont.
Abstract index surveys, ca. 1860-1957 Ibid.
N: USIGS 1 reel
P: CaOTA
2710

ROCHESTER, Ont.
Assessment rolls, 1863-1899; collectors'
rolls, 1859-1895; council minutes, 1853-
1899; deeds, 1847-1876 Ibid.
N: USIGS 13 reels
P: CaOTA
2711

ROMNEY TOWNSHIP, Ont.
Collectors' rolls, 1891-1899; council minutes,
1895-1900; deeds, 1847-1877 Ibid.
N: USIGS 5 reels
P: CaOTA
2712

ST. CATHERINES, Ont.
Assessment and collectors' rolls, 1854-1899;
council minutes, 1845-1899; deeds, 1847-1876
Ibid.
N: USIGS 36 reels
P: CaOTA
2713

ST. MARYS, Ont.
Council minutes, 1889-1900; deeds, 1851-1876
Ibid.
N: USIGS 14 reels
P: CaOTA
2714

ST. THOMAS, Ont.
Assessment (tax) rolls, 1856-1900; collector
rolls, 1856-1857; council minutes, 1852-1904;
deeds, 1854-1876 Ibid.
N: USIGS 25 reels
P: CaOTA
2715

ST. VINCENT TOWNSHIP, Ont.
Deeds, 1847-1876 Ibid.
N: USIGS 11 reels
P: CaOTA
2716

SALTFLEET TOWNSHIP, Ont.
Assessment rolls, 1803-1899; collector
rolls, 1803-1899; council minutes, 1850-1899;
deeds, 1847-1878 Ibid.
N: USIGS 12 reels
P: CaOTA
2717

SANDWICH, Ont.
Assessment rolls, 1870-1884; council
minutes, 1878-1899; deeds, 1853-1880 Ibid.
N: USIGS 8 reels
P: CaOTA
2718

SANDWICH EAST, Ont.
Assessment rolls, 1870-1890 Ibid.
N: USIGS 2 reels
P: CaOTA
2719

SANDWICH EAST TOWNSHIP, Ont.
Deeds, 1861-1876; deed index, 1882 Ibid.
N: USIGS 7 reels
P: CaOTA
2720

SANDWICH SOUTH TOWNSHIP, Ont.
Assessment rolls, 1894-1897 Ibid.
N: USIGS 1 reel
P: CaOTA
2721

SANDWICH TOWNSHIP, Ont.
Deeds, 1847-1860 Ibid.
N: USIGS 4 reels
P: CaOTA
2722

SANDWICH WEST, Ont.
Assessment rolls, 1870-1898 Ibid.
N: USIGS 2 reels
P: CaOTA
2723

SANDWICH WEST TOWNSHIP, Ont.
Council minutes, 1868-1899; deeds, 1861-1876
Ibid.
N: USIGS 8 reels
P: CaOTA
2724

SARAWAK TOWNSHIP, Ont.
Deeds, 1858-1877 Ibid.
N: USIGS 2 reels
P: CaOTA
2725

SARNIA, Ont.
Assessment rolls, 1857-1899; council
minutes, 1856-1899; deeds, 1851-1876
Ibid.
N: USIGS 28 reels
P: CaOTA
2726

SARNIA TOWNSHIP, Ont.
Assessment and collector rolls, 1850-1899;
council minutes, 1850-1900; deeds, 1847-1875
Ibid.
N: USIGS 12 reels
P: CaOTA
2727

SAUGEEN TOWNSHIP, Ont.
Deeds, 1856-1876 Ibid.
N: USIGS 4 reels
P: CaOTA
2728

SCARBORO TOWNSHIP, Ont.
Deeds, 1847-1877 Ibid.
N: USIGS 8 reels
P: CaOTA
2729

SCOTT TOWNSHIP, Ont.
Deeds, 1808-1878 Ibid.
N: USIGS 6 reels
P: CaOTA
2730

SCUGOG TOWNSHIP, Ont.
Deeds, 1817-1879 Ibid.
N: USIGS 4 reels
P: CaOTA
2731

SEAFORTH, Ont.
Deeds, 1860-1875 Ibid.
N: USIGS 5 reels
P: CaOTA
2732

SELKIRK, Ont.
Index of surveys, 1861-1957 Ibid.
N: USIGS 1 reel
P: CaOTA
2733

SENECA TOWNSHIP, Ont.
Deeds, 1847-1876; patent grants, 1846-1867
Ibid.
N: USIGS 7 reels
P: CaOTA
2734

SHAKESPEARE, Ont.
Deeds, 1854-1952 Ibid.
N: USIGS 3 reels
P: CaOTA
2735

SHELBURNE, Ont.
Deeds, 1866-1880 Ibid.
N: USIGS 2 reels
P: CaOTA
2736

SHERBROOKE TOWNSHIP, Ont.
Deeds, 1827-1885 Ibid.
N: USIGS 4 reels
P: CaOTA
2737

SHREWSBURY, Ont.
Deeds, 1853-1888 Ibid.
N: USIGS 2 reels
P: CaOTA
2738

SIMCOE, Ont.
Assessment rolls and collector rolls, 1882-
1899; council minutes, 1851-1899; deeds, 1850-
1876 Ibid.
N: USIGS 10 reels
P: CaOTA
2739

SOMBRA, Ont.
Deeds, 1854-1868 Ibid.
N: USIGS 1 reel
P: CaOTA
2740

SOMBRA TOWNSHIP, Ont.
Assessment and collector rolls, 1887-1889;
council minutes, 1851-1900; deeds, 1847-1876
Ibid.
N: USIGS 11 reels
P: CaOTA
2741

SOUTH CAYUGA TOWNSHIP, Ont.
Deeds, 1837-1878; patent grants, 1852-1862
Ibid.
N: USIGS 5 reels
P: CaOTA
2742

SOUTH DORCHESTER TOWNSHIP, Ont.
Assessment rolls, 1859-1899; collectors'
rolls, 1859-1899; council minutes, 1885-1898;
deeds, 1847-1876; voters' list, 1878 Ibid.
N: USIGS 12 reels
P: CaOTA
2743

SOUTH DUMFRIES TOWNSHIP, Ont.
Assessment and collectors' rolls, 1884-1899;
council minutes, 1819-1901; deeds, 1819-1877;
histories and genealogical notes, n.d. Ibid.
N: USIGS 17 reels
P: CaOTA
2744

SOUTH EASTHOPE TOWNSHIP, Ont.
Assessment rolls, 1880-1899; council
minutes, 1886-1901; deeds, 1847-1879 Ibid.
N: USIGS 9 reels
P: CaOTA
2745

SOUTH NORWICH TOWNSHIP, Ont.
Deeds, 1847-1875 Ibid.
N: USIGS 8 reels
P: CaOTA
2746

SOUTH WATERLOO TOWNSHIP, Ont.
Deeds, 1862 Ibid.
N: USIGS 1 reel
P: CaOTA
2747

SOUTHAMPTON, Ont.
Deeds, 1852-1880 Ibid.
N: USIGS 4 reels
P: CaOTA
2748

SOUTHWOLD TOWNSHIP, Ont.
Assessment rolls, 1856-1899; council
minutes, 1850-1900; deeds, 1847-1876 Ibid.
N: USIGS 22 reels
P: CaOTA
2749

SPARTA, Ont.
Index of surveys before 1876 Ibid.
N: USIGS 1 reel
P: CaOTA
2750

SPEYSIDE, Ont.
Index of surveys, 1844-1958 Ibid.
N: USIGS 1 reel
P: CaOTA
2751

STAFFA, Ont.
Index of surveys, 1839-1957 Ibid.
N: USIGS 1 reel
P: CaOTA
2752

STAMFORD TOWNSHIP, Ont.
Deeds, 1796-1877 Ibid.
N: USIGS 11 reels
P: CaOTA
2753

STANLEY TOWNSHIP, Ont.
Deeds, 1847-1876 Ibid.
N: USIGS 7 reels
P: CaOTA
2754

STAYNER, Ont.
Index of surveys, 1867-1958 Ibid.
N: USIGS 3 reels
P: CaOTA
2755

STEPHEN TOWNSHIP, Ont.
Deeds, 1847-1876 Ibid.
N: USIGS 7 reels
P: CaOTA
2756

STRATFORD, Ont.
Assessment rolls, 1855-1899; council
minutes, 1853-1901; deeds, 1850-1875 Ibid.
N: USIGS 26 reels
P: CaOTA
2757

STRATHROY, Ont.
Assessment rolls, 1880-1899; council
minutes, 1874-1899; deeds, 1847-1902 Ibid.
N: USIGS 27 reels
P: CaOTA
2758

STREETSVILLE, Ont.
Deeds, 1853-1879 Ibid.
N: USIGS 1 reel
P: CaOTA
2759

STROMNESS, Ont.
Index of surveys, 1855-1958 Ibid.
N: USIGS 1 reel
P: CaOTA
2760

SULLIVAN TOWNSHIP, Ont.
Deeds, 1848-1877 Ibid.
N: USIGS 4 reels
P: CaOTA
2761

SUNNIDALE TOWNSHIP, Ont.
Deeds, 1847-1877; patent grants, 1834-1865
Ibid.
N: USIGS 10 reels
P: CaOTA
2762

SUTTON, Ont.
Deeds, 1851-1870 Ibid.
N: USIGS 1 reel
P: CaOTA
2763

SYDENHAM TOWNSHIP, Ont.
Deeds, 1847-1877 Ibid.
N: USIGS 8 reels
P: CaOTA
2764

TARA, Ont.
Index of surveys, 1858-1957 Ibid.
N: USIGS 1 reel
P: CaOTA
2765

TAVISTOCK, Ont.
Deeds, 1851-1885 Ibid.
N: USIGS 2 reels
P: CaOTA
2766

TAY TOWNSHIP, Ont.
Deeds, 1847-1877 Ibid.
N: USIGS 7 reels
P: CaOTA
2767

TECUMSETH TOWNSHIP, Ont.
Deeds, 1847-1876; patent grants, 1820-1865
Ibid.
N: USIGS 12 reels
P: CaOTA
2768

TEESWATER, Ont.
Deeds, 1875-1882 Ibid.
N: USIGS 2 reels
P: CaOTA
2769

THAMESVILLE, Ont.
By-laws, 1874-1899; council minutes,
1874-1904; deeds, 1865-1881; vital records,
1895-1907 Ibid.
N: USIGS 6 reels
P: CaOTA
2770

THEDFORD, Ont.
Council minutes, 1886-1902; deeds, 1860-1879
Ibid.
N: USIGS 2 reels
P: CaOTA
2771

THORAH TOWNSHIP, Ont.
Deeds, 1822-1876 Ibid.
N: USIGS 5 reels
P: CaOTA
2772

THORNBURY, Ont.
Index of surveys, 1878-1957 Ibid.
N: USIGS 1 reel
P: CaOTA
2773

THOROLD, Ont.
Deeds, 1852-1877 Ibid.
N: USIGS 8 reels
P: CaOTA
2774

THOROLD TOWNSHIP, Ont.
Deeds, 1798-1876 Ibid.
N: USIGS 9 reels
P: CaOTA
2775

TILBURY, Ont.
Deeds, 1851-1885 Ibid.
N: USIGS 2 reels
P: CaOTA
2776

TILBURY NORTH TOWNSHIP
Assessment rolls, 1892-1899; council
minutes, 1892-1899 Ibid.
N: USIGS 2 reels
P: CaOTA
2777

TILBURY WEST TOWNSHIP, Ont.
Assessment rolls, 1870-1888; assessment
rolls and collectors' rolls, 1889-1899;
council minutes, 1886-1899; deeds, 1809-1876
Ibid.
N: USIGS 11 reels
P: CaOTA
2778

TILLSONBURG, Ont.
Deeds, 1872-1875 Ibid.
N: USIGS 2 reels
P: CaOTA
2779

TINY TOWNSHIP, Ont.
Deeds, 1847-1876; patent grants, 1822-1865
Ibid.
N: USIGS 9 reels
P: CaOTA
2780

TORONTO GORE TOWNSHIP, Ont.
Deeds, 1826-1881 Ibid.
N: USIGS 4 reels   2781
P: CaOTA

TORONTO TOWNSHIP, Ont.
Deeds, 1807-1876 Ibid.
N: USIGS 12 reels   2782
P: CaOTA

TOSSORONTIO TOWNSHIP, Ont.
Deeds, 1847-1875; patent grants, 1822-1865 Ibid.
N: USIGS 6 reels   2783
P: CaOTA

TOWNSEND TOWNSHIP, Ont.
Council minutes, 1862-1899; deeds, 1840-1876
Ibid.
N: USIGS 14 reels   2784
P: CaOTA

TRAFALGAR TOWNSHIP, Ont.
Deeds, 1847-1876 Ibid.
N: USIGS 12 reels   2785
P: CaOTA

TROWBRIDGE, Ont.
Deeds, 1857-1953 Ibid.
N: USIGS 3 reels   2786
P: CaOTA

TUCKERSMITH TOWNSHIP, Ont.
Deeds, 1847-1876 Ibid.
N: USIGS 7 reels   2787
P: CaOTA

TURNBERRY TOWNSHIP, Ont.
Deeds, 1855-1876 Ibid.
N: USIGS 6 reels   2788
P: CaOTA

TYRCONNELL, Ont.
Index of surveys, 1876 Ibid.
N: USIGS 1 reel   2789
P: CaOTA

USBORNE TOWNSHIP, Ont.
Deeds, 1848-1876 Ibid.
N: USIGS 6 reels   2790
P: CaOTA

UXBRIDGE, Ont.
Deeds, 1873-1876 Ibid.
N: USIGS 2 reels   2791
P: CaOTA

UXBRIDGE TOWNSHIP, Ont.
Deeds, 1805-1876 Ibid.
N: USIGS 9 reels   2792
P: CaOTA

VAUGHAN TOWNSHIP, Ont.
Deeds, 1847-1877 Ibid.
N: USIGS 12 reels   2793
P: CaOTA

VESPRA TOWNSHIP, Ont.
Deeds, 1847-1877; patent grants, 1821-1865 Ibid.
N: USIGS 11 reels   2794
P: CaOTA

VIENNA, Ont.
Council minutes, 1897-1900; deeds, 1854-1879
Ibid.
N: USIGS 5 reels   2795
P: CaOTA

WAINFLEET TOWNSHIP, Ont.
Deeds, 1797-1876 Ibid.
N: USIGS 8 reels   2796
P: CaOTA

WALKERTON, Ont.
Deeds, 1871-1876 Ibid.
N: USIGS 3 reels   2797
P: CaOTA

WALKERVILLE, Ont.
Council minutes, 1890-1899 Ibid.
N: USIGS 1 reel   2798
P: CaOTA

WALLACEBURG, Ont.
Council minutes, 1875-1888; deeds, 1851-1875
Ibid.
N: USIGS 6 reels   2799
P: CaOTA

WALLACETOWN, Ont.
Index of surveys, before 1876 Ibid.
N: USIGS 1 reel   2800
P: CaOTA

WALLACE TOWNSHIP, Ont.
Assessment and collector rolls, 1857-1899;
council minutes, 1858-1900; deeds, 1856-1875;
vital records, 1896-1907; voters' lists, 1877-
1898 Ibid.
N: USIGS 10 reels   2801
P: CaOTA

WALPOLE TOWNSHIP, Ont.
Deeds, 1798-1840, 1847-1876; patent grants,
1796-1862 Ibid.
N: USIGS 14 reels   2802
P: CaOTA

WALSINGHAM TOWNSHIP, Ont.
Deeds, 1840-1876 Ibid.
N: USIGS 13 reels   2803
P: CaOTA

WANSTEAD, Ont.
Deeds, 1860-1867 Ibid.
N: USIGS 1 reel   2804
P: CaOTA

WARDSVILLE, Ont.
Deeds, 1868-1900 Ibid.
N: USIGS 4 reels   2805
P: CaOTA

WARWICK TOWNSHIP, Ont.
Assessment and collector rolls, 1856-1898;
council minutes, 1850-1899; deeds, 1847-1875
Ibid.
N: USIGS 13 reels   2806
P: CaOTA

WATERDOWN, Ont.
Assessment rolls, 1880-1899; index of surveys,
1796-1875 Ibid.
N: USIGS 2 reels   2807
P: CaOTA

WATERFORD, Ont.
Council minutes, 1878-1899 Ibid.
N: USIGS 1 reel   2808
P: CaOTA

WATERLOO, Ont.
Deeds, 1857-1877 Ibid.
N: USIGS 4 reels   2809
P: CaOTA

WATERLOO TOWNSHIP, Ont.
Deeds, 1847-1875 Ibid.
N: USIGS 15 reels   2810
P: CaOTA

WATFORD, Ont.
Deeds, 1862-1883 Ibid.
N: USIGS 1 reel   2811
P: CaOTA

WAWANOSH TOWNSHIP, Ont.
Deeds, 1847-1876 Ibid.
N: USIGS 9 reels   2812
P: CaOTA

WELLAND, Ont.
Deeds, 1853-1876 Ibid.
N: USIGS 10 reels   2813
P: CaOTA

WELLANDPORT, Ont.
Deeds, 1859-1865 Ibid.
N: USIGS 1 reel   2814
P: CaOTA

WELLESLEY TOWNSHIP, Ont.
Deeds, 1849-1875 Ibid.
N: USIGS 6 reels   2815
P: CaOTA

WEST DOVER TOWNSHIP, Ont.
Deeds, 1847-1886 Ibid.
N: USIGS 2 reels   2816
P: CaOTA

WEST FLAMBOROUGH TOWNSHIP, Ont.
Assessment and collector rolls, 1861-1899;
council minutes, 1866-1899; deeds, 1816-1876
Ibid.
N: USIGS 17 reels   2817
P: CaOTA

WEST GARAFRAXA TOWNSHIP, Ont.
Deeds, 1822-1824 Ibid.
N: USIGS 13 reels   2818
P: CaOTA

WEST GWILLIMBURY TOWNSHIP, Ont.
Deeds, 1847-1880; patent grants, 1803-1864
Ibid.
N: USIGS 11 reels   2819
P: CaOTA

WEST LUTHER TOWNSHIP, Ont.
Deeds, 1847-1876 Ibid.
N: USIGS 6 reels   2820
P: CaOTA

WEST MONKTON, Ont.
Deeds, 1857-1920 Ibid.
N: USIGS 3 reels   2821
P: CaOTA

WEST NISSOURI TOWNSHIP, Ont.
Abstracts of titles, 1821-1853; assessment
rolls, 1853-1899; deeds, 1830-1904 Ibid.
N: USIGS 33 reels   2822
P: CaOTA

WEST OXFORD TOWNSHIP, Ont.
Deeds, 1847-1877 Ibid.
N: USIGS 9 reels   2823
P: CaOTA

WEST WILLIAMS TOWNSHIP, Ont.
Assessment and collection rolls, 1865-1899;
council minutes, 1869-1919; deeds, 1863-1902
Ibid.
N: USIGS 14 reels   2824
P: CaOTA

WEST ZORRA TOWNSHIP, Ont.
Deeds, 1847-1876 Ibid.
N: USIGS 7 reels   2825
P: CaOTA

WESTMINSTER TOWNSHIP, Ont.
Assessment rolls, 1870-1899; council minutes,
1817-1913; deeds, 1847-1901; wills, 1866-1888
Ibid.
N: USIGS 39 reels   2826
P: CaOTA

WESTON, Ont.
Deeds, 1852-1865 Ibid.
N: USIGS 1 reel   2827
P: CaOTA

WHEATLEY, Ont.
Deeds, 1842-1900 Ibid.
N: USIGS 3 reels   2828
P: CaOTA

WHITBY, Ont.
Deeds, 1854-1876 Ibid.
N: USIGS 8 reels   2829
P: CaOTA

WHITBY TOWNSHIP, Ont.
Deeds, 1800-1875 Ibid.
N: USIGS 14 reels   2830
P: CaOTA

WHITCHURCH TOWNSHIP, Ont.
Deeds, 1797-1876 Ibid.
N: USIGS 12 reels   2831
P: CaOTA

WILLOUGHBY TOWNSHIP, Ont.
Deeds, 1796-1877 Ibid.
N: USIGS 6 reels   2832
P: CaOTA

WILMOT TOWNSHIP, Ont.
Deeds, 1798-1815, 1847-1876 Ibid.
N: USIGS 10 reels   2833
P: CaOTA

WINDHAM TOWNSHIP, Ont.
Council minutes, 1836-1899; deeds, 1840-1876
Ibid.
N: USIGS 13 reels   2834
P: CaOTA

WINDSOR, Ont.
Assessment rolls, 1854-1899; council minutes,
1854-1899; deeds, 1853-1876 Ibid.
N: USIGS 29 reels   2835
P: CaOTA

WINGHAM, Ont.
Deeds, 1862-1877 Ibid.
N: USIGS 3 reels   2836
P: CaOTA

WOODHOUSE TOWNSHIP, Ont.
Council minutes, 1873-1899; deeds, 1840-1876
Ibid.
N: USIGS 9 reels   2837
P: CaOTA

WOODSTOCK, Ont.
Deeds, 1847-1875 Ibid.
N: USIGS 10 reels   2838
P: CaOTA

WOOLWICH TOWNSHIP, Ont.
Deeds, 1819-1875 Ibid.
N: USIGS 10 reels   2839
P: CaOTA

WORSOW, Ont.
Index of surveys, 1858-1947 Ibid.
N: USIGS 1 reel   2840
P: CaOTA

WROXETER, Ont.
Deeds, 1860-1877 Ibid.
N: USIGS 2 reels   2841
P: CaOTA

WYOMING, Ont.
Assessment rolls, 1876-1898; council minutes,
1877-1899; deeds, 1857-1883 Ibid.
N: USIGS 6 reels   2842
P: CaOTA

YARMOUTH TOWNSHIP, Ont.
Council minutes, 1850-1901; deeds, 1847-1876
Ibid.
N: USIGS 21 reels   2843
P: CaOTA

YORK, Ont.
Index of surveys, 1841-1957 Ibid.
N: USIGS 1 reel   2844
P: CaOTA

YORK TOWNSHIP, Ont.
Deeds, 1796-1876; index of surveys, to 1958 Ibid.
N: USIGS 67 reels   2845
P: CaOTA

ZONE TOWNSHIP, Ont.
Deeds, 1847-1878 Ibid.
N: USIGS 6 reels   2846
P: CaOTA

Church Records

AILSA CRAIG, Ont. PRESBYTERIAN CHURCH
Minutes, 1887-1893; records, 1869-1956 Ibid.
N: USIGS 2 reels   2847
P: CaOTA

AMHERSTBURG, Ont. CHRIST CHURCH
(Anglican)
Parish register, 1829-1912 Ibid.
N: MiD-B   2848

AMHERSTBURG, Ont. PRESBYTERIAN CHURCH
Records, 1831-1899 Ibid.
N: USIGS 1 reel   2849
P: CaOTA

ATWOOD, Ont. PRESBYTERIAN CHURCH
Records, 1863-1904 Ibid.
N: USIGS 1 reel   2850
P: CaOTA

AVONTON, Ont. AVON PRESBYTERIAN
CHURCH
Records, 1859-1900 Ibid.
N: USIGS 1 reel   2851
P: CaOTA

BELMONT, Ont. PRESBYTERIAN CHURCH
Records, 1862-1900 Ibid.
N: USIGS 1 reel   2852
P: CaOTA

CAMLACHIE, Ont. PRESBYTERIAN CHURCH
Records, 1852-1900 Ibid.
N: USIGS 1 reel   2853
P: CaOTA

CARLUKE, Ont. PRESBYTERIAN CHURCH
Records, 1845-1899 Ibid.
N: USIGS 1 reel   2854
P: CaOTA

CHATHAM, Ont. PRESBYTERIAN CHURCH
Records, 1848-1925 Ibid.
N: USIGS 2 reels   2855
P: CaOTA

CHATHAM, Ont. ST. PAUL'S ANGLICAN
CHURCH
Register, 1829-1841 Ibid.
N: MiD   2856

CRIEFF, Ont. KNOX PRESBYTERIAN CHURCH
Baptismal records, 1855-1899; marriage
records, 1897-1899 Ibid.
N: USIGS 1 reel   2857
P: CaOTA

DRESDEN, Ont. PRESBYTERIAN CHURCH
Minutes, 1881-1919 Ibid.
N: USIGS 1 reel   2858
P: CaOTA

EAST TILBURY TOWNSHIP, Ont.
PRESBYTERIAN CHURCH
Records, 1879-1900 Ibid.
N: USIGS 1 reel   2859
P: CaOTA

EAST WILLIAMS TOWNSHIP, Ont.
PRESBYTERIAN CHURCH
Marriages, 1856-1899 Ibid.
N: USIGS 1 reel   2860
P: CaOTA

ELORA, Ont. CHALMERS PRESBYTERIAN
CHURCH (Disbanded)
Baptismal records, 1856-1899; communion
roll, 1859-1895; session minute book, 1856-
1899 Ibid.
N: USIGS 1 reel   2861
P: CaOTA

ELORA, Ont. KNOX PRESBYTERIAN CHURCH
Baptismal records, 1837-1899; communion
rolls, 1854-1887; marriage records, 1856-
1899; session minute book, 1837-1850, 1859-
1899 Ibid.
N: USIGS 1 reel   2862
P: CaOTA

FERGUS, Ont. ST. ANDREWS PRESBYTERIAN
CHURCH
Baptismal records, 1845-1899 Ibid.
N: USIGS 1 reel   2863
P: CaOTA

FINGAL, Ont. PRESBYTERIAN CHURCH
Records, 1857-1900 Ibid.
N: USIGS 1 reel   2864
P: CaOTA

FOREST, Ont. PRESBYTERIAN CHURCH
Records, 1884-1909 Ibid.
N: USIGS 1 reel   2865
P: CaOTA

GUELPH, Ont. KNOX PRESBYTERIAN CHURCH
Baptismal records, 1853-1899; financial
records, 1870-1895 Ibid.
N: USIGS 1 reel   2866
P: CaOTA

GUELPH, Ont. ST. ANDREWS PRESBYTERIAN
CHURCH
Baptismal records, 1858-1899; congregational
records, 1856-1900; marriage records, 1858-
1899; session minute book, 1832-1899 Ibid.
N: USIGS 2 reels   2867
P: CaOTA

HAMILTON, Ont. PRESBYTERIAN CHURCH
Records, 1841-1899 Ibid.
N: USIGS 5 reels   2868
P: CaOTA

INGERSOLL, Ont. METHODIST CHURCH
Marriages, 1900-1902 Ibid.
N: USIGS 1 reel   2869
P: CaOTA

KOMOKA, Ont. PRESBYTERIAN CHURCH
Records, 1873-1899 Ibid.
N: USIGS 1 reel   2870
P: CaOTA

LEAMINGTON, Ont. KNOX PRESBYTERIAN
CHURCH
Records, 1889-1908 Ibid.
N: USIGS 1 reel   2871
P: CaOTA

LISTOWEL, Ont. KNOX PRESBYTERIAN
CHURCH
Records, 1869-1900 Ibid.
N: USIGS 1 reel   2872
P: CaOTA

LONDON TOWNSHIP, Ont. PRESBYTERIAN
CHURCH
Records, 1868-1912 Ibid.
N: USIGS 1 reel   2873
P: CaOTA

LONDON TOWNSHIP, Ont. ST. JAMES
PRESBYTERIAN CHURCH
Records, 1858-1903 Ibid.
N: USIGS 1 reel   2874
P: CaOTA

MERRITTON, Ont. ST. ANDREW'S
PRESBYTERIAN CHURCH
Records, 1867-1899 Ibid.
N: USIGS 1 reel   2875
P: CaOTA

MILVERTON, Ont. BURNS PRESBYTERIAN
CHURCH
Records, 1861-1900 Ibid.
N: USIGS 1 reel   2876
P: CaOTA

MITCHELL, Ont. KNOX PRESBYTERIAN
CHURCH
Records, 1856-1900 Ibid.
N: USIGS 1 reel   2877
P: CaOTA

MOLESWORTH, Ont. ST. ANDREW'S
PRESBYTERIAN CHURCH
Records, 1869-1900 Ibid.
N: USIGS 1 reel   2878
P: CaOTA

MORRISTON, Ont. DUFFS PRESBYTERIAN
CHURCH
Baptismal records, 1840-1899; congregational
minute book, 1835-1899; marriage records,
1840-1899 Ibid.
N: USIGS 1 reel   2879
P: CaOTA

NORTH MORNINGTON, Ont. BURNS
PRESBYTERIAN CHURCH
Marriages, 1896-1900 Ibid.
N: USIGS 1 reel   2880
P: CaOTA

PERTH, Ont. ST. ANDREWS CHURCH
Register of births, marriages and deaths,
1830-1887 Ibid.
N: CaOOA 25 feet   2881

PETROLIA, Ont. ST. ANDREWS PRESBYTERIAN
CHURCH
Records, 1858-1900 Ibid.
N: USIGS 1 reel   2882
P: CaOTA

POINT EDWARD, Ont. PRESBYTERIAN CHURCH
Records, 1872-1903 Ibid.
N: USIGS 1 reel   2883
P: CaOTA

PORT DOVER, Ont. KNOX PRESBYTERIAN
CHURCH
Records, 1849-1899 Ibid.
N: USIGS 1 reel   2884
P: CaOTA

PUCE, Ont. ST. ANDREWS PRESBYTERIAN
CHURCH
Records, 1881-1904 Ibid.
N: USIGS 1 reel   2885
P: CaOTA

ST. CATHERINES, Ont. PRESBYTERIAN
CHURCH
Baptisms and marriages, 1860-1899 Ibid.
N: USIGS 1 reel   2886
P: CaOTA

ST. MARYS, Ont. PRESBYTERIAN CHURCH
Marriages (First Church), 1896-1900;
marriages (Knox Church), 1896-1900 Ibid.
N: UslGS 2 reels 2887
P: CaOTA

ST. THOMAS, Ont. ALMA STREET
PRESBYTERIAN CHURCH
Records, 1890-1900 Ibid.
N: UslGS 1 reel 2888
P: CaOTA

ST. THOMAS, Ont. KNOX PRESBYTERIAN
CHURCH
Records, 1896-1900 Ibid.
N: UslGS 2889
P: CaOTA

SANDWICH, Ont. ST. JOHN'S CHURCH
(Anglican)
Church wardens' book, 1821-1857 Ibid.
N: MiD 2890

SARNIA, Ont. PRESBYTERIAN CHURCH
Records, 1843-1903 Ibid.
N: UslGS 1 reel 2891
P: CaOTA

SHAKESPEARE, Ont. PRESBYTERIAN CHURCH
Records, 1857-1899 Ibid.
N: UslGS 1 reel 2892
P: CaOTA

SIMCOE, Ont. PRESBYTERIAN CHURCH
Records, 1849-1899 Ibid.
N: UslGS 1 reel 2893
P: CaOTA

STRATHROY, Ont. ST. ANDREWS
PRESBYTERIAN CHURCH
Records, 1863-1913 Ibid.
N: UslGS 1 reel 2894
P: CaOTA

THAMESVILLE, Ont. PRESBYTERIAN CHURCH
Records, 1866-1909 Ibid.
N: UslGS 1 reel 2895
P: CaOTA

THEDFORD, Ont. PRESBYTERIAN CHURCH
Baptisms and marriages, 1866-1915 Ibid.
N: UslGS 1 reel 2896
P: CaOTA

UPPER CANADA CLERGY CORPORATION
Minutes, 1819-1835
N: CaOTA 50 feet 2897
P: CaOTA

WALLACEBURG, Ont. PRESBYTERIAN CHURCH
Baptisms and marriages, 1882-1905 Ibid.
N: UslGS 1 reel 2898
P: CaOTA

WARWICK, Ont. PRESBYTERIAN CHURCH
Records, 1854-1905 Ibid.
N: UslGS 1 reel 2899
P: CaOTA

WATERTOWN, Ont. PRESBYTERIAN CHURCH
Baptisms, 1878-1901 Ibid.
N: UslGS 1 reel 2900
P: CaOTA

WEST WILLIAMS TOWNSHIP, Ont. WILLIAMS
PRESBYTERIAN CHURCH
Church history, n.d. Ibid.
N: UslGS 1 reel 2901
P: CaOTA

WINDSOR, Ont. PRESBYTERIAN CHURCH
Records, 1857-1900 Ibid.
N: UslGS 1 reel 2902
P: CaOTA

WOODSTOCK, Ont. METHODIST CHURCH
Marriages, 1896-1912 Ibid.
N: UslGS 1 reel 2903
P: CaOTA

WOODSTOCK, Ont. PRESBYTERIAN CHURCH
Marriages, 1907-1919 Ibid.
N: UslGS 1 reel 2904
P: CaOTA

YARMOUTH TOWNSHIP, Ont. PRESBYTERIAN
CHURCH

Baptisms, 1889-1900 Ibid.
N: UslGS 1 reel 2905
P: CaOTA

Personal Papers

ANDERSON, Capt. THOMAS GUMMERSALL
Papers, 1814-1822 WHi
N: WHi 25 feet 2906
P: CaOTA

BULGER, ANDREW, 1789-1858
Papers, 1814-1849, 14 items CaOOA
DCO: MnHi 2907

CROOKSHANK, GEORGE, Receiver General
Crookshank-Lambert letters, 1801-1861
CaOTA
N: CaOTA 40 feet 2908

DICKSON, ROBERT, 1765-1823
Papers, 1790-1822 CaOOA WHi
DCO: MnHi 1 box 2909

FAIRHOLME FAMILY
Papers, 1834-1845 priv.
N: CaOOA 20 feet 2910

[FARIES, HUGH?], 1779-1852
Diary, Rainy River, 1804, 40 p. CaOOA
DCO: MnHi 2911

FARMAR, HUGH HOVELL
Letters re: intended emigration from
Ireland to Upper Canada, 1783-1820 priv.
N: CaOOA 20 feet 2912

FARR, CHARLES COBBOLD, 1851-1914
Autobiography (typescript) priv.
N: CaOOA 25 feet 2913

GRUBBE FAMILY
History, 1783-1934
N: CaOTA 25 feet 2914
P: CaOTA

JOHNSON, Capt. WILLIAM
Diaries, 1832-1850
N: CaOTA 25 feet 2915
P: CaOTA

LUNDY, Rev. F. J., Rector of Grimsby, Ontario
Diaries, 1849-1867 (5 years missing) priv.
N: CaOTA 4 reels 2916

McNEILLEDGE, ALEXANDER, 1792-1874
Diaries, 1837-1875 CaONHi
N: CaOOA 3 reels 2917

MILNE, DAVID
Letters from James Clarke, 1923-1940
CaOOA
N: CaOOA 1 reel* 2918

MORRISON, JAMES J., 1861-1936
Memoirs as secretary of the Ontario Grange,
1907, 1914-1933 (typescript) CaOOA
N: CaOOA 1 reel 2919

PATTESON, THOMAS CHARLES
Family correspondence, 1858-1863,
1875 priv.
N: CaOTA 50 feet 2920

ROBINSON, GEORGE
Diary, Asiatic cholera, June-Sept., 1832
priv.
N: CaOOA 12 feet 2921
P: CaOOa

ROBINSON, Sir JOHN BEVERLEY, Bart.,
1791-1863
Diaries, 1815-1817 priv.
N: CaOTA 50 feet 2922

ROBINSON, Sir JOHN BEVERLEY, Bart.,
1791-1863
Letters to J. B. Robinson and Emma Walker,
1803-1822; Autograph letters and portraits
priv.
N: CaOTA 1 reel 2923

ROBINSON, PETER
Papers re: the Irish settlement in the Bathurst

District and Peterborough County, Upper Canada,
1823, 1825 CaOTA
N: CaOTA 2 reels 2924

ROWELL, NEWTON WESLEY, 1867-1941
Correspondence and papers, 1887-1941 CaOOA
N: CaOOA 17 reels * 2925

SMITH, ELIAS
Letter book, 1799-1880 MH-BA
N: CaOOA 1 reel 2926

SMITH, Sir HENRY
Sporting register, 1864-1908
N: CaOTA 10 feet 2927

SPARKS, NICHOLAS, 1792-1862
Respondents' exhibits, 1839-1848, in
Exchequer court suit for trespass on
Ordnance lands at Ottawa priv.
N: CaOOA 20 feet 2928

STRACHAN, JOHN, Bp., 1778-1867
Autobiography and diary to 1799; letters
and documents, mainly from Strachan to
Rev. A.N. Bethune, 1835-1866
N: CaOTA 50 feet 2929

WILSON, Rev. EDWARD FRANCIS, 1844-1915
Autobiography and family history priv.
N: CaOTA 50 feet 2930
P: CaOTA

WOOD, ALEXANDER
Letter book, 1822-1829
N: CaOTA 50 feet 2931

Business Papers

CASE, WILLIAM, 1776-1848
Account books, medical practice, Hamilton,
Ont., 1825-1867 priv.
N: CaOOA 2932

TORONTO TRADES AND LABOUR COUNCIL
Minutes, 1881-1893 Canadian Labour Congress
N: CaOOA 1 reel 2933

TORONTO TRADES ASSEMBLY
Minutes, 1871-1878 Canadian Labour Congress
N: CaOOA 1 reel 2934

WRIGHT, RUGGLES, ca. 1798-1863
Lumbering and real estate papers, 1816-1862
priv.
N: CaOOA 1 reel 2935
P: CaOOA

Collections

CANADA. PUBLIC ARCHIVES
Material re: Nils G. Szoltevki or Von Schoultz
and the attack at Point Windmill, Prescott,
Ont., 1838 CaOOA
DCO: NSyU 75 p. 2936

FEDERATED WOMEN'S INSTITUTES OF CANADA.
ONTARIO
Tweedsmuir Histories (13 local histories of towns
or townships)
N: CaOTA 2 reels 2937

LENNOX AND ADDINGTON HISTORICAL SOCIETY,
Napanee, Ont.
Collections Ibid.
N: CaOOA 22 reels 2938
P: Ibid.

FUR TRADE AND THE WEST

Government Records

BATTLEFORD INDIAN AGENCY, Sask.
Pay lists, treaty money to Indians after Riel
Rebellion, 1885 Ibid.
N: CaACG 1 reel 2939

BUREAU OF SOCIAL RESEARCH OF THE
GOVERNMENTS OF MANITOBA,
SASKATCHEWAN, AND ALBERTA
Ukrainian Rural Communities: Investigation,
1916   CaSRA
N: CaMWP   2940

CANADA. DEPT. OF JUSTICE
Records re: Louis Riel, 1873-1886   CaOOA
N: CaOOA 400 feet
P: CaSSA   2941

CANADA. DEPT. OF THE INTERIOR
Orders in Council, 1864-1905   Dept. of
Natural Resources, Regina, Sask.
N: CaSSA 1100 feet   2942

CANADA. GOVERNOR GENERAL, 1768-1807
Papers re: fur trade   CaOOA
DCO: MnHi 1 box   2943

GREAT BRITAIN. ARMY. DE MEURON'S
REGIMENT
Pay list, Dec. 1815- Sept. 1816
DCO: CaMWPA 130 p.   2944

GREAT BRITAIN. COLONIAL OFFICE
Papers re: Palliser expedition, 1857-1862
UKLPRO
N: UKLPRO 1 reel
P: CaSRA   2945

GREAT BRITAIN. COLONIAL OFFICE.C.O.134
Hudson's Bay. Original correspondence,
1675-1759, 3 v.   UKLPRO
N: CaOOA
DCO: DLC   2946

GREAT BRITAIN. COLONIAL OFFICE. C.O. 135
Hudson's Bay. Entry books, 1670-1789, 4 v.
UKLPRO
N: CaOOA 1 reel   2947

HOBBEMA INDIAN AGENCY, Alta.
Lists of half-breeds who have withdrawn
from Indian treaty, July 12, 1886, June 1,
1888, for Alberta and Saskatchewan, 45 p.
Ibid.
PP: CaACG   2948

NORTHWEST TERRITORIES, Canada. ADVISORY
COUNCIL
Minutes on matters of finance, 1888-1891
CaSSA
N: CaSRA 8 feet   2949

NORTHWEST TERRITORIES, Canada. COUNCIL
Bills and unpublished sessional papers, 1887-
1887   Sasketchewan Legislative Assembly
Office
N: CaSRA 2 reels   2950

NORTHWEST TERRITORIES, Canada. COUNCIL
Orders in council, 1892-1899; indexes and
registers of orders in council, 1892-1905
CaSRL
N: CaSRA 2 reels
P: CaSSA   2951

NORTHWEST TERRITORIES, Canada.
EXECUTIVE COMMITTEE
Minutes, 1892-1897   CaSSA
N: CaSRA 20 feet   2952

NORTHWEST TERRITORIES, Canada.
LEGISLATIVE ASSEMBLY
Bills, petitions, unpublished sessional papers,
and select committee reports, 1888-1905
Sasketchewan Legislative Assembly Office
N: CaSRA 6 reels
P: CaSSA   2953

NORTHWEST TERRITORIES, Canada.
LIEUTENANT GOVERNOR
Proclamations and orders, nos. 1-2425, 1885-
1897   Sasketchewan Executive Council Office
N: CaSRA 2 reels   2954

Church Records

ANGLICAN CHURCH IN CANADA. DIOCESES.
RUPERT'S LAND
Letters Patent of erection of see, May 21, 1849
DCO: CaMWPA 11 p.   2955

CHURCH MISSIONARY SOCIETY, 1799-
Papers re: Rupert's Land and North West
Pacific missions, 1821-1924   UKLCMH
N: CaOOA 52 reels   2956

KEEWATIN (Vicariat Apostolique)
Archives   Ibid.
N: CaOOSJ   2957

Personal Papers

ASKIN, JOHN, 1739-1815
Papers, 1791-1812   MiD-B
N: ? 1 reel
P: MiD-B   2958

CHABOILLEZ, CHARLES, 1772-1812
Journal, Aug. 1797-June 1798, expedition to
Winnipeg and Pembina rivers   CaOOA
N: CaOOA 20 feet   2959

CHABOILLEZ, CHARLES JEAN BAPTISTE,
1736-1808
Journal, 1797-1798, 71 p.   CaQMM
DCO: MnHi   2960

CHARLEBOIS, Mgr. OVIDE
Papiers   Vicariat Apostolique de Keewatin
N: CaOOSJ   2961

CLAUS, DANIEL
Papers, 1716-1780   CaOOA
DCO: DLC 2 v.
N: WHi   2962

CLOUSTON, JAMES STEWART
Papers re: Hudson's Bay Co., 1838-1850,
72 p.   priv.
N: CaOOA 10 feet   2963

CONNOR, THOMAS, b. ca. 1780, North West
Company trader
Diary, 1804-1805, 33 p.   CaOOA
DCO: MnHi   2964

COWAN, WILLIAM, surgeon
Diaries, Fort Garry, 1852-1855, 1862-1871;
Moose Factory, 1856-1862; return to
England, 1862-1865   CaOOA
N: CaOOA 1 reel
P: CaMWPA CaOOA   2965

CROOKS, RAMSAY, 1787-1859
Correspondence, 1813-1828   priv.
DCO: NN 2 v.   2966

ERMATINGER, EDWARD, 1797-1876
In-letters, 1820-1874, 2 v.   CaOOA
N: CaOOA 55 feet
P: CaBViPA CU-B UHi   2967

FISHER, HENRY, Hudson's Bay trader
Correspondence, 1826-1867   Catholic
Archdiocese of Manitoba, St. Boniface, Man.
N: MnHi 2 reels   2968

HARGRAVE FAMILY
Papers, 1821-1886   CaOOA
N: CaOOA 12 reels   2969

HECTOR, Sir JAMES, 1834-1906
Papers re: Palliser expedition, 1857-1862
NzDOU
N: ? 2 reels
P: CaSRA   2970

JACOB, SAMUEL, 1760-1827
Business papers [English and Yiddish]; letters
from Canada, 1763-1798   CaOOA
N: CaOOA
P: NNYi   2971

LA VÉRENDRYE, PIERRE GAULTIER DE
VARENNES, Sieur de, 1685-1749
Papers, 1735-1748, 4 items   CaOOA
Catholic Archdiocese of St. Boniface, Man.
priv.
DCO: MnHi   2972

LOWE, THOMAS
Papers, letters, journals and accounts with
Hudson's Bay Company, 1841-1863   priv.
N: CaBViPA   2973

McGILLIVRAY, WILLIAM, 1764?-1825
Journal, 1793, 50 p.   CaQMM
DCO: MnHi   2974

MACKENZIE, Sir ALEXANDER, 1763-1820
Journal of voyage from Athabaska to Arctic
Ocean, 1789   UKLBM
N: WaPS 1 reel   2975

McKENZIE, RODERICK, ca. 1761-1844
Papers, 1786-1808   CaOOA CaQMM
DCO: MnHi 1 box   2976

McLEOD, JOHN, 1788-1859
Papers, 1811-1842   CaOOA
N: MnHi 1 reel   2977

McLEOD, JOHN, 1788-1859
Papers, 1823-1849   CaOOA
N: CaOOA 1 reel
P: CU-B CaBViPA UHi   2978

NAVARRE, ROBERT, 1709-1791
Journal...Pontiac's Rebellion (transcript)
CaOOA
N: CaOOA 25 feet   2979

POND, PETER, 1740-1807
Papers, 1773-1777   CaOT MiD-B NBuHi
DCO: MnHi 1 box   2980

RADISSON, PIERRE ESPRIT, ca. 1620-1710, and
GROSEILLIERS, MÉDARD CHOUART, Sieur de,
1618-ca. 1685
Papers, 1618-1694   CaQQA ICHi ICN M-Ar
FrBN UKLBM UKO Mayor, Charly-sur-Marne
DCO: MnHi 1 box   2981

SELKIRK, THOMAS DOUGLAS, 5th EARL of,
1771-1820
Papers, 1802-1833 (transcript)   CaOOA
N: CaOOA 20 reels
P: CaBViPA CaMWPA   2982

SELKIRK, THOMAS DOUGLAS, 5th EARL of,
1771-1820
Papers, 1806-1824   DNA priv.
DCO: MnHi 1 box   2983

SIFTON, Sir CLIFFORD, 1861-1929
Papers, 1889-1926   CaOOA
N: CaOOA 202 reels   2984

THOMPSON, DAVID, 1770-1857
Narrative of explorations, 1784-1812   CaOT
CaOTA
N: CaOOA 90 feet   2985

THOMPSON, DAVID, 1770-1857
Papers, 1797-1798, 1804, 1820-1843   CaOOA
CaOTA
DCO: MnHi 1 box   2986

TRUDEAU, JEAN BAPTISTE
Journal, 1795   CaQQLa-Ar
N: CaQQLa 1 reel   2987

UMFREVILLE, EDWARD, of Northwest Company
Diary, 1784   CaQMM
DCO: MnHi 1 box   2988

Business Papers

GRANT, CAMPION, AND COMPANY, Montreal
Papers, 1792-1794, 43 items   CaQMSS
DCO: MnHi   2989

HUDSON'S BAY COMPANY, 1670-
Papers, selections, 1679-1842
MnU UKLPRO General Register House,
Edinburgh Beaver House, London
DCO: MnHi 1 box
N: MnHi 2 reels   2990

HUDSON'S BAY COMPANY, 1670-
Proceedings, 1866-1947; report to governor,
1863-1899   UKLHB
N: WaU 4 reels   2991

HUDSON'S BAY COMPANY, 1670-
Records, 1670-1870   UKLHB
N: CaOOA 1600 reels*
P: CaOOA   2992

Collections

CANADA. PUBLIC ARCHIVES
Claus papers, 1761-1796; Indian records, 1723-1746; Monckton papers, 1760-1761; Board of Trade transcripts, 1696-1749; Registre du Fort Dusquesne; extracts from Joncaire papers, and Fonds Verreau (transcript)   CaOOA
N: unknown 2 reels   2993
P: NjP PHarH

ROYAL GEOGRAPHICAL SOCIETY, London
Papers re: Palliser expedition, selections, 1856-1860   UKLGS
N: CaSRA 15 feet   2994

MANITOBA

Government Records

CANADA. DEPT. OF TRANSPORT
Winnipeg shipping registers, 1875-1887   CaOOA
N: CaMWPA 75 feet   2995

U.S. DEPT. OF STATE
Letters received from the agent for Red River affairs, 1867-1870   DNA
N: DNA 1 reel [T-23]   2996
P: CaMWPA

Provincial Records

MANITOBA. BOUNDARY COMMISSION, 1872
Note book and journal of orders   priv.
DCO: CaMWPA 98 p.   2997

Church Records

NORWAY HOUSE, Man. WESLEYAN METHODIST CHAPEL
Baptism register, 1840-1854, 108 p.   CaMWPA
DCO: MnHi   2998

PORTAGE LA PRAIRIE, Man. ST. MARY'S CHURCH (Anglican)
Registers, 1855-1883   Ibid.
N: CaMWPA 30 feet   2999

ST. BONIFACE, Man. (Archdiocese)
Correspondence, 1861-1868   Ibid.
N: MnHi 1 reel   3000

Personal Papers

BEGG, ALEXANDER, 1839-1897
Red River journals, Nov., 1869-July, 1870   CaOOA
N: CaOOA 15 feet   3001

CADOTTE, JEAN BAPTISTE, 1761-1818
Letter and contracts, 1795-1796, 8 p.   CaOOA
DCO: CaMWPA   3002

CUNNINGHAM, ROBERT
Correspondence and papers, 1872-1875, 20 items   priv.
N: CaMWPA 4 feet   3003

Journal of trip into Canada via the Red River   CaQMM
N: ?   3004
P: MnU

LAURIER, Sir WILFRID, 1841-1919
Papers re: Manitoba schools   CaOKQ
N: CaOOA 3 reels   3005

LA VÉRENDRYE, PIERRE GAULTIER DE VARENNES, Sieur de, 1685-1749

Letter and contract, 1735, 1748   MnHi
DCO: CaMWPA CaOOA 5 p.   3006

McCREADY, S. B.
Manitoba scrapbook, 1880-1940; diary, 1888-1893   priv.
N: CaMWPA 25 feet   3007

MACDONALD, Sir JOHN ALEXANDER, 1815-1891
Letters to Sidney Smith and H. H. Smith, 1857-1891, 126 items   CaOOA
DCO: CaMWPA   3008

MacDONELL, MILES, 1769-1828
Correspondence, 1812-1816, 5 items   CaOOA
DCO: MnHi   3009

McKENZIE, KENNETH, of Burnside, Man.
Diary of Red River Troubles, Jan. 25-Nov. 18, 1870   priv.
N: CaMWPA 10 feet   3010

MORRIS, ALEXANDER, 1826-1889
Papers, 1873-1877   CaMWPA
N: CaOOA 2 reels   3011
P: CaSRA

MORRIS, ALEXANDER, 1826-1889
Papers, including those of William Morris   CaOKQ
N: CaOOA 2 reels   3012

SISSONS, THOMAS, Jr., of Portage la Prairie, Man.
Diary, 1873-1899   priv.
N: CaMWPA 50 feet   3013

SPENCE, THOMAS, 1832-1900
"Red River troubles," 1869-1870   CaMWPA; (transcript) 149 p.   CaOOA
N: CaOOA   3014

TAYLOR, JAMES WICKES, 1819-1893
Papers, 1842-1894   MnHi
N: MnHi 8 reels   3015
P: CaMWP CaOOA NNC

TRAILL, WALTER J. S.
Correspondence, 1864-1880   priv.
N: CaMWPA 50 feet*   3016

Business Papers

HENDRY, JOHN, farmer, of Virden, Man.
Journal and account books, 1907-1938, 300 p.   priv.
N: CaMWPA   3017

McDOUGALL, Rev. G. M., of Portage la Prairie, Man.
Account book, 1874-1889   priv.
N: CaMWPA 10 feet   3018

WINNIPEG, Man. CITIZENS
Petition to Governor General, asking that the Canadian Pacific Railway cross the Red River at Winnipeg, 1875   CaMWPA
N: CaMWPA   3019

SASKATCHEWAN

Government Records

CANADA. DEPT. OF PUBLIC WORKS
Correspondence re: Swan River barracks, 1875-1879   Ibid.
N: CaSRA 30 feet   3020

CANADA. DEPT. OF THE INTERIOR
File no. 41345, York Farmers' Colonization Company   CaOORD
N: CaSSA 90 feet   3021

CANADA. DEPT. OF THE INTERIOR
Files re: Saskatoon colonization and Regina townsite   CaOORD
N: CaSSA 300 feet   3022

CANADA. DEPT. OF THE INTERIOR
Records re: North-West Territories and Manitoba, 1870-1883   Ibid.
N: CaSRA 2 reels   3023

CANADA. DEPT. OF THE INTERIOR. DOMINION LANDS BRANCH
File re: Regina townsite, 1882-1899   Ibid.
N: CaSRA 1 reel   3024
P: CaSRA   not duplicate of N.

Provincial Records

SASKATCHEWAN. ARCHIVES, Regina
Pamphlets, theses, local history material re: Western Canada, 1895-1956
N: CaSRA 4 reels   3025

SASKATCHEWAN. ARCHIVES, Regina
Reminiscences and extracts from diaries of pioneers in North-West Territories and Saskatchewan   priv.
N: CaSRA 3 reels   3026

SASKATCHEWAN. DEBT ADJUSTMENT BOARD, Yorkton Judicial District
Records, 1932-1940   [dest.]
N: CaSRA 23 reels 16 mm.   3027

SASKATCHEWAN. DEPT. OF EDUCATION
Reports and other records, 1885-1891   CaSSA Ibid.
N: CaSSA 100 feet   3028

SASKATCHEWAN. DEPT. OF HIGHWAYS
Bridge files, 1893-   Ibid.   [dest.]
N: CaSRA 47 reels 16 mm.   3029

SASKATCHEWAN. DEPT. OF MUNICIPAL AFFAIRS
Assessment roll and register, Local Improvement Districts 601-639   Ibid.
N: CaSSA 500 feet   3030

SASKATCHEWAN. DEPT. OF MUNICIPAL AFFAIRS
List of urban and rural municipal officers, 1907-1948   Ibid.
N: CaSSA 100 feet   3031

SASKATCHEWAN. EXECUTIVE COUNCIL
Oaths book, 1905-   Ibid.
N: CaSSA 20 feet   3032

SASKATCHEWAN. EXECUTIVE COUNCIL OFFICE
Provincial election returns, 1905-1948   Ibid.
N: CaSRA 110 feet   3033

SASKATCHEWAN. GOLDEN JUBILEE COMMITTEE
Correspondence, 1952-1955   CaSRA
N: CaSRA 3 reels 16 mm.   3034

SASKATCHEWAN. LEGISLATIVE ASSEMBLY
Oaths book, 1903-1950   Ibid.
N: CaSRA 10 feet   3035

SASKATCHEWAN. LEGISLATIVE LIBRARY
Place names of Saskatchewan   CaSRL
N: CaSRA 10 feet   3036

SASKATCHEWAN. PROVINCIAL MEDIATION BOARD
Agricultural Land Survey (Rural Municipality 2-622), 1943   Ibid.
N: CaSSA 1800 feet   3037

SASKATCHEWAN. REGIONAL INSPECTOR OF SCHOOLS
Histories of 35 Sask. Indian reserves, compiled by Indian schools, 1955   Ibid.
N: CaSRA 1 reel   3038

SASKATCHEWAN. RELIEF COMMISSION
Records, 1931-1934   Ibid.
N: CaSSA 75 feet   3039

SASKATCHEWAN. SCHOOL DISTRICTS
Local histories celebrating the Golden Jubilee of Saskatchewan, 1955, 850 items   Ibid.
N: CaSRA 35 reels   3040

SASKATCHEWAN. TREASURY DEPARTMENT
Province of Saskatchewan hail insurance contracts, 1905-1907   Ibid.
N: CaSRA 2 reels   3041

SASKATCHEWAN. TREASURY DEPARTMENT
Record of seed grain liens, 1908-1910   Ibid.
N: CaSRA 70 feet   3042

Local Records

ALBEMARLE, Sask.
School District No. 2845 daily register, 1914
priv.
N: CaSSA 1 foot   3043

ARCOLA, Sask.
Records: Town, 1901-1916; School District
No. 637, 1902-1924   Ibid.
N: CaSSA 415 feet   3044

BATTLEFORD, Sask.
School District No. 71 records, 1887-1912   Ibid.
N: CaSRA 110 feet   3045

BEAVERLODGE, Sask. LOCAL DEVELOPMENT
AREA
Miscellaneous records (Uranium City and
district), 1956   Ibid.
N: CaSRA 2 reels   3046

BUCK LAKE, Sask.
School District No. 331 records, 1913-1955
Ibid.
N: CaSSA 20 feet   3047

FORT QU'APPELLE, Sask.
School District No. 26 records, 1885-1921;
Overseer's letter book, 1898-1902   Ibid.
N: CaSSA 50 feet   3048

GRENFELL, Sask.
Minutes, by-laws, and other records, 1904-1926
Ibid.
N: CaSSA 100 feet   3049

KISBEY, Sask. BROCK (Rural Municipality No. 64)
Records, 1898-1908   Ibid.
N: CaSSA 75 feet   3050

LANGENBURG (Rural Municipality No. 181), Sask.
Minute books, 1897-1918   Ibid.
N: CaSSA 30 feet   3051

LLOYDMINSTER, Sask.
Village minutes and correspondence, 1904
priv.
N: CaSSA 7 feet   3052

MAPLE CREEK, Sask.
Records, 1398-1916   Ibid.
N: CaSSA 300 feet   3053

MARRIOTT (Rural Municipality No. 317), Sask.
Minutes, 1910-1955; financial statements, 1943-
1955   Ibid.
N: CaSRA 1 reel   3054

MELFORT, Sask., BOARD OF TRADE
Records, 1905-1913   Ibid.
N: CaSRA 50 feet   3055

MOOSE JAW, Sask.
Council minutes, 1884-1911; by-laws,
1885-1909   Ibid.
N: CaSSA 300 feet   3056

MOOSE JAW, Sask. DISTRICT COURT
Returns of convictions, 1913-1943   [dest.]
N: CaSRA 2 reels 16 mm.   3057

MOOSOMIN, Sask.
Records, 1889-1915   Ibid.
N: CaSSA 1000 feet   3058

MYLOR, Sask.
School District No. 1079 records, 1904-1945
priv.
N: CaSSA 40 feet   3059

NORTH QU'APPELLE (Rural Municipality No.
187), Sask.
Minutes, 1884-1921   Ibid.
N: CaSSA 100 feet   3060

PRINCE ALBERT, Sask.
Minutes and other records, 1885-1918   Ibid.
N: CaSSA 1400 feet   3061

PRINCE ALBERT, Sask.
School District No. 3 records, 1897-1906   Ibid.
N: CaSSA 50 feet   3062

QU'APPELLE, Sask.
School District No. 2 records, 1904-1943   Ibid.
N: CaSSA 150 feet   3063

REGINA, Sask.
Council minutes and by-laws, 1884-1921   Ibid.
N: CaSSA 600 feet   3064

ST. ANDREWS (Rural Municipality No. 287), Sask
Voters' list, 1916   priv.
N: CaSSA 1 foot   3065

SALTCOATS, Sask.
Records: Town, 1894-1927; Rural Municipality
No. 213, 1898-1912; School District No. 140,
1907-1911   Ibid.
N: CaSSA 70 feet   3066

SOUTH QU'APPELLE (Rural Municipality No.
157), Sask.
Records, 1884-1915   Ibid.
N: CaSSA 400 feet   3067

SUMMERBURY, Sask.
School District No. 33 records, 1886-1951   Ibid.
N: CaSSA 50 feet   3068

SWIFT CURRENT, Sask.
Records, 1904-1937   Ibid.
N: CaSSA 300 feet   3069

SWIFT CURRENT (Rural Municipality No. 137),
Sask.
Records, 1905-1911   Ibid.
N: CaSSA 200 feet   3070

WHITEWOOD, Sask.
Records, 1893-1917; School District No. 57
records, 1894-1922; Statute Labor and Local
Improvement District No. 123 records,
1897-1910; Local Improvement District
No. 153 and Rural Municipality of Willowdale
No. 153 records, 1910-1913   Ibid.
N: CaSSA 600 feet   3071

WIDE AWAKE, Sask.
School District No. 54 records, 1886-1949
Ibid.
N: CaSSA 30 feet   3072

YORKTON, Sask.
Council minutes and other records, 1894-1914
Ibid.
N: CaSSA 500 feet   3073

YORKTON, Sask.
Records of Rural Municipalities of Wallace
(No. 243) and Orkney (No. 244), and of
Statute Labor Districts, 1898-1923   Ibid.
N: CaSSA 100 feet   3074

Church Records

ANGLICAN CHURCH IN CANADA. DIOCESES.
QU'APPELLE
Records, 1883-1957   Anglican Church Synod
Office, Regina
N: CaSRA 6 reels   3075

INDIAN HEAD, Sask. UNITED CHURCH
(Methodist)
Miscellaneous items from cornerstone, 1898
Ibid.
N: CaSRA 15 feet   3076

TOGO, Sask. UNITED CHURCH. MYLOR
APPOINTMENT
Account book, 1923-1951   priv.
N: CaSSA 30 feet   3077

Personal Papers

ASHTON, E. J.
Reminiscences upon coming to Lloydminster,
1903   priv.
N: CaSSA 20 feet   3078

BEATTY, REGINALD, 1854-1928, homesteader
Diary, 1885-1886, 1896-1898   priv.
N: CaSRA 22 feet   3079

BODEN, BERNARD D'ESTE
Letters re: Barr Colony, 1903-1907   priv.
N: CaSSA 30 feet   3080

BRADSHAW, J. E., of Prince Albert, Sask.
Political scrapbook, 1907-1917   priv.
N: CaSSA 70 feet   3081

BROOKS, EDWIN JACKSON, 1848-1939
Letters re: pioneer experiences, Indian Head,
Sask., 1882-1884   CaSRA
N: CaSRA 50 feet   3082

BROWN, Mrs. ANNIE G.
Diary, 1910-1915   priv.
N: CaSSA 80 feet   3083

CLARKE, WILLIAM WALLACE
Diary while snow-bound at Touchwood Hills,
1875   Prince Albert Historical Society
N: CaSSA 4 feet   3084

COWAN, N.
Memoirs of a lumberjack, 1903-1907   priv.
N: CaSSA 5 feet   3085

DAVIN, NICHOLAS FLOOD, 1843-1901
Newspaper articles and pamphlets, 1866-1897
priv.
N: CaSRA 1 reel   3086

EDWARDS, GEORGE
Letters re: farmers' organizations, 1926-1949
priv.
N: CaSSA 4 feet   3087

FITZGERALD, THOMAS
Papers re: homestead, school lands, and local
Roman Catholic church, 1820-1952   priv.
N: CaSSA 3 feet   3088

GILCHRIST, F.C., 1859-1896, homesteader
and Fisheries Inspector
Diary re: Fort Qu'Appelle and district, 1878-
1896   priv.
N: CaSRA 1 reel   3089

HARRISON, HERBERT M., pioneer farmer
Diary re: Baljennie district, 1903-1954   priv.
N: CaSRA 2 reels   3090

HAYES, CATHERINE (SIMPSON), 1856-1945
Papers, 1888-1941   priv.
N: CaSRA 70 feet   3091

HOLTBY, ROBERT
Diary of coming to Canada, 1903   priv.
N: CaSSA 6 feet   3092

HORRELL, J., of North Battleford, Sask.
Diary, 1907-1946   priv.
N: CaSSA 20 feet   3093

JONES, NATHANIEL
Correspondence and pamphlets re:
Barr Colony, 1903   priv.
N: CaSSA 8 feet   3094

LAVOIE, PHILIPPE E., M.D., 1886-1953
Papers re: Île à la Crosse settlement, 1935-
1953   priv.
N: CaSRA 20 feet   3095

LLOYD, GEORGE EXTON
Papers, 1902-1949   priv.
N: CaSSA 15 feet   3096

LORENTZ, P., of Drinkwater, Sask.
Diary, 1911-1947   priv.
N: CaSSA 30 feet   3097

MACDONALD, Sir JOHN ALEXANDER, 1815-1891
Papers re: Regina townsite, 1882-1883   CaOOA
N: CaSRA 15 feet   3098

MacKENZIE, WILLIAM LYON, 1860-1917,
bridge engineer, Canadian Northern Railway
Diary and addresses, 1900-1908   priv.
N: CaSRA 40 feet   3099

MARTIN, ROBERT
Diary re: coming to Western Canada, 1882
priv.
N: CaSSA 8 feet   3100

MARTIN, WILLIAM MELVILLE, 1876-
Papers re: soldiers' settlement, 1919-1922
Saskatchewan Executive Council Office [dest.]
N: CaSRA 9 reels   3101

MEYERS, WILLIAM FREDERICK
Diary and homestead file, 1882-1884 CaSSA
N: CaSRA 10 feet   3102

MIDDLETON, GAVIN, homesteader
Diary re: Carnduff district, 1882-1884 priv.
N: CaSRA 8 feet   3103

NICOL, ALEX
Accounts with the Barr Colony, 1903, 1908
priv.
N: CaSSA 1 foot   3104

NISBET, Rev. JAMES
Letters re: journey to site of Prince Albert,
1866 CaOTV
N: CaSSA 2 feet   3105

PATRICK, Dr. F. A.
Political reminiscences, 1891-1919 priv.
N: CaSSA 10 feet   3106

PEARCE, WILLIAM, surveyor
Papers, 1883-1928 priv.
N: CaSRA 1 reel   3107

RACKHAM, STANLEY
Diary, including Barr Colony experiences,
1900-1911 priv.
N: CaSSA 20 feet   3108

RENDELL, Mrs. ALICE
Letters re: Barr Colony settlement, 1903-1905
priv.
N: CaSSA 2 feet   3109

SCOTT, WALTER, 1867-1938
Papers re: construction of Legislative Building,
1906-1914 priv.
N: CaSSA 50 feet   3110

THOMSON, ROBERT K.
Diary at Moose Jaw, Sask., 1882 priv.
N: CaSSA 3 feet   3111

WATT, GEORGE, 1866-1943
Diaries, 1904-1931 CaSRA
N: CaSRA 4 reels   3112

WILDE, THOMAS, 1860-1941, homesteader
Diary re: Moosomin district, 1902-1940 priv.
N: CaSRA 2 reels   3113

Business Papers

ARCOLA, Sask. BOARD OF TRADE AND
BUSINESS CLUB
Minutes, 1907, 1925-1935 Arcola
N: CaSSA 70 feet   3114

ENTERPRISE CO-OPERATIVE ASSOCIATION,
Richmound, Sask.
Records, 1918-1954 priv.
N: CaSSA 15 feet   3115

ETHELTON GRAIN GROWERS' ASSOCIATION,
Ethelton, Sask.
Records, 1919-1925 priv.
N: CaSSA 10 feet   3116

MATADOR LAND AND CATTLE COMPANY
Correspondence re: ranch operations, 1905-
1916 Ibid.
N: CaSRA 12 feet
P: CaSSA   3117

QU'APPELLE MUNICIPAL ELEVATOR Co.,
Qu'Appelle, Sask.
Records South Qu'Appelle Rural
Municipality No. 157
N: CaSSA 70 feet   3118

SASKATCHEWAN CO-OPERATIVE ELEVATOR
Co., Ltd.
By-laws, revised, 1925 priv.
N: CaSSA   3119

SASKATCHEWAN GRAIN GROWERS'
ASSOCIATION. ALBEMARLE LOCAL
Minute book, 1921-1922 priv.
N: CaSSA 2 feet   3120

SASKATCHEWAN GRAIN GROWERS'
ASSOCIATION. RICHMOUND BRANCH
Minute books, 1913-1915 priv.
N: CaSSA 10 feet   3121

SASKATCHEWAN PURCHASING COMPANY,
Broadview, Sask.
Records, 1914 priv.; Saskatchewan
Registrar of Joint Stock Companies
N: CaSRA 54 feet   3122

TRADES AND LABOUR COUNCIL, Regina, Sask.
Minutes, 1907-1913 Ibid.
N: CaSRA 39 feet   3123

WELWYN FARMERS' ELEVATOR COMPANY,
Welwyn, Sask.
Letter book, records, papers, 1903-1942 priv.
N: CaSRA 60 feet   3124

WHEELER, ARTHUR JAMES, of Bank End, Sask.
Farming diary, 1904-1951 priv.
N: CaSSA 12 feet   3125

Collections

SASKATCHEWAN. ARCHIVES, Regina
Questionnaires completed by Saskatchewan
Pioneers, 1953-1955, 20 forms, 166 p.
CaSRA
PP: CaACG   3126

SASKATCHEWAN. ARCHIVES, Saskatoon
Homemakers' Clubs local histories: Conquest,
Ethelton, Mantario, Pelly, Pense v.p.
N: CaSSA 87 feet   3127

Institutions

CANADIAN RED POLL ASSOCIATION
Minute book, 1907-1956 priv.
N: CaSSA 50 feet   3128

COLLEGE OF PHYSICIANS AND SURGEONS
OF THE NORTHWEST TERRITORIES
Register, 1886-1908; minute book, 1893-1908
priv.
N: CaSSA 45 feet   3129

GRENFELL, Sask. MECHANICS AND LITERARY
INSTITUTE
Minutes, 1892-1915 Grenfell
N: CaSSA 10 feet   3130

LOCAL ASSOCIATION OF RURAL MUNICIPALITIES
OF NORTHEASTERN SASKATCHEWAN
Minutes and correspondence, 1921-1923 Ibid.
N: CaSSA 8 feet   3131

MONET AGRICULTURAL SOCIETY, Hughton, Sask.
Minutes, 1919-1930 Ibid.
N: CaSSA 10 feet   3132

SASKATCHEWAN ASSOCIATION OF RURAL
MUNICIPALITIES
Minutes of meetings and convention reports,
1906-1948 CaSSA
N: CaSSA 140 feet   3133

SASKATCHEWAN URBAN MUNICIPALITIES
ASSOCIATION
Convention programs and reports, 1909-1921,
1935, 1938, 1943 Ibid.
N: CaSSA 40 feet   3134

SASKATCHEWAN VETERANS CIVIL SECURITY
CORPS
Outgoing correspondence, 1940-1945 Ibid.
N: CaSRA 2 reels 16 mm.   3135

TOUCHWOOD AGRICULTURAL SOCIETY,
Touchwood, Sask.
Minutes, 1911-1930 priv.
N: CaSSA 15 feet   3136

WOMEN'S MUSICAL CLUB, Regina, Sask.
Minutes and miscellaneous papers, 1907-1957
Ibid.
N: CaSRA 2 reels   3137

School Records

SASKATCHEWAN SCHOOL TRUSTEES
ASSOCIATION
Records, 1908-1944 Ibid.
N: CaSSA 70 feet   3138

ALBERTA

Provincial Records

ALBERTA. DEPARTMENT OF AGRICULTURE
Cattle brands, 1880-1883, 95 p. Ibid.
DCO: CaACG   3139

Church Records

CHURCH OF JESUS CHRIST OF LATTER-DAY
SAINTS. ALBERTA
Ward and branch records: Alberta Stake;
Barnwell, Burdette, Calgary, Diamond City,
Lethbridge, Picture Butte, Raymond, Rose-
berry, Rosemary, Stirling, Taber, Welling
Wards; Champion, Coutts, Edmonton, Gleichen,
Manyberries, Tyrell's Lake, Warner Branches
USIC
N: USIGS 52 reels   3140

Personal Papers

DOUGLASS, J. L.
Journal, 1886, re: trip from England to
Montreal, Calgary area, New York, back to
England, 45 p. priv.
N: CaACG 1 reel
P: CaACG   3141

GRAHAM, DONALD
Papers, 1867-1890 priv.
N: CaACG 1 reel
P: CaACG   3142

HARDISTY, RICHARD
Personal letters, 1845-1889, 20 items priv.
DC: CaACG   3143

LEAVITT, EDWARD JENKINS, Mormon pioneer
of Caldwell and Glenwood, Alberta
Autobiography, 1875-? priv.
N: CaACG 1 reel
P: CaACG   3144

LONGMAN, CHARLES
Diary during Riel rebellion, 1885, 2 p. priv.
PP: CaACG   3145

McEWAN, JOHN H.
Biographical and personal papers, 1953-1957,
28 p. priv.
PP: CaACG   3146

MacGREGOR, JAMES G.
Letter re: Negro settlements at Breton,
Wildwood, and Amber Valley, Alberta priv.
DCO: CaACG   3147

PINKHAM, MARY
Papers re: Anglican missionaries, ca. 1883-
1956 priv.
N: CaACG 1 reel   3148

REED, GORDON
Letters re: Crowfoot's pass on C. P. R.,
1956-1957, 2 items priv.
PP: CaACG   3149

STEEL, F. M.
Report and letters re: Snyder musk ox survey,
1935, 70 p. priv.
PP: CaACG   3150

STEINHAUER, Rev. ROBERT B.
Diary re: Methodist missions in Alberta,
1887-1925 priv.
N: CaACG 1 reel   3151

WOODRUFF, JEREMIAH, Mormon pioneer of
Caldwell and Cardston, Alberta
Autobiography, 1885- ? priv.
N: CaACG 1 reel   3152
P: CaACG

Business Papers

BROKOVSKI, EDWARD, trader
Letter book, 1878-1896 priv.
N: CaACG 1 reel   3153

JACKSON, HASKELL G., rancher
Diaries, 1909-1942 priv.
N: CaACG 1 reel   3154
P: CaACG

BRITISH COLUMBIA

Government Records

GREAT BRITAIN. ADMIRALTY
Pacific Station records, 1848-1860, 1 v.
CaBViPA
N: CaOOA 85 feet   3155

GREAT BRITAIN. ADMIRALTY. Adm. 50
Admirals' journals re: Northwest Pacific
Coast, 1843-1854 UKLPRO
N: CaOOA 3 reels   3156

GREAT BRITAIN. COLONIAL OFFICE. C.O. 60
British Columbia. Correspondence, 1858-1871,
44 v. UKLPRO
N: CaOOA 34 reels   3157

GREAT BRITAIN. COLONIAL OFFICE. C.O. 61
British Columbia. Acts, 1858-1869, 1 v.
UKLPRO
N: CaOOA 65 feet   3158

GREAT BRITAIN. COLONIAL OFFICE. C.O. 63
British Columbia. Government gazettes, 1863-
1925, 10 v. UKLPRO
N: CaOOA 1863-1871, 4 v. 3 reels   3159

GREAT BRITAIN. COLONIAL OFFICE. C.O. 64
British Columbia. "Blue Books," i.e. statis-
tics, 1860-1870, 11 v. UKLPRO
N: CaOOA 2 reels   3160

GREAT BRITAIN. COLONIAL OFFICE. C.O. 305
Vancouver Island. Original correspondence,
1846-1866, 30 v. UKLPRO
N: CaOOA 19 reels   3161

GREAT BRITAIN. COLONIAL OFFICE. C.O. 306
Vancouver Island. Acts, 1853-1866, 1 v.
UKLPRO
N: CaOOA 40 feet   3162

GREAT BRITAIN. COLONIAL OFFICE. C.O. 307
Vancouver Island. Sessional papers, 1860-1866,
2 v. UKLPRO
N: CaOOA 2 reels   3163

GREAT BRITAIN. COLONIAL OFFICE. C.O. 308
Vancouver Island. Government Gazettes, 1864-
1866, 1 v. UKLPRO
N: CaOOA 40 feet   3164

GREAT BRITAIN. COLONIAL OFFICE. C.O. 381
Colonies General. Entry books, Series II,
1740-1872, 77 v. UKLPRO
N: CaOOA British Columbia and Vancouver
Island material 40 feet   3165

GREAT BRITAIN. COLONIAL OFFICE. C.O. 398
British Columbia. Entry books, 1858-1871,
7 v. UKLPRO
N: CaOOA 3 reels   3166

GREAT BRITAIN. COLONIAL OFFICE. C.O. 410
Vancouver Island. Entry books, 1849-1867,
2 v. UKLPRO
N: CaOOA 1 reel   3167

GREAT BRITAIN. COLONIAL OFFICE. C.O. 478
Vancouver Island. "Blue Books," i.e. statis-
tics, 1863-1865, 3 v. UKLPRO
N: CaOOA 70 feet   3168

Provincial Records

BRITISH COLUMBIA. ATTORNEY GENERAL
Company registration files Ibid.
N: CaBViPA 83 reels   3169

BRITISH COLUMBIA. ATTORNEY GENERAL
Inquisitions, 1862-1918 Ibid.
N: CaBViPA 32 reels   3170

BRITISH COLUMBIA. DEPT. OF MUNICIPAL
AFFAIRS
By-laws of villages and municipalities,
1924-1957 Ibid.
N: CaBViPA 6 reels   3171

BRITISH COLUMBIA. PROVINCIAL
SECRETARY
Orders in Council, 1872-1957 Ibid.
N: CaBViPA 156 reels   3172

Local Records

CRANBROOK, B.C.
Police records, 1899-1904 Ibid.
N: CaBViPA 1 reel   3173

FORT KAMLOOPS, B.C.
Accounts, 1863-1864 priv.
N: CaBViPA 2 reels   3174

Church Records

CHURCH OF JESUS CHRIST OF LATTER-DAY
SAINTS. BRITISH COLUMBIA
Records: New Westminster branch,
Vancouver Ward USlC
N: USlGS 2 reels   3175

METHODIST CHURCH (Canada). VANCOUVER
ISLAND AND BRITISH COLUMBIA
District meetings, 1860-1885 Ibid.
N: CaBViPA 1 reel   3176

UNITED CHURCH OF CANADA. CONFERENCES.
BRITISH COLUMBIA
Minutes, 1925-1954 Ibid.
N: CaBViPA 3 reels   3177

VICTORIA, B.C. ST. ANDREW'S CATHEDRAL
Vital records, 1849-1924 Ibid.
N: CaBViPA 1 reel   3178

VICTORIA, B.C. ST. ANDREWS PRESBYTERIAN
CHURCH
Records, 1866-1953 Ibid.
N: CaBViPA 5 reels   3179

WILLIAMS LAKE, B.C. ST. JOSEPH'S MISSION
Vital records, 1866-1943 Ibid.
N: CaBViPA 2 reels   3180

Personal Papers

BRYANT, C.
Diary, 1856-1892; letters, 1870-1894 priv.
N: CaBViPA 1 reel   3181

BUSHBY, A.T.
Journal, Aug., - Oct., 1864 priv.
N: CaBViPA 1 reel   3182

CORNWALL, C.F.
Diary, 1862-1873 priv.
N: CaBViPA 1 reel   3183

DOUGLAS, Sir JAMES, 1803-1877
Letters, 1855-1869 priv.
N: CaBViPA 1 reel   3184

FRASER, PAUL
Journal, Aug., 1850 - June, 1855 priv.
N: CaBViPA 1 reel   3185

HOLMES, W. W.
Some memories of the construction of the C.P.R
in the Fraser Canyon priv.
N: OrHi 8 frames   3186

HORNE, ADAM
Diary, 1854-1856, 1868 priv.
N: CaBViPA   3187

JOLI DE LOTBINIÈRE, Sir HENRI
Letters, 1901-1906 priv.
N: CaBViPA 1 reel   3188

MANSON, WILLIAM
Kamloops and Calumet journal, Jan., 1859-
Nov., 1862 priv.
N: CaBViPA 1 reel   3189

MOFFAT, H.H.
Kamloops journal, July, 1867 - July, 1870;
Shuswap accounts, Jan - Dec., 1867 priv.
N: CaBViPA 1 reel   3190

O'REILLY, PETER
Diaries, 1866-1898 priv.
N: CaBViPA 2 reels   3191

PICARD, E.
Reminiscences, West Kootenay, B.C.,
1886-1926 (typescript) priv.
N: CaOOA 1 reel   3192

REDGRAVE, STEPHEN
Diary of overland journey to British
Columbia, 1862 priv.
N: CaBViPA 1 reel   3193

ROBERTS, Rev. R.J.
Diaries, 1847-1904 priv.
N: CaBViPA 4 reels   3194

ROBSON, EBENEZER
Diaries, 1857-1910 priv.
N: CaBViPA 3 reels   3195

SMITH, MARCUS
Diary, 1872-1889 priv.
N: CaBViPA 1 reel   3196

STUART, JOHN, 1779-1847
Journal, Rocky Mountain House, 1805-1806
CaBViPA
N: CaOOA 5 feet   3197

TOLMIE, S.F.
Diary, 1830-1842 priv.
N: CaBViPA   3198

TRAILL, E.W.E.
Letters, July, 1889 - Dec., 1892 priv.
N: CaBViPA 1 reel   3199

WORK, JOHN, 1792-1861
Journals, 1823-1835, 1851 CaBViPA
N: CaOOA 2 reels   3200
P: CaBViPA

Business Papers

LAMPSON AND DICKSON
Journal, May, 1825-June, 1826, Mar.-Oct., 1867
priv.
N: CaBViPA   3201

Collections

BRITISH COLUMBIA. ARCHIVES
Diaries, 1836-1916 v.p.
N: CaBViPA 2 reels   3202

BRITISH COLUMBIA. ARCHIVES
Vital records: Fort St. James, 1893-1948;
Barkerville, 1869-1901; Lillooet, 1861-1917;
Stuart's Lake, 1867-1870; Casslar Cassiar,
1878-1905 v.p.
N: CaBViPA 2 reels   3203

ROSS, DONALD, collector
Papers CaBViPA
N: CaOTV 1 reel   3204

Institutions

BRITISH CAMPAIGNERS ASSOCIATION,
British Columbia
Minutes, 1908-1935 Ibid.
N: CaBViPA   3205

BRITISH COLUMBIA LAW SOCIETY
Records, 1869-1890 Ibid.
N: CaBViPA 1 reel   3206

NATURAL HISTORY SOCIETY OF BRITISH
COLUMBIA
Minutes, 1895-1929 Ibid.
N: CaBViPA 1 reel   3207

NEW WESTMINSTER, B. C. ROYAL COLUMBIAN
HOSPITAL
Records, 1862-1926 Ibid.
N: CaBViPA 2 reels   3208

SEAMEN'S INSTITUTE OF BRITISH COLUMBIA
Minutes, 1909-1927 Ibid.
N: CaBviPA 1 reel   3209

SOCIÉTÉ D'ÉTRANGÈRES, British Columbia
Archives, 1854-1866 priv.
N: CaBViPA 1 reel   3210

UNION OF BRITISH COLUMBIA MUNICIPALITIES
Minutes, 1905-1908 Ibid.
N: CaBViPA   3211

School Records

CACHE CREEK BOARDING SCHOOL,
Cache Creek, B.C.
Records, 1873-1929 Ibid.
N: CaBViPA   3212

Ships' Logs

With ships' logs are included journals, diaries,
and other records of voyages.

BRITISH COLUMBIA. ARCHIVES
Ships' logs: 1785, 1792-1796, 1819-1872 v.p.
N: CaBViPA 1 reel   3213

BRITISH WEST INDIES

Government Records

GREAT BRITAIN. COLONIAL OFFICE. C. O. 318
West Indies, original correspondence, 1624-
1808, v. 1-2 UKLPRO
DCO: DLC   3214

GREAT BRITAIN. HIGH COURT OF ADMIRALTY.
H.C.A. 49
Court of vice-admiralty proceedings: piracy
cases, 1722-1739; Jamaica, 1747-1748; New
York, 1775-1782 UKLPRO
DCO: DLC   3215

RODNEY, GEORGE BRYDGES RODNEY,
1st BARON, 1719-1792
Report on West Indies, 1762, 27 p. NN
N: CU   3216

BAHAMAS

Government Records

GREAT BRITAIN. COLONIAL OFFICE. C.O. 23
Bahamas, original correspondence, 1696-1737
UKLPRO
DCO: DLC   3217

Church Records

NEW YORK (Archdiocese). ARCHIVES
Bahama Island material in the Archives of the
Archdiocese of New York and Archives of Mt.
St. Vincent-on-the-Hudson, New York
N: MnCS 50 feet 16 mm.   3218

BARBADOS

Government Records

GREAT BRITIAN. COLONIAL OFFICE. C.O. 28
Barbados, original correspondence, selections,
1761-1815 UKLPRO
DCO: DLC   3219

GRENADA

Government Records

GREAT BRITAIN. COLONIAL OFFICE. C.O. 101
Grenada, original correspondence, 1777-1779
UKLPRO
DCO: DLC 3 v.   3220

JAMAICA

Government Records

GREAT BRITAIN. COLONIAL OFFICE. C.O. 137
Jamaica, original correspondence, 1689-1783
UKLPRO
DCO: DLC   3221

Local Records

ST. THOMAS IN THE VALE, Jamaica
Poll tax roll, 1789-1802 priv.
N: DHU 1 reel   3222
P: DHU

OLD PROVIDENCE ISLAND

Government Records

GREAT BRITAIN. COLONIAL OFFICE. C.O. 124
Records of Governor and Company of Adventur-
ers of Old Providence Island, 1630-1650, 2 v.
UKLPRO
N: CU-B 1 reel   3223
P: CU-B

ST. VINCENT

Government Records

GREAT BRITAIN. COLONIAL OFFICE. C.O. 260
St. Vincent, original correspondence,
selections, 1776-1778, 1786 UKLPRO
DCO: DLC   3224

VIRGIN ISLANDS

Government Records

GREAT BRITAIN. COLONIAL OFFICE. C.O. 314
Virgin Islands, original correspondence, 1711-
1791, v. 1 UKLPRO
DCO: DLC   3225

DANISH WEST INDIES

Government Records

CURAÇAO
Vital records, 1714-1831 NeHAR
N: USlGS 5 reels   3226

NEDERLANDSCHE WEST-INDISCHE COMPAGNIE
Selected items, 1623-1624; proceedings, 1655-
1665; records of Amsterdam Chamber, 1635-
1636, 1646-1676; records of Zeeland Chamber,
1635-1646 NeHAR
N: DLC 5 reels   3227

NETHERLANDS. ALGEMEEN RIJKSARCHIEF
Documents re: West Indische Companie,
1597-1795 NeHAR
N: CU-B 217 reels   3228

NETHERLANDS WEST INDIES
Vital records: St. Eustatius, St. Martin, and
Saba Islands, 1710-1832 NeHAR
N: USlGS 1 reel   3229

Church Records

DUTCH GUIANA [SURINAM]
Parish registers of Surinam Kolonie [Dutch
Guiana]: Dutch Reformed Church, 1747-1801;
Lutheran and Catholic, 1742-1830; Jewish,
1742-1817; Reformed Church, 1687-1828;
Evangelical Lutheran, 1743-1828; Portuguese
Jewish, 1777-1828; High Dutch Jewish, 1773-
1838; Evangelical Brothers, 1779-1828;
Portuguese Israelites, 1662-1833; also civil
marriage records, 1816-1827; vital records
of Paramaribo, 1723-1827 NeHAR
N: USlGS 12 reels   3230

DUTCH WEST INDIES

Census

DENMARK. CENSUS, 1841
Census returns: Virgin Islands (St. Thomas,
St. John, St. Croix) DaKR
N: USlGS 9 reels   3231

DENMARK. CENSUS, 1846
Census returns: Virgin Islands (St. Thomas,
St. John, and St. Croix) DaKR
N: USlGS 8 reels   3232

DENMARK. CENSUS, 1857
Census returns: Virgin Islands (St. Croix,
St. John, St. Thomas) DaKR
N: USlGS 5 reels   3233

Government Records

DANISH WEST INDIES
Customs journals and miscellaneous customs
records: Christiansted, Frederiksted, and
Salt River Bay, 1745-1799 DNA
N: DNA 23 reels [T-39]   3234

DANISH WEST INDIES
Letters from Governor Frederik Moth,
1732-1736 DaKR
N: DaKR 1 reel   3235
P: DNA

DANISH WEST INDIES
Vital records of St. Thomas and St. John
Islands, 1691-1899, books 1-13; vital records
of St. Croix, 1740-1865, books 1-11 DaKL
N: USlGS 6 reels   3236

Church Records

NEDERLANDSCHE HERVORMEDE KERK, St.
Croix, Virgin Islands

Vital records, 1764-1814, books 1-3 DaKL
N: USlGS 1 reel   3237

UNITED STATES

Bibliography

AMERICAN ANTIQUARIAN SOCIETY
Checklist of manuscripts, 1956 MWA
N: MHi 6 feet   3238

AMERICAN GEOGRAPHICAL SOCIETY OF NEW
YORK. LIBRARY
Research catalog, 1940 Ibid.
N: CU 26 reels 16 mm.   3239

BLATHWAYT, WILLIAM, 1645-1741
Calendar of papers in the Sir Thomas Phillips
collection, 1645-1741 CSmH
N: ViWI 1 reel   3240

CALIFORNIA. UNIVERSITY. BANCROFT
LIBRARY
List of microfilms re: British investments in
North and Central America CU-B
N: WHi 1 reel   3241

HOWELL, E. VERNON, 1872-1931, collector
Papers re: Henri Harrisse and Samuel L.
Barlow, 1871-1914, 45 sheets NN
DCO: NcU   3242

RICH, OBADIAH, 1777-1850
Letters to Henry Stevens re: sale of Americana,
Sept., 1847 - Aug., 1848; statement of accounts
MiU-C
DCO: NN   3243

U.S. LIBRARY OF CONGRESS. CENSUS
LIBRARY PROJECT
References on the different censuses DLC
N: DLC 1 reel   3244

U. S. WORKS PROGRESS ADMINISTRATION
Index of WPA Historical Records Survey of
"Manuscripts Accessions" edited and compiled
by Margaret Eliot, 1940
N: DLC 1 reel   3245

Census

U.S. VETERANS ADMINISTRATION
Special schedules of the eleventh census of the
United States enumerating Union veterans and
widows of Union veterans of the Civil War,
1890 DNA
N: DNA 118 reels [M-123]   3246

Constitutional Documents

BUTLER, PIERCE, 1744-1822
Papers re: Constitutional Convention, 1787
priv.
DCO: DLC*   3247

MADISON, JAMES, Pres. U. S., 1751-1836
Manuscript notes of debates in the Federal
Convention, 1787 DLC
N: DLC 1 reel   3248

PATERSON, WILLIAM, 1745-1806
Notes re: the U.S. Constitution, 1787,
51 p. priv.
DCO: DLC   3249

WILSON, JAMES, 1742-1798
Papers re: the Constitutional Convention,
1787 PHi
DCO: DLC   3250

Amendments

U.S. CONGRESS
Proposal for first twelve amendments to U.S.
Constitution and related papers Ibid.
DCO: DLC   3251

U.S. CONGRESS
Thirteenth Amendment to the Constitution,
1865 NNP
DCO: DLC   3252

Government Records

GREAT BRITAIN. ADMIRALTY. Adm. 7
Miscellanea, Law officers' opinions, 1733-
1783 UKLPRO
DCO: DLC   3253

GREAT BRITAIN. COLONIAL OFFICE. C.O.1
Colonial papers, general series, 1574-1697,
68 v. UKLPRO
N: DLC 30 reels   3254
P: DLC

GREAT BRITAIN. COLONIAL OFFICE. C.O.5
Selections re: America and West Indies
UKLPRO
DCO: DLC
N: DLC 95 reels   3255
P: DLC

GREAT BRITAIN. COLONIAL OFFICE. C.O.323
Colonies (general), (formerly Plantations,
general), Board of Trade correspondence,
American selections, 1750-1768 UKLPRO
DCO: DLC   3256

GREAT BRITAIN. COLONIAL OFFICE. C.O.389
Board of Trade (Commercial). Entry books,
opinions of counsel, 1736-1738 UKLPRO
DCO: DLC   3257

GREAT BRITAIN. COLONIAL OFFICE. C.O.390
Board of Trade, miscellanea, selected
customs house accounts, 1675-1731 UKLPRO
DOC: DLC   3258

GREAT BRITAIN. COMMISSIONERS OF
CUSTOMS IN AMERICA
Records and minutes, 1762-1770 MH MHi
N: CU 2 reels   3259

GREAT BRITAIN. CUSTOMS AND EXCISE.
Customs 3
Ledgers of imports and exports, selections re:
exports to Virginia and Maryland, 1697-1703
UKLPRO
DCO: DLC   3260

GREAT BRITAIN. CUSTOMS AND EXCISE.
Customs 16
Accounts, ledgers of imports and exports,
America, 1768-1773, 262 ff. UKLPRO
DCO: DLC NcU   3261

GREAT BRITAIN. HIGH COURT OF ADMIRALTY
H.C.A. 1
Indictments, 1604, 1619-1634, 1648-1809,
v. 5, 7-27, 55 UKLPRO
DCO: DLC   3262

GREAT BRITAIN. HOME OFFICE. H.O.49
Law officers' letter books. Correspondence
between Secretaries of State and Law officers,
American selections, 1762-1795 UKLPRO
DCO: DLC   3263

GREAT BRITAIN. TREASURY. Treasury 1
In-letters, 1768-1771, 1776 UKLPRO
DCO: DLC   3264

GREAT BRITAIN. TREASURY. Treasury 28
Letters re: America, 1763-1797 UKLPRO
DCO: DLC   3265

GREAT BRITAIN. TREASURY. Treasury 29
Minute books, 1765-1784 UKLPRO
N: DLC 8 reels   3266
P: DLC

GREAT BRITAIN. TREASURY. Treasury 64
Law officers' opinions, 1763-1783 UKLPRO
DCO: DLC   3267

GREAT BRITAIN. WAR OFFICE. W.O. 1
Secretary at War, in-letters, American
selections, 1755-1817 UKLPRO
DCO: DLC   3268

HOME OWNERS' LOAN CORPORATION
General administrative correspondence,

1933-1936 DNA
N: DNA 482 reels 16 mm.   3269

NORTHWEST TERRITORY, U.S.
Executive journal, 1788-1801 OHi
N: OHi 1 reel   3270
P: OHi

UNITED STATES
The Federal Register, 1936-1958 DNA
N: DNA 102 reels [M-190]   3271

U.S. ADJUTANT - GENERAL'S OFFICE
Registers of enlistments in the United States
Army, 1798-1914 DNA
N: DNA 81 reels [M-233]   3272

U.S. ADJUTANT-GENERAL'S OFFICE
Report of expedition to the plains, March 25 -
May 7, 1867, 164 p. DNA
N: KU   3273

U.S. BUREAU OF CUSTOMS
Enrollments of vessels, licenses, and bills of
sale, 1870-1956 DNA
N: De 22 reels 16mm.   3274

U.S. BUREAU OF LABOR STANDARDS
Index to Labor Organization registration
case files, 1945-1948 DNA
N: DNA 6 reels 16 mm.   3275

U. S. BUREAU OF LABOR STATISTICS
Collective bargaining agreements, 1941-
1947 Ibid.
N: NIC-I 244 reels   3276

U.S. BUREAU OF RECLAMATION
Project histories and reports of Reclamation
Bureau Projects, 1902-1925: Belle Fourche,
S.D., 1905-1919; Blackfeet (Indian), Mont.,
1910-1923; Boise, Ida., 1902-1918; Flathead
(Indian), Mont., 1909-1923; Fort Peck
(Indian), Mont., 1909-1923; Grand Valley,
Col., 1903-1923; Huntley, Mont., 1904-1919;
Jackson Lake Enlargment, Wyo., 1902-1916;
King Hill, Ida., 1914-1924; Klamath, Ore.-
Cal., 1903-1925; Lower Yellowstone,
Mont.-N.D., 1904-1921; Milk River, Mont.
1902-1919; Minidoka, Ida., 1903-1919;
Okanogan, Wash., 1905-1919; Shoshone, Wyo.,
1909-1919; Sun River, Mont., 1910-1919;
Umatilla, Ore., 1905-1919; Yakima, Wash.,
1902-1919; General reports, 1909-1916 DNA
N: DNA 141 reels [M-96]   3277

U.S. BUREAU OF REFUGEES, FREEDMEN, AND
ABANDONED LANDS
Selected letters, 1865-1868 DNA
N: NNC 1 reel   3278

U.S. BUREAU OF THE MINT
Letters sent by the director of the U.S. Mint
at Philadelphia, 1795-1817 DNA
N: DNA 1 reel [M-64]   3279

U.S. CIVILIAN CONSERVATION CORPS
Monthly statistical progress reports,
1933-1942 DNA
N: DNA 193 reels   3280

U.S. COAST GUARD
Assistance reports, 1916-1940 DNA
N: DNA 280 reels 16 mm.   3281

U.S. COAST GUARD
Casualty and wreck reports, 1913-1939 DNA
N: DNA 28 reels 16 mm.   3282

U.S. COAST GUARD
Lighthouse deeds and contracts, 1790-1816
DNA
N: DNA 2 reels [M-94]   3283
P: MoIT

U.S. COAST GUARD
Lighthouse letters, 1792-1809 DNA
N: DNA 3 reels [M-63]   3284
P: MoIT

U.S. COMMISSION ON INDUSTRIAL RELATIONS
Reports, 1912-1915 DNA
N: DNA 15 reels [T-4]   3285

U.S. COMMISSIONER OF CORPORATIONS
Report on the Petroleum Industry, Part III,

Foreign Trade, 1909 DNA
N: DNA 1 reel [T-154] 3286

U.S. COMMISSIONER OF THE REVENUE
Letters sent, 1792-1807 DNA
N: DNA 3 reels [T-256] 3287

U.S. CONGRESS
Army- McCarthy hearings (Blue, transcript)
Ibid.
N: DLC 4 reels 16 mm. 3288

U.S. CONGRESS. SENATE
Territorial papers, 1789-1873 DNA
N: DNA 20 reels [M-200] 3289

U.S. CONTINENTAL CONGRESS
Department of State cash book, 1785-1795 DNA
DCO: DLC 3290

U.S. CONTINENTAL CONGRESS
Papers, 1774-1789 DNA
N: DNA 56 reels [M-247] 3291

U.S. CONTINENTAL CONGRESS
Papers, including those of John Holker,
1777-1822 DLC
N: NNC 2 reels 3292

U.S. CONTINENTAL CONGRESS
Reports of the Board of Treasury, 1785-1787,
3 v. NN
DCO: DLC 3293

U.S. CONTINENTAL CONGRESS. 1774
Journal, manuscript transcript, Sept. 5-
Oct. 26, 1774 priv.
N: DLC 1 reel* 3294
P: DLC

U.S. CONTINENTAL CONGRESS. 1774
Proceedings, manuscripts, 1774 R
N: NcU 26 frames 3295

U.S. DEPT. OF AGRICULTURE
Letters sent by the Assistant Secretaries of
Agriculture, 1889-1894 DNA
N: DNA 16 reels [M-122] 3296

U.S. DEPT. OF LABOR
Subject Index to General Files of the Chief Clerk,
1907-1942 DNA
N: DNA 1 reel 16 mm. 3297

U.S. DEPT. OF LABOR. WAGE AND HOUR AND
PUBLIC CONTRACTS DIVISION
Wage data gathered by inspectors in connection
with eight region V inspection cases, 1938-1944
DNA
N: DNA 9 reels 3298

U.S. DEPT. OF STATE
Documents re: Henry Adams, 1863-1865 DNA
N: ICU 1 reel 3299

U.S. DEPT. OF STATE
Domestic letters, 1784-1861: "American
Letters,"1784-1792; "Domestic Letters,"
1792-1861 DNA
N: DNA 51 reels [M-40] 3300

U.S. DEPT. OF STATE
Port facilities forms DS
N: DLC 1 reel 3301

U.S. DEPT. OF STATE
Records concerning the publication and distrib-
ution of the Laws, 1826-1829 DNA
N: DNA 1 reel [T-266] 3302

U.S. DEPT. OF STATE
Registers of correspondence, 1870-1906 DNA
N: DNA 71 reels [M 17] 3303

U.S. DEPT. OF STATE
Treaty with Wyandots, 1795 DS
DCO: DLC 1 portfolio 3304

U.S. DEPT. OF THE INTERIOR
Records relating to wagon roads, 1857-1887
DNA
N: DNA 16 reels [M-95] 3305
P: CoHi

U.S. EXECUTIVE COUNCIL
Minutes, July 11, 1933-Nov. 13, 1934 DNA
N: DNA 1 reel [T-37] 3306

U.S. EXTENSION SERVICE
Annual narrative and statistical reports [from
county agents and state extension service
officers], 1908-1944 DNA
N: DNA 3,585 reels 16 mm. 3307

U.S. FARM CREDIT ADMINISTRATION
Statistical reports on Farmers' Marketing and
Purchasing Cooperatives, 1913-1942 DNA
N: DNA 38 reels 3308

U.S. GENERAL ACCOUNTING OFFICE
"Miscellaneous Treasury accounts," 1790-
1800 DNA
N: DNA 47 reels [M-235] 3309

U.S. GENERAL LAND OFFICE
Journal and report of James Leander Cathcart
and James Hutton, agents appointed by the
Secretary of the Navy to survey timber re-
sources between the Mermentau and Mobile
Rivers, Nov., 1818 - May, 1819 DNA
N: DNA 1 reel [M-8] 3310
P: A-Ar
PP: LNHT

U.S. GENERAL LAND OFFICE
Letters sent to surveyors general, 1796-1860
DNA
N: DNA 18 reels [M-27] 3311

U.S. GENERAL LAND OFFICE
Miscellaneous letters sent, 1796-1860 DNA
N: DNA 89 reels [M-25] 3312
P: IaU

U.S. GEOLOGICAL SURVEY
Letters received by John Wesley Powell,
director of the geographical and geological
survey of the Rocky Mountain Region, 1869-
1879 DNA
N: DNA 10 reels [M-156] 3313
P: UHi

U.S. GEOLOGICAL SURVEY
Letters sent, 1879-1895 DNA
N: DNA 29 reels [M-152] 3314

U.S. GEOLOGICAL SURVEY
Registers of letters received, 1879-1901 DNA
N: DNA 16 reels [M-157] 3315
P: WaU

U.S. GEORGE WASHINGTON BICENTENNIAL
COMMISSION
Card index to pictures collected by the
Commission DNA
N: DNA 1 reel [T-271] 3316

U.S. INDUSTRIAL COMMISSION, 1898-1902
Minutes, 1898-1902 DNA
N: DNA 1 reel [T-10] 3317

U.S. INTERSTATE COMMERCE COMMISSION
Annual reports filed by Common Carriers
under its jurisdiction, 1888-1914 DNA
N: DNA 1,348 reels 16 mm. 3318

U.S. MARITIME COMMISSION
Vessel movement cards of the U.S. Shipping
Board and the U.S. Maritime Commission,
1917-1940 DNA
N: DNA 6 reels 16 mm. 3319

U.S. NATIONAL ARCHIVES
Publications, 1935-1958 DNA
N: DNA 10 reels [M-248] 3320

U.S. NATIONAL EMERGENCY COUNCIL
Proceedings, 1933-1936 DNA
N: DNA 1 reel [T-38] 3321

U.S. NATIONAL RECOVERY ADMINISTRATION
Document series, 1933-1936 DNA
N: DNA 186 reels 16 mm. [M-213] 3322

U.S. NATIONAL RESOURCES PLANNING BOARD
Reports, 1936-1943 DNA
N: DNA 5 reels [M 120] 3323

UNITED STATES NAVAL ASTRONOMICAL
EXPEDITION, 1849-1852
Correspondence, 1848-1852 DNA
N: DNA 1 reel [T-54] 3324

U.S. OFFICE OF EXPLORATIONS AND SURVEYS
Correspondence concerning Isaac Stevens'

survey of a northern route for the Pacific
Railway, 1853-1861 DNA
N: DNA 1 reel [M-126] 3325
P: WaU

U.S. OFFICE OF INDIAN AFFAIRS
Letter book of the Creek Trading House, 1795-
1816 DNA
N: DNA 1 reel [M-4] 3326
P: A-Ar

U.S. OFFICE OF INDIAN AFFAIRS
Letters of Tench Coxe, Commissioner of the
Revenue, relating to the procurement of
military, naval and Indian supplies, 1794-1796
DNA
N: DNA 1 reel [M-74] 3327

U.S. OFFICE OF INDIAN AFFAIRS
Letters received by the Office of Indian Affairs,
1824-1881 DNA
N: DNA 603 reels [M-234] 3328

U.S. OFFICE OF INDIAN AFFAIRS
Letters received by the Superintendent of
Indian Affairs, 1806-1824 DNA
N: DNA 1 reel [T-58] 3329

U.S. OFFICE OF INDIAN AFFAIRS
Letters sent, 1824-1869 DNA
N: DNA 90 reels [M-21] 3330
P: IaU KHi

U.S. OFFICE OF INDIAN AFFAIRS
Letters sent by the Secretary of War relating
to Indian Affairs, 1800-1824 DNA
N: DNA 6 reels [M-15] 3331
P: KHi

U.S. OFFICE OF INDIAN AFFAIRS
Letters sent by the Superintendent of Indian
Trade, 1807-1823 DNA
N: DNA 6 reels [M-16] 3332
P: CSmH 1809-1824 TM

U.S. OFFICE OF INDIAN AFFAIRS
Records of Chicsaw Bluffs factory, 1796-1819;
Illinois Bayou factory, 1818-1819; Spadre Bluffs
factory, 1820-1824 DNA
N: DNA 1 reel 3333
P: TM

U.S. OFFICE OF INDIAN AFFAIRS
Registers of letters received by the Office of
Indian Affairs, 1824-1880 DNA
N: DNA 126 reels [M-18] 3334
P: KHi

U.S. OFFICE OF PRICE ADMINISTRATION
Fact finding in price control DNA
N: DNA 1 reel 3335

U.S. OFFICE OF PRICE ADMINISTRATION
Studies and reports, 1941-1946 DNA
N: DNA 2 reels [M-164] 3336

U.S. OFFICE OF THE CHIEF OF ENGINEERS
Letters relating to internal improvements,
1824-1830 DNA
N: DNA 3 reels [M-65] 3337
P: MoIT

U.S. OFFICE OF THE CHIEF OF ENGINEERS
Letters sent by the Topographical Bureau
and by successor divisions, 1829-1870 DNA
N: DNA 37 reels [M-66] 3338
P: MoIT WaU

U.S. PATENT OFFICE
Patent drawings, 1828-1836 DNA
N: DNA 3 reels 3339

U.S. POST OFFICE DEPT.
Mail routes registers, 1850-1870 DNA
N: WaU 1 reel 3340

U.S. PRESIDENT
Index to executive orders - alphabetical, ca.
1855-1938 DNA
N: DNA 19 reels [T-277] 3341

U.S. PRESIDENT
Index to executive orders - numerical, ca.
1855-1938 DNA
N: DNA 6 reels [T-278] 3342

U.S. PRESIDENT
Index to presidential proclamations,

1789-ca. 1938 DNA
N: DNA 2 reels [T-279]   3343

U.S. PRESIDENT, 1861-1865 (Lincoln)
Presidential proclamations, 1861-1865 DNA
N: I 1 reel   3344

U.S. PUBLIC WORKS ADMINISTRATION
Completed non-federal project case files,
1933-1945 DNA
N: DNA 8,859 reels 16 mm   3345

U.S. PUBLIC WORKS ADMINISTRATION
Investigative case files, 1933-1942 DNA
N: DNA 824 reels 16 mm.   3346

U.S. REVENUE-CUTTER SERVICE
Scrapbook, 1850-1915 CtNlCG
N: CtNCG 1 reel   3347

U.S. RURAL ELECTRIFICATION ADMINISTRATION
Project case files Alabama through Virginia,
1935-1937 DNA
N: DNA 75 reels   3348

U.S. SOIL CONSERVATION SERVICE
Vendor case files (for land purchased for
resettlement), 1933-1939 DNA
N: DNA 292 reels 16 mm.   3349

U.S. SUPREME COURT
Case papers, 1792-1807 DNA
N: DNA 11 reels   3350

U.S. SUPREME COURT
Minutes, 1790-1947; Dockets, 1791-1950;
Attorney rolls, 1790-1951 DNA
N: DNA 72 reels [M-215-217]   3351

U.S. TREASURY DEPT.
Circulars on the customs, Oct. 2, 1789-June
30, 1796 DLC
N: ICU 1 reel   3352

U.S. TREASURY DEPT.
Correspondence of the Secretary of the
Treasury with collectors of customs,
1789-1833 DNA
N: DNA 39 reels [M-178]   3353

U.S. TREASURY DEPT.
Embargo circulars, July 10, 1807-Mar. 3,
1809 DNA
N: ICU 1 reel   3354

U.S. TREASURY DEPT.
Letters and reports received by the Secretary
of the Treasury from special agents, 1854-1861
DNA
N: DNA 3 reels [M-177]   3355
P: MoIT

U.S. TREASURY DEPT.
Letters received by the Secretary of the
Treasury from collectors of customs, 1833-
1869 DNA
N: DNA 226 reels [M-174]   3356

U.S. TREASURY DEPT.
Letters sent by the Secretary of the Treasury
to collectors of customs at Pacific ports,
1850-1878 DNA
N: DNA 5 reels [M-176]   3357

U.S. TREASURY DEPT.
Records of the Commissioners of Claims
(Southern Claims Commission), 1871-1880 DNA
N: DNA 14 reels [M-87]   3358

U.S. TREASURY DEPT. SECRET SERVICE
DIVISION
Agents' daily reports, 1864-1936 [including
some transcripts and abstracts. Reports under
50 years old are restricted.] DNA
N: DNA 843 reels 16 mm.*   3359

U.S. WAR DEPT.
Letters received by the Secretary of War,
registered series, 1803-1860 DNA
N: DNA 189 reels [M221]   3360

U.S. WAR DEPT.
Letters received by the Secretary of War,
unregistered series, 1789-1860 DNA
N: DNA 22 reels [M-222]   3361

U.S. WAR DEPT.
Material re: National Road, 1832-1841,

57 items DNA
N: OHi   3362

U.S. WEATHER BUREAU
Weather reports, 1819-1892 DNA
N: DNA 562 reels   3363

U.S. WORKS PROGRESS ADMINISTRATION
Records of W.P.A. and predecessor agencies,
1933-1944 [chiefly central office records, but
containing some field records] DNA
N: DNA 17,7000 reels 16 mm.   3364

Personal Papers

ABERT, CHARLES
Journal, 1861-1863, and letters   priv.
N: DLC 1 reel   3365

ADAMS, ABIGAIL (SMITH), 1744-1818
Letters to her sister, Elizabeth Peabody
Shaw DLC
N: FU 1 reel   3366

ADAMS, HENRY, 1838-1918
Harvard class record book, 1873-1877 priv.
N: CSmH   3367

ADAMS, HENRY, 1838-1918
Letters to George Bancroft, Francis Parkman,
and Charles Dean, 1874-1887 MHi
N: ICU 1 reel   3368

ADAMS, HENRY, 1838-1918
Letters to Worthington C. Ford, 1886-1898
NN
N: ICU   3369

ADAMS, JOHN, Pres. U.S., 1735-1826
Correspondence with Richard Rush, 1811-1822
MHi
DCO: PHi   3370

ADAMS, JOHN, Pres. U.S., 1735-1826
Letters, 1795-1893, 1 v. Robert Treat Crane
Collection priv.
DCO: NN   3371

ADAMS, SAMUEL, 1722-1803
Correspondence, 1769-1793 NN
DCO: DLC 19 v.   3372

ADAMS FAMILY
Papers, 1750-1870 MHi
N: MHi 608 reels   3373
P: CSmH CU CtY DLC DNA DeU FU GEU ICU
   IU IaU MCM MH MWA MdBJ MeB MiU MnU
   MoIT NIC NNC NRU NcD NhD NjP OU OrU
   PPAmP PPiU PSt RPB TxHR ViU ViWI WaU

These are fully described in a series of pamphlets that are provided with the films.

ANDERSON, RICHARD CLOUGH, Jr., 1788-1826
Diary, 1803-1826 priv.
N: DLC NcU 550 frames   3374

ANDERSON - AITKEN - DORMAN FAMILIES
Letters, 1832-1879, 40 items priv.
N: DLC 1 reel   3375

ANTHONY, SUSAN BROWNELL, 1820-1906
Letters to Mrs. Dall, 1853-1890, 25 items
N: CU 1 reel   3376

ATKINSON, GEORGE FRANCIS, 1854-1918
Letters, 1885-1892, 27 items
John Henry Comstock papers NIC
N: NcU 1 reel   3377

BANCROFT, GEORGE, 1800-1891
Correspondence, 1820-1880 DLC priv.
N: DLC 2 reels   3378

BARTON, CLARA, 1821-1912
Diaries, Aug., 1903-June,1904, Jan.-Dec.,1910
American Red Cross
N: DLC 1 reel   3379

BELL, JOHN, 1797-1869
Papers, 1838-1860 DLC
N: ICU 1 reel   3380

BELL, JOHN, 1797-1869
Papers, 1847-1861 NcU
N: ICU 1 reel   3381

BIDDLE, Commodore JAMES, 1783-1848
Letters
N: PHi 7 reels   3382

BIDDLE, NICHOLAS, 1786-1844
Letter books, 1823-1840 DLC
N: MH-BA 4 reels   3383

BIDDLE, NICHOLAS, 1786-1844
Papers, 1775-1846 DLC
N: DLC 46 reels   3384
P: ICU PPiU WHi NNC

BIRNEY, JAMES GILLESPIE, 1792-1857
Selected letters DLC
N: DLC 1 reel   3385

BLACK, JEREMIAH SULLIVAN, 1810-1883
Papers, 1813-1904, 75 v. DLC
N: DLC 36 reels   3386
P: CSmH CU DLC ICU IHi NIC NjP NNC
   TxU

BLATHWAYT, WILLIAM, 1645-1741
Papers, 1674-1715 ViWC
N: ViWC 6 reels   3387
P: ViWC

BLEDSOE, ALBERT TAYLOR
Letters ViU
N: NcD 1 reel   3388

BOND, WILLIAM
Papers, 1768-1833 priv.
N: DLC 1 reel   3389

BOONE, DANIEL, 1734-1820
Letter, 1809, 1 item LNHT
Lithograph: LNHT   3390

BORAH, WILLIAM EDGAR, 1865-1940
Scrapbooks, 55 v. IdU
N: DLC 11 reels   3391

BOUDINOT, ELIAS, 1740-1821
Journey to Boston, 1809 NjP
M: ViWI 1 reel   3392

BOUDINOT, ELIAS, 1740-1821
Papers, 1736-1821 PHi
N: NjP 1 reel   3393
P: PHi

BOUDINOT, ELIAS, 1740-1821
Papers, 1773-1785 DLC
N: NjP 1 reel   3394

BOUDINOT, ELIAS, 1740-1821
Papers (transcripts) DLC
N: DLC 1 reel   3395

BOUQUET, HENRY, 1719-1765
Last will and testament MdAA
DCO: DLC 1 box   3396

BOUQUET, HENRY, 1719-1765
Will and inventory of property, 1765 UKLBM
N: ?   3397
P: MiU

BOURNE, SYLVANUS
Letters from Thomas Jefferson, Henry
Tazwell, et al. priv.
DCO: DLC 9 letters   3398

BRADLEY, Rev. DAN BEACH, 1804-1873
Journals, 1832-1873, 25 v. OO
N: DLC 18 reels   3399
P: DLC 18 reels

BRAGG, BRAXTON, 1817-1876
Letters to his wife, 1861-1863 priv.
DCO: DLC 1 portfolio   3400

BRAGG, BRAXTON, 1817-1876
Papers, 1861-1865 OClWHi
N: OClWHi 4 reels   3401

BRANDEIS, LOUIS DEMBITZ, 1856-1941
Correspondence with Woodrow Wilson,
1912-1923 priv.
DCO: DLC 1 box   3402

BRIGGS, ISAAC
Papers DLC
N: DLC 1 reel   3403

BRINK, FRANCIS G., 1893-
Field notes, 1941-1942; travel notes,
1941-1945 priv.
N: DLC 2 reels   3404

BRISTOW, BENJAMIN HELM, 1832-1896
Correspondence, selections, 1873-1884 DLC
N: OFH 1 reel   3405

BROOKS, WILLIAM E.
In-letters re: Woodrow Wilson, 1927-1929 priv.
DCO: DLC 1 portfolio   3406

BRYAN, GUY MORRISON, 1821-1901
Letters from R. B. Hayes, 1850-1892 TxU
N: OFH 1 reel   3407

BRYANT, JOHN E.
Letters to R. B. Hayes OFH
N: OFH 1 reel   3408

BUCHANAN, JAMES, Pres. U.S., 1791-1868
Papers, 1836-1846 PHi
N: NNC 1/2 reel   3409

BULLOCK, RUFUS BROWN, 1834-1907
Letters to R. B. Hayes OFH
N: OFH 1 reel   3410

BUTLER, NICHOLAS MURRAY, 1862-1947
Correspondence with Woodrow Wilson,
1902-1911 NNC
DCO: DLC 1 box   3411

CABELL, JOSEPH C.
Letters to Thomas Jefferson, 1810-1826 priv.
N: DLC 1 reel*   3412

CABLE, GEORGE WASHINGTON, 1844-1925
Correspondence with Charles W. Chesnutt,
1889-1923 TNF
N: T 1 reel   3413

CABLE, GEORGE WASHINGTON, 1844-1925
Letters, 1889-1921 TNF
N: TNF 1 reel   3414

CABLE, GEORGE WASHINGTON, 1844-1925
Papers, 1884-1917, 58 items priv.
N: NcD 1 reel   3415

CALHOUN, JOHN CALDWELL, 1782-1850
Papers, 1801-1850, 30,000 items v.p.
N: ScU-S
P: ScU-S
DCO: ScU-S   3416

CALHOUN, JOHN CALDWELL, 1782-1850
Papers, 1818-1846 MiD-B
N: MiD-B 1 reel   3417

CALHOUN, JOHN CALDWELL, 1782-1850
Papers, 1819-1850 DLC
N: DNA 6 reels [T-16]   3418

CAMERON, SIMON, 1779-1889
In-letters and business papers, 1836-1892,
4,100 items PHarHi
N: PHarH 10 reels   3419

CAMPBELL, GEORGE WASHINGTON, 1769-1848
Papers, 1804-1886 priv.
DCO: DLC 3 boxes   3420

CAPELLEN VAN DE POL, JOHAN DERK
van der, Baron
Papers, 1768-1783 NeHAR
N: DLC 1 reel   3421

CAREY, MATTHEW, 1760-1869
Diary, 1791-1796, 1820-1821, 275 p. priv.
N: PHi   3422

CARROLL, CHARLES, 1737-1832
Letters to Thomas Jefferson priv.
N: CSmH 42 frames   3423

CARTER, THOMAS HENRY
Papers, 1895-1911 DLC
N: DLC 1 reel   3424

CARVER, JONATHAN, 1710-1780
Papers, 1759-1770 DLC UKLBM UKLPRO
priv.
DCO: MnHi 1 box   3425

CASS, LEWIS, 1780-1866
Papers, 1819-1842 DNA
N: PPAmP 57 reels   3426

CAZENOVE, LEWIS A.
Letters to Eleuthère duPont, 1824-1848 priv.
N: DLC 1 reel   3427

CHANDLER, WILLIAM EATON, 1835-1917
Letters to R. B. Hayes OFH
N: OFH 76 frames   3428

CHANDLER, WILLIAM EATON, 1835-1917
Papers, 1876-1882 DLC
N: OFH 4 reels   3429

CHANNING, WILLIAM HENRY, 1810-1884
Four letters to Parke Godwin, 1846-1857 NN
N: IU   3430

CHASE, SALMON PORTLAND, 1808-1873
In-letters, 1836-1842, 1846, 1871, 24 items
priv.
DCO: DLC 1 box   3431

CHASE, SALMON PORTLAND, 1808-1873
Letters and journal, 1861-1862 DLC
N: MH-BA 1 reel   3432

CHASE, SALMON PORTLAND, 1808-1873
Papers DLC
N: FU 2 reels   3433

CHASE, SALMON PORTLAND, 1808-1873
Papers, 1826-1873 PHi
N: FU   3434

CLARK, WILLIAM, 1770-1838
Papers, selections, 1812-1839 KHi
N: MnHi 2 reels   3435

CLAY, CASSIUS MARCELLUS, Jr., 1810-1903
The life, memoirs, writings, and speeches of
Cassius M. Clay priv.
N: KyU 1 reel   3436

CLAY, CASSIUS MARCELLUS, Jr., 1810-1903
Papers, 1817-1877 priv.
N: DLC 1 reel   3437

CLAY, HENRY, 1777-1852
Letters, n.d. priv.
N: KyHi 1 reel   3438

CLAY, HENRY, 1777-1852
Papers, 1807-1852 MiD-B
N: MiD-B 1 reel   3439

CLAY FAMILY
Papers Ashland
N: KyU
P: KyHi KyU   3440

COLFAX, SCHUYLER, 1823-1885
Correspondence with Horace Greeley, 1842-
1880 NN
N: In 1 reel   3441

COLFAX, SCHUYLER, 1823-1885
Letters, 1838-1880 DLC
N: In 1 reel   3442

COMLY, JAMES M., 1832-1887
Correspondence with R. B. Hayes, 1865-1888
OHi
N: OFH   3443

CONNOR, HENRY W.
In-letters, 1843-1850 priv.
DCO: DLC 1 box   3444

COOKE, PHILIP ST. GEORGE, 1809-1895
Papers and clippings, 1837-1942 priv.
N: NcU 280 frames   3445

COOPER, SAMUEL, 1798-1876
Family papers, 1780-1893, 87 items; recollec-
tions of 1818-1852, 1 v. priv.
N: NcU 1 reel   3446

CRÈVECOEUR, SAINT-JOHN DE, 1735-1813
In-letters, 1786-1790, 81 items priv.
N: DLC 1 reel   3447

CRITTENDEN, JOHN JORDAN, 1787-1863
Papers, 1841-1844 DLC
N: NjP 1 reel   3448

CURRY, JABEZ LAMAR MONROE, 1825-1903
Letters to R. B. Hayes OFH
N: OFH 20 frames   3449

CURRY, JABEZ LAMAR MONROE, 1825-1903
Papers A-Ar
N: DLC 4 reels   3450

CURRY, JABEZ LAMAR MONROE, 1825-1903
Papers DLC
N: OFH 2 reels   3451

CURRY, JABEZ LAMAR MONROE, 1825-1903
Papers priv.
N: A-Ar 1 reel   3452

CURTIS, GEORGE WILLIAM, 1824-1892
Letters to R. B. Hayes OFH
N: OFH 14 frames   3453

CUSHING, CALEB, 1800-1879
Letters, 1837-1873, 27 items MiD NN
DCO: DLC   3454

DANA, RICHARD HENRY, 1815-1882
Diary, 1830-1859 MHi
N: NNC 1 reel   3455

DAVIS, DAVID, 1815-1886
Papers, 1840-1885, 15,000 items v.p. priv.
N: priv. 10 reels*
P: INS
DCO: ICHi   3456

DAVIS, JEFFERSON, 1808-1889
Letter to W. H. Kernan, n.d., 1 p. priv.
DCO: GAHi   3457

DAVIS, JEFFERSON, 1808-1889
Letters, 1863-1883 (selections) NcU
N: AU   3458

DAVIS, JEFFERSON, 1808-1889
Letters to Sidney Root and his family priv.
DCO: GAHi 120 p.   3459

DEPEW, CHAUNCEY MITCHELL, 1834-1928
Letters received, 1865-1926 DGW
DCO: DLC 1 box   3460

DICKINSON, EMILY, 1830-1886
Papers MA
N: DFo 3 reels
P: DFo HiU   3461

DINWIDDIE, ROBERT, 1693-1770
Correspondence re: American colonies, 1751-
1758 (typescript) CU
N: CU 1 reel
P: C DLC OCl   3462

DIX, JOHN ADAMS, 1798-1879
Letters, 1831-1882 DLC PHi
N: NNC 1 reel   3463

DOHERTY, HUGH
Letters to Parke Godwin, 1843-1875 NN
N: IU   3464

DONNELLY, IGNATIUS, 1831-1901
Papers, 1890-1896 MnHi
N: MnHi 15 reels
P: CU NNC   3465

DOTY, JAMES DUANE, 1799-1865
Papers re: Northwest Territory, 1777,
1822-1843
N: ? 1 reel
P: WHi   3466

EARLY, JUBAL ANDERSON, 1816-1894
Miscellaneous papers, 1838-1890 priv.
N: DLC 1 reel   3467

EATON, WILLIAM, 1764-1811
Letters, 1801-1807, 4 items NN
N: CSmH   3468

EATON, WILLIAM, 1764-1811
Papers, 1789-1808 DLC
N: CSmH 58 frames   3469

EDWARDS, JONATHAN, 1703-1758
Papers MNtCA
N: MNtCA 11 reels
P: MNtCA   3470

EDWARDS, JONATHAN, 1703-1758
Selected manuscripts, including "On Faith" and
"Efficatious Grace" CtY
N: ICU 1 reel   3471

EISENHOWER, DWIGHT DAVID, Pres. U.S., 1890-
Miscellaneous individual documents; e.g., 1st
proclamation to Austria priv.
DCO: DLC 1 portfolio   3472

ELIOT, JOHN, 1604-1690
Miscellaneous manuscripts DLC
N: NNC 1 reel   3473

ELY, RICHARD THEODORE, 1854-1943
Papers, 1894-1942 WU
N: NNC 1 reel   3474

EMERSON, RALPH WALDO, 1803-1882
Notes on his journals and letters, 1824-1866
priv.
N: NNC 17 reels*   3475

EMERSON, RALPH WALDO, 1803-1882
Papers priv.
N: NNC 6 reels *   3476

EMERSON, WILLIAM, 1803-1882
Papers, 1767-1867 priv.
N: ? 6 reels*   3477
P: NNC

EVARTS, JEREMIAH, 1781-1831
Papers, 1784-1831, 20 items priv.
DCO: DLC   3478

EVERETT, EDWARD, 1794-1865
Correspondence re: Mount Vernon, 1857-1861
MHi
N: MHi 1 foot   3479
P: Mount Vernon Ladies' Association

FARROW, HENRY P.
Letters to R. B. Hayes OFH
N: OFH 1 reel   3480

FIDLER, Rev. NOAH
Journal, 1801-1805 priv.
DCO: DLC 1 box   3481

FILSON, JOHN
Diaries, 1785-1786 WHi
N: In   3482

FINLAY, HUGH, ca. 1731-1801
Journal, 1773-1774 DNA
N: DNA 1 reel [T-268]   3483

FISH, HAMILTON, 1808-1893
Diary, Dec., 1876 - Mar., 1877, v.7 DLC
N: OFH 1 reel   3484

FISH, HAMILTON, 1808-1893
In-letters, 1846-1861, 55 items priv.
N: ViU   3485
P: ViU

FISKE, JOHN, 1842-1901
Letters, 1860-1899 CSmH
N: NNC 1 reel   3486

FITZHUGH, WILLIAM
Letter book, 1679-1699 priv.
DCO: DLC 1 v.   3487

FORCE, PETER, 1790-1868
Papers DLC
N: DLC 11 reels   3488
P: TxU

FRANKFURTER, FELIX, 1882-
Office files as Chairman of the War Labor
Policies Board, 1918-1919 DNA
N: DNA 1 reel   3489

FRANKLIN, BENJAMIN, 1706-1790
Autobiography (holograph), 1771-1788, 130 ll.
CSmH
DCO: NN   3490

FRANKLIN, BENJAMIN, 1706-1790
General P.O. ledger: "Ledger of B. Franklin,"
1776-1778 DNA
N: DNA 1 reel [T-269]   3491

FRANKLIN, BENJAMIN, 1706-1790
Letters to Joseph Galloway, 1766-1775, 60 p.
MiU-C
N: MiU-C 1 reel*   3492
P: NjP

FRANKLIN, BENJAMIN, 1706-1790
Papers, 1642-1810, ca. 15,000 items PPAmP
N: PPAmP 64 reels   3493

The entire papers of Franklin are held by Yale
and the American Philosophical Society, either
as originals or some form of duplication.

FRANKLIN, BENJAMIN, 1706-1790
Papers, Henry M. Stevens collection DLC
N: DLC 22 reels   3494

FREMONT, JOHN CHARLES, 1813-1890
Correspondence and papers, 1862-1889 OFH
N: CU-B 1 reel   3495

FULLER, MELVILLE WESTON, 1833-1910
Papers v.p.
DCO: ICHi 2 filing drawers   3496

GAGE, THOMAS, 1721-1787
Papers re: Pennsylvania, 1763-1775 MiU-C
N: PHarH 4 1/2 reels*   3497
P: PPiU

GALLATIN, ALBERT, 1761-1849
Miscellaneous papers re: Pennsylvania, Indians,
1748-1803, 64 items NHi
DCO: PHarH   3498

GARFIELD, JAMES ABRAM, Pres. U.S., 1831-
1881
Diaries, 1872-1881 DLC
N: OFH 2 reels   3499

GARFIELD, JAMES ABRAM, Pres. U.S.,
1831-1881
Letters from William E. Dodge, 1868-1881,
6 items DLC
N: NNC   3500

GARFIELD, JAMES ABRAM, Pres. U.S.,
1831-1881
Letters to R. B. Hayes OFH
N: OFH 18 frames   3501

GARFIELD, JAMES ABRAM, Pres. U.S.,
1831-1881
Papers, Mar.-Dec., 1876 DLC
N: OFH 1 reel   3502

GATES, HORATIO, 1728-1806
Papers, 1726-1803, 30 boxes NHi
N: NHi 13 reels   3503
P: NHi

GERRY, ELBRIDGE, Jr.
Diary of a journey from Cambridge, Mass.,
to Washington, D. C., May 3-Aug 3, 1813,
173 p. NN
DCO: NN   3504

GIDDINGS, JOSHUA REID, 1795-1864
Giddings-Julian papers, 1839-1896 DLC
N: CU 3 reels   3505

GILMAN, DANIEL COIT, 1831-1908
Papers (selections) MdBJ
N: OFH 5 reels   3506

GLENN, J.H.
A memorandum of the first part of my life,
1799-1823, 167 p. priv.
N: DLC   3507

GODWIN, PARKE, 1816-1904
Letters to Charles Anderson Dana, 1844-1846,
25 items NN
N: IU   3508

GOLDMAN, EMMA, 1869-1940
Letters to Dr. F. G. Heiner, 1934 priv.
N: ICN 1/2 reel   3509

GORGAS, JOSIAH, 1818-1863
Journal, 1857-1864 (typescript) priv.
N: NcU 202 frames   3510

GRANT, ULYSSES SIMPSON, Pres. U.S.,
1822-1885
Manuscripts in André DeCoppet Collection NjP
N: NjP 1 reel   3511

GRATZ FAMILY
Papers, Joseph Henry Collection OCAJA
N: PHi 8 reels   3512
DCO: NNAJHi

GRAY, HORACE, 1828-1902
Letters, 1845-1902, 368 items DUSC
N: DLC 1 reel   3513

GREBLE, EDWIN
Letters, 1858-1870, 12 items priv.
N: DLC   3514

GREELEY, HORACE, 1811-1872
Correspondence with Hamilton Fish, 33 items
DLC
DCO: OU   3515

GREELEY, HORACE, 1811-1872
Letters, 120 items DLC
DCO: OU   3516

GREELEY, HORACE, 1811-1872
Letters, 1840-1870 MB
N: NRU 1 reel   3517

GREELEY, HORACE, 1811-1872
Letters, 1840-1872 DLC
N: NRU 1 reel   3518

GREELEY, HORACE, 1811-1872
Letters, 1841-1872 CtY
N: NRU 1 reel   3519

GREELEY, HORACE, 1811-1872
Letters, 1845-1871 CSmH
N: NRU 1 reel   3520

GREELEY, HORACE, 1811-1872
Letters to Margaret Fuller, 1847-1849,
14 items MH
DCO: OU   3521

GREELEY, HORACE, 1811-1872
Letters to Abraham Lincoln, 1858-1865
41 items DLC
DCO: OU   3522

GREELEY, HORACE, 1811-1872
Seven articles, 7 letters to Henry Clay, 1846-
1849 DLC
N: IU   3523

GREENE, NATHANIEL, 1742-1786
Letters to Col. James Abeel, 1779-1780,
5 letters [unk.]
DC: DeHi 6 p.   3524

HAMILTON, ALEXANDER, 1757-1804
Official papers of, and relating to, Alexander
Hamilton, 1776-1816 DNA
N: NNC 11 reels [T-267]   3525
P: DNA

HAMILTON, ALEXANDER, 1757-1804
Papers, 1749-1849, 113 v. DLC
N: DLC 46 reels   3526
P: CU ICU MnU N NNC NjP WHi

HAMILTON, ALEXANDER, 1757-1804
School exercises DLC
N: ViWI 1 reel   3527

HAMMOND, JAMES HENRY, 1807-1864
Papers, 1823-1875 DLC
N: DLC 20 reels   3528
P: ICU NNC

HARLAN, JOHN MARSHALL, 1833-1911
Papers, 1864-1911 KyU-L
N: KyU 11 reels   3529

HARMAR, JOSIAH, 1753-1813
Papers, 1790 MiU-C
N: OHi 1 reel   3530

HARPER, ROBERT GOODLOE, 1765-1825
Papers and correspondence, 1790-1823 DLC
N: ICU   3531

HARRIS, TOWNSEND, 1804-1878
Journals and papers, 1855-1861 NNCoCi
N: NNCoCi 3 reels   3532

HARRISON, WILLIAM HENRY, Pres. U.S.,
1773-1841
Letters to his wife, Anna Symmes Harrison,
1819-1847 priv.
N: DLC 41 p.   3533

HARRISON, WILLIAM HENRY, Pres. U.S., 1773-
1841
Papers, 1785-1827 DLC
N: OHi 3 reels   3534
P: OHi

HARRISON, WILLIAM HENRY, Pres. U.S.,
1773-1841
Papers (selections) CSmH
N: OHi 1 reel   3535

HAY, JOHN, 1838-1905
Diaries and notebooks, 1861-1870 RPB
N: RPB 1 reel   3536
P: DLC

HAY, JOHN, 1838-1905
  Papers, 1832-1873 IU
  N: RPB   3537
  P: RPB

HAYES, LUCY WEBB, 1851-1886
  Papers OFH
  N: OFH 7 reels   3538

HAYES, RUTHERFORD BIRCHARD, Pres. U.S.,
  1822-1893
  Children's papers, 1870-1889 OFH
  N: NIC 1 reel   3539

HAYES, RUTHERFORD BIRCHARD, Pres. U.S.,
  1822-1893
  Correspondence as governor of Ohio, 1868-
  1872, 1876-1877
  N: OHi reels   3540

HAYES, RUTHERFORD BIRCHARD, Pres.U.S.,
  1822-1893
  Papers, 1829-1895 (selections) OFH
  N: MnHi 3 reels   3541

HAYES, RUTHERFORD BIRCHARD, Pres. U.S.,
  1822-1893
  Papers re: Japan (selections) OFH
  N: OFH 11 frames   3542

HAYES, RUTHERFORD BIRCHARD, Pres., U.S.,
  1822-1893
  Scrapbooks, Railroad Strike of 1877 OFH
  N: OFH 1 reel   3543

HAYES, RUTHERFORD BIRCHARD, Pres. U.S.,
  1822-1893
  Scrapbooks, Southern affairs OFH
  N: OFH 1 reel   3544

HAYES, RUTHERFORD BIRCHARD, Pres. U.S.,
  1822-1893
  Selected papers re: election of 1876 OFH
  N: OFH 5 reels   3545
  P: CU DLC ICU IU MH NN NNC NcD PU

HERNDON, WILLIAM, 1818-1891
  Correspondence with Theodore Parker
  re: nomination of Lincoln, 1854-1859, 68 items
  priv.
  N: IaU   3546

HEWITT, ABRAM STEVENS, 1822-1903
  Narrative... presidential election and
  electoral commission, 1876-1877 NHi
  N: OFH 1 reel   3547

HILL, DANIEL HARVEY, 1821-1889
  Papers priv.
  N: ArU 1 reel   3548

HILL, DANIEL HARVEY, 1821-1889
  Papers, 1816-1924 Nc-Ar
  N: ArU 4 reels   3549

HITCHCOCK, GILBERT MONELL, 1859-1934
  Papers, 1915-1935 DLC
  N: DLC 1 reel   3550

HOLCOMBE, JAMES P., 1820-1873
  Letter to Judah P. Benjamin, Nov. 16, 1864
  DLC
  N: IU   3551

HOLMES, OLIVER WENDELL, Sr., 1809-1894
  Correspondence, 1887-1891, 8 items
  St. Croix Historical Society, Hudson, Wis.
  N: MHi 8 feet   3552

HONYMAN, Dr. ROBERT
  Diary, 1776-1782 DLC
  N: CSmH   3553

HOOVER, HERBERT CLARK, Pres. U.S., 1874-
  Papers re: federal regulation of radio,
  1922-1932 priv.
  N: WHi 1 reel (also Verifax)   3554

HOWELLS, MRS. JOSEPH A.
  Manuscript: "Domestic Life of William Dean
  Howells" OFH
  N: OFH   3555

HOWELLS, WILLIAM DEAN, 1837-1920
  Letters, 1860-1914
  N: OHi   3556

HOWELLS, WILLIAM DEAN, 1837-1920
  Letters to Hamlin Garland, 1888-1894 CLSU

N: CLSU 1 reel   3557
P: CLSU

HOWELLS, WILLIAM DEAN, 1873-1920
  Manuscript: "Novel-Writing and Novel-
  Reading" OFH
  N: OFH   3558

HOWELLS, WILLIAM DEAN, 1837-1920
  Papers, 1857-1914 OFH
  N: OFH 1 reel   3559

HUBBARD, EDMUND W.
  Letters and papers DLC
  N: DLC 1 reel   3560

HUGHES, CHARLES EVANS, 1862-1948
  "Biographical notes" re: Charles Evans
  Hughes priv.*
  N: DLC 1 reel*   3561

HUGHES, CHARLES EVANS, 1862-1948
  Letters to his parents RPB priv.
  N: DLC 2 reels*   3562

HUNT FAMILY
  Papers, 1881-1924 priv.
  N: DLC 2 reels   3563

INGERSOLL, ROBERT GREEN, 1833-1899
  Letters to Rutherford B. Hayes, 1876-1893,
  14 items OFH
  N: I   3564

INMAN, ARTHUR
  Diaries, 1918-1941 (with introduction
  covering years 1894-1918) priv.
  N: DLC 8 reels*   3565

IRVING, WASHINGTON, 1783-1859
  Miscellaneous manuscripts v.p.
  DCO: CtY*
  N: CtY 2 reels   3566

JACKSON, ANDREW, Pres. U.S., 1767-1845
  Letters to W. B. Lewis, 1826-1845, 25 items
  NNP
  DCO: NN   3567

JACKSON, ANDREW, Pres. U.S., 1767-1845
  Papers, 1775-1860, 157 v. DLC
  N: DLC 74 reels   3568
  P: DLC FU ICU NNC T WHi

JACKSON, ANDREW, Pres. U.S., 1767-1845
  Papers at "The Hermitage," 1822-1837,
  26 items Ibid.
  N: TNJ 1 reel   3569
  P: T

JACKSON, THOMAS JONATHAN, 1824-1863
  Papers, 1845-1860, 109 items priv.
  DCO: DLC   3570

JAY, JOHN, 1745-1829
  Correspondence, 1776-1794, 55 items
  Windsor Castle
  N: DLC 1 reel   3571
  P: DLC
  PP: DLC

JAY, JOHN, 1745-1829
  Letter book, 1779-1782 CSmH
  DCO: DLC 1 box   3572

JAY, JOHN, 1745-1829
  Papers, 1715-1862 NNC
  N: NNC 7 reels   3573
  P: NNC

JEFFERSON, THOMAS, Pres. U.S., 1743-1826
  Catalogue of President Jefferson's library, in
  his handwriting, as arranged by himself, n.d.
  MHi
  N: ICU 1 reel   3574

JEFFERSON, THOMAS, Pres. U.S., 1743-1826
  Correspondence with John Ledyard, 1786-
  1810, 7 items DLC
  N: CSmH 1 reel   3575

JEFFERSON, THOMAS, Pres. U.S., 1743-1826
  Jefferson's catalogue of books for the University
  of Virginia Library, 1825 ViU
  N: ICU 1 reel   3576

JEFFERSON, THOMAS, Pres. U.S., 1743-1826
  Letters to Edmund Bacon, 1806-1817, 23 items
  MHi

N: CSmH 26 frames   3577

JEFFERSON, THOMAS, Pres. U.S., 1743-1826
  Papers CSmH CU MHi MiU-C MoSHi
  NHi NNC NNP PHi PPAmP Vi ViHi ViW
  ViWC priv.
  N: DLC 65 reels   3578
  P: DLC

JEFFERSON, THOMAS, Pres. U.S., 1743-1826
  Papers NHi
  N: NHi 1 reel   3579
  P: DLC

JEFFERSON, THOMAS, Pres. U.S., 1743-1826
  Papers NHi
  N: NHi 2 reels   3580
  P: NHi

JEFFERSON, THOMAS, Pres. U.S., 1743-1826
  Papers Thomas Jefferson Memorial
  Foundation, Charlottesville, Va.
  N: ViU   3581
  P: ViU

JEFFERSON, THOMAS, Pres. U.S., 1746-1826
  Papers v.p.
  N: NjP   3582

The entire papers of Jefferson are at Princeton
in one form or another of duplication, and can
be checked by the film of "control cards" of
52 reels.

JEFFERSON, THOMAS, Pres. U.S., 1743-1826
  Papers, 1651-1826, 238 v. DLC
  N: DLC 101 reels   3583
  P: CSt CU CoD ICU MH MnU MoU NN NNC
  NcD NjP PPAmP ViU WaU

JEFFERSON, THOMAS, Pres. U.S.,
  1743-1826
  Papers, 1776-1824, 194 items PPAmP
  N: PPAmP 1 reel   3584

JEFFERSON, THOMAS, Pres. U.S., 1743-1826
  Papers, 1784-1824, 11 items priv.
  DCO: NcU 11 items   3585

JOHNSON, ANDREW, Pres.U.S., 1808-1875
  Papers, 1848, 1865-1868 OFH
  N: OFH 1 reel   3586

JOHNSON, ANDREW, Pres., U.S., 1808-1875
  Papers, 1866-1868 MiD-B
  N: MiD-B 1 reel   3587

JOHNSON, ANDREW, Pres. U.S., 1808-1875
  Pardon issued to S. B. Hoyt, Sept. 13, 1865, 3p.
  priv.
  DCO: GAHi   3588

JOHNSON, REVERDY, 1796-1876
  Papers, 1830-1876 DLC
  N: NNC 1 reel   3589

JOHNSTON, JOHN, 1775-1861
  Papers as Indian agent, 1806-1828 DNA
  N: OHi 3 reels   3590
  P: OHi

KEARNY, STEPHEN WATTS, 1794-1848
  Letters, 1807-1848, 12 items priv.
  DCO: NmSM   3591

KEIFER, JOSEPH WARREN, 1836-1932
  Letters to R. B. Hayes OFH
  N: OFH 25 frames   3592

KEY, DAVID McKENDREE, 1824-1900
  Papers NcU priv.
  N: OFH 612 frames   3593

KINGSBURY, JACOB, 1755-1837
  Papers DLC ICHi
  N: MiD-B 2 reels   3594

KINGSBURY, JACOB, 1755-1837
  Papers, 1727-1856 DLC
  N: OHi 1 reel   3595

KNOX, HENRY, 1750-1806
  Correspondence with General Lincoln,
  General Wadsworth, Major North and Mr.
  Carrington, Feb.-June 1788 MHi
  N: MHi 10 feet   3596

KNOX, HENRY, 1750-1806
    Selected letters, 1780-1805 MHi
    N: MAnP 3 reels*
                                            3597

KOCHTITZKY, OTTO, 1855-
    Memoirs, 1931 (typescript)   priv.
    N: MoHi NcU
                                            3598

KORAES, ADAMANTIOS, 1748-1833
    Correspondence with Thomas Jefferson, July-
    Dec.,1823, Jan. 30, 1825 DLC
    N: ICU 1 reel
                                            3599

LAFAYETTE, MARIE JOSEPH DU MOTIER,
    MARQUIS DE, 1757-1834
    Correspondence with Nicholas Fish, Jan.,1825-
    Apr.,1831 priv.
    N: NHi
                                            3600

LAFAYETTE, MARIE JOSEPH DU MOTIER,
    MARQUIS DE, 1757-1834
    Lafayette-Leclerc papers, 1780-1789 ViWC
    N: ViWC 4 reels
    P: ViWC
                                            3601

LAFAYETTE, MARIE JOSEPH DU MOTIER,
    MARQUIS DE, 1757-1834
    Letters to Washington, 1777-1799 PEaL
    N: NHi 1 reel
                                            3602

LANE, FRANKLIN KNIGHT, 1864-1921
    Papers, 1908-1919 CU-B
    N: CU-B 2 reels
    P: NNC
                                            3603

LATROBE, BENJAMIN HENRY, 1764-1820
    Diary, visit to Mount Vernon, July, 1796,
    15 p. OFH
    N: DLC
    PP: DLC
                                            3604

LATROBE, BENJAMIN HENRY, 1764-1820
    Extracts from diary, 1796 OFH
    N: DLC 1 reel
                                            3605

LEAHY, WILLIAM DANIEL, 1875-1959
    Diary, 1897-1931 DLC
    N: DLC 1 reel*
                                            3606

LEAR, TOBIAS, 1762-1816
    Diary, 1799, 1801, 58 p.   priv.
    DCO: MiU-C
                                            3607

LEDYARD, JOHN, 1751-1789
    Papers priv.
    DCO: NhD 3 v.
                                            3608

LEE, RICHARD HENRY, 1732-1794
    Letters, 1777-1791, 25 items DLC
    N: ViU
    P: ViU
                                            3609

LEE, ROBERT EDWARD, 1807-1870
    Letter to Col. Blount re: holding Guinea's
    Depot (Va.), May 4, 1863, 1 p.   priv.
    DCO: GAHi
                                            3610

LEE, ROBERT EDWARD, 1807-1870
    Letter to J. A. Seddon, asking for supplies,
    Nov. 10, 1863, 2 p.   priv.
    DCO: CSbC
                                            3611

LEE, ROBERT EDWARD, 1807-1870
    Letters, 1861-1867, 7 items   priv.
    DCO: WvU
                                            3612

LEE, ROBERT EDWARD, 1807-1870
    Letters, invoice book, papers
    Debutts-Ely Collection
    N: ? 1 reel
    P: DLC*
                                            3613

LEGENDRE, CHARLES W.
    Papers, 1866-1892 DLC
    N: DLC 7 reels
    P: FU
                                            3614

LIEBER, FRANCIS, 1800-1872
    Correspondence, 1827-1871 MH
    N: CSmH 501 frames
                                            3615

LIEBER, FRANCIS, 1800-1872
    Letters, 1806-1858, 23 items CSmH
    N: NcU 1 reel
                                            3616

LIEBER, FRANCIS, 1800-1872
    Letters to Hamilton Fish, 1857-1872 DLC
    N: CSmH 390 frames
                                            3617

LIEBER, FRANCIS, 1800-1872
    Papers priv.
    N: NcU
                                            3618

LIEBER, FRANCIS, 1800-1872
    Papers, 1834-1876, 2 v. DLC
    N: CSmH 638 frames
                                            3619

LIEBER, FRANCIS, 1800-1872
    Vierzehn Wein und Wonnelieder IU
    N: CSmH
                                            3620

LINCOLN, ABRAHAM, Pres. U.S., 1809-1865
    Lincoln legals C.H. Clinton (De Witt Co.)
    N: I 1 reel 16 mm.
                                            3621

LINCOLN, ABRAHAM, Pres. U.S., 1809-1865
    Lincoln's scrapbook of Lincoln-Douglas debates
    DLC
    N: DLC 15 feet
                                            3622

LINCOLN, ABRAHAM, Pres. U.S., 1809-1865
    Notes from the Hayes Papers OFH
    N: OFH 19 frames
                                            3623

LINCOLN, ABRAHAM, Pres. U.S., 1809-1865
    Papers, Herndon-Weik Collection DLC
    N: DLC 14 reels
    P: InU MBU MiD RPB WaPS
                                            3624

LINCOLN, ABRAHAM, Pres. U.S., 1809-1865
    Papers, Robert Todd Lincoln Collection,
    1790-1916, 154 v. DLC
    N: DLC 99 reels
    P: CStbS CU FU I IC ICHi ICU INS N NNC NRU
       NhD RPB TxU WaPS WaU
                                            3625

LINCOLN, ABRAHAM, Pres. U.S., 1809-1865
    Plan for purchasing Delaware slaves, Nov.,
    1861 CSmH
    DCO: DeHi 32 p.
                                            3626

LINCOLN, ABRAHAM, Pres. U.S., 1809-1865
    Telegrams, 1864-1865 DNA
    N: I 1 reel
                                            3627

LONGSTREET, JAMES, 1821-1904
    Papers, 1875-1904 priv.
    DCO: NcU 19 items
                                            3628

LORD, WILLIAM WILBERFORCE
    Papers, 1858-1926 NN
    N: WaU 1 reel
                                            3629

LOVEJOY, ELIJAH PARISH, 1802-1837
    Papers, 1828-1837, 8 items v.p.
    DCO: MeWC*
                                            3630

LYON, LUCIUS, 1800-1851
    In-letters, 1833-1836, 7 items priv.
    DCO: DLC
                                            3631

McARTHUR, DUNCAN, 1772-1839
    Papers, 1783-1840 DLC
    N: ? 20 reels
    P: OHi
                                            3632

McCLELLAN, GEORGE BRINTON, 1826-1885
    Papers DLC
    N: MiEM 25 reels
                                            3633

McCLELLAN, GEORGE BRINTON, 1826-1885
    Papers, 1852-1855 DLC
    DCO: MnHi 1 box
                                            3634

MACLURE, WILLIAM, 1763-1840
    Correspondence with Marie D. Fretageot,
    1820-1833, 409 items InNhW
    N: InNhW 1 reel
    P: In
                                            3635

MACLURE, WILLIAM, 1763-1840
    Journals and notebooks, 1802-1825 InNhW
    N: PPAmP
                                            3636

MACLURE, WILLIAM, 1763-1840
    Letters to Benjamin Silliman, 1817-1838,
    31 items CtY
    N: PPAmP
                                            3637

McCOSH, JAMES, 1811-1894
    Letters to R. B. Hayes OFH
    N: OFH 20 frames
                                            3638

McGRATH, EARL J., 1902-
    Public papers, 1949-1953 priv.
    N: MoIT
                                            3639

MACON, NATHANIEL, 1758-1837
    Papers, 1773-1843 Nc-Ar
    N: KyU 20 feet
                                            3640

MADISON, JAMES, Pres. U.S., 1751-1836
    Correspondence with Cutts family priv.
    N: ? 1 reel
    P: DLC
                                            3641

MADISON, JAMES, Pres. U.S., 1751-1836
    In-letters, 1808-1812 NjP
    N: DLC 1 reel
                                            3642

MADISON, JAMES, Pres. U.S., 1751-1836
    Madison items from the Continental Congress
    Papers, 1776, 1781-1788 DLC
    N: DNA 1 reel [T-270]
                                            3643

MADISON, JAMES, Pres. U.S., 1751-1836
    Papers
    N: DLC 39 reels
                                            3644

MALLORY, STEPHEN RUSSELL, 1813-1873
    Papers, 1846-1872, 93 items priv.
    N: NcU 1 reel
                                            3645

MANN, HORACE, 1796-1859
    Papers, especially letters, 1857-
    1859, v. p.
    DCO: OYesA 233 items
                                            3646

MARCY, WILLIAM LEARNED, 1786-1857
    Papers, 1832-1847 DLC
    N: NNC 1 reel
                                            3647

MARSHALL, JOHN, 1755-1835
    Journal, 1856-1857, 369 p.   priv.
    N: ViU
    P: ViU
                                            3648

MARSHALL, JOHN, 1755-1835
    Papers DLC
    N: NNC 3 reels
                                            3649

MASON, CHARLES, 1730-1787
    Journal during the survey of the Mason and
    Dixon Line, 1763-1768 DNA
    N: DNA 1 reel [M-86]
    P: De DeHi DeU NcU WvU
                                            3650

MASON, GEORGE, 1725-1792
    Papers DLC
    N: DLC 1 reel
                                            3651

MAURY, MATTHEW FONTAINE, 1806-1873
    Testimonial fund papers, 1865-1888, 15 items
    priv.
    N: NcU 36 frames
                                            3652

MEDILL, WILLIAM, 1802-1865
    Papers priv.
    N: DLC 1 reel
                                            3653

MINTO, WALTER, 1753-1796
    Papers, 1757-1799, 28 items MiU-C
    N: PPAmP
                                            3654

MONROE, JAMES, Pres. U.S., 1758-1831
    Correspondence, 1807-1816 NN
    N: FU 1 reel
                                            3655

MONROE, JAMES, Pres. U.S., 1758-1831
    In-letters DLC
    N: FU 1 reel
                                            3656

MONROE, JAMES, Pres. U.S., 1758-1831
    In-letters FU
    N: FU 1 reel
                                            3657

MONROE, JAMES, Pres. U.S., 1758-1831
    Letters, 1812-1825, 12 items priv.
    DCO: NPV
                                            3658

MONROE, JAMES, Pres. U.S., 1758-1831
    Papers NN
    N: FU 1 reel
                                            3659

MONROE, JAMES, Pres. U.S., 1758-1831
    Papers, Laurence G. Hoss Collection priv.
    N: DLC 2 reels
                                            3660

MORGAN, LEWIS HENRY, 1818-1881
    Personal papers, 1840-1881
    N: NRU 11 reels
                                            3661

MORRIS, GOUVERNEUR, 1752-1816
    Letter to James Morris, 1790 NHi
    N: NHi
                                            3662

MORRIS, ROBERT, 1734-1806
    Marine board letter book MdAN
    N: PHi 1 reel
                                            3663

MORRIS, ROBERT, 1734-1806
Papers, 1774-1837 CSmH
N: NNC 2 reels   3664

MORRIS, ROBERT, 1734-1806
Papers, 1775-1829 DLC
N: DLC 12 reels   3665
P: NNC

MORRIS, ROLAND SLETOR, 1874-1945
In-letters, 1910-1920 priv.
N: DLC 1 reel   3666
PP: DLC

MORSE, SAMUEL FINLEY BREESE, 1791-1872
Case of Samuel F.B. Morse and Alfred Vail
versus O.J. Smith in the Superior Court of
New York (including letters from Amos Kendall)
priv.
N: KyU 35 feet   3667

MORSE, SAMUEL FINLEY BREEZE, 1791-1872
Papers, 1816-1869 priv.
N: DLC 1 reel   3668

MOSBY, JOHN SINGLETON, 1833-1916
Letters, 1861-1886 priv.
DCO: DLC 1 v.   3669

MOSES, MIRIAM GRATZ
Papers: Series II, 1837-1862, 195 items;
Series III, 1842-1853, 27 items NcU
N: NcU 1 reel   3670
DCO: OCJA

MYERS, WILLIAM STARR, 1877-1956
Diary, 1887-1902, 5v. NjP
N: NcU 2 reels   3671

OSSOLI, SARAH MARGARET FULLER, Marchesa
d', 1810-1850
Papers MB
N: NhD 2 reels   3672

PALMER, ALEXANDER MITCHELL, 1872-1936
In-letters, 1910-1920 priv.
DCO: DLC 1 box   3673

PARTRIDGE, ALDEN, 1785-1854
Papers, 1805-1916 VtNN
N: NcU 4 reels   3674

PATERSON, WILLIAM, 1745-1806
Papers, 1783-1804   NN
N: NjP 1 reel   3675

PENN, WILLIAM, 1644-1718
Journal A, 1701-1710 P
N: PHarH   3676

PENN, WILLIAM, 1644-1718
Papers, 1672?-1712 UKLFS
DCO: PHi 2 v.   3677

PENN, WILLIAM, 1644-1718
Papers, 1672-1718, 6 items v.p.
DCO: PSC-F   3678

PENN, WILLIAM, 1644-1718
Selected material PHi
N: NB 4 reels   3679

PERRY, MATTHEW CALBRAITH, 1794-1858
Letter books, 1843-1845 DNA
N: DNA 1 reel [M-206]   3680
P: DeU

PHILLIPS, ULRICH B.
Manuscripts of lectures priv.
N: CtY   3681

PICKERING, TIMOTHY, 1745-1829
Correspondence with Samuel Hodgdon, 1780-
1784 DNA
N: NNC 2 reels   3682

PICKERING, TIMOTHY, 1745-1829
Letters to Allen McLane, 1798-1799,
3 items MHi
N: DeU 1 reel   3683

PIERCE, FRANKLIN, Pres. U.S., 1804-1869
Mexican War journal, 1847 CSmH
DCO: NhD   3684

PIERCE, FRANKLIN, Pres. U.S., 1804-1869
Papers, 1844 DLC
N: NjP 1 reel   3685

PIKE, JAMES SHEPARD
Correspondence with W.P.Fessenden and
Salmon P. Chase, 1850-1881 MeCa
N: ViU   3686

PIKE, ZEBULON MONTGOMERY, 1779-1813
Notebook of maps, traverse tables, and
meteorological observations, 1805-1807 DNA
N: DNA 1 reel [T-36]   3687

PINCKNEY, THOMAS, 1750-1828
Papers, ca. 1771-1826, 12 folders priv.
DCO: ScHi   3688

PLITT, GEORGE
Correspondence with James Buchanan, J.W.
Forney, and others, 1836-1859 priv.
DCO: DLC*   3689
N: DLC 1 reel
PP: DLC

POLK, JAMES KNOX, Pres. U.S., 1795-1849
Index to papers in Tennessee Archives T
N: DLC 1 reel   3690

POLK, JAMES KNOX, Pres. U.S., 1795-1849
Papers, 1775-1849, 165 v. DLC
N: DLC 53 reels   3691
P: FU ICU LU NjP NRU TxU

POLLARD, ISAAC, Sr.
Diary, 1850-1855; diary of Isaac Pollard, Jr.,
1860 priv.
N: DLC 1 reel   3692
P: DLC

PROCTOR, WILBUR HUNTINGTON
Diary, Jan., 1864-Apr., 1874 priv.
N: DLC 1 reel   3693
P: DLC

PULITZER, JOSEPH, 1847-1911
Correspondence St. Louis Post-Dispatch
N: NNC 4 reels   3694
P: MoS

RANDOLPH, JOHN, of Roanoke, 1773-1833
Letters, 1798-1830, 87 items DLC
N: ViU   3695

RANDOLPH, JOHN, of Roanoke, 1773-1833
Letters, 1800-1863, 80 items priv.
N: NcU 1 reel   3696

RANDOLPH, JOHN, of Roanoke, 1773-1833
Letters to Hermanus Bleecker, 1812-1828,
46 items ViU
N: DLC 1 reel   3697
PP: DLC

RANDOLPH, JOHN, of Roanoke, 1773-1833
Material assembled by W.C. Cabell
Bruce-Randolph Collection Vi
N: Vi 6 reels   3698
P: Vi

REED, JOSEPH, 1741-1785
Papers, 1757-1842, 11 v. NHi
N: NHi 3 reels   3699
P: PHarH

RICE, LUTHER, 1783-1836
Journal, 1808-1812, 1815-1820; ledger book,
1819-1826; memorandum book, 1815 DGW
N: DGW   3700
P: NNUT TxFwSB

ROGERS, ROBERT, 1751-1795
Papers, 1760-1841 CaQMSS DNA NN
UKLPRO
DCO: MnHi 1 box   3701

ROOSEVELT, FRANKLIN DELANO, Pres. U.S.,
1882-1945
Correspondence with Lord Tweedsmuir, Mar.
30, 1936-June 17, 1939, 62 p. NHyR
N: CaOKQ   3702

ROOSEVELT, FRANKLIN DELANO, Pres. U.S.,
1882-1945
Material from speech files, 1937, 1940, 1941,
1943 NHyR
N: WaU   3703

ROOSEVELT, FRANKLIN DELANO, Pres. U.S.,
1882-1945
Papers re: Russian-American relations
NHpR   N: CSt 1 reel   3704

ROOSEVELT, FRANKLIN DELANO, Pres. U.S.,
1882-1945
Press conferences, 1933-1945, 25 v.
NHyR
N: NHyR 12 reels   3705
P: CU

ROOSEVELT, THEODORE, Pres. U.S.,
1858-1919
Letters to his sister, Anna Roosevelt Cowles,
1870-1919 priv.
N: DLC 3 reels*   3706

ROOSEVELT, THEODORE, Pres. U.S., 1858-1919
Letters to Orville H. Platt, 1903-1906, 11 items
Ct
DCO: Ct   3707

ROOSEVELT, THEODORE, Pres. U.S., 1858-1919
Papers DLC
N: DLC 315 reels*   3708

ROWAN, STEPHEN CLEGG, 1808-1890
Papers, 1826-1890 DNA
N: DNA 1 reel [M-180]   3709

RUTLEDGE, JOHN, 1739-1800
Account book, 1761-1786 priv.
N: DLC 1 reel   3710

SARGENT, WINTHROP, 1753-1820
Papers, 1771-1865 OHi
N: OHi 6 reels   3711
P: OHi

SATOLLI, FRANCESCO, Cardinal, 1839-1910
Manuscript re: tour of U.S.A., 1896
Collegio di Sant'Anselmo, Rome
N: MnCS   3712

SCHINER, MICHAEL
Diary, 1813-1863 DLC
N: DHU 1 reel   3713

SCHURZ, CARL, 1829-1906
Papers, 1876-1881 DLC
N: OFH 14 reels   3714

SEWARD, WILLIAM HENRY, 1801-1872
In-letters, 1856-1881 NRU
N: PHarH 10 feet   3715

SHERMAN, JOHN, 1823-1900
In-letters, 1848-1893, 500 items priv.
N: DLC 1 reel   3716

SHERMAN, JOHN, 1823-1900
Selected correspondence, 1848-1876 DLC
N: OFH 81 frames   3717

SHERMAN, WILLIAM TECUMSEH, 1820-1891
Letters, 38 items I
N: CoU   3718

SHERMAN, WILLIAM TECUMSEH, 1820-1891
Letters, 1872-1882 MiU-C
N: CoU   3719

SHERMAN, WILLIAM TECUMSEH, 1820-1891
Letters to General B. H. Grierson, 1867-
1881 ICN
DCO: CoU   3720

SHERMAN, WILLIAM TECUMSEH, 1820-1891
Papers, selections, 1865-1878; letters to
Philip Sheridan, 1868-1887 DLC
N: CoU   3721

SMET, Rev. PIERRE JEAN DE, 1801-1873
Selected documents DAL-Adj Gen
N: CoU 1 reel   3722

SMITH, JOSEPH, 1805-1844
Day book, store at Nauvoo, June, 1842-June,
1844
N: CtY   3723

SOUTHARD, SAMUEL LEWIS, 1787-1872
Papers, 1808-1848 priv.
DCO: DLC 29 items   3724

SOWLE, CORNELIUS
Correspondence with John Jacob Astor, 1811-
1820 priv.
N: DLC 1 reel   3725

STANTON, EDWIN McMASTERS, 1814-1869
Papers priv.
N: NNC 1 reel   3726

STANTON, EDWIN McMASTERS, 1814-1869
Papers, 1831-1870 DLC
N: CU 14 reels   3727

STEFFENS, LINCOLN, 1866-1936
Autobiography (manuscript) NNC
N: NNC 3 reels   3728

STEPHENS, ALEXANDER HAMILTON, 1812-1883
Correspondence, 1834-1872 NNCSH
N: NjP NNCSH ViU 6 reels   3729
P: ArU DLC GU MdBJ MH NcD NcU NjP
   NRU ViU WaU

STEPHENS, ALEXANDER HAMILTON, 1812-1883
Papers, 1845-1879 DLC NcD
N: GEU 6 reels   3730

STEUBEN, Baron F.W.L.G.A. von, 1730-1794
Letter from Steuben, N.Y., re: missionary
sent from Connecticut, Sept. 3, 1793
Missionary Society of Conn., Hartford
DCO: Ct   3731

STEVENS, ISAAC INGALLS
Letters, 1856-1860 CtY
N: WaU 2 reels   3732

STILLMAN, GEORGE
Correspondence, diary, military papers,
1775-1804   priv.
DCO: DLC 50 items   3733

STIMSON, HENRY LEWIS, 1867-1950
Diary and miscellaneous papers, 1910-1933
CtY
N: ? 4 reels   3734
P: CtY

STOCKTON, ROBERT FIELD, 1795-1866
Correspondence with George Bancroft,
Secretary of Navy, 1843-1847 DNA
N: DNA 1 reel   3735
P: CLO

STORY, JOSEPH, 1779-1845
Manuscripts re: Daniel Webster speeches,
ca. 1830, 14 p. DLC
N: NhD   3736

STORY, JOSEPH, 1779-1845
Papers, 1804-1843 DLC
N: DLC 5 reels   3737

STORY, JOSEPH, 1779-1845
Scrapbook containing newspaper clippings, etc.,
1846 MH-L
N: NNC 1 reel   3738

STRAUS, OSCAR SOLOMON, 1850-1926
Correspondence DLC
N: DLC 1 reel   3739

STRAUS, OSCAR SOLOMON, 1850-1926
Letters DLC
N: NNC 10 reels   3740

STRONG, GEORGE TEMPLETON, 1820-1875
Diary, 1835-1875 NNC
N: ? 3 reels   3741
P: NN

SUMNER, CHARLES, 1811-1874
Letters re: Western Freedmen's Aid
Commission, 1866-1870, 20 p. MH
N: NNC   3742

TALLMADGE, BENJAMIN, 1754-1835
Papers, 1774-ca.1840 priv.
N: DLC 1 reel   3743

TAPPAN, BENJAMIN, 1775-1857
Papers, 1799-1852, ca. 60 items priv.
N: DLC 2 reels   3744

TAYLOR, ZACHARY, Pres. U.S., 1784-1850
Autobiography Taylor Papers DLC
N: DLC 1 reel   3745

TAYLOR, ZACHARY, Pres. U.S., 1784-1850
Letters re: Fort Snelling, 1828-1830, 5 items
DLC DNA KyHi
DCO: MnHi   3746

TAYLOR, ZACHARY, Pres. U.S., 1784-1850
Papers, 1841-1887 (also of Richard Taylor,
1826-1879), 422 items priv.
N: NcU 1 reel   3747

THOMAS, GEORGE HENRY, 1816-1870
Papers, 1848-1893 CSmH
N: NN 115 frames*   3748

THOMSON, CHARLES, 1729-1824
Notes on Stamp Act Congress, First
Continental Congress, 1774-1777, 1789 MdHi
DCO: DLC   3749

TILDEN, SAMUEL JONES, 1814-1886
Papers, 1876-1879 NN
N: OFH 4 reels   3750

TILGHMAN, TENCH, 1744-1786
Papers, 1775-1786 priv.
DCO: DLC 1 box   3751

TRUMBULL, LYMAN, 1813-1896
Papers, 1855-1872, 77 v. DLC
N: DLC 22 reels   3752
P: CSmH CU I ICU NIC NNC ScU TxU

TUGWELL, REXFORD GUY, 1891-
Papers NHyR
N: MBU 1 reel   3753

TYLER, JOHN, Pres. U.S., 1790-1862
Miscellaneous material priv.
DCO: DLC   3754

UNDERWOOD, OSCAR WILDER, 1862-1929
Letters, 1900-1928, ca. 200 items priv.
N: ViU   3755

UNDERWOOD, OSCAR WILDER, 1862-1929
Papers, 1842-1931, 259 items A-Ar
N: NcU 374 frames   3756

VALLANDIGHAM, CLEMENT LAIRD, 1820-1871
Letters (selections) DLC
N: CoU   3757

VAN BUREN, MARTIN, Pres. U.S., 1782-1862
Papers, 1787-1868 DLC
N: DLC 31 reels   3758
P: FU NNC NRU

VAUGHAN, SAMUEL
Diary, June-Sept.,1787 priv.
N: DLC 1 reel   3759
PP: DLC

WADSWORTH, JEREMIAH, 1743-1804
Correspondence priv.
DCO: DLC 2 boxes   3760

WAGER, JOHN PHILIP
Diary, 1812-1814   DLC
N: DLC 1 reel   3761

WAITE, MORRISON REMICK, 1816-1888
Letters to R. B. Hayes OFH
N: OFH 8 frames   3762

WASHINGTON, GEORGE, Pres. U.S., 1732-1799
Diaries, 1795, 1798 NNC
N: NNC 1 reel   3763

WASHINGTON, GEORGE, Pres. U.S., 1732-1799
General Washington's orders, Aug. - Nov.,1782,
Revolutionary War Orders, v. 64 DNA
N: DNA 1 reel   3764

WASHINGTON, GEORGE, Pres. U.S., 1732-1799
Letter to the Earl of Loudon, Jan. 10, 1757
CSmH
N: PPiU   3765

WASHINGTON, GEORGE, Pres. U.S., 1732-1799
Letters Chateau de Rochambeau, France
DCO: DLC 35 sheets   3766

WASHINGTON, GEORGE, Pres. U.S., 1732-1799
Memorandum or journal of letters & c...
submitted... by the heads of the departments...
Jan. 5, 1793 - Feb. 21, 1797 Washington
Papers, v. 337 DLC
N: ICU   3767

WASHINGTON, GEORGE, Pres. U.S., 1732-1799
Orderly book: Valley Forge, Jan. 1-Apr. 15,
1778; elsewhere, Apr. 17, 1779-Aug. 8, 1779
priv.
N: IaU 278 frames   3768

WASHINGTON, GEORGE, Pres. U. S., 1732-1799
Papers, v.d. v.p.
N: DLC

DCO: DLC   3769

As completely as possible all known Washington
items have been collected in one form or another
of photocopy at the Library of Congress, to supplement its holding of originals.

WASHINGTON, GEORGE, Pres. U.S., 1732-1799
Papers, 1752-1825 NNP
DCO: DLC NN 2 v.   3770

WATTERSON, HENRY, 1840-1921
Papers, 1828-1920 DLC
N: NNC 16 reels   3771

WEBSTER, DANIEL, 1782-1852
In-letters, 1833-1843 DLC
N: PU 1174 frames   3772

WEBSTER, DANIEL, 1782-1852
Introduction and notes for Reply to Hayne,
1830, 14 p. DLC
N: NhD   3773

WEBSTER, DANIEL, 1782-1852
Letters, 1820-1843, 20 items CtY
N: NhD   3774

WEBSTER, DANIEL, 1782-1852
Letters to Thomas A. Merrill, 1802-1807, 1851,
15 items (collected by Mattie Holton Wilcox)
NhD
N: NcU 1 reel   3775

WEBSTER, DANIEL, 1782-1852
Reply to Hayne, drafts, 1830 MB
N: NhD   3776

WEBSTER, NOAH, 1758-1843
Letters NN
N: CtY 1 reel   3777
P: CtY

WEED, THURLOW, 1797-1882
In-letters DLC
N: NRU 3 reels   3778

WEED, THURLOW, 1797-1882
Papers NHi
N: NRU   3779

WELLES, GIDEON, 1802-1878
Diary, trip from Hartford, Connecticut,to
Illinois, 1841 NjP
N: NjP 1 reel   3780

WELLES, GIDEON, 1802-1878
Papers, 1833-1847 DLC
N: NNC 1/4 reel   3781

WHITE, WILLIAM ALLEN, 1868-1944
Papers, 1899-1939 DLC
N: ICU 9 reels   3782
P: KHi

WILDER, ANNA
Correspondence, 1776-1838 priv.
DCO: DLC 1 folio   3783

WILKES, CHARLES, 1798-1877
Papers re: exploring expedition, 1837-1847,
5 v. KHi
N: KHi 1 reel   3784
P: KHi

WILLIAMS, JOHN L.,Jr.
Letters, 1846-1862, 9 items priv.
DCO: DLC   3785

WILLIAMS, ROGER, 1603?-1683
Papers, 1629-1682, 564 p. MHi RHi v.p.
DCO: CSmH Ct CtY DLC ICN IEN IU
     MSaE MWA MiU NHi NN NNUT
     OClWHi RHi RPJCB
N: CU 1 reel   3786

WILSON, ELLEN AXSON
Correspondence with Woodrow Wilson priv.
N: DLC 1 reel*   3787

WILSON, HENRY, 1812-1875
Papers DLC
N: MBU 1 reel   3788

WILSON, HENRY, 1812-1875
Papers, 1856-1875 OFH
N: OFH 97 frames   3789

WILSON, JAMES HARRISON, 1837-1925
Correspondence, 1867-1918 CoHi

N: CoHi 14 reels NNC 25 reels 11 16 mm.
P: I PHarH TxWB   3790

WILSON, WOODROW, Pres. U.S., 1856-1924
  Correspondence with George Harvey, Feb. 3,
  1906-Jan. 12, 1912 (transcript) DLC
  N: NjP 1 reel   3791

WILSON, WOODROW, Pres. U.S., 1856-1924
  Correspondence with Frank L. Polk, 1915-
  1920, 30 items priv.
  DCO: NN   3792

WILSON, WOODROW, Pres. U.S., 1856-1924
  Letters to Edwin A. Alderman, 1903-1921 ViU
  DCO: DLC 1 box   3793

WILSON, WOODROW, Pres. U.S., 1856-1924
  Letters to Richard Heath Dabney, 1902-
  1922 ViU
  DCO: DLC   3794

WILSON, WOODROW, Pres. U.S., 1856-1924
  Letters to Joseph Edward Davies, 1918 priv.
  DCO: DLC 1 box   3795

WILSON, WOODROW, Pres. U.S., 1856-1924
  Letters to Otis A. Glazebrook, 1912-1914 priv.
  DCO: DLC 1 box   3796

WILSON, WOODROW, Pres. U.S., 1856-1924
  Letters to Horace S. Scudder, 1889-1893 priv.
  DCO: DLC 1 box   3797

WILSON, WOODROW, Pres. U.S., 1856-1924
  Notes of lectures in jurisprudence and politics,
  1903-1904 (taken by Homer Charles Zink)
  priv.
  N: NjP 1 reel   3798

WILSON, WOODROW, Pres. U.S., 1856-1924
  Petition of W. Wilson to practice law, 1882
  C.H. Atlanta
  DCO: GAHi   3799

WINANT, JOHN GILBERT, 1889-1947
  Papers, 1916-1947 NNC
  N: NNC 4 reels   3800

WIRT, WILLIAM, 1772-1834
  Letters, 1805-1828
  N: ViU   3801

WOOLLEY, ROBERT W.
  In-letters, 49 items priv.
  N: DLC 1 reel*   3802

WRIGHT, ORVILLE, 1871-1948
  Scrapbooks, 1903-1948 DLC
  N: DLC 10 reels
  P: ODa   3803

ZUENDT FAMILY
  Papers, 1697-1899 priv.
  N: DLC 1 reel   3804

Art History

Personal Papers

ARCHAMBAULT, A. MARGARETTA
  Papers, 1900-1925 PHi
  N: MiDA-A 4 reels   3805

AUDUBON, JOHN JAMES, 1785-1851
  Diary, Apr.-Dec., 1826 priv.
  N: NHi 1 reel   3806

AUDUBON, JOHN JAMES, 1785-1851
  Papers, journals, and correspondence, 1822-
  1845 PPAmA
  N: MiDA-A 2 reels   3807

BIDDLE, GEORGE
  Papers, 1933-1944 PPMA
  N: MiDA-A   3808

BIRCH, WILLIAM RUSSELL
  Autobiography PHi
  N: MiDA-A   3809

BORGLUM, GUTZON, 1871-1941
  Correspondence, 1908-1953 priv.
  N: DLC 1 reel*
  PP: DLC   3810

BRADY, MATHEW B., 1823-1896
  Register, 1870-1875 DLC

N: DLC 1 reel   3811
P: DLC

COPLEY, JOHN SINGLETON, 1738-1815
  Correspondence, 1756-1815 MB
  N: DLC 1 reel   3812

COPLEY, JOHN SINGLETON, 1738-1815
  Letters, 1774-1799, ca.45 items CSmH
  N: MHi   3813

COPLEY, JOHN SINGLETON, 1738-1815
  Papers, 355 p. DLC
  N: DLC
  P: MWA   3814

EICHOLTZ, JACOB
  Day book, 1809-1817 PHi
  N: MiDA-A   3815

EVANS, DAVID
  Day books, 1774-1812 PHi
  N: MiDA-A   3816

GOBRECHT, CHRISTIAN, 1784-1844
  Papers, 1822-1902 PHi
  N: MiDA-A 66 frames   3817

GREEN, ELIZABETH SHIPPEN
  Scrapbooks, 1904-1912 PP
  N: MiDA-A 2 reels   3818

LAWSON, ALEXANDER
  Scrapbooks, 2v. PPAN
  N: MiDA-A 1 reel   3819

NEAGLE, JOHN
  Commonplace book PHi
  N: MiDA-A 1 reel   3820

OAKLEY, VIOLET
  Scrapbooks, 1898-1925 priv.
  N: MiDA-A 1 reel   3821

ORD, GEORGE.
  Correspondence with Titian Ramsey Peale,
  1827-1854. PHi
  N: MiDA-A   3822

PEALE, CHARLES WILLSON, 1741-1827
  Letters, 1821-1823, 130 p. PHi
  N: MiDA-A 65 frames   3823

PEALE, REMBRANDT, 1778-1860
  Notes of the painting room, ca. 1850 PHi
  N: MiDA-A 246 frames   3824

PELLETREAU, ELIAS, 1726-1810, silversmith
  Account book, 1759-1805, 109 p. priv.
  DCO: NN   3825

REMINGTON, FREDERIC, 1861-1909
  Letters and papers, 1880-1909 NOg NOgR
  N: NN 1 reel *
  P: NN   3826

RICHARDSON, JOSEPH, Jr.
  Day book, 1796-1801; ledger, 1796-1831 PHi
  N: MiDA-A 204 frames   3827

ROLLINSON, WILLIAM, 1762-1842, engraver
  Diary, voyage to Liverpool and New York,
  1788-1789, 66 p. priv.
  DCO: MiU-C   3828

SARTAIN, JOHN, 1808-1897
  Letter press book, 1875-1876 PHi
  N: MiDA-A 2 reels   3829

SARTAIN, WILLIAM, 1843-1924
  Autobiography, ca. 1910, 92 p. PPPM
  N: MiDA-A 96 frames   3830

SMITH, RUSSELL
  Diary, 1883-1892 PHi
  N: MiDA-A   3831

STUART, GILBERT CHARLES, 1755-1828
  Letter to Gov.Jonathan Trumbull re: portrait
  of Gen.Washington, ordered for state of Conn.,
  Feb.,1801 PHi
  PP: Ct   3832

TRUMBULL, JOHN, 1756-1843
  Papers DLC NHi
  N: CtY 5 reels   3833

TRUMBULL, JOHN, 1756-1843
  Records in Dept. of State, 1796-1841 DNA
  N: CtY 1 reel   3834

TUCKER, THOMAS
  Papers re: manufacture of porcelain PPPM
  N: MiDA-A   3835

WEST, BENJAMIN
  Accounts, 1790-1804, 1810-1811; sketch books,
  1790-1807; estate papers, 1814-1819 PHi
  N: MiDA-A 125 frames   3836

WHISTLER, JAMES ABBOTT McNEILL, 1834-1903
  Letters to Lantin-Latour, 1863-1871 DLC
  N: DLC 1 reel   3837

Institutions

AMERICAN ACADEMY OF FINE ARTS,
  New York
  Papers, 1802-1839 NHi
  N: CtY 1 reel   3838

AMERICAN PHILOSOPHICAL SOCIETY
  Curator's catalogue, 1769-1900;
  Peale, Audubon,and other material
  re: art PPAmP
  N: MiDA-A 9 reels   3839

AMERICAN PHILOSOPHICAL SOCIETY
  Peale-Sellers papers PPAmP
  N: PPAmP   3840

ARTISTS' FUND SOCIETY OF PHILADELPHIA
  Minutes, 1835-1843; miscellaneous papers,
  1836-1858 PHi
  N: MiDA-A 194 frames   3841

CARL SCHURZ MEMORIAL FOUNDATION
  American artists' biographical index,1900-1920
  Ibid.
  N: MiDA-A   3842

DETROIT INSTITUTE OF ARTS
  Photographs in recorder's file, as of 1952; ac-
  cession cards, 1882-1949; index cards, 1905-
  1952 MiDA-A
  N: MiDA 12 reels 5 16 mm.   3843

DREXEL INSTITUTE OF TECHNOLOGY
  Miscellaneous records,1892-1905 PPD
  N: MiDA-A 1 reel   3844

GRAPHIC ASSOCIATION OF PHILADELPHIA
  Minutes, 1849-1855, 1 v. PHi
  N: MiDA-A 76 frames   3845

MONTICELLO
  Architectural records Ibid.
  N: NcU 1 reel 32 colored slides   3846

NATIONAL ART ASSOCIATION.
  Record book, 1858-1860, 1 v. PHi
  N: MiDA-A 49 frames   3847

PENNSYLVANIA. ACADEMY OF FINE ARTS
  Records and papers, 1809-1955 Ibid.
  N: MiDA-A 30 reels   3848

PENNSYLVANIA. HISTORICAL SOCIETY
  Harriet Sartain collection, 1834-1917 PHi
  N: MiDA-A 4 reels   3849

PENNSYLVANIA. HISTORICAL SOCIETY
  Manuscripts on American Art PHi
  N: MiDA-A 12 reels   3850

PHILADELPHIA. CENTENNIAL EXHIBITION,
  1876
  Records PHi
  N: MiDA-A 27 frames   3851

PHILADELPHIA. GREAT CENTRAL FAIR FOR
  THE U.S. SANITARY COMMISSION
  Records, manuscript and printed PHi
  N: MiDA-A 80 frames   3852

U.S. MINT, Philadelphia
  Register of the medal dies of theU.S., com-
  piled by Franklin Peale, 1841, 1 v. PHi
  N: MiDA-A 27 frames   3853

U.S. NAVY DEPT.
  Pictorial inventory of prints and paintings, 1955
  DN
  N: DN 2 reels   P: MSaP   3854

Business Papers

AMERICAN FUR COMPANY
  Correspondence and accounts, 1803-1848

MiD-B
N: MiD-B 3 reels
P: CaOOA WHi WaU   3855

AMERICAN FUR COMPANY
Letter books, account books, miscellaneous
papers, 1827-1848 NHi
N: NHi 20 reels   3856
P: CU CaOOA ICU WHi WaU

AMERICAN FUR COMPANY
Papers DLC DNA ICN priv.
DCO: MnHi 16 boxes   3857

AMERICAN FUR COMPANY. NORTHERN
DEPARTMENT
Account books, 1817-1834 CaOOA
N: CaOOA 2 reels   3858
P: ICU WHi

AMSTERDAM. GEMEENTE-ARCHIEF
Documents re: Compagnie de Cerès, 1791-
1825 Archief Brants, Ibid.
N: DLC 3 reels   3859

BRESLAU, Germany. STADTARCHIV
Material on American trade, 1798-1848 Ibid.
DCO: DLC 220 sheets   3860

CANADA. PUBLIC ARCHIVES
[Railway and American business material]
Package marked 1857 United States railways,
stocks, and statistics, 1840-1852, 59 p. CaOOA
N: MnU   3861

CHAMBERLAYNE, WILLIAM
Account book, 1790-1810 priv.
DCO: DLC 1 folder   3862

DUMAS, C. W. F.
Papers, 1775-1795 Ne HAR
N: DLC 3 reels   3863

HAGUE. ECONOMISCH-HISTORISCH ARCHIEF
Business letters from America: van der Kemp
in Philadelphia to Stadnitski en van Heukelom
in Amsterdam, 1824-1841; from New York to
Daniel Crommelin & Zoonen, 1847-1860 Ibid.
N: DLC 2 reels   3864

HEYL, ERIK
Sketch histories of 117 Great Lakes and
East Coast steamers priv.
N: MSaP 1 reel 16 mm.   3865

HOUSTON (ALEXANDER) AND COMPANY,
Glasgow, Scotland
Letterbooks, 1776-1781 UKE
N: DLC 1 reel   3866
P: DLC

ROBINSON, JESSE H.
Diary re: Telegraph Co., 1867 priv.
N: DLC 1 reel   3867

ROGERS, HENRY J., 1811-1879
Selected papers re: Telegraph Co., 1844-1875
priv.
N: DLC 1 reel   3868

U.S. NATIONAL ARCHIVES
Documents re: fur trade, Indian affairs, the
Far West, 1818-1832 DNA
N: CU-B 5 reels   3869

U.S. WAR DEPT.
Items re: fur trade, 1823-1830 DNA
N: priv. 1 reel   3870
P: CU-B

WRIGHT, GEORGE F.
Fur trade correspondence William G. Ewing
Papers In
N: WHi 1 reel   3871

Collections

AMERICAN PHILOSOPHICAL SOCIETY
Cherokee medicinal and magical texts PPAmP
N: PPAmP   3872

AMSTERDAM. UNIVERSITEIT
Selections: Situation des finances de l'État de
Pennsylvanie et de l'État de Massachusetts,
1790; journal of Samuel Fuller; Brieven, Hand-
schriften, Schenking Diedrichs, 1744-1864 Ibid.
N: DLC 10 reels   3873

AVIGNON, France. BIBLIOTHÈQUE
MUNICIPALE
Manuscrits, selections, v. 1330, 2750
DCO: DLC 320 sheets   3874

BERLIN. PREUSSISCHE STAATSBIBLIOTHEK
Nachlass A. H. Francke: Correspondence with
America, 1692-1826 Ibid.
DCO: DLC 1119 sheets   3875

BERN (Canton), Switz. STAATSARCHIV
American material, 57 ll. SzBeA
DCO: DLC   3876

BRAY, DR. THOMAS, collector, 1656-1730
Americana Sion College, London
DCO: DLC   3877

BRITISH MUSEUM
Selections from: Cottonian, Egerton, Harleian,
Hargrave, King's, Lansdowne, Sloane, Stowe,
and Additional manuscripts, and Briefs or
Church Briefs UKLBM
DCO: DLC   3878

CARPENTRAS, France. BIBLIOTHÈQUE
MUNICIPALE
Manuscrits, selections, v. 590, 833, 1775,
1777, 1806, 1821 Ibid.
DCO: DLC 204 sheets   3879

DENMARK. RIGSARKIVET
Selections re: America, 1559-1720 DaKR
N: DLC 16 reels   3880
P: DLC

DRINKWATER, ALPHEUS W., collector
Telegraphic news dispatches of flights of
Orville and Wilbur Wright, May, 1908, 20 p.
priv.
N: NcU   3881
DCO: NcU

DUBLIN. UNIVERSITY. TRINITY COLLEGE
American material (including Icelandic
manuscripts) IrD
DCO: DLC   3882

FLORENCE. BIBLIOTECA NAZIONALE CENTRALE
Manuscripts: Codici Palatini, 479 a, 479 b;
Miscellanea, II, II., 538; II, III, 500; Classe
XIII, P. Cod. 5 Ibid.
N: DLC 2 reels   3883

GLASGOW. UNIVERSITY
Hunterian manuscripts: Journal of Captain
Durben of Arnold's attack on Quebec; petition
of Arthur Dobbs to Frederick, Prince of Wales
Ibid.
DCO: DLC   3884

GREAT BRITAIN. PARLIAMENT. HOUSE OF
LORDS
Committee books, manuscripts, and bills:
material of American interest Ibid.
N: DLC   3885
PP: DLC

HAGUE. KONINKLIJKE BIBLIOTHEEK
Letters of William Temple, 1664; letters of
W. E. H. Lecky; memoirs of Sirtema van
Grovestius, 1823; letters of J. L. Motley;
Latin manuscripts attributed to Franklin;
papers of van Wely family; description of
territories and islands of North India; Diary
of Cornelis Stout, 1678; journal of Reeps,
1692-1694 Ibid.
N: DLC 9 reels   3886

HOGENDORP, G. K. van
American papers, 1773-1786 NeHAR
N: DLC 4 reels   3887

INSTITUT DE FRANCE. BIBLIOTHÈQUE
Selections: manuscrits, collections Godefroy
and Moulin Ibid.
DCO: DLC 89,879 sheets   3888

JEFFERSON, THOMAS, Pres. U.S., 1743-1826,
collector
Marine hospital papers, 1801-1808, 26 items
DLC
N: LNHT   3889

LONDON (City)
Material re: transportation to the colonies,
1717-1737 UKLGU
DCO: DLC   3890

LYONS. BIBLIOTHÈQUE DE L'ACADÉMIE
Manuscrits, selections, v.158, 236 Ibid.
DCO: DLC 399 sheets   3891

LYONS, France. BIBLIOTHÈQUE MUNICIPALE
Manuscrits, selections, v.394, 813, 1503,
1518 Ibid.
DCO: DLC 173 sheets   3892

MacDONALD, A.J., d. 1854
Materials for a history of communities in
the U.S. CtY
N: CtY 1 reel   3893

MURPHY, JOHN B., collector
Presidential wills, Adams, J.Q.-Roosevelt,
Franklin v.p.
DCO: DLC 1 box   3894

NANCY, France. BIBLIOTHÈQUE PUBLIQUE
Manuscrits, selections, v. 698 Ibid.
DCO: DLC 12 sheets   3895

NORTH CAROLINA. UNIVERSITY. BUREAU OF
PUBLIC RECORDS, COLLECTION, AND
RESEARCH
Early state records, v.d. v.p.
N: DLC   3896
P: NcU-BPR

This large collection contains both printed
matter and manuscripts. It is carefully ana-
lyzed in A Guide to the Microfilm Collection of
Early State Records and its Supplement.
Positives may be purchased from the Library
of Congress.

PARIS. BIBLIOTHÈQUE DE L'ARSENAL
Manuscripts, selections, archives de la Bastille
FrPA
DCO: DLC 12,839 ll.   3897

PARIS. BIBLIOTHÈQUE MAZARINE
Manuscripts, selections, v. 1533, 1616,
1833, 1850, 1912, 1963-1964, 2006, 2404,
2626, 2764, 2778-2779, 2884, 3192, 3205,
3292, 3450-3453, 3455, 3749, 3783 Ibid.
DCO: DLC 9542 sheets   3898

PARIS. BIBLIOTHÈQUE NATIONALE
Selections from manuscripts: Américains;
Anglais; Français; Français, Nouvelles
Acquisitions; Latins; Mexicains; Collections
Angrand; Baluze, Clairambault; Mélanges de
Colbert; Cinq Cents de Colbert; Dupuy; Joly
de Fleury; Moreau FrBN
DCO: DLC 98481 sheets   3899

PARIS. BIBLIOTHÈQUE SAINTE GENEVIÈVE
Manuscripts, selections, v. 529-534, 543, 710,
1798, 1805-1809, 2036, 2088, 2127, 2342, 2551,
3002, 3507-3508 Ibid.
DCO: DLC 3249 sheets   3900

PARIS. MUSÉE D'HISTOIRE NATURELLE
Manuscripts, selections, v. 71-73, 177, 293,
328, 335, 357, 380, 382-385, 395, 417, 444-
445, 691, 763, 841, 940, 944, 948, 1072, 1081-
1082, 1140, 1151, 1194, 1225, 1261-1262, 1267,
1314, 1443, 1743-1749, 1797-1806, 1896-1898,
1935, 1961, 1965-1970, 1980, 1997-1998 Ibid.
DCO: DLC 9542 sheets   3901

[PRIVATE COLLECTOR]
Papers re: science in British American
colonies, 1672-1766, 12 items priv.
DCO: DLC   3902

RAFINESQUE, CONSTANTINE SAMUEL, 1783-
1840
Ancient monuments of North and South America
(manuscript), 1822-1825, 125 p. PU
N: PPAmP   3903

ROYAL SOCIETY OF LONDON
Material of American interest, 1662-1794
UKLR
DCO: DLC   3904

SIMMONS, JAMES F., 1809-1873
In-letters from American statesmen priv.
N: DLC 1 reel   3905
P: DLC

SOCIETY OF THE CINCINNATI
Letters from Washington, L'Enfant, and
Lafayette DLC
N: DLC 1 reel*   3906

STEWART, Sir WILLIAM DRUMMOND
Correspondence re: America, 1838-1848   priv.
N: OkU   3907

STOCKHOLM. KUNGLIGA BIBLIOTEKET
Letters from Presidents of the U.S. and
other distinguished Americans   SvSK
N: DLC 1 reel   3908
PP: DLC

TOULON, France. BIBLIOTHÈQUE DU PORT
Manuscrits, ancienne côte 997 /3A A2584
Ibid.
DCO: DLC 161 sheets   3909

VATICAN. ARCHIVIO DEL SEGRETARIO
DI STATO
American material: Lettere de Vescovi,
Prelati, e Governatori, nos. 20, 93, 96,
383; selections from Nunziatura di: Flandra,
v. 18, 24, 44, 45, 49, 50, 57, 135; Francia,
v. 48, 53, 54, 130, 131, 180, 181, 452, 462,
491-493, 509, 510, 555, 556, 562-570;
Inghilterra, v. 4, 6, 7, 12; Pace, v. 49, 50,
54, 57; Portogallo, v.1A, 4, 12; Spagna, v.1-8,
10, 11, 14, 16, 17, 19, 22, 28-36, 38, 39,
62-65, 244A, 245-247, 271-273, 306, 308,
310, 357, 435, 436; Principe et titolati,
v. 115, 116, 118   Ibid.
N: DLC 2 reels and 761 feet   3910
P: DLC
PP: DLC of 761 feet

VATICAN. ARCHIVIO SEGRETO
Acta Miscellanea,v. 3 (old designation Acta
Camerarii, no. 48); Acta Miscellanea,
Armadii VI, v.42, VIII,v. 59; 81;XIII, v.
155; XIII, v. 54; XV, v.62, XLII, v. 17-19;
LIII, v. 33; Albani Collection, v. 165;
Regesta Vaticana, v. 1196-1197, 1199-
1200   Ibid.
N: DLC 10 reels   3911
P: DLC

VATICAN. BIBLIOTECA BOLOGNETTI
Selections: v. 24, 38, 116, 117, 143   Ibid.
N: DLC 2 reels   3912
P: DLC

VATICAN. BIBLIOTECA VATICANA
Selections: Barberini, v. 241, 324, 1496-1497,
2136, 2626, 2893, 2897, 3453, 3463, 3544,
3560, 3584-3585, 3603-3605, 3615, 4431, 4592,
5118, 5208, 5264, 5312, 5327, 5341-5342,
8509, 8577, 8583, 8634-8636, 8646, 8650;
Ottobani, v. 597, 2245, 2417, 2432, 2604,
2708; Palatine, v. 1361; Queen of Sweden,
650-651, 659, 793, 1608, 2105-2107;Urbinate
v. 696, 829, 833-834, 836, 849, 854, 860-
861, 865, 897, 1039, 1041, 1048-1049,
1053-1054, 1060, 1062, 1064, 1072, 1075-
1083, 1085-1087, 1113-1114, 1743; Bibliotheca
Vaticana, v. 3738, 3773, 6227, 6559, 7750,
8638, 9201, 8064, 9450, 9452 I, 9452 II, 9565,
10364   Ibid.
N: DLC 769 feet   3913
PP: DLC

VATICAN. BIBLIOTECA VATICANA
Selections: FF Vat. Lib., v. 11, no. 901
[formerly Archivio Segreto, Armadii VI,
v. 34]; Ottobani, v. 2441, 2447, 2486, 2516,
2700, 2723, 3140, 3189, 3206, 3227   Ibid.
N: DLC 2 reels   3914
P: DLC

VENICE. BIBLIOTECA NAZIONALE MARCIANA
Codici e manuscritti: Francesi, v. 277;
Italiani, nos. 5084-5086, 5396, 7829 (old
designations, Class IV, Cod. DX-DXIII, DXVI;
Class VII, Cod. DCCCCIII); Latini, no. 3843
(old designation, Class X, Cod. CX); Relazioni
Inghilterra, Battista Agnese, v. 5067, 5120;
Giorgio Sideri, v. 5451   Ibid.
N: DLC 9 reels   3915
P: DLC

VERONA. BIBLIOTECA COMMUNALE
Manuscripts nos. Cl.St. 50; Ubication 1206,
Busta XIII-16   Ibid.
N: DLC 1 reel   3916

VIENNA. NATIONALBIBLIOTHEK
Handschriftensammlung: nr. 335, 337, 623,
5542, 7474, 7984, 12925   Ibid.
Glass plate negatives: DLC   3917

VIENNA. NATIONALBIBLIOTHEK
Handschriftensammlung: nr. 5620, 5880,
5880e, 5887, 6122, 6130, 6136, 6388,
6393, 6496, 6740, 6765, 6831, 8546,
10303, 10777, 10927, 12486, 12613   Ibid.
DCO: DLC 1564 sheets   3918

WASSENAER FAMILY (Netherlands)
Extracts from resolutions of the West India
Company and the States General, 1628, 1638
NeHAR
N: DLC 1 reel   3919

(DOCTOR) WILLIAMS' LIBRARY, London
American material in Baxter letters, Baxter
treatises, and Roger Morrice manuscripts
UKLDW
DCO: DLC   3920

Foreign Affairs

ABERDEEN, GEORGE HAMILTON GORDON,
4th EARL of, 1784-1860
Correspondence with Sir Robert Peel and
Queen Victoria (selections)   UKLBM
N: DLC 7 reels   3921

ARGENTINE REPUBLIC. ARCHIVO GENERAL
DE LA NACIÓN
Correspondence with consuls and agents in
the U.S., 1810-1823; foreign relations,
U.S., 1811-1854; diplomatic correspondence
of General Alvear, 1823-1852; Alvear
mission, 1823-1825, 1833, 1837-1852   Ibid.
N: DLC 1 reel and 291 feet   3922
P: DLC
PP: DLC 291 feet

AUSTRIA. FINANZMINISTERIUM. ARCHIV
Selections: Präsidialakten der finanzmin-
isteriums, 1815-1855; Präsidialakten der
allgemeinen Hofkammer, 1831-1847; Akten
des Kommersenates, 1837   Ibid.
DCO: DLC 1234 sheets   3923

AUSTRIA. HAUS-, HOF-, UND STAATS-
ARCHIV
Ministerium des Aussern, selections,
1815-1894 [Politisches Archiv, 1815-1824,
1848-1894; Actes de haute Police, 1849-
1886; Handelpolitische Abteilung, 1849-1866;
Administrative Registeratur, 1841-1894];
Staatskanzlei, selections, reports from
various countries, 1776-1852   Ibid.
DCO: DLC 26324 sheets   3924

AUSTRIA. HAUS-, HOF-, UND STAATSARCHIV
Selections: Commerzliterale, 1754-1811;
Commerzkammer, 1814-1830; Commerz-
Kommission, 1816-1824; Commerz-
Präsidialakten, 1819-1823   Ibid.
DCO: DLC 1233 sheets   3925

AUSTRIA. KRIEGSARCHIV
Selections: Alte Feldakten: Kriege fremder
Mächte, 1776-1790; Memoiren, 1819-1824;
Nachlass Moering, 1842-1843; Marinereferat,
1867   Ibid.
DCO: DLC 901 sheets   3926

AUSTRIA. MINISTERIUM DES INNERN [UND
JUSTIZ-MINISTERIUM] ARCHIV
Präsidialakten des Handelsministeriums,
selections, 1850-1891   Ibid.
DCO: DLC 359 sheets   3927

BAYARD, JAMES ASHTON, 1767-1816
Notes on the Commissioners at Ghent, 1814,
14 p.   DeHi
DC: DeHi   3928

BERLIN. KÖNIGLICH GEHEIMES STAATSARCHIV
American selections: Acta betreffend den
Americanischen Handel und Krieg, 1776-1783;
Kabinetts-Ministerium, 1778-1828; Kabinetts-
Ministerium-Nachlasse, 1774-1797, 1836-
1839; Auswärtiges Amt, 1817-1876 [Amerika,
1817-1850; Central Bureau, 1838-1867;
Handelssachen Generalia, 1819-1821, 1834-
1876; Handelssachen, Nordamerika, 1818-
1869; Handelssachen, Sud-und Mittelamerika,
1821-1878 [Haiti, 1821-1878; Mexiko, 1823-
1867; Cuba, 1827-1877]; Preussiche Consulate
ausser Europa, 1802-1862]; Auswanderung Generalia, 1816-1869; Auswanderung ausser Europa,

1819-1869; Gemischte Differenzen, 1838-1872;
Justiz, 1834-1856; Nachrichten ausser Europa,
1826-1880; Neutralitat, 1857-1861; Ministerium
des Innern, Auswanderung, 1849-1857; Gesand-
schaft Hamburg, material re: Genesee Association, 1792; Justiz-Ministerium, emigration
material, 1818-1846; Civil Cabinet, Acta, 1838-
1839   Ibid.
DCO: DLC 67861 sheets   3929

BREMEN, Germany. STAATSARCHIV
Durchmarsch von hessichen Truppen nach
Amerika, 1736-1784; Verhältnisse der
Hansastädte mit den Vereinigten Staaten,
1790-1868; mit Texas, 1837-1845; Consular
records: Baltimore, 1797-1842; New York,
1815-1866; New Orleans, 1817-1866; Philadelphia, 1827-1868; Alexandria, 1828-1852;
Boston, 1828-1867; Charleston, 1828-1867;
Savannah, 1830-1865; Mobile, 1842-1866;
Richmond, Norfolk, and Petersburg, 1844-
1866; Galveston, 1846-1867; St. Louis, 1846-
1862; San Francisco, 1850-1868; Cincinnati,
1853-1864; Indianola, 1853-1868; Key West,
1860-1867; Angabebücher der auf der Weser
ankommenden Schiffe, 1782-1791, 1800-
1802, 1816-1817   Ibid.
N: DLC 72 reels   3930
P: DLC

CHILE. ARCHIVO NACIONAL
Correspondence with Homan Allen and other
U.S. agents; correspondence in Archivo
Carrera, 1816-1818   Ibid.
N: DLC 83 feet   3931
PP: DLC

FRANCE. ARCHIVES DE LA MARINE. Série B-7
Pays étrangers, commerce et consulats.
Lettres reçues, selections, 1664-1789   FrAN
DCO: DLC 892 sheets   3932

FRANCE. DIRECTOIRE EXÉCUTIF. Séries
AF-III, AF-IV
Correspondence with French agents in the U.S.,
1793-1798; material re: Louisiana purchase,
1799-1813   FrAN
N: DLC 3 reels   3933
P: DLC

FRANCE. LÉGATION. U.S.
Minutes, 1777-1796, v. 1-3   FrAN
DCO: DLC 1288 sheets   3934

FRANCE. MINISTÈRE DES AFFAIRES
ÉTRANGÈRES
Correspondance politique, Angleterre,
selections, 1775-1782   FrAN
N: DLC 1632 feet   3935
PP: DLC

FRANCE. MINISTÈRE DES AFFAIRES
ÉTRANGÈRES
Correspondance politique, États-Unis, 1850-
1857, 13 v.   FrAN
N: CU-B*   3936
P: CU-B

FRANCE. MINISTÈRE DES AFFAIRES
ÉTRANGÈRES
Correspondance politique, États-Unis,
selections   FrAN
N: DLC 22 reels and 2044 feet   3937
P: DLC
PP: DLC

FRANCE. MINISTÈRE DES AFFAIRES
ÉTRANGÈRES
Correspondance politique des Consuls, États-
Unis, 1849-1871, 16 v.   FrAN
N: CU-B*   3938
P: CU-B

FRANCE. MINISTÈRE DES AFFAIRES
ÉTRANGÈRES
Material re: Treaty of Paris, 1782-1783   Ibid.
DCO: MiU-C 1 foot   3939

FRANCE. MINISTÈRE DES AFFAIRES
ÉTRANGÈRES
Mémoires et documents, Amérique, Angle-
terre, États-Unis, France [American items]
(selections)   FrAN
N: DLC 3978 feet   3940
PP: DLC

FRANCE. MINISTÈRE DES AFFAIRES
ÉTRANGÈRES. Série B I

Consular correspondence and records: Boston, 1779-1792; Charleston, 1784-1792; New York, 1783-1792; Norfolk, 1784-1792; Philadelphia, 1778-1792; Williamsburg, 1784-1787 FrAN
N: DLC 9 reels
P: DLC
3941

FRANCE. MINISTÈRE DES AFFAIRES ÉTRANGÈRES. Série B 3
Selected miscellaneous records, cartons, 439-449, 451, 457 FrAN
N: DLC 11 reels
P: DLC
3942

GARAMAN, Comte GEORGE DE
Journal re: French Legation in Washington, 1812-1813; autobiography priv.
N: DLC 1 reel
P: DLC
3943

GREAT BRITAIN. ADMIRALTY. Adm. 13
Instructions to Rear-Admiral Sir Houston Stewart, Commander-in-Chief of North American and West Indian station, 1857, 1860 UKLPRO
DCO: DLC
3944

GREAT BRITAIN. BOARD OF TRADE. B.T. 5
Minutes, 1784-1838 UKLPRO
N: DLC 17 reels
P: DLC
3945

GREAT BRITAIN. BOARD OF TRADE. B.T. 6
Miscellanea, selections, 1789-1828 UKLPRO
N: DLC 6 reels
P: DLC
3946

GREAT BRITAIN. FOREIGN OFFICE. F.O. 4
United States of America, general correspondence (mainly consular), 1783-1791, v. 2-10 UKLPRO
N: DLC 6 reels
P: DLC
3947

GREAT BRITAIN. FOREIGN OFFICE. F.O. 5
United States of America, Series II, 1851-1865 UKLPRO
N: CU-B 13 reels
3948

GREAT BRITAIN. FOREIGN OFFICE. F.O. 5
United States of America, general correspondence, selections, 1859-1881 UKLPRO
N: DLC 81 reels
P: DLC
3949

GREAT BRITAIN. FOREIGN OFFICE. F.O. 5
United States of America, general correspondence, Series II, selections, 1807-1876 UKLPRO
DCO: DLC
3950

GREAT BRITAIN. FOREIGN OFFICE. F.O. 27
France, general correspondence, selections re: Treaty of Paris, 1782-1783 UKLPRO
DCO: DLC
3951

GREAT BRITAIN. FOREIGN OFFICE. F.O. 83
Law officers' reports, America, 1781-1876, 23 v. UKLPRO
DCO: DLC
3952

GREAT BRITAIN. FOREIGN OFFICE. F.O. 95
Miscellanea, series I, selections re: Jay's Treaty, 1794, and treaty of 1806 UKLPRO
DCO: DLC
3953

GREAT BRITAIN. FOREIGN OFFICE. F.O. 97
Supplement to General correspondence, selections re: Treaty of Paris, 1782-1783; Citizen Genêt, 1793; Maine Boundary dispute, 1837-1843 UKLPRO
DCO: DLC
3954

GREAT BRITAIN. FOREIGN OFFICE. F.O. 115
United States of America, correspondence, of British Diplomatic representatives, selections, 1791-1902 UKLPRO
N: DLC 500 reels
P: DLC
3955

GREAT BRITAIN. FOREIGN OFFICE. F.O. 116
United States of America, letterbooks, 1791-1823, 10 v. UKLPRO
N: DLC 3 reels
P: DLC
3956

GREAT BRITAIN. HIGH COURT OF ADMIRALTY. H.C.A. 32

Prize papers, selections UKLPRO
DCO: DLC 8 v.
3957

GREAT BRITAIN. PRIVY COUNCIL. P.C. 2
Registers, American selections, 1784-1815 UKLPRO
DCO: DLC
3958

GREAT BRITAIN. TREASURY. T. 28
Various letters relating to America, 1763-1797, 2 v. UKLPRO
DCO: DLC
3959

HAMBURG, Germany. COMMERZBIBLIOTHEK
Konsulatsberichte aus U.S.A. Ibid.
N: DLC 3 reels
3960

JACKSON, FRANCIS JAMES, 1770-1814
Instructions from Foreign Office and despatches to Foreign Office, 1809 UKLPRO
DCO: DLC
3961

LANSING, ROBERT, 1864-1928
Diaries, and selected papers, 1916-1919 DLC
N: CSt-H 2 reels
3962

LISTON, Sir ROBERT
Papers, 1795-1803 UKE
N: DLC 1 reel
P: DLC
3963

MEXICO. ARCHIVO GENERAL DE LA NACIÓN
Marina: selections, 1770, 1775-1820, 1836-1837 MxAGN
DCO: DLC 7566 sheets
3964

MEXICO. ARCHIVO GENERAL DE LA NACIÓN
Oficio de Seria, 1807-1818 MxAGN
DCO: DLC 1056 sheets
3965

MILLER, DAVID HUNTER, 1875-1932
Diary of the Paris Conference NNC
N: NNC 10 reels
3966
P: CCH CaOT DLC IU MMiW MdBJ MiU-L MnU MoU NIC NN NNC NRU OU PPT WaU

NAPLES (Kingdom). LEGAZIONE. U.S.
Correspondence, 1847-1860 ItNAS
N: DLC 3 reels
P: DLC
3967

NETHERLANDS. ALGEMEEN RIJKSARCHIEF
Legatie Archieven: reports re: St. Eustatius and troubles between England, France, and Spain, 1777-1780; van Berckel's American mission, 1783-1789; van Polanen's mission, 1795-1802; from Dutch Ministers in the U.S., 1825-1870; material written in 1857 re: American Revolution NeHAR
N: DLC 6 reels
3968

NETHERLANDS. DEPARTMENT VAN BUITENLANDSCHE ZAKEN (Department of Foreign Affairs)
Documents in numbered series re: U.S., 1796-1870 NeHAR
N: DLC 20 reels
3969

NETHERLANDS. MINISTER IN THE U.S.
Despatches, chronological series, 1813-1879 NeHAR
N: DLC 40 reels
3970

NETHERLANDS. REPRESENTATIVES IN U.S.
Instructions received, 1831-1882 NeHAR
N: DLC 17 reels
3971

NETHERLANDS (United Provinces, 1581-1795)
Admiraliteits colleges, selections of American interest, 1735-1792 NeHAR
N: DLC 6 reels
3972

NETHERLANDS (United Provinces, 1581-1795) STATEN GENERAAL
Resolutions and despatches from ministers and consuls of American interest, 1775-1796 NeHAR
N: DLC 18 reels
3973

NETHERLANDS (Batavian Republic, 1795-1806). RAAD VAN AZIATISCHE BEZITTINGEN [Council of Asiatic Colonies]
Letters from Heineken, Dutch consul at Philadelphia, 1802-1803 NeHAR
N: DLC 1 reel
3974

OLDENBURG, Germany. STAATSARCHIV
Anhalt-Zerbst troops in the Revolution,

1778-1789; emigration material, 1790-1850; Consular correspondence, general, 1830-1860; Baltimore, 1860-1867; Boston, 1859-1867; Charleston, 1859; Cincinnati, 1861-1867; Chicago, 1858-1868; Galveston, 1858-1868; Havana, 1864-1867; Louisville, 1860-1867; Milwaukee, 1859-1867; New Orleans, 1859-1867; New York, 1860; Philadelphia, 1858-1867; St. Louis, 1859-1869; San Francisco, 1859-1869; Savannah, 1859-1869; Auswanderung, 1858-1860 Ibid.
N: DLC 40 reels
P: DLC
3975

POLANEN, van, Dutch commercial agent in U.S.
Papers, 1808-1811 NeHAR
N: DLC 1 reel
3976

RUSSIA (Empire). MINISTERSTVO INOSTRANNYKH DEL [Ministry of Foreign Affairs]
Negotiations for treaty of 1832 with U.S.; documents re: transfer of Alaska Ibid.
DCO: DLC 401 ll.
3977

SARDINIA (Kingdom)
American foreign affairs material: Corti Straniere, Lettere Ministri ItTAS
N: DLC 54 reels
P: DLC
3978

SCHWERIN, Germany. GROSSHERZOGLICHES GEHEIMES UND HAUPTARCHIV
Consular records from America, 1789-1844; emigration material, 1837-1864; die Einfuhr von Kolonialprodukten während der Kontinentalsperre, 1809-1810; die Beförderung von Insassen des Landes Landarbeitshauses Güstrow nach Amerika, 1824-1856 Ibid.
N: DLC 12 reels
P: DLC
3979

SPEIGEL, L.P. van de, collector
Letters of Rudolph van Dorsten, consul at Philadelphia, 1790-1791; of Heineken, consul at Philadelphia, 1792; annotations on American independence and copy of secret instructions to Dutch Minister in U.S., 1783 NeHAR
N: DLC 2 reels
3980

SULLIVAN, JAMES, 1744-1808
Papers re: Passamaquoddy and St. Croix river boundary, 1796-1799 MHi
N: NN 1 reel
3981

TUSCANY
Affari Esteri: despatches of Tuscan ambassador in Paris, 1776-1783; selections re: U.S. treaty with France and proposed treaty with Tuscany, 1778-1785 ItFAS
N: DLC 6 reels
P: DLC
3982

U.S. CONSULATE. BOMA, Belgian Congo
Post records: instructions to and despatches from U.S. Consuls in Boma, 1906-1908 DNA
N: DNA 2 reels [T-48]
3983

U.S. CONTINENTAL CONGRESS
Foreign letters of the Continental Congress and the Dept. of State, Jan. 14, 1785-Dec. 23, 1790 DNA
N: DNA 1 reel [M-61]
3984

U.S. CONTINENTAL CONGRESS
Ledgers covering expenses of Agents in Europe, 1776-1787 DNA
N: DNA 2 reels [T-244]
3985

U.S. DEPT. OF STATE
Communications received from A.B. Steinberger, 1872-1875 DNA
N: DNA 2 reels [M-37, T-28, 29]
3986

U.S. DEPT. OF STATE
Communications received from Special Agent, A. Dudley Mann, 1846-1852 DNA
N: DNA 1 reel [M-37, T-14]
3987

U.S. DEPT. OF STATE
Communications from Special Agents S.L. Phelps, W. Scott Lord, Frederick F. Low, Willard B. Tisdale, James O. Broadhead, Manton Marble, W.H. Schnetze, and E.O. Shakespeare, 1882-1886 DNA
N: DNA 1 reel [M-37, T-32]
3988

U.S. DEPT. OF STATE
Consular despatches, 1785-1906: Acapulco, 1823-1906; Algiers, 1785-1817; Amoy, 1844-1906; Bombay, 1838-1906; Buenaventura, 1867-1885; Buenos Aires, 1811-1906; Callao, 1854-1906; Canton, 1790-1906; Cap Haitien, 1801-1813; Chefoo, 1863-1906; Chinkiang, 1864-1902; Chunking, 1896-1906; Ciudad Juarez (Paso del Norte), 1850-1906; Foochow, 1849-1906; Frankfort on the Main, 1861-1869; Hanchow, 1904-1906; Hankow, 1861-1906; Hong Kong, 1844-1906; Honolulu, 1820-1903; Kanagawa, 1861-1897; La Guaira, 1810-1836; Lima, 1823-1854; Liverpool, 1853-1857; Macao, 1849-1869; Mazatlán, 1826-1906; Monrovia, 1852-1906; Monterey, Upper California, 1834-1848; Monterrey, Mexico, 1849-1906; Montevideo, 1821-1906; Nagasaki, 1860-1906; Nanking, 1902-1906; Newchwang, 1865-1906; Ningpo, 1853-1896; Panamá, 1823-1906; Puerto Rico, 1821-1899 (San Juan, 1821-1899; Guayama, 1828-1850; Ponce, 1828-1866, 1877-1885, Mayagüez, 1828-1850, 1880-1892); St. Bartholomew, 1799-1828; St. Petersburg, 1803-1809; Santa Fe, 1830-1846; Seoul, 1886-1906; Shanghai, 1847-1906; Swatow, 1860-1881; Sydney, New South Wales, 1836-1906; Tamsui, 1898-1906; Tientsin, 1868-1906; Valparaiso, 1812-1906; Venice, 1854-1870; Veracruz, 1822-1906; Virgin Islands (St. Thomas), 1805-1821; Yokohama, 1897-1906 DNA
N: DNA 1026 reels   3989

U.S. DEPT. OF STATE
Consular instructions, 1801-1834 DNA
N: DNA 7 reels [M-78]   3990

U.S. DEPT. OF STATE
Despatches from U.S. consuls in Aleppo, 1835-1840 DNA
N: DNA 1 reel [T-188]   3991

U.S. DEPT. OF STATE
Despatches from U.S. consuls in Alexandria, 1835-1873 DNA
N: DNA 7 reels [T-45]   3992

U.S. DEPT. OF STATE
Despatches from U.S. consuls; Amoor River, 1856-1874 DNA
N: DNA 2 reels [T-111]   3993

U.S. DEPT. OF STATE
Despatches from U.S. consuls in Amsterdam, 1807-1829 DNA
N: DNA 1 reel [T-182]   3994

U.S. DEPT. OF STATE
Despatches from U.S. consuls in Antung, 1904-1906 DNA
N: DNA 1 reel [T-112]   3995

U.S. DEPT. OF STATE
Despatches from U.S. consuls in Antwerp, 1802-1835 DNA
N: DNA 1 reel [T-181]   3996

U.S. DEPT. OF STATE
Despatches from U.S. consuls in Apia, 1843-1906 DNA
N: DNA 27 reels [T-27]   3997

U.S. DEPT. OF STATE
Despatches from U.S. consuls in Barcelona, 1797-1857, 1895-1899, 1902-1906 DNA
N: DNA 7 reels [T-121]   3998

U.S. DEPT. OF STATE
Despatches from U.S. consuls in Batavia, 1818-1906 DNA
N: DNA 14 reels [T-95]   3999

U.S. DEPT. OF STATE
Despatches from U.S. consuls in Batum, 1890-1906 DNA
N: DNA 1 reel [T-162]   4000

U.S. DEPT. OF STATE
Despatches from U.S. consuls in Bay of Islands and Auckland, 1839-1906 DNA
N: DNA 13 reels [T-49]   4001

U.S. DEPT. OF STATE
Despatches from U.S. consuls in Bermuda, 1818-1832 DNA
N: DNA 1 reel [T-262]   4002

U.S. DEPT. OF STATE
Despatches from U.S. consuls in Bilbao, 1791-1875 DNA
N: DNA 1 reel [T-183]   4003

U.S. DEPT. OF STATE
Despatches from U.S. consuls in Birmingham, 1869-1882 DNA
N: DNA 1 reel [T-247]   4004

U.S. DEPT. OF STATE
Despatches from U.S. consuls in Bogotá, 1851-1899 DNA
N: DNA 1 reel [T-116]   4005

U.S. DEPT. OF STATE
Despatches from U.S. consuls in Boma, 1888-1895 DNA
N: DNA 1 reel [T-47]   4006

U.S. DEPT. OF STATE
Despatches from U.S. consuls in Bordeaux, 1783-1809, 1886-1891 DNA
N: DNA 3 reels [T-164]   4007

U.S. DEPT. OF STATE
Despatches from U.S. consuls in Bradford, 1883-1888 DNA
N: DNA 1 reel [T-165]   4008

U.S. DEPT. OF STATE
Despatches from U.S. consuls in Bremen, 1794-1853, 1882-1890 DNA
N: DNA 7 reels [T-184]   4009

U.S. DEPT. OF STATE
Despatches from U.S. consuls in Bristol, 1792-1850 DNA
N: DNA 3 reels [T-185]   4010

U.S. DEPT. OF STATE
Despatches from U.S. consuls in Brunai, 1862-1868 DNA
N: DNA 1 reel [T-110]   4011

U.S. DEPT. OF STATE
Despatches from U.S. consuls in Brussels, 1893-1906 DNA
N: DNA 1 reel [T-166]   4012

U.S. DEPT. OF STATE
Despatches from U.S. consuls in Butaritari, 1888-1892 DNA
N: DNA 1 reel [T-89]   4013

U.S. DEPT. OF STATE
Despatches from U.S. consuls in Cadiz, 1791-1816 DNA
N: DNA 3 reels [T-186]   4014

U.S. DEPT. OF STATE
Despatches from U.S. consuls in Cagliari, 1802-1825 DNA
N: DNA 1 reel [T-187]   4015

U.S. DEPT. OF STATE
Despatches from U.S. consuls in Cairo, 1864-1906 DNA
N: DNA 24 reels [T-41]   4016

U.S. DEPT. OF STATE
Despatches from U.S. consuls in Calcutta, 1843-1906 DNA
N: DNA 17 reels [T-189]   4017

U.S. DEPT. OF STATE
Despatches from U.S. consuls in Canea, 1858-1874 DNA
N: DNA 1 reel [T-190]   4018

U.S. DEPT. OF STATE
Despatches from U.S. consuls in Cape Town, 1799-1842 DNA
N: DNA 2 reels [T-191]   4019

U.S. DEPT. OF STATE
Despatches from consuls in Cap Haitien, 1814-1834 DNA
N: DNA 2 reels [M-9; T-5,6]   4020

U.S. DEPT. OF STATE
Despatches from U.S. consuls in Cartagena, Colombia, 1822-1829, 1851-1857 DNA
N: DNA 2 reels [T-192]   4021

U.S. DEPT. OF STATE
Despatches from U.S. consuls in Chihuahua, 1901-1906 DNA
N: DNA 1 reel [T-167]   4022

U.S. DEPT. OF STATE
Despatches from U.S. consuls in Christiania, 1886-1901 DNA
N: DNA 2 reels [T-122]   4023

U.S. DEPT. OF STATE
Despatches from U.S. consuls in Christiansand, 1810-1819 DNA
N: DNA 1 reel [T-235]   4024

U.S. DEPT. OF STATE
Despatches from U.S. consuls in Colón, 1852-1857 DNA
N: DNA 1 reel [T-193]   4025

U.S. DEPT. OF STATE
Despatches from U.S. consuls in Constantinople, 1820-1850, 1887-1892 DNA
N: DNA 4 reels [T-194]   4026

U.S. DEPT. OF STATE
Despatches from U.S. consuls in Copenhagen, 1792-1832 DNA
N: DNA 3 reels [T-195]   4027

U.S. DEPT. OF STATE
Despatches from U.S. consuls in Cork, 1851-1856, 1880-1886 DNA
N: DNA 2 reels [T-196]   4028

U.S. DEPT. OF STATE
Despatches from U.S. consuls in Curaçao, 1793-1838, 1882-1887 DNA
N: DNA 2 reels [T-197]   4029

U.S. DEPT. OF STATE
Despatches from U.S. consuls in Dublin, 1790-1850 DNA
N: DNA 1 reel [T-199]   4030

U.S. DEPT. OF STATE
Despatches from U.S. consuls in Dundee, 1834-1857, 1881-1882 DNA
N: DNA 3 reels [T-200]   4031

U.S. DEPT. OF STATE
Despatches from U.S. consuls in Elsinore, 1792-1838 DNA
N: DNA 1 reel [T-201]   4032

U.S. DEPT. OF STATE
Despatches from U.S. consuls in Falmouth, 1790-1834 DNA
N: DNA 2 reels [T-202]   4033

U.S. DEPT. OF STATE
Despatches from U.S. consuls in Fayal, 1795-1850 DNA
N: DNA 3 reels [T-203]   4034

U.S. DEPT. OF STATE
Despatches from U.S. consuls in Florence, 1890-1896 DNA
N: DNA 1 reel [T-204]   4035

U.S. DEPT. OF STATE
Despatches from U.S. consuls in Funchal, 1793-1850 DNA
N: DNA 2 reels [T-205]   4036

U.S. DEPT. OF STATE
Despatches from U.S. consuls in Galveston, 1832-1846 DNA
N: DNA 2 reels [T-151]   4037

U.S. DEPT. OF STATE
Despatches from U.S. consuls in Genoa, 1799-1857, 1864-1870 DNA
N: DNA 6 reels [T-64]   4038

U.S. DEPT. OF STATE
Despatches from U.S. consuls in Georgetown, British Guiana, 1801-1854 DNA
N: DNA 5 reels [T-198]   4039

U.S. DEPT. OF STATE
Despatches from U.S. consuls in Gibraltar, 1791-1829 DNA
N: DNA 3 reels [T-206]   4040

U.S. DEPT. OF STATE
Despatches from U.S. consuls in Glasgow,
1801-1823 DNA
N: DNA 1 reel [T-207]   4041

U.S. DEPT. OF STATE
Despatches from U.S. consuls in Gothenburg,
1800-1888 DNA
N: DNA 2 reels [T-276]   4042

U.S. DEPT. OF STATE
Despatches from U.S. consuls in Guadeloupe,
1802-1850 DNA
N: DNA 2 reels [T-208]   4043

U.S. DEPT. OF STATE
Despatches from U.S. consuls in Guayaquil,
1826-1857 DNA
N: DNA 2 reels [T-209]   4044

U.S. DEPT. OF STATE
Despatches from U.S. consuls in Guaymas,
1889-1892 DNA
N: DNA 1 reel [T-210]   4045

U.S. DEPT. OF STATE
Despatches from U.S. consuls in Hakodate,
1856-1878 DNA
N: DNA 2 reels [T-113]   4046

U. S. DEPT. OF STATE
Despatches from U.S. consuls in Hamburg,
1790-1832, 1842-1847, 1850-1853,
1879-1885, 1899-1901   DNA
N: DNA 9 reels [T-211]   4047

U.S. DEPT. OF STATE
Despatches from U.S. consuls in Havana,
1783-1832, 1838, 1840-1841, 1843-1844,
1853-1854, 1863-1865, 1896-1902   DNA
N: DNA 18 reels [T-20]   4048

U. S. DEPT. OF STATE
Despatches from U.S. consuls in Havre,
1789-1846, 1850-1854 DNA
N: DNA 5 reels [T-212]   4049

U.S. DEPT. OF STATE
Despatches from U.S. consuls in Hesse-Cassel,
1835-1850 DNA
N: DNA 1 reel [T-213]   4050

U.S. DEPT. OF STATE
Despatches from U.S. consuls in Hilo,
1853-1872 DNA
N: DNA 4 reels [T-133]   4051

U.S. DEPT. OF STATE
Despatches from U.S. consuls in Hobart,
1842-1906 DNA
N: DNA 4 reels [T-127]   4052

U.S. DEPT. OF STATE
Despatches from U.S. consuls in Iloilo,
1878-1886 DNA
N: DNA 1 reel [T-109]   4053

U.S. DEPT. OF STATE
Despatches from U.S. consuls in Kingston,
Jamaica, 1796-1844, 1860-1868, 1898-1899
DNA
N: DNA 11 reels [T-31]   4054

U.S. DEPT. OF STATE
Despatches from U.S. consuls in Lahaina,
1850-1871 DNA
N: DNA 3 reels [T-101]   4055

U.S. DEPT. OF STATE
Despatches from U.S. consuls in Lauthala,
1844-1890 DNA
N: DNA 7 reels [T-25]   4056

U.S. DEPT. OF STATE
Despatches from U.S. consuls in Leghorn,
1793-1850 DNA
N: DNA 3 reels [T-214]   4057

U.S. DEPT. OF STATE
Despatches from U.S. consuls in Leipzig,
1826-1850 DNA
N: DNA 3 reels [T-215]   4058

U.S. DEPT. OF STATE
Despatches from U.S. consuls in Levuka and

Suva, 1891-1906 DNA
N: DNA 1 reel [T-108]   4059

U.S. DEPT. OF STATE
Despatches from U.S. consuls in Lisbon,
1791-1826 DNA
N: DNA 4 reels [T-180]   4060

U.S. DEPT. OF STATE
Despatches from U.S. consuls in Liverpool,
1812-1825, Jan.-June,1867, 1878-1880, 1889-
1891 DNA
N: DNA 4 reels [M-141; T-3,35,41, 46]   4061

U.S. DEPT. OF STATE
Despatches from U.S. consuls in London,
1790-1812, 1817-1827, 1844-1846,
May,1881-Feb., 1882, April,1883-Nov., 1884,
Nov.,1902-Sept., 1903 DNA
N: DNA 8 reels [T-168]   4062

U.S. DEPT. OF STATE
Despatches from U.S. consuls in Londonderry,
1835-1850 DNA
N: DNA 1 reel [T-216]   4063

U.S. DEPT. OF STATE
Despatches from U.S. consuls in Lyons,
1885-1886 DNA
N: DNA 1 reel [T-169]   4064

U.S. DEPT. OF STATE
Despatches from U.S. consuls in Málaga,
1793-1838 DNA
N: DNA 2 reels [T-217]   4065

U.S. DEPT. OF STATE
Despatches from U.S. consuls in Malta,
1801-1850 DNA
N: DNA 2 reels [T-218]   4066

U.S. DEPT. OF STATE
Despatches from U.S. consuls in Manchester,
1847-1862 DNA
N: DNA 1 reel [T-219]   4067

U.S. DEPT. OF STATE
Despatches from U.S. consuls in Manila,
1817-1899 DNA
N: DNA 12 reels [T-43]   4068

U.S. DEPT. OF STATE
Despatches from U.S. consuls in Manzanillo,
1855-1906 DNA
N: DNA 3 reels [T-15]   4069

U.S. DEPT. OF STATE
Despatches from U.S. consuls in Maracaibo,
1834-1835, 1851-1864, 1886-1887, 1891-1892
DNA
N: DNA 5 reels [T-62]   4070

U.S. DEPT. OF STATE
Despatches from U.S. consuls in Marseilles,
1790-1857, 1867-1869, 1888-1890, 1905-1906
DNA
N: DNA 10 reels [T-220]   4071

U.S. DEPT. OF STATE
Despatches from U.S. consuls in Matamoros,
1826-1871 DNA
N: DNA 5 reels [T-18]   4072

U.S. DEPT. OF STATE
Despatches from U.S. consuls in Medan-Padang,
1853-1898 DNA
N: DNA 2 reels [T-106]   4073

U.S. DEPT. OF STATE
Despatches from U.S. consuls in Melbourne,
1852-1906 DNA
N: DNA 16 reels [T-102]   4074

U.S. DEPT. OF STATE
Despatches from U.S. consuls in Mérida,
1883-1897 DNA
N: DNA 3 reels [T-29]   4075

U.S. DEPT. OF STATE
Despatches from U.S. consuls in Milan,
1874-1884 DNA
N: DNA 1 reel [T-170]   4076

U.S. DEPT. OF STATE
Despatches from U.S. consuls in Minatitlán,
1853-1869 DNA
N: DNA 1 reel [T-221]   4077

U.S. DEPT. OF STATE
Despatches from U.S. consuls in Montreal,
1889-1892 DNA
N: DNA 1 reel [T-222]   4078

U.S. DEPT. OF STATE
Despatches from U.S. consuls in Moscow,
1857-1906 DNA
N: DNA 4 reels [T-97]   4079

U.S. DEPT. OF STATE
Despatches from U.S. consuls in Mozambique,
1854-1894 DNA
N: DNA 1 reel [T-171]   4080

U.S. DEPT. OF STATE
Despatches from U.S. consuls in Mukden,
1904-1906 DNA
N: DNA 1 reel [T-105]   4081

U.S. DEPT. OF STATE
Despatches from U.S. consuls in Munich,
1856-1866 DNA
N: DNA 2 reels [T-261]   4082

U.S. DEPT. OF STATE
Despatches from U.S. consuls in Nantes,
1790-1850 DNA
N: DNA 1 reel [T-223]   4083

U.S. DEPT. OF STATE
Despatches from U.S. consuls in Naples,
1796-1832, 1850-1857, 1895-1903 DNA
N: DNA 3 reels [T-224]   4084

U.S. DEPT. OF STATE
Despatches from U.S. consuls in New Orleans,
1796-1807 DNA
N: DNA 1 reel [T-225]   4085

U.S. DEPT. OF STATE
Despatches from U.S. consuls in Newcastle,
New South Wales, 1887-1906 DNA
N: DNA 6 reels [T-92]   4086

U.S. DEPT. OF STATE
Despatches from U.S. consuls in Nouméa,
1887-1905 DNA
N: DNA 2 reels [T-91]   4087

U.S. DEPT. OF STATE
Despatches from U.S. consuls in Odessa,
1870-1883, 1891-1895 DNA
N: DNA 3 reels [T-117]   4088

U.S. DEPT. OF STATE
Despatches from U.S. consuls in Osaka and
Hiogo, 1868-1873, 1891-1894 DNA
N: DNA 2 reels [T-155]   4089

U.S. DEPT. OF STATE
Despatches from U.S. consuls in Paramaribo,
1799-1834, 1858-1863 DNA
N: DNA 2 reels [T-226]   4090

U.S. DEPT. OF STATE
Despatches from U.S. consuls in Paris,
1790-1813 DNA
N: DNA 4 reels [T-1]   4091

U.S. DEPT. OF STATE
Despatches from U.S. consuls in Petropavlovsk,
1875-1878 DNA
N: DNA 1 reel [T-104]   4092

U.S. DEPT. OF STATE
Despatches from U.S. consuls in Plymouth,
1793-1835 DNA
N: DNA 1 reel [T-228]   4093

U.S. DEPT. OF STATE
Despatches from U.S. consuls in Ponape,
Oct. 13, 1890-Apr. 23, 1892 DNA
N: DNA 1 reel [T-90]   4094

U.S. DEPT. OF STATE
Despatches from U.S. consuls in Port Louis,
Mauritius, 1794-1906 DNA
N: DNA 19 reels [T-118]   4095

U.S. DEPT. OF STATE
Despatches from U.S. consuls in Puerto Cabello,
1851-1859 DNA
N: DNA 1 reel [T-229]   4096

U.S. DEPT. OF STATE
Despatches from U.S. consuls in Rio de
Janeiro, 1887-1889 DNA
N: DNA 1 reel [T-172]   4097

U.S. DEPT. OF STATE
Despatches from U.S. consuls in
Rio Grande do Sul, 1829-1897 DNA
N: DNA 7 reels [T-145]   4098

U.S. DEPT. OF STATE
Despatches from U.S. consuls in Rome,
1801-1833, 1847-1850 DNA
N: DNA 2 reels [T-231]   4099

U.S. DEPT. OF STATE
Despatches from U.S. consuls in Rotterdam,
1802-1835 DNA
N: DNA 1 reel [T-232]   4100

U.S. DEPT. OF STATE
Despatches from U.S. consuls in Saigon,
1889-1906 DNA
N: DNA 1 reel [T-103]   4101

U.S. DEPT. OF STATE
Despatches from U.S. consuls in St. Christopher,
1894-1906 DNA
N: DNA 1 reel [T-234]   4102

U.S. DEPT. OF STATE
Despatches from U.S. consuls in St. Croix,
1791-1850 DNA
N: DNA 3 reels [T-233]   4103

U.S. DEPT. OF STATE
Despatches from U.S. consuls in St. Eustatius,
1793-1838 DNA
N: DNA 1 reel [T-236]   4104

U.S. DEPT. OF STATE
Despatches from U.S. consuls in St. George's,
Bermuda, 1878-1901 DNA
N: DNA 1 reel [T-173]   4105

U.S. DEPT. OF STATE
Despatches from U.S. consuls in St. Johns,
Newfoundland, 1852-1906 DNA
N: DNA 9 reels T-129]   4106

U.S. DEPT. OF STATE
Despatches from U.S. consuls in San Dimas,
1871-1873 DNA
N: DNA 1 reel [T-259]   4107

U.S. DEPT. OF STATE
Despatches from U.S. consuls in San José,
Costa Rica, 1852-1857 DNA
N: DNA 1 reel [T-35]   4108

U.S. DEPT. OF STATE
Despatches from U.S. consuls in San Juan del Sur,
1858-1862, 1868-1881   DNA
N: DNA 2 reels [T-152]   4109

U.S. DEPT. OF STATE
Despatches from U.S. consuls in San Salvador,
1899-1901 DNA
N: DNA 1 reel [T-237]   4110

U.S. DEPT. OF STATE
Despatches from U.S. consuls in Santiago de
Cuba, 1893-1903 DNA
N: DNA 4 reels [T-55]   4111

U.S. DEPT. OF STATE
Despatches from U.S. consuls in
Santo Domingo, 1861-1871 DNA
N: DNA 3 reels [T-56]   4112

U.S. DEPT. OF STATE
Despatches from U.S. consuls in Sheffield,
1864-1877 DNA
N: DNA 9 reels [T-248]   4113

U.S. DEPT. OF STATE
Despatches from U.S. consuls in Singapore,
1833-1906 DNA
N: DNA 26 reels [T-128]   4114

U.S. DEPT. OF STATE
Despatches from U.S. consuls in Smyrna,
1802-1838 DNA
N: DNA 1 reel [T-238]   4115

U.S. DEPT. OF STATE
Despatches from U.S. consuls in Southampton,
1790-1829 DNA
N: DNA 1 reel [T-239]   4116

U.S. DEPT. OF STATE
Despatches from U.S. consuls in Stettin,
1901-1906 DNA
N: DNA 1 reel [T-59]   4117

U.S. DEPT. OF STATE
Despatches from U.S. consuls in Stockholm,
1810-1897 DNA
N: DNA 7 reels [T-230]   4118

U.S. DEPT. OF STATE
Despatches from U.S. consuls in Tabasco,
1830-1850 DNA
N: DNA 1 reel [T-240]   4119

U.S. DEPT. OF STATE
Despatches from U.S. consuls in Tahiti,
1836-1906 DNA
N: DNA 10 reels [T-26]   4120

U.S. DEPT. OF STATE
Despatches from U.S. consuls in Talcahuano,
1836-1895 DNA
N: DNA 5 reels [T-115]   4121

U.S. DEPT. OF STATE
Despatches from U.S. consuls in Tamatave,
1890-1892 DNA
N: DNA 1 reel [T-60]   4122

U.S. DEPT. OF STATE
Despatches from U.S. consuls in Tampico,
1843-1850 DNA
N: DNA 1 reel [T-241]   4123

U.S. DEPT. OF STATE
Despatches from U.S. consuls in Tangier,
1838-1848, 1886-1888, 1893-1895 DNA
N: DNA 4 reels [T-161]   4124

U.S. DEPT. OF STATE
Despatches from U.S. consuls in Tetuán,
1877-1888 DNA
N: DNA 1 reel [T-156]   4125

U.S. DEPT. OF STATE
Despatches from U.S. consuls in Texas,
1825-1844 DNA
N: DNA 1 reel [T-153]   4126

U.S. DEPT. OF STATE
Despatches from U.S. consuls in Trieste,
1800-1832 DNA
N: DNA 1 reel [T-242]   4127

U.S. DEPT. OF STATE
Despatches from U.S. consuls in Trinidad,
1824-1890 DNA
N: DNA 7 reels [T-148]   4128

U.S. DEPT. OF STATE
Despatches from U.S. consuls in Tripoli,
1796-1885 DNA
N: DNA 11 reels [T-40]   4129

U.S. DEPT. OF STATE
Despatches from U.S. consuls in Turin,
1894-1906 DNA
N: DNA 1 reel [T-174]   4130

U.S. DEPT. OF STATE
Despatches from U.S. consuls in Vancouver, B.C.,
1890-1906 DNA
N: DNA 5 reels [T-114]   4131

U.S. DEPT. OF STATE
Despatches from U.S. consuls in Victoria, B.C.,
1862-1884 DNA
N: DNA 5 reels [T-130]   4132

U.S. DEPT. OF STATE
Despatches from U.S. consuls in Vienna,
1830-1857 DNA
N: DNA 2 reels [T-243]   4133

U.S. DEPT. OF STATE
Despatches from U.S. consuls in Vladivostok,
1898-1906 DNA
N: DNA 1 reel [T-107]   4134

U.S. DEPT. OF STATE
Despatches from U.S. consuls in Winnipeg,
1869-1906 DNA
N: DNA 10 reels [T-24]   4135

U.S. DEPT. OF STATE
Despatches from U.S. consuls in Zanzibar,
1836-1906 DNA
N: DNA 11 reels [T-100]   4136

U.S. DEPT. OF STATE
Despatches from U.S. ministers to Austria,
1845-1849, 1854-1869 DNA
N: DNA 4 reels [T-157]   4137

U.S. DEPT. OF STATE
Despatches from U.S. ministers to Belgium,
1892-1894 DNA
N: DNA 1 reel [M-193; T-31]   4138

U.S. DEPT. OF STATE
Despatches from U.S. ministers to Bolivia,
1848-1872, 1890-1892, 1900-1902 DNA
N: DNA 7 reels [T-51]   4139

U.S. DEPT. OF STATE
Despatches from U.S. ministers to Central
America, 1824-1906 DNA
N: DNA 93 reels   4140

U.S. DEPT. OF STATE
Despatches from U.S. ministers to Chile,
1851-1853, 1890-1896 DNA
N: DNA 9 reels [T-2]   4141

U.S. DEPT. OF STATE
Despatches from U.S. ministers in Colombia,
1845-1849, 1902-1905 DNA
N: DNA 3 reels [T-33]   4142

U.S. DEPT. OF STATE
Despatches from U.S. ministers to Cuba,
May-Aug., 1903 DNA
N: DNA 1 reel [T-158]   4143

U.S. DEPT. OF STATE
Despatches from U.S. ministers to the
Dominican Republic, 1903-1906 DNA
N: DNA 3 reels [T-99]   4144

U.S. DEPT. OF STATE
Despatches from U.S. ministers to Ecuador,
1848-1866 DNA
N: DNA 7 reels [T-50]   4145

U.S. DEPT. OF STATE
Despatches from U.S. ministers to Greece,
July,1903-Apr., 1904 DNA
N: DNA 1 reel [T-159]   4146

U.S. DEPT. OF STATE
Despatches from U.S. ministers to Haiti,
1862-1889, 1891-1906 DNA
N: DNA 45 reels [M-82, T-1-23, 26-47] 4147

U.S. DEPT. OF STATE
Despatches from U.S. ministers in Hawaii,
1845-1900 DNA
N: DNA 34 reels [T-30]   4148

U.S. DEPT. OF STATE
Despatches from U.S. ministers to Persia,
1883-1906 DNA
N: DNA 11 reels [M-223]   4149

U.S. DEPT. OF STATE
Despatches from U.S. ministers to Peru,
1826-1864, Nov., 1892-July,1893 DNA
N: DNA 20 reels [T-52]   4150

U.S. DEPT. OF STATE
Despatches from U.S. ministers to Sweden and
Norway, 1891-1893 DNA
N: DNA 1 reel [M-45 - T-22]   4151

U.S. DEPT. OF STATE
Despatches from U.S. ministers to Switzerland,
Apr.-Dec., 1854, 1856-1857, 1901-1903 DNA
N: DNA 3 reels [T-98]   4152

U.S. DEPT. OF STATE
Despatches from U.S. ministers to Venezuela,
1872-1906 DNA
N: DNA 40 reels [M-79; T-21-60]   4153

U.S. DEPT. OF STATE
Diplomatic and consular instructions, 1791-
1801 DNA
N: DNA 5 reels [M-28]   4154

U.S. DEPT. OF STATE
Diplomatic despatches: Argentina, 1817-1906; Belgium, 1832-1862; Brazil, 1809-1906; Chile, 1896-1905; China, 1843-1906; Denmark, 1811-1812, 1827-1861; Dominican Republic, 1883-1892; France, 1789-1869; German States and Germany, 1799-1906; Great Britain, 1792-1906; Haiti, 1889-1891; Italian States and Italy, 1832-1906; Japan, 1855-1906; Korea, 1883-1905; Mexico, 1823-1906; Paraguay and Uruguay, 1858-1906; Portugal, 1790-1801, 1822-1826; Russia, 1808-1906; Siam, 1882-1906; Spain, 1792-1906; Special agents, 1794-1837; Sweden and Norway, 1814-1825; Turkey, 1818-1906; Venezuela, 1835-1872   DNA
N: DNA 1324 reels   4155

U.S. DEPT. OF STATE
Diplomatic instructions, 1801-1906: all countries, 1801-1833; American states, 1829-1833; Argentina, 1843-1906; Austria, 1837-1906; Balkan states, 1868-1906; Barbary Powers, 1834-1906; Belgium, 1832-1906; Bolivia, 1848-1906; Brazil, 1833-1906; Central American states, 1833-1906; Chile, 1833-1906; China, 1843-1906; Colombia, 1834-1906;Cuba, 1902-1906; Denmark, 1833-1906; Ecuador, 1848-1906; Egypt, 1875-1886; France, 1829-1906; German states, 1835-1869; Germany, 1868-1906; Great Britain, 1829-1906; Haiti and Santo Domingo, 1862-1906; Hawaii, 1848-1900; Italy, 1838-1906; Japan, 1855-1906; Korea, 1883-1905; Liberia, 1863-1906; Mexico, 1833-1906; Netherlands, 1833-1888; Netherlands and Luxemburg, 1888-1906; Panama, 1903-1906; Papal States, 1848-1868; Paraguay and Uruguay, 1858-1906; Persia, 1833-1906; Peru, 1833-1906; Portugal, 1833-1906; Russia, 1833-1906; Siam, 1882-1906; Spain, 1833-1906; Special missions, 1823-1906; Sweden and Norway, 1834-1906; Switzerland, 1853-1906; Texas, 1837-1845; Turkey, 1823-1906; Two Sicilies, 1838-1861; Venezuela, 1835-1900 DNA
N: DNA 174 reels [M-77]   4156

U.S. DEPT. OF STATE
Instructions to U.S. visitors to Vienna, 1875-1877, v. 2   DNA
N: DNA 1 reel   4157
P: CLO

U.S. DEPT. OF STATE
Minutes of Treaty Conferences between U.S. and Japanese representatives, and Treaty Drafts, Mar. 11 - July 22, 1872   DNA
N: DNA 1 reel [T-119]   4158

U.S. DEPT. OF STATE
Miscellaneous letters, 1789-1825   DNA
N: DNA 66 reels [M-179]   4159

U.S. DEPT. OF STATE
Miscellaneous letters, Aug. 1-17, 1880   DNA
N: DNA 1 reel [T-63]   4160

U.S. DEPT. OF STATE
Notes received from the Legation of the Argentine Republic in the U.S., 1811-1906 DNA
N: DNA 4 reels [M-47]   4161

U.S. DEPT. OF STATE
Notes received from the Austrian Legation in the U.S., 1820-1848   DNA
N: DNA 1 reel [M-48]   4162

U.S. DEPT. OF STATE
Notes received from the Belgian Legation in the U.S., 1832-1906   DNA
N: DNA 12 reels [M-194]   4163

U.S. DEPT. OF STATE
Notes received from the Brazilian Legation in the U.S., 1824-1906   DNA
N: DNA 8 reels [M-49]   4164

U.S. DEPT. OF STATE
Notes received from the British Legation in the U.S., 1791-1825   DNA
N: DNA 14 reels [M-50]   4165

U.S. DEPT. OF STATE
Notes received from the British Legation in the U.S., Jan. 2-Dec. 29, 1852, Apr. 20, 1865-Feb. 11, 1873, Jan. 2-Oct. 30, 1880, June 1,

1895-Mar. 30, 1901 DNA
N: DNA 28 reels [T-28]   4166

U.S. DEPT. OF STATE
Notes received from Central American Legations in the U.S., 1823-1861 DNA
N: DNA 5 reels [T-34]   4167

U.S. DEPT. OF STATE
Notes received from the Chilean Legation in the U.S., 1811-1853   DNA
N: DNA 1 reel [M-73]   4168

U.S. DEPT. OF STATE
Notes received from the Chinese Legation in the U.S., 1868-1906   DNA
N: DNA 6 reels [M-98]   4169

U.S. DEPT. OF STATE
Notes received from the Colombian Legation in the U.S., 1810-1834   DNA
N: DNA 1 reel [M-51]   4170

U.S. DEPT. OF STATE
Notes received from the Danish Legation in the U.S., 1801-1832; register, 1812-1849 DNA
N: DNA 1 reel [M-52]   4171

U.S. DEPT. OF STATE
Notes received from the French Legation in the U.S., 1789-1826   DNA
N: DNA 7 reels [M-53]   4172

U.S. DEPT. OF STATE
Notes received from the French Legation in the U.S. 1870-1872, 1904-1906   DNA
N: DNA 3 reels [M-53; T 32, 45, 46]   4173

U.S. DEPT. OF STATE
Notes received from the Hawaiian Legation in the U.S., 1841-1899   DNA
N: DNA 4 reels [T-160]   4174

U.S. DEPT. OF STATE
Notes received from the Italian Legation in the U.S., 1861-1906   DNA
N: DNA 18 reels [M-202]   4175

U.S. DEPT. OF STATE
Notes received from the Japanese Legation in the U.S., 1858-1906   DNA
N: DNA 9 reels [M-163]   4176

U.S. DEPT. OF STATE
Notes received from the Korean Legation in the U.S., 1883-1906   DNA
N: DNA 1 reel [M-166]   4177

U.S. DEPT. OF STATE
Notes received from the Legation of the Kingdom of Two Sicilies in the U.S., 1826-1860   DNA
N: DNA 2 reels [M-55]   4178

U.S. DEPT. OF STATE
Notes received from the Legations of the German States and Germany in the U.S., 1869-1871, 1894-1895   DNA
N: DNA 3 reels [M-58; T- 9, 10, 24]   4179

U.S. DEPT. OF STATE
Notes received from the Mexican Legation in the U.S., 1816-1831   DNA
N: DNA 1 reel [M-54]   4180

U.S. DEPT. OF STATE
Notes received from the Netherlands Legation in the U.S., 1784-1861   DNA
N: DNA 1 reel [M-56]   4181

U.S. DEPT. OF STATE
Notes received from the Portuguese Legation in the U.S., 1796-1830   DNA
N: DNA 2 reels [M-57]   4182

U.S. DEPT. OF STATE
Notes received from the Prussian Legation in the U.S., 1817-1848   DNA
N: DNA 1 reel [M-58]   4183

U.S. DEPT. OF STATE
Notes received from the Russian Legation in the U.S., 1809-1826   DNA
N: DNA 1 reel [M-39]   4184

U.S. DEPT. OF STATE
Notes received from the Siamese Legation

in the U.S., 1876-1906 DNA
N: DNA 1 reel [T-161]   4185

U.S. DEPT. OF STATE
Notes received from the Spanish Legation in the U.S., 1790-1826   DNA
N: DNA 11 reels [M-59]   4186

U.S. DEPT. OF STATE
Notes received from the Swedish Legation in the U.S., 1813-1848   DNA
N: DNA 2 reels [M-60]   4187

U.S. DEPT. OF STATE
Notes received from the Tunisian Legation in the U.S., 1805-1806   DNA
N: DNA 1 reel [M-67]   4188

U.S. DEPT. OF STATE
Notes received from the Venezuelan Legation in the U.S., 1835-1906   DNA
N: DNA 1 reel [T-93]   4189

U.S. DEPT. OF STATE
Notes to Foreign Legations in the United States, 1834-1906   DNA
N: DNA 93 reels [M-99]   4190

U.S. DEPT. OF STATE
Notes to foreign ministers and consuls in the U.S., 1793-1834   DNA
N: DNA 5 reels [M-38]   4191

U.S. DEPT. OF STATE
Records of negotiations connected with the Treaty of Ghent, 1813-1815   DNA
N: DNA 2 reels [M-36]   4192

U.S. DEPT. OF STATE
Registers of correspondence, 1870-1906 DNA
N: DNA 71 reels [M-17]   4193

U.S. DEPT. OF STATE
"South American Missions": Communications received from Special Agents Caesar A.Rodney, Theodorick Bland, John Graham, and H.M. Brackenridge, 1817-1819 DNA
N: DNA 1 reel [T-19]   4194

U.S. LEGATION. CHILE
Records, 1893-1905   DNA
N: DNA 14 reels [M-20]   4195

U.S. LEGATION. FRANCE
Records, 1835-1842   DNA
N: DNA 10 reels [M-14]   4196

U.S. LEGATION. NAPLES (Kingdom)
Correspondence with Neapolitan Foreign Office, 1816-1824   ItNAS
N: DLC 5 reels   4197

U.S. LIBRARY OF CONGRESS
European treaties bearing on the U.S., 1492-1715   v.p.
DCO: DLC 7 boxes   4198

U.S. NATIONAL ARCHIVES
List of United States diplomatic representatives, 1778-1820   DNA
N: DLC 1 reel   4199

U.S. TREATIES, etc., 1817-1825 (Monroe)
Treaty of peace with Algiers, Dec. 22, 1818, 39 p. [in English and Algerian]
DCO: NN   4200

U.S. TREATIES, etc., 1858-1865 (Buchanan and Lincoln)
Treaties, 1858-1864   DNA
N: I 1 reel   4201

VENICE. SENATO
Deliberations, 1774-1784, 1787; Dispacci al Senate, selections: Francia, Inghilterra, Spagna; Relazioni, Francia, Busta 10, 29 ItVAS
N: DLC 29 reels   4202
P: DLC

Immigration

AMBERG, Germany. BAYERISCHES STAATSARCHIV
Kammer des Innern: emigration to North

America, 1832-1846; annual surveys of
emigration to North America, 1843-1861 Ibid.
N: DLC 3 reels   4203
P: DLC

BERGEN, Norway. STATSARKIVET
Stavanger Amt No. 678: Documents re:
emigration Ibid.
N: DLC 50 feet   4204

BREMEN. HANDELSKAMMER. ARCHIV
Auswanderer, 1841-1873; Auswanderer Con-
vention mit den Vereinigten Staaten, 1868-
1876; Handel mit den Vereinigten Staaten Ibid.
N: DLC 11 reels   4205
P: DLC

BRESLAU, Ger. PREUSSICHES STAATSARCHIV
Emigration material re: Schwenkenfelders
and others, 1718-1880 Ibid.
DCO: DLC 1736 sheets   4206

COBURG, Ger. BAYERISCHE STAATSARCHIV-
ALIENABTEILUNG
Unterstützungen zur Auswanderung nach
Amerika, 1834-1873 Ibid.
N: DLC 2 reels   4207
P: DLC

CONCORDIA HISTORICAL
INSTITUTE, St. LOUIS, Mo.
Papers re: Saxon immigration,
early 19th cent., 7 items MoSC
DCO: MoSC   4208

DARMSTADT, Germany. HESSICHES
STAATSARCHIV
Emigration material, 1630-1804, 1843-1867
Ibid.
N: DLC 12 reels   4209
P: DLC

DONAU, Germany. BAYERISCHES
STAATSARCHIV
Auswanderungen nach Amerika, 1839-1852;
Auswanderungen nach überseeischen Staaten,
1839-1860 Ibid.
N: DLC 12 reels   4210
P: DLC

DRESDEN, Germany. SÄCHSICHES
HAUPTSTAATSARCHIV
Emigration material, including plan for
Lutheran Seminary and Elb-Americkanische
Compagnie, 1706-1851 Ibid.
N: DLC 33 reels   4211
P: DLC

DÜSSELDORF. PREUSSICHE STAATSARCHIV
Trade and emigration material, 1816-1849
Ibid.
N: DLC 6 reels   4212
P: DLC

FRANKFURT AM MAIN, Germany. REICHSARCHIV
Bund and Reich material on emigration and
other relations with the United States, 1848-
1850, 1854-1859 Ibid.
DCO: DLC 704 sheets   4213

FRANKFURT AM MAIN, Germany.
STADTARCHIV
Emigration material, 1773-1805, 1817-1867;
Zollverein trade negotiations with the U.S.,
1838-1857; Thurn und Taxis postal negotiations
with the U.S., 1853-1855 Ibid.
DCO: DLC 1488 sheets   4214

FRANKFURT AM MAIN, Germany.
STADTBIBLIOTHEK
Soc. Ff. Auswanderer. 503, 1852-1879 Ibid.
DCO: DLC 161 sheets   4215

GRABAU, J. A. A.
Immigration papers, March 10, 1843
4 p. priv.
DCO: MoSC   4216

GREIZ, Germany. THÜRINGISCHES
STAATSARCHIV
Übersiedelung verschiedener Individulen nach
Nordamerika Ibid.
N: DLC 3 reels   4217
P: DLC

HAMBURG, Germany. STAATSARCHIV
Auswandererlisten Direkt, 1850-1872;
Auswandererlisten Indirekt, 1855-1873;
Kurzer Bericht über den Aufenhalt de la
Fayettes in Hamburg, 1797; official trade
material, 1778-1854 Ibid.
N: DLC 92 reels   4218
P: DLC

HISTORISCHER VEREIN VON SCHWABEN UND
NEUBURG, Neuburg an der Donau, Germany
Akten des amerikanischen Auswanderungs-
vereins, 1849 Ibid.
N: DLC 2 reels   4219
P: DLC

KARLSRÜHE, Germany. GENERAL-
LANDESARCHIV
Emigration material, 1737-1787, 1818-1859
Ibid.
N: DLC 16 reels   4220
P: DLC
PP: DLC

KOBLENZ, Germany. PREUSSISCHES
STAATSARCHIV
Nassau-Saarbrücken, Sany-Altenkirchen, and
Grafschaft Sponheim emigration material, 1709-
1785; Rheinprovinz emigration material, 1843-
1858 Ibid.
DCO: DLC 2653 sheets   4221

KÖNIGSBERG, Germany. PREUSSISCHES
STAATSARCHIV
Emigration material, 1686-1827 Ibid.
DCO: DLC 58 sheets   4222

LANDSHUT, Germany. BAYERISCHES
STAATSARCHIV
Auswanderungen nach Amerika, 1839-1869
Ibid.
N: DLC 1 reel   4223
P: DLC

MAGDEBURG, Germany. KÖNIGLICHES
STAATSARCHIV
Mansfelder and Saxon emigration material,
1753, 1766, 1801-1804; summary Ibid.
DCO: DLC 241 sheets   4224

MANNHEIM, Germany. STÄDTISCHES ARCHIV
Emigration material, 1709-1804 Ibid.
N: DLC 5 feet   4225
PP: DLC

MUNICH. GEHEIMES STAATSARCHIV
Emigration material, 1683, 1768, 1816-1866;
trade negotiations, 1838-1845; reports of Comte
d'Haslang, Ambassador in England, 1757-1787
Ibid.
N: DLC 55 reels and 10 feet   4226
P: DLC
PP: DLC of the 10 feet

NEUBURG AN DER DONAU, Germany.
BAYERISCHES STAATSARCHIV
Auswanderungen nach Amerika, 1839-1852;
Auswanderungen nach überseeischen Staaten,
1839-1860 Ibid.
N: DLC 12 reels   4227
P: DLC

NORWAY. DEPARTEMENTET FOR SOSIALE
SAKER
Material re: emigration laws of 1845, 1869,
and 1897 Ibid.
N: DLC 77 feet   4228

NORWAY. RIGSARKIVET
Historiografish Samling, "America-letters ":
letters re: Quakers of Stavanger; documents
re: emigration, 1835-1857 NoOR
N: DLC 163 feet   4229

OSNABRÜCK, Germany. STAATSARCHIV
Durchmarsch Hannoverischen-Hessischer
Truppen, 1740-1776; postal material, 1779-
1782; emigration material, 1803-1879; Aufruf
an deutsche Verlandsfreunde behuf revolution-
ärer Verbindungen, 1839-1852 Ibid.
N: DLC 35 reels   4230
P: DLC

ROTTERDAM. GEMMENTE-ARCHIEF
Documents re: emigration of Palatines to
America Ibid.
N: DLC 2 reels   4231

RUDOLSTADT, Germany. STAATSARCHIV
Das Auswanderungswesen, 1846-1897 Ibid.
N: DLC 1 reel   4232
P: DLC

SPEYER, Germany. BAYERISCHES STAATS-
ARCHIV
Kurpfalz emigration material, 1685-1779 Ibid.
N: DLC 8 feet   4233
PP: DLC

STETTIN, Germany. KÖNIGLICH PREUSSISCHES
STAATSARCHIV
Emigration material, 1853-1855; trade
material, 1777, 1815-1846 Ibid.
DCO: DLC 868 sheets   4234

STUTTGART, Germany. WÜRTTEMBERGISCHES
STAATSARCHIV
Emigration material, 1709-1717 Ibid.
N: DLC 1 reel   4235
P: DLC

U.S. IMMIGRATION AND NATURALIZATION
SERVICE
Chronological index to ship and passenger
arrivals at New York, N.Y., 1897-1906 DNA
N: DNA 29 reels   4236

U.S. IMMIGRATION AND NATURALIZATION
SERVICE
Crew lists of vessels arriving at Brunswick,
Ga., 1904-1906 DNA
N: DNA 1 reel   4237

U.S. IMMIGRATION AND NATURALIZATION
SERVICE
Crew lists of vessels arriving at
Pensacola, Fla., 1905-1906 DNA
N: DNA 1 reel   4238

U.S. IMMIGRATION AND NATURALIZATION
SERVICE
Crew lists of vessels arriving at Tampa, Fla.,
1904-1906 DNA
N: DNA 1 reel   4239

U.S. IMMIGRATION AND NATURALIZATION
SERVICE
Passenger and crew lists of vessels arriving
at Gulfport, Miss., 1904-1906 DNA
N: DNA 2 reels   4240

U.S. IMMIGRATION AND NATURALIZATION
SERVICE
Passenger and crew lists of vessels arriving at
Mobile, Ala., 1903-1906 DNA
N: DNA 3 reels   4241

U.S. IMMIGRATION AND NATURALIZATION
SERVICE
Passenger and crew lists of vessels arriving at
New York, N.Y., 1897-1906 DNA
N: DNA 823 reels   4242

U.S. IMMIGRATION AND NATURALIZATION
SERVICE
Passenger lists of vessels arriving at
Key West, Fla., 1898-1906 DNA
N: DNA 7 reels   4243

U.S. IMMIGRATION AND NATURALIZATION
SERVICE
Passenger lists of vessels arriving at
Miami, Fla., 1898-1906 DNA
N: DNA 3 reels   4244

U.S. IMMIGRATION AND NATURALIZATION
SERVICE
Passenger lists of vessels arriving at
New Bedford, Mass., 1902-1906 DNA
N: DNA 3 reels   4245

U.S. IMMIGRATION AND NATURALIZATION
SERVICE
Passenger lists of vessels arriving at
New Orleans, La., 1903-1906 DNA
N: DNA 12 reels   4246

U.S. IMMIGRATION AND NATURALIZATION
SERVICE
Passenger lists of vessels arriving at
Pascagoula, Miss., 1903-1906 DNA
N: DNA 1 reel   4247

U.S. IMMIGRATION AND NATURALIZATION
SERVICE
Passenger lists of vessels arriving at
Philadelphia, Pa., 1883-1906 DNA
N: DNA 34 reels   4248

U.S. IMMIGRATION AND NATURALIZATION
SERVICE
Passenger lists of vessels arriving at Portland,
Me., 1893-1906 DNA
N: DNA 5 reels   4249

U.S. IMMIGRATION AND NATURALIZATION
SERVICE
Passenger lists of vessels arriving at Tampa,
Fla., 1898-1906 DNA
N: DNA 2 reels   4250

WEIMAR, Germany. THÜRINGISCHES
STAATSARCHIV
Emigration material, 1833-1857 Ibid.
N: DLC 4 reels   4251
P: DLC

WIESBADEN, Germany. PREUSSISCHES
STAATSARCHIV
Dillenburg, Hesse-Homburg, and Nassau
emigration material, 1697-1876 Ibid.
DCO: DLC 5059 sheets   4252

WÜRZBURG, Germany. BAYERISCHES
STAATSARCHIV
Emigration material, 1754-1855; Geistliche
Mission nach Amerika, 1788-1797; passage of
Anspach troops, 1777; recruitment for English,
1780-1782 Ibid.
N: DLC 10 reels and 75 feet   4253
P: DLC
PP: DLC of the 75 feet

ZÜRICH, Switz. (Canton). STAATSARCHIV
Emigration material, 22 ll. SzZ
DCO: DLC   4254

Labor

AMERICAN FEDERATION OF LABOR
Out-letters of Pres. William Green,
1926-1952 Ibid.
N: DAF 43 reels   4255
P: NIC-I

UNITED MINE WORKERS OF AMERICA,
District 12
Papers Ibid.
N: NIC-I 7 reels   4256

Military Affairs

Colonial Wars

CONNECTICUT. ARCHIVES
Selected papers re: Colonial Wars, 1675-1775
Ct
N: USIGS 7 reels   4257
P: Ct

GREAT BRITAIN. ADMIRALTY
Roster of Americans joining British warships
at Port Royal, Jamaica, before the attack
on Cartagena, 1741 UKLPRO
DCO: DLC also transcripts
N: Bibliofilm 1 reel   4258
P: CtY

GREAT BRITAIN. ADMIRALTY
Secretary's department, American selections:
Prize Office letters, 1704-1705; Solicitor's
department letters, 1700-1783; letters from
Doctors' Commons, 1731-1782; intelligence,
1797-1803; reports of courts martial, 1775-
1781, 1812-1815 UKLPRO
DCO: DLC   4259

GREAT BRITAIN. ADMIRALTY. Adm. 2
Secretary's department, out-letters re:
America, 1689-1815 UKLPRO
DCO: DLC 30 v.   4260

French and Indian War

ABERCROMBY, JAMES, 1706-1781
Papers, 1758 CSmH
N: PHarH 1/2 reel*   4261

AMHERST, JEFFREY AMHERST, 1st BARON,
1717-1797
Papers, American selections, 1756-1764
W.O. 34 UKLPRO
DCO: DLC 23 v.   4262

BRADDOCK, EDWARD, 1695-1755
Order books, 1753-1755 ICN
N: PBL 1 reel   4263

CONNECTICUT. ARCHIVES
French and Indian War records, 1758-1780 Ct
N: USIGS 2 reels   4264
P: Ct

CUMBERLAND, WILLIAM AUGUSTUS, DUKE
of, 1721-1765
Papers, selections, 1754-1757 Windsor
Castle
N: DLC 2 reels   4265
P: DLC

Diary of British-American soldier in French
and Indian War, July 30 - Nov. 2, 1758 priv.
N: DLC 1 reel   4266
PP: DLC

FISHER, SAMUEL
Diary of operations around Lake George,
1758 priv.
DCO: DLC   4267

GREAT BRITAIN. COLONIAL OFFICE. C.O. 117
Havana, original correspondence, 1762-1763
UKLPRO
DCO: DLC   4268

GRUBBS, SAMUEL
Orderly book of [his] company, 1759 CSmH
N: PPiU 1 reel   4269

HENDERSON, WILLIAM, soldier
Journal, 1758-1759 NBu
N: NN 54 frames   4270

HUTCHINS, THOMAS, 1730-1789
Diary, 1762, 10 p. CaOOA
DCO: MnHi   4271

LOUDON, JOHN CAMPBELL, 4th EARL of,
1705-1782
Papers re: Pennsylvania, 1754-1760 CSmH
N: PHarH 2 reels*   4272

MONYPENNY, Maj. ALEXANDER
Diary, Cherokee wars with colonists, 1761
OkTG
N: OkTG 1 reel   4273

PELL, ROBERT, collector
French documents re: Fort Ticonderoga, Apr.
24, 1757-Nov. 30, 1758 v.p.
N: NFt 1 reel   4274

ROGERS, ROBERT, 1731-1795
Journal, 1760-1761, ...capitulation of
Western French posts, 27 p. Chalmers
Papers, NN
DC: NN   4275

SPAULDING, Lieutenant
Diary of activities near Lake George, 1758
priv.
DCO: DLC 17 p.   4276

American Revolution

ANDRÉ, JOHN, 1751-1780
Papers found in his boots when captured, 1780
N
DCO: DLC 1 box NN   4277

ASSOCIATED LOYALISTS. BOARD OF
DIRECTORS
Minutes, Jan., 1781 - June, 1782 MiU-C
N: NjP 1 reel*   4278

BAMBERG, Germany. BAYERISCHES
STAATSARCHIV
Material on American Revolution, 1776-1783,
and on emigration, 1816-1851 Ibid.
N: DLC 12 reels   4279
P: DLC
PP: DLC

BAYREUTH, Germany. HISTORISCHER
VEREIN VON OBERFRANKEN
Diary of Stephan Popp, 1777-1783; diary of
Jäger-Lieutenant von Failitzsch, 1777-1783;
line of march of oboe-player Georg Adam
Stang, 1777-1783 Ibid.
N: DLC 2 reels   4280
P: DLC

BEVAN, DAVIS
Orderly book, Continental Army, Valley Forge,
May 22-23, 1778; miscellaneous military
records, 1779-1780, 87 p. priv.
DCO: NN   4281

CANADA. PUBLIC ARCHIVES
Rolls of regiments of Loyalists, 1775-1783
CaOOA
DCO: DLC 21 portfolios   4282

CASTRIES, ARMAND CHARLES AUGUSTIN DE
LA CROIX, duc DE, 1756-1842
Journal de mon voyage en Amérique, 1780,
76 p. Paris, Dépôt Général des Fortifications
DCO: MiU-C   4283

CLINTON, Sir HENRY, 1738-1795
Papers re: Pennsylvania, 1775-1778 MiU-C
N: PHarH 20 feet*   4284

COLBRATH, WILLIAM
Diary at Fort Schuyler [Fort Stanwix], N.Y.,
Apr. 17 - Aug. 23, 1777, 21 ll. priv.
DCO: NN   4285

CONNECTICUT. ARCHIVES
Records re: Revolutionary War, 1763-1820 Ct
N: USIGS 60 reels   4286
P: Ct

CONNECTICUT. ARCHIVES
Revolutionary War papers from private
collections Ct
N: USIGS 3 reels   4287
P: Ct

CONNECTICUT. ARCHIVES
Revolutionary War papers: orderly books of
various officers; papers re: procedure of
Connecticut towns
N: USIGS 12 reels   4288
P: Ct

DAY, BENJAMIN
"Account book of General Woodford's Brigade,"
Philadelphia, May 8, 1777 priv.
N: PHi 1 reel   4289

DELAWARE
Revolutionary War claims and settlements with
the United States, 1776-1787, 88 p. De
N: De   4290

DELAWARE. MILITARY COMMISSARY
Accounts, 1781-1783, 40 p. De
N: De   4291

DORCHESTER, Sir GUY CARLETON, 1st
VISCOUNT
Headquarters papers UKLPRO
N: ViWC 30 reels   4292
P: ViU
DCO: NN

EELS, JEREMIAH B.
Diary while imprisoned, New York City,
Mar. 14-Nov. 24, 1777; miscellaneous
accounts, 1776-1781, 21 p. priv.
DCO: NN   4293

ELIZA (Privateer)
Prize money receipts for capture of Brigantine
William, 1782-1783 [unk.]
DCO: Ct   4294

ESTAING, CHARLES HENRI, COMTE D',
1729-1794
Journal du siège de Savannah, 1779, 60 p.
Dépôt Général des Fortifications, Paris
DCO: MiU-C   4295

FENNO, JOHN
Orderly book at siege of Boston, 1775   MHi
DCO: DLC   4296

GALLOWAY, JOSEPH, 1731-1803
Selected papers, including: "Plan of Union,
1774" Duane Papers NHi; letters, 4 items,
178? DLC; "Plan for facilitating the reduction
of His Majesty's revolted colonies" MiU-C
N: NjP 1 reel   4297

GEORGE III, King of Great Britain, 1738-1820
Originalbriefe betragend Stellung eines Jäger-
korps nach Amerika, 1776-1777   GeMSA
DCO: DLC 27 sheets   4298

GLEASON, SAMUEL
Journal, kept at Roxbury, Mass., 1775
Farmington Village Library, Conn.
DCO: Ct   4299

GREAT BRITAIN. ADJUTANT GENERAL'S
OFFICE
Orderly book, 1776-1784   MiD-B
N: MiD-B 1 reel   4300

GREAT BRITAIN. ADMIRALTY. Adm. 1.
Admirals' despatches, American selections,
1781-1815, 20 v.   UKLPRO
DCO: DLC   4301

GREAT BRITAIN. ADMIRALTY. Adm. 51
Captains' logs, selections   UKLPRO
N: DLC 14 reels   4302
P: DLC

GREAT BRITAIN. ARMY
Muster rolls of Loyalist regiment, Md. and
Penn., 1777-1783   MdAA
N: MdAA   4303

GREAT BRITAIN. ARMY. INFANTRY. 55th
REGIMENT
Rosters, captured on Staten Island, 1776,
86 p.   Ct
DCO: Ct   4304

GREAT BRITAIN. ARMY. PROVINCIAL TROOPS
(America)
List of officers in the Provincial forces, ca.
1783   priv.
DCO: NN 13 p.   4305

GREAT BRITAIN. AUDIT OFFICE. A.O. 12
American Loyalist claims, series I, 1776-
1831, 146 v.   UKLPRO
N: DLC 30 reels   4306

GREAT BRITAIN. AUDIT OFFICE. A.O. 13
Selected American Loyalist claims, 1778-1784
UKLPRO
DCO: DLC   4307

GREAT BRITAIN. COLONIAL OFFICE. C.O. 5
America and West Indies, orginal correspondence: correspondence between the Command-
ers-in-chief in America and the American Secretary, 1781-1782, 1016 p.   UKLPRO
DCO: MiU-C   4308

GREAT BRITAIN. HIGH COURT OF ADMIRALTY
H.C.A. 24
Papers of the New York Court of Vice
Admiralty, 1778-1783   UKLPRO
DCO: DLC   4309

GREAT BRITAIN. HIGH COURT OF ADMIRALTY
H.C.A. 32
Prize papers, New York Court of Vice Admir-
alty, 1776-1783   UKLPRO
DCO: DLC   4310

GREAT BRITAIN. LOYALIST COMMISSION.
A.O. 12
Books and papers, 1777-1790   UKLPRO
UKLRI; transcripts, 60 v.   NN
N: NN 24 reels   4311

GREAT BRITAIN. PUBLIC RECORD OFFICE
Venetian Archives, transcripts of Venetian
State Papers re: the American Revolution,
1 v.   UKLPRO
N: DLC 1 reel   4312

GREAT BRITAIN. TREASURY. Treasury 50
Documents re: American refugees, 1790-1835,

56 v. UKLPRO
N: CaOOA 7 reels   4313

GREAT BRITAIN. WAR OFFICE. W.O. 4
Secretary at War, outletters: American
letter books, 1763-1784   UKLPRO
DCO: DLC   4314

GREAT BRITAIN. WAR OFFICE. W.O. 28
Headquarters records, 1777-1783   UKLPRO
DCO: DLC   4315

GREY, CHARLES, 1st EARL, 1729-1807
Orderly book, 1778, 1 v.
N: NjR   4316

HANAU, Germany. HESSISCHER GESCHICHTS-
VEREIN
American Revolutionary material: Journal
des Hessen-Hanauischen Regiment 1ten
Bataillons, Mar.-June, 1776; Tagbuch gefürt
von den grenadier Johannes Reuber, 1776-
1806 Ibid.
DCO: DLC 204 sheets   4317

HANNOVER, Germany. KÖNIGLICHES
STAATSARCHIV
Ministerium des Auswärtige Gelegenheit,
1755-1865 [Troops for America, including
Royal American Regiment, 1755-1790;
American relations, 1796-1865; Policei-
Sachen, Revolutionäre Bewegungen in Amerika
in Beziehung auf Deutschland, 1847-1853];
Finanzministerium, American trade, 1840-
1861; General Commando, Durchmärsche
Truppen nach Amerika, 1775-1784; Land-
drostei Hannover, Auswanderungen nach
Amerika, 1830-1868; Ministerium der Innern,
Bestrebungen unter den Deutschen Amerikas
zur Revolutionierung Deutschlands, 1847-
1852 Ibid.
N: DLC 24 reels   4318
P: DLC

HEATH, Maj. Gen. WILLIAM, 1737-1814
Orderly book, 1777-1778   DNA
N: DNA 1 reel [T-42]   4319

HESSE-CASSEL. HEER. FELDJÄGER-KORPS
Diary, 1777-1784, 238 p.   GeMaSA
N: NSiHi   4320

HESSE-CASSEL. HEER. FUSILIER REGIMENT
VON ALT-LOBERG
Diary, 1776-1783, 308 p.   GeMaSA
N: NSiHi   4821

HESSE-CASSEL. HEER. GARNISON-REGIMENT
VON HUYN (later VON BENNING REGIMENT)
Diary, 1776-1783, 150 p.   GeMaSA
N: NNWML   4322

HESSE-CASSEL. HEER. GARNISON-REGIMENT
VON WISSENBACH (later VON KNOBLOCH)
Diary, 1776-1783, 628 p.   GeMaSA
N: NSiHi   4323

HESSE-CASSEL. HEER. GRENADIER
BATAILLON BLOCK (later VON LENERKE)
Diary, 1776-1784, 43 p.   GeMaSA
N: NNW   4324

HESSE-CASSEL. HEER. GRENADIER
BATAILLON PLATTE
Diary, 1776-1784, 443 p.   GeMaSA
N: NSiHi   4325

HESSE-CASSEL. HEER. GRENADIER
BATAILLON VON MINNIGERODE (later VON
LOEWENSTEIN)
Diary, 1776-1784, 375 p.   GeMaSA
N: NSiHi   4326

HESSE-CASSEL. HEER. LEIB INFANTERIE
REGIMENT (later ERBPRINZ REGIMENT)
Diary, 1776-1784, 132 p.   GeMaSA
N: NNWML 1 reel   4327

HESSE-CASSEL. HEER. (NEUES) LEIB
INFANTERIE REGIMENT
Diary, 1779-1784, 96 p.   GeMaSA
N: NSiHi   4328

HESSE-CASSEL. HEER. REGIMENT PRINZ
FRIEDRICH

Diary, 1776-1783, 271 p.   GeMaSA
N: NSiHi   4329

HESSE-CASSEL. HEER. REGIMENT VON
BISCHAUSEN
Diary, 1776-1783, 84 p.   GeMaSA
N: NSiHi   4330

HESSE-CASSEL. HEER. REGIMENT VON
DONOP
Diary, 1776-1784, 70 p.   GeMaSA
N: NSiHi   4331

HESSE-CASSEL. HEER. REGIMENT VON
KNYPHAUSEN
Diary, 1776-1783, 157 p.   GeMaSA
N: NSiHi   4332

HESSE-CASSEL. HEER. REGIMENT VON
MIRBACH
Diary, 1777-1780, 428 p.   GeMaSA
N: NSiHi   4333

HESSE-CASSEL. HEER. REGIMENT VON
TRUMBACH (later VON BODE)
Diary, 1776-1783, 296 p.   GeMaSA
N: NSiHi   4334

HISTORISCHER VEREIN FÜR MITTELFRANKEN,
Ansbach, Germany
Diary of German soldier in America, 1777;
songs at departure of Ansbach-Bayreuth
troops, 1777; amounts paid officers, 1794-1795;
instructions to troops, 1779-1784 ms. 485-487
Ibid.
N: DLC 2 reels   4335

HOWE, JOHN, British spy
Journal, 1775-1813 NhHi
N: ViWI 1 reel   4336

HOWE, ROBERT, 1732-1785
Orderly book, 1776-1778 priv.
N: IaU 93 frames   4337

HOWE, ROBERT, 1732-1785
Orderly book, West Point, Feb. 23-May 28,
1780 DLC
N: DLC 1 reel   4338

HOWE, ROBERT, 1732-1785
Orderly book when in command of the Southern
Department, June, 1776-July, 1778 priv.
N: DLC 1 reel   4339

HUNTER, ANDREW, 1732-1823
War diary, 1776-1779 NjP
N: NjP 1 reel   4340

JENKINS, JOHN
Journal re: Sullivan Expedition, 1778-1781
priv.
N: PHarH 4 feet   4341

KASSEL, Germany. LANDESBIBLIOTHEK
Diaries and journals of Hessian soldiers
during service in America, 1776-1785 Ibid.
DCO: DLC 560 sheets   4342

KENDALL, Capt. CURTIS
Revolutionary War muster roll, 1 v.
N: ViU   4343
P: ViU

KISSAM, JOHN, Major, Queens Co., N.Y.
Loyalist militia
Papers re: military affairs, June, 1777-Apr.,
1782 (transcript)
DCO: NN 66 p.   4344

LIVINGSTON, HENRY, Jr.
Journal of Canadian campaign with the Conti-
nental Army, Aug. 25-Dec. 22, 1775 priv.
DCO: NN 32 ll.   4345

McDOUGALL, ALEXANDER, 1732-1786
Orderly book, 1776   NHi
N: NHi   4346

MALSBURG, Captain FRIEDRICH VON DER,
Hessian officer
Diary, Feb.-Dec., 1776, 162 p.   GeMaSA
N: NNWML   4347

MARBURG, Germany. HESSEN-KASSELSCHES
ARCHIV
American selections: Kriegsachen, 1775-1789

[Acc. 1930/5, formerly Heeresarchiv, Rep. 15 A, Kap. XXXIII, XXXIV, O.W.S. 1247-1249, 1268]; Kriegstagebücher, Ordrebücher, und Kriegsberichte, 1776-1784; Kriegsministerium, Engl. Subsidien Gelder, 1776-1784; Kabinetts-Ministerium, monatliche Listen, 1776-1784; Fürstlich Waldeckisches Kabinett, englische-waldeckische Soldregiments, 1776-1784; Ministerium des Auswärtigen, material on relations with the U.S.; Ministerium des Innern, emigration material, 1821, 1823, 1867 Ibid.
DCO: DLC 37879 sheets   4348

MARTIN, Captain, Hessian officer
Diary, July-Dec., 1778, 55 p. GeMaSA
N: NSiHi   4349

MARYLAND
Revolutionary War records, 1776-1796 MdAA
N: MdAA 2 reels   4350

MARYLAND HISTORICAL SOCIETY
Unpublished revolutionary records, 1775-1783, 6 v. (typescript) MdHi
N: USIGS 2 reels   4351

MASSACHUSETTS. ARCHIVES
Revolutionary War rolls M-Ar
N: M-Ar 6 reels   4352

MÜNSTER, Germany. PREUSSISCHES STAATSARCHIV
Durchmärsche Hessischer Truppen, 1777-1803; trade and emigration material, 1815-1873 Ibid.
N: DLC 12 reels   4353
P: DLC

NASON, Lt. NATHANIEL
Orderly book and returns of provisions, clothing, and equipment, Col. Vose's Light Infantry, Yorktown Campaign, Feb.-Oct., 1781 DNA
N: DNA 1 reel [T-281]   4354

NEUWIED, Germany. FÜRSTLICH WIEDISCHES ARCHIV
Acta die Correspondenz mit den Grafen von Schwerin während der Campagne in Britannien und Amerika, 1777-1782; Korrespondenz mit Waldo und Palairet re: settlement in Massachusetts [Maine], 1757-1766, 1774; Prinz Max von Wied, Tagebuch der Reise in Nordamerika, 1832-1834; Briefe, 1832-1834 Ibid.
DCO: DLC 1412 sheets   4355

NÜRNBERG, Germany. BAYERISCHES STAATS-ARCHIV
Material on Schwenkenfeld, 1526, 1529; Ansbach-Bayreuth troops in Revolution, 1777-1781; emigration material, 1811-1860; Mexican War soldiers, 1851, 1853-1861 Ibid.
N: DLC 12 reels   4356
P: DLC

OLIVER, PETER, 1713-1791
The origin and progress of the American Rebellion to the year 1776 UKLBM; (typescript), 238 p. MHi
N: CU typescript   4357

PACA, WILLIAM, 1740-1799
Letters, 1778-1786; also letter from Major Galvan describing Green Springs, Va., battle PHi
N: NjP 1 reel   4358

PANTON, Rev. GEORGE, British Army Chaplain
In-letters re: Samuel Seabury and British reaction to American Revolution
N: CtY   4359

PEEBLES, Lt. JOHN, of 42nd regiment
Journals during American Revolution UKENRH
N: DLC 1 reel   4360
P: DLC

PENNSYLVANIA. HISTORICAL SOCIETY
Letters re: Revolutionary prisoners of war PHi
N: NcD 1 reel   4361

PIERPONT MORGAN LIBRARY, New York
Autograph letters and documents by American and British leaders, at siege of Yorktown, 1781, 2 v. NNP
N: NNP 1 reel*   4362
P: NNP

QUICKEL, Capt. MICHAEL
Company accounts, 1776 PYHi
N: PYHi   4363

SAWYER, EBENEZER, Revolutionary soldier
Diary of march from near Berwick, Me., to West Point and return, June 8, 1778-Apr. 6, 1779; accounts, 1779-1780 priv.
DCO: NN 24 ll.   4364

SONS OF THE AMERICAN REVOLUTION
Membership applications to 1951, 167 v. Ibid.
N: USIGS 401 reels   4365
P: USIGS

SOWELL, JOSEPH
Journal kept on board H.M.S. Milford, Oct., 1775-Oct., 1776 UKLPRO
DCO: DLC   4366

SPAIN. ARCHIVO GENERAL DE SIMANCAS
Marina: papers re: naval operations in the West Indies, 1780-1783 Ibid.
N: ILC 494 feet   4367
PP: DLC

TILGHMAN, TENCH, 1744-1786
Diary and accounts for Indian Commission and operations at Yorktown, 1775, 1781 priv.
DCO: DLC 20 sheets   4368

TREAT, ROBERT, Revolutionary soldier
Diary re: Saratoga Campaign, Aug. 19-Oct. 2, 1777 priv.
DCO: Ct   4369

TWISS, JOHN, Jr., Revolutionary soldier
Journal re: march from Bethlem, Conn., to Boston, Mass., Aug. 11-Dec. 8, 1775, 38 p. Ct
DCO: Ct   4370

U.S. ADJUTANT-GENERAL'S OFFICE
Index to compiled service records of Volunteer soldiers of the Revolution from North Carolina DNA
N: DNA 2 reels 16 mm. [M-257]   4371

U.S. ADJUTANT-GENERAL'S OFFICE
Revolutionary War rolls, 1775-1783 DNA
N: DNA 137 reels [M-246]   4372

U.S. ARMY. 19th REGIMENT
Orderly book, Col. Charles Webb, Nov., 1775-July, 1776, 257 p. Ct
DCO: Ct   4373

U.S. CONGRESS
Reports on the claims of the heirs of the Comte de Rochambeau, 1842 DLC
N: DLC 1 reel   4374
P: DLC

U.S. CONTINENTAL CONGRESS. MEDICAL COMMITTEE
Report on the hospital, 1777-1782 DNA
N: NjP 1 reel   4375

U.S. LIBRARY OF CONGRESS
Papers re: Revolutionary prisoners of war DLC
N: NcD 1 reel   4376

U.S. NAVY BOARD OF THE EASTERN DEPT.
Papers William Vernon Papers RNHi
N: ? 1 reel   4377
P: RHi

U.S. VETERANS ADMINISTRATION
Pension records, veterans in the Ticonderoga-Crown Point expedition, May, 1775 DNA
N: VtHi 4 reels   4378
P: VtHi

VIRGINIA
Revolutionary War claims, pensions, land bounties in Ohio and Kentucky Vi
N: Vi 67 reels   4379
P: USIGS

WEEDON, GEORGE
Correspondence with officers of U.S. Army, 1777-1786, 153 items priv.
N: PPAmP   4380

WENTWORTH, BENNING, 1696-1770
Original town grants; claim to Lords of Treasury for land losses in the Revolution UKLPRO
N: VtHi 2 reels   4381

WOLFENBÜTTEL, Germany. LANDESHAUPT-ARCHIV
Brunswick-Lüneburg troops in the Revolution, 1775-1785; Riedesel papers, 1776-1783; records of St. Louis Consulate, 1854-1859 Ibid.
N: DLC 48 reels   4382
P: DLC

WOOLWICH, Eng. ROYAL ARTILLERY INSTITUTION. LIBRARY
Correspondence of British officers in command of New York City, 1778-1780 UKGwRA
N: DLC 1 reel   4383
P: DLC

From 1790 to 1812

BARBEE, THOMAS
Orderly book, 1794 priv.
DCO: MiU-C   4384

HARMAR, JOSIAH, 1753-1813
Orderly book: expedition against Indians, Fort Washington, 1790 priv.
N: PHarH 10 feet   4385

PINKHAM, ANDREW
Journal kept on U.S.F. President, 1799 priv.
N: DLC 1 reel   4386

RODGERS, JOHN, 1773-1838
In-letters re: Mediterranean-North African area, 1802-1804 priv.
N: NN 1 reel*   4387

U.S. NAVY DEPT.
Letters received by the Secretary of the Navy from Captains ("Captains' Letters"), 1807-1861, 1866-1885 DNA
N: DNA 407 reels [M-125]   4388
P: PPiU

U.S. NAVY DEPT.
Letters received by the Secretary of the Navy from Commanders, 1804-1886 DNA
N: DNA 124 reels [M-147]   4389
P: PPiU

U.S. NAVY DEPT.
Letters received by the Secretary of the Navy from officers below the rank of commander, ("Officers' Letters"), 1802-1865 DNA
N: DNA 400 reels [M-148]   4390

U.S. NAVY DEPT.
Letters sent by the Secretary of the Navy to officers ("Officers, Ships of War"), 1798-1868 DNA
N: DNA 86 reels [M-149]   4391
P: PPiU 58 reels

U.S. NAVY DEPT.
Miscellaneous letters received by the Secretary of the Navy, 1807-1815 DNA
N: DNA 61 reels [M-124]   4392

U.S. SUPREME COURT
Records of prize cases heard by the Committees of the Continental Congress, 1776-1780, and the Court of Appeals in Cases of Capture, 1780-1787 DNA
N: DNA 15 reels [M-162]   4393

U.S. WAR DEPT.
Letters sent concerning Naval affairs, 1790-1798 DNA
N: DNA 1 reel [T-250]   4394

U.S. WAR DEPT.
Letters sent relating to military affairs, 1800-1861 DNA
N: DNA 43 reels [M-6]   4395
P: MoIT

U.S. WAR DEPT.
Letters sent to the President by the Secretary
of War, 1800-1863 DNA
N: DNA 6 reels [M-127]   4396
P: MoIT

U.S. WAR DEPT.
Registers of letters received by the Office of
the Secretary of War, 1800-1860 DNA
N: DNA 96 reels [M-22]   4397
P: MoIT

WAYNE, ANTHONY, 1745-1796
Orderly books, no. 2-6, 1793-1794 KyLoF
N: KyU 50 feet   4398
P: KyU

WAYNE, ANTHONY, 1745-1796
Papers, 1794 PPPrHi
N: OHi 1 reel   4399

WAYNE, ANTHONY, 1745-1796
Papers and orderly books, 1795-1796 MiD-B
N: MiD-B 1 reel   4400

War of 1812

Account of campaign and death of Zebulon M.
Pike priv.
N: OkU   4401

CAMP, Col. JOSEPH
Papers re: War of 1812, 24 ll. priv.
DCO: Ct   4402

CANADA. PUBLIC ARCHIVES
Colonial records, 1807-1814; War of 1812
manuscripts CaOOA
N: ? 2 reels   4403
P: OHi

CONNECTICUT. ARCHIVES
Selected papers re: War of 1812, 1812-1819
Ct
N: USlGS 2 reels   4404
P: Ct

CONSTITUTION (U.S. Frigate)
Log, Feb. 1, 1812 - Dec. 13, 1813 DNA
N: DNA 1 reel [T-123]   4405

CUSHING, DANIEL LEWIS
Orderly book, U.S. Army, Fort Meigs, 1813,
92 p. OT
N: OHi OT   4406

GREAT BRITAIN. ADMIRALTY. Adm. 1
Captains' letters, American selections,
1812-1815 UKLPRO
DCO: DLC   4407

GREAT BRITAIN. ADMIRALTY. Adm. 50
Admirals' journals, 1812-1815 (selections)
UKLPRO
N: DLC 3 reels   4408
P: DLC

HAIRSTON, GEORGE, 1750-1827
Records re: War of 1812, 1813-1814, 3 v.
NcU
N: NcU 3 reels   4409

HARRINGTON, HENRY WILLIAM, naval officer
Diary, War of 1812 priv.
N: Nc-Ar 1 reel   4410

KENTUCKY. ADJUTANT GENERAL
Roster, War of 1812; roster of Kentucky
military officers, 1812-1816 KyHi
N: KyHi 2 reels 1 16 mm.   4411

LEWISTON, FORT
Log in War of 1812, Sept., 1814-Jan., 1815
Lewes, Del.
DC: DeHi 23 p.   4412

MILLER, JACOB
Movement of troops from Bellefonte to
Buffalo, N.Y., 1812-1813 priv.
N: PHarH 5 feet   4413

Narrative re: conduct of British, War of
1812, 1813, 38 p. (dedicated to Gen. T. M.
Forman)
N: MdAA   4414

NIAGARA, FORT
Garrison orders, Nov. 15, 1812-Dec. 16, 1813;
returns of prisoners taken at Fort Niagara and
Fort George, 83 p.
DCO: NN   4415

PIATT, JOHN H., U.S. Commissary General
Letterbook, 1812-1814 DLC
N: NcD   4417

PENNSYLVANIA INFANTRY. TANNEHILL'S
BRIGADE, 1812-1814
Orderly book of Niagara River campaign, 1812-
1814 priv.
N: PHarH 5 feet   4416

PRESIDENT (U.S. Frigate)
Log, April - Oct., 1813 priv.
N: NN 1 reel   4418

SOCIETY OF THE WAR OF 1812
General membership applications, 1877-1925
Ibid.
N: USlGS 14 reels   4419
P: USlGS

U.S. ARMY
Pay roll, Maj. Gen. John Cocke's division,
East Tennessee Volunteers, Oct., 1813-Feb.,
1814, 112 p. priv.
N: A-Ar 1 reel   4420

VIRGINIA
Militia muster rolls - War of 1812 Vi
N: Vi 7 reels 16 mm.   4421
P: USlGS Vi

From 1815 to 1861

ALABAMA. MILITIA. 1836 (Creek War)
Carded records of military service of Capt.
William Donaldson Mounted Co. DNA
N: A-Ar 1 reel   4422

BIDDLE, JAMES, 1783-1848
Journal kept aboard the U.S.S. Ontario,
Oct., 1817 - Mar., 1818 DNA
N: DNA 1 reel [T-22]   4423

DAVIS, General WILLIAM WATTS HART
Journal describing treaty with Navajos,
Oct., 1854 priv.
DCO: DLC   4424

DEBLOIS, CHARLES J.
Journal as Captain's Clerk aboard the U.S.S.
Macedonian, Sept., 1818-July, 1819 DNA
N: DNA 1 reel [T-68]   4425

DORNIN, Lt. THOMAS A., 1800-1874
Journal kept aboard the U.S.S. Brandywine and
U.S.S. Falmouth, 1826-1834 DNA
N: DNA 1 reel [T-67]   4426

GAUNTT, Lt. CHARLES, ca. 1790-1855
Journal kept aboard the U.S.S. Macedonian,
1818-1821 DNA
N: DNA 1 reel [T-66]   4427

HAMBLETON, JOHN N., chaplain
Journal of the voyage of the U.S.S. Nonsuch
up the Orinoco, July 11 - Aug. 24, 1819 DNA
N: DNA 1 reel [M-83]   4428

HUDSON, WILLIAM LEVERRETH, 1794-1862
Journal kept on U.S.S. Peacock, 1840-1842
priv.
N: NcU 298 frames   4429

MARCY, RANDOLPH B.
Documents from Office of Adjutant General
and Department of the West DNA
N: OkU   4430

STUART, JAMES EWELL BROWN, 1833-1864
Diaries, pocket, 1858-1860, 200 p. ViU
N: ?   4431
P: KU

STUART, JAMES EWELL BROWN, 1833-1864
Journal on expeditions against the Kiowas and
Comanches, May 15-Aug. 11, 1860, 68 p. CtY
N: KU   4432

U.S. ADJUTANT-GENERAL'S OFFICE
Records relating to the United States Military
Academy, 1812-1867 DNA
N: DNA 29 reels [M-91]   4433
P: MoIT

U.S. NAVY DEPT.
Letters received by the Secretary of the Navy
from Commanding Officers of Squadrons
("Squadron Letters"), 1841-1886: East India,
1841-1861; Brazil, 1841-1861; Pacific,
1841-1886; Mediterranean, 1842-1861; Home,
1842-1861; African, 1843-1861; Eastern,
1853; Potomac Flotilla, 1861-1865; Atlantic
Blockading, 1861; Gulf Blockading, 1861-1862;
West India, 1861-1864; Mississippi, 1861-1865;
South Atlantic Blockading, 1861-1865; North
Atlantic Blockading, 1861-1865; West Gulf
Blockading, 1862-1865; East Gulf Blockading,
1862-1865; Mortar Flotilla, 1862; James
River Flotilla, 1862; South Atlantic, 1865-
1885; European, 1865-1885; Atlantic, 1865-
1866; Gulf, 1865-1867; Asiatic, 1865-1885;
Special, 1865-1866; North Atlantic, 1866-
1885; Training, 1882-1885 DNA
N: DNA 300 reels [M-89]   4434
P: PPiU 271 reels, 1841-1846

U.S. VETERANS ADMINISTRATION
Index to pension claims based on disabilities
incurred in service in the "Old Wars," 1815-
1861; claims filed, 1815-1926 DNA
N: DNA 8 reels 16 mm.   4435

U.S. VETERANS ADMINISTRATION
Index to pension claims, Indian Wars, 1817-
1898; claims filed, 1892-1926 DNA
N: DNA 21 reels 16 mm.   4436

U.S. WAR DEPT.
Census of Creek Indians, 1832 DNA
N: DNA 1 reel [T-275]   4437

U.S. WAR DEPT.
Confidential and unofficial letters sent by the
Secretary of War, 1814-1847 DNA
N: DNA 2 reels [M-7]   4438
P: MoIT

U.S. WAR DEPT.
Reports to Congress, 1830-1870 DNA
N: DNA 1 reel [T-13]   4439

Mexican War

KEARNY, STEPHEN WATTS, 1794-1848
Papers, 1810-1848 MoSHi
N: CLU 1 reel   4440

LANE, JOSEPH
Letterbook, Mexican War " Reports and
Letters " OrHi
N: OrHi 64 frames   4441

MATTHEWS, WILLIAM
Mexican War diary, 1846-1847, 29 p. priv.
DCO: PHarH   4442

MEGINNESS, JOHN F.
Mexican War diary, 1848
N: PHarH 1 reel   4443

NAUVOO LEGION
Papers, 1846-1858 Recorder's office, Salt
Lake City
N: Universal Microfilm Co.   4444
P: UPB

TIPTON, J.W.H., private, 1st Tennessee
Mounted Volunteers, 1822-1894
Journal, July, 1846-April, 1847 priv.
N: T 1 reel   4445

U.S. ADJUTANT-GENERAL'S OFFICE
Orders of General Zachary Taylor to the Army
of Occupation in the Mexican War, 1845-1847
DNA
N: DNA 3 reels [M-29]   4446
P: MoIT

U.S. ADJUTANT-GENERAL'S OFFICE
Records of the 10th Military Department,
1846-1851 DNA
N: DNA 7 reels [M-210]   4447

U.S. GENERAL ACCOUNTING OFFICE
Selected records re: Fremont Expeditions and

the California Battalion, 1842-1854; claims,
1846-1891   DNA
N: DNA 3 reels [T-135]   4448

U.S. VETERANS ADMINISTRATION
Index to pension claims - Mexican War:
claims filed, 1887-1926   DNA
N: DNA 13 reels 16 mm.   4449

WILEY, BENJAMIN L.
Mexican War diary, July-Dec., 1847   ICarbS
N: ICarbS 1 reel   4450
P: I

Civil War - Bibliography

BAKER, Brig. Gen. LAFAYETTE C.; and
TURNER, Maj. LEVI C., Judge Advocate
Index to files [of the above] relating to investi-
gations of fraud and subversive activity during
the Civil War, 1862-1865   DNA
N: DNA 1 reel   4451

BRADY, MATHEW B., 1823-1896
Register of persons for whom photographs
were made, Jan., 1863-Dec., 1865, 2 v.   NN
N: NN 1 reel   4452

U.S. WAR DEPT.
List of photographs and photographic negatives
relating to the War for the Union, 1861-1865
(War Dept. Subject Catalogue No. 5, 1897)
DNA
N: DNA 1 reel [T-251]   4453

Civil War - Government Records

ARKANSAS. CONFEDERATE PENSION BOARD
Record of Confederate Veterans and Widows
Ibid.
N: ArHi   4454
P: ArHi

CONFEDERATE STATES OF AMERICA. ARMY
Office of the Adjutant and Inspector General's
Office: Records, Part of Chap. I.A., 1861-
1865   DNA
N: DNA 77 reels   4455

CONFEDERATE STATES OF AMERICA. ARMY
Quartermasters' Department: Letters and
telegrams sent, 1861-1865   DNA
N: DNA 9 reels [T-131]   4456

CONFEDERATE STATES OF AMERICA. ARMY
South Carolina service records, n.d.   DNA
DCO: Sc-Ar 18000 items   4457

CONFEDERATE STATES OF AMERICA. ARMY
OF TENNESSEE
Register of surgeons   priv.
N: DLC 1 reel   4458

CONFEDERATE STATES OF AMERICA. DEPT.
OF JUSTICE
Opinions of the Attorney-General, 1861-1865,
1 v.   NN
N: NcU 1 reel   4459

CONFEDERATE STATES OF AMERICA.
ORDNANCE WORKS, Tyler, Texas
Letters sent by Lt. Col. G.H. Hill,
1864-1865   DNA-CR
N: DNA 1 reel [M-119]   4460

EARLY Co., Ga.
Confederate pensions, 1861-1865   C.H.
Blakeley
N: G-Ar 1 reel   4461

GEORGIA. ADJUTANT GENERAL
Georgia Confederate military records   Ibid.
N: G-Ar 27 reels   4462

MARSHALL Co., Tenn.
Muster roll of volunteers in Confederate ser-
vice   C.H. Lewisburg
N: T 1 reel   4463

U.S. ARMY. 7TH CORPS
Orders and circulars, 1863-1865, 37 items
priv.
N: ArHi   4464
P: ArHi ArU

U.S. ARMY. SIGNAL CORPS
Mathew Brady collection of Civil War photo-
graphs, 1861-1865   DNA
N: DNA 4 reels [T-252]   4465

U.S. GENERAL ACCOUNTING OFFICE
Civil War direct assessment lists: Tennessee,
1865-1866   DNA
N: DNA 6 reels [T-227]   4466

U.S. VETERANS ADMINISTRATION
Index to pension claims - Civil, Spanish-
American, and certain Indian Wars, and
in the Regular Establishment: claims
filed, 1861-1934   DNA
N: DNA 691 reels 16 mm.   4467

U.S. WAR DEPT.
Correspondence of General W.T. Sherman,
1863-1883   DNA
N: CoU   4468

VIRGINIA
Confederate service records of Virginia
soldiers, 1861-1865   Vi
N: Vi 42 reels   4469
P: USIGS

Civil War - Personal Papers

ARCHER, H.S., Confederate soldier
Civil War diary, 1862-1864   TNV
N: ICU 1 reel   4470
P: CStbS

AVERY, PHINEAS ORLANDO, 1838-1916,
Fourth Illinois Cavalry
Letters, 1861-1864   priv.
N: NbHi 1 reel   4471

AYERS, ALEXANDER MILLER, 1827-1902,
125th Illinois
Civil War letters to his wife, 1862-1865,
181 items   priv.
N: GEU 1 reel*   4472

BARNETT, JAMES W.
Letters of the C.S.A., 1862, 42 p.   priv.
N: A-Ar   4473

BASS, W.J., b. 1845
Civil War diary, 1861-1865, 65 p.   CtY
N: NNC 1 reel*   4474
P: MH NjP

BLOOMFIELD, ALPHEUS S.
Civil War letters and papers, re: Battery A,
1st Ohio Volunteer Light Infantry, Sept., 1864-
July, 1865   priv.
N: ? 1 reel   4475
P: DLC

BROTHERTON FAMILY
Civil War letters, scrapbook of William H.
Brotherton's political career, 1862-1908,
46 items   priv.
N: GEU 1 reel   4476

BROWN, A. FRANK, clerk, Confederate
government in Kentucky
Scrapbook of writings, 1861   priv.
N: KyU 10 feet   4477

BROWN, CAMPBELL
Military reminiscences, 1861-1865, 201 p.   T
N: T   4478
DCO: NcU

BROWN, WILSON W.
Manuscript, narrative of escape from Confeder-
ates after the great locomotive chase in Georgia, 1862, 232 p.   priv.
N: OT   4479

CAMPBELL, GIVEN
Journal, last march of Jefferson Davis,
Apr. 18-May 10, 1865   priv.
N: ? 1 reel   4480
P: DLC

CAMPBELL, WILLIAM W.
Account of prison experiences in Confederacy,
1861-1864   priv.
N: WHi 1 reel   4481

CARUTHERS, W.A., Confederate soldier
Diary, 1861-1864   priv.
N: T 1 reel   4482

CHAMPION, SYDNEY S., Colonel, Mississippi
Volunteer Cavalry
Civil War correspondence with his wife   priv.
N: NcD 1 reel   4483

CHAMPLAIN, WILLIAM ERVING
Civil War letters, 1862-1864, 8 items   priv.
DCO: NPV   4484

Civil War diary (anonymous)   priv.
N: Nc-Ar 1 reel   4485

Civil War diary (anonymous), 1864-1865   priv.
N: PHarH 5 feet   4486

CLOSE, PETER, Union soldier
Diary, 1862 [in French]   priv.
N: T 1 reel   4487

COLEMAN, Mrs. ANN MARY (CRITTENDEN),
1813-1891
Civil War scrapbook, 1856-1865, 7 p.   KyU
N: KyU   4488

COON, DAVID, 1822-1864
Letters to his wife and children, 1864 (typescript)
priv.
N: DLC 1 reel   4489

COONS, CHARLES EDWARD, Confederate soldier
Letters to Eliza Jane Moore, 1863-1865   priv.
N: KyU 5 feet   4490

COX, AZELLE D.
Civil War diary   [unk.]
N: ViU   4491
P: ViU

COX, EUGENE
Civil War diary, 1861-1862, 2v.   priv.
N: ViU   4492
P: ViU

DANIELLY, FRANCIS McDADE, Company K,
14th Alabama Regiment
Civil War letters to his wife   priv.
N: A-Ar 1 reel   4493

DANTZLER, DANIEL DAVID
Diary, last months of the Civil War (typescript)
priv.
N: KyU 2 feet   4494

DAVIS, WILLIAM H., Company C, 9th Tennessee
Regiment
Letters and diaries, 1862-1865, 13 items   priv.
N: GEU 1 reel   4495

Diary of unknown Confederate soldier, 1861
priv.
N: ViU   4496
P: ViU

DURANT, GEORGE BENJAMIN
Civil War scrapbook, 1861-1865   priv.
N: KyU 10 feet   4497

ENSLOW, CHARLES CALVIN
Excerpts of letters to his wife, 1862-65   priv.
DCO: DLC 1 box   4498

FAHNESTOCK, ALLEN L., 86th Illinois Infantry
Diary, 1862-1865   priv.
N: Nc-Ar 1 reel   4499

FANCHER, J.A.P., Confederate soldier
Diary, Jan., 1864-Nov., 1865   priv.
N: T 1 reel   4500

FEAMSTER, THOMAS L., Confederate soldier
in W. Va.
Diary, 1861, 1864-1865   priv.
N: WvU 1 reel   4501

FLEMING, JOHN, 1845-1924
Civil War recollections, 1861-1864   priv.
N: PHarH 1 reel   4502
P: NHi

FORBES, STEPHEN ALFRED, 1844-1930
Material on Grierson Raid, 1903-1928, 15
items   priv.
N: IU   4503
P: I

FREY, EMIL, Captain, Union Army
Letters to family in Switzerland, 1860-1865
Baseler Staatsarchiv
N: MoSHi 1 reel*   4504

FURNAS, ROBERT WILKINSON, 1824-1905,
2nd Nebraska Volunteer Cavalry

Journal, 1862-1863 NbHi
N: NbHi 1 reel
4505

GILLIS FAMILY
Letters, chiefly while in Confederate service,
1859-1865, 16 items   priv.
N: GEU 1 reel
4506

GORDON, JOHN BROWN, 1832-1904
Amnesty oath, Sept. 15, 1865, 1 p.   DNA
DCO: GAHi
4507

GORDON, SAMUEL M., Co. H, 25th Ohio
Regiment
Diary, in West Virginia, 1861 priv.
N: GEU 1 reel
4508

GORDON, WILLIAM WASHINGTON, 1834-1912
Diary, 1864-1865 NcU
N: NcU 1 reel
4509

GRANT, CHARLES N.
Civil War letters (typescript) priv.
N: KyU 15 feet*
4510

GREENHOW, MARY (Mrs. HUGH LEE),
Confederate spy
Diary, Winchester, Va., Mar.-Sept., 1862,
May, 1863-Nov., 1865 priv.
N: DLC
PP: DLC
4511

GRIMES, Mrs. SOPHIA HARDIN
Civil War scrapbook priv.
N: KyU 10 feet
4512

GRUBB, J. G.
Journal of war time, 1865, 513 p.   priv.
N: WaU
4513

GUERRANT, EDWARD OWINGS, 1838-1916
Autograph book, 1863-1865, Confederate
prisoners, Johnson's Island priv.
N: KyU 5 feet
4514

HALSEY, EDWIN L.
Papers re: Civil War, 1862-1865, 48 items
priv.
N: NcU 1 reel
4515

HAND, GEORGE O.
Civil War diary, 1861-1864 priv.
DCO: DLC
4516

HARDEE, WILLIAM JOSEPH, 1815-1873
Letters, June-Aug., 1864, 235 p.   A-Ar
N: A-Ar
4517

HARDIN, Mrs. R.A. (HETTIE L. IRWIN)
Civil War reminiscences, n.d.   priv.
N: T 1 reel
4518

HARGIS, O.P., b. 1846
Reminiscences re: Civil War
(typescript)   priv.
N: NcU 20 frames
4519

HARMSEN, CHARLES
Two papers re: Confederate Commissary Dept.
and Bureau of Nitre and Mining, May 1, Aug.
23, 1865, 2 p.   GAHi
DCO: GAHi
4520

HARRIS, F. M.
Civil War journal, 1864; miscellaneous
college material, 183 p.   priv.
DCO: InGrD
4521

HARRIS, ISHAM G., Gov. Tenn.
Out-letter book re: Confederate Government
and Army, May, 1861 - March, 1862 TKL
N: T 1 reel
4522

HARRISON, WILLIAM
Diary, Oct., 1864 - May, 1865, Company D. 39,
N. J. Volunteers priv.
N: ?
P: NHi
4523

HARWOOD, J.C., Union soldier
Diary, 1863-1864 priv.
N: T 1 reel
4524

HASKELL, Lt. Col. CHARLES T., Confederate
soldier
Reminiscences, 69 p. (typescript) priv.
N: WHi
4525

HATHAWAY, LELAND, b. 1834, Capt.
Confederate Army

Civil War recollections, 1864-1865, 9 v.   priv.
N: NcU 665 frames
4526

HATHAWAY, LELAND, b. 1834, Capt.
Confederate Army
Papers re: Civil War KyU
N: KyU 75 feet
4527

HATTON, JOHN WILLIAM LORD
Memoir of the First Maryland Battery,
1861-1865 priv.
N: DLC 1 reel
4528

HAWSE, Capt. JASPER, 14th Va. Infantry
Diary, 1861-1863 (typescript) priv.
N: ViU
4529

HEG, HANS CHRISTIAN, 1829-1863, Col., 15th
Wisconsin Infantry
Civil War letters, 1862-1863 WHi
N: MnHi 1 reel
4530

HINES, THOMAS HENRY, 1838-1898, Confederate
soldier
Papers, 1809-1889 priv.
N: KyU 1 reel
4531

HODGES, JAMES, Union soldier
Papers, 1863-1865 priv.
N: DLC 1 reel
P: DLC
4532

HOSPES, ADOLPHUS CONRAD, 1st Minnesota
Regiment
Letters, 1861-1863 priv.
N: WHi 1 reel
4533

HULSE, DANIEL M.
Civil War letters, 1861-1864 priv.
N: NNC 1 reel
4534

JOBE, T. JEFFERSON, Confederate soldier
Civil War diary, May 26 - Aug. 6, 1861 priv.
N: ArHi
P: ArHi
4535

KEENE, HENRY S., 6th Wisconsin Infantry
Diary, 1861-1864 (typescript) priv.
N: NNC
4536

LONDON, HENRY A.
Civil War diary priv.
N: Nc-Ar 1 reel
4537

LONGSTREET, JAMES, 1821-1904
In-letters re: Gettysburg, 16 items priv.
N: NcD
4538

McCORMICK, R. LAIRD
Civil War diary, 1863-1864 priv.
N: PHarH 20 feet
4539

MACKEY, LEONIDAS WILLIAM, Lt. C.S.A.
Letter re: conditions of Confederate forces
before Atlanta, July 5, 1864, 2 p.   priv.
DCO: GAHi
4540

MARCY, JOHN S., defendant
Court martial, Morris Island, 1864, 26 p.
DAL
N: NhD
4541

MATTHEWS, STANLEY, 1824-1889
Civil War letters, 1861-1865, 95 items OCHP
N: OFH 1 reel
P: OCHP
4542

MAURY FAMILY
Diary re: Confederate history, 1861-1865 priv.
N: G-Ar
4543

MEREDITH, WILLIAM TUCKEY, b. 1839
Letters to Mary Watson, Nov., 1863-Dec., 1864,
from U.S.S. Hartford priv.
N: NjP 1 reel
4544

MERRILEES, JOHN
Civil War diaries, 1862-1865, 3 v.   ICHi
N: ICHi 3 reels
4545

MILLIGAN, SAMUEL, Unionist of East Tennessee
Memoir, 1863 - ca. 1869 priv.
N: T 1 reel
4546

MONTGOMERY, THOMAS, 1841-1907
Civil War letters, 1862-1867 priv.
N: MnHi 1 reel
4547

MORRISON, DELIA
Civil War diary, 1862-1865 (typescript) priv.
N: KyU 10 feet
4548

NAPOLEON, LUCIAN
Civil War diary [unk.]
N: ViU
P: ViU
4549

NORTON, JOHN ALSTON, b. 1845
Manuscript books re: Civil War, 2 v.   priv.
N: NcU 1 reel
4550

O'BRYAN, JOSEPH BRANCH, Company B, 1st
Tennessee Infantry
Letters to his sisters, 1861-1865, 34 items
priv.
N: T 1 reel
4551

OLDHAM, KIE
Selected Documents re: Confederacy, 1861-
1864 ArHi
N: ArHi 1 reel
P: ArHi ArU
4552

PEARCE, Brig. Gen. NICHOLAS B., C.S.A.
Reminiscences, 1861 ArHi
N: ArHi 1 reel
P: ArHi ArU
4553

PELHAM, JOHN, Confederate soldier
Letters, 26 p.   priv.
N: A-Ar
4554

PERRY FAMILY
Papers re: Civil War priv.
N: KyU 5 feet
4555

POATES, Mrs. LEMUEL
Civil War diary, 1863-1865 priv.
N: NIC 1 reel
4556

RAY, Lt. LAVENDER R., 1842-1916, C.S.A.
cavalry
Papers, 1861-?, 1 v.   G-Ar
N: GEU 1 reel
4557

REYNOLDS, WILLIAM C.
Confederate Army diaries and records, 1860-
1861 KyU
N: KyU 5 feet
4558

RICHMANN, F.W.
Recommendation from Governor Medill of
Ohio, Apr. 16, 1856; orders from General
Grant, July 1, 1862 MoSC priv.
DCO: MoSC 3 p.
4559

SANDERSON, JOHN P.
Reports on the Order of American Knights,
1864 DNA
N: MoSHi 1 reel
4560

SAVAGE, THOMAS A.
Civil War diary priv.
N: Nc-Ar 1 reel
4561

SHENANDOAH (Confederate Privateer)
Log, 1864-1865, 2 v.   Nc-Ar
N: DLC NcU 1 reel
4562

SHERMAN, AMOS B.
Civil War journal, 1861-1863 priv.
N: WaU 1 reel
4563

SILVIS, WILLIAM L., 8th Minnesota Infantry
Diary, 1864 priv.
N: MnHi 1 reel
4564

SPAULDING, OLIVER L.
Civil War diaries, 1862-1865, 100 p.   priv.
DCO: DLC
4565

STALEY, JOSIAH
Civil War letters, 1862-1864 priv.
N: OHi
P: OHi
4566

STEVENS, HAZARD, 1842-1918
Civil War letters and papers WaU
N: ? 2 reels
P: DLC
4567

STONE, THOMAS R., Confederate soldier
Civil War diary, May 5, 1861-July, 1862 priv.
N: ArHi
P: ArHi
4568

STONE, WILLIAM JOHNSON, 1841-1923,
Confederate soldier
Papers, 1864-1923 priv.
N: KyU 25 feet
4569

STOUT, SAMUEL HOLLINGSWORTH, 1822-1903,
Confederate surgeon

Papers, 1847-1903 priv.
N: GEU 4 reels   4570

STOUT, SAMUEL HOLLINGSWORTH, 1822-1903,
Confederate surgeon
Papers, 1847-1911, 820 items priv.
N: NcD 5 reels   4571

STOUT, SAMUEL HOLLINGSWORTH, 1822-1903,
Confederate surgeon
Papers, 1847-1903, with other reports of
Confederate medical officers NcD
N: NcD 3 reels   4572

STRICKLER, G.B., and JONES, J.H.B.
Diary and notebook of Co. I, 4th Virginia
Infantry, 1862-1864, 134 p. priv.
N: ?   4573
P: ViU

STUART, GEORGE HAY
Papers re: Christian and Sanitary
Commissions, 1860-1866 DLC
N: NNC 1 reel   4574

TALLMAN, WILLIAM HENRY HARRISON,
1840-1893
Civil War reminiscences, 1861-1865 priv.
N: KyU 30 feet*   4575

TAYLOR FAMILY, of Virginia
Letters re: 10th Virginia Cavalry, 1864 priv.
N: ?   4576
P: ViU   230 frames

THIOT, CHARLES HENRY, 1822-1865
Papers, Civil War letters, 1861-1865, 21 items
priv.
N: GEU 1 reel   4577

TILGHMAN, TENCH F.
Diary re: last days of Confederacy, flight of
Jefferson Davis, Jan. 1 - June 30, Sept. 25, 26,
1865 priv.
N: MdAA NcU 1 reel   4578

TUTTLE, JOHN W.
Civil War journal, 1860-1867 KyU
N: KyU   4579
P: KyU

TYLER, GEORGE H.
Diary during siege of Vicksburg, Mar. - Nov.,
1863 priv.
N: NjP 1 reel   4580

TYRREL, TRUMAN, 1842-1906, 29th Wisconsin
Infantry
Civil War diary, 1864 priv.
N: MnHi 1 reel   4581

VAN METER, MARY E.
Civil War diary, 1862-1863 (transcript) priv.
N: KyU 3 feet   4582

VAN RENSSELAER, SARAH K. (PENDLETON)
Civil War diary, 1862-1869 priv.
N: NHi 1 reel   4583

VORDELL, Major WILLIAM GILDERSLEEVE,
Confederate Army
Letters to his wife, Jane Dickson (Bell), 1862-
1863, 51 items priv.
N: T 1 reel   4584

WADDELL, Col. JAMES DANIEL, 1832-1881,
20th Georgia Regiment
Letters to his wife, 1862-1864, 14 items priv.
N: GEU 1 reel   4585

WATKINS FAMILY
Papers, including Civil War letters of Nathan-
iel Watkins, 1852-1889 ViW
N: NjP 1 reel   4586

WATSON, ROBERT
Civil War diary, 1863-1865 priv.
N: NIC 1 reel   4587

WATTERS, RICHARD P., d. 1862, Rome Light
Guards, 8th Georgia Regiment
Letters, 1861-1862, 22 items priv.
N: GEU 1 reel   4588

WEAVER, HENRY CLAY
Letters to Cornelia Wiley, 1861-1865 priv.
N: DLC 1 reel   4589

WEBB, HOWELL
Autograph book, 1863-1864, as Johnson's
Island prisoner priv.
N: NcU 1 reel   4590

WHITE, GEORGE, Confederate surgeon
Letters to his wife, 1846-1864 (typescript) priv.
N: ?   4591
P: KyU

WHITE, J. C., Union soldier
Letters to J. S. Woods, 1861-1863 KyU
N: KyU 2 feet   4592

WILSON, JAMES HARRISON, 1837-1925
Journals, 1861-1865 DeHi
N: De 555 frames   4593

YOUNG, JOHN, Private, 4th Minnesota
Infantry
Civil War papers, 1862-1864 priv.
N: MnHi 1 reel   4594

Civil War - Collections

BROOKS, WILLIAM E., collector
Civil War diaries (transcript): Gen. Charles
H. Howard, Mar., 1862-Sept., 1864; Marcus B.
DeWitt, Chaplain 8th Tenn., Mar., 1863-May,
1863; Alexander R. Boteler, Aide to J.E.B.
Stuart, May 2-5, 1864 priv.
N: DLC 1 reel   4595

COVER, RAY L., collector
Miscellaneous papers, 1759-1865, including
material on the care of wounded and prisoners
after the Battle of Gettysburg priv.
N: PHarH 4 feet   4596

DUKE UNIVERSITY
Correspondence of Johnson's Island prisoners
NcD
N: OFH 44 frames   4597

JUSTICE, ALEXANDER, collector
Fort Macon material, 1861, 1 v. NcU
N: NcU 80 frames   4598

NORTH CAROLINA. UNIVERSITY
Johnson's Island papers, 1864-1865 NcU
N: OFH 128 frames   4599

OHIO HISTORICAL SOCIETY. MUSEUM
Records of Confederate soldiers who died at
Camp Chase, n.d. OHi
N: GAHi 1 reel   4600

PALMER, WILLIAM P., collector
Material re: Civil War, 1861-1865, 1868,
31 items OClWHi
N: priv. 1 reel   4601
P: GHi NcU

U.S. WAR DEPT.
Compiled service records of Confederate soldiers serving in organizations raised directly
by the Confederate government DNA
N: DNA 5 reels 16 mm. [M-258]   4602

U.S. WAR DEPT.
Consolidated index to compiled service records
of Confederate soldiers DNA
N: DNA 535 reels 16 mm. [M-253]   4603

U.S. WAR DEPT. COLLECTION OF
CONFEDERATE RECORDS
Records relating to Confederate Naval and
Marine personnel DNA
N: DNA 7 reels 16 mm. [M-260]   4604

Civil War - Organizations

ALABAMA INFANTRY. 19th REGIMENT
["THE CHEROKEES"]
Muster roll priv.
N: A-Ar   4605

ALABAMA INFANTRY. 26th REGIMENT
History of Co. H, 101 p. priv.
N: A-Ar 1 reel   4606

ALABAMA INFANTRY. 39th REGIMENT
Muster Roll of Co. E priv.
N: A-Ar 1 reel   4607

ALABAMA INFANTRY. 39th REGIMENT
Roster, Co. F, "Capt. A.H. Flewelin Co.,"
1862 A-Ar
N: A-Ar   4608

ARKANSAS INFANTRY. 3rd REGIMENT
Muster rolls, 1861-1864 DLC
N: ArHi 50 feet   4609

Federal Army officers in unidentified Confederate
prison: Autograph book priv.
N: GEU 1 reel   4610

UNITED CONFEDERATE VETERANS. VIRGINIA
DIVISION. CAMP 14
Minutes, 1910-1930, 1 v. priv.
N: ViU   4611
P: ViU

UNITED STATES SANITARY COMMISSION
Papers, 1851-1871 NN
N: NNC 15 reels   4612

From 1861 to 1917

BROWN, E. B.
Journal re: expedition against Sitting Bull,
1876-1877, 42 p. [unk.]
DCO: DLC   4613

CRESSON, CHARLES CLEMENT, Lt. 1st U.S.
Cavalry
Diary, punitive expedition against Indians in
Idaho, June 4-Aug. 10, 1878 priv.
DCO: NN 23 ll.   4614

CROOK, GEORGE, 1829-1890
Correspondence, 1864-1908, 632 items OFH
N: OrU   4615

DRAKE, Col. SAMUEL ADAMS, 1833-1905
Recollections of the Old Army in Kansas, 34 p.
CtY
N: KU   4616

GRIERSON, BENJAMIN HENRY, 1826-1911
Letters, military papers, 1868-1872 priv.
N: OkHi 3 reels   4617

HARDMAN, Lt. P.U., 7th U.S. Cavalry
Diary re: Indian campaigns, battle of Washita,
1868 priv.
N: OkU   4618

RENO, MARCUS ALBERT, 1835-1889, defendant
Proceedings of court of inquiry re: Little Big
Horn, 1879 (typescript and clippings) DNA
N: ICU 1 reel   4619

SHERIDAN, PHILIP HENRY, 1831-1888
Sheridan-Sherman correspondence, 1868-1882,
2 v. DLC
N: CSdS 1 reel   4620

U.S. ADJUTANT-GENERAL'S OFFICE
Affairs on the Rio Grande and the Texas Fron-
tier, 1875-1881 (Consolidated file #1653) DNA
N: DNA 6 reels [T-32]   4621
P: MiEM

U.S. ADJUTANT-GENERAL'S OFFICE
Correction Division reports, 1912-1939
N: DNA-W 61 reels   4622

U.S. ADJUTANT-GENERAL'S OFFICE
Papers relating to Marcus A. Reno, Captain,
U.S. Army, 1857-1898 DNA
N: DNA 1 reel   4623

U.S. ADJUTANT-GENERAL'S OFFICE
Post returns, Camp Randall, Wis., 1863-1866
DNA
N: WHi 1 reel   4624

U.S. ARMY. MILITARY COMMISSION
Proceedings re: Sioux War, 1862 DNA
Judge Advocate General
DCO: MnHi 3 boxes   4625

U.S. NAVY DEPT. BUREAU OF YARDS AND
DOCKS
Index to plans, 1876-1941 DNA
N: DNA 22 reels 16 mm.   4626

U.S. NAVY DEPT. BUREAU OF
YARDS AND DOCKS
Plans of plants, machinery and structures,
1876-1941 DNA
N: DNA 497 reels   4627

Mexican Border

U.S. ADJUTANT-GENERAL'S OFFICE
Final report re: Mexican Border, 1916-1917
DNA
N: DNA 1 reel   4628
P: CLO

World War I

ALLIED AND ASSOCIATED POWERS (1914-1920).
SUPREME WAR COUNCIL
Records, 1918-1919 (typescript)   DNA
N: CSt-H 2 reels   4629

ARPIN, EDMUND P.
World War I diary   priv.
N: WHi   4630

HENDERSON, Capt. THOMAS P., of Williamson
Co., Tenn.
Diary, July, 1917 - March, 1919   priv.
N: T 1 reel   4631

LYNCH, JOHN B., 406th Telegraph Bureau, A.E.F.
Letters, 1917-1919   priv.
N: DLC 1 reel   4632

QUICK, ERNEST E., compiler
Dansville's part in the World War   priv.
N: N 3 reels
P: N 2 reels   4633

U.S. GENERAL STAFF
Calendar of significant World War I documents
selected by the Historical Branch, Army War
College, 1917-1919   DNA
N: DNA 36 reels   4634

U.S. NAVY DEPT. BUREAU OF YARDS AND
DOCKS
Correspondence re: Navy yards and stations,
1916-1925   DNA
N: DNA 379 reels 16 mm.   4635

From 1919 to 1941

U.S. ADJUTANT-GENERAL'S OFFICE
Indexes to the A.G.O. central files, 1917-
1939   DNA
N: DNA 1,950 reels 16 mm.   4636

U.S. ARMY AIR FORCES. OFFICE OF FLYING
SAFETY
Aircraft Accident Reports (AF Form 14) and
Airplane Flight Reports (WD Air Corps form
No. 1); Aircraft Accident Classification Com-
mittee Proceedings; Reports of Board of Offi-
cers convened to investigate accidents, Jan.,
1918 - Dec., 1940
N: DNA-W 38 reels   4637

U.S. NAVY DEPT.
Letters received by the Office of Inventions,
offering suggestions on submarine safety,
1927-1936   DNA
N: DNA 10 reels 16 mm.   4638

U.S. NAVY DEPT. BUREAU OF YARDS AND
DOCKS
Contracts correspondence, 1925-1942   DNA
N: DNA 138 reels 16 mm.   4639

U.S. NAVY DEPT. BUREAU OF YARDS AND
DOCKS
General correspondence, 1925-1942   DNA
N: DNA 320 reels 16 mm.   4640

World War II

AGUIRRE, JOSÉ ANTONIO DE
Diary re: residence in Berlin and escape to
Sweden and South America, 1941-1945   priv.
N: DLC 2 reels*   4641

ALLIED FORCES. ALLIED FORCE
HEADQUARTERS
General records, 1942-1947
N: DNA-W 1648 reels   4642

ALLIED FORCES. SUPREME HEADQUARTERS
Records, 1942-1947   DNA-W
N: DNA-W 1970 reels   4643

ALLIED MILITARY GOVERNMENT
Records (Italy): Region I (Sicily); Region III,
Nov., 1943 - Jan., 1947
N: DNA-W 762 reels   4644

BRAEUTIGAM, OTTO
Diary while in German Foreign Affairs Section
of Dr. A. Rosenberg's special service, 1941-
1943   priv.
N: DLC 1 reel*
P: DLC   4645

COLORADO COLLEGE. COBURN LIBRARY
World War II scrap books   CoCC
N: CoHi 6 reels   4646

INTERNATIONAL MILITARY TRIBUNAL FOR THE
FAR EAST
Transcript of proceedings, Jan. 7 and Oct. 1,
1947   Ibid.
N: DLC 1 reel   4647

KENTUCKY. UNIVERSITY
Records seized from Germans, World War II
Ibid.
N: KyU 4 reels   4648

McCRIGHT, EWELL R.
Urkunden Stalag Luft 3 für die ältesten offiziere
DLC
N: DLC 1 reel   4649

STILWELL, JOSEPH WARREN, 1883-1946
"Black and white books," Dec. 7, 1941- Apr.
18, 1943; diary, Dec. 7, 1941-Dec. 5, 1944
CSt-H
N: CSt-H 1 reel*   4650

U.S. ADJUTANT-GENERAL'S OFFICE
Cross reference sheets to classified
correspondence and other papers, 1940-1947
N: DNA-W 1539 reels   4651

U.S. ADJUTANT-GENERAL'S OFFICE
Cross reference sheets to unclassified
records, 1940-1945
N: DNA-W 1525 reels   4652

U.S. ADJUTANT-GENERAL'S OFFICE
Joint Army-Navy pre-induction test
report sheets, April, 1943-
N: DNA-W 31 reels   4653

U.S. ARMY. AMERICAN FORCES IN GERMANY,
1918-1923
American Military Government of Occupied
Germany, 1918-1920. Report of the officer in
charge of civil affairs, Third Army, and
American Forces in Germany, 1920, v. 1
(typescript)
N: CSt-H 1 reel   4654

U.S. ARMY. SIXTH AND TWELFTH ARMY
GROUPS
Administrative files, 1943-1945
N: DNA-W 28 reels   4655

U.S. ARMY AIR FORCES
Incoming and outgoing messages of the
Air Adjutant General (theater or geographic
files), Apr., 1941-Dec., 1944
N: DNA-W 425 reels   4656

U.S. COUNCIL OF NATIONAL DEFENSE.
ADVISORY COMMISSION
Numbered document file of the Advisory
Commission to the Council of National Defense,
1940-1941   DNA
N: DNA 2 reels [M-187]   4657

U.S. COUNCIL OF NATIONAL DEFENSE.
ADVISORY COMMISSION
Press releases of the Advisory Commission to
the Council of National Defense, June 3, 1940-
Jan. 15, 1941   DNA
N: DNA 1 reel [M-185]   4658

U.S. COUNCIL OF NATIONAL DEFENSE.
ADVISORY COMMISSION
Progress reports of the Advisory Commission
to the Council of National Defense, July 24,
1940 - May 28, 1941   DNA
N: DNA 1 reel [M-186]   4659

U.S. DEPT. OF JUSTICE. ANTITRUST DIVISION
Collection of 10 confidential reports submitted
to B.E.W., OEWA (Enemy branch)   Ibid.
N: DLC 1 reel   4660

U.S. LIBRARY OF CONGRESS
Leaflets and newspapers containing Japanese
propaganda issued in the Philippines and a file
of guerrilla propaganda from the same area,
prior to Aug., 1945
N: DLC 1 reel   4661

U.S. NAVY DEPT. BUREAU OF NAVAL
PERSONNEL
Muster rolls of ships, aircraft squadrons,
and shore activities, 1939-1954   DNA
N: DNA 20,395 reels 16 mm.   4662

U.S. NAVY DEPT. BUREAU OF YARDS AND
DOCKS
Specifications correspondence, 1925-1942
DNA
N: DNA 479 reels 16 mm.   4663

U.S. OFFICE OF PRODUCTION MANAGEMENT.
COUNCIL
Numbered document file of the Council of the
Office of Production Management, Dec. 21,
1940-Jan. 15, 1942   DNA
N: DNA 1 reel [M-195]   4664

U.S. OFFICE OF STRATEGIC SERVICES
Captured German documents, various dates,
1943-1944 [unk.]
N: DLC 1 reel   4665

U.S. OFFICE OF STRATEGIC SERVICES
Microfilm secret file   Ibid.
N: DLC 44 reels   4666

U.S. OFFICE OF STRATEGIC SERVICES.
RESEARCH AND ANALYSIS BRANCH
R & A and OIR reports, 1944   Dept. of State
Reference Division
N: FU 7 reels   4667

U.S. OFFICE OF STRATEGIC SERVICES.
RESEARCH AND ANALYSIS BRANCH
Reports 28, 44, 109, 204, 207, 215 B, 354,
624, 647, 650, 665, 659   DLC
N: DLC
P: DLC incomplete   4668

U.S. OFFICE OF STRATEGIC SERVICES.
RESEARCH AND ANALYSIS BRANCH
Reports 583, 665 A, 764, 1007.1, 3315, 3327,
3499, 4501   DS
N: DLC
P: DLC   4669

U.S. SUPPLY PRIORITIES AND ALLOCATIONS
BOARD
Numbered document file of the Supply
Priorities and Allocations Board, Sept. 2,
1941-Jan. 15, 1942   DNA
N: DNA 1 reel [M-196]   4670

U.S. WAR DEPT.
Background material used in compilation
of the Summary Technical Reports compiled
by the Division of War Research, Columbia
University v. p.
N: DNA-W 486 reels   4671

U.S. WAR DEPT. SPECIAL SERVICE DIVISION
AND MORALE SERVICES DIVISION
Questionnaires returned by military personnel,
1941-1945 v. p.
N: DNA-W 44 reels   4672

U.S. WAR RELOCATION AUTHORITY
Relocation center final accountability rosters,
1944-1946   DNA
N: DNA 10 reels   4673

U.S. WARTIME CIVIL CONTROL ADMINIS-
TRATION
Evacuees' social data registration forms, 1942
DNA
N: DNA 29 reels 16 mm.   4674

U.S. WARTIME CIVIL CONTROL ADMINIS-
TRATION
Master index of evacuees, 1942-1943   DNA
N: DNA 26 reels 16 mm.   4675

U.S. WARTIME CIVIL CONTROL ADMINIS-
TRATION
Vital statistics, change of residence cards,
summary tabulations and lists of evacuees,
and evacuees' movement lists   DNA
N: DNA 5 reels 16 mm.   4676

Religion

AMERICAN BOARD OF COMMISSIONERS FOR
FOREIGN MISSIONS
Index to archives   MH
N: ?   P: WHi   4677

AMERICAN HOME MISSIONARY SOCIETY
Correspondence, 1822-1893 ICU
N: CaOTV 2 reels   4678

AMERICAN HOME MISSIONARY SOCIETY
Correspondence, 1849-1893 ICT
N: MnHi 24 reels   4679

ASBURY, FRANCIS, Bp., 1745-1816
Letters, 100 items   Emory University Theol.
Library
N: GEU-T 3/4 reel   4680
P: NcLjHi

ASBURY, FRANCIS, Bp., 1745-1816
Letters, 1768-1816 NjMD IEG   Baltimore
Methodist Hist. Society
N: NjMD 1 reel   4681
P: NNUT

BACKUS, ISAAC, 1724-1806
Letters and miscellaneous papers MNtCA
N: MNtCA 2 reels   4682
P: NcD NNUT

BOEHM, HENRY
Journals, 1800-1830 NjMD
N: NjMD 1 reel   4683
P: NcD NcLjHi

CARROLL, JOHN, Abp., 1735-1815
Letters relating to Catholic doctrine, 1785 priv.
DCO: DLC 1 folder   4684

CHURCH OF JESUS CHRIST OF LATTER-DAY
SAINTS
Record of members and annual genealogical
reports, L.S.D. missions, U.S. and Canada,
1907-1954 USlC
N: USlGS 24 reels   4685
P: USlGS

FRIENDS, SOCIETY OF (Primitive)
Miscellaneous records and epistles
N: PSC-F 2 reels   4686
P: PSC-F

GARRETTSON, FREEBORN, 1752-1827
Autobiography, 1779; journal, 1779-1826 NjMD
N: NjMD 1 reel   4687
P: WaU

GREEN, THOMAS MARSHAL, 1837-1904
Papers re: Presbyterianism MoHi
N: KyU 2 reels   4688

HALLE, Germany. MISSIONSBIBLIOTHEK
DES WAISENHAUSES
Muhlenberg diaries, 1742, 1748, 1752, 1753,
1759-1760, 1779, 1782 Ibid.
N: DLC 2 reels   4689
P: DLC

HALLE, Germany. MISSIONSBIBLIOTHEK
DES WAISENHAUSES
Saltzburger emigrants to Georgia, records,
1733-1748; reports of Virginia Parish, 1736-
1738; of three Pennsylvania parishes, 1733-
1769 ; Pennsylvania correspondence and
records, 1743-1807; Nova Scotia community,
records, 1776-1787 Ibid.
DCO: DLC 11317 sheets   4690

HASKINS, THOMAS
Journal, 1773-1777   DLC
N: ICU 1/2 reel   4691
P: NcLjHi

HAVEN, GILBERT, Bishop of M. E. Church
(North), 1821-1880
Letters from Mexico and Atlanta, 1873-1875,
20 items   NIC
N: GEU 1 reel   4692

HERRNHUT, Germany. ARCHIV DER BRÜDER-
UNITÄT
Records of Georgia, Pennsylvania, and
New York, including material on David and
Anna Nitschman, Spangenberg, and Conrad
Wieser, 1733-1895; Labrador records,
1750-1908 Ibid.
DCO: DLC 15453 sheets   4693

JESUITS
Auszüge aus Briefen von Jesuiten in America,
1611-1685; Briefen der Jesuiten in Amerika
über Missionsangelegenheiten, 1633-1760
Hauptstaatsarchiv, Munich
N: DLC 4 reels   4694
P: DLC

METTEN, Germany (Benedictine Abbey).
ARCHIVES
American Benedictine materials Ibid.
N: ?   4695
P: MnCS 32 mm.

PILMORE, JOSEPH, 1739-1825
Journal, 1769-1774 Methodist Episcopal
Church. Philadelphia Annual Conference;
(typescript)   ICU
N: ICU   of typescript   4696

PRESBYTERIAN CHURCH. BOARD OF FOREIGN
MISSIONS
In-letters from missionaries: Africa, 1837-
1901; India, 1833-1899; Japan, 1859-1899;
Latin America, 1854-1899; Persia (Iran), 1870-
1900; Syria, 1870-1900; Korea, 1884-1900;
Thailand, 1840-1900; China, 1837-1900;
miscellaneous, 1833-1904 [dest.]
N: PPPrHi 219 reels   4697
P: NNPr

PRESBYTERIAN HISTORICAL SOCIETY,
Philadelphia
American Indian correspondence of
Presbyterian missionaries, 1841-1856
PPPrHi
N: OkTU 15 reels   4698

SOCIETY FOR THE PROPAGATION OF THE
GOSPEL IN FOREIGN PARTS
Annual reports, 1719-1784 [gaps] Ibid.
N: DLC 2 reels   4699

SOCIETY FOR THE PROPAGATION OF THE
GOSPEL IN FOREIGN PARTS
Contemporary copies of letters (A. ms.), 1702-
1736; original letters (B. ms.), 1702-1799;
journals, 1783-1794; journal, appendix B,
1701-1711; minutes, 1833-1901; Standing
Committee journals, 1701-1758; Standing
Committee minutes, 1757-1782 Ibid.
N: DLC 127 reels   4700
P: DLC

SOUTHERN BAPTIST CONVENTION. HISTORICAL
COMMISSION
Basic Baptist historical materials, v. d.   v. p.
N: TNSB   4701

These materials are fully listed in the Historical
Commission's Microfilm Catalogue, Basic Baptist
Historical Materials, 1959 edition. See p. 15-25
for Church Records and Manuscripts.

U.S. LIBRARY OF CONGRESS
Mormon diaries, journals, and life
sketches DLC
N: CU-B 13 reels   4702

WHATCOAT, RICHARD, Bp., 1736-1806
Journal, 1789-1800 DLC
N: ICU 1 reel   4703
P: ICU

WILMER, RICHARD HOOKER, Bp. (Episcopal),
1816-1900
Letters of consent to consecration, 1862;
sketches of signatories: Bishops Lay, Gregg,
Routledge, Polk, John, Atkinson, and Davis
priv.
N: A-Ar 1 reel   4704

WOOLMAN, JOHN, 1720-1772
Journal, manuscript, and deeds   NjR
N: PSC-F   4705
P: PSC-F

Ships' Logs

With ship's logs are included journals, diaries,
and other records of voyages. Logs, which are
the official records of vessels, are listed under
the vessels' names. Journals, which are personal
documents, even though they are sometimes
called supplementary logs, are listed under the
names of their authors.

BARNEY, JOSEPH N.
Log and personal diary, 1839, 1849-1852, 210 p.
NcU
N: NcU 1 reel   4706

EDWARD (Bark)
Logbook, Dec. 11, 1844-Feb. 5, 1846 priv.
N: DLC 1 reel   4707

HALSEY, ELISHA L.
Journal kept on ship Angelique, 1833-1835
priv.
N: NcU 324 frames   4708

KNAPP, JOHN
Journal kept on board H. M. S. Rose to
Boston and return, 1683-1684 Egerton 2526
UKLBM
N: CtY 1 reel*   4709

SAMARIA (Schooner)
Log, Nehemiah H. Radcliff, Master priv.
N: DLC 1 reel   4710

SAVANNAH (Steamer)
Log book, Mar.-Dec., 1819 DSI
DCO: GHi   4711

Slavery

FRIENDS, SOCIETY OF (Anti-Slavery).
INDIANA YEARLY MEETING
Minutes of the women's meeting, 1843-1857
N: InRE 1/2 reel   4712
P: In

GREAT BRITAIN. FOREIGN OFFICE. F.O. 84
Slave trade correspondence, 1839-1845 (select-
ions) UKLPRO
DCO: DLC   4713

JOHN RYLANDS LIBRARY, Manchester, Eng.
Slave trade material, 1744-1787 UKMR
DCO: DLC   4714

KIEL, Germany. PREUSSISCHES STAATSARCHIV
Trade material, 1772-1805, slave trade
material, 1619-1849; candidates in theology
about to preach in America, 1844-1845 Ibid.
N: DLC 7 reels   4715
P: DLC

LÜBECK, Germany. STAATSARCHIV
Trade material, 1782-1868; slave trade
material, 1837-1868 Ibid.
N: DLC 9 reels   4716
P: DLC

U.S. DEPT. OF THE INTERIOR
Records relating to the suppression of the
African Slave Trade and Negro colonization,
1854-1872 DNA
N: DNA 10 reels [M-160]   4717
P: DeU

U.S. FEDERAL WRITERS' PROJECT
Slave narratives: interviews with former slaves
in Alabama, Arkansas, Florida, Georgia, Indiana, Kansas, Kentucky, Maryland, Mississippi, Missouri, North Carolina, Ohio, Oklahoma,
South Carolina, Tennessee, Texas, and Virginia,
1936-1938, 17 v.   DLC
N: DLC 11 reels   4718
P: DLC

U.S. LIBRARY OF CONGRESS
Newspaper articles re: slavery and Hinton
Rowan Helper's "The Impending Crisis of
the South," 1857-1909 DLC
N: NNC 1 reel   4719

U.S. NAVY DEPT.
Correspondence of the Secretary of the Navy
relating to African Colonization, 1819-1844
DNA
N: DNA 2 reels [M-205]   4720

NEW ENGLAND

Government Records

NEW ENGLAND CONFEDERATION, 1643-1702
Records, 1643-1702 Ct
N: USlGS 1 reel   4721

Church Records

FRIENDS, SOCIETY OF. NEW ENGLAND
YEARLY MEETING
Minutes, 1863-1885
N: PSC-F   4722
P: PSC-F

MAINE

Census

U.S. CENSUS. FIFTH, 1830
Population schedules, Maine DNA
N: DNA 7 reels
P: USIGS
4723

U.S. CENSUS. SIXTH, 1840
Population schedules, Maine DNA
N: DNA 7 reels
P: USIGS
4724

U.S. CENSUS. SEVENTH, 1850
Population schedules, Maine DNA
N: DNA 6 reels
P: USIGS
4725

U.S. CENSUS. EIGHTH, 1860
Population schedules, Maine DNA
N: DNA 6 reels
P: USIGS
4726

U.S. CENSUS. NINTH, 1870
Population schedules, Maine DNA
N: DNA 7 reels
P: USIGS
4727

U.S. CENSUS. TENTH, 1880
Population schedules, Maine DNA
N: DNA 18 reels
P: USIGS
4728

State Records

MAINE
Brides' index to marriages, 1895-1953 Me
N: USIGS 111 reels
4729

MAINE
Deaths of World War II veterans Me
N: USIGS 1 reel
4730

MAINE
Mortality records, 1850, 1860, 1870 Me
N: USIGS 3 reels
4731

MAINE
Vital records index, to 1922 Me
N: USIGS 149 reels
4732

MAINE. LAND OFFICE
Deeds of public lands, 1824-1861 Me
N: USIGS 4 reels
4733

MAINE. SECRETARY OF STATE
Primary election returns, 1912-1952 Ibid.
N: Me 3 reels
P: MeBa
4734

MASSACHUSETTS
Revolutionary War land grants in Maine Me
N: USIGS 13 reels
4735

MASSACHUSETTS. LAND AGENT IN MAINE
Deeds of public lands, 1780-1860 Me
N: USIGS 6 reels
4736

County Records

AROOSTOOK Co., Me.
Deeds, 1839-1866; probate records, 1839-1905;
marriages, 1839-1892 C.H. Houlton
N: USIGS 30 reels
4737

AROOSTOOK Co., Me. NORTHERN DISTRICT
Deeds, 1846-1867 C.H. Fort Kent
N: USIGS 4 reels
4738

CUMBERLAND Co., Me.
Land records, 1760-1860 C. H. Portland
N: USIGS 162 reels
4739

FRANKLIN Co., Me.
Deeds and mortgages, 1838-1894; probate
records, 1838-1891 C.H. Farmington
N: USIGS 42 reels
4740

HANCOCK Co., Me.
Deeds, 1791-1861; probate records, 1791-1899
C.H. Ellsworth
N: USIGS 78 reels
4741

KENNEBEC Co., Me.
Probate records, 1799-1886; deeds, 1799-1860;
marriages, 1828-1887; census, 1881
C.H. Augusta
N: USIGS 255 reels
4742

KNOX Co. (formerly EASTERN DISTRICT
LINCOLN Co.), Me.
Vital records, 1836-1860 C.H. Rockland
N: USIGS 20 reels
4743

LINCOLN Co., Me.
Land records, 1761-1860; probate records,
1760-1861 C.H. Wiscasset
N: USIGS 172 reels
4744

OXFORD Co., Me.
Probate records, 1805-1872; deeds, eastern
district, 1806-1862 C.H. South Paris
N: USIGS 82 reels
4745

OXFORD Co., Me. WESTERN DISTRICT
Deeds, 1799-1865 C.H. Fryeburg
N: USIGS 25 reels
4746

PENOBSCOT Co., Me.
Probate records, 1816-1893; deeds, 1814-1860;
marriage records, 1827-1888 C.H. Bangor
N: USIGS 225 reels
4747

PISCATAQUIS Co, Me.
Probate records, 1838-1884; deeds, 1838-1862;
marriage records, 1838-1889 C.H. Dover-
Foxcroft
N: USIGS 32 reels
4748

SAGADAHOC Co., Me.
Probate records, 1854-1901; deeds, 1826-1863
C.H. Bath
N: USIGS 61 reels
4749

SOMERSET Co., Me.
Probate records, 1810-1885; commissioners'
records, 1833-1844, 1848; marriage records,
1834-1890; deeds, 1809-1861 C.H. Skowhegan
N: USIGS 70 reels
4750

WALDO Co., Me.
Probate records, 1826-1899; deeds, 1791-1850;
homestead exemptions, 1850-1954; marriage
records, 1802-1887; state copies of census, 1850-
1880 C.H. Belfast
N: USIGS 127 reels
4751

WASHINGTON Co., Me. NORTHERN DISTRICT
Deeds, 1802-1839; probate records, 1826-1839
C. H. Houlton (Aroostook Co.)
N: USIGS 4 reels
4752

YORK Co., Me.
Land records, 1642-1860; probate records,
1687-1860 C.H. Alfred
N: USIGS 207 reels
4753

Town and City Records

ADDISON, Me.
Town records, 1757-1892; marriages,
1853-1892 Ibid.
N: USIGS 1 reel
4754

ALBANY, Me.
Vital records, to 1944 Ibid.
N: USIGS 1 reel
4755

ALBION, Me.
Town and vital records, to 1892 Ibid.
N: USIGS 1 reel
4756

ALEXANDER, Me.
Marriages, 1858-1926 Ibid.
N: USIGS 1 reel
4757

ALNA, Me.
Town and vital records, to 1892 Ibid.
N: USIGS 1 reel
4758

ALTON, Me.
Vital records, 1855-1940 Ibid.
N: USIGS 1 reel
4759

AMHERST, Me.
Vital records, 1783-1891 Ibid.
N: USIGS 1 reel
4760

AMITY, Me.
Town and vital records, 1862-1882, with some

marriage records Ibid.
N: USIGS 1 reel
4761

ANSON, Me.
Town and vital records, to 1890 Ibid.
N: USIGS 1 reel
4762

APPLETON, Me.
Vital records, to 1892 Ibid.
N: USIGS 1 reel
4763

ARGYLE, Me.
Vital records, to 1892 Augusta
N: USIGS 1 reel
4764

ARROWSIC, Me.
Vital records, to 1892 Ibid.
N: USIGS 1 reel
4765

ATKINSON, Me.
Vital records, 1753-1901 Ibid.
N: USIGS 1 reel
4766

AUBURN, Me.
Vital records, 1786-1954 Ibid.
N: USIGS 15 reels 16 mm.
4767

AUGUSTA, Me.
Town and vital records, to 1892 Ibid.
N: USIGS 3 reels
4768

AVON, Me.
Vital records, 1766-1850 Ibid.
N: USIGS 1 reel
4769

BAILEYVILLE, Me.
Vital records, 1861-1939 Ibid.
N: USIGS 1 reel
4770

BALDWIN, Me., see FLINTSTOWN PLANTATION,
4855, under this same heading

BANGOR, Me.
Town records, 1795-1833; vital records, 1775-
1892 Ibid.
N: USIGS 4 reels
4771

BATH, Me.
Vital records, to 1892 Ibid.
N: USIGS 1 reel
4772

BEDDINGTON, Me.
Town and vital records, 1792-1892 Ibid.
N: USIGS 1 reel
4773

BELFAST, Me.
Town records, 1768-1838; vital records, 1773-
1903 Ibid.
N: USIGS 3 reels
4774

BELGRADE, Me.
Vital records, to 1892 Ibid.
N: USIGS 1 reel
4775

BELMONT, Me.
Town and vital records, 1855-1883 Ibid.
N: USIGS 1 reel
4776

BENTON, Me.
Vital records, to 1892 Ibid.
N: USIGS 1 reel
4777

BERWICK, Me.
Town records, 1701-1776 (transcript),
215 p. NNNG
N: USIGS 1 reel
4778

BINGHAM, Me.
Vital records, to 1892 Ibid.
N: USIGS 1 reel
4779

BOOTHBAY, Me.
Vital records, to 1892 Ibid.
N: USIGS 1 reel
4780

BOWDOIN, Me.
Vital records, to 1892 Ibid.
N: USIGS 1 reel
4781

BOWDOINHAM, Me.
Vital records, to 1892 Ibid.
N: USIGS 2 reels
4782

BOWERBANK, Me.
Vital records, 1832-1932 Ibid.
N: USIGS 1 reel
4783

BRADFORD, Me.
Town records, 1819-1854; vital records, 1863-
1940 Ibid.
N: USIGS 1 reel
4784

BRADLEY, Me.
Vital records, 1805-1893; militia roll, 1880-1893 Ibid.
N: USIGS 1 reel   4785

BREMEN, Me.
Vital records, to 1892 Ibid.
N: USIGS 1 reel   4786

BREWER, Me.
Vital records, 1743-1943 Ibid.
N: USIGS 3 reels   4787

BRIGHTON, Me.
Town and vital records, to 1892 Ibid.
N: USIGS 1 reel   4788

BRISTOL, Me.
Town and vital records, to 1900 Ibid.
N: USIGS 2 reels   4789

BROOKTON, Me.
Vital records, to 1892 Augusta
N: USIGS 1 reel   4790

BROWNVILLE, Me.
Vital records, 1812-1868 Ibid.
N: USIGS 1 reel   4791

BUCKSPORT, Me.
Vital records, 1775-1907 Ibid.
N: USIGS 1 reel   4792

BURLINGTON, Me.
Vital records, 1769-1893 Ibid.
N: USIGS 1 reel   4793

BURNHAM, Me.
Vital records, 1821-1891 Ibid.
N: USIGS 1 reel   4794

CALAIS, Me.
Vital records, to 1892 Ibid.
N: USIGS 1 reel   4795

CAMBRIDGE, Me.
Vital records, to 1892 Ibid.
N: USIGS 1 reel   4796

CANAAN, Me.
Vital records, to 1910 Ibid.
N: USIGS 1 reel   4797

CARIBOU, Me.
Town and vital records, 1848-1929 Ibid.
N: USIGS 1 reel   4798

CARMEL, Me.
Vital records, 1760-1891 Ibid.
N: USIGS 1 reel   4799

CARTHAGE, Me.
Vital records, 1824-1891 Ibid.
N: USIGS 1 reel   4800

CARY PLANTATION, Me.
Vital records, 1862-1882 Ibid.
N: USIGS 1 reel   4801

CASTINE, Me.
Town records, 1856-1891; vital records, 1796-1891 Ibid.
N: USIGS 1 reel   4802

CASTLE HILL, Me.
Vital records, 1855-1892 Ibid.
N: USIGS 1 reel   4803

CENTERVILLE, Me.
Vital records, 1770-1888 Ibid.
N: USIGS 1 reel   4804

CHAPMAN, Me.
Vital records, 1868-1891 Ibid.
N: USIGS 1 reel   4805

CHARLESTON, Me.
Town records, 1811-1891; vital records, 1809-1897 Ibid.
N: USIGS 1 reel   4806

CHARLOTTE, Me.
Vital records, 1816-1892 Ibid.
N: USIGS 1 reel   4807

CHELSEA, Me.
Vital records, to 1892 Ibid.
N: USIGS 1 reel   4808

CHERRYFIELD, Me.
Vital records, 1854-1939 Ibid.
N: USIGS 1 reel   4809

CHESTER, Me.
Vital records, 1788-1943 Ibid.
N: USIGS 1 reel   4810

CHESTERVILLE, Me.
Vital records, 1788-1907 Ibid.
N: USIGS 1 reel   4811

CHINA, Me.
Town records, 1796-1832; vital records to 1892 Ibid.
N: USIGS 2 reels   4812

CLIFTON, Me.
Vital records, 1848-1892 Ibid.
N: USIGS 1 reel   4813

CLINTON, Me.
Vital records, to 1892 Ibid.
N: USIGS 1 reel   4814

COLUMBIA, Me.
Vital records, 1752-1860; militia roll, 1880-1917 Ibid.
N: USIGS 1 reel   4815

COLUMBIA FALLS, Me.
Vital records, 1863-1891 Ibid.
N: USIGS 1 reel   4816

CONCORD, Me.
Vital records, to 1892 Ibid.
N: USIGS 1 reel   4817

COOPER, Me.
Marriages, 1878-1930; militia roll, 1887-1909 Ibid.
N: USIGS 1 reel   4818

CORINNA, Me.
Vital records, 1707-1891 Ibid.
N: USIGS 1 reel   4819

CORINTH, Me.
Vital records, 1785-1895 Ibid.
N: USIGS 1 reel   4820

CORNVILLE, Me.
Vital records, to 1892 Ibid.
N: USIGS 1 reel   4821

COXHALL (now LYMAN), Me.
Proprietors' records, 1781-1790 Alfred
N: USIGS 1 reel   4822

CRAWFORD, Me.
Vital records, 1827-1900 Ibid.
N: USIGS 1 reel   4823

CRYSTAL PLANTATION, Me.
Vital records, to 1892 Augusta
N: USIGS 1 reel   4824

CUSHING, Me.
Vital records, to 1892 Ibid.
N: USIGS 1 reel   4825

CUTLER, Me.
Vital records, 1844-1896 Ibid.
N: USIGS 1 reel   4826

DAMARISCOTTA, Me.
Vital records, to 1892 Ibid.
N: USIGS 1 reel   4827

DANFORTH, Me.
Vital records, 1860-1891 Ibid.
N: USIGS 1 reel   4828

DANVILLE, Me.
Vital records, to 1887 Ibid.
N: USIGS 1 reel   4829

DEERING (now part of PORTLAND), Me.
Town records, 1811-1892 Portland
N: Microfilm Service Corp
P: MeP   4830

DENNISTOWN, Me.
Vital records, 1840-1892 Ibid.
N: USIGS 1 reel   4831

DENNYSVILLE, Me.
Vital records, 1790-1917 Ibid.
N: USIGS 1 reel   4832

DETROIT, Me.
Town and vital records, to 1892 Ibid.
N: USIGS 1 reel   4833

DEXTER, Me.
Vital records, 1761-1897 Ibid.
N: USIGS 1 reel   4834

DIXMONT, Me.
Vital records, 1800-1894 Ibid.
N: USIGS 1 reel   4835

DOVER-FOXCROFT, Me.
Vital records, 1790-1930 Ibid.
N: USIGS 1 reel   4836

DRESDEN, Me.
Early town records; vital records, to 1892 Ibid.
N: USIGS 1 reel   4837

DREW, Me.
Vital records, 1853-1928 Ibid.
N: USIGS 1 reel   4838

DURHAM, Me.
Vital records, to 1892 Ibid.
N: USIGS 1 reel   4839

EAST MACHIAS, Me.
Vital records, 1709-1900 Ibid.
N: USIGS 1 reel   4840

EAST POND PLANTATION, Me
Town and vital records, 1821-1839 Smithfield
N: USIGS 1 reel   4841

EASTPORT, Me.
Vital records, 1760-1892 Ibid.
N: USIGS 6 reels   4842

EDDINGTON, Me.
Vital records, 1802-1922 Ibid.
N: USIGS 1 reel   4843

EDGECOMB, Me.
Town and vital records, to 1892 Ibid.
N: USIGS 1 reel   4844

EDINBURG, Me.
Town and vital records, 1835-1899 Ibid.
N: USIGS 1 reel   4845

EDMUNDS, Me.
Vital records, to 1892 Augusta
N: USIGS 1 reel   4846

EMBDEN, Me.
Vital records, to 1892 Ibid.
N: USIGS 1 reel   4847

ETNA, Me.
Vital records, 1742-1910 Ibid.
N: USIGS 1 reel   4848

EUSTIS, Me.
Marriage records, 1871-1892 Madrid
N: USIGS 1 reel   4849

FAIRFIELD, Me.
Vital records, to 1867 Ibid.
N: USIGS 1 reel   4850

FALMOUTH, Me.
Proprietors' records, 1718-1826 (transcript) priv.
N: USIGS 1 reel   4851

FARMINGDALE, Me.
Vital records, to 1892 Vienna
N: USIGS 1 reel   4852

FARMINGTON, Me.
Vital records, to 1892 Ibid.
N: USIGS 1 reel   4853

FAYETTE, Me.
Vital records, to 1892 Vienna
N: USIGS 1 reel   4854

FLINTSTOWN PLANTATION (now BALDWIN), Me.
Proprietors' records book, 147 p. (transcript) priv.
N: USIGS 1 reel   4855

FORT FAIRFIELD, Me.
Vital records, 1847-1892 Ibid.
N: USIGS 1 reel   4856

FRANKLIN PLANTATION, Me.
Vital records, to 1892 Augusta
N: USIGS 1 reel   4857

FREEDOM, Me.
Town records, 1777-1844; vital records, 1777-1892 Ibid.
N: USIGS 1 reel   4858

FREEMAN, Me.
Vital records, 1837-1877 Strong
N: USIGS 1 reel 4859

FRENCHVILLE, Me.
Town and vital records, 1869-1892 Ibid.
N: USIGS 1 reel 4860

FRIENDSHIP, Me.
Town and vital records, to 1889 Ibid.
N: USIGS 1 reel 4861

GARDINER, Me.
Vital records, to 1892 Vienna
N: USIGS 1 reel 4862

GARLAND, Me.
Births, 1854-1950 Ibid.
N: USIGS 1 reel 4863

GEORGETOWN, Me.
Town and vital records, to 1940 Ibid.
N: USIGS 1 reel 4864

GLENBURN, Me.
Vital records, 1800-1888 Ibid.
N: USIGS 1 reel 4865

GOULDSBORO, Me.
Town records, 1801-1895; vital records, 1772-1898 Ibid.
N: USIGS 1 reel 4866

GREENBUSH, Me.
Vital records, 1794-1931 Ibid.
N: USIGS 1 reel 4867

GREENE, Me.
Vital records, to 1892 Ibid.
N: USIGS 1 reel 4868

GREENVILLE, Me.
Vital records, 1820-1892 Ibid.
N: USIGS 1 reel 4869

GUILFORD, Me.
Vital records, 1770-1932 Ibid.
N: USIGS 1 reel 4870

HALLOWELL, Me.
Town and vital records, 1761-1812 Augusta
N: USIGS 1 reel 4871

HAMMOND PLANTATION, Me.
Vital records, 1864-1954 Ibid.
N: USIGS 1 reel 4872

HANCOCK, Me.
Town records, 1828-1853; vital records, 1828-1891 Ibid.
N: USIGS 1 reel 4873

HARMONY, Me.
Town and vital records, to 1892 Ibid.
N: USIGS 1 reel 4874

HARPSWELL CENTER, Me.
Church and justice of the peace records, 1753-1853 (transcript) NNNG
N: USIGS 1 reel 4875

HARRINGTON, Me.
Vital records, 1851-1892 Ibid.
N: USIGS 1 reel 4876

HARTLAND, Me.
Vital records, to 1892 Ibid.
N: USIGS 1 reel 4877

HERMON, Me.
Marriage records, 1872-1891 Ibid.
N: USIGS 1 reel 4878

HERSEYS, Me.
Vital records, 1864-1914 Ibid.
N: USIGS 1 reel 4879

HODGDON, Me.
Vital records, 1837-1940 Ibid.
N: USIGS 2 reels 4880

HOPE, Me.
Vital records, to 1892 Ibid.
N: USIGS 1 reel 4881

HOULTON, Me.
Town records, 1826-1857; vital records, 1828-1892 Ibid.
N: USIGS 1 reel 4882

HOWLAND, Me.
Vital records, 1798-1937 Ibid.
N: USIGS 1 reel 4883

HUDSON, Me.
Vital records, 1856-1892; militia roll, 1880-1917 Ibid.
N: USIGS 1 reel 4884

INDUSTRY, Me.
Vital records, to 1892 Ibid.
N: USIGS 4885

JACKSON BROOK, Me.
Vital records, 1857-1889 Ibid.
N: USIGS 1 reel 4886

JAY, Me.
Town records, 1795-1822; vital records, 1795-1891 Ibid.
N: USIGS 1 reel 4887

JEFFERSON, Me.
Town and vital records, to 1892 Ibid.
N: USIGS 1 reel 4888

JONESBORO, Me.
Vital records, 1786-1890 Ibid.
N: USIGS 1 reel 4889

KENDUSKEAG, Me.
Vital records, 1852-1891 Ibid.
N: USIGS 1 reel 4890

KINGFIELD, Me.
Vital records, to 1892 Ibid.
N: USIGS 1 reel 4891

KINGMAN, Me.
Marriage records, to 1892 Augusta
N: USIGS 1 reel 4892

KINGSBURY, Me.
Town and vital records, to 1875 Ibid.
N: USIGS 1 reel 4893

KNOX, Me.
Town records, 1777-1845; vital records, 1777-1896 Ibid.
N: USIGS 1 reel 4894

LA GRANGE, Me.
Vital records, 1833-1891; militia roll, 1880-1913 Ibid.
N: USIGS 1 reel 4895

LAKEVILLE PLANTATION, Me.
Vital records, 1862-1955 Ibid.
N: USIGS 1 reel 4896

LEE, Me.
Town records, 1780-1853; vital records, 1780-1945 Ibid.
N: USIGS 1 reel 4897

LEEDS, Me.
Vital records, to 1892 Ibid.
N: USIGS 1 reel 4898

LETTER E PLANTATION, Me.
Vital records, to 1892; bills of sale and mortgage of personal property records, 1844-1849; militia records, 1880 Augusta
N: USIGS 1 reel 4899

LEVANT, Me.
Vital records, 1769-1917; militia roll, 1881-1917 Ibid.
N: USIGS 1 reel 4900

LEWISTON, Me.
Vital records, to 1900 Ibid.
N: USIGS 3 reels 4901

LIBERTY, Me.
Vital records, 1864-1891 Ibid.
N: USIGS 1 reel 4902

LIMESTONE, Me.
Vital records, to 1935 Ibid.
N: USIGS 1 reel 4903

LINCOLN, Me.
Vital records, 1829-1892 Ibid.
N: USIGS 2 reels 4904

LINCOLNVILLE, Me.
Vital records, 1786-1892 Ibid.
N: USIGS 1 reel 4905

LINNEUS, Me.
Town records, 1840-1892; vital records, 1784-1892 Ibid.
N: USIGS 1 reel 4906

LISBON, Me.
Vital records, to 1892 Ibid.
N: USIGS 1 reel 4907

LITCHFIELD, Me.
Town and vital records, to 1892 Vienna
N: USIGS 1 reel 4908

LIVERMORE, Me.
Vital records, to 1892 Ibid.
N: USIGS 1 reel 4909

LOWELL, Me.
Vital records, 1854-1939 Ibid.
N: USIGS 1 reel 4910

LUBEC, Me.
Vital records, 1819-1892 Ibid.
N: USIGS 1 reel 4911

LYMAN, Me., see COXHALL, Me., 4822, under this same heading

MACHIAS, Me.
Town records, 1773-1799; vital records, 1773-1891 Ibid.
N: USIGS 1 reel 4912

MACHIASPORT, Me.
Vital records, 1859-1891 Ibid.
N: USIGS 1 reel 4913

MACWAHOC, Me.
Town and vital records, 1851-1862, 1864-1896 Ibid.
N: USIGS 1 reel 4914

MADRID, Me.
Vital records, to 1891 Ibid.
N: USIGS 1 reel 4915

MANCHESTER, Me.
Vital records, to 1892; death records, to 1908 Vienna
N: USIGS 1 reel 4916

MAPLETON, Me.
Vital records, 1855-1891 Perham
N: USIGS 1 reel 4917

MARS HILL, Me.
Vital records, 1786-1892 Ibid.
N: USIGS 1 reel 4918

MARSHFIELD, Me.
Vital records, 1757-1892 Ibid.
N: USIGS 1 reel 4919

MATINICUS, Me.
Town and vital records, to 1892 Wiscasset
N: USIGS 1 reel 4920

MATTAWAMKEAG, Me.
Vital records, 1860-1891 Ibid.
N: USIGS 1 reel 4921

MAXFIELD, Me.
Town records, 1825-1890; vital records, 1825-1891 Ibid.
N: USIGS 1 reel 4922

MEDFORD, Me.
Marriage records, to 1892 Augusta
N: USIGS 1 reel 4923

MEDWAY, Me.
Vital records, 1856-1940 Ibid.
N: USIGS 1 reel 4924

MERCER, Me.
Vital records, to 1892 Ibid.
N: USIGS 1 reel 4925

MILFORD, Me.
Marriages, 1864-1891 Ibid.
N: USIGS 1 reel 4926

MILLBRIDGE, Me.
Town records, 1848-1868; marriage records, 1848-1891 Ibid.
N: USIGS 1 reel 4927

MILO, Me.
Vital records, 1802-1891 Ibid.
N: USIGS 1 reel 4928

MINOT, Me.
Vital records, to 1892 Ibid.
N: USIGS 1 reel   4929

MONHEGAN, Me.
Town and vital records, to 1889 Ibid.
N: USIGS 1 reel   4930

MONMOUTH, Me.
Town records, to 1857; vital records, to 1892
Vienna
N: USIGS 1 reel   4931

MONROE, Me.
Vital records, 1778-1892 Ibid.
N: USIGS 1 reel   4932

MONSON, Me.
Vital records, 1635-1890 Ibid.
N: USIGS 1 reel   4933

MONTICELLO, Me.
Vital records, 1860-1896 Ibid.
N: USIGS 1 reel   4934

MONTVILLE, Me.
Town records, 1785-1856; vital records,
1785-1891 Ibid.
N: USIGS 1 reel   4935

MORRILL, Me.
Vital records, 1781-1891 Ibid.
N: USIGS 1 reel   4936

MOSCOW, Me.
Vital records, to 1892 Ibid.
N: USIGS 1 reel   4937

MOUNT VERNON, Me.
Town and vital records, to 1892 Vassalboro
N: USIGS 1 reel   4938

NEW PORTLAND, Me.
Vital records, to 1892 Ibid.
N: USIGS 1 reel   4939

NEW SHARON, Me.
Vital records, 1797-1953 Ibid.
N: USIGS 1 reel   4940

NEW SWEDEN, Me.
Vital records, 1872-1900; cemetery records,
1875-1954 Ibid.
N: USIGS 1 reel   4941

NEWBURG, Me.
Vital records, 1830-1939 Ibid.
N: USIGS 1 reel   4942

NEWCASTLE, Me.
Town and vital records, to 1892 Ibid.
N: USIGS 1 reel   4943

NEWPORT, Me.
Vital records, 1858-1891 Ibid.
N: USIGS 1 reel   4944

NOBLEBORO, Me.
Town and vital records, to 1892 Ibid.
N: USIGS 1 reel   4945

NORRIDGEWOCK, Me.
Town and vital records, to 1892 Ibid.
N: USIGS 1 reel   4946

NORTH HAVEN, Me.
Town and vital records, to 1892 Ibid.
N: USIGS 1 reel   4947

NORTHFIELD, Me.
Personal property records, 1878-1902; vital
records, 1822-1907; minutes of town meetings,
1838-1892 Ibid.
N: USIGS 1 reel   4948

OAKFIELD, Me.
Vital records, 1882-1891 Ibid.
N: USIGS 1 reel   4949

OAKLAND, Me.
Vital records, to 1892 Vassalboro
N: USIGS 1 reel   4950

OLD TOWN, Me.
Vital records, 1820-1891 Ibid.
N: USIGS 1 reel   4951

ORLAND, Me.
Vital records, 1765-1920 Ibid.
N: USIGS 1 reel   4952

ORNO, Me.
Town and vital records, 1806-1838; vital
records, 1806-1826, 1830-1907 Ibid.
N: USIGS 2 reels   4953

ORRINGTON, Me.
Vital records, 1772-1944 Ibid.
N: USIGS 1 reel   4954

PALMYRA, Me.
Vital records, to 1892 Ibid.
N: USIGS 1 reel   4955

PARKMAN, Me.
Vital records, 1782-1941 Ibid.
N: USIGS 1 reel   4956

PASSADUMKEAG, Me.
Births, 1844-1954 Ibid.
N: USIGS 1 reel   4957

PATRICKTOWN PLANTATION, Me., see
SOMERVILLE, Me, 4999, under this same
heading

PATTEN, Me.
Vital records, 1821-1918 Ibid.
N: USIGS 1 reel   4958

PEJEPSCOT, Me.
Vital records, 1700-1850, 268 p. (part type-
script) NNNG
N: USIGS 1 reel   4959

PEMBROKE, Me.
Vital records, to 1892 Ibid.
N: USIGS 1 reel   4960

PENOBSCOT, Me.
Vital records, 1732-1892 Ibid.
N: USIGS 1 reel   4961

PERHAM, Me.
Vital records, 1855-1891 Ibid.
N: USIGS 1 reel   4962

PERKINS, Me.
Vital records, to 1916; miscellaneous court
records; militia roll, 1880 Augusta
N: USIGS 1 reel   4963

PERRY, Me.
Vital records, to 1892 Ibid.
N: USIGS 1 reel   4964

PHILLIPS, Me.
Vital records, to 1892 Ibid.
N: USIGS 1 reel   4965

PHIPPSBURG, Me.
Vital records, to 1892 Ibid.
N: USIGS 1 reel   4966

PITTSFIELD, Me.
Town and vital records, to 1892 Ibid.
N: USIGS 1 reel   4967

PITTSTON, Me.
Town and vital records, to 1841; vital records,
to 1892 Ibid.
N: USIGS 2 reels   4968

PLEASANT RIDGE, Me.
Town and vital records, to 1897 Ibid.
N: USIGS 1 reel   4969

PLYMOUTH, Me.
Vital records, 1795-1891 Ibid.
N: USIGS 1 reel   4970

POLAND, Me.
Vital records, to 1892; marriage records, to
1937 Ibid.
N: USIGS 1 reel   4971

PORTAGE LAKE PLANTATION, Me.
Town and vital records, 1875-1892 Ibid.
N: USIGS 1 reel   4972

PRENTISS, Me.
Vital records, 1841-1939 Ibid.
N: USIGS 1 reel   4973

PRESQUE ISLE, Me.
Vital records, 1859-1892 Ibid.
N: USIGS 1 reel   4974

PRINCETON, Me.
Vital records, 1861-1889 Ibid.
N: USIGS 1 reel   4975

PROSPECT, Me.
Vital records, 1725-1850 NNNG
N: USIGS 1 reel   4976

PROSPECT, Me.
Vital records, 1756-1891 Ibid.
N: USIGS 1 reel   4977

RANGELEY, Me.
Vital records, to 1892 Ibid.
N: USIGS 1 reel   4978

READFIELD, Me.
Vital records, to 1892 Vienna
N: USIGS 1 reel   4979

RICHMOND, Me.
Vital records, to 1892 Ibid.
N: USIGS 1 reel   4980

ROBBINSTON, Me.
Vital records, 1857-1937 Ibid.
N: USIGS 1 reel   4982

RIPLEY, Me.
Vital records, to 1892 Ibid.
N: USIGS 1 reel   4981

ROCKLAND, Me.
Vital records, to 1892 Ibid.
N: USIGS 1 reel   4983

ROCKPORT, Me.
Town records, to 1821; vital records, to 1892
Ibid.
N: USIGS 2 reels   4984

ROME, Me.
Town records, to 1847; vital records, to 1892
Vassalboro
N: USIGS 1 reel   4985

SAINT ALBANS, Me.
Vital records, to 1892 Ibid.
N: USIGS 1 reel   4986

SAINT GEORGE, Me.
Vital records, to 1892 Ibid.
N: USIGS 1 reel   4987

SANGERVILLE, Me.
Vital records, 1793-1891 Ibid.
N: USIGS 1 reel   4988

SEARSMONT, Me.
Vital records, 1854-1891 Ibid.
N: USIGS 1 reel   4989

SEBEC, Me.
Vital records, 1813-1853 Ibid.
N: USIGS 1 reel   4990

SHERMAN, Me.
Vital records, 1800-1892; town census records,
1870, 1880; miscellaneous records, 1869-1922
Ibid.
N: USIGS 1 reel   4991

SHIRLEY, Me.
Vital records, 1797-1883 Ibid.
N: USIGS 1 reel   4992

SIDNEY, Me.
Vital records, to 1892 Vassalboro
N: USIGS 1 reel   4993

SILVER RIDGE PLANTATION, Me.
Vital records, 1859-1891 Ibid.
N: USIGS 1 reel   4994

SKOWHEGAN, Me.
Vital records, to 1892 Ibid.
N: USIGS 5 reels   4995

SMITHFIELD, Me.
Town and vital records, to 1892 Ibid.
N: USIGS 1 reel   4996

SMYRNA, Me.
Town records, to 1909; vital records, to 1869;
marriage records, 1869-1909 Ibid.
N: USIGS 1 reel   4997

SOLON, Me.
Vital records, to 1907 Ibid.
N: USIGS 1 reel   4998

SOMERVILLE, (formerly PATRICKTOWN
PLANTATION), Me.
Vital records, to 1892 Ibid.
N: USIGS 1 reel   4999

SOUTH THOMASTON, Me.
Vital records, to 1892 Ibid.
N: USlGS 1 reel   5000

SOUTHPORT, Me.
Vital records, to 1892 Ibid.
N: USlGS 1 reel   5001

SPRINGFIELD, Me.
Vital records, 1834-1897 Ibid.
N: USlGS 1 reel   5002

STACYVILLE PLANTATION, Me.
Town and vital records, 1860-1876 Ibid.
N: USlGS 1 reel   5003

STARKS, Me.
Vital records, to 1892 Ibid.
N: USlGS 1 reel   5004

STETSON, Me.
Vital records, 1803-1894 Ibid.
N: USlGS 1 reel   5005

STEUBEN, Me.
Vital records, 1769-1900 Ibid.
N: USlGS 1 reel   5006

STOCKTON SPRINGS, Me.
Vital records, 1832-1891 Ibid.
N: USlGS 1 reel   5007

STRONG, Me.
Vital records, to 1892 Ibid.
N: USlGS 1 reel   5008

SULLIVAN, Me.
Town records, 1789-1848; vital records,
1745-1891; militia roll, 1881-1917 Ibid.
N: USlGS 1 reel   5009

SWANVILLE, Me.
Vital records, 1812-1891 Ibid.
N: USlGS 1 reel   5010

TEMPLE, Me.
Vital records, to 1892 Ibid.
N: USlGS 1 reel   5011

THOMASTON, Me.
Town records, 1776-1887; vital records, to
1892 Warren
N: USlGS 2 reels   5012

THORNDIKE, Me.
Town records, 1776-1885; vital records, 1776-
1894 Ibid.
N: USlGS 1 reel   5013

TOPSFIELD, Me.
Vital records, to 1892 Augusta
N: USlGS 1 reel   5014

TRESCOTT, Me.
Vital records, to 1892 Augusta
N: USlGS 1 reel   5015

TROY, Me.
Vital records, 1825-1915 Ibid.
N: USlGS 1 reel   5016

TURNER, Me.
Town records, 1787-1817; vital records, 1787-
1893 Ibid.
N: USlGS 3 reels   5017

UNION, Me.
Vital records, to 1892 Ibid.
N: USlGS 1 reel   5018

UNITY, Me.
Town records, 1802-1835; vital records, 1797-
1891 Ibid.
N: USlGS 1 reel   5019

VASSALBORO, Me.
Town records, 1764-1845; vital records, to
1892 Ibid.
N: USlGS 1 reel   5020

VEAZIE, Me.
Vital records, 1852-1894 Ibid.
N: USlGS 1 reel   5021

VIENNA, Me.
Vital records, to 1892 Ibid.
N: USlGS 1 reel   5022

VINALHAVEN, Me.
Town and vital records, to 1892 Ibid.
N: USlGS 1 reel   5023

WALDOBORO, Me.
Town and vital records, to 1892; cemetery
records, 1785-1906 Ibid.
N: USlGS 2 reels   5024

WALES, Me.
Vital records, to 1900 Ibid.
N: USlGS 1 reel   5025

WALLAGRASS, Me.
Town and vital records, 1866-1894 Ibid.
N: USlGS 1 reel   5026

WARREN, Me.
Vital records, to 1892 Ibid.
N: USlGS 1 reel   5027

WASHBURN, Me.
Vital records, 1855-1891 Perham
N: USlGS 1 reel   5028

WASHINGTON, Me.
Vital records, to 1892 Ibid.
N: USlGS 1 reel   5029

WATERBORO, Me.
Proprietors' records, 1781-1790 Alfred
N: USlGS 1 reel   5030

WATERVILLE, Me.
Vital records, to 1892 Ibid.
N: USlGS 22 reels   5031

WAYNE, Me.
Town and vital records, to 1892 Vienna
N: USlGS 1 reel   5032

WEBSTER, Me.
Vital records, to 1892 Ibid.
N: USlGS 1 reel   5033

WELD, Me.
Vital records, to 1892 Ibid.
N: USlGS 1 reel   5034

WELLINGTON, Me.
Town and vital records, to 1892 Ibid.
N: USlGS 1 reel   5035

WESLEY, Me.
Vital records, 1840-1891; militia roll, 1885-
1909 Ibid.
N: USlGS 1 reel   5036

WEST BATH, Me.
Vital records, to 1936 Ibid.
N: USlGS 1 reel   5037

WEST GARDINER, Me.
Vital records, to 1892 Vienna
N: USlGS 1 reel   5038

WESTON, Me.
Vital records, 1814-1892 Ibid.
N: USlGS 1 reel   5039

WESTPORT, Me.
Town and vital records, to 1945 Ibid.
N: USlGS 1 reel   5040

WHITEFIELD, Me.
Town and vital records, to 1892 Ibid.
N: USlGS 1 reel   5041

WHITING, Me.
Vital records, 1814-1891 Ibid.
N: USlGS 1 reel   5042

WHITNEYVILLE, Me.
Births, 1861-1891 Ibid.
N: USlGS 1 reel   5043

WILLIMATIC, Me.
Vital records, 1859-1939 Ibid.
N: USlGS 1 reel   5044

WILTON, Me.
Town and vital records, to 1892 Ibid.
N: USlGS 1 reel   5045

WINDSOR, Me.
Vital records, to 1892 Ibid.
N: USlGS 1 reel   5046

WINN, Me.
Vital records, 1863-1917 Ibid.
N: USlGS 1 reel   5047

WINSLOW, Me.
Marriages, 1795-1833 (typescript) NNNG
N: USlGS   5048

WINSLOW, Me.
Town and vital records, to 1892 Vassalboro
N: USlGS 1 reel   5049

WINTERPORT, Me.
Vital records, 1860-1894 Ibid.
N: USlGS 1 reel   5050

WINTHROP, Me.
Vital records, to 1892 Ibid.
N: USlGS 2 reels   5051

WISCASSET, Me.
Town records, 1752-1839; vital records, 1752-
1945 Ibid.
N: USlGS 2 reels   5052

WOODLAND, Me.
Vital records, 1874-1891 Ibid.
N: USlGS 1 reel   5053

WOOLWICH, Me.
Town records, 1760-1828; vital records, 1760-
1892 Ibid.
N: USlGS 2 reels   5054

Church Records

BELFAST, Me. FIRST BAPTIST CHURCH
Records, 1809-1839 Ibid.
N: USlGS 1 reel   5055

DAVIS, Rev. C. D., Paris, Me.
Church records, 1838-1852 (typescript) NNNG
N: USlGS   5056

LEWISTON, Me. ST. PETER AND ST. PAUL
CHURCH (Catholic)
Church records, 1870-1953 Ibid.
N: USlGS 14 reels   5057

NEW SWEDEN, Me. LUTHERAN CHURCH
Church records, 1870-1929; record of
members, 1870-1892 Ibid.
N: USlGS 1 reel   5058

VAN BUREN, Me. ST. BRUNO'S PARISH
Birth records, 1838-1893 (transcript) Ibid.
N: USlGS 1 reel   5059

WELLS, Me. FIRST CHURCH OF CHRIST
Register, 1701-1811, 1 box MeHi
DCO: DLC   5060

Personal Papers

ASHBURTON, ALEXANDER BARING, 1st
BARON, 1774-1848
Papers, 1790-1840 UKLPRO
N: DLC 1 reel*
P: MAnP   5061

MERRILL, Dr. F. W.
Book of births, Winn, Me., 1873-1918 priv.
N: USlGS   5062

NEW HAMPSHIRE

Bibliography

NEW HAMPSHIRE. SECRETARY OF STATE
Catalogue of town records Nh
N: USlGS 1 reel   5063

Census

U.S. CENSUS. SECOND, 1800
Population schedules, New Hampshire NhHi
N: USlGS 2 reels   5064
P: NhHi

U.S. CENSUS. FIFTH, 1830
Population schedules, New Hampshire DNA
N: DNA 5 reels   5065

U.S. CENSUS. SIXTH, 1840
Population schedules, New Hampshire DNA
N: DNA 4 reels   5066
P: USlGS

U.S. CENSUS. SEVENTH, 1850
Population schedules, New Hampshire DNA
N: DNA 4 reels
P: USIGS   5067

U.S. CENSUS. SEVENTH TO TENTH, 1850-1880
Mortality schedules, New Hampshire Nh
N: USIGS 2 reels   5068
P: Nh

U.S. CENSUS. EIGHTH, 1860
Population schedules, New Hampshire DNA
N: DNA 3 reels
P: USIGS   5069

U.S. CENSUS. NINTH, 1870
Population schedules, New Hampshire DNA
N: DNA 3 reels
P: USIGS   5070

U.S. CENSUS. TENTH, 1880
Population schedules, New Hampshire DNA
N: DNA 10 reels   5071

State Records

NEW HAMPSHIRE (Colony)
Probate records, 1655-1771, 26 v. NhHi
N: USIGS 11 reels   5072
P: NhHi

NEW HAMPSHIRE (Colony)
Province deeds, 1671-1771 NhHi C.H. Exeter
N: USIGS 80 reels   5073

NEW HAMPSHIRE
Revolutionary pensioners' records, 64v. NhHi
N: USIGS 26 reels   5074
P: NhHi

County Records

BELKNAP Co., N.H.
Probate records, 1841-1865; deeds, 1771-1851
C.H. Laconia
N: USIGS 22 reels   5075

CARROLL Co., N.H.
Probate records, 1840-1870; deeds, 1841-1851
C.H. Ossipee
N: USIGS 15 reels   5076

CHESHIRE Co., N.H.
Wills, 1771-1869; administrations, 1823-1869;
dowers' claims, 1814-1886; guardianship
papers, 1824-1853; deeds, 1770-1860
C.H. Keene
N: USIGS 114 reels   5077

COOS Co., N.H.
Original deeds (partly burnt), 1772-1887; copies
of original deeds, 1772-1887 C.H. Lancaster
N: USIGS 34 reels   5078

GRAFTON Co., N.H.
Deeds, 1773-1850; probate records, 1773-1854
C.H. Woodsville
N: USIGS 132 reels   5079

HILLSBORO Co., N.H.
Probate records, 1771-1859; execution of
lawsuits, 1813-1859; deeds, 1771-1851 C.H.
Nashua
N: USIGS 185 reels   5080

MERRIMACK Co., N.H.
Probate records, 1823-1875; deeds, 1823-1861
C.H. Concord
N: USIGS 70 reels   5081
P: Ibid.

ROCKINGHAM Co., N.H.
Probate records, 1771-1862; deeds, 1770-1852
C.H. Exeter
N: USIGS 141 reels   5082

STRAFFORD Co., N.H.
Probate records, 1773-1876; deeds, 1773-1851
C.H. Dover
N: USIGS 131 reels   5083

SULLIVAN Co., N.H.
Probate records, 1827-1902; deeds, 1827-1850
C.H. Newport
N: USIGS 34 reels   5084

Town Records

CAMPTON, N.H.
Town and vital records, ca. 1768-1834; tax
records, 1823-1843 Ibid.
N: USIGS 1 reel   5085

CENTER HARBOR, N.H.
Town and vital records, 1797-1820 Ibid.
N: USIGS 1 reel   5086

DORCHESTER, N.H.
Proprietors' records, 1772-1848 Ibid.
DCO: NhD 1 box   5087

EXETER, N.H.
Town records, 1636-1829; vital records, 1657-
1853; tax records, 1763-1830 Ibid.
N: USIGS 6 reels   5088

GRANTHAM, N.H.
Vital records, 1788-1850 Ibid.
N: USIGS 1 reel   5089

HANOVER, N.H.
Proprietors' records, 1761-1847; town and
vital records, 1760-1845; highway allotments
and surveys, 1777-1889 NhD
DCO: NhD 5 v.   5090

HANOVER, N.H.
Vital records, 1762-1847 Ibid.
DCO: NhD
N: USIGS 1 reel   5091

HENNIKER, N.H.
Proprietors' records, in transcript; town
records, 1769-1819; vital records, 1756-
1820; town census, 1835 Ibid.
N: USIGS 1 reel   5092

HOOKSETT, N.H.
Town and vital records, containing military
enlistments, 1822-1859 Ibid.
N: USIGS 1 reel   5093

JAFFREY, N.H.
Town records, 1802-1825; vital records, 1805-
1886; cemetery records, n.d. Ibid.
N: US:GS 1 reel   5094

KEENE, N.H.
Town records, 1753-1825 Ibid.
N: USIGS 1 reel   5095

LEE, N.H.
Town account book, 1809-1825 Ibid.
N: USIGS 1/2 reel   5096

MILAN, N.H.
Vital records, 1822-1881 Ibid.
N: USIGS 1 reel   5097

NEW HAMPSHIRE. SECRETARY OF STATE
Town records, 1636-1907 (transcript) Ibid.
N: USIGS 435 reels   5098
P: Nh

NORTHWOOD, N.H.
Vital records, 1780-1824 (transcript) Ibid.
N: USIGS 1 reel   5099

ROCHESTER, N.H.
Town records, 1737-1885 Ibid.
N: USIGS 1 reel   5100

ROXBURY, N.H.
Town records, 1812-1831 Ibid.
N: USIGS 1 reel   5101

SALISBURY, N.H.
Vital records, 1797-1845 Ibid.
N: USIGS 1 reel   5102

SANDWICH, N.H.
Vital records, 1797-1820 Ibid.
N: USIGS 1 reel   5103

SPRINGFIELD, N.H.
Vital records, 1794-1850 Ibid.
N: USIGS 1 reel   5104

STODDARD, N.H.
Vital records, 1773-1850 Ibid.
N: USIGS 1 reel   5105

WEARE, N.H.
Vital records, kept by Daniel Morre, town clerk,
March 26, 1811, 32 p. (typescript) NNNG
N: USIGS   5106

WHITEFIELD, N.H.
Town records, 1804-1850; vital records, 1795-
1867 Ibid.
N: USIGS 1 reel   5107

WINCHESTER, N.H.
Proprietors' records, 1733-1800; town records,
1732-1803; vital records, 1736-1849; city licenses,
1810-1838 Ibid.
N: USIGS 1 reel   5108

Church Records

EAST DERRY, N.H. CONGREGATIONAL CHURCH
Records, 1740-1837, 2 v. Ibid.
N: CtY 2 reels   5109

FRIENDS, SOCIETY OF. DARTMOUTH [N.H.]
MONTHLY MEETING
Births and deaths, 1765-1841; minutes, 1698-
1792 RPMB
N: USIGS 1 reel   5110
P: PSC-F

FRIENDS, SOCIETY OF. SOUTH KINGSTON
[N.H.] MONTHLY MEETING
Births, deaths, and marriages, 1740-1892;
men's minutes, 1743-1864; women's minutes,
1743-1872 RPMB
N: USIGS   5111
P: PSC-F

HOLDERNESS, N.H. EPISCOPAL CHURCH
Records, 1790-1844 (transcript) N
N: USIGS 1 reel   5112

LONDONDERRY, N.H. PRESBYTERIAN CHURCH
East Parish records, 1742-1837, v. 1-3 Ibid.
N: PPPrHi 2 reels   5113

LONDONDERRY, N.H. PRESBYTERIAN CHURCH
Records, 1723-1760 Ibid.
N: CtY 1 reel   5114

LONDONDERRY, N.H. PRESBYTERIAN
CHURCH
West Parish records, 1736-1821 Ibid.
N: PPPrHi 1 reel   5115

NEW HAMPSHIRE. HISTORICAL SOCIETY
Church and cemetery records, n.d. (typescript)
NhHi
N: USIGS 11 reels   5116
P: NhHi

NEW HAMPSHIRE. STATE LIBRARY
Church records, 1713-1885; family records,
mortality schedules, 1850, 1860, 1870, 1880;
death records of Rindge Nh
N: USIGS 10 reels   5117

Personal Papers

GOFFE, JOSEPH, 1766-1846
Dialogues and exercises MWA
DCO: NhD 1 box   5118

OCCOM, SAMSON, 1723-1792
Diary priv.
DCO: NhD 3 v.   5119

Collections

LANCASTER, DANIEL
Biographical dictionary of New Hampshire
(manuscript), 7v. NHi
N: ? 1 reel   5120
P: MWA

College Records

DARTMOUTH COLLEGE
Great issues course, sample journals, 1952,
11 v. NhD
N: NhD 1 reel   5121

DARTMOUTH COLLEGE. TRUSTEES
Records, 1770-1909 Ibid.
DCO: NhD 5 v.   5122

VERMONT

Census

U.S. CENSUS. FIFTH, 1830
Population schedules, Vermont   DNA
N: DNA 6 reels   5123
P: USIGS

U.S. CENSUS. SIXTH, 1840
Population schedules, Vermont   DNA
N: DNA 5 reels   5124
P: USIGS

U.S. CENSUS. SEVENTH, 1850
Population schedules, Vermont   DNA
N: DNA 4 reels   5125
P: USIGS

U.S. CENSUS. EIGHTH, 1860
Population schedules, Vermont   DNA
N: DNA 3 reels   5126
P: USIGS

U.S. CENSUS. NINTH, 1870
Population schedules, Vermont   DNA
N: DNA 3 reels   5127
P: USIGS

U.S. CENSUS. TENTH, 1880
Population schedules, Vermont   DNA
N: DNA 11 reels   5128

State Records

VERMONT. GENERAL ASSEMBLY
Journals and proceedings, 1778
DCO: VtU   5129

VERMONT. SECRETARY OF STATE
General index to Vermont vital records, to
1870   Vt-S
N: USIGS 287 reels   5130

County Records

Vermont county records include those of the
probate districts into which some Vermont
counties are divided.

ADDISON Co., Vt.
New Haven District probate records, 1824-1857
C.H. Vergennes
N: USIGS 4 reels   5131
P: Vt-PR

BENNINGTON Co., Vt.
Bennington District probate records, 1778-
1851; deeds, 1782-1832   C.H. Bennington
N: USIGS 7 reels   5132
P: Vt-PR

BENNINGTON Co., Vt.
Manchester District probate records,
1779-1850   C.H. Manchester
N: USIGS 5 reels   5133
P: Vt-PR

CALEDONIA Co., Vt.
Probate records, 1796-1855; guardian records,
1839-1857   C.H. St. Johnsbury
N: USIGS 9 reels   5134
P: Vt-PR

CHITTENDEN Co., Vt.
Chittenden District probate records, 1795-
1857; guardianship records, 1818-1856
C.H. Burlington
N: USIGS 14 reels   5135
P: Vt-PR

ESSEX Co., Vt.
Essex District probate records, 1791-1855;
deeds, 1793-1854, 10 v.   C.H. Guildhall
N: USIGS 2 reels   5136
P: Vt-PR

FRANKLIN Co., Vt.
Deeds, 1797-1852; Franklin District probate

records, 1796-1848   C.H. St. Albans
N: USIGS 16 reels   5137
P: Vt-PR

GRAND ISLE Co., Vt.
Grand Isle District probate records,
1796-1854   C.H. North Hero
N: USIGS 4 reels   5138
P: Vt-PR

LAMOILLE Co., Vt.
Lamoille District probate records,
1837-1859   C.H. Hyde Park
N: USIGS 3 reels   5139
P: Vt-PR

ORANGE Co., Vt.
Bradford District probate records, 1781-1852
C.H. Wells River
N: USIGS 4 reels   5140
P: Vt-PR

ORANGE Co., Vt.
Randolph District probate records, 1792-1850;
land records, 1771-1832; tax records, 1789-
1832; miscellaneous records, 1770-1781
C.H. Chelsea
N: USIGS 4 reels   5141
P: Vt-PR

ORLEANS Co., Vt.
Orleans District probate records, 1796-1855;
land records, 1799-1949   C.H. Newport
N: USIGS 3 reels   5142
P: Vt-PR

RUTLAND Co., Vt.
Fair Haven District probate records,
1797-1823   C.H. Fair Haven
N: USIGS 2 reels   5143
P: Vt-PR

RUTLAND Co., Vt.
Rutland District probate records, 1784-1850;
deeds, 1774-1822   C.H. Rutland
N: USIGS 9 reels   5144
P: Vt-PR

WASHINGTON Co., Vt.
Jefferson District probate records, 1811-1814;
Washington District probate records, 1815-
1857   C.H. Montpelier
N: USIGS 8 reels   5145
P: Vt-PR

WINDHAM Co., Vt.
Marlboro District probate records, 1781-1850;
guardian records, 1821-1849   C.H. Brattleboro
N: USIGS 11 reels   5146
P: Vt-PR

WINDHAM Co., Vt.
Westminster District probate records,
1781-1851   C.H. Bellows Falls
N: USIGS 7 reels   5147
P: Vt-PR

WINDSOR Co., Vt.
Land records, 1784-1794; Hartford District
probate records, 1783-1851   C.H. Woodstock
N: USIGS 10 reels   5148
P: Vt-PR

WINDSOR Co., Vt.
Windsor District probate records, 1787-1850;
guardian records, 1805-1855   C.H. Ludlow
N: USIGS 11 reels   5149
P: Vt-PR

Town Records

Vermont town records are listed in the sequence
of age. First come the records of the Proprietors
to whom the town's land was originally granted.
These are followed by the records of the town
itself. Records of births, marriages, and deaths
come next, combined into vital records. When
vital records were kept in the same book as the
town records, a joint entry is made of town and
vital records.

ACTON (now TOWNSHEND), Vt.
Town and vital records, 1801-1841;
land records, 1801-1841   Ibid.
N: USIGS 1 reel   5150
P: Vt-PR

ADDISON, Vt.
Town records, 1784-1858; land records,
1784-1855; vital records, 1784-1855   Ibid.
N: USIGS 4 reels   5151
P: Vt-PR

ALBANY, Vt.
Land records, 1806-1852; vital records,
1800-1874   Ibid.
N: USIGS 5 reels   5152
P: Vt-PR

ALBURG, Vt.
Land records, 1792-1852; vital records,
1842-1868; cemetery records, 1792-1870   Ibid.
N: USIGS 6 reels   5153
P: Vt-PR

ANDOVER, Vt.
Town and vital records, 1781-1861;
land records, 1780-1856   Ibid.
N: USIGS 5 reels   5154

ARLINGTON, Vt.
Land records, 1780-1860; vital records,
1773-1931   Ibid.
N: USIGS 6 reels   5155
P: Vt-PR

ATHENS, Vt.
Proprietors' records, 1779-1786;
land records, 1787-1864; vital records,
1779-1869   Ibid.
N: USIGS 5 reels   5156
P: Vt-PR

BAKERSFIELD, Vt.
Land records, 1792-1849; vital records,
1792-1868   Ibid.
N: USIGS 4 reels   5157
P: Vt. PR

BALTIMORE, Vt.
Town records, 1794-1844; land records,
1794-1897   Ibid.
N: USIGS 1 reel   5158
P: Vt-PR

BARNARD, Vt.
Town records, 1761-1819; land records,
1781-1853; vital records, 1774-1871   Ibid.
N: USIGS 8 reels   5159
P: Vt-PR

BARNET, Vt.
Proprietors' records, 1785-1861; land
records, 1783-1852   Ibid.
N: USIGS 8 reels   5160
P: Vt-PR

BARRE, Vt.
Land records, 1793-1851; vital records,
1791-1880   Ibid.
N: USIGS 6 reels   5161
P: Vt-PR

BARTON, Vt.
Proprietor's records, 1789-1820;
land records, 1797-1874; vital records,
1857-1870   Ibid.
N: USIGS 5 reels   5162
P: Vt-PR

BELVIDERE, Vt.
Town and vital records, 1797-1812; land
records, 1797-1861; vital records, 1795-1855;
cemetery records, 1797-1870   Ibid.
N: USIGS 2 reels   5163
P: Vt-PR

BENNINGTON, Vt.
Town and vital records, 1741-1930;
land records, 1741-1851   Ibid.
N: USIGS 14 reels   5164
P: Vt-PR

BENSON, Vt.
Proprietors' records, 1784-1786; town and
vital records, 1788-1863; vital records,
1786-1850; vital records, 1787-1863   Ibid.
N: USIGS 9 reels   5165
P: Vt-PR

BERKSHIRE, Vt.
Proprietors' records, 1794-1812; town and
vital records, 1800-1855; land records,
1794-1852   Ibid.
N: USIGS 9 reels   5166
P: Vt-PR

BERLIN, Vt.
Proprietors' records, 1785-1802; land
records, 1791-1852 Montpelier
N: USIGS 4 reels   5167
P: Vt-PR

BETHEL, Vt.
Land records, 1779-1851; vital records,
1785-1857; cemetery records, 1785-1857
Ibid.
N: USIGS 6 reels   5168
P: Vt-PR

BLOOMFIELD, Vt.
Proprietors' records, 1767-1802; land
records, 1803-1854 Ibid.
N: USIGS 1 reel   5169
P: Vt-PR

BOLTON, Vt.
Proprietors' records, 1763-1791;
land records, 1789-1851 Ibid.
N: USIGS 4 reels   5170
P: Vt-PR

BRADFORD, Vt.
Town records, 1775-1852; land records,
1775-1852; vital records, 1800-1875 Ibid.
N: USIGS 9 reels   5171
P: Vt-PR

BRAINTREE, Vt.
Proprietors' records, 1780-1801;
town and vital records, 1780-1858;
land records, 1788-1849 Ibid.
N: USIGS 6 reels   5172
P: Vt-PR

BRANDON, Vt.
Land records, 1785-1852; marriage records,
1819-1909 Ibid.
N: USIGS 10 reels   5173
P: Vt-PR

BRATTLEBORO, Vt.
Town and vital records, 1779-1915;
land records, 1783-1851; cemetery records,
1779-1857 Ibid.
N: USIGS 11 reels   5174
P: Vt-PR

BRIDGEWATER, Vt.
Land records, 1781-1894; vital records,
1773-1869 Ibid.
N: USIGS 7 reels   5175
P: Vt-PR

BRIDPORT, Vt.
Town and vital records, 1782-1873; land
records, 1785-1851 Ibid.
N: USIGS 7 reels   5176
P: Vt-PR

BRISTOL, Vt.
Town and vital records, 1790-1830;
land records, 1792-1850 Ibid.
N: USIGS 7 reels   5177
P: Vt-PR

BROOKFIELD, Vt.
Proprietors' records, 1783-1785; land records,
1786-1850; vital records, 1779-1904 Ibid.
N: USIGS 8 reels   5178
P: Vt-PR

BROOKLINE, Vt.
Town and vital records, 1795-1857; land
records, 1795-1853 Ibid.
N: USIGS 3 reels   5179
P: Vt-PR

BROWNINGTON, Vt.
Land records, 1797-1852; vital records,
1861-1867 Ibid.
N: USIGS 1 reel   5180
P: Vt-PR

BRUNSWICK, Vt.
Proprietors' records, 1786-1825; land
records, 1793-1851 Ibid.
N: USIGS 2 reels   5181
P: Vt-PR

BURKE, Vt.
Town and vital records, 1796-1850;
land records, 1799-1854; cemetery
records, 1796-1866 Ibid.
N: USIGS 5 reels   5182
P: Vt.

BURLINGTON, Vt.
Proprietors' records, 1763-1872; land
records, 1763-1850; vital records, 1789-1863;
cemetery records, 1789-1870 Ibid.
N: USIGS 13 reels   5183
P: Vt-PR

CABOT, Vt.
Land records, 1788-1852; vital records,
1788-1872; cemetery records, 1788-
1870 Ibid.
N: USIGS 5 reels   5184
P: Vt-PR

CALAIS, Vt.
Proprietors' records, 1780-1788; town and
vital records, 1795-1904; land records,
1790-1853; vital records, 1781-1905;
cemetery records, 1781-1870 Ibid.
N: USIGS 6 reels   5185
P: Vt-PR

CAMBRIDGE, Vt.
Land records, 1784-1850; vital records,
1785-1882 Jeffersonville
N: USIGS 7 reels   5186
P: Vt-PR

CANAAN, Vt.
Land records, 1797-1851 Ibid.
N: USIGS 2 reels   5187
P: Vt-PR

CASTLETON, Vt.
Land records, 1784-1851; vital records,
1784-1861 Ibid.
N: USIGS 7 reels   5188
P: Vt-PR

CAVENDISH, Vt.
Town and vital records, 1782-1856; land
records, 1761-1851 Ibid.
N: USIGS 7 reels   5189
P: Vt-PR

CHARLESTON, Vt.
Proprietors' records, 1780-1830; town records,
1780-1830; land records, 1806-1849; vital
records, 1803-1870 Ibid.
N: USIGS 4 reels   5190
P: Vt-PR

CHARLOTTE, Vt.
Proprietors' records, 1763-1820, town and
vital records, 1787-1876; land records,
1787-1851 Ibid.
N: USIGS 6 reels   5191
P: Vt-PR

CHELSEA, Vt.
Land records, 1784-1850; vital records,
1784-1857 Ibid.
N: USIGS 8 reels   5192
P: Vt-PR

CHESTER, Vt.
Town and vital records, 1763-1853; land
records, 1763-1853 Ibid.
N: USIGS 7 reels   5193
P: Vt-PR

CHITTENDEN, Vt.
Town and vital records, 1793-1851; land
records, 1789-1854 Ibid.
N: USIGS 6 reels   5194
P: Vt-PR

CLARENDON, Vt.
Land records, 1778-1853; vital records,
1783-1825, 1827-1833 Ibid.
N: USIGS 7 reels   5195
P: Vt-PR

COLCHESTER, Vt.
Proprietors' records, 1763-1820; town and
vital records, 1797-1861; land records,
1774-1851; cemetery records, 1763-1870 Ibid.
N: USIGS 7 reels   5196
P: Vt-PR

CONCORD, Vt.
Town and vital records, 1784-1851; land
records, 1794-1850 Ibid.
N: USIGS 4 reels   5197
P: Vt-PR

CORINTH, Vt.
Land records, 1780-1852; vital records,
1757-1864 Ibid.

N: USIGS 5 reels   5198
P: Vt-PR

CORNWALL, Vt.
Proprietors' records, 1761-1855; town and
vital records, 1790-1855; land records,
1784-1856 Ibid.
N: USIGS 9 reels   5199
P: Vt-PR

CRAFTSBURY, Vt.
Proprietors' records, 1781-1803; land records,
1792-1852; vital records, 1781-1900 Ibid.
N: USIGS 4 reels   5200
P: Vt-PR

DANBY, Vt.
Proprietors' records, 1762-1791; land
records, 1771-1854; vital records,
1771-1854 Ibid.
N: USIGS 8 reels   5201
P: Vt-PR

DANVILLE, Vt.
Town and vital records, 1793-1866; deeds,
1788-1851; vital records, 1793-1950;
cemetery records, 1798-1880 Ibid.
N: USIGS 8 reels   5202
P: Vt-PR

DERBY, Vt.
Land records, 1790-1852; vital records,
indices, 1790-1905 Derby Center
N: USIGS 5 reels   5203
P: Vt-PR

DERBY, Vt., see SALEM, Vt., 5321, under this
same heading

DORSET, Vt.
Land records, 1770-1852; vital records,
1868-1888 Ibid.
N: USIGS 7 reels   5204
P: Vt-PR

DOVER, Vt.
Town and vital records, 1789-1852; land
records, 1789-1853 Ibid.
N: USIGS 4 reels   5205
P: Vt-PR

DUMMERSTON, Vt.
Land records, 1781-1853; vital records,
1761-1882 Ibid.
N: USIGS 6 reels   5206
P: Vt-PR

DUXBURY, Vt.
Land records, 1770-1853; vital records,
1800-1834 Ibid.
N: USIGS 4 reels   5207
P: Vt-PR

EAST HAVEN, Vt.
Proprietors' records, 1810-1811; land records,
1845-1856 Ibid.
N: USIGS 1 reel   5208
P: Vt-PR

EDEN, Vt.
Town and vital records, 1802-1852; land
records, 1802-1852; vital records, 1860-1891
Ibid.
N: USIGS 3 reels   5209
P: Vt-PR

ELMORE, Vt.
Land records, 1786-1853; vital records,
1803-1870; cemetery records, 1803-1870 Ibid.
N: USIGS 3 reels   5210
P: Vt-PR

ENOSBURG, Vt.
Town and vital records, 1799-1858; land
records, 1780-1850; cemetery records,
1780-1870 Ibid.
N: USIGS 8 reels   5211
P: Vt-PR

ESSEX, Vt.
Proprietors' records, 1763-1808;
town and vital records, 1786-1861; land
records, 1786-1851 Ibid.
N: USIGS 7 reels   5212
P: Vt-PR

FAIRFAX, Vt.
Town and vital records, 1787-1845; land

records, 1763-1850 Ibid.
N: USIGS 5 reels 5213
P: Vt-PR

FAIRFAX, Vt.
Vital records, 1754-1868 (transcript) NNNG
N: USIGS 1 reel 5214
P: Vt-RC

FAIRFIELD, Vt.
Town records, 1763-1841; land records,
1763-1851; vital records, 1780-1858 Ibid.
N: USIGS 8 reels 5215
P: Vt-PR

FAIRHAVEN, Vt.
Land records, 1794-1854 Ibid.
N: USIGS 2 reels 5216
P: Vt-PR

FAIRLEE, Vt.
Town records, 1792-1875; land records, 1761-
1856; vital records, 1792-1863 Ibid.
N: USIGS 5 reels 5217
P: Vt-PR

FAYSTON, Vt.
Town and vital records, 1805-1843; land
records, 1782-1853 Moretown
N: USIGS 4 reels 5218
P: Vt-PR

FERRISBURG, Vt.
Proprietors' records, 1785-1799; town and
vital records, 1793-1859; land records,
1787-1852 Ibid.
N: USIGS 7 reels 5219
P: Vt-PR

FLETCHER, Vt.
Land records, 1790-1854; vital records,
1790-1867 Ibid.
N: USIGS 5 reels 5220
P: Vt-PR

FRANKLIN, Vt.
Land records, 1795-1850; vital records,
1795-1867; cemetery records, 1795-1870 Ibid.
N: USIGS 4 reels 5221
P: Vt-PR

GEORGIA, Vt.
Proprietors' records, 1763-1808; town and
vital records, 1798-1862; land records, 1788-
1851; vital records, 1792-1867; cemetery
records, 1792-1870; church records, 1812-
1827 Ibid.
N: USIGS 7 reels 5222
P: Vt-PR

GLASTONBURY, Vt.
Town and vital records, 1834-1896; land
records, 1833-1855 Bennington
N: USIGS 1 reel 5223
P: Vt-PR

GLOVER, Vt.
Land records, 1797-1854; vital records,
1857-1867 Ibid.
N: USIGS 3 reels 5224
P: Vt-PR

GOSHEN, Vt.
Land records, 1813-1856 Ibid.
N: USIGS 2 reels 5225
P: Vt-PR

GOSHEN GORE DISTRICT, Vt.
Land records, 1821-1851 St. Johnsbury
N: USIGS 1 reel 5226
P: Vt-PR

GRAFTON, Vt.
Town and vital records, 1781-1862; land
records, 1781-1851 Ibid.
N: USIGS 5 reels 5227
P: Vt-PR

GRANBY, Vt.
Town and vital records, 1798-1833; land
records, 1779-1866 St. Johnsbury
N: USIGS 3 reels 5228
P: Vt-PR

GRAND ISLE, Vt.
Land records, 1799-1867; vital records,
1761-1896 Ibid.
N: USIGS 4 reels 5229
P: Vt-PR

GRANVILLE, Vt.
Proprietors' records, 1782-1785; land
records, 1785-1849; vital records, 1851-1868
Ibid.
N: USIGS 5 reels 5230
P: Vt-PR

GREENSBORO, Vt.
Town and vital records, 1832-1870;
land records, 1831-1854; cemetery records,
1793-1870 Ibid.
N: USIGS 3 reels 5231
P: Vt-PR

GROTON, Vt.
Town records, 1817-1854; land records,
1797-1854; vital records, 1771-1929 Ibid.
N: USIGS 6 reels 5232
P: Vt-PR

GUILDHALL, Vt.
Town and vital records, 1799-1831;
land records, 1784-1858 Ibid.
N: USIGS 5 reels 5233
P: Vt-PR

GUILFORD, Vt.
Town and vital records, 1781-1890; land
records, 1754-1851; vital records, 1754-1804
Ibid.
N: USIGS 7 reels 5234
P: Vt-PR

HALIFAX, Vt.
Town and vital records, 1772-1865; land
records, 1772-1853 Ibid.
N: USIGS 8 reels 5235
P: Vt-PR

HANCOCK, Vt.
Town and vital records, 1792-1861; land
records, 1792-1853 Ibid.
N: USIGS 5 reels 5236
P: Vt-PR

HARDWICK, Vt.
Town records, 1795-1863; land records,
1796-1850; vital records, 1795-1863 Ibid.
N: USIGS 6 reels 5237
P: Vt-PR

HARTFORD, Vt.
Town and vital records, 1764-1859; land
records, 1765-1850; vital records, 1788-1801
White River Junction
N: USIGS 7 reels 5238
P: Vt-PR

HARTLAND, Vt.
Town and vital records, 1777-1867; land
records, 1778-1851 Ibid.
N: USIGS 9 reels 5239
P: Vt-PR

HIGHGATE, Vt.
Town and vital records, 1794-1895; land
records, 1763-1851 Ibid.
N: USIGS 9 reels 5240
P: Vt-PR

HINESBURG, Vt.
Proprietors' records, 1762-1853; land
records, 1762-1853; vital records,
1790-1906 Ibid.
N: USIGS 7 reels 5241
P: Vt-PR

HOLLAND, Vt.
Land records, 1804-1859; vital records,
1829-1867 Ibid.
N: USIGS 2 reels 5242
P: Vt-PR

HUBBARDTON, Vt.
Land records, 1771-1855; vital records,
1770-1896 Ibid.
N: USIGS 7 reels 5243
P: Vt-PR

HUNTINGTON, Vt.
Proprietors' records, 1763-1808; town and
vital records, 1846-1892; land records,
1791-1849; vital records, 1775-1852 Ibid.
N: USIGS 6 reels 5244
P: Vt-PR

HYDE PARK, Vt.
Land records, 1790-1853; vital records,

1789-1947 Ibid.
N: USIGS 5 reels 5245
P: Vt-PR

IRA, Vt.
Land records, 1771-1865; vital records,
1857-1896; index, 1793-1905 Ibid.
N: USIGS 4 reels 5246
P: Vt-PR

IRASBURG, Vt.
Proprietors' records, 1801-1807; town and
vital records, 1803-1892; land records,
1805-1855; vital records, 1857-1869;
cemetery records, 1801-1870 Ibid.
N: USIGS 5 reels 5247
P: Vt-PR

ISLE LA MOTTE, Vt.
Town and vital records, 1791-1864; land
records, 1792-1855; vital records, 1792-1898
Ibid.
N: USIGS 2 reels 5248
P: Vt-PR

JAMAICA, Vt.
Town and vital records, 1790-1879; land
records, 1781-1850 Ibid.
N: USIGS 7 reels 5249
P: Vt-PR

JAY, Vt.
Town and vital records, 1859-1879; land
records, 1828-1853; vital records,
1846-1868 Ibid.
N: USIGS 3 reels 5250
P: Vt-PR

JERICHO, Vt.
Proprietors' records, 1785-1802; town
records, 1785-1802; land records, 1790-1853;
vital records, 1785-1850 Ibid.
N: USIGS 5 reels 5251
P: Vt-PR

JOHNSON, Vt.
Land records, 1828-1853; vital records,
1766-1866 Ibid.
N: USIGS 6 reels 5252
P: Vt-PR

KIRBY, Vt.
Land records, 1810-1859 St. Johnsbury
N: USIGS 2 reels 5253
P: Vt-PR

LANDGROVE, Vt.
Land records, 1800-1853 Ibid.
N: USIGS 1 reel 5254
P: Vt-PR

LEICESTER, Vt.
Land records, 1799-1851; vital records,
1786-1847 Ibid.
N: USIGS 6 reels 5255
P: Vt-PR

LEMINGTON, Vt.
Land records, 1762-1854 Ibid.
N: USIGS 1 reel 5256
P: Vt-PR

LINCOLN, Vt.
Land records, 1782-1854; vital records,
1868-1903 Ibid.
N: USIGS 5 reels 5257
P: Vt-PR

LONDONDERRY, Vt.
Town and vital records, 1785-1894; land
records, 1782-1852 Ibid.
N: USIGS 7 reels 5258
P: Vt-PR

LOWELL, Vt.
Land records, 1812-1835; vital records,
1809-1866 Ibid.
N: USIGS 3 reels 5259
P: Vt-PR

LUDLOW, Vt.
Land records, 1761-1851; vital records,
1768-1901 Ibid.
N: USIGS 7 reels 5260
P: Vt-PR

LUNENBERG, Vt.
Town and vital records, 1803-1856; land

records, 1781-1853 Ibid.
N: USIGS 5 reels   5261
P: Vt-PR

LYNDON, Vt.
   Town and vital records, 1793-1891; land
   records, 1792-1850 Lyndonville
   N: USIGS 4 reels   5262
   P: Vt-PR

MAIDSTONE, Vt.
   Proprietors' records, 1761-1829; town records,
   1827-1891; land records, 1788-1857; vital
   records, 1761-1829 Ibid.
   N: USIGS 3 reels   5263
   P: Vt-PR

MANCHESTER, Vt.
   Land records, 1766-1850 Ibid.
   N: USIGS 6 reels   5264
   P: Vt-PR

MANSFIELD (now STOWE), Vt.
   Town and vital records, 1815-1844;
   land records, 1815-1851 Stowe
   N: USIGS 1 reel   5265
   P: Vt-PR

MARLBORO, Vt.
   Town records, 1781-1857; land records,
   1778-1852; vital records, 1770-1857 Ibid.
   N: USIGS 6 reels   5266
   P: Vt-PR

MARSHFIELD, Vt.
   Town and vital records, 1800-1883; land
   records, 1800-1853; cemetery records,
   1800-1869 Ibid.
   N: USIGS 5 reels   5267
   P: Vt-PR

MENDON, Vt.
   Land records, 1799-1850; vital records,
   1868-1902 Ibid.
   N: USIGS 4 reels   5268
   P: Vt-PR

MIDDLEBURY, Vt.
   Land records. 1788-1852; vital records,
   1783-1901 Ibid.
   N: USIGS 8 reels   5269
   P: Vt-PR

MIDDLESEX, Vt.
   Town and vital records, 1790-1851;
   land records, 1788-1851 Ibid.
   N: USIGS 6 reels   5270
   P: Vt-PR

MIDDLETOWN SPRINGS. Vt.
   Land records, 1785-1850; vital records,
   1800-1867 Ibid.
   N: USIGS 6 reels   5271
   P: Vt-PR

MILTON, Vt.
   Town and vital records, 1795-1811; land
   records, 1788-1854; vital records.
   1797-1857 Ibid.
   N: USIGS 9 reels   5272
   P: Vt-PR

MONKTON. Vt.
   Town and vital records. 1798-1905; land
   records. 1786-1850; vital records,
   1786-1824 Ibid.
   N: USIGS 8 reels   5273
   P: Vt-PR

MONTGOMERY, Vt.
   Town and vital records. 1802-1850; land
   records, 1802-1849; vital records.
   1792-1868 Ibid.
   N: USIGS 4 reels   5274
   P: Vt-PR

MONTPELIER. Vt.
   Land records, 1788-1853 Ibid.
   N: USIGS 8 reels   5275
   P: Vt-PR

MOORETOWN, Vt.
   Town and vital records, 1773-1800 Bradford
   N: USIGS 1 reel   5276
   P: Vt-PR

MORETOWN, Vt.
   Proprietors' records, 1762-1806; land records,

1800-1852; vital records, 1777-1918 Ibid.
N: USIGS 5 reels   5277
P: Vt-PR

MORGAN, Vt.
   Land records, 1780-1846 Ibid.
   N: USIGS 2 reels   5278
   P: Vt-PR

MORGAN, Vt.
   Town records, 1805-1856, 32 p. (transcript)
   NNNG
   N: USIGS 1 reel   5279
   P: Vt-PR

MORRISTOWN, Vt.
   Town and vital records, 1784-1888; land
   records, 1795-1851; cemetery records,
   1795-1870 Ibid.
   N: USIGS 6 reels   5280
   P: Vt-PR

MOUNT HOLLY, Vt.
   Town and vital records, 1792-1907; land
   records, 1792-1852 Ibid.
   N: USIGS 7 reels   5281
   P: Vt-PR

MOUNT TABOR, Vt.
   Land records, 1788-1852; vital records,
   1788-1895 Ibid.
   N: USIGS 4 reels   5282
   P: Vt-PR

NEW HAVEN, Vt.
   Town and vital records, 1791-1864; land
   records, 1786-1857 Ibid.
   N: USIGS 9 reels   5283
   P: Vt-PR

NEWARK, Vt.
   Land records, 1808-1858 Ibid.
   N: USIGS 2 reels   5284
   P: Vt-PR

NEWBURY, Vt.
   Town and vital records, 1784-1855; land
   records, 1782-1851 Ibid.
   N: USIGS 7 reels   5285
   P: Vt-PR

NEWFANE, Vt.
   Land records, 1782-1854; land records.
   1771-1867 Ibid.
   N: USIGS 7 reels   5286
   P: Vt-PR

NEWPORT, Vt.
   Proprietors' records, 1789-1835; town and
   vital records, 1800-1876; land records,
   1797-1851 Ibid.
   N: USIGS 3 reels   5287
   P: Vt-PR

NORTH HERO, Vt.
   Town and vital records, 1832-1882; land
   records, 1795-1854; vital records,
   1857-1896 Ibid.
   N: USIGS 4 reels   5288
   P: Vt-PR

NORTHFIELD, Vt.
   Proprietors' records, 1783-1787; town and
   vital records, 1795-1857; land records,
   1795-1851 Ibid.
   N: USIGS 8 reels   5289
   P: Vt-PR

NORWICH, Vt.
   Town and vital records, 1761-1890;
   land records. 1781-1852; church records.
   1804-1846 Ibid.
   N: USIGS 7 reels   5290
   P: Vt-PR

ORANGE, Vt.
   Proprietors' records, 1785-1812; land
   records, 1786-1852; vital records, 1800-1856;
   cemetery records, 1796-1870 Ibid.
   N: USIGS 7 reels   5291
   P: Vt-PR

ORWELL, Vt.
   Proprietors' records, 1784-1794; town and
   vital records, 1792-1851; land records,
   1792-1851; cemetery records, 1784-1870 Ibid.
   N: USIGS 11 reels   5292
   P: Vt-PR

PANTON, Vt.
   Proprietors' records, 1761-1837; town records,
   1784-1879; land records, 1784-1849; vital
   records, 1784-1879 Ibid.
   N: USIGS 2 reels   5293
   P: Vt-PR

PAWLET, Vt.
   Land records, 1782-1853; vital records,
   1768-1897 Ibid.
   N: USIGS 6 reels   5294
   P: Vt-PR

PEACHAM, Vt.
   Proprietors' records, 1780-1791; land
   records, 1783-1850; vital records, 1783-1884
   Ibid.
   N: USIGS 6 reels   5295
   P: Vt-PR

PERU, Vt.
   Proprietors' records, 1787-1856;
   land records, 1802-1850 Ibid.
   N: USIGS 3 reels   5296
   P: Vt-PR

PITTSFIELD, Vt.
   Town and vital records, 1793-1862; land
   records, 1793-1854 Ibid.
   N: USIGS 3 reels   5297
   P Vt-PR

PITTSFORD, Vt.
   Land records, 1761-1852; vital records,
   1756-1869 Ibid.
   N: USIGS 12 reels   5298
   P: Vt-PR

PLAINFIELD, Vt.
   Town and vital records, 1793-1908; land
   records, 1793-1854 Montpelier
   N: USIGS 4 reels   5299
   P: Vt-PR

PLYMOUTH, Vt.
   Town and vital records, 1830-1858; land
   records, 1761-1854; cemetery records,
   to 1870 Ibid.
   N: USIGS 8 reels   5300
   P: Vt-PR

POMFRET, Vt.
   Land records, 1769-1852; vital records,
   1770-1868 Ibid.
   N: USIGS 8 reels   5301
   P: Vt-PR

POWNAL, Vt.
   Town and vital records, 1830-1850; land
   records, 1760-1850; vital records, 1760-1787
   Ibid.
   N: USIGS 8 reels   5302
   P: Vt-PR

PUTNEY, Vt.
   Proprietors' records, 1753-1762; town and
   vital records, 1770-1851; land records,
   1770-1851 Ibid.
   N: USIGS 8 reels   5303
   P: Vt-PR

PUTNEY, Vt.
   Town records, 1740-1850 (transcript) NNNG
   N: USIGS   5304
   P: NNNG

RANDOLPH, Vt.
   Land records, 1783-1850; vital records,
   1785-1861 Ibid.
   N: USIGS 7 reels   5305
   P: Vt-PR

READING, Vt.
   Town and vital records, 1785-1858; land
   records, 1760-1851 Ibid.
   N: USIGS 11 reels   5306
   P: Vt-PR

READSBORO, Vt.
   Town and vital records, 1794-1864; land
   records, 1797-1854 Ibid.
   N: USIGS 7 reels   5307
   P: Vt-PR

RICHFORD, Vt.
   Town and vital records, 1799-1871; land
   records, 1800-1854 Ibid.
   N: USIGS 6 reels   5308
   P: Vt-PR

RICHMOND, Vt.
Town and vital records, 1795-1856; land records, 1795-1851; cemetery records, 1795-1870 Ibid.
N: USIGS 5 reels 5309
P: Vt-PR

RIPTON, Vt.
Proprietors' records, 1781-1860; town and vital records, 1781-1870; land records, 1836-1850 Ibid.
N: USIGS 3 reels 5310
P: Vt-PR

ROCHESTER, Vt.
Proprietors' records, 1781-1821; town and vital records, 1788-1860; land records, 1788-1860 Ibid.
N: USIGS 5 reels 5311
P: Vt-PR

ROCKINGHAM, Vt.
Town records, 1752-1761; town and vital records, 1779-1860; land records, 1779-1860; vital records, 1839-1870 Bellows Falls
N: USIGS 9 reels 5312
P: Vt-PR

ROXBURY, Vt.
Town and vital records, 1796-1851; land records, 1796-1851; cemetery records, 1722-1857 Ibid.
N: USIGS 5 reels 5313
P: Vt-PR

ROYALTON, Vt.
Land records, 1784-1851; vital records, 1784-1854 Ibid.
N: USIGS 7 reels 5314
P: Vt-PR

RUPERT, Vt.
Land records, 1780-1850 Ibid.
N: USIGS 5 reels 5315
P: Vt-PR

RUTLAND, Vt.
Land records, 1792-1851; vital records, 1857-1875 Ibid.
N: USIGS 9 reels 5316
P: Vt-PR

RYEGATE, Vt.
Town and vital records, 1799-1886; land records, 1781-1849; vital records, 1770-1915; cemetery records, 1781-1870 Ibid.
N: USIGS 7 reels 5317
P: Vt-PR

ST. ALBANS, Vt.
Town and vital records, 1788-1844; land records, 1790-1850; vital records, 1790-1844 Ibid.
N: USIGS 9 reels 5318
P: Vt-PR

ST. GEORGE, Vt.
Land records, 1813-1856; vital records, 1813-1850 Ibid.
N: USIGS 1 reel 5319

ST. JOHNSBURY, Vt.
Land records, 1787-1852; vital records, 1807-1853 Ibid.
N: USIGS 7 reels 5320
P: Vt-PR

SALEM (now DERBY), Vt.
Land records, 1820-1852 Derby Center
N: USIGS 1 reel 5321
P: Vt-PR

SALISBURY, Vt.
Proprietors' records, 1786-1859; town and vital records, 1786-1859; land records, 1786-1859 Ibid.
N: USIGS 4 reels 5322
P: Vt-PR

SANDGATE, Vt.
Land records, 1775-1854 Ibid.
N: USIGS 4 reels 5323
P: Vt-PR

SEARSBURG, Vt.
Land records, 1820-1853; vital records,

1820-1952; cemetery records, 1820-1870 Ibid.
N: USIGS 2 reels 5324
P: Vt-PR

SHAFTSBURY, Vt.
Proprietors' records, 1760-1815; town and vital records, 1718-1906; land records, 1779-1851; cemetery records, 1766-1910 Ibid.
N: USIGS 11 reels 5325
P: Vt-PR

SHARON, Vt.
Town and vital records, 1768-1880; land records, 1761-1881 Ibid.
N: USIGS 6 reels 5326
P: Vt-PR

SHEFFIELD, Vt.
Town and vital records, 1796-1856; land records, 1793-1852 Ibid.
N: USIGS 4 reels 5327
P: Vt-PR

SHELBURNE, Vt.
Town and vital records, 1799-1875; land records, 1783-1849; cemetery records, 1799-1870 Ibid.
N: USIGS 5 reels 5328
P: Vt-PR

SHELDON, Vt.
Town and vital records, 1794-1840; land records, 1794-1852; vital records, 1840-1898 Ibid.
N: USIGS 6 reels 5329
P: Vt-PR

SHERBURNE, Vt.
Land records, 1761-1851 Ibid.
N: USIGS 3 reels 5330
P: Vt-PR

SHOREHAM, Vt.
Land records, 1789-1851; vital records, 1857-1896; cemetery records, v.d.; miscellaneous records, 1784-1832 Ibid.
N: USIGS 8 reels 5331
P: Vt-PR

SHREWSBURY, Vt.
Town records, 1772-1868; land records, 1782-1851; vital records, 1772-1908 Ibid.
N: USIGS 7 reels 5332
P: Vt-PR

SOMERSET, Vt.
Land records, 1795-1857 Ibid.
N: USIGS 2 reels 5333
P: Vt-PR

SOUTH HERO, Vt.
Town and vital records, 1817-1869; land records, 1783-1854; vital records, 1857-1896; cemetery records, 1784-1870 Ibid.
N: USIGS 7 reels 5334
P: Vt-PR

SPRINGFIELD, Vt.
Town and vital records, 1730-1880; land records, 1778-1852 Ibid.
N: USIGS 10 reels 5335
P: Vt-PR

STAMFORD, Vt.
Land records, 1777-1850; vital records, 1812-1816 Ibid.
N: USIGS 6 reels 5336
P: Vt-PR

STARKSBORO, Vt.
Proprietors' records, 1792-1877; town and vital records, 1797-1851; land records, 1796-1849 Ibid.
N: USIGS 5 reels 5337
P: Vt-PR

STERLING, Vt.
Town and vital records, 1806-1834; land records, 1832-1852 Morrisville
N: USIGS 1 reel 5338
P: Vt-PR

STOCKBRIDGE, Vt.
Town records, 1802-1854; land records, 1761-1851; vital records, 1797-1854 Gaysville
N: USIGS 10 reels 5339
P: Vt-PR

STOWE, Vt.
Town and vital records, 1814-1856; land records, 1795-1850; vital records, 1797-1857 Ibid.
N: USIGS 5 reels 5340
P: Vt-PR

STOWE, Vt., see MANSFIELD, Vt., 5265

STRAFFORD, Vt.
Town and vital records, 1761-1904; land records, 1784-1850 Ibid.
N: USIGS 7 reels 5341
P: Vt-PR

STRATTON, Vt.
Proprietors' records, 1783-1795; land records, 1792-1853; vital records, 1788-1867; cemetery records, 1783-1870 Ibid.
N: USIGS 5 reels 5342
P: Vt-PR

SUDBURY, Vt.
Proprietors' records, 1773-1836; land records, 1783-1852; vital records, 1788-1859; cemetery records, 1788-1870 Ibid.
N: USIGS 6 reels 5343
P: Vt-PR

SUNDERLAND, Vt.
Proprietors' records, 1761-1918; land records, 1760-1857; vital records, 1760-1918 Ibid.
N: USIGS 5 reels 5344
P: Vt-PR

SUTTON, Vt.
Town and vital records, 1794-1940; land records, 1791-1852; cemetery records, 1791-1870 Ibid.
N: USIGS 5 reels 5345
P: Vt-PR

SWANTON, Vt.
Proprietors' records, 1790-1805; town and vital records, 1790-1823; land records, 1790-1851 Ibid.
N: USIGS 9 reels 5346
P: Vt-PR

THETFORD, Vt.
Land records, 1778-1850; vital records, 1768-1904 Ibid.
N: USIGS 9 reels 5347
P: Vt-PR

TINMOUTH, Vt.
Land records, 1771-1855; vital records, 1802-1904; church records, 1804-1866 Ibid.
N: USIGS 5 reels 5348
P: Vt-PR

TOPSHAM, Vt.
Town and vital records, 1792-1855; land records, 1794-1849 Waits River
N: USIGS 6 reels 5349
P: Vt-PR

TOWNSHEND, Vt.
Proprietors' records, 1753-1801; town and vital records, 1787-1869; land records, 1780-1850; vital records, 1780-1869 Ibid.
N: USIGS 8 reels 5350
P: Vt-PR

TOWNSHEND, Vt., see ACTON, Vt., 5150

TROY, Vt.
Town and vital records, 1802-1842; land records, 1806-1854 Ibid.
N: USIGS 3 reels 5351
P: Vt-PR

TUNBRIDGE, Vt.
Town and vital records, 1785-1878; land records, 1761-1852; church records, 1792-1864 Ibid.
N: USIGS 7 reels 5352
P: Vt-PR

UNDERHILL, Vt.
Town and vital records, 1797-1866; land records, 1795-1850; vital records, 1797-1865; cemetery records, 1795-1870 Ibid.
N: USIGS 7 reels 5353
P: Vt-PR

VERGENNES, Vt.
Town and vital records, 1792-1844; land

records, 1793-1854 Ibid.
N: USIGS 6 reels   5354
P: Vt-PR

VERNON, Vt.
Town records, 1820-1876; land records,
1774-1876; vital records, 1774-1876 Ibid.
N: USIGS 7 reels   5355
P: Vt-PR

VERSHIRE, Vt.
Land records, 1791-1853; vital records,
1793-1857 Ibid.
N: USIGS 5 reels   5356
P: Vt-PR

VICTORY, Vt.
Proprietors' records, 1798-1802; land
records, 1841-1854 St. Johnsbury
N: USIGS 1 reel   5357
P: Vt-PR

WAITSFIELD, Vt.
Land records, 1795-1856; vital records,
1789-1856; church records, 1796-1855 Ibid.
N: USIGS 5 reels   5353
P: Vt-PR

WALDEN, Vt.
Town and vital records, 1801-1865; land
records, 1794-1850 Ibid.
N: USIGS 4 reels   5359
P: Vt-PR

WALLINGFORD, Vt.
Land records, 1762-1854; vital records, 1883-
1904; miscellaneous records, 1770-1890 Ibid.
N: USIGS 7 reels   5360
P: Vt-PR

WALTHAM, Vt.
Town and vital records, 1842-1861; land
records, 1797-1864 Ibid.
N: USIGS 3 reels   5361
P: Vt-PR

WARDSBORO, Vt.
Land records, 1787-1850; vital records,
1790-1906 Ibid.
N: USIGS 5 reels   5362
P: Vt-PR

WARREN, Vt.
Town and vital records, 1798-1874; land
records, 1798-1849 Ibid.
N: USIGS 4 reels   5363
P: Vt-PR

WASHINGTON, Vt.
Town and vital records, 1795-1864;
land records, 1793-1853 Ibid.
N: USIGS 7 reels   5364
P: Vt-PR

WATERBURY, Vt.
Proprietors' records, 1763-1796; town and
vital records, 1796-1854; land records,
1790-1850; vital records, 1761-1942 Ibid.
N: USIGS 7 reels   5365
P: Vt-PR

WATERFORD, Vt.
Land records, 1793-1849; land records,
1793-1856; cemetery records, 1782-1869 Ibid.
N: USIGS 5 reels   5366
P: Vt-PR

WATERVILLE, Vt.
Town and vital records, 1807-1864; land
records, 1824-1855; vital records,
1857-1867 Ibid.
N: USIGS 3 reels   5367
P: Vt-PR

WEATHERSFIELD, Vt.
Town and vital records, 1772-1880; land
records, 1781-1853; cemetery records,
1772-1940 Perkinsville
N: USIGS 10 reels   5368
P: Vt-PR

WELLS, Vt.
Land records, 1779-1857 Ibid.
N: USIGS 4 reels   5369
P: Vt-PR

WEST FAIRLEE, Vt.
Town and vital records, 1797-1851; land

records, 1797-1852 Ibid.
N: USIGS 4 reels   5370
P: Vt-PR

WEST HAVEN, Vt.
Land records, 1795-1852; vital records,
1868-1896
N: USIGS 4 reels   5371
P: Vt-PR

WESTFIELD, Vt.
Land records, 1805-1900; vital records,
1802-1872 Ibid.
N: USIGS 3 reels   5372
P: Vt-PR

WESTFORD, Vt.
Land records, 1793-1850 Ibid.
N: USIGS 6 reels   5373
P: Vt-PR

WESTMINSTER, Vt.
Proprietors' records, 1736-1767; land records,
1786-1852; vital records, 1786-1857 Ibid.
N: USIGS 9 reels   5374
P: Vt-PR

WESTMORE, Vt.
Proprietors' records, 1800-1805; land
records, 1803-1853 Ibid.
N: USIGS 1 reel   5375
P: Vt-PR

WESTON, Vt.
Land records, 1800-1854; vital records,
1795-1852 Ibid.
N: USIGS 6 reels   5376
P: Vt-PR

WEYBRIDGE, Vt.
Land records, 1789-1850; vital records,
1774-1875 Ibid.
N: USIGS 4 reels   5377
P: Vt-PR

WHEELOCK, Vt.
Land records, 1796-1852 Ibid.
N: USIGS 4 reels   5378
P: Vt-PR

WHITING, Vt.
Land records, 1783-1863; vital records,
1783-1863 Ibid.
N: USIGS 4 reels   5379
P: Vt-PR

WHITINGHAM, Vt.
Town and vital records, 1781-1909;
land records, 1780-1851; vital records,
1780-1803; cemetery records, 1770-1870
Ibid.
N: USIGS 8 reels   5380
P: Vt-PR

WILLIAMSTOWN, Vt.
Proprietors' records, 1781-1787; town and
vital records, 1784-1798; land records,
1784-1851; vital records, 1789-1869 Ibid.
N: USIGS 6 reels   5381
P: Vt-PR

WILLISTON, Vt.
Proprietors' records, 1763-1804; land
records, 1772-1854; vital records,
1772-1811, 1816-1865 Ibid.
N: USIGS 7 reels   5382
P: Vt-PR

WILMINGTON, Vt.
Proprietors' records, 1794-1875; town and
vital records, 1794-1875; land records,
1766-1855; vital records, 1766-1803 Ibid.
N: USIGS 8 reels   5383
P: Vt-PR

WINDHAM, Vt.
Town and vital records, 1796-1860; land
records, 1796-1850 Ibid.
N: USIGS 3 reels   5384
P: Vt-PR

WINDSOR, Vt.
Land records, 1761-1851; vital records,
1765-1851 Ibid.
N: USIGS 11 reels   5385
P: Vt-PR

WINHALL, Vt.
Land records, 1796-1853; vital records,

1796-1853 Ibid.
N: USIGS 3 reels   5386
P: Vt-PR

WOLCOTT, Vt.
Land records, 1787-1853; vital records,
1794-1875; cemetery records, 1794-1870 Ibid.
N: USIGS 4 reels   5387
P: Vt-PR

WOODBURY, Vt.
Land records, 1797-1853; vital records,
1803-1883; cemetery records, 1800-1870 Ibid.
N: USIGS 4 reels   5388
P: Vt-PR

WOODFORD, Vt.
Town and vital records, 1792-1850; land
records, 1792-1850 Ibid.
N: USIGS 4 reels   5389
P: Vt-PR

WOODSTOCK, Vt.
Land records, 1779-1850; vital records,
1754-1868 Ibid.
N: USIGS 9 reels   5390
P: Vt-PR

WORCESTER, Vt.
Land records, 1803-1838; vital records,
1803-1882; cemetery records, 1803-1870
Ibid.
N: USIGS 3 reels   5391
P: Vt-PR

Church Records

FRIENDS, SOCIETY OF. DANBY [Vt.]
MONTHLY MEETING
Births and deaths, 1795-1876; minutes,
1795-1878; removals, 1828-1857; women's
minutes, 1815-1861 NNSF
N: USIGS 3 reels   5392
P: PHC PSC-F

FRIENDS, SOCIETY OF. FERRISBURG [Vt.]
MONTHLY MEETING
Minutes, 1801-1849; register, 1829-1846;
women's minutes, 1801-1855 NNSF
N: USIGS 2 reels   5393
P: PHC PSC-F

FRIENDS, SOCIETY OF. FERRISBURG [Vt.]
MONTHLY MEETING
Records, 1755-1881 Ibid.
N: USIGS 1 reel   5394

FRIENDS, SOCIETY OF. LINCOLN [Vt.]
MEETING
Vital records, 1758-1862, 54 p. Ibid.
DCO: N
N: USIGS   5395

FRIENDS, SOCIETY OF. STARKSBOROUGH [Vt.]
MONTHLY MEETING
Men's minutes, 1813-1838 NNSF
N: USIGS   5396
P: PHC PSC-F

HARTLAND, Vt. CHURCH OF CHRIST
Record books, 1779-1827, nos. 1-2 VtHi
N: USIGS 5 reels   **5397**

SANDGATE, Vt. CONGREGATIONAL CHURCH
Records, 1775-1867, 35 p. (transcript) N
N: USIGS   5398

Personal Papers

ALLEN, IRA, 1751-1814
Papers, 1767-1814 N
DCO: VtU   5399

BULLOCK FAMILY
Papers re: Guilford, Vt., 1760-1850 priv.
N: VtHi 1 reel   5400

CRAFTS, SAMUEL CHANDLER, 1768-1853
Plans [land records] Vt-PR
N: Vt-PR 1 reel   5401
P: VtU

MORRILL, JUSTIN SMITH, 1810-1898
Letters on Vermont politics, 1852-1857,
43 items DLC
N: VtU 90 frames   5402

TYLER, ROYALL, 1757-1826
Correspondence and legal papers re: the
Royall Tyler collection VtHi
N: Vt-PR 2 reels *
P: VtHi
5403

WASHINGTON, GEORGE, Pres. U.S., 1732-1799
Papers re: Vermont DLC
N: VtHi 1 reel
5404

WILLIAMS, SAMUEL, 1743-1817
Philosophical lectures on the constitution,
duty, and religion of man, 387 p. VtHi
N: VtHi 1 reel 16 mm.
5405

Business Papers

FARRAND,   of Fairfield, Vt.
Account book, 1839-1860 priv.
N: VtHi 25 feet
5406

Collections

U.S. LIBRARY OF CONGRESS
Papers of Vermont, miscellany DLC
N: VtHi 3 reels
5407

MASSACHUSETTS

Census

MASSACHUSETTS. SECRETARY OF STATE
Census, 1855 M-Ar
N: M-Ar 33 reels
5408

MASSACHUSETTS. SECRETARY OF STATE
Census, 1865 M-Ar
N: M-Ar 32 reels
5409

U.S. CENSUS. FIFTH, 1830
Population schedules, Massachusetts DNA
N: DNA 10 reels
5410

U.S. CENSUS. SIXTH, 1840
Population schedules, Massachusetts DNA
N: DNA 11 reels
P: USIGS
5411

U.S. CENSUS. SEVENTH, 1850
Population schedules, Massachusetts DNA
N: DNA 9 reels
P: USIGS
5412

U.S. CENSUS. SEVENTH, 1850
Population schedules, Massachusetts M-Ar
N: M-Ar 22 reels
5413

U.S. CENSUS. EIGHTH, 1860
Population schedules, Massachusetts DNA
N: DNA 12 reels
P: USIGS
5414

U.S. CENSUS. NINTH, 1870
Population schedules, Massachusetts DNA
N: DNA 15 reels
P: USIGS
5415

U.S. CENSUS. NINTH, 1870
Population schedules, Massachusetts M-Ar
N: M-Ar 20 reels
5416

U.S. CENSUS. TENTH, 1880
Population schedules, Massachusetts DNA
N: DNA 50 reels
5417

Government Records

U.S. BUREAU OF CUSTOMS
Index to passenger lists of vessels arriving at
Boston, 1848-1891 DNA
N: DNA 282 reels 16 mm. [M-265]
5418

U.S. BUREAU OF MARINE INSPECTION AND
NAVIGATION
Certificates of registry, enrollment, and
license issued by the collector of customs at
Edgartown, Mass., 1815-1913 DNA
N: DNA 9 reels [M-130]
5419

U.S. CUSTOMS HOUSE, GLOUCESTER, Mass.
Register of ships, 1847-1849 (partly burnt)
DNA
N: MSaP 10 feet
5420

U.S. CUSTOMS HOUSE, SALEM, Mass.
Impost books, 1789-1797, 1807-1811,
1816-1824 MSaE
N: MSaP 3 reels
5421

U.S. CUSTOMS HOUSE, SALEM, Mass.
Records, 1795, 1807-1811 MSaE
N: MSaP 2 reels
5422

U.S. CUSTOMS HOUSE, SALEM AND BEVERLY
Register of ships, 1792-1800 DNA
N: MAaP 1 reel
5423

U.S. MARINE BOARD
Letter book, Boston, 1778 MdAN
N: PHi 1 reel
5424

State Records

MASSACHUSETTS. COURT OF ADMIRALTY AND
COURT OF VICE ADMIRALTY
Records, 1718-1750, 1765-1772
Mass. Supreme Court
DCO: DLC 3 boxes
5425

MASSACHUSETTS. GENERAL COURT
Fast Day proclamations, 1673/4-1678 M-Ar
N: MHi 1 frame
5426

MASSACHUSETTS. SUPERINTENDENT OF
ALIEN PASSENGERS
Passenger lists, 1849-1891 M-Ar
N: M-Ar 70 reels
5427

County Records

FRANKLIN Co., Mass.
Deeds, 1802-1826 C.H. Greenfield
N: USIGS 10 reels
5428

HAMPSHIRE Co., Mass.
Vital records, 1638-1696; "Waste book,"
1663-1667 MSCV
DCO: Ct
N: USIGS 1 reel
5429

Town and City Records

BOSTON, Mass.
Indentures of poor apprentices, 1734-1805
Ibid.
N: Ibid. 2 reels
P: ViWI
5430

BOSTON, Mass.
Town records, 1634-1822; selectmen's
records, 1701-1822; city records, 1822-1914
Ibid.
N: MB 174 reels
P: M
5431

BRIGHTON, Mass.
Town records, 1807-1874 City Clerk, Boston
N: MB 2 reels
P: MB
5432

CHARLESTOWN, Mass.
Town records, 1629-1847 City Clerk, Boston
N: MB 13 reels
P: MB
5433

DORCHESTER, Mass.
Town records, 1632-1870 City Clerk, Boston
N: MB 16 reels
P: MB
5434

EAST GRANVILLE, Mass.
Death records, 1739-1863 (transcript) Ct
N: USIGS
5435

HYDE PARK, Mass.
Town records, 1868-1912 City Clerk, Boston
N: MB 4 reels
P: MB
5436

NEW BEDFORD, Mass.
Taxation rate, 1771, 23 p. MH-BA
N: CU 1 reel
5437

QUINCY, Mass.
Town records, 1791-1891 Ibid.
N: MHi 2 reels
5438

ROXBURY, Mass.
Town of Roxbury street records, 3 v.

Boston, Mass.
N: NNU 1 reel
5439

ROXBURY, Mass.
Town records, 1648-1846; city records, 1846-
1849 City Clerk, Boston
N: MB 13 reels
P: MB
5440

ROXBURY, Mass.
Town records, 17th and 18th cents. Boston
N: NNU 4 reels
P: NNU 1 reel
5441

SWANSEA, Mass.
Index to town records RHi
N: USIGS 2 reels
5442

WEST ROXBURY, Mass.
Town records, 1851-1874 City Clerk, Boston
N: MB 3 reels
P: MB
5443

Church Records

BOSTON. ST. PAUL'S CHURCH
Vital records, 1801-1839 Ct
N: USIGS
P: Ct
5444

CANTON, Mass.
Church records, 1717-1799 (transcribed by
Elijah Dunbar) Ibid.
N: MHi 10 feet
5445

FRIENDS, SOCIETY OF. BOLTON [Mass.]
MONTHLY MEETING
Men's minutes, 1799-1881; women's minutes,
1799-1884 RPMB
N: USIGS
P: PSC-F
5446

FRIENDS, SOCIETY OF. EAST HOOSACK
[Mass.] MONTHLY MEETING
Births and deaths, 1783-1842; minutes,
1783-1820, 1833-1843; women's minutes,
1783-1845 NNSF
N: USIGS 3 reels
P: PHC PSC-F
5447

FRIENDS, SOCIETY OF. HAMPTON [Mass.]
MONTHLY MEETING
Minutes, 1701-1804 RPMB
N: USIGS
P: PSC-F
5448

FRIENDS, SOCIETY OF. NANTUCKET [Mass.]
MONTHLY MEETING
Births, deaths, and marriages, 1792-1885;
marriage certificates, 1755; minutes,
1708-1839 RHi
N: RHi 4 reels
P: USIGS
5449

FRIENDS, SOCIETY OF. NANTUCKET [Mass.]
MONTHLY MEETING
Births, deaths, removals, and disownments,
1708-1914; marriages, 1709-1817; men's
minutes, 1708-1873
N: PSC-F
P: PSC-F
5450

FRIENDS, SOCIETY OF. NANTUCKET [Mass.]
MONTHLY MEETING
Births and deaths, 1845-1867; marriages,
1845-1867; men's minutes, 1845-1867;
women's minutes, 1845-1867 RPMB
N: USIGS
P: PSC-F
5451

FRIENDS, SOCIETY OF. NANTUCKET [Mass.]
MONTHLY MEETING
Marriage certificates, books 1-2; minutes,
v. 1-5; record book [vital records]; Northern
District minutes and marriage certificates;
Nova Scotia Meeting minutes; Otis Group
yearly meeting, 1863
Nantucket Historical Association, Nantucket,
Mass.
N: RHi
P: PHC
5452

FRIENDS, SOCIETY OF. NANTUCKET [Mass.]
MONTHLY MEETING FOR THE NORTHERN
DISTRICT
Marriages, 1795-1828; removals, 1744-1828
N: PSC-F
P: PSC-F
5453

FRIENDS, SOCIETY OF. NEW BEDFORD
[Mass.] MONTHLY MEETING
Births and deaths, 1793-1947; marriages,
1699-1792; men's minutes, 1792-1850;
removals, 1792-1887; women's minutes,
1792-1850 Ibid.
N: USIGS
P: PSC-F   5454

FRIENDS, SOCIETY OF. PEMBROKE [Mass.]
MONTHLY MEETING
Men's minutes, 1702-1876; women's minutes,
1676-1876 RPBM
N: USIGS
P: PSC-F   5455

FRIENDS, SOCIETY OF. RICHMOND [Mass.]
MONTHLY MEETING
Epistles, removals, 1793-1836; denials,
1820-1836; list of members, 1792-1850; men's
minutes, 1792-1835; women's minutes,
1792-1850 RPBM
N: USIGS
P: PSC-F   5456

FRIENDS, SOCIETY OF. SANDWICH [Mass.]
MONTHLY MEETING
Births and deaths, 1750-1850; births, deaths,
and marriages, 1646-1761, 1802-1916;
marriages, 1762-1841; men's minutes,
1672-1852; women's minutes, 1802-1861 Ibid.
N: USIGS
P: PSC-F   5457

FRIENDS, SOCIETY OF. SEABROOK [Mass.]
MONTHLY MEETING
Men's minutes, 1700-1875; women's minutes,
1701-1888 RPMB
N: USIGS
P: PSC-F   5458

FRIENDS, SOCIETY OF. SEABROOK AND
AMESBURY [Mass.] MONTHLY MEETING
Minutes, 1844-1888
N: USIGS
P: PSC-F   5459

FRIENDS, SOCIETY OF. SWANSEA [Mass.]
MONTHLY MEETING
Acknowledgements and denials, 1787-1801;
births and deaths, 1784-1843; list of those
travelling in New England Yearly Meetings,
1656-1891; marriages, 1733-1821; membership, 1720-1875; men's minutes, 1732-1888;
removals, 1803-1837; women's minutes,
1732-1878 RPMB
N: USIGS
P: PSC-F   5460

GRAVES, Rev. J.
Letter to Episcopal Church in Providence, July
13, 1776   William Clark papers MBD
N: MBD 4 frames   5461

HARTWELL, Rev. JOHN
Pastor's record book: Leverett, Mass., 1859-
1863; Becket, Mass., 1864-1870; Southbury,
Conn., 1872-1878 Ct
N: USIGS 1 reel   5462

MIDDLEBORO, Mass. THIRD CALVINISTIC
BAPTIST CHURCH
Records, 1761-1932 Ibid.
N: MNtCA 1 reel   5463

NEWTON THEOLOGICAL INSTITUTION, Newton
Center, Mass. TRUSTEES
Records, 1826-1901 MNtCA
N: MNtCA 1 reel   5464

PLAINFIELD, Mass. CONGREGATIONAL CHURCH
Church records, 1785-1841 Ct
N: USIGS 1 reel   5465

PROTESTANT EPISCOPAL CHURCH IN THE
U.S.A. DIOCESES. MASSACHUSETTS
Records of New England churches: originals,
1761-1811; transcripts, 1602-1908 MBD
N: MBD 1 reel
P: WaU   5466

STERLING (formerly LANCASTER), Mass.
SECOND CHURCH
Record book, 1744-1813, 216 p. Ibid.
DCO: MWA   5467

WEST GRANVILLE, Mass. SECOND CHURCH
OF CHRIST (Congregational)

Church records, 1739-1863 Ct
N: USIGS 1 reel   5468

WEST QUINCY, Mass. SWEDISH BAPTIST
CHURCH
Records [Swedish and English], 1885-1922,
7 v. Ibid.
N: Ibid. 1 reel
P: MNtCA *   5469

Personal Papers

ALCOTT, BRONSON, 1799-1888
Diaries and letters, 1826-1882 MCo
N: MCo 30 reels*
P: MCo   5470

ALLEN FAMILY
Correspondence of Elisha Lee Allen, Jonathan
Allen, Thomas Allen, William Allen, John
Breck, John Codman, Eleazar Wheelock Ripley,
and Love (Allen) Ripley NNF
N: ? 1 reel
P: MPB   5471

AMORY FAMILY
Papers, 1709-1807 priv.
N: MHi 5 reels
P: CSmH   5472

BARRELL, JOSEPH, d. 1804
Letter book, 1791-1797   MH
N: MHi 1 reel   5473

BASS, EDWARD, Bp., 1726-1803
Correspondence, 1778-1784, 12 items MBD
N: MBD 23 frames   5474

BELCHER, JONATHAN, 1681-1757
Letterbooks, 1723/4-1755 MHi
N: NjP 7 reels   5475

BELCHER, JONATHAN, 1681-1757
Manuscript commonplace book, 1727 MH
N: CU 1 reel   5476

BEMIS, GEORGE, 1816-1878
Letters, 1859-1862, 23 items   priv.
N: MHi 1 reel   5477

BRADFORD, WILLIAM, 1590-1657, Gov.
Plymouth
Letter to John Winthrop, Oct. 11, 1645
Wakeman Collection CtSoP
Ph: CtSoP   5478

BURR, ESTHER, 1731-1758
Journal, 1754-1757
N: MHi   5479

CHANDLER, SAMUEL, 1713-1775
Diary, 1746, 1749-1758, 1761-1764 MSaE;
1769-1772 priv.
N: MHi 1 reel   5480

CHANNING, WILLIAM ELLERY, 1780-1842
In-letters RHi
N: RPB 1 reel   5481

CHANNING, WILLIAM ELLERY, 1780-1842
Letter to Harmanus Bleeker, Feb. 7, 1842
CSmH
N: RPB   5482

CHANNING, WILLIAM ELLERY, 1818-1901
Journal, 1852-1867, 6v.   MH
N: RPB 4 reels   5483

COBB, DAVID, 1748-1830
Correspondence with Robert Treat Paine,
1770-1781 Paine Papers MHi
N: MAnP 1/2 reel   5484

COE, GEORGE SIMMONS, 1817-1896
Correspondence with Salmon Portland Chase,
1861-1862 DNA
N: MH-BA 1 reel   5485

COOLIDGE, Mrs.
Letters, 1845-1847 Mss. Heard V-B-121
MH-B
N: MSaP 1 reel   5486

CUSHING, THOMAS, and FRYE, PETER
Letters, 1774-1778 MHi
N: MHi 5 1/2 feet   5487

DIXON, FREDERICK
In-letters, as editor of the *Christian Science
Monitor*, 1914-1918, 67 items DLC
DCO: NN   5488

GREEN, JACOB, 1722-1790
Diary, 1751-1787 NjP
N: MHi 4 feet   5489

GREEN, JACOB, 1722-1790
Meditations about quitting his job, Dec. 1, 1768
N: MHi 1 1/2 feet   5490

GURNEY, THOMAS
Shorthand dictionary, 1790 NN
N: MSaP 1 reel   5491

HALE, ROBERT, 1668-1719
Letters, 1691-1755, 23 items MWA
DCO: MnHi   5492

HAWLEY, JOSEPH, 1723-1788
Papers (including those of Northampton, Mass.,
Committee of Public Safety, 1653-1789), 1 v.
NN
N: CU 1 reel   5493

HEARD, AUGUSTINE, 1785-1868
Foreign letters, 1808-1864 MH-B
N: MSaP 1 reel   5494

HEARD, AUGUSTINE, 1785-1868
Letters, 1841-1843 Mss. Heard v. C-8 MH-B
N: MSaP 1 reel   5495

HUTCHINSON, THOMAS, 1711-1780
Correspondence, 1740-1774, 7 items PHi
N: RPB   5496

HUTCHINSON, THOMAS, 1711-1780
Correspondence, 1741-1743, 1761-1770,
v. 25, 26 "Massachusetts Archives" M-Ar
N: M-Ar
P: CSmH   5497

HUTCHINSON, THOMAS, 1711-1780
Correspondence, 1766-1791 MiU-C
N: MHi 45 feet   5498

HUTCHINSON, THOMAS, 1711-1780
Correspondence, 1766-1782, 10 items PPAmP
N: RPB   5499

HUTCHINSON, THOMAS, 1711-1780
Correspondence, 1771-1774, v.25-27
"Massachusetts Archives" M-Ar
N: RPB 2 reels   5500

HUTCHINSON, THOMAS, 1711-1780
Correspondence, 29 items CSmH
N: RPB   5501

JUDD, SYLVESTER, 1789-1860
The Judd manuscripts, v. 1-3, 5-7, 5b MNF
N: Porter-Phelps-Huntington Foundation,
Hadley 2 reels
RN: MNF   5502

JUDD, SYLVESTER, 1789-1860
The Judd manuscripts, v. 1-2 MNF
N: MNF Northampton 1 reel
P: MNF   5503

JUDSON, ADONIRAM, 1788-1850
Letters, 17 items MNtCA
N: MNtCA 1 reel
P: MNtCA   5504

LAWRENCE, AMOS, 1786-1852
Letters   Robinson papers MHi
N: KU 193 frames
DCO: KU   505

LONGFELLOW, STEPHEN
Diaries, 1771-1795 MHi
N: MHi 1 reel   5506

MacGILL, CHARLES
Papers re: Fort Warren, Boston, Dec., 1861-
Dec., 1862 NcD
N: MBU 1 reel   5507

MAYHEW, JONATHAN, 1720-1766
Sermons, 1749-1764, 8 items CSmH
N: MBU 1 reel   5508

O'CONNOR, JAMES FRANCIS THADDEUS, 1884-
Diary, 1933-1940 priv.
N: MH 2 reels   5509

OSSOLI, SARAH MARGARET (FULLER),
MARCHESA D', 1810-1850
Papers MB
N: NcD 2 reels   5510

PARKMAN, FRANCIS, 1823-1893
Correspondence with Abbé Casgrain, 1866-1896
MH
N: MHi 20 feet   5511

PRINCE, THOMAS, 1687-1758
Manuscripts and sermons, 1717-1785 v.p.
N: WaU 1 reel   5512

PYNCHON, JOHN, 1626-1702
Hampshire records of births, marriages, and
deaths, 1651-1674, 238 p.   MSCV
N: MSCV*   5513

PYNCHON, JOHN, 1626-1702
Waste book for Hampshire Co., Mass., 1663-
1676, 156 p.   MSCV
N: MSCV*   5514
P: MSCV

SARGENT, WINTHROP, 1753-1820
Correspondence, 1790-1820 (originals and
transcripts) TxHR
N: MHi 3 reels   5515
P: TxHR

SEARS, BARNAS, 1802-1880
Notes of his lectures, Oct., 1838-   MNtCA
N: MNtCA 1 reel   5516

SEWALL, SAMUEL, 1652-1730
Journal, 1683 et seq. MH
N: MHi 1 reel   5517

SLATTERY, CHARLES LEWIS, Bp., 1867-1930
Correspondence with Bishop Whipple and
others, 1882-1922, 67 items priv.
N: MBD 150 frames   5518
P: MnHi

STUART, MOSES, 1780-1852
Papers MNtCA
N: MNtCA 5 reels   5519

THACHER, PETER, 1651-1727, Milton, Mass.
Journal, 1678/9-1681/2, 1698-1699, 130 p.
(typescript) MH
N: MHi   5520

TURNER, SIDNEY
Journals and letters, 1864-1869, 3 v. priv.
N: MH   5521

VERY, JONES, 1813-1880
Letters to Ralph Waldo Emerson, 1838-1846
MWeC
N: NNC 1 reel   5522

VERY, JONES, 1813-1860
Manuscript sermons, 1846-1862 RPB
N: NNC 1 reel   5523

WENDELL FAMILY
Correspondence, 1682-1794, of Jacob
Wendell of Boston, Mass., Abraham
Wendell of New York, and John Wendell of
Portsmouth, N.H. priv.
DCO: NN 1 box   5524

WILLIAMS, WILLIAM
Diary DLC
N: MWA 1 reel   5525

WINTHROP, JOHN, 1714-1779
Papers, 1744-1769 MH
DCO: DLC 1 box, 1 portfolio   5526

Business Papers

BACKUS (ELIJAH) AND SONS
Iron works correspondence, 1763-1813, 1 v.
MH-BA
N: CU 1 reel   5527

BARTLETT, WILLIAM
Farming accounts, Westhampton, Mass.,
1704-1756 MH-BA
N: CU   5528

BOSTON MANUFACTURING COMPANY
Statements of affairs, 1853-1888 MH
N: PU   5529

BROMFIELD, HENRY
Foreign marketing cash book (Boston), 1750-
1756 MH-BA
N: CU 1 reel   5530

CLARK, ROBERT
Boston ship registers, 1789-1829 (typescript)
priv.
N: CtY   5531

COOK, C., Jr.
Shipping correspondence, 1833-1835 priv.
N: MSaP 15 feet   5532

ERVING, JOHN
Shipping accounts (Boston), 1733-1745,
1 v. MH-BA
N: CU   5533

FOSTER, HOPESTILL
Lumber account book (Boston), 1759-1772, 1v.
MH-BA
N: CU 1 reel   5534

HULL, JOHN
General store account book (Boston), 1685-
1689, 1 v. MH-BA
N: CU 1 reel   5535

LLOYD, HENRY, Boston merchant
Foreign marketing (West Indies),
1765-1767, 553 p. MH-BA
N: CU   5536

NASH, JACOB
General labor account book (Boston), 1705-1710,
1 v. MH-BA
N: CU 1 reel   5537

NEW ENGLAND MUTUAL LIFE INSURANCE
COMPANY, Boston
Papers, 1850-1857, 11 p. priv.
DCO: MnHi   5538

PYNCHON, JOHN, 1626-1702
Account books, 1651-1697, 6 v. MSCV
N: MSCV *   5539

PYNCHON, JOHN, Jr., 1646-1721
Account book, 1669-1674, 155 p. MSCV
N: MSCV*   5540

REA, DANIEL
Tailoring accounts (Boston), 1736-1784, 3 v.
MH-BA
N: CU 2 reels   5541

RUSSELL, JAMES
Shipping accounts (Charlestown, Mass.), 1747-
1754, 1 v. MH-BA
N: CU 1 reel   5542

SHOVE, GEORGE
General store account book (Dighton, Mass.),
1768-1799, 1 v. MH-BA
N: CU 1 reel   5543

SPEARE, DEERING, AND YEATON
Ship dimension book, 1852
Penobscot Maritime Museum
N: MSaP 15 feet   5544

STURGIS, SAMUEL
Shipping accounts for whaling vessels (Boston),
1733-1785, 1 v. MH
N: CU 1 reel   5545

TILDEN, D., master mariner
Diary re: shipping at Boston and Scituate,
Feb.-Dec., 1769, 1 v. NN
N: CU 1 reel   5546

WENDELL, BARRETT, 1855-1921
History of Lee, Higginson and Co., 1848-1918
MHi
N: MH-BA 1 reel   5547

Collections

MASSACHUSETTS. ARCHIVES
"Massachusetts Archives" otherwise known
as Felt Collection, 1628-1775 M-Ar
N: M-Ar   5548

MASSACHUSETTS. ARCHIVES
"Massachusetts Archives" otherwise known
as Felt Collection, 1628-1700 M-Ar
DCO: MHi   5549

NORTH CAROLINA. UNIVERSITY. LIBRARY
Papers re: Fort Warren, Boston NcU
N: MBU 1 reel   5550

Institutions

BOSTON. FIRE SOCIETY
Minutes and articles, 1741-1805 MHi
N: CU 1 reel   5551

BOSTON. PROPRIETORS OF LOUISBOURG SQUARE
Records, 1826-1944 MH
N: ? 1 reel   5552
P: DLC

BOSTON. SUN FIRE SOCIETY
Articles, 1765, 1 p. MHi
N: CU   5553

BOSTON. UNION FIRE CLUB
Rules and orders, 1772, 2 p. MHi
N: CU   5554

School Records

IPSWICH, Mass. GRAMMAR SCHOOL. FEOFFEES
Records, 1652-1763 Ibid.
DCO: MHi   5555

PHILLIPS ACADEMY, Andover, Mass. TRUSTEES
Minutes, 1778-1921 MAnP
N: MAnP 1 reel*   5556

ROXBURY LATIN SCHOOL, West Roxbury, Mass.
(formerly ROXBURY, Mass. SCHOOL. FEOF-
FEES and ROXBURY, Mass. GRAMMAR
SCHOOL IN THE EASTERLY PART OF THE
TOWN OF ROXBURY)
"Old school book," 1645-1788 Ibid.
DCO: M-Ar MHi   5557

Ships' Logs

With ships' logs are included journals, diaries,
and other records of voyages. Logs, which are
the official records of vessels, are listed under
the vessels' names. Journals, which are personal
documents, even though they are sometimes
called supplementary logs, are listed under the
names of their authors.

GRAND TURK (Brig)
Log, Boston to Mediterranean, 1815, 91 p.
MeHi   5558
N: MSaP

HECTOR (Brig)
Log, Leghorn to Calcutta, 1806 DNA
N: MSaP 20 feet   5559

JAMES, MALACHI
Sea journals, Jan. 19, 1759-July 1, 1761
priv.
N: MHi 10 feet   5560

RHODE ISLAND

Census

RHODE ISLAND (Colony)
Census, 1742
N: RHi   5561

U.S. CENSUS. FIFTH, 1830
Population schedules, Rhode Island DNA
N: DNA 2 reels   5562
P: USIGS

U.S. CENSUS. SIXTH, 1840
Population schedules, Rhode Island DNA
N: DNA 2 reels   5563
P: USIGS

U.S. CENSUS. SEVENTH, 1850
Population schedules, Rhode Island DNA
N: DNA 2 reels   5564
P: USIGS

U.S. CENSUS. EIGHTH, 1860
Population schedules, Rhode Island   DNA
N: DNA 2 reels   5565

U.S. CENSUS. NINTH, 1870
Population schedules, Rhode Island   DNA
N: DNA 2 reels   5566

U.S. CENSUS. TENTH, 1880
Population schedules, Rhode Island   DNA
N: DNA 8 reels   5567

Town Records

LITTLE COMPTON, R.I.
Proprietors' records, town records, n.d.
N: RHi 2 reels   5568

NEWPORT, R.I.
Fees collected at the Post Office, 1771-1775,
95 p.   NN
N: CU   5569

NEWPORT, R.I.
Vital records, 1638-1808, 143 p.   NNNG
N: NNNG
P: USIGS   5570

SOUTH KINGSTON, R.I.
Vital records, 1782-1840, 77 p. (typescript
from Nailer Tom Hazard's diary)   NNNG
N: NNNG
P: USIGS   5571

WARWICK, R.I.
Land evidences (deed abstracts), 1669-1734
RHi
N: USIGS 2 reels
P: RHi   5572

Church Records

FRIENDS, SOCIETY OF. FALL RIVER [R.I.]
MONTHLY MEETING
Marriages, 1845-1862   RPMB
N: USIGS
P: PSC-F   5573

FRIENDS, SOCIETY OF. NEWPORT [R.I.]
MONTHLY MEETING
Men's minutes, 1676-1874; women's minutes,
1690-1868   RPBM
N: USIGS 5 reels
P: PSC-F   5574

FRIENDS, SOCIETY OF. PROVIDENCE [R.I.]
MONTHLY MEETING
Births, deaths, and burials, 1783-1898;
men's minutes, 1783-1800, 1841-1881;
women's minutes, 1783-1881   RPMB
N: USIGS
P: PSC-F   5575

FRIENDS, SOCIETY OF. RHODE ISLAND
MONTHLY MEETING
Births, 1638-1812; deaths, 1647-1875;
marriages, 1643-1888; removals, 1786-1899;
testifications and manumissions, 1773-1799
RPMB
N: USIGS
P: PSC-F   5576

FRIENDS, SOCIETY OF. SMITHFIELD [R.I.]
MONTHLY MEETING
Births and deaths, 1765-1857; denials and
removals, 1783-1873; denials, intentions
of marriage, and removals, 1886-1920;
marriages, 1725-1905; men's minutes, 1718-
1903; ministers and elders, 1783-1858;
women's minutes, 1718-1892   RPMB
N: USIGS
P: PSC-F   5577

FRIENDS, SOCIETY OF. SOUTH KINGSTON
[R.I.] MONTHLY MEETING
Births and deaths, 1755-1944; men's
minutes, 1845-1879   priv.
N: USIGS 1 reel
P: PSC-F   5578

FRIENDS, SOCIETY OF. SOUTH KINGSTON AND
GREENWICH [R.I.] MONTHLY MEETING
Men's minutes, 1844-1863; women's minutes,

1844-1862   Ibid.
N: USIGS   5579
P: PSC-F

FRIENDS, SOCIETY OF. SWANSEY [R.I.]
MONTHLY MEETING
Minutes, 1844-1850; women's minutes,
1844-1863   priv.
N: USIGS 1 reel
P: PSC-F   5580

NEWPORT, R.I. FIRST BAPTIST CHURCH
Records, 1772-1791   RNHi
N: USIGS   5581

NEWPORT, R.I. TRINITY CHURCH
Records, 1709-1799   RNHi
N: USIGS 1 reel   5582

Personal Papers

BROWN, MOSES, 1738-1836
Correspondence, 1769-1826   PHi priv.
N: RPB 2 reels
P: RPB   5583

BROWN, MOSES, 1738-1836
Correspondence with English Friends, 1789-
1833, 10 items   UKLF
N: RPB   5584

BROWN, MOSES, 1738-1836
Letters, 1775-1823   priv.
N: RHi 1 reel   5585

BUSHNELL, HORACE, 1802-1876
Sermons in manuscript   CtY-D
N: RPB 1 reel   5586

DROWNE, WILLIAM, 1793-1874
Sketch of Dr. Solomon Drowne, 1873-1874   RHi
N: RPB   5587

ROBINSON, GIFFORD S.
Correspondence, 1862-1864   RPB
N: RPB   5588

WAYLAND, FRANCIS, 1796-1865
Letters to Rev. Daniel S. Wayland, 1840-1855
RPB
N: RPB 1 reel   5589

WHIPPLE, ABRAHAM
Letter books, 1779-1786   priv.
N: RHi 1 reel
P: RHi   5590

Institutions

PROVIDENCE, R.I. SWAN POINT CEMETERY
Records, n.d.   RHi
N: USIGS 8 reels   5591

Ships' Logs

BOY (Ship)
Log, 1836-1838   priv.
N: RHi 1 reel
P: RHi   5592

MERCURY (Ship)
Log, 1820-1825   priv.
N: RHi 1 reel   5593

CONNECTICUT

Census

U.S. CENSUS. FIFTH, 1830
Population schedules, Connecticut   DNA
N: DNA 6 reels   5594

U.S. CENSUS. SIXTH, 1840
Population schedules, Connecticut   DNA
N: DNA 4 reels
P: USIGS   5595

U.S. CENSUS. SEVENTH, 1850
Population schedules, Connecticut   DNA
N: DNA 12 reels
P: USIGS   5596

U.S. CENSUS. EIGHTH, 1860
Population schedules, Connecticut   DNA
N: DNA 5 reels
P: USIGS   5597

U.S. CENSUS. NINTH, 1870
Population schedules, Connecticut   DNA
N: DNA 5 reels   5598

U.S. CENSUS. TENTH, 1880
Population schedules, Connecticut   DNA
N: DNA 17 reels   5599

Government Records

U.S. CUSTOMS HOUSE, NEW HAVEN, Conn.
List of foreigners inward, 1762-1801   DNA
N: ViWI 18 frames   5600

State Records

CONNECTICUT (Colony)
Land records, 1640-1846   Ct
N: USIGS 3 reels
P: Ct   5601

CONNECTICUT
Records of school districts, 1820-1864   Ct
N: USIGS 2 reels
P: Ct   5602

CONNECTICUT. ADJUTANT GENERAL
General orders, 1792-1823, 176 p.   Ct
DCO: Ct   5603

CONNECTICUT. COMMISSIONERS ON CONNECT-
ICUT-MASSACHUSETTS BOUNDARY, 1695
Report by John Butcher and William Whiting,
commissioners, Aug., 1695   M-Ar
DCO: Ct   5604

CONNECTICUT. CONSTITUTIONAL CONVEN-
TION, 1788
Document signed by 128 delegates, ratifying
the U.S. Constitution   DNA
PP: Ct   5605

County Records

FAIRFIELD Co., Conn.
Wills, 1648-1757; vital records, 1790-1855;
cemetery records, 1790-1855   NNNG
N: USIGS 4 reels   5606

NEW LONDON Co., Conn.
Records of trials, 1661-1700, v. 1-6   Ct
N: USIGS
P: Ct   5607

Town Records

Connecticut town records have been combined into
three sets: Proprietors' records, town records,
and the records of the probate districts, which
are usually but not always coterminous with the
towns under which they are listed.

ANDOVER, Conn.
Land records, 1848-1854   Salem, Conn.
N: USIGS 1 reel
P: Ct   5608

ASHFORD, Conn.
Proprietors' records, 1705-1770; land records,
1714-1855; probate records, 1830-1858
Warrenville
N: USIGS 15 reels
P: Ct   5609

AVON, Conn.
Land records, 1830-1867; probate records,
1836-1874   Ibid.
N: USIGS 3 reels
P: Ct   5610

BARKHAMSTED, Conn.
Proprietors' records, 1729-1833; land records, 1781-1861; probate records, 1819-1854   Ibid.
N: USIGS 11 reels   5611
P: Ct

BERLIN, Conn.
Land records, 1783-1850; probate records, 1835-1854   New Britain
N: USIGS 16 reels   5612
P: Ct

BETHANY, Conn.
Land records, 1832-1881   Ibid.
N: USIGS 3 reels   5613
P: Ct

BETHLEHEM, Conn.
Land records, 1787-1904   Ibid.
N: USIGS 7 reels   5614
P: Ct

BLOOMFIELD, Conn.
Land records, 1835-1854   Ibid.
N: USIGS 2 reels   5615
P: Ct

BOLTON, Conn.
Land records, 1719-1851   Ibid.
N: USIGS 6 reels   5616
P: Ct

BOZRAH, Conn.
Land records, 1786-1850; probate records, 1843-1889   Fitchville
N: USIGS 4 reels   5617
P: Ct

BRANFORD, Conn.
Land records, 1645-1851   Ibid.
N: USIGS 14 reels   5618
P: Ct

BRIDGEPORT, Conn.
Land records, 1821-1852   Ibid.
N: USIGS 11 reels   5619
P: Ct

BRISTOL, Conn.
Land records, 1785-1859; probate records, 1830-1852; vital records, 1785-1871   Ibid.
N: USIGS 16 reels   5620
P: Ct

BROOKFIELD, Conn.
Land records, 1788-1858   Ibid.
N: USIGS 8 reels   5621
P: Ct

BROOKLYN, Conn.
Land records, 1786-1852; probate records, 1833-1859   Ibid.
N: USIGS 5 reels   5622
P: Ct

BURLINGTON, Conn.
Land records, 1806-1857; probate records, 1835-1861   Ibid.
N: USIGS 8 reels   5623
P: Ct

CANAAN, Conn.
Land records, 1737-1853; probate district records, 1847-1860   Falls Village, North Canaan
N: USIGS 12 reels   5624
P: Ct

CANTERBURY, Conn.
Land records, 1703-1855; probate district records, 1835-1855   Ibid.
N: USIGS 14 reels   5625
P: Ct

CANTON, Conn.
Land records, 1809-1851; probate district records, 1841-1855   Collinsville
N: USIGS 4 reels   5626
P: Ct

CHAPLIN, Conn.
Land records, 1822-1854   Ibid.
N: USIGS 2 reels   5627
P: Ct

CHATHAM, Conn.
Land records, 1767-1873   East Hampton
Probate records, 1824-1853   Portland
N: USIGS 15 reels   5628

CHESHIRE, Conn.
Land records, 1780-1851; probate records, 1829-1858   Ibid.
N: USIGS 14 reels   5629
P: Ct

CHESTER, Conn.
Land records, 1836-1865   Ibid.
Proprietors' records, 1730-1753   Ct
N: USIGS 3 reels   5630
P: Ct

CLINTON, Conn.
Land records, 1838-1873   Ibid.
N: USIGS 2 reels   5631
P: Ct

COLCHESTER, Conn.
Proprietors' records, 1713-1805; land records, 1702-1862; probate district records, 1741-1851   Ibid.
N: USIGS 21 reels   5632
P: Ct

COLEBROOK, Conn.
Land records, 1771-1854   Ibid.
N: USIGS 7 reels   5633
P: Ct

COLEBROOK, Conn.   WEST SCHOOL DISTRICT
Register, 1839-1859   Ct
N: USIGS   5634
P: Ct

COLUMBIA, Conn.
Land records, 1804-1874; minutes and vital records, 1804-1841   Ibid.
N: USIGS 4 reels   5635
P: Ct

CORNWALL, Conn.
Proprietors' records, 1730-1887; land records, 1740-1856; probate records, 1847-1860   Ibid.
N: USIGS 10 reels   5636
P: Ct

COVENTRY, Conn.
Land records, 1710-1854; probate records, 1849-1856   Ibid.
Deeds, 1692-1840   Ct
N: USIGS 15 reels   5637
P: Ct

DANBURY, Conn.
Land records, 1777-1861; probate records, 1739-1851   Ibid.
N: USIGS 32 reels   5638
P: Ct

DARIEN, Conn.
Land records, 1820-1850   Ibid.
N: USIGS 2 reels   5639
P: Ct

DERBY, Conn.
Land records, 1667-1852   Ibid.
N: USIGS 18 reels   5640
P: Ct

DURHAM, Conn.
Land records, 1698-1857   Ibid.
N: USIGS 10 reels   5641
P: Ct

EAST HADDAM, Conn.
Land records, 1704-1860; probate district records, 1832-1855   Ibid.
N: USIGS 16 reels   5642
P: Ct

EAST HARTFORD, Conn.
Land records, 1783-1851   Ibid.
N: USIGS 11 reels   5643
P: Ct

EAST HAVEN, Conn.
Land records, 1785-1852   Ibid.
N: USIGS 6 reels   5644
P: Ct

EAST LYME, Conn.
Land records, 1839-1861; probate records, 1843-1858   Ibid.   5645
N: USIGS 2 reels
P: Ct

EAST WINDSOR, Conn.
Land records, 1768-1830   Ct
Land records, 1826-1864   Broadbrook

Probate records, 1781-1855   Warehouse Point
N: USIGS 21 reels   5646
P: Ct

EASTFORD, Conn.
Probate records, 1847-1867   Ibid.
N: USIGS 1 reel   5647
P: Ct

EASTON, Conn.
Land records, 1845-1860   Ibid.
N: USIGS 1 reels   5648
P: Ct

ELLINGTON, Conn.
Land records, 1786-1854   Ibid.
Probate records, 1826-1854   Rockville
N: USIGS 9 reels   5649
P: Ct

ENFIELD, Conn.
Proprietors' records, 1680-1775; land records, 1693-1853; probate records, 1831-1856   Thompsonville
N: USIGS 14 reels   5650
P: Ct

FAIRFIELD, Conn.
Land records, 1731-1860; probate records, 1747-1852   Ibid.
Proprietors' records, 1749-1750; land records, 1649-1732; probate records, 1648-1755   Ct
N: USIGS 46 reels   5651
P: Ct

FARMINGTON, Conn.
Land records, 1645-1857; probate district records, 1769-1860   Ibid.
N: USIGS 35 reels   5652
P: Ct

FRANKLIN, Conn.
Land records, 1716-1858   Ibid.
N: USIGS 4 reels   5653
P: Ct

GLASTONBURY, Conn.
Land records, 1690-1853   Ibid.
N: USIGS 15 reels   5654

GOSHEN, Conn.
Land records, 1739-1859   Ibid.
N: USIGS 12 reels   5655
P: Ct

GRANBY, Conn.
Land records, 1786-1868; probate records, 1807-1850   Ibid.
N: USIGS 15 reels   5656
P: Ct

GREENWICH, Conn.
Land records, 1640-1856   Ibid.
N: USIGS 16 reels   5657
P: Ct

GRISWOLD, Conn.
Land records, 1815-1851   Ibid.
N: USIGS 3 reels   5658
P: Ct

GROTON, Conn.
Land records, 1708-1852; probate records, 1839-1850   Ibid.
N: USIGS 13 reels   5659
P: Ct

GUILFORD, Conn.
Proprietors' records, 1703-1926; land records, 1645-1852; probate records, 1720-1852   Ibid.
N: USIGS 35 reels   5660
P: Ct

GUILFORD, Conn.
Vital records (marked "Thos. Fitch's Book") 1816-1842, 1865, 1874   Ct
N: USIGS   5661
P: Ct

HADDAM, Conn.
Land records, 1673-1857; probate records, 1830-1855   Ibid.
N: USIGS 17 reels   5662
P: Ct

HAMDEN, Conn.
Land records, 1786-1861   Ibid.
N: USIGS 13 reels   5663
P: Ct

HAMPTON, Conn.
    Land records, 1786-1855; probate records,
    1836-1858 Ibid.
    N: USIGS 6 reels   5664
    P: Ct

HARTFORD, Conn.
    Proprietors' records, 1639-1688; land records,
    1685-1851; probate records, 1635-1850 Ibid.
    N: USIGS 62 reels   5665
    P: Ct

HARTFORD, Conn.
    Proprietors' records, 1659-1857; probate
    records, 1649-1677 Ct
    N: USIGS 2 reels   5666
    P: Ct

HARTLAND, Conn.
    Proprietors' records, 1734-1760; land records,
    1760-1859; probate records, 1836-1850 Ibid.
    N: USIGS 8 reels   5667
    P: Ct

HARWINTON, Conn.
    Proprietors' records, 1729-1748; land records,
    1738-1879; probate district records, 1835-1854
    Ibid.
    N: USIGS 11 reels   5668
    P: Ct

HEBRON, Conn.
    Land records, 1713-1851; probate records,
    1789-1851 Ibid.
    N: USIGS 20 reels   5669
    P: Ct

KENT, Conn.
    Proprietors' records, 1738-1802; land records,
    1735-1856; probate records, 1837-1858 Ibid.
    N: USIGS 14 reels   5670
    P: Ct

KILLINGLY, Conn.
    Land records, 1709-1851; probate records,
    1849-1854 Danielson
    N: USIGS 18 reels   5671
    P: Ct

KILLINGWORTH, Conn.
    Land records, 1664-1854; probate records,
    1834-1852 Ibid.
    N: USIGS 16 reels   5672
    P: Ct

LEBANON, Conn.
    Land records, 1685-1869; probate records,
    1826-1853 Ibid.
    N: USIGS 17 reels   5673

LEBANON, Conn.
    Vital records, 1638-1886 Ct
    N: USIGS   5674
    P: Ct

LEDYARD, Conn.
    Land records, 1834-1853; probate records,
    1837-1857 Ibid.
    N: USIGS 3 reels   5675

LISBON, Conn.
    Land records, 1786-1852 Ibid.
    N: USIGS 3 reels   5676
    P: Ct

LITCHFIELD, Conn.
    Proprietors' records, 1723-1807; land records,
    1719-1853; probate records, 1743-1850 Ibid.
    N: USIGS 34 reels   5677
    P: Ct

LYME, Conn.
    Church records, 1731-1780; town records,
    1672-1685, 45 p. NNNG
    N: USIGS   5678

LYME, Conn.
    Land grants and earmarks, 1665-1948;
    land records, 1662-1872 Ibid.
    N: USIGS 21 reels   5679
    P: Ct

MADISON, CONN.
    Church records, 1791-1822; town records,
    1787-1882, 188 p. NNNG
    N: USIGS   5680
    P: Ct

MADISON, Conn.
    Land records, 1826-1885; probate records,
    1834-1856 Ibid.
    N: USIGS 5 reels   5681
    P: Ct

MANCHESTER, Conn.
    Land records, 1823-1871 Ibid.
    N: USIGS 5 reels   5682
    P: Ct

MANSFIELD, Conn.
    Proprietors' records, 1702-1752; land records,
    1708-1852; probate records, 1831-1851 Ibid.
    N: USIGS 18 reels   5683
    P: Ct

MARLBOROUGH, Conn.
    Land records, 1803-1878 Ibid.
    N: USIGS 3 reels   5684
    P: Ct

MARLBOROUGH, Conn.
    Records of deaths, 1718-1900 Ct
    N: USIGS   5685
    P: Ct

MERIDEN, Conn.
    Land records, 1806-1854; probate records,
    1836-1854 Ibid.
    N: USIGS 8 reels   5686
    P: Ct

MIDDLEBURY, Conn.
    Land records, 1807-1873 Ibid.
    N: USIGS 4 reels   5687
    P: Ct

MIDDLETOWN, Conn.
    Land records, 1640-1853; probate records,
    1752-1855 Ibid.
    N: USIGS 45 reels   5688
    P: Ct

MILFORD, Conn.
    Fundamental documents, 13 items Ct
    DCO: Ct   5689

MILFORD, Conn.
    Land records, 1639-1852; probate records,
    1832-1853 Ibid.
    N: USIGS 19 reels   5690
    P: Ct

MONROE, Conn.
    Land records, 1823-1858 Ibid.
    N: USIGS 4 reels   5691
    P: Ct

MONTVILLE, Conn.
    Land records, 1786-1871 Ibid.
    N: USIGS 8 reels   5692
    P: Ct

MONTVILLE, Conn.
    Marriage records, 1820-1855 Ct
    N: USIGS   5693
    P: Ct

NAUGATUCK, Conn.
    Land records, 1844-1854 Ibid.
    N: USIGS 2 reels   5694
    P: Ct

NEW CANAAN, Conn.
    Land records, 1801-1857 Ibid.
    N: USIGS 10 reels   5695
    P: Ct

NEW HARTFORD, Conn.
    Land records, 1739-1853; probate records,
    1834-1852 Ibid.
    N: USIGS 11 reels   5696
    P: Ct

NEW HAVEN, Conn.
    Marriage records, 1835-1854, v. 6, 527 p. Ct
    N: USIGS   5697
    P: Ct

NEW HAVEN, Conn.
    Proprietors' records, 1724-1771; land records,
    1679-1850; probate records, 1647-1856 Ibid.
    N: USIGS 103 reels   5698
    P: Ct

NEW HAVEN, Conn.
    Register of American seamen in District of
    New Haven, June-Dec., 1801; collection of Naval

papers, 1826, 1830, 33 p. Ct
    N: USIGS   5699
    P: Ct

NEW LONDON, Conn.
    Land records, 1664-1854; probate records,
    1675-1852 Ibid.
    N: USIGS 39 reels   5700

NEW LONDON, Conn., see also HURLBUTT,
    RALPH, 6285, under CONNECTICUT,
    Personal Papers

NEW MILFORD, Conn.
    Land records, 1707-1858; probate records,
    1787-1853 Ibid.
    N: USIGS 35 reels   5701
    P: Ct

NEWTOWN, Conn.
    Land records, 1712-1852; probate records,
    1810-1850 Ibid.
    N: USIGS 27 reels   5702
    P: Ct

NEWTOWN, Conn.
    Town records, 1700-1875, 146 p. (typescript)
    NNNG
    N: USIGS   5703

NORFOLK, Conn.
    Proprietors' records, 1754-1772; land records,
    1758-1855; probate records, 1778-1856 Ibid.
    N: USIGS 13 reels   5704
    P: Ct

NORTH BRANFORD, Conn.
    Land records, 1831-1854 Ibid.
    N: USIGS 2 reels   5705
    P: Ct

NORTH DERBY, Conn.
    Deeds, 1726-1758, 106 p., v. 1 Oxford
    N: USIGS   5706

NORTH HAVEN, Conn.
    Land records, 1779-1877 Ibid.
    N: USIGS 9 reels   5707
    P: Ct

NORTH STONINGTON, Conn.
    Land records, 1813-1850; probate records,
    1835-1858 Ibid.
    N: USIGS 5 reels   5708
    P: Ct

NORWALK, Conn.
    Land records, 1652-1853; probate records,
    1802-1851 Ibid.
    N: USIGS 25 reels   5709
    P: Ct

NORWICH, Conn.
    Land records, 1659-1850; probate records,
    1748-1852 Ibid.
    N: USIGS 41 reels   5710
    P: Ct

OLD LYME, Conn.
    Probate district records, 1829-1866 Ibid.
    N: USIGS 1 reel   5711
    P: Ct

ORANGE, Conn.
    Land records, 1822-1858 West Haven
    N: USIGS 4 reels   5712
    P: Ct

OXFORD, Conn.
    Land records, 1798-1858 Ibid.
    N: USIGS 9 reels   5713
    P: Ct

PLAINFIELD, Conn.
    Land records, 1701-1851; probate records,
    1747-1850 Ibid.
    N: USIGS 18 reels   5714
    P: Ct

PLYMOUTH, Conn.
    Land records, 1795-1853; probate records,
    1833-1855 Terryville
    N: USIGS 11 reels   5715
    P: Ct

POMFRET, Conn.
    Land records, 1686-1852; probate records,
    1753-1857 Ibid.
    N: USIGS 18 reels   P: Ct   5716

PORTLAND, Conn.
Land records, 1841-1857 Ibid.
N: USIGS 2 reels 5717
P: Ct

PRESTON, Conn.
Land records, 1687-1854 Ibid.
N: USIGS 12 reels 5718
P: Ct

PRESTON, Conn.
Town records, 1706-1743; baptisms, 1668-
1754, 184 p. NNNG
N: USIGS 5719

PROSPECT, Conn.
Land records, 1827-1854 Ibid.
N: USIGS 2 reels 5720
P: Ct

REDDING, Conn.
Land records, 1767-1861; probate records,
1839-1856 Ibid.
N: USIGS 12 reels 5721
P: Ct

RIDGEFIELD, Conn.
Land records, 1709-1854; probate records,
1841-1855 Ibid.
N: USIGS 14 reels 5722
P: Ct

ROCKY HILL, Conn.
Land records, 1843-1866 Ibid.
N: USIGS 1 reel 5723
P: Ct

ROXBURY, Conn.
Land records, 1796-1855; probate records,
1842-1859 Ibid.
N: USIGS 9 reels 5724
P: Ct

SALEM, Conn.
Land records, 1819-1880; probate records,
1842-1872 Ibid.
N: USIGS 3 reels 5725
P: Ct

SALISBURY, Conn.
Deeds, 1747-1762; tax lists, 1746-1761; town
meeting, 1741-1750, 328 p. NNNG
N: USIGS 5726

SALISBURY, Conn.
Proprietors' records, 1739-1835; land records,
1741-1861; probate records, 1847-1856 Ibid.
N: USIGS 15 reels 5727
P: Ct

SAYBROOK, Conn.
Land records, 1648-1859 Deep River
Probate records, 1780-1852 Chester
N: USIGS 24 reels 5728
P: Ct
DCO: Ct

SAYBROOK, Conn.
Land records, 1648-1793 Deep River
DCO: Ct 6 v. 5729

SHARON, Conn.
Proprietors' records, 1739-1871; land records,
1739-1865; probate records, 1757-1855 Ibid.
N: USIGS 27 reels 5730
P: Ct

SHELTON, Conn.
Land records, 1789-1856 Ibid.
N: USIGS 8 reels 5731
P: Ct

SHERMAN, Conn.
Land records, 1803-1855 Ibid.
N: USIGS 4 reels 5732
P: Ct

SIMSBURY, Conn.
Land records, 1666-1851; probate records,
1769-1852 Ibid.
N: USIGS 27 reels 5733
P: Ct

SOMERS, Conn.
Land records, 1729-1854; probate records,
1834-1853 Ibid.
N: USIGS 7 reels 5734
P: Ct

SOUTH WINDSOR, Conn.
Land records, 1845-1878 Ibid.
N: USIGS 2 reels 5735
P: Ct

SOUTHBURY, Conn.
Deeds, 1786-1882 South Britain
N: USIGS 8 reels 5736
P: Ct

SOUTHINGTON, Conn.
Land records, 1779-1851; probate records,
1825-1851 Ibid.
N: USIGS 12 reels 5737
P: Ct

STAFFORD, Conn.
Land records, 1727-1852; probate records,
1769-1852 Stafford Springs
N: USIGS 23 reels 5738

STAMFORD, Conn.
Land records, 1630-1852; probate records,
1728-1851 Ibid.
N: USIGS 27 reels 5739
P: Ct

STERLING, Conn.
Land records, 1794-1859 Orenco
N: USIGS 4 reels 5740
P: Ct

STONINGTON, Conn.
Land records, 1665-1850; probate records,
1767-1855 Ibid.
N: USIGS 21 reels 5741
P: Ct

STRATFORD, Conn.
Land records, 1652-1866; probate district
records, 1840-1853 Ibid.
Probate district records, 1782-1851 Bridgeport
N: USIGS 29 reels 5742
P: Ct

SUFFIELD, Conn.
Land records, 1677-1722, 1754-1858; probate
records, 1821-1853 Ibid.
N: USIGS 16 reels 5743
P: Ct

THOMPSON, Conn.
Land records, 1785-1853; probate records,
1832-1851 North Grosvenor Dale
N: USIGS 11 reels 5744
P: Ct

TOLLAND, Conn.
Land records, 1713-1850; probate records,
1830-1853 Ibid.
N: USIGS 13 reels 5745
P: Ct

TORRINGTON, Conn.
Land records, 1733-1851; probate records,
1847-1857 Ibid.
N: USIGS 5746
P: Ct 9 reels

TRUMBULL, Conn.
Land records, 1798-1855 Ibid.
N: USIGS 6 reels 5747
P: Ct

UNION, Conn.
Land records, 1733-1858 Ibid.
N: USIGS 4 reels 5748
P: Ct

VERNON, Conn.
Land records, 1808-1863 Rockville
N: USIGS 4 reels 5749
P: Ct

VOLUNTOWN, Conn.
Land records, 1696-1851; probate records,
1830-1851 Ibid.
N: USIGS 8 reels 5750
P: Ct

WALLINGFORD, Conn.
Land records, 1670-1854; probate records,
1776-1855 Ibid.
N: USIGS 31 reels 5751
P: Ct

WARREN, Conn.
Land records, 1786-1879 Ibid.
N: USIGS 5 reels 5752
P: Ct

WASHINGTON, Conn.
Land records, 1779-1855; probate records,
1832-1855 Ibid.
N: USIGS 9 reels 5753
P: Ct

WATERBURY, Conn.
Land records, 1672-1850; probate records,
1779-1851 Ibid.
N: USIGS film 36 reels 5754
P: Ct

WATERFORD, Conn.
Land records, 1801-1856 Ibid.
N: USIGS 5 reels 5755
P: Ct

WATERTOWN, Conn.
Land records, 1780-1858; probate records,
1834-1860 Ibid.
N: USIGS 14 reels 5756

WESTBROOK, Conn.
Land records, 1840-1885 Ibid.
N: USIGS 1 reel 5757
P: Ct

WESTON, Conn.
Land records, 1787-1879 Ibid.
Probate records, 1832-1858 Bridgeport
N: USIGS 15 reels 5758
P: Ct

WESTPORT, Conn.
Land records, 1835-1877; probate records,
1835-1854 Ibid.
N: USIGS 4 reels 5759
P: Ct

WETHERSFIELD, Conn.
Cemetery records, 1887-1947 Ct
N: USIGS 5760
P: Ct

WETHERSFIELD, Conn.
Charter, 1685 Ct
DCO: Ct 5761

WETHERSFIELD, Conn.
Justice of the Peace Court proceedings,
1773-1785, 48 p. priv.
DCO: NN 5762

WETHERSFIELD, Conn.
Land records, 1635-1859 Ibid.
N: USIGS 23 reels 5763
P: Ct

WILLINGTON, Conn.
Land records, 1727-1855 Ibid.
N: USIGS 7 reels 5764
P: Ct

WILTON, Conn.
Land records, 1802-1851 Ibid.
N: USIGS 9 reels 5765
P: Ct

WINCHESTER, Conn.
Land records, 1744-1857; probate records,
1838-1851 Winsted
N: USIGS 10 reels 5766
P: Ct

WINDHAM, Conn.
Land records, 1686-1854; probate records,
1719-1867
N: USIGS 36 reels 5767
P: Ct

WINDSOR, Conn.
Proprietors' records, 1650-1787; land records,
1640-1857 Ibid.
N: USIGS 23 reels 5768
P: Ct

WOLCOTT, Conn.
Land records, 1796-1863 Ibid.
N: USIGS 5 reels 5769
P: Ct

WOODBRIDGE, Conn.
Land records, 1784-1924 Ibid.
N: USIGS 11 reels 5770
P: Ct

WOODBURY, Conn.
Land records, 1659-1863; probate records,
1719-1850 Ibid.
N: USIGS 34 reels P: Ct 5771

WOODSTOCK, Conn.
Land records, 1749-1855; probate records,
1831-1853 Ibid.
N: USIGS 13 reels   5772
P: Ct

Church Records

ANDOVER, Conn. FIRST CONGREGATIONAL
CHURCH
Vital records, 1747-1932, v. 1-2 Ct
N: USIGS   5773
P: Ct

ANSONIA, Conn. CHRIST CHURCH (Episcopal)
Records, 1834-1941, v. 1-7 Ct
N: USIGS   5774
P: Ct

ASHFORD, Conn. WESTFORD CONGREGATIONAL
CHURCH
Records, 1768-1937, 2 v. Ct
DCO: Ct   5775

AVON, Conn. CONGREGATIONAL CHURCH
(formerly THIRD CHURCH OF FARMINGTON)
Records, 1818-1921, v. 1-8 Ct
N: USIGS   5776
P: Ct

AVON, Conn. WEST AVON CONGREGATIONAL
CHURCH
Minutes, 1840-1889 Ct
N: USIGS   5777
P: Ct

BANTAM, Conn. ST. PAUL'S CHURCH (Episcopal)
Vital records, 1799-1916 Ct
N: USIGS   5778
P: Ct

BAPTISTS. CONNECTICUT. ASHFORD ASSO-
CIATION MINISTERIAL CONFERENCE
Minutes, 1846-1903, v. 2 Ct
N: USIGS   5779
P: Ct

BARKHAMSTED, Conn. FIRST CONGREGATIONAL
CHURCH
Records, 1781-1914, v. 1-4 Ct
N: USIGS   5780
P: Ct

BARKHAMSTED, Conn. PLEASANT VALLEY
METHODIST EPISCOPAL CHURCH
Vital records, 1850-1952 Ct
N: USIGS   5781
P: Ct

BARKHAMSTED, Conn. ST. PAUL'S CHURCH
(Episcopal) AT RIVERTON (formerly THE
EPISCOPAL SOCIETY OF UNION CHURCH
IN HITCHCOCKSVILLE)
Vital records, 1828-1937, v. 1-2 Ct
N: USIGS   5782
P: Ct

BERLIN, Conn. EAST BERLIN METHODIST
CHURCH
Vital records, 1871-1939, v. 1 Ct
N: USIGS   5783
P: Ct

BERLIN, Conn. FIRST CONGREGATIONAL
CHURCH
Vital records, 1775-1922, v. 1-3 Ct
N: USIGS   5784
P: Ct

BERLIN, Conn. KENSINGTON CONGREGATIONAL
CHURCH (formerly FARMINGTON SECOND
SOCIETY)
Vital records, 1709-1889, v. 1-2 Ct
N: USIGS   5785
P: Ct

BERLIN, Conn. KENSINGTON METHODIST
CHURCH
Vital records, 1858-1941, v. 1-3 Ct
N: USIGS   5786
P: Ct

BERLIN, Conn. METHODIST CHURCH
Records, 1812-1895, v. 1-4 Ct
N: USIGS   5787
P: Ct

BERLIN, Conn. WORTHINGTON ECCLESIAS-
TICAL SOCIETY
Records, 1772-1928, 2 v. Ct
N: USIGS   5788
P: Ct

BETHANY, Conn. CHRIST CHURCH (Episcopal)
Records, 1799-1896, v. 1-5 Ct
N: USIGS   5789
P: Ct

BETHANY, Conn. CONGREGATIONAL CHURCH
Minutes, 1762-1842, v. 1-2 Ct
N: USIGS   5790
P: Ct

BETHEL, Conn. ST. THOMAS' CHURCH (Epis-
copal)
Records, 1847-1903, v. 1-2 Ct
N: USIGS   5791
P: Ct

BETHLEHEM, Conn. CHRIST CHURCH (Episco-
pal)
Records, 1807-1905, v. 1-4 Ct
N: USIGS   5792
P: Ct

BETHLEHEM, Conn. CONGREGATIONAL CHURCH
Vital records, 1738-1850, v. 1-2 Ct
N: USIGS   5793
P: Ct

BETHLEHEM, Conn. METHODIST CHURCH
Vital records, 1859-1924 Ct
N: USIGS 1 reel   5794
P: Ct

BLOOMFIELD, Conn. CONGREGATIONAL CHURCH
Records, 1738-1918, v. 1-7 Ct
N: USIGS   5795
P: Ct

BLOOMFIELD, Conn. ST. ANDREW'S CHURCH
(Episcopal)
Records, 1743-1936, v. 1-2 Ct
N: USIGS   5796
P: Ct
DCO: Ct

BOLTON, Conn. CONGREGATIONAL CHURCH
Records, 1725-1922 Ct
N: USIGS   5797
P: Ct

BOZRAH, Conn. BOZRAHVILLE CONGREGATIONAL
CHURCH
Vital records, 1828-1890,. v. 1-3 Ct
N: USIGS   5798

BOZRAH, Conn. ECCLESIASTICAL SOCIETY AND
CONGREGATIONAL CHURCH (formerly NEW
CONCORD SOCIETY IN NORWICH)
Records, 1737-1845, v. 2-4 Ct
N: USIGS   5799
P: Ct

BOZRAH, Conn. FITCHVILLE BAPTIST CHURCH
Vital records, 1887-1932 Ct
N: USIGS   5800
P: Ct

BRANFORD, Conn. FIRST CONGREGATIONAL
CHURCH
Vital records, 1687-1899, v. 1-5 Ct
N: USIGS   5801
P: Ct
DCO: Ct

BRANFORD, Conn. TRINITY CHURCH (Episcopal)
Records, 1784-1895, v. 1-2 Ct
N: USIGS   5802
P: Ct

BRIDGEPORT, Conn. UNITED CONGREGATION-
AL CHURCH (formerly STRATFIELD SOCIETY)
Records, 1693-1911, 10 v. Ct
N: USIGS 4 reels   5803
P: Ct

BRIDGEWATER, Conn. CONGREGATIONAL
CHURCH
Vital records, 1809-1919 Ct
N: USIGS   5804
P: Ct

BRIDGEWATER, Conn. ST. MARK'S
CHURCH (Episcopal)
Vital records, 1810-1916, v. 1-2 Ct
N: USIGS   5805
P: Ct

BRISTOL, Conn. CONGREGATIONAL CHURCH
Records, 1742-1876 Ct
N: USIGS 2 reels   5806
P: Ct
DCO: Ct

BRISTOL, Conn. PROSPECT METHODIST
EPISCOPAL CHURCH
Vital records, 1849-1916 Ct
N: USIGS   5807
P: Ct

BRISTOL, Conn. TRINITY CHURCH (Episcopal)
Records, 1834-1949 Ct
N: USIGS   5808
P: Ct

BROAD BROOK, Conn. GRACE
EPISCOPAL CHURCH
Vital records, 1845-1909 Ct
N: USIGS   5809
P: Ct

BROOKFIELD, Conn. ST. PAUL'S
CHURCH (Episcopal)
Records, 1707-1930, v. 1-6 Ct
N: USIGS 2 reels   5810
P: Ct

BROOKLYN, Conn. FIRST BAPTIST CHURCH
Minutes, 1828-1934, v. 1-3 Ct
N: USIGS   5811
P: Ct

BROOKLYN, Conn. FIRST CONGREGATIONAL
CHURCH
Records, 1731-1913, v. 1-4 Ct
N: USIGS   5812
P: Ct

BROOKLYN, Conn. FIRST TRINITARIAN
CONGREGATIONAL CHURCH
Records, 1734-1897, v. 1-6 Ct
N: USIGS   5813
P: Ct

CANAAN, Conn. CHRIST CHURCH (Episcopal)
Vital records, 1846-1893 Ct
N: USIGS   5814
P: Ct

CANAAN, Conn. FALLS VILLAGE
CONGREGATIONAL CHURCH
Vital records, 1858-1941 Ct
N: USIGS   5815
P: Ct

CANAAN, Conn. FIRST ECCLESIASTICAL
SOCIETY AND CONGREGATIONAL CHURCH
Records, 1741-1852, v. 1-3 Ct
N: USIGS   5816
P: Ct

CANAAN, Conn., and STILLWATER, N.Y.
CHURCH OF CHRIST
Vital records, 1752-1817 Ct
N: USIGS   5817
P: Ct

CANTERBURY, Conn. FIRST
CONGREGATIONAL CHURCH
Vital records, 1711-1821 Ct
N: USIGS   5818
P: Ct

CANTERBURY, Conn. SECOND
CONGREGATIONAL CHURCH
Vital records, 1770-1850 Ct
N: USIGS   5819
P: Ct

CANTERBURY, Conn. WESTMINSTER ECCLESI-
ASTICAL SOCIETY AND CONGREGATIONAL
CHURCH
Records, 1770-1878, v. 1-2 Ct
N: USIGS   5820
P: Ct

CANTON, Conn. CONGREGATIONAL CHURCH
Records, 1746-1953 Ct
N: USIGS 2 reels   5821
P: Ct

CHAPLIN, Conn. ECCLESIASTICAL SOCIETY
Minutes, 1809-1906 Ct
N: USIGS   5822
P: Ct

CHESHIRE, Conn. CONGREGATIONAL CHURCH
Records, 1724-1917 Ct
N: USIGS 2 reels
P: Ct
5823

CHESHIRE, Conn. ST. PETER'S CHURCH
(Episcopal)
Records, 1797-1923, v. 1-4 Ct
N: USIGS
P: Ct
5824

CHESTER, Conn. CONGREGATIONAL CHURCH
Records, 1741-1929, v. 1-8 Ct
N: USIGS
P: Ct
5825

CHESTER, Conn. FIRST BAPTIST CHURCH
Records, 1886-1941, v. 1-2 Ct
N: USIGS
P: Ct
5826

CHESTER, Conn. ST. LUKE'S MISSION
(Episcopal)
Vital records, 1898-1930 Ct
N: USIGS 1 reel
P: Ct
5827

CLINTON, Conn. CHURCH OF THE HOLY
ADVENT
Records, 1873-1936, v. 1-2 Ct
N: USIGS
P: Ct
5828

CLINTON, Conn. METHODIST
EPISCOPAL CHURCH
Records, 1829-1936, v. 1-5 Ct
N: USIGS
P: Ct
5829

COLCHESTER, Conn. BAPTIST CHURCH
Minutes, 1835-1953, v. 1-2 Ct
N: USIGS
P: Ct
5830

COLCHESTER, Conn. CALVARY CHURCH
(Episcopal)
Vital records, 1864-1936 Ct
N: USIGS
P: Ct
5831

COLCHESTER, Conn. FIRST BAPTIST CHURCH
Records, 1780-1939, v. 1-2 Ct
N: USIGS
P: Ct
5832

COLCHESTER, Conn. FIRST
CONGREGATIONAL CHURCH
Records, 1702-1937, v. 1-6 Ct
N: USIGS
P: Ct
5833

COLCHESTER, Conn. SECOND
CONGREGATIONAL CHURCH
Vital records, 1729-1811, v. 1-2 Ct
N: USIGS
P: Ct
5834

COLCHESTER, Conn. THIRD BAPTIST CHURCH
Minutes, 1809-1875 Ct
N: USIGS
P: Ct
5835

COLCHESTER, Conn. WESTCHESTER
ECCLESIASTICAL SOCIETY
Records, 1728-1835, v. 1-2 Ct
N: USIGS
P: Ct
5836

COLEBROOK, Conn. COLEBROOK RIVER
BURYING GROUND ASSOCIATION
Records, 1828-1884 Ct
N: USIGS
P: Ct
5837

COLEBROOK, Conn. CONGREGATIONAL CHURCH
Records, 1783-1939, v. 1-7 Ct
N: USIGS
P: Ct
5838

COLEBROOK RIVER, Conn. UNION CHURCH
SOCIETY
Records, 1828-1884 Ct
N: USIGS
P: Ct
5839

COLLINSVILLE, Conn. METHODIST EPISCOPAL
CHURCH
Vital records, 1866-1873 Ct
N: USIGS
P: Ct
5840

COLLINSVILLE, Conn. TRINITY CHURCH
(Episcopal)
Records, 1873-1924, v. 1-4 Ct
N: USIGS
P: Ct
5841

COLUMBIA, Conn. CONGREGATIONAL CHURCH
(formerly NORTHWEST OR CRANK SOCIETY
IN LEBANON)
Records, 1722-1725, 1737-1917, v. 1-6 Ct
N: USIGS
P: Ct
5842

CONGREGATIONAL CHURCH. CONNECTICUT.
LITCHFIELD SOUTH ASSOCIATION
Minutes, 1795-1930, v. 1-2 Ct
N: USIGS 1 reel
P: Ct
5843

CORNWALL, Conn. FIRST METHODIST
EPISCOPAL CHURCH
Records, 1839-1898 Ct
N: USIGS
P: Ct
5844

CORNWALL HOLLOW, Conn. BAPTIST CHURCH
Minutes, 1843-1935 Ct
N: USIGS
P: Ct
5845

CROMWELL, Conn. BAPTIST CHURCH
(formerly MIDDLETOWN SECOND
BAPTIST CHURCH)
Records, 1802-1920, v. 1-2 Ct
N: USIGS
P: Ct
5846

CROMWELL, Conn. FIRST CONGREGATIONAL
CHURCH (formerly MIDDLETOWN SECOND
OR NORTH OR UPPER SOCIETY)
Vital records, 1715-1875, v. 1-2 Ct
N: USIGS
P: Ct
5847

CRYSTAL LAKE, Conn. METHODIST
EPISCOPAL CHURCH
Vital records, 1792-1949 Ct
N: USIGS
P: Ct
5848

DANBURY, Conn. FIRST CONGREGATIONAL
CHURCH
Records, 1754-1930, v. 1-2, 5-12
N: USIGS
P: Ct
5849

DANBURY, Conn. KING STREET
CHRISTIAN CHURCH
Minutes, 1830-1914, v. 1-2 Ct
N: USIGS
P: Ct
5850

DANBURY, Conn. ST. JAMES
EPISCOPAL CHURCH
Records, 1812-1923, v. 2-7 Ct
N: USIGS 2 reels
P: Ct
5851

DANBURY, Conn. SECOND OR CALVARY
CONGREGATIONAL CHURCH
Records, 1851-1906 Ct
N: USIGS
P: Ct
5852

DANIELSON, Conn. WESTFIELD
CONGREGATIONAL CHURCH
Records, 1801-1936 Ct
N: USIGS 2 reels
P: Ct
5853

DARIEN, Conn.
Church records, to 1850, 135 p. (abstracts)
NNNG
N: USIGS
5854

DEEP RIVER, Conn. ST. PETER'S MISSION
(Episcopal)
Vital records, 1895-1912 Ct
N: USIGS
P: Ct
5855

DERBY, Conn. METHODIST EPISCOPAL
CHURCH (formerly BIRMINGHAM
METHODIST EPISCOPAL CHURCH)
Records, 1828-1935, v. 1-6 Ct
N: USIGS
P: Ct
5856

DURHAM, Conn. CHURCH OF THE EPIPHANY
Vital records, 1850-1940, v. 1 Ct
N: USIGS
P: Ct
5857

DURHAM, Conn. CONGREGATIONAL CHURCH
Records, 1756-1938, v. 1-8 Ct
N: USIGS
P: Ct
5858

EAST CANAAN, Conn. SECOND CHURCH OF
CHRIST
Records, 1767-1942, v. 1-3 Ct
N: USIGS
P: Ct
5859

EAST GRANBY, Conn. COPPER HILL
METHODIST CHURCH
Vital records, 1858-1941 Ct
N: USIGS
P: Ct
5860

EAST HADDAM, Conn. FIRST BAPTIST
SOCIETY
Minutes, 1809-1875 Ct
N: USIGS
P: Ct
5861

EAST HADDAM, Conn. FIRST CONGREGATIONAL
CHURCH AND ECCLESIASTICAL SOCIETY
Records, 1702-1927, v. 1-4, 6 Ct
N: USIGS
P: Ct
5862

EAST HADDAM, Conn. MOODUS METHODIST
CHURCH
Records, 1840-1922, v. 1-5 Ct
N: USIGS
P: Ct
5863

EAST HADDAM, Conn. ST. STEPHEN'S CHURCH
(Episcopal)
Records, 1791-1913, v. 1-6 Ct
N: USIGS
P: Ct
5864

EAST HADDAM, Conn. SECOND CONGRE-
GATIONAL CHURCH AND ECCLESIASTICAL
SOCIETY
Records, 1733-1931, v. 1-6 Ct
N: USIGS
P: Ct
5865

EAST HADDAM AND HADLYME, Conn.
BAPTIST SOCIETIES
Minutes, 1844-1874 Ct
N: USIGS
P: Ct
5866

EAST HAMPTON, Conn.
CONGREGATIONAL CHURCH
Records, 1747-1930, v. 1-10 Ct
N: USIGS
P: Ct
5867

EAST HAMPTON, Conn. HADDAM NECK
CONGREGATIONAL CHURCH
Records, 1740-1944, v. 1-12 Ct
N: USIGS
P: Ct
5868

EAST HARTFORD, Conn. FIRST CONGREGATION-
AL CHURCH AND ECCLESIASTICAL SOCIETY
Records, 1699-1912 Ct
N: USIGS
P: Ct
5869

EAST HARTLAND, Conn. EAST AND WEST
HARTLAND CONGREGATIONAL CHURCHES
Vital records, 1768-1922, v. 1 Ct
N: USIGS
P: Ct
5870

EAST HARTLAND, Conn. FIRST
CHURCH (Congregational)
Records, 1731-1896 Ct
N: USIGS
P: Ct
5871

EAST HARTLAND, Conn. FIRST ECCLESIASTICAL
SOCIETY AND CONGREGATIONAL CHURCH
Records, 1768-1914, v. 1-4 Ct
N: USIGS
P: Ct
5872

EAST HAVEN, Conn. CHRIST CHURCH
(Episcopal)
Minutes, 1788-1839, v. 1-2 Ct
N: USIGS
P: Ct
5873

EAST HAVEN, Conn. FIRST CONGREGATIONAL
CHURCH [THE OLD STONE CHURCH]
Records, 1755-1905, v. 1-3 Ct
N: USlGS
P: Ct   5874

EAST WINDSOR, Conn. BROAD BROOK
CONGREGATIONAL CHURCH
Records, 1851-1907, v. 1-2 Ct
N: USlGS
P: Ct   5875

EAST WINDSOR, Conn.
FIRST CHURCH OF CHRIST
Records, 1695-1853 Ct
N: USlGS
P: Ct   5876

EAST WINDSOR, Conn. FIRST
CONGREGATIONAL CHURCH
Vital records, 1803-1932, v. 1-2 Ct
N: USlGS
P: Ct   5877

EAST WINDSOR, Conn. FIRST ECCLESIASTICAL
SOCIETY (formerly NORTH OR FOURTH
SOCIETY)
Minutes, 1752-1933, v. 1-3, 5 Ct
N: USlGS
P: Ct   5878

EASTFORD, Conn. BAPTIST CHURCH (formerly
NORTH ASHFORD BAPTIST CHURCH)
Minutes, 1850-1938 Ct
N: USlGS
P: Ct   5879

EASTFORD, Conn. EASTFORD CONGRE-
GATIONAL CHURCH
Records, 1778-1941, v. 1-5 Ct
N: USlGS
P: Ct   5880

EASTON, Conn. CHRIST CHURCH (Episcopal)
Minutes, 1784-1898 Ct
N: USlGS
P: Ct   5881

EASTON (formerly NORTH FAIRFIELD), Conn.
ECCLESIASTICAL SOCIETY AND CONGRE-
GATIONAL CHURCH
Records, 1762-1930, v. 1-3 Ct
N: USlGS
P: Ct   5882

ELLINGTON, Conn.
CONGREGATIONAL CHURCH
Records, 1785-1941, v. 1-4, 7 Ct
N: USlGS 2 reels
P: Ct
DCO: Ct   5883

ENFIELD, Conn. FIRST
CONGREGATIONAL CHURCH
Records, 1770-1907, v. 1-5 Ct
N: USlGS
P: Ct   5884

ESSEX, Conn. CENTERBROOK ECCLESIASTICAL
SOCIETY AND CONGREGATIONAL CHURCH
(formerly SAYBROOK SECOND SOCIETY)
Records, 1722-1931, v. 1-5 Ct
N: USlGS
P: Ct   5885

ESSEX, Conn. FIRST BAPTIST CHURCH AND
SOCIETY (formerly of SAYBROOK)
Records, 1810-1896, v. 1-3 Ct
N: USlGS
P: Ct   5886

ESSEX, Conn. FIRST
CONGREGATIONAL CHURCH
Records, 1852-1941, v. 1-2 Ct
N: USlGS
P: Ct   5887

ESSEX, Conn. ST. JOHN'S CHURCH (Episcopal)
Records, 1790-1938, v. 1-4 Ct
N: USlGS
P: Ct   5888

FAIR HAVEN, Conn. FIRST CONGREGATIONAL
CHURCH
Vital records, 1830-1894 Ct
N: USlGS
P: Ct
DCO: Ct   5889

FAIRFIELD, Conn. FIRST
CONGREGATIONAL CHURCH
Vital records, 1694-1806 Ct
N: USlGS
P: Ct   5890

FAIRFIELD, Conn. GREENFIELD HILL OR
NORTHWEST SOCIETY AND CHURCH
Records, 1668-1881, v. 1-3 Ct
N: USlGS
P: Ct   5891

FAIRFIELD, Conn. ST. PAUL'S
CHURCH (Episcopal)
Records, 1853-1947, v. 1-3, 5 Ct
N: USlGS
P: Ct   5892

FAIRFIELD, Conn. STRATFIELD
BAPTIST CHURCH
Records, 1751-1938, v. 1-8 Ct
N: USlGS
P: Ct   5893

FARMINGTON, Conn. FIRST CONGREGATIONAL
CHURCH
Records, 1652-1938 Ct
N: USlGS 2 reels
P: Ct   5894

FARMINGTON, Conn. FIRST SOCIETY
Tax abatements, 1777-1780, 2 v. Ct
DCO: Ct   5895

FARMINGTON, Conn. ST. JAMES' CHURCH
(Episcopal)
Vital records, 1873-1937, v. 1-3 Ct
N: USlGS
P: Ct   5896

FITCHVILLE, Conn. UNION CONGREGATIONAL
CHURCH
Minutes, 1852-1867 Ct
N: USlGS
P: Ct   5897

FLANDERS, Conn. BAPTIST COMMUNITY
CHURCH (formerly LYME FIRST BAPTIST
CHURCH)
Records, 1752-1859, v. 1-3 Ct
N: USlGS
P: Ct   5898

FRANKLIN, Conn. CONGREGATIONAL CHURCH
(formerly NORWICH WEST FARMS OR
SECOND SOCIETY)
Minutes, 1730-1883 Ct
N: USlGS
P: Ct   5899

FRANKLIN, Conn. CONGREGATIONAL CHURCH
(formerly SECOND CHURCH IN NORWICH)
Vital records, 1718-1932 Ct
N: USlGS
P: Ct   5900

FRANKLIN, Conn. SECOND ECCLESIASTICAL
SOCIETY
Records, 1813-1864 Ct
N: USlGS
P: Ct   5901

FRIENDS, SOCIETY OF. GREENWICH [Conn.]
MONTHLY MEETING
Births and deaths, 1690-1900; marriages,
1704-1883; minutes, 1699-1898 RPMB
N: USlGS
P: PSC-F   5902

FRIENDS, SOCIETY OF. WEST HARTFORD
[Conn.] MONTHLY MEETING
Vital records, 1800-1823 Ct
N: USlGS 1 reel
P: Ct   5903

FRIENDS, SOCIETY OF. WEST HARTFORD
[Conn.] MONTHLY MEETING
Vital records, 1805-1828 NNSF
N: USlGS
P: PHC   5904

GLASTONBURY, Conn. BUCKINGHAM
CONGREGATIONAL CHURCH INC.
(formerly EASTBURY SOCIETY)
Records, 1731-1873, v. 1-2 Ct
N: USlGS
P: Ct   5905

GLASTONBURY, Conn. EAST GLASTONBURY
METHODIST CHURCH
Records, 1795-1911, v. 1-4 Ct
N: USlGS
P: Ct   5906

GLASTONBURY, Conn. FIRST CONGREGA-
TIONAL CHURCH
Records, 1731-1924, v. 1-5 Ct
N: USlGS
P: Ct   5907

GLASTONBURY, Conn. ST. JAMES' CHURCH
(Episcopal)
Records, 1857-1941, v. 1-4 Ct
N: USlGS
P: Ct   5908

GLASTONBURY, Conn. ST. LUKE'S CHURCH
(Episcopal)
Records, 1806-1949, v. 1-2, 5-8 Ct
N: USlGS
P: Ct   5909

GOSHEN, Conn. FIRST CHURCH OF CHRIST
(Congregational)
Records, 1791-1854, v. 1-2 Ct
N: USlGS
P: Ct   5910

GOSHEN, Conn. NORTH
CONGREGATIONAL CHURCH
Records, 1828-1853 Ct
N: USlGS
P: Ct   5911

GRANBY, Conn. FIRST CONGREGATIONAL
CHURCH (formerly NORTH WEST SOCIETY
OF SIMSBURY)
Records, 1739-1887, 1895-1919, v. 1-8 Ct
N: USlGS
P: Ct   5912

GREENS FARMS, Conn.
Parish records Ibid.
N: CtY 4 reels   5913

GREENWICH, Conn.
Church records (abstract), up to 1850, 220 p.
NNNG
N: USlGS   5914

GREENWICH, Conn. STANWICH
CONGREGATIONAL CHURCH
Vital records, 1796-1834 Ct
N: USlGS
P: Ct   5915

GRISWOLD, Conn. FIRST CONGREGATIONAL
CHURCH (formerly NORTH OR SECOND
CHURCH IN PRESTON)
Records, 1720-1857, 1863-1878, v. 1-5 Ct
N: USlGS
P: Ct   5916

GROTON, Conn. FIRST
CONGREGATIONAL CHURCH
Vital records, 1727-1811 Ct
N: USlGS
P: Ct   5917

GROTON, Conn. NOANK BAPTIST CHURCH
Minutes, 1843-1892, v. 1-2 Ct
N: USlGS
P: Ct   5918

GROTON, Conn. POQUONOC
BRIDGE BAPTIST CHURCH
Minutes, 1856-1921 Ct
N: USlGS
P: Ct   5919

GUILFORD, Conn. CHRIST EPISCOPAL CHURCH
Records, 1744-1909, v. 1-3 Ct
N: USlGS
P: Ct   5920

GUILFORD, Conn. FIRST ECCLESIASTICAL
SOCIETY AND CONGREGATIONAL CHURCH
Records, 1717-1921 Ct
N: USlGS 2 reels
P: Ct   5921

GUILFORD, Conn. METHODIST EPISCOPAL
CHURCH
Records, 1855-1901, v. 1-2 Ct
N: USlGS
P: Ct   5922

HADDAM, Conn. FIRST CONGREGATIONAL
CHURCH
Records, 1700-1908, v. 1-2, 4-8 Ct
N: USIGS
P: Ct
5923

HADDAM, Conn. HADDAM CONGREGATIONAL
CHURCH
Vital records, 1756-1799 Ct
N: USIGS
P: Ct
5924

HADDAM, Conn. HADDAM MISSION (Episcopal)
(includes missions of Shailerville, Tylerville,
and Maromas)
Vital records, 1876-1934 Ct
N: USIGS
P: Ct
5925

HADDAM, Conn. ST. JAMES' CHURCH (Episcopal)
Vital records, 1860-1931, v. 1-2 Ct
N: USIGS
P: Ct
5926

HADLYME, Conn. GRACE CHAPEL (Episcopal)
Vital records, 1899-1925, v. 1 Ct
N: USIGS
P: Ct
5927

HADLYME, Conn. HADLYME ECCLESIASTICAL
SOCIETY AND CONGREGATIONAL CHURCH
Records, 1742-1932, v. 1-5 Ct
N: USIGS
P: Ct
5928

HAMDEN, Conn. GRACE CHURCH (Episcopal)
Records, 1790-1927, v. 1-4 Ct
N: USIGS
P: Ct
5929

HAMDEN, Conn. PLAINS METHODIST EPISCOPAL
CHURCH
Minutes, 1897-1903, 1937-1953, v. 3-4 Ct
N: USIGS
P: Ct
5930

HAMDEN, Conn. WHITNEYVILLE CONGREGA-
TIONAL CHURCH (formerly EAST PLAIN
CHURCH)
Records, 1795-1915, v. 1-5 Ct
N: USIGS
P: Ct
5931

HAMPTON, Conn. BAPTIST CHURCH
Minutes, 1770-1844, v. 1-5 Ct
N: USIGS
P: Ct
5932

HAMPTON, Conn. FIRST CONGREGATIONAL
CHURCH
Records, 1723-1879, v. 1-3 Ct
N: USIGS
P: Ct
5933

HARTFORD, Conn. ASYLUM BAPTIST CHURCH
Minutes, 1869-1936, v. 1-2, 5 Ct
N: USIGS
P: Ct
5934

HARTFORD, Conn. BLUE HILLS BAPTIST
CHURCH (formerly FIRST BAPTIST CHURCH
OF WINDSOR)
Records, 1810-1899, v. 1-2 Ct
N: USIGS
P: Ct
5935

HARTFORD, Conn. CENTRAL BAPTIST CHURCH
Minutes, 1923-1931 Ct
N: USIGS
P: Ct
5936

HARTFORD, Conn. CHRIST CHURCH (Episcopal)
Records, 1795-1840, 1848-1877, 1887-1927 Ct
N: USIGS
P: Ct
5937

HARTFORD, Conn. CHURCH OF THE GOOD SHEP-
HERD (Episcopal)
Records, 1864-1935, v. 1-9 Ct
N: USIGS 2 reels
P: Ct
5938

HARTFORD, Conn. FIRST BAPTIST CHURCH
Vital records, 1789-1909, v. 1-3 Ct
N: USIGS
P: Ct
5939

HARTFORD, Conn. FIRST INDEPENDENT UNI-
VERSALIST CHURCH
Vital records, 1824-1923, v. 1 Ct
N: USIGS
P: Ct
5940

HARTFORD, Conn. FIRST PRESBYTERIAN
CHURCH
Minutes, 1851-1924, v. 1-6 Ct
N: USIGS
P: Ct
5941

HARTFORD, Conn. FOURTH CONGREGATIONAL
CHURCH (formerly "FREE CHURCH")
Vital records, 1832-1907, v. 1-3 Ct
N: USIGS
P: Ct
5942

HARTFORD, Conn. GRACE CHURCH (Episcopal)
Records, 1863-1937, v. 1-6 Ct
N: USIGS
P: Ct
5943

HARTFORD, Conn. NORTH AND PARK CONGRE-
GATIONAL CHURCH
Records, 1824-1926, v. 1-4, 7 Ct
N: USIGS
P: Ct
5944

HARTFORD, Conn. NORTH METHODIST CHURCH
Records, 1871-1926, v. 1-3, 5 Ct
N: USIGS
P: Ct
5945

HARTFORD, Conn. PEARL STREET CONGRE-
GATIONAL CHURCH
Vital records, 1851-1913, v. 1-3 Ct
N: USIGS
P: Ct
5946

HARTFORD, Conn. ST. JAMES CHURCH (Epis-
copal)
Records, 1868-1947, v. 1-6, 9 Ct
N: USIGS
P: Ct
5947

HARTFORD, Conn. ST. JOHN'S CHURCH (Episcopal)
Records, 1841-1925, v. 1-2, 4-8 Ct
N: USIGS 2 reels
5948

HARTFORD, Conn. ST. PAUL'S CHURCH (Epis-
copal)
Records, 1850-1879, v. 1-2 Ct
N: USIGS
P: Ct
5949

HARTFORD, Conn. ST. THOMAS' CHURCH (Epis-
copal)
Vital records, 1871-1920, v. 1-4 Ct
N: USIGS
P: Ct
5950

HARTFORD, Conn. SECOND CONGREGATIONAL
CHURCH AND SECOND ECCLESIASTICAL
SOCIETY
Records, 1792-1862, 1868-1914, v. 1-3, A-B
Ct
N: USIGS
P: Ct
5951

HARTFORD, Conn. SOUTH BAPTIST CHURCH
Minutes, 1834-1928, v. 1-10 Ct
N: USIGS
P: Ct
5952

HARTFORD, Conn. TRINITY CHURCH (Episcopal)
Records, 1859-1936, v. 1-7 Ct
N: USIGS 2 reels
P: Ct
5953

HARTFORD, Conn. WETHERSFIELD AVENUE
CONGREGATIONAL CHURCH
Records, 1868-1914, v. 1-3 Ct
N: USIGS
P: Ct
5954

HARTFORD, Conn. WINDSOR AVENUE CONGRE-
GATIONAL CHURCH
Records, 1865-1908, v. 1, 3-5 Ct
N: USIGS
P: Ct
5955

HARWINTON, Conn. FIRST CONGREGATIONAL
CHURCH
Vital records, 1791-1861 Ct
N: USIGS
P: Ct
5956

HEBRON, Conn. FIRST CONGREGATIONAL
CHURCH
Minutes, 1787-1915, v. 1-2 Ct
N: USIGS
P: Ct
5957

HEBRON, Conn. GILEAD ECCLESIASTICAL
SOCIETY
Minutes, 1748-1941; vital records, 1752-1943,
v. 1-2 Ct
N: USIGS
P: Ct
5958

HEBRON, Conn. ST. PETER'S CHURCH (Episcopal)
Records, 1787-1905 Ct
N: USIGS
P: Ct
5959

HIGGANUM, Conn. CONGREGATIONAL CHURCH
Vital records, 1844-1893 Ct
N: USIGS
P: Ct
5960

HOCKANUM, Conn. SOUTH CONGREGATIONAL
CHURCH
Vital records, 1877-1923, 1925-1940, v. 1-3 Ct
N: USIGS
P: Ct
5961

HOTCHKISS, FREDERICK WILLIAM, 1762-1844
Papers re: Saybrook church priv.
N: CtY
5962

IVORYTON, Conn. ALL SAINTS' CHURCH (Epis-
copal)
Vital records, 1904-1941 Ct
N: USIGS
P: Ct
5963

JEWETT CITY, Conn. METHODIST EPISCOPAL
CHURCH
Records, 1844-1930, v. 1-4 Ct
N: USIGS
P: Ct
5964

JEWETT CITY, Conn. SECOND CONGREGATIONAL
CHURCH
Vital records, 1825-1861, v. 1 Ct
N: USIGS
P: Ct
5965

JONES, Rev. DAVID E., pastor
Records: Congregational Church, Roxbury,
Conn., 1871-1886; Broad Brook Congregational
Church, 1886-1898; Ellington Congregational
Church, Taylor, Penn., 1898-1920;
miscellaneous records, 1875-1918 Ct
N: USIGS
P: Ct
5966

KENT, Conn. CONGREGATIONAL CHURCH
Vital records, 1739-1915, v. 1-2 Ct
N: USIGS
P: Ct
5967

KILLINGLY, Conn. DANIELSON METHODIST
EPISCOPAL CHURCH
Records, 1842-1889, v. 1-4, 33 Ct
N: USIGS
P: Ct
5968

KILLINGLY, Conn. FIRST CONGREGATIONAL
CHURCH
Minutes, 1790-1858 Ct
N: USIGS
P: Ct
5969

KILLINGLY, Conn. SOUTH CONGREGATIONAL
CHURCH, Breakneck Hill
Vital records, 1746-1755 Ct
N: USIGS
P: Ct
5970

KILLINGWORTH, Conn. EMMANUEL CHURCH
(Episcopal) (formerly KILLINGWORTH AND
NORTH BRISTOL EPISCOPALIAN SOCIETIES,
united as THE UNION SOCIETY in 1800 and
named EMMANUEL CHURCH in 1869)
Vital records, 1800-1883 Ct
N: USIGS
P: Ct
5971

KILLINGWORTH, Conn. FIRST CONGREGATIONAL
CHURCH
Records, 1735-1893, v. 1-4 Ct
N: USIGS
P: Ct
5972

KILLINGWORTH, Conn. SECOND PARISH
Records, 1739-1839, 52 p. NNNG
N: USIGS
P: Ct   5973

LEBANON, Conn. EXETER CONGREGATIONAL
CHURCH
Records, 1709-1914, v. 1-3 Ct
N: USIGS
P: Ct   5974

LEBANON, Conn. FIRST ECCLESIASTICAL
SOCIETY AND CONGREGATIONAL CHURCH
Records, 1700-1873, v. 1-5 Ct
N: USIGS
P: Ct   5975

LEBANON, Conn. GOSHEN CONGREGATIONAL
CHURCH
Records, 1728-1895, 2 v. Ct
N: USIGS 1 reel
P: Ct   5976

LEBANON, Conn. ORANGE BAPTIST CHURCH
Minutes, 1818-1881 Ct
N: USIGS
P: Ct   5977

LEDYARD, Conn. CONGREGATIONAL CHURCH
Vital records, 1810-1897 Ct
N: USIGS
P: Ct   5978

LISBON, Conn. NEWENT CONGREGATIONAL
CHURCH
Records, 1724-1932, v. 1-6 Ct
N: USIGS
P: Ct   5979

LITCHFIELD, Conn. FIRST CONGREGATIONAL
CHURCH
Records, 1886-1938 Ct
N: USIGS
P: Ct   5980

LITCHFIELD, Conn. FIRST ECCLESIASTICAL
SOCIETY
Minutes, 1768-1927, v. 1-2 Ct
N: USIGS
P: Ct   5981

LITCHFIELD, Conn. FIRST EPISCOPAL
SOCIETY
Minutes, 1784-1896, v. 1 Ct
N: USIGS
P: Ct   5982

LITCHFIELD, Conn. FIRST METHODIST CHURCH
Records, 1790-1917, v. 1-3, 7 Ct
N: USIGS
P: Ct   5983

LITCHFIELD, Conn. ST. MICHAEL'S CHURCH
(Episcopal)
Vital records, 1750-1870, v. 1-2 Ct
N: USIGS
P: Ct   5984

LYME, Conn. FIRST CONGREGATIONAL
CHURCH [THIRD OR NORTH OR HAMBURG
SOCIETY]
Vital records, 1787-1932, v. 1-2, 4
N: USIGS
P: Ct   5985

LYME, Conn. NORTH LYME BAPTIST CHURCH
Minutes, 1810-1903, v. 1-4 Ct
N: USIGS
P: Ct   5986

MADISON, Conn. FIRST
CONGREGATIONAL CHURCH
Records, 1707-1917, v. 1-11 Ct
N: USIGS
P: Ct   5987

MADISON, Conn. METHODIST
EPISCOPAL CHURCH
Vital records, 1839-1923, v. 1 Ct
N: USIGS
P: Ct   5988

MADISON, Conn. ROCKLAND
METHODIST EPISCOPAL CHURCH
Vital records, 1833-1906 Ct
N: USIGS
P: Ct   5989

MANCHESTER, Conn. FIRST
CONGREGATIONAL CHURCH
Records, 1772-1917 Ct
N: USIGS 1 reel   5990

MANCHESTER, Conn. METHODIST CHURCH
Vital records, 1850-1941, v. 1, 4-5 Ct
N: USIGS
P: Ct   5991

MANCHESTER, Conn. ST. MARY'S CHURCH
(Episcopal)
Vital records, 1876-1924, v. 1-4 Ct
N: USIGS
P: Ct   5992

MANCHESTER, Conn. SECOND
CONGREGATIONAL CHURCH
Records, 1851-1941 Ct
N: USIGS 1 reel   5993

MANSFIELD, Conn. FIRST
CONGREGATIONAL CHURCH
Records, 1710-1894, v. A, 1-3 Ct
N: USIGS
P: Ct   5994

MANSFIELD, Conn. STORRS COMMUNITY
CHURCH (formerly NORTH MANSFIELD
CONGREGATIONAL CHURCH)
Vital records, 1784-1824 Ct
N: USIGS
P: Ct   5995

MANSFIELD, Conn. STORRS CONGREGATIONAL
CHURCH (formerly MANSFIELD SECOND
[NORTH] CHURCH)
Records, 1737-1929, v. 1-3 Ct
N: USIGS
P: Ct   5996

MARLBOROUGH, Conn.
CONGREGATIONAL CHURCH
Vital records, 1749-1855 Ct
N: USIGS
P: Ct   5997

MERIDEN, Conn. CENTER
CONGREGATIONAL CHURCH
Records, 1846-1915, v. 1-3 Ct
N: USIGS
P: Ct   5998

MERIDEN, Conn. FIRST BAPTIST CHURCH
Minutes, 1786-1822, 1837-1852, v. 1-2 Ct
N: USIGS
P: Ct   5999

MERIDEN, Conn. FIRST
CONGREGATIONAL CHURCH
Vital records, 1729-1937, v. 2-4 Ct
N: USIGS
P: Ct   6000

MERIDEN, Conn. MAIN STREET BAPTIST
CHURCH (formerly WEST MERIDEN BAPTIST
CHURCH)
Records, 1861-1936 Ct
N: USIGS
P: Ct   6001

MERIDEN, Conn. ST. ANDREW'S
EPISCOPAL CHURCH
Records, 1789-1929, v. 1-8, 12 Ct
N: USIGS 2 reels   6002
P: Ct

MIDDLE HADDAM, Conn.
CHRIST CHURCH (Episcopal)
Records, 1794-1912, v. 1, 3, 4 Ct
N: USIGS
P: Ct   6003

MIDDLE HADDAM, Conn.
CONGREGATIONAL CHURCH
Marriage records, 1740-1824 NNNG
N: USIGS   6004

MIDDLE HADDAM, Conn.
SECOND ECCLESIASTICAL SOCIETY
Records, 1854-1932, v. 1-2, 6-7 Ct
N: USIGS
P: Ct   6005

MIDDLEBURY, Conn.
CONGREGATIONAL CHURCH
Records, 1796-1915, v. 1-3 Ct
N: USIGS
P: Ct   6006

MIDDLEBURY, Conn.
METHODIST EPISCOPAL CHURCH
Records, 1834-1922, v. 1-3, 6-7 Ct
N: USIGS
P: Ct   6007

MIDDLEFIELD, Conn.
CONGREGATIONAL CHURCH
Records, 1744-1940, v. 1-5 Ct
N: USIGS
P: Ct   6008

MIDDLEFIELD, Conn.
ST. PAUL'S CHURCH (Episcopal)
Vital records, 1873-1911, v. 1 Ct
N: USIGS
P: Ct   6009

MIDDLETOWN, Conn. CHURCH OF THE HOLY
TRINITY (Episcopal) (formerly CHRIST CHURCH)
Records, 1750-1947, v. 1-2, B-Z Ct
N: USIGS 6 reels   6010
P: Ct

MIDDLETOWN, Conn. FIRST BAPTIST CHURCH
Records, 1795-1914, v. 1-5 Ct
N: USIGS
P: Ct   6011

MIDDLETOWN, Conn. FIRST CONGREGATIONAL
CHURCH
Records, 1668-1871, v. 1-5 Ct
N: USIGS
P: Ct   6012

MIDDLETOWN, Conn. FIRST UNIVERSALIST
CHURCH
Minutes, 1846-1911 Ct
N: USIGS
P: Ct   6013

MIDDLETOWN, Conn. SECOND CHURCH
OF CHRIST COVENANT
Records, 1828, 9 p. NNNG
N: USIGS   6014

MIDDLETOWN, Conn.
SOUTH CONGREGATIONAL CHURCH
Records, 1787-1909, v. 1-2, 4-5 Ct
N: USIGS
P: Ct   6015

MILFORD, Conn. FIRST CONGREGATIONAL
CHURCH
Records, 1784-1926, v. 1-5 Ct
N: USIGS
P: Ct   6016

MILFORD, Conn. PLYMOUTH CONGREGATION-
AL CHURCH (formerly SECOND CONGRE-
GATIONAL CHURCH IN MILFORD)
Records, 1851-1926, v. 2-4 Ct
N: USIGS
P: Ct   6017

MILFORD, Conn. PLYMOUTH ECCLESIASTICAL
SOCIETY [MILFORD SECOND SOCIETY]
Minutes, 1760-1930 Ct
N: USIGS
P: Ct   6018

MILTON, Conn. CHURCH OF CHRIST
(Congregational)
Records, 1798-1898, v. 1-2 Ct
N: USIGS
P: Ct   6019

MILTON, Conn. ST. PETER'S CHURCH
(Episcopal) (formerly ST. GEORGE'S CHURCH)
Records, 1764-1868, v. 1-4 Ct
N: USIGS
P: Ct   6020

MILTON, Conn. TRINITY CHURCH (Episcopal)
Vital records, 1832-1940, 2 v. Ct
N: USIGS 1 reel
P: Ct   6021

MONROE, Conn. CONGREGATIONAL CHURCH
(formerly NEW STRATFORD SOCIETY)
Minutes, 1762-1812 Ct
N: USIGS 1 reel   6022

MONROE, Conn. ST. PETER'S CHURCH
(Episcopal)
Minutes, 1823-1908 Ct
N: USIGS
P: Ct   6023

MONTVILLE, Conn. CONGREGATIONAL
CHURCH (formerly NEW LONDON NORTH
PARISH)
Records, 1722-1919, v. 1-4 Ct
N: USlGS
P: Ct
6024

MONTVILLE, Conn. FIRST ECCLESIASTICAL
SOCIETY (formerly NEW LONDON NORTH
PARISH)
Minutes, 1721-1837 Ct
N: USlGS
P: Ct
6025

MOOSUP, Conn. METHODIST EPISCOPAL
CHURCH
Vital records, 1842-1932, v. 1-3 Ct
N: USlGS
P: Ct
6026

MOOSUP, Conn. UNION BAPTIST CHURCH
AND ECCLESIASTICAL SOCIETY (formerly
FIRST BAPTIST CHURCH)
Records, 1792-1931, v. 1-5 Ct
N: USlGS
P: Ct
6027

MORRIS, Conn. CONGREGATIONAL CHURCH
Records, 1748-1892 Ct
N: USlGS
P: Ct
6028

MYSTIC, Conn. ST. MARK'S CHURCH (Episcopal)
Vital records, 1859-1920, v.1-2 Ct
N: USlGS
P: Ct
6029

NAUGATUCK, Conn. CONGREGATIONAL CHURCH
Vital records, 1781-1901, v.1-3 Ibid.
N: USlGS
P: Ct
6030

NEW BRITAIN, Conn. FIRST BAPTIST CHURCH
(formerly FIRST BAPTIST CHURCH IN BERLIN)
Records, 1821-1922, v. 1-5 Ct
N: USlGS
P: Ct
6031

NEW CANAAN, Conn. CONGREGATIONAL
CHURCH
Vital records, 1733-1899, v.1-2 Ct
N: USlGS
P: Ct
6032

NEW FAIRFIELD, Conn. NEW FAIRFIELD
SOUTH CONGREGATIONAL CHURCH
Records, 1742-1900, v. 1-3 Ct
N: USlGS
P: Ct
6033

NEW HARTFORD, Conn. BAKERSVILLE
METHODIST EPISCOPAL CHURCH
Records, 1827-1858, 1861-1930, v.1 Ct
N: USlGS
6034

NEW HARTFORD, Conn. CONGREGATIONAL
CHURCH
Records, 1739-1867 Ct
N: USlGS
P: Ct
6035

NEW HAVEN, Conn. CHRIST CHURCH (Episcopal)
Records, 1837-1939, v. 1-6 Ct
N: USlGS 2 reels
P: Ct
6036

NEW HAVEN, Conn. CHURCH OF THE REDEEMER
(formerly CHAPEL STREET CONGREGATIONAL
CHURCH)
Records, 1838-1933, v. 1-4 Ct
N: USlGS
P: Ct
6037

NEW HAVEN, Conn. FIRST BAPTIST CHURCH
Records, 1816-1941, v.1-11 Ct
N: USlGS
P: Ct
6038

NEW HAVEN, Conn. FIRST CHURCH OF
CHRIST AND ECCLESIASTICAL SOCIETY
Vital records, 1639-1911, v. 1-6, 9 Ct
N: USlGS 1 reel
P: Ct
6039

NEW HAVEN, Conn. FIRST ECCLESIASTICAL
SOCIETY
Records, 1715-1880, v. 1-3 Ct
N: USlGS   P: Ct
6040

NEW HAVEN, Conn. HOPE BAPTIST CHURCH
Vital records, 1887-1902, v. 1-2 Ct
N: USlGS
6041

NEW HAVEN, Conn. ST. PAUL'S CHURCH
(Episcopal)
Vital records, 1845-1940, v. 1-5 Ct
N: USlGS
P: Ct
6042

NEW HAVEN, Conn. ST. THOMAS'S CHURCH
(Episcopal)
Records, 1848-1931, v. 1-8 Ct
N: USlGS 2 reels
P: Ct
6043

NEW HAVEN, Conn. SECOND BAPTIST CHURCH
Records, 1842-1865, v. 1-3 Ct
N: USlGS
6044

NEW HAVEN, Conn. TRINITY CHURCH
(Episcopal)
Vital records, 1767-1939, v. 1-7 Ct
N: USlGS 2 reels
P: Ct
6045

NEW LONDON, Conn. FEDERAL STREET
METHODIST EPISCOPAL CHURCH (New
England Southern Conference)
Records, 1816-1918, v. 1-4 Ct
N: USlGS
P: Ct
6046

NEW LONDON, Conn. FIRST BAPTIST CHURCH
AND SOCIETY
Records, 1804-1909, v. 1-5 Ct
N: USlGS
P: Ct
6047

NEW LONDON, Conn. FIRST CHURCH OF
CHRIST (Congregational)
Records, 1670-1888, v. 1-5, 7-10 Ct
N: USlGS
P: Ct
6048

NEW LONDON, Conn. FIRST CONGREGATIONAL
CHURCH
Records, 1670-1780, 1860-1903, 1908-1916,
v. 1-5 Ct
N: USlGS
P: Ct
6049

NEW LONDON, Conn. ST. JAMES CHURCH
(Episcopal)
Records, 1725-1874, v. 1-2 Ct
N: USlGS
P: Ct
6050

NEW LONDON, Conn. SECOND CONGREGA-
TIONAL CHURCH
Records, 1835-1922, v. 1-2 Ct
N: USlGS
P: Ct
6051

NEW MILFORD, Conn. CONGREGATIONAL
CHURCH
Records, 1753-1938, v. 1-8 Ct
N: USlGS
P: Ct
6052

NEWINGTON, Conn. CHURCH OF CHRIST
(Congregational)
Records, 1716-1927, v. 1-2, 4-5 Ct
N: USlGS
P: Ct
6053

NEWINGTON, Conn. GRACE CHURCH
(Episcopal)
Records, 1871-1940, v. 1-3 Ct
N: USlGS
P: Ct
6054

NEWTOWN, Conn. CONGREGATIONAL CHURCH
Records of baptisms and marriages,
1800-1875 Ct
N: USlGS
P: Ct
6055

NEWTOWN, Conn. FIRST CONGREGATIONAL
CHURCH
Records, 1715-1951, v. 1-9 Ct
N: USlGS 2 reels
P: Ct
6056

NEWTOWN, Conn. METHODIST EPISCOPAL
CHURCH (New York East Conference)
Vital records, 1805-1932, v. 1 Ct
N: USlGS   P: Ct
6057

NEWTOWN, Conn. ST. JOHN'S CHURCH
(Episcopal)
Vital records, 1880-1913 Ct
N: USlGS
P: Ct
6058

NEWTOWN, Conn. TRINITY CHURCH (Episcopal)
Records, 1764-1792, 1818-1921, v. 1-5 Ct
N: USlGS
P: Ct
6059

NORFOLK, Conn. CHURCH OF CHRIST
(Congregational)
Records, 1760-1928, v. 1-4, 6-8 Ct
N: USlGS
P: Ct
6060

NORTH BRANFORD, Conn. CONGREGATIONAL
CHURCH
Vital records, 1768-1805, 1809-1867, v. 2-3 Ct
N: USlGS 1 reel
P: Ct
6061

NORTH BRANFORD, Conn. ZION CHURCH
(Episcopal)
Vital records, 1812-1875, v. 1-2 Ct
N: USlGS
P: Ct
6062

NORTH COVENTRY, Conn. SECOND
CONGREGATIONAL CHURCH
Records, 1740-1910, v. 1-6 Ct
N: USlGS
P: Ct
6063

NORTH GOSHEN, Conn. METHODIST EPISCOPAL
CHURCH
Records, 1840-1940, v. 1-2 Ct
N: USlGS
P: Ct
6064

NORTH GRANBY, Conn. FIRST UNIVERSALIST
SOCIETY
Records, 1832-1881, 1896-1912, v. 1-2 Ct
N: USlGS
P: Ct
6065

NORTH GUILFORD, Conn. ST. JOHN'S CHURCH
(Episcopal)
Records, 1748-1868, v. 1-3 Ct
N: USlGS
P: Ct
6066

NORTH GUILFORD, Conn. SECOND
CONGREGATIONAL CHURCH
Records, 1720-1859, v. 1-4, 6 Ct
N: USlGS
P: Ct
6067

NORTH HAVEN, Conn. CONGREGATIONAL
CHURCH
Vital records, 1716-1910, v. 1-3 Ct
N: USlGS
P: Ct
6068

NORTH HAVEN, Conn. ST. JOHN'S CHURCH
(Episcopal)
Records, 1759-1858 Ct
N: USlGS
P: Ct
6069

NORTH MADISON, Conn. CONGREGATIONAL
CHURCH
Records, 1754-1877, v. 1-4 Ct
N: USlGS
P: Ct
6070

NORTH MADISON, Conn. GERMAN LUTHERAN
IMMANUEL CHURCH
Records, 1898-1922, v. 1-3 Ct
N: USlGS
P: Ct
6071

NORTH STONINGTON, Conn. "BREAKNECK"
CONGREGATIONAL CHURCH
Records, 1746-1754 Ct
N: USlGS
P: Ct
6072

NORTH STONINGTON, Conn. CONGREGATIONAL
CHURCH
Records, 1720-1887 Ct
N: USlGS
P: Ct
6073

NORTHFIELD, Conn. TRINITY CHURCH
(Episcopal)
Records, 1793-1892, v. 1-2 Ct
N: USlGS
P: Ct
6074

NORTHFORD, Conn. CONGREGATIONAL CHURCH
Records, 1750-1926, v. 1-3 Ct
N: USIGS   6075
P: Ct

NORTHFORD, Conn. ST. ANDREW'S CHURCH
(Episcopal)
Records, 1763-1899, v. 1-3 Ct
N: USIGS   6076
P: Ct

NORTHVILLE, Conn. BAPTIST CHURCH
Minutes, 1814-1939, v. 1-4 Ct
N: USIGS   6077
P: Ct

NORWALK, Conn. ST. PAUL'S CHURCH
(Episcopal)
Records, 1741-1925, v. 1-11 Ct
N: USIGS 2 reels   6078
P: Ct

NORWICH, Conn. CHRIST CHURCH (Episcopal)
Records, 1746-1901, v. A, 1-6 Ct
N: USIGS   6079
P: Ct

NORWICH, Conn. FALLS CONGREGATIONAL
CHURCH
Minutes, 1827-1842 Ct
N: USIGS   6080
P: Ct

NORWICH, Conn. FIRST BAPTIST CHURCH
Records, 1800-1944, v. 1-6 Ct
N: USIGS 2 reels   6081
P: Ct

NORWICH, Conn. FIRST CONGREGATIONAL
CHURCH
Vital records, 1660-1916, v. 1-6 Ct
N: USIGS   6082
P: Ct

NORWICH, Conn. FIRST UNIVERSALIST CHURCH
Minutes, 1838-1941, v. 1-3 Ct
N: USIGS   6083
P: Ct

NORWICH, Conn. FIRST UNIVERSALIST
SOCIETY (formerly the SOCIETY OF UNITED
CHRISTIAN FRIENDS)
Minutes, 1836-1946, v. 1-3 Ct
N: USIGS   6084
P: Ct

NORWICH, Conn. FOURTH CONGREGATIONAL
CHURCH [GREENVILLE CONGREGATIONAL
CHURCH]
Vital records, 1833-1857, v. 1 Ct
N: USIGS   6085
P: Ct

NORWICH, Conn. SECOND CONGREGATIONAL
CHURCH [CHELSEA CHURCH]
Records, 1760-1918, v. 1-3 Ct
N: USIGS   6086
P: Ct

NORWICH, Conn. TAFTVILLE CONGREGATION-
AL ECCLESIASTICAL SOCIETY AND CHURCH
Records, 1867-1916, v. 1-2 Ct
N: USIGS   6087
P: Ct

OLD GREENWICH, Conn. FIRST
CONGREGATIONAL CHURCH
Records, 1798-1936, v. 1-6 Ct
N: USIGS   6088
P: Ct

OLD LYME, Conn. FIRST BAPTIST CHURCH
Records, 1842-1924, v. 1-3 Ct
N: USIGS   6089
P: Ct

OLD LYME, Conn. FIRST CONGREGATIONAL
CHURCH (formerly FIRST SOCIETY OF LYME)
Minutes, 1721-1876 Ct
N: USIGS   6090
P: Ct

OLD LYME, Conn. FIRST ECCLESIASTICAL
SOCIETY AND CONGREGATIONAL CHURCH
Records, 1731-1784, v. 1-4 Ct
N: USIGS   6091
P: Ct

OLD MYSTIC, Conn. FIRST BAPTIST CHURCH
Vital records, 1754-1899, v. 1-4 Ct
N: USIGS   6092
P: Ct

OLD SAYBROOK, Conn. CONGREGATIONAL
CHURCH
Records, 1736-1935, v. 1-3, 5 Ct
N: USIGS   6093
P: Ct

OLD SAYBROOK, Conn. GRACE EPISCOPAL
CHURCH
Vital records, 1815-1948, v. 1-3 Ct
N: USIGS   6094
P: Ct

ORANGE, Conn. CONGREGATIONAL CHURCH
(formerly NORTH MILFORD PARISH)
Records, 1804-1929, v. 1-5 Ct
N: USIGS   6095
P: Ct

OXFORD, Conn. CONGREGATIONAL CHURCH
Records, 1741-1929, v. 1-4 Ct
N: USIGS   6096
P: Ct

OXFORD, Conn. ST. PETER'S CHURCH
(Episcopal)
Vital records, 1845-1948 Ct
N: USIGS   6097
P: Ct

PENDLETON HILL, Conn. FIRST
BAPTIST CHURCH
Records, 1754-1905, v. 1-4 Ct
N: USIGS   6098
P: Ct

PINE MEADOW, Conn. ST. JOHN'S CHURCH
(Episcopal)
Vital records, 1850-1904, v. 1-3 Ct
N: USIGS   6099
P: Ct

PLAINFIELD, Conn. CENTRAL VILLAGE
CONGREGATIONAL CHURCH
Vital records, 1846-1941 Ct
N: USIGS   6100
P: Ct

PLAINFIELD, Conn. FIRST CONGREGATIONAL
CHURCH
Records, 1747-1879, v. 1-2 Ct
N: USIGS   6101
P: Ct

PLAINFIELD, Conn. NORTH PLAINFIELD
ECCLESIASTICAL SOCIETY
Minutes, 1845-1941 Ct
N: USIGS   6102
P: Ct

PLAINFIELD, Conn. PACKERVILLE BAPTIST
CHURCH
Records, 1828-1928, v. 1-3 Ct
N: USIGS   6103
P: Ct

PLAINFIELD, Conn. ST. PAUL'S
CHURCH (Episcopal)
Vital records, 1856-1893, v. 1 Ct
N: USIGS   6104
P: Ct

PLAINFIELD, Conn. WAUREGAN
CONGREGATIONAL CHURCH
Vital records, 1856-1941 Ct
N: USIGS   6105
P: Ct

PLAINVILLE, Conn. BAPTIST CHURCH
Minutes, 1851-1934, v. 1-3 Ct
N: USIGS   6106
P: Ct

PLAINVILLE, Conn. CONGREGATIONAL
CHURCH
Records, 1839-1926, v. 1-5 Ct
N: USIGS   6107
P: Ct

PLYMOUTH, Conn. CONGREGATIONAL
CHURCH
Vital records, 1765-1810, v. 1-2 Ct
N: USIGS 1 reel   6108
P: Ct

PLYMOUTH, Conn. ST. MATTHEW'S CHURCH
(Episcopal)
Records, 1744-1891, v. 1-3 Ct
N: USIGS   6109
P: Ct

PLYMOUTH, Conn. ST. PETER'S
CHURCH (Episcopal)
Records, 1784-1910, 1915, v. 1-5 Ct
N: USIGS   6110
P: Ct

POMFRET, Conn. CATHOLIC REFORMED
CHRISTIAN CHURCH
Vital records, 1792-1798 Ct
N: USIGS   6111
P: Ct

POMFRET, Conn. CHRIST CHURCH (Episcopal)
Vital records, 1826-1889, v. 1-2 Ct
N: USIGS   6112
P: Ct

POMFRET (and ABINGTON), Conn. SECOND
SOCIETY (Congregational)
Records, 1749-1923, v. 1-3 Ct
N: USIGS   6113
P: Ct

POMFRET (and BROOKLYN), Conn. TRINITY
CHURCH (Episcopal)
Vital records, 1771-1866, v. 1-4 Ct
N: USIGS   6114
P: Ct

PORTLAND, Conn. CENTRAL CONGREGATION-
AL CHURCH
Vital records, 1851-1888, v. 1-2 Ct
N: USIGS   6115
P: Ct

PORTLAND, Conn. FIRST CONGREGATIONAL
CHURCH
Records, 1710-1925, v. 1-10 Ct
N: USIGS   6116
P: Ct

POQUENTANUCK, Conn. ST. JAMES CHURCH
(Episcopal)
Records, 1814-1899, v. 1-4 Ct
N: USIGS   6117
P: Ct

POQUONOCK, Conn. SECOND
CONGREGATIONAL CHURCH
Vital records, 1771-1782 Ct
N: USIGS   6118
P: Ct

PRESTON, Conn. FIRST CONGREGATIONAL
CHURCH
Vital records, 1757-1845 Ct
N: USIGS   6119
P: Ct

PRESTON, Conn. FIRST ECCLESIASTICAL
SOCIETY AND CONGREGATIONAL CHURCH
Records, 1698-1887, v. 1-3 Ct
N: USIGS   6120
P: Ct

PRESTON, Conn. LONG SOCIETY (formerly
EAST NORWICH SOCIETY)
Church records, 1757-1938 Ct
N: USIGS   6121
P: Ct

PROSPECT, Conn. CONGREGATIONAL CHURCH,
(formerly COLUMBIA SOCIETY)
Records, 1797-1937, v. 1-3 Ct
N: USIGS   6122
P: Ct

PROTESTANT EPISCOPAL CHURCH IN THE U.S.A.
CONVENTIONS. CONNECTICUT, 1774, 1776
Papers, 1774-1783, 6 items MBD
N: MBD 14 frames   6123

PUTNAM, Conn. BAPTIST CHURCH
Records, 1847-1941, v. 1-5 Ct
N: USIGS   6124
P: Ct

PUTNAM, Conn. CONGREGATIONAL CHURCH
Records, 1848-1933, v. 1-4 Ct
N: USIGS
P: Ct   6125

PUTNAM (formerly NORTH KILLINGLY), Conn.
EAST PUTNAM CONGREGATIONAL CHURCH
Records, 1715-1904   Ct
N: USIGS   6126
P: Ct

PUTNAM, Conn. FIRST CONGREGATIONAL
CHURCH (formerly PUTNAM HEIGHTS
SOCIETY)
Vital records, 1711-1829 (typescript) Ct   6127
N: USIGS
P: Ct

QUAKER FARMS, Conn. CHRIST CHURCH
(Episcopal)
Vital records, 1845-1948, v. 1-2 Ct
N: USIGS   6128
P: Ct

REDDING, Conn. CONGREGATIONAL CHURCH
AND ECCLESIASTICAL SOCIETY
Records, 1729-1882, v. 1-4 Ct
N: USIGS   6129
P: Ct

RIDGEFIELD, Conn. FIRST CONGREGATIONAL
CHURCH
Records, 1761-1915, v. 1-8 Ct
N: USIGS   6130
P: Ct

ROCKVILLE, Conn. FIRST CONGREGATIONAL
CHURCH
Records, 1837-1888, v. 1, 3 Ct
N: USIGS   6131
P: Ct

ROCKVILLE, Conn. METHODIST
EPISCOPAL CHURCH
Vital records, 1834-1937 Ct
N: USIGS   6132
P: Ct

ROCKVILLE, Conn. ROCKVILLE FIRST
BAPTIST CHURCH
Records, 1842-1939, v. 1-10 Ct
N: USIGS   6133
P: Ct

ROCKVILLE, Conn. ST. JOHN'S CHURCH
(Episcopal)
Vital records, 1827-1879, 1888-1938, v. 1-3
Ct
N: USIGS   6134
P: Ct

ROCKVILLE, Conn. SECOND CONGREGATIONAL
CHURCH
Records, 1848-1888, v. 1-3 Ct
N: USIGS   6135
P: Ct

ROCKVILLE, Conn. UNION CONGREGATIONAL
CHURCH
Records, 1888-1945, v. 1-3 Ct
N: USIGS   6136
P: Ct

ROCKY HILL, Conn. CONGREGATIONAL
CHURCH
Records (abstracts), 1722-1855 Ct
N: USIGS   6137
P: Ct

ROXBURY, Conn. CONGREGATIONAL CHURCH
AND ECCLESIASTICAL SOCIETY
Records, 1742-1930, v. 1-3, 7 Ct
N: USIGS   6138
P: Ct

SALISBURY, Conn. CONGREGATIONAL CHURCH
Records, 1744-1941, v. 1-3 Ct
N: USIGS   6139
P: Ct
DCO: Ct

SALISBURY, Conn. ST. JOHN'S CHURCH
(Episcopal)
Records, 1823-1883, v. 1-4 Ct
N: USIGS   6140
P: Ct

SCOTLAND, Conn. BRUNSWICK SEPARATE
CHURCH (Congregational)
Minutes, 1776-1846 Ct
N: USIGS   6141
P: Ct

SCOTLAND, Conn. CONGREGATIONAL CHURCH
Records, 1732-1915, v. 1-4 Ct
N: USIGS   6142
P: Ct

SEYMOUR, Conn. TRINITY CHURCH (Episcopal)
(formerly UNION CHURCH AT HUMPHREYS-
VILLE)
Records, 1797-1853, v. 1-4 Ct
N: USIGS   6143
P: Ct

SCOTLAND, Conn., CONGREGATIONAL CHURCH,
see TALLMAN, pastor, 6191, under this same
heading

SHARON, Conn. CHRIST CHURCH (Episcopal)
Minutes, 1809-1932 Ct
N: USIGS   6144
P: Ct

SHARON, Conn. FIRST CHURCH OF CHRIST
(Congregational)
Records, 1755-1879, v. 1-2 Ct
N: USIGS   6145
P: Ct

SHELTON, Conn. CONGREGATIONAL CHURCH
Vital records, 1892-1922, v. 1 Ct
N: USIGS   6146
P: Ct

SHELTON, Conn. HUNTINGTON CONGREGATION-
AL CHURCH AND ECCLESIASTICAL SOCIETY
Records, 1717-1946, v. 1-6 Ct
N: USIGS 2 reels   6147
P: Ct

SHELTON, Conn. ST. PAUL'S CHURCH
(Episcopal)
Records, 1755-1907, v. 1-4 Ct
N: USIGS   6148
P: Ct

SHELTON, Conn. WHITE HILLS BAPTIST
CHURCH
Minutes, 1838-1932, v. 1-2 Ct
N: USIGS   6149
P: Ct

SHERMAN, Conn. NORTH CONGREGATIONAL
CHURCH (formerly NEW FAIRFIELD NORTH
SOCIETY)
Records, 1744-1921, v. 1-5 Ct
N: USIGS   6150
P: Ct

SHERMAN, Conn. SHERMAN CONGREGATIONAL
CHURCH
Records, 1786-1949 Ct
N: USIGS   6151
P: Ct

SIMSBURY, Conn. METHODIST CHURCH
Vital records, 1857-1926, v. 1 Ct
N: USIGS   6152
P: Ct

SOMERS, Conn. CONGREGATIONAL CHURCH
Records, 1727-1890, v. 1-5 Ct
N: USIGS   6153
P: Ct

SOMERS, Conn. SOMERSVILLE
CONGREGATIONAL CHURCH
Minutes, 1871-1939, v. 1-3 Ct
N: USIGS   6154
P: Ct

SOUTH COVENTRY, Conn. FIRST
CONGREGATIONAL CHURCH
Records, 1768-1936, v. 1-7 Ct
N: USIGS   6155
P: Ct

SOUTH COVENTRY, Conn. FIRST
ECCLESIASTICAL SOCIETY
Minutes, 1740-1798 Ct
N: USIGS   6156
P: Ct

SOUTH GLASTONBURY, Conn.
CONGREGATIONAL CHURCH
Records, 1836-1950, v. 1, 2, 4 Ct
N: USIGS 2 reels   6157
P: Ct

SOUTH KILLINGLY, Conn. CONGREGATIONAL
CHURCH
Records, 1746-1835 Ct
N: USIGS   6158
P: Ct

SOUTH NORWALK, Conn. FIRST METHODIST
EPISCOPAL CHURCH
Vital records, 1850-1869, 1883-1890, v. 1-2 Ct
N: USIGS   6159
P: Ct

SOUTH NORWALK, Conn. SOUTH NORWALK
CONGREGATIONAL CHURCH
Sunday School minutes, 1838-1847 Ct
N: USIGS   6160
P: Ct

SOUTH NORWALK, Conn. TRINITY CHURCH
(Episcopal)
Vital records, 1867-1948, v. 1-6 Ct
N: USIGS   6161
P: Ct

SOUTH WINDSOR, Conn. FIRST CONGREGATIONAL
CHURCH
Records, 1694-1898, v. 1-2, 5 Ct
N: USIGS   6162
P: Ct

SOUTH WINDSOR, Conn. WAPPING
METHODIST EPISCOPAL CHURCH
Vital records, 1843-1936, v. 2-5 Ct
N: USIGS   6163
P: Ct

SOUTHBURY, Conn. CHURCH OF THE
EPIPHANY (Episcopal)
Vital records, 1863-1940 Ct
N: USIGS   6164
P: Ct

SOUTHBURY, Conn. CONGREGATIONAL CHURCH
Records, 1732-1922, v. 1-2, 4 Ct
N: USIGS   6165
P: Ct
DCO: Ct v. 3

SOUTHBURY, Conn. MISSION OF THE GOOD
SHEPARD (Episcopal)
Vital records, 1921-1929 Ct
N: USIGS   6166
P: Ct

SOUTHBURY, Conn. SOUTH BRITAIN
CONGREGATIONAL CHURCH
Records, 1766-1884, v. 1-2, 4-5 Ct
N: USIGS   6167
P: Ct

SOUTHBURY, Conn. SOUTHBURY AND SOUTH
BRITAIN METHODIST EPISCOPAL CHURCH
Vital records, 1832-1896 Ct
N: USIGS   6168
P: Ct

SOUTHBURY, Conn. SOUTHBURY METHODIST
EPISCOPAL CHURCH
Vital records, 1847-1938 Ct
N: USIGS 1 reel   6169
P: Ct

SOUTHINGTON, Conn. FIRST CONGREGATIONAL
CHURCH
Records, 1728-1930, v. 1-4, 6 Ct
N: USIGS   6170
P: Ct

SOUTHINGTON, Conn. ST. PAUL'S CHURCH
(Episcopal)
Records, 1876-1941, v. 1, 4-5 Ct
N: USIGS   6171
P: Ct

SPRAGUE, Conn. HANOVER CONGREGATIONAL
CHURCH
Records, 1761-1915, v. 1-4 Ct
N: USIGS   6172
P: Ct

STAFFORD, Conn. FIRST UNIVERSALIST
CHURCH
Records, 1814-1917, v. 1-3 Ct
N: USIGS   6173
P: Ct

STAFFORD SPRINGS, Conn. FIRST
CONGREGATIONAL CHURCH

Records, 1757-1892, v. 1-4 Ct
N: USIGS
P: Ct   6174

STAFFORD SPRINGS, Conn. GRACE CHURCH
(Episcopal)
Records, 1872-1922, v. 1-2 Ct
N: USIGS
P: Ct   6175

STAFFORD SPRINGS, Conn. STAFFORD
SPRINGS CONGREGATIONAL CHURCH
Records, 1850-1936, v. 1-4, 6-8 Ct
N: USIGS
P: Ct   6176

STAFFORD SPRINGS, Conn. STAFFORD
SPRINGS METHODIST EPISCOPAL CHURCH
Records, 1830-1949, v. 1, 6, 8-9 Ct
N: USIGS
P: Ct   6177

STAFFORDVILLE, Conn. CONGREGATIONAL
CHURCH AND ECCLESIASTICAL SOCIETY
Minutes, 1852-1914, v. 1-4 Ct
N: USIGS
P: Ct   6178

STAFFORDVILLE, Conn. METHODIST
EPISCOPAL CHURCH
Records, 1866-1946, v. 1-6 Ct
N: USIGS
P: Ct   6179

STAMFORD, Conn. FIRST CONGREGATIONAL
CHURCH
Records, 1747-1907, v. 1-5 Ct
N: USIGS
P: Ct   6180

STAMFORD, Conn. NORTH STAMFORD
CONGREGATIONAL CHURCH
Records, 1782-1928, v. 1-4 Ct
N: USIGS
P: Ct   6181

STONINGTON, Conn. FIRST CONGREGATIONAL
CHURCH AND ECCLESIASTICAL SOCIETY
Records, 1674-1925, v. 1-10 Ct
N: USIGS 3 reels
P: Ct   6182

STONINGTON, Conn. SECOND
CONGREGATIONAL CHURCH
Records, 1809-1929, v. 1-2 Ct
N: USIGS
P: Ct   6183

STRATFORD, Conn. CHRIST CHURCH
(Episcopal)
Records, 1722-1932, v. 1-4, 8, 12 Ct
N: USIGS
P: Ct   6184

STRATFORD, Conn. FIRST CONGREGATIONAL
CHURCH
Records, 1688-1927, v. 2-6 Ct
N: USIGS
P: Ct   6185

STRATFORD, Conn. FIRST ECCLESIASTICAL
SOCIETY
Minutes, 1847-1914, v. 1-3 Ct
N: USIGS
P: Ct   6186

STRATFORD, Conn. FIRST METHODIST
EPISCOPAL CHURCH
Records, 1813-1931, v. 1, 3-6 Ct
N: USIGS
P: Ct   6187

SUFFIELD, Conn. CALVARY CHURCH
(Episcopal)
Records, 1865-1933, v. 1-3 Ct
N: USIGS
P: Ct   6188

SUFFIELD, Conn. FIRST CONGREGATIONAL
CHURCH SOCIETY
Minutes, 1776-1812 Ct
N: USIGS
P: Ct   6189

SUFFIELD, Conn. SECOND ECCLESIASTICAL
CHURCH
Minutes, 1792-1858 Ct
N: USIGS
P: Ct   6190

TALLMAN, pastor, Congregational Church,
Scotland, Conn.
Note book (vital records), 1844-1869 Ct
N: USIGS
P: Ct   6191

TARIFFVILLE, Conn. TRINITY CHURCH
(Episcopal)
Vital records, 1849-1936, v. 1-2 Ct
N: USIGS
P: Ct   6192

THOMASTON, Conn. FIRST CONGREGATIONAL
CHURCH
Records, 1728-1921 Ct
N: USIGS
P: Ct   6193

THOMPSON, Conn. CONGREGATIONAL
CHURCH
Records, 1730-1756, 23 p. Ibid.
N: USIGS
DCO: NNNG 23 p.   6194

THOMPSONVILLE, Conn. ST. ANDREW'S
CHURCH
Vital records, 1844-1920, v. 1-5 Ct
N: USIGS
P: Ct   6195

TOLLAND, Conn. BAPTIST CHURCH
Records, 1807-1904, v. 1-3, 5 Ct
N: USIGS
P: Ct   6196

TOLLAND, Conn. CONGREGATIONAL CHURCH
Minutes, 1806-1928, v. 1-2, 6 Ct
N: USIGS
P: Ct   6197

TOLLAND, Conn. METHODIST EPISCOPAL
CHURCH
Vital records, 1832-1912, v. 1-5 Ct
N: USIGS
P: Ct   6198

TORRINGTON, Conn. FIRST CONGREGATIONAL
CHURCH AND ECCLESIASTICAL SOCIETY
Records, 1741-1775, 1787-1901, v. 1-5, 8 Ct
N: USIGS
P: Ct   6199

TORRINGTON, Conn. TORRINGTON
ECCLESIASTICAL SOCIETY
Minutes, 1757-1849 Ct
N: USIGS
P: Ct   6200

TRUMBULL, Conn. CHRIST CHURCH (Episcopal)
Vital records, 1787-1923 Ct
N: USIGS
P: Ct   6201

TRUMBULL, Conn. CONGREGATIONAL
CHURCH
Records, 1761-1891, v. 2-4 Ct
N: USIGS
P: Ct   6202

UNION, Conn. CONGREGATIONAL CHURCH
Records, 1759-1922, v. 1-3 Ct
N: USIGS
P: Ct   6203

UNIONVILLE, Conn. CHRIST CHURCH
(Episcopal)
Vital records, 1846-1883 Ct
N: USIGS
P: Ct   6204

VERNON (formerly NORTH BOLTON), Conn.
FIRST CONGREGATIONAL CHURCH
Vital records, 1762-1940, v. 1-2 Ct
N: USIGS
P: Ct   6205

VOLUNTOWN, Conn. FIRST CONGREGATIONAL
CHURCH
Vital records, 1723-1836 Ct
N: USIGS
P: Ct   6206

VOLUNTOWN, Conn. FIRST PRESBYTERIAN
CHURCH
Records, 1723-1764 Ct
N: USIGS
P: Ct   6207

VOLUNTOWN, Conn. LINE CHURCH (formerly
FIRST CONGREGATIONAL CHURCH)
Records, 1779-1902 Ct
N: USIGS
P: Ct   6208

VOLUNTOWN, Conn. VOLUNTOWN AND STERL-
ING CONGREGATIONAL CHURCH (formerly
THE LINE CHURCH (Presbyterian))
Records, 1723-1914, v. 1-4 Ct
N: USIGS 2 reels
P: Ct   6209

WALLINGFORD, Conn. FIRST BAPTIST
CHURCH
Records, 1790-1939, v. 1-4 Ct
N: USIGS 3 reels
P: Ct   6210

WALLINGFORD, Conn. FIRST
CONGREGATIONAL CHURCH
Vital records, 1758-1894, v. 1-3 Ct
N: USIGS
P: Ct   6211

WALLINGFORD, Conn. METHODIST CHURCH
Records, 1895-1941, v. 1-3 Ct
N: USIGS
P: Ct   6212

WALLINGFORD, Conn. ST. PAUL'S PROTES-
TANT EPISCOPAL CHURCH (formerly "UNION
CHURCH")
Vital records, 1832-1900 Ct
N: USIGS
P: Ct   6213

WALLINGFORD, Conn. SECOND BAPTIST
CHURCH
Minutes, 1790-1822 Ct
N: USIGS
P: Ct   6214

WAPPING, Conn. SECOND CONGREGATIONAL
CHURCH
Records, 1830-1936, v. 1-3 Ct
N: USIGS
P: Ct   6215

WAPPING, Conn. WAPPING FEDERATED
CHURCH (now WAPPING COMMUNITY CHURCH)
Minutes, 1924-1936 Ct
N: USIGS
P: Ct   6216

WAREHOUSE POINT, Conn. METHODIST
EPISCOPAL CHURCH
Vital records, 1830-1912, v. 1-3 Ct
N: USIGS
P: Ct   6217

WAREHOUSE POINT, Conn. ST. JOHN'S
PARISH (Episcopal)
Records, 1803-1926, v. 1-8 Ct
N: USIGS
P: Ct   6218

WARREN, Conn. CHURCH OF CHRIST
(Congregational)
Records, 1757-1931, v. 2, 5 Ct
N: USIGS
P: Ct   6219

WASHINGTON, Conn. FIRST CONGREGATIONAL
CHURCH
Minutes, 1741-1919, v. 1-2 Ct
N: USIGS
P: Ct
DCO: Ct   6220

WASHINGTON, Conn. ST. ANDREW'S CHURCH
(Episcopal)
Records, 1784-1939, v. 1-5 Ct
N: USIGS
P: Ct   6221

WATERBURY, Conn. FIRST CONGREGATIONAL
CHURCH
Records, 1795-1895, v. 3-4, 7-10 Ct
N: USIGS
P: Ct   6222

WATERBURY, Conn. ST. JOHN'S PROTESTANT
EPISCOPAL CHURCH (formerly ST. JAMES
AND FIRST EPISCOPAL SOCIETY)
Records, 1761-1927, v. 1-7 Ct
N: USIGS 2 reels
P: Ct   6223

WATERFORD, Conn. CHRIST CHURCH
(Episcopal)
Vital records, 1850-1913 Ct
N: USIGS   6224
P: Ct

WATERFORD, Conn. FIRST BAPTIST CHURCH
Vital records, 1786-1878, v. 1-2 Ct
N: USIGS   6225
P: Ct

WATERFORD, Conn. SECOND BAPTIST CHURCH
Vital records, 1835-1916 Ct
N: USIGS   6226
P: Ct

WATERTOWN, Conn. CHRIST CHURCH (Episcopal)
Records, 1784-1911, v. 1-3, 8-11 Ct
N: USIGS 2 reels   6227
P: Ct

WATERTOWN, Conn. FIRST ECCLESIASTICAL
SOCIETY AND CONGREGATIONAL CHURCH
Records, 1785-1887, v. 1-3 Ct
N: USIGS   6228
P: Ct

WATERTOWN, Conn. METHODIST CHURCH
Vital records, 1853-1941, v. 1-5 Ct
N: USIGS   6229
P: Ct

WATERTOWN (and BETHLEHEM), Conn.
METHODIST EPISCOPAL SOCIETY
Minutes, 1820-1826 Ct
N: USIGS   6230
P: Ct

WEST ASHFORD, Conn. THE BAPTIST CHURCH
OF CHRIST
Records, 1765-1863, 4 v. Ct
N: USIGS   6231
P: Ct

WEST GOSHEN, Conn. METHODIST CHURCH
Minutes, 1832-1841, v. 1 Ct
N: USIGS   6232
P: Ct

WEST GRANBY, Conn. METHODIST CHURCH
Records, 1844-1939, v. 1-3 Ct
N: USIGS   6233
P: Ct

WEST HADDAM, Conn. PONSET METHODIST
CHURCH
Vital records, 1916-1930 Ct
N: USIGS   6234
P: Ct

WEST HARTFORD, Conn. CONGREGATIONAL
CHURCH
Records, 1713-1933, v. 1-9 Ct
N: USIGS 3 reels   6235
P: Ct

WEST HARTFORD, Conn. FIRST BAPTIST
CHURCH
Minutes, 1858-1940, v. 1-2 Ct
N: USIGS   6236
P: Ct

WEST HARTFORD, Conn. ST. JAMES' CHURCH
(Episcopal)
Vital records, 1875-1940, v. 1-2 Ct
N: USIGS   6237
P: Ct

WEST HARTLAND, Conn. CONGREGATIONAL
CHURCH (formerly HARTLAND SECOND
SOCIETY)
Records, 1762-1901, v. 1-2 Ct
N: USIGS   6238
P: Ct

WEST HARTLAND, Conn. SECOND CHURCH
(Congregational)
Records, 1781-1912 Ct
N: USIGS   6239
P: Ct

WEST HAVEN, Conn. CHRIST CHURCH
(Episcopal)
Vital records, 1851-1879 Ct
N: USIGS   6240
P: Ct

WEST HAVEN, Conn. FIRST CONGREGATIONAL
CHURCH

Records, 1724-1918, v. 1-2, 5-6, 12 Ct
N: USIGS   6241
P: Ct

WEST STAFFORD, Conn. SECOND
CONGREGATIONAL CHURCH
Vital records, 1780-1848, 1864-1895, v. 1, 7
Ct
N: USIGS   6242
P: Ct

WEST WOODSTOCK, Conn. CONGREGATIONAL
CHURCH
Records, 1743-1937, v. 1-5 Ct
N: USIGS   6243
P: Ct
DCO: Ct

WESTBROOK, Conn. FIRST CONGREGATIONAL
CHURCH
Vital records, 1724-1838 Ct
N: USIGS   6244
P: Ct

WESTFIELD, Conn. THIRD CONGREGATIONAL
CHURCH
Records, 1773-1916, v. 1-5 Ct
N: USIGS   6245
P: Ct

WESTON, Conn. EMMANUEL CHURCH
(Episcopal)
Minutes, 1845-1942 Ct
N: USIGS   6246
P: Ct

WESTON, Conn. NORTHFIELD CONGREGATION-
AL CHURCH AND SOCIETY
Records, 1757-1941, v. 1-7 Ct
N: USIGS   6247
P: Ct

WESTPORT, Conn. SAUGATUCK CONGREGA-
TIONAL CHURCH
Records, 1830-1926, v. 1-5 Ct
N: USIGS   6248
P: Ct

WETHERSFIELD, Conn. BAPTIST
CHURCH AND SOCIETY
Minutes, 1816-1919, v. 1-2 Ct
N: USIGS   6249
P: Ct

WETHERSFIELD, Conn. FIRST
CONGREGATIONAL CHURCH
Records, 1694-1908 Ct
DCO: Ct   6250
N: USIGS
P: Ct

WETHERSFIELD, Conn. FIRST SOCIETY
(Ecclesiastical)
Minutes, 1734-1846, v. 3 Ct
N: USIGS   6251
P: Ct

WILLIAMS, JOHN, Bp. (Protestant Episcopal)
Journal of his official acts, 1851-1899, v. 1-5
Ct
N: USIGS 1 reel   6252
P: Ct

WILLINGTON, Conn. CONGREGATIONAL CHURCH
Records, 1759-1911, v. 1-5 Ct
N: USIGS   6253
P: Ct

WILTON, Conn. ST. MATHEW'S EPISCOPAL
SOCIETY
Records, 1802-1892, v. 1-2 Ct
N: USIGS   6254
P: Ct

WINCHESTER, Conn. FIRST
CONGREGATIONAL CHURCH
Records, 1784-1927, v. 1-4 Ct
N: USIGS   6255
P: Ct

WINCHESTER, Conn. FIRST ECCLESIASTICAL
SOCIETY AND CONGREGATIONAL CHURCH
Records, 1768-1908, v. 1-5 Ct
N: USIGS 2 reels   6256

WINCHESTER, Conn. SECOND
CONGREGATIONAL CHURCH

Records, 1853-1952, v. 1-6 Ct
N: USIGS   6257
P: Ct

WINDHAM, Conn. FIRST CONGREGATIONAL
CHURCH
Records, 1700-1924, v. 1-2 Ct
N: USIGS   6258
P: Ct

WINDHAM, Conn. ST. PAUL'S
EPISCOPAL CHURCH
Records, 1832-1925, v. 1-3 Ct
N: USIGS   6259
P: Ct

WINDSOR, Conn. FIRST CONGREGATIONAL
CHURCH
Records, 1739-1932, v. 1-4, 14-16 Ct
N: USIGS   6260
P: Ct

WINDSOR, Conn. NORTH WINDSOR
CONGREGATIONAL CHURCH
Vital records, 1761-1794 Ct
N: USIGS   6261
P: Ct

WINDSOR, Conn. TRINITY METHODIST
EPISCOPAL CHURCH
Vital records, 1840-1912 Ct
N: USIGS   6262
P: Ct

WINSTED, Conn. FIRST CONGREGATIONAL
CHURCH
Vital records, 1778-1869 Ct
N: USIGS   6263
P: Ct

WINSTED, Conn. ST. JAMES
CHURCH (Episcopal)
Records, 1848-1953, v. 1-8 Ct
N: USIGS 3 reels   6264
P: Ct

WINSTED, Conn. TRINITY METHODIST
EPISCOPAL CHURCH
Minutes, 1835-1923, v. 1 Ct
N: USIGS   6265
P: Ct

WOLCOTT, Conn. ALL SAINTS'
CHURCH (Episcopal)
Records, 1811-1869, v. 1-3 Ct
N: USIGS   6266
P: Ct

WOLCOTT, Conn. CONGREGATIONAL CHURCH
AND ECCLESIASTICAL SOCIETY
Records, 1773-1922 Ct
N: USIGS   6267
P: Ct

WOODBURY, Conn. METHODIST CHURCH
Records, 1838-1941, v. 1-2 Ct
N: USIGS   6268
P: Ct

WOODBURY, Conn. ST. PAUL'S CHURCH (Epis-
copal)
Records, 1765-1923, v. 1-4 Ct
N: USIGS   6269
P: Ct

WOODSTOCK, Conn. EAST WOODSTOCK METH-
ODIST CHURCH
Vital records, 1827-1920, v. 1 Ct
N: USIGS   6270
P: Ct

WOODSTOCK, Conn. FIRST CONGREGATIONAL
CHURCH
Records, 1727-1926, v. 1-5 Ct
N: USIGS   6271
P: Ct

Personal Papers

BELLAMY, JOSEPH, 1719-1790
Correspondence, 1739-1759, 445 p.
(transcripts) PPPrHi
N: NjP 1 reel   6272
P: CtHC

BELLAMY, JOSEPH, 1719-1790
Papers, 1740-1790 priv.
N: NjP 1 reel   P: CtHC   6273

BLAKESLEE, ABRAHAM, 1761-1813, North
Haven, Conn.
Notebook of family records Ct
N: USIGS
P: Ct   6274

BOURNE, RANDOLPH SILLIMAN, 1886-1918
Letters to Alyse Gregory, 1913-1918, 42 items
CtY
N: CtY 1 reel   6275
P: NNC

BROWN, WILLIAM C.
Diary, 1777-1900 Ct
DCO: Ct part containing vital records
N: USIGS 1 reel   6276
P: Ct

BULKLEY, JONATHAN, of Mill River, Fairfield,
Conn.
Journal, 1802-1826, 198 p. CtSoP
DCO: NN   6277

CHAPMAN, HERMAN H., b. 1874
Papers, 1900-1940 CtY-F
N: MnHi 5 reels   6278

CLEGG, JAMES, 1679-1755
Diary, 1709-1755 priv.
N: CtY
P: CtY   6279

FISH, JOSEPH, 1706-1781
Correspondence; especially with Ezra Stiles,
ca. 100 letters CtY
N: MHi 13 feet*   6280

GIBBS, JOSIAH WILLARD, 1839-1903
Letters to Daniel Coit Gilman, 1879-1888,
9 items   MdBJ
N: CtY   6281

HAYDEN FAMILY, of Windsor, Conn.
Papers   William Gregg Foundation, Granite-
ville, S. C.
N: DLC 1 reel   6282

HEDGES, CORNELIUS, 1831-1907
Diary at Yale, Oct., 1851-Nov., 1852 priv.
N: CtY 1 reel   6283

HUNTINGTON, MARY ANN, of Norwich, Conn.
Sermon text book, 1826-1846 Ct
N: USIGS
P: Ct   6284

HURLBUTT, RALPH
Records as Justice of the Peace, New London,
Conn., 1807-1837 Ct
N: USIGS
P: Ct   6285

INGERSOLL, JARED, 1722-1781
An historical account of some affairs relating
to the church, 1740, 19 p. CtY
N: WaU   6286

JARVIS, ABRAHAM, Bp., 1739-1813
Family correspondence, 1799-1850, 42 items
Episcopal Diocese of Connecticut
N: CtY   6287

MORSE, JEDIDIAH, 1761-1826, of Woodstock, Conn.
Autobiography Ct
N: USIGS
P: Ct   6288

PERKINS, NATHAN, 1748-1838
Notebook
N: CtY 2 reels   6289

PETERS, Rev. SAMUEL
Correspondence with Rev. John Tyler re:
Bishop Seabury, 1783-1806, 7 items Seabury
Society for the Preservation of the Glebe House,
Woodbury, Conn.
DCO: Ct   6290

PIERSON, ABRAHAM, deacon, Killingworth, Conn.
Note book, 1787-1802 Ct
N: USIGS
P: Ct   6291

ROOT FAMILY, of Farmington, Conn.
Deeds and land papers, 1673-1893, 16 items
priv.
DCO: Ct   6292

SEABURY, SAMUEL, Bp., 1729-1796
Papers
N: CtY 3 reels   6293

SHAW, NATHANIEL, 1735-1782
Papers CtY
N: CtY 60 reels   6294

STILES, EZRA, 1727-1795
In-letters, 1749-1788, 75 items
N: CtY   6295

STODDARD, AMOS, 1762-1813
Autobiography (typescript) priv.
N: CtY   6296

THOMLINSON, Rev. J.
Diary, 1715-1722
N: CtY   6297

TRUMBULL, JOSEPH, 1737-1778
Correspondence, 1760-1867, 5 v., index Ct
DCO: Ct   6298

WADSWORTH, JEREMIAH, 1743-1804
Correspondence, 1779-1794, 67 items CtHWad
DCO: Ct   6299

WADSWORTH, JEREMIAH, 1743-1804
Letters, 1777-1818, 19 items priv.
N: DLC 2 reels   6300

WELLS, HORACE, 1815-1848
Documents re: discovery of anesthesia,
1852-1894, 31 items Ct priv.
DCO: Ct   6301

WINTHROP, JOHN, Jr., 1606-1676
Petition...for a charter for the Colony of
Connecticut..., 1661   UKLPRO
PP: Ct   6302

WOLCOTT, ROGER, Gov. Conn., 1679-1767
Letters, 1750-1754, 80 items MHi
DCO: DLC   6303

Business Papers

ALLEN, JOEL, 1755-1825
Account book, 1787-1792 priv.
N: CtY 1 reel   6304

EMMONS, MARSH, of Hartland, Conn.
Tailor's account book, 1830-1858 Ct
N: USIGS
P: Ct   6305

LASSELL, JOSHUA, of Windham, Conn.
Account book, 1744-1750 Ct
DCO: Ct   6306

OSBORN, LUCIUS S., 1832-1882, of Beacon
Falls and Humphreyville, Conn.
Account book, 156 p. priv.
N: USIGS
P: UPB   6307

RUSSELL, NOADIAH, 1659-1713
Account book, 1703-1713 priv.
N: CtY 1 reel   6308

Collections

BOARDMAN, WILLIAM F. J., collector
Manuscripts re: Boardman-Seymour families
and miscellaneous papers, 1601-1835 Ct
N: USIGS 7 reels   6309
P: Ct

CONNECTICUT. ARCHIVES
Land and school records brought together by
private collectors Ct
N: USIGS 4 reels   6310
P: Ct

CONNECTICUT. ARCHIVES
Militia records, 1678-1820   Ct
N: USIGS 18 reels   6311
P: Ct

CONNECTICUT. ARCHIVES
Militia records, 1775, 1777, 1779, 1786-1931;
Charles P. Heartman's collection of Connect-
icut military papers, 1788-1824 Ct
N: USIGS 4 reels   6312
P: Ct

CONNECTICUT. ARCHIVES
Records re: civil officers' records, 1669-1756
Ct
N: USIGS 3 reels   6313
P: Ct

CONNECTICUT. ARCHIVES
Records re: land lotteries and divorces,
1755-1789 Ct
N: USIGS 2 reels   6314
P: Ct

CONNECTICUT. ARCHIVES
Records re: Susquehanna settlers, 1771-1797;
Western lands, 1783-1819 Ct
N: USIGS 2 reels   6315
P: Ct

CONNECTICUT. ARCHIVES
Records re: transactions between Connecticut
and Indians, 1647-1789 Ct
N: USIGS 1 reel   6316
P: Ct

CONNECTICUT. STATE LIBRARY
Barbour collection of vital records, prior to
1850 Ct
N: USIGS 98 reels   6317
P: Ct

CONNECTICUT. STATE LIBRARY
Indian deeds, 1636-1664 Ct
DCO: Ct   6318
N: USIGS 1 reel

GAY, JULIUS, collector
Papers re: Farmington, Conn., 1777-1827,
39 items priv.
DCO: Ct   6319

HARRISON, JOHN H., compiler
Notebook re: vital statistics, 1831-1886 Ct
N: USIGS 1 reel   6320
P: Ct

NEW HAVEN COLONY HISTORICAL SOCIETY,
New Haven
Manuscripts Ct
N: USIGS 33 reels   6321

SEABURY SOCIETY, Woodbury, Conn.
Papers re: Bishop Seabury, Rev. Jeremiah
Leaming, John Rutgers Marshall, 1765-1787,
7 items Ibid.
DCO: Ct   6322

WINTHROP, ROBERT CHARLES, 1809-1894,
collector
Connecticut manuscripts, 1631-1794, 4 v. Ct
N: USIGS 1 reel   6323
P: Ct

WYLLYS, SAMUEL, collector
Papers re: witchcraft trials in Connecticut,
1662-1693, 70 p. Ct
DCO: Ct   6324
N: USIGS
P: Ct

Institutions

CONNECTICUT. STATE LIBRARY
Vital records after 1850 Ct
N: USIGS 1 reel   6325
P: Ct

CONNECTICUT LAND COMPANY
Articles of association, 1795-1797 Ct
N: Ct 1 reel   6326

CONNECTICUT LAND COMPANY
Records Ibid.
N: Ibid. 3 reels   6327
P: OClWHi

FRANKLIN, Conn. EAST FRANKLIN CEMETERY
Trustees records, 1864-1934 Ct
N: USIGS   6328
P: Ct

GRANBY, Conn. WEST GRANBY BURYING
GROUNDS
Records, 1810-1908 Ct
N: USIGS   6329
P: Ct

NORTH MEADOW ASSOCIATION, Hartford, Conn.
Proprietors' records, 1792-1931 Ct
N: USIGS 1 reel   6330

WARREN, Conn. WARREN SOCIETY
Minutes, 1750-1823 Ct
N: USIGS
P: Ct
6331

School Records

HOPKINS GRAMMAR SCHOOL, New Haven, Conn.
Records, 1683-1919 Ibid.
N: CtY 2 reels
6332

WOODSTOCK, Conn. NORTH SCHOOL DISTRICT
Records, 1798-1905 Ct
DCO: Ct
6333

Ships' Logs

HURON (Sealing vessel) of New Haven
Logbook, Jan.,1821- Apr.,1822
N: DLC 1 reel*
6334

NEW YORK

Census

U.S. CENSUS. THIRD, 1810
Population schedules, New York DNA
N: DNA 12 reels
6335

U.S. CENSUS. FIFTH, 1830
Population schedules, New York DNA
N: DNA 34 reels
P: NNNG USIGS
6336

U.S. CENSUS. SIXTH, 1840
Population schedules, New York DNA
N: DNA 28 reels
P: NNNG USIGS
6337

U.S. CENSUS. SEVENTH, 1850
Population schedules, New York DNA
N: DNA 70 reels
P: NNNG USIGS
6338

U.S. CENSUS. EIGHTH, 1860
Population schedules, New York DNA
N: DNA 38 reels
P: USIGS
6339

U.S. CENSUS. NINTH, 1870
Population schedules, New York DNA
N: DNA 57 reels
6340

U.S. CENSUS. TENTH, 1880
Population schedules, New York DNA
N: DNA 145 reels
6341

Government Records

U.S. BUREAU OF CUSTOMS
Passenger lists of vessels arriving at New
York, 1820-1897 DNA
N: DNA 675 reels [M-237]
6342

U.S. BUREAU OF THE PUBLIC DEBT
New York state loan office, register of loan
office certificates, 1777-1781; register of public debt certificates, 1784-1787, 396 p. DNA
N: NNC
6343

U. S. PRIZE COURT, New York
Papers, 1861-1865 Ibid.
N: NNC 47 reels
6344

State Records

NEW YORK (Colony). SUPREME COURT
OF JUDICATURE
Minute books, 1704-1773 Ibid.
N: DLC 5 reels
6345

NEW YORK (State)
Probate letters of administration, 1778-1797 N
N: USIGS 2 reels
6346

NEW YORK (State)
Wills and probate records, 1787-1822 N
N: USIGS 2 reels
6347

NEW YORK (State). ADJUTANT-GENERAL'S
OFFICE
Veterans'bonus cards, World War I N
N: N 97 reels
6348

NEW YORK (State). COMMISSIONERS OF
CONFISCATION ACT OF 1782
Depositions. Westchester Co. priv.
N: NIC 1 reel
6349

NEW YORK (State). COMMISSIONERS ON THE
NEW YORK-CONNECTICUT BOUNDARY
Boundary between N.Y. and Conn., 1908-1912,
2 v. Ct
Blueprint negative: Ct
6350

NEW YORK (State). COURT OF CHANCERY
Common orders, 1830-1847; minutes, 1783-
1847; record of orders, 1701-1708, 1720-
1770; wills tried, 1779-1847, v. 1-3 N
N: USIGS 24 reels
6351

NEW YORK (State). DEPT. OF LABOR
Beauty Service Minimum Wage Board.
Verbatim minutes, 1947 Ibid.
N: NIC-I 1 reel
6352

NEW YORK (State). DEPT. OF LABOR
Cleaning and Dyeing Minimum Wage Board.
Verbatim minutes, 1947 Ibid.
N: NIC-I 1 reel
6353

NEW YORK (State). DEPT. OF LABOR
Confectionery Minimum Wage Board.
Verbatim minutes, 1947 Ibid.
N: NIC-I 1 reel
6354

NEW YORK (State). DEPT. OF LABOR
Hotel Minimum Wage Board.
Verbatim minutes, 1947 Ibid.
N: NIC-I 1 reel
6355

NEW YORK (State). DEPT. OF LABOR
Restaurant Minimum Wage Board.
Verbatim minutes, 1947 Ibid.
N: NIC-I 1 reel
6356

NEW YORK (State). DEPT. OF STATE
Miscellaneous land records, 1799-1849
N: N 250 reels
6357

NEW YORK (State). DEPT. OF STATE. LAND
BUREAU
Land papers: loose papers called "Original
land grants" and "Land under water," 1799-
1949 Ibid.
N: N 250 reels
6358

NEW YORK (State). GOVERNOR (Franklin D.
Roosevelt, 1882-1945)
Official correspondence, 1929-1932 NHyR
N: NHyR 263 reels
P: N
6359

NEW YORK (State). GOVERNOR (Herbert
H. Lehman, 1878-)
Official correspondence, 1933-1942
Executive Department
N: N 106 reels
6360

NEW YORK (State). GOVERNOR (Thomas
E. Dewey, 1902-)
Official correspondence, 1943-1954
Executive Department
N: N 280 reels
P: N 208 reels incomplete
6361

NEW YORK (State). SUPREME COURT
Wills tried, 1818-1829 N
N: USIGS 1 reel
6362

County Records

CLINTON Co., N.Y.
Wills, Book A, 1807-1833 C.H. Plattsburg
N: USIGS 1 reel
6363

WESTCHESTER Co. and Town, N.Y.
Minutes of Mayor's court, 1696-1734; of Court
of Sessions, 1657-1678, 1691-1696; town
meetings, 1665-1691, 1746-1775 NHi
N: NHi
6364

YATES Co., N.Y. POOR HOUSE
Rules and by-laws, 1830-1868 Yates Co. Hist.
Soc.
N: Ibid. 1 reel
P: NNC
6365

Town and City Records

BEDFORD TOWNSHIP, N.Y.
Record book, 1683-1709 Ibid.
DCO: NN NNNG
6366

HISTORICAL RECORDS SURVEY. NEW YORK
(State)
Transcripts of early New York town records,
v. 1 Ibid.
N: WaU 1 reel
6367

NEW YORK (City), N.Y.
Index to old records of municipalities and corporations consolidated with New York, 26 p.
(typescript) NNQ
N: USIGS
6368

SALEM, N.Y.
Town clerk's records, 1779-1834, 250 p. priv.
DCO: NN
6369

WESTCHESTER, N.Y.
Borough records New York City, Comptroller's
Office
N: ? 2 reels
P: NNU
6370

Church Records

ATHENS, N.Y. TRINITY CHURCH (Episcopal)
Records, 1807-1825, 86 p. Ibid.
DCO: N
N: USIGS
6371

CHASE, Rev. HENRY, New York City, N.Y.
Baptism register, 1822-1858, 143 p. NNNG
N: USIGS
6372

CLAVERACK, N.Y. REFORMED CHURCH
Records, 1800-1881, 555 p. Ibid.
DCO: N
N: USIGS
6373

ELMHURST (formerly NEWTON), N.Y.
NEWTON PRESBYTERIAN CHURCH
Records, 1727-1882 NNNG
N: USIGS
6374

FRIENDS, SOCIETY OF. ALBANY [N.Y.]
MONTHLY MEETING
Register, 1841-1915; men's minutes, 1840-
1894; women's minutes, 1840-1869 NNSF
N: USIGS 1 reel
P: PHC PSC-F
6375

FRIENDS, SOCIETY OF. AMAWALK [N.Y.]
MONTHLY MEETING
Births and deaths, 1798-1905; certificates,
1828-1911; marriages, 1798-1884; men's
minutes, 1828-1886; women's minutes,
1812-1867 NNSF
N: USIGS 3 reels
P: PHC PSC-F
6376

FRIENDS, SOCIETY OF. BETHPAGE [N.Y.]
PREPARATIVE MEETING
Minutes, 1774-1802 NNSF
N: USIGS 1 reel
P: PHC PSC-F
6377

FRIENDS, SOCIETY OF. BRIDGEWATER [N.Y.]
MONTHLY MEETING
Births, deaths, and removals, 1817-1861;
men's minutes, 1817-1861; women's minutes,
1817-1860 NNSF
N: USIGS 2 reels
P: PHC PSC-F
6378

FRIENDS, SOCIETY OF. BUTTERNUTS [N.Y.]
MONTHLY MEETING
Births and deaths, 1788-1869; men's
minutes, 1810-1855; women's minutes,
1810-1857 NNSF
N: USIGS 2 reels
P: PHC PSC-F
6379

FRIENDS, SOCIETY OF. CHAPPAQUA [N.Y.]
MONTHLY MEETING
Births, deaths, and marriages, 1756-1908;
men's minutes, 1828-1864; removals,
1828-1898; women's minutes, 1785-1797,
1817-1871 NNSF
N: USIGS 3 reels   6380
P: PHC PSC-F

FRIENDS, SOCIETY OF. CHATHAM [N.Y.]
MONTHLY MEETING
Marriages and removals, 1819-1867; men's
minutes, 1819-1887; women's minutes,
1819-1863 NNSF
N: USIGS 1 reel   6381
P: PHC PSC-F

FRIENDS, SOCIETY OF. COEYMANS [N.Y.]
Records: deaths, 1828-1856; discipline of yearly meetings, 1810, 1839; marriage intentions of
women's meeting, 1799-1867; marriages, 1829-
1853; monthly meetings, 1799-1842; preparative meetings, 1789-1851; removals, 1830-
1867 N
N: USIGS   6382

FRIENDS, SOCIETY OF. COEYMANS [N.Y.]
MONTHLY MEETING
Births and deaths, 1761-1856; marriages, 1829-
1867; minutes, 1828-1867; women's minutes,
1799-1867; vital records, 1812-1867 NNSF
N: USIGS 3 reels   6383
P: PHC PSC-F

FRIENDS, SOCIETY OF. COLLINS [N.Y.]
MONTHLY MEETING
Births and deaths, 1829-1851; men's minutes,
1820-1850; removals, 1833-1865; women's
minutes, 1830-1853 NNSF
N: USIGS 3 reels   6384
P: PHC PSC-F

FRIENDS, SOCIETY OF. CORNWALL [N.Y.]
MONTHLY MEETING
Births and deaths, 1810-1823; marriages,
1828-1938; minutes, 1788-1871; women's
minutes, 1700-1858 NNSF
N: USIGS 4 reels   6385
P: PHC PSC-F

FRIENDS, SOCIETY OF. CREEK [N.Y.]
MONTHLY MEETING
Births and deaths, 1787-1886; minutes, 1803-
1877; women's minutes, 1803-1883 NNSF
N: USIGS 4 reels   6386
P: PSC-F

FRIENDS, SOCIETY OF. DE RUYTER [N.Y.]
MONTHLY MEETING
Births and deaths, 1809-1862; minutes, 1820-
1852; women's minutes, 1842-1880 NNSF
N: USIGS 1 reel   6387
P: PHC PSC-F

FRIENDS, SOCIETY OF. DUANESBURG [N.Y.]
MONTHLY MEETING
Births and deaths,1810-1912; marriages
and removals,1806-1912; men's minutes,
1806-1849; minutes, 1806-1827; women's
minutes, 1806-1867 NNSF
N: USIGS 2 reels   6388
P: PHC PSC-F

FRIENDS, SOCIETY OF. EASTON [N.Y.]
MONTHLY MEETING
Births and deaths, 1790-1950; marriages,
1789-1936; minutes, 1813-1946; register,
1846-1929; removals, 1790-1898; women's
minutes, 1793-1885 Ibid.
N: USIGS   6389
P: PHC PSC-F

FRIENDS, SOCIETY OF. ELBA [N.Y.] MONTHLY
MEETING
Men's minutes, 1837-1868 NNSF
N: USIGS 1/3 reel   6390
P: PHC PSC-F

FRIENDS, SOCIETY OF. FARMINGTON [N.Y.]
MONTHLY MEETING
Births and deaths, 1802-1867; men's minutes,
1803-1877; women's minutes, 1803-1867 NNSF
N: USIGS 5 reels   6391
P: PHC PSC-F

FRIENDS, SOCIETY OF. FARNHAM [N.Y]
MONTHLY MEETING
Births and deaths, 1841-1884; minutes,
1842-1878 NNSF
N: USIGS 1/2 reel   6392
P: PHC PSC-F

FRIENDS, SOCIETY OF. FLUSHING [N.Y.]
MONTHLY MEETING
Births and deaths, 1640-1880; certificates,
1670-1760; first register, n.d.; marriages,
1764-1821; minutes, 1671-1872; register,
1805-1906; removals, 1670-1760; 1788-1798,
1805-1877; women's minutes, 1771-1865
NNSF
N: USIGS 8 reels   6393
P: PHC PSC-F

FRIENDS, SOCIETY OF. GALWAY [N.Y.]
MONTHLY MEETING
Vital records, 1828; minutes, 1820-1866;
women's minutes, 1802-1865 Ibid.
N: USIGS
P: PHC PSC-F   6394

FRIENDS, SOCIETY OF. GRANVILLE [N.Y.]
MONTHLY MEETING
Vital records, 1795-1876 NNSF
N: USIGS 1 reel   6395

FRIENDS, SOCIETY OF. HAMBURG [N.Y.]
MONTHLY MEETING
Births and deaths, 1759-1866; minutes,
1814-1856; women's minutes, 1814-1851 NNSF
N: USIGS   6396
P: PHC PSC-F

FRIENDS, SOCIETY OF. HARTLAND [N.Y.]
MONTHLY MEETING
Births and deaths, 1821-1862; minutes,
1821-1855; women's minutes, 1821-1854
NNSF
N: USIGS 2 reels   6397
P: PHC PSC-F

FRIENDS, SOCIETY OF. HECTOR [N.Y.]
MONTHLY MEETING
Women's minutes, 1847-1862 NNSF
N: USIGS 1 reel   6398
P: PSC-F

FRIENDS, SOCIETY OF. HUDSON [N.Y.]
MONTHLY MEETING
Births and deaths, 1810-1905; marriages
and removals, 1794-1905; minutes, 1793-1872;
women's minutes, 1793-1849 NNSF
N: USIGS 4 reels   6399
P: PHC PSC-F

FRIENDS, SOCIETY OF. JERICHO [N.Y.]
MONTHLY MEETING
Births and deaths, 1790-1938; catalog of
records NNSF
N: USIGS 1 reel   6400
P: PHC PSC-F

FRIENDS, SOCIETY OF. LE RAY [N.Y.]
MONTHLY MEETING
Births and deaths, 1815-1838; minutes,
1815-1842; women's minutes, 1815-1847
NNSF
N: USIGS 2 reels   6401
P: PSC-F

FRIENDS, SOCIETY OF. LOWVILLE [N.Y.]
MONTHLY MEETING
Births and deaths, 1825-1859 NNSF
N: USIGS 1/3 reel   6402

FRIENDS, SOCIETY OF. MARLBOROUGH [N.Y.]
MONTHLY MEETING
Minutes, 1804-1868; register, 1800-1885;
removals, 1804-1863; vital records, 1804-1885;
women's minutes, 1804-1852 NNSF
N: USIGS 5 reels   6403
P: PHC PSC-F

FRIENDS, SOCIETY OF. MILTON AND
GALWAY [N.Y.] MONTHLY MEETING
Men's minutes, 1828-1855; removals,
1828-1861; women's minutes, 1828-1861
NNFS
N: USIGS   6404
P: PSC-F PHC

FRIENDS, SOCIETY OF. NEW YORK [N.Y.]
MONTHLY MEETING
Births and deaths, 1770-1904; burials, 1848-
1878; index to minutes, 1834-1867; list of
members, 1801-1805; marriages, 1828-1876;
memorials, 1707-1820; men's minutes, 1804-
1855; register, 1805-1849; removals, 1798-
1902; women's minutes, 1806-1868 NNSF
N: USIGS 15 reels   6405
P: PHC PSC-F

FRIENDS, SOCIETY OF. NEW YORK [N.Y.]
YEARLY MEETING
Record of membership, 1828; list of members,

1828 NNSF
N: USIGS 1 reel   6406
P: PHC PSC-F

FRIENDS, SOCIETY OF. NINE PARTNERS [N.Y.]
MONTHLY MEETING
Vital records 1781-1898; men's minutes,
1769-1851; women's minutes, 1794-1862
NNSF
N: USIGS   6407
P: PHC PSC-F

FRIENDS, SOCIETY OF. OBLONG [N.Y.]
MONTHLY MEETING
Vital records, 1745-1783, 1786-1893; men's
minutes, 1757-1896; removals, 1781-1911;
women's minutes, 1796-1873 NNFS
N: USIGS 6 reels   6408
P: PHC PSC-F

FRIENDS, SOCIETY OF. OSWEGO [N.Y.]
MONTHLY MEETING
Vital records, 1799-1933; men's minutes,
1799-1804, 1809-1815, 1828-1875; women's
minutes, 1799-1876 NNFS
N: USIGS 4 reels   6409
P: PHC PSC-F

FRIENDS, SOCIETY OF. PERU [N.Y.]
MONTHLY MEETING
Vital records, 1766-1866; men's minutes,
1799-1867; removals, 1799-1866; women's
minutes, 1799-1868 NNSF
N: USIGS 3 reels   6410
P: PHC PSC-F

FRIENDS, SOCIETY OF. PLAINS [N.Y.]
MONTHLY MEETING
Births and deaths, 1760-1876; men's minutes,
1838-1876; removals, 1828-1863; women's
minutes, 1814-1851 NNSF
N: USIGS 2 reels   6411
P: PHC PSC-F

FRIENDS, SOCIETY OF. PROSPECT
PARK [N.Y.]
Burial register, 1828-1865 NNSF
N: USIGS 1 reel   6412
P: PHC PSC-F

FRIENDS, SOCIETY OF. PURCHASE [N.Y.]
MONTHLY MEETING
Births and deaths, 1700-1931; men's minutes,
1725-1883; register, 1828-1907; testifications,
1781-1789; women's minutes, 1828-1877
NNSF
N: USIGS 4 reels   6413
P: PHC PSC-F

FRIENDS, SOCIETY OF. QUEENSBURY [N.Y.]
MONTHLY MEETING
Births and deaths, 1828-1877; marriages
and removals, 1800-1844; men's minutes,
1800-1878; women's minutes, 1800-1863 NNSF
N: USIGS 4 reels   6414
P: PHC PSC-F

FRIENDS, SOCIETY OF. RENSSELAERVILLE
[N.Y.] MONTHLY MEETING
Births and deaths, 1828-1867; minutes,
1814-1833; removals, 1814-1837; women's
minutes, 1814-1853 NNSF
N: USIGS   6415
P: PHC PSC-F

FRIENDS, SOCIETY OF. SARATOGA [N.Y.]
MONTHLY MEETING
Births and deaths, 1787-1877; marriages,
1778-1790; marriages and removals, 1794-
1862; men's minutes, 1778-1851; removals,
1778-1784; women's minutes, 1784-1884
NNSF
N: USIGS 3 reels   6416
P: PHC PSC-F

FRIENDS, SOCIETY OF. SCIPIO [N.Y.]
MONTHLY MEETING
Births and deaths, 1828-1868; marriages and
removals, 1809-1898; men's minutes, 1808-
1856; register, 1820-1879; removals, 1828-
1924; women's minutes, 1808-1862 NNSF
N: USIGS 3 reels   6417
P: PHC PSC-F

FRIENDS, SOCIETY OF. SMYRNA [N.Y.]
MONTHLY MEETING
Men's minutes, 1836-1883; women's minutes,
1836-1895 NNSF
N: USIGS   6418
P: PHC PSC-F

FRIENDS, SOCIETY OF. TROY [N.Y.]
MONTHLY MEETING
Certificates, 1813-1903; men's minutes,
1813-1906; vital records, 1813-1911;
women's minutes, 1813-1878 NNFS
N: USlGS 6419
P: PHC

FRIENDS, SOCIETY OF. VERONA [N.Y.]
MONTHLY MEETING
Women's minutes, 1842-1870 NNFS
N: USlGS 6420
P: PHC

FRIENDS, SOCIETY OF. WESTBURY [N.Y.]
MONTHLY MEETING
Certificates, 1799-1898; indexes, 1697-1898;
men's minutes, 1697-1850; vital records,
1730-1868; women's minutes, 1704-1858
Ibid.
N: USlGS 6421
P: N PHC

FRIENDS, SOCIETY OF. WESTBURY AND
JERICHO [N.Y.] MONTHLY MEETING
Men's and women's joint minutes, 1836-1909;
men's minutes, 1828-1836; vital records,
1828-1928; women's minutes, 1828-1874
Ibid.
N: USlGS 6422
P: PHC

FRIENDS, SOCIETY OF. WESTERN [N.Y.]
MONTHLY MEETING
Men's minutes, 1843-1871; vital records,
1843-1871; women's minutes, 1843-1867
Ibid.
N: USlGS 6423
P: PHC

HAMBURG, Germany. STAATSARCHIV
Official documents of the council on ecclesias-
tical affairs of the Lutheran parishes of the
Augsburg Confession in New York, 1724-1760;
postal material, 1788-1820 Ibid.
N: DLC 176 feet 6424
PP: DLC

IROQUOIS NATION. ONONDAGA TRIBE
Doctrines, 1735-1815 BeBM
DCO: NSyU 99 p. 6425

MONTGOMERY, N.Y. REFORMED DUTCH
CHURCH
Vital records, 1734-1807 (typescript) priv.
N: N 6426

NEW YORK. BETH HAMEDRASH HAGADOL
Registers, 1873-1945 [in Yiddish] NNYi
N: NNYi 600 feet 6427

NEW YORK. DUTCH REFORMED CHURCH
Records, 1649-1698, 1726-1811, 402 p. NNNG
N: USlGS 6428

NEW YORK. SHEARITH ISRAEL CONGREGATION
Records, 1730- Ibid.
N: Ibid. 300 feet 6429
P: NNYi

NEW YORK. TRINITY CHURCH
Minutes of board of managers for the building
of the church, Jan., 1695 - June, 1697 O.S.,
18 ll. Ibid.
DCO: NN 6430

NEW YORK GENEALOGICAL AND BIOGRAPHICAL
SOCIETY
Transcripts of Church records NNNG
N: USlGS 10 reels 6431
P: N

PRESBYTERIAN CHURCH IN THE U.S.A.
SYNODS. NEW YORK
Minutes, 1745-1758 PHi
N: PPPrHi 1 reel 6432

PRESBYTERIAN CHURCH IN THE U.S.A.
SYNODS. NEW YORK AND NEW JERSEY
Records, 1810-1882 Ibid.
N: Ibid. 2 reels 6433
P: PPPrHi

PRESBYTERIAN CHURCH IN THE U.S.A.
SYNODS. NEW YORK AND PHILADELPHIA
Minutes, 1758-1788 PHi
N: PPPrHi 1 reel 6434

SHARP, JOHN
Proposal for the advancement of religion in
New York, presented to the Society for the
Propagation of the Gospel, 1713, 39 ll. NN
DCO: NN 6435

SOCIETY FOR THE PROPAGATION OF THE
GOSPEL
Colonial letters: Westchester County, N.Y.
Ibid.
N: NNU 2 reels 6436

TUCKAHOE, N.Y. ST. JOHN'S CHURCH (Epis-
copal)
Register, 1853-1939 Ibid.
N: NN 1 reel * 6437

VOSBURGH, ROYDEN WOODWARD, collector
New York church records, v.d. (typescript)
NNNG
N: USlGS 61 reels 6438

WINGDALE (formerly DOVER), N.Y. FIRST
BAPTIST CHURCH OF CHRIST
First record book, 1757-1844 Ibid.
N: MWA 10 feet 6439

Personal Papers

ADAMS, JAMES TRUSLOW, 1878-1949
Correspondence with publisher, Little, Brown
& Co. Ibid.
N: NNC 1 reel 6440

ALBERTSON, RALPH, b. 1866
Papers priv.
N: NNC 1 reel 6441

ALDEN-DAY-PERKINS-WILLIAMS FAMILIES
Letters, 1784-1856 priv.
N: NIC 1 reel 6442

ALEXANDER, WILLIAM, 1726-1783, known as
the EARL of STIRLING
Papers, 1717-1783 NHi
N: NHi 2 reels 6443
P: CSmH 1753-1773

ALLEN, WILLIAM H., b. 1874
Papers priv.
N: NNC 1 reel 6444

ANDERSON, ALEXANDER, 1775-1870
Diaries, 1793-1799 priv.
N: NNC 1 reel 6445

ANSORGE, MARTIN C., b. 1882
Papers priv.
N: NNC 1 reel 6446

ARMSTRONG, JOHN, 1758-1842
Letters priv.
N: NHi 6447

BAILEY, LIBERTY HYDE, 1858-1954
Correspondence, 1894-1935 MH priv.
N: NIC 1 reel 6448

BALDWIN, JOSEPH CLARK, b. 1897
Papers priv.
N: NNC 1 reel 6449

BARTHOLOMEW, PAIGE, 1860-1944
Correspondence, 1884-1889, 44 items NIC
Electrocopies: MnHi 6450

BARWICK, ROBERT
Journal, 1775-1776 NNC
N: NNC 1 reel 6451

BEADLE, ERASTUS
Diary, journey from Buffalo, N.Y., to Nebraska, and return, Mar. 9-Oct. 1, 1857, 184 p.
priv.
DCO: NN 6452

BECKER, Lt. CHARLES F., 1870-1915
Testimony in the Rosenthal murder case priv.
N: NNC 1 reel 6453

BELKNAP, MRS. S. YANCEY, b. 1895
Papers priv.
N: NNC 1 reel 6454

BELLOWS, HENRY WHITNEY, 1814-1882
Papers, 1861-1882 MH
N: NNC 12 reels 6455

BELMONT, Mrs. E.R., b. 1879
Papers priv.
N: NNC 2 reels* 6456
P: NNC

BISHOP, PERCY POE, b. 1877
Casemates (recollections), 1952, 410 p.
(typescript) NNC
N: NNC 6457

BRADISH, LUTHER
Selected correspondence re: James F. Cooper
NHi
N: OU 6458

BREWER, WILLIAM HENRY
Papers, 1852-1909 CtY
N: NIC 1 reel 6459

BURLINGHAM, CHARLES C., b. 1885
Papers priv.
N: NNC 2 reels * 6460

BURNETT, WILLIAM, d. 1808
Letterbook, 1786-1803 NHi
N: NHi 1 reel 6461
P: MiD-B

CHAMPFLEURY, JULES, 1821-1889
Journals and Notes, 1853-1888 NNC
N: NNC 1 reel 6462

CLINTON, DeWITT, Gov. N.Y., 1769-1828
Papers, 1785-1828, 24 v. NNC
N: N 8 reels 6463

COLDEN, CADWALLADER, 1688-1776
Papers NHi
N: NNC 2 reels 6464

COLDEN, CADWALLADER, 1688-1776
Scientific papers NHi
N: NHi 2 reels 6465

COLLINS, JOSEPH, b. 1866
Papers, 1911-1933 priv.
N: NNC 1 reel 6466
P: NNC

CORNELL, EZRA, 1807-1874
Letters, 1843-1874 NIC
N: NIC 2 reels 6467

COUDERT, FREDERIC RENÉ, 1871-1955
Papers priv.
N: NNC 7 reels* 6468

DAVIS, MALCOLM W., b. 1889
Papers priv.
N: NNC 1 reel* 6469
P: NNC

DEAN, THOMAS, Indian agent of
Brotherton, N.Y.
Papers, 1814-1836 priv.
N: WHi 1 reel 6470

DEW, THOMAS RODERICK, 1802-1846
Papers, 1846 ViW
N: NNC 1 reel 6471

DEXTER, SIMON NEWTON, 1785-1862
Letters, 1800-1862 priv.
N: NIC 2 reels 6472

DOTY, MARIA (WING)
Journal, 1859-1862 priv.
N: NPV 6473

DUANE, JAMES, 1733-1797
Papers, 1680-1853, 10 boxes NHi
N: NHi 3 reels 6474

DUER, CAROLINE K., 1865-1956
Papers, 1915-1918 priv.
N: NNC 1 reel 6475
P: NNC

EARLE, GENEVIEVE, 1883-1956
Papers, 1935-1950 NNC
N: NNC 1 reel 6476
P: NNC

EDDY, JOHN HARTSHORNE, 1783-1817
Diary, journey New York to Oswego, with
Commissioners to examine internal navigation
between Hudson River and Lakes Ontario and
Erie, June 30-July 18, 1810, 130 p. ICN
DCO: NN 6477

EDGAR, WILLIAM
    Papers, 1750-1870, 11 v.   priv.
    DCO: NN   6478

FABIAN, BELA, b. 1889
    Papers priv.
    N: NNC 1 reel *   6479
    P: NNC

FISH, NICHOLAS, 1758-1833
    Papers, 1776-1793 v.p.
    DCO: DLC 8 items   6480

FLOYD FAMILY
    Papers, late 18th and early 19th cents.   priv.
    N: NHi 1 reel   6481

GARDINER, JOHN LYON, of Gardiner's Island,
    N. Y.
    Memorandum book, 1790-1809; farm register,
    1790-1809, 106 p.   priv.
    DCO: NN   6482

GARNSEY, DANIEL
    Diaries, 1789-1790 priv.
    N: N 1 reel   6483

GAY, SIDNEY HOWARD, 1814-1888
    In-letters, 1862-1865 NNC
    N: ?   6484
    P: NNC 7 reels

GAY, SIDNEY HOWARD, 1814-1888
    Papers, 1835-1862
    N: NNC 1 reel   6485

GRANDIN, EGBERT BRATT, of Palmyra, N.Y.
    Journal, 1831-1840 priv.
    N: MiD-B   6486

GRIEG, JOHN
    Papers, 1794-1860 priv.
    N: NIC 18 reels   6487
    P: NIC

HALLETT, SAMUEL
    Diaries, 1857-1858 priv.
    N: NIC 1 reel   6488
    P: NIC

HARTSHORNE, WILLIAM, Quaker
    Diary, journey, New York to Detroit, to treat
    with the Indians, May 4-Sept. 17, 1793, 108 p.
    N.Y. Friends Yearly Meeting
    DCO: NN   6489

HAWLEY, JOSEPH ROSWELL, 1826-1905
    Correspondence, 1861-1865, 1870-1890 priv.
    N: NNC 1 reel*   6490

HAWLEY, JOSEPH ROSWELL, 1826-1905
    Papers DLC
    N: NNC 2 reels*   6491

HETTRICK, JOHN T., b. 1868
    Papers priv.
    N: NNC 1 reel   6492
    P: NNC

HOLMES, SAMUEL LEEK
    Courtship correspondence with Huldah Bolton,
    Feb.-July, 1821, 38 items priv.
    N: NN   6493

HOLT, JOSEPH, 1807-1894
    Papers, Dec.,1860-May,1861 DLC
    N: NNC 1 reel   6494

HONE, PHILIP, 1780-1851
    Diary, 1826-1851, 28 v. NHi
    N: NHi 8 reels   6495

HOSACK, DAVID, 1769-1835
    Correspondence with Jared Sparks, 1824-1835
    MH
    N: NNC 1 reel   6496

HOSACK, DAVID, 1769-1835
    Letters, 1802-1834 DLC PHi PU
    N: NNC 3 reels   6497

HOSACK, DAVID, 1769-1835
    Letters to Thomas Parke, 1803-1819, 4 items
    MH
    N: NNC   6498

HOSACK, DAVID, 1769-1835
    Six letters to Thomas Jefferson and Timothy
    Pickering, 1806-1825 MH
    N: NNC   6499

JAMES, EDWIN P.
    Diary and note book, 1820-1824 NNBon
    N: NN 1 reel*   6500

LAMB, JOHN, 1735-1800
    Papers, 1762-1795 NHi
    N: NHi 3 reels   6501

LASKER, ALBERT D., 1880-1952
    Papers priv.
    N: NNC 1 reel*   6502
    P: NNC

LAZARUS, REUBEN A., b. 1895
    Papers priv.
    N: NNC 2 reels*   6503
    P: NNC

LEDYARD FAMILY
    Papers, 1793-1916 priv.
    N: NIC 4 reels   6504

LIVINGSTON, GILBERT, 1742-1806
    Family correspondence, 1724-1836 NN
    N: CU 2 reels   6505

LIVINGSTON, PHILIP, 1740-1810
    Papers, including those of Peter Van Brugh
    Livingston, 1541-1859 priv.
    DCO: NN 3 v.   6506

LIVINGSTON FAMILY
    Papers, 1580-1821, including partial copy of
    autobiography of Rev. John Livingston, 1603-
    1682, 5 v. priv.
    N: NHi   6507
    P: NHi

LIVINGSTON FAMILY
    Papers, 1630-1929 NHpR
    N: NHpR ? 12 reels   6508
    P: N

LIVINGSTONE FAMILY
    Papers, 1865-1942, 13 items priv.
    N: DLC 1 reel   6509
    P: DLC

LOCKLEY, FREDERIC E., 1824-1905
    Memoirs priv.
    N: NHi   6510
    P: NHi

McCLELLAN, GEORGE BRINTON, Jr., 1865-
    1945
    Papers, 1894-1917 DLC
    N: NNC 2 reels   6511

McDOUGALL, ALEXANDER, 1732-1786
    Papers, 1757-1795 NHi
    N: NHi 4 reels   6512

MacKAY, AENEAS
    Diary, 1810-1815 (typescript) priv.
    N: NHi   6513

McKESSON, JOHN, 1734-1796
    Selected papers re: Indians NHi
    N: NHi 1 reel   6514

MARKHAM AND PUFFER FAMILIES
    Papers, 1861-1882 priv.
    N: NIC 1 reel   6515

MARVIN, LANGDON P., b. 1876
    Papers priv.
    N: NNC 1 reel   6516
    P: NNC

MILLEDOLER, PHILIP, 1775-1852
    Papers, selections NHi
    N: NHi 1 reel   6517

MITCHELL, WESLEY CLAIR, 1874-1948
    Diary, 1905-1948 priv.
    N: NNC 4 reels*   6518
    P: NNC

MORGAN, EDWIN DENNISON, 1811-1883
    Letters to Charles Sumner, 1863-1869 priv.
    N: NNC 1 reel   6519

MORRIS, GEORGE SYLVESTER, 1840-1889
    Miscellaneous manuscripts, 1857-1887, 16 items
    MiU
    N: NNC 2 reels   6520

MURRAY, WILLIAM VANS, 1762-1803
    Papers, 1784-1805 DLC NjP
    N: CSmH 3 reels   6521

MURRAY, WILLIAM VANS, 1762-1803
    Papers, 1784-1805 PHi
    N: CSmH 3 reels   6522

    New York diary, 1775 DLC
    N: ViWI   6523

NORTON, JOHN
    Letter book, ca. 1805-1810
    N: N 1 reel   6524

OLMSTED, FREDERICK LAW, 1822-1903
    Papers, 1861-1863, 1891 priv.
    N: NNC 1 reel   6525

OSGOOD, JAMES RIPLEY, 1836-1892
    Letters to Benjamin Holt Ticknor, 1870-1892
    DLC
    N: NNC 1 reel   6526

PARISH, DAVID
    Letter books, 1802-1816, 6 v.   priv.
    N: NHi 2 reels   6527

PECK, ALPHONSO R., 1813-1883
    Correspondence, 1849-1851, 6 items NIC
    DCO: MnHi   6528

PENDLETON, NATHANIEL, 1756-1821
    Papers, 1782-1819 NHi
    N: NHi 1 reel   6529

PETERS, Rev. SAMUEL
    Correspondence, 8 v.   Protestant Episcopal
    Church Archives, NHi
    N: NHi 3 reels   6530

PHELPS, ANSON GREENE, 1781-1853
    Diary, 1806-1807, 1816-1853, 1287 p. priv.
    N: NN   6531
    P: CtY   DLC

PICKENS, ANDREW, 1739-1817
    Papers, 1785-1795 CSmH
    N: NNC 1 reel   6532

POTTER-WILKINSON FAMILIES
    Papers, 1768-1815 priv.
    N: NIC 1 reel   6533

PRENDERGAST, WILLIAM A., 1867-1954
    Papers priv.
    N: NNC 3 reels*   6534
    P: NNC

PRICE, JOSEPH M., 1870-1949
    Papers, 1909-1943 NNC
    N: NNC 1 reel   6535
    P: NNC

QUIGG, MURRAY T., 1891-1956
    Papers priv.
    N: NNC 1 reel   6536
    P: NNC

REYNOLDS, JACKSON E., b. 1873
    Papers priv.
    N: NNC 1 reel   6537
    P: NNC

ROBERTSON, ARCHIBALD, 1745-1813
    Diaries, 1765-1780, 6 v. NN
    N: NN 1 reel*   6538
    P: NN

RODGERS, CLEVELAND, b. 1885
    Papers priv.
    N: NNC 1 reel   6539
    P: NNC

RYAN, JOHN AUGUSTINE, 1869-1945
    Papers DCU
    N: NNC 1 reel   6540

SAXE, MARTIN, b. 1874
    Papers priv.
    N: NNC 1 reel   6541
    P: NNC

SMITH, WILLIAM, 1728-1793
    Diary, 1753-1783 NN
    N: NN 2 reels   6542
    P: ViWI

SPRING, Mrs. PRESTON B.
    Records of families, 1895 priv.
    N: NHi   6543

STEPHENS, JAMES, 1825-1901, Fenian
    Diary while in U.S. raising funds and
    volunteers, 1858-1860 UKBeRO
    DCO: NN 37 ll.   6544

THACHER, THOMAS D., b. 1881
    Papers priv.
    N: NNC 1 reel *   6545
    P: NNC

THOMPSON, CHARLES
Journals and letters, 1844-1851 priv.
N: NHi 6546

VALK, JACOB R., b. 1781
Diary, 1792-1854 priv.
N: NNC 6547

VAN KLEFFENS, Mme. EELCO N.
Diaries, 1942-1956 priv.
N: NNC 8 reels*
P: NNC 6548

VASSAR, MATTHEW, 1792-1868
Letters, 1830-1867, 18 items NN NRU priv.
DCO: NPV 6549

VEILLER, LAWRENCE, b. 1872
Papers, 1898-1941 priv.
N: NNC 1 reel
P: NNC 6550

WADSWORTH FAMILY, of New York
Papers, 1793-1873 priv.
N: NRU 17 reels* 6551

WARNER, CHARLES DUDLEY, 1829-1900
Correspondence with Daniel Willard Fiske
NIC
N: NIC 4 reels
P: NNC 6552

WASHBURN, STANLEY, b. 1878
Papers priv.
N: NNC 2 reels*
P: NNC 6553

WEBB, JAMES WATSON, 1802-1884
Correspondence, 1834-1877 NRU
N: CtY
P: CtY 6554

WHITE, RICHARD GRANT, 1821-1885
In-letters, 1847-1884 NNC
N: NNC 1 reel 6555

WHITE, RICHARD GRANT, 1821-1885
Papers, 1821-1885 (typescript) NNC
N: NNC 1 reel 6556

WILKINSON, JEMIMA, 1752-1819
Papers, 1771-1849 priv.
N: NIC 1 reel
P: NIC 6557

WRIGHT, REUBEN, of Canandaigua, N.Y.
Daybook, 1791-1793 priv.
N: PHarH 10 feet 6558

WRIGHT, SILAS, 1795-1847
Papers, 1836-1846 PHi
N: NNC 1/2 reel 6559

Business Papers

ASTOR, JOHN JACOB
Business papers, 1792-1892 MH-BA
N: WHi 13 reels
P: WyU 6560

BANCKER, GERARD
Survey books, of New York City and environs,
1780-1815, v. 1, 2, 4, 5 NHi
DCO: NN 6561

BEEKMAN, GERARD G., New York merchant
Letter book, 1752-1770 NHi
N: CU 6562

BROOKES, JOSHUA
Journal during business trip in the U.S.,
Apr., 1798-Dec., 1803 priv.
N: NN 1 reel 6563

CLOPPER, CORNELIUS
Account book, 1751-1787, 1 v. NHi
N: CU 1 reel 6564

CORNELL PAPERBOARD PRODUCTS COMPANY
Sales Manual, n.d. priv.
N: NIC 1 reel 6565

DEALL, SAMUEL
Account books, 1758-1775, 2 v. NHi
N: CU 1 reel 6566

FARMERS' LOAN AND TRUST COMPANY, Ithaca,
N.Y.
Correspondence, 1831-1854 priv.
N: NIC 5 reels 6567

FONDA, JELLES
Account book (Mohawk Co.), 1761-1774 priv.
N: NIC 1 reel
P: NIC 6568

GILFORD (SAMUEL) SHIPPING Co.
Account book (New York), 1763-1774 NHi
N: CU 1 reel 6569

HIBERNIA IRON WORKS
Accounts and inventory, 1767-1781, 6 items,
1 v. William Alexander Papers NHi
N: CU 6570

HOLLAND LAND COMPANY
Account books for Range 2, Township 10, and
Range 12, Township 3, 1802-1842, 1819-1835
Holland Land Office Museum, Batavia
N: NIC 2 reels 6571

LANSING, J.J.
Account book (Albany, N.Y.), 1742-1769, 1 v.
[portions in Dutch] NHi
N: CU 6572

LIVINGSTON, GILBERT, 1742-1806
Building account book (New York), 1770-1772
NHi
N: CU 1 reel 6573

LIVINGSTON, ROBERT R., 1746-1813
Account book (Clermont), 1761-1787 NHi
N: CU 1 reel 6574

MARIUS, JACOB
New Amsterdam account book, 1658-1659;
Amsterdam accounts, 1712-1713; New York
accounts, 1775-1783, 1 v. [portions in Dutch]
NN
N: CU 1 reel 6575

MILLER, ELIAS B., of Chenango Falls, N.Y.
Papers, 1776-1857, 1 v. priv.
DCO: NN 6576

NEW YORK. MERCHANTS
Memorial to Governor Colden, 1761; Custom
House receipts, 1763, 1 v. NN
N: CU 1 reel 6577

NEW YORK AND ERIE RAILROAD COMPANY
Letterbook, 1846-1847 priv.
N: NIC 1 reel 6578

NEW YORK THEATRE COMPANY, New York, N.Y.
Minute book, 1885-1894, 2 v. NN
N: MH 1 reel 6579

NICOLL, CHARLES
Shipments to the West Indies, 1762-1763,
1 v. NHi
N: CU 1 reel 6580

NICOLL AND ALLAIRE
Account book (New York), 1757-1759, 1 v.
NHi
N: CU 1 reel 6581

PHELPS-DODGE COMPANY
Business records re: orders and contracts
with Navy commissioners' office and Watervliet
and Alleghany arsenals, 1832-1842 DNA
N: NNC 2 reels 6582

PRYOR, J. EDWARD, builder
Account book (New York), 1762-1767, 2 v.
NHi
N: CU 1 reel 6583

PULTENEY ESTATE
Letterbook, 1801-1812, priv.
N: NIC 1 reel 6584

PULTNEY LAND COMPANY
Letterbook no. 7, 1819-1824
N: NRU 6585

SAGE, HENRY WILLIAMS, 1814-1897
Sage & Co. letter impression copy books,
1885-1897 priv.
N: NIC 28 reels 6586

SANDERS, BARENT
Day book (Albany), 1723-1731, 1 v. NHi
N: CU 1 reel 6587

SANDERS, JOHN
Account book (Schenectady), 1730-1751 NHi
N: CU 1 reel 6588

SANDERS, ROBERT
Day book (Albany), 1735-1741, 1 v. NHi
N: CU 1 reel 6589

SCHOONMAKER, EGBERT
Account book (Saugerties, N.Y.), 1765-1797
NHi
N: CU 1 reel 6590

SCHYLER
Account books (Kingston, N.Y.), 1711-1729,
1756-1798 [large portions in Dutch] NN
N: CU 1 reel 6591

SCHYLER, Mrs. ANN ELIZABETH
Ledger (New York), 1732-1769 NHi
N: CU 1 reel 6592

SNYDER, BENJAMIN
Account books (Churchland, N.Y.), 1768-1795,
3 v. NHi
N: CU 1 reel 6593

TOWNSEND, SAMUEL
Account book, 1746-1752 NHi
N: CU 1 reel 6594

VASSAR, MATHEW, 1792-1868
Autobiographical fragments, business
recollections NPV priv.
N: NPV 1 reel 6595

VASSAR (M.) AND COMPANY, brewers
Account book, Apr., 1810-Mar., 1811 priv.
N: NPV 6596

WENDELL, EVERT
Account book; day book (Albany, N.Y.),
1708-1753, 1 v. NHi
N: CU 1 reel 6597

WENDELL, EVERT
Ledger (Albany), 1720-1733 NHi
N: CU 1 reel 6598

WENDELL, JOHANNES EVERT
Account book (Schenectady, N.Y.), 1738-1741
NHi
N: CU 1 reel 6599

WESTERVELT, HARMAN C.
Notes on Merchants' Exchange, Custom House,
etc., 1805-1809, 1 v. NN
N: CU 1 reel 6600

WICK, JOHN
Accounts (Southampton, N.Y.), 1688-1718,
1 v. NN
N: CU 1 reel 6601

WILLIAMS (ROBERT) INDIAN PURCHASE
Book of records of the division of the Plain
Land, 1748, included with the purchase and
patent, ...made by Robert Williams in 1648,
1 v. NNaHi
DC: NN 6602

WITTER, THOMAS
Account book, 1747-1768; sloop "Deborah"
1748-1763, 1 v. NHi
N: CU 1 reel 6603

Collections

ADIRONDACK MUSEUM, Blue Mountain Lake, N.Y.
Adirondack material, v.d. v.p.
N: NBmA 2500 frames 6604

ANDREWS, WAYNE, ed.
Calendar of the Albert Gallatin collection, 1950
NHi
N: NHi 1 reel
P: CU 6605

NEW YORK. STATE LIBRARY
Freedom train documents, 84 items Ibid.
N: N 2 reels 6606

NEW YORK. STATE LIBRARY
Shaker collection N
N: N 9 reels
P: OClWHi 6607

TENNENBAUM, Dr. JOSEPH, collector
New York Anti-Nazi boycott movement, sundry
material, 1933-1945 priv.
N: NNYi 400 feet 6608

TENNENBAUM, Dr. JOSEPH, collector
U.S.A. Anti-Nazi boycott movement material,
1933-1941 NNYi
N: NNYi 1 reel 6609

WHITESIDE, PHINEAS and JOHN, collectors
Collection, 1769-1938 priv.
N: NIC 1 reel   6610

College Records

JEWETT, MILO P.
Papers re: Vassar College, 1828-1882,
29 items NPV
DCO: NPV   6611

Institutions

NATIONAL CIVIL SERVICE REFORM LEAGUE
Scrapbook, 1923-1947 priv.
N: NIC 1 reel   6612

NEW YORK. CHAMBER OF COMMERCE OF THE
STATE OF NEW YORK
Minutes, 1768-1858, 4 v. Ibid.
DCO: NN   6613

PHI BETA KAPPA. NEW YORK. BETA
CHAPTER (New York University)
Minutes, 1858-1944 Ibid.
N: NNU 1 reel   6614

TAMMANY SOCIETY
Constitution, with signatures of members,
1789-1916, 280 p. Ibid.
DCO: NN   6615

Ships' Logs

With ships' logs are included journals, diaries,
and other records of voyages. Logs, which are
the official records of vessels, are listed under
the vessels' names. Journals, which are personal
documents, even though they are sometimes
called supplementary logs, are listed under the
names of their authors.

CLAPP, BENJAMIN
Diary of voyages from New York, 1811-1821
priv.
N: CtY 1 reel   6616

EDEN (Ship)
Log, England to Maryland, 1771 NN
N: CU 1/2 reel   6617

MERCURY (Snow)
Log, New York to Falmouth, 1771 NN
N: CU 1/2 reel   6618

OTHELLO (Brig)
Trade on board, June, 1764- July, 1765 (signed
Thomas Rogers), 1 v. NHi
N: CU 1 reel   6619

SPIES, FRANCIS
Journal, voyage, New York to Manila, in ship
Herald, 1830-1831 priv.
N: NN 1 reel*   6620

PENNSYLVANIA

Census

U.S. CENSUS. SECOND, 1800
Population schedules, Pennsylvania DNA
N: DNA 10 reels   6621

U.S. CENSUS. FOURTH, 1820
Population schedules, Pennsylvania DNA
N: DNA 19 reels   6622

U.S. CENSUS. FIFTH, 1830
Population schedules, Pennsylvania DNA
N: DNA 24 reels   6623
P: PHi USlGS

U.S. CENSUS. SIXTH, 1840
Population schedules, Pennsylvania DNA
N: DNA 22 reels   6624
P: PHi USlGS

U.S. CENSUS. SEVENTH, 1850
Population schedules, Pennsylvania DNA
N: DNA 23 reels   6625
P: PHi USlGS

U.S. CENSUS. EIGHTH, 1860
Population schedules, Pennsylvania DNA
N: DNA 29 reels   6626
P: USlGS

U.S. CENSUS. NINTH, 1870
Population schedules, Pennsylvania DNA
N: DNA 46 reels   6627
P: USlGS

U.S. CENSUS. TENTH, 1880
Population schedules, Pennsylvania DNA
N: DNA 124 reels   6628

Government Records

GREAT BRITAIN. BOARD OF TRADE
Report on 19 acts passed by Pennsylvania
Assembly, 1758-1759, 40 p. UKLPRO
DCO: NHi
N: PHarH   6629

U.S. BUREAU OF CUSTOMS
Impost books of the Collector of Customs at
Philadelphia, 1789-1804 DNA
N: DNA 6 reels [T-255]   6630

U.S. INTERNAL REVENUE SERVICE
Federal direct tax records, Delaware and York
Counties, Pennsylvania, 1798 DNA
N: DNA 3 reels [T-146]   6631

State Records

PENNSYLVANIA (Colony)
Immigrant lists, 1728-1775 P
DCO: PHi   6632

PENNSYLVANIA
Naturalization records, 1798-1852 C.H. Read-
ing
N: USlGS 4 reels   6633

PENNSYLVANIA. ATTORNEY GENERAL
Opinions, 1889-1950 Ibid.
N: PPT-L 7 reels   6634

PENNSYLVANIA. COURT OF OYER AND
TERMINER
Dockets, 1778-1800 Ibid.
N: PPT-L 1 reel   6635

PENNSYLVANIA - MARYLAND BOUNDARY
DISPUTE
Minutes, Mar. 15 - Nov. 24, 1750 PHi
DCO: DeHi 19 p.   6636

County Records

ADAMS Co., Pa.
Draft books, A, B, C, D, 1765-1832
C.H. Gettysburg
N: PYHi 1 reel   6637

ADAMS Co., Pa.
Wills, 1800-1851; orphans' court records, 1800-
1835; deeds, 1800-1851; tax lists, 1799-1842;
vital records, 1852-1950; census records, 1830,
1850 C.H. Gettysburg
N: USlGS 54 reels   6638

BERKS Co., Pa.
Commission books, 1783-1854, v. 1-4
C.H. Reading
N: USlGS 2 reels   6639

BERKS Co., Pa.
Deeds, 1717-1867; tax lists, 1753-1856 PRHi
N: USlGS 8 reels   6640

BERKS Co., Pa.
Names of persons who took oath of Allegiance,
1777-1778, 250 p.   PPGen
N: USlGS   6641

BERKS Co., Pa.
Wills, 1752-1859; orphans' court proceedings,
1752-1857; deeds, 1752-1850; vital records,
1852-1855, 1871-1906 C.H. Reading
N: USlGS 90 reels   6642

BUCKS Co., Pa.
Minute book, Common Pleas and Quarter
Sessions, 1684-1730 C.H. Doylestown
N: ? 1 reel   6643
P: PHi

CHESTER Co., Pa.
Charge to Grand Jury, 1766, by Judge
John Morton, 2 p. NN
N: NhD   6644

CHESTER Co., Pa.
Court records, 1681-1712; wills, 1714-1854;
letters of attorney, 1774-1816; orphans' court
records, 1716-1850; deeds, 1688-1850; warrants
and surveys, 1701-1727 C.H. West Chester
N: USlGS 45 reels   6645

CHESTER Co., Pa.
Provincial court minutes, 1756-1778; tax
transcripts, 1715-1850; vital records, 1852-
1855; septennial census, 1842-1857 PWcHi
N: USlGS 96 reels   6646

CUMBERLAND Co., Pa.
Wills, 1750-1877; letters of administration,
1750-1880; orphans' court records, 1751-
1863; deeds, 1750-1850; tax lists, 1750-
1850; vital records, 1852-1855, 1886-1930
C.H. Carlisle
N: USlGS 88 reels   6647

DAUPHIN Co., Pa.
Miscellaneous church records and family
records, n.d. PHarHi
N: USlGS 1 reel   6648

DAUPHIN Co., Pa.
Wills, 1785-1875; orphans' court dockets, 1785-
1852; deeds, 1785-1850; tax lists, 1785-1850;
vital records, 1852-1950 C.H. Harrisburg
N: USlGS 185 reels   6649

DELAWARE Co., Pa.
Recognizance book, 1835-1886; wills, 1789-
1892; orphans' court docket, 1790-1865;
deeds, 1770-1826 C.H. Media
N: USlGS 29 reels   6650

DELAWARE Co., Pa.
Tax transcripts, townships formerly in
Chester Co., 1781-1789 PWcHi
N: USlGS 1 reel   6651

LANCASTER Co., Pa.
Court minute books, 1729-1844; wills, 1729-
1870; orphans' court records, 1742-1850;
deeds, 1729-1835; tax lists, 1750-1814
C.H. Lancaster
N: USlGS 98 reels   6652

LANCASTER Co., Pa.
Quarter sessions docket, 1721-1801
C.H. Lancaster
N: PPT-L 1 reel   6653

LEBANON Co., Pa.
Wills, 1813-1881; orphans' court records, 1813-
1855; deeds, 1813-1850; tax lists, 1842-1849;
vital records, 1852-1855, 1885-1950; military
records, 1800-1932; census, 1850, 1860 C.H.
Lebanon
N: USlGS 75 reels   6654

MERCER Co., Pa.
Records, 1803-1814 C.H. Mercer
N: PHarH 58 feet   6655

MONTGOMERY Co., Pa.
Wills, 1784-1800, 1807-1863; orphans' court
records, 1784-1818, 1825-1850; deeds, 1784-
1820; tax lists, 1785-1846 C.H. Norristown
N: USlGS 109 reels   6656

NORTHAMPTON Co., Pa.
Wills, deeds, correspondence, treasurer's
accounts, 1727-1851; tax lists and assessments, 1761-1793, 1808-1815; papers,
warrants, and surveys, 1734-1879 PHi
N: USlGS 19 reels   6657

PERRY Co., Pa.
Wills, 1820-1880; orphans' court records,
1820-1854; deeds, 1820-1851; tax lists, 1820-
1846; vital records, 1852-1950 C.H. New
Bloomfield
N: USlGS 42 reels   6658

PHILADELPHIA Co., Pa.
Quarter sessions docket, 1760-1784; mayor's
court docket, 1759-1764 C.H. Philadelphia
N: PPT-L 2 reels   6659

PHILADELPHIA Co., Pa.
Wills, 1683-1693, 1699-1802, 1806, 1809,
1811, 1813, 1815, 1818, 1824, 1826-1829,
1831, 1833, 1836, 1838, 1840-1901; orphans'
court records, 1719-1852; deeds, 1683-1821
C.H. Philadelphia
N: USIGS 284 reels   6660

PHILADELPHIA Co., Pa. COMMISSIONERS
Journals of proceedings, March 29, 1718-
Aug. 1765 [unk.]
N: PHi 1 reel   6661

YORK Co., Pa.
County commissioners' minutes, 1749-1780;
Revolutionary records; non-associators' fines
and class lists, 1777, 1781 C.H. York
N: PYHi 4 reels   6662

YORK Co., Pa.
Taxables, 1768-1800 C.H. York
N: PYHi 18 reels
P: USIGS   6663

YORK Co., Pa.
Wills, 1749-1858; orphans' court dockets, 1749-
1861; deeds, 1749-1768, 1771-1859; vital records,
1877-1907 C.H. York
N: USIGS 76 reels   6664

Town and City Records

BIRMINGHAM TOWNSHIP, Delaware Co., Pa.
Death register, 1804-1838 PWcHi
N: USIGS   6665

ELK TOWNSHIP, Clarion Co., Pa.
Poor board and tax records, 1880-1891 Ibid.
N: PHarH 9 feet   6666

FORT PITT (now PITTSBURGH), Pa.
Daybook, 1765-1767 PPiHi
N: PHarH 30 feet   6667

GOSHEN, Pa.
Town book, 1718-1870 PWcHi
DCO: PHi 309 p.   6668

HARRISON TOWNSHIP, Potter Co., Pa.
Records, 1823-1880 priv.
N: PHarH 8 1/2 feet   6669

NEW SALEM, Pa.
Borough council minutes, 1876-1893 PYHi
N: PYHi
P: USIGS   6670

PHILADELPHIA
Port accounts, 1781-1788 PHarH
N: ? 1 reel
P: PHi   6671

PITTSBURGH. POINT PARK COMMISSION
Report re: site of Fort Pitt, 1943 Ibid.
N: PHarH 1/2 reel   6672

STRABAN TOWNSHIP, Pa.
Supervisors' record book, 1749-1900 Ibid.
N: PYHi   6673

WRIGHTSVILLE, Pa. BOROUGH COUNCIL
Minutes, 1834-1896 PYHi
N: PYHi 1 reel
P: USIGS   6674

Church Records

ABBOTSTOWN, Pa. EMMANUEL REFORMED
CHURCH
Register, 1768-1880 Ibid.
N: PYHi
P: USIGS   6675

ABBOTSTOWN, Pa. ST. JOHN'S LUTHERAN
CHURCH
Records, 1837-1850 Ibid.
N: PYHi
P: USIGS   6676

ARENDTSVILLE, Pa. ZION CHURCH [ARENDT'S]
Union register, 1786-1874 Ibid.
N: PYHi
P: USIGS   6677

BARREN HILL, Pa. GERMAN PROTESTANT
EVANGELICAL CONGREGATION OF
ST. PETER
Constitution, 1765 priv.
N: USIGS   6678

BAUER, Pastor, Lutheran Congregation,
Lehighton, Chester Co., Pa.
Records, 1841-1893 C.H. West Chester
N: USIGS 1 reel   6679

BRODBECK, Pa. ST. JACOB'S UNION [STONE]
CHURCH
Register, 1756-1856 [in German] Ibid.
N: PYHi
P: USIGS   6680

BROWNSVILLE, Pa. REDSTONE BAPTIST
CHURCH
Records of Philadelphia and Bucks Co., Pa.,
and Burlington, N.J., Baptists PWcHi
N: USIGS 2 reels   6681

CAMPBELLSTOWN, Pa. EVANGELICAL
LUTHERAN CHURCH
Records, 1794-1889 PMtAL
N: USIGS   6682

CARLISLE, Pa. FIRST PRESBYTERIAN CHURCH
Records, 1785-1920 PHarH
N: PHarH 155 feet   6683

CARLISLE, Pa. PRESBYTERIAN CHURCH
Minutes, 1785 Ibid.
N: PHi 1 reel   6684

CATHCART, Rev. ROBERT
Abstracts of vital records from private
register as Presbyterian minister at York
and Hopewell, Pa., 1793-1837 PYHi
N: USIGS
P: PYHi   6685

CENTRE SQUARE, Pa. ST. JOHN'S LUTHERAN
CHURCH
Records, 1773-1835 PMtAL
N: USIGS 1 reel   6686

CHADDS FORD, Pa. BRANDYWINE BAPTIST
CHURCH
Record PChHi
N: USIGS   6687

CHANCEFORD, Pa. ST. LUKE'S LUTHERAN
CHURCH
Records, 1888-1941 Ibid.
N: PYHi
P: USIGS   6688

CHANCEFORD, Pa. ST. LUKE'S [STEHLI'S]
UNITED EVANGELICAL CONGREGATION
Records, 1777-1833 [in German] Ibid.
N: PYHi
P: USIGS   6689

CHANCEFORD TOWNSHIP, Pa. ST. LUKE'S
[STAHLEY'S] LUTHERAN CHURCH
Trustees' records, 1772-1833 [in German];
registers, 1868-1943 Ibid.
N: PYHi
P: USIGS (trustee's records only)   6690

CHAPMAN, Pa. BOTSCHAFTS LUTHERAN
CHURCH
Records, 1776-1876 PMtAL
N: USIGS   6691

COATESVILLE, Pa. HEPHZIBAH BAPTIST
CHURCH
Records, n.d. PCHi
N: USIGS 1 reel   6692

CODORUS, Pa. SHAFFER'S [ZION'S] LUTHERAN
AND REFORMED CHURCH
Protocol, 1861-1909 Ibid.
N: PYHi   6693

CODORUS, Pa. STEITZ [BETHLEHEM UNION]
CHURCH
Registers, 1794-1839 Ibid.
N: PYHi
P: USIGS   6694

COMPANIONVILLE, Pa. ST. JOHN'S CHURCH
(Episcopal)
Vital statistics, 1736-1839, 17 p. NNNG
N: USIGS 1 reel   6695

CONEWAGO, Pa. DUTCH REFORMED CHURCH
Records, 1769-1803 PYHi
N: PYHi   6696

CONEWAGO, Pa. DUTCH REFORMED CHURCH
Records, 1769-1800 priv.
N: USIGS 1 reel   6697

CONEWAGO, Pa. DUTCH REFORMED CHURCH
Vital records, 1773-1793 NNNG
N: USIGS   6698

CONEWAGO, Pa. QUICKEL'S UNION CHURCH
[ZION] (Lutheran and Reformed)
Register, 1765-1905 Ibid.
N: PYHi 2 reels   6699
P: USIGS (to 1833)

CONEWAGO CHAPEL (Catholic), Adams Co., Pa.
Register, 1790-1835 PyHi
N: PYHi
P: USIGS   6700

DALLASTOWN, Pa. ST. JOHN'S [BLYMIRE'S
UNION] CHURCH
Registers, 1766-1834 Ibid.
N: PYHi
P: USIGS   6701

DEININGER, Rev. C.J., York Co., Pa.
Private register, 1853-1885 PYHi
N: PYHi
P: USIGS   6702

DOVER, Pa. SALEM [STRAYER'S] LUTHERAN
CHURCH
Registers, 1761-1916 Ibid.
N: PYHi
P: USIGS (to 1873)   6703

DRYVILLE, Pa. CHRIST CHURCH
Records, 1738-1911, 1 v. [in German] PMtAL
N: USIGS 1 reel   6704

EARLINGTON, Pa. LITTLE ZION CHURCH
(Lutheran)
Records, 1753-1909 [in German] PMtAL
N: USIGS 1 reel   6705

EAST BERLIN, Pa. HOLY TRINITY CHURCH
(Lutheran)
Register, 1822-1884, 2 v. Ibid.
N: PYHi 1 reel   6706
P: USIGS

EAST COVENTRY, Pa. BROWNBACK CHURCH
Records, 1722-1786 PWcHi
N: USIGS 1 reel   6707

EAST NANTMEAL, Pa. BAPTIST CHURCH
Records, n.d. PWcHi
N: USIGS 1 reel   6708

EASTON, Pa. ST. JOHN'S LUTHERAN CHURCH
Records, n.d. [in German] PMtAL
N: USIGS 1 reel   6709

ELIZABETHTOWN, Pa. CHRIST CHURCH
(Lutheran)
Records, 1771-1886, 3 v. PMtAL
N: USIGS 1 reel   6710

FAUST, Rev. JACOB N., York Co., Pa.
Private register, 1898-1929 PYHi
N: PYHi
P: USIGS   6711

FOGELSVILLE, Lehigh Co., Pa. FOGELSVILLE
[WEISSENBURG] LUTHERAN CHURCH
Records, 1754-1862 [in German] PMtAL
N: USIGS 1 reel   6712

FRANKLIN, Pa. FLOHR'S LUTHERAN AND
REFORMED CONGREGATION
Records, 1855-1888 PGL
N: USIGS   6713

FRANKLIN, Pa. FLOHR'S LUTHERAN CHURCH
Register, 1887-1935 Ibid.
N: PYHi
P: USIGS (to 1895)   6714

FREDERICK, Pa. EVANGELICAL LUTHERAN
CHURCH
Records, 1741-1910 PGL
N: USIGS   6715

FREYSVILLE, Pa. EMANUEL REFORMED
CHURCH
Register, 1867-1936 Ibid.
N: PYHi
P: USlGS   6716

FREYSVILLE, Pa. FREYSVILLE EVANGELICAL
LUTHERAN CHURCH
Register, 1871-1889 Ibid.
N: PYHi
P: USlGS   6717

FREYSVILLE, Windsor Township, Pa.
EMANUEL REFORMED AND LUTHERAN
[FREY'S] CHURCH
Register, 1809-1832, 1861-1862 Ibid.
N: PYHi
P: USlGS   6718

FRIEDENSVILLE, Pa. FRIEDENS LUTHERAN
CHURCH
Records, 1763-1925 [in German, with English
translation], 6 v. PMtAL
N: USlGS 1 reel   6719

FRIEDENSVILLE, Pa. JERUSALEM CHURCH
(Lutheran)
Records, 1759-1792 [in German] PMtAL
N: USlGS 1 reel   6720

FRIEDENSVILLE, Pa. JERUSALEM REFORMED
CHURCH
Records, 1848-1874 [in German] PMtAL
N: USlGS 1 reel   6721

FRIENDS, SOCIETY OF. ABINGTON [Pa.]
MONTHLY MEETING
Births and deaths, 1682-1809; men's
minutes, 1682-1937 PSC-F
N: PSC-F
P: PSC-F USlGS   6722

FRIENDS, SOCIETY OF. ABINGTON [Pa.]
QUARTERLY MEETING
Men's minutes, 1825-1930
N: USlGS
P: PSC-F   6723

FRIENDS, SOCIETY OF. ABINGTON [Pa.]
QUARTERLY MEETING
Ministers' and elders' minutes, 1786-1863,
1896-1931; women's minutes, 1786-1852,
1856-1897
N: PSC-F
P: PSC-F   6724

FRIENDS, SOCIETY OF (Hicksite). ABINGTON
[Pa.] MONTHLY MEETING
Marriages, 1685-1721, 1745-1947; marriages
(out), 1870-1947; membership, 1809-1938;
removals, 1827-1837 Ibid.
N: USlGS
P: PSC-F   6725

FRIENDS, SOCIETY OF. BART [Pa.]
PREPARATIVE MEETING
Minutes, 1887-1905, 1912, 1913, 1916, 1925
PSC-F
N: PSC-F
P: PSC-F   6726

FRIENDS, SOCIETY OF. BIRMINGHAM [Pa.]
MONTHLY MEETING
Marriages, 1816-1839; men's minutes, 1815-
1936 PSC-F
N: PSC-F
P: PSC-F USlGS   6727

FRIENDS, SOCIETY OF. BRADFORD [Pa.]
MONTHLY MEETING
Births and deaths, 1828-1899; marriages,
1828-1872; men's minutes, 1756-1757, 1828-
1896; removals, 1828-1887; women's minutes,
1828-1886 PSC-F
N:PSC-F
P: PSC-F   6728

FRIENDS, SOCIETY OF. BRADFORD [Pa.]
MONTHLY MEETING
Extracts of: marriage and removal records,
ca. 1737 Media Institute of Science (Painter
Collection)
N: PSC-F   6729

FRIENDS, SOCIETY OF. BRADFORD [Pa.]
MONTHLY MEETING
Records, 1737-1764, 256 p. PHC
N: PPY   6730

FRIENDS, SOCIETY OF. BUCKINGHAM [Pa.]
MONTHLY MEETING
Births and deaths, 1750-1920; births, deaths,
and marriages, 1702-1807; marriages,
1802-1947; removals sent, 1778-1936
Newtown National Bank, Newtown, Pa.
N: USlGS
P: PSC-F   6731

FRIENDS, SOCIETY OF. BYBERRY [Pa.]
MONTHLY MEETING
Births, 1740-1879; deaths, 1736-1823;
disendowments, acknowledgments, 1813-1821;
Friends in the ministry, 1810-1821; marriages,
1811-1886; men's minutes, 1831-1863;
removals, 1810-1852; sufferings, 1809-1838;
miscellaneous certificates, 1833-1854 PSC-F
N: USlGS
P: PSC-F   6732

FRIENDS, SOCIETY OF. CALN [Pa.]
PREPARATIVE MEETING
Men's minutes, 1850-1887 PSC-F
N: PSC-F
P: PSC-F   6733

FRIENDS, SOCIETY OF. CALN [Pa.]
QUARTERLY MEETING
Joint sessions minutes, 1901-1936; men's
minutes, 1828-1900; ministers' and elders'
minutes, 1877-1937; minutes, 1901-1936;
women's minutes, 1828-1894 PSC-F
N: PSC-F
P: PSC-F   6734

FRIENDS, SOCIETY OF. CAMBRIDGE [Pa.]
PREPARATIVE MEETING
Minutes, 1831-1845; women's minutes,
1831-1842 PSC-F
N: PSC-F
P: PSC-F   6735

FRIENDS, SOCIETY OF. CATAWISSA [Pa.]
MONTHLY MEETING
Births and deaths, 1790-1901; marriages,
1797-1802; men's minutes, 1796-1808 PSC-F
N: PSC-F
P: PSC-F USlGS   6736

FRIENDS, SOCIETY OF. CATAWISSA [Pa.]
PREPARATIVE MEETING
Marriages, 1796-1802; men's minutes,
1801-1815; Shamokin preparative meeting
minutes, 1857-1859 PSC-F
N: PSC-F
P: PSC-F   6737

FRIENDS, SOCIETY OF. CENTRE [Pa.]
MONTHLY MEETING
Minutes, 1868-1906 MdFBH
N: PSC-F
P: PSC-F   6738

FRIENDS, SOCIETY OF. CENTRE [Pa.]
PREPARATIVE MEETING
Minutes, 1824-1828 PSC-F
N: PSC-F
P: PSC-F   6739

FRIENDS, SOCIETY OF. CENTRE Co.[Pa.]
MONTHLY MEETING
Marriages, 1804-1893; minutes, 1841-1936;
removals, 1825-1923 Ibid.   6740
N: ICU 1 reel
P: USlGS

FRIENDS, SOCIETY OF. CHESTER [Pa.]
MONTHLY MEETING
Deed and trustee arrangements, n. d.; list of
members, 1885-1934; membership; 1827-1947
Ibid.
N: PSC-F
P: PSC-F   6741

FRIENDS, SOCIETY OF. CHESTER [Pa.]
MONTHLY MEETING
Marriages, 1828-1910; membership books,
1827-1880, 1885-1947; men's minutes, 1827-
1926; removals, 1828-1915; women's minutes,
1695-1779, 1827-1854
N: PSC-F 2 reels   6742
P: PSC-F USlGS

FRIENDS, SOCIETY OF (Orthodox). CHESTER
[Pa.] MONTHLY MEETING
Accounts, 1692-1706; acknowledgments, 1700-
1733; births, 1677-1711; births and deaths,
1677-1925; list of members, 1827-1884; mar-

riages, 1692-1928; men's minutes, 1681-1941;
removals, 1688-1733, 1765-1936, synopsis,
trusts, deeds, etc., 1736-1826; women's
minutes, 1780-1919
N: PSC-F   6743
P: PSC-F USlGS

FRIENDS, SOCIETY OF. CHICHESTER [Pa.]
PREPARATIVE MEETING
Women's minutes, 1843-1858, 1873-1899
PSC-F
N: PSC-F 1/2 reel   6744
P: PSC-F USlGS

FRIENDS, SOCIETY OF. COLUMBIA [Pa.]
PREPARATIVE MEETING
Births and deaths, 1816-1837; burying ground
committee minutes, 1814-1817; minutes,
1812-1829 PSC-F
N: PSC-F   6745
P: PSC-F

FRIENDS, SOCIETY OF. CONCORD [Pa.]
MONTHLY MEETING
Births and deaths, 1680-1916; marriages,
1679-1934; men's minutes, 1684-1875;
women's minutes, 1715-1813 PSC-F
N: PSC-F 3 reels   6746
P: PSC-F USlGS

FRIENDS, SOCIETY OF. CONCORD [Pa.]
MONTHLY MEETING
Day-book, 1821-1824; graveyard records,
1831-1867; membership, 1824-1869; removals,
1814, 1827-1913 PSC-F
N: USlGS 2 reels   6747

FRIENDS, SOCIETY OF. CONCORD [Pa.]
MONTHLY MEETING
Membership, 1744-1949 PSC-F
N: PSC-F   6748
P: PSC-F

FRIENDS, SOCIETY OF. CONCORD [Pa.]
QUARTERLY MEETING
Men's minutes, 1813-1881; women's minutes,
1827-1871
N: PSC-F 3 reels   6749
P: PSC-F USlGS

FRIENDS, SOCIETY OF. DARBY [Pa.]
MONTHLY MEETING
Births and burials, 1682-1939; list of
members, 1828-1848; marriages, 1694-1848;
men's minutes, 1684-1763, 1827-1849;
removals, 1682-1939; women's minutes,
1684-1849 PSC-F
N: PSC-F   6750
P: PSC-F USlGS

FRIENDS, SOCIETY OF. DARBY [Pa.]
MONTHLY MEETING
Marriages, 1849-1943; membership, 1808;
removals, 1751-1924; sufferings, 1775-1819
N: USlGS   6751
P: PSC-F

FRIENDS, SOCIETY OF. DARBY [Pa.]
MONTHLY MEETING
Minutes, 1763-1950; women's minutes, 1827-
1891 Ibid.
N: PSC-F   6752
P: PSC-F

FRIENDS, SOCIETY OF (Primitive). DEER
CREEK [Pa.] MONTHLY MEETING
Marriages and removals, 1857-1859;
ministers' and elders' minutes, 1842-1852;
minutes, 1854-1865 Ibid.
N: PSC-F   6753
P: PSC-F

FRIENDS, SOCIETY OF. DOE RUN [Pa.]
PREPARATIVE MEETING
Minutes, 1822-1946; women's minutes,
1887-1893
N: PSC-F   6754
P: PSC-F USlGS

FRIENDS, SOCIETY OF. EXETER [Pa.]
MONTHLY MEETING
Births and deaths, 1715-1885; marriages,
1743-1873; men's minutes, 1737-1808, 1829-
1901; minutes, 1901-1921; removals, 1739-
1797, 1830-1881; women's minutes, 1737-1789,
1827-1894 PSC-F
N: PSC-F 4 reels   6755
P: PSC-F USlGS

FRIENDS, SOCIETY OF. EXETER [Pa.]
MONTHLY MEETING
Minutes, 1737-1765, 564 p.   PHC
N: PPY   6756

FRIENDS, SOCIETY OF. FALLOWFIELD [Pa.]
MONTHLY MEETING
Births, 1762-1911; deaths, 1794-1921;
marriages, 1811-1937; minutes, 1907-1938;
removals, 1865-1914 PSC-F
N: USIGS 2 reels   6757
P: PSC-F USIGS

FRIENDS, SOCIETY OF. FALLOWFIELD [Pa.]
MONTHLY MEETING
Men's minutes, 1811-1884; removals,
1811-1865 PSC-F
N: PSC-F 1 reel   6758
P: PSC-F   USIGS

FRIENDS, SOCIETY OF. FALLS [Pa.]
MONTHLY MEETING
Marriages, 1827-1936; memberships, 1804-
1943 Newtown National Bank, Newtown, Pa.
N: USIGS   6759
P: PSC-F

FRIENDS, SOCIETY OF. FALLS [Pa.]
MONTHLY MEETING
Removals received, 1683-1743; removals
sent, 1828-1881 PSC-F
N: USIGS   6760
P: PSC-F

FRIENDS, SOCIETY OF (Primitive). FALLS
[Pa.] MONTHLY MEETING
Births and deaths, 1860-1943; burials,
1847-1876; marriages, 1863-1933; ministers'
and elders' minutes, 1870-1878; minutes,
1866-1943; removals, 1775-1883
N: PSC-F   6761
P: PSC-F

FRIENDS, SOCIETY OF. FISHING CREEK [Pa.]
PREPARATIVE MEETING
Minutes, 1838-1894; women's minutes, 1863-
1893 PSC-F
N: PSC-F   6762
P: PSC-F

FRIENDS, SOCIETY OF. GOSHEN [Pa.]
MONTHLY MEETING
Certificates to meeting, 1878-1903; marriages,
births, and deaths, 1825-1938; memberships,
1799-1947; minutes, 1722-1798, 1827-1937
PWcHi
N: USIGS 5 reels   6763

FRIENDS, SOCIETY OF. GOSHEN [Pa.]
MONTHLY MEETING
Men's minutes, 1747-1762 PSC-F
N: USIGS   6764
P: PSC-F

FRIENDS, SOCIETY OF. GOSHEN [Pa.]
PREPARATIVE MEETING
Minutes, 1808-1814, 1827-1850
N: USIGS   6765
P: PSC-F

FRIENDS, SOCIETY OF. GREEN STREET [Pa.]
MONTHLY MEETING
Births, 1775-1936; deaths, 1775-1940;
marriages, 1817-1856; membership,
1815-1862; removals, 1816-1933 PSC-F
N: USIGS   6766
P: PSC-F

FRIENDS, SOCIETY OF. GWYNEDD [Pa.]
MONTHLY MEETING
Births, 1764-1921; deaths, 1805-1921;
marriages, 1793-1917; minutes, 1848-1897;
removals, 1779-1856 PSC-F
N: USIGS   6767
P: PSC-F

FRIENDS, SOCIETY OF. GWYNEDD [Pa.]
MONTHLY MEETING
Men's minutes, 1801-1848; women's minutes,
1827-1841
N: USIGS   6768
P: PSC-F

FRIENDS, SOCIETY OF. GWYNEDD [Pa.]
PREPARATIVE MEETING
Men's minutes, 1798-1920; women's minutes,
1810-1893 PSC-F
N: PSC-F 1 reel   6769
P: PSC-F USIGS

FRIENDS, SOCIETY OF. HOMEVILLE [Pa.]
PREPARATIVE MEETING
Minutes, 1877-1917 PSC-F
N: PSC-F   6770
P: PSC-F

FRIENDS, SOCIETY OF. HORSHAM [Pa.]
MONTHLY MEETING
Births and burials, 1782-1889; men's minutes,
1782-1806; removals, 1782-1821
N: PSC-F   6771
P: PSC-F USIGS

FRIENDS, SOCIETY OF. HORSHAM [Pa.]
MONTHLY MEETING
Marriages, 1827-1871; membership,
1845-1881
N: USIGS   6772
P: PSC-F

FRIENDS, SOCIETY OF. HORSHAM [Pa.]
MONTHLY MEETING
Marriages, 1871-1894 PSC-F
N: PSC-F   6773
P: PSC-F USIGS

FRIENDS, SOCIETY OF. HORSHAM [Pa.]
MONTHLY MEETING
Minutes, 1806-1905 PSC-F
N: PSC-F   6774
P: PSC-F USIGS

FRIENDS, SOCIETY OF. KENNETT [Pa.]
MONTHLY MEETING
Births and deaths, 1706-1898; marriages,
1718-1821; men's minutes, 1686-1839; removals,
1751-1875; sufferings, 1757-1791; women's
minutes, 1789-1821, 1827-1844
N: PSC-F 2 reels   6775
P: PSC-F USIGS

FRIENDS, SOCIETY OF. KENNETT [Pa.]
MONTHLY MEETING
Membership, 1825-1944   PSC-F
N: USIGS   6776
P: PSC-F

FRIENDS, SOCIETY OF. KENNETT [Pa.]
MONTHLY MEETING
Membership by preparative meetings, 1851
PSC-F
N: PSC-F   6777
P: PSC-F

FRIENDS, SOCIETY OF. LANSDOWNE [Pa.]
MONTHLY MEETING
History of establishment PSC-F
N: PSC-F   6778
P: PSC-F

FRIENDS, SOCIETY OF. LANSDOWNE [Pa.]
MONTHLY MEETING
Membership, 1901-1947 PSC-F
N: USIGS   6779
P: PSC-F

FRIENDS, SOCIETY OF. LANSDOWNE [Pa.]
MONTHLY MEETING
Men's minutes, 1898-1937; First Day School
records, 1898-1913
N: PSC-F   6780
P: PSC-F USIGS

FRIENDS, SOCIETY OF. LONDON GROVE [Pa.]
MONTHLY MEETING
Births and deaths, 1738-1895; marriages,
1792-1946; memberships, 1805-1947; men's
minutes, 1792-1867; removals, 1792-1871
PSC-F
N: USIGS   6781
P: PSC-F

FRIENDS, SOCIETY OF. MAKEFIELD [Pa.]
MONTHLY MEETING
Births, 1797-1928; births and deaths,
1793-1890; marriages, 1820-1946; member-
ship, 1819, 1841-1925; men's minutes,
1820-1847; removals, 1820-1946 Newtown
National Bank, Newtown, Pa.
N: USIGS   6782
P: PSC-F

FRIENDS, SOCIETY OF. MENALLEN [Pa.]
MONTHLY MEETING
Births and deaths, 1775-1857 Ibid.
N: USIGS   6783
P: PSC-F

FRIENDS, SOCIETY OF. MENALLEN [Pa.]
MONTHLY MEETING
Minutes, 1780-1811 Ibid.
N: PSC-F   6784
P: PSC-F

FRIENDS, SOCIETY OF. MERION [Pa.]
PREPARATIVE MEETING
Burials, 1702-1708; deaths, 1702-1808; men's
minutes, 1702-1705, 1832-1834, 1854-1859,
1862-1940; women's accounts, 1848-1869;
women's meetings, 1819-1836, 1848-1884;
women's minutes, 1809-1836, 1849-1884
PSC-F
N: PSC-F   6785
P: PSC-F

FRIENDS, SOCIETY OF. MIDDLETOWN
[Bucks Co., Pa.] MONTHLY MEETING
Births and deaths, 1715-1806
N: USIGS   6786
P: PSC-F

FRIENDS, SOCIETY OF. MIDDLETOWN
[Bucks Co., Pa.] MONTHLY MEETING
Men's minutes, 1683-1939; women's
minutes, 1683-1893
N: PSC-F 2 reels   6787
P: PSC-F USIGS

FRIENDS, SOCIETY OF (Hicksite).
MIDDLETOWN [Bucks Co., Pa.] MONTHLY
MEETING
Acknowledgments, 1683-1759; births,
1671-1946; condemnations, 1686-1947; deaths,
1671-1946; marriages, 1682-1915; removals,
1671-1743, 1835-1945 Ibid.
N: USIGS   6788
P: PSC-F

FRIENDS, SOCIETY OF. MILLVILLE [Pa.]
HALF YEARLY MEETING
Ministers' and elders' minutes, 1836-1898;
minutes, 1834-1912; women's minutes,
1834-1893 PSC-F
N: PSC-F   6789
P: PSC-F

FRIENDS, SOCIETY OF. MILLVILLE [Pa.]
MONTHLY MEETING
Births and deaths, 1788-1907; removals,
1897-1907; statistical reports, 1898-1935
PSC-F
N: USIGS   6790
P: PSC-F

FRIENDS, SOCIETY OF. MOUNT [Pa.]
PREPARATIVE MEETING
Minutes, 1808-1850; women's minutes,
1844-1847 PSC-F
N: PSC-F   6791
P: PSC-F

FRIENDS, SOCIETY OF. MUNCY [Pa.]
MONTHLY MEETING (name changed to
FISHING CREEK, 1855)
Men's minutes, 1832-1867 Ibid.
N: PSC-F   6792
P: PSC-F USIGS

FRIENDS, SOCIETY OF. NEW GARDEN [Pa.]
MONTHLY MEETING
Births and deaths, 1768-1897; men's minutes,
1914-1938; sufferings, 1777-1787; women's
minutes, 1778-1786 Ibid.
N: PSC-F   6793
P: PSC-F

FRIENDS, SOCIETY OF. NEW GARDEN [Pa.]
MONTHLY MEETING
Marriages and removals, 1832-1904
C.H. Easton, Md.
N: USIGS   6794
P: PSC-F

FRIENDS, SOCIETY OF. NEW GARDEN [Pa.]
MONTHLY MEETING
Members, 1807-1940
N: USIGS   6795
P: PSC-F

FRIENDS, SOCIETY OF. NEW GARDEN [Pa.]
MONTHLY MEETING
Minutes, 1718-1746, 352 p.   PHC
N: PPY   6796

FRIENDS, SOCIETY OF. NEW GARDEN [Pa.]
MONTHLY MEETING
Minutes, 1827-1872 PSC-F
N: PSC-F   P: PSC-F   6797

FRIENDS, SOCIETY OF. NOTTINGHAM [Pa.]
MONTHLY MEETING
Extracts from minutes, 1730-1825 Media
Institute of Science (Painter Collection)
N: PSC-F   6798

FRIENDS, SOCIETY OF (Primitive). NOTTING-
HAM [Pa.] QUARTERLY MEETING
Minutes, 1861-1868 Ibid.
N: PSC-F   6799
P: PSC-F

FRIENDS, SOCIETY OF (Primitive).
NOTTINGHAM AND LITTLE BRITAIN [Pa.]
MONTHLY MEETING
Minutes, 1864-1890 Ibid.
N: PSC-F   6800
P: PSC-F

FRIENDS, SOCIETY OF. PENNSBURY [Pa.]
PREPARATIVE MEETING
Minutes, 1818-1827 PSC-F
N: PSC-F   6801
P: PSC-F

FRIENDS, SOCIETY OF (Primitive).
PENNSYLVANIA GENERAL MEETING
Committee on publications' minutes, 1872-
1908; marriages, 1866-1898; ministers' and
elders' minutes, 1876-1907; minutes, 1860-
1925
N: PSC-F   6802
P: PSC-F

FRIENDS, SOCIETY OF. PHILADELPHIA [Pa.]
MONTHLY MEETING
Births, 1783-1826; births and deaths,
1827-1903; burials, 1806-1826; grave books,
1806-1827; marriages, 1828-1925; marriages
not under care of meeting, 1847-1908;
memberships, 1827-1940; removals,
1828-1865; removals received, 1822-1827
N: USIGS   6803
P: PSC-F

FRIENDS, SOCIETY OF. PHILADELPHIA [Pa.]
MONTHLY MEETING
Minutes, 1682-1714 PHC
N: PPY   6804

FRIENDS, SOCIETY OF. PHILADELPHIA [Pa.]
MONTHLY MEETING (Cherry Street)
Births and deaths, 1686-1807; men's
minutes, 1833-1907; removals, 1684-1758;
removals received, 1823-1827; removals
sent, 1828-1865; women's minutes, 1827-
1899 Ibid.
N: PSC-F   6805
P: PSC-F USIGS

FRIENDS, SOCIETY OF. PHILADELPHIA [Pa.]
MONTHLY MEETING (Cherry Street)
Minutes, 1920-1946 Ibid.
N: PSC-F   6806
P: PSC-F

FRIENDS, SOCIETY OF. PHILADELPHIA [Pa.]
MONTHLY MEETING (Spruce Street)
Births and deaths, 1686-1807, 1833-1902;
list of members, 1833-1902; membership,
1864-1888; men's minutes, 1833-1903;
ministers' and elders' minutes, 1845-1897;
overseers' minutes, 1852-1871; removals,
1684-1758, 1833-1902; women's minutes,
1833-1893
N: PSC-F   6807
P: PSC-F

FRIENDS, SOCIETY OF. PHILADELPHIA [Pa.]
PREPARATIVE MEETING (Spruce Street)
Minutes, 1867-1894; women's minutes,
1818-1823, 1843-1851, 1863-1893 PSC-F
N: PSC-F   6808
P: PSC-F

FRIENDS, SOCIETY OF. PHILADELPHIA [Pa.]
QUARTERLY MEETING
Home influence association minutes, 1896-
1900; First-day school organization
treasurer's accounts, 1902-1907; First-day
school union minutes, 1888-1917; men's
minutes, 1828-1891; ministers' and elders'
minutes, 1835-1908; minutes, 1891-1920;
Visiting committee minutes, 1909-1914;
women's minutes, 1828-1905 PSC-F
N: PSC-F   6809
P: PSC-F

FRIENDS, SOCIETY OF. PHILADELPHIA [Pa.]
YEARLY MEETING
Committee on Indian Affairs minutes, 1838-
1850, 1893-1901; Executive Committee on
Indian Affairs minutes, 1876-1883; Sub-Com-
mittee on Indian Affairs minutes, 1841-1847,
1893-1894 PSC-F
N: PSC-F   6810
P: PSC-F

FRIENDS, SOCIETY OF. PHILADELPHIA [Pa.]
YEARLY MEETING
Epistles, 1827-1828; General committee, 1827-
1841; men's minutes, 1827-1917; ministers' and
elders' minutes, 1827-1913; Representative committee, 1841-1858, 1875-1916; women's minutes,
1827-1923 PSC-F
N: PSC-F   6811
P: PSC-F

FRIENDS, SOCIETY OF. PHILADELPHIA [Pa.]
YEARLY MEETING
Men's minutes, 1681-1827 Ibid.
N: USIGS   6812
P: PHC PSC-F

FRIENDS, SOCIETY OF (Free Quakers). PHILA-
DELPHIA [Pa.] YEARLY MEETING
Certificates and visiting minutes, 1781-1786;
Epistles, 1781-1786; memorial and remon-
strance (against disarmament); minutes and
accounts, 1781-1786
N: PSC-F   6813

FRIENDS, SOCIETY OF (Orthodox).
PHILADELPHIA [Pa.] YEARLY MEETING
Men's minutes, 1681-1827; minutes, 1828-1845
N: USIGS   6814
P: PSC-F

FRIENDS, SOCIETY OF (Primitive). PHILADEL-
PHIA [Pa.] MONTHLY MEETING
Births and deaths, 1865-1903; ministers' and
elders' minutes, 1867-1903; minutes, 1866-
1903; removals, 1868-1900 Ibid.
N: PSC-F   6815
P: PSC-F

FRIENDS, SOCIETY OF. PIKELAND [Pa.]
PREPARATIVE MEETING
Minutes, 1838-1854 PSC-F
N: PSC-F   6816
P: PSC-F

FRIENDS, SOCIETY OF. PLYMOUTH [Pa.]
MONTHLY MEETING
Men's minutes, 1790-1816, 1827-1853 Ibid.
N: USIGS   6817
P: PSC-F

FRIENDS, SOCIETY OF. PLYMOUTH [Pa.]
PREPARATIVE MEETING
Men's minutes, 1790-1816, 1827-1897;
women's minutes, 1810-1865 PSC-F
N: PSC-F   6818
P: PSC-F

FRIENDS, SOCIETY OF. PLYMOUTH [Pa.]
PREPARATIVE MEETING
Minutes, 1897-1915
N: PSC-F*   6819
P: PSC-F

FRIENDS, SOCIETY OF. PLYMOUTH [Pa.]
PREPARATIVE MEETING
Women's minutes, 1866-1893 Ibid.
N: PSC-F   6820
P: PSC-F

FRIENDS, SOCIETY OF. PROVIDENCE
[Montgomery Co., Pa.] PREPARATIVE
MEETING
Minutes, 1812-1866 PSC-F
N: PSC-F 1/2 reel   6821
P: PSC-F USIGS

FRIENDS, SOCIETY OF. PROVIDENCE
[Montgomery Co., Pa.] UNITED MONTHLY
MEETING
Membership, 1934-1947 PSC-F
N: USIGS   6822
P: PSC-F

FRIENDS, SOCIETY OF. RADNOR [Pa.]
MONTHLY MEETING
Births and burials, 1684-1729, 1813-1918;
marriages and removals, 1684-1917;
memorials, 1683-1697; men's minutes,
1684-1686, 1693-1704, 1712-1804, 1812-1825,

1827-1936; ministers' and elders' minutes,
1872-1938; removals, 1700-1817; sufferings,
1776-1779; treasury accounts, 1810-1932;
women's minutes 1827-1887 PSC-F
N: PSC-F   6823
P: PSC-F

FRIENDS, SOCIETY OF. RADNOR [Pa.]
MONTHLY MEETING
Ministers' and elders' minutes, 1756-1803
PSC-F
N: PSC-F   6824
P: PSC-F

FRIENDS, SOCIETY OF. RADNOR [Pa.]
MONTHLY MEETING
Minutes, 1686-1740, 328 p. PHC
N: PPY   6825

FRIENDS, SOCIETY OF. RADNOR [Pa.]
PREPARATIVE MEETING
Women's minutes, 1871-1882 PSC-F
N: PSC-F   6826
P: PSC-F

FRIENDS, SOCIETY OF. RICHLAND [Pa.]
MONTHLY MEETING
Births and deaths, 1686-1880; membership,
1800-1948; removals, 1791-1940 Richland
Meeting House (Hicksite)
N: USIGS   6827
P: PSC-F

FRIENDS, SOCIETY OF. RICHLAND [Pa.]
MONTHLY MEETING
Burials, 1818-1897; marriages, 1742-1942
PSC-F
N: USIGS   6828
P: PSC-F

FRIENDS, SOCIETY OF. RICHLAND [Pa.]
MONTHLY MEETING
Men's minutes, 1742-1898; women's minutes,
1744-1826 PSC-F
N: PSC-F   6829
P: PSC-F USIGS

FRIENDS, SOCIETY OF. ROARING CREEK [Pa.]
MONTHLY MEETING
Men's minutes, 1814-1917 Ibid.
N: USIGS   6830
P: PSC-F

FRIENDS, SOCIETY OF. ROARING CREEK,
CATAWISSA, AND BERWICH [Pa.] MEETINGS
Births and deaths, 1790-1901 Ibid.
N: USIGS   6831
P: PSC-F

FRIENDS, SOCIETY OF. SADSBURY [near
Christiana, Pa.] MONTHLY MEETING
Births and burials, 1733-1894; marriages,
1738-1903; men's minutes, 1737-1882;
removals, 1764-1828
N: PSC-F   6832
P: PSC-F

FRIENDS, SOCIETY OF. SADSBURY [near
Christiana, Pa.] MONTHLY MEETING
Gravestone inscriptions, 1822-1901; removals
received, 1770-1792 PSC-F
N: USIGS   6833
P: PSC-F

FRIENDS, SOCIETY OF. SADSBURY [near
Christiana, Pa.] MONTHLY MEETING
Minutes, 1737-1756 PHC
N: PPY   6834

FRIENDS, SOCIETY OF. SADSBURY [near
Christiana, Pa.] PREPARATIVE MEETING
Joint minutes, 1891-1925; men's minutes,
1828-1850
N: PSC-F   6835
P: PSC-F

FRIENDS, SOCIETY OF. UPPER DUBLIN [Pa.]
PREPARATIVE MEETING
Joint minutes, 1885-1940; men's minutes,
1814-1885; women's minutes, 1814-1885
N: PSC-F   6836
P: PSC-F

FRIENDS, SOCIETY OF (Orthodox). UWCHLAN
[Lionville, Pa.] MONTHLY MEETING
Births and burials, 1721-1899; marriages,

1830-1899; minutes, 1857-1900; men's
minutes, 1796-1799, 1828-1857; ministers'
and elders' minutes, 1782-1789; removals,
1828-1881; women's minutes, 1828-1882
N: PSC-F   6837
P: PSC-F   USIGS

FRIENDS, SOCIETY OF. VALLEY [Chester Co.,
Pa.] PREPARATIVE MEETING
Men's minutes, 1808-1939; women's minutes,
1814-1828, 1842-1896
N: PSC-F   6838
P: PSC-F

FRIENDS, SOCIETY OF. VINCENTOWN [Pa.]
PREPARATIVE MEETING
Minutes, 1830-1855   PSC-F
N: PSC-F   6839
P: PSC-F

FRIENDS, SOCIETY OF. WARRINGTON [Pa.]
MONTHLY MEETING
Births and deaths, 1727-1899; digest of
records, 1747-1856; marriages, 1748-1854;
minutes, 1747-1785, 1805-1823   Ibid.
N: USIGS   6840
P: PSC-F

FRIENDS, SOCIETY OF. WILLISTOWN [Pa.]
PREPARATIVE MEETING
First day school minutes, 1882-1886,
1894-1899, 1908-1923; deeds and accounts,
1830-1832, 1874-1935; library record,
1844-1846, 1866-1870; women's minutes,
1870-1906   Ibid.
N: USIGS   6841
P: PSC-F

FRIENDS, SOCIETY OF. WILLISTOWN [Pa.]
PREPARATIVE MEETING
Minutes, 1867-1889, 1906-1934   Ibid.
N: PSC-F   6842
P: PSC-F

FRIENDS, SOCIETY OF. WRIGHTSTOWN [Pa.]
MONTHLY MEETING
Births and deaths, 1716-1901; burials,
1845-1887; marriages, 1730-1760, 1827-1916;
membership, 1827; removals sent, 1786-
1836   Newtown National Bank, Newtown, Pa.
N: USIGS   6843
P: PSC-F

FRIENDS, SOCIETY OF. YORK [Pa.]
MONTHLY MEETING
Marriage certificates, 1786-1823; removal
certificates, 1786-1848   Ibid.
N: PYHi   6844
P: USIGS

FRIENDS, SOCIETY OF. YORK [Pa.]
MONTHLY MEETING
Removals, 1787-1851
N: USIGS   6845
P: PSC-F

GERMANTOWN, Pa. ST. MICHAEL's
LUTHERAN CHURCH
Records, 1741-1841, 3 v. [in German]   PMtAL
N: USIGS   1 reel   6846

GERMANY TOWNSHIP, Pa. ST. JOHN'S
LUTHERAN CHURCH
Records, 1763-1924   Ibid.
N: PYHi   6847

GETTYSBURG, Pa. CHRIST [COLLEGE] CHURCH
(Lutheran)
Register, 1819-1861   Ibid.
N: PYHi   6848
P: USIGS

GETTYSBURG, Pa. EVANGELICAL LUTHERAN
CONGREGATION OF CHRIST'S CHURCH
Records, 1837-ca.1850   PGL
N: USIGS   6849

GLEN RUN, Pa. BAPTIST CHURCH
Records, 1832-1947   PChHi
N: USIGS   1 reel   6850

GREAT VALLEY, Pa. ST. PETER'S PARISH
Records, c. 1774   PWcHi
N: USIGS   1 reel   6851
P: PHi

GREENWICH, Pa. DUNKELS CHURCH
(Reformed)
Records, 1746-1832   PLF
N: USIGS   1 reel   6852

HANOVER, Pa. EMANUEL REFORMED CHURCH
Register, 1771-1856 [in German]   PYHi
N: PYHi   6853
P: USIGS

HANOVER, Pa. ST. MATTHEW'S LUTHERAN
CHURCH
Records, 1743-1831   PGL
N: USIGS   6854

HANOVER, Pa. ST. MATTHEW'S LUTHERAN
CHURCH
Registers, 1743-1831   PYHi
N: PYHi   6855
P: USIGS

HEIDELBERG, Pa. BETHEL REFORMED
CHURCH [SMITH'S STATION]
Register, 1873-1935   Ibid.
N: PYHi   6856
P: USIGS

HEIDELBERG [UNIONVILLE], Pa. UNION
LUTHERAN CHURCH
Records, 1768-1850 [in German, with
English translation]   PMtAL
N: USIGS   1 reel   6857

HILL CHURCH, Lebanon Co., Pa.
Records, 1730-1839   PHarH
N: PHarH   15 feet   6858

HISTORICAL SOCIETY OF THE EVANGELICAL
AND REFORMED CHURCH, Franklin and
Marshall College, Lancaster, Pa.
Church and cemetery records, re: Eastern
Pa., Md., N.J.   Ibid.
N: USIGS   4 reels   6859

HISTORICAL SOCIETY OF THE EVANGELICAL
AND REFORMED CHURCH, Franklin and
Marshall College, Lancaster, Pa.
Family, church, and cemetery records, Pa.
Ibid.
N: USIGS   5 reels   6860

HOPEWELL, Pa. ST. JOHN'S [SADLER'S]
LUTHERAN CHURCH
Register, 1791-1859   Ibid.
N: PYHi   6861
P: USIGS

HUNTINGDON, Pa. CHRIST CHURCH (Episcopal)
Vestry book, 1760-1880   Ibid.
N: PYHi   6862
P: USIGS

HUNTINGDON, Pa. LOWER BERMUDIAN
[CHRIST] LUTHERAN CHURCH
Records, 1829-1880   PYHi
N: PYHi   6863
P: USIGS

HUNTINGDON, Pa. LOWER BERMUDIAN UNION
CHURCH
Records, 1745-1909 (part in transcript)   PYHi
N: PYHi   6864
P: USIGS

HUNTINGDON, Pa. UPPER BERMUDIAN
LUTHERAN CHURCH
Register, 1791-1943   PYHi
N: PYHi   6865
P: USIGS

JACKSON TOWNSHIP, Pa. ROTH'S LUTHERAN
CHURCH
Minute books, 1888-1911   Ibid.
N: PYHi   6866
P: USIGS (to 1897)

JACKSON TOWNSHIP, Pa. ROTH'S REFORMED
[PIGEON HILLS, TRINITY] CHURCH
Records, 1818-1936   Ibid.
N: PYHi   6867
P: USIGS

JEFFERSON, Pa. JEFFERSON LUTHERAN
AND REFORMED CHURCH
Records, 1841-1858   Ibid.
N: PYHi   6868

JERSEY SHORE, Pa. BAPTIST CHURCH
Record, n.d.   PChHi
N: USIGS   1 reel   6869

JONESTOWN, Pa. LUTHERAN CHURCH
Church records, 1783-1881, 2 v.   PMtAL
N: USIGS   1 reel   6870

KREIDERSVILLE, Pa. ZION STONE LUTHERAN
CHURCH
Records, 1750-1873, 3 v.   PMtAL
N: USIGS   1 reel   6871

KREUTZ CREEK, Pa. LUTHERAN CHURCH
Registers, 1757-1870   Ibid.
N: PYHi   6872
P: USIGS

LANCASTER, Pa. FIRST REFORMED CHURCH
Records, n.d.   Ibid.
N: USIGS   3 reels   6873

LANCASTER, Pa. HOLY TRINITY LUTHERAN
CHURCH
Records, 1728-1850, 4 v.   PMtAL
N: USIGS   1 reel   6874

LANCASTER, Pa. REFORMED CHURCH OF ST.
PAUL'S
Records, 1847-1947   PLF
N: USIGS   2 reels   6875

LANCASTER, Pa. ST. PETER'S REFORMED
CHURCH
Register, 1906-1947   priv.
N: USIGS   6876

LANCASTER, Pa. ST. STEPHEN'S EVANGELI-
CAL LUTHERAN CHURCH
Records, 1874-1947   priv.
N: USIGS   6877

LEBANON, Pa. BINDNAGELS EVANGELICAL
LUTHERAN CONGREGATION
Deeds and miscellaneous records, during the
18th century   PLebHi
N: USIGS   6878

LEBANON, Pa. SALEM LUTHERAN CHURCH
Vital records, 1773-1876   Ibid.
N: USIGS   2 reels   6879

LITTLESTOWN, Pa. CHRIST REFORMED CHURCH
Registers, 1747-1926   Ibid.
N: PYHi   2 reels   6880
P: USIGS

LITTLESTOWN, Pa. ST. JOHN'S LUTHERAN
CHURCH
Records, 1763-1924   Ibid.
N: PYHi   6881

LOBACHVILLE, Pa. ST. PAUL'S LUTHERAN
CHURCH
Records, 1833-1901   PMtAL
N: USIGS   1 reel   6882

LOGANS VALLEY, Pa. ANTIS LUTHERAN
CHURCH (formerly SALEM LUTHERAN
CHURCH)
Vital records, 1805-1877   Ct
N: USIGS   1 reel   6883

LOWER PROVIDENCE, Pa. BAPTIST CHURCH
Records, n.d.   PChHi
N: USIGS   2 reels   6884

LOWER SUGARLOAF, Pa. EVANGELICAL
CHRISTIAN CHURCHES (Lutheran and
Reformed Faith)
Vital records, 1882-1894   Ibid.
N: USIGS   1 reel   6885

LOWER WINDSOR, Pa. CANADOCHLY
EVANGELICAL CHURCH
Registers, ca. 1814-1919 [part in German]
Ibid.
N: PYHi   6886
P: USIGS

LOWER WINDSOR, Pa. CANADOCHLY
[CONEJOHELA] EVANGELICAL LUTHERAN
CHURCH
Register, 1754-1873 [in German]   Ibid.
N: PYHi   6887
P: USIGS

LUTHERAN AND REFORMED UNION CONGRE-
GATION, Lower Bermudian, Adams Co., Pa.
Records, original and translation   PGL
N: USIGS   6888

MANCHESTER, Pa. MANCHESTER UNION
CHURCH and CEMETERY
Records, 1822-1933, 5 v.   Ibid.
N: PYHi   6889
P: USIGS

METHODIST EPISCOPAL CHURCH. CONFERENCES.
EAST BALTIMORE. SHREWSBURY CIRCUIT,
York Co., Pa.
Records, 1867-1934, 5 v. Ibid.
N: PYHi
P: USIGS   6890

METHODIST EPISCOPAL CHURCH. CONFER-
ENCES. PHILADELPHIA (Old Kent Circuit)
Vital records, 1853-1869: Bond, Chestertown,
Kennedyville, Locust Grove, Salem, Fairlee,
Sudlersville, and Union at Warton MdHi
N: USIGS 1 reel   6891

MORAVIAN CHURCH. PROVINCES. NORTHERN
PROVINCE. ARCHIVES COMMITTEE,
Bethlehem, Pa.
Diaries of various missions, western Pennsyl-
vania and Ohio, 1765-1821; letters, 1749-1822
Ibid.
N: PHarH 5 reels   6892

MOSELEM, Pa. ZION LUTHERAN CHURCH
Records, 1759-1858, 2 v. PMtAL
N: USIGS 1 reel   6893

MT. JOY, Pa. MARK'S GERMAN REFORMED
AND EVANGELICAL LUTHERAN CHURCH
Register, 1836-1926 PYHi
N: PYHi
P: USIGS   6894

NEW BRITAIN, Pa. BAPTIST CHURCH
Records, n.d. PChHi
N: USIGS 1 reel   6895

NEW HOLLAND, Pa. TRINITY LUTHERAN
CHURCH
Records, 1730-1949 Ibid.
N: USIGS 1 reel   6896

NEW OXFORD, Pa. GERMAN REFORMED
CHURCH
Register, 1822-1846 Ibid.
N: PYHi
P: USIGS   6897

NEW TRIPOLI, Pa. EBENEZER LUTHERAN
CHURCH
Church records, 1768-1862 PMtAL
N: USIGS 1 reel   6898

NORTH CODORUS TOWNSHIP, Pa. LISCHY'S
CHURCH (Lutheran)
Records, 1798-1863 Ibid.
N: PYHi   6899

NORTH CODORUS TOWNSHIP, Pa. ST. PAUL'S
[ZIEGER'S] LUTHERAN CHURCH
Register, 1771-1854 Ibid.
N: PYHi
P: USIGS   6900

NORTH and SOUTH HAMPTON, Pa.
DUTCH REFORMED CHURCH
Records, 1710-1820 priv.
N: USIGS 1 reel   6901

NORTH WALES, Pa. ST. PETER'S LUTHERAN
CHURCH
Records, 1789-1891, 2 v. [in German] PMtAL
N: USIGS 1 reel   6902

NORWEGIAN, Pa. PINESWAMP [RAPPS]
LUTHERAN CHURCH
Records, 1811-1828 [in German with English
translation] PMtAL
N: USIGS 1 reel   6903

PARADISE TOWNSHIP, Pa. HOLTZSCHWAMM
REFORMED [PARADISE] CHURCH
Registers, 1833-1934 Ibid.
N: PYHi
P: USIGS   6904

PETERSBURG, Pa. HUNTINGTON LUTHERAN
CHURCH
Records, 1839-1902 Ibid.
N: PYHi
P: USIGS   6905

PHILADELPHIA, Pa. FIRST BAPTIST CHURCH
Records, 1746-1946 PChHi
N: USIGS 3 reels   6906

PHILADELPHIA, Pa. FIRST REFORMED CHURCH
Vital records, 1748-1831 (transcript) Ibid.
N: USIGS 1 reel   6907

PHILADELPHIA, Pa. OLD ZION GERMAN
LUTHERAN CHURCH
Vital records, 1745-1867, v. 1-8 [in German]
PMtAL
N: USIGS 3 reels   6908

PHILADELPHIA, Pa. ST. MICHAEL'S ZION
LUTHERAN CHURCH
Records, 1753-1764, 1817 [in German] PMtAL
N: USIGS 1 reel   6909

PHILADELPHIA, Pa. TENTH BAPTIST CHURCH
Records, ca. 1838-1947 PChHi
N: USIGS 1 reel   6910

PHILADELPHIA, Pa. THIRD BAPTIST CHURCH
Records, n.d. PChHi
N: USIGS 1 reel   6911

PIKE, Pa. ST. JOSEPH'S LUTHERAN CHURCH
Records, 1741-1887, 2 v. [in German] PMtAL
N: USIGS 1 reel   6912

PIKELAND, Pa. ZION'S LUTHERAN CHURCH
Records, 1745-1881, 2 v. [in German] PMtAL
N: USIGS 1 reel   6913

POTTSTOWN, Pa. IMMANUEL LUTHERAN
CHURCH
Records, 1777-1872 [in German] PMtAL
N: USIGS 1 reel   6914

PRESBYTERIAN CHURCH IN THE U.S.A.
PRESBYTERIES. PHILADELPHIA
Minutes, 1733-1746 PHi
N: PPPrHi 1 reel   6915

READING, Pa. FIRST REFORMED CHURCH
Records, 1755-1949 Ibid.
N: USIGS 3 reels   6916

READING, Pa. TRINITY LUTHERAN CHURCH
Records, 1752-1862, 4 v. [in German] PMtAL
N: USIGS 2 reels   6917

READING, Pa. TRINITY LUTHERAN CHURCH
Records, 1838-1930 Ibid.
N: USIGS 3 reels   6918

RED HILL, Pa. ST. PAUL'S LUTHERAN
CHURCH
Records, 1739-1867, 3 v. [in German] PMtAL
N: USIGS   6919

REHRERSBERG, Pa. ALTALAHA LUTHERAN
CHURCH
Records, 1757-1852 [in German] PMtAL
N: USIGS 1 reel   6920

ROSSVILLE, Pa. ST. MICHAEL'S EVANGELICAL
LUTHERAN CHURCH
Registers, 1864-1890 Ibid.
N: PYHi
P: USIGS   6921

ST. MATTHEW'S LUTHERAN CHURCH
[KELLER'S CHURCH], Bucks Co., Pa.
Records [in German], 1751-1870 PMtAL
N: USIGS 1 reel   6922

SCHAEFFERSTOWN, Pa. ST. LUKE'S CHURCH
Records, n.d. PWcHi
N: USIGS 1 reel   6923

SHREWSBURY CIRCUIT EVANGELICAL ASSOCIA-
TION, Pa.
Records, 1885-1903 PyHi
N: PYHi
P: USIGS   6924

SHREWSBURY, Pa. CHRIST LUTHERAN CHURCH
Register, 1843-1941 Ibid.
N: PYHi 2 reels
P: USIGS   6925

SHREWSBURY, Pa. JERUSALEM [FISSEL'S]
LUTHERAN AND REFORMED CHURCH
Register, 1801-1863 [in German] Ibid.
N: PYHi
P: USIGS   6926

SHREWSBURY, Pa. ST. PAUL'S [SOLOMON'S]
REFORMED CHURCH
Register, 1850-1891 Ibid.
N: PYHi   6927

SPRINGFIELD, Pa. SALEM EVANGELICAL AND
GERMAN REFORMED CHURCH
Records, 1870-1911, 1922 Ibid.
N: PYHi
P: USIGS   6928

SPRINGFIELD TOWNSHIP, Pa. FRIEDENSAAL
[SCHUSTER'S, WHITE] LUTHERAN CHURCH
Register, 1755-1829 Ibid.
N: PYHi
P: USIGS   6929

SPRINGFIELD TOWNSHIP, Pa. ST. PETER'S
[THE YELLOW] REFORMED CHURCH
Register, 1784-1849; financial record, 1783-
1822 Ibid.
N: PYHi   6930
P: USIGS (registers only)

SPRING GARDEN, Pa. MT. ZION [SPRING GAR-
DEN] EVANGELICAL LUTHERAN CHURCH
Register, 1853-1900 Ibid.
N: PYHi
P: USIGS   6931

STABEN, Pa. CONEWAGO [GREAT] PRESBYTER-
IAN CHURCH
Register, 1832-1849 Ibid.
N: PYHi
P: USIGS   6932

STARVIEW, Pa. CHRIST [HOOVER'S, STAR-
VIEW] UNION REFORMED AND LUTHERAN
CHURCH
Registers, 1821-1892 [part in German] Ibid.
N: PYHi
P: USIGS   6933

STOEVER, Rev. JOHN CASPER
Records, 1730-1779 PHi
N: PYHi   6934

STOUCHSBURG, Pa. CHRIST LUTHERAN
CHURCH
Records, 1743-1851, v. 1-2 PMtAL
N: USIGS 1 reel   6935

STRASBURG, Pa. ST. MICHAEL'S LUTHERAN
CHURCH
Records, 1754-1865, 2 v. PMtAL
N: USIGS 1 reel   6936

TINICUM, Pa. CHRIST LUTHERAN CHURCH
Records, 1760-1862, 1866-1909, 3 v. PMtAL
N: USIGS 1 reel   6937

TRAPPE, Pa. AUGUSTUS LUTHERAN CHURCH
Records, 1729-1843, 2 v. [in German] PMtAL
N: USIGS 1 reel   6938

TROY, Pa. FIRST BAPTIST CHURCH
Records, n.d. PChHi
N: USIGS 1 reel   6939

UPPER MAHONEY, Pa. ST. JACOB'S
LUTHERAN AND REFORMED CHURCH
Records, 1803-1880 priv.
N: USIGS   6940

UPPER SALFORD, Pa. OLD GOSHENHOPPEN
LUTHERAN CHURCH
Records, 1732-1828 [in German] PMtAL
N: USIGS   6941

UPPER SAUCON, Pa. ST. PAUL'S LUTHERAN
AND REFORMED CHURCH [BLUE CHURCH]
Records, 1740-1892 [in German, part trans-
lated in English] PMtAL
N: USIGS 2 reels   6942

VINCENT, Pa. VINCENT BAPTIST CHURCH
Records, 1737-1947 (typescript) PWcHi
N: USIGS 1 reel   6943

WARRINGTON TOWNSHIP, Pa. ST. JOHN'S
[OLD BRICK] LUTHERAN CHURCH
Records, 1823-1899 Ibid.
N: PYHi   6944
P: USIGS (to 1863)

WASHINGTON, Pa. BARREN'S EVANGELICAL
REFORMED CHURCH (Salem)
Registers, 1865-1898 Ibid.
N: PYHi 1 reel
P: USIGS   6945

WASHINGTON, Pa. ST. PAUL'S [SOWER'S OR RED RUN] UNION CHURCH
Union register, 1845-1886   Ibid.
N: PYHi
P: USlGS   6946

WAYNE, Pa.   GREAT VALLEY BAPTIST CHURCH
Records, n.d.   PChHi
N: USlGS 2 reels   6947

WAYNESBORO, Pa.   CHURCH OF JESUS CHRIST OF LATTER-DAY SAINTS
Ward records: Fairview, 1940-1948   USlC
N: USlGS 1 reel   6948

WEISEL, Pa.   PEACE LUTHERAN CHURCH
Records, 1750-1880 [in German]   PMtAL
N: USlGS 1 reel   6949

WEST CHESTER, Pa.   METHODIST EPISCOPAL CHURCH
Records, 1866-1946   PWcHi
N: USlGS 2 reels   6950

WEST MANCHESTER, Pa.   NEIMAN'S [SHILOH] EVANGELICAL LUTHERAN AND REFORMED CHURCH
Register, 1844-1945, 5 v.   Ibid.
N: PYHi
P: USlGS   6951

WEST MANCHESTER, Pa.   ST. PAUL'S [WOLF'S] LUTHERAN CHURCH
Registers, 1773-1835, 1847-1900   Ibid.
N: PYHi
P: USlGS   6952

WEST MANCHESTER, Pa.   ST. PAUL'S [WOLF'S] REFORMED CHURCH
Registers, 1764-1936   Ibid.
N: PYHi
P: USlGS   6953

WEST MANHEIM, Pa.   ST. DAVID'S [SHERMAN'S] REFORMED CHURCH
Register, 1783-1869 [part in German]   Ibid.
N: PYHi
P: USlGS   6954

WEST PIKELAND, Pa.   ST. PETER'S LUTHERAN CHURCH
Records, 1771-1880, 2 v. [in German]   PMtAL
N: USlGS 1 reel   6955

WINDSOR, Pa.   ST. PAUL'S LUTHERAN CONGREGATION
Records, 1766-1891 [part in German, with English translation]   C. H. West Chester
N: USlGS 1 reel   6956

WRIGHTSVILLE, Pa.   METHODIST CHURCH
Register, 1876-1908   Ibid.
N: PYHi
P: USlGS   6957

YORK, Pa.   CHRIST LUTHERAN CHURCH
Records, ca. 1733-1894, 3 v. [part in German]   Ibid.
N: PYHi 2 reels   6958
P: USlGS

YORK, Pa.   DUKE STREET CHURCH (Methodist Episcopal)
Records, 1865-1945   Ibid.
N: PYHi   6959
P: USlGS

YORK, Pa.   FIRST AND TRINITY REFORMED CHURCH
Records, 1763-1852 [part in German]   Ibid.
N: PYHi   6960
P: USlGS

YORK, Pa.   FIRST BAPTIST CHURCH
Register, 1891-1907   Ibid.
N: PYHi   6961
P: USlGS

YORK, Pa.   FIRST MORAVIAN CHURCH
Records, 1751-1900 [mostly in German]   Ibid.
N: PYHi 4 reels   6962
P: USlGS

YORK, Pa.   FIRST PRESBYTERIAN CHURCH
Register, 1793-1917   Ibid.
N: PYHi   6963
P: USlGS

YORK, Pa.   FIRST REFORMED CHURCH
Register, 1745-1887, 4 v.   Ibid.
N: PYHi   6964

YORK, Pa.   FIRST UNITED BRETHREN CHURCH
Records, 1866-1942   Ibid.
N: PYHi   6965
P: USlGS

YORK, Pa.   ST. JOHN'S CHURCH (Episcopal)
Records, 1767, 1784-1878   Ibid.
N: PYHi   6966
P: USlGS

YORK, Pa.   ST. JOHN'S EVANGELICAL LUTHERAN CHURCH
Records, 1874-1930   Ibid.
N: PYHi   6967
P: USlGS

YORK, Pa.   ST. LUKE'S LUTHERAN CHURCH
Register, 1888-1941   Ibid.
N: PYHi   6968
P: USlGS

YORK, Pa.   ST. PAUL'S ENGLISH EVANGELICAL LUTHERAN CHURCH
Register, 1836-1856   Ibid.
N: PYHi   6969
P: USlGS

YORK, Pa.   ST. PAUL'S EVANGELICAL LUTHERAN CHURCH
Records, 1836-1941   Ibid.
N: PYHi   6970
P: USlGS

YORK, Pa.   UNION EVANGELICAL CHURCH
Registers, 1874-1933, 3 v.   Ibid.
N: PYHi   6971
P: USlGS

YORK, Pa.   ZION LUTHERAN CHURCH
Register, 1849-1940   Ibid.
N: PYHi   6972
P: USlGS

YORKANA, Pa.   UNITED EVANGELICAL CHURCH
Records, 1903-1943 [part in German]   Ibid.
N: PYHi   6973
P: USlGS

Personal Papers

ADDISON, ALEXANDER, 1759-1807
Correspondence, 1786-1787   PPiU
N: PPiU 1 reel   6974

ADLUM, JOHN, ca. 1759-ca. 1785
Memoirs re: York Co., Pa., and Revolution priv.
N: PHarH 17 feet   6975

BARRINGER, RUFUS
Diary, 1770-1774 (typescript)   Nc-Ar
N: PHarH 5 1/2 feet   6976

BARTRAM, JOHN, 1699-1777
Papers, 4 v.   PHi
N: ViWI 2 reels   6977

BINGHAM, WILLIAM, 1752-1804
Correspondence with David Cobb and William Merrick, 1793-1803
DCO: PHi 1 v.   6978

BLAND, RICHARD, 1710-1776
Papers, 1753-1776   PHi
N: WaU 1 reel   6979

BROOKE, GEORGE, ca. 1779-1827
Papers   PRHi
N: PHarH 1 reel   6980

BURD, Col. JAMES
Journal, 1757-1758   priv.
N: PHi 1 reel   6981

CARTER and HENRY FAMILIES
Miscellaneous papers, 1756-1877   priv.
N: PHarH 30 feet   6982

CHANDLER, ELIZABETH M.
Letters from Jane Howell, 1830-1842   MiU
N: PHarH 40 feet   6983

CHENEY, THOMAS, Squire
Docket, ca. 1780   PWcHi
N: USlGS   6984

CLARK, WILLIS GAYLORD, 1808-1841, and CLARK, LEWIS GAYLORD, 1829-1868
Letters, 156 p.   PHi
N: NN   6985

COLT, JUDAH, of Erie, Pa.
Diaries, 1761-1832 (typescript)   priv.
N: PHarH 25 feet   6986

COOKE, JAY, 1821-1905
Correspondence, 1868-1873   PHi
N: MnHi 1 reel   6987

COOPER, Dr. JOHN
Papers, 1769-1843   priv.
DCO: PHarH 12 items   6988

COPE, EDWARD DRINKER
Field diaries, Paris journal, 1872-1892   NNM
N: PPAmP   6989

CORNPLANTER, JESSE
Indian songs in Seneca dialect   PPAmP
N: PPAmP 72 frames   6990

CUTHBERTSON, Rev. JOHN
Diary, 1751-1791   priv.
N: PHarH 2 reels   6991

DARLINGTON, WILLIAM, of West Chester, Pa.
Papers, 1800-1862   priv.
N: NHi 7 reels   6992
P: NHi

DUNGLISON, ROBLEY
Diary   PPC
N: PPAmP 811 frames   6993

DUNLAP, JOHN, 1747-1812
Register of estate, 1809; register of southern lands   priv.
DCO: PHi 322 p.   6994

DU PONCEAU, PETER STEPHEN, 1760-1844
Letters to Albert Gallatin, 1801-1843, 43 items   NHi
N: PPAmP   6995

DU SIMITIERE, PIERRE EUGENE, 1736-1784
Papers re: Pennsylvania, 1660-1770   PP
N: WHi 1 reel   6996

ELDRED, EDWARD I., of Hugo's Corner, Pa.
Justice of the Peace docket, 1808-1846   priv.
N: PHarH 12 feet   6997

ELKINTON, JOSEPH, Quaker missionary to the Indians
Journal, 1815-1864, 616 p. (WPA transcript)
N: PHarH   6998

EVANS, LEWIS
Letter re: Palatines, 1754   priv.
N: PPAmP   6999

FISHER, JOHN, of York, Pa.
Letters, 1792   PYHi
N: PYHi   7000

FRANKLIN, JOHN
Papers, 1754-1828, 114 items   PHarH
N: PHarH   7001

GREGG, DAVID M.
Manuscript biographies of Joseph Heister, Frederick A. Muhlenberg, and Andrew Gregg priv.
N: PPAmP   7002

GRUBB, Capt. JOHN
Journal re: establishment of Camp Erie at Presque Isle, 1795   PErH
N: PHarH 1 1/2 feet   7003

HALLOWELL, HENRY CLAY
Reminiscences, 1893
N: ?   7004
P: PSC-F

HAMTRAMCK, JOHN FRANCIS
Letters, 1792-1796   Anthony Wayne Papers PHi
N: MiD-B   7005

HARMAR, JOSIAH, 1753-1813
Papers, 1775-1798   MiU-C
N: PHarH 2 reels*   7006
P: PPiU

HARRIS, Mrs. PLINY
    Journal re: farm life, 1851-1853 [unk.]
    N: PHarH 4 feet   7007

HAYES, PATRICK
    Papers re: naval affairs   priv.
    N: PPAmP 1 reel   7008

HAZARD, SAMUEL, merchant of Philadelphia,
    1714-1758
    Letterbook, 1749-1758, 650 letters, and 6 let-
    ters of a later date from Ebenezer Hazard
    NjP
    N: PHi 1 reel   7009

HERSHEY, BENJAMIN
    Family correspondence, 1832-1863 priv.
    N: PHarH 1 reel   7010

HESS, JOHAN CONRAD, of Lower Sugarloaf, Pa.
    Will, n.d.   priv.
    N: USIGS   7011

HICKS, ELIAS
    Miscellaneous papers   priv.
    DCO: PSC-F   7012

HOPKINSON FAMILY
    Papers, 1737-1842 PHi
    DCO: PHi 18 v.   7013

HORSMANDEN, DANIEL
    Papers re: Six Nations Indians, 1714-1747 NHi
    N: PHarH 40 feet   7014

HUNTER, GEORGE
    Journals, 1769-1809 PPAmP
    N: PPAmP 1 reel   7015

JACKSON, HALLIDAY, Quaker missionary to the
    Seneca Indians
    Papers, 1793-1845 PWcHi
    N: PHarH 2 reels   7016

KING, ALFRED
    Papers re: Erie War of the Gauges, 1853-1855,
    44 items priv.
    DCO: PHarH   7017

LACOCK, JOHN KENNEDY
    Papers, notes, and pictures, n.d. priv.
    N: PHarH 85 feet   7018

LEHNER, GEORGE
    Journal re: railroad journey from Chambers-
    burg to Indianapolis, 1862 priv.
    N: PHarH 5 feet   7019

LEININGER, JOHANN JAKOB
    License from Pennsylvania ministerium, Jan. 13,
    1827, 1 p. PLT
    DCO: MoSC   7020

Le RAY De CHAUMONT FAMILY
    Papers re: Bradford Co., Pa., 1811-1832
    Bradford Co. Historical Society
    N: PHarH 25 feet   7021

LLOYD, DAVID, 1656-1731/2
    Papers, 1686-1731 PHi
    N: WHi 1 reel   7022

LOGAN, JAMES, 1674-1751
    Journals and papers, 1709-1711 MH
    N: CSmH   7023

LOGAN, JAMES, 1674-1751
    Papers, 1681-1751 PHi
    N: CSmH 10 reels   7024

LOGAN, JAMES, 1674-1751
    Papers, 5 items v.p.
    DCO: PSC-F   7025

MATTERN, J. G.
    Papers   priv.
    N: ?
    P: PSC-F   7026

MOON, MOSES
    Account of journeys to Black River, N.Y.,
    1803-1804, 1811 priv.
    DCO: PSC-F 26 p.   7027

MORGAN, EDWIN D.
    Papers, 1856-1877, 92 ll. N
    DCO: PHarH   7028

MORGAN, GEORGE
    Letter books as agent for U.S. Commissioners
    for Indian Affairs, 1775-1779 PPi
    N: PHarH 1 reel   7029

MORGAN, GEORGE
    Papers PHi
    N: PHi 1 reel   7030

MUHLENBERG, F.A.
    Diary, re: records of Trinity Lutheran Church,
    Reading, Pa., 1770-1773 [in German] PMtAL
    N: USIGS 1 reel   7031

MUHLENBERG, FREDERICK A.C., 1750-1801
    Papers, 1780-1784 PPAmP
    N: PPAmP   7032

MÜHLENBERG, HENRY, 1711-1787
    Journals PPAmP
    N: PPAmP   7033

MUHLENBERG FAMILY
    Papers, n.d.   priv.
    N: PPAmP 11 reels   7034

NICHOLSON, JOHN
    Letter books, 1795-1797 PHi
    N: PHarH 4 reels   7035

NILES, HENRY, of York Co., Pa.
    Diary, 1868-1900 PYHi
    N: PYHi 2 reels   7036
    P: USIGS

PARRISH, JASPER
    Papers re: Indian affairs, 1812-1823 NBuHi
    N: PHarH   7037

PEMBERTON, JAMES
    Journal re: trip to South Carolina, 1745 priv.
    N: ?   7038
    P: PSC-F

PENN FAMILY
    Papers, 1684-1788, including accounts of
    William Penn with Samuel Carpenter, 1684-
    1709 NBuHi
    N: PHarH   7039

PIERCE, MARIS B., leader of Seneca Nation
    Papers, 1787-1874 NBuHi
    N: PHarH   7040

PORTER, JEREMIAH, 1804-1893
    Journals, 1836-1879, 10 v. ICU
    N: PPPrHi   7041

POST, CHRISTIAN FREDERICK
    Diary, Apr. 1-June 30, 1760 PHi
    N: PHarH 10 feet   7042

POST, CHRISTIAN FREDERICK
    Journal of trip to the Great Council of the
    Different Indian Nations, 1760, 52 p. priv.
    N: PPAmP   7043

PROUD, ROBERT
    Manuscripts PSC-F
    N: PSC-F   7044
    P: PSC-F

RHODES, WILLIAM, of Fort Jackson, Pa.
    Papers, 1785-1794, 1832 priv.
    N: DLC 1 reel   7045

RITTENHOUSE FAMILY
    Letters, 1755-1841 priv.
    DCO: PHi 61 p.   7046

ROBINSON, MONCURE
    Letter book, 1875-1876 priv.
    N: PHarH 30 feet   7047

SCHLATTER, WILLIAM
    Letters, 1814-1825 priv
    N: PHi 1 reel   7048

SCHOFIELD, W.S., schoolteacher
    Diary, 1862-1863 priv.
    N: PHarH 5 1/2 feet   7049

SHAW, JOSEPH A.
    Letters, 1862-1864 priv.
    N: PHarH   7050

SHIPPEN FAMILY
    Miscellaneous letters, ca. 1800 priv.
    N: PHi 1 reel   7051

SHIPPEN FAMILY
    Papers, 1725-1812, including diary of Joseph
    Shippen, June-July, 1755 priv.
    N: PHarH 7 feet   7052
    P: DLC

SIMMONS, HENRY, Jr.
    Journal of Quaker missionary to the Indians,
    1796-1800 priv.
    N: PHarH 7 1/2 feet   7053

SIMPSON, JAMES T.
    Diaries, 1862-1864 priv.
    N: PHarH   7054

SLIFER, ELI, 1818-1888
    Letters, 1862-1863 priv.
    N: PHarH 1 1/2 feet   7055

SLIFER, ELI, 1818-1888
    Slifer-Dill papers, political and military
    communications, 1850-1870, 3652 letters
    PCarD
    N: PHarH 6 reels   7056
    P: PCarD PHi

SMALL, DAVID, of York, Pa., 1809-1885
    Papers priv.
    N: PYHi   7057
    P: USIGS

SPECK, FRANK G.
    Papers priv.
    N: PPAmP 4 reels   7058

SWIFT, Mrs. ELIZABETH DARLING, of
    Pittsburgh, Pa.
    Correspondence of wife of clergyman, 1790-
    1871, 115 items PHarH
    N: PHarH   7059

THORNTON, WILLIAM
    Papers DLC
    N: PPAmP 6 reels   7060

TONKIN, R. DUDLEY
    Scrapbook re: the "Last Raft," 1938 priv.
    N: PHarH 10 feet   7061

TOWNSEND, RICHARD
    Journal, 1804-1848 priv.
    N: PSC-F   7062
    P: PSC-F

    Unidentified traveler: Diary, journey from
    Norristown, Pa., to Bethlehem, Pa., Sept. 29 -
    Oct. 14, 1820 priv.
    DCO: NN 20 ll.   7063

VALENTINE, ROBERT
    Diary, 1781-1784
    N: PSC-F   7064
    P: PSC-F

VAUGHAN, SAMUEL
    Diary...of a trip through Fort Pitt, Va., Md.,
    Penn., 1787 priv.
    DCO: DLC   7065

WEISER, JOHANN CONRAD, 1696-1760
    Indian affairs letters PHi
    N: PPiU   7066

WHITE, BARCLAY I.
    Journal, v. 1-3 priv.
    N: PSC-F   7067
    P: PSC-F

WILSON, WILLIAM B.
    Diary, 1817-1871 priv.
    N: PHi 4 v.   7068

YOUNG, WILLIAM
    Memoirs PHi
    N: MWA 10 feet   7069

ZIEBER, EUGENIA
    Letters, 1848-1850   Or-Ar
    N: PHarH 3 feet   7070

                    Business Papers

ANDERSON, C.M., Greenburg, Pa.
    Ledger, 1842-1889 PGr
    N: PHarH 20 feet   7071

BANK OF NORTH AMERICA, Philadelphia
    Records, 1781-1792 PHi
    N: NNC   7072

BELL TELEPHONE COMPANY OF
    PENNSYLVANIA
    Letter books, 1886-1892 Ibid.
    N: PHarH 2 reels   7073

BERKS TITLE INSURANCE Co., Reading, Pa.
Indentures issued, 1749-1913 Ibid.
N: USIGS 1 reel   7074

BERRY-ANSHUTZ FAMILY
Papers, including iron furnace material,
1791-1936 (typescript) priv.
N: PHarH 45 feet   7075

BUCHER FAMILY, Alexandria, Pa.
Papers and store ledgers, 1768-1837 priv.
N: PHarH 1 reel   7076

CARTER, JOHN J., 1861-1917
Diaries (including material on Carter Oil Co.)
priv.
N: PHarH 5 reels   7077

CHEVALIER, JOHN
Ledger (Philadelphia) [with Peter Chevalier],
1770-1781 priv.
N: PHarH 15 feet   7078

CORBETT, C.A.
Journals re: lumbering, 1870, 1882 priv.
N: PHarH 2 1/2 feet   7079

CORNWALL ORE BANKS
Reports, 1866-1871 PHi
N: PHarH 10 feet   7080

COURIER, newspaper, Conneautville, Pa.
Office ledger, 1854-1860 priv.
N: PHarH 3 1/2 feet   7081

DALLETT, JOHN
Letterbooks of the "Red D" Line, 1840-1861
priv.
N: PU*   7082

DANIEL, JOHN
Account book priv.
N: PHi 1 reel   7083

DOBBINS, DANIEL
Papers re: ship building, 1800-1899 NBuHi
N: PHarH   7084

DYSART, CORNELIUS, M.D.
Record books re: prescription and methods of
treating diseases, 1804-1828 PYHi
N: PYHi   7085

Exports from Philadelphia and inlet trade from
Delaware to Philadelphia, 1770-1774, 1 v. NN
N: CU 1 reel   7086

FOXBURY, Pa. TAVERN
Register, 1853-1854 priv.
N: PHarH   7087

HALL, DAVID
Papers and account books, 1745-1767
PPAmP
N: PPAmP   7088

HAND, Col. EDWARD
Manuscript account book, ca. 1750 priv.
N: PHi 1 reel   7089

HARBOR CREEK INSURANCE Co., Erie, Pa.
Records, 1858-1915 Ibid.
N: PHarH 1 reel   7090

HAYES, WILLIAM
Daybook, ca. 1756-1795 OHi
N: PHarH 20 feet   7091

HOFFMAN, JOHANNES WILHELM
Diary and account book, kept in Germany
and York Co., Pa., 1732-1760 priv.
N: DLC 1 reel   7092

HOLLAND LAND Co.
Records, 1795-1804 PMCHi
N: PHarH 2 reels   7093

JAMESTOWN AND FRANKLIN RAILROAD
Papers, 1835-1868 priv.
N: PHarH 8 feet   7094

Ledger re: coal business, Shippenville, Pa.,
1895-1897 priv.
N: PHarH 16 feet   7095

LYNN, A.M., Emlenton, Pa.
Store ledger, 1874-1914 priv.
N: PHarH 7 feet   7096

MARY ANN FURNACE
Waste book, 1762-1763; day book, 1763-1764
PHi
N: PYHi   7097

MEREDITH, REESE
Commercial correspondence (Philadelphia),
1751-1769, 1 v. NN
N: CU 1 reel   7098

MORRIS, CADWALADER
Bills of lading of shipments from Philadelphia
to Havana and Kingston, 1764-1770, 1 v. NN
N: CU 1 reel   7099

NORTHUMBERLAND BRIDGE Co., Pa.
Minute book, 1811-1816 priv.
N: PHarH 10 feet   7100

PENNSYLVANIA POPULATION COMPANY
Minutes and account books, 1792-1815 PMCHi
N: PHarH 1 reel   7101

A Philadelphia merchant's account book, 1748-
1750 priv.
DCO: NN 25 p.   7102

SHIPPEN, WILLIAM, of Shippenville, Pa.
Store ledger, 1827-1828 priv.
N: PHarH 20 feet   7103

STOEHR, DANIEL, of York Co., Pa.
Account books, 1787-1864, 2 v. priv.
N: PYHi   7104

Store account (Greensburg, Pa.), 1798-1802
(Anonymous) PGr
N: PHarH 35 feet   7105

TRIMBLE, JAMES H., Beaver Co., Pa.
Store accounts, 1816-1866 priv.
N: PHarH 2 reels   7106

UNITED STATES HOTEL, Erie, Pa.
Register, 1811 NBuHi
N: PHarH   7107

VAUGHAN, SAMUEL, merchant
Diary re: tour of the United States, 1787 DLC
N: PHarH 20 feet   7108

VENSELL FAMILY
Business records, 1863-1894 priv.
N: PHarH 30 feet   7109

WHITE HILL OIL WELLS, Clarion Co., Pa.
Records, 1885 priv.
N: PHarH 1 foot   7110

WILLOW GROVE HOTEL, on old Lincoln Highway
between Bedford and Everett, Pa.
Registers, 1845-1853 priv.
N: PHarH   7111

WILSON, WILLIAM, Fort Franklin, Pa.
Daybook, 1797 priv.
N: PHarH 9 feet   7112

Collections

BAIR, ROBERT C., collector
Personarum: materials re: Chanceford, its
lands, and peoples, 3 v. PYHi
N: PYHi 1 reel   7113

BASEL, Switz. STAATSARCHIV
Material re: emigration to Pennsylvania SzB
N: DLC 87 feet   7114
PP: DLC

BRITISH MUSEUM
"Historical papers and travels," material re:
Palatines   Harleian 7021 UKLBM
N: N 1 reel   7115

CANADA. PUBLIC ARCHIVES
Selections re: Western Pennsylvania CaOOA
N: PHarH 2 reels   7116
P: PPiU

CHICAGO HISTORICAL SOCIETY
Pennsylvania material, 1754-1903 ICHi
N: PHarH 50 feet   7117

CORNELL UNIVERSITY. LIBRARY. COLLECTION
OF REGIONAL HISTORY
Pennsylvania material, 1765-1958 NIC
N: PHarH 120 feet   7118
DCO: PHarH 81 items

DURANG, CHARLES
Scrapbooks re: Philadelphia history, 1749-1855
PU
N: PU   7119
P: NNU PU

FRANKLIN AND MARSHALL COLLEGE
Church and family records of Lehigh, Berks,
and Bucks Cos., Pa., 1756-1866, 1869-1907
Ibid.
N: USIGS 2 reels   7120

GREAT BRITAIN. PUBLIC RECORD OFFICE
Pennsylvania material, 1689-1810 UKLPRO
N: PHarH 1 1/2 reels   7121

HISTORICAL SOCIETY OF BERKS COUNTY, Pa.
Church and vital records of Pennsylvania, n.d.
PRHi
N: USIGS 18 reels   7122

HISTORICAL SOCIETY OF MONTGOMERY Co.,
Pa.
Church, Town,and family records, n.d. Ibid.
N: USIGS 14 reels   7123

HISTORICAL SOCIETY OF WESTERN
PENNSYLVANIA, Pittsburgh
Denny-O'Hara papers, 1784-1912: papers of
Ebenezer Denny, Harmar Denny, and James
O'Hara (military contractor); Josiah
Harmar's regimental book, 1786-1789;
Captain Stanton Shole's military journal,
1812-1814 PPiHi
N: PHarH 7 reels   7124
P: OHi

INDIANA HISTORICAL SOCIETY
Pennsylvania material InHi
N: PHarH 1 reel   7125

NEW YORK (Colony)
Land grants on the Delaware River, with
surveys, 1667-1689, 225 ll. N
DCO: PHarH   7126

NEW YORK (City). PUBLIC LIBRARY
Pennsylvania material, 1620-1850 NN
N: PHarH 5 reels   7127
DCO: PHarH 52 items

NEW YORK HISTORICAL SOCIETY
Material on land companies and land specula-
tion, 1796-1808 NHi
N: PHarH 15 feet   7128

NEW YORK HISTORICAL SOCIETY
Pennsylvania material, 1682-1820 NHi
N: PHarH 1 reel   7129
DCO: PHarH 49 p.

O'RIELLY, HENRY, collector
Pennsylvania and Iroquois items, 1790-1820
NHi
N: PHarH 2 reels   7130

PENNSYLVANIA. HISTORICAL AND MUSEUM
COMMISSION
Records of Virginia counties in present-day
Southwestern Pennsylvania (West August
District and Yohogania County), 1775-1780
PPiU Washington Co. Historical Society
N: PHarH 60 feet   7131

PENNSYLVANIA. HISTORICAL AND MUSEUM
COMMISSION
Selections re: Indians of Pennsylvania DNA
CaOOA PHi
N: PHarH 1 reel   7132
DCO: PHarH 1 cubic foot

PENNSYLVANIA. HISTORICAL SOCIETY
Church, town,and family records PHi
N: USIGS 18 reels   7133

PENNSYLVANIA. HISTORICAL SOCIETY
Material on land companies and land specula-
tion, 1770-1842 PHi
N: PHarH 2 1/2 reels   7134

PENNSYLVANIA. HISTORICAL SOCIETY
Papers re: York County PHi
N: PYHi 1 reel   7135

PENNSYLVANIA. HISTORICAL SOCIETY
Penn-Hamilton Correspondence, 1748-1770
PHi
N: PPiU 1 reel   7136

PHILADELPHIA. LIBRARY COMPANY
Constitution and by-laws, 1824 PPL
N: PHi 1 reel   7137

PHILADFLPHIA. LIBRARY COMPANY
Minute book, 1760, 1 v. PPL
N: PHi 1 reel   7138

U.S. COURT OF CLAIMS
Brief history of the origin and migration of the Delaware, Stockbridge, Christian, and Munsee Indians   Court of Claims, No. H-226, v.1, pt.2 DNA
N: PHarH 40 feet   7139

WESTERN RESERVE HISTORICAL SOCIETY, Cleveland, Ohio
Selections re: Pennsylvania, 1786-1813, 31 items OClWHi
DCO: PHarH   7140

WISCONSIN HISTORICAL SOCIETY, Madison, Wis.
Newspaper excerpts re: labor in Pennsylvania, 1827-1939 WHi
N: PHarH 2 reels   7141

Institutions

PENNSYLVANIA. HISTORICAL SOCIETY
Minutes, 1848-1849 PHi
N: PHi 1 reel   7142

PHILADELPHIA SOCIETY FOR PROMOTING AGRICULTURE
Minutes, 1785, 1 v. PU
N: PHi 1 reel   7143

SOCIETY FOR THE IMPROVEMENT OF ROADS AND INLAND NAVIGATION
Journal, 1791-1793, 57 p. priv.
DCO: PHarH   7144

UNION LEAGUE OF AMERICA. COUNCIL No. 1, York Co., Pa.
Constitution, by-laws, and minutes Ibid.
N: PYHi 1 reel   7145

School and College Records

BRADFORD SCHOOL DISTRICT, McKean Co., Pa.
Records, 1837-1845 McKean Co. Historical Society, Bradford, Pa.
N: PHarH 4 1/2 feet   7146

CONEWAGO, Pa. SCHOOL DISTRICT
Treasurers' accounts, 1875-1935 PYHi
N: PYHi 2 reels   7147
P: USlGS

HISTORICAL SOCIETY OF YORK Co., Pa.
School attendance records, Cumberland and York Cos., 1771-1774, 1826-1835 PYHi
N: PYHi   7148
P: USlGS

WASHINGTON AND JEFFERSON COLLEGE
Records, 1820-1947 PWW
N: PHarH 3 reels   7149

NEW JERSEY

Census

U.S. CENSUS. FIFTH, 1830
Population schedules, New Jersey DNA
N: DNA 5 reels   7150
P: PHi

U.S. CENSUS. SIXTH, 1840
Population schedules, New Jersey DNA
N: DNA 5 reels   7151
P: PHi USlGS

U.S. CENSUS. SEVENTH, 1850
Population schedules, New Jersey DNA
N: DNA 5 reels   7152
P: PHi USlGS

U.S. CENSUS. EIGHTH, 1860
Population schedules, New Jersey DNA
N: DNA 7 reels   7153
P: USlGS

U.S. CENSUS. NINTH, 1870
Population schedules, New Jersey DNA
N: DNA 9 reels   7154

U.S. CENSUS. TENTH, 1880
Population schedules, New Jersey DNA
N: DNA 32 reels   7155

Government Records

U.S. DISTRICT COURT. NEW JERSEY
Bankruptcy case files (Act of 1867), 1867-1878 DNA
N: DNA 91 reels 16 mm.   7156

U.S. DISTRICT COURT. NEW JERSEY
Minutes, 1789-1850; dockets, 1863-1944; minutes of the former circuit court, 1796-1911; dockets of the former circuit court, 1862-1911 DNA
N: DNA 96 reels 16 mm.   7157

State Records

BOARD OF GENERAL PROPRIETORS OF THE EASTERN DIVISION OF NEW JERSEY
Minutes, 1685-1866 Surveyor General, Perth Amboy
N: Bibliofilm 3 reels   7158
P: NjP

COUNCIL OF PROPRIETORS OF THE WESTERN DIVISION OF NEW JERSEY
Concessions and agreements, 1676/7; minutes, 1688-1951 Ibid.
N: NjR 4 reels   7159

NEW JERSEY (Colony)
Court of Common Rights of Chancery, D. 2, Liber 2, 1684, 901 p. Ibid.
N: Bibliofilm 1 reel   7160
P: NjP

NEW JERSEY (Colony)
Liber AAA of deeds, 1680; Commissions, acts of assembly, etc., 1682-1703; Book C, patents; Commissions AAA, 1703-1774 Nj-S
N: Bibliofilm 3 reels   7161
P: NjP USlGS USlGS also has deeds, patents, commissions, 1666-1682)

NEW JERSEY
Tax ratable manuscripts, 1773-1822 Nj
N: Nj 25 reels   7162
P: Nj

NEW JERSEY. CONVENTION, 1787
Minutes - Ratification of Federal Constitution, Dec., 1787, 44 p. Nj
DCO: Nj 44 p.   7163

NEW JERSEY. SUPREME COURT
Declaration of intentions of Aliens, Feb., 1852-Oct., 1869 Ibid.
N: Bibliofilm   7164
P: NjP 1 reel

NEW JERSEY. SUPREME COURT
Docket, May, 1738-Nov., 1784 Ibid.
N: Bibliofilm 3 reels   7165
P: NjP

NEW JERSEY. SUPREME COURT
Lib. A. for judgments, 1755-1758 Ibid.
N: Bibliofilm 1 reel   7166
P: NjP

NEW JERSEY. SUPREME COURT
Minutes, 1681-1783; docket, 1738-1748 Ibid.
N: Bibliofilm 12 reels   7167
P: NjP

NEW JERSEY. SUPREME COURT
Records of naturalization, November term, 1851. Minors Ibid.
N: Bibliofilm 2 reels   7168
P: NjP

NEW JERSEY. TREASURER OF THE EASTERN DIVISION
Correspondence with Morris County Loan Office, 1776-1838, 414 p. C.H. Morristown
N: Bibliofilm 1 reel   7169
P: NjP card

County Records

ESSEX Co., N.J.
Road book A, 1698-1804 C.H. Newark
N: Bibliofilm 1 reel   7170
P: NjP

MORRIS Co., N.J.
Proceedings of justices and freeholders, 1786-1823, 661 p. C.H. Morristown
N: Bibliofilm   7171
P: NjP card

SOMERSET Co., N.J. BOARD OF CHOSEN FREEHOLDERS
Minutes, 1772-1810, 360 p. C.H. Somerville
N: Bibliofilm   7172
P: NjP USlGS

SOMERSET Co., N.J. COMMISSIONER OF ROADS AND HIGHWAYS
Old road book, 1745-1776, 138 p. C.H. Somerville
N: Bibliofilm 1 reel   7173
P: NjP USlGS

Town Records

BURLINGTON, N.J.
Township minutes, 1693-1780, 101 p. Ibid.
N: Bibliofilm   7174
P: NjP USlGS 1 reel

CHESTER TOWNSHIP, N.J.
"Ponsoking," 1692-1823 Ibid.
N: Bibliofilm 1 reel   7175

FRANKLIN TOWNSHIP, Somerset Co., N.J.
Poor book, 1764-1841 Ibid.
N: NjR 180 frames   7176

MIDDLETOWN, N.J.
Account book, 1723-1728; book of mortgages; books of estrays, 3 v. NHi
N: CU 1 reel   7177

PISCATAWAY TOWNSHIP, N.J.
Records, 1682-1933, 2 v. Ibid.
N: NjR 1 reel   7178

WOODBRIDGE TOWNSHIP, N.J.
Freeholders' book, Liber "A," 1668-1717 Ibid.
N: Bibliofilm 1 reel   7179
P: NjP USlGS

Church Records

NEW JERSEY, CHURCH RECORDS, see also HOLLAND SOCIETY OF NEW YORK, 7256, under NEW JERSEY, Collections

CHURCH OF JESUS CHRIST OF LATTER-DAY SAINTS. NEW JERSEY
Ward records: East Orange USlC
N: USlGS 1 reel   7180

CRANBURY, N.J. FIRST PRESBYTERIAN CHURCH
Records, 1745-1954 Ibid.
N: NjR 3 reels   7181
P: NjR USlGS

CRANBURY, N.J. SECOND PRESBYTERIAN CHURCH
Records, 1838-1935 First Presbyterian Church, Cranbury, N.J.
N: NjR 2 reels   7182
P: NjR USlGS

DANVILLE, N.J. PRESBYTERIAN CHURCH
Record book, 1831-1867 Ibid.
N: PPPrHi 1 reel   7183

FRIENDS, SOCIETY OF. BURLINGTON [N.J.] MONTHLY MEETING
Minutes, 1676-1737, 577 p.   PHC
N: PPY   7184

FRIENDS, SOCIETY OF (Orthodox). BURLINGTON [N.J.] MONTHLY MEETING
Births and deaths, 1682-1800; removals received, 1675-1749 PSC-F
N: USlGS   7185
P: PSC-F

FRIENDS, SOCIETY OF. CAPE MAY [N.J.] PREPARATIVE MEETING
Minutes, 1794-1817 PSC-F
N: PSC-F   7186
P: PSC-F

FRIENDS, SOCIETY OF. CHESTER [N.J.]
MONTHLY MEETING
Account book, 1829-1890; births and deaths,
1726-1820; list of members, 1804; marriages,
1804-1867; membership book, 1754-1882;
men's minutes, 1804-1949; ministers' and
elders' minutes, 1847-1905; women's
minutes, 1827-1900 PSC-F
N: PSC-F 1 reel   7187
P: PSC-F USlGS

FRIENDS, SOCIETY OF. CHESTER [N.J.]
MONTHLY MEETING
Marriages, 1867-1950; minutes, 1940-1953
PSC-F
N: PSC-F   7188
P: PSC-F

FRIENDS, SOCIETY OF. CHESTER [N.J.]
MONTHLY MEETING
Men's minutes, 1940-1949
N: PSC-F   7189
P: PSC-F

FRIENDS, SOCIETY OF. CHESTER [N.J.]
PREPARATIVE MEETING
Account book, 1849-1913; men's minutes,
1827-1914; women's minutes, 1827-1835,
1846-1897
N: PSC-F   7190
P: PSC-F USlGS

FRIENDS, SOCIETY OF. CHESTER [N.J.]
PREPARATIVE MEETING
Minutes, 1914-1950
N: PSC-F   7191
P: PSC-F

FRIENDS, SOCIETY OF. CHESTERFIELD [N.J.]
MONTHLY MEETING
Births, deaths, and marriages, 1679-1750;
removals, 1677-1773; acknowledgments and
miscellaneous papers, 1682-1890; miscellan-
eous papers, 1750-1920; deeds, 1781-1885
Chesterfield Meeting House (Hicksite)
N: USlGS   7192
P: PSC-F

FRIENDS, SOCIETY OF. CHESTERFIELD [N.J.]
MONTHLY MEETING
Marriages, 1684-1847; memorandum signed by
John Woolman, 1762; men's minutes, 1684-1917;
women's minutes, 1688-1878 Ibid.
N: PSC-F 4 reels   7193
P: PSC-F USlGS

FRIENDS, SOCIETY OF. EVESHAM [N.J.]
MONTHLY MEETING
Births and deaths, 1693-1886; marriages,
1760-1794, 1827-1878; membership, 1760-
1884; men's minutes, 1760-1884; ministers'
and elders' minutes, 1862-1884; womens'
minutes, 1828-1884 PSC-F
N: PSC-F 1 reel   7194
P: PSC-F USlGS

FRIENDS, SOCIETY OF. EVESHAM [N.J.]
MONTHLY MEETING
First[-second] book of marriages, 420 p.
N: PPY   7195

FRIENDS, SOCIETY OF. EVESHAM [N.J.]
PREPARATIVE MEETING
Men's minutes, 1854-1884; women's minutes,
1847-1884
N: PSC-F   7196
P: PSC-F

FRIENDS, SOCIETY OF. GREENWICH [N.J.]
MONTHLY MEETING
Men's minutes, 1827-1862 PSC-F
N: USlGS   7197
P: PSC-F

FRIENDS, SOCIETY OF. HADDONFIELD [N.J.]
MONTHLY MEETING
Births and deaths, 1771-1855; joint minutes,
1903-1942; men's minutes, 1827-1942; min-
isters' and elders' minutes, 1828-1854, 1883-
1938; women's minutes, 1828-1903
N: PSC-F   7198
P: PSC-F USlGS

FRIENDS, SOCIETY OF. HADDONFIELD [N.J.]
MONTHLY MEETING
Minutes, 1693-1705, 1710-1731, 347 p. PHC
N: PPY   7199

FRIENDS, SOCIETY OF. HADDONFIELD [N.J.]
PREPARATIVE MEETING
Joint minutes, 1926-1941; men's minutes,
1848-1907; women's minutes, 1838- 1856,
1864-1903
N: PSC-F   7200
P: PSC-F

FRIENDS, SOCIETY OF. HADDONFIELD [N.J.]
QUARTERLY MEETING
Men's minutes, 1827-1916; ministers' and
elders' minutes, 1828-1930; minutes, 1916-
1945; women's minutes, 1827-1903
N: PSC-F   7201
P: PSC-F USlGS

FRIENDS, SOCIETY OF. HARDWICK AND
RANDOLPH [N.J.] MONTHLY MEETING
Births and deaths, 1710-1861; marriages, 1714-
1855; minutes, 1797-1855; removals, 1792-
1847; women's minutes, 1823-1849 NNSF
N: USlGS 2 reels   7202
P: PHC PSC-F

FRIENDS, SOCIETY OF. LITTLE EGG
HARBOR [N.J.] MONTHLY MEETING
Minutes, 1715-1762 PHC
N: PPY   7203

FRIENDS, SOCIETY OF. MAURICE
RIVER [N.J.] MONTHLY MEETING
Births and deaths, 1728-1841; marriages,
1805-1844; men's minutes, 1804-1823;
women's minutes, 1833-1854 PSC-F
N: USlGS 1 reel   7204

FRIENDS, SOCIETY OF. MAURICE
RIVER [N.J.] MONTHLY MEETING
Ministers' and elders' minutes, 1830-1854
PSC-F
N: PSC-F   7205
P: PSC-F

FRIENDS, SOCIETY OF. MAURICE
RIVER [N.J.] PREPARATIVE MEETING
Women's minutes, 1809-1834 PSC-F
N: PSC-F   7206
P: PSC-F USlGS

FRIENDS, SOCIETY OF. MOUNT HOLLY [N.J.]
MONTHLY MEETING
Births, 1747-1890; burials, 1776-1930;
marriages, 1678-1940; membership,
1776-1942; minutes, 1776-1852; removals,
1827-1924 PSC-F
N: PSC-F 2 reels   7207
P: PSC-F

FRIENDS, SOCIETY OF. NEWTON
[Camden, N.J.] PREPARATIVE MEETING
Men's minutes, 1828-1838, 1847-1913;
women's minutes, 1845-1903
N: PSC-F   7208
P: PSC-F

FRIENDS, SOCIETY OF. QUAKERTOWN [N.J.]
MONTHLY MEETING
Births, 1703-1803; births, burials, and
removals, 1759-1921; marriages, 1752-1866;
minutes, 1744-1905; sufferings and removals,
1807-1864; women's minutes, 1744-1885 PSC-F
N: PSC-F 1 reel   7209
P: PSC-F

FRIENDS. SOCIETY OF. QUAKERTOWN [N.J.]
PREPARATIVE MEETING
Minutes, 1801-1823 PSC-F
N: PSC-F   7210
P: PSC-F USlGS

FRIENDS, SOCIETY OF. RAHWAY AND
PLAINFIELD [N.J.] MONTHLY MEETING
Births and deaths, 1705-1892; marriages,
1713-1889; men's minutes, 1777-1781, 1784-
1858; removals and marriages, 1770-1894;
women's minutes, 1723-1850 NNSF
N: USlGS 6 reels   7211
P: PHC PSC-F

FRIENDS, SOCIETY OF. RANCOCAS [N.J.]
PREPARATIVE MEETING
Minutes, 1799-1881; women's minutes,
1853-1882 Ibid.
N: PSC-F   7212
P: PSC-F

FRIENDS, SOCIETY OF. SALEM [N.J.]
MONTHLY MEETING
Marriages, 1827-1946; memberships,

1895-1947; men's minutes, 1827-1863 PSC-F
N: USlGS 1 reel   7213
P: PSC-F

FRIENDS, SOCIETY OF. SALEM [N.J.]
MONTHLY MEETING
Minutes, 1676-1740, 449 p. PHC
N: PPY   7214
P: USlGS

FRIENDS, SOCIETY OF. SHREWSBURY [N.J.]
MONTHLY MEETING
Births and deaths, 1650-1742; marriages,
1828-1902; men's minutes, 1732-1756, 1786-
1855; women's minutes, 1828-1837 NNSF
N: USlGS 1 reel   7215
P: PHC PSC-F

FRIENDS, SOCIETY OF. UPPER PENNS
NECK [N.J.] PREPARATIVE MEETING
Minutes, 1796-1867; women's minutes,
1842-1867 PSC-F
N: PSC-F   7216
P: PSC-F

FRIENDS, SOCIETY OF. UPPER SPRINGFIELD
[near Juliustown, N.J.] MONTHLY MEETING
Marriages, 1830-1943; men's minutes, 1828-
1857; minutes, 1857-1927; removals, 1828-
1912; women's minutes, 1806-1812 Ibid.
N: PSC-F 1 reel   7217
P: PSC-F USlGS

FRIENDS, SOCIETY OF. UPPER SPRINGFIELD
[near Juliustown, N.J.] MONTHLY MEETING
Membership, 1919; minutes, 1857-1927 Ibid.
N: USlGS   7218
P: PSC-F

FRIENDS, SOCIETY OF. WESTERN [Westfield,
N.J.] QUARTERLY MEETING
Men's minutes, 1819-1892; ministers' and
elders' minutes, 1763-1877; women's minutes,
1758-1897
N: PSC-F   7219
P: PSC-F

FRIENDS, SOCIETY OF. WESTFIELD [N.J.]
PREPARATIVE MEETING
Men's minutes, 1801-1897; women's minutes,
1801-1901
N: PSC-F   7220
P: PSC-F

FRIENDS, SOCIETY OF. WOODBRIDGE [N.J.]
MONTHLY MEETING
Men's minutes, 1686-1788 NNSF
N: USlGS   7221
P: PHC

FRIENDS, SOCIETY OF. WOODBURY [N.J.]
MONTHLY MEETING
Minutes, 1827-1870 PSC-F
N: PSC-F   7222
P: PSC-F

FRIENDS, SOCIETY OF. WOODSTOWN [N.J.]
MONTHLY MEETING
Births, 1756-1896; deaths, 1789-1897;
marriages, 1794-1896; minutes, 1821-1891
PSC-F
N: USlGS   7223
P: PSC-F

FRIENDS, SOCIETY OF. WOODSTOWN [N.J.]
MONTHLY MEETING
Minutes, 1904-1917
N: PSC-F*   7224
P: PSC-F

FRIENDS, SOCIETY OF. WOODSTOWN (or
PILESGROVE) [N.J.] MONTHLY
MEETING
Men's minutes, 1794-1821 PSC-F
N: PSC-F   7225
P: PSC-F USlGS

HAZEN, N.J. FIRST PRESBYTERIAN CHURCH
Records, 1787-1906, 3 v. Ibid.
N: NjR 1 reel   7226

KINGSTON, N.J. PRESBYTERIAN CHURCH
Records, 1791-1932 Ibid.
N: NjR 2 reels   7227
P: NjR USlGS

MARLBORO TOWNSHIP, N.J. FIRST REFORMED
CHURCH OF FREEHOLD
Records, 1709-1851, 2 v. Monmouth County
Historical Association
N: NjR 1 reel   7228

NEW BRUNSWICK, N. J. FIRST BAPTIST CHURCH
   Records, 1809-1934 Ibid.
   N: NjR 2 reels   7229

NEWARK, N. J. PARK PRESBYTERIAN CHURCH
   Records, 1825-1949 Ibid.
   N: ?
   P: PPPrHi   7230

OLDWICK, N. J. EVANGELICAL LUTHERAN
   ZION CHURCH
   Records, 1749-1900 Ibid.
   N: NjR 3 reels   7231

PARSIPPANY, N. J. PRESBYTERIAN CHURCH
   Records, 1745-1910 Ibid.
   N: NjR 3 reels
   P: NjR USlGS   7232

PASSAIC, N. J. FIRST PROTESTANT REFORMED
   DUTCH CHURCH AT ACQUACKANONK
   Records, 1692-1944 Ibid.
   N: Ibid. 2 reel
   P: Ibid.
   RN: NjR   7233

PENNINGTON, N. J. FIRST PRESBYTERIAN
   CHURCH
   Record book Nj
   N: Nj 1/4 of a reel   7234

PENNS NECK, N.J. ST. GEORGE'S SWEDISH
   LUTHERAN CHURCH (later ST. GEORGE'S)
   (Episcopal)
   Record book, 1750? Ibid.
   N: PP   7235

SCOTCH PLAINS, N. J. BAPTIST CHURCH
   Records, 1747-1941 Ibid.
   N: NjR 3 reels
   P: NjR USlGS   7236

SPOTSWOOD, N. J. ST. PETER'S CHURCH
   Records, 1761-1911 Ibid.
   N: NjR 2 reels
   P: NjR USlGS   7237

SWEDESBORO, N.J. SWEDISH EVANGELICAL
   LUTHERAN CHURCH (later TRINITY CHURCH)
   (Episcopal)
   Record book, 1712-1755? Ibid.
   N: PP
   P: PHi   7238

WASHINGTON, N. J. FIRST PRESBYTERIAN
   CHURCH
   Records, 1787-1955 Ibid.
   N: NjR 2 reels   7239

Personal Papers

BRECKINRIDGE, JOSEPH CABELL, 1788-1823
   Letters from Princeton, 1806-1813, 175 p.
   DLC
   N: NjP   7240

CHRYSTIE, JOHN, 1788-1813
   Papers, 1770-1817 priv.
   N: NjP 1 reel   7241

DOUGLASS, MABEL (SMITH)
   Correspondence re: establishment and early
   history of N. J. State College for Women, 1910-
   1938 NjNbDNj
   N: NjR 4 reels   7242

FIDLER, DANIEL, 1772-1842
   Papers, 1790-1831 NjMD
   N: NjMD 1 reel   7243

GIBSON, JAMES
   Journal, 1786 PHi
   N: NjP 1 reel   7244

GREEN, ASHBEL, 1762-1848
   Life of John Witherspoon (manuscript) NjHi
   N: NjP 1 reel   7245

HENRY, JOSEPH, 1797-1878
   Letters and papers, 1834-1877 CtY MH-G
   NNC PPAmP
   N: NjP 7 reels   7246

HUNT, HENRY, 1773-1835
   Correspondence, 1803-1834 ICU
   N: NjP 1 reel   7247

LIVINGSTON, WILLIAM, 1723-1790
   Papers, 1695-1822, 55 v., 11 boxes MHi
   N: MHi 13 reels   7248
   P: CtY NNC Nj NjHi NjR

RANKIN, EDWARD ERASTUS, 1820-1889
   Wanderbuch, 1846- priv.
   N: NjP 1 reel*   7249

SMITH, CHARLES P., 1819-1883
   Reminiscences; journal of participation in
   legislative sessions, 1855-1857, 902 p. Nj
   N: Nj   7250
   P: NjR

SNOWDEN, GILBERT TENNENT
   Journal, 1783-1795 PPPrHi
   N: NjP 1 reel   7251

SPAFFORD, HORATIO GATES, 1778-1832
   Correspondence, 1809-1827 DLC MHi
   NHi PHi
   N: NjP 4 reels   7252

WINTER, WILLIAM, 1836-1917
   Letters to Lawrence Hutton, 1880-1903 NjP
   N: NjP 1 reel   7253

WRIGHT, HENDRICK BRADLEY, 1808-1881
   Papers, 1821-1881 PHi
   N: NjP 14 reels   7254

Business Papers

LEEDS, WILLIAM
   Account book (Shrewsbury, N.J.), 1722-1733
   NHi
   N: CU 1 reel   7255

Collections

HOLLAND SOCIETY OF NEW YORK
   New Jersey cemetery, church, and marriage
   records Ibid.
   N: USlGS 6 reels   7256
   P: Ibid.

College Records

MARSHALL, ISAAC ROBERTS, d. 1812
   Diary kept while a student in the College of
   New Jersey, 1805-1807 priv.
   N: NjP   7257

PRINCETON UNIVERSITY. TRUSTEES
   Minutes, 1748-1868, 4 v. NjP
   N: NjP   7258
   P: NjP

SPENCER, WILLIAM, 1848-1920
   Diaries, account books, as student at Prince-
   ton and Edgehill School, 1865-1870 priv.
   N: NjP 1 reel   7259

STRAWBRIDGE, GEORGE, 1784-1859
   Memoirs re: Class 1802, Princeton NjP
   N: DeU 1 reel   7260

DELAWARE

Census

DELAWARE
   Census taken by Swedish pastors, 1754 SvSR
   DCO: DeHi 13 p.   7261

U.S. CENSUS. SECOND, 1800
   Population schedules, Delaware DNA
   N: DNA 1 reel   7262
   P: LM TxD USlGS

U.S. CENSUS. FIFTH, 1830
   Population schedules, Delaware DNA
   N: DNA 2 reels   7263
   P: PHi TxD USlGS

U.S. CENSUS. SIXTH, 1840
   Population schedules, Delaware DNA
   N: DNA 1 reel   7264
   P: CL De DeWi PHi USlGS

U.S. CENSUS. SEVENTH, 1850
   Population schedules, Delaware DNA
   N: DNA 3 reels   7265
   P: PHi USlGS

U.S. CENSUS. EIGHTH, 1860
   Population schedules, Delaware DNA
   N: DNA 1 reel   7266
   P: USlGS

U.S. CENSUS. NINTH, 1870
   Population schedules, Delaware DNA
   N: DNA 2 reels   7267

U.S. CENSUS. TENTH, 1880
   Population schedules, Delaware DNA
   N: DNA 5 reels   7268

Government Records

GREAT BRITAIN. CUSTOMS AND EXCISE.
   Customs 16
   Customs papers (Delaware Bay Area), 1768-
   1773, 267 p. UKLPRO
   N: De   7269

U.S. ARMY
   Fort Delaware records: official reports, 1848-
   1854; construction instructions, 1848-1864;
   journals and reports, Aug.-Dec., 1829; floor
   plans
   N: De 1 reel, and 17 film strips   7270

State Records

DELAWARE
   Apprentice indentures, 1760-1850; petitions of
   servants and slaves, 1779-1844; manumissions,
   1780-1827 De
   N: De 3 reels   7271

DELAWARE
   Births, 1861-1913; baptisms, 1759-1890;
   marriage bonds, 1680-1850, 1889-1894; deaths,
   1855-1910 De
   N: De 105 reels   7272
   P: USlGS

DELAWARE
   Documents re: ratification of the Federal
   Constitution, 1787 De
   N: De 1 reel   7273
   P: De

DELAWARE. STATE AUDITOR
   Account book, 1784-1800, 332 p. De
   N: De 167 frames   7274

County Records

Delaware county records are listed collectively,
unless they appear to have special value to the
researcher. Separate listing is always given to
wills, deeds, and vital records. In order that
researchers may differentiate between materials
the originals of which are held at county courthouses and materials the originals of which are
held at the state archives, an exception has been
made to the usual alphabetical listing. Courthouse
material always precedes archival material.

KENT Co., Del.
   Chancery court records, 1806-1877; wills,
   1680-1860; orphans' court records, 1766-1774,
   1784-1791, 1800-1808, 1817-1822, 1826-1831,
   1833-1835, 1838-1845, 1847; deeds, 1680-1688,
   1699-1764, 1768-1785, 1791-1792, 1794-1797,
   1800-1801, 1804-1806, 1808-1821, 1823-1825,
   1827-1839, 1841-1850; misc. deeds and bonds,
   1723-1730; land records, 1680-1743, 1793-1844
   C.H. Dover
   N: De 63 reels   7275
   P: USlGS

KENT Co., Del.
   Court records, 1680-1725; guardians' accounts,
   ca. 1750-1850; land records, 1683-1774; tax
   lists, 1726-1850; naturalization papers, ca.
   1834-1870 De
   N: De 23 reels   7276
   P: USlGS

KENT Co., Del.
   Orphans' court records, 1718-1722; wills,
   1860- ; deeds, 1850-
   N: De   7277

NEW CASTLE Co., Del.
Chancery court records, 1786-1852; wills, 1682-1854; guardians' accounts, 1803-1869; orphans' court records, 1742-1761, 1778-1915; deeds, 1787-1850; land records, 1647-1769; apprentice indentures, 1846-1854 C.H. Wilmington
N: De 47 reels   7278

NEW CASTLE Co., Del.
Court records, 1831- ; wills, 1854- ; guardians' accounts, 1869- ; orphans' court, 1915- ; deeds, 1850- ; land records, 1769-
C.H. Wilmington
N: De   7279

NEW CASTLE Co., Del.
Deeds, 1673-1743, 1748-1787 C.H. Wilmington
N: Ibid.   7280
P: De DeU USIGS

NEW CASTLE Co., Del.
Land warrants, 1671-1776 C.H. Wilmington
N: De 2 reels   7281
P: DeU USIGS

NEW CASTLE Co., Del.
Proprietors' land records, n.d.; tax lists, 1738-1852 De
N: De 9 reels   7282
P: USIGS

NEW CASTLE Co., Del.
Records, 1676-1699 De
DCO: PHi 4 v.   7283

SUSSEX Co., Del.
Chancery court records, 1817-1836; guardians' account, n.d.; orphans' court records, 1728-1802; land records, 18th century; tax lists, ca. 1767-1850; apprentice indentures, 1828-1930; cemetery records, n.d. De
N: De 27 reels   7284
P: USIGS

SUSSEX Co., Del.
Court records, 1749-1852; wills, 1682-1718, 1751-1851; orphans' court records, 1770-1857; land records, 1693-1733, 1742-1814, 1817-1825, 1827-1828, 1830-1835, 1837-1839, 1841-1842, 1844-1850 C.H. Georgetown
N: De 46 reels   7285
P: USIGS

SUSSEX Co., Del.
Court records, 1852- ; wills, 1851- ; guardians' records, 1846- ; orphans' court records, 1857- ; deeds, 1850-   De
N: De   7286

SUSSEX Co., Del.
Orphans' court records, 1728-1743 De
DCO: PHi 158 p.   7287

Church Records

BALTIMORE MILLS, Del. GRACE CHURCH
Registrar
N: De   7288

BETHEL CHURCH (African Methodist Episcopal), Del.
Trustees' minute book, 1865-1872 Ibid.
N: De   7289

BLACKBIRD, Del. OLD UNION METHODIST EPISCOPAL CHURCH
Records, 1804-1906 (WPA transcript) De
N: De   7290
P: USIGS

BLADES, Del. EPWORTH AND ASBURY CHURCH (Methodist Episcopal)
Records, 1908-1935 (WPA transcript) De
N: De   7291
P: USIGS

BRIDGEVILLE, Del. ST. MARY'S CHURCH (Episcopal)
Records, 1890-1939 (WPA transcript) De
N: De   7292
P: USIGS

BRIDGEVILLE, Del. UNION METHODIST EPISCOPAL CHURCH
Records, 1898-1939 (WPA transcript) De
N: De   7293
P: USIGS

BROADCREEK, Del. CHRIST CHURCH (Episcopal)
Records, 1853-1865 (WPA transcript) De
N: De   7294
P: USIGS

CANNON, Del. CANNON METHODIST PROTESTANT CHURCH
Records, 1905-1939 (WPA transcript) De
N: De   7295
P: USIGS

CECIL CIRCUIT (Methodist Episcopal), New Castle Co., Del.
Register, 1848-1869 (WPA transcript) De
N: De   7296
P: USIGS

CHESTER BETHEL METHODIST EPISCOPAL CHURCH, Faulk Road, Brandywine Hundred, Del.
Records, 1875-1940 (WPA transcript) De
N: De   7297
P: USIGS

CLARKSVILLE, Del. ST. GEORGE'S METHODIST EPISCOPAL CHURCH
Records, 1907-1914 (WPA transcript) De
N: De   7298
P: USIGS

CLAYMONT, Del. CHURCH OF ATONEMENT
Records, 1870-1910 (WPA transcript) De
N: De   7299
P: USIGS

COOLSPRING AND INDIAN RIVER CONGREGATION (Presbyterian), Sussex Co., Del.
Session minutes, 1756-1848 (WPA transcript) De
N: De   7300
P: USIGS

DAGSBORO, Del. PRINCE GEORGE CHAPEL (Episcopal)
Parish register, 1790-1844 Ibid.
N: De   7301

DELAWARE. HALL OF RECORDS
Miscellaneous church records, n.d. (WPA transcript) De
N: De   7302
P: USIGS

DELMAR, Del. FIRST METHODIST EPISCOPAL CHURCH
Records, 1869-1941 (WPA transcript) De
N: De   7303
P: USIGS

DELMAR, Del. MT. OLIVE METHODIST EPISCOPAL CHURCH
Records, 1889-1941 (WPA transcript) De
N: De   7304
P: USIGS

ELLENDALE, Del. ELLENDALE METHODIST EPISCOPAL CHURCH
Records, 1907-1940 (WPA transcript) De
N: De   7305
P: USIGS

FARMINGTON, Del. FARMINGTON METHODIST EPISCOPAL CHURCH
Records, 1879-1914 (WPA transcript) De
N: De   7306
P: USIGS

FELTON, Del. FELTON METHODIST EPISCOPAL CHURCH
Records re: Manship, Willis, Maston's, Viola, 1865-1914 (WPA transcript) De
N: De   7307
P: USIGS

FRANKFORD, Del. BLACKWATER PRESBYTERIAN CHURCH
Records, 1778-1828 (WPA transcript) De
N: De   7308
P: USIGS

FRANKFORD, Del. FRANKFORD METHODIST EPISCOPAL CHURCH
Records, 1876-1900 (WPA transcript) De
N: De   7309
P: USIGS

FRANKFORD CIRCUIT CHURCHES (Methodist Episcopal), Del.
Records, 1868-1900 (WPA transcript) De
N: De   7310
P: USIGS

FREDERICA METHODIST EPISCOPAL CHURCH, Kent Co., Del.
Records, 1780-1914 (WPA transcript) De
N: De   7311
P: USIGS

FRIENDS, SOCIETY OF. CAMDEN [Del.] MONTHLY MEETING
Births, 1745-1913; deaths, 1757-1947; marriages, 1789-1941 PSC-F
N: PSC-F 75 feet   7312
P: De PSC-F USIGS

FRIENDS, SOCIETY OF. CAMDEN [Del.] MONTHLY MEETING
Removals, 1836-1893 PSC-F
N: PSC-F   7313
P: PSC-F

FRIENDS, SOCIETY OF. CENTRE [Del.] MONTHLY MEETING
Extracts of: birth, death, and marriage records, ca. 1868 Painter Collection Media Institute of Science
N: PSC-F   7314

FRIENDS, SOCIETY OF. CENTRE [Del.] MONTHLY MEETING
Men's minutes, 1808-1921, 2 v.; women's minutes, 1808-1893, 2 v. PSC-F
N: PSC-F   7315
P: PSC-F

FRIENDS, SOCIETY OF. CENTRE [Del.] PREPARATIVE MEETING
Minutes, 1808-1876
N: PSC-F*   7316
P: PSC-F

FRIENDS, SOCIETY OF. DUCK CREEK [Del.] MONTHLY MEETING
Births and burials, 1705-1757, 1778-1846; manumissions, 1774-1792; marriages, 1705-1757; men's minutes, 1705-1830; women's minutes, 1711-1830; removals, 1773-1836 PSC-F
N: PSC-F 2 reels   7317
P: PSC-F USIGS

FRIENDS, SOCIETY OF. HOCKESSIN [Del.] PREPARATIVE MEETING
Minutes, 1818-1886
N: PSC-F*   7318
P: PSC-F

FRIENDS, SOCIETY OF. MOTHERKILL [Del.] MONTHLY MEETING
Marriages and removals, 1789-1832; men's minutes, 1788-1830; women's minutes, 1788-1845 Ibid.
N: PSC-F   7319
P: PSC-F USIGS

FRIENDS, SOCIETY OF. WILMINGTON [Del.] MONTHLY MEETING
Births, 1731-1851; births and deaths, 1740-1851; burial permits, 1834-1947; marriages, 1750-1938; membership, 1748- ca. 1914; removals, 1751-1937 Wilmington Meeting House (Hicksite)
N: USIGS   7320
P: PSC-F

FRIENDS, SOCIETY OF. WILMINGTON [Del.] MONTHLY MEETING
Men's minutes, 1750-1901; women's minutes, 1750-1891 Ibid.
N: PSC-F   7321
P: PSC-F USIGS

FRIENDS, SOCIETY OF. WILMINGTON [Del.] MONTHLY MEETING
Ministers' and elders' minutes, 1757-1769, 1772-1863 PSC-F
N: PSC-F   7322
P: PSC-F USIGS

GEORGETOWN, Del. GEORGETOWN CIRCUIT CHURCHES (Methodist Episcopal)
Records re: Cokesbery, Sandhill, St. John, and Bethesda, 1892-1914 (WPA transcript) De
N: De   7323
P: USIGS

GEORGETOWN, Del. GEORGETOWN PROTESTANT CHURCH (Methodist)
Records, 1898-1916 (WPA transcript) De
N: De   7324
P: USIGS

GEORGETOWN, Del. PRESBYTERIAN CHURCH
Records, 1859-1913 (WPA transcript) De
N: De
P: USIGS   7325

GEORGETOWN, Del. ST. PAUL'S CHURCH
(Episcopal)
Records, 1840-1914 (WPA transcript) De
N: De
P: USIGS   7326

GEORGETOWN, Del. ST. PAUL'S CHURCH
(Episcopal)
Register, 1885-1939 Ibid.
N: De   7327

GEORGETOWN, Del. WESLEY METHODIST
CHURCH
Records, 1858-1915 (WPA transcript) De
N: De
P: USIGS   7328

GEORGETOWN, Del. ZOAR CIRCUIT METHODIST
EPISCOPAL CHURCH
Records, 1897-1913 (WPA transcript) De
N: De
P: USIGS   7329

GLASGOW, Del. BETHEL AND GLASGOW
METHODIST EPISCOPAL CHURCH
Records, 1872-1893 (WPA transcript) De
N: De
P: USIGS   7330

GLASGOW, Del. METHODIST EPISCOPAL
CHURCH
Records, 1860-1924 (WPA transcript) De
N: De
P: USIGS   7331

GLASGOW, Del. PENGADER PRESBYTERIAN
CHURCH
Records, 1900-1913 (WPA transcript) De
N: De
P: USIGS   7332

GREENWOOD, Del. GREENWOOD CIRCUIT
CHURCH (Methodist Episcopal)
Records, 1838-1931 (WPA transcript) De
N: De
P: USIGS   7333

GUMBORO, Del. GUMBORO CIRCUIT METHODIST
EPISCOPAL CHURCH
Records, 1891-1938 (WPA transcript) De
N: De
P: USIGS   7334

HARBESON, Del. HARBESON CIRCUIT CHURCH
(Methodist Episcopal)
Records re: Beaver Dam, Reynolds, Weiglands,
1897-1950 (WPA transcript) De
N: De
P: USIGS   7335

HARRINGTON, Del. HARRINGTON METHODIST
EPISCOPAL CHURCH
Records, 1865-1917 (WPA transcript) De
N: De
P: USIGS   7336

HARRINGTON, Del. HARRINGTON METHODIST
PROTESTANT CIRCUIT CHURCH
Records, 1838-1911 (WPA transcript) De
N: De
P: USIGS   7337

HARRINGTON, Del. HARRINGTON METHODIST
PROTESTANT CHURCH
Records, 1880-1917 (WPA transcript) De
N: De
P: USIGS   7338

HOCKESSIN, Del. HOCKESSIN CHURCH
(Methodist Episcopal)
Records, 1884-1917 (WPA transcript) De
N: De
P: USIGS   7339

HOUSTON, Del. HOUSTON METHODIST
EPISCOPAL CHURCH
Records, 1892-1936 (WPA transcript) De
N: De
P: USIGS   7340

LAUREL, Del. CENTENARY CHURCH
(Methodist Episcopal)
Records, 1879-1914 (WPA transcript) De
N: De
P: USIGS   7341

LAUREL, Del. MT. PLEASANT METHODIST
EPISCOPAL CHURCH
Records, 1893-1925 (WPA transcript) De
N: De
P: USIGS   7342

LAUREL, Del. ST. PHILLIP'S CHAPEL
(Episcopal)
Records, 1835-1887 (WPA transcript) De
N: De
P: USIGS   7343

LAUREL, Del. ST. PHILLIP'S CHURCH
(Episcopal)
Records, 1889-1911 (WPA transcript) De
N: De
P: USIGS   7344

LAWES METHODIST EPISCOPAL CHURCH, Kent
Co., Del.
Records, 1888-1921 (WPA transcript) De
N: De
P: USIGS   7345

LEWES, Del. BETHEL METHODIST EPISCOPAL
CHURCH
Records, 1860-1933 (WPA transcript) De
N: De
P: USIGS   7346

LEWES, Del. GROOME MEMORIAL METHODIST
PROTESTANT CHURCH
Records, 1904-1940 (WPA transcript) De
N: De
P: USIGS   7347

LEWES, Del. LEWES PRESBYTERIAN CHURCH
Records, 1737-1856 (WPA transcript) De
N: De
P: USIGS   7348

LEWES, Del. ST. PETER'S CHURCH (Episcopal)
Records, 1708-1797 (WPA transcript) De
N: De
P: USIGS   7349

LEWES, Del. ST. PETER'S CHURCH (Episcopal)
Records, 1731-1948, 7 v. Ibid.
N: De   7350

LINCOLN, Del. METHODIST EPISCOPAL CHURCH
Records, 1871-1939 (WPA transcript) De
N: De
P: USIGS   7351

MERMAID, Del. EBENEZER METHODIST
EPISCOPAL CHURCH
Records, 1897-1913 (WPA transcript) De
N: De
P: USIGS   7352

METHODIST CHURCH (United States). CIRCUITS.
BRIDGEVILLE, Del.
Records, 1832-1939 (WPA transcript) De
N: De
P: USIGS   7353

METHODIST CHURCH (United States). CIRCUITS.
CHRISTIANA, Del.
Records re: Newark, Salem, Red Lion, Glas-
gow, Ebenezer, Cooch's Bridge, 1807-1921
(WPA transcript) De
N: De
P: USIGS   7354

METHODIST CHURCH (United States). CIRCUITS
(Mission). SUSSEX, Del.
Records re: Providence, Trinity, Shiloh,
St. Paul's, 1865-1902 (WPA transcript) De
N: De
P: USIGS   7355

MILFORD, Del. CHRIST CHURCH (Episcopal)
Records, 1880-1914 (WPA transcript) De
N: De
P: USIGS   7356

MILFORD, Del. FIRST METHODIST PROTESTANT
CHURCH
Records, 1910-1940 (WPA transcript) De
N: De
P: USIGS   7357

MILFORD, Del. PRESBYTERIAN CHURCH
Records, 1849-1888 (WPA transcript) De
N: De
P: USIGS   7358

MILLSBORO, Del. ST. MARK'S CHURCH
(Episcopal)
Records, 1848-1929 (WPA transcript) De
N: De
P: USIGS   7359

MILLWOOD, Del. MILLWOOD METHODIST
EPISCOPAL CHURCH
Records, 1888-1915 (WPA transcript) De
N: De
P: USIGS   7360

MILTON, Del. FIRST METHODIST PROTESTANT
CHURCH
Records, 1874-1940 (WPA transcript) De
N: De
P: USIGS   7361

MILTON, Del. MILTON METHODIST EPISCOPAL
CHURCH
Records, 1863-1910 (WPA transcript) De
N: De
P: USIGS   7362

MT. PLEASANT AND NEWARK UNION METHO-
DIST EPISCOPAL CHURCH (formerly MT.
PLEASANT METHODIST EPISCOPAL
CHURCH), Del.
Records, 1838-1913 (WPA transcript) De
N: De
P: USIGS 2 reels   7363

NASSAU, Del. NASSAU CIRCUIT METHODIST
EPISCOPAL CHURCH
Records re: Whites, Zion, Ebenezer, and
Connelly's, 1880-1941 (WPA transcript) De
N: De
P: USIGS   7364

NEW CASTLE, Del. BETHEL BAPTIST PRIMITIVE
CHURCH
Records, 1821-1925 (WPA transcript) De
N: De
P: USIGS   7365

NEW CASTLE, Del. NEW CASTLE CHURCH
(Methodist Episcopal)
Records, 1839-1866 (WPA transcript) De
N: De
P: USIGS   7366

NEW CASTLE, Del. WELSH TRACT BAPTIST
CHURCH
Records, 1804-1850 (WPA transcript) De
N: De
P: USIGS   7367

NEWARK, Del. HEAD OF CHRISTIANA
PRESBYTERIAN CHURCH
Records, 1781-1933 (WPA transcript) De
N: De
P: USIGS   7368

NEWARK, Del. VILLAGE PRESBYTERIAN
CHURCH
Records, 1835-1854 (WPA transcript) De
N: De
P: USIGS   7369

OLD DRAWERS CHURCH, Del.
Records, 1732-1909, 300 ll. DeHi
DCO: DeHi   7370

PRESBYTERIAN CHURCH IN THE U.S.A.
PRESBYTERIES. NEW CASTLE, Del.
Minutes, v.1, 3-4 PHi
N: PPPrHi   7371

RED LION METHODIST EPISCOPAL CHURCH,
New Castle Co., Del.
Records, 1881-1904 (WPA transcript) De
N: De
P: USIGS   7372

REHOBOTH, Del. METHODIST EPISCOPAL
CHURCH
Records, 1909-1941 (WPA transcript) De
N: De 7373
P: USIGS

RELIANCE, Del. GETHSEMANE PROTESTANT
CHURCH (Methodist)
Records, 1852-1938 (WPA transcript) De
N: De 7374
P: USIGS

ROCKLAND, Del. MT. LEBANON METHODIST
EPISCOPAL CHURCH
Records, 1869-1914 (WPA transcript) De
N: De 7375
P: USIGS

ROXANNA, Del. ROXANNA CIRCUIT CHURCH
(Methodist Episcopal)
Records, 1856-1872 (WPA transcript) De
N: De 7376
P: USIGS

ST. JOHN'S CHURCH (Episcopal), Greenville,
Little Creek Hundred, Del.
Records, 1842-1912 (WPA transcript) De
N: De 7377
P: USIGS

SEAFORD, Del. CANNON CHARGE METHODIST
EPISCOPAL CHURCH
Records, 1896-1913 (WPA transcript) De
N: De 7378
P: USIGS

SEAFORD, Del. ST. JONES METHODIST
EPISCOPAL CHURCH
Records, 1866-1920 (WPA transcript) De
N: De 7379
P: USIGS

SEAFORD, Del. ST. LUKE'S CHURCH
(Episcopal)
Records, 1835-1919 (WPA transcript) De
N: USIGS 7380

SEAFORD, Del. SEAFORD PROTESTANT CHURCH
(Methodist)
Records, 1887-1914 (WPA transcript) De
N: De 7381
P: USIGS

STEPNEY PARISH (Episcopal), Wicomico Co.,
Del.
Records, 1714-1772 (WPA transcript) De
N: De 7382
P: USIGS

WILLIAMSVILLE, Del. SOUND THREE CHURCHES
Records, 1784, 1868, 1891 (WPA transcript) De
N: De 7383
P: USIGS

WILMINGTON, Del. ASBURY METHODIST
EPISCOPAL CHURCH
Records, 1766-1911 (WPA transcript) De
N: De 2 reels 7384
P: USIGS

WILMINGTON, Del. BRANDYWINE METHODIST
EPISCOPAL CHURCH
Records, 1835-1839, 1846-1847, 1849-1852,
1855, 1857-1904, 1906-1913, 1918 (WPA trans-
cript) De
N: De 7385
P: USIGS

WILMINGTON, Del. COOKMAN METHODIST
EPISCOPAL CHURCH
Records, 1889-1933 (WPA transcript) De
N: De 7386
P: USIGS

WILMINGTON, Del. EAST LAKE METHODIST
EPISCOPAL CHURCH
Records, 1894-1923 (WPA transcript) De
N: De 7387
P: USIGS

WILMINGTON, Del. EPWORTH METHODIST
EPISCOPAL CHURCH
Records, 1842, 1853, 1855-1856, 1867-1920,
1928, 1934 (WPA transcript) De
N: De 7388
P: USIGS

WILMINGTON, Del. FIRST METHODIST
EPISCOPAL CHURCH
Records, 1905-1932 (WPA transcript) De
N: De 7389
P: USIGS

WILMINGTON, Del. FIRST PRESBYTERIAN
CHURCH
List of burials, 1760-1899 (WPA transcript)
De
N: De 7390
P: USIGS

WILMINGTON, Del. GRACE METHODIST
EPISCOPAL CHURCH
Records, 1866-1915 (WPA transcript) De
N: De 7391
P: USIGS

WILMINGTON, Del. GREENHILL PRESBYTERIAN
CHURCH
Records, 1851-1917 (WPA transcript) De
N: De 7392
P: USIGS

WILMINGTON, Del. HANOVER PRESBYTERIAN
CHURCH
Records, 1772-1915 (WPA transcript) De
N: De 7393
P: USIGS

WILMINGTON, Del. HOLY TRINITY
[OLD SWEDES] CHURCH
Church record, 1750-1885, 917 p. De
N: USIGS 1 reel 7394

WILMINGTON, Del. HOLY TRINITY [OLD
SWEDES] CHURCH
Records, 1697-1890 De
N: De 4 reels 7395
P: USIGS

WILMINGTON, Del. KINGSWOOD METHODIST
EPISCOPAL CHURCH
Records, 1885-1937 (WPA transcript) De
N: De 7396
P: USIGS

WILMINGTON, Del. KIRKWOOD METHODIST
EPISCOPAL CHURCH
Records, 1898-1915 (WPA transcript) De
N: De 7397
P: USIGS

WILMINGTON, Del. MADELEY METHODIST
EPISCOPAL CHURCH
Records, 1890-1926 (WPA transcript) De
N: De 7398
P: USIGS

WILMINGTON, Del. MT. SALEM METHODIST
EPISCOPAL CHURCH
Records, 1847-1863 (WPA transcript) De
N: De 7399
P: USIGS

WILMINGTON, Del. NEWARK UNION MEETING
HOUSE
Records, 1845-1913 (WPA transcript) De
N: De 7400
P: USIGS

WILMINGTON, Del. OLIVET PRESBYTERIAN
CHURCH
Records, 1867-1915 (WPA transcript) De
N: De 7401
P: USIGS

WILMINGTON, Del. ST. PAUL'S METHODIST
EPISCOPAL CHURCH
Records, 1868-1906 (WPA transcript) De
N: De 7402
P: USIGS

WILMINGTON, Del. SCOTT METHODIST
EPISCOPAL CHURCH
Records, 1815, 1834, 1840, 1843-1923, 1925,
1932, 1935 (WPA transcript) De
N: De 7403
P: USIGS

WILMINGTON, Del. UNION METHODIST
EPISCOPAL CHURCH
Records, 1816, 1828, 1831, 1833-1834,
1836, 1839, 1841-1844, 1847-1924, 1928

(WPA transcript) De
N: De 2 reels 7404
P: USIGS

WILMINGTON, Del. WESLEY METHODIST
EPISCOPAL CHURCH
Records, 1884-1903 (WPA transcript) De
N: De 7405
P: USIGS

WILMINGTON, Del. WESTMINSTER PRESBY-
TERIAN CHURCH
Records, 1886-1915 (WPA transcript) De
N: De 7406
P: USIGS

Personal Papers

AYRES, ROBERT ?
Journal, 1787-1788 PPiHi
N: PHaH 7407
P: NjM D

BOYNTON, LUCIUS CYRUS
Journal of residence in New England, Delaware,
and Virginia, 1835-1853 DeU
N: DLC 1 reel 7408

BROBSON, WILLIAM P.
Diary of Wilmington events, 1825-1828 PHarH
N: DeU 1 reel 7409
P: DeHi

CARTER, ELIZABETH L.
Diary, 1789-1797 priv.
N: De 258 frames 7410

COPE, T. P.
Letterbook, 1816-1853 De
N: De 357 frames 7411
P: DeHi

DARLINGTON, WILLIAM, 1728-1863
Journal re: trip to Baltimore, 1803 NHi
N: DeU 1 reel 7412

FISHER, JOHN
Letters to the Rodneys, 1794-1822,
17 items NHi
DC: DeHi 34 p. 7413

FORMAN, MARTHA BROWN (OGLE), 1788-1864
Diary, 1814-1860 MdHi
N: DeU 1 reel 7414

GARRETT, THOMAS
Letters, 1850-1869, 11 items MB
DC: DeHi 24 p. 7415

HOLT, RYVES
Letters, 1734-1752, 5 items PHi
DC: DeHi 10 p. 7416

HOUSTON, Mrs. LYDIA B.
Diaries, 1862-1864, 1873-1875 priv.
N: De 146 frames 7417

KENNEDY, JOHN PENDLETON, 1795-1870
Account of trip to Richmond with Louis McLane,
March 13-26, 1838, 5 l. priv. ?
DCO: DeU 7418

LAMMOT, D.
Letters to E. I. duPont, 1825-1838, 7 items
PKSL
DC: DeHi 7 p. 7419

McDOWELL, Rev. ALEXANDER, 1730-1805
Family papers (transcript) priv.
N: De 1 reel 50 feet 7420
P: DeU

McLANE, ALLAN, 1746-1829
Correspondence with Louis McLane MHi
N: DeU 1 reel 7421

McLANE, ALLAN, 1746-1829
Letters NHi
DC: DeHi 3 v. 7422

McLANE, LOUIS, 1786-1857
Letters, 1806-1848 PCarlD ScCle priv.
DCO: DeU 277 ll. 7423

McLANE, LOUIS, 1786-1857
Letters, 1832-1836 MiU-C
N: DeU 1 reel   7424

McLANE, LOUIS, 1786-1857
Papers, 1784-1883 priv.
N: DeU 5 reels   7425

McLANE, LOUIS, 1786-1857
Papers, 1786-1857 CoHi
N: DeU 3 reels   7426
P: CoHi

READ, JOHN, 1688-1756
Family papers, 1735-1906, 1 v. DLC
N: DeU 1 reel   7427

RISING, JOHAN CLASSON, 1617-1672
Manuscripts re: New Sweden, 1650 -   SvUU
N: DeU 1 reel   7428

RISING, JOHAN CLASSON, 1617-1672
Papers re: three lower counties, 1629-1774
PHi
N: DeU 1 reel   7429

RUMSEY FAMILY
Papers, 1776-1777 DLC
DC: DeHi 56 p.   7430

STORRS, HENRY RANDOLPH, 1787-1837
Journal NBuHi
N: DeU 2 reels   7431

SULLIVAN, ISAAC
Diary, 1818-1844 De
N: De 21 frames   7432

SULLIVAN, LEVI
Diary, 1840-1865 De
N: De 3 frames   7433

SWEDBERG, JESPER, Bp., 1653-1735
Swecia Nova, America Illuminata (manu-
script), 1727 SvSR
N: PHi 1 reel   7434

WALLIS FAMILY, of Muncy, Pa.
Papers priv.
N: ? 7 reels   7435
P: PHi

WHITE FAMILY, Delaware
Correspondence, 1860-1875 priv.
N: DeU 1 reel   7436

WILLIAMS, JAMES MERRILL, b. 1842
Journal, 1864-1893 NcU
N: DeU 1 reel   7437

Business Papers

LEBANON [Del.] MERCHANT
Shipping accounts, 1868-1912 priv.
N: De 1186 frames   7438

LEWES [Del.] MERCHANT
Ledgers, 1822-1879 priv.
N: De 309 frames   7439

LYNCH, ELIJAH
Business records (Lewes, Del.), 1828-1897
priv.
N: De 1436 frames   7440

MARRINER, SIMON
Tavern and tailor accounts (Lewes, Del.),
1799-1819 priv.
N: De 124 frames   7441

MARSHALL, JOHN
Account of pilots' fees, 1827-1837 priv.
N: De 45 frames   7442

NEILL, HENRY
General store account book (Lewes, Del.),
1785-1797 priv.
N: De 160 frames   7443

OCEAN HOUSE, Lewes, Del.
Ledger book, 1847-1853 priv.
N: De 50 frames   7444

WEST, ROBERT
Account book (Lewes, Del.), 1807-1809 priv.
N: De 240 frames   7445

WEST, SAMUEL
General store ledger (Lewes, Del.), 1772-
1775; accounts of pilots' fees and supplies,
1812-1819 priv.
N: De 30 frames   7446

Collections

GREAT BRITAIN. PUBLIC RECORD OFFICE
Documents re: New Castle Co., Del.,
Loyalists UKLPRO
DC: DeHi 116 p.   7447

U.S. LIBRARY OF CONGRESS
Delaware papers: Colonial and Revolutionary
documents, 1-17, 4 v. DLC
N: DeU 2 reels   7448

School and College Records

DELAWARE
Material re: schools under the Dutch, 1655-
1673 N
DC: DeHi   7449

NEWARK ACADEMY, Newark, Del., 1783-1947
Trustees' minutes, 1783-1947 DeU
N: De 1 reel   7450
P: DeU

Ships' Logs

With ships' logs are included journals, diaries,
and other records of voyages. Journals, which
are personal documents, are listed under the
name of the author.

MARTIN, JOHN
Journal kept on whale ship Lucy-Ann of
Wilmington, Del., 1841-1843 ICHi
N: DeHi 1 reel   7451

MARYLAND

Census

U.S. CENSUS. FIFTH, 1830
Population schedules, Maryland DNA
N: DNA 6 reels   7452
P: MdAA PHi USIGS

U.S. CENSUS. SIXTH, 1840
Population schedules, Maryland DNA
N: DNA 5 reels   7453
P: USIGS

U.S. CENSUS. SEVENTH, 1850
Population schedules, Maryland DNA
N: DNA 6 reels   7454
P: USIGS

U.S. CENSUS. EIGHTH, 1860
Population schedules, Maryland DNA
N: DNA 8 reels   7455
P: USIGS

U.S. CENSUS. NINTH, 1870
Population schedules, Maryland DNA
N: DNA 8 reels   7456

U.S. CENSUS. TENTH, 1880
Population schedules, Maryland DNA
N: DNA 26 reels   7457

Government Records

U.S. CUSTOMS HOUSE, BALTIMORE
Carpenters' certificates, 1790-1832 MdHi
N: MSaP 2 reels   7458

U.S. CUSTOMS HOUSE, BALTIMORE
Entrances and clearances, 1782-1824 DNA
N: DNA 1 reel [T-257]   7459

U.S. TREASURY DEPT.
Direct tax of 1798, Maryland, Anne Arundel Co.
MdAA
N: MdAA   7460

State Records

MARYLAND (Colony)
Port of entry papers, 1742-1775 MdAA
N: MdAA 1 reel   7461

MARYLAND (Colony). CHARTER
Charter of Maryland, granted by Charles I,
1632, 23 p. UKP-L
N: MdAA   7462

MARYLAND (Colony). COURT OF VICE
ADMIRALTY
Record book, 1754-1775 MdAA
N: MdAA   7463

MARYLAND
Militia rolls, 1813-1814 MdAA
N: MdAA 1 reel   7464

MARYLAND
Patents, certificates and warrants, 1637-1852
MdAA
N: USIGS 81 reels   7465

MARYLAND
Pension claims, 1855-1857 MdAA
N: MdAA   7466

MARYLAND
Requests for absentee ballots by persons in
military service, 1944 MdAA
N: MdAA 1 reel   7467

MARYLAND. GENERAL ASSEMBLY. HOUSE OF
DELEGATES
Report [in part] on Penitentiary by Joint Com-
mittee of Legislature, 1838 MdAA
N: MdAA 1 reel   7468

MARYLAND. HALL OF RECORDS COMMISSION
Colonial records of Maryland, 1635-1891 MdAA
N: USIGS 257 reels   7469
P: CSmH DLC MdAA UKLBM

MARYLAND. HALL OF RECORDS COMMISSION
Gibson papers, 1755-1832, nos. 1-64 MdAA
N: MdAA 1 reel   7470

MARYLAND. HALL OF RECORDS COMMISSION
Habersham papers - F. Scott Key, 1768-1858
MdAA
N: MdAA   7471

MARYLAND. HALL OF RECORDS COMMISSION
Rideout papers, nos. 1-564 MdAA
N: MdAA 1 reel   7472

County Records

Maryland county records are listed collectively,
unless they appear to have special value to the
researcher. Separate listing is always given to
wills, deeds, and vital records. In order that
researchers may differentiate between materials,
the originals of which are held at county courthouses, and materials, the originals of which are
held at the state archives, an exception has been
made to the usual alphabetical listing. Courthouse
material always precedes archival material.

ALLEGANY Co., Md.
Wills, 1851- ; orphans' court records, 1791-;
chattel and miscellaneous records, 1951-
C.H. Cumberland
N: MdAA   7473

ALLEGANY Co., Md.
Wills, 1790-1850; inventories, 1791-1851; administrators' records, 1791-1855; guardians'
records, 1793-1867; orphans' court records,
1791-1852; land records, 1791-1850; marri-

age licenses book, 1847-1865 C.H. Cumberland
N: USlGS 35 reels　　　　　　　　7474
P: MdAA

ANNE ARUNDEL Co., Md.
Court minutes, 1725,1733,1748, 1752, 1754-1755, 1766, 1774-1775, 1793-1797 [1 reel]; wills, 1777- ; inventories, 1853- ; accounts, 1850- ; orphans' court records, 1852- ; land records, 1844, 1855-　C.H. Annapolis
N: MdAA　　　　　　　　　　7475

ANNE ARUNDEL Co., Md.
Guardians' bonds, 1801-1820　MdAA
N: USlGS 1 reel　　　　　　　　7476
P: MdAA

ANNE ARUNDEL, Co., Md.
Mortality schedules, 1850-1880　MdHi
N: USlGS　　　　　　　　　　7477

ANNE ARUNDEL Co., Md.
Wills, 1777-1820; deeds, 1666-1778; land records, 1778-1789　MdAA
N: MdAA 4 reels　　　　　　　7478
P: USlGS

ANNE ARUNDEL Co., Md.
Wills, 1817-1864; inventories, 1777-1853; administrators' records, 1777-1851; guardian s' records, 1780-1856; orphans' court records, 1784-1852; deeds, 1789-1850; marriage records, 1777-1851, 1875-1886　C.H. Annapolis
N: USlGS 60 reels　　　　　　7479
P: MdAA

BALTIMORE Co., Md.
Court records, 1777-1850; wills, 1675-1852; inventories, 1665-1850; administrators' records, 1711-1852; guardians' records, 1777-1852; land records, 1779-1849　C.H. Baltimore
N: USlGS 298 reels　　　　　　7480
P: MdAA　land records only

BALTIMORE Co., Md.
Land records, 1659-1800; marriage licenses, 1777-1851　MdAA
N: USlGS 48 reels　　　　　　7481
P: MdAA

BALTIMORE Co., Md.
Records of taxables and levies, 1690-1705 C.H. Towson
N: MdAA　　　　　　　　　　7482

BALTIMORE Co., Md.
Wills, 1851- ; orphans' court records, 1851- ; land records, 1659-1800, 1851-1922 C.H. Towson
N: MdAA　　　　　　　　　　7483

CALVERT Co., Md.
Court records, 1882- ; wills, 1882- ; inventories, 1882- ; accounts, 1882- ; land records, ca. 1840-1880, 1882　C.H. Prince Frederick
N: MdAA　　　　　　　　　　7484

CAROLINE Co., Md.
Wills, 1853-1885, 1898- ; orphans' court records, 1828- ; land records, 1851-
C.H. Denton
N: MdAA　　　　　　　　　　7485

CAROLINE Co., Md.
Wills, 1688-1855; inventories, 1697-1850; administrators' records, 1703-1851; distribution of estates, 1812-1853; guardians' records, 1787-1866; land records, 1774-1851; marriage records, 1774-1865　C.H. Denton
N: USlGS 38 reels　　　　　　7486
P: MdAA

CARROLL Co., Md.
Wills, 1852-; orphans' court proceedings, 1837-
C.H. Westminster
N: MdAA　　　　　　　　　　7487

CARROLL Co., Md.
Wills, 1837-1852; inventories, 1837-1852; administrators' records, 1837-1853; guardians' records, 1837-1865; land records, 1837-1850　C.H. Westminster
N: USlGS 14 reels　　　　　　7488
P: MdAA

CECIL Co., Md.
Wills, 1852- ; orphans' court proceedings, 1798-1834, 1836; land records, 1918- ; marriage licenses, 1840-1863　C.H. Elkton
N: MdAA　　　　　　　　　　7489

CECIL Co., Md.
Wills, 1675-1853; inventories, 1675-1792, 1795-1830, 1833-1850; administrators' and guardians' accounts, 1676-1797, 1802-1859; land records, 1673-1850; marriage licenses, 1777-1863　C.H. Elkton
N: USlGS 69 reels　　　　　　7490
P: MdAA　after ca. 1780

CHARLES Co., Md.
Wills, 1850- ; inventories, 1852- ; administrators' accounts, 1950- ; accounts, 1851- ; orphans' court proceedings, 1853- ; corporation records, 1952- ; equity records, 1948-1951, 1954; mortgages, 1950- ; chattel records, 1950　C.H. La Plata
N: MdAA　　　　　　　　　　7491

CHARLES Co., Md.
Wills, 1665-1825; orphans' court records, 1824-1827; land records, 1658-1701, 1703-1790　MdAA
N: USlGS 19 reels　　　　　　7492
P: MdAA

CHARLES Co., Md.
Wills, 1825-1850; inventories, 1673-1775, 1791-1852; administrators' accounts, 1708-1806, 1825-1851; guardians' accounts, 1790-1823; orphans' court records, 1791-1824, 1827-1853; land records, 1790-1810, 1813-1850　C.H. La Plata
N: USlGS 39 reels　　　　　　7493
P: MdAA

DORCHESTER Co., Md.
Court judgments, 1788-1800; wills, 1852- ; orphans' court proceedings, 1843-　C.H. Cambridge
N: MdAA　　　　　　　　　　7494

DORCHESTER Co., Md.
Land records, 1669-1780, 1782-1788; marriage licenses, 1780-1850　MdAA
N: USlGS　　　　　　　　　　7495
P: MdAA　marriage records

DORCHESTER Co., Md.
Land records, 1788-1851　C.H. Cambridge
N: USlGS 24 reels　　　　　　7496

FREDERICK Co., Md.
Court minutes, 1763-1766, 1768; equity court records, 1919-; judgments, 1748-1750, 1763-1766; wills, 1855-; orphans' court proceedings, 1777-　C.H. Frederick
N: MdAA　　　　　　　　　　7497

FREDERICK CO., Md.
Land records, 1748-1789; marriage licenses, 1779-1797　MdAA
N: USlGS 15 reels　　　　　　7498

FREDERICK Co., Md.
Wills, 1744-1854; inventories, 1749-1851; administrators' records, 1750-1853; guardians' records, 1778-1853; land records, 1790-1851
C.H. Frederick
N: USlGS 30 reels　　　　　　7499
P: MdAA but administrators' records only after 1799

GARRETT Co., Md.
Wills, 1873- ; orphans' court proceedings, 1873-1912, 1934-　C.H. Oakland
N: USlGS　　　　　　　　　　7500

HARFORD Co., Md.
Wills, 1853- ; orphans' court, 1800-1822; 1828-1838, 1842-　C.H. Bel Air
N: MdAA　　　　　　　　　　7501

HARFORD Co., Md.
Wills, 1775-1853; inventories, 1777-1852; administrators' records, 1774-1851; guardians' records, 1778-1902; land records, 1773-1850; marriage licenses, 1774-1886　C.H. Bel Air
N: USlGS 49 reels　　　　　　7502
P: MdAA but land records only from 1790

HOWARD Co., Md.
Wills, 1840-1862; inventories, 1840-1854; administrators' records, 1840-1870; guardians' records, 1840-1893; orphans' court proceedings, 1840-1849; land records, 1839-1850; license book, 1840-1850　C.H. Ellicott City
N: USlGS 10 reels　　　　　　7503
P: MdAA

HOWARD Co., Md.
Wills, 1863- ; orphans' court proceedings,

1840- ; land records, 1850-1918; chattel records, 1952　C.H. Ellicott City
N: MdAA　　　　　　　　　　7504

KENT Co., Md.
Wills, 1799-1854; inventories, 1788-1850; administrators' records, 1790-1850; guardians' records, 1790-1860; land records, 1790-1850
C.H. Chestertown
N: USlGS 37 reels　　　　　　7505
P: MdAA

KENT Co., Md.
Chancery records, 1939- ; wills, 1854- ; guardians' records, 1788-1798; orphans' court proceedings, 1803- ; marriage records, 1865-1888　C.H. Chestertown
N: MdAA　　　　　　　　　　7506

KENT Co., Md.
Court records, 1656-1662; marriage records, 1796-1866　MdHi
N: USlGS　　　　　　　　　　7507

KENT Co., Md.
Wills, 1669-1798; inventories, 1709-1788; administrators' records, 1664-1789; land records, 1648-1790　MdAA
N: MdAA　　　　　　　　　　7508
P: USlGS

KENT AND QUEEN ANNE COUNTIES, Md.
Marriages, 1763-1845　MdHi
N: USlGS　　　　　　　　　　7509

MONTGOMERY Co., Md.
Wills, 1777-1851, orphans' court proceedings, 1779-1855; land records, 1777-1851
C.H. Rockville
N: USlGS 30 reels　　　　　　7510
P: MdAA land records only from 1791

MONTGOMERY Co., Md.
Wills, 1852- ; orphans' court proceedings, 1855-　C.H. Rockville
N: MdAA　　　　　　　　　　7511

PRINCE GEORGE'S Co., Md.
Wills, 1854-1871, 1873- ; inventories, 1848- ; guardians' records, 1791-1828; orphans' court proceedings and guardian bonds, 1806-1812, 1824-1874, 1876-1903, 1908- ; administration accounts, 1849- ; land records, 1895-1922, 1948- ; marriage licenses, 1777-1884
C.H. Upper Marlboro
N: MdAA　　　　　　　　　　7512

PRINCE GEORGE'S Co., Md.
Wills, 1698-1854; inventories and accounts, 1696-1854; administrators' records, 1698-1857; guardians' records, 1703-1858; land records, 1789-1791, 1793-1794, 1796-1797, 1799-1801, 1803-1806, 1808, 1810-1812, 1815-1816, 1818-1819, 1821-1825, 1827, 1830-1831, 1833-1836, 1838, 1840, 1844-1845, 1847-1850
C.H. Upper Marlboro
N: USlGS 46 reels　　　　　　7513
P: MdAA land records; wills after 1833; inventories after 1792; guardians' records, 1789 and after 1808; administrators' records after 1784

PRINCE GEORGE'S Co., Md.
Land records, 1696-1789; marriage licenses, 1777-1818　MdAA
N: USlGS 10 reels　　　　　　7514
P: MdAA

QUEEN ANNE'S Co., Md.
Wills, 1791-1810, 1815-1837; inventories, 1795-1851; administrators' records, 1790-1857; guardians' records, 1798-1864; land records, 1788-1852　C.H. Centerville
N: USlGS 38 reels　　　　　　7515
P: MdAA

QUEEN ANNE'S Co., Md.
Wills, 1856- ; inventories, 1796, 1851-1855, 1857- ; administrators' records, 1853- ; guardians' records, 1853- ; orphans' court proceedings, 1799-1820, 1822- ; manumission record, 1849-1863; land records, 1852-1892, 1906- ; accounts of sales, 1823-1842, 1844-1852, 1855-1890　C.H. Centreville
N: MdAA　　　　　　　　　　7516

QUEEN ANNE'S Co., Md.
Wills, 1734-1791; inventories, 1739-1750, 1774-1791; administrators' records, 1741-1790; guardians' records, 1778-1800; deeds, 1714-1789　MdAA
N: USlGS 16 reels　　　　　　7517

ST. MARY'S Co., Md.
Wills, 1658-1857; inventories, 1795-1850; administrators' records, 1782-1852; guardians' records, 1779-1862; orphans' court records, 1807-1852; land records, 1781-1851
C. H. Leonardtown
N: MdAA 32 reels   7518

ST. MARY'S Co., Md.
Wills, 1857- ; inventories, 1859- ; administrators' records, 1808- ; orphans' court proceedings, 1777-1801, 1852- ; land records, 1950- ; assessment books, 1793-1794, 1796, 1801, 1806, 1812, 1821, 1826; militia enrollment, 1794 C. H. Leonardtown
N: MdAA   7519

SOMERSET Co., Md.
Wills, 1664-1722, 1777-1859; inventories, 1730-1850; administrators' records, 1751-1776, 1778-1851; guardians' accounts, 1828-1850; land records, 1790-1850
C. H. Princess Anne
N: USlGS 44 reels   7520
P: MdAA

SOMERSET Co., Md.
Wills, 1859- ; orphans' court proceedings, 1811-1836, 1838- C. H. Princess Anne
N: MdAA   7521

SOMERSET Co., Md.
Court records, 1665-1731; deeds, 1665-1790; land records, 1665-1850; vital records, 1650-1720; cattle marks, 1717-1723 MdAA
N: USlGS 13 reels   7522

SOMERSET Co., Md.
Marriage licenses, 1796-1831 MdHi
N: USlGS   7523

TALBOT Co., Md.
Wills, 1665-1862; inventories, 1635-1710, 1725-1829, 1834-1851; administrators' records, 1664-1860; distributions of estates, 1783-1821, 1825-1857; guardians' records, 1664-1878; land records, 1692-1850 C. H. Easton
N: USlGS 65 reels   7524
P: MdAA wills from 1848, guardians' records from 1845, land records from 1784

TALBOT Co., Md.
Wills, 1848- ; inventories, administrators' accounts, 1861; guardians' accounts, 1879-1901; orphans' court proceedings, 1852- ; distribution and releases, 1858-1897; releases, 1897
C. H. Easton
N: MdAA   7525

TALBOT Co., Md.
Land records, 1665-1673, 1676-1692 MdAA
N: USlGS 3 reels   7526

TALBOT Co., Md.
Miscellaneous marriage licenses, 1738-1751, 1794-1810 MdHi
N: USlGS   7527

WASHINGTON Co., Md.
Wills, 1777-1863; inventories, 1778-1823, 1828-1850; administrators' records, 1778-1856; guardians' records, 1776-1872; land records, 1777-1850; marriage records, 1799-1860 C. H. Hagerstown
N: USlGS 76 reels   7528
P: MdAA

WASHINGTON Co., Md.
Wills, 1850-; orphans' court proceedings, 1806-; marriage records, 1799-1886 C. H. Hagerstown
N: MdAA   7529

WICOMOCO Co., Md.
Wills, 1867- ; orphans' court proceedings, 1867-1944 C. H. Salisbury
N: MdAA   7530

WORCESTER Co., Md.
Court proceedings, 1806-1851; wills, 1790-1851; inventories, 1804-1851; administrators' records, 1792-1853; guardians' accounts, 1825-1856; land records, 1749-1815, 1818-1850 C. H. Snow Hill
N: USlGS   7531
P: MdAA wills only from 1806

WORCESTER Co., Md.
Court proceedings, 1782-1789; wills, 1665-1790; inventories, 1668-1789; administrators'

bonds, 1667-1793; land records, 1742-1760
MdAA
N: USlGS 9 reels   7532

WORCESTER Co., Md.
Marriage licenses, 1795-1865, 335 p. MdHi
N: USlGS   7533

City Records

BALTIMORE, Md.
Wills, 1852; orphans' court proceedings, 1850-; land records, 1850-1856; block books, 1851-
C. H. Baltimore
N: MdAA   7534

BALTIMORE, Md.
Marriage records, 1851-1856 MdHi
N: USlGS   7535

BALTIMORE, Md. BOARD OF SUPERVISORS OF ELECTIONS
Election returns, 1896-1936, 1956 Ibid.
N: Ibid. 8 reels   7536
P: MdBE

Town Records

BLADENSBURG, Md.
Record book, 1742-1836 priv.
N: MdAA   7537

CENTERVILLE, Md. TOWN COMMISSIONERS
Proceedings, 1776-1919 MdAA
N: MdAA 1 reel   7538

Church Records

ACCOKEEK, Md. ST. JOHN'S PARISH [PISATAWAY PARISH] (Episcopal)
Records, 1691-1805 MdHi
N: USlGS   7539

ALBERTON, Md. ST. ALBAN'S CHAPEL
Parish register, 1894-1918 MdAA
N: MdAA   7540

ALL FAITH'S PARISH (Episcopal), St. Mary's Co., Md.
Records, 1692-1892 MdAA
N: MdAA 2 reels   7541

ALL HALLOWS PARISH (Episcopal), Anne Arundel Co., Md.
Records, 1689-1956 MdAA
N: MdAA 2 reels   7542

ALL HALLOWS PARISH (Episcopal), Worcester Co., Md.
Records, 1844-1954 MdAA
N: MdAA 1 reel   7543

ALL SAINTS' PARISH (Episcopal), Calvert Co., Md.
Vestry minutes, 1703-1717, 1720-1753 MdAA
N: MdAA 1 reel   7544

ALL SAINTS PARISH (Episcopal), Frederick Co., Md.
Vital records, 1727-1863 MdHi
N: USlGS   7545

ALL SAINTS' PARISH (Episcopal), Talbot Co., Md.
Records, 1875-1950 MdAA
N: MdAA 1 reel   7546

ALLEN, Dr. ETHAN
Historical notes of Eastern Shore parishes (Episcopal) in Caroline, Cecil, Dorchester, Kent, Queen Anne's, Somerset, Talbot, and Worcester Counties and on Kent Island, v. 1-6
MdAA
N: MdAA 3 reels   P: USlGS   7547

ANNAPOLIS, Md. PRESBYTERIAN CHURCH
Records, 1870-1943 MdAA
N: MdAA 1 reel   7548

ANNAPOLIS, Md. ST. ANNE'S PARISH
Parish register, 1708-1785, 1858-1952, v. I-VII
MdAA
N: MdAA 3 reels   7549
P: MdAA

ANNAPOLIS, Md. ST. ANNE'S PARISH
Records, 1687-1818 MdHi
N: UslGS   7550

ARUNDEL CIRCUIT METHODIST PROTESTANT CHURCH, Md.
Records, 1830-1894 MdHi
N: USlGS   7551

BALTIMORE, Md. ASSOCIATE REFORMED CONGREGATION
Vital records, 1812-1865, 539 p. MdHi
N: USlGS   7552

BALTIMORE, Md. CATHEDRAL (Catholic)
Burial records of churches, 1793-1874, 3 v., 1352 p. MdHi
N: USlGS   7553

BALTIMORE, Md. CHRIST CHURCH (Episcopal)
Vital records, 1828-1871 MdHi
N: USlGS   7554

BALTIMORE, Md. CHURCH OF THE HOLY INNOCENTS (Episcopal)
Parish registers, 1899-1925 MdAA
N: MdAA 1 reel   7555

BALTIMORE, Md. CRANMER CHAPEL (Episcopal) (since 1870, CHURCH OF OUR SAVIOUR)
Vestry proceedings, 1844-1865 MdAA
N: MdAA 1 reel   7556

BALTIMORE, Md. ENGLISH LUTHERAN CHURCH
Parish register, 1857-1924 MdHi
N: USlGS   7557

BALTIMORE, Md. FIRST GERMAN REFORMED CHURCH
Registers, 1768-1851, v. 1-2 MdHi
N: USlGS   7558

BALTIMORE, Md. FIRST PRESBYTERIAN CHURCH
Vital records, 1767-1879 MdHi
N: USlGS   7559

BALTIMORE, Md. GERMAN EVANGELICAL REFORMED CHURCH
Records [partly in German script], 1798-1850
MdHi
N: USlGS   7560

BALTIMORE, Md. LIGHT STREET METHODIST EPISCOPAL CHURCH
Vital records, 1794-1835 MdHi
N: USlGS   7561

BALTIMORE, Md. MEMORIAL CHURCH OF THE HOLY COMFORTER [ST. MATTHEW'S CHAPEL] (Episcopal)
Parish register, 1875-1922 MdAA
N: MdAA   7562

BALTIMORE, Md. NEW JERUSALEM CHURCH (Swedenborgian)
Vital records, 1793-1862 MdHi
N: USlGS   7563

BALTIMORE, Md. RAPSBURG MISSION (Episcopal)
Parish register, 1907 MdAA
N: MdAA   7564

BALTIMORE, Md. ST. ANDREW'S CHURCH (Episcopal)
Lauraville Parish register, 1891-1907 MdAA
N: MdAA   7565

BALTIMORE, Md. ST. CLEMENT'S CHURCH (Episcopal) (near Rosedale)
Parish register, 1892-1895 MdAA
N: MdAA   7566

BALTIMORE, Md. ST. MARK'S CHURCH (Episcopal)
Records, 1847-1914 MdAA
N: MdAA 1 reel   7567

BALTIMORE, Md. ST. PAUL'S CHURCH (Episcopal)
Parish registers, 1710-1837, v. 1-2, 1376 p.
MdHi
N: USlGS   7568

BALTIMORE, Md. ST. PETER'S CHURCH (Episcopal)
Vital records, 1803-1885 MdHi
N: USlGS   7569

BALTIMORE, Md. ST. STEPHEN'S CHURCH
(Episcopal)
Records, 1857-1892 MdAA
N: MdAA 1 reel 7570

BALTIMORE, Md. SECOND BAPTIST CHURCH
Records PChHi
N: USIGS 1 reel 7571

BALTIMORE, Md. TRINITY CHURCH (Episcopal)
Records, 1802-1819, 1845-1904 MdAA
N: MdAA 2 reels 7572

BALTIMORE, Md. TRINITY CHURCH (Episcopal)
Records, 1806-1818 MdHi
N: USIGS 7573

BALTIMORE, Md. ZION GERMAN LUTHERAN
CHURCH
Vital records, 1789-1849, 1097 p. MdHi
N: USIGS 7574

BARRY, Rev. J. WILSON
Summary of history of Trinity Parish, Charles
Co., Md., 1750-1906 DLC
N: USIGS 7575

CAMBRIDGE, Md. DORCHESTER PARISH
Records, 1818-1892 MdHi
N: USIGS 7576

CAMBRIDGE, Md. DORCHESTER PARISH and
GREAT CHOPTANK PARISH [CHRIST CHURCH]
(Episcopal)
Register, 1738-1903 MdHi
N: USIGS 7577

CAMBRIDGE, Md. GREAT CHOPTANK PARISH
Records, 1788-1886 MdHi
N: USIGS 7578

CEDARCROFT, Md. CHAPEL OF THE NATIVITY
(Episcopal)
Parish register, 1912-1921 MdAA
N: MdAA 1 reel 7579

CENTREVILLE, Md. ST. PAUL'S PARISH
(Episcopal)
Records, 1837-1940 MdAA
N: MdAA 1 reel 7580

CHRIST CHURCH (Episcopal), Calvert Co., Md.
Minutes of the Brotherhood of St. Andrew,
1917-1928; records, 1685-1939 MdAA
N: MdAA 1 reel 7581

CHRIST CHURCH PARISH (Episcopal), Anne Arun-
del Co., Md.
Records, 1692-1957 MdAA
N: MdAA 1 reel 7582

CHRIST CHURCH PARISH (Episcopal), Queen
Anne's Co., Md.
Records, 1801-1909, 1912-1954 MdAA
N: MdAA 1 reel 7583

CHURCH HILL, Md. ST. LUKE'S PARISH
(Episcopal)
Records, 1722-1850, 648 p. MdHi
N: USIGS 7584

CHURCH OF JESUS CHRIST OF LATTER-DAY
SAINTS. MARYLAND
Branch and ward records: Baltimore and
Greenbelt, 1940-1948 USIC
N: USIGS 2 reels 7585

CORRUNA, Md. EMMANUEL CHURCH
(Episcopal)
Parish register, 1889-1908 MdAA
N: MdAA 1 reel 7586

COVENTRY PARISH (Episcopal), Somerset Co.,
Md.
Records, 1745-1828, 1848-1915 MdAA
N: MdAA 1 reel 7587

COVENTRY PARISH (Episcopal), Somerset Co.,
Md.
Records, 1734-1811, 1837-1898 MdHi
N: USIGS 7588

DAVIDSONVILLE, Md. ALL HALLOW'S PARISH
(Episcopal)
Records, 1685-1899 MdHi
N: USIGS 7589

DORCHESTER COUNTY AND DORCHESTER
PARISH, Md.

Vital records, 1743-1770, 1819-1853 MdHi
N: USIGS 7590

DURHAM PARISH (Episcopal), Charles Co., Md.
Vestry records, 1774-1824 DLC MdHi
N: USIGS 7591
P: MdAA

EASTON, Md. TRINITY CATHEDRAL
(Episcopal)
Records, 1869-1956 MdAA
N: MdAA 7592

FREDERICK, Md. EVANGELICAL LUTHERAN
CHURCH
Records, 1742-1807, 1810-1850, v. 1-5 MdHi
N: USIGS 7533

FREDERICK, Md. EVANGELICAL REFORMED
CHURCH
Records, 1746-1833, v. 1 (typescript) PLF
N: USIGS 7594

FREDERICK, Md. GERMAN REFORMED
CHURCH
Vital records, 1753-1900, v. 1-3, 1323 p.
MdHi
N: USIGS 7595

FREDERICK, Md. REFORMED CHURCH
Records (typescript) PLF
N: USIGS 7596

FREELAND, Md. CHAPEL OF THE HOLY
CROSS (Episcopal)
Parish register, 1888-1923 MdAA
N: MdAA 7597

FRIENDS, SOCIETY OF. BALTIMORE [Md.]
MONTHLY MEETING
Births and burials (membership), 1805-1844;
marriages, 1830-1937; minutes [copies of],
1792-1814; removals, 1829-1867; women's
minutes, 1814-1828 MdFBH
N: PSC-F 7598
P: PSC-F

FRIENDS, SOCIETY OF. BALTIMORE [Md.]
MONTHLY MEETING
Membership, 1807-1837 MdFBSR
N: PSC-F 7599
P: PSC-F

FRIENDS, SOCIETY OF. BALTIMORE [Md.]
QUARTERLY MEETING
Minutes, 1807-1823 MdFBH
N: PSC-F 7600
P: PSC-F

FRIENDS, SOCIETY OF. BALTIMORE [Md.]
YEARLY MEETING
Catalog of materials in the vault Ibid.
N: PSC-F 7601
P: PSC-F

FRIENDS, SOCIETY OF. BALTIMORE [Md.]
YEARLY MEETING
Minutes of meeting for sufferings, 1827-1877
MdFBH
N: PSC-F 7602
P: PSC-F

FRIENDS, SOCIETY OF (Primitive).
BALTIMORE [Md.] YEARLY MEETING
Meeting for sufferings, 1856-1868; men's
minutes, 1854-1868; ministers' and elders'
minutes, 1855-1865; women's minutes,
1854-1858 Ibid.
N: PSC-F 7603
P: PSC-F

FRIENDS, SOCIETY OF. CECIL [Md.]
MONTHLY MEETING
Births and deaths, 1668-1913; marriages,
1698-1784; men's minutes, 1698-1840;
women's minutes, 1765-1848 PSC-F
N: PSC-F 2 reels 7604
P: PSC-F USIGS

FRIENDS, SOCIETY OF. DEER CREEK [Md.]
MONTHLY MEETING
Births and deaths, 1761-1823 MdFBSR
N: PSC-F 7605
P: PSC-F

FRIENDS, SOCIETY OF. DEER CREEK [Md.]
MONTHLY MEETING

Births, deaths, marriages, and removals,
1817-1911; minutes, 1819-1845 Ibid.
N: PSC-F 7606
P: PSC-F

FRIENDS, SOCIETY OF. DUNNINGS CREEK
[Md.] QUARTERLY MEETING
Women's minutes, 1840-1905 MdFBH
N: PSC-F 7607
P: PSC-F

FRIENDS, SOCIETY OF. GUN POWDER [Md.]
MONTHLY MEETING
Births, deaths, and membership, 1716-1859
MdFBSR
N: PSC-F 7608
P: PSC-F

FRIENDS, SOCIETY OF. GUN POWDER [Md.]
PREPARATIVE MEETING
Minutes, 1829-1852 [includes deaths of North
Carolinians, 1719-1791] MdFBH
N: PSC-F 7609
P: PSC-F

FRIENDS, SOCIETY OF. INDIAN SPRING [Md.]
PREPARATIVE MEETING
Minutes, 1829-1840 MdFBH
N: PSC-F 7610
P: PSC-F

FRIENDS, SOCIETY OF. LITTLE FALLS [Md.]
MONTHLY MEETING
Births and deaths, 1738-1848; marriages,
1818-1873; removals, 1815-1871 MdFBSR
N: PSC-F 7611
P: PSC-F

FRIENDS, SOCIETY OF. MARYLAND HALF-
YEAR'S MEETING
Women's minutes, 1677-1790 MdFBH
N: PSC-F 7612
P: PSC-F

FRIENDS, SOCIETY OF. NORTHWEST
FORK [Md.] MONTHLY MEETING
Marriages and removals, 1832-1904 Ibid.
N: PSC-F 7613
P: PSC-F

FRIENDS, SOCIETY OF. NORTHWEST FORK
[Md.] MONTHLY MEETING
Marriages, 1801-1826; minutes, 1800-1855
C.H. Easton (Talbot Co.)
N: USIGS 7614
P: PSC-F

FRIENDS, SOCIETY OF. NOTTINGHAM [Md.]
MONTHLY MEETING
Births and deaths, 1691-1883; marriages,
1730-1889; men's minutes, 1730-1778;
removals, 1764-1855; women's minutes, 1740-
1778 Ibid.
N: Ibid. 7615
P: PSC-F

FRIEND'S SOCIETY OF. PATUXENT [Md.]
MONTHLY MEETING
Minutes, 1871-1918 MdFBH
N: PSC-F 7616
P: PSC-F

FRIENDS, SOCIETY OF. SANDY SPRING [Md.]
MONTHLY MEETING
Births, deaths, and membership, 1730-1895
MdFBSR
N: PSC-F 7617
P: PSC-F

FRIENDS, SOCIETY OF. SOUTHERN [Md.]
HALF-YEARLY MEETING
Minutes, 1759-1822; women's minutes,
1756-1816 PSC-F
N: PSC-F 7618
P: PSC-F USIGS

FRIENDS, SOCIETY OF. THIRD HAVEN [Md.]
Records, 1668, 1676-1765, 1784-1797 MdHi
N: USIGS 2 reels 7619

FRIENDS, SOCIETY OF. THIRD HAVEN [Md.]
MONTHLY MEETING
Births, 1665-1930; deaths, 1675-1941; index
to records, 1676-1897; marriages, 1668-1935;
men's minutes, 1676-1871; Nicholite births,
1760-1820; Nicholite marriages, 1767-1800;
removals sent, 1798-1912 PSC-F
N: USIGS 7620
P: PSC-F

FRIENDS, SOCIETY OF. WARRINGTON [Md.]
MONTHLY MEETING
Births and deaths, ca. 1731-1876; minutes,
1747-1763, 1805-1823   PYHi
N: PYHi
P: USIGS   7621

FRIENDS, SOCIETY OF. WEST RIVER [Md.]
QUARTERLY MEETING
Minutes, 1710-1775; women's minutes, 1703-
1774   MdFBH
N: PSC-F
P: PSC-F   7622

GARRISON FOREST, Md. ST. THOMAS PARISH
(Episcopal)
Records, 1728-1891, 421 p.   MdHi
N: USIGS   7623

GIBSON, ALEXANDER E.
Marriage register (Episcopal church), 1851-
1896   MdAA
N: MdAA 1 reel   7624

GIBSON, Rev. FRANK M.
Private vital church records (Episcopal), 1883-
1925   MdAA
N: MdAA 1 reel   7625

GRAYTON, Md. OLD DURHAM CHURCH
Proceedings of the vestry, 1824-1927   Ibid.
N: DLC 1 reel   7626

GREEN HILL CHURCH (Episcopal), Howard Co.
(formerly Anne Arundel Co.), Md.
Records, 1711-1857, 254 p.   MdHi
N: USIGS   7627

HAGERSTOWN, Md. REFORMED CHURCH
Vital records, 1766-1809   MdHi
N: USIGS   7628

HAGERSTOWN, Md. REFORMED CHURCH
Vital records, 1771-1944   PLF
N: USIGS 2 reels   7629

HAGERSTOWN, Md. ZION REFORMED CHURCH
Vital records, 1807-1849   MdHi
N: USIGS   7630

HILLSBORO, Md. ST. JOHN'S PARISH
(Episcopal)
Records, 1746-1858, 280 p.   MdHi
N: USIGS   7631

HOLY TRINITY PARISH (Episcopal), Talbot Co.,
Md.
Records, 1850-1853, 1898-1908, 1910-1930,
1946-1951   MdAA
N: MdAA   7632

HUGGINS, JAMES A.
Notes; Chapel of Ease, Dorchester Co., Md.
MdAA
N: MdAA   7633

HUNTERSVILLE, Md. ALL FAITH CHURCH
Vestry proceedings,etc., 1692-1820   DLC
N: USIGS   7634

I.U. PARISH (Episcopal), Kent Co., Md.
Records, 1861-1957   MdAA
N: MdAA 1 reel   7635

JERUSALEM LUTHERAN CHURCH, Carroll Co.,
Md.
Parish register, ca., 1793-1881   MdHi
N: USIGS   7636

JESSUP (formerly HOOVERSVILLE), Md.
ST. MARY'S CHURCH (Episcopal)
Parish register, 1871-1907   MdAA
N: MdAA   7637

JOPPA (later KINGVILLE), Md. ST. JOHN'S
PARISH (Episcopal)
Records, 1696-1851   MdHi
N: USIGS   7633

KING AND QUEEN PARISH (Episcopal), St.
Mary's Co., Md.
Records, 1839-1881   MdAA
N: MdAA 1 reel   7639

KING AND QUEEN PARISH, St. Mary's Co., Md.
Vestry minutes, 1799-1838   DLC
N: USIGS
P: MdAA   7640

LAUREL, Md. ST. PHILLIP'S PARISH
(Episcopal)
Vital records, 1846-1868   MdHi
N: USIGS   7641

LEELAND, Md. ST. BARNABAS CHURCH
(Episcopal)
Records, 1686-1773   MdHi
N: USIGS
P: MdAA   7642

LEELAND, Md. ST. PAUL'S PARISH (Episcopal)
Register, 1733-1879   MdHi
N: USIGS   7643

LEONARDTOWN, Md. ST. ANDREW'S
PARISH (Episcopal)
Records, 1736-1896   MdHi
N: USIGS
P: MdAA   7644

LEONARDTOWN, Md. ST. ANDREW'S PARISH
(Episcopal)
Vestry minutes, 1917-1944   MdAA
N: MdAA   7645

MacFARLAND, Rev. MALCOLM
Diary and register of St. Mark's Church (Epis-
copal), Baltimore, Md., 1841-1861   MdAA
N: MdAA 1 reel   7646

MANCHESTER, Md. REFORMED AND
LUTHERAN CHURCH
Record book, 1760-1836   PYHi
N: PYHi
P: USIGS   7647

MANCHESTER, Md. ZION LUTHERAN CHURCH
Vital records, 1783-1853   MdHi
N: USIGS   7648

MARTIN, Rev. HARRY
Register of Somerset Parish (Episcopal),
Somerset Co., Md., 1886-1893   MdAA
N: MdAA   7649

MARYLAND HISTORICAL SOCIETY
Records of Catholic congregations in Charles
County, 1793-1861: Upper and Lower Zachiah,
Mattawoman,and St. Mary's Bryantown   MdHi
N: USIGS   7650

MASON, HENRY M.
Diary re: St. Peter's Parish (Episcopal),
Talbot Co., Md., 1837-1868   MdAA
N: MdAA   7651

METHODIST CHURCH (United States).
CIRCUITS. HARFORD, Md.
Vital records, 1809-1876   MdHi
N: USIGS 1 reel   7652

MIDDLEHAM CHAPEL (Episcopal), Calvert Co.,
Md.
Register, 1900-1946, 1948-1957   MdAA
N: MdAA   7653

MIDDLETOWN, Md. ZION CHURCH (Lutheran)
Registers, 1779-1825   MdHi
N: USIGS   7654

MIDDLETOWN, Md. ZION LUTHERAN CHURCH
Registers, 1779-1827   Ibid.
N: PYHi
P: USIGS   7655

MILES RIVER PARISH (Episcopal), Talbot Co.,
Md.
Records, 1880-1894, 1903, 1906-1956   MdAA
N: MdAA 2 reels   7656

MT. CALVARY CHURCH (Episcopal), Howard
Co., Md.
Parish register, 1842-1923, 1936, 1940   MdAA
N: MdAA 1 reel   7657

NORTH SASSAFRAS PARISH, Md. ST.
STEPHEN'S CHURCH (Episcopal)
Records, 1693-1899   MdAA
N: MdAA   7658

ODENTOWN, Md. ST. PETER'S CHURCH
[ELLICOTT'S CHAPEL] (Episcopal)
Parish register, 1848-1918   MdAA
N: MdAA 1 reel   7659

PERRYMAN, Md. ST. GEORGE'S PARISH
Records, 1681-1799   MdHi
N: USIGS   7660

PIPE CREEK, Md. ST. BENJAMIN'S [KRIDER'S]
EVANGELICAL LUTHERAN CHURCH
Registers, 1766-1837   Ibid.
N: PYHi
P: USIGS   7661

PIPE CREEK, Md. ST. BENJAMIN'S [KRIDER'S]
LUTHERAN CHURCH
Records, 1763-1836   MdHi
N: USIGS   7662

POCOMOKE PARISH (Episcopal), Worcester Co.,
Md.
Records, 1855-1930   MdAA
N: MdAA 1 reel   7663

PORT REPUBLIC, Md. CHRIST CHURCH
PARISH (Episcopal)
Vital records, 1688-1847   MdHi
N: USIGS   7664

PRINCE GEORGE'S PARISH, Montgomery Co., Md.
Register, 1792-1845, v. 1   DLC
N: USIGS   7665

PRINCE GEORGE'S PARISH (Episcopal),
Montgomery Co., Md.
Records, 1711-1845   MdAA
N: MdAA   7666

PRINCE GEORGE'S PARISH (Episcopal), Montgo-
mery Co., Md.
Vital records, 1792-1845   MdHi
N: USIGS   7667

PROTESTANT EPISCOPAL CHURCH IN THE
U.S.A. DIOCESES. EASTON. NORTHERN
CONVOCATION
Book, 1880-1902   MdAA
N: MdAA 1 reel   7668

PROTESTANT EPISCOPAL CHURCH IN THE
U.S.A. SOUTHERN QUARTERLY MEETING
Minutes, 1834-1880   MdAA
N: MdAA 1 reel   7669

QUEEN ANNE PARISH (Episcopal), Prince
George's Co., Md.
Register, 1705/6-1773   DLC
N: USIGS
P: MdAA   7670

QUEEN ANNE PARISH (Episcopal), Prince
George's Co., Md.
Vital records, 1686-1777   MdAA
N: MdAA   7671

RIDOUT, Dr. JOHN
Brief history of Presbyterian Church,
Annapolis, Md.   MdAA
N: MdAA   7672

ROCK CREEK, Md. PRINCE GEORGE'S PARISH
(Episcopal)
Records, 1726-1832   MdHi
N: USIGS   7673

ROSSVILLE, Md. CHURCH OF THE HOLY
COMFORTER (Episcopal)
Parish register, 1896-1910   MdAA
N: MdAA 1 reel   7674

ST. BARNABAS CHURCH (Episcopal), Prince
George Co., Md.
Vestry records, 1705/6-1773; vital records,
1686-1777   Ibid.
N: MdAA 1 reel   7675

ST. JAMES PARISH (Episcopal), Anne Arundel
Co., Md.
Records, 1682-1869, 1120 p.   MdHi
N: USIGS   7676

ST. JAMES and ST. JOHN PARISHES (Episcopal),
Baltimore Co., Md.
Registers, 1787-1883. v.1-2   MdHi
N: USIGS   7677

ST. JOHN'S PARISH, Charles and Prince George's
Counties, Md.
Records, 1784-1878   DLC
N: USIGS   7678

ST. JOHN'S PARISH, Charles and Prince George's
Counties, Md. CHRIST CHURCH (Episcopal)
Vestry minutes, 1824-1934   MdAA
N: MdAA 2 reels   7679

ST. JOHN'S PARISH, Harford Co., Md.

ST. JOHN'S CHURCH (Episcopal)
Records, 1787-1895 MdHi
N: USIGS   7680

ST. JOHN'S PARISH (Episcopal), Harford Co.,
Md.
Records, 1792-1891 MdHi
N: USIGS   7681

ST. JOHN'S PARISH (Episcopal), Prince
George's Co., Md.
Records, 1784-1874   MdAA
N: MdAA 1 reel   7682

ST. MARGARET'S WESTMINSTER PARISH,
Anne Arundel Co., Md.
Parish register, 1680-1885 MdAA
N: MdAA 1 reel
P: MdAA   7683

ST. MARK'S PARISH (Episcopal), Frederick Co.,
Md.
Vestry records, 1829-1916 MdAA
N: MdAA   7684

ST. MARK'S PARISH, Frederick Co., Md.
ST. MARK'S CHURCH (Episcopal)
Records, 1789, 1801, 1806-1830 MdAA
N: MdAA 1 reel   7685

ST. MARY ANNE'S PARISH (Episcopal), Cecil Co.,
Md.
Records, 1711-1799, 1824-1931 MdAA
N: MdAA   7686

ST. MARY ANNE'S PARISH (Episcopal), Cecil Co.,
Md.
Vital records, 1687-1837 MdHi
N: USIGS   7687

ST. MARY'S WHITE CHAPEL PARISH (Episcopal),
Caroline Co., Md.
Register, 1951-1956 MdAA
N: MdAA 1 reel   7688

ST. MICHAEL'S CHURCH (Episcopal), Talbot
Co., Md.
Records, 1627-1831 Ibid.
N: PHi 1 reel   7689

ST. MICHAEL'S PARISH (Episcopal), Talbot Co.,
Md.
Records, 1672-1704, 1731-1859 MdHi
N: USIGS   7690

ST. MICHAEL'S PARISH, Talbot Co., Md.
CHRIST CHURCH (Episcopal)
Records, 1852-1933 Ibid.
N: MdAA 1 reel   7691

ST. PAUL'S PARISH (Episcopal), Calvert Co.,
Md.
Parish register, 1841-1938 MdAA
N: MdAA 1 reel   7692

ST. PAUL'S PARISH (Episcopal), Kent Co., Md.
Records, 1679-1956 MdAA
N: MdAA 2 reels   7693

ST. PAUL'S PARISH (Episcopal), Kent Co., Md.
Records, 1650-1818 MdHi
N: USIGS   7694

ST. PAUL'S PARISH (Episcopal), Prince George's
Co., Md.
Vestry minutes, 1733-1819 DLC
N: USIGS
P: MdAA   7695

ST. PAUL'S PARISH (Episcopal), Queen Anne's
Co., Md.
Records, 1694-1819, v. 1-2, 563 p. MdHi
N: USIGS   7696

ST. PAUL'S -BY-THE-SEA PARISH (Episcopal),
Worcester Co., Md.
Records, 1918-1932, 1935-1957 MdAA
N: MdAA 1 reel   7697

ST. PETER'S CHAPEL (Episcopal), Calvert Co.,
Md.
Register, 1900-1947 MdAA
N: MdAA   7698

ST. PETER'S PARISH (Episcopal), Montgomery
Co., Md.
Vital records, 1797-1854 MdHi
N: USIGS   7699

ST. PETER'S PARISH (Episcopal),
Talbot Co., Md.
Records, 1681-1948 MdAA
N: MdAA 3 reels   7700

ST. PETER'S PARISH (Episcopal),
Talbot Co., Md.
Records, 1681-1855, v. 1-2, 917 p.   MdHi
N: PHi USIGS   7701

ST. STEPHEN'S PARISH, Cecil Co., Md.
Records, 1687-1837 MdHi
N: PHi 1 reel   7702

ST. STEPHEN'S [NORTH SASSAFRAS] PARISH
(Episcopal), Cecilton and Earleville, Cecil
Co., Md.
Vestry proceedings, 1693-1804, v. 1-2 MdHi
N: USIGS   7703

SALEM GERMAN REFORMED CHURCH, Conoco-
cheague District, Md.
Records of births, etc. (fragmentary), 1771-
1802 MdHi
N: USIGS   7704

SALEM REFORMED CHURCH, Franklin Co., Md.
Register, 1793-1834 Ibid.
N: PYHi
P: USIGS   7705

SAMUEL'S LUTHERAN AND REFORMED CHURCH,
Somerset Co., Md.
Records, 1784-1793 PGL
N: USIGS   7706

SHREWSBURY PARISH (Episcopal), Kent Co.,
Md.
Records, 1687-1945; "The Judgment" MdAA
N: MdAA 3 reels   7707

SHREWSBURY PARISH (Episcopal), Kent Co., Md.
Records, 1702-1882, v. 1-3, 1067 p. MdHi
N: USIGS   7708

SILVER RUN, Md. ST. MARY'S LUTHERAN
CHURCH
Register, ca. 1784-1851 PYHi
N: PYHi 1 reel
P: USIGS   7709

SILVER RUN, Md. ST. MARY'S REFORMED
CHURCH
Records, 1762-1866 Ibid.
N: PYHi
P: USIGS   7710

SOMERSET PARISH (Episcopal), Somerset Co.,
Md.
Records, 1689-1956 MdAA
N: MdAA 3 reels   7711

SPRINGHILL PARISH (Episcopal), Wicomico Co.,
Md.
Records, 1832-1944 MdAA
N: MdAA   7712

STEPNEY PARISH, Wicomico Co., Md.
Records, 1738-1838 MdAA
N: MdAA   7713

STEPNEY PARISH (now BIVALVE), Md.
GREENHILL CHURCH (Episcopal)
Records, 1703-1890 MdHi
N: USIGS   7714

STEWART, Rev. HENSEY JOHN
Journal re: Stepney Parish (Episcopal),
Wicomico Co., Md., 1840-1845 MdAA
N: MdAA   7715

SUNDERLAND, Md. ALL SAINTS CHURCH
(Episcopal)
Vestry proceedings, 1702-1753 MdHi
N: USIGS   7716

TRINITY CHURCH, Charles Co., Md.
Records, 1794-1856 DLC
N: USIGS   7717

TRINITY PARISH (Episcopal), Anne Arundel and
Howard Cos., Md.
Records, 1866-1909 MdAA
N: MdAA   7718

TRINITY PARISH, Charles Co., Md.
Records, 1750-1856 DLC
N: USIGS   7719

TRINITY PARISH (Episcopal), Charles Co., Md.
Records, 1654-1726, 1749-1797 MdHi
N: USIGS   7720

TRINITY PARISH (Episcopal), Charles Co., Md.
Records and history, 1750-1906 MdAA
N: MdAA 2 reels   7721

TRINITY PARISH, Charles Co., Md. TRINITY
CHURCH (Episcopal)
Records, 1729-1804, 1817-1922 MdAA
N: MdAA 1 reel   7722

VIENNA PARISH, Md. ST. PAUL'S CHURCH
(Episcopal)
Records, 1869-1957 MdAA
N: MdAA 2 reels   7723

WALKERSVILLE, Md. GLADE REFORM
CHURCH CHARGE
Register, 1863-1865 MdHi
N: USIGS   7724

WESTERN RUN, Md. ST. JOHN'S CHURCH
(Episcopal)
Vestry minutes, 1820-1891 MdAA
N: MdAA   7725

WESTERN RUN PARISH, Md. ST. JOHN'S CHURCH
IN THE VALLEY (Episcopal)
Records, 1782-1854 MdHi
N: USIGS   7726

WESTMINSTER PARISH, Md. ST. MARGARET'S
CHURCH (Episcopal)
Records, ca. 1699 - ca. 1885 MdHi
N: MdAA 1 reel   7727

WESTMINSTER PARISH, Md.
ST. MARGARET'S CHURCH (Episcopal)
Register, 1673-1885, 832 p. MdHi
N: USIGS   7728

WHITEMARSH PARISH (Episcopal), Talbot Co.,
Md.
Parish register, 1857-1954 MdAA
N: MdAA 1 reel   7729

WILLIAM AND MARY'S PARISH, St. Mary's Co.,
Md.
Records, 1798-1923 DLC
N: USIGS   7730

WINTER'S CHURCH, Frederick Co. (now
ST. LUKE'S, Carroll Co.), Md.
Records, 1783-1873 PGL
N: USIGS   7731

WOODSTOCK COLLEGE OF BALTIMORE
COUNTY, Md.
Land records of St. Indigoes and Newtown res-
idences; Fenwick, Sewall, Brent, and Brooke
papers; miscellaneous papers, rent rolls, St.
Mary's Co.   MdAA
N: MdAA 1 reel   7732

WORCESTER PARISH (Episcopal), Worcester Co.,
Md.
Register, 1846-1893 MdAA
N: MdAA 1 reel   7733

WORCESTER PARISH , Md. ST. MARTINS
CHURCH (Episcopal)
Records, 1722-1840 MdAA
N: MdAA 1 reel   7734

WYE PARISH (Episcopal), Queen Anne's Co., Md.
Records, 1859-1957 MdAA
N: MdAA 1 reel   7735

ZION PARISH (Episcopal), Frederick Co., Md.
Records, 1820-1911 MdAA
N: MdAA   7736

Personal Papers

ARMSTRONG, ALEXANDER
Selected speeches and addresses priv.
N: MdAA 1 reel   7737

BROOKBANK, SPENCER
Family deeds, patents, re: St. Mary's Co.,
1743, 1771, 1787 MdAA
N: MdAA   7738

CALLISTER, HENRY
Correspondence, 1741-1780, 4 v. MdBD
DCO: NN
N: CU 1 reel   7739

CALVERT FAMILY, Md.
Rent rolls, 1639-1762; Calvert papers, 1516-
1768; Fort Cumberland muster rolls, 1757-
1758; early settlers, 1633-1680 MdHi
N: USIGS 7 reels   7740

CHALMERS, GEORGE
Maryland papers, 1619-1812 NN
N: MdBE   7741

DENT, GEORGE B., St. Mary's Co., Md.
Surveyors' books and other family records,
1869-1872, 1874-1907 MdAA
N: MdAA 1 reel   7742

DuBOIS MARTIN, FRANÇOIS AUGUSTIN
Papers MdHi
N: NjP 1 reel   7743

EMORY, Gen. THOMAS
Diary, 1837 MdAA
N: MdAA 1 reel   7744

GOUGH, HARRY DORSEY
Letter book, 1790-1797 MdHi
N: WaU film strip   7745

HAMILTON, Dr. ALEXANDER, 1712-1756
Itinerarium, 1744, 278 p. CsmH
N: ViWI   7746

HANCOCK, JAMES E., of Baltimore, Md.
Fort McHenry, Baltimore priv.
N: MdAA   7747

HUME, FANNIE PAGE
Diary, 1861, 1862 priv.
N: NcU 2 reels   7748

LIND, E. G.
Diary, 1855-1856; accounts, 1855-1902
MdBP
DCO: DLC 1 box   7749

LUX, WILLIAM
Letter book (Baltimore), 1763-1768 NHi
N: CU 1 reel   7750

McHENRY, JAMES, 1783-1816
Papers, 1798-1812 MdAN
N: NjP 1 reel   7751

POWELL, WILLOUGHBY
Autobiography priv.
N: MdAA 1 reel   7752

SCHOEPF, JOHANN DAVID
Travels in Confederation, 1783-1784 [trans.
from German] MdBE
N: MdAA 1 reel   7753

Business Papers

BOHEMIA MANOR, Md.
Day book, 1735/6-1760
DCO: priv.
N: De   7754

BRICE, JOHN, Deputy Notary Public, Annapolis,
Md., collector
Declarations by masters of vessels re: parti-
culars of voyages, 1734-1743 MdHi
N: MdAA   7755

CUMBERLAND VALLEY R.R. COMPANY
Report of William Minor Roberts, 1835-1836
MdAA
N: MdAA   7756

PINKNEY, ROBERT
Account book, 1764-1766 MdAA
N: MdAA 1 reel   7757

U.S. LIBRARY OF CONGRESS
Maryland and Virginia mercantile accounts,
1761 DLC
N: NjP 1 reel   7758

Collections

JONES, Mrs. STEPHEN, collector
Fenwick-Taney family papers re: land
records, St. Mary's Co., Md., 1789, 1796,
1799, 1801, 1817, 1818, 1820, 1842 MdAA
N: MdAA 1 reel   7759

MARYLAND HISTORICAL SOCIETY
Records of marriages in Maryland and Delaware,
1777-1804, 703 p. Ibid.
N: USIGS   7760

Institutions

SOCIETY OF THE ARK AND DOVE
Membership applications, 1910-1953 Ibid.
N: USIGS 1 reel   7761
P: USIGS

SOCIETY OF THE WAR OF 1812 and ASSOCIATION
OF THE DESCENDANTS OF THE DEFENDERS
OF BALTIMORE
Applications, 4 v. MdHi
N: USIGS 2 reels   7762
P: MdAA

TUESDAY CLUB, Annapolis, Md.
Records, May 27, 1755- Feb. 10, 1756 DLC
N: NhD 1 reel   7763

UNION SOCIETY OF JOURNEYMEN CORD-
WAINERS, Baltimore
Constitution, by-laws, and minutes,
1806-1909 MdAA
N: ViWI 40 frames   7764

School Records

BALTIMORE, Md. Mrs. CALLISTER'S SCHOOL
Records, 1783-1788   Callister papers MdAA
N: MdAA   7765

CHARLOTTE HALL SCHOOL, Charlotte Hall,
Md. TRUSTEES
Minutes, 1774-1805 MdAA
N: MdAA   7766

DISTRICT OF COLUMBIA

Census

U.S. CENSUS. SECOND, 1800
Population schedules, District of Columbia
DNA
N: DNA 1 reel   7767
P: USIGS

U.S. CENSUS. FOURTH, 1820
Population schedules, District of Columbia
DNA
N: DNA 1 reel   7768
P: USIGS

U.S. CENSUS. FIFTH, 1830
Population schedules, District of Columbia
DNA
N: DNA 1 reel   7769
P: PHi TxD USIGS

U.S. CENSUS. SIXTH, 1840
Population schedules, District of Columbia
DNA
N: DNA 1 reel   7770
P: USIGS

U.S. CENSUS. SEVENTH, 1850
Population schedules, District of Columbia
DNA
N: DNA 2 reels   7771
P: USIGS

U.S. CENSUSES. SEVENTH TO TENTH, 1850-
1880
Agricultural, manufacturing, social statistics
schedules, District of Columbia NcD
N: NcD 1 reel   7772

U.S. CENSUS. EIGHTH, 1860
Population schedules, District of Columbia
DNA
N: DNA 1 reel   7773
P: USIGS

U.S. CENSUS. NINTH, 1870
Population schedule, District of Columbia
DNA
N: DNA 1 reel   7774

U.S. CENSUS. TENTH, 1880
Defectives, dependents, delinquents,
paupers and indigents, special manufacturing
schedules, District of Columbia NcD
N: NcD   7775

U.S. CENSUS. TENTH, 1880
Population schedules, District of Columbia
DNA
N: DNA 4 reels   7776

Government Records

DISTRICT OF COLUMBIA. COMMISSIONERS
Proceedings, 1791-1802 DNA
N: DNA 1 reel [T-69]   7777

Church Records

CHURCH OF JESUS CHRIST OF LATTER-DAY
SAINTS. WASHINGTON, D.C.
Ward and branch records: Washington USIC
N: USIGS   7778

Personal Papers

GREEN, BERNARD RICHARDSON
Journal of operations on the building of the
Library of Congress, 1888-1893 priv.
DCO: DLC   7779

RIGGS FAMILY
Papers, 1854-1858 priv.
N: DLC 1 reel*   7780

Business Papers

GIDEON, JACOB AND GEORGE S., merchants,
Washington, D.C.
Account books, 1845-1849 DLC
N: I 1 reel   7781

Collections

GREEN, BERNARD C., compiler
Scrapbooks [Washingtoniana] priv.
N: DLC 1 reel   7782

Institutions

FREEMASONS. WASHINGTON, D.C.
Charters of Washington Lodges, 1802-1947,
50 p. priv.
N: DLC   7783
PP: DLC

THE SOUTH

Personal Papers

ALLEN-SIMPSON FAMILY
Papers, 1857-1878, 103 items priv.
N: NcU 1 reel   7784

ALLISON, J. MACK, Jr.
Diary, 1943 (typescript), 14 p. priv.
N: NcU 1 reel   7785

BACON, HENRY, 1822-1891
Diary, 1876-1877, 1880-1886, 1888-1891, 6 v.
priv.
N: NcU 522 frames   7786

BALL, HENRY WARING, 1858-1934
Diaries, 1884-1928, 13 v. priv.
N: NcU 1 reel   7787

BALL, WILLIAM J.
Books, 1804-1890, 3 v. priv.
N: NcU 186 frames   7788

BASINGER, WILLIAM STARR, 1827-1910
Reminiscences and family papers, 1896-1932
(typescript) priv.
N: NcU 1 reel   7789

BAYNE-GAYLE FAMILY
Papers: journal of Sarah Anne Gayle, 1827-

1831; Hugh A. Bayne memoirs, 1870-1928,
3 v.   priv.
N: NcU 206 frames and 3 reels   7790

BERRY, ELIZA USHER
Papers and book, 1830-1843, 7 items priv.
N: NcU 65 frames   7791

BLACKBURN, GEORGE
Records, 1816-1864 priv.
N: NcU 110 frames   7792

BROOKS, JOHN STANLEY, d. 1864
Letters, 1861-1864, 24 items priv.
N: NcU 1 reel   7793

BROUN, JOHN PETER
Papers, 1819-1934 priv.
N: NcU 1 reel   7794

BROWN, JOHN W., 1800-?
Diary, 1821-1822, 1852-1865 (typescript),
341 p. priv.
N: NcU 300 frames   7795

BUCK, IRVING A.
Papers, 1860-1865 priv.
N: NcU 96 frames   7796

BUTLER, LUCY WOOD (Mrs. WADDY B.)
Papers, including diary, 1859-1863, 178 p.
(typescript) priv.
N: NcU   7797

CALDER, WILLIAM, b. 1844
Diary, 1861, 1865, 2 v. priv.
N: NcU 83 frames   7798

CALDER, WILLIAM, b. 1844
Papers, 1861-1865 NcD
N: NcD   7799

CARMOUCHE, ANNIE JETER
Papers and reminiscences,1853-1915, 40 items
and 266 p. priv.
N: NcU 396 frames   7800

CARR, OBED W.
Diaries: 1873, 1879-1881, 1883-1884 priv.
N: NcD   7801

CASWELL, WILLIAM RICHARD, 1809-1862
Papers, 1805-1900 priv.
N: NcU 514 frames   7802

CHAPRON, JOHN M.
Papers and lettercopy book, 1800-1944, 156
items and 1 v. priv.
N: NcU 390 frames   7803

CHESTER, MARY JANE
Papers, 1840-1847, 82 items priv.
N: NcU 166 frames   7804

CHINA, ALFRED J.
Papers, 1837-1901 priv.
N: NcD 1 reel   7805

CHOTARD, ELIZA WILLIAMS
Autobiography, 1868, 32 p. (typescript) priv.
N: NcU   7806

CLARKE, MAXWELL TROAX
Papers, 1854-1890, 80 items priv.
DCO: NcU   7807

CLAXTON, ALEXANDER, ca. 1790-1841
Letters to Francis Sorrel, 1832-1839 (type-
script) priv.
N: NcU 1 reel   7808

COBB-HUNTER FAMILY
Papers, 1819-1904, 154 items, 6 v. priv.
N: NcU 480 frames   7809

COFFEE, AARON
Papers, 1840-1878, 20 items priv.
N: NcU 58 frames   7810

COGGIN, J.R.
Papers, 1813-1847 priv.
N: Nc-Ar 1 reel   7811

COGHILL, J.F., 1842-1926
Letters, 1862-1864, 14 items priv.
N: NcU 1 reel   7812

COLCOCK, WILLIAM FERGUSON, 1804-1889
Autobiography, 52 p. priv.
N: NcU 33 frames   7813

COLMER, GEORGE, 1807-1878
Diary, 1842-1878 LNHT
N: LSU 2 reels   7814
P: NcU

COPELAND, DAVID THOMAS
Diary, 1884-1888 priv.
N: NcU 192 frames   7815

COTTRELL, JOSEPH BENSON, 1829-1895
Diary, scrapbook, 1854-1892 priv.
N: NcU 194 frames   7816

CRAFT-FORT-THORNE FAMILIES
Papers, 1820-1878, 111 items, 4 pamphlets,
1 v. priv.
N: NcU 414 frames   7817

DAVIS, HAYNE, 1868-1942
Papers re: Practical Peace League
(typescript) priv.
N: NcU 56 frames   7818

DAWSON, NATHANIEL HENRY RHODES, 1829-
1895
Papers, 1851-1917 priv.
N: NcU 550 frames   7819

DEAVER, S.O.
Diary, 1886-1895 priv.
N: NcU 102 frames   7820

DEVEREUX, MARGARET MORDECAI
Letters, 1837-1856, 60 items priv.
N: NcU 1 reel   7821

DOCKERY FAMILY
Papers re: Alfred and Wm. Alfred, 4 items
priv.
N: NcU 1 reel   7822

DOUGLAS FAMILY
Papers, 1837-1859, 61 items priv.
N: NcU 164 frames   7823

DRANE, ANTHONY
Papers, 1820-1863, 24 items priv.
N: NcD   7824

DUPRE, LAURENT
Papers, 1862, 1865-1866, 27 items priv.
N: NcU 48 frames   7825

ELLWOOD, CHARLES A.
Scrapbook NcD
N: NcD   7826
P: NcD

ERWIN, GEORGE PHIFER
Papers priv.
N: NcU 147 frames   7827

EUBANK, HENRY
Diary priv.
N: Nc-Ar 1 reel   7828

FARMER, JOHN
Papers, 1760-1891 priv.
N: Nc-Ar 1 reel   7829

FISHBURNE, CLEMENT DANIEL, b. 1832
Recollections, ca. 1830-ca. 1875, written
ca. 1885 ViU
Transcript in typescript, 168 p. priv.
N: NcU 170 frames of typescript   7830

FORREST FAMILY
Papers, 1847-1898, re: French Forrest, 1796-
1866, and Douglas Forrest, 1837-1902 priv.
N: NcU 2 reels   7831

FORT FAMILY
Papers, 1812-1883, 88 items priv.
N: NcU 1 reel   7832

FRONTIS, STEPHEN, 1792-1867
Autobiography, 1792-1820 priv.
N: NcU 64 frames   7833

FUNSTEN, DAVID, 1819-1866
Family papers, 1811-1902 (typescript)
priv.
N: NcU 1 reel   7834

GARNETT-WISE FAMILIES
Papers, 1624-1884, 67 items priv.
N: NcU 1 reel   7835

GAYLE-CRAWFORD FAMILY
Papers and books, 1826-1895, 11 v., 19 items
priv.
N: NcU 1 reel   7836

GILLIS, MARCELLIN, b. 1824
Papers, 1825-1925, 461 items priv.
N: NcU 1108 frames   7837

GILMER, MORGAN S.
Papers (typescript) priv.
N: NcD 1 reel   7838

GRATTAN, MARY E.
Papers, 1861-1865, 15 items priv.
N: NcU   7839

GRIFFITHS, THOMAS
Journal, 1767-1768 Etruria Museum,
Hanley, England
N: NcU 24 frames   7840

GRIFFITHS, THOMAS
Journal of visit to the Cherokees, 1767 priv.
N: Nc-Ar   7841

GRIMBALL, JOHN BERKLEY
Diary, 1832-1883; papers, 1871-1874 priv.
N: NcD 2 reels   7842

GRIMBALL, META MORRIS
Diary, Dec., 1860-Feb., 1866 priv.
N: NcD 1 reel   7843

GUNTER-POELLNITZ FAMILY
Papers, 1853-1881, 15 items priv.
N: NcU 1 reel   7844

HABERSHAM, ROBERT
Diary, 1831-1832 (typescript) priv.
N: NcU 1 reel   7845

HAIGH, WILLIAM HOOPER, 1823-1870
Diary, 1841-1844 (typescript) NcU
N: NcU 1 reel   7846

HAMILTON, ELI SPINKS
Letters, 1861-1864, 38 items priv.
N: NcU 1 reel   7847

HAMILTON, JAMES, 1786-1857
Papers, 1810-1862, 40 items
priv.
N: NcU 1 reel*   7848

HAMILTON, W. S.
Papers, 1783-1888, 1924 L
N: NcU 6 reels   7849

HARALSON, ELIZABETH WOOD
Papers, 1772-1951, 118 p. (typescript) priv.
N: NcU 125 frames   7850

HARALSON, HERNDON, b. 1757
Diary, 1837-1847, 130 p.; index, 12 p. priv.
N: NcU of index
DCO: NcU of diary   7851

HARDAWAY, ROBERT ARCHELAUS, b. 1829
Book, 1844-1897 (typescript) priv.
N: NcU 384 frames   7852

HARPER, GEORGE W.F., 1834-1921
Diaries, 1846-1921 NcU
N: NcU 7 reels   7853

HARPER, KENTON, 1801-1867
Papers, 1838-1949 priv.
N: NcU 328 frames   7854
P: NcU

HARRINGTON, HENRY WILLIAM, b. 1793
Diary, 1826-1864, 64 p. (ditto copy) priv.
N: NcU 1 reel   7855

HAYNE, PAUL HAMILTON
Letters to Bayard Taylor, 1859-1878 NIC
N: NcD 1 reel   7856

HEDGECOCK, WILLIAM M.
Letters, 1861-1863, 41 items priv.
N: NcU 65 frames   7857

HENTZ FAMILY
Papers, 1826-1865, 23 items priv.
N: NcU 1 reel   7858

HEYWARD-FERGUSON FAMILY
Papers, 1806-1923, 216 items, 2 pamphlets,
10 v. priv.
N: NcU 1 reel   7859

HILL, FREDERICK JONES
Medical notes, 1812 priv.
N: NcU 1 reel   7860

HINES, CHARLES
Papers priv.
N: Nc-Ar 1 reel   7861

HINES, JOHN WILSON, 1841-1915
Papers, 1862-1866, 1872, 73 items priv.
N: NcU 1 reel   7862

HOLMES, EMMA E., 1838-1910
Diary, 1861-1866, 3 v. v.1-2 NcD;

(typescript) priv.; v. 3 priv.
N: NcU of priv. 7863

HOOK, JOHN, 1745-1808
Letters, 1727-1823; diaries, 1770-1773, 1795, 1799, 1802, 1807 NcD
N: NcD 6 reels 7864

HOOPER, JOHN
Letters, 1863-1865, 213 p. (typescript) priv.
N: NcU 1 reel 7865

HOPKINSON, JOSEPH, 1770-1842
Papers (selected letters from William Gaston), 1822-1841, 10 items PPGen
DCO: NcU 7866

HUGUENIN-JOHNSTON FAMILY
Papers, 1827-1866, 32 items priv.
N: NcU 1 reel 7867

HUME, FANNIE PAGE, 1838-1865
Diaries, 1861-1862, 2 v. priv.
N: NcU 2 reels 7868

IREDELL, CADWALLADER J.
Papers, 1862-1865, 64 items NcU
N: NcU 1 reel 7869

JACKSON-McKINNE FAMILY
Papers, 1817-1871, 19 items priv.
N: NcU 151 frames 7870

JANIN, EUGENE
Papers, 1854-1866, 14 items CSmH
DCO: NcU 7871

JENKINS, DONELSON CAFFERY, b. 1841
Diary, 1862-1865 priv.
N: NcU 66 frames 7872

JOHNSTON, CHARLES W.
Papers, 1820-1853, 23 items priv.
N: NcU 1 reel 7873

JONES, CADWALLADER, b. 1843
Papers, 1859-1925, 200 items NcU
N: NcU 1 reel 7874

JONES, CATESBY AP ROGER, 1821-1877
Journal, 1843-1845 priv.
N: NcU 1 reel 7875

KEAN-PRESCOTT FAMILY
Papers, 1779-1881 priv.
N: NcU 137 frames 7876

KENNEDY, FRANCIS MILTON
Diary, 1853-1864, 64 p. (typescript) priv.
N: NcU 70 frames
P: NcU 7877

KENNEDY, JOHN PENDLETON, 1795-1870
Journal, 1829-1839, May-Oct., 1856 (voyage to England and Continent) priv.
N: NcD 1 reel 7878

KEY, DAVID McKENDREE, 1824-1900
Papers, 1839-1901 priv.
N: NcU 905 frames 7879

KURTZ, GEORGE W.
Books, 1861-1865, 2 v. priv.
N: NcU 71 frames 7880

LAW, EVANDER McIVOR, 1836-1920
Papers, 1860-1864, 479 items priv.
N: NcU 900 frames 7881

LAWSON, JOHN, d. 1712
Letters, 1701-1711, 5 items Sloane papers UKLBM
N: NcU 1 reel 7882

LAY, HENRY CHAMPLIN
Diary, 1862-1865, 2 v. NcU
N: NcU 1 reel 7883

LEE, EDWIN G., 1835-1870
Diary, 1864-1865, 1 v. priv.
N: NcU 65 frames 7884

LEE-MARSHALL FAMILY
Papers, 1811-1870, 15 items priv.
N: NcU 1 reel 7885

LEROY, JAMES A.
Letters, 1906-1908 ICN
N: NcD 7886

LESESNE, JOSEPH W., 1811-1856
Papers, 1833-1848, 16 items priv.
N: NcU
DCO: NcU 13 pages 7887

LESTER-GRAY FAMILY
Documents re: Joseph Glover Baldwin priv.
N: NcU 7888

LONDON, JOHN, 1747-1816
Journal, 1776 (typescript) priv.
N: NcU 1 reel 7889

LONDON FAMILY
Papers, 1881-1933, 8 v. priv.
N: NcU 2 reels 7890

LYONS, JAMES, 1802-1882
Papers, 1821, 15 items priv.
N: NcU 46 frames 7891

McCLELLAN-STONEBRAKER-McCARTNEY FAMILIES
Papers and books, 1822-1866 priv.
N: NcU 352 frames 7892

McDONALD, CHARLES J., 1793-1860
Papers, 1830-1860, 7 items priv.
N: NcU 7893

McDOWELL, WILLIAM WALLACE, 1824-1893
Papers, 1805-1886, 33 items priv.
N: NcU 91 frames 7894

McINTOSH, A. C.
Papers, 1848-1849, 22 items priv.
N: NcU 1 reel 7895

McINTOSH, DAVID GREGG, 1836-1916
Papers, 1910, 134 p. (typescript) priv.
N: NcU 140 frames* 7896

McIVER, ANNA R.
Papers, 1840-1853, 1866, 1880, 102 items priv.
N: NcU 1 reel 7897

McIVER, GEORGE WILLCOX, 1858-1947
Autobiography, 2 v. (typescript) priv.
N: NcU 480 frames 7898

McQUEEN, JOSEPH PICKENS, 1854-1904
Papers, 1856-1867 priv.
DCO: NcU 8 items 7899

MALLORY, JAMES
Diary, 1843-1877, 2 v. priv.
N: NcU 380 frames 7900

MANEY, LEWIS M.
Papers, 1862-1867, 5 items priv.
DCO: NcU 7901

MANIGAULT, LOUIS
Book, 1861-1866, 1 v. priv.
N: NcU 1 reel 7902

MARTIN, ROBERT CAMPBELL, b. 1839
Papers, 1855-1865 priv.
N: NcU 2 reels 7903

MAURICE, CHARLES STEWART
Letters, 1862-1865, 62 items priv.
N: NcU 130 frames 7904

MAYO, PETER HELMS, b. 1836
Recollections, 133 p. (typescript) priv.
N: NcU 136 frames 7905

MERCER FAMILY
Papers, 1861-1864, 73 p. (typescript) priv.
N: NcU 7906

MERIWETHER, ELIZABETH AVERY, 1824-1916
Recollections, 1825-1916, 371 p. (typescript) priv.
N: NcU 382 frames 7907

MILES, WILLIAM PORCHER, 1822-1899
Papers, 1782-1907 NcU
N: NcU 4 reels 7908

MILNER FAMILY
Papers, 1820-1919, 45 items priv.
N: NcU 1 reel 7909

MONTGOMERY, JOHN J., d. 1911
Papers re: his aeronautical experiments, 1885-1947, 32 items [unk.]
DCO: NcU 7910

MOORE, HARRIETT ELLEN, 1842-1918
Diary, 1863 priv.
N: NcU 1 reel 7911

MUIR, JAMES and JOHN
Letters, 1781-1789, 20 items priv.
N: NcU 7912

NORTON, SUSANNAH R. (GIBSON)
Papers, 1754-1882, 63 items priv.
N: NcD 7913

PAGE, RICHARD L., 1807-1901
Logs, 1825-1864, 5 v. priv.
N: NcU 679 frames 7914

PENICK, DANIEL A., 1797-1870
Diary and 6 letters, 1821-1857 NcU
N: NcU 7915

PETTIT, WILLIAM B., 1825-1905
Papers, 1850-1928 priv.
N: NcU 560 frames 7916

PFOHL, CHRISTIAN THOMAS, 1838-1909
Papers, 1860-1864 priv.
N: NcU 209 frames 7917

POCHÉ, FELIX PIERRE, 1836-1895
Diary, 1863-1865, 10 v. priv.
N: NcU 342 frames 7918

POLK, LUCIUS J.
Papers, 1818-1876, 39 items priv.
N: NcU 1 reel 7919

POOL FAMILY
Scrapbook priv.
N: NcU 1 reel 7920

PRUDEN, WILLIAM DOSSEY, 1847-1918
Papers, 1812-1919 priv.
N: NcU 592 frames 7921

RACE, OLIVIA CORINNE (KITTREDGE), 1835-1916
Diary, 1870-1873, 2 v. priv.
N: NcU 206 frames 7922

RAINEY, ISAAC N., b. 1844
Reminiscences, 1925, 45 p. (typescript) priv.
N: NcU 48 frames 7923

RANDOLPH, V. M.
Diary, 1819-1820 priv.
N: NcU 68 frames 7924

RANDOLPH-YATES FAMILY
Papers, 1815-1864, 44 items NcU
N: NcU 7925

REEVE, EDWARD PAYSON, 1832-1898
Papers, 1852-1948, 503 items priv.
N: NcU 1 reel 7926

REID, ROBERT RAYMOND, 1789-1841
Diary, 1833, 1835, 55 p. (typescript) priv.
N: NcU 1 reel 7927

RICE FAMILY, of North and South Carolina
Papers, 1816-1823, 22 items priv.
N: DLC 1 reel 7928

RIVES, MARY ELIZABETH, 1829-1900
Diary, 1865-1899, 360 p. (typescript) priv.
N: NcU 1 reel 7929

ROLINSON, JOHN W., 1827-1906
Book, 1845-1905 priv.
N: NcU 74 frames 7930

ROYALL, EDWARD MANLY, b. 1828
Papers, 1821-1865, 1928, 35 items priv.
N: NcU 1 reel 7931

SAMFORD FAMILY
Diaries, 1884-1946, 5 v., 10 items priv.
N: NcU 1 reel 7932

SCHENCK, NICHOLAS W., b. 1830
Reminiscences, ca. 1830-1911, 1 v. priv.
N: NcU 142 frames 7933

SCHUTTE, WILLIAM CONRAD, 1737-1806
Family papers, 1741-1844 priv.
N: NcU 298 frames 7934

SCOTT, JAMES
Virginia and North Carolina papers, 1771-1810; Kentucky papers, 1789-1839 Or
N: Or-Ar 29 feet 16 mm.
P: Or-Ar 7935

SCOTT, THOMAS
Journal, 1789-1799 priv.
N: priv. 1/2 reel
P: NcLjHi 7936

SCOTT, WALTER T., 1827?-1879
Diary, 1877-1878, 4 v. priv.
N: NcU 174 frames 7937

SEABROOK, WHITEMARSH B.
Letters, 1849-1852 DLC.
N: NcU 1 reel   7938

SHEPPARD, LOUISA C.
Recollections, 1860-1865, 70 p. (typescript)
priv.
N: NcU   7939

SHURLEY, JOHN R.
Diary, 1847-1862 priv.
N: NcU 30 frames   7940

SILER, JESSE R., 1793-1876
Recollections, 1814-1862, 1 v. priv.
N: NcU 30 frames   7941

SIMS, WILLIAM HENRY
Papers, 1857, 1860; diary, 1865, 3 items
priv.
N: NcU 53 frames   7942

SLAGLE, ELAM L.
Papers, 1847-1854 priv.
N: NcU 35 frames   7943

SMITH, BENJAMIN BOSWORTH, Bp., 1794-1884
Papers, 1835-1934 NNUT PPPEHi priv.
N: priv. 2 reels
P: NcU   7944

SMITH, GEORGE GILMAN, 1836-1913
Diary, 1868-1910, 28 v. priv.
N: NcU 3 reels   7945

SMITH, Rev. JACOB HENRY, 1820-1897
Diary, 1860-1897 priv.
N: NcU 876 frames   7946

SPENCER, CHARLES, 1841-1917
Diary, 1862-1865, 4 v. priv.
N: NcU 340 frames   7947

SPRING, GARDINER
Papers, 1806-1865 CtY PHi
N: NcD 2 reels   7948

STOWELL, CALVIN, b. 1836
Scrapbook and letters, 1855-1872, 1907-1914
priv.
N: NcU 1 reel   7949

STRANGE, ROBERT, 1823-1877
Papers, 1837-1865, 22 items; letters,
1796-1854 priv.
N: NcU 1 reel   7950

STRUDWICK, ANNIE
Diary and letter, 1862-1864 priv.
N: NcU 74 frames   7951

TALLICHET, ALBERT
Papers, 1841-1873, 21 items priv.
N: NcU 88 frames   7952

TAYLOR, ALFRED, b. 1823
Journals, 1851-1909, 3 v. priv.
N: NcU 520 frames   7953

THOMAS, JAMES JEFFERSON
Autograph book, 1851 NjP
N: NcD   7954

TWEED, ROBERT, 1821-1898
Papers, 1843-1864, 52 items priv.
N: NcU 192 frames   7955

WALKER, JOHN, b. 1785
Diary, 1840-1866, 5 v. priv.
N: NcU 3 reels   7956

WALLER, GEORGE E.
Letters, 1858-1864, 37 items priv.
N: NcU 112 frames   7957

WEAKLEY, THOMAS PORTER
Diary and letters, 1863-1865 priv.
N: NcU 1 reel   7958

WEAKLEY, THOMAS PORTER
Papers, 1830-1864, 25 items priv.
N: NcU 1 reel   7959

WEBB-MOORE FAMILIES
Papers, 1792-1807, 1839-1866, 1878, 1885
priv.
N: NcU 53 frames   7960

WELLFORD, ROBERT, 1753-1823
Diary, 1794-1819, 5 v. and 6 letters priv.
N: NcU 1 reel   7961

WHEELER, JOHN HILL, 1806-1882
Diaries and miscellaneous papers,
1854-1882 DLC
N: NcU 5 reels   7962

WHITE, MAUNSELL
Papers, 1805-1860, 81 items priv.
N: NcU 1 reel   7963

WHITE-WELLFORD-TALIAFERRO-MARSHALL
FAMILY
Papers, 1804-1927, 14 v., 298 items priv.
N: NcU 3 reels   7964

WHITMORE, CHARLES
Diary, 1834-1864 priv.
N: NcU 1 reel   7965

WHITTLE FAMILY
Papers, 1753-1922, 156 items, 4 v. priv.
N: NcU 2 reels   7966

WILEY, CALVIN H.
Papers priv.
N: Nc-Ar 1 reel   7967

WOOD, JOHN TAYLOR, 1830-1904
Scrapbook and family notes, 1848-1893 priv.
N: NcU 1 reel   7968

WORTHINGTON, AMANDA DOUGHERTY, b. 1805
Papers and diary, 1819-1878, 95 items, 2 v.
priv.
N: NcU 452 frames*   7969

WRIGHT-GREEN FAMILY
Papers, 1798, 1807, 1817-1867 priv.
N: NcU 215 frames*   7970

Collections

DRAPER, LYMAN COPELAND, 1815-1891,
collector
Draper manuscripts WHi
N: WHi 133 reels   7971
P: DLC GEU GU ICU KU KyU NjP T TM TNJ
Wv-Ar

These are fully described in a pamphlet that is
provided with the films.

SPAIN. ARCHIVO GENERAL DE INDIAS, Seville
Audiencias. Santo Domingo, selections chiefly
re: Florida and Louisiana, 1531-1832 SpAGI
DCO: DLC 63079 sheets   7972

Slavery

DUKE UNIVERSITY
Letters re: slave insurrections in the ante-
bellum South, 1765-1840 Henry Watson
collection NcD
N: NN 93 frames   7973

MOORE, ALBERT R., collector
Manumission records, 1829, 17 p. priv.
DCO: NcU   7974

WEST VIRGINIA

Census

U.S. CENSUS. NINTH, 1870 DNA
Population schedules, West Virginia DNA
N: DNA 5 reels   7975

U.S. CENSUS. TENTH, 1880
Population schedules, West Virginia DNA
N: DNA 18 reels   7976

State Records

VIRGINIA
West Virginia vital statistics, 1853-1862 Vi
N: Vi 10 reels   7977
P: USlGS WvU

WEST VIRGINIA. STATE TREASURER
Records, 1861-1867 Ibid.
N: WvU 1 reel   7978

County Records

MONONGALIA Co., W.Va.
Tax book, 1855 priv.
N: WvU 1 reel   7979

Church Records

BRIDGEPORT, W. Va. SIMPSON CREEK
BAPTIST CHURCH
Records, n.d. PChHi
N: USlGS   7980

CLARKSBURG, W.Va. FIRST PRESBYTERIAN
CHURCH
Minutes, 1829-1870 Ibid.
N: WvU 1 reel   7981

FRIENDS, SOCIETY OF. ELK HORN [W.Va.]
MONTHLY MEETING
Membership, 1908-1923 MdFBH
N: PSC-F   7982
P: PSC-F

LESAGE, W. Va. GREENBOTTOM BAPTIST
CHURCH
Records, n.d. PChHi
N: USlGS 1 reel   7983

Personal Papers

ALLEN, WALTER, et al., defendants
Miners' treason trial papers, 1921-1923
C.H. Charles Town (Jefferson Co., W.Va.)
N: WvU 4 reels   7984

BOGGS, IRA BROOKS, 1890-1955
Writings on West Virginia 4-H work, 1927-
1956 priv.
N: WvU 1 reel   7985

BROWN, JOHN, 1800-1859, defendant
Entries, Oct. - Nov., 1859, re: trial
C.H. Charles Town (Jefferson Co.,W.Va.)
DCO: WvU 65 items   7986

COLE, HARRY OUTEN, 1874-1950, engineer
[Autobiographical sketch] priv.
N: WvU 1 reel   7987

DAVIS, HENRY GASSAWAY, 1823-1916
Papers, 1867-1916 priv.
N: WvU 1 reel   7988

GOFF, NATHAN, Jr., 1842-1920
Letters to R. B. Hayes when Goff was
Secretary of the Navy, 1881, 17 items OFH
DCO: WvU   7989

JACKSON, WILLIAM A.
Papers, 1892-1930 WvU
N: WvU 2 reels   7990

McKOWN, SARAH MORGAN, of Berkeley Co.,
W. Va.
Diaries, 1860-1899, 39 items priv.
N: WvU 2 reels   7991

MORGAN, ZACKQUILL II, d. 1814, defendant
Court papers, Amelia Tansey vs. Zackquill
Morgan II, 1803-1806 priv.
DCO: WvU 29 p.   7992

PIERPONT, FRANCIS H., 1814-1899
Letters to Lincoln from Reorganized Govern-
ment of Virginia, 1861-1864 DLC
N: WvU 1 reel   7993

RANDOLPH, WILLIAM M., of Moorefield, W. Va.
Pocket diary, 1853-1854 priv.
N: WvU 1/2 reel   7994

SMITH, LETTIE, of Grant and Tucker Cos., W. Va.
Pocket diary, 1864-1870 priv.
N: WvU 1/2 reel   7995

WARD, HENRY DANS, rector and school teacher
Diary, 1843-1862 priv.
N: WvU 1 reel   7996

Business Papers

CLARK, A.B.
General store account book, 1873-1875 priv.
N: WvU 1 reel   7997

FAIRFAX, GEORGE W.
Business papers, 1808-1898, including
Preston Co., W. Va., court books, 1839-1866
priv.
N: WvU 1 reel   7998

HANSON, THOMAS
Surveying journal, Apr.-Aug., 1774 DLC
N: WvU 1 reel   7999

HARMISON, CHARLES
Land papers, 1755-1913 priv.
DCO: WvU 1 folder   8000

HAYMOND FAMILY
Surveys of Monongalia and Harrison Cos., W.
Va., 1784-1789, 1795-1796, 1816, 1834-1836,
1843, 1903 priv.
N: WvU 1 reel   8001

THOMAS, WILLIAM, of Blacksville, W. Va.
Ledgers and account books of store and grist
mill, 1850-1908, 3 items   priv.
N: WvU 1 reel   8002

A West Virginia merchant's day book, Jan. 1,
1795 - Dec. 31, 1798   priv.
N: WvU 2 reels   8003

WHITE SULPHUR SPRING HOTEL, W. Va.
Records and accounts, 1816-1817, 1827-
1828, 1830-1831, 1896, 1898, 5 v. Old
White Museum, White Sulphur Springs, W. Va.
N: ViU   8004

Collections

MARTINSBURG, W. Va. PUBLIC LIBRARY
Martinsburg and Berkeley County papers,
1781-1953 WvMa
N: WvU 1 reel   8005

MATHERS, MAX, compiler
Monongalia County scrapbook, 1838-1951 priv.
N: WvU 1 reel   8006

WEST VIRGINIA PULP AND PAPER COMPANY
Reports re: timberlands, Pocahontas,
Randolph, and Webster Cos., 1920 Ibid.
N: WvU 1 reel   8007

College Records

WEST VIRGINIA UNIVERSITY. COLLEGE OF
AGRICULTURE. AGRICULTURAL EXTENSION
DIVISION
Archives, 1912, 1915-1950 Ibid.
N: WvU 47 reels   8008

WEST VIRGINIA UNIVERSITY. GRADUATE SCHOOL
Archives, 1910-1950 Ibid.
N: WvU 1 reel   8009

VIRGINIA

Census

U.S. CENSUS. THIRD, 1810
Population schedules, Virginia DNA
N: DNA 6 reels   8010

U.S. CENSUS. FIFTH, 1830
Population schedules, Virginia DNA
N: DNA 13 reels   8011
P: AB USIGS

U.S. CENSUS. SIXTH, 1840
Population schedules, Virginia DNA
N: DNA 10 reels   8012
P: USIGS

U.S. CENSUS. SEVENTH, 1850
Population schedules, Virginia DNA
N: DNA 12 reels   8013
P: USIGS

U.S. CENSUS. EIGHTH, 1860
Population schedules, Virginia DNA
N: DNA 14 reels   8014
P: USIGS ViU

U.S. CENSUS. NINTH, 1870
Agriculture schedule, Virginia Vi
N: Vi 4 reels   8015
P: Vi USIGS

U.S. CENSUS. NINTH, 1870
Death schedule, Virginia Vi
N: Vi 1 reel   8016
P: Vi

U.S. CENSUS. NINTH, 1870
Industry schedule, Virginia Vi
N: Vi 1 reel   8017
P: Vi

U.S. CENSUS. NINTH, 1870
Population schedules, Virginia DNA
N: DNA 13 reels   8018
P: USIGS

U.S. CENSUS. NINTH, 1870
Population schedules, Virginia Vi
N: Vi 21 reels   8019
P: USIGS Vi

U.S. CENSUS. NINTH, 1870
Social statistics schedules, Virginia Vi
N: Vi 1 reel   8020
P: USIGS Vi

U.S. CENSUS. TENTH, 1880
Population schedules, Virginia DNA
N: DNA 45 reels   8021

VIRGINIA
Mortality records, year ending June, 1870 Vi
N: Vi 1 reel   8022
P: USIGS

Government Records

FRANCE. CONSULAT, NORFOLK, Va.
Papers, 1784-1866 MiD-B
N: MiD-B   8023
P: NcD

U.S. DISTRICT COURT. VIRGINIA (Eastern
District)
Papers relating to the trial of Aaron Burr
and Harman Blennerhassett, 1807 DNA
N: DNA 1 reel [T-265]   8024

State Records

VIRGINIA (Colony)
Proceedings of the Commission re: Northern
Neck, 1736 priv.
N: PHi 1 reel   8025

VIRGINIA
Land grants and supporting papers, 1623-1923,
including Northern Neck grants, 1690-1862, and
military grants, since French and Indian War
Vi
N: USIGS 356 reels   8026
P: Vi

VIRGINIA
Miscellaneous wills, 1675-1884 CSmH
N: CSmH   8027
P: USIGS 1 reel

VIRGINIA
Miscellaneous Virginia court records CSmH
N: CSmH 4 reels   8028
P: USIGS

VIRGINIA
Personal property tax lists, 1782-1841 Vi
N: Vi 20 reels   8029
P: USIGS

VIRGINIA
Tax lists of various counties, 1782-1863 Vi
N: Vi 82 reels   8030
P: USIGS

VIRGINIA. JAMES RIVER NAVAL OFFICE
Manifest book, 1773-1775   Vi
N: Vi 1 reel   8031
P: Vi

VIRGINIA. LAND OFFICE
Record books, 1623-1950 Vi
N: Vi 368 reels   8032
P: Vi

VIRGINIA. MILITIA
Commissioned officers of 2nd Virginia militia,
1806 priv.
DCO: DLC   8033

County Records

Virginia county records are listed collectively,
unless they appear to have special value to the
researcher. Separate listing is always given to
court order books, wills, deeds, vital records,
and muster rolls. In order that researchers may
differentiate between materials the originals of
which are held at county courthouses and materials the originals of which are held at the state
archives, an exception has been made to the
usual alphabetical listing. Courthouse material
always precedes archival material.

ACCOMACK Co., Va.
Court order books, 1666-1787; court records,
1797-1872; wills, 1632-1645, 1663-1767; deeds,
1632-1645, 1663-1783, 1860-1865; vital records,
1774-1806, 1853-1896 C.H. Accomac
N: Vi 56 reels   8034
P: USIGS Vi

ACCOMACK Co., Va.
Court order books, 1767-1860; court records,
1727-1842; wills, 1715-1729, 1767-1892; deeds,
1715-1729, 1767-1892; marriage records, 1774-
1853; vestry orders, 1723-1784; naval officer's
book of entries and clearances, 1785 Vi
N: Vi 85 reels   8035
P: USIGS Vi

ALBEMARLE Co., Va.
Court order books, 1744-1831; court records,
1830-1866; wills, 1748-1867; deeds, 1758-1866;
vital records, 1780-1903 C.H. Charlottesville
N: Vi 60 reels   8036
P: USIGS Vi

ALBEMARLE Co., Va.
Deeds, 1804-1807, 1819-1822, 1824-1826;
marriage bonds, 1780-1805; marriage
register, 1806-1868 Vi
N: Vi 3 reels   8037
P: USIGS Vi

ALLEGHANY Co., Va.
Court order books, 1822-1883; guardian bonds,
1825-1871; wills, 1822-1876; deeds, 1822-1873;
land records, 1822-1946; marriage register,
1822-1916 C.H. Covington
N: Vi 16 reels   8038
P: USIGS Vi

AMELIA Co., Va.
Court order books, 1735-1866; wills, 1734-
1865; deeds, 1734-1869; vital records, 1854-
1918; muster roll, 1861-1865   C.H. Amelia
Courthouse
N: Vi 54 reels   8039
P: USIGS Vi

AMHERST Co., Va.
Court order books, 1766-1868; court records,
1761-1930; wills, 1761-1870; deeds,
1761-1865; marriage records, 1854-1900
C.H. Amherst
N: Vi 39 reels   8040
P: USIGS Vi

AMHERST Co., Va.
Marriage register, 1763-1852 Vi
N: Vi 1 reel   8041
P: USIGS Vi

APPOMATOX Co., Va.
Personal property tax lists, 1845-1863 Vi
N: Vi 2 reels   8042
P: USIGS Vi

ARLINGTON Co. (formerly ALEXANDRIA Co.), Va.
Court order books, 1780-1799, 1801-1827; court
records, 1786-1868; wills, 1800-1878; deeds,
1801-1865; vital records, 1850-1896
C.H. Arlington
N: Vi 30 reels   8043
P: USIGS Vi

ARLINGTON Co. (formerly ALEXANDRIA Co.), Va.
Court records, 1786-1846 Vi
N: Vi 7 reels   8044
P: USIGS Vi

AUGUSTA Co., Va.
Court order books, 1745-1867; court records,
1787-1906; wills, 1745-1865; deeds, 1745-1866;
vital records, 1785-1900; court martial records, 1756-1796; court of enquiry records,

1807-1864; muster roll, 1861-1865 C. H.
Staunton
N: Vi 110 reels   8045
P: USIGS Vi

AUGUSTA Co. , Va.
List of tithables for 1777 Vi
N: Vi 1 reel   8046
P: USIGS Vi

BATH Co. , Va.
Court order books, 1791-1873; court records,
1791-1897; wills, 1791-1876; deeds, 1791-1874;
vital records, 1791-1895 C.H. Warm Springs
N: Vi 21 reels   8047
P: USIGS Vi

BEDFORD Co. , Va.
Court order books, 1754-1865; wills, 1763-1888;
deeds, 1754-1865; vital records, 1754-1949;
muster roll, 1861-1865 C. H. Bedford
N: Vi 67 reels   8048
P: USIGS Vi

BLAND Co. , Va.
Court order books, 1861-1869; wills,
1861-1904; deeds, 1861-1870; marriage
records, 1861-1929 C.H. Bland
N: Vi 6 reels   8049
P: USIGS Vi

BOTETOURT Co. , Va.
Court order books, 1770-1867; court records,
1774-1914; wills, 1770-1869; deeds, 1770-
1869; vital records, 1787-1913 C.H. Fincastle
N: Vi 41 reels   8050
P: USIGS Vi

BOTETOURT Co. , Va.
Marriage records, 1770-1853 Vi
N: Vi 2 reels   8051
P: USIGS Vi

BRUNSWICK Co. , Va.
Court order books, 1732-1864; court records,
1732-1860; wills, 1732-1865; deeds,
1732-1869; vital records, 1750-1901
C.H. Lawrenceville
N: Vi 54 reels   8052
P: USIGS Vi

BRUNSWICK Co. , Va.
Marriage register, 1751-1853 Vi
N: Vi 1 reel   8053
P: USIGS Vi

BUCHANAN Co. , Va.
Personal property tax list, 1859-1863 Vi
N: Vi 1 reel   8054
P: USIGS Vi

BUCKINGHAM Co. , Va.
List of tithables for 1773-1774; personal
property tax lists, 1782-1863; surveyors'
platt books, 1762-1814 Vi
N: Vi 9 reels   8055
P: USIGS Vi

BUCKINGHAM Co. , Va.
Miscellaneous documents, 1805-1873 CSmH
N: USIGS 1 reel   8056
P: USIGS

CAMPBELL Co. , Va.
Court order books, 1782-1869; court records,
1783-1924; wills, 1782-1878; deeds, 1782-1869;
marriage register, 1782-1936 C.H. Rustburg
N: Vi 38 reels   8057
P: USIGS

CAROLINE Co. , Va.
Court order books, 1804-1866; court records,
1809-1866; wills, 1814-1863; deeds,
1836-1840, 1846-1865; vital records,
1864-1932 C.H. Bowling Green
N: Vi 15 reels   8058
P: USIGS Vi

CAROLINE Co. , Va.
Court order books, 1732-1804, 1822-1824;
court records, 1729-1845; marriage records,
1787-1853; proceedings, Committee of Safety,
1774-1776; personal property tax lists, 1783-
1863 Vi
N: Vi 21 reels   8059
P: USIGS Vi

CARROLL Co. , Va.
Court order books, 1842-1867; surveyors'

records, 1842-1910; wills, 1842-1875; deeds,
1842-1867; vital records, 1853-1913
C. H. Hillsville
N: Vi 14 reels   8060
P: USIGS Vi

CHARLES CITY Co. , Va.
Court records, 1831-1879; wills, 1808-1920;
deeds, 1789-1867; vital records, 1762-1931;
muster rolls, 1861-1865 C.H. Charles City
N: Vi 13 reels   8061
P: USIGS Vi

CHARLES CITY Co. , Va.
Court order books, 1655-1762; court records,
1762-1879; wills, 1689-1690, 1763-1774,
1789-1808; deeds, 1689-1690, 1763-1774 Vi
N: Vi 8 reels   8062
P: USIGS Vi

CHARLOTTE Co. , Va.
Court order books, 1765-1868; court records,
1765-1880; wills, 1765-1867; deeds, 1765-1870;
marriage register, 1782-1900
C.H. Charlotte
N: Vi 41 reels   8063
P: USIGS Vi

CHESTERFIELD Co. , Va.
Court order books, 1749-1865; wills,
1749-1865; deeds, 1749-1866; marriage
register, 1855-1896; muster roll, 1812,
1861-1865 C.H. Chesterfield
N: Vi 56 reels   8064
P: USIGS Vi

CHESTERFIELD Co. , Va.
Marriage register, 1771-1853 Vi
N: Vi 1 reel   8065
P: USIGS Vi

CLARKE Co. , Va.
Court order books, 1836-1858; court records,
1836-1904; wills, 1836-1878; deeds, 1836-1866;
marriage records, 1836-1933; muster roll,
1861-1865 C.H. Berryville
N: Vi 14 reels   8066
P: USIGS Vi

CRAIG Co. , Va.
Court order books, 1851-1863; platt book,
1851-1932; wills, 1851-1867; deeds, 1851-1884;
vital records, 1864-1937; muster roll,
1861-1865 C.H. New Castle
N: Vi 8 reels   8067
P: USIGS Vi

CULPEPER Co. , Va.
Court records, 1763-1869; wills, 1749-1870;
deeds, 1749-1864; vital records, 1850-1917
C.H. Culpeper
N: Vi 50 reels   8068
P: USIGS Vi

CULPEPER Co. , Va.
Wills, 1749-1791; marriage registers,
1781-1853; militia list, Jan., 1781 Vi
N: Vi 4 reels   8069
P: USIGS Vi

CUMBERLAND Co. , Va.
Court order books, 1749-1869; court records,
1769-1860; wills, 1749-1887; deeds, 1749-1868;
vital records, 1853-1919 C. H. Cumberland
N: Vi 38 reels   8070
P: USIGS Vi

DINWIDDIE Co. , Va.
Court records, 1819-1906; wills, 1830-1875;
deeds, 1819-1871; vital records, 1850-1916
C. H. Dinwiddie
N: Vi 22 reels   8071
P: USIGS Vi

DINWIDDIE Co. , Va.
Court order book, 1789-1791; platt book, 1755-
1865; deeds, 1833-1837 Vi
N: Vi 2 reels   8072
P: USIGS Vi

ELIZABETH CITY Co. , Va.
Court order books, 1731-1747, 1755-1757;
court records, 1737-1748, 1756-1769, 1803-
1813, 1819-1824, 1827-1861; wills, 1689-1756;
deeds, 1689-1756; marriage registers, 1865-
1908 C.H. Hampton
N: Vi 15 reels   8073
P: USIGS Vi

ELIZABETH CITY Co. , Va.
Court records, 1684-1699, 1701-1904; wills,
1684-1699, 1701-1904; deeds, 1684-1699, 1701-
1904 Vi
N: Vi 14 reels   8074
P: USIGS Vi

ESSEX Co. , Va.
Confederate veterans' records, 1861-1865;
Daughters of the Confederacy records, 1898-
1948 C.H. Tappahannock
N: Vi 1 reel   8075
P: USIGS

ESSEX Co. , Va.
Court order books, 1716-1723, 1802-1809;
court records, 1731-1796, 1843-1856; vital
records, 1804-1891 C. H. Tappahannock
N: Vi 13 reels   8076
P: USIGS Vi

ESSEX Co. , Va.
Court order books, 1695-1702, 1723-1801,
1809-1863; court records, 1731-1760, 1796-
1814, 1816-1820, 1824-1825, 1827, 1831, 1834-
1902; wills, 1692-1902; deeds, 1692-1867 Vi
N: Vi 99 reels   8077
P: USIGS Vi

ESSEX Co. , see also (OLD) RAPPAHANNOCK Co. ,
8137, under this same heading

FAIRFAX Co. , Va.
Court order books, 1749-1867; court records,
1742-1856; wills, 1742-1866; deeds, 1742-1865;
vital records, 1853-1933; muster roll, 1861-
1865 C.H. Fairfax
N: Vi 43 reels   8078
P: USIGS Vi

FAIRFAX Co. , Va.
Minute book, 1822-1823 C. H. Arlington
N: Vi 1 reel   8079
P: USIGS Vi

FAIRFAX Co. , Va.
Court order books, 1722-1774; deeds, 1772-
1773 Vi
N: Vi 3 reels   8080
P: USIGS Vi

FLOYD Co. , Va.
Court order books, 1831-1864; court records,
1831-1866; wills, 1831-1873; deeds, 1831-1870;
vital records, 1843-1925 C.H. Floyd
N: Vi 13 reels   8082
P: USIGS Vi

FAUQUIER Co. , Va.
Court order books, 1832-1846; court records,
1759-1882; wills, 1759-1865; deeds, 1759-1866;
vital records, 1759-1906; muster roll, 1861-
1865 C. H. Warrenton
N: Vi 71 reels   8081
P: USIGS Vi

FLUVANNA Co. , Va.
Court order books, 1777-1867; court records,
1794-1852; wills, 1777-1867; deeds, 1777-1867;
vital records, 1781-1923 C. H. Palmyra
N: Vi 25 reels   8083
P: USIGS Vi

FRANKLIN Co. , Va.
Court order books, 1786-1865; court records,
1789-1865; wills, 1786-1866; deeds, 1786-1866;
vital records, 1786-1915 C.H. Rocky Mount
N: Vi 40 reels   8084
P: USIGS Vi

FREDERICK Co. , Va.
Court order books, 1743-1856; court records,
1736-1841; wills, 1743-1865; deeds, 1743-1867;
vital records, 1773-1907; militia records, 1796-
1821; muster roll, 1861-1865 C.H. Winchester
N: Vi 116 reels   8085
P: USIGS Vi

GILES Co. , Va.
Court order books, 1806-1868; court records,
1807-1872; wills, 1806-1873; deeds, 1806-1870;
vital records, 1806-1913 C.H. Pearisburg
N: Vi 20 reels   8086
P: USIGS Vi

GLOUCESTER Co. , Va.
Court minutes, 1820-1825, 1833-1842, 1858-
1867; surveyors' books, 1733-1810, 1817-
1852; personal property tax list, 1782-1861 Vi

N: Vi 6 reels   8087
P: USIGS Vi

GLOUCESTER Co., Va.
    Sheriff's tax book, 1770-1771 priv.
    N: ViU   8088
    P: ViU

GOOCHLAND Co., Va.
    Court order books, 1728-1871; court records,
    1794-1822; wills, 1728-1871; deeds, 1728-1868;
    vital records, 1852-1901; muster roll, 1861-
    1865 C.H. Goochland
    N: Vi 39 reels   8089
    P: USIGS Vi

GOOCHLAND Co., Va.
    Marriage register, 1730-1853 Vi
    N: Vi 1 reel   8090
    P: USIGS Vi

GRAYSON Co., Va.
    Court order books, 1793-1865; court records,
    1793-1933; wills, 1796-1869; deeds, 1793-1868;
    vital records, 1793-1906 C.H. Independence
    N: Vi 20 reels   8091
    P: USIGS V1

GREENE Co., Va.
    Court order books, 1842-1864; wills, 1838-1925;
    deeds, 1841-1873; vital records, 1838-1944;
    C.H. Stanardsville
    N: Vi 11 reels   8092
    P: USIGS Vi

GREENSVILLE Co., Va.
    Court order books, 1781-1866; court records,
    1796-1877; wills, 1781-1876; deeds, 1781-1874;
    vital records, 1853-1901 C.H. Emporia
    N: Vi 24 reels   8093
    P: USIGS Vi

GREENSVILLE Co., Va.
    Marriage register, 1781-1853, 280 p. Vi
    N: Vi   8094
    P: USIGS Vi

HALIFAX Co., Va.
    Court order books, 1752-1821; court records,
    1751-1901; wills, 1752-1865; deeds, 1752-1867;
    vital records, 1753-1889 C.H. Halifax
    N: Vi 84 reels   8095
    P: USIGS Vi

HANOVER Co., Va.
    Wills, 1785-1895; vital records, 1853-1897
    C.H. Hanover
    N: Vi 2 reels   8096
    P: USIGS Vi

HANOVER Co., Va.
    Court records, 1733-1735, 1783-1792; wills,
    1733-1735, 1783-1792; deeds, 1733-1735,
    1783-1792; personal property tax lists, 1782-
    1863 Vi
    N: Vi 8 reels   8097
    P: USIGS Vi

HENRICO Co., Va.
    Court order books, 1781-1816; court records,
    1792-1867; wills, 1787-1869; deeds, 1781-1876;
    vital records, 1781-1831, 1853-1870
    C.H. Richmond
    N: Vi 76 reels   8098
    P: USIGS Vi

HENRICO Co., Va.
    Court order books, 1678-1701, 1707-1709, 1737-
    1746, 1755-1769; court records, 1650-1807;
    wills, 1677-1787, 1832, 1843; deeds, 1677-1787;
    Colonial records, 1677-1739 Vi
    N: Vi 18 reels   8099
    P: USIGS Vi

HENRY Co., Va.
    Court order books, 1777-1820; court records,
    1777-1904; wills, 1777-1867; deeds, 1777-1867;
    vital records, 1778-1913 C.H. Martinsville
    N: Vi 36 reels   8100
    P: USIGS Vi

HENRY Co., Va.
    Marriage register, 1778-1849 Vi
    N: Vi 1 reel   8101
    P: USIGS Vi

HIGHLAND Co., Va.
    Court order books, 1847-1873; wills, 1847-1924;
    deeds, 1847-1870; vital records, 1853-1951

C.H. Monterey
    N: Vi 7 reels   8102
    P: USIGS Vi

ISLE OF WIGHT Co., Va.
    Court order books, 1746-1866; court records,
    1767-1861; wills, 1636-1902; deeds, 1688-1866;
    vital records, 1853-1900 C.H. Isle of Wight
    N: Vi 46 reels   8103
    P: USIGS Vi

ISLE OF WIGHT Co., Va.
    Marriage register, 1771-1853, 795 p. Vi
    N: Vi   8104
    P: USIGS Vi

JAMES CITY Co., Va.
    Land owners (James City and James City
    Island), 1619-1779; tax book, 1768-1769;
    personal property tax lists, 1782-1861 Vi
    N: Vi 5 reels   8105
    P: USIGS Vi

JAMES CITY Co., Va.
    Petitions to the General Assembly, 1777-1861
    Vi
    N: Vi 1 reel   8106
    P: Vi

KING AND QUEEN Co., Va.
    Court order books, 1831-1874; court records,
    1831-1851; wills, 1864-1893; court minutes,
    1858-1866; personal property tax, 1782-1863
    Vi
    N: Vi 12 reels   8107
    P: USIGS

KING GEORGE Co., Va.
    Court order books, 1735-1869; court records,
    1721-1874; wills, 1752-1901; deeds, 1721-1868;
    marriages, 1656-1930 C.H. King George
    N: Vi 43 reels   8108
    P: USIGS Vi

KING GEORGE Co., Va.
    Court order books, 1721-1734, 1751-1765,
    1789-1812 Vi
    N: Vi 4 reels   8109
    P: USIGS Vi

KING WILLIAM Co., Va.
    Court records, 1701-1885; deeds, 1701-1885;
    personal property tax, 1782-1863 Vi
    N: Vi 22 reels   8110
    P: USIGS Vi

LANCASTER Co., Va.
    Court order books, 1831-1866; wills,1860-1925;
    deeds, 1841-1885; vital records, 1849-1870
    C.H. Lancaster
    N: Vi 8 reels   8111
    P: USIGS Vi

LANCASTER Co., Va.
    Court order books, 1655-1854; court records,
    1793-1842; wills, 1652-1850; deeds, 1652-1849;
    marriage register, 1715-1852; deaths, 1853-
    1870 Vi
    N: Vi 38 reels   8112
    P: USIGS

LEE Co., Va.
    Court order books, 1808-1867; court records,
    1794-1944; wills, 1793-1888; deeds, 1793-1869;
    vital records, 1830-1916 C.H. Jonesville
    N: Vi 22 reels   8113
    P: USIGS Vi

LOUDOUN Co., Va.
    Court order books, 1757-1812; court records,
    1759-1801; wills, 1757-1866; deeds, 1757-1865;
    vital records, 1760-1914 C.H. Leesburg
    N: Vi 99 reels   8114
    P: USIGS Vi

LOUDOUN Co., Va.
    Court minutes and Revolutionary War claims,
    1780-1783; miscellaneous court records; mil-
    itia records, 56th and 57th regiments, 1793-
    1809 C.H. Winchester (Frederick Co.)
    N: Vi 2 reels   8115
    P: USIGS Vi

LOUISA Co., Va.
    Court order books, 1742-1866; court records,
    1743-1870; wills, 1745-1901; deeds, 1742-1865;
    vital records, 1864-1941; muster rolls,
    1861-1865 C.H. Louisa
    N: Vi 44 reels   8116
    P: USIGS Vi

LOUISA Co., Va.
    Marriage register, 1766-1861 Vi
    N: Vi 1 reel   8117
    P: USIGS Vi

LUNENBURG Co., Va.
    Court order books, 1746-1865; court records,
    1791-1870; wills, 1746-1851; deeds, 1746-
    1869; vital records, 1746-1929 C.H.
    Lunenburg
    N: Vi 20 reels   8118
    P: USIGS

MADISON Co., Va.
    Court order books, 1793-1863; court records,
    1796-1888; wills, 1793-1866; deeds, 1793-1871;
    marriage records, 1793-1905 C.H. Madison
    N: Vi 28 reels   8119
    P: USIGS Vi

MATHEWS Co., Va.
    Tax lists, 1781-1862; platt book, 1817-1921 Vi
    N: Vi 7 reels   8120
    P: USIGS Vi

MECKLENBURG Co., Va.
    Court order books, 1765-1858; court records,
    1766-1865; wills, 1765-1866; deeds, 1765-1870;
    marriage records, 1765-1929 C.H. Boydton
    N: Vi 52 reels   8121
    P: USIGS Vi

MIDDLESEX Co., Va.
    Will indices, 1675-1950; deed indices, 1675-
    1897; vital records, 1663-1763, 1853-1904;
    muster roll, 1861-1865 C.H. Saluda
    N: Vi 6 reels   8122
    P: USIGS Vi

MIDDLESEX Co., Va.
    Court order books, 1673-1726, 1732-1737,
    1740-1786, 1794-1795, 1813-1865; court
    records, 1752-1850; wills, 1675-1860; deeds,
    1679-1865; marriage records, 1740-1896 Vi
    N: Vi 57 reels   8123
    P: USIGS Vi

MONTGOMERY Co., Va.
    Court order books, 1773-1867; wills, 1796-
    1874; deeds, 1773-1868; vital records, 1854-
    1902 C.H. Christiansburg
    N: Vi 34 reels   8124
    P: USIGS Vi

MONTGOMERY Co., Va.
    Marriage register, 1777-1853, 656 p. Vi
    N: Vi   8125
    P: USIGS Vi

NANSEMOND Co., Va.
    Personal property tax lists, 1815-1861 Vi
    N: Vi 6 reels   8126
    P: USIGS Vi

NELSON Co., Va.
    Court order books, 1808-1868; wills, 1808-1867;
    deeds, 1808-1867; vital records, 1808-1926
    C.H. Lovington
    N: Vi 20 reels   8127
    P: USIGS Vi

NELSON Co., Va.
    Marriage register, 1808-1878, 307 p. Vi
    N: Vi   8128
    P: USIGS Vi

NEW KENT Co., Va.
    Personal property tax lists, 1782-1863 Vi
    N: Vi 3 reels   8129
    P: USIGS Vi

NORFOLK Co., Va.
    Court order books, 1719-1734, 1776-1779,
    1801-1810; court records, 1751-1884;
    minute books, 1743-1868; wills, 1637-1675,
    1719-1734, 1742-1903; deeds, 1637-1865;
    vital records, 1782-1790, 1817-1917
    C.H. Portsmouth
    N: Vi 84 reels   8130
    P: USIGS Vi

NORFOLK Co., Va.
    Court order books, 1675-1686, 1719-1722,
    1742-1801; wills, 1646-1685, 1703-1706, 1718-
    1719, 1721-1734, 1740-1783, 1836-1868; deeds,
    1646-1706, 1708-1719, 1721-1765, 1836-1868 Vi
    N: Vi 13 reels   8131
    P: USIGS Vi

NORTHAMPTON Co., Va.
Court records, 1632-1640, 1815-1887; wills, indices, 1632-1950; deeds, indices, 1632-1917; marriage registers, 1853-1922 C.H. Eastville
N: USIGS 9 reels
P: USIGS Vi
8132

NORTHAMPTON Co., Va.
Court order books, 1640-1651, 1655-1865; court minutes, 1754-1783; court records, 1718-1828; wills, 1640-1740, 1750-1792, 1811-1901; deeds, 1640-1867; tithables, 1662-1664, 1675-1677; vital records, 1706-1870 Vi
N: Vi 58 reels
P: USIGS Vi
8133

NORTHUMBERLAND Co., Va.
Court order books, 1861-1871; court records, 1839-1873; wills, 1839-1872; deeds, 1839-1866; vital records, 1735-1850, 1853-1917
C.H. Heathsville
N: Vi 14 reels
P: USIGS Vi
8134

NORTHUMBERLAND Co., Va.
Court order books, 1650-1861; court records, 1652-1672, 1706-1729, 1738-1749, 1788-1843; wills, 1749-1839; deeds, 1650-1652, 1749-1839; vital records, 1650-1810, 1850-1853 Vi
N: Vi 60 reels
P: USIGS Vi
8135

NOTTOWAY Co., Va.
Court order books, 1793-1854; court records, 1840-1860; wills, 1789-1845; deeds, 1789-1842; marriage records, 1784-1815, 1865-1897
C.H. Nottoway
N: Vi 16 reels
P: USIGS Vi
8136

(OLD) RAPPAHANNOCK Co. (now ESSEX Co.), Va.
Court order books, 1656-1692; wills, 1656-1692; deeds, 1656-1692 Vi
N: Vi 6 reels
P: USIGS Vi
8137

ORANGE Co., Va.
Court order books, 1734-1777, 1801-1856; court records, 1764-1885; wills, 1735-1864; deeds, 1734-1865; vital records, 1757-1912
C.H. Orange
N: Vi 42 reels
P: USIGS Vi
8138

ORANGE Co., Va.
Wills, 1735-1801 Vi
N: Vi 2 reels
P: USIGS Vi
8139

PAGE Co., Va.
Court records, 1831-1886; wills, 1831-1866; deeds, 1831-1867; vital records, 1831-1906;
C.H. Luray
N: Vi 24 reels
P: USIGS Vi
8140

PATRICK Co., Va.
Court order books, 1791-1864; court records, 1832-1875; wills, 1791-1867; deeds, 1791-1866; vital records, 1791-1912; muster roll, 1861-1865 C.H. Stuart
N: Vi 24 reels
P: USIGS Vi
8141

PITTSYLVANIA Co., Va.
Court order books, 1767-1866; court records, 1737-1866; wills, 1767-1880; deeds, 1767-1866; vital records, 1767-1896; muster roll, 1861-1865 C.H. Chatham
N: Vi 71 reels
P: USIGS Vi
8142

POWHATAN Co., Va.
Court order books, 1777-1860; wills, 1777-1868; deeds, 1777-1898; vital records, 1853-1935 C.H. Powhatan
N: Vi 35 reels
P: USIGS Vi
8143

POWHATAN Co., Va.
Marriage register, 1777-1853, 301 p. Vi
N: Vi
P: USIGS Vi
8144

PRINCE EDWARD Co., Va.
Court order books, 1754-1869; court records, 1764-1869; wills, 1754-1869; deeds, 1754-1866; vital records, 1754-1949; muster roll, 1861-

1865 C.H. Farmville
N: Vi 42 reels
P: USIGS Vi
8145

PRINCE GEORGE Co., Va.
Court order books, 1811-1814; court records, 1794-1879; deeds, 1842-1846, 1851-1858; vital records, 1865-1904; muster roll, 1861-1865 C.H. Prince George
N: Vi 5 reels
P: USIGS Vi
8146

PRINCE GEORGE Co., Va.
Court records, 1714-1720; court minutes, 1737-1740; wills, 1711-1728, 1759-1792; deeds, 1711-1728, 1759-1792; platt books, 1711-1728, 1759-1792; personal property tax list, 1782-1863 Vi
N: Vi 11 reels
P: USIGS Vi
8147

PRINCE WILLIAM Co., Va.
Court order books, 1754-1757, 1761-1769, 1804-1806, 1812-1814, 1846-1850; court records, 1752-1873; wills, 1734-1872; deeds, 1732-1869; vital records, 1859-1946 C.H. Manassas
N: Vi 35 reels
P: USIGS Vi
8148

PRINCE WILLIAM Co., Va.
Deeds, 1731-1732, 404 p.; personal property tax list, 1782-1861 Vi
N: Vi 1 reel
8149

PRINCESS ANNE Co., Va.
Court records, 1717-1894; wills, 1714-1735, 1783-1794; deeds, 1691-1747; marriage records, 1786-1850, 1853-1939 C.H. Princess Anne
N: Vi 25 reels
P: USIGS Vi
8150

PRINCESS ANNE Co., Va.
Court order books, 1691-1709, 1717-1728, 1737-1753, 1762-1769; wills, 1691-1735, 1740-1747, 1769-1772, 1774-1777, 1779-1871; deeds, 1691-1735, 1740-1865 Vi
N: Vi 41 reels
P: USIGS Vi
8151

PULASKI Co., Va.
Court order books, 1839-1862; court records, 1839-1876; wills, 1840-1871; deeds, 1839-1867; vital records, 1839-1933 C.H. Pulaski
N: Vi 12 reels
P: USIGS Vi
8152

RAPPAHANNOCK Co., Va.
Court order books, 1833-1871; court records, 1833-1871; wills, 1833-1866; deeds, 1833-1867; vital records, 1833-1870 C.H. Washington
N: Vi 24 reels
P: USIGS Vi
8153

RAPPAHANNOCK Co., 1656-1692, see (OLD) RAPPAHANNOCK Co., 8137, under this same heading.

RICHMOND Co., Va.
Court order books, 1692-1694, 1752-1762, 1858-1871; court records, 1824-1866; deeds, 1850-1868; marriage records, 1824-1850
C.H. Warsaw
N: Vi 9 reels
P: USIGS Vi
8154

RICHMOND Co., Va.
Court order books, 1692-1861; court records, 1710-1849; wills, 1699-1787, 1789-1879; deeds, 1692-1832, 1835-1850; vital records, 1853-1906, 1912-1917 Vi
N: Vi 59 reels
8155

ROANOKE Co., Va.
Court order books, 1838-1868; court records, 1838-1868; wills, 1838-1870; deeds, 1838-1869; vital records, 1838-1919 C.H. Salem
N: Vi 23 reels
P: USIGS Vi
8156

ROCKBRIDGE Co., Va.
Court order books, 1778-1821; court records, 1778-1867; wills, 1778-1874; deeds, 1778-1868; vital records, 1782-1913; muster roll, 1861-1865 C.H. Lexington
N: Vi 55 reels
P: USIGS
8157

ROCKBRIDGE Co., Va.
Court records, 1794-1848; fee book, 1841-1842 NcD
N: USIGS   P: NcD
8158

ROCKINGHAM Co., Va.
Court records, 1761-1876; wills, 1803-1863; deeds, 1778-1863; vital records, 1778-1904
C.H. Harrisonburg
N: Vi 54 reels
P: USIGS Vi
8159

ROCKINGHAM Co., Va.
Personal property tax lists, 1782-1863 Vi
N: Vi 14 reels
P: USIGS Vi
8160

ROCKINGHAM Co., Va.
Court records, 1796-1845; tax lists, 1789-1845 NcD
N: USIGS 4 reels
8161

RUSSELL Co., Va.
Court order books, 1786-1867; court records, 1786-1908; wills, 1803-1866; deeds, 1787-1869; vital records, 1853-1908 C.H. Lebanon
N: Vi 26 reels
P: USIGS Vi
8162

SCOTT Co., Va
Personal property tax lists, 1815-1863; land tax lists, 1815-1863 Vi
N: Vi 11 reels
P: USIGS Vi
8163

SHENANDOAH Co., Va.
Court order books, 1772-1774, 1781-1786, 1795-1811; court records, 1785-1921; wills, 1772-1866; deeds, 1772-1867; vital records, 1772-1915; muster roll, 1861-1865
C.H. Woodstock
N: Vi 67 reels
P: USIGS Vi
8164

SMYTH Co., Va.
Court order books, 1832-1866; court records, 1833-1890; wills, 1832-1873; deeds, 1832-1865; vital records, 1832-1915 C.H. Marion
N: Vi 17 reels
P: USIGS Vi
8165

SOUTHAMPTON Co., Va.
Court order books, 1749-1849; court records, 1751-1870; wills, 1749-1896; deeds, 1749-1870; vital records, 1850-1899 C.H. Courtland
N: Vi 43 reels
P: USIGS Vi
8166

SOUTHAMPTON Co., Va.
Marriage records, 1750-1853 Vi
N: Vi 2 reels
P: USIGS Vi
8167

SPOTSYLVANIA Co., Va.
Court order books, 1724-1798, 1807-1810, 1821-1871; court records, 1796-1831; wills, 1722-1824, 1830-1869; deeds, 1722-1774, 1782-1865; marriages, 1853-1935
C.H. Spotsylvania
N: Vi 42 reels
P: USIGS Vi
8168

SPOTSYLVANIA Co., Va.
Court minutes, 1784-1787, 1799-1807, 1810-1821; court order books, 1792-1798, 1824-1826; court records, 1756-1771, 1846-1889; wills, 1815-1820, 1830-1833, 1836-1838, 1843-1846, 1852-1856, 1869-1876; deeds, 1814-1817, 1821-1822, 1865-1869; marriages, 1795-1853 Vi
N: Vi 25 reels
8169

STAFFORD Co., Va.
Court order books, 1790-1793, 1806-1809; court records, 1827-1837, 1852-1873; deeds, 1780-1873; vital records, 1853-1927; muster roll, 1861-1865 C.H. Stafford
N: Vi 8 reels
P: USIGS Vi
8170

STAFFORD Co., Va.
Court order books, 1664-1693, 1722-1728, 1748-1764, 1780-1786; court records, 1680-1681; wills, 1664-1693, 1722-1728, 1748-1764, 1780-1786; deeds, 1664-1693, 1722-1728, 1748-1764, 1780-1786; personal property tax lists, 1783-1861 Vi
N: Vi 17 reels
P: USIGS Vi
8171

SURRY Co., Va.
Court order books, 1671-1874; court records, 1672-1906; wills, 1652-1875; deeds, 1652-1873; vital records, 1853-1939; militia records, 1840-1861 C.H. Surry
N: Vi 53 reels
P: USIGS Vi
8172

SURRY Co., Va.
Wills, 1645-1686; deeds, 1645-1686; marriage

register, 1768-1853 Vi
N: Vi 2 reels
P: USIGS   8173

SUSSEX Co., Va.
Court order books, 1754-1864; court records,
1754-1866; wills, 1754-1864; deeds, 1754-
1864; vital records, 1850-1901 C.H. Sussex
N: Vi 33 reels
P: USIGS Vi   8174

SUSSEX Co., Va.
Marriage register, 1754-1853, 502 p. Vi
N: Vi
P: USIGS Vi   8175

TAZEWELL Co., Va.
Court order books, 1800-1871; court records,
1801-1891; wills, 1800-1866; deeds, 1800-1869;
vital records, 1853-1920 C.H. Tazewell
N: Vi 20 reels
P: USIGS Vi   8176

WARREN Co., Va.
Court records, 1836-1872; wills, 1836-1904,
deeds, 1836-1871; vital records, 1836-1917;
muster roll, 1861-1865 C.H. Front Royal
N: Vi 18 reels
P: USIGS Vi   8177

WARWICK Co., Va.
Court minutes, 1748-1762; Overseers of the
Poor records, 1786-1860; personal property
tax list, 1782-1861 Vi
N: Vi 2 reels
P: USIGS Vi   8178

WASHINGTON Co., Va.
Court records, 1776-1870; wills, 1777-1903;
deeds, 1778-1866; vital records, 1795-1902;
muster roll, 1861-1865 C.H. Abingdon
N: Vi 36 reels
P: USIGS Vi   8179

WESTMORELAND Co., Va.
Court order books, 1819-1867; court records,
1723-1917; wills, 1723-1868; deeds, 1723-1868;
vital records, 1826-1895 C.H. Montross
N: Vi 11 reels
P: USIGS Vi   8180

WESTMORELAND Co., Va.
Court order books, 1662-1669, 1690-1764,
1776-1860; court records, 1809-1856; wills,
1653-1671, 1691-1709, 1712-1859; deeds,
1653-1671, 1691-1709, 1712-1859; deaths,
1853, 1857-1896; register of Free Negroes,
1828-1849; fiduciary book, 1742-1789 Vi
N: Vi 65 reels
P: USIGS Vi   8181

WISE Co., Va.
Court order book, 1856-1861; surveyors' book,
1856-1924; wills, 1856-1884; deeds, 1856-1866;
vital records, 1856-1908 C.H. Wise
N: Vi 6 reels
P: USIGS Vi   8182

WYTHE Co., Va.
Court order books, 1790-1865; court records,
1790-1910; wills, 1790-1865; deeds,
1790-1867; vital records, 1790-1919; muster
roll, 1861-1865 C.H. Wytheville
N: Vi 36 reels
P: USIGS Vi   8183

YORK Co., Va.
Court order books, 1633-1851; court records,
1694-1860; wills, 1633-1901; deeds, 1633-1866;
marriage records, 1772-1849, 1852-1928;
claim for losses, 1781 C.H. Yorktown
N: Vi 44 reels
P: USIGS Vi   8184

YORK Co., Va.
Marriage bonds and consents, 1772-1849 Vi
N: Vi 1 reel
P: USIGS Vi   8185

City Records

ABINGDON, Va.
Trustees' minutes, 1789-1861 Ibid.
N: ViU
P: ViU   8186

ALEXANDRIA, Va.
Deeds, 1783-1865; marriage register,
1870-1905 Vi
N: Vi 43 reels
P: USIGS Vi   8187

ALEXANDRIA, Va.
Proceedings of Board of Trustees, 1749-
1767 Ibid.
DCO: DLC 1 box   8188

DUMFRIES, Va. DISTRICT COURT
Records at large, 1798-1799 ViWC
N: ViWC 90 feet
P: ViWC   8189

FREDERICKSBURG, Va.
Hustings court order books, 1789-1871; court
records, 1790-1869; wills, 1782-1817, 1828-
1868; deeds, 1782-1869; marriage records,
1781-1939 Ibid.
N: Vi 40 reels
P: USIGS Vi   8190

LOUISA, Va. TOWN COUNCIL
Minutes, 1873-1903, 1 v. priv.
N: ViU
P: ViU   8191

LYNCHBURG, Va.
Court order books, 1805-1866; wills, 1809-
1876; deeds, 1805-1872; vital records, 1853-
1909; muster roll, 1861-1865 Ibid.
N: Vi 34 reels
P: USIGS Vi   8192

LYNCHBURG, Va.
Marriage register, 1805-1853 Vi
N: Vi 1 reel
P: USIGS Vi   8193

LYNCHBURG, Va.
Tax book, 1813-1816 priv.
N: ViU
P: ViU   8194

NORFOLK, Va.
Borough registers, 1756-1762, 1783-1810, re:
ships' cargoes damaged and sold   priv.
N: ViU   8195

NORFOLK, Va.
Court order books, 1761-1872; court records,
1850-1910; wills, 1784-1910; deeds, 1784-1866;
vital records, 1792-1804; Borough register,
1682; loose papers re: Confederate soldiers
Ibid.
N: Vi 59 reels   8196

PETERSBURG, Va.
Chancery order books, 1831-1865; Hustings
court minutes, 1784-1867; court records,
1806-1866; wills, 1784-1901; deeds, 1784-
1866; vital records, 1784-1910; militia records,
1853-1855; fee book, 1763 Ibid.
N: Vi 44 reels
P: USIGS Vi   8197

PORTSMOUTH, Va.
Chancery order books, 1866-1874; court
minutes, 1858-1869; court records, 1858-
1905; wills, 1858-1913; deeds, 1858-1869;
vital records, 1858-1901 Ibid.
N: Vi 11 reels
P: USIGS Vi   8198

RICHMOND, Henrico Co., Va.
Common Council records, 1782-1883 Vi
N: Vi 13 reels
P: 8199

RICHMOND, Henrico Co., Va.
Courtney's marriage register and index,
1816-1865 Vi
N: Vi
P: USIGS   8200

RICHMOND, Henrico Co., Va.
Court order books, 1782-1817; court minutes,
1793-1866; wills, 1810-1866; deeds,
1782-1865; marriage register, 1853-1878
C.H. Richmond
N: Vi 96 reels
P: USIGS Vi   8201

STAUNTON, Va.
Court order books, 1839-1870; minutes,
1796-1865; wills, 1802-1879; deeds, 1802-
1867; vital records, 1802-1926; historical
records of early laws and ordinances Ibid.
N: Vi 13 reels
P: USIGS Vi   8202

WAYNESBORO, Va.
Municipal records, 1844-1864, 1888-1912 Ibid.
N: ViU 1 1/2 reels
P: ViU   8203

WAYNESBORO, Va.
Session books, 1840-1908 priv.
N: ViU
P: ViU   8204

WILLIAMSBURG, Va.
Petitions to the General Assembly, 1775-1852;
land tax and personal property tax books, 1782-
1861 Vi
N: Vi 2 reels
P: Vi   8205

YORKTOWN, Va.
Hustings court records, 1787-1793 Ibid.
N: Vi 1 reel
P: USIGS Vi   8206

Church Records

ABINGDON PARISH (Episcopal), Gloucester Co.,
Va.
Registers, 1678-1761, 1830-1916 Vi
N: Vi 2 reels
P: USIGS Vi   8207

ALBEMARLE PARISH (Episcopal), Surry and
Sussex Cos., Va.
Parish register, 1739-1778; vestry book,
1742-1787 Vi
N: Vi 1 reel
P: USIGS Vi   8208

ALEXANDRIA, Va. ST. PAUL'S CHURCH
(Episcopal)
Records, 1827-1933 Vi
N: Vi 2 reels
P: USIGS Vi   8209

ANTRIM PARISH (Episcopal), Halifax Co., Va.
Vestry book, 1752-1817 Vi
N: Vi 1 reel
P: USIGS Vi   8210

AUGUSTA PARISH (Episcopal), Augusta Co., Va.
Vestry book, 1746-1780 Vi C.H. Staunton
N: Vi 2 reels
P: USIGS Vi   8211

BATH PARISH (Episcopal), Dinwiddie Co., Va.
Parish register, 1727-1797 Vi
N: Vi 1 reel
P: USIGS Vi   8212

BATTLE RUN BAPTIST CHURCH, Culpeper Co.,
Va.
Records, 1827-1852, 149 p. Vi
N: Vi
P: USIGS Vi   8213

BEAVER DAM BAPTIST CHURCH, Isle of Wight Co.
Records, 1828-1894, 481 p. Vi
N: USIGS   8214

BETHEL PRESBYTERIAN CHURCH, Augusta
Co., Va.
Session books, 1817-1869 Ibid.
N: ViU
P: ViU   8215

BLISSLAND PARISH (Episcopal), New Kent Co., Va.
Vestry book, 1721-1786 Vi
N: Vi 1 reel
P: USIGS Vi   8216

BRISTOL PARISH (Episcopal), Prince George
and Dinwiddie Cos., Va.
Parish register, 1720-1792; vestry book,
1720-1789 Vi
N: Vi 1 reel
P: USIGS Vi   8217

CAMBDEN PARISH (Episcopal), Pittsylvania Co., Va.
Vestry book, 1767-1852 C.H. Chatham
DCO: Vi 308 p.
N: USIGS of original and DCO 2 reels   8218
P: USIGS

CAMERON PARISH (Episcopal), Loudon Co., Va.
List of tithables, 1758-1799 C.H. Leesburg
N: Vi 1 reel
P: USIGS Vi   8219

CHARLES RIVER and YORK HAMPTON
PARISHES (Episcopal), York Co., Va.
Parish register, 1648-1800 Vi
N: Vi 1 reel
P: USIGS Vi   8220

CHARLOTTE COURT HOUSE, Va. ASHCAMP
BAPTIST CHURCH
Minutes, 1813-1870 Vi
N: Vi 1 reel   8221
P: USlGS Vi

CHRIST CHURCH PARISH (Episcopal),
Lancaster Co., Va.
Vestry books, 1739-1870, 239 p. Vi
N: Vi   8222
P: USlGS

CHRIST CHURCH PARISH (Episcopal),
Middlesex Co., Va.
Parish register, 1653-1814; vestry book,
1663-1767 Vi
N: Vi 2 reels   8223
P: USlGS Vi

CHURCH OF JESUS CHRIST OF LATTER-DAY
SAINTS. VIRGINIA
Records: Washington stake, 1947-1948;
Alexandria branch, Arlington and Richmond
wards USlC
N: USlGS 4 reels   8224

CHURCHVILLE, Va. ST. PETER'S
EVANGELICAL LUTHERAN CHURCH
Records, 1790-1892 Ibid.
N: USlGS 2 reels   8225

CUMBERLAND PARISH(Episcopal), Lunenburg Co.,
Va.
Vestry book, 1747-1831, 238 p.
N: Vi   8226
P: USlGS Vi

DETTINGEN PARISH (Episcopal), Prince
William Co., Va.
Vestry books, 1745-1802, 301 p. Vi
N: Vi   8227
P: USlGS

EBENEZER CHURCH (Baptist), Loudoun Co., Va.
Book, 1804-1896 C.H. Winchester
N: Vi   8228
P: USlGS Vi

ELIZABETH CITY, Va.
Parish vestry book, 1751-1883 Ibid.
DCO: DLC 1 v.   8229

ELIZABETH RIVER PARISH (Episcopal), Norfolk
Co., Va.
Vestry book, 1749-1761, 47 p. Vi
N: Vi   8230
P: USlGS

ERMENTROUT CHURCH (Lutheran),
Rockingham Co., Va.
Records, 1798-1863, 172 p. Vi
N: Vi   8231
P: USlGS

FREDERICK PARISH(Episcopal), Frederick Co.,Va.
Vestry book, 1764-1818, 321 p. Vi
N: Vi   8232
P: USlGS

FREDERICKSBURG, Va. ST. GEORGE'S PARISH
Vestry minutes, 1723-1745 ViU
N: ViU   8233
P: USlGS ViU

FREDERICKSVILLE PARISH (Episcopal),
Louisa Co., Va.
Vestry book, 1742-1787, 179 p. Vi
N: Vi   8234
P: USlGS Vi

FRIENDS, SOCIETY OF. CEDAR CREEK [Va.]
MONTHLY MEETING
Minutes, 1739-1773 MdFBH
N: PSC-F   8235
P: PSC-F

FRIENDS, SOCIETY OF. CHUCATUCK [Va.]
MEETING
Records, 1684-1755, 115 p. Vi
N: Vi   8236
P: USlGS Vi

FRIENDS, SOCIETY OF. HENRICO Co., Va.
Records, 1699-1834, 951 p. Vi
N: Vi   8237
P: USlGS

FRIENDS, SOCIETY OF. HOPEWELL [Va.]
MEETING

Records, 1830-1895, 814 p. Vi
N: Vi   8238
P: USlGS

FRIENDS, SOCIETY OF. SOUTH RIVER [Va.]
MONTHLY MEETING
Records, 1757-1858 Vi
N: USlGS 3 reels   8239

FRIENDS, SOCIETY OF. VIRGINIA YEARLY
MEETING
Men's minutes, 1737-1758
N: PSC-F   8240
P: PSC-F

FRIENDS, SOCIETY OF. VIRGINIA YEARLY
MEETING
Records, 1702-1858 (1724-1737 lost by fire);
women's minutes, 1763-1825 MdFBH
N: PSC-F   8241
P: PSC-F

FRIENDS, SOCIETY OF. WHITE OAK SWAMP
[Va.] MONTHLY MEETING
Records, 1757-1824, 1101 p. Vi
N: Vi   8242
P: USlGS Vi

FRYING PAN BAPTIST CHURCH, Loudoun Co., Va.
Minutes, 1791-1879 C.H. Winchester (Frederick Co.)
N: Vi   8243
P: USlGS Vi

GERMAN REFORMED CHURCH, Loudoun Co., Va.
Records, 1789-1859, 167 p. Vi
N: Vi   8244
P: USlGS Vi

HEBRON LUTHERAN CHURCH, Madison Co., Va.
History, records, 1754-1866 C.H. Madison
N: Vi 1 reel   8245
P: USlGS Vi

HENRICO PARISH, Va. ST. JOHN'S EPISCOPAL
CHURCH
Records, 1730-1887, 1133 p. Vi
N: Vi   8246
P: USlGS

HUNGARS PARISH, Northampton Co., Va.
Vestry book, 1758-1782 C.H. Northampton
N: Vi   8247
P: USlGS Vi

IMMANUEL EPISCOPAL CHURCH, Hanover Co.,
Va.
Records, 1815-1926, 202 p. Vi
N: Ni   8248
P: USlGS

IVY, Va. ST. PAUL'S CHURCH
Parish register, 1848-1936, 1 v. priv.
N: ViU   8249
P: ViU

KINGSTON PARISH, Gloucester Co., Va.
Tithables, 1774-1775 Vi
N: Vi   8250
P: USlGS

KINGSTON PARISH CHURCH (Episcopal),
Mathews Co., Va.
Records, 1679-1796, 356 p. Vi
N: Vi   8251
P: USlGS Vi

LEAVELL, Rev. W.T.
Private register of ministry in Va., 1840-1899
Vi
N: Vi 1 reel   8252
P: USlGS

LEXINGTON PARISH (Episcopal), Amherst Co., Va.
Vestry book, 1779-1880, 126 p. Vi
N: Vi   8253
P: USlGS

LOVETTSVILLE, Va. NEW JERUSALEM
LUTHERAN CHURCH
Records, 1784-1836 PGL
N: USlGS   8254

LUNENBERG PARISH(Episcopal), Richmond Co.,Va.
Register, 1790-1800, 49 p. Vi
N: Vi   8255
P: USlGS Vi

LYNNHAVEN PARISH (Episcopal), Princess
Anne Co., Va.
Vestry book, 1723-1892, 381 p. Vi
N: Vi   P: USlGS Vi   8256

MIDDLETON PARISH, Williamsburg, Va.
Register, 1662-1797 Vi
N: Vi   8257
P: USlGS Vi

NEW JERUSALEM CHURCH (Lutheran),
Loudon Co., Va.
Records, 1784-1836, 296 p. Vi
N: Vi   8258
P: USlGS Vi

NEWPORT NEWS, Va. ST. PAUL'S CHURCH
(Episcopal)
Parish register, 1880-1900, 223 p. Vi
N: Vi   8259
P: USlGS Vi

NEWPORT PARISH (Episcopal), Isle of Wight
Co., Va.
History; vestry book, 1724-1772, 252 p.
C.H. Isle of Wight
N: Vi   8260
P: USlGS Vi

NEWPORT PARISH, Va. CHRIST CHURCH
(Episcopal)
Vestry proceedings, 1836-1894, with historical
sketch, 1606-1826, 234 p. C.H. Isle of Wight
N: Vi   8261
P: USlGS

NORTH FARNHAM PARISH (Episcopal),
Richmond Co., Va.
Register, 1672-1800, 266 p. Vi
N: Vi   8262
P: USlGS Vi

OVERWHARTON PARISH (Episcopal),
Stafford Co., Va.
Register, 1724-1774; vestry book, 1815-1820,
218 p. Vi
N: Vi   8263
P: USlGS Vi

PETSWORTH PARISH (Episcopal), Gloucester
Co., Va.
Vestry book, 1677-1793, 412 p. Vi
N: Vi   8264
P: USlGS Vi

PINE CHURCH (Lutheran), Shenandoah Co., Va.
Records, 1783-1896, 291 p. Vi
N: Vi   8265
P: USlGS Vi

PROTESTANT EPISCOPAL CHURCH IN THE
U.S.A. VIRGINIA
Historical and geographical accounts of
parishes, n.d., 177 p. Vi
N: Vi   8266
P: USlGS

RALEIGH PARISH CHURCH (Episcopal), Amelia
Co., Va.
Vestry book, 1790-1926, 300 p. Vi
N: Vi   8267
P: USlGS Vi

RAPPAHANNOCK CHRISTIAN CHURCH,
Essex Co., Va.
Records, 1832-1895, 144 p. Vi
N: Vi   8268
P: USlGS Vi

RICHMOND, Va. ST. JAMES' CHURCH
(Episcopal)
Records, 1837-1889, 943 p. Vi
N: Vi   8269
P: USlGS Vi

RICHMOND Va. SEVENTH STREET CHRISTIAN
CHURCH
Records, 1832-1851, 124 p. Vi
N: Vi   8270
P: USlGS Vi

RIVANNA PARISH CHURCH (Episcopal), Fluvanna
Co., Va.
Register, 1849-1939, 337 p. Vi
N: Vi   8271
P: USlGS Vi

RUSSEL PARISH CHURCH (Episcopal), Bedford
Co., Va.
Records, 1825-1839, 1841-1853, 79 p. Vi
N: Vi   8272
P: USlGS Vi

ST. ANDREW'S PARISH (Episcopal),
Brunswick Co., Va.
Vestry book, 1732-1797, 204 p. Vi
N: Vi
P: USIGS Vi   8273

ST. ANN'S PARISH (Episcopal), Albemarle Co.,
Va.
Vestry book, 1772-1785; Overseers to the Poor
accounts, 1786-1809, 184 p. Vi
N: Vi
P: USIGS Vi   8274

ST. GEORGE'S PARISH (Episcopal), Accomac Co.,
Va.
Records, 1763-1787, 137 p. Vi
N: Vi
P: USIGS Vi   8275

ST. GEORGE'S PARISH (Episcopal), Spotsylvania
Co., Va.
Vestry book, 1726-1743, 58 p. Vi
N: Vi
P: USIGS   8276

ST. JAMES' NORTHAM PARISH (Episcopal),
Goochland Co., Va.
Vestry book, 1744-1850, 289 p. Vi
N: Vi
P: Vi USIGS   8277

ST. JOHN'S CHURCH (Episcopal), Hampton, Va.
Records, 1751-1889, 532 p. Vi
N: Vi
P: USIGS   8278

ST. JOHN'S CHURCH (Lutheran), Shenandoah
Co., Va.
Records, 1849-1915, 365 p. Vi
N: Vi
P: USIGS Vi   8279

ST. LUKE'S CHURCH (Lutheran), Rockingham
Co., Va.
Records, 1880-1898, 96 p. Vi
N: Vi
P: USIGS   8280

ST. MARK'S PARISH (Episcopal), Culpeper
Co., Va.
Records, 1730-1785, 1794-1797, 466 p. Vi
N: USIGS   8281

ST. PATRICK'S PARISH (Episcopal), Prince
Edward Co., Va.
Vestry book, 1755-1774, 90 p. Vi
N: Vi
P: USIGS Vi   8282

ST. PAUL'S PARISH (Episcopal), Hanover Co.,
Va.
Vestry book, 1705-1785, 446 p. Vi
N: Vi
P: USIGS Vi   8283

ST. PAUL'S PARISH (Episcopal), King George
Co., Va.
Parish register, 1716-1793, 237 p. Vi
N: Vi
P: USIGS Vi   8284

ST. PETER'S PARISH (Episcopal),
New Kent Co., Va.
Records, 1685-1778, 438 p. Vi
N: Vi
P: USIGS Vi   8285

ST. STEPHEN'S CHURCH, Hamner Parish, Va.
Records, 1841-1853 Vi
N: Vi
P: USIGS Vi   8286

ST. THOMAS CHURCH (Episcopal), Orange Co.,
Va.
Parish register, 1856-1926, 178 p. Vi
N: Vi
P: USIGS Vi   8287

SHELBURNE PARISH (Episcopal), Loudoun
Co., Va.
Vestry book, 1771-1805, 72 p. Vi
N: Vi
P: USIGS Vi   8288

SOLOMON'S CHURCH (Lutheran), Shenandoah
Co., Va.
Records, 1793-1851, 269 p. Vi
N: Vi
P: USIGS Vi   8289

SOUTH FARNHAM PARISH (Episcopal), Essex
Co., Va.
Vestry book, 1739-1876, 148 p. Vi
N: Vi   P: USIGS Vi   8290

SOUTHAM PARISH (Episcopal), Powhatan Co., Va.
Vestry book, 1745-1836, 547 p. Vi
N: Vi
P: USIGS Vi   8291

STRATTON MAJOR PARISH (Episcopal), King
and Queen Co., Va.
Vestry book, 1729-1783, 151 p. Vi
N: Vi
P: USIGS Vi   8292

SUFFOLK PARISH (Episcopal), Nansemond Co.,
Va.
Vestry book, 1749-1856, 154 p. Vi
N: Vi
P: USIGS Vi   8293

TIMBERVILLE, Va. RADER'S [ROEDER'S]
LUTHERAN CHURCH
Records, 1772-1908, 315 p.; register, 1787-
1796, 73 p. Vi
N: Vi
P: USIGS Vi   8294

TINKLING SPRING PRESBYTERIAN CHURCH,
Augusta Co., Va.
Register and session books, 1741-1908, 3 v.
Ibid.
N: ViU   8295

UPPER NANSEMOND PARISH (Episcopal),
Nansemond Co., Va.
Vestry book, 1744-1793, 297 p. Vi
N: Vi
P: USIGS Vi   8296

WARE PARISH, Gloucester Co., Va.
Register, 1830-1916 Vi
N: USIGS 1 reel
P: Vi   8297

WAYNESBORO, Va. BETHANY LUTHERAN
CHURCH
Parish register, 1771-1845 Ibid.
N: ViU
P: ViU   8298

WICOMICO PARISH (Episcopal), Northumberland
Co., Va.
Vestry book, 1703-1795, 230 p. Vi
N: Vi
P: USIGS Vi   8299

WILLIAMSBURG, Va. BRUTON PARISH
(Episcopal)
Records, 1662-1797, 1827-1908, 433 p. Vi
N: Vi   8300
P: USIGS Vi

WINCHESTER GERMAN REFORMED CHURCH,
Frederick Co., Va.
Records, 1789-1897, 732 p. Vi
N: Vi
P: USIGS Vi   8301

WOODVILLE BAPTIST CHURCH, Rappahannock
Co., Va.
Records, 1852-1947 Ibid.
N: ViU   8302

ZION CHURCH (Lutheran), Floyd Co., Va.
Register, 1793-1855, 107 p. Vi
N: Vi
P: USIGS Vi   8303

ZION'S CHURCH (Lutheran), Wythe Co., Va.
Records, 1791-1930, 166 p. Vi
N: Vi
P: USIGS Vi   8304

Personal Papers

ABERCROMBY, JAMES
Letter book, 1746-1773 Vi
N: Vi 1 reel
P: Vi   8305

ALEXANDER and GRAHAM FAMILIES
Papers, 1814-1861 priv.
DCO: DLC 1 box   8306

AMBLER, ELIZABETH JACQUELINE
Correspondence with Mrs. Ann Fisher
(the Carrington Letters), 1796-1823, 1v. priv.
N: ViU   8307
P: ViU

AMBLER, ELIZABETH JACQUELINE
Letters, 1781-1823 priv.
DCO: DLC 1 v.   8308

BALL, JOSEPH
Letter book, 1743-1759 DLC
N: DLC 1 reel   8309

BALLOU FAMILY, of Virginia
Papers, 1736-1889 priv.
N: DLC 1 reel   8310
P: DLC

BARBOUR, JAMES, Gov. Va., 1775-1842
Correspondence, 1792-1848 NN
N: ViU   8311
P: ViU

BARTON, BENJAMIN SMITH, 1766-1815
Journal [visit to Virginia], 1802, 142 p. DLC
DCO: DLC   8312

BEERS, NATHAN
Diary, 1777-1782 DLC
N: ViWI 1 reel   8313

BRECKINBRIDGE-WATTS FAMILIES
Letters, 1794-1862 priv.
N: ViU   8314
P: ViU

BROWNE, Mrs. CHARLOTTE
Journal of a voyage from London to Virginia,
1754-1757, 1 v. priv.
DCO: DLC   8315

BURNET, DAVID T.
Correspondence, 1836-1837 priv.
N: ViU   8316
P: ViU

BURWELL, WILLIAM A.
Private memoirs, 1804-1810 DLC
N: ViWI 1 reel   8317

BYRD, SAMUEL POWELL
Papers, 1828-1858 ViWC
N: ViWC 100 feet   8318
P: ViWC

BYRD, WILLIAM, II, 1674-1744
Journal of Commissioners to establish the Vir-
ginia-North Carolina boundary, 1728 UKLBM
DCO: DLC 1 box   8319

BYRD, WILLIAM, II, 1674-1744
Letters and literary exercises, 1696-1726;
diary, 1739-1741, 2 v. NcU
N: NcU 1 reel   8320
DCO: NcU

BYRD, WILLIAM, II, 1674-1744
Manuscripts, 1727-1728 ViWC
N: ViWC 100 feet   8321

BYRD FAMILY
Manuscript, ca. 1728, 1 v. priv.
N: PHi 1 reel   8322

CAMPBELL, DAVID, Gov. Va., 1779-1859
Papers, 1774-1904, 8032 items, 32 v. NcD
N: ? 18 reels   8323
P: WHi

CAMPBELL-PRESTON FAMILIES
Papers re: southwestern Virginia, 1741-1825
DLC
N: DLC 7 reels   8324
P: ViU

CARTER, LANDON
Diary, 1766-1767 MiU
N: ViU   8325
P: ViU

CARTER, ROBERT, of Nomini Hall
Letterbooks, 1761-1769, 2 items ViWC
N: ViWC 85 feet   8326
P: ViWC

COCKE FAMILY
Papers re: John Hartwell Cocke and Charles
Cary Cocke, 776 items, 22 v. priv.
N: NcU 4 reels   8327

COOKE, PHILIP PENDLETON
Letters to John Pendleton Kennedy, 1845-1846
priv.
N: NcD 1 reel   8328

CORBIN, RICHARD
Papers, 1746-1818 ViWC
N: ViWC 100 feet   P: ViWC   8329

CRAIG, JOHN
Diary, 1740-1749, 1v. priv.
N: ViU   8330

DANIEL, J. R. V.
Diary, 1869, 1873 priv.
N: Vi 1 reel   8331
P: Vi

DANIEL FAMILY
Diaries, notebooks, and papers, 2 v. priv.
N: ViU   8332
P: ViU

EPPES, JOHN WAYLES
Correspondence NcD
N: ViU   8333
P: ViU

FAIRFAX FAMILY, of Virginia
Survey and affidavits re: Fairfax estate
v. p.
N: DLC   8334
DCO: DLC

FLETCHER, ELIJAH, 1789-1858
Letters, 1808-1856, 200 p. InHi
DC: ViSWC*   8335

GILPIN, JOSHUA, 1765-1840
Journals and notebooks, 1790-1833, 62 v. P
N: PHarH 3 1/2 reels   8336
P: DeHi

GILPIN, JOSHUA, 1765-1840
Letterbook ViU
N: ViU   8337
P: DeHi

GRAY, M. R.
Diary, 1822-1829, 1 v. priv.
N: ViU   8338
P: ViU

HOOK, JOHN
Letterbook, 1758-1784, 1 v.
N: ViU   8339
P: ViU

HOTCHKISS-McCULLOUGH FAMILIES
Papers ViU
N: DLC 6 reels   8340

HOWARD, ELIZA
Diary, 1857, 1860, 1868, 30 p. priv.
N: ViU   8341
P: ViU

HULLIHAN, WALTER O.
Letters, 1858-1866 priv.
N: ViU   8342
P: ViU

HUNDLEY FAMILY
Papers, 1838-1900 priv.
N: ViU   8343
P: ViU

IRBY, RICHARD
Papers and accounts, 1844-1901, 5 v. priv.
N: ViU   8344
P: ViU

JONES, HENRY B.
Papers, 1842-1870, 7 v. priv.
N: ViU   8345
P: ViU

KELLAND, JOHN
Correspondence, 1862-1877 priv.
N: ViU   8346
P: ViU

KEYES, SUSAN WOOD, of Winchester, Va., b. 1837
Journal, 1849 priv.
N: NcD 1 reel   8347

LEE, BERTRAM TAMBLYN
Letters to Miles Poindexter, 1923-1936 ViU
N: DLC 1 reel   8348

LEE, THOMAS SIM
Letters and receipts, 1771-1820 priv.
DCO: DLC 26 items   8349

LEE, WILLIAM, of "Greenspring"
Letterbook, 1769-1776, 1 v.
N: ViU   8350
P: ViU

LEE FAMILY
Papers
N: CtY 1 reel   8351

LEE FAMILY, of Virginia
Papers (Armes collection) priv.
DCO: DLC 2 boxes*   8352

LEWIS, JOSEPH T.
Letters, 1768-1824 priv.
N: ViU   8353
P: ViU

LEWIS FAMILY
Papers, 1780-1835, 240 items ICU
N: ViU 4 reels   8354

MOFFATT, THOMAS
Diary, 1775-1777 DLC
N: ViWi   8355

NELSON, WILLIAM, 1711-1772
Letter book, including letters of Thomas
Nelson, 1766-1775 Vi
N: Vi 1 reel   8356
P: Vi

NELSON FAMILY, of Virginia
Papers, ca. 1743-1789
Brock Collection CSmH
N: ViU   8357

NORTON FAMILY
Papers, 1752-1827 ViWC
N: ViWC 90 feet   8358
P: ViWC

PAGE, JOHN
Papers, 1776-1805, 38 items CSmH NcD
N: ViWI 2 reels   8359

PAGE, MANN, Jr.
Papers, 1775-1869 ViWC
N: ViWC 100 feet   8360
P: ViWC

PEACHY FAMILY
Papers, 1809-1815 ViWC
N: ViWC 90 feet   8361
P: ViWC

PENDLETON, EDMUND, 1721-1803
Letters, 1776-1779, 48 items NcU
N: NcU ViWC   8362

POINDEXTER, MILES
Papers, 1897-1937, 550,000 items ViU
N: ViU 180 reels   8363
P: WaU

PRESTON FAMILY, of Virginia
Papers, 1727-1896 priv.
N: DLC 15 reels   8364

RANDOLPH-HUBBARD FAMILIES
Letters, 1840-1861, 46 items priv.
N: ViU   8365
P: ViU

RIGSBY FAMILY
Papers re: western Virginia, 1855-1889 priv.
N: KyU 1 reel   8366

ROLFE, JOHN, 1585-1622
True relation of the state of Virginia, 1616
17 p. priv.
DCO: MiU-C   8367

SEELY, SYLVANUS, d. 1821
Diaries, 1768-1821, 30 v. priv.
N: NjP 5 reels   8368
P: ViWI

SLAUGHTER, PHILIP
Diary, 1807-1816 priv.
N: Vi 1 reel   8369
P: Vi

SMITH, Dr. AUGUSTINE
Papers, 1779-1843 ViWC
N: ViWC 75 feet   8370
P: ViWC

SPENCER, WILLIAM
Diary, 1790 ViWC
N: ViWC 90 feet   8371

STEVENSON, Mrs. SARAH COLES
Letters to her family, 1836-1841 NcD
N: ViU   8372

STRACHEY, WILLIAM, fl. 1609-1618
The historie of Travaile into Virginia Britanniae,
1618   Sloane 1622 UKLBM
N: DFo 1 reel   8373

STRACHEY, WILLIAM, fl. 1609-1618
The historie of travaile into Virginia Britannia,
1612-1618   Ashmole 1758 UKO
N: DFo 1 reel   8374

TALIAFERRO, WILLIAM BOOTH, 1822-1898
Papers, 1805-1901 ViW; (typescript) priv.
N: NcU 840 frames of typescript   8375

TAYLOR, Col. FRANCIS, of Orange Co., Va.
Diary, 1786-1799 Vi
N: Vi 1 reel   8376
P: Vi

TAZEWELL, LITTLETON WALLER, Gov. Va.,
1774-1860
Book, 192 p. priv.
N: NcU 96 frames   8377

TOULMIN, HARRY
Letters, 1793-1811, 21 items DLC
N: CSmH 1 reel   8378

TUCKER, GEORGE, 1775-1861
Correspondence, 1822-1859 DLC
N: ViU   8379
P: ViU

TUCKER, GEORGE, 1775-1861
Letters and papers ViU
N: MoSW 1 reel   8380

TUCKER, NATHANIEL BEVERLY, 1784-1851
Papers, 1821-1851 ViWC
N: ViWC 2 reels   8381

VAN LEW, ELIZABETH
Papers, 1862-1901 NN
N: Vi   8382

WASHINGTON, HENRY A.
Correspondence re: his edition of Jefferson's
writings ViWC
N: ViWC 15 feet   8383
P: ViWC

WETZEL FAMILY, Madison and Greene Cos., Va.
Letters, 1830-1898 priv.
N: ViU   8384

WICKHAM, JOHN
Diaries, memorandum books, and
correspondence, 1790-1830 priv.
N: ViU 3 reels   8385

WILSON, BENJAMIN
Papers re: Virginia, 1788-1859, 50 items
priv.
N: KyU 10 feet   8386

WISE, HENRY ALEXANDER, Gov. Va., 1806-1876
Papers, 1833-1876, 37 items priv.
N: NcU 1 reel   8387

Business Papers

BLAND, EDWARD
Legal account book, 1806-1827   priv.
N: ViU   8388
P: ViU

BOGLE FAMILY, Glasgow
Papers re: trade between Glasgow and Virginia,
1729-1787   UKGM
N: ViU   8389

BUMGARDNER, JACOB
Business papers, 1770-1930 priv.
N: ViU 1 reel   8390
P: ViU

BURWELL-MILLWOOD FAMILIES
Store and farm accounts, 1789-1870, 7 v.
[unk.]
N: ViU   8391

CARTER, Dr. JAMES
Account book, 1752-1773 ViWC
N: ViWC 50 feet   8392
P: ViWC

CARTER, ROBERT, of Nomini Hall
Waste-book, 1773-1783; account book, 1784-
1785 ViWC
N: ViWC 2 reels   P: ViWC   8393

CHARLTON, EDWARD
  Account book, 1769-1773 ViWC
  N: ViWC 100 feet   8394
  P: ViWC

CRAIG, ALEXANDER
  Account book, 1749-1763 ViWC
  N: ViWC 100 feet   8395
  P: ViWC

DOUGLAS, JOHN
  Liquidation document for Neil Jamieson and
  Co., 1799, 6 p.
  N: CU 1 reel   8396

DUNN, Dr. THOMAS HENRY
  Medical account books, 1852-1853, 1855, 1857
  Vi
  N: Vi 1/3 reel   8397
  P: USIGS

FONTAINE, EDMUND
  Letter book re: C & O RR., 1843-1850 Vi
  N: Vi   8398

GALT, JOHN MINSON
  Account books, 1771-1780 (with William
  Pasteur), 1782-1783 ViWC
  N: ViWC 2 reels   8399
  P: ViWC

GILMER FAMILY
  Account books and letters, 1762-1832 priv.
  N: ViU   8400
  P: ViU

GREENE, THOMAS
  Ledger, 1828-1874, containing abstracts of
  data substantiating clients' claims to service in
  Revolutionary War Vi
  N: Vi 1 reel   8401
  P: USIGS

HARWOOD, HUMPHREY
  Account book, 1776-1794 ViWC
  N: ViWC 90 feet   8402
  P: ViWC

JAMIESON, NEIL
  Business papers, 1757-1762, 1 v. DLC
  N: NjP 1 reel   8403

JERDONE, FRANCIS
  Account book, 1751-1752 ViWC
  N: ViWC 90 feet   8404
  P: ViWC

JONES, ELLIOTT P.
  General merchandise account books (with
  John J. Wake), 1859-1862; Milton Plantation
  account books, 1856-1861 Vi
  N: Vi 2/3 reel   8405
  P: USIGS

LIBERTY (Brig)
  Account book, 1838 (typescript) Vi
  N: Vi   8406
  P: USIGS

LYNCHBURG PLOW Co., Lynchburg, Va.
  Minute book, 1896-1926 Ibid.
  N: ViU   8407

McFARLAND, FRANCIS, 1788-1871
  Diaries and account books, 1815-1871, 23 v.
  priv.
  N: ViU   8408
  P: ViU

McFARLAND, FRANCIS, 1788-1871
  Diary, 1815-1871, 21 v. and 1 letter priv.
  N: NcU 850 frames   8409

McWANE, HENRY EDWARD, Sr.
  Diaries, 1891-1914, 17 v.; papers re: Lynch-
  burg Foundry Co.   priv.
  N: ViU   8410

MADISON, JAMES, Sr.
  Account book, 1744-1757, 1v. priv.
  N: ViU   8411
  P: ViU

MERCER, JOHN, of Marlborough, Va., 1704-1768
  Land book, 1728-1765 Vi
  N: Vi 1 reel   8412
  P: Vi

MERCER, JOHN, of Marlborough, Va., 1704-1768
  Ledgers, 1725-1737, 1744-1749, 2 v. PDoHi
  N: PDoHi P: PDoHi   8413

MOUNT AIRY PLANTATION, Virginia
  Books, 1805-1855, 3 v. priv.
  N: NcU 1 reel   8414

MURRELL, JOHN D.
  Account book, 1819-1830, 1 v. priv.
  N: ViU   8415
  P: ViU

PRINCIPIO COMPANY
  Accounts and letters re: Potomac Iron Works,
  1768-1769, 1 v. NN
  N: CU 1 reel   8416

ROSE, ROBERT
  Account book, ca. 1727-1733 ViWC
  N: ViU 84 frames   8417
  P: ViWI

ROSE, ROBERT
  Account book and diary, 1747-1750 ViWC
  N: ViWC 20 feet   8418
  P: ViWC

SAVAGE, NATHANIEL LYTTLETON, Virginia
  planter
  Account book, 1768-1785, 1 v. NN
  N: CU 1 reel   8419

SOUTHALL, TURNER
  Receipt book, 1776-1780 ViWC
  N: ViWC 90 feet   8420
  P: ViWC

SWEET SPRINGS HOTEL, Monroe, Va.
  Records, 1855-1906, 3 v. priv.
  N: ViU   8421
  P: ViU

WASHINGTON, GEORGE, Pres. U.S., 1732-1799
  Surveys, 1750, 1773 priv.
  DC: WvU   8422

WESTOVER PLANTATION, Virginia
  Journal, 1858-1864, 1 v. priv.
  N: NcU 160 frames   8423

WHITE HILL PLANTATION, Virginia
  Books, 1817-1859, 5 v. priv.
  N: NcU 2 reels   8424

WOODFORD, WILLIAM
  Letter book re: shipping between England and
  Virginia, 1723-1737 KyU
  N: KyU 15 feet   8425

Collections

CABELL, NATHANIEL FRANCIS, collector
  Letters and manuscripts on agriculture,
  1749-1879, 133 items Vi
  N: ViU   8426

CABELL, NATHANIEL FRANCIS, collector
  Virginia Agriculture Papers, 1722-1879 Vi
  N: Vi 1 reel   8427
  P: Vi

COLONIAL WILLIAMSBURG, INC.
  Bowyer-Hubard papers, 1767-1816 ViWC
  N: ViWC 75 feet   8428
  P: ViWC

COLONIAL WILLIAMSBURG, INC.
  Spotswood papers, 1646-1830 ViWC
  N: ViWC 1 reel 28 feet   8429
  P: ViWC

COLONIAL WILLIAMSBURG, INC.
  Waller collection, 1737-1912 ViWC
  N: ViWC 10 feet   8430
  P: ViWC

FRENCH, S. BASSETT, compiler
  Virginia biographical sketches, n.d. Vi
  N: USIGS 4 reels   8431
  P: Vi

KOONTZ, LOUIS KNOTT, collector
  Correspondence re: Virginia frontier, ca. 1752-
  1951 v.p.
  N: CLU 68 reels   8432

VIRGINIA COLONIAL RECORDS PROJECT
  Virginia records and papers, 1580-1750 v.p.
  N: Vi   8433
  P: ViU ViWI

The Virginia Colonial Records Project has filmed,

in Great Britain and Europe, all items concerned
with Virginia it could discover. This material has
been fully described and indexed in reports made
by the Project, of which a few copies are still available for institutions.

College Records

WILLIAM AND MARY COLLEGE, Williamsburg, Va.
  Board of visitors' minutes, 1860-1902 ViW
  N: ViW 1 reel*   8434

WILLIAM AND MARY COLLEGE, Williamsburg, Va.
  Bursar's accounts, ledgers, etc.,
  1754-1891 ViW
  N: ViW 1 reel*   8435

WILLIAM AND MARY COLLEGE, Williamsburg, Va.
  Faculty minutes, 1817-1945 ViW
  N: ViW 3 reels*   8436

WILLIAM AND MARY COLLEGE, Williamsburg,
  Va.
  Faculty reports to visitors, 1831-1835; account
  book of Thomas R. Dew, 1836-1846; student
  matriculation books, 1827-1920 ViW
  N: ViW 1 reel*   8437

Institutions

CHARLOTTESVILLE, Va. LYCEUM
  Minute book, 1845-1846, 1 v. priv.
  N: ViU   8438
  P: ViU

DEMOCRATIC PARTY. VIRGINIA. STATE
  COMMITTEE
  Correspondence and lists of delegates, 1932,
  4 v. Ibid.
  N: ViU   8439
  P: ViU

FREEMASONS. WILLIAMSBURG, Va.
  Minutes of Lodge, 1773-1779 Ibid.
  DCO: DLC 1 box   8440

MUTUAL ASSURANCE SOCIETY OF VIRGINIA
  Declarations, 1796-1867 Ibid.
  N: Vi 23 reels   8441
  P: Vi

PETERSBURG, Va. BLANDFORD CEMETERY
  Interments, 1843-1943 Ibid.
  N: Vi 2 reels   8442
  P: USIGS Vi

RICHMOND, Va. HOLLYWOOD CEMETERY
  Burial register, 1847-1955; burial register of
  Confederate Dead from Lee Camp Soldiers
  Home, Richmond, 1894-1946 Ibid.
  N: Vi 4 reels   8443
  P: USIGS Vi

RICHMOND, Va. SHOCKOE CEMETERY
  Records, 1822-1955 Ibid.
  N: Vi 4 reels   8444
  P: USIGS Vi

WOMAN'S CHRISTIAN TEMPERANCE UNION.
  VIRGINIA
  Minute books, 1883-1887 priv.
  N: ViU DLC   8445
  P: ViU

NORTH CAROLINA

Census

U.S. CENSUS. SECOND, 1800
  Population schedules, North Carolina DNA
  N: DNA 6 reels   8446

U.S. CENSUS. THIRD, 1810
  Population schedules, North Carolina DNA
  N: DNA 6 reels   8447

U.S. CENSUS. FOURTH, 1820
  Population schedules, North Carolina DNA
  N: DNA 6 reels   8448

U.S. CENSUS. FIFTH, 1830
Population schedules, North Carolina DNA
N: DNA 8 reels   8449
  P: KyU USIGS

U.S. CENSUS. SIXTH, 1840
Population schedules, North Carolina DNA
N: DNA 6 reels   8450
  P: AB USIGS

U.S. CENSUS. SEVENTH, 1850
Population schedules, North Carolina DNA
N: DNA 8 reels   8451
  P: AB USIGS

U.S. CENSUS. SEVENTH TO NINTH, 1850-1870
Agriculture schedules, North Carolina NcD
N: Nc-Ar   8452

U.S. CENSUS. SEVENTH TO NINTH, 1850-1870
Industry schedules, North Carolina NcD
N: Nc-Ar   8453

U.S. CENSUS. SEVENTH TO NINTH, 1850-1870
Social statistics schedules, North Carolina
NcD
N: Nc-Ar   8454

U.S. CENSUS. EIGHTH, 1860
Population schedules, North Carolina DNA
N: DNA 9 reels   8455
  P: USIGS

U.S. CENSUS. EIGHTH TO NINTH, 1860-1870
Mortality schedules, North Carolina NcD
N: Nc-Ar   8456

U.S. CENSUS. NINTH, 1870
Population schedules, North Carolina DNA
N: DNA 12 reels   8457
  P: USIGS

U.S. CENSUS. TENTH, 1880
Population schedules, North Carolina DNA
N: DNA 39 reels   8458

Government Records

U.S. ADJUTANT-GENERAL'S OFFICE
Index to compiled service records of Volunteer
soldiers from North Carolina during the Cherokee
Removal DNA
N: DNA 1 reel 16 mm. [M-256]   8459

U.S. ADJUTANT-GENERAL'S OFFICE
Index to compiled service records of Volunteer
soldiers of the War of 1812 from North Carolina
DNA
N: DNA 5 reels 16 mm. [M-250]   8460

U.S. DEPT. OF THE INTERIOR
Report by Special Agent, O. M. McPherson,
on condition and tribal rights of the Indians of
Robeson and adjoining counties, 1914, 252 p.
Nc-Ar
N: USIGS   8461

U.S. OFFICE OF INDIAN AFFAIRS
Cherokee Indian agency, North Carolina, Chero-
kee Reservation census roll, Jan. 1, 1940 Ibid.
N: DLC 1 reel   8462

U.S. PATENT OFFICE
Correspondence re: Daniel Lee Ibid.
N: NcD 2 reels   8463

U.S. PATENT OFFICE
Selected letters from the Department of
Agriculture re: Daniel Lee, 1839-1857,
33 items DNA
N: NcD 1 reel   8464

**U.S. WAR DEPT. COLLECTION OF
CONFEDERATE RECORDS**
Index to compiled service records of Confed-
erate soldiers from North Carolina DNA
N: DNA 43 reels 16 mm. [M-230]   8465

State Records

NORTH CAROLINA (Colony). COURT OF CLAIM
Land records, 1755-1774 Nc-S
N: USIGS 2 reels   8466

**NORTH CAROLINA (Colony). COURT OF VICE
ADMIRALTY**
Records, 1728-1737, 1739-1758
DCO: DLC 389 p.   8467

NORTH CAROLINA
Land grants, 1735-1853; marriage records,
1879-1886 Nc-Ar
N: USIGS 5 reels   8468

NORTH CAROLINA
Tax lists, 1755: Beaufort, Cumberland,
Currituck, Granville, New Hanover, Orange,
Tyrrell counties; list of taxables, Dobbs
County, 1769 Nc-S
N: USIGS 1 reel   8469

NORTH CAROLINA
Tax lists: Anson, 1763; Beaufort, 1764; Bladen,
1763; Brunswick, 1769; Caswell, 1777; Craven,
1720, 1769; Granville, 1769; Onslow, 1769, 1770;
Pasquotank, 1754, 1769; Pitt, 1762 Nc-S
N: USIGS 1 reel   8470

NORTH CAROLINA
Wills, 1663-1789, 35 v.; wills and court
records, 1679-1773 Nc-Ar
N: USIGS 15 reels   8471

NORTH CAROLINA. BOARD OF AGRICULTURE
Minutes, 1887-1953 Ibid.
N: Nc-Ar 2 reels   8472

County Records

North Carolina county records are listed collectively, unless they appear to have special value to the
researcher. Separate listing is always given to
minute books, wills and/or probate records, deeds,
vital records, and muster rolls. In order that researchers may differentiate between materials the
originals of which are held at county courthouses
and materials the originals of which are held at the
state archives, an exception has been made to the
usual alphabetical listing. Courthouse material
always precedes archival material.

ALAMANCE Co., N.C.
Marriage records, 1854-1868, 58 p. Nc-Ar
N: USIGS   8473

ALBEMARLE Co., N.C.
State papers, 1678-1739, 2 v. Nc-Ar
  USIGS 2 reels   8474

ANSON Co., N.C.
Court minutes, 1771-1776, 1848-1858; wills,
1751-1942; deeds, 1749-1838 C.H. Wadesboro
N: USIGS 29 reels   8475
  P: Nc-Ar

ANSON Co., N.C.
Land entries, 1778-1795, 315 p. Nc-Ar
N: USIGS 1 reel   8476

ASHE Co., N.C.
Wills, 1800-1858; deeds, 1800-1869; marriage
records, 1851-1866 C.H. Jefferson
N: USIGS 49 reels   8477
  P: Nc-Ar wills to 1842

ASHE Co., N.C.
Court minutes, 1806-1866; deeds and grants,
1778-1849; wills and equity dockets,
1806-1829 Nc-Ar
N: USIGS 10 reels   8478

BEAUFORT Co., N.C.
Court minutes, 1756-1761, 1785-1786, 1809-
1814, 1824-1829, 1832-1838, 1841-1868
C.H. Washington
N: USIGS 8 reels   8479
  P: Nc-Ar

BEAUFORT Co., N.C.
Deeds, mortgages, and bills of sale, 1784, 1803-
1807; tax lists, 1784 Nc-Ar
N: USIGS 1 reel   8480

BEAUFORT Co., N.C.
Land entries, 1778-1795; lists of taxables,
1779, 1786, 1789 Nc-S
N: USIGS 2 reels   8481

BERTIE Co., N.C.
Wills, 1761-1942; deeds, 1722-1822 C.H.
Windsor

N: USIGS 33 reels   8482
  P: Nc-Ar deeds from 1721

BERTIE Co., N.C.
Court records, 1801-1868; wills, 1728-1744,
1749-1844; deeds,1714-1855 Nc-Ar
N: USIGS 12 reels   8483

BLADEN Co., N.C.
Wills, 1760-1942; deeds, 1770-1869; marriage
records, 1868-1872 C.H. Elizabethtown
N: USIGS 28 reels   8484
  P: Nc-Ar

BLADEN Co., N.C.
Deeds, 1738-1780 Nc-Ar
N: USIGS 2 reels   8485

BRUNSWICK Co., N.C.
Court minutes, 1859-1866; wills, 1780-1946;
deeds, 1764-1849; marriage register, 1850-
1904 C.H. Southport
N: USIGS 8 reels   8486

BRUNSWICK Co., N.C.
Court minutes, 1850-1859, 1866-1868; wills,
1781-1847, 1850-1859, 1866-1868 Nc-Ar
N: USIGS 2 reels   8487

BUNCOMBE Co., N.C.
Court minutes, 1792-1832; wills, 1831-1864;
deeds, 1789-1868; marriage records, 1851-
1889 C.H. Asheville
N: USIGS 23 reels   8488

BUNCOMBE Co., N.C.
Land entries, 1794-1822 Nc-S
N: USIGS 2 reels   8489

BURKE Co., N.C.
Wills, 1793-1905; deeds, 1789-1856 Nc-Ar
N: USIGS 3 reels   8490

BUTE Co., N.C.
Wills, 1760-1800; land entries, 1778-1779;
tax list, 1771 Nc-Ar
N: USIGS 4 reels   8491

CABARRUS Co., N.C.
Court minutes, 1795-1805, 1819-1845; wills,
1842-1868; deeds, 1788-1868 C.H. Concord
N: USIGS 11 reels   8492
  P: Nc-Ar

CABARRUS Co., N.C.
Court minutes, 1793-1797 Nc-Ar
N: USIGS 1 reel   8493

CAMDEN Co., N.C.
Wills, 1822-1869; deeds, 1777-1867; marriage
records, 1848-1867, 1873-1911 C.H. Camden
N: USIGS 13 reels   8494
  P: Nc-Ar

CAMDEN Co., N.C.
Court records, 1800-1870; land entries, 1778-
1795 Nc-Ar
N: USIGS 4 reels   8495

CARTERET Co., N.C.
Wills, 1745-1942; deeds, 1778-1852
C.H. Beaufort
N: USIGS 15 reels   8496
  P: Nc-Ar

CARTERET Co., N.C.
Court minutes, 1723-1747; wills, 1717-1887;
deeds, 1721-1815 Nc-Ar
N: USIGS 15 reels   8497

CASWELL Co., N.C.
Wills, 1777-1908, deeds, 1777-1841; marriage
records, 1852-1867; delayed birth certificates,
1941-1946 C.H. Yanceyville
N: USIGS 24 reels   8498
  P: Nc-Ar

CASWELL Co., N.C.
Court minutes, 1777, 1854-1856; wills, 1772-
1864; deeds, 1778-1863 Nc-Ar
N: USIGS 4 reels   8499

CATAWBA Co., N.C.
Wills, 1843-1868; deeds, 1842-1874; marriage
records, 1851-1866 C.H. Newton
N: USIGS 5 reels   8500

CHATHAM Co., N.C.
Court minutes, 1842-1868; wills, 1780-1924;
deeds, 1771-1840; marriage registers, 1852-
1867 C.H. Pittsboro

N: USIGS 17 reels   8501
P: Nc-Ar

CHATHAM Co., N.C.
Wills, 1782-1857; deeds, 1778-1799 Nc-Ar
N: USIGS 4 reels   8502

CHEROKEE Co., N.C.
Deeds, 1839-1866 C.H. Murphy
N: USIGS 5 reels   8503

CHOWAN Co., N.C.
Court order books, 1780-1830; court records,
1687-1890; wills, 1760-1941; deeds, 1699-1814;
vital records, 1750-1817 C.H. Edenton
N: USIGS 68 reels   8504
P: Nc-Ar

CHOWAN Co., N.C.
Court records, 1724-1846; wills, 1694-1866;
deeds, 1714-1735 Nc-Ar
N: USIGS 4 reels   8505

CLEVELAND Co., N.C.
Court records, 1844-1868; wills, 1841-1867;
deeds, 1841-1865; marriage records, 1851-
1865 C.H. Shelby
N: USIGS 4 reels   8506

COLUMBUS Co., N.C.
Wills, 1847-1865; deeds, 1807-1865;
marriage records, 1853-1868 C.H.
Whitesville
N: USIGS   8507

COLUMBUS Co., N.C.
Court minutes, 1838-1846 Nc-Ar
N: USIGS 1 reel   8508

CRAVEN Co., N.C.
Wills, 1700-1942; deeds, 1708-1868
C.H. New Bern
N: USIGS 43 reels   8509
P: Nc-Ar

CRAVEN Co., N.C.
Wills, 1737-1891; deeds, 1716-1891 Nc-Ar
N: USIGS 19 reels   8510

CUMBERLAND Co., N.C.
Court minutes, 1844-1860; wills, 1754-1942;
deeds, 1754-1848; census, 1840, 1850 C.H.
Fayetteville
N: USIGS 42 reels   8511

CUMBERLAND Co., N.C.
Court records, 1766-1837; wills, 1757-1869;
deeds, 1757-1815 Nc-Ar
N: USIGS 3 reels   8512

CURRITUCK Co., N.C.
Court minutes, 1821-1830; court records,
1834-1840, 1855-1867; wills, 1761-1941; deeds,
1719-1850 C.H. Currituck
N: USIGS 19 reels   8513

CURRITUCK Co., N.C.
Guardian accounts, 1830-1870; wills, 1772-1827,
1830-1884 Nc-Ar
N: USIGS 8 reels   8514

DAVIDSON Co., N.C.
Wills, 1822-1868; deeds, 1823-1865; marriage
records, 1822-1938 C.H. Lexington
N: USIGS 9 reels   8515
P: Nc-Ar

DAVIE Co., N.C.
Deeds, 1837-1868; marriage records, 1851-
1865 C.H. Mocksville
N: USIGS 3 reels   8516
P: Nc-Ar

DOBBS Co., N.C.
Wills, 1767; deeds, 1765-1769, 1778-1797 Nc-Ar
N: USIGS 2 reels   8517

DUPLIN Co., N.C.
Wills, 1750, 1760-1942; deeds, 1754-1860;
tax lists, 1811-1817 C.H. Kenansville
N: USIGS 29 reels   8518
P: Nc-Ar

DUPLIN Co., N.C.
Court minutes, 1784-1852; wills, 1761-1804;
tax lists, 1783-1817 Nc-Ar
N: USIGS 7 reels   8519

EDGECOMBE Co., N.C.
Wills, 1760-1942; deeds, 1759-1830 C.H.
Tarboro
N: USIGS 27 reels   8520

EDGECOMBE Co., N.C.
Wills, 1733-1753, 1758-1830; deeds, 1732-1741
Nc-Ar
N: USIGS 9 reels   8521

FRANKLIN Co., N.C.
Court minutes, 1854-1860; wills, 1785-1943;
deeds, 1778-1896 C.H. Louisburg
N: USIGS 29 reels   8522
P: Nc-Ar

FRANKLIN Co., N.C.
Wills, 1787-1839; deeds, 1797-1799, 1814;
tax lists, 1798 Nc-Ar
N: USIGS 5 reels   8523

GATES Co., N.C.
Wills, 1780-1867; deeds, 1776-1872
C.H. Gatesville
N: USIGS 12 reels   8524
P: Nc-Ar

GATES Co., N.C.
Wills, 1762-1805, 1808-1867; bonds, 1810-1812,
1823-1825 Nc-Ar
N: USIGS 7 reels   8525

GRANVILLE Co., N.C.
Court records, 1754-1868; wills, 1746-1943;
deeds, 1746-1826; marriage records, 1746-
1880; tax lists, 1786-1791 C.H. Oxford
N: USIGS 53 reels   8526
P: Nc-Ar

GRANVILLE Co., N.C.
Land entries, 1778-1796 Nc-Ar
N: USIGS 1 reel   8527

GREENE Co., N.C.
Wills, 1839-1845 Nc-Ar
N: USIGS 2 reels   8528

GUILFORD Co., N.C.
Court minutes, 1826-1852; wills, 1771-1943;
deeds, 1771-1835 C.H. Greensboro
N: USIGS 27 reels   8529

GUILFORD Co., N.C.
Deeds, 1779-1795 Nc-Ar
N: USIGS 1 reel   8530

HALIFAX Co., N.C.
Court records, 1832-1868; wills, 1759-1943;
deeds, 1732-1825 C.H. Halifax
N: USIGS 26 reels   8531

HALIFAX Co., N.C.
Wills, 1755-1854; land entries, 1778-1795
Nc-Ar
N: USIGS 4 reels   8532

HAYWOOD Co., N.C.
Court minutes, 1809-1868; wills, 1829-1878;
deeds, 1809-1865; marriage records, 1852-
1868 C.H. Waynesville
N: USIGS 8 reels   8533
P: Nc-Ar

HENDERSON Co., N.C.
Court minutes, 1838-1868; wills, 1838-1882;
deeds, 1838-1870; marriage records, 1851-
1872 C.H. Hendersonville
N: USIGS 7 reels   8534
P: Nc-Ar

HERTFORD Co., N.C.
Wills, 1830-1866 C.H. Winton
N: USIGS 1 reel   8535

HYDE Co., N.C.
Wills, 1765-1868; deeds, 1716-1869
C.H. Swanquarter
N: USIGS 20 reels   8536
P: Nc-Ar

HYDE Co., N.C.
Court records, 1781-1869; wills, 1781-1869;
deeds, 1778-1795 Nc-Ar
N: USIGS 1 reel   8537

IREDELL Co., N.C.
Wills, 1790-1867; deeds, 1788-1869 C.H.
Statesville

N: USIGS 16 reels   8538
P: Nc-Ar

IREDELL Co, N.C.
Land entries, 1789-1794, 35 p.   Nc-Ar
N: USIGS   8539

JOHNSTON Co., N.C.
Wills, 1760-1897; deeds, 1762-1869
C.H. Smithfield
N: USIGS 16 reels   8540
P: Nc-Ar

JOHNSTON Co., N.C.
Wills, 1759-1863; deeds, 1759-1795; court
martial minutes, 1759-1779 Nc-Ar
N: USIGS 14 reels   8541

JONES Co., N.C.
Wills, 1778-1868; deeds, 1784-1804, 1813,
1819-1867; marriage records, 1851-1874
C.H. Trenton
N: USIGS 9 reels   8542
P: Nc-Ar

JONES Co., N.C.
Court records, 1809-1829; wills, 1760-1842;
land entries, 1779-1795 Nc-Ar
N: USIGS 2 reels   8543

LENOIR Co., N.C., see HINES, LOVIT, collector,
8655, under NORTH CAROLINA, Collections

LINCOLN Co., N.C.
Wills, 1824-1869; deeds, 1779-1869; marriage
records, 1851-1869 C.H. Lincolnton
N: USIGS 19 reels   8544
P: Nc-Ar

LINCOLN Co., N.C.
Court records, 1779-1782; land entries, 1783-
1795 Nc-Ar
N: USIGS 2 reels   8545

MACON Co., N.C.
Court records, 1829-1875; wills, 1829-1853;
deeds, 1829-1865; marriage records, 1829-
1949 C.H. Franklin
N: USIGS 9 reels   8546
P: Nc-Ar

McDOWELL Co., N.C.
Court minutes, 1843-1867; wills, 1843-1865;
deeds, 1843-1866; marriage records, 1851-
1869 C.H. Marion
N: USIGS 4 reels   8547
P: Nc-Ar

MARTIN Co., N.C.
Wills, 1774-1867; deeds, 1774-1867
C.H. Williamston
N: USIGS 10 reels   8548
P: Nc-Ar

MECKLENBURG Co., N.C.
Court records, 1774-1869; wills, 1763-1929;
deeds, 1755-1845; marriage records, 1850-1888
C.H. Charlotte
N: USIGS 25 reels   8549
P: Nc-Ar

MECKLENBURG Co., N.C.
Wills, 1749-1869; guardian bonds, 1780-1873
Nc-Ar
N: USIGS 4 reels   8550

MONTGOMERY Co., N.C.
Land entries, 1779-1796; tax lists, 1782 Nc-Ar
N: USIGS 1 reel   8551

MOORE Co., N.C.
Land entries, 1784-1795; court records,
1784-1795 Nc-Ar
N: USIGS 1 reel   8552

NASH Co., N.C.
Wills, 1776-1943; deeds, 1778-1831
C.H. Nashville
N: USIGS 32 reels   8553
P: Nc-Ar

NASH Co., N.C.
Wills, 1778-1859; guardian accounts, 1827-1838;
land entries, 1778-1796 Nc-Ar
N: USIGS 4 reels   8554

NEW HANOVER Co., N.C.
Court minutes, 1843-1845, 1847-1850, 1859-
1868; wills, 1734-1741, 1747-1942; deeds,

1734-1741, 1744-1917 C.H. Wilmington
N: USIGS 38 reels
P: Nc-Ar   8555

NEW HANOVER Co., N.C.
Court records, 1746-1858; wills, 1732-1864
Nc-Ar
N: USIGS 4 reels   8556

NORTHAMPTON Co., N.C.
Wills, 1741-1871; deeds, 1741-1868; marriage
records, 1851-1865 C.H. Jackson
N: USIGS 17 reels
P: Nc-Ar   8557

NORTHAMPTON Co., N.C.
Land entries, 1778-1794; wills, 1762-1808;
orphans' estates, 1781-1802 Nc-Ar
N: USIGS 2 reels   8558

ONSLOW Co., N.C.
Wills, 1765-1939; deeds, 1712-1839
C.H. Jacksonville
N: USIGS 17 reels
P: Nc-Ar   8559

ONSLOW Co., N.C.
Wills, 1746-1863; guardians' records, 1754-
1867 Nc-Ar
N: USIGS 5 reels   8560

ORANGE Co., N.C.
Court minutes, 1856-1861; wills, 1752-1946;
deeds, 1755-1840 C.H. Hillsboro
N: USIGS 19 reels
P: Nc-Ar   8561

ORANGE Co., N.C.
Wills, 1753-1865; deeds, 1753-1795 Nc-Ar
N: USIGS 7 reels   8562

PASQUOTANK Co., N.C.
Wills, 1752-1941; deeds, 1745-1831; divisions
of land, 1793-1885 C.H. Elizabeth City
N: USIGS 25 reels
P: Nc-Ar   8563

PASQUOTANK Co., N.C.
Court records, 1757-1785; wills, 1720-1867;
deeds, 1700-1747, 1755-1766, 1778-1793; vital
records, 1691-1797; apprenticeship indentures,
1823 Nc-Ar
N: USIGS 8 reels   8564

PERQUIMANS Co., N.C.
Court minutes, 1827-1868; wills, 1761-1941;
deeds, 1681-1841 C.H. Hertford
N: USIGS 28 reels
P: Nc-Ar   8565

PERQUIMANS Co., N.C.
Wills, 1711-1805; vital records, 1659-1739
Nc-Ar
N: USIGS 4 reels   8566

PERSON Co., N.C.
Wills, 1847-1867; deeds, 1791-1869; marriage
records, 1851-1867 C.H. Roxboro
N: USIGS 14 reels
P: Nc-Ar   8567

PERSON Co., N.C.
Wills, 1792-1876; land entries, 1792-1796
Nc-Ar
N: USIGS 7 reels   8568

PERSON COUNTY, N.C. WARDENS OF THE
POOR
Records, 1792-1831 NcU
Records, 1831-1868 C.H. Roxboro
N: NcU 1 reel   8569

PITT Co., N.C.
Wills, 1858-1866; deeds, 1762-1866; marriage
records, 1851-1866 C.H. Greenville
N: USIGS 15 reels
P: Nc-Ar   8570

PITT Co., N.C.
Wills, 1762-1851; deeds, 1793-1797; taxables,
1778-1779 Nc-Ar
N: USIGS 1 reel   8571

RANDOLPH Co., N.C.
Court minutes, 1779-1868; wills, 1779-1923;
deeds, 1779-1848; marriage records, 1788-
1789, 1801-1809, 1845-1871 C.H. Asheboro
N: USIGS 22 reels   P: Nc-Ar   8572

RANDOLPH Co., N.C.
Land entries, 1783-1795; list of taxables, 1779,
205 p. Nc-Ar
N: USIGS   8573

RICHMOND Co., N.C.
Wills, 1779-1868; deeds, 1784-1869; marriage
records, 1780-1864, 1872-1891
C.H. Rockingham
N: USIGS 25 reels   8574

RICHMOND Co., N.C.
Land entries and grants, 1780-1795; immigrant
records; tax books, 1792-1793; list of taxables,
1790, 1793-1812, 408 p. Nc-Ar
N: USIGS   8575

ROBESON Co., N.C.
Wills, 1787-1865; deeds, 1786-1865; marriage
records, 1851-1866 C.H. Lumberton
N: USIGS
P: Nc-Ar   8576

ROBESON Co., N.C.
Wills, 1783-1851, 4 v.; deeds, 1792-1793, 1797-
1798, 1801-1802 Nc-Ar
N: USIGS 3 reels   8577

ROCKINGHAM Co., N.C.
Wills, 1804-1865; deeds, 1785-1866
C.H. Wentworth
N: USIGS 24 reels
P: Nc-Ar   8578

ROCKINGHAM Co., N.C.
Court minutes, 1786-1808, 941 p. Nc-Ar
N: USIGS   8579

ROWAN Co., N.C.
Court minutes, 1753-1868; wills, 1757-1942;
deeds, 1753-1833; census, 1850, 1860
C.H. Salisbury
N: USIGS 87 reels
P: Nc-Ar   8580

ROWAN Co., N.C.
Wills, 1743-1868, 24 v.; land entries, 1778-
1795; tax lists, 1802-1804, 1807 Nc-Ar
N: USIGS 10 reels   8581

RUTHERFORD Co., N.C.
Wills, 1782-1868; deeds, 1779-1867; marriage
records, 1851-1868 C.H. Rutherfordton
N: USIGS 14 reels
P: Nc-Ar TxD deeds to 1853   8582

RUTHERFORD Co., N.C.
Wills, 1784-1833; land entries and grants, 1782-
1797; guardian accounts, 1840-1850 Nc-Ar
N: USIGS 3 reels   8583

SAMPSON Co., N.C.
Court minutes, 1794-1851; wills, 1820-1922;
deeds, 1745-1839; marriage register, 1867-
1875 C.H. Clinton
N: USIGS 15 reels
P: Nc-Ar   8584

STANLY Co., N.C.
Wills, 1841-1865; deeds, 1841-1869 C.H.
Albemarle
N: USIGS 3 reels   8585

STOKES Co., N.C.
Wills, 1792-1865; deeds, 1790-1865
C.H. Danbury
N: USIGS 9 reels
P: Nc-Ar   8586

STOKES Co., N.C.
Court minutes, 1790-1800; inventories of es-
tates, 1790-1809; land entries, 1790-1795
Nc-Ar
N: USIGS 3 reels   8587

SURRY Co., N.C.
Wills, 1771-1867; deeds, 1771-1867; marriage
records, 1853-1867 C.H. Dobson
N: USIGS 47 reels
P: Nc-Ar   8588

SURRY Co., N.C.
Wills, 1777-1796; land entries, 1778-1795;
lists of taxables, 1771, 1772, 1782 Nc-Ar
N: USIGS 2 reels   8589

TRYON Co., N.C.
Court minutes, 1769-1779 Nc-Ar
N: USIGS 1 reel   8590

TYRRELL Co., N.C.
Wills, 1750-1865; deeds, 1736-1873; marriage
records, 1851-1868 C.H. Columbia
N: USIGS 12 reels
P: Nc-Ar   8591

TYRRELL Co., N.C.
Guardians' bonds, 1739-1871; wills, 1744-1836;
register of lands, 1747-1748; land entries, 1778-
1796 Nc-Ar
N: USIGS 5 reels   8592

UNION Co., N.C.
Wills, 1841-1867; deeds, 1842-1869; marriage
records, 1851-1870 C.H. Monroe
N: USIGS 6 reels   8593

WAKE Co., N.C.
Wills, 1771-1902; deeds, 1785-1842 C.H. Raleigh
N: USIGS 6 reels
P: Nc-Ar   8594

WAKE Co., N.C.
Wills, 1778-1794; deeds, 1778-1794; census,
1880 Nc-Ar
N: USIGS 3 reels   8595

WARREN Co., N.C.
Court minutes, 1806-1868; wills, 1764-1943;
deeds, 1764-1827 C.H. Warrenton
N: USIGS 37 reels
P: Nc-Ar   8596

WARREN Co., N.C.
Court records, 1782-1825; wills, 1780-1825
Nc-Ar
N: USIGS 6 reels   8597

WASHINGTON Co., N.C.
Deeds, 1799-1869; marriage records, 1851-
1884 C.H. Plymouth
N: USIGS 6 reels
P: Nc-Ar   8598

WASHINGTON Co., N.C.
Deeds, 1800-1801 Nc-Ar
N: USIGS 1 reel   8599

WAYNE Co., N.C.
Court minutes, 1820-1867; wills, 1807-1922;
deeds, 1780-1848; marriage licenses, 1851-
1868 C.H. Goldsboro
N: USIGS 21 reels
P: Nc-Ar   8600

WAYNE Co., N.C.
Court records, 1787-1851; wills, 1776-1851;
land records, 1780-1795 Nc-Ar
N: USIGS 7 reels   8601

WILKES Co., N.C.
Wills, 1800-1868; deeds, 1778-1869 C.H.
Wilkesboro
N: USIGS 14 reels
P: Nc-Ar   8602

WILKES Co., N.C.
Court minutes, 1778-1785, 1796-1797; wills,
1778-1899; deeds, 1778-1854; Civil War
claims and pensions, 1853-1902 Nc-Ar
N: USIGS 22 reels   8603

YANCEY Co., N.C.
Court minutes, 1834-1870; wills, 1834-1869;
deeds, 1833-1863 C.H. Burnsville
N: USIGS 5 reels
P: Nc-Ar   8604

Town and City Records

HIGH POINT, N.C.
Commissioner's minute book, 1859-1862 Ibid.
N: Nc-Ar 1 reel   8605

YANCEYVILLE, N.C. REGISTER OF DEEDS
Miscellaneous record book, 569 p. Ibid.
N: ?
P: ICN   8606

Church Records

BEAR CREEK CHURCH, Stanly Co., N.C.
Records, 1802-1828, 75 p. priv.
N: NcU 56 frames   8607

CLARKTON, N.C. BROWN MARSH
PRESBYTERIAN CHURCH
Records, 1796-1927 Ibid.
N: USlGS 1 reel   8608

EDENTON, N.C. ST. PAUL'S CHURCH
Vestry proceedings, 1701-1841 (transcript)
Nc-Ar
N: USlGS 1 reel   8609

FLAT RIVER PRIMITIVE BAPTIST CHURCH,
Person Co., N.C.
Indexes to minute books 1 to 3, 1786-1945,
53 p. priv.
N: USlGS   8610
P: Nc-Ar

LEWIS FORK BAPTIST ASSOCIATION, Wilkes Co.,
N.C.
Minutes, 1836-1870 Ibid.
N: Nc-Ar 1 reel   8611

LEXINGTON, N.C. PILGRIM CHURCH
Records Ibid.
N: Nc-Ar 2 reels   8612

LEXINGTON, N.C. PILGRIM GERMAN
REFORM CHURCH
Records, 1759-1897, 113 p. Vi
N: Vi   8613
P: USlGS 1 reel

LUTHERAN CHURCH. SYNODS. NORTH
CAROLINA and TENNESSEE
Records, 1813, 1818, 1820, 1825, 1828
[in German] priv.
N: T 1 reel   8614

MILLS RIVER, N.C. FRENCH BROAD BAPTIST
CHURCH
Minutes, 1835-1862; church records, 1862-
1924 Ibid.
N: Nc-Ar 2 reels   8615

PRIMITIVE BAPTIST CHURCH, Caswell Co., N.C.
Records of churches: Bush Arbor; Country
Line, 1869-1917; Lynches Creek, 1799-1856;
Prospect Hill, 1864-1945 C.H. Yanceyville
N: USlGS 1 reel   8616

ST. GABRIEL'S PARISH, Duplin Co., N.C.
Wardens' records, 1799-1817 Nc-Ar
N: USlGS 1 reel   8617

ST. GEORGE'S PARISH, Northampton Co., N.C.
Wardens' records, 1773-1814 Nc-Ar
N: USlGS 1 reel   8618

ST. JAMES PARISH, N.C.
Records, 1811-1852 Ibid.
N: Nc-Ar   8619

ST. JOHN'S PARISH, Beaufort, N.C.
Vestry book, 1742-1843 Nc-Ar
N: USlGS 1 reel   8620

WHEELEY'S PRIMITIVE BAPTIST CHURCH,
Person Co., N.C.
Minute books 1 and 2, 1790-1898, 304 p. priv.
N: USlGS   8621
P: Nc-Ar

Personal Papers

ARCHDALE, JOHN, 1642-1717
Papers, 1694-1706 C.O. 289 UKLPFO
DCO: DLC   8622
DCO: NcU 1 v.

BONHAM, Rev. NEHEMIAH, of Haywood Co., N.C.
Diary, 1829-1838 priv.
N: Nc-Ar 1 reel   8623

DOBBS, ARTHUR, 1689-1765
Papers, 1569-1845 (including family papers)
UKBeRO priv.
N: IrNL 3 reels   8624
P: NcU

DOBBS, ARTHUR, 1689-1765
Papers, 1758-1763 Amherst papers, W.O. 34,
v. 35,36 UKLPRO
DCO: NcU 184 items   8625

GENNETT, ANDREW, IV
Autobiography, 1938-1939 priv.
N: NcD 1 reel*   8626

GRAHAM, WILLIAM ALEXANDER, Gov. N.C.,
1804-1875
Papers (selections) Nc-Ar
N: OFH 56 frames   8627

HOGG, GAVIN, of Raleigh, N.C.
Papers, 1810-1901, 250 items priv.
N: NcD 1 reel   8628

McLEAN, ANGUS WILTON, Gov. N.C., 1870-1935
In-letters, 2 v. NcD
N: NcD 1 reel*   8629

McLEAN, ANGUS WILTON, Gov. N.C., 1870-1935
Papers, 1912-1933 priv.
N: NcU 421 frames   8630

SMALLWOOD, CHARLES, M.D., of Bertie Co.,
N.C., b. 1828
Diaries, 1843-1865, 1875, 1894, 2 v. priv.
N: NcU 154 frames   8631

SMALLWOOD, CHARLES, M.D., of Bertie Co.,
N.C., b. 1828
Diary, 1884-1896 priv.
N: Nc-Ar 1 reel   8632

THOMAS, WILLIAM HOLLAND, of
Waynesboro, N.C.
Papers, 1820-1931 priv.
N: NcD 2 reels   8633

WILLIAMSON, HUGH
Letters, 1778-1815 priv.
N: Nc-Ar 1 reel   8634

Business Papers

BARRINGER, RUFUS
Account book, 1837-1842 priv.
N: NcU 1 reel   8635

BELL, Dr. J.E.
Account book, 1809-1871 priv.
N: Nc-Ar   8636

CLARK AND CARNAL, Plymouth, N.C.
Letterbook, 1814-1815, 1 v. priv.
N: NcU 97 frames   8637

FLINN, ANDREW
"Green River" plantation book, 1840 priv.
N: NcU 1 reel   8638

FREELAND, JOHN JAY, of Hillsboro, N.C.
General store account books, 1852-1856 priv.
N: T 1 reel   8639

GAILLARD, PETER
Plantation books, 1799-1851, 3 v. priv.
N: NcU 1 reel   8640

HARRIS, DAVID GOLIGHTLY
Farm journals, 1855-1870, 7v. priv.
N: NcU 1 reel   8641

LEWIS, CHARLES
Account book, 1854 NcD
N: NcD 1 reel   8642

MASSENBURG, NICHOLAS B.
Farm journal, 1847-1851, 1 v. priv.
N: priv. 208 frames   P: NcU   8643

MEEK, S.M.
Journals and ledger, 1835-1858, 1 v. priv.
N: NcU 1 reel   8644

MERCHANTS BANK, Newbern, N.C.
Records, 1835-1869 Ibid.
N: Nc-Ar 1 reel   8645

METCALFE, CLIVE, 1863-1924
Diary-plantation journal, 1888-1893, 3 v.
priv.
N: NcU 200 frames   8646

MITCHELL, ROBERT, of Wilkes Co., N.C.
Account book, 1855-1874 priv.
N: Nc-Ar 1 reel   8647

NORTH CAROLINA RAILWAY COMPANY
Directors' minutes, 1904-1952; cash book,
1897-1951 Ibid.
N: Nc-Ar 1 reel   8648

PALMER, JOHN
Account books, 1750-1756, 1778-1784, 2 v.
priv. N: NcU 1 reel   8649

PERRY, JOHN
Accounts, 1829-1862 priv.
N: Nc-Ar   8650

STONEY-PORCHER FAMILY
Plantation diary and records, 1799-1862, 7 v.,
9 items priv.
N: NcU 1 reel   8651

WAYSIDE HOME, High Point, N.C.
Register, 1863-1864 priv.
N: G-Ar   8652

WILKES, RICHARD A.L., b. 1799
Account book, 1820-1863 priv.
N. NcU 1 reel   8653

Collections

CLARK, LULAH ANDERSON, collector
Papers of Anderson, Hall, and Farr families,
1853-1863, 1879, 10 items and 1 v. priv.
N: NcU 60 frames   8654

HINES, LOVIT, collector
Lenoir County, N.C., material, 1732-1914
Nc-Ar
N: USlGS 2 reels   8655

HOYT, WILLIAM HENRY, 1884-1957, collector
Papers re: Peter Stuart Ney and Michel Ney
v.p. [U.S., Scotland, France]
N: NcU ca. 75 reels   8656
DCO: NcU being processed

NORTH CAROLINA. ARCHIVES
Early records: Colonial America, 1629-
1753; North Carolina, 1628-1839 v.p.
N: Nc-Ar 5 reels   8657

NORTH CAROLINA. ARCHIVES
Miscellaneous microfilm collection: Skinner,
McRae, Wooley, and Duberry Papers, 1774-
1869; Little Collection; Blount Collection,
1780-1834; Bond Collection, 1755-1905;
Spanish records; W.R. Freeman Collection,
1812-1874; Steele Papers, 1756-1874; Led-
better Papers, 1830-1865; Crozer diary and
letters, Mar. 13-Apr. 30, 1865; Tryon
journal, 1771; Lilley Collection, 1785-1880;
Beaver Papers v.p.
N: Nc-Ar 14 reels   8658

NORTH CAROLINA. UNIVERSITY. LIBRARY
Scrapbook on desegregation, 1954-1955
NcU
N: NIC   8659

Institutions

AMERICAN FREE PRODUCE ASSOCIATION
Minutes, 1838-1846 MH
N: NcD 1 reel   8660
P: PHC

CUPOLA HOUSE, Edenton, N.C.
Papers, 1695-1884 Shepherd-Pruden Memor-
ial Library, Edenton, N.C.
N: NcU 5 reels   8661

FAYETTEVILLE LIGHT INFANTRY, Fayetteville,
N.C.
Minute book, 1793-1844
N: Nc-Ar 2 reels   8662

SPEW MARROW AGRICULTURAL CLUB
Papers priv.
N: Nc-Ar 1 reel   8663

School and College Records

BASSETT, JOHN SPENCER, 1867-1928
Papers regarding...controversy over...views
and writings while a teacher at Trinity College...
NcD
N: NNC 1 reel   8664

CABARRUS Co., N.C. BOARD OF EDUCATION
Minutes, 1841-1888 Ibid.
N: Nc-Ar 1 reel   8665

NORTH CAROLINA. STATE COLLEGE OF
AGRICULTURE AND ENGINEERING,
West Raleigh
Trustees' minutes, 1887-1932 Ibid.
N: Nc-Ar 2 reels   8666

SOUTH CAROLINA

Census

U.S. CENSUS. SECOND, 1800
Population schedules, South Carolina DNA
N: DNA 4 reels   8667

U.S. CENSUS. THIRD, 1810
Population schedules, South Carolina DNA
N: DNA 3 reels   8668

U.S. CENSUS. FOURTH, 1820
Population schedules, South Carolina DNA
N: DNA 4 reels   8669

U.S. CENSUS. FIFTH, 1830
Population schedules, South Carolina DNA
N: DNA 5 reels   8670
P: AB USIGS

U.S. CENSUS. SIXTH, 1840
Population schedules, South Carolina DNA
N: DNA 4 reels   8671
P: AB USIGS

U.S. CENSUS. SEVENTH, 1850
Agriculture schedules, South Carolina Sc-Ar
N: Sc-Ar 2 reels   8672

U.S. CENSUS. SEVENTH, 1850
Population schedules, South Carolina DNA
N: DNA 6 reels   8673
P: AB

U.S. CENSUS. SEVENTH TO NINTH,
1850-1870
Deaths, South Carolina Sc-Ar
N: Sc-Ar 2 reels   8674

U.S. CENSUS. SEVENTH TO NINTH, 1850-1870
Products of industry, South Carolina Sc-Ar
N: Sc-Ar 1 reel   8675

U.S. CENSUS. SEVENTH TO NINTH,
1850-1870
Social statistics, South Carolina Sc-Ar
N: Sc-Ar 1 reel   8676

U.S. CENSUS. EIGHTH, 1860
Agriculture schedules, South Carolina Sc-Ar
N: Sc-Ar 2 reels   8677

U.S. CENSUS. EIGHTH, 1860
Population schedules, South Carolina DNA
N: DNA 6 reels   8678
P: FU

U.S. CENSUS. NINTH, 1870
Agriculture schedules, South Carolina Sc-Ar
N: Sc-Ar 2 reels   8679

U.S. CENSUS. NINTH, 1870
Population schedules, South Carolina DNA
N: DNA 8 reels   8680
P: Sc-Ar USIGS

U.S. CENSUS. TENTH, 1880
Agriculture schedules, South Carolina Sc-Ar
N: Sc-Ar 9 reels   8681

U.S. CENSUS. TENTH, 1880
Defective, dependent, and delinquent classes,
South Carolina Sc-Ar
N: Sc-Ar 1 reel   8682

U.S. CENSUS. TENTH, 1880
Manufactures, South Carolina Sc-Ar
N: Sc-Ar 1 reel   8683

U.S. CENSUS. TENTH, 1880
Mortality, South Carolina Sc-Ar
N: Sc-Ar 1 reel   8684

U.S. CENSUS. TENTH, 1880
Population schedules, South Carolina DNA
N: DNA 27 reels   8685

State Records

SOUTH CAROLINA (Colony). COMMISSIONERS
OF FORTIFICATION
Journal, 1755-1770 ScHi
N: ScHi 1 reel   8686

SOUTH CAROLINA (Colony). COURT OF VICE
ADMIRALTY
Minutes, 1716-1763
DCO: DLC 9 boxes   8687

SOUTH CAROLINA (Colony). SECRETARY OF
THE PROVINCE
Records, 1671-1754 Sc-Ar
N: USIGS 5 reels   8688
P: Sc-Ar

SOUTH CAROLINA
Court records, 1771-1787; land grants, 1671-
1719; mortgages, 1734-1860; marriage settlements, 1785-1889; miscellaneous records, 1774-
1868 Sc-Ar
N: USIGS 102 reels   8689
P: Sc-Ar

SOUTH CAROLINA
Land grants, 1731-1775, 1784-1882; plats, 1733-
1861 Sc-S
N: USIGS 57 reels   8690
P: Sc-Ar

County Records

South Carolina county records are listed collectively, unless they appear to have special value to the
researcher. Separate listing is always given to
minute books, wills and/or probate records, deeds,
vital records, and muster rolls. In order that researchers may differentiate between materials the
originals of which are held at county courthouses
and materials the orginals of which are held at the
state archives, an exception has been made to the
usual alphabetical listing. Courthouse material
always precedes archival material

ABBEVILLE Co., S.C.
Probate records, 1787-1868; land plats, 1784-
1788 C.H. Abbeville
N: USIGS 10 reels   8691
P: Sc-Ar

ANDERSON Co., S.C.
Court records, 1819-1882; probate records,
1791-1880; deeds, 1789-1864; marriage records,
1911-1956; plat books, 1803-1864; Confederate
veterans' records, n.d.; free school journal,
1831-1847; account book of private company,
1849-1852 C.H. Anderson
N: USIGS 441 reels   8692

BARNWELL Co., S.C.
Wills, 1787-1836, 1850-1865; deeds, 1789-1851
C.H. Barnwell
N: Sc-Ar 4 reels   8693
P: USIGS

CHARLESTON Co., S.C.
Bills of sale of Negro slaves, 1799-1872;
wills, 1671-1868 (transcript) Sc-Ar
N: USIGS 38 reels   8694
P: Sc-Ar

CHARLESTON Co., S.C.
Charters, 1874-1892; court records, 1888-1947;
probate records, 1840-1949; deeds and land
records, 1719-1721, 1724-1726, 1737, 1744-
1745, 1753-1754, 1765-1950; tax records,
1859-1949 C.H. Charleston
N: Sc-Ar 498 reels   8695

CHARLESTON Co., S.C.
Probate records, 1687-1754 (WPA transcript);
land records, 1719-1873; citizenship petitions
and dowers, 1796-1905 C.H. Charleston
N: USIGS 186 reels   8696
P: Sc-Ar

CHARLESTON Co., S.C.
Wills (old), 1692-1868; with miscellaneous re-
cords ScHi
N: USIGS 13 reels   8697

CHARLESTON DISTRICT, S.C.
Chancery court records, 1800-1863
C.H. Charleston
N: USIGS 187 reels   P: Sc-Ar   8698

CHESTER Co., S.C.
Probate records, 1787-1868; deeds, 1785-1867
C.H. Chester
N: USIGS 29 reels   8699
P: Sc-Ar

EDGEFIELD Co., S.C.
Wills, 1787-1866; deeds, 1787-1866; inventories,
1803-1813, 1816-1832 C.H. Edgefield
N: Sc-Ar 28 reels   8700
P: USIGS

FAIRFIELD Co., S.C.
Wills, 1787-1857; deeds, 1785-1866
C.H. Winnsboro
N: USIGS 19 reels   8701
P: Sc-Ar

GREENVILLE Co., S.C.
Equity bills, 1822-1823; probate records, 1787-
1899; deeds, 1786-1865 C.H. Greenville
N: USIGS 28 reels   8702
P: Sc-Ar

HORRY Co., S.C.
Court records, 1803-1873; deeds, 1803-1939
C.H. Conway
N: USIGS 3 reels   8703
P: Sc-Ar

KERSHAW Co., S.C.
Wills, 1782-1824, 1840-1868; deeds, 1791-1866
C.H. Camden
N: USIGS 10 reels   8704
P: Sc-Ar

LANCASTER Co., S.C.
Land plats, 1829-1882; court records, 1822-
1871; probate records, 1820-1870; wills, 1865-
1892; deeds, 1787-1867 C.H. Lancaster
N: USIGS 19 reels   8705
P: Sc-Ar

LAURENS Co., S.C.
Court records, 1800-1865; marriage records,
1911-1951 C.H. Laurens
N: USIGS 12 reels   8706
P: SC-Ar

LAURENS Co., S.C.
Wills, 1788-1823, 1833-1861; deeds,
1785-1800, 1803-1867 C.H. Laurens
N: Sc-Ar 11 reels   8707
P: USIGS

LEXINGTON Co., S.C.
Deeds, 1839-1867; probate records, 1851-1893
C.H. Lexington
N: USIGS 7 reels   8708
P: Sc-Ar

MARION Co., S.C.
Wills, 1800-1888; deeds, 1800-1864
C.H. Marion
N: USIGS 9 reels   8709
P: Sc-Ar

MARLBORO Co., S.C.
Wills, 1787-1881; deeds, 1786-1797, 1802-1868
C.H. Bennettsville
N: USIGS 9 reels   8710
P: Sc-Ar

NEWBERRY Co., S.C.
Equity court records, 1818-1870 C.H. New-
berry
N: USIGS 101 reels   8711

NEWBERRY Co., S.C.
Wills, 1787-1949; deeds, 1773-1949; mortgages,
1918-1949; plats, 1906-1937; miscellaneous
records, 1886-1949 C.H. Newberry
N: Sc-Ar 63 reels   8712

PENDLETON Co. (later ANDERSON Co.), S.C.
Minutes, 1790-1793; naturalization papers,
1806-1825 C.H. Anderson
N: USIGS 1 reel   8713

PICKENS Co., S.C.
Wills, 1830-1860; deeds, 1826-1866 C.H.
Pickens
N: Sc-Ar 6 reels   8714
P: USIGS

PICKENS Co., S.C.
Citizenship petitions, 1823-1860 Charleston
N: USIGS 1 reel   8715
P: Sc-Ar

RICHLAND Co., S.C.
Court records, 1793-1870; wills, 1865-1941;
probate records, 1806-1888; estate papers,
early to 1955 C.H. Columbia
N: USIGS 147 reels   8716
P: Sc-Ar

SPARTANBURG Co., S.C.
Court records, 1804-1864; pension applications
and rolls of Civil War veterans and widows
C.H. Spartanburg
N: USIGS 11 reels   8717

SUMTER So., S.C.
Court records, 1802-1950; deeds, 1801-1948;
probate court records, 1800-1951; mortgages,
1904-1949; plats, 1785-1948   C.H. Sumter
N: Sc-Ar 124 reels   8718

WILLIAMSBURG Co., S.C.
Wills, 1806-1879; deeds, 1806-1865   C.H.
Kingstree
N: USIGS 5 reels   8719
P: Sc-Ar

Town and City Records

CHARLESTON, S.C.
Births, 1877-1901   Ibid.
N: Ibid. 22 reels   8720
P: Sc-Ar   USIGS

CHARLESTON, S.C.
Deaths, 1821-1886; marriages, 1877-1887   Ibid.
N: USIGS 54 reels   8721
P: Sc-Ar   USIGS

CHARLESTON, S.C.   BOARD OF POLICE
Proceedings, 1780   UKLPRO
N: Sc-Ar 1 reel   8722

CHARLESTON, S.C.   CITY COUNCIL
Proceedings, 1821-1822, 1857-1861, 1865-1870,
1876-1880   Ibid.
N: Sc-Ar 4 reels   8723

COLUMBIA, S.C.
Land records, 1704-1775   Ibid.
N: USIGS 9 reels   8724

ST. JOHN'S PARISH, Berkeley Co., S.C.
Minute book of road commissioners, 1760-1798
ScHi
N: USIGS 1 reel   8725
P: Sc-Ar

Church Records

BAPTISTS. SOUTH CAROLINA
Records, 1737-1955   priv.
N: ScU 24 reels   8726

BAPTISTS. SOUTH CAROLINA
Records, 1791-1953   ScGrvF
N: USIGS 20 reels   8727

BAPTISTS. SOUTH CAROLINA
Records, n.d. (WPA transcript)   ScU
N: USIGS 10 reels   8728

CHARLESTON, S.C. CHRIST CHURCH PARISH
Records, 1700-1847   Ibid.
N: USIGS 1 reel   8729

CHARLESTON, S.C. CIRCULAR INDEPENDENT
[CONGREGATIONAL] CHURCH
Records, 1732-1872   ScHi
N: USIGS 1 reel   8730
P: ScHi

CHARLESTON, S.C. CONGREGATIONAL CHURCH
Records, 1695-1916   ScU
N: ScU 4 reels   8731

CHARLESTON, S.C. GERMAN CHURCH
Record book, 1765-1787   Ibid.
N: USIGS 1 reel   8732

CHARLESTON, S.C. INDEPENDENT OR
CONGREGATIONAL CHURCH
Record books and register, 1730-1935
(WPA transcript) ScU-SC
N: USIGS 3 reels   8733

CHARLESTON, S.C. INDEPENDENT OR
CONGREGATIONAL CHURCH
Records, 1732-1913   Ibid.
N: USIGS 1 reel   8734

CHARLESTON, S.C. ST. JOHN'S
COLLETON PARISH
Records, 1734-1917   Ibid.
N: USIGS 2 reels   8735

CHARLESTON, S.C. ST. PETER'S CHURCH
Receipt and account book, 1886-1912   ScHi
N: USIGS   8736

CHARLESTON, S.C. ST. PHILIP'S
PARISH (Episcopal)
Records, 1713-1801, 1804-1812,
1823-1835   Ibid.
N: USIGS 1 reel   8737
P: ScHi

CHARLESTON, S.C. ST. STEPHEN'S AND
ST. JOHN'S BERKELEY PARISH
Records, 1754-1890 (orig. dest. - early years
transcribed in 1850)   Ibid.
N: USIGS 1 reel   8738
P: ScHi

CHURCH OF JESUS CHRIST OF LATTER-DAY
SAINTS. SOUTH CAROLINA
Ward and branch records: Augusta, Columbia,
Charleston, Darlington, Greenville, Gaffney,
Hartsville, Ridgeway, Society Hill, Spartanburg,
Sumpter, Winnsboro, 1947-1948   USIC
N: USIGS 12 reels   8739

ELIZABETH BAPTIST CHURCH, Mt. Croghan,
Chesterfield Co., S.C.
Minutes   Ibid.
N: Nc-Ar 1 reel   8740
P: Nc-Ar

FRIENDS, SOCIETY OF. CHARLESTON [S.C.]
Minutes, 1719-1769 (typescript)   ScHi
N: USIGS 1 reel   8741
P: ScHi

HOPEWELL ASSOCIATE REFORMED
PRESBYTERIAN CHURCH, Chester Co., S.C.
Records, 1833-1910, 248 p.   ScU
N: USIGS   8742

LUTHERAN CHURCH. SOUTH CAROLINA
Records, 1767-1937   ScU
N: ScU 4 reels   8743

LUTHERAN CHURCH. SOUTH CAROLINA
Records, 1778-1937   Columbia
N: USIGS 3 reels   8744

METHODIST CHURCH (United States).
SOUTH CAROLINA
Records, 1810-1931 (WPA transcript)   ScU-SC
N: USIGS 2 reels   8745

METHODIST CHURCH (United States).
SOUTH CAROLINA
Records, 1817-1938   ScU
N: ScU 2 reels   8746

ORANGEBURGH [ORANGEBURG], S.C. CHURCH
OF THE REDEEMER
Register, 1739-1885   ScHi
N: USIGS 1 reel   8747

PHILLIPS, Rev. EDWARD, Charleston, S.C.
Records of marriages and burials, 1822-1866
ScHi
N: USIGS   8748

PRESBYTERIAN CHURCH IN THE U.S.
SOUTH CAROLINA
Records, 1740-1949   ScU
N: ScU 7 reels   8749

PRESBYTERIAN CHURCH IN THE U.S.
SOUTH CAROLINA
Records, 1740-1937 (WPA transcript)   ScU
N: USIGS 3 reels   8750

PROTESTANT EPISCOPAL CHURCH IN THE
U.S.A. DIOCESES. SOUTH CAROLINA
Records, 1693-1912   Ibid.
N: USIGS 8 reels   8751

PROTESTANT EPISCOPAL CHURCH IN THE
U.S.A. SOUTH CAROLINA
Records, 1693-1936 (WPA transcript)   ScU
N: USIGS 5 reels   8752

ST. HELENA PARISH, Beaufort Co., S.C.
Records, 1725-1825
N: USIGS 1 reel   8753

SULLIVANS ISLAND (formerly MOULTRIEVILLE),
S.C. CHAPEL OF THE HOLY CROSS
Records, 1891-1926   Ibid.
N: USIGS 1 reel   8754

TRAPIER, Rev. PAUL
Private register, 1827-1856, re: St. Mark's,
St. Stephen's, St. Michael's, and Calvary
churches, vicinity of Charleston, S.C., and
St. James' Church, James Island, S.C.   ScHi
N: USIGS 1 reel   8755

UNION ASSOCIATE REFORM PRESBYTERIAN
CHURCH, Chester Co., S.C.
Records, 1752-1939, 207 p.   ScU
N: USIGS   8756

Personal Papers

ALLSTON-PRINGLE-HILL FAMILY
Papers, 1847-1921, 165 items   ScHi
N: NcU 1 reel   8757

DeFOREST, JOHN WILLIAM, b. 1826
Letters and reports to Freedmen's Bureau
from Greenville, S.C., Oct., 1866-Dec., 1867,
48 p.   DNA
N: CtY   8758

MANIGAULT, M.I., of Charleston, S.C.
Papers, 1790-1820   priv.
N: NcD 1 reel   8759

NASH, B.R., of Sumter, S.C.
Papers, 1892-1901, 25 items   priv.
N: NcD   8760

PERRY, BENJAMIN FRANKLIN, Gov. S.C.,
1805-1886
Correspondence, 1861-1864   priv.
N: A-Ar 1 reel   8761

PERRY, BENJAMIN FRANKLIN, Gov. S.C., 1805-
1886
Papers, 1822-1872   priv.
N: NcU 480 frames   8762

PINCKNEY, CHARLES COTESWORTH, 1812-1899
Papers, 1886-1891   CLU
N: NcU 18 feet   8763

PINCKNEY, ELIZA LUCAS (Mrs. CHARLES),
1723-1793
Letterbook, 1739-1762   priv.
N: DLC 1 reel   8764
PP: DLC

PINCKNEY, ELIZA LUCAS (Mrs. CHARLES),
1723-1793
Letterbooks, 1739-1762   ScHi
N: ScHi 1 reel*   8765

SCHIRMER, JACOB F., 1803-1880
Diaries, containing vital records, 1826-1886
ScHi
N: USIGS 3 reels   8766
P: Sc-Ar   USIGS

WADLINGTON, THOMAS B., of Newbury, S.C.
Papers, 1758-1925, 290 items   priv.
N: NcD   8767

Business Papers

BELIN, ALLARD
Almanacs with notes on rice culture, 1792,
1797, 1798, 3 v.   priv.
N: NcU   8768

BUTLER, WILLIAM
Observations on culture of rice, 1786   priv.
N: NcU 23 frames   8769

Store ledger, Spartanburg Co., S.C., 1837-
1857   priv.
N: KyHi   USIGS   8770

Collections

SOUTH CAROLINA. ARCHIVES
British Public Record Office transcripts,
1710-1782, 31 v.   Sc-Ar
N: Sc-Ar 6 reels   8771
P: MiEM

SOUTH CAROLINA HISTORICAL SOCIETY,
Charleston, S.C.
Cemetery and church records of South Carolina,
n.d.   Ibid.
N: USIGS 2 reels   8772

Institutions

CHARLESTON, S.C. CHAMBER OF COMMERCE
Records, 1784-1863 ScHi
N: ScHi 1 reel   8773

CHARLESTON, S. C. ORPHAN'S HOUSE
Records, 1790-1947 ScHi
N: USlGS 5 reels   8774
P: ScHi

CHARLESTON LIBRARY SOCIETY, Charleston,
S.C.
Treasurer's records priv.
N: NcD 1 reel   8775

DARLINGTON AGRICULTURAL SOCIETY,
Darlington, S.C.
Minutes, 1846-1949 ScD
N: ScU 1 reel   8776

FELLOWSHIP SOCIETY, Charleston, S.C.
Minute books, ledgers, treasurer's
account book, newspapers, etc., 1762-1947
Ibid.
N: ScU 17 reels   8777

MEDICAL SOCIETY OF SOUTH CAROLINA,
Charleston, S.C.
Records, 1789-1833 Ibid.
N: ScU 1 reel   8778

SOCIETY FOR THE RELIEF OF THE WIDOWS
AND ORPHANS OF THE CLERGY OF THE
PROTESTANT EPISCOPAL CHURCH,
Charleston, S.C.
Records, 1762-1861 ScHi
N: USlGS 2 reels*   8779
P: ScHi

SUMTER, S. C. BOROUGH HOUSE
Papers re: W. W. Anderson and Thomas Childs,
1815-1910, 20 v. priv.
N: NcU 3 reels   8780

WINYAH INDIGO SOCIETY, Georgetown, S.C.
Records, 1788-1918 Ibid.
N: ScU 2 reels   8781

GEORGIA

Census

GEORGIA. CENSUS
Forsyth Co., 1845; Laurens Co., 1838; Newton
Co., 1838; Tattnall Co., 1838; Warren Co.,
1845; Dooly Co., 1845; Jasper Co., 1852
G-Ar
N: G-Ar 1 reel   8782
P: USlGS

U.S. CENSUS. FOURTH, 1820
Population schedules, Georgia DNA
N: DNA 5 reels   8783
P: G-Ar 2 reels

U.S. CENSUS. FIFTH, 1830
Population schedules, Georgia DNA
N: DNA 6 reels   8784
P: A-Ar G-Ar GHi

U.S. CENSUS. SIXTH, 1840
Population schedules, Georgia DNA
N: DNA 5 reels   8785
P: AB Ga-Ar GHi USlGS

U.S. CENSUS. SEVENTH, 1850
Agriculture, social statistics schedules,
Georgia NcD
N: NcD 4 reels   8786
P: NNC

U.S. CENSUS. SEVENTH, 1850
Population schedules, Georgia DNA
N: DNA 23 reels   8787
P: AB Ga-Ar GHi USlGS

U.S. CENSUS, EIGHTH, 1860
Agriculture, social statistics schedules,
Georgia NcD
N: NcD 4 reels   P: NNC   8788

U.S. CENSUS. EIGHTH, 1860
Population schedules, Georgia DNA
N: DNA 8 reels   8789
P: Ga-Ar USlGS

U.S. CENSUS. NINTH, 1870
Agriculture, social statistics schedules,
Georgia NcD
N: NcD 1 reel   8790

U.S. CENSUS. NINTH, 1870
Population schedule, Georgia DNA
N: DNA 13 reels   8791
P: Ga-Ar USlGS

U.S. CENSUS. TENTH, 1880
Agriculture, defectives, dependents, and
delinquents, manufacturing schedules,
Georgia NcD
N: NcD 2 reels   8792

U.S. CENSUS. TENTH, 1880
Population schedules, Georgia DNA
N: DNA 40 reels   8793
P: Ga-Ar

Government Records

GREAT BRITAIN. AUDIT OFFICE. A.O. 12, 13
Georgia loyalist claims UKLPRO
N: G-Ar 5 reels   8794

U.S. CONTINENTAL CONGRESS
Georgia state papers, 1777-1788 DLC
N: GHi 1 reel   8795

State Records

GEORGIA (Colony). CHARTER
Royal charter of the Colony of Georgia, granted
by George II, June 9, 1732, 20 p. UKLPRO
DCO: GAHi   8796

GEORGIA (Colony). TRUSTEES
Proceedings, 1732-1738 OkTG
N: OkTG 1 reel   8797

GEORGIA (Colony). TRUSTEES
Records, 1732-1752 G-Ar
N: G-Ar   8798

GEORGIA
Colonial records of the state of Georgia, v.
XX, XXVII-XXXIX, 1732-1785 G-Ar
N: G-Ar 9 reels   8799

GEORGIA
Conveyances, 1750-1761, 1766-1778, 1783-
1802; mortgages, 1755-1822; probate records,
1754-1777; bonds, 1755-1813; commissions,
1754-1827; proclamations, 1754-1823; marks
and brands, 1755-1793 G-Ar
N: G-Ar 26 reels   8800

GEORGIA
Military commissions, 1798-1860; military
records, 1798-1899 G-Ar
N: G-Ar 21 reels   8801

GEORGIA
Passports, 1785-1820; records of Benjamin
Hawkins, agent of Indian Affairs; American
State Papers (WPA transcripts) G
N: A-Ar   8802

GEORGIA
Passports, through the Indian Territory, 1785-
1820 G-Ar
N: LM 1 reel   8803

GEORGIA
Surveyors' field notes G-Ar
N: G-Ar 18 reels   8804

GEORGIA
Tax digest, 1787-1867 G-Ar
N: G-Ar 56 reels   8805

GEORGIA
Tax digests, 1860 series G-Ar
N: G-Ar 13 reels   8806

GEORGIA
Tax digests, 1870 series (Applin and Burke
Cos.) G-S
N: G-Ar 67 reels   8807

GEORGIA. COUNCIL OF SAFETY
Records, 1775-1776 G-Ar
N: G-Ar   8808

GEORGIA. SURVEYOR GENERAL
Land office records, maps, surveys, field
notes, grants, 1756-1850 Ibid.
N: G-Ar 220 reels   8809

County Records

Georgia county records are listed collectively,
unless they appear to have special value to the
researcher. Separate listing is always given to
minute books, wills and/or probate records, deeds,
vital records, and muster rolls. In order that researchers may differentiate between materials the
originals of which are held at county courthouses
and materials the originals of which are held at the
state archives, an exception has been made to the
usual alphabetical listing. Courthouse material
always precedes archival material.

BALDWIN Co, Ga.
Tax lists, 1818-1819, 1821, 76 p. (typescript)
G-Ar
N: 1 reel   8810

BIBB Co., Ga.
Marriages and wills prior to 1860, 76 p.
(typescript) G-Ar
N: USlGS   8811

CAMDEN Co., Ga.
Court records, 1794-1888; probate records,
1795-1829, 1868-1916; land records, 1784-1837;
marriages, 1819-1831; Spanish censuses, 1793,
1813; tax digests, 1819-1863; citizenships, 1793-
1860; affidavits- slaves brought into state, 1818-
1847; registration of free persons of color,
1819-1847 C. H. Woodbine
N: G-Ar 11 reels   8812

CHATHAM Co., Ga.
Court records, 1782-1837; wills, 1775-1839;
land records, 1785-1842; marriage records,
1805-1866; register of free persons of color,
1826-1835; store account book, 1783-1796;
state census, 1845; aliens' records, 1801-1906
C. H. Savannah
N: G-Ar 22 reels   8813

CHATHAM Co., Ga.
Abstracts of wills, 1817-1826 (typescript);
marriages, 1805-1852, 353 p. G-Ar
N: USlGS   8814

CLARK Co., Ga.
Abstracts of: wills, bonds, marriages, 1802-
1828, 111 p. (typescript) G-Ar
N: USlGS   8815

DECATUR Co., Ga.
Plat books, I, II, n.d. C.H. Bainbridge
N: G-Ar 1 reel   8816

EARLY Co., Ga.
Court records, 1820-1916; probate records,
1822-1958; land records, 1831-1866, 1868-1929;
vital records, 1820-1915; tax digest, ca. 1850;
voters' lists, 1896, 1898, 1900; annual returns,
1850-1906; record of charter, 1890-1955; marks,
brands, and estrays, 1822-1849, 1851-1870, 1880-
1955 C.H. Blakeley
N: G-Ar 79 reels   8817

EFFINGHAM Co., Ga.
Wills, 1829-1859; land records, 1786-1819,
1822-1859; miscellaneous records, 1791-1834;
plat books, A-D C.H. Springfield
N: G-Ar 5 reels   8818

EFFINGHAM Co., Ga.
Marriage records, 1750-1875, 73 p. (typescript)
priv.
N: USlGS   8819

ELBERT Co., Ga.
Superior court minutes, 1791-1794 C.H.
Elberton
N: G-Ar 1 reel   8820

ELBERT Co., Ga.
Marriages, 1804-1829 (typescript) G-Ar
N: USlGS   8821

EMANUEL Co., Ga.
Court records, 1819-1898; probate records,
1812-1892; land records, 1858-1867, 1903-1907;

vital records, 1817-1899; registrations of free persons of color, 1855; tax digest, 1841; cattle brands and marks   C.H. Swainsboro
N: G-Ar 7 reels   8822

FRANKLIN Co., Ga.
Wills, 1848-1899; letters of administration, 1855-1865; deeds, 1785-1860, 1870-1878; marriage book, 1805-1882; homestead book, 1868-1904 C.H. Carnesville
N: G-Ar 19 reels   8823

FRANKLIN Co., Ga.
Marriage license book [abstracts], 1805-1850 (transcript); court of ordinary minutes, including wills, inventories, bonds, and settlement of estates, 1786-1856; deeds, 1786-1792, 1794-1853 G-Ar
N: USIGS 12 reels   8824

GLYNN Co., Ga.
Probate records, 1792-1809; deeds, 1859-1869 C.H. Brunswick
N: G-Ar 2 reels   8825

GREENE Co., Ga.
Court records, 1790-1909; probate records, 1786-1921; land records, 1784-1852, 1857-1882; marriage records, 1786-1908; Confederate pension roll, 1861-1864 C.H. Greensboro
N: G-Ar 89 reels   8826

HANCOCK Co., Ga.
Tax returns, 1795, 1802, 1813, 367 p. (typescript) G-Ar
N: USIGS   8827

HARALSON Co., Ga.
Court records, 1855-1905; wills, 1865-1919; land records, 1830-1934; marriages, 1865-1909; voters' registers, 1896-1897; guardians' records, 1857-1933; administrators' records, 1856-1937; licenses for liquor selling, 1856-1896; tax digest, 1866-1885, 1892-1899 C.H. Buchanan
N: G-Ar 71 reels   8828

JACKSON Co., Ga.
Court records, 1796-1831; marriages, 1806-1860 C.H. Jefferson
N: G-Ar 3 reels   8829

JASPER Co., Ga.
Court records, 1807-1920; probate records, 1797-1924; land records, 1807-1920; marriages, 1808-1900; tax digest, 1871-1899; Confederate pensions, v.d.; physicians' license book, 1881-1911 C.H. Monticello
N: G-Ar 108 reels   8830

JASPER Co., Ga.
Persons entitled to draw land in 1825, 24 p. (typescript) G-Ar
N: USIGS   8831

JONES Co., Ga.
Tax digest, 1811; marriages, 1811-1828; abstracts of will books, 1809-1890 (typescript) G-Ar
N: USIGS 1 reel   8832

LAURENS Co., Ga.
Wills, 1809-1869; marriages, 1809-1855; land lottery, 1819; family records and histories, 219 p. (typescript) G-Ar
N: USIGS   8833

LIBERTY Co., Ga.
Court records, 1784-1884; deeds, 1777-1783, 1785-1874; vital records, 1784-1895; Riceboro Store account book, 1816-1817 C.H. Hinesville
N: G-Ar 12 reels   8834

McINTOSH Co., Ga.
Tax digest, 1862 G-Ar
N: G-Ar 1 reel   8835

MONROE Co., Ga.
Court orders, court records, 1824- ; probate records, 1825- ; deeds, 1822-1910; land records, 1839- ; tax digest, 1828, 1853-1883; marriages, 1824- ; physicians' register, 1881-1915; Confederacy records, 1861-1865, 1898 C.H. Forsyth
N: G-Ar 160 reels   8836

MONTGOMERY Co., Ga.
Court records, 1807-1868; deeds, 1794-1856, 1858-1872 C.H. Mount Vernon
N: G-Ar 7 reels   8837

MORGAN Co., Ga.
Court records, 1808-1921; probate records, 1808-1904; land records, 1806-1956; tax records, 1808-1899 [gaps]; marriages, 1866-1907; slave register, 1818-1824; Confederate records, n.d.; oaths for selling liquor, 1840-1846 C.H. Madison
N: G-Ar 142 reels   8838

NEWTON Co., Ga.
Wills, 1823-1851; marriages, 1822-1846 C.H. Covington
N: G-Ar 1 reel   8839

OGLETHORPE Co., Ga.
Court records, 1794-1922; probate records, 1793-1927; land records, 1794-1901; annual returns, 1798-1903; indentures of apprenticeship, 1896-1903; vital records, 1793-1808, 1875-1876; census, 1800; tax records, 1794-1895; Confederate army rolls, 1881-1931; pauper records, 1851-1888; poor-school records, 1829; physicians' list, 1881-1944; license to sell liquor, 1869-1889; stud liens, 1889-1906 C.H. Lexington
N: G-Ar 149 reels   8840

PULASKI Co., Ga.
Deeds, 1807-1811 C.H. Hawkinsville
N: G-Ar 1 reel   8841

RICHMOND Co., Ga.
Court records, 1790-1898; probate records, 1777-1905; accounts, 1793-1796, 1799-1900; land records, 1853-1870; marriages, 1806-1900; tax records, 1831, 1849-1862, 1867-1879; store account book, 1795-1796 C.H. Augusta
N: G-Ar 131 reels   8842

RICHMOND Co., Ga.
Marriages, 1802-1852 (typescript) G-Ar
N: USIGS   8843

SCREVEN Co., Ga.
Court records, 1811-1875; probate records, 1836-1902; land records, 1794-1864; vital records, 1837-1881; cemetery records, n.d. C.H. Sylvania
N: G-Ar 11 reels   8844

SCREVEN Co., Ga.
Vital records, 1859-1878; cemetery records, v. 1-2 (DAR transcript) G-Ar
N: G-Ar 2 reels   8845

STEWART Co., Ga.
Court records, 1827-1859; probate records, 1831-1890; marriages, 1825-1895; estray book, 1837-1859 C.H. Lumpkin
N: G-Ar 10 reels   8846

TALIAFERRO Co., Ga.
Court records, 1826-1836; wills, 1826-1834; guardian bonds, 1826-1878; land lottery, 1832; roster of militia men, 1827 C.H. Crawfordville
N: G-Ar 2 reels   8847

TATTNALL Co., Ga.
Court records, 1805-1839, 1841-1868; probate records, 1836-1840, 1850-1898; plat books, 1835-1881; marriages, 1832-1856, 1858-1867 C.H. Reidsville
N: G-Ar 2 reels   8848

TELFAIR Co., Ga.
Court records, 1831-1863, 1869; wills, 1869-1921; marriage book, 1810-1856; treasury book, 1841-1854 C.H. McRae
N: G-Ar 1 reel   8849

THOMAS Co., Ga.
Court records, 1826-1907; probate records, 1826-1957; land records, 1826-1911; annual returns, 1845-1849, 1853-1901; exemptions, 1874-1912; voters' register, 1898; marriages, 1826-1921; physicians' register, 1844-1957 C.H. Thomasville
N: G-Ar 172 reels   8850

TWIGGS Co., Ga.
Tax digest, 1818, 1826, 1830, 1833, 1853, 150 p. (typescript) G-Ar
N: USIGS   8851

WARREN Co., Ga.
Court records, 1794-1842; probate records, 1794-1861; deeds, 1812-1814; marriages, 1794-1853; miscellaneous records, 1815-1853 C.H. Warrenton
N: G-Ar 7 reels   8852

WEBSTER Co., Ga.
Estate records, 1854-1914; administrators' and guardians' bonds, 1854-1914 C.H. Preston
N: G-Ar 2 reels   8853

WILKES Co., Ga.
Court records, 1792-1910; wills, 1786-1925; land records, 1785-1901; homestead records, 1868-1956; tax digest, 1807, 1813-1860, 1867; marriages, 1806-1905; indentures and apprenticeship, 1866-1938; records of persons of color, 1818-1826; Confederate records, 1861-1865; physicians' and dentists' records, 1881-1951 C.H. Washington
N: G-Ar 173 reels   8854

City Records

COLUMBUS, Ga.
Commissioners' minutes, Jan., 1828-July, 1828 Ibid.
N: G-Ar 1 reel   8855

ST. MARY'S, Camden Co., Ga.
Record book, 1841-1861, found on board U.S.S. Wabash G-Ar
N: G-Ar 1 reel   8856

Church Records

ANTIOCH BAPTIST CHURCH, Morgan Co., Ga.
Records, 1809-1902 C.H. Madison
N: G-Ar 1 reel   8857

BAPTIST CHURCH, Early Co., Ga.
Records, 1837-1894 C.H. Blakely
N: G-Ar 1 reel   8858

BAPTISTS. GEORGIA. GEORGIA BAPTIST ASSOCIATION
Minutes, 1803-1860, 1867-1942 Ibid.
N: G-Ar 4 reels   8859

BAPTISTS. GEORGIA. MORGAN Co.
Records, 1834-1951 C.H. Madison
N: G-Ar 1 reel   8860

BETHANY BAPTIST CHURCH, ?, Ga.
Church roll, 1788-1866, 23 p. Ibid.
N: GU 1 reel   8861

BETHEL BAPTIST CHURCH, Jasper Co., Ga.
Records, 1853-1900 Ibid.
N: G-Ar 1 reel   8862

BETHEL BAPTIST COUNTY CHURCH, Heard Co., Ga.
Records, 1828-1901 Ibid.
N: G-Ar 1 reel   8863

BETHEL CHURCH, Screven Co., Ga.
Rolls, n.d. C.H. Sylvania
N: G-Ar   8864

BETHLEHEM BAPTIST CHURCH, Washington Co., Ga.
Minutes, 1791-1912, 1 v. priv.
N: G-Ar 1 reel   8865

CHURCH OF CHRIST, Bersheba, Henry Co., Ga.
Records, 1838-1900 G-Ar
N: G-Ar 1 reel   8866

CHURCH OF JESUS CHRIST OF LATTER-DAY SAINTS. GEORGIA
Ward and branch records: Axson, Waycross
N: USIGS 2 reels   8867

COUNTY LINE BAPTIST CHURCH, Oglethorpe Co., Ga.
Minutes and history, 1807-1918, 5 v. C.H. Lexington
N: H-Ar 1 reel   8868

CRAWFORDVILLE, Ga. BAPTIST CHURCH
Roll, 1831-1900   C.H. Crawfordville (Taliaferro Co.)
N: G-Ar 1 reel   8869

DARIEN, Ga. BAPTIST CHURCH
Records, 1794-1856, v. 1-2 priv.
N: G-Ar 1 reel   8870

EPISCOPAL CHURCH, Camden Co., Ga.
Records re: Missions and Christ Church, Frederica, St. Simons, 1912-1956 priv.
N: G-Ar   8871

FORSYTH CIRCUIT METHODIST CHURCH,
Monroe Co., Ga.
Minutes quarterly conference, 1835-1863
C. H. Forsyth
N: G-Ar   8872

GOSHEN BAPTIST CHURCH, Lincoln Co., Ga.
Records, n.d., 2 v.   Ibid.
N: G-Ar 1 reel   8873

HARDMAN'S BAPTIST CHURCH, De Kalb Co., Ga.
Records, 1825-1885   G-Ar
N: G-Ar 1 reel   8874

KIOKEE BAPTIST CHURCH, Columbia Co., Ga.
Records, 1790-1817, 1820-1849, 1875- , 3 v.
Ibid.
N: G-Ar 1 reel   8875

LONG CREEK BAPTIST CHURCH, Warren Co.,
Ga.
Records, 1786-1951, 4v.   C. H. Warrenton
N: G-Ar 1 reel   8876

MARS HILL CHURCH, Clarke Co., Ga.
Church roll, 1799-1896?, 43 p.   Ibid.
N: GU 1 reel   8877

METHODIST CHURCH, Monroe Co., Ga.
Records, 1835-1899   C. H. Forsyth   8878

METHODIST CHURCH (United States). GEORGIA.
SCREVEN CO.
Records, n.d.   C. H. Sylvania
N: G-Ar   8879

METHODIST EPISCOPAL CHURCH, SOUTH,
Camden Co., Ga.
Records, 1807-1918, 7 v.   priv.
N: G-Ar 1 reel   8880

METHODIST EPISCOPAL CHURCH, SOUTH,
Early Co., Ga.
Records, 1894-1951   C. H. Blakeley
N: G-Ar 1 reel   8881

METHODIST EPISCOPAL CHURCH, SOUTH, St.
Mary's, Ga.
Records, 1839-1930 (including Zion Church,
Kingsland, 1887-1930), 7v.   priv.
N: G-Ar 1 reel   8882

MIDWAY CONGREGATIONAL CHURCH, Liberty
Co., Ga.
Records, n.d., 9 v.   Ibid.
N: G-Ar 1 reel   8883

MIDWAY, Ga. CONGREGATIONAL CHURCH
Vital records, 1754 - ca. 1868, 413 p.
(typescript)   G-Ar
N: USlGS 1 reel   8884

MONTICELLO, Jasper Co., Ga. BAPTIST
CHURCH
Records, 1865-1906   Ibid.
N: G-Ar 1 reel   8885

MONTICELLO, Jasper Co., Ga. METHODIST
CHURCH
Records, 1878-1924   Ibid.
N: G-Ar 1 reel   8886

MONTICELLO, Jasper Co., Ga. PRES-
BYTERIAN CHURCH
Records, 1829-1905   Ibid.
N: G-Ar 1 reel   8887

MONTICELLO STATION CHURCH, Jasper Co.,
Ga.
Register, 1878-1899   Ibid.
N: G-Ar 1 reel   8888

PHILLIPS MILL BAPTIST CHURCH, Wilkes Co.,
Ga.
Records, 1785-1948   priv.
N: G-Ar   8889

PLEASANT GROVE CHURCH (Methodist Episcopal,
South), Early Co., Ga.
Records, 1902-1930   C. H. Blakely
N: G-Ar 1 reel   8890

PROTESTANT EPISCOPAL CHURCH IN THE
U.S.A. DIOCESES. GEORGIA
Journals of annual conventions, 1906-1956   Ibid.
N: G-Ar 4 reels   8891

PROVIDENCE BAPTIST CHURCH, Jefferson Co.,
Ga.
Records, n.d., 4 v.   Ibid.
N: G-Ar 1 reel   8892

RICHLAND CHURCH (Baptist), Twiggs Co., Ga.
Records, 1812-1906, 3 v.   Ibid.
N: G-Ar 1 reel   8893

ST. MARY'S, Ga. FIRST PRESBYTERIAN
CHURCH
Parish register, 1808-1819, 1842-1905   priv.
N: G-Ar 1 reel   8894

ST. MARY'S, Ga. FIRST PRESBYTERIAN
CHURCH
Records, 1808-1919   C. H. Woodbine
N: G-Ar   8895

ST. MARY'S, Ga. PRESBYTERIAN CHURCH
Records, 1807-1918   C. H. Woodbine (Cam-
den Co.)
N: G-Ar   8896

SARDIS BAPTIST CHURCH, Burke Co., Ga.
Records, n.d.   Ibid.
N: G-Ar 1 reel   8897

SARDIS BAPTIST CHURCH, Wilkes Co., Ga.
Records, 1805-1851, 4 v.   priv.
N: G-Ar 1 reel   8898

SAVANNAH, Ga. ST. JOHN THE BAPTIST
CHURCH (Catholic)
Parish register, 1796-1816   Ibid.
N: G-Ar 1 reel   8899

SHILOH BAPTIST CHURCH, Greene Co., Ga.
Records, 1839   C. H. Greensboro
N: G-Ar 1 reel   8900

SHILOH (formerly LITTLE RIVER, BAPTIST
CHURCH), Jasper Co., Ga.
Records, 1870-1931   Ibid.
N: G-Ar 1 reel   8901

STONE CREEK CHURCH (Baptist), Twiggs Co.,
Ga.
Minutes, 1808-1954, 5 v.   Ibid.
N: G-Ar 1 reel   8902

WASHINGTON, Wilkes Co., Ga. BAPTIST
CHURCH
Records, 1827-1948   priv.
N: G-Ar 4 reels   8903

Personal Papers

BACON, AUGUSTUS OCTAVIUS, 1839-1914
Diary, 1853, 1861, 1868, 3 v.   priv.
N: NcU 186 frames   8904

BENNING, HENRY LEWIS, 1814-1875
Papers, 1818-1897   priv.
N: NcU 178 frames   8905

BLACKSHEAR, JAMES APPLETON, 1841-1867
Diaries, 1861-1867, 4 v.   priv.
N: GEU 1 reel   8906

BULLOCH, ARCHIBALD
Papers, 1769-1777, 12 items   DNA MiU-C
NN
DCO: GHi   8907

COUPER, JOHN, 1759-1850
Family papers, 1827-1923   priv.
N: NcU 180 frames   8908

EARLY, PETER
Land grant, Bulloch Co., Ga., to Moses
Goodman, Nov. 15, 1813, 3 p.   priv.
DCO: GAHi   8909

HABERSHAM FAMILY, of Georgia
Papers, 1850-1892   DLC
N: GU 1 reel   8910

HAMMOND, OCTAVIA S.
Letter to Mrs. [George] Adair, Feb. 10, 1865,
4 p.   priv.
DCO: GAHi   8911

HAWKINS, BENJAMIN
Correspondence and journal, 1795-1818
PPAmP
N: GU 2 reels   8912

JOHNSON, W. G.
Diary, 1874-1890   C. H. Lexington (Oglethorpe
Co., Ga.)
N: G-Ar   8913

McINTOSH, LACHLAN, 1725-1806
Papers, 1763-1796, 63 items   DLC DNA
MiU-C NHi NcD PHi WHi
DCO: GHi   8914

McINTOSH, LACHLAN, 1725-1806
Peter Force transcripts, 1776-1789   DLC
N: GHi 1 reel   8915

MACKAY-STILES FAMILY
Robert Mackay letters, 1795-1849, 197 items
GHi
Mackay, Stiles, Couper, and Wylly letters,
diaries, and records, 1775-1926, 2 v. (type-
script)   priv.
N: NcU 3 reels   8916

MAIER, JOHN
Letter re: exhibition of his art works, 1871;
resolution of Royal Arch Masons on his death,
1879, 2 items, 3 p.   priv.
DCO: GAHi   8917

ROWLAND, KATE B. (WHITEHEAD, Mrs.
CHARLES M. ROWLAND)
Journals, Augusta, Ga., 1863-1865, 1877-1878,
3 v.   priv.
N: GEU 1 reel   8918

TIFT, NELSON, 1810-1891
Diary, 1835-1851, 1856 (typescript)   priv.
N: NcU 189 frames   8919

TIFT, NELSON, 1810-1891
Journal, 1835-1856, 151 p.   C. H. Albany, Ga.
(Dougherty Co.)
N: GU 1 reel   8920

WALLACE-OWENS FAMILY
Papers, 1787-1885   priv.
N: NcU 378 frames   8921

Business Papers

COUPER, JAMES HAMILTON, 1794-1866
Plantation records, Hopeton Plantation,
Glynn Co., 1818-1854, 4 v.   NcU
N: GU 1 reel   8922

HOPETON PLANTATION, Glynn Co., Ga.
Account books, 1818-1841, 62 p.   NcU
DCO: DLC   8923

KELVIN GROVE, Georgia
Plantation book, 1853-1857, 1 v.   priv.
N: NcU 60 frames   8924

McKINLEY, WILLIAM, Georgia planter
Account book, 1832-1863, 246 p.   priv.
N: NcU 200 frames   8925

ROSWELL MANUFACTURING CO., Roswell, Cobb
Co., Ga.
Stockholders' minutes, 1840-1900   C. H.
Marietta
N: G-Ar   8926

Collections

U.S. WAR DEPT. COLLECTION OF
CONFEDERATE RECORDS
Index to compiled service records of Confed-
erate soldiers from Georgia   DNA
N: DNA 67 reels 16 mm. [M-226]   8927

College Records

GEORGIA. UNIVERSITY. TRUSTEES
Minutes, 1794-1834   Ibid.
N: G-Ar   8928

MONROE FEMALE COLLEGE
Records, n.d.   C. H. Forsyth (Monroe Co.)
N: G-Ar   8929

TIFT COLLEGE, Forsyth, Ga.
Records, n.d.   C. H. Forsyth (Monroe Co.)
N: G-Ar 1 reel   8930

Institutions

JEKYLL ISLAND CLUB
Records, 1886-1942 priv.
N: G-Ar   8931

MAGNOLIA LODGE, Early Co., Ga.
History; treasurers' records, n.d. C.H.
Blakely
N: G-Ar 1 reel   8932

OAK GROVE CEMETERY ASSOCIATION,
Camden Co., Ga.
Records, 1910-1923 priv.
N: G-Ar 1 reel   8933

PLANTERS' CLUB, Hancock Co., Ga.
Letters, 1842-1847 C.H. Sparta
N: NcU 1 reel   8934

FLORIDA

Census

ALACHUA Co., Fla.
Census book, 1875 F
N: USIGS 1 reel   8935

U.S. CENSUS. FIFTH, 1830
Population schedules, Florida DNA
N: DNA 1 reel   8936
P: FSaHi

U.S. CENSUS. SIXTH, 1840
Population schedules, Florida DNA
N: DNA 1 reel   8937
P: AB USIGS

U.S. CENSUS. SEVENTH, 1850
Population schedules, Florida DNA
N: DNA 3 reels   8938
P: AB USIGS

U.S. CENSUS. EIGHTH, 1860
Population schedules, Florida DNA
N: DNA 2 reels   8939
P: USIGS

U.S. CENSUS. NINTH, 1870
Population schedules, Florida DNA
N: DNA 2 reels   8940

U.S. CENSUS. TENTH, 1880
Population schedules, Florida DNA
N: DNA 8 reels   8941

Government Records

GREAT BRITAIN. AUDIT OFFICE. A.O. 1
Declared accounts, East and West Florida,
1767-1786 UKLPRO
DCO: DLC   8942

GREAT BRITAIN. AUDIT OFFICE. A.O. 16
East Florida, General record book, 1764-1776
UKLPRO
DCO: DLC   8943

GREAT BRITAIN. TREASURY. Treasury 50
Miscellanea, American sufferers and East
Florida orders, 1789-1795 UKLPRO
DCO: DLC   8944

GREAT BRITAIN. TREASURY. Treasury 50
Miscellanea, documents relating to refugees,
East Florida, 1789-1795 UKLPRO
DCO: DLC   8945

GREAT BRITAIN. TREASURY
Treasury Solicitor papers, East Florida
claims, 1786-1820 UKLPRO
DCO: DLC   8946

SPAIN. ARCHIVO GENERAL DE SIMANCAS
Guerra Moderna: selections re: expedition
from Cadiz to the West Indies, 1780; Florida,
Louisiana, and the Internal Provinces, 1787-
1801 Ibid.
N: DLC 1277 feet   8947
PP: DLC

U.S. ADJUTANT-GENERAL'S OFFICE
Index to compiled service records of Volunteer
Union soldiers from Florida DNA
N: DNA 1 reel 16 mm. [M-264]   8948

U.S. DEPT. OF STATE
Territorial papers: Florida, 1777-1824 DNA
N: DNA 11 reels [M-116]   8949

U.S. WAR DEPT.
Records of the Dept. of Florida, 1840-1843
DNA
N: DNA 4 reels   8950

State Records

FLORIDA. COMPTROLLER
Pension claims of Confederate veterans and
their widows, 1885-1955 Ibid.
N: USIGS 168 reels   8951

County Records

FLORIDA. COUNTIES
Tax rolls, 1839-1891 F
N: USIGS 66 reels   8952

City Records

ST. AUGUSTINE, Fla.
Marriage licenses, 1785-1800 DLC
DCO: FSaHi   8953

Church Records

CHURCH OF JESUS CHRIST OF LATTER-DAY
SAINTS. FLORIDA
Ward and branch records: Gainesville, Jackson-
ville, Lake City, Palataka, Sanderson USIC
N: USIGS 7 reels   8954

ST. AUGUSTINE, Fla. (Diocese, Catholic)
Marriage records, 1784-1801 (typescript) priv.
N: USIGS 1 reel   8955

ST. AUGUSTINE, Fla. CATHEDRAL (Catholic)
Baptisms, 1594-1799; confirmations, 1606,
1735-1763; marriages, 1594-1763, 1787-1795;
burials, 1623-1763 Ibid.
DCO: FSaHi   8956

Personal Papers

CLEMENTS, BENJAMIN
Survey of St. Augustine, field note book,
1834-1835 FSaHi
N: DLC 1 reel   8957

DANIEL, RICHARD POTTS, 1828-1915
Journal, 1855-1858, 1 v. priv.
N: NcU 80 frames   8958

LE CONTE, JOHN EATON
Observations on the soil and climate of East
Florida, 1822, 24 p. DNA
N: PPAmP 14 frames   8959

SMITH, BUCKINGHAM, 1810-1871
Papers [Florida selections], 1500-1786 NHi
N: NHi 3 reels   8960

TUTTLE, Lt. STEPHEN
Correspondence re: fortifications and wall of
St. Augustine, 1833 DNA
N: DLC 1 reel   8961

Collections

CAMPS, PEDRO, Father, d. 1790, compiler
"Golden Book of the Minorcans": baptisms,
1768-1777, New Smyrna, Fla.; baptisms, 1777-
1784, 1791-1804; marriages, 1776-1784, St.
Augustine, Fla. St. Augustine Cathedral Archives
N: DLC 1 reel   P: FSaHi   8962

DAUGHTERS OF THE AMERICAN REVOLUTION.
FLORIDA CHAPTER
Church, cemetery, and vital records, ca. 1823-
1903 (transcripts) Ibid.
N: USIGS 8 reels   8963

LOWERY, WOODBURY, collector
Florida history, 1566-1680, transcripts from
Spanish, French, and English Archives, v. 2-9
Castillo de San Marcos National Monument
N: DLC 8 reels   8964
P: FSaHi v. 3-9 only

ST. JOHN'S Co., Fla. ARCHIVES
Patriot's war manuscripts: letters, 1812 (Span-
ish, with translation); claims for losses, 1812-
1813 Castillo de San Marcos National Monument
N: DLC 1812 frames   8965
P: FSaHi

U.S. WAR DEPT. COLLECTION OF
CONFEDERATE RECORDS
Compiled service records of Confederate
soldiers from Florida DNA
N: DNA 103 reels 16 mm. [M-251]   8966

U.S. WAR DEPT. COLLECTION OF
CONFEDERATE RECORDS
Index to compiled service records of
Confederate soldiers from Florida DNA
N: DNA 9 reels 16 mm. [M-225]   8967

U.S. WORKS PROGRESS ADMINISTRATION.
VETERANS' GRAVES REGISTRATION
PROJECT
Register of deceased veterans buried in
Florida Ibid.
N: USIGS 1 reel   8968

Institutions

SEMINOLE NATION. MICCOSUKEE TRIBE
Contract with Morton Silver, 1954-1958 Ibid.
DC: DLC 1 folder   8969

ALABAMA

Census

U.S. CENSUS. FIFTH, 1830
Population schedules, Alabama DNA
N: DNA 4 reels   8970
P: A-Ar AB USIGS

U.S. CENSUS. SIXTH, 1840
Population schedules, Alabama DNA
N: DNA 4 reels   8971
P: A-Ar AB AU USIGS

U.S. CENSUS. SEVENTH, 1850
Agricultural and industrial statistics, Madison
Co., Ala., 70 p. A-Ar
N: A-Ar   8972

U.S. CENSUS. SEVENTH, 1850
Population schedules, Alabama DNA
N: DNA 19 reels   8973
P: A-Ar AB USIGS

U.S. CENSUS. EIGHTH, 1860
Agricultural, industrial, and social statistics,
Alabama - Madison Co., 71 p. A-Ar
N: A-Ar   8974
P: FU

U.S. CENSUS. EIGHTH, 1860
Population schedules, Alabama DNA
N: DNA 7 reels   8975
P: A-Ar AB USIGS

U.S. CENSUS. NINTH, 1870
Population schedules, Alabama DNA
N: DNA 10 reels   8976
P: A-Ar AB USIGS

U.S. CENSUS. TENTH, 1880
Population schedules, Alabama DNA
N: DNA 35 reels   8977
P: A-Ar AB

Government Records

U.S. ADJUTANT-GENERAL'S OFFICE
Index to compiled service records of Volunteer
soldiers from Alabama during the Cherokee
Removal DNA
N: DNA 1 reel 16 mm. [M-243]   8978
P: A-Ar

U.S. ADJUTANT-GENERAL'S OFFICE
Index to compiled service records of Volunteer
soldiers of the Florida War from Alabama DNA
N: DNA 1 reel 16 mm. [M-245]   8979
P: A-Ar

U.S. ADJUTANT-GENERAL'S OFFICE
Index to compiled service records of Volunteer
soldiers of the Creek War from Alabama DNA
N: DNA 2 reels 16 mm. [M-244]   8980

U.S. COURT OF COMMISSIONERS OF
ALABAMA CLAIMS
Opinions, insurance tables, script valuation,
and the act of June 3, 1884, 100 p.   priv.
N: A-Ar 1 reel   8981

U.S. GENERAL LAND OFFICE
Inventory and finding list of records, 1737-
1893, now at AU
N: A-Ar 3 reels   8982

U.S. GENERAL LAND OFFICE
Record of the Evidence Board under the Act of
1803: South of Tennessee, East of Pearl River,
1803-1809 DNA
N: DNA 1 reel   8983

U.S. IMMIGRATION AND NATURALIZATION
SERVICE
Passenger lists of vessels arriving at Mobile,
1830-1862 DNA
N: A-Ar 1 reel   8984

U.S. POST OFFICE, Kinston, Ala.
Post office records, Dec., 1894-Sept., 1899,
118 p. Ibid.
N: A-Ar   8985

State Records

ALABAMA
Election returns, 1819 A-Ar
N: AU 3 reels   8986

ALABAMA
Medical register, 1878-1938, 577 p.   priv.
N: A-Ar   8987

ALABAMA
Plat books and field notes: Northern Alabama;
Southern Alabama; Conecuh, St. Stephens, and
Sparta districts; boundary lines, townships 14-
18, Range 8 East   A-Ar
N: A-Ar 6 reels   8988

ALABAMA
Presidential election returns, 1824-1892;
Confederate presidential election returns,
1861 A-Ar
N: A-Ar 1 reel   8989

ALABAMA. COMPTROLLER OF PUBLIC
ACCOUNTS
Report, 1841, 1851, 1858, 1859
N: AU   8990

ALABAMA. DEBT COMMISSIONER
Letter book, Jan., 1875 - May, 1876, 207 p.
A-Ar
N: A-Ar   8991

ALABAMA. EXECUTIVE DEPARTMENT
Answers to letters, Nov., 1821-Jan.,1823,
61 p. A-Ar
N: A-Ar   8992

County Records

Alabama county records are listed collectively,
unless they appear to have special value to the
researcher. Separate listing is always given to

minute books, wills and/or probate records, deeds,
vital records, and muster rolls. In order that researchers may differentiate between materials the
originals of which are held at county courthouses
and materials the originals of which are held at the
state archives, an exception has been made to the
usual alphabetical listing. Courthouse material
always precedes archival material.

AUTAUGA Co., Ala.
Assessment of taxes, 1852, 1873, 294 p.
C.H. Prattville
N: A-Ar 1 reel   8993

BIBB Co. (formerly CAHABA Co.), Ala.
Court records, 1818-1834, 1869, 1875-1876;
State Treasury records, 1819-1822, 1831;
marriage records, 1820-1834 C.H. Center-
ville
N: A-Ar 8 reels   8994

BLOUNT Co., Ala.
Court records, 1820-1832; miscellaneous
records, 1820-1829 C.H. Oneonta
N: A-Ar 2 reels   8995

CHEROKEE Co., Ala.
Material from departmental files C.H. Centre
N: A-Ar 1 reel   8996

CLARKE Co., Ala.
Court records, 1823-1844, 1505 p.; deeds,
1819-1821, 1823-1834, 338 p.; marriage
records, 1814-1834, 274 p.; tract book, 501 p.;
marks and brands, 1813-1952, 210 p.
C.H. Grove Hill
N: A-Ar 4 reels   8997

DALE Co., Ala.
Cemetery records, 134 p.   C.H. Ozark
N: A-Ar   8998

ESCAMBIA Co., Ala.
Index to records on film held by Gulf State
Oil Co., 13 p.
N: A-Ar   8999

FRANKLIN Co., Ala.
Registration book, July-Aug., 1867, 467 p.
C.H. Russellville
N: A-Ar 1 reel   9000

GREENE Co., Ala.
Wills and estates, Revolutionary soldiers,
n.d., 100 p. (WPA transcript) T
N: USIGS   9001

JACKSON Co., Ala.
Wills, deeds, marriages, and miscellaneous data,
n.d., 101 p. (WPA transcript) T
N: USIGS   9002

JEFFERSON Co., Ala.
Circuit court records, 1820-1825, 52 p. C.H.
Birmingham
N: A-Ar   9003

JEFFERSON Co., Ala.
Marriage records, ca. 1818-1831, 100 p.
(WPA transcript) T
N: USIGS   9004

LAWRENCE Co., Ala.
Marriage records, 1818-1823, 117 p. C.H.
Moulton
N: A-Ar   9005

LAWRENCE Co., Ala.
Wills, marriages, notes, n.d., 42 p.
(WPA transcript) T
N: USIGS   9006

LIMESTONE Co., Ala.
Chancery records, wills, deeds, marriage
records, Revolutionary War pensions, n.d.,
95 p. (WPA transcript) T
N: USIGS   9007

LOWNDES Co., Ala.
Wills, 1830-1940; marriage records, 1830-
1851, 1855-1871 C.H. Hayneville
N: A-Ar 5 reels   9008

MADISON Co., Ala.
Court records, 1802-1823; marriages, 1819-
1828 C.H. Huntsville
N: A-Ar 5 reels   9009

MADISON Co., Ala.
Court records, n.d.; wills, n.d.; deeds, n.d.;
marriages, 1809-1817; early land patents, n.d.;
notes from 1850 census, 95 p. (WPA transcript)
T
N: USIGS   9010

MADISON Co., Ala., see KELLEY, Rev.
GEORGE A., 9065, under ALABAMA,
Personal Papers

MOBILE Co., Ala.
Probate Court records, 1715-1884; deeds, 1813,
1817-1823; marriage bonds, 1835-1840; naturalization minutes, 1833-1871; Spanish land grants;
miscellaneous records, 1819-1826 C.H. Mobile
N: A-Ar 9 reels   9011

MONROE Co., Ala.
Orphans' court minutes, 1816-1821, 190 p.
C.H. Monroeville
N: A-Ar   9012

MONTGOMERY Co., Ala.
Court records, 1816-1836 C.H. Montgomery
N: A-Ar 1 reel   9013

PIKE Co., Ala.
Court records, 1828-1849, 1872-1879; wills,
1837-1876; census, 1850, 1866; marriage
records, 1830-1859; bonds of county officials,
1829-1846; sales of estates, 1842-1856; books
of estrays, 1838-1881; inventory records, 1833-
1837 C.H. Troy
N: A-Ar 4 reels   9014

TALLADEGA Co., Ala.
Court minutes, 1833-1848, 371 p.
C.H. Talladega
N: A-Ar   9015

TUSCALOOSA Co., Ala.
Wills, orphans' court records, deeds, and
marriages, n.d., 376 p. (WPA transcript) T
N: USIGS   9016

WASHINGTON Co., Ala.
Wills, 1820-1889 C.H. Chatom
N: A-Ar 3 reels   9017

City Records

MOBILE, Ala.
Aldermen's records, 1829-1832; city
documents, 1815-1859, 425 p. Ibid.
N: A-Ar 1 reel   9018

Church Records

ALPINE BAPTIST CHURCH, Talladega Co., Ala.
Records, 1832-1949, 519 p. Ibid.
N: A-Ar   9019

BAPTISTS. ALABAMA. COOSA RIVER
BAPTIST ASSOCIATION
Minutes, 1834-1918   priv.
N: A-Ar 3 reels   9020

BAPTISTS. ALABAMA. MOBILE BAPTIST
ASSOCIATION
Minutes, 1873-1952 Ibid.
N: A-Ar 1 reel   9021

BAPTISTS. ALABAMA. PINE BARREN BAPTIST
ASSOCIATION
Minutes, 1857-1869 Ibid.
N: A-Ar 1 reel   9022

BAPTISTS. ALABAMA STATE CONVENTION
Minutes, 1823, 1824, 1827, 1829, 1834-1841
N: A-Ar 1 reel   9023

BEULAH BAPTIST CHURCH, Pickens Co., Ala.
Records, 1833-1952 Ibid.
N: A-Ar 1/2 reel   9024

BURNT CORN, Ala. BETHANY CHURCH
Records, 1821-1885, 1897-1956 Ibid.
N: A-Ar 2 reels   9025

CARLOWVILLE, Ala. CENTRE RIDGE BAPTIST
CHURCH
Minutes, 1931 Ibid.
N: A-Ar   9026

CROPWELL, Ala. BAPTIST CHURCH
Records, 1889-1923, 38 p. Ibid.
N: A-Ar   9027

EUTAW, Ala. BEULAH BAPTIST CHURCH
Minutes, 1833-1932 Ibid.
N: A-Ar 1 reel   9028

FAYETTEVILLE (formerly FT. WILLIAMS), Ala.
FT. WILLIAMS BAPTIST CHURCH
Records, 1833-1909, 573 p. Ibid.
N: A-Ar   9029

FRISCO, Ala. SALEM BAPTIST CHURCH
Minutes, 1817-1911, 145 p. Ibid.
N: A-Ar   9030

GOOD HOPE [FIRST BAPTIST] CHURCH,
Talladega Co., Ala.
Records, 1836-1876, 68 p. Ibid.
N: A-Ar   9031

JACKSONVILLE, Ala. ST. LUKE'S CHURCH
(Episcopal)
Records, 1848-1949, 176 p. Ibid.
N: A-Ar   9032

JACKSONVILLE BAPTIST CHURCH, Talladega
Co., Ala.
Records, 1835-1919, 339 p. Ibid.
N: A-Ar   9033

MOUNT ZION BAPTIST CHURCH, Benton (now
Calhoun) Co., Ala.
Minutes, 1834-1876 Ibid.
N: A-Ar 1 reel   9034

NEW HOPEWELL BAPTIST CHURCH
Benton (now Calhoun) Co., Ala.
Records, 1832-1848 Ibid.
N: A-Ar   9035

NOTASULGA, Ala. BAPTIST CHURCH
Minutes, 1850-1919, 554 p. Ibid.
N: A-Ar 1 reel   9036

NOTASULGA, Ala. BETHLEHEM PRIMITIVE
BAPTIST CHURCH
Minutes, 1908-1934 Ibid.
N: A-Ar 1 reel   9037

PHILLIPS, JOHN W., D.D.
Sermons and articles A-Ar
N: A-Ar 1 reel   9038

PISGAH CHURCH, Cherokee Co., Ala.
Church book, 1844-1855, 100 p. priv.
N: A-Ar   9039

PLEASANT GROVE, Ala. CUMBERLAND
PRESBYTERIAN CHURCH
Records, 1885 Ibid.
N: A-Ar 1 reel   9040

PROVIDENCE BAPTIST CHURCH, Dallas Co., Ala.
Minutes, 1821-1920, 300 p. Ibid.
N: A-Ar   9041

SCOTTSBORO, Ala. PLEASANT GROVE
PRESBYTERIAN CHURCH
Minutes and records, 1885-1907 Ibid.
N: A-Ar   9042

SUMMERFIELD, Ala. METHODIST CHURCH
Records, 1845-1948 Ibid.
N: A-Ar   9043

TALLASSAHATCHEE BAPTIST CHURCH,
Talladega Co., Ala.
Records, 1833-1857, 1859-1897, 1907-1935,
591 p. Ibid.
N: A-Ar 2 reels   9044

Personal Papers

BASSETT, Dr. JOHN J.
Letters, 1835-1836 priv.
N: A-Ar 1 reel   9045

BLISS, R. L.
Letters, 1861-1865, 150 p. priv.
N: A-Ar   9046

BRINDLEY, ASA A.
Diary, letters, papers, 1853-1883 priv.
N: A-Ar 1 reel   9047

BROWN-STONE FAMILY, of East Alabama
Papers, 1861-1869, 15 items priv.
N: GEU 1 reel   9048

BURRUS, Rev. J.C., 1821-1910
Sermons, Notasulga, Ala., 1846-1857,
76 p. priv.
N: A-Ar   9049

CLAY, CLEMENT CLAIBORNE, Gov. Ala, 1816-
1882
Correspondence, 17 letters priv.
N: A-Ar   9050

CLAY, CLEMENT CLAIBORNE, Gov. Ala., 1816-
1882
Papers, 1861-1870, 6 items NcD
DCO: MnHi   9051

CLAY-CLOPTON, VIRGINIA CAROLINE
(TUNSTALL)
Clippings, day books, etc., re: Huntsville,
Ala., 2 cartons priv.
N: NcD   9052

COLLIER-SHAFFER FAMILY
Papers re: Virginia and Alabama, 1859-1865,
19 items priv.
N: GEU 1 reel   9053

COOPER, WILLIAM, b. 1802
Diary, 1865, 1872 A-Ar
N: NcU 1 reel   9054

COOPER, WILLIAM, of Tuscumbia, Ala.
Diary, 1862-1886, 215 p. NcU
N: A-Ar 1 reel   9055

FITZPATRICK, BENJAMIN, Gov. Ala., 1802-1869
Correspondence and papers, 1821-1869 priv.
N: A-Ar 1 reel   9056

GAGE, CHARLES PINCKNEY
Will, 1869, 8 p. AMob
N: AU   9057

GORGAS, SOLOMON ATKINSON, b. 1815
Diary, 1850-1851, 59 p. (typescript) priv.
N: NcU 1 reel   9058

GOULD, WILLIAM PROCTOR, d. 1862
Personal and farm diary (Alabama), 1828-
1856, 5 v. (mimeograph) priv.
N: NcU 1 reel   9059

GOULD, WILLIAM PROCTOR, d. 1862
Provisions furnished Choctaws, 1813; diary,
1847-1850, 1856-1862 priv.
N: A-Ar   9060

HAYS, CHARLES
Letters and papers priv.
N: A-Ar   9061

HOOD, R. JACOMB
Letter to Emile Erlanger and Company, London,
1877, 5 p. DBRE
N: AU 5 frames   9062

HOWARD, MILFORD W.
Autobiography, 1956, 178 p. priv.
N: A-Ar 1 reel   9063

IRVIN FAMILY
Papers, 31 p. priv.
N: A-Ar   9064

KELLEY, Rev. GEORGE A.
Papers re: Madison Co., Ala., 1819-1829
priv.
N: A-Ar 1 reel   9065

KELLY, JOHN
Administration papers, Mobile Probate court,
Nov. 14, 1855 C.H. Mobile
N: A-Ar   9066

McKEE, JOHN
Letters re: Choctaw Agency, 1814 priv.
N: A-Ar   9067

MILES, MARGARETT JOSEPHINE (Mrs. GILLIS),
of Lowndesboro, Ala.
Diary, 1860-1868 priv.
N: NcD 1 reel   9068

MOORE, A.B., Gov. Ala.
Correspondence with Bell, 1861-1862 priv.
N: A-Ar   9069

O'NEAL, EMMET, Gov. Ala.
Scrap books re: Alamo graft priv.
N: A-Ar 2 reels   9070

OWEN, Dr. THOMAS M.
In-letters priv.
N: A-Ar 1 reel   9071

PARSON, LEWIS E., Gov. Ala.
Correspondence, 4 letters priv.
N: A-Ar   9072

PEGUES, REBECCA ANN EVANS
Diary, 1833-1859 priv.
N: A-Ar 1 reel   9073

PEGUES, REBECCA ANN EVANS
Diary and Journal, 1837-1884 A-Ar
N: ScU 1 reel   9074

PICTON, Mrs. ELIZA GOULD MEANS
Reminiscences priv.
N: A-Ar   9075

ROBERTSON, Maj. RICHARD M., of Selma, Ala.
Papers, 1867-1880 priv.
N: NcD 1 reel   9076

SAUNDERS, GEORGE B., of Livingston, Ala.
Private papers and letters, 1842-1867 priv.
N: A-Ar 1 reel   9077

SHORTER, JOHN GILL, Gov. Ala., 1818-1872
Correspondence priv.
N: A-Ar 1 reel   9078

TERRELL-DABNEY FAMILIES
Papers priv.
N: A-Ar   9079

TORREY, RUFUS C.
Letters to James Dellet, 1843-1845 priv.
N: A-Ar 1 reel   9080

WITHERS, Dr. ROBERT WALKER, of
Greensboro, Ala.
Papers priv.
N: NcD   9081

YANCEY, WILLIAM LOWNDES, 1814-1863
Correspondence and papers priv.
N: A-Ar 1 reel   9082

YEARGAN, ROBERT R., of Mellow Valley, Ala.
Diary, 1864-1870 priv.
N: A-Ar 1 reel   9083

Business Papers

COFFEE, JOHN, 1772-1833
Order books, 1812-1813, 1814-1815, 203 p.
First National Bank, Huntsville, Ala.
DCO: NcU   9084

COMER, JOHN FLETCHER
Farm journal, 1846-1847, 197 p. NcU
N: AU   9085

GOWDEY, SAMUEL M.
Business papers, 1832-1839; journal, 1839-1844
priv.
N: A-Ar   9086

MATTHEWS, GEORGE, Gov. Ala.
Estate records, 316 p. priv.
N: A-Ar   9087

Collections

BLUE, MATTHEW P., collector
M.P. Blue collection A-Ar
N: AU 6 reels   9088

LEWIS, BURWELL BOYKIN, collector
Burwell Boykin Lewis collection, 1843-1894
NcU
N: AU 2 reels   9089

WESTENHAVER, Mrs. MARYLINE C., collector
Papers of the Hammond and Cauthen families
N: A-Ar 1 reel   9090

Institutions

ALABAMA BIBLE SOCIETY
1st and 2nd Annual report   Ibid.
N: A-Ar   9091

ALABAMA DENTAL ASSOCIATION
Membership and Laws, 1841-1941   priv.
N: A-Ar 1 reel   9092

ALABAMA LIBRARY ASSOCIATION
Proceedings, 1904   AMob
N: AU   9093

ALABAMA STATE MEDICAL ASSOCIATION
Minutes, 1850, 1851, 1869   Ibid.
N: A-Ar 1 reel*   9094

CHOCTAW NATION
Muster rolls, 1837, 21 p.   DNA
N: A-Ar 1 reel   9095

HUNTSVILLE, Ala. STATE BRANCH BANK
Protest book, 1831-1837   Ibid.
N: A-Ar 1 reel   9096

JEFFERSON MANLY FAULKNER SOLDIER'S
HOME OF ALABAMA, Mountain Creek, Ala.
Record book, 1824-1934   priv.
N: A-Ar 1 reel   9097

MOBILE, Ala. PINE CREST CEMETERY
Interment records, 1907-1951, 300 p.   Ibid.
N: A-Ar 1 reel   9098

MONTGOMERY, Ala. GREENWOOD CEMETERY
Interment records, 1907-1950, 266 p.   Ibid.
N: A-Ar 1 reel   9099

MONTGOMERY, Ala. OAKWOOD CEMETERY
Records of Confederate dead, 1861-1864, 39 p.;
interment records, 1876-1910, 1919-1948   Ibid.
N: A-Ar 3 reels   9100

PROMOTERS SOCIETY, Mt. Meigs, Montgomery,
Ala.
Constitution and minutes, 1847-1849, 168 p.
Ibid.
N: A-Ar   9101

UNITED DAUGHTERS OF THE CONFEDERACY.
FLORENCE, Ala., CHAPTER
Historical records   Ibid.
N: A-Ar   9102

Ships' Logs

With ship's logs are included journals, diaries,
and other records of voyages.

CLARK, EBENEZER
Log book, Pascagoula and Mobile, 1838-1850
priv.
N: AU   9103

FOSTER, MINNIE C.
Scrapbook re: river boats, Alabama River
priv.
N: A-Ar 1 reel   9104

MISSISSIPPI

Bibliography

MISSISSIPPI WRITERS
Bibliography, n.d.   priv.
N: Ms-Ar 1 reel   9105

Census

MISSISSIPPI (Ter.)
Census, 1803-1816   Ms-Ar
N: LU 1 reel   9106

U.S. CENSUS. FOURTH, 1820
Population schedules, Mississippi   DNA
N: DNA 2 reels   P: LM   9107

U.S. CENSUS. FIFTH, 1830
Population schedules, Mississippi   DNA
N: DNA 2 reels   9108
P: USIGS

U.S. CENSUS. SIXTH, 1840
Population schedules, Mississippi   DNA
N: DNA 3 reels   9109
P: AB USIGS

U.S. CENSUS. SEVENTH, 1850
Population schedules, Mississippi   DNA
N: DNA   9110
P: AB LM USIGS

U.S. CENSUS. EIGHTH, 1860
Population schedules, Mississippi   DNA
N: DNA 6 reels   9111
P: FU USIGS

U.S. CENSUS. NINTH, 1870
Population schedules, Mississippi   DNA
N: DNA 10 reels   9112

U.S. CENSUS. TENTH, 1880
Population schedules, Mississippi   DNA
N: DNA 32 reels   9113

Government Records

U.S. POST OFFICES. MISSISSIPPI
Postmasters' registers, 1832-1930   Ibid.
N: Ms-Ar 1 reel   9114

State Records

MISSISSIPPI. COMMISSIONERS OF PUBLIC
BUILDINGS
Journal, 1836-1840   Ms-Ar
N: Ms-Ar 1 reel   9115

MISSISSIPPI-TENNESSEE BOUNDARY
COMMISSIONS
Journal, 1837   Ms-Ar
N: Ms-Ar 1 reel   9116

Church Records

MONROE PRESBYTERIAN CHURCH, Pontotoc
Co., Miss.
Records, 1823-1925   G-S
N: G-S 1 reel   9117
P: Ms-Ar

NATCHEZ, Miss. TRINITY EPISCOPAL CHURCH
Records, 1822-1890   Ibid.
N: Microphoto 1 reel   9118
P: Ms-Ar

Personal Papers

ALCORN, JAMES LUSK, Gov. Miss., 1816-1894
Papers, 1850-1949, 30 items   Southern His-
torical Collection NcU
N: NNF 1 reel   9119
P: NNF

ALLEN, JAMES
Papers, 1788-1796   Ms-Ar;
1856-1869   priv.
N: NcU 500 frames   9120

ATKIN, EDMOND
Manuscript, 1753   DLC
N: Ms-Ar 1 reel   9121

CATHCART, JAMES LEANDER
Correspondence, 1801-1802, 10 items   NN
N: CSmH   9122

QUITMAN, JOHN ANTHONY, 1798-1858
Papers, 1843   ViU
N: Ms-Ar 1 reel   9123

REDWOOD-CANNON FAMILY, of Lowndes Co.,
Miss.
Papers, 1843-1865, 20 items   priv.
N: GEU 1 reel*   9124

SHARKEY, H. CLAY
Papers, 1867-1931   priv.
N: Ms-Ar 1 reel   9125

SOMERVILLE, NELLIE NUGENT
Papers, 1896-1951   MCR
N: Ms-Ar 1 reel   9126

SPEIGHT, LAMON
Family papers, 1784-1870   priv.
N: Ms-Ar 1 reel   9127

Business Papers

LEIGH, PETER RANDOLPH, 1820-1870
Plantation journal and account book, "The
Mountain," Mississippi, 1852-1864, 1 v.   priv.
N: CU 1 reel   9128

NEWSTEAD PLANTATION, Washington Co.,
Miss.
Diary, 1857-1882, 9 v.   priv.
N: NcU 1 reel   9129

WRIGHT AND FREEMAN, funeral directors,
Hattiesburg, Miss.
Records, n.d. (typescript)   priv.
N: USIGS   9130

Collections

MISSISSIPPI. DEPT. OF ARCHIVES AND
HISTORY
Mississippi provincial archives, English
dominion, 1763-1780 [Dunbar Rowland
transcripts from UKLPRO]   Ms-Ar
N: A-Ar 5 reels   9131
P: AU

MISSISSIPPI. DEPT. OF ARCHIVES AND
HISTORY
Mississippi provincial archives, French
dominion, 1678-1763. [Dunbar Rowland
transcripts of France. Archives des Colonies. Série C 13. Correspondence générale, Louisiane]   Ms-Ar
N: A-Ar 10 reels   9132
P: AU

MISSISSIPPI. DEPT. OF ARCHIVES AND
HISTORY
Mississippi provincial archives, Spanish dom-
inion, 1783-1820 (some transcripts)   Ms-Ar
N: A-Ar 5 reels   9133

MISSISSIPPI. DEPT. OF ARCHIVES AND HISTORY
Spanish records, 1781-1798   Ms-Ar
N: Ms-Ar 1 reel   9134

U.S. WAR DEPT. COLLECTION OF
CONFEDERATE RECORDS
Index to compiled service records of Confed-
erate soldiers from Mississippi   DNA
N: DNA 45 reels 16 mm. [M-232] 9135

Institutions

ELLISVILLE, Miss. OLD AND NEW ELLISVILLE
CEMETERIES
Records, n.d. (typescript)   priv.
N: USIGS   9136

JACKSON, Miss. GREENWOOD CEMETERY
Records, 1862-1915   Ibid.
N: Ms-Ar 1 reel   9137

LOUISIANA

Census

ORLEANS (Ter.)
Census, 1806   LNHT
DCO: LNHT 1 item   9138

U.S. CENSUS. THIRD, 1810
Population schedules, Louisiana   DNA
N: DNA 1 reel   9139
P: LM

U.S. CENSUS. FOURTH, 1820
Population schedules, Louisiana DNA
N: DNA 3 reels
P: LM   9140

U.S. CENSUS. FIFTH, 1830
Population schedules, Louisiana DNA
N: DNA 3 reels
P: LM   9141

U.S. CENSUS. SIXTH, 1840
Population schedules, Louisiana DNA
N: DNA 3 reels USlGS
P: LM USlGS   9142

U.S. CENSUS. SEVENTH, 1850
Agriculture, social statistics schedules,
Louisiana NcD
N: NcD 1 reel   9143

U.S. CENSUS. SEVENTH, 1850
Population schedules, Louisiana DNA
N: DNA 5 reels
P: LM USlGS   9144

U.S. CENSUS. EIGHTH, 1860
Agriculture, social statistics schedules,
Louisiana NcD
N: NcD 2 reels
P: NNC   9145

U.S. CENSUS. EIGHTH, 1860
Population schedules, Louisiana DNA
N: DNA 5 reels
P: FU LM USlGS   9146

U.S. CENSUS. NINTH, 1870
Agriculture, social statistics schedules,
Louisiana NcD
N: NcD 2 reels
P: NNC   9147

U.S. CENSUS. NINTH, 1870
Population schedules, Louisiana DNA
N: DNA 8 reels
P: LM   9148

U.S. CENSUS. TENTH, 1880
Agriculture, defectives and dependents, manu-
facturing schedules, Louisiana NcD
N: NcD 1 reel   9149

U.S. CENSUS. TENTH, 1880
Population schedules, Louisiana DNA
N: DNA 28 reels
P: LM   9150

Government Records

FRANCE. ARCHIVES DES COLONIES.
Série C-13-A
Correspondance générale. Louisiane, 1694-
1781 FrAN
N: CaOOA 36 reels   9151

FRANCE. ARCHIVES DES COLONIES.
Série C-13-A
Correspondance générale, Louisiane,
selections, v. 5. FrAN
DCO: DLC 35 sheets   9152

FRANCE. ARCHIVES DES COLONIES.
Série C-13-C
Mémoires et documents relatives à la
Louisiane, 1673-1782, 4 v. FrAN
N: CaOOA 4 reels   9153

FRANCE. ARCHIVES DES COLONIES.
Série C-13-C
Mémoires et documents relatives à la
Louisiane, selections, v.1,4 FrAN
N: DLC 2 feet
P: DLC   9154

SPAIN. ARCHIVO GENERAL DE INDIAS, Seville
Ministerio de Ultramar: selections re:
Louisiana and Florida, 1771-1772 SpAGI
DCO: DLC 37 sheets   9155

SPAIN. ARCHIVO HISTÓRICO NACIONAL, Madrid
Consejo de Indias: Residencias: Don Louis de
Unzaga y Amezaga as Governor of New Orleans,
1786-1789; Baron de Carondelet, as Governor
of Louisiana, 1797; Estaban Miró as Governor,
and charges against him, 1805 Ibid.
N: DLC 4 reels   9156

SWEDEN. RIKSARKIVET
Notes et renseignements sur la Louisiane.
Cahier 5: Mississippi Campagne SvSR
N: OCHP 1 reel   9157

U.S. ADJUTANT-GENERAL'S OFFICE
Index to compiled service records of Volunteer
soldiers of the War of 1812 from Louisiana
organizations DNA
N: DNA 3 reels 16 mm. [M-229]   9158

U.S. ADJUTANT-GENERAL'S OFFICE
Index to compiled service records of Volunteer
soldiers of the War of 1837-1838 from Louisiana
DNA
N: DNA 1 reel 16 mm. [M-241]   9159

U.S. ADJUTANT-GENERAL'S OFFICE
Index to compiled service records of Volunteer
soldiers of the Florida War from Louisiana
DNA
N: DNA 1 reel 16 mm. [M-239]   9160

U.S. ADJUTANT-GENERAL'S OFFICE
Index to compiled service records of Volunteer
soldiers of the War with Spain from Louisiana
DNA
N: DNA 1 reel 16 mm. [M-240]   9161

U.S. BUREAU OF CUSTOMS
New Orleans Collector of Customs, letters,
1804-1807, 16 items DNA
N: LNHT 1 reel   9162

U.S. BUREAU OF CUSTOMS
Passenger lists of vessels arriving at New
Orleans, 1820-1902 DNA
N: DNA 93 reels 16 mm. [M-259]   9163

U.S. DEPT. OF STATE
Territorial papers: Orleans territory,
1764-1813 DNA
N: DNA 13 reels [T-260]   9164

State Records

LOUISIANA (Province). GOVERNOR (Spanish)
Despatches, 1766-1791, 25 v. SpAGI
DCO: LNHT NN   9165

LOUISIANA (Province). SUPERIOR COUNCIL
Legal records, 1717-1773; miscellaneous
records, 1738-1748 L-M
N: L-M 76 reels   9166

ORLEANS (Ter.). COUNCILLORS
Election report, 1805 LNHT
DCO: LNHT 1 item   9167

County Records

NATCHITOCHES PARISH, La.
Deeds and other recorded instruments, 1732-
1767 C.H. Natchitoches
N: LNaN   9168

OPELOUSAS and ATTAKAPAS DISTRICTS, La.
Brand book, 1760-1888 LLafS
N: LLafS 620 frames
P: LLafS   9169

City Records

NEW ORLEANS
Census, 1803, 1 p. DNA
DCO: LNHT   9170

NEW ORLEANS
Ordinances, 1866- ; real estate assessments,
1858- ; arrest books, 1881- Ibid.
N: LN   9171

NEW ORLEANS. CITIZENS
Petition, 1803 LNHT
DCO: LNHT 1 item   9172

NEW ORLEANS. MAYOR, 1936-1938
Robert S. Maestri correspondence, subject
and cross files Ibid.
N: LN 31 reels 16 mm.   9173

Church Records

CHURCH OF JESUS CHRIST OF LATTER-DAY
SAINTS. LOUISIANA
Ward and branch records: New Orleans, La.,
1849-1850 USlC
N: USlGS 1 reel   9174

NEW ORLEANS. URSULINE CHAPEL
Mortgage and baptismal records,
1834-1915 Ibid.
N: LNHT 1 reel
P: LNHT   9175

VIOLET, La. OUR LADY OF LOURDES CHURCH
Register of baptisms, marriages, and deaths,
1787-1887 Ibid.
N: LNHT 1 reel   9176

Personal Papers

AIME, GABRIELLE
Journal of a voyage and notes, 1847-1867
L-M
N: L-M 1 reel   9177

BARROW, DAVID CRENSHAW
Family papers, 1834-1893, 699 items and
4 v. priv.
N: NcU 2 reels   9178

BARROW FAMILY
Bartholomew Barrow daybook, 1811-1814;
R.R. Barrow residence plantation journal
(Louisiana), 252 p. NcU
N: NcU 1 reel   9179

BOSSIER, PLACIDE
Diary, 1860 priv.
N: LNaN   9180

BOULIGNY, FRANCISCO
Memoria sobre la Luisiana, 1776 SpBN
N: LNHT 1 reel   9181

CARLETON, MARK, 1866-1925
Papers, field notes on sugar cane, 1897-1901
LU
N: NbHi 1 reel   9182

CLOUTIER, FULBERT
Diary, 1865 priv.
N: LNaN   9183

D'ARTAGUETTE, DIRON
Journal of events in Louisiana, Sept., 1722-
Sept., 1723 FrAN
N: LNHT 1 reel   9184

FISK FAMILY
Papers, 1813-1897 LNHT
N: LNHT 1 reel*   9185

KING, GRACE, 1852-1932
Papers, including the Charles Gayarré
papers, 1781-1933, 1338 items LSU
N: NcU 5 reels   9186

LAMY, LOUIS MICHEL
Will, 1811
DCO: LNHT 1 piece   9187

LANDRETH, JOHN
Journal of expedition to the Gulf Coast,
Nov., 1818-May, 1819, 250 p. DNA
N: DNA 1 reel [T-12]
P: LU   9188

LEONARD, JOHN W.
Letter re: Constitutional Convention, Oct. 24,
1910 LNHT
DCO: LNHT 1 item   9189

LOCKETT, SAMUEL H.
Louisiana as it is, 1872 LNHT
N: LNHT 1 reel   9190

MATHER, JAMES
Letter, 1811
DCO: LNHT 1 item   9191

NICHOLLS FAMILY, New Orleans
Memoirs, 1847-1877 priv.
N: priv. 1 reel
P: LNHT   9192

POMBE, RAPHAEL
Letters, 1880, 4 items MH
DCO: LNHT   9193

PONTALBA, JOSEPH XAVIER DE, Baron
Letters to Governor Miró, 1792-1795 LNHT
N: LNHT 1 reel   9194
P: LNHT

PONTALBA, JOSEPH XAVIER DE, Baron
Letters to his wife, 1796 LNHT
N: LNHT 1 reel   9195
P: LNHT

RIDDELL, Dr. JOHN LEONARD, 1807-1865
Journals, 1831-1849 LNHT
N: LNHT 1 reel*   9196

ROUQUETTE, ADRIEN, 1813-1887
Letters and poems, 184? InNd
N: LNHT 1 reel   9197

SILLIMAN, BENJAMIN, 1779-1864
Journey to New Orleans, 1845 CtY
N: LNHT 1 reel   9198

URQUHART FAMILY
Papers, 1821-1874 LNHT
N: LNHT 1 reel*   9199

WADE, HENRY F.
Papers, 1843-1939 LNHT
N: LNHT 1 reel   9200

WHARTON, THOMAS KELAH
Diaries, 1853-1862 NN
N: LNHT 1 reel*   9201

Business Papers

AIME, VALCOUR
Sugar plantation journal, accounts, and diary,
1821-1860 L-M
N: L-M   9202

EVAN HALL PLANTATION, La.
Account book, 1772-1835 priv.
N: NcU 1 reel   9203

LOUISIANA. STATE UNIVERSITY AND AGRICUL-
TURAL AND MECHANICAL COLLEGE. DEPT.
OF ARCHIVES
Plantation papers (part typescript) LU
N: NNC 10 reels   9204

WARMOTH, HENRY CLAY, 1842-1931
Papers (Magnolia Plantation, La., Journal),
1856-1863 NcU
N: NcU 623 frames   9205

Collections

TULANE UNIVERSITY OF LOUISIANA. SCHOOL
OF MEDICINE
Yellow Fever Papers, 1859-1952 LNHT-M
DCO: LNHT 16 items   9206

U.S. LIBRARY OF CONGRESS
Louisiana miscellaneous collection, 1731-1928
DLC
N: LNHT 3 reels   9207

U.S. LIBRARY OF CONGRESS
Material on history of Louisiana, 1750-
1780 v.p.
DCO: DLC
N: CSt 12 reels   9208

Ships' Logs

With ships' logs are included journals, diaries,
and other records of voyages.

STEVENS, S. GLEASON
Log book and diary, 1845 RPB
N: LNHT 1 reel   9209

TEXAS

Bibliography

HISTORICAL RECORDS SURVEY. TEXAS
Cumulative Index to Biographical Studies of
Texas TxU
N: TxD 2 reels   9210

Census

U.S. CENSUS. SEVENTH, 1850
Population schedules, Texas DNA
N: DNA 7 reels   9211
P: USIGS

U.S. CENSUS. EIGHTH, 1860
Population schedules, Texas DNA
N: DNA 7 reels   9212
P: FU USIGS

U.S. CENSUS. NINTH, 1870
Population schedules, Texas DNA
N: DNA 9 reels   9213

U.S. CENSUS. TENTH, 1880
Population schedules, Texas DNA
N: DNA 47 reels   9214

Government Records

GREAT BRITAIN. FOREIGN OFFICE. F.O. 75
Consular Despatches from Texas, 1840-1845,
23 v. UKLPRO
N: CU-B   9215
P: CU-B

TEXAS (Republic). ADJUTANT GENERAL
Muster roll of the soldiers of the Republic of
Texas, 1834-1846, 347 p. General Land
Office, Austin
DCO: TxD   9216

TEXAS (Republic). CUSTOMS HOUSE,
GALVESTON
Records, 1836-1845 TxG
N: DLC 1 reel   9217
P: DLC

County Records

CHEROKEE Co., Texas
Marriage records, 1864-1870 C.H. Rusk
N: TxD 1 reel   9218

FANNIN Co., Texas
Marriage records, 1838-1870 C.H. Bonham
N: TxD 1 reel   9219

FAYETTE Co., Texas
Marriage records, 1838-1871 C.H. La Grange
N: TxD 1 reel   9220

NACOGDOCHES Co., Texas
Marriage records, 1837-1871
C.H. Nacogdoches
N: TxD 1 reel   9221

NUECES Co., Texas
Wills, 1855-1900; marriages, 1857-1900
C.H. Corpus Christi
N: DLC 1 reel   9222

PARKER Co., Texas
Marriage records, 1874-1886
C.H. Weatherford
N: TxD 1 reel   9223

RED RIVER Co., Texas
Marriage records, 1845-1877
C.H. Clarksville
N: TxD 1 reel   9224

ROBERTSON Co., Texas
Marriage records, 1838-1875 C.H. Franklin
N: TxD 1 reel   9225

SAN AUGUSTINE Co., Texas
Marriage records, 1837-1880
C.H. San Augustine
N: TxD 1 reel   9226

WASHINGTON Co., Texas
Marriage records, 1837-1870
C.H. Brenham
N: TxD 1 reel   9227

Church Records

BAPTISTS. TEXAS. SWEETWATER BAPTIST
ASSOCIATION
Minutes, 1885-1894 TxAbH
N: TxAbH 1 reel   9228

CHURCH OF JESUS CHRIST OF LATTER-DAY
SAINTS. TEXAS
Ward records: El Paso USIC
N: USIGS   9229

Personal Papers

HOLLEY, Mrs. MARY AUSTIN
Papers, 1808-1846 TxU
N: KyU 1 reel   9230

JEMISON, ROBERT, IV
Diary re: scouting trip to Texas, 1854, 34 p.
priv.
N: A-Ar   9231

REAGAN, JOHN HENNINGER, 1818-1905
Papers TxU
N: NNC 8 reels   9232

SHACKELFORD, Captain JOHN
Texas War letters priv.
N: A-Ar 1 reel   9233

Business Papers

SNYDER (D.H. and J.W.) COMPANY
Papers, 1870-1900
N: TxU 1 reel   9234
P: WyU

Collections

BRAUNFELS, Germany. FÜRST ZU SOLMISCHES
ARCHIV
Registratur des Texas-Vereins: Records,
1842-1864 Ibid.
DCO: DLC 17301 sheets   9235

U.S. WAR DEPT. COLLECTION OF
CONFEDERATE RECORDS
Index to compiled service records of Confed-
erate soldiers from Texas DNA
N: DNA 41 reels 16 mm. [M-227]   9236

Institutions

THE TEXAS ASSOCIATION
Minutes, May, 1844-1845 KyLo
N: ? 20 feet   9237
P: KyU

OKLAHOMA

Government Records

U.S. ADJUTANT-GENERAL'S OFFICE
Fort Sill, Okla., Post returns, 1869-1917
DNA
N: DNA 3 reels   9238

U.S. DEPT. OF THE INTERIOR
Material on Cherokee mineral licenses and
oil leases, 1890-1898; Kiowa military and
Federal relations, 1865-1925 Ibid.
N: OkHi 1 reel   9239

County Records

PONTOTOC Co., Okla.
  County and probate court records (Chickasaw Nation), 1887-1904   C.H. Ada
  N: OkU   9240

Personal Papers

BYINGTON, CYRUS, 1793-1868
  Letters, 1819-1870   OkTG
  N: OkTG 1 reel   9241

CANTON, FRANK
  Correspondence and papers, 1849-1927
  N: OkU 1 reel   9242
  P: WyU

DREW, JOHN
  Papers on the Cherokee Indians   priv.
  N: OkHi 1 reel   9243

HUNTER, GEORGE
  Journal, expedition to Red and Washita Rivers, 1804, 107 p.   priv.
  N: PPAmP   9244

LATROBE, CHARLES JACOB, 1801-1875
  Diary, Mar. 7, 1832-May 19, 1834   OkTG
  N: OkTG 1 reel   9245

LOUGHRIDGE, ROBERT McGILL, 1809-1900
  Correspondence, 1841-1886   PPPrHi
  N: OkTU 2 reels   9246

MARCY, RANDOLPH B.
  Papers re: forts in Oklahoma, 1848-1852   priv.
  N: OkU   9247

PORTER, JEREMIAH, 1804-1893
  Personal journals, 1831-1833   priv.
  N: OkU   9248

ROSS, JOHN, 1790-1866
  Papers re: Cherokee matters, 1814-1877   OkTG
  N: OkTG 10 reels   9249

Institutions

OKLAHOMA HISTORICAL SOCIETY
  Material on Peyote cult of Pawnee Indians   OkHi
  N: OkHi 1 reel   9250

ARKANSAS

Census

U.S. CENSUS. FIFTH, 1830
  Population schedules, Arkansas   DNA
  N: DNA 1 reel   9251
  P: USIGS

U.S. CENSUS. SIXTH, 1840
  Population schedules, Arkansas   DNA
  N: DNA 1 reel   9252
  P: ArU USIGS

U.S. CENSUS. SEVENTH, 1850
  Population schedules, Arkansas   DNA
  N: DNA 7 reels   9253
  P: ArU USIGS

U.S. CENSUS. EIGHTH, 1860
  Population schedules, Arkansas   DNA
  N: DNA 5 reels   9254
  P: ArU USIGS

U.S. CENSUS. NINTH, 1870
  Population schedules, Arkansas   DNA
  N: DNA   9255
  P: ArU USIGS

U.S. CENSUS. TENTH, 1880
  Population schedules, Arkansas   DNA
  N: DNA 23 reels   9256
  P: ArU

Government Records

U.S. OFFICE OF INDIAN AFFAIRS
  Letter book of the Arkansas Trading House, 1805-1810   DNA
  N: DNA 1 reel [M-142]   9257
  P: TM

Territorial Records

ARKANSAS (Ter.). GOVERNOR, 1825-1828
  Message and letter book, 1825-1828, 72 l.   ArHi
  N: ArHi 1 reel   9258
  P: ArHi ArU

ARKANSAS (Ter.). MILITARY COMMISSION
  Register, 1820-1836, 1 v.   ArHi
  N: ArHi 1 reel   9259
  P: ArHi ArU

State Records

ARKANSAS. CONSTITUTIONAL CONVENTION, 1874
  Proceedings, 1874   ArHi
  N: ArHi DLC 1 reel   9260
  P: DLC

County Records

ARKANSAS Co., Ark.
  Court records, 1797-1844; tax assessment lists, 1819-1849; deeds, Book B, 1813-1818   C.H. De Witt
  N: ArHi 3 reels   9261
  P: ArHi ArU

CLARK Co., Ark.
  Court records, 1820-1860; marriage records books, 1821-1867, A-D   C.H. Arkadelphia
  N: ArHi 1 reel   9262

CONWAY Co., Ark.
  Court docket, 1837-1848; letters of administration, 1825-1859   C.H. Morrilton
  N: Ar-Hi 309 frames   9263

CRAWFORD CO., Ark.
  Tax records, 1821-1834, 1839-1847   C.H. Van Buren
  N: ArHi 910 frames   9264

CRITTENDEN Co., Ark.
  Wills, 1826-1903; probate court books, 1837-1871; grantor index, A-M, 1827-1909; grantee index, A-D, 1827-1907   priv.
  N: TM 3 reels*   9265

CRITTENDEN Co., Ark. ABSTRACT AND TITLE COMPANY
  Grantor Index, A-M; will books A and B   Ibid.
  N: ArHi 1 reel   9266
  P: ArHi

HEMPSTEAD Co., Ark.
  Court of common pleas records, 1819-1822   ArHi
  N: ArHi 122 frames   9267

INDEPENDENCE Co., Ark.
  Land survey, 1848-1873; Marriage Record Book A   C.H. Batesville
  N: ArHi 2 reels   9268
  P: ArHi

PULASKI Co., Ark.
  County records, 1850-1893   C.H. Little Rock
  N: ArHi 37 reels   9269
  P: ArHi

PULASKI Co., Ark., see BEEBE, ROSWELL, 9287, under ARKANSAS, Personal Papers

SALINE Co., Ark.
  Marriage records, books A-C, 1836-1875   C.H. Benton
  N: ArHi 1 reel   9270
  P: ArHi

VAN BUREN Co., Ark.
  Probate records books, A and B; letters of administration, 1859-1900; marriage record books, 1877-   C.H. Clinton
  N: ArHi 250 feet   9271

WASHINGTON Co., Ark.
  Sheriff's census, 1829, 1865   C.H. Fayetteville
  N: ArHi 1 reel   9272
  P: ArHi

City Records

ARKADELPHIA, Ark.
  Digest of city ordinances, 1899   Ibid.
  N: ArHi 62 frames   9273

CONWAY, Ark.
  Municipal court records, 1887-1896, 404 p.   priv.
  N: ArHi 1 reel   9274
  P: ArHi ArU

Church Records

ARKADELPHIA, Ark. FIRST METHODIST CHURCH
  Minutes, 1858-1866; register, 1913-1959   Ibid.
  N: ArHi 33 feet   9275

BAPTISTS. ARKANSAS. ASSOCIATION OF BAPTIST CHURCHES, MOUNT VERNON DISTRICT
  Minutes, 1853-1928   Ibid.
  N: Ar-Hi 150 feet   9276

BAPTISTS. ARKANSAS. ASSOCIATION OF BAPTIST CHURCHES, SALINE Co.
  Minutes, 1848-1903   Ibid.
  N: ArHi 190 frames   9277

CYPRESS VALLEY BAPTIST CHURCH, Lee Co., Ark.
  Records, to 1861   Ibid.
  N: ArHi 102 frames   9278

DWIGHT MISSION, Ark.
  Records, 1819-1840   MH
  N: ArHi* 1 reel   9279
  P: ArU

GARNETT CUMBERLAND PRESBYTERIAN CHURCH, Lincoln Co., Ark.
  Minutes, 1883-1894
  N: ArHi 1 reel   9280
  P: ArHi

METHODIST CHURCH (United States). CONFERENCES. ARKANSAS
  Records, 1836-1889   Ibid.
  N: ArHi 1 reel   9281
  P: ArHi

MOUNT OLIVE BAPTIST CHURCH, Ashley Co., Ark.
  Records, 1859-1885   priv.
  N: ArHi 1 reel   9282
  P: ArHi

SYLVANIA PRESBYTERIAN CHURCH, East Arkansas Presbytery, Ark.
  Records, 1878-1953   Ibid.
  N: ArHi 1 reel   9283
  P: ArU

Personal Papers

ADAMS, ELIZA
  Diary, 1859-1863   priv.
  N: ArHi   9284

ADAMS, LAURA
  Diary (extracts), 1859
  N: ArHi 1 reel   9285
  P: ArHi

BARROW, JOHN C.
Papers   priv.
N: ArHi 1/2 reel
P: ArHi
9286

BEEBE, ROSWELL, Arkansas Internal Improvement Commissioner
In-letters re: railroads in Arkansas, ca. 1840
priv.
N: ArHi 104 frames
9287

BEEBE, ROSWELL, Arkansas Internal Improvement Commissioner
Letter to Pulaski Co. Court, June 10, 1851
priv.
N: ArHi 1 reel
P: ArHi ArU
9288

BROWN, JOHN W.
Diary, 1821-1865   priv.
N: ArHi 75 feet
9289

CUNNINGHAM FAMILY
Papers of John Henry and Edward   ArHi
N: ArHi 1 reel
P: ArHi ArU
9290

DAVIS, JEFFERSON, Gov. Ark., 1862-1913
Speeches and miscellaneous items   priv.
N: ArU 1 reel
9291

DELONY FAMILY, of Hempstead Co., Ark.
Records   priv.
N: ArHi
P: ArHi
9292

DeWITT, MARCUS B.
Selected documents, 1819-1830   priv.
N: ArHi 1 reel*
9293

FAGOT, ANDRÉ
Notarial records, Arkansas Post, 1809-1812
[in French]
N: ArHi 1 reel
P: ArHi ArU
9294

FLANAGIN, HARRIS, 1817-1874
Papers, 1862-1874   ArHi
N: ArHi 1 reel
P: ArHi ArU
9295

GILLET, ORVILLE
Papers, 1861-1865   ArHi
N: ArHi
P: ArHi ArU
9296

GRAVES, L. H.
Diary, 1861-1864 (typescript) priv.
N: ArU 1 reel
9297

HANEY, J. H.
Diary, 1861-1865   priv.
N: ArHi 516 frames
P: ArHi
9298

JORDAN, CHARLES F.
Diary, to 1865   priv.
N: ArHi 128 frames
9299

KANNADY, J. R.
Diary (extracts), 1861-1880 (transcript) priv.
N: ArHi 31 frames
9300

NOLAND, C. F. M.
Letters   priv.
N: ArHi*
9301

NORWOOD, HAL LEE, 1871-
Scrap books priv.
N: ArU 1 reel
9302

PIKE, ALBERT, 1809-1891
Letters, 1849-1882, 15 items   ArHi
N: ArHi 1 reel
P: ArHi ArU
9303

TAYLOR FAMILY, Ark.
Papers, 1883-1935   ArHi
N: ArHi 10 feet
9304

TRIMBLE, ROBERT WILSON
Papers priv.
N: ArHi 1/2 reel
P: ArHi
9305

TRULOCK FAMILY
Papers, to 1861 priv.
N: ArHi 81 frames *
9306

WILLIAMS, DAVID C.
Papers ArHi
N: ArHi 1 reel
P: ArHi ArU
9307

WOODRUFF, WILLIAM EDWARD, 1795-1885
Papers, 1825-1872 ArHi
N: ArHi 1 reel
P: ArHi ArU
9308

Business Papers

BORKMAN, JACOB
Day book, 1839 priv.
N: ArHi 20 ft.
9309

LITTLE ROCK PRINTING COMPANY,
Little Rock, Ark.
Directors' proceedings, 1872-1874   priv.
N: ArHi 1 reel
P: ArHi
9310

PERNOT, Dr. HENRI CHARLES
Account books, 1852-1862   ArHi
N: ArHi 1 reel
P: ArHi ArU
9311

WILLIAMS (DAVID C.) COMPANY
Papers ArHi
N: ArHi 1 reel
P: ArU
9312

Collections

CHICAGO HISTORICAL SOCIETY
Arkansas manuscripts ICHi
N: ArU 1 reel
9313

ILLINOIS. STATE LIBRARY
Letters illustrative of Arkansas history, 1838-
1865, 88 items I
DCO: ArU
9314

MISSOURI. HISTORICAL SOCIETY, St. Louis
Arkansas manuscripts MoSHi
N: ArU 1 reel
9315

NEWBERRY LIBRARY, Chicago
Arkansas manuscripts ICN
N: ArU 1 reel
9316

WISCONSIN. STATE HISTORICAL SOCIETY
Arkansas manuscripts, 1861-1899 WHi
N: ArU 1 reel
9317

Institutions

ARKANSAS POST, Ark.
Records, 1720-1787 (typescript and trans-
lation) priv.
N: ArHi 2 reels
P: ArHi
9318

COLLEGE OF PHYSICIANS AND SURGEONS OF
LITTLE ROCK AND PULASKI COUNTY, Ark.
Minutes, 1873-1885 Ibid.
N: Ar-Hi 1 reel
P: Ar-Hi
9319

LITTLE ROCK AESTHETIC CLUB
Proceedings, 1883-1946 Ibid.
N: ArHi 3 reels
P: ArHi
9320

LITTLE ROCK-PULASKI CO. MEDICAL SOCIETY
Minutes, 1872-1885, 333 p. ArHi
N: ArHi 1 reel
P: ArHi ArU
9321

UNION LEAGUE OF AMERICA. ARKANSAS
STATE COUNCIL.
Records, 1871-1872 priv.
N: ArHi
P: ArHi
9322

Ships' Logs

With ships' logs are included journals, diaries,
and other records of voyages.

BRACELETT (Steamer)
Portage Book
N: ArHi
P: ArU
9323

TENNESSEE

Census

U.S. CENSUS. FIFTH, 1830
Population schedules, Tennessee   DNA
N: DNA 9 reels
P: TM USIGS
9324

U.S. CENSUS. SIXTH, 1840
Population schedules, Tennessee   DNA
N: DNA 8 reels
P: AB TM USIGS
9325

U.S. CENSUS. SEVENTH, 1850
Agriculture, manufacturing, social statistics
schedules, Tennessee NcD
N: NcD 7 reels
P: LU NNC
9326

U.S. CENSUS. SEVENTH, 1850
Population schedules, Tennessee   DNA
N: DNA 11 reels
P: AB TM TxD USIGS
9327

U.S. CENSUS. EIGHTH, 1860
Agriculture, manufacturing, social statistics
schedules, Tennessee   NcD
N: NcD 7 reels
9328

U.S. CENSUS. EIGHTH, 1860
Population schedules, Tennessee   DNA
N: DNA 9 reels
P: USIGS
9329

U.S. CENSUS. NINTH, 1870
Agriculture, manufacturing, social statistics
schedules, Tennessee NcD
N: NcD 2 reels
9330

U.S. CENSUS. NINTH, 1870
Population schedules, Tennessee   DNA
N: DNA 14 reels
P: USIGS
9331

U.S. CENSUS. TENTH, 1880
Agriculture, defectives, dependents and de-
linquents, and manufacturing schedules,
Tennessee NcD
N: NcD 3 reels
9332

U.S. CENSUS. TENTH, 1880
Population schedules, Tennessee   DNA
N: DNA 44 reels
9333

Government Records

U.S. BUREAU OF REFUGEES, FREEDMEN,
AND ABANDONED LANDS
Selected records of Tennessee Field Office,
1865-1872 DNA
N: DNA 73 reels
P: T
9334

U.S. GENERAL LAND OFFICE
Lists of North Carolina land grants in
Tennessee, 1778-1791 DNA
N: DNA 1 reel [M-68]
P: TM
9335

U.S. OFFICE OF INDIAN AFFAIRS
Records of the Cherokee Indian Agency in
Tennessee, 1801-1835 DNA
N: DNA 14 reels [M-208]
9336

County Records

Tennessee county records are listed collectively,
unless they appear to have special value to the

researcher. Separate listing is always given to court minutes, wills and/or probate records, deeds, vital records, and muster rolls. In order that researchers may differentiate between materials the originals of which are held at county courthouses and materials the originals of which are held at the state archives, an exception has been made to the usual alphabetical listing. Courthouse material always precedes archival material.

ANDERSON Co., Tenn.
Court records, 1801-1819; probate records, 1830-1841; marriage records, 1838-1858 (WPA transcript) T
N: USlGS 2 reels   9337

BEDFORD Co., Tenn.
Court records, 1837-1855; will book, v.1; marriage records, 1861-1864 (WPA transcript) T
N: USlGS 10 reels   9338

BENTON Co., Tenn.
Court records, 1842-1854; marriage records, 1846-1851 (WPA transcript) T
N: USlGS 3 reels   9339

BLEDSOE Co., Tenn.
Court records, 1810-1824, 1834-1846; deeds, 1807-1826, 1829-1854 (WPA transcript) T
N: USlGS 7 reels   9340

BLOUNT Co., Tenn.
Court records, 1795-1811, 1814-1818; marriage records, 1754-1870; will book, 1799-1858; entry taker's book, 1824-1826 (WPA transcript) T
N: USlGS 7 reels   9341

BRADLEY Co., Tenn.
Court records, 1837-1859 (WPA transcript) T
N: USlGS 8 reels   9342

CAMPBELL Co., Tenn.
Court minutes, 1813-1820, 1834-1846; probate records, 1807-1841, 1860-1880; deeds, 1806-1810; land entries, 1825-1833; marriage records, 1838-1860 (WPA transcript) T
N: USlGS 5 reels   9343

CANNON Co., Tenn.
Court records, 1836-1841; marriage records, 1850-1866; will book, 1836-1895 (WPA transcript) T
N: USlGS 3 reels   9344

CARROLL Co., Tenn.
Court records, 1821-1859; marriage records, 1838-1860; will book, 1822-1864 (WPA transcript) T
N: USlGS 10 reels   9345

CARTER Co., Tenn.
Court records, 1804-1805, 1819-1829; probate records, 1794-1847 (WPA transcript) T
N: USlGS 6 reels   9346

CHEATHAM Co., Tenn.
Court records, 1856-1860; marriage records, 1856-1897; probate records, 1856-1871 (WPA transcript) T
N: USlGS 3 reels   9347

CLAIBORNE Co., Tenn.
Court records, 1801-1824; wills, 1837-1850; deeds, 1801-1865; marriage records, 1838-1868 (WPA transcript) T
N: USlGS 9 reels   9348

CLAY Co., Tenn.
Marriage records, 1871-1873 (WPA transcript) T
N: USlGS 2 reels   9349

COCKE Co., Tenn.
Deeds, 1856-1860, 27 p. (WPA transcript) T
N: USlGS   9350

COFFEE Co., Tenn.
Court records, 1836-1841; marriage records, 1853-1886; probate records, 1833-1868 (WPA transcript) T
N: USlGS 2 reels   9351

CROCKETT Co., Tenn.
Marriage records, 1872-1888 (WPA transcript) T
N: USlGS 2 reels   9352

CUMBERLAND Co., Tenn.
Land records, 1856-1897 (WPA transcript) T
N: USlGS 2 reels   9353

DAVIDSON Co., Tenn.
Court minutes, 1783-1803; wills, 1784-1805; land records, 1784-1793; marriage records, 1838-1847, 2885 p.   C.H. Nashville
N: Nc-Ar   9354

DAVIDSON Co., Tenn.
Court records, 1798-1809; probate records, 1784-1816, 1821-1826, 1832-1836; land records, 1784-1793, 1820; marriage records, 1838-1847 (WPA transcript) T
N: USlGS 19 reels   9355

DECATUR Co., Tenn.
Probate records, 1846-1860; deed book, 1846-1854; survey book, 1846-1860; record book, 1854-1857; marriage records, 1869-1898 (WPA transcript) T
N: USlGS 4 reels   9356

DeKALB Co., Tenn.
Court records, 1837-1849; will book, 1838-1854; marriage records, 1848-1859 (WPA transcript) T
N: USlGS 4 reels   9357

DICKSON Co., Tenn.
Court records, 1804-1815, 1839-1845; will books, 1804-1908; marriage records, 1838-1848 (WPA transcript) T
N: USlGS 4 reels   9358

DYER Co., Tenn.
Court records, 1848-1856; wills, 1853-1893; deed book, 1824-1827; entry book, 1820-1855; marriage records, 1860-1880 (WPA transcript) T
N: USlGS 6 reels   9359

FAYETTE Co., Tenn.
Court records, 1824-1829; marriage records, 1838-1857; will book, 1836-1854 (WPA transcript) T
N: USlGS 5 reels   9360

FENTRESS Co., Tenn.
Court records, 1842-1844; land records, 1824-1838 (WPA transcript) T
N: USlGS 3 reels   9361

FRANKLIN Co., Tenn.
Court records, 1832-1843; deed book, 1808-1810; marriage records, 1838-1875; will book, 1808-1876 (WPA transcript) T
N: USlGS 7 reels   9362

GIBSON Co., Tenn.
Court records, 1824-1832, 1834-1847; probate records, 1825-1841, 1846-1852; marriage records, 1824-1860 (WPA transcript) T
N: USlGS 7 reels   9363

GILES Co., Tenn.
Court records, 1813, 1816-1817, 1823-1827, 1833; marriage records, 1865-1870; wills, 1830-1857 (WPA transcript) T
N: USlGS 9 reels   9364

GRAINGER Co., Tenn.
Court records, 1796-1816; probate records, 1833-1854; marriage records, 1796-1857; tax records, 1814-1815 (WPA transcript) T
N: USlGS 7 reels   9365

GREENE Co., Tenn.
Court minutes, 1783-1796, 159 p.
C.H. Greeneville
N: Nc-Ar   9366

GREENE Co., Tenn.
Court records, 1783-1796, 1802-1832; probate records, 1828-1842; tax book, 1809-1817 (WPA transcript) T
N: USlGS 21 reels   9367

GRUNDY Co., Tenn.
Probate records, 1838-1895; marriage records, 1850-1874 (WPA transcript) T
N: USlGS 4 reels   9368

HAMBLEN Co., Tenn.
Marriage records, 1870-1882, 38 p. (WPA transcript) T
N: USlGS   9369

HAMILTON Co., Tenn.
Court records, 1860-1867; deeds, 1796-1848; probate records, 1864-1870; marriage records, 1857-1870; entry taker's book, 1824-1897 (WPA transcript) T
N: USlGS 14 reels   9370

HARDEMAN Co., Tenn.
Court records, 1823-1829; probate records, 1823-1838; marriage records, 1823-1852, 1860-1870 (WPA transcript) T
N: USlGS 8 reels   9371

HARDIN Co., Tenn.
Court records, 1820-1849; marriage records, 1867-1868 (WPA transcript) T
N: USlGS 3 reels   9372

HAWKINS Co., Tenn.
Wills, 1797-1886; deeds, 1788-1800; miscellaneous records, 1306 p.
C.H. Rogersville
N: Nc-Ar   9373

HAWKINS Co., Tenn.
Court records, 1810-1845; deeds, 1788-1800; marriage records, 1820-1846; will book, 1797-1886 (WPA transcript) T
N: USlGS 7 reels   9374

HAYWOOD Co., Tenn.
Court records, 1823-1831, 1834-1840; marriage records, 1859-1866; will book, 1826-1839 (WPA transcript) T
N: USlGS 7 reels   9375

HENDERSON Co., Tenn.
Will book, 1895-1932 (WPA transcript) T
N: USlGS 3 reels   9376

HENRY Co., Tenn.
Court records, 1824-1828, 1832-1849; probate records, 1844-1856; tax book, 1827-1835 (WPA transcript) T
N: USlGS 8 reels   9377

HICKMAN Co., Tenn.
Court records, 1844-1855; deed book, 1808-1813; probate records, 1844-1852 (WPA transcript) T
N: USlGS 3 reels   9378

HUMPHREYS Co., Tenn.
Court records, 1842-1850; deed book, 1810-1816; probate records, 1838-1844; marriage records, 1864-1868 (WPA transcript) T
N: USlGS 4 reels   9379

JACKSON Co., Tenn.
Church and family records, n.d., 117 p.; ranger book, 1817-1860, 68 p.; miscellaneous records, 1810-1909 (WPA transcript) T
N: USlGS   9380

JEFFERSON Co., Tenn.
Court minutes, 1792-1802; wills, 1792-1810; grant book, 1792-1794; marriage records, 1792-1870, 778 p.   C.H. Dandridge
N: Nc-Ar   9381

JEFFERSON Co., Tenn.
Court records, 1792-1860; will books, 1792-1844; probate records, 1805-1832, 1836-1846; marriage records, 1792-1870; tax records, 1822-1830; scholastic population, 1841-1861 (WPA transcript) T
N: USlGS 15 reels   9382

JOHNSON Co., Tenn.
Probate records, 1827-1867; marriage records, 1838-1860; tax records, 1836-1839 (WPA transcript) T
N: USlGS 2 reels   9383

KNOX Co., Tenn.
Court minutes, 1793-1809; wills, 1792-1803; guardian book, 1792-1821; marriage records, 1792-1837, 3333 p.   C.H. Knoxville
N: Nc-Ar   9384

KNOX Co., Tenn.
Court records, 1792-1866; probate records, 1792-1821; estate books, 1812-1830; marriage records, 1792-1864; tax records, 1844-1845 (WPA transcript) T
N: USlGS 27 reels   9385

LAUDERDALE Co., Tenn.

Court minutes, 1836-1861; marriage records, 1838-1866; probate records, 1837-1855 (WPA transcript) T
N: USlGS 5 reels   9386

LAWRENCE Co., Tenn.
Court records, 1818-1823, 1848-1871; marriage records, 1838-1866; probate records, 1829-1847; road record book, 1853-1883 (WPA transcript) T
N: USlGS 5 reels   9387

LAWRENCE Co., Tenn.
Justice of the Peace books, 1818-1822 T
N: T 1 reel   9388

LEWIS Co., Tenn.
Court records, 1846-1870; guardian bonds, 1846-1874, 434 p. (WPA transcript) T
N: USlGS   9389

LINCOLN Co., Tenn.
Court records, 1811-1812, 1814, 1817; probate records, 1810-1824, 1827-1850; marriage records, 1838-1860 (WPA transcript) T
N: USlGS 4 reels   9390

McMINN Co., Tenn.
Court records, 1819-1829; marriage records, 1821-1864; probate records, 1828-1834, 1838-1848 (WPA transcript) T
N: USlGS 6 reels   9391

McNAIRY Co., Tenn.
Deeds, 1823-1845; marriage records, 1861-1869 (WPA transcript) T
N: USlGS 3 reels   9392

MACON Co., Tenn.
Court records, 1843-1874 (WPA transcript) T
N: USlGS 1 reel   9393

MADISON Co., Tenn.
Court records, 1821-1854; probate records, 1822-1879; marriage records, 1838-1871; tax book, 1822-1832 (WPA transcript) T
N: USlGS 16 reels   9394

MARION Co., Tenn.
Deed books, 1819-1830 (WPA transcript) T
N: USlGS 2 reels   9395

MARSHALL Co., Tenn.
Court minutes, 1836-1840; wills, 1835-1855; marriage records, 1838-1865 (WPA transcript) T
N: USlGS 4 reels   9396

MAURY Co., Tenn.
Court records, 1808-1929 (WPA transcript) T
N: USlGS 6 reels   9397

MEIGS Co., Tenn.
Court records, 1836-1846; probate records, 1836-1850; marriage records, 1838-1902; school book, 1838-1848 (WPA transcript) T
N: USlGS 6 reels   9398

MONROE Co., Tenn.
Court records, 1827-1842; marriage records, 1838-1845, 1847-1852, 1856-1868; will book, 1825-1869 (WPA transcript) T
N: USlGS 3 reels   9399

MONTGOMERY Co., Tenn.
Court records, 1805-1825; marriage records, 1838-1854; probate records, 1797-1818 (WPA transcript) T
N: USlGS 9 reels   9400

MORGAN Co., Tenn.
Court minutes, 1824-1827; marriage records, 1862-1887 (WPA transcript) T
N: USlGS 3 reels   9401

OBION Co., Tenn.
Court records, 1824-1848 (WPA transcript) T
N: USlGS 2 reels   9402

OVERTON Co., Tenn.
Court records, 1815-1856 (WPA transcript) T
N: USlGS 2 reels   9403

PERRY Co., Tenn.
Court records, 1826-1841 (WPA transcript) T
N: USlGS 2 reels   9404

POLK Co., Tenn.
Court records, 1840-1848 (WPA transcript) T
N: USlGS 3 reels   9405

PUTNAM Co., Tenn.
Court minutes, 1842-1856; tax book, 1854-1855 (WPA transcript) T
N:USlGS 6 reels   9406

RHEA Co., Tenn.
Court records, 1823-1844; probate records, 1825-1860; marriage records, 1808-1890; deeds, 1808-1809 (WPA transcript) T
N: USlGS 5 reels   9407

ROANE Co., Tenn.
Tax lists, 1848-1849; marriage registers, 1838-1876 C.H. Kingston
N: T 1 reel   9408

ROANE Co., Tenn.
Court minutes, 1801-1823; deeds, 1801-1860; probate records, 1801-1860; Revolutionary War pension applications, 1793-1855; marriage records, 1801-1838 (WPA transcript) T
N: USlGS 13 reels   9409

ROANE Co., Tenn., see McCLELLAN, JOHN, 9492, under TENNESSEE, Business Papers

ROBERTSON Co., Tenn.
Court records, 1796-1824; probate records, 1796-1821; marriage records, 1829-1860 (WPA transcript) T
N: USlGS 11 reels   9410

ROBERTSON Co., Tenn., see DORSEY, A.L., collector, 9494, under TENNESSEE, Collections

RUTHERFORD Co., Tenn.
Court minutes, 1804-1830; probate records, 1804-1832; marriage records, 1804-1845; tax records, 1809-1813, 1849 (WPA transcript) T
N: USlGS 15 reels   9411

SCOTT Co., Tenn.
Court minutes, 1850-1855; deeds, 1859-1861; marriage records, 1854-1880 (WPA transcript) T
N: USlGS 3 reels   9412

SEQUATCHIE Co., Tenn.
Court records, 1858-1874; probate records, 1858-1895; marriage records, 1858-1874 (WPA transcript) T
N: USlGS 3 reels   9413

SEVIER Co., Tenn.
Marriage records, 1856-1873, 114 p. (WPA transcript) T
N: USlGS   9414

SHELBY Co., Tenn.
Court minutes, 1820-1859; probate records, 1824-1862; vital records, 1820-1865; wills, 1830-1862 (WPA transcript) T
N: USlGS 14 reels   9415

SMITH Co., Tenn.
Court records, 1799-1835; probate records, 1805-1823 (WPA transcript) T
N: USlGS 12 reels   9416

STEWART Co., Tenn.
Court records, 1804-1807, 1811-1819; marriage records, 1838-1848; deeds, 1789-1818; tax book, 1808-1812 (WPA transcript) T
N: USlGS 4 reels   9417

SULLIVAN Co., Tenn.
Deeds, 1775-1802, 339 p. C.H. Blountville
N: Nc-Ar   9418

SULLIVAN Co., Tenn.
Will book, 1830-1870; deeds, 1775-1815, 1834-1838; marriage records, 1861-1870 (WPA transcript) T
N: USlGS 5 reels   9419

SUMNER Co., Tenn.
Court minutes, 1787-1805; wills, 1789-1822; tax lists, 1787-1794; marriage records, 1787-1838, 1358 p. C.H. Gallatin
N: Nc-Ar   9420

SUMNER, Co., Tenn.
Court records, 1787-1805; will books, 1789-1842; marriage records, 1787-1838; tax records, 1787-1794 (WPA transcript) T
N: USlGS 5 reels   9421

TIPTON, Co., Tenn.
Court records, 1823-1853; marriage records, 1840-1860; will book, 1824-1859 (WPA transcript) T
N: USlGS 7 reels   9422

UNION Co., Tenn.
Court minutes, 1854-1858 (WPA transcript) T
N: USlGS 7 reels   9423

VAN BUREN Co., Tenn.
Court records, 1840; marriage records, 1840-1861 (WPA transcript) T
N: USlGS 4 reels   9424

WARREN Co., Tenn.
Probate records, 1808-1844; marriage records, 1852-1864; deeds, 1808-1826 (WPA transcript) T
N: USlGS 5 reels   9425

WASHINGTON Co., Tenn.
Court minutes, 1778-1804; wills, 1779-1858, 2374 p. C.H. Jonesboro
N: Nc-Ar   9426

WASHINGTON Co., Tenn.
Court minutes, 1778-1817, 1819-1847; wills, 1779-1860; tax list, 1814-1815; marriage records, 1838-1846 (WPA transcript) T
N: USlGS 17 reels   9427

WAYNE Co., Tenn.
Court records, 1837-1840; wills, 1848-1857; marriage records, 1857-1898 (WPA transcript) T
N: USlGS 3 reels   9428

WEAKLEY Co., Tenn.
Court minutes, 1827-1846, 1853-1857; wills, 1828-1861; land records, 1794-1844; marriage records, 1846-1854 (WPA transcript) T
N: USlGS 9 reels   9429

WHITE Co., Tenn.
Court minute books, 1848-1853 C.H. Sparta
N: T 1 reel   9430

WHITE Co., Tenn.
Court records, 1806-1820, 1824-1827, 1835-1841; wills, 1810-1828, 1831-1840; tax book, 1811-1815; marriage records, 1838-1860 (WPA transcript) T
N: USlGS 10 reels   9431

WILLIAMSON Co., Tenn.
Minutes, 1800-1817; wills, 1800-1837; marriage records, 1800-1837 (WPA transcript) T
N: USlGS 6 reels   9432

WILSON Co., Tenn.
Court minutes, 1803-1807, 1809-1819, 1822-1824; wills, 1803-1819; grant book, 1807-1809; marriage records, 1802-1840 (WPA transcript) T
N: USlGS 6 reels   9433

City Records

MEMPHIS, Tenn., see GRAHAM, WILLIAM A., 9463, under TENNESSEE, Personal Papers

MORRISTOWN, Tenn.
History of Morristown, 1867-1936 (WPA transcript) T
N: USlGS 1 reel   9434

RUGBY, Tenn., see HUGHES, THOMAS, 9465, under TENNESSEE, Personal Papers

Church Records

ASHWOOD, Tenn. ST. JOHN'S CHURCH (Episcopal)
Records, 1822-1848 priv.
N: T   9435

BAPTIST CHURCH, Bledsoe Co., Tenn.
Minutes, 1882-1938, 48 p. (WPA transcript) T
N: USlGS   9436

BAPTISTS. TENNESSEE. EAST TENNESSEE
ASSOCIATION
Minutes, 1841-1872, 140 p. (WPA transcript)
T
N: USlGS   9437

BOSTON, Tenn. DISCIPLES OF CHRIST
Church records, 1855-1888 Ibid.
N: T 1 reel   9438

CHRISTIANBURG BAPTIST CHURCH, Monroe Co.,
Tenn.
Minutes, 1828-1917, 259 p. (WPA transcript) T
N: USlGS   9439

COLUMBIA, Tenn. ZION CHURCH
Records, 1808-1939
N: TNJ   9440

CONGER, ISAAC, Methodist circuit rider
Diary, 1813 T
N: T 1 reel   9441

FRANKLIN, Tenn. ST. PAUL'S CHURCH
(Episcopal)
Records, 1827-1854 Ibid.
N: T 1 reel   9442

FRIENDS, SOCIETY OF. BLOUNT Co.[Tenn.]
FRIENDSVILLE MEETING
Manuscript records, n.d., v.1
N: TU   9443

GUTHRIE, Rev. ROBERT HENDERSON
Diary, 1874-1875, 36 p. (WPA transcript) T
N: USlGS   9444

LA GRANGE, Tenn. IMMANUEL CHURCH
(Episcopal)
Minutes, 1848 (WPA transcript) T
N: USlGS   9445

MARYVILLE, Tenn. FIRST BAPTIST CHURCH
Minutes, 1886-1899, 57 p. (WPA transcript) T
N: USlGS   9446

MEMPHIS, Tenn. CHURCHES
Records, 1828-1938 Ibid.
N: priv. 5 reels   9447
P: TM

METHODIST CHURCH (United States).
CONFERENCES. TENNESSEE
Records, 1812-1892 Ibid.
N: T 2 reels   9448

NASHVILLE, Tenn. CHRIST CHURCH (Episcopal)
Records, 1829-1929
N: TNJ   9449

NASHVILLE, Tenn. CHRIST EPISCOPAL CHURCH
Vital records, 1829-1858 Ibid.
N: T 1 reel   9450

NASHVILLE, Tenn. FIRST BAPTIST CHURCH
Records, 1820-1910 Ibid.
N: TNJ   9451

NASHVILLE, Tenn. FIRST PRESBYTERIAN
CHURCH
Records, 1833-1929 Ibid.
N: TNJ   9452

NEW PROVIDENCE, Tenn. CUMBERLAND
PRESBYTERIAN CHURCH
Records, 1838-1920 priv.
N: T 1 reel   9453

POLK, LEONIDAS, Bp., 1806-1864
Papers, 1767-1934 TSewU
N: NcU 3 reels 3944 frames   9454
P: TNJ TSewU TxU

PULASKI, Tenn. FIRST PRESBYTERIAN
CHURCH AND MASONIC HALL
Records, 1828-1830, 6 p. (WPA transcript) T
N: USlGS   9455

ST. JOHN'S PARISH, Maury Co., Tenn.
Register, 1842-1848 priv.
N: NcU 1 reel   9456

SINKING CREEK BAPTIST CHURCH, Carter Co.,
Tenn.
Records, 1783-1879 (WPA transcript) T
N: USlGS   9457

Personal Papers

BILLS, JOHN HOUSTON, 1800-1871
Letterbook, 1842-1846, 245 p. (typescript)
priv.
N: NcU 248 frames   9458

BLANC, HENRY WILLIAM
Diary, 1881, 212 p. priv.
N: NcU 1 reel   9459
P: TSewU

CHEATHAM, BENJAMIN FRANKLIN, 1820-1886
Papers, 1834-1893 priv.
N: NcU 394 frames   9460

FORTUNE, T. THOMAS
Scrapbook priv.
N: TNF 1 reel   9461

FOSTER FAMILY
Letters, 1817-1852, 283 items priv.
N: T 1 reel   9462

GRAHAM, WILLIAM A.
Papers: selections re: Memphis, June, 1826-
Sept., 1833 NcU
N: TM filmstrip*   9463

HOOKE, Miss JOSEPHINE HORTENSE
Diary, Aug., 1863 - Apr., 1864, 24 p. (WPA
transcript) T
N: USlGS   9464

HUGHES, THOMAS, 1822-1896
Papers re: Rugby, Tenn., 1872-1938, 200
items T
N: NcU 720 frames T 1 reel   9465

JOHNSON, CAVE
Correspondence with James Buchanan, 1824-
1868, 67 items PHi
N: PHi 1 reel   9466
P: T

LANGSTON, JOHN MERCER, 1829-1897
Papers, 1854-1896 TNF
N: TNF 1 reel   9467
P: DHU DLC

LAUGHLIN, SAMUEL HERVEY
Memoir, 1845 priv.
N: T 1 reel   9468

LIVINGSTON, CATHERINE (KATE)
Diary, 1859-1868, 156 p. (WPA transcript) T
N: USlGS   9469

McGAVOCK, RANDAL WILLIAM, 1826-1863
Papers, 1797-1897, 75 items NcU
N: T 1 reel   9470

MILLSAPS, ADLY M.
Letters, 1833-1850, 26 items priv.
N: T 1 reel   9471

MURPHY, L.W., Sr.
Field notes re: Tennessee - Mississippi
Line, ca. 1894 priv.
N: T 1 reel   9472

NICHOLSON, A.O.P.
Correspondence, 1838-1872, 128 items NHi
N: NHi 1 reel   9473
P: T

NICKOLDS, MARY L., 1859-1947
Diary re: yellow fever in Memphis priv.
N: KyU 6 feet   9474

OTEY, JAMES HERVEY, Bp., 1800-1863
Diary, 1840-1863, 14 v. TSewU
N: ? 1 reel   9475
P: TxU

OTEY, JAMES HERVEY, Bp, 1800-1863
Diary while Bishop of the Diocese of
Tennessee, 1855 TNJ
N: TNJ 1 reel   9476
P: T

OTEY, JAMES HERVEY, Bp., 1800-1863
Papers, 1835-1884, 27 items TSewU
N: ?   9477
P: TxU

OVERTON, JOHN, 1766-1833
Papers, 1785-1854 THi
N: TNJ 2 reels   9478
P: T

OVERTON, JOHN, 1766-1833
Papers, 1790-1840, 461 items priv.
N: TNJ   9479
P: NcU 2 reels

PISE, DAVID, b. 1815
Journals, 1836-1868 TSewU
N: NcU 566 frames   9480

POLK, WILLIAM
Papers re: land divisions in Tenn., n.d. priv.
N: T   9481

QUINTARD, CHARLES TODD, Bp., 1824-1898
Diaries, 1864-1898 priv.
N: TSewU 8 reels   9482
P: TxU

QUINTARD, CHARLES TODD, Bp., 1824-1898
Diaries and papers, 1864-1898 priv.
N: NcU 7 reels   9483
P: NcU

RHEA, JOHN
Letters to Jefferson, Madison, Monroe, and
Jackson, 1805-1831, 35 items DLC
N: T 1 reel   9484

SHANNON, AUGUSTINE F.
Journal, 1848-1850, 62 p. (WPA transcript) T
N: USlGS   9485

STRICKLER, CHRISTINA
Journal re: trip from Shelbyville to Niagara
Falls, New York, Boston, Philadelphia,
Washington, etc., June 19-Aug. 25, 1851
priv.
N: T 1 reel   9486

STRICKLER, MARY
Journal of trip from Nashville to New York,
Boston, Albany, Buffalo, Philadelphia, May-
Aug., 1847 priv.
N: T 1 reel   9487

Business Papers

BILLS, JOHN HOUSTON
Diary re: plantation near Bolivar, Tenn.,
1843-1871 priv.
N: TNJ 2 reels   9488
P: T

BUCK, ISAAC NEWTON
Account book and papers of store near White
Plains, Tenn., 1836-1850 priv.
N: T 1 reel   9489

CINCINNATI, CUMBERLAND GAP AND
CHARLESTON R.R., Tenn.
Minutes, 1854-1860, 57 p. (WPA transcript) T
N: USlGS   9490

COOKE, RICHARD F.
Survey book (Putnam Co., Tenn.), 1825-1839,
398 p. (WPA transcript) T
N: USlGS   9491

McCLELLAN, JOHN
Surveyor's book (Roane Co., Tenn.), 1808-1810,
219 p. (WPA transcript) T
N:USlGS   9492

METCALFE, ILAI, Robertson Co., Tenn.
Account book, 1806-1840, 49 p. (WPA
transcript) T
N: USlGS   9493

Collections

DORSEY, A.L., collector
Material re: Robertson Co., Tenn., 1862-1938
TS
N: T 1 reel   9494

FLEMING, SAM M., collector
Papers on the McEwen family and Tennessee
history, 1787-1930 priv.
N: NcU 170 frames   9495

U.S. WAR DEPT. COLLECTION OF
CONFEDERATE RECORDS
Index to compiled service records of Confed-
erate soldiers from Tennessee DNA
N: DNA 48 reels 16 mm. [M-231]   9496

Institutions

CHATTANOOGA, Tenn. NATIONAL CEMETERY
Interment records, 1863-1939, 341 p.
(WPA transcript) T
N: USlGS   9497

School Records

ABBE INSTITUTE, Lebanon, Tenn.
School records, 1855-1860 priv.
N: T 1 reel   9498

MAURY ACADEMY, Jefferson Co., Tenn.
Minutes, 1818-1860, 27 p. (WPA transcript) T
N: USlGS   9499

KENTUCKY

Census

U.S. CENSUS. THIRD, 1810
Population schedules, Kentucky DNA
N: DNA 5 reels   9500

U.S. CENSUS. FOURTH, 1820
Population schedules, Kentucky DNA
N: DNA 14 reels   9501

U.S. CENSUS. FIFTH, 1830
Population schedules, Kentucky DNA
N: DNA 10 reels   9502
P: USlGS

U.S. CENSUS. SIXTH, 1840
Population schedules, Kentucky DNA
N: DNA 7 reels   9503
P: USlGS

U.S. CENSUS. SEVENTH, 1850
Agriculture, manufacturing, social statistics
schedules, Kentucky NcD
N: NcD 7 reels   9504
P: NNC

U.S. CENSUS. SEVENTH, 1850
Population schedules, Kentucky DNA
N: DNA 9 reels   9505
P: USlGS

U.S. CENSUS. EIGHTH, 1860
Agriculture, manufacturing, social statistics
schedules, Kentucky NcD
N: NcD 7 reels   9506
P: NNC TNS

U.S. CENSUS. EIGHTH, 1860
Population schedules, Kentucky DNA
N: DNA 10 reels   9507
P: USlGS

U.S. CENSUS. NINTH, 1870
Agriculture, manufacturing, social statistics
schedules, Kentucky NcD
N: NcD 8 reels   9508
P: TNS

U.S. CENSUS. NINTH, 1870
Population schedules, Kentucky DNA
N: DNA 13 reels   9509
P: USlGS

U.S. CENSUS. TENTH, 1880
Agriculture; defectives, dependents, and de-
linquents; manufacturing schedules, Kentucky
NcD
N: NcD 20 reels   9510
P: TNS

U.S. CENSUS. TENTH, 1880
Population schedules, Kentucky DNA
N: DNA 46 reels   9511

Government Records

U.S. COPYRIGHT OFFICE
Copyright register for Louisville, Ky., 1860-
1870 DLC
N: KyU 15 feet   9512

U.S. DISTRICT COURT. KENTUCKY
Court orders, 1789-1800 C.H. Harrodsburg
N: KyU 1 reel   9513
P: USlGS

State Records

KENTUCKY
County tax lists, origin to 1875 (some gaps,
Boyle, Carlisle, Knott, Leslie, McCreary
not included) KyHi
N: USlGS 476 reels   9514
P: KyHi KyU

KENTUCKY. COURT OF APPEALS
General index books, 1864-1936, 10 v. Ibid.
N: KyU 5 reels   9515

KENTUCKY (District). SUPERIOR COURT
Order book, 1783-1786 Harrodsburg
Historical Society
N: KyU 1 reel   9516
P: KyHi KyU

KENTUCKY. GENERAL ASSEMBLY
Legislative documents, 1837-1840 KyU
N: DLC 1 reel   9517

VIRGINIA
General index to land grants in Kentucky,
1779-1801, 690 p. Vi
N: USlGS   9518

County Records

Kentucky county records are listed collectively,
unless they appear to have special value to the
researcher. Separate listing is always given to
court order books, wills, deeds, vital records,
and muster rolls.

BOURBON Co., Ky.
Marriage bonds, 1786-1794 C.H. Paris
N: KyU 1 reel   9519
P: KyHi USlGS

CLARK Co., Ky.
Marriage records, 1793-1800 (typescript)
priv.
N: KyU 2 feet   9520

CLARK Co., Ky.
Scrapbook KyU
N: KyU 6 feet   9521

FAYETTE Co., Ky.
Court records, 1788-1800, 8 v. (transcripts
of burnt records); wills, 1793-1952; deeds,
1794-1953 C.H. Lexington
N: KyU 319 reels   9522
P: USlGS

FRANKLIN Co., Ky.
Deed book A, 1795-1804 C.H. Frankfort
N: KyHi 1 reel   9523

GARRARD Co., Ky.
Court order books, 1797-1810; wills, 1797-
1811; deeds, 1797-1807; depositions, 1813-
1827 C.H. Lancaster
N: KyU 6 reels   9524
P: USlGS

HART Co., Ky.
Order book, 1819-1823 C.H. Munfordville
N: KyU 15 feet   9525

HART Co., Ky., see CANN, ROY A., collector,
9703, under KENTUCKY, Collections

JEFFERSON Co., Ky.
Order books, 1784-1785; minute books, 1784-
1785, 1790-1793, 1795-1829; wills, 1784-1833;
deeds, 1783-1790; division books, 1784-1785
C.H. Louisville
N: KyU 5 reels   9526
P: USlGS

JESSAMINE Co., Ky.
Wills, 1797-1813; deeds, 1799-1804
C.H. Nicholasville
N: KyU 2 reels   9527
P: USlGS

KENTUCKY Co., Va. (now state of KENTUCKY)
Clerk's record, April 7, 1779 ICU
N: KyHi 1 reel in part   9528

LINCOLN Co., Ky.
Court order books, 1781-1794; wills, 1781-
1804; deeds, 1781-1791 C.H. Stamford
N: KyU 4 reels   9529
P: USlGS

MASON Co., Ky.
Tax list, 1794-1809 KyHi
N: NcD 1 reel   9530

NELSON Co., Ky.
Court minutes; marriage records, 1785-1885;
miscellaneous records, 1782-1830; tithables,
1785-1823; tavern keepers' bonds, prior to
1801-1824 C.H. Bardstown
N: ? 11 reels   9531
P: KyHi

NELSON Co., Ky.
Court order books, 1785-1816, 1822-1825;
court records, 1780-1870; deeds, 1814-1822;
wills, 1785-1890 C.H. Bardstown
N: priv.   9532
P: KyBgW KyLo

NELSON Co., Ky.
Court order books, 1790-1791; wills, 1790-
1807; deeds, 1784-1795 C.H. Bardstown
N: KyU 2 reels   9533
P: USlGS

NELSON Co., Ky.
Tithes, order books, 1785-1788 C.H. Bards-
town
N: KyHi 1 reel   9534

PIKE Co., Ky.
Circuit court records, 1860-1867
C.H. Pikeville
N: KyU 5 reels   9535

WARREN Co., Ky.
Tax lists, 1797-1805 C.H. Bowling Green
DCO: KyBgW 297 p.   9536

WARREN Co., Ky.
Records, 1779-1860
N: ? 39 reels   9537
P: KyU

City Records

BARDSTOWN, Ky.
Journal and day book, 1805, 1807
C.H. Bardstown
N: priv.   9538
P: KyBgW KyLoU

COVINGTON, Ky.
Minute book B, 1826-1832 Christopher Gist
Historical Society, Covington, Ky.
N: KyHi 1 reel   9539

FALMOUTH, Ky. BOARD OF TRUSTEES
Minutes, 1879-1883, 433 p. KyU
N: KyU 20 feet   9540

LEXINGTON, Ky.
Trustees' records, 1782-1836, 1840-1843,
1851-1854; Park Commissioners' minutes,
1922-1956 Ibid.
N: KyU 4 reels   9541
P: KyU

LOUISVILLE, Ky.
Petition for establishing, May 1, 1780 ICU
N: KyHi 1 reel in part   9542

WINCHESTER Ky. BOARD OF TRUSTEES
Minutes, 1794-1806 KyU
N: KyU 5 feet   9543

Church Records

BAPTIST CHURCH, Hart Co., Ky., see CANN,
ROY A., collector, 9703, under KENTUCKY,
Collections

BAPTIST CHURCH ON GREEN RIVER, Ky.
Record book, 1803-1841 KyU
N: KyU 10 feet   9544

BARDSTOWN, Ky. FIRST PRESBYTERIAN
CHURCH
Records, 1810-1916, 3 v. C.H. Bardstown
N: KyU   9545
P: KyBgW KyLoU KyU

BEECH GROVE BAPTIST CHURCH, Owen Co.,
Ky.
Minutes, 1897-1956 priv.
N: KyU 40 feet   9546

BETHEL PRESBYTERIAN CHURCH, Fayette Co.,
Ky.
Session record, 1823-1900 KyU
N: KyU 50 feet   9547

CANE RIDGE CHRISTIAN CHURCH, Bourbon Co.,
Ky.
List of members, 1838-1916 KyU
N: KyU 10 feet   9548

CHERRY SPRINGS CHURCH, Scott Co., Ky.
Records, 1857-1903 priv.
N: KyU 15 feet   9549

CHURCH HISTORICAL SOCIETY, Philadelphia, Pa.
Papers, 1794-1952: Bishops Benjamin Bosworth
Smith, Charles Edward Woodcock, George David
Cummins, and Thomas Underwood Dudley Ibid.
N: ? 40 feet Ibid.   9550
P: KyU

CLEAR CREEK PRESBYTERIAN CHURCH,
Jessamine Co., Ky.
Record book, 1828-1876 KyU
N: KyU 15 feet   9551

CONCORD PRESBYTERIAN CHURCH,
Nicholas Co., Ky.
Session record book, 1822-1886 Ibid.
N: KyU 20 feet   9552

DANVILLE, Ky. FIRST PRESBYTERIAN CHURCH
Records, 1827-1830, 1852-1868 KyU
N: KyU 2 reels   9553

DANVILLE, Ky. SECOND PRESBYTERIAN CHURCH
Records, 1858-1915, 1937-1951 KyU
N: KyU 50 feet   9554

EBENEZER, Ky. PRESBYTERIAN CHURCH
Minutes, 1867-1924 priv.
N: KyU 1 reel   9555

EBENEZER ASSOCIATE REFORMED
PRESBYTERIAN CHURCH, Jessamine Co., Ky.
Record book, 1840-1886 KyU
N: KyU 25 feet   9556

FALL, Rev. PHILIP S.
Letters and papers, 1826-?
KyHi Frankfort Christian Church
N: KyHi 2 reels   9557

FOUR MILE BAPTIST CHURCH, Campbell Co.,
Ky.
Records, 1819-1873 KyU
N: KyU 30 feet   9558

FRIENDSHIP AND LULBEGRUD BAPTIST
CHURCHES, Clark Co., Ky.
Record books, 1793-1903, 5 v. Clark Co.
Historical Society
N: KyU 1 reel   9559

GUNPOWDER BAPTIST CHURCH, Boone Co., Ky.
Minutes, 1902-1931 Ibid.
N: KyHi 1 reel   9560

HAZELGREEN, Ky. FIRST PRESBYTERIAN
CHURCH

Records, 1882-1901 KyU
N: KyU 5 feet   9561

JUNCTION CITY, Ky. BOYLE PRESBYTERIAN
CHURCH
Records, 1900-1931 KyU
N: KyU   9562

LAIR PRESBYTERIAN CHURCH, Bourbon Co., Ky.
Records, 1908-1939 KyU
N: KyU 10 feet   9563

LEXINGTON, Ky. CENTRAL CHRISTIAN CHURCH
Records, 1853-1952 KyU
N: KyU 4 reels   9564

LOUISVILLE, Ky. LOUISVILLE PRESBYTERIAN
CHURCH
Records, 1899-1950 KyU
N: KyU   9565

LULBEGRUD BAPTIST CHURCH, Clark Co., Ky.,
see FRIENDSHIP AND LULBEGRUD BAPTIST
CHURCHES, 9559, under this same heading

MAYSLICK, Ky. MAYSLICK PRESBYTERIAN
CHURCH
Record book, 1850-1953 KyU
N: KyU 25 feet   9566

METHODIST CHURCH (United States).
CIRCUITS. MURRAY, Ky.
Records, 1832-1878, 1886-1912 priv.
N: KyU 25 feet   9567

MIDWAY, Ky. PRESBYTERIAN CHURCH
Records, 1832-1948, 4 v. KyU
N: KyU 75 feet   9568

MT. HOREB PRESBYTERIAN CHURCH, Fayette
Co., Ky.
Records, 1827-1917 Ibid.
N: KyU 1 reel   9569

MOUNT PLEASANT BAPTIST CHURCH,
Jessamine Co., Ky.
Record books, 1801-1867 priv.
N: KyU 30 feet   9570

MT. VERNON, Ky. McFARLAND MEMORIAL
CHURCH (Presbyterian)
Records, 1915-1936 KyU
N: KyU   9571

MUDDY FORK CHURCH (Baptist), Ky., see
TURNER, THOMAS O., 9584, under this
same heading

OWINGSVILLE, Ky. MENIFEE MEMORIAL
CHURCH
Minute book, 1876-1902 Ibid.
N: KyU 15 feet   9572

PARIS, Ky. FIRST PRESBYTERIAN CHURCH
Records, 1859-1933, including those of Second
Presbyterian and Clintonville Presbyterian
Churches Ibid.
N: KyU 1 reel   9573

PRESBYTERIAN CHURCH IN THE U.S.A.
PRESBYTERIES. KENTUCKY
Records: Ebenezer, Guerrant, Lexington-
Ebenezer, Louisville, Paducah, Transylvania,
West Lexington presbyteries, 1787-1951 Ibid.
N: KyU 25 reels   9574

QUICKSAND, Ky. REGULAR BAPTIST CHURCH
Records, 1858-1888 KyU
N: KyU 3 feet   9575

SALEM, Ky. PRESBYTERIAN CHURCH
Session minutes, 1892-1955 KyU
N: KyU 10 feet   9576

SHAKERS
Records of Shaker colonies in Kentucky
KyHMHi KyLoF OClWHi
N: KyU 19 reels   9577

SHAKERS, Pleasant Hill, Ky.
Papers Ibid.
N: ? 3 reels   9578

SHAKERS, South Union, Ky.
Journal, 1906-1909 priv.
N: KyU 35 feet   9579

SPOON RIVER REGULAR BAPTIST ASSOCIATION,
Madison Co., Ky.
Minutes, 1834 C.H. Richmond (Madison Co.)
N: KyHi   9580

SPRINGFIELD, Ky. PRESBYTERIAN CHURCH
Session book, 1828-1870 Ibid.
N: KyU 25 feet   9581

STAMPING GROUND, Ky. BAPTIST CHURCH
Records, 1795-1958 Ibid.
N: KyU 3 reels*   9582

SWIFT'S CAMP CHURCH (Baptist), Morgan Co.,
Ky.
Record, 1848-1852 KyU
N: KyU 7 feet   9583

TURNER, THOMAS O.
Papers, 1895-1952, includes minutes Muddy
Fork Church (Baptist) priv.
N: KyU 30 feet   9584

WATTS, EDWARD COMBS
Papers re: Kentucky Methodist history priv.
N: KyU 50 feet   9585

Personal Papers

ALEXANDER FAMILY
Papers, 1824-1896 priv.
N: KyU 4 reels   9586

ALLYN, FRANCIS
Papers, 1814-1828, including 2 letters from
Marquis de Lafayette KyU
N: KyU 10 feet   9587

BALLARD, ADDISON M.
Diary, 1839-1853 KyHi
N: KyHi 1 reel   9588

BALLARD, RAY
Papers (Knox Co. land record book, Civil War
letter), 1819-1919 priv.
N: KyU 20 feet   9589

BARLOW, EDWARD CALLISTUS
Papers, 1858-1896 KyU
N: KyU 25 feet   9590

BARLOW FAMILY
Papers priv.
N: KyU 20 feet   9591

BEALL, WILLIAM KENNEDY
Journal, July-Aug., 1812 (typescript) priv.
N: KyU 10 feet   9592

BEARD, Mrs. EUGENIA
Papers, including John Payne Campbell
papers, 1856-1866; Samuel Gibson papers;
Minnie H. Gibson papers; Le Compte family
papers priv.
N: KyU 50 feet   9593

BEAUCHAMP FAMILY
Papers, 1820-1928 KyU
N: KyU 60 feet   9594

BLAKELEY, STEPHENS
Papers re: Goebel affair, 1900 priv.
N: KyU 3 feet   9595

BOYD FAMILY
Papers, 1830-1915, including 21 letters from
Millard Fillmore and 3 from James Buchanan
to Anne Dixon Boyd priv.
N: KyU 1 reel*   9596

BRECKINRIDGE, JOHN, 1760-1806
Notes on Kentucky Constitutional Convention,
1799 DLC
N: KyU 10 feet   9597

BROCK, ZELL
Scrapbook re: history of New Liberty, Ky.
KyU
N: KyU 10 feet   9598

BROWN, WILLIAM LITTLE
Diary, 1810-1813 (typescript) NN
N: KyU 10 feet   9599

BUCKNER, SIMON BOLIVAR
Letters to his wife, during march to Fort

Atkinson, Oct.-Nov., 1881, 9 items priv.
DCO: KyBgW   9600

BURBRIDGE, STEPHEN GANO, 1831-1894
Correspondence, 1862-1865, 20 items priv.
N: KyU *   9601

CAMDEN, JOHNSON NEWLON, 1865-
Papers, 1912-1940 KyU
N: KyU 35 feet   9602

CARRELL, SAMUEL E.
Diaries and commonplace book, 1835-1841 KyU
N: KyU 25 feet   9603

CARSON FAMILY
Letters and papers, ca. 1830-1850 KyHi
N: KyHi 1 reel   9604

CARTER, LILLARD HARVEY, b. 1867
Scrapbook, n.d. KyU
N: KyU 15 feet   9605

CHENAULT FAMILY
Letters and papers C.H. Richmond
(Madison Co.)
N: KyHi 1 reel   9606

CLAY FAMILY
Papers re: Cassius M. Clay, ca. 1850-1913
priv.
N: KyU 50 feet   9607

COMPTON, JOHN P.
Letters, 1835-1836 priv.
N: KyU 1 foot   9608

CRAIG, JEFFERSON T.
Diary, 1853-1856 KyGe
N: KyU 20 feet   9609

CROSBY FAMILY
Papers, 1806-1889, including letters to and
from Horace Holley and his wife priv.
N: KyU 3 reels   9610

CURRY, H. W.
Record of sale of estate, October 25, 1848 KyU
N: KyU 7 feet   9611

DEMAREE, JOHN O.
Papers re: Henry and Shelby Cos., 1874-1906
priv.
N: KyU 15 feet   9612

DILLS, JOHN
Family letters, 1843-1898 priv.
N: KyU 25 feet   9613

DOUGLASS, GEORGE L., 1808-1889
Papers, 1825-(1889) 1924 priv.
N: KyU 4 reels   9614
P: KyU

FACKLER FAMILY
Papers, 1792-1941, including history of Boyle
Co., Ky. priv.
N: KyU 1 reel   9615

FERGUSON, BRUCE
Scrapbook re: Goebel affair, 1900 KyU
N: KyU 15 feet   9616

FISHER FAMILY
Papers re: Fort William, Ky., 1797-1884 KyU
N: KyU 30 feet   9617

FORSYTHE FAMILY, Pikesville, Ky.
Papers, 1841-1898 priv.
N: KyU 1 reel   9618

FOX, JOHN, 1862-1919
Letters to M[icajah Fible], 1883-1889 KyU
N: KyU 10 feet   9619

GAINES FAMILY
Papers re: New Liberty, Ky. priv.
N: KyU 10 feet   9620

GAYLE, Mrs. JUNE
Papers re: Jefferson inaugural KyU
N: KyU 2 feet   9621

GAYLE, JUNE WARE, 1865-1901
Scrapbook re: his career priv.
N: KyU 8 feet   9622

GOEBEL, WILLIAM F., d. 1900
Court records and other papers re: Goebel

assassination, 1900-1907 C.H. Georgetown
(Scott Co., Ky.)
N: KyHi 8 reels   9623

GOEBEL FAMILY
Letters, 1880-1942 KyU
N: KyU 2 reels   9624

GRUNDY FAMILY
Letters and documents, 1784-1867, 16 items
priv.
N: KyU 3 feet   9625

GUERRANT FAMILY
Papers, 1850-1896 priv.
N: KyU 5 reels   9626

HALY, PERCY, d. 1937
Scrapbook priv.
N: KyU 15 feet   9627

HAMMER, VICTOR
Papers, 3 fragments KyU
N: KyU 30 feet   9628

HARBESON, BEN
Scrapbook KyU
N: KyU 20 feet   9629

HARDIN, LIZZIE
Diary, 1860-1865 Pioneer Museum, Harrods-
burg, Ky.
N: KyU 15 feet   9630
P: NcU

HART, JAMES G.
Medical records, 1873-1900, 7 v. priv.
N: KyU 40 feet   9631

HINES FAMILY, of Warren Co., Ky.
Letters and papers, 1814-1870, 77 p. priv.
DCO: KyBgW   9632

HOLT, FELIX
Letters to Mrs. Louis Holt Dick, 1933-1954
priv.
N: KyU 3 feet   9633

HOWE, JOSEPH P., itinerant preacher
Diary in Kentucky, 1795-1816 priv.
N: ?   9634
P: KyBgW

HUNT-MORGAN FAMILY
Papers, 1854-1899 priv.
N: KyU 40 feet   9635

JAMES, OLLIE MURRAY, 1871-1918
Papers, 1912-1916 priv.
N: KyU 60 feet   9636

JAMES, OLLIE MURRAY, 1871-1918
Papers, including two letters from Woodrow
Wilson KyU
N: KyU 20 feet   9637

JEFFRIES, LUTHER C.
Papers re: move from Kentucky to Texas,
1848-1891 priv.
N: KyU 2 reels   9638

JOHNSON, THOMAS
Letters, 1861-1865 priv.
N: KyU 5 feet 16 mm.   9639

JOHNSTON, JAMES (and THOMAS)
Papers, 1813-1891 KyU
N: KyU 30 feet   9640

JONES FAMILY, of Bourbon Co., Ky
Diaries, 1855-1889, 34 v. priv.
N: KyU 4 reels   9641

JULIAN, CHARLES, 1774-1837
Journal, 1800-1818 priv.
N: KyU 10 feet   9642

LAFFERTY, Mrs. MAUDE WARD
Papers re: Hoffman family priv.
N: KyU 10 feet   9643

LESLIE, PRESTON HOPKINS, 1819-1907
Scrapbook priv.
N: KyU 3 feet   9644

LESTER, W.S.
Letters re: Goebel affair KyU
N: KyU 7 feet   9645

LEWIS, JOSEPH H., 1824-1904
Papers KyU
N: KyU 2 feet   9646

LISTON FAMILY
Papers priv.
N: KyU 5 feet   9647

LOGAN, G. W.
Letters, 1853-1867 priv.
N: KyU 30 feet*   9648

LONG FAMILY
Papers, 1829-1934 priv.
N: KyU 50 feet   9649

LOVE, WILLIAM THOMAS [SALT RIVER TOM],
b. 1854
Memoir of William Thomas Love, 1858-Feb.,
1908 KyU
N: KyU 1 reel   9650

LYLE, JOHN
Diary, 1801-1803 (typescript) ICU
N: KyU 6 feet   9651

McAFEE, ROBERT
Journal, 1796-1803 [unk.]
N: KyHi 1 reel   9652

MANLEY, BASIL, 1825-1892
Letterbooks, 1852-1893, 22 v. KyLoS
N: NcU 11 reels   9653

MEANS FAMILY
Papers, including Seaton family KyU
N: KyU 1 reel   9654

MILWARD, JOSEPH U.
Diary, 1892 priv.
N: KyU 10 feet   9655
P: KyU

NORTHCUTT, WILLIAM BROOKS
Diary (War of 1812 and later) KyHi
N: KyHi 1 reel   9656

PETTIT, THOMAS STEVENSON, 1843-1931
Papers, 1864-1932 priv.
N: KyU 20 feet   9657

POLSGROVE, JAMES
Scrapbook and papers, 1894-1942 KyU
N: KyU 1 reel   9658

POWERS, CALEB, 1869-1932
Letters to Mrs. Lulie Clay Brock, 1902-1905
KyU
N: KyU 20 feet   9659

PREWITT, JOHN M.
Papers re: Montgomery Co., Ky., n.d. priv.
N: KyU 10 feet   9660

RANNEY, WILLIAM W.
Family papers, 1858-1927 KyU
N: KyU 10 feet   9661

RHEA, ALBERT G.
Scrapbook KyU
N: KyU 10 feet   9662

RICHARDSON, JAMES M., b. 1858
Letters, 1881-1919, 38 items priv.
N: KyU 10 feet   9663

ROGERS, JAMES, of Bourbon Co., Ky.
Family papers, 1800-1849 priv.
N: KyU 7 reels   9664

RUSSELL, S.M.
Side lights on the Goebel assassination priv.
N: KyU 1 foot   9665

RUST, JACOB WARD, b. 1819
Autobiography priv.
N: KyU 25 feet   9666

SCOTT, CHARLES, 1739-1813
Journal, n.d. KyLoF
N: KyU   9667
P: KyU

SCOTT, ROBERT W., b. 1808
Memoranda itineris: Frankfort, Ky., to
Philadelphia and Washington, Sept., 1829-
Feb., 1830; Lake Washington, Miss., to

Florida and New Orleans, Jan., 1836 priv.
N: KyU 10 feet   9668

SEBASTIAN, BENJAMIN
Letters re: Spaniards and navigation rights
on the Mississippi, 1795-1807, 27 items priv.
DCO: KyBgW 58 p.   9669

SEBASTIAN, BENJAMIN
Papers, 1806-1807, includes letter from Henry
Clay priv.
N: KyU 5 feet   9670

SHELBY, ISAAC, 1750-1826
Autobiography ICU
N: KyHi 1 reel   9671

SHELBY FAMILY
Papers, 1738-1862 DLC
N: KyU 4 reels   9672

SPEIGHT-OATIS FAMILY
Family papers and letters, 1784-1870
(some transcripts) LU
N: KyHi 1 reel   9673

SPENCER, I.J.
Scrapbook of references collected by his
daughter, Mrs. Julia Hoge (Spencer) Ardery
priv.
N: KyU 50 feet   9674

STAPLES, CHARLES R.
Memorandum of conversation with T.S.
Logwood re: Bath and Menifee County feuds,
May 22, 1930 priv.
N: KyU 10 feet   9675

STUBBLEFIELD, VERNON C.
Papers re: Nathaniel Stubblefield's invention
of the wireless KyU
N: KyU 5 feet   9676

STUBBLEFIELD FAMILY, of Mason Co., Ky.
Papers, 1797-1892 priv.
N: KyU 50 feet   9677

SWEENEY, JOSEPH A.
Journal and account book re: trip from Va.
into Ky., Ill., and Mo., 1820-1821 priv.
N: KyU 2 feet   9678

TARVIN, A.E.
Scrapbook, 1920-1937 KyU
N: KyU 25 feet   9679

TURNER, DANIEL
Papers, 1808-1908 priv.
N: KyU 15 feet   9680

WAIT, CYRENIUS
Papers, 1809-1925, 296 items priv.
N: KyU 50 feet   9681

WEAR FAMILY
Papers, 1840-1897 KyU
N: KyU 5 feet   9682

WEBB-FORD FAMILY
Diaries, 1852-1916 KyU
N: KyU 1 reel   9683

WHITE, MAUNSEL
Papers, 1802-1883 priv.
N: KyU 75 feet   9684

WOODSON, UREY, 1859
Papers, 1876-1945 priv.
N: KyU 10 feet   9685

WOODWARD, AUGUSTUS E., 1830-1860
Diary re: operation of farm and slave labor,
Feb. 1-Aug. 22, 1856 (transcript) priv.
N: KyU 5 feet   9686

YEISER, PHILIP, 1809-
Diary, 1856-1857, 1859, 1860-1863, 1864-1875,
1877-1878, 1880-1886, 1888 priv.
N: KyU 50 feet   9687

ZOLLICOFFER, General FELIX
Biography and clippings priv.
N: KyU   9688

Business Papers

BELLS MINES, Sturgis, Ky.
Day book and account book, 1864-1866, 285 p.

KyU
N: KyU 10 feet   9689

BERRY FAMILY
Papers re: farm operation, 1855-1905 priv.
N: KyU 1 reel   9690

CLAY, C.F., Bourbon Co., Ky.
Plantation day book, 1878-1879, 1881-1882,
1886-1887 priv.
N: KyU 20 feet   9691

DUPEYSTER FAMILY
Account books, 1865-1881, 3 v. KyU
N: KyU 70 feet   9692

GREEN FAMILY
Papers re: development of Western Union
Telegraph Company, 1837-1883 priv.
N: KyU 1 reel   9693

GREENSBURG, Ky. STORE
Account book, 1825-1829 KyU
N: KyU 30 feet   9694

HUNT, JOHN W.
Day book, July-September, 1796 priv.
N: KyU 10 feet   9695

KENTUCKY UNION LAND COMPANY
Papers, 1885-1906 priv.
N: KyU 10 feet*   9696

LONSDALE, WALTON & COMPANY, Mills
Point, Ky.
Ledger and letters, 1834-1873 priv.
N: KyU 10 feet   9697

SHELBY, EVAN (and ISAAC)
Land grants, 1780; survey, 1782 ICU
N: KyHi 1 reel in part   9698

SMITH, General ENOCH, Sr.
Survey book, 1780-1792 priv.
N: KyHi 1/2 reel   9699

STEDMAN, EBENEZER HIRAM, d. 1885, of
Georgetown, Ky.
Memoirs of early papermaking in Kentucky
addressed to Col. S.I.M. Major KyU
N: KyU 2 feet   9700

STEDMAN, EBENEZER HIRAM, d. 1885, of
Georgetown, Ky.
Paper mill diary, 1858 priv.
N: OHi 1 reel   9701

WELLS, Mrs. PEARL (OOTS)
Account books of Oots cooperage firm, 1880-
1901 KyU
N: KyU 50 feet   9702

Collections

CANN, ROY A., collector
Papers, 1829-1943, including records:
Munfordville Presbyterian Church; Baptist
Church, Hart Co.; history of Hart Co. KyU
N: KyU 2 reels   9703

GILLISS, WALTER, compiler
Notes re: LeGrand family, 1909 KyU
N: KyU 10 feet   9704

LOUISVILLE COURIER JOURNAL
Clipping file, 50,000 items KyLoCj
N: KyLoCj (filmsort jackets)   9705

MASON Co., Ky., HISTORICAL SOCIETY
Papers, ca. 1777-1877 Ibid.
N: KyU 2 reels   9706
P: DLC

YANCEY, Mrs. EVA
Scrapbook re: history of Gwenton, Ky. priv.
N: KyU 10 feet   9707

Institutions

CLARK COUNTY MEDICAL SOCIETY (formerly
WINCHESTER ACADEMY OF MEDICINE AND
SURGERY), Winchester, Ky.

Records, 1879-1916 KyWi
N: KyU 25 feet   9708

FREEMASONS. LANCASTER, Ky. CHAPTER
NO. 104
Record book, 1853-1874 KyU
N: KyU 10 feet   9709

KU KLUX KLAN, Pond Creek, Ky.
Membership roll, 1926-1927 KyU
N: KyU 10 feet   9710

PEWEE VALLEY, Ky. CONFEDERATE HOME
Records Ibid.
N: KyHi 5 reels 3 16 mm.   9711

School and College Records

BOURBON ACADEMY, Bourbon Co., Ky.
Minute book, 1799-1855 priv.
N: KyU 16 feet   9712

FERGUSON, MARY
Reminiscences of Science Hill School, Shelby-
ville, Ky., 1857 KyU
N: KyU 1 foot   9713

MORTON SCHOOL, Lexington, Ky.
Notes priv.
N: KyU 10 feet   9714

TRANSYLVANIA UNIVERSITY, Lexington, Ky.
Papers, 1795-1826 PPPrHi
N: KyU 2 reels   9715

OHIO

Census

U.S. CENSUS. FOURTH, 1820
Population schedules, Ohio DNA
N: DNA 10 reels   9716

U.S. CENSUS. FIFTH, 1830
Population schedules, Ohio DNA
N: DNA 17 reels   9717

U.S. CENSUS. SIXTH, 1840
Population schedules, Ohio DNA
N: DNA 18 reels   9718
P: USIGS

U.S. CENSUS. SEVENTH, 1850
Population schedules, Ohio DNA
N: DNA 20 reels   9719
P: USIGS

U.S. CENSUS. EIGHTH, 1860
Population schedules, Ohio DNA
N: DNA 27 reels   9720
P: USIGS

U.S. CENSUS. NINTH, 1870
Population schedules, Ohio DNA
N: DNA 29 reels   9721

U.S. CENSUS. TENTH, 1880
Mortality schedules, Ohio, counties A-G O
N: OC1WHi 1 reel   9722

U.S. CENSUS. TENTH, 1880
Population schedules, Ohio DNA
N: DNA 91 reels   9723

Government Records

U.S. DISTRICT COURT. OHIO (Southern
District)
Record relating to the proposed trials of
Aaron Burr and Herman Blennerhasset, Aug. 1,
1805-Jan. 21, 1808 DNA
N: OCHP 1 reel   9724

U.S. POST OFFICE DEPT.
Ohio postmaster records, 1832-1930 DNA
N: OHi 1 reel   9725

State Records

OHIO
Ohio canal boat list book, 1839-1857   OHi
N: OHi 1 reel   9726

OHIO. BUREAU OF CODE REVISION
Work sheets of Ohio revised code, 1953   Ohio
Legislative Service Commission
N: Ibid. 15 reels 16 mm.*   9727

OHIO. GOVERNOR
Governors' papers, 1797-1882   OHi
N: OHi 72 reels   9728
P: OHi

County Records

ADAMS Co., Ohio
Inventory of estates, 1816-1826   C.H. Lima
OHi
N: OHi 1 reel   9729
P: OHi

BELMONT Co., Ohio
Will books, A, B, C, to 1827 C.H. St. Clairs-
ville
N: priv. 1 reel*   9730
P: O

CLERMONT Co., Ohio
Marriages, 1800-1821 C.H. Batavia
N: OClWHi 1 reel   9731

COSHOCTON Co., Ohio
Wills, 1811-1852; marriages, 1811-1837
C.H. Coshocton
N: OClWHi 1 reel   9732

CRAWFORD Co., Ohio
Marriages, 1831-1864 (transcript) OClWHi
N: priv. 1 reel*   9733
P: O

DEFIANCE Co., Ohio
Marriages, 1848-1865 C.H. Defiance
N: OClWHi 1 reel   9734

DELAWARE Co., Ohio
Treasurer's records, 1813-1819; school
districts' records, 1827-1837 Ibid.
N: priv.   9735
P: OFH

GEAUGA Co., Ohio
Marriages, 1806-1860 (transcript) OClWHi
N: priv. 1 reel*   9736
P: O

LUCAS Co., Ohio. BOARD OF ELECTIONS
Abstract of votes cast, Nov., 1952 OT
N: OT 60 leaves   9737

MORGAN Co., Ohio
Wills, 1819-1852 C.H. McConnelsville
N: priv. 1/2 reel   9738
P: O*

MUSKINGUM Co., Ohio
Marriages, 1804-1865 C.H. Zanesville
N: OClWHi 1 reel   9739

MUSKINGUM Co., Ohio
Wills, 1804-1852 C.H. Zanesville
N: priv. 1 1/2 reels   9740
P: O*

PAULDING Co., Ohio
Marriages, 1839-1879; wills, 1852-1873(?)
C.H. Paulding
N: priv. 1 reel*   9741
P: O

PERRY Co., Ohio
Marriages, 1818-1875 (transcript)   OClWHi
N: priv. 1 reel*   9742
P: O

PERRY Co., Ohio
Wills, 1819-1863 C.H. New Lexington
N: priv. 1 reel   9743
P: O

PORTAGE Co., Ohio
Marriages, Probate court C.H. Ravenna
N: priv. 3 reels*   9744
P: O

TUSCARAWAS Co., Ohio
Marriages, 1808-1844 C.H. New Philadelphia
N: priv. 1/2 reel*   9745

WARREN Co., Ohio
Court records, 1803- ; births, 1867-1908;
deaths, 1881-1908; soldiers' discharges
C.H. Lebanon
N: OLeWHi   9746
P: OLeWHi

WARREN Co., Ohio
Marriages, 1803-1854 C.H. Lebanon
N: OLeWHi 1 reel   9747

WASHINGTON Co., Ohio
Marriages, 1825-1864 C.H. Marietta
N: OClWHi 1 reel   9748

City Records

ANDERSON TOWNSHIP, Ohio
Records, 1820-1838 priv.
N: OCHP 1 reel   9749

Church Records

CENTRAL COLLEGE, Ohio. PRESBYTERIAN
CHURCH
Records, 1843-1879 priv.
N: OHi 1 reel   9750

DELAWARE, Ohio. FIRST PRESBYTERIAN
CHURCH
Records, 1819-1835 priv.
N: OFH   9751

FRIENDS, SOCIETY OF. OHIO
Papers, 1798-1853 CSmH
N: OHi 1 reel   9752

FRIENDS, SOCIETY OF. OHIO YEARLY
MEETING
Minutes held at Short Creek House, 1813
Friends Boarding School, Barnesville, Ohio
N: OHi   9753

FRIENDS, SOCIETY OF. OHIO YEARLY
MEETING, Mount Pleasant, Ohio
Ohio minutes, 1813-1821
N: OHi   9754

FRIENDS, SOCIETY OF. PLAINFIELD [Ohio]
MONTHLY MEETING
Marriage certificates, 1822-1893; ministers'
and elders' minutes, 1828-1842; removals,
1849-1898; women's minutes, 1813-1880
N: PSC-F   9755
P: PSC-F

FRIENDS, SOCIETY OF (Primitive). SALEM
[Ohio] MONTHLY MEETING
Minutes, 1865-1888 Ibid.
N: PSC-F   9756
P: PSC-F

FRIENDS SOCIETY OF (Primitive). SALEM
[Ohio] MONTHLY MEETING, see WARREN
Co. HISTORICAL SOCIETY, 9823, under
OHIO, Collections

WESTERN RESERVE HISTORICAL SOCIETY
Shaker papers OClWHi
N: OClWHi 7 reels   9757
P: KyBgW

Personal Papers

ANDREWS, JOSEPH GARDNER
Journal re: Fort Defiance, 1795 DLC
N: OHi 1 reel   9758

BACKUS, JAMES,1764-1816
Journal, 1787-1791   OHi
N: OHi 1 reel   P: OHi   9759

BELL, JOHN, 1796-1869
Court martial at Lower Sandusky [Fremont],
Ohio, 1844 OHi
N: OFH 1 reel   9760

BICKHAM, WILLIAM DENISON, 1827-1894
Correspondence, 1875-1891 priv.
N: OFH 84 frames   9761

BINGHAM, JOHN ARMOR, 1815-1900
Correspondence, selections priv.
N: OFH 31 frames   9762

BROWN, ETHAN ALLEN, Gov. Ohio, 1766-1852
In-letters, 1806-1844 O
N: NcD 1 reel   9763

BROWN, ETHAN ALLEN, Gov. Ohio, 1766-1852
Letters, 1806-1844 OHi
N: OHi   9764

BROWNE, SYMMES
Selected papers OCHP
N: NcD 1 reel   9765

BURTS, Dr. A.T.
Papers OClWHi
N: OClWHi 1/2 reel   9766

COX, JACOB DOLSON, 1828-1900
Diary, Apr.,1864-May,1865, 106 p. OO
N: ?   9767
P: OCl

COX, SAMUEL SULLIVAN, 1824-1889
Papers RPB
N: OFH 3 reels   9768

CRAIG, ISAAC 1742?-1826
Papers   PPi
N: OHi 3 reels   9769
P: OHi

CRANE, HART
Letters to G. B. Munson, 1919-1928   OU
N: OU   9770

CURTIS, HENRY BARNES, b. 1799
Letters, selections priv.
N: OFH 1 reel   9771

DAWSON, MOSES, 1768-1844
Letters to Andrew Jackson, 1828-1844 DLC
N: OCHP 1 reel   9772

DRAKE, DANIEL, M.D., 1785-1852
Letters to his daughter-in-law, Margaret,
Nov., 1848- Oct., 1852, 20 items OCHP
N: OCHP 1 reel   9773

DUPERRONT BABY FAMILY
Papers re: Ohio country, 1752-1794 CaQMU
N: PHarH 20 feet   9774

FIELDS, DOROTHY LOUISE
Sketch of the life of David G. Burnet, 1941
ViU
N: priv. 1 reel   9775
P: OCHP

FINLEY, JAMES BRADLEY, 1811-1852
In-letters, 1811-1853 ODW
N: ?   9776
P: ICU 2 reels

FISHER, JOSEPH
Memoirs, 1825-1844, 76 p. priv.
N: OHi   9777

FORCE, JOHN
Journal, 1811-1812 NjHi
N: NjR 1 reel   9778
P: O

GEMEINLEIND, JOHANN, of Gnadenhutten, Ohio
Diaries and records, 1799-1869 priv.
N: OHi 2 reels   9779

GORDON, LEWIS S.
In-letters, ca. 1850, 57 p. priv.
N: OHi   9780

GREEN, SAMUEL ABBOTT, 1830-1918
Papers, selections TNP
N: OFH 2 reels   9781

HALSTEAD, MURAT, 1829-1908
Correspondence, 1861-1902   priv.
N: OFH   1 reel   9782

HARRISON, WILLIAM, 1685-1713
Letters to Henry Watkins, 1711-1713,
92 items OU
N: OU   9783

HEATON, JAMES
Old-time letters, 1813-1839 DLC
N: OCHP 320 frames   9784

HOWE, HENRY
Reminiscences of travel in New York, New
Jersey, Virginia, and Ohio, 1840-1847, 85 p.
OHi
N: ViWi   9785

HUNTINGTON, SAMUEL, Gov. Ohio, 1765-1817
Papers, 1785-1824 O
N: OHi 1 reel 16 mm.*   9786
P: O

KEELER, LUCY ELLIOT, 1864-1930
Letters, D. J. Ryan Collection OHi
N: OFH 1 reel   9787

KELLOGG, MINER KILBOURNE, 1814-1899
Private journal and other papers, 1835-1848 In
N: In 1 reel*   9788
P: OCHP

KIMBALL, H. I.
Letters to R. B. Hayes OFH
N: OFH 1 reel   9789

McNEMAR, RICHARD
Diary, 1805-1835, 5 v. DLC
N: ODa 1 reel   9790

MARBLE, MANTON MALONE, 1835-1917
Papers, 1876-1878 DLC
N: OFH 3 reels   9791

MARSH, CUTTING
Diaries, Nov., 1829-Apr., 1830, 103 p.   WHi
N: OT   9792

MEEK, ADA P.
Family letters, 1808-1851, 58 items   priv.
N: OHi   9793

MEIGS, RETURN JONATHAN, 1740-1823
Letter to Edward Tiffin, 1806 priv.
N: OHi   9794

MEIGS, RETURN JONATHAN, Gov. Ohio,
1764-1824
Papers, 1772-1855 DLC
N: OHi 1 reel   9795

MEIGS, RETURN JONATHAN, Gov. Ohio,
1764-1824
Papers as governor, 1812-1814 O
N: OHi 2 reels 16 mm.*   9796
P: O

MOLER, JOHN E.
Journal, 1837-1859 priv.
N: OHi 1 reel   9797

O'HARA, JAMES, 1752-1819
Papers, 1785-1794 InHi
N: OHi 1 reel   9798

OSBORN, CHARLES
Journal, 1832-1833, 210 p.   priv.
N: OHi 2 reels   9799

PLATT FAMILY, of Columbus, Ohio
Letters and diaries OFH
N: OFH 1 reel   9800

PUTNAM, RUFUS, 1738-1824
Journal, 1784, 276 p.   priv.
N: OHi   9801

PUTNAM, RUFUS, 1738-1824
Memoir of the Putnam family, 161 p.   priv.
N: OHi   9802

RAWSON, EUGENE ALLEN
Letters, 1840-1864 priv.
N: OFH 1 reel   9803

RYAN, DANIEL JOSEPH, 1855-1923
Correspondence, selections OHi
N: OFH 1 reel   9804

ST. CLAIR, ARTHUR, 1734-1818
Papers, 1788-1815 O
Microcards : 119 items   9805

SHORT, WILLIAM
Correspondence, 1784-1792 DLC MH PHi
N: OU 1036 frames   9806

SMITH, JOHN, 1735-1824
Papers in the defense of..., 1805-1823 OCHP
N: OCHP 1 reel*   9807
P: OCHP

SMITH, WILLIAM HENRY, 1833-1896
Memoirs, 1880-1889 OHi
N: OFH   9808

SMITH, WILLIAM HENRY, 1833-1896
Papers, 1855-1907 InHi
N: OFH 6 reels   9809

STIMSON, RODNEY M., 1824-
Scrapbook on R. B. Hayes OMM
N: OFH   9810

SYMMES, JOHN CLEVE, 1742-1814
Correspondence re: Miami purchase, 1788-
1796 priv.
N: ? 1 reel   9811
P: DLC

TORRENCE, AARON
Papers, 1792-1793   OCHP
N: OHi 1 reel   9812

TUPPER, SAMUEL, Indian agent
Letters from U. S. trading house, [Lower]
Sandusky, Ohio, 1807-1812 OClWHi
N: OFH   9813

WILEY, CALVIN H.
Papers, selections Nc-Ar
N: OFH 206 frames   9814

WILLIAMS, MILO G., 1804-1880
Reminiscences of Cincinnati from his diary,
v. 1, 1878, 267 p. OUU
N: OCHP 1 reel   9815

WOOD, ELEAZER DERBY, 1783-1814
Papers, 1808-1814 WHi
N: OHi 1 reel   9816

WORTHINGTON, THOMAS, Gov. Ohio, 1773-1827
Diary no. 23, Sept. 14, 1822-Aug. 25, 1823
N: OHi 1 reel   9817

WORTHINGTON, THOMAS, Gov. Ohio, 1773-1827
Papers, 1796-1827; letterbooks, 1801-1824
priv.
N: DLC 3 reels   9818

WORTHINGTON, THOMAS, Gov. Ohio, 1773-1827
Papers, 1796-1827 O
N: OHi 3 reels 16 mm.*   9819
P: O

ZEISBERGER, DAVID
Journal, 1781-1797 OCHP
N: OHi 1 reel   9820

Business Papers

NASH, SAMUEL, of Berlin, Ohio
Cash books, 1853-1859 priv.
N: OHi   9821

OLIVER HOUSE, Toledo, Ohio
Manuscript day book, 1862, 1879 priv.
N: OT   9822

Collections

WARREN COUNTY HISTORICAL SOCIETY
Lebanon cemetery records; Friends' marriage
records OLeWHi
N: OLeWHi 1 reel   9823
P: O OLeWHi

College Records

LANE THEOLOGICAL SEMINARY, Cincinnati, Ohio
Letters and papers, 1829-1932, 27 folders ICP
N: ICU   9824
P: PPPrHi 3 reels

Institutions

PEABODY EDUCATION FUND
Papers, selections TNP
N: OFH   9825

Ships' Logs

BEY CITTY (Schooner)
Log, Mar. 25-Nov. 15, 1859, 119 p.   priv.
N: priv.   9826
P: OCl

HANS CROCKER (Ship)
Log, Apr. 22-Nov. 28, 1862
Milwaukee County Historical Society
N: OCl   9827

INDIANA

Census

U.S. CENSUS. FIFTH, 1830
Population schedules, Indiana DNA
N: DNA 7 reels   9828
P: InLPU USIGS

U.S. CENSUS. SIXTH, 1840
Population schedules, Indiana DNA
N: DNA 8 reels   9829
P: USIGS

U.S. CENSUS. SEVENTH, 1850
Population schedules, Indiana DNA
N: DNA 10 reels   9830
P: ICN In USIGS

U.S. CENSUS. EIGHTH, 1860
Population schedules, Indiana DNA
N: DNA 13 reels   9831
P: USIGS

U.S. CENSUS. NINTH, 1870
Population schedules, Indiana DNA
N: DNA 19 reels   9832

U.S. CENSUS. TENTH, 1880
Population schedules, Indiana DNA
N: DNA 62 reels   9833

Government Records

U.S. CUSTOMS HOUSE, COVINGTON, Ind.
Statement of cargo, 1860-1864 Ibid.
N: In 1 reel   9834

State Records

INDIANA. ATTORNEY GENERAL, 1925-1929
Depositions re: Ku Klux Klan In
N: In 3 reels   9835

INDIANA. AUDITOR OF STATE
Vouchers, 1818-1870 In-Ar
N: In 39 reels   9836

INDIANA. CONSTITUTIONAL CONVENTION,
1850-1851
Credentials In
N: In 50 feet   9837

INDIANA. DEPARTMENT OF PUBLIC
INSTRUCTION

Correspondence of superintendents Ibid.
N: In 25 reels   9838

INDIANA. GENERAL ASSEMBLY. HOUSE OF
   REPRESENTATIVES
   Journal, 1813, 1814-1816, 1822 In
   N: In 1 reel   9839

INDIANA. GOVERNOR, 1818-1823
   Executive proceedings In
   N: In 1 reel   9840

INDIANA. INSURANCE DEPARTMENT
   Annual statements of companies doing
   business, 1862 - In
   N: In in process   9841

County Records

ALLEN Co., Ind.
   Court order books, 1824-1839; court
   records, 1839-1849; probate records,
   1825-1855; deeds, 1824-1853; marriages,
   1847-1880 C.H. Fort Wayne
   N: In 9 reels   9842

CRAWFORD Co., Ind.
   Probate records, 1818-1903; deed indices,
   1819-1878; marriages, 1818-1900 C.H.
   English
   N: In 10 reels   9843
   P: In

DEARBORN Co., Ind.
   Probate records, 1826-1913; vital records,
   1826-1836, 1882-1906 C.H. Lawrenceburg
   N: In 16 reels   9844
   P: In

DECATUR Co., Ind.
   Probate records, 1822-1906; deed indices,
   1822-1901; marriages, 1822-1905 C.H.
   Greensburg
   N: In 24 reels   9845
   P: In

DUBOIS Co., Ind.
   Wills, 1841-1902; vital records, 1839-1902;
   naturalizations, 1852-1906 C.H. Jasper
   N: In 26 reels   9846
   P: In

FAYETTE Co., Ind.
   Probate records, 1819-1900; deed indices,
   1816-1903; fee book, 1852-1911; vital records,
   1819-1904 C.H. Connersville
   N: In 4 reels   9847
   P: In

FLOYD Co., Ind.
   Probate records, 1818-1900; deeds, 1818-
   1829; deed indices, 1803-1904; vital records,
   1819-1907 C.H. New Albany
   N: In 18 reels   9848
   P: In

FOUNTAIN Co., Ind.
   Wills, 1827-1899 C.H. Covington
   N: In 4 reels   9849
   P: In

FULTON Co., Ind.
   Marriage records, 1836-1905 C.H. Rochester
   N: In 10 reels   9850

HAMILTON Co., Ind.
   Probate records, 1823-1901; deed indices,
   1825-1901 C.H. Noblesville
   N: In 20 reels   9851
   P: In

HANCOCK Co., Ind.
   Probate records, 1828-1902; deed indices,
   1827-1905 C.H. Greenfield
   N: In 10 reels   9852
   P: In

HARRISON Co., Ind.
   Probate records, 1814-1900; deed indices,
   1809-1901 C.H. Corydon
   N: In 18 reels   9853
   P: In

HENRY Co., Ind.
   Wills, 1822-1901; deed indices, 1824-1905;
   marriages, 1828-1852 C.H. New Castle
   N: In 18 reels   9854

JACKSON Co., Ind.
   Probate records, 1847-1909; deed indices,
   1815-1900; marriages, 1816-1902 C.H.
   Brownstown
   N: In 26 reels   9855
   P: In

LAWRENCE Co., Ind.
   Probate records, 1818-1918; deed indices,
   1819-1904; vital records, 1818-1901
   C.H. Bedford
   N: In 28 reels   9856
   P: In

MADISON Co., Ind.
   Wills, 1879-1901; deed indices, 1827-1901
   C.H. Anderson
   N: In 14 reels   9857
   P: In

MONROE Co., Ind.
   Probate records, 1818-1904; deed indices,
   1817-1905; marriages, 1818-1852 C.H.
   Bloomington
   N: In 14 reels   9858
   P: In

MORGAN Co., Ind.
   Probate records, 1822-1904; deed indices,
   1822-1903; marriages, 1822-1901 C.H.
   Martinsville
   N: In 22 reels   9859
   P: In

OHIO Co., Ind.
   Probate records, 1842-1901; deed indices,
   1844-1899; vital records, 1844-1900
   C.H. Rising Sun
   N: In 6 reels   9860
   P: In

RANDOLPH Co., Ind.
   Court records, 1826-1881; probate records,
   1819-1900; deed indices, 1820-1901; vital
   records, 1819-1937 C.H. Winchester
   N: In 30 reels   9861
   P: In

RUSH Co., Ind.
   Probate records, 1822-1907; deed indices,
   1822-1907; marriages, 1822-1901 C.H.
   Rushville
   N: In 18 reels   9862
   P: In

SCOTT Co., Ind.
   Probate records, 1820-1923; deed indices,
   1820-1910; marriages, 1877-1908 C.H.
   Scottsburg
   N: In 10 reels   9863
   P: In

SHELBY Co., Ind.
   Probate records, 1822-1906; deed indices,
   1822-1902; marriages, 1822-1952 C.H.
   Shelbyville
   N: In 20 reels   9864
   P: In

WASHINGTON Co., Ind.
   Probate records, 1814-1902; deed indices,
   1814-1911 C.H. Salem
   N: In 16 reels   9865
   P: In

WAYNE Co., Ind.
   Wills, 1812-1900; deed indices, 1816-1910;
   marriages, 1811-1860 C.H. Richmond
   N: In 15 reels   9866
   P: In

Church Records

CHURCH OF JESUS CHRIST OF LATTER-DAY
   SAINTS. INDIANA
   Ward and branch records: South Shore USIC
   N: USIGS 1 reel   9867

FRIENDS, SOCIETY OF. INDIANA YEARLY
   MEETING. COMMITTEE ON INDIAN
   AFFAIRS
   Minutes, 1821-1856 InRE
   N: In 1/2 reel   9868
   P: InRE

FRIENDS, SOCIETY OF. RICHMOND [Ind.]
   YEARLY MEETING
   Extracts from minutes, 1854-1871 Ibid.
   N: KU   9869

FRIENDSHIP, Ind. BEAR CREEK CHURCH
   Records, n.d. PChHi
   N: USIGS 1 reel   9870

METHODIST CHURCH (United States). CONFER-
   ENCES. INDIANA. CHARLESTOWN CIRCUIT
   Steward's book, 1830-1848, 215 p. InGrD
   DCO: InGrD   9871

METHODIST CHURCH (United States). CONFER-
   ENCES. INDIANA. SILVER CREEK CIRCUIT
   Secretary's book, 1809-1830, 137 p. InGrD
   DCO: InGrD   9872

OXFORD, Ind. OXFORD PRESBYTERIAN CHURCH
   Papers re: centennial celebration, Aug. 20-23,
   1953 Ibid.
   N: PPPrHi 1 reel   9873

Personal Papers

BOND, EDWARD
   Papers, 1782-1820 In
   N: Nc-Ar   9874

EGGLESTON, EDWARD, 1837-1902
   Papers, 1804-1907 NIC
   N: In   9875

EWING, GEORGE WASHINGTON
   Correspondence, 1803-1866 DLC
   N: In   9876

EWING, WILLIAM GRIFFITH, 1801-1854
   Papers, 1851-1856 In
   N: MnHi 1 reel   9877

GRAHAM, JOHN KENNEDY
   Papers, 1802-1841 priv.
   N: InHi 229 frames   9878

HESTER, FRANCIS ASBURY, 1822-1906
   Diary of a circuit rider, 1840-1888 InGrD
   N: In 1 reel   9879
   P: InGrD

INGHAM, JONAS, b. 1746
   Life and opinions priv.
   N: InRE 1 reel   9880

JACKSON, JOHN GEORGE, 1777-1825, and MEIGS,
   RETURN JONATHAN, 1764-1824
   Letters and papers, 1781-1832 InU
   N: InU 1 reel*   9881
   P: InU

JULIAN, GEORGE WASHINGTON, 1817-1899
   Papers, 1865-1880; diary, 1869-1878 In
   N: CU 2 reels   9882

M'COY, JOHN, 1782-1859, of Clark Co., Ind.
   Diary, July, 1847-Apr., 1852, 275 p. (typescript)
   priv.
   N: DLC   9883
   P: NN

MacDONALD, Capt. DONALD
   Diaries of journeys to New Harmony, Ind.,
   1824-1826 priv.
   N: In   9884

REED FAMILY, of Indiana and Kentucky
   Papers, 1795-1891 priv.
   N: DLC 1 reel   9885

SPARKS, WILLIAM TENNIS, 1849-?
   Reminiscences ViU
   N: InU 3 reels   9886

TIPTON, JOHN, 1786-1839
   Journal, May 15-July 30, 1821 In
   Blueprint: InU 45 p.   9887

Business Papers

WABASH LAND COMPANY
Papers, 1773-1793   PHi
DCO: DLC 1 box   9888

Institutions

CONGREGATIONAL HOME MISSIONARY SOCIETY
Papers re: Indiana, 1826-1832 ICU-T
N: MoSW 1 reel   9889

NEW HARMONY COMMUNITY, New Harmony, Ind.
Correspondence, 1814-1830, 269 items InNhW
N: InNhW 1 reel   9890
P: In

NEW HARMONY COMMUNITY, New Harmony, Ind.
Records, 1825-1828 InNhW
N: IU-H 2 reels   9891
P: In

NEW HARMONY COMMUNITY, New Harmony, Ind.,
see MacDONALD, Capt. DONALD, 9884, under
INDIANA, Personal Papers

University Records

PURDUE UNIVERSITY, Lafayette, Ind.
BOARD OF TRUSTEES
Minutes, Oct. 20, 1865 -   InLPU
N: InLPU   9892

ILLINOIS

Census

U.S. CENSUS. FIFTH, 1830
Population schedules, Illinois   DNA
N: DNA 4 reels   9893
P: USIGS

U.S. CENSUS. SIXTH, 1840
Population schedules, Illinois   DNA
N: DNA 5 reels   9894
P: USIGS

U.S. CENSUS. SEVENTH, 1850
Population schedules, Illinois   DNA
N: DNA 22 reels   9895
P: ICN USIGS

U.S. CENSUS. EIGHTH, 1860
Population schedules, Illinois   DNA
N: DNA 18 reels   9896
P: USIGS

U.S. CENSUS. NINTH, 1870
Population schedules, Illinois   DNA
N: DNA 26 reels   9897

U.S. CENSUS. TENTH, 1880
Population schedules, Illinois   DNA
N: DNA 89 reels   9898

State Records

ILLINOIS. COMMITTEE ON HERRIN MASSACRE,
1922
Stenographic transcript I-Ar
N: ICHi 2 reels   9899

County Records

GALLATIN Co., Ill.
Census, 1830; marriages, 1813-1838; settle-
ment of estates, 1821-1838, 75 p. (typescript)
NNNG
N: USIGS 2 reels   9900

RANDOLPH Co., Ill.
Court records, 1801-1849; County Clerk's
records, 1801-1849; probate records, 1809-
1849; marriage records, 1809-1850; French
royal notaries, 1718-1797; private and
public papers, 1720-1816   I-Ar
N: I-Ar 49 reels   9901
P: I-Ar

SHELBY Co., Ill.
Marriages, 1827-1831, 1854-1871; deaths,
1877-1892   C.H. Shelbyville
N: USIGS 1 reel   9902

WILLIAMSON Co., Ill., see PAISLEY, OLDHAM,
editor, 9927, under ILLINOIS, Collections

City Records

CHICAGO, Ill., see NORTH CAROLINA. UNIVER-
SITY, 9926, under ILLINOIS, Collections

NAUVOO, Hancock Co., Ill.
Tax list, 1840, 1842, 1850; school records,
1842-1845 USIC
N: USIC 2 reels   9903
P: USIGS

Church Records

CHURCH OF JESUS CHRIST OF LATTER-DAY
SAINTS. ILLINOIS
Ward and branch records: Aurora, Batavia,
Chain-O-Lakes, Lima, Logan Square, North
Shore, Rockford, University, West Suburban
USIC
N: USIGS 9 reels   9904

GLEN ELLYN, Ill. FIRST PRESBYTERIAN
CHURCH
Records, 1928-1950 Ibid.
N: ICP 30 feet 16 mm.   9905

PRESBYTERIAN CHURCH IN THE U.S.A.
PRESBYTERIES. ROCK RIVER, Ill.
Records, 1847-1945 Ibid.
N: ICP 1 reel   9906

Personal Papers

CLARKE, ROBERT
Letters, 1870-1890 OFH
N: IU   9907

EVANS, Rev. WALTER A.
Private register of vital records, 1889-1900
priv.
N: USIGS 1 reel   9908

FORSYTH, JOHN, of Illinois
Diary, 1861 priv.
N: NcU 1 reel   9909

LAMON, WARD HILL, 1828-1893
Papers, 1860-1891 CSmH
N: I 3 reels   9910

LAWLER, MICHAEL KELLY
Papers, 1819-1879 ICarbS
N: ICarbS 1 reel   9911
P: I

MATTESON, LYDIA O., and HUBBARD, MARY H.
Letters, 1854, 1858-1859 NHi
N: NHi 1 reel   9912
P: I

MILLER, WILLIAM, 1782-1849
Correspondence, 1812-1849, 800 items
N: ICU 4 reels*   9913
P: IAurC

MORAN, BENJAMIN, 1820-1886
Diary, 1857-1875, 43 v. DLC
N: ICU 10 reels   9914

PECK, JOHN MASON, 1789-1858
Manuscript journal, 1854-1858 priv.
N: ICU 1 reel   9915

PORTER, JEREMIAH, 1804-1893
Diary, 1831-1832, 60 p.   ICHi
DCO: MnHi   9916

STEVENS, WALLACE, 1879-
Letters to Ronald Latimer, 1934-1938 priv.
N: ICU 1 reel   9917

TROWBRIDGE, J.
Grammar of the Delaware language MiU
N: ICU   9918

WRIGHT, SAMUEL G.
Abstract of Ministerial Labors in Knox and
Stark Counties, Ill., 1840-1844 priv.
N: I 1 reel   9919

YOUNG, S. GLENN, 1887-1925
Reports and other materials re: Young
DJ DNA
N: ICHi 1/2 reel   9920

Business Papers

IRWIN AND CORNEAU, druggists, Springfield, Ill.
Account book, 1847-1850, 330 p. priv.
N: ?   9921
P: I

MUDD, HENRY T., merchant, of Pittsfield, Ill.
Account book, n.d. priv.
N: USIGS   9922

THORNTON, JOEL, justice of the peace, Pike
Co., Ill.
Account book, 1836-1870 priv.
N: USIGS   9923

Collections

HASTINGS, ROBERT NICHOLS, collector
Papers on the Fundamentalist controversy in
the Presbyterian Church NNUT
N: ICP 5 reels *   9924
P: ICP

ILLINOIS STATE HISTORICAL SOCIETY
Material on Black Hawk War, 1837 DNA WHi
N: I 8 reels some pos.   9925

NORTH CAROLINA. UNIVERSITY
Gordon papers re: Chicago, 1745-1936 NcU
N: ICHi 2 reels   9926

PAISLEY, OLDHAM, editor, Marion Republican
Scrapbooks re: Herrin Massacre and other
Williamson Co., Ill., events, 1922-1930, 13 v.
N: IMar   9927
PP: ICHi

College Records

BEMIS, EDWARD
Newspaper clippings and letters re: resignation
from the faculty of the University of Chicago,
1895-1896 ICU
N: NNC 1 reel   9928

MICHIGAN

Census

U.S. CENSUS. FOURTH, 1820
Michigan Territorial census Mi
N: Mi 1 reel   9929
P: DNA

U.S. CENSUS. FIFTH, 1830
Population schedules, Michigan DNA
N: DNA 1 reel   9930

U.S. CENSUS. SIXTH, 1840
Population schedules, Michigan DNA
N: DNA 3 reels   9931
P: USIGS

U.S. CENSUS. SEVENTH, 1850
Population schedules, Michigan DNA
N: DNA 4 reels
P: USIGS   9932

U.S. CENSUS. EIGHTH, 1860
Population schedules, Michigan DNA
N: DNA 10 reels
P: USIGS   9933

U.S. CENSUS. NINTH, 1870
Population schedules, Michigan DNA
N: DNA 14 reels
P: USIGS   9934

U.S. CENSUS. TENTH, 1880
Population schedules, Michigan DNA
N: DNA 46 reels   9935

Government Records

U.S. ADJUTANT-GENERAL'S OFFICE
Fort Mackinac, Michigan, Post returns,
1816-1895 DNA
N: DNA 3 reels   9936

U.S. OFFICE OF INDIAN AFFAIRS
Records of the Michigan Superintendency of
Indian Affairs, 1814-1851 DNA
N: DNA 71 reels [M-1]
P: MiEM   9937

County Records

BRANCH Co., Mich.
Marriage records, 1833-1869 C.H. Coldwater
N: USIGS 1 reel   9938

GENESEE Co., Mich.
Marriage records, 1836-1856 C.H. Flint
N: USIGS 1 reel
P: MiD-B   9939

IONIA Co., Mich.
Marriage records, 1837-1867 C.H. Ionia
N: USIGS 1 reel
P: MiD-B   9940

KENT Co., Mich.
Cemetery records (transcript) MiGr
N: USIGS 1 reel   9941

LAPEER Co., Mich.
Marriage records, 1831-1885 C.H. Lapeer
N: USIGS 1 reel   9942

LENAWEE Co., Mich.
Marriage records, 1852-1864 C.H. Adrian
N: USIGS 1 reel
P: MiD-B   9943

NEWAYGO Co., Mich.
Marriage records, 1852-1866 C.H. White
Cloud
N: USIGS 1 reel
P: MiD-B   9944

OAKLAND Co., Mich.
Marriages, 1827-1849, 124 p. (transcript)
NNNG
N: USIGS   9945

OTTAWA Co., Mich.
Cemetery records C.H. Grand Haven
N: USIGS 1 reel   9946

SANILAC Co., Mich.
Marriage records, 1849-1887 C.H. Sandusky
N: USIGS 1 reel   9947

WASHTENAW Co., Mich.
Marriage records, 1832-1870 C.H. Ann Arbor
N: USIGS 1 reel   9948

WAYNE Co., Mich.
Cemetery records, n.d., 191 p. NNNG
N: USIGS 1 reel   9949

WAYNE Co., Mich.
Letters from suicides, 1927-1932 Detroit
Coroner's Office
N: CoU 100 frames   9950

WAYNE Co., Mich. CIRCUIT COURT
Journal, ca. 1820, 1823-1828; calendar, 1823-
1828; judgment records, 1823-1836 C.H.
Detroit [Board of Auditors]
N: MiU-L 5 reels
P: MiU-L   9951

City Records

MACKINAC, Mich.
Impost book MiU
N: MiD-B   9952

MACKINAC ISLAND, Mich.
Marriage records, 1821-1831 (typed
transcript) [unk.]
N: MiD-B 1 reel   9953

MANCHESTER, Mich., see ENGLISH, ALBERT D.,
9970, under MICHIGAN, Personal Papers

Church Records

AMERICAN HOME MISSIONARY SOCIETY
Papers re: Michigan, 1825-1846 ICT
N: ICT 6 reels
P: MiEM   9954

DEARBORN, Mich. CHRIST CHURCH (Episcopal)
Treasurer's book, 1875-1886 Ibid.
N: MiD-B
P: MiD-B   9955

DEARBORN, Mich. METHODIST EPISCOPAL
CHURCH
Secretary's book, 1851-1914 Ibid.
N: MiD-B
P: MiD-B   9956

DEARBORN, Mich. ST. ALPHONSUS
CHURCH (Catholic)
Records, 5 v. Ibid.
N: MiD-B   9957

FRANKENMUTH, Mich. LUTHERAN CHURCH
Gemeinde-ordnung, Feb., 1848, 9 p. MoSC
DCO: MoSC   9958

FRIENDS, SOCIETY OF. BATTLE CREEK [Mich.]
MONTHLY MEETING
Births and deaths, 1838-1872; men's minutes,
1838-1872; removals, 1838-1868; women's
minutes, 1838-1869 NNSF
N: USIGS 2 reels
P: PHC PSC-F   9959

KELLY, Fr. PATRICK, collector
Baptisms and marriages, var. towns west of
Pontiac, Mich., through Livingston, Oakland,
and Ingham Counties, 1843-1859 priv.
N: USIGS 1 reel   9960

MONROE, Mich. ST. ANTOINE
CHURCH (Catholic)
Record book, 1794-1840; register, 1830-1839
Ibid.
N: MiD-B   9961

WHITE PIGEON, Mich. CONGREGATIONAL
CHURCH
Records, 1848 Ibid.
N: MiD-B
P: MiD-B   9962

WHITE PIGEON, Mich. FIRST PRESBYTERIAN
CHURCH
Records, 1830-1943 Ibid.
N: MiD-B
P: MiD-B   9963

Personal Papers

BARBEAU, PETER, 1800-1882
Papers, 1789-1864 MiSs
N: MiSs 8 reels
P: MnHi   9964

BARTHE, CHARLES ANDRE, 1722-1786
Diary, 1765-1766 MiD-B
N: MiD-B 1 reel   9965

BURNETT, WILLIAM, Fur Trader, St. Joseph,
Mich.
Letter book, 1786-1803 NHi
N: NHi 1 reel
P: NHi   9966

DeFOREST, JOHN WILLIAM, b. 1826
Papers (Boltwood Family), 1856-1867 MiD-B
N: MiD-B 2 reels   9967

DORR, EBENEZER, 1762-1847
Papers, 1793-1797 MiD-B
N: MiD-B 1 reel   9968

EDWARDS, ABRAHAM E.
Papers and ledgers, 1817-1823, v. 1-2 InWHi;
v.3 MiD-B
N: MiD-B 1 reel   9969

ENGLISH, ALBERT D.
Papers re: Tecumseh and Manchester, Mich.,
1828-1929, 68 v. priv.
N: MiD-B   9970

FELCH, ALPHEUS, 1804-1896
Papers, and diary, 1833 MiD-B
N: MiD-B 1 reel   9971

GORDON, JOHN MONTGOMERY
Diary of a trip to Michigan, July-Oct., 1836
priv.
N: MiD-B 1 reel   9972

GRAEBNER, J.H.P.
"Die fraenkischen Colonien des Saginaw
Thales im Staate Michigan," 49 p. MoSC
DCO: MoSC   9973

HUBBARD, BELA
Field notes, 2 notebooks MiU-H
N: MiD-B 1 reel   9974

HUNT, TIMOTHY DWIGHT
Michigan marriage records, 1849-1894
CSaT
N: MiD-B   9975

JACKER, EDWARD
Papers, 1823-1887 MiD-B
N: MiD-B   9976

JOHNSTON, GEORGE, 1796-1861
Papers, 1819-1858, 37 items MiSau
DCO: MnHi   9977

MacKINTOSH, ALEXANDER
Diaries re: journeys from Detroit to Scotland
and return, 1827, 1835 MiD-B
N: MiD-B 2 reels   9978

MORISON, DANIEL
Papers, 1769 MiD-B
N: MiD-B 1 reel   9979

PORTEOUS, JOHN, d. 1799
Papers, journals, 1762-1771 MiD-B
N: MiD-B 2 reels   9980

RANKIN, FRANCIS H., Sr.
Diary, 1874 MiFli
N: priv. 1/2 reel*
P: MiFli   9981

RICHARD, Father GABRIEL, 1767-1832
Letters, 1796-1809 priv.
N: MiD-B   9982

RICHARD, Father GABRIEL, 1767-1832
Papers, 1784-1836 MiD-B
N: MiD-B 1 reel   9983

ROOT, REBECCA FISH, 1770-1856
Papers, diary, memoranda, 1828-1850 MiD-B
N: MiD-B 1 reel   9984

TROWBRIDGE, CHARLES CHRISTOPHER, 1800-
1883
Accounts of Twaatwaa or Miami Indians, 1824
MiD-B
N: MiD-B 1 reel   9985

TROWBRIDGE, CHARLES CHRISTOPHER, 1800-
1883
Papers and journal, 1820 MiD-B
N: MiD-B 1 reel   9986

WARD, EBER
    Papers, 1801-1875 priv.
    N: MiD-B 2 reels
    P: MiD-B   9987

WORMELEY, KATHARINE PRESCOTT, 1830-1908
    Letters, 1861-1363 Mi-H
    N: NNC 4 reels   9988

Business Papers

DEQUINDRE, [ANTOINE?], of Detroit
    Daybook for store, 1815-1818 Monroe
    County Historical Society
    N: MiD-B   9989

MACKINTOSH, ANGUS
    Inventory book, 1819-1821 priv.
    N: MiD-B 1 reel   9990

Collections

DETROIT. PUBLIC LIBRARY. BURTON HISTORICAL COLLECTION
    Black Hawk War material, 1832 MiD-B
    N: MiD-B 1 reel   9991

DETROIT NEWS
    Scrapbook history of Isle Royale National
    Park movement, 1921-1946 Ibid.
    N: MiD-B   9992

FLINT, Mich. PUBLIC LIBRARY
    Genesee County obituaries, 1898-1940 MiFli
    N: MiFli 8 reels*   9993

Ships' Logs

CHIPPEWA (Schooner)
    Log book, 1793-1795 MiD-B
    N: MiD-B   9994

WISCONSIN

Census

U.S. CENSUS. SIXTH, 1840
    Population schedules, Wisconsin DNA
    N: DNA 1 reel
    P: USIGS   9995

U.S. CENSUS. SEVENTH, 1850
    Population schedules, Wisconsin DNA
    N: DNA 3 reels
    P: USIGS   9996

U.S. CENSUS. EIGHTH, 1860
    Population schedules, Wisconsin DNA
    N: DNA 9 reels
    P: USIGS   9997

U.S. CENSUS. NINTH, 1870
    Population schedules, Wisconsin DNA
    N: DNA 12 reels   9998

U.S. CENSUS. TENTH, 1880
    Population schedules, Wisconsin DNA
    N: DNA 37 reels   9999

Government Records

U.S. ADJUTANT-GENERAL'S OFFICE
    Post returns, Fort Crawford, Wis., 1817-
    1856, 3 v. DNA
    N: WHi 1 reel   10000

U.S. COPYRIGHT OFFICE
    Wisconsin copyright records, 1848-1870 DLC
    N: WHi 1 reel   10001

U.S. WAR DEPT. QUARTERMASTER GENERAL
    Papers re: Forts Howard, Crawford, and
    Winnebago, 1819-1888 DNA
    N: WHi 3 reels   10002

U.S. WEATHER BUREAU
    Wisconsin reports, 1820-1852 DNA
    N: WHi 1 reel   10003

Church Records

BARAGA, Rev. IRANEUS FREDERIC, 1797-1868
    Baptismal records (with those of other Catholic
    priests) at La Pointe and Bayfield Missions,
    1835-1887 Holy Family Church, Bayfield,
    Wis.
    N: WHi 1 reel   10004

CATHOLIC CHURCH. WISCONSIN
    Records, 1801-1870 Wilten Abbey, Austria
    N: WHi 1 reel   10005

CHURCH OF JESUS CHRIST OF LATTER-DAY
SAINTS. WISCONSIN
    Ward and branch records: Milwaukee Ward,
    1927-1948; Milwaukee South Branch, 1936-1948;
    Racine Branch, 1937-1948 USlC
    N: USIGS 3 reels   10006

LA POINTE, Wis. LA POINTE MISSION CHURCH
    Papers, 1833-1867, 26 p. IChi
    DCO: MnHi   10007

WOOD RIVER, Wis. SWEDISH BAPTIST CHURCH
    Records, 1869-1912 [in Swedish] priv.
    N: WHi   10008

Personal Papers

ANDERSON, RASMUS BJORN, 1842-1936
    Correspondence, 1875-1909 priv.
    N: WHi 1 reel   10009

ARCHIQUETTE, JOHN
    Diary, in Oneida language, 1868-1874
    N: WHi 1 reel   10010

BAILEY, ANTOINETTE GRIPPEN (Mrs. JAMES
MONROE), 1834-1931
    Papers priv.
    N: WHi 1 reel   10011

BARLAND, THOMAS, 1809-1896
    Letters re: settlement in Wisconsin, 1852-1853,
    7 items priv.
    N: MnHi   10012

BORTH, HENRY F., 1883-
    Biography (manuscript) of Frank Borth priv
    N: WHi 1 reel   10013

BOYD, THOMAS B., Indian agent
    Letters from Prairie du Chien, 1837-1843
    Winnebago, Neb., Indian agency
    N: WHi 1 reel   10014

BUTTIES, ANSON W., railroad engineer,
1821-1906
    Papers, 1846-1856 priv.
    N: WHi 1 reel   10015

COLE, CHARLES D., 1806-1847
    Papers, 1831-1847 priv.
    N: WHi 1 reel   10016

CUSHING, CALEB, 1800-1879
    Papers re: Wisconsin, 1846-1872 DLC
    N: WHi   10017

DANIELS, JOHN
    Papers, 1797-1866 priv.
    N: WHi 1 reel   10018

DAVIS, HENRY C., surveyor for Northern
Pacific RR
    Diary, 1870 priv.
    N: WHi 1 reel   10019

DOTY, JAMES DUANE, 1799-1865
    Letter books, 1829-1836, 2 v. CSmH
    N: CSmH
    P: MiU-L   10020

DOTY, JAMES DUANE, 1799-1865
    Letters to John Jacob and William B. Astor,
    1835-1856 MH-BA   N: WHi 1 reel   10021

DOTY, JAMES DUANE, 1799-1865
    Papers, 1820-1856 CSmH
    N: WHi 1 reel   10022

DYE, ASEL GORDON, of Sheboygan, Wis.
    Diary, 1836-1841, 1855 priv.
    N: WHi 2 reels   10023

EMERSON, R   H
    Diary re: emigration from England to
    Wisconsin, 1859 priv.
    N: WHi 1 reel   10024

ESTERLY, GEORGE W., 1890-1893
    Autobiography (typescript) priv.
    N: WHi 1 reel   10025

FRIMAN, WILLIAM, Swedish immigrant
    Correspondence re: Wisconsin, 1848-1877
    priv.
    N: WHi 1 reel*   10026

FRISCH, JOHN G., dentist
    Scrapbook re: fluoridation, 1944-1952 priv.
    N: WHi 1 reel   10027

JOHNSON, Rev. SAMUEL ROOSEVELT,
1802-1873
    Letters to Bishop Kemper and others,
    1836-1870 NNG
    N: WHi 1 reel   10028

LAPHAM, INCREASE ALLEN, 1811-1875
    Diaries, 1827-1833, and correspondence WHi
    N: WHi 4 reels   10029
    P: KyLoF ?

LLOYD, HENRY DEMAREST, 1847-1903
    Correspondence, 1873-1883 priv.
    N: WHi 1 reel   10030

VAN CLEVE, BENJAMIN
    Biographical memorandum, 1773-1802 priv.
    N: WHi 1 reel   10031

VILAS, LEVI BAKER, 1811-1879
    Papers, 1830-1872 priv.
    N: WHi 1 reel   10032

WASHBURN, AMASA CORNWALL
    Diary re: Great Lakes trips and return to
    Vermont, 1831-1833 priv.
    N: WHi 1 reel   10033

WEBER, FRANK J., 1849-1943
    Correspondence, 1927-1935 priv.
    N: WHi 1 reel   10034

WILCOX, ROY PORTER, 1873-1946
    Four speeches, 1916, 1918 priv.
    N: WHi 1 reel   10035

ZAITZ, ANTHONY W.
    Papers re: proposed State educational television,
    1951-1954 priv.
    N: WHi 1 reel   10036

Business Papers

ASTOR, JOHN JACOB, 1763-1848
    Green Bay land record books, 1835-1867 MH-B
    N: WHi 1 reel   10037

BANK OF MILWAUKEE
    Minute book, 1837-1842; papers and correspondence of Alexander and John Mitchell, presidents
    of the bank, 1847-1906 WHi
    N: MH-BA 1 reel   10038

CENTER, ALEXANDER J.
    Field notes, survey, Fort Crawford to Fort
    Howard, 1832 DNA
    N: WHi 1 reel   10039

CHAPMAN, JAMES, 1857-1930, of Bayfield, Wis.
    Account book, 1862-1874 Bayfield Public
    Library
    N: WHi 1 reel   10040

COUMBE, WARNER R., M.D., of Richland
Center, Wis.
    Records re: patients and farm tenants,
    1901-1908, 1919-1920 priv.
    N: WHi 1 reel   10041

FIELD, WILLIAM, 1804-1858, of New
  Diggings, Wis.
  Account books, 1836-1873 priv.
  N: WHi 1 reel   10042

HAMMONDS AND HEUSTON, General merchandise
  firm
  Day book, 1852-1853 priv.
  N: WHi 1 reel   10043

MATTOX, ROBERT CLARK, 1858-1937
  Account book, 1888-1906 priv.
  N: WHi 1 reel   10044

WISCONSIN MARINE AND FIRE INSURANCE
  COMPANY
  Records and papers, 1839-1853 WHi
  N: MH-BA 1 reel   10045
  P: MH-BA

Collections

HASKIN, HARLEY THEODORE, collector
  Family papers, 1851, 1864, 1865; diary of
  Dilton, Wis., 1864-1866 priv.
  N: Or-Ar 62 frames   10046

HAWKINS, S. N., compiler
  Material re: Hawkins Settlement, St. Croix Co.,
  Wis., 1855, 47 p. priv.
  N: USIGS 1 reel   10047

WISCONSIN. STATE HISTORICAL SOCIETY
  Selections from Labor manuscripts: Janesville,
  Wis., U.A.W. Local 121, Minute book, June,
  1834-Oct., 1836; U.A.W. Local 95, Minute book,
  March, 1934- Sept., 1935 WHi
  N: MiU   10048

College Records

BUCK, SOLON JUSTUS, b. 1884
  Letters re: student life at University of
  Wisconsin, 1901-1906 priv.
  N: WHi 1 reel   10049

ELY, RICHARD THEODORE, 1854-1943
  Proceedings, University of Wisconsin
  Regents' investigation, 1894 WHi
  N: WHi 1 reel   10050

Institutions

FOND DU LAC COUNTY MEDICAL SOCIETY,
  Fond du Lac, Wis.
  Minutes, 1902-1935 Ibid.
  N: WHi 1 reel   10051

HARDWARE MUTUAL CASUALTY Co.
  Records re: Wisconsin Medical Society's
  plan for group accident and health insurance,
  1944-1957 Ibid.
  N: WHi 6 reels   10052

WISCONSIN CENTENNIAL AUTOMOTIVE
  COMMITTEE, Inc.
  Papers
  N: WHi 1 reel   10053

MINNESOTA

Census

MINNESOTA
  State census, 1870 MnHi
  N: DNA 13 reels   10054

U.S. CENSUS. SEVENTH, 1850
  Population schedules, Minnesota DNA
  N: DNA 1 reel   10055
  P: USIGS

U.S. CENSUS. EIGHTH, 1860
  Population schedules, Minnesota DNA
  N: DNA   10056
  P: USIGS

U.S. CENSUS. NINTH, 1870
  Population schedules, Minnesota DNA
  N: DNA 1 reel   10057
  P: USIGS

U.S. CENSUS. TENTH, 1880
  Population schedules, Minnesota DNA
  N: DNA 24 reels   10058

Government Records

U.S. GENERAL LAND OFFICE
  Land grants in regard to St. John's Abbey DNA
  N: MnCS 33 frames   10059

U.S. NATIONAL ARCHIVES
  War Department papers re: Minnesota, 1805-
  1927 DNA
  N: MnHi 1 reel   10060
  DCO: MnHi 1 box

Church Records

ANOKA, Minn. FIRST UNIVERSALIST SOCIETY
  Papers, 1867-1900 priv.
  N: MnHi 4 reels   10061

BENEDICTINES
  Abbots Primate. Correspondence re: St. John's
  Abbey Collegio di S. Anselmo, Rome
  N: MnCS 1 reel 32 mm.   10062

BUREAU OF CATHOLIC INDIAN MISSIONS,
  Washington, D.C.
  St. John's and Benedictine materials re: Minne-
  sota Indians, to 1900 Ibid.
  N: MnCS 1 reel 32 mm.   10063

CHASKA, Minn. MORAVIAN CHURCH
  Papers, 1864-1877, 24 items PBM
  DCO: MnHi   10064

CLAREMONT, Minn. FIRST CONGREGATIONAL
  CHURCH
  Papers, 1894-1910 priv.
  N: MnHi 2 reels   10065

EXCELSIOR, Minn. CONGREGATIONAL CHURCH
  Papers, 1853-1924 priv.
  N: MnHi 6 reels   10066

GIDNEY, Rev. JOSEPH BENJAMIN
  Baptist vital records (churches in Wisconsin,
  Iowa, California, Minnesota), 1875-1906,
  34 p. priv.
  DCO: MnHi   10067

HEISS, MICHAEL, Abp., 1818-1890
  Correspondence to Rome re: German question,
  1886
  N: MnCS 32 mm.   10068

LAKE ELMO, Minn. ST. PAUL'S EVANGELICAL
  CHURCH
  Records [in German], 1855-1937 Ibid.
  N: MnHi 1 reel   10069

LATROBE, Pa. ST. VINCENT ARCHABBEY.
  ARCHIVES
  Materials re: St. John's Abbey Ibid.
  N: MnCS 80 feet   10070

MINNESOTA HISTORICAL SOCIETY
  Selected data on religious affairs of Minnesota
  Indians MnHi
  N: MnCS 30 feet 32 mm.   10071

PRESBYTERIAN CHURCH IN THE U.S.A. (New
  school). PRESBYTERIES. MINNESOTA
  Minutes, 1850-1869 Ibid.
  N: PPPrHi 1 reel   10072

PRESBYTERIAN CHURCH IN THE U.S.A.
  (New school). SYNODS. MINNESOTA
  Minutes, 1858-1869 Ibid.
  N: PPPrHi 1 reel   10073

PRESBYTERIAN CHURCH IN THE U.S.A. (Old
  school). PRESBYTERIES. ST. PAUL, Minn.
  Records, 1855-1870 Ibid.
  N: PPPrHi 1 reel   10074

PRESBYTERIAN CHURCH IN THE U.S.A.
  (Reunited). PRESBYTERIES
  Records, 1870-1884 Ibid.
  N: PPPrHi 1 reel   10075

ST. PAUL, Minn. CATHEDRAL OF ST. PAUL
  Record books, 1840-1857, 3 v. Ibid.
  DCO: MnHi   10076

SMITH, BERNARD, O.S.B., 1818-1890
  Correspondence, 1840-1890 Abbey of St.
  Paul's Outside the Walls, Rome
  N: MnCS 15 reels   10077

WIMMER, BONIFACE, O.S.B., 1809-1887
  Letters to Abbot Angelo Pescetelli, O.S.B.
  Abbey of St. Paul's Outside the Walls, Rome.
  N: MnCS 2 reels   10078

Personal Papers

ANDREWS, JAMES A., 1845-1930
  Papers, 1852-1920 priv.
  N: MnHi 1 reel   10079

AYER, ELIZABETH TAYLOR, 1803-1898
  Papers, 1868-1885 priv.
  N: MnHi 1 reel   10080

BARRICK, NIMROD, b. 1851
  Diaries, 1871-1932, 14 v. priv.
  N: MnHi 1 reel   10081

BELL, JAMES HUGHES, 1825-1892
  Papers, 1845-1892 priv.
  N: MnHi 2 reels   10082

BOSSHARD, HENRY, 1811-1877
  Correspondence, 1866-1879 WHi
  DCO: MnHi 1 box   10083

BOURLAND, JAMES A.
  Papers re: Red River Valley, 1841-1896 priv.
  N: DLC 3 reels   10084

BREWSTER, CHARLES G., b. 1832
  Diary, 1852-1859 priv.
  N: MnHi 1 reel   10085

BROUSE, JOHN ANDREW, 1808-1893
  Diary, 1827-1858 priv.
  N: MnHi 4 reels*   10086

BURNS, ROBERT, 1832-1891
  Letterbook, 1862-1865 priv.
  N: MnHi 1 reel   10087

BUTTON, GEORGE I.
  Letters, 1859, 3 items La Crosse County
  Historical Society
  DCO: MnHi   10088

CHRISTENSEN, OTTO AUGUST, 1870-1918
  Papers, 1870-1949 priv.
  N: MnHi 1 reel   10089

CLAPP, MOSES EDWIN, 1851-1929
  Papers, 1873-1929 priv.
  N: MnHi 1 reel   10090

COLHOUN, JAMES EDWARD, 1798-1889
  Diary, 1823 priv.
  N: MnHi 1 reel   10091

DAVIS, CHARLES E.
  Letters, 1859-1865 priv.
  N: MnHi 1 reel   10092

DAVIS, EDWARD E., 1st Minnesota infantry
  Letters, 1859-1860 priv.
  N: CtY   10093

DREW, BENJAMIN, 1812-1903
  Diary, 1858-1859 MnS
  N: MnHi 1 reel   10094

EDGAR, WILLIAM CROWELL, 1856-1932
  Papers, 1885-1923 MnM
  N: MnHi 1 reel   10095

FAIRCHILD, LUCIUS, 1831-1896
Papers, 1855-1892, 19 items   WHi
DCO: MnHi   10096

FAST, Mrs. HERMANN J., 1865-1930
Diary, 1914-1920 [in German]   priv.
N: MnHi 2 reels   10097

FLANDREAU, CHARLES EUGENE, 1828-1903
Papers, 1856-1863 DNA
N: MnHi 1 reel   10098

FOGG, FREDERIC A., 1850-1930
Papers, 1876-1920   priv.
N: MnHi 1 reel   10099

GALTIER, LUCIAN, 1811-1866
Papers, 1864-1866, 2 items   St. Paul Catholic
Historical Society
DCO: MnHi   10100

GEYER, CHARLES A., 1809-1853
Letters, 1842-1846, 14 items   priv.
DCO: MnHi   10101

GRACE, THOMAS LANGDON, Bp., 1814-1897
Diary, 1861, 3 p.   St. Paul Catholic Historical
Society
DCO: MnHi   10102

GRANT, SAMUEL C.
Correspondence, 1868-1872   priv.
N: MnHi 1 reel   10103

GRIFFIN, THOMAS HENRY, 1836-1922
Papers, 1878-1883, 1899-1909   priv.
N: MnHi 13 reels   10104

HARRIS, JOHN S., 1826-1901
Papers, 1849-1909   priv.
N: MnHi 6 reels   10105

HUTCHINSON, ASA B., 1823-1884
Papers, 1844-1899   priv.
N: MnHi 2 reels   10106

JANZEN, CORNELIUS, 1840-1914
Annals, 1862-1913   priv.
N: MnHi 1 reel   10107

KEMPER, JACKSON, 1789-1870
Papers, 1841-1843, 5 items   WHi
DCO: MnHi   10108

KENNICOTT, ROBERT, 1835-1866
Correspondence, 1852-1867   priv.
DCO: MnHi 1 box
N: MnHi 3 reels   10109

KINNEY, JAY P., 1875-
Papers   NIC
N: NIC
P: MnSF   10110

KREBS, KARL GOTTLIEB, 1829-1909
Autobiography, 1908, 43 p.   priv.
DCO: MnHi   10111

LANGFORD, NATHANIEL, 1832-1911
Diary, 1863   MnHi
N: ? 1 reel*
P: MtU   10112

LAPHAM, INCREASE ALLEN, 1811-1875
Correspondence, 1856-1858   WHi
N: MnHi 1 reel   10113

LA PLANTE, EDWARD, 1900-
Papers, 1941-1944   priv.
N: MnHi 1 reel   10114

LINDEGARD, AXEL
Papers, 1861-1931 priv.
N: MnHi 1 reel   10115

LORAS, MATIAS, 1792-1858
Correspondence, 1843-1850   Chancery
Office, Archdiocese of Dubuque
DCO: MnHi 1 box   10116

MILLS, JOSEPH T., 1811-1897
Diary, 1856   WHi
N: MnHi 1 reel   10117

MILLS, LUCIUS D., 1848-1936
Diaries, 1872-1936, 36 v.   priv.
N: MnHi 4 reels   10118

NICOLET, JOSEPH NICHOLAS, 1786-1843
Papers, 1808-1842   DLC NN PHi WHi
DCO: MnHi 1 box   10119

PECK, SIMON LEWIS, 1844-1935
Diary, 1867   priv.
N: MnHi 1 reel   10120

PELAMOURGES, JOHN ANTHONY MARIE, Bp.,
1806-1875
Papers, 1858   St. Paul Catholic Historical
Society
DCO: MnHi 2 items   10121

PIERZ, FRANCIS, 1785-1880
Papers   St. Paul Catholic Historical
Society   MnStjosS
DCO: MnHi 1 box   10122

RAMSAY, ALEXANDER
Correspondence, selections re: R.B. Hayes
MnHi
N: OFH   10123

REDINGTON, EDWARD S., 1820-1888
Diary, 1850   priv.
N: MnHi 1 reel   10124

ROBERTSON, RUSSEL K.
Correspondence re: Minnesota, 1852-1854,
9 items   NIC
DCO: MnHi   10125

ROLLINS, IRVING WASHINGTON, 1829-1895
Papers, 1848-1897   priv.
N: MnHi 3 reels   10126

ROLVAAG, OLE EDUART, 1876-1931
Papers, 1896-1934   priv.
N: MnHi   10127

SNELLING, HENRY HUNT, 1816-1897
Reminiscences   ICN
DCO: MnHi 1 v.   10128

SNELLING, JOSIAH, 1782-1827
Diary, 1827   priv.
N: MnHi 1 reel   10129

STONE, EDWARD MARTIN, 1805-1883
Diary, 1822-1831   priv.
N: MnHi 1 reel   10130

STORER, DANIEL M., 1828-1905
Diary, 1841-1905
N: MnHi 1 reel   10131

STUNTZ, ALBERT C., 1825-1914
Diary, 1858-1882   WHi
N: MnHi 1 reel   10132

SUCKLEY, GEORGE, 1830-1869
Correspondence, 1853-1854, 8 items   CSmH
DCO: MnHi   10133

TREADWELL, JOHN N., 1828-1913
Letter, 1858   priv.
DCO: MnHi   10134

TROWBRIDGE, CHARLES CHRISTOPHER,
1799-1883
Diary re: Cass Expedition, 1820   priv.
N: MnHi 1 reel   10135

ULLMANN, Mrs. JOSEPH, 1832-1899
Reminiscences re: St. Paul, 1855-1866, 162 p.
priv.
DCO: MnHi   10136

VANDERBURGH, CHARLES, 1829-1898
Letters, 1856   priv.
N: MnHi 1 reel   10137

WOOD, WILLIAM H., 1817-1870
Papers, 1865-1913   priv.
N: MnHi 1 reel   10138

Business Papers

LAWRENCE, JOHN H., 1858-1935
Farm account book, 1889-1934   priv.
N: MnHi 1 reel   10139

SHAW (PERCY M., Jr.) AND COMPANY,
Duluth, Minn.
Correspondence, 1895-1925   priv.
DCO: MnHi 1 box   10140

WASHBURN, CADWALLADER COLDEN, 1818-1882
Business correspondence, 1869, 19 items   WHi
DCO: MnHi   10141

Institutions

LITCHFIELD, Minn.   LITCHFIELD CEMETERY
ASSOCIATION
Records, 1870-1935   Ibid.
N: MnHi 1 reel   10142

NORTHFIELD LYCEUM, Northfield, Minn.
Papers, 1856-1860, 1863   priv.
N: MnHi 6 reels   10143

POMONA GRANGE No. 12, Hennepin Co., Minn.
Records, 1881-1895   priv.
N: MnHi 4 reels   10144

ST. PAUL, Minn.   OAKLAND CEMETERY
ASSOCIATION
Records, 1854-1937   priv.
N: MnHi 275 reels   10145

IOWA

Census

U.S. CENSUS. SIXTH, 1840
Population schedules, Iowa   DNA
N: DNA 1 reel
P: USIGS   10146

U.S. CENSUS. SEVENTH, 1850
Population schedules, Iowa   DNA
N: DNA 2 reels
P: USIGS   10147

U.S. CENSUS. EIGHTH, 1860
Population schedules, Iowa   DNA
N: DNA 8 reels
P: USIGS   10148

U.S. CENSUS. NINTH, 1870
Population schedules, Iowa   DNA
N: DNA 13 reels   10149

U.S. CENSUS. TENTH, 1880
Population schedules, Iowa   DNA
N: DNA 47 reels   10150

State Records

IOWA. SECRETARY OF STATE
Election records, 1839-1890   Ibid.
N: IaU 3 reels   10151

Church Records

CHURCH OF JESUS CHRIST OF LATTER-DAY
SAINTS. IOWA
Ward and branch records: Zahahemla   USIC
N: USIGS 1 reel   10152

EVANGELICAL LUTHERAN SYNOD OF IOWA
AND OTHER STATES
Papers, 1853, 3 items   priv.
DCO: MnHi   10153

FRANKLIN, Iowa.   LUTHERAN CHURCH
Parish register, 1849-1901   Ibid.
N: USIGS 1 reel   10154

ST. PETER'S CHURCH (German Evangelical),
Lee Co., Iowa
Records, 1849-1901   Ibid.
N: USIGS 1 reel   10155

Personal Papers

BEACH, JOHN, U. S. Indian agent for Sac
and Fox Indians
Letterbook, 1840-1847 DLC
N: IaU   10156

GRAVES, JULIUS K.
Journal: Dubuque, Iowa,to New Mexico
and return, 1865-1866, 200 p.   priv.
N: IaU   10157

JONES, GEORGE W.,1804-1896
Correspondence, 1838 Ia-HA
N: MnHi 1 reel   10158

NOSSAMAN, WELCH, b. 1851
Life story of pioneer life in Iowa and
Colorado, 1933, 203 p.   priv.
N: IaU   10159

RECK, MICHAEL
Papers, 1866-1874, 21 items   IaDU-Sem
DCO: MnHi   10160

STREET, JOSEPH MONTFORD, 1782-1840
Correspondence, 1828-1839   Ia-HA
N: MnHi 4 reels   10161

WIER-FOSTER FAMILY, of Iowa
Letters, 1847-1888, 49 items   priv.
N: OrU   10162

Business Papers

WALCOTT SAVINGS BANK, Walcott, Ia.
Minutes, 1893-1930; mortgage register,
1893-1913   Ibid.
N: IaU 436 frames   10163

Institutions

GRAND ARMY OF THE REPUBLIC. DEPT.
OF IOWA
G. A. R. Letters (addressed to the department
commanders and adjutant generals), 1889-1900
Ibid.
N: ? 2 reels   10164
P: IaU

THE WEST

Overland Journeys

Government Records

U. S. COMMISSIONERS ON THE ROAD FROM
MISSOURI TO NEW MEXICO (Santa Fé Trail)
Report, 1827   DNA
N: KHi 24 frames   10165
P: NmU

Personal Papers

ARMSTRONG, J.E.
Diary, 1849, Overland journey from Ohio   OHi
N: NbHi 1 reel   10166

BISHOP, FRANCIS MARION
Diary, journey from Chicago to Salt Lake
City and down the Green and Colorado Rivers,
1870-1871, 103 p. (typescript)   priv.
DCO: NN   10167

BRADLEY, GEORGE Y.
Diary, first Powell expedition down Green
and Colorado Rivers, Mar. 24-Aug. 30, 1869,
40 p.   DLC
DCO: NN   10168

BROWN, JOSEPH C.
Survey field notes for Santa Fé Trail,
1825-1827   DNA
N: KHi 15 feet   10169
P: KHi

BURTON, HENRY W.
Overland diary, 1849   priv.
N: CoHi 1 reel   10170

CHADWICK, SAMUEL
Diary, journey from Marshall, Wisconsin,to
California, Mar. 23, 1852 - Sept. 12, 1852;
miscellaneous papers, 1843-1852   priv.
DCO: NN 96 ll.   10171

CLEAVER, BENJAMIN
Plains diary, Aug. 14- Sept. 24, 1848   priv.
N: Or-Ar 1 reel   10172

CLOUGH, AARON, 1840?-1865
Notebook, Oceola, Iowa,and overland diary,
May 15.- Dec. 15, 1862, 1 v.   priv.
N: OrHi 65 frames   filmstrip   10173

COLEMAN, LEW
Diary . . . Kansas to Fort Dodge (Denver City),
1866 priv.
N: WaPS 1 reel   10174

COOPER, ARVAZENA ANGELINE (SPILLMAN),
1845-1929
Overland journey, Missouri to Oregon, 1863
Multnomah Chapter, DAR
N: OrHi 38 frames   10175

DUNIWAY, ABIGAIL SCOTT
Journal of trip to Oregon, 1852 (typescript)
OrHi
N: OrHi 10 feet   10176

EDDY, JAMES A.
Overland diary (Albany, Ill., to Aspen, Col.),
1886 priv.
N: priv.   10177
P: CoHi 1 reel

EGAN, HOWARD, 1815-1878
Journal, westward expedition, 1847, 180 p.
N: CtY   10178

FLETCHER FAMILY
Account of trip to Oregon, 1864   priv.
N: WyHi   10179

GAYLORD, ORANGE
Level book, n.d. , ; copy of diary of trip across
the plains, Mar. 7-Aug. 25, 1853 priv.
N: Or-Ar 42 frames 16 mm. [Loan microfilm
#18]   10180

GOLDSMITH, S.
Winslow letters re: death of George Winslow,
1849, on overland trail   priv.
N: NbHi 1 reel   10181

GREEN, ROBERT
Journey to California gold fields, 1849   priv.
N: PHarH 5 1/2 feet   10182

HINMAN, C. G.
Journal...Groveland Bell Wagon trip ... Peoria
to California Gold Fields, 1849-1850 CoD
N: CoD 1 reel *   10183

HOFFMAN, WILLIAM
Diary, 1853-1885; overland journey, 1853   priv.
N: OrHi 49 frames   10184

HOLT, W.M.
Overland journey, Washington, Arkansas,to
California, 1852 (typescript)   priv.
N: ArHi 21 frames   10185

JOHNSON, JOHN LAWRENCE, 1830-1916
Diary, crossing the plains, Apr. 1- Sept. 14,
1851   priv.
N: Or-Ar 10 feet   10186

JOHNSON, JOHN PETER RASMUS, 1824-1910
Journal, overland journey, July 25-Sept. 30,
1864 priv.
N: UPB   10187
P: UPB

KING, A. D.
Diary of overland journey from Arkansas to
California, July 6, 1849- Mar. 19, 1850,
84p. ArU
DCO: NN   10188

KORZENBORN, HENRY
Journal of trip West, May-Sept. , 1850
(typescript)   priv.
N: KyU 10 feet   10189

KRIPPS, BOLIVAR
Letters re: trip from St. Joseph to California,
1849, 6 items   CoD
N: CoD   10190

LONG, STEPHEN HARRIMAN, 1784-1864
Journals, 1823   MnHi
N: priv. 1 reel*   10191
P: CU-B

LOVELAND, CYRUS CLERK, d. 1885
Diary, overland journey, Missouri to California,
1850, 96 ll.   C
DCO: C   10192

MARTIN, THOMAS SALATHIEL, b. 1818
Narrative of Frémont Expedition to California,
1845-1846   CU-B
N: CU-B 1 reel   10193

PENGRA, Mrs. BYNON J.
Diary, Illinois to Oregon, 1853 (transcript)
priv.
N: OrHi 10 feet   10194

RAYMOND, ALMIRA, 1827-1880
Album (farewell and friendship messages,
journey to Oregon) , 1839-1840 priv.
N: OrHi 10 feet   10195

SAWYERS, WILLIAM MONTGOMERY, cattle
driver
Memorandum of trip from Llano Co. , Texas
to Cheyenne, Wyoming Ter. , Mar. 19- May 17,
1877; pension record for service in Civil War;
biographical data priv.
N: Or-Ar 143 frames 16 mm.   10196

SHIRE, WILLIAM
Overland trail diary, 1862 [unk.]
DCO: priv. 14 p.
N: WyHi   10197

SIBLEY, G.C.
Diary on Santa Fé Trail, 1825   DNA
N: KHi 10 feet   10198
P: KHi

SMITH, JEDEDIAH STRONG, 1799-1831
Journal, 1822-1828   DLC
N: DLC 1 reel   10199
P: UHi

SMITH, JEDEDIAH STRONG, 1799-1831
Letters [unk.]
DCO: priv.
N: priv. ? 1 reel   10200
P: UHi

SMITH, SIDNEY
Diary, overland journey, Peoria party, 1839
OrFP
N: OrHi? 27 frames   10201
P: OrHi UHi

SPOONER, E.A.
Overland trail diary, 1849-1850   KHi
N: KHi 48 frames   10202
P: KHi

STEPHENS FAMILY, of Hayesville, Ore.
Journal re: arrival from Missouri and
founding of Hayesville, 1849   priv.
N: Or-Ar 40 frames   10203

TROWBRIDGE, SABIN
Letters to wife, Sarah, 1850-1852; Constitution
of the Palestine Co. ; journal of westward
expedition, 1850 [unk.]
N: MoSHi 10 feet*   10204

WALKER, WILLIAM EVERETT, 1808-1868?
Diary: Maryland, Ohio, Missouri, and Oregon,
1829-1862 priv.
N: ? 20 feet   10205
P: OrHi

Collections

CALIFORNIA. UNIVERSITY. BANCROFT
LIBRARY
Diaries of overland journeys to California,
1849-1874   v.p.
N: CU-B 1 reel*   10206

YALE UNIVERSITY
William R. Coe Collection of Western Americana,
1800-1953 CtY
N: CtY 21 reels   10207
P: WyU

MISSOURI

Census

U.S. CENSUS. FIFTH, 1830
Population schedules, Missouri DNA
N: DNA 2 reels   10208
P: MoS USIGS

U.S. CENSUS. SIXTH, 1840
Population schedules, Missouri DNA
N: DNA 4 reels   10209
P: MoS USIGS

U.S. CENSUS. SEVENTH, 1850
Population schedules, Missouri DNA
N: DNA 7 reels   10210
P: MoS USIGS

U.S. CENSUS. EIGHTH, 1860
Population schedules, Missouri DNA
N: DNA 13 reels   10211
P: MoS USIGS

U.S. CENSUS. NINTH, 1870
Population schedules, Missouri DNA
N: DNA 20 reels   10212
P: MoS

U.S. CENSUS. TENTH, 1880
Population schedules, Missouri DNA
N: DNA 71 reels   10213
P: MoS

Government Records

U.S. OFFICE OF INDIAN AFFAIRS
Records of the St. Louis Superintendency,
1807-1855 KHi
N: KHi 6 reels   10214
P: KHi

State Records

MISSOURI. GENERAL ASSEMBLY.
COMMITTEE ON MORMON DIFFICULTIES
Journal and papers, 1838-1839 Ibid.
N: CtY 1 reel   10215

County Records

JACKSON Co., Mo.
Records of County Clerk, 1827-1839 C.H.
Independence
N: Ibid.   10216
P: UPB

MACON Co., Mo.
Letters of administration, 1839-1855
C.H. Macon
N: USIGS 1 reel   10217

Church Records

CHURCH OF JESUS CHRIST OF LATTER-DAY
SAINTS. MISSOURI
Branch records: Dry Hill, 1847, 1855-1859
USIC
N: USIGS 1 reel   10218

CONGREGATIONAL HOME MISSIONARY SOCIETY
Papers re: Missouri, 1825-1840 ICU-T
N: MoSW 1 reel   10219

DANVILLE PRESBYTERIAN CHURCH,
Montgomery Co., Mo.
Minute book and roll, 1843-1877 priv.
N: MoSHi*   10220

FREEDOM BAPTIST CHURCH, Montgomery Co.,
Mo.
Minute book, 1824-1868 priv.
N: MoSHi*   10221

PIEPER, F.
Letter to Pittsburgh Pastoral Conference
[Missouri Synod], March 4, 1931, 1 p.
MoSC
DCO: MoSC   10222

Personal Papers

ADAMS, JOHN, b. 1796
Journal, 1796-1839, 100 p. MoSHi
N: MoSHi   10223
P: I

BAIERLEIN, E.R.
Luther's Catechism in the Chippewa language,
ca. 1852, 43 p. MoSC
DCO: MoSC   10224

BAUER, F.
Letters to G.M. Grossmann, Sept. 20, 21,
1855, 3 p. MoSC
DCO: MoSC   10225

BERKENMEYER, W.C.
Chronicle, 1731-1750, 2 v. PGHi
DCO: MoSC   10226

BIEWEND, ADOLPH
Papers, 1837-1896, 8 items priv.
DCO: MoSC   10227

BLOW, SUSAN, 1872-19--
Letters to William Torrey Harris [unk.]
N: MoSHi 2 reels   10228

BUENGER, JOHANN FRIEDRICH
Letters, 1842, 1859, 4 items MoSC
DCO: MoSC   10229

CHOUTEAU, PIERRE, Jr., 1789-1865
Papers, 1811-1843, 48 items MoSHi
DCO: MnHi   10230

FAGG, THOMAS JEFFERSON CLARK, 1822-1916
Two fragments of memoir priv.
N: MoSHi 3 feet*   10231

FALCKNER, JUSTUS
Copy of ordination certificate, 1703;
in-letters, 1703 PPLT
DCO: MoSC   10232

FIELD, ELIZA RIDDLE
Correspondence with Sol Smith and
Noah M. Ludlow, 1865-1890 MH
N: MoSHi 1 reel*   10233

FUELLKRUS, EMMA
Letters to Ernst Fuellkrus, Oct. 23, 1892,
May 12, 1900 MoSC
DCO: MoSC   10234

GEYER, CHARLES A.
Letters to George Engelmann, 1842-1846,
13 items MoSB
N: MoSHi 12 feet*   10235

GRAEBNER, A.L.
Diary, Oct. 3, 1863-Jan. 14, 1864, 20 p. MoSC
DCO: MoSC   10236

HAUPT, CHRISTIANINE ROSINE
Letter to Christian Gottfried Haupt, March 21,
1840, 2 p. MoSC
DCO: MoSC   10237

HELMUTH, JUSTUS HEINRICH CHRISTIAN
Ordinationschein (Ordination certificate),
Aug. 3, 1768 PLT
DCO: MoSC   10238

JONES FAMILY, of Montgomery Co., Mo.
Letters and documents, 1841-1897 priv.
N: MoSHi*   10239

KILIAN, JOHANN
Letters, June 22, 1877, Sept. 9, 1878;
Verantwortung in Thesen, Aug. 1877 Serbin
Archives, Austin, Tex.
DCO: MoSC   10240

KOENIG, EMILIE (LOHMANN)
Letters, July 19, 1853, Sept. 28, 1853,
3 items priv.
DCO: MoSC   10241

LAKIN, BENJAMIN, 1767-1849
Journal, 1797-1820 ICU-T
N: MoSW 1 reel   10242

LOEBER, GOTTHOLD HEINRICH
In-letters, 1830, 1834, 1849, 3 items, 12 p.
MoSC
DCO: MoSC   10243

MUDD, HENRY T.
Family letters, Pittsfield, Ill., Kirkwood, Mo.,
1850-1879 MoHi
N: Or-Ar 1005 frames 16 mm.   10244

RICHMANN, F.W.
Letters, Dec. 11, 1851 (one undated); certificate
of membership in Missouri Synod MoSC
DCO: MoSC   10245

SCHIEFERDECKER, GEORG ALBERT
Letter to Dr. R. Demme, n.d., 4 p. PPLT
DCO: MoSC   10246

STEPHAN, MARTIN
Papers, 1839, 59 p. MoSC C.H. Perryville
(Perry Co.)
DCO: MoSC   10247

TRENHOLM, GEORGE A.
Papers, 4 v. DLC
N: MoSW   10248

WALKER, JOHN J., postmaster, St. Louis
Letters, 1830-1834 ViU
N: MoSHi 4 feet*   10249

WALTHER, C.F.W.
Papers, 1811, 1841-1849, 1872, 1877
(6 items); letters, 1833-1885, including
Sauer collection (34 items) MoSC
DCO: MoSC   10250

Business Papers

BAKER, SYLVESTER MARION, b. 1813
Store ledger, Danville, Mo., 1840-1850 priv.
N: MoSHi*   10251

BOGY, JOSEPH
Letter books, 1823-1842; account book, 1837-
1841; treasurer's accounts, Ste. Genevieve Co.,
Mo., 1833-1841 priv.
N: MoSHi 1 reel*   10252

BREWER'S UNION OF ST. LOUIS
Minutes, 1898-1940 [unk.]
N: MoU 1 reel*   10253

FULKERSON, ROBERT C.
Account book - Lautre Lick, 1837-1838;
Justice of Peace Records, 1843-1859 ICU
N: MoSHi 1 reel*   10254

MISSOURI FUR Co., St. Louis
Papers, 1812-1814 KHi
N: MnHi 1 reel   10255

PERRY, JOHN D.
Historical data re: building Union Pacific
Railway, 1864 KHi
N: MoSHi 20 feet*   10256

YATES, T.S.
Store account book, Fulton, Mo., 1831-1832
MoU
N: MoU 1 reel*   10257

KANSAS

Census

KANSAS. BOARD OF AGRICULTURE
Census records, 1875 KHi
N: KHi 20 reels   10258
P: KHi

KANSAS. SECRETARY OF STATE
Census records, Kansas Territory, 1855 KHi
N: KHi 1 reel   10259
P: KHi

KANSAS. SECRETARY OF STATE
Census records, 1865 KHi
N: KHi 8 reels
P: KHi
10260

KANSAS. SECRETARY OF STATE
Census records, 1870 KHi
N: KHi 22 reels
P: KHi
10261

U.S. CENSUS. EIGHTH, 1860
Population schedules, Kansas DNA
N: DNA 2 reels
P: USlGS
10262

U.S. CENSUS. NINTH, 1870
Population schedules, Kansas DNA
N: DNA 5 reels
10263

U.S. CENSUS. TENTH, 1880
Population schedules, Kansas DNA
N: DNA 29 reels
10264

Government Records

U.S. DEPT. OF STATE
Territorial papers: Kansas, 1854-1861 DNA
N: DNA 2 reels
10265

U.S. POST OFFICE DEPARTMENT
Postal Records of the State of Kansas, 1841-
1930 DNA
N: DNA 1 reel
P: KHi
10266

U.S. WAR DEPT.
Selected records re: Kansas and Nebraska,
1853-1860 DNA
N: KU 1 reel
10267

State Records

KANSAS. ADJUTANT GENERAL'S OFFICE
Enrollment of soldiers under the Act of 1883,
1883 KHi
N: KHi 7 reels
P: KHi
10268

KANSAS. INSURANCE COMMISSION
Records, 1870-1948 KHi
N: KHi 622 reels
P: KHi
10269

KANSAS. LIVESTOCK SANITARY COMMISSIONER
Records, 1884-1934 KHi
N: KHi 6 reels
P: KHi
10270

KANSAS. SECRETARY OF STATE
Election returns, 1861-1930 KHi
N: KHi 36 reels
P: KHi
10271

County Records

DICKINSON Co., Kan.
Records, 1861-1888 C.H. Abilene
N: KHi 80 feet
P: KHi
10272

SHAWNEE Co., Kan.
Records, 1855-1898 C.H. Topeka
N: KHi 40 feet
P: KHi
10273

City Records

ABILENE, Kan.
Records, 1869-1876 Ibid.
N: KHi 20 feet
P: KHi
10274

EUDORA, Kan., CITY COUNCIL
General diary, Oct., 1859-May, 1860 Ibid.
N: KU 1 reel
10275

WICHITA, Kan.
Records, 1870-1889
N: Ibid. 2 reels 16 mm.
P: KHi
10276

Church Records

AMERICAN HOME MISSIONARY SOCIETY
Papers re: Kansas, 1854-1877, 1892-1893 ICT
N: ICT 12 reels
P: KHi KU
10277

ATCHISON, Kan. ST. BENEDICT'S ABBEY.
ARCHIVES
St. John's Abbey material, 246 items Ibid.
N: MnCS 16 mm.
10278

FINK, LOUIS MARIA, Bp., 1834-1904
Records, letters to Ludwig Missions Verein,
1857-1910, 216 items Munich, Ludwig Missions
Verein Archives
N: KAS*
10279

FRIENDS, SOCIETY OF. RICHMOND [Ind.]
YEARLY MEETING
Reports of the Indian Committee re: Friends'
mission among the Shawnees of Kansas, 1854-
1871, 30 p. Ibid.
N: KU
10280

IRVIN, SAMUEL M., 1812-1887, Indian missionary
Diary, Ioway Indian Mission, Highland, Kansas,
1841-1842, 1844, 1849, 65 p. KHi
N: KHi KU 25 feet
P: KHi PPPRHi
10281

NEWMAN, HERMAN, collector
Historical material on the early history of
Friends in Kansas priv.
N: KU 250 frames
10282

PRESBYTERIAN HISTORICAL SOCIETY
Philadelphia, Pa.
American Indian correspondence, Kansas,
1833-1864, 1883-1884 PPPrHi
N: PPPrHi 6 reels
P: KHi
10283

PROTESTANT EPISCOPAL CHURCH IN THE
U.S.A. DIOCESES. KANSAS
Records, 1861-1926 Ibid.
N: KHi 50 feet
P: KHi
10284

SIMERWELL, ELIZABETH
Diaries re: Indian Mission, 1852-1861 priv.
N: KHi 56 frames
P: KHi
10285

TOPEKA, Kan. FIRST BAPTIST CHURCH
Records, 1857-1948 Ibid.
N: KHi 2 reels
P: KHi
10286

TOPEKA, Kan. FIRST CONGREGATIONAL
CHURCH
Records, 1855-1927 Ibid.
N: KHi 1 reel
P: KHi
10287

TOPEKA, Kan. FIRST PRESBYTERIAN
CHURCH
Records, 1859-1931 Ibid.
N: KHi 1 reel
P: KHi
10288

WIMMER, BONIFAZ, Archabbot, 1809-1887
Letters to Angelo Pescitelli, Abbot, 1851-1880
Rome, Abbey of St. Paul outside the Walls
N: KAS 2 reels *
10289

WIMMER, BONIFAZ, Archabbot, 1809-1887
Letters to the Abbots of Metten, 1832-1887,
274 items Germany, Abbey of Metten
N: KAS *
10290

WOLF, INNOCENT, Abbot, 1843-1922
Letters to the Abbots of Metten, 1887-1898,
57 items Germany, Abbey of Metten
N: KAS*
10291

Personal Papers

BALES, ELEAZER
Journal, trip through Kansas and Canada,
1859 priv.
N: PSC-F 1 reel
10292

CRAWFORD, SAMUEL J., 1835-1913
Letters re: Indian affairs, 1889-1891 KU
N: KU 92 frames
10293

CURTIS, SAM S.
Letters, 73 p. CtY
N: KU
10294

DINSMOOR, SILAS
Papers, 1794-1853 NhD
N: KHi 4 reels*
P: KHi
10295

FREY, WILLIAM
Papers, 1869-1881 NN
N: KHi 50 feet
10296

GRIFFING, JAMES SAYRE, 1822-1882, pioneer
missionary
Papers, 1841-1899 KHi
N: KHi 1 reel *
10297

HENNEY, FRED
Scrapbook...82 years in Hutchinson, Kan.,
1871-1953, 498 p. priv.
N: KU
10298

HYATT, THADDEUS, 1816-1901
Papers, 1858-1859, 1875-1876 KHi priv.
N: KHi 3 reels
P: KHi
10299

REINHART, HERMAN F.
Papers and diaries, 1832-1882 KHi
N: KHi 50 feet
P: KHi Or-Ar
10300

Business Papers

GRINTER, MOSES
Account book (Indian trade), 1855-1882 KHi
N: KHi 20 feet
P: KHi
10301

HODGES BROTHERS LUMBER Co.,
Olathe, Kan.
Business records, 1888-1900 KHi
N: KHi 4 reels
P: KHi
10302

MOORE, JOHN THOMAS, storekeeper
Account and inventory book, 1858-1860 priv.
N: KU 92 frames
10303

College Records

WASHBURN COLLEGE, Topeka, Kan.
Records, 1865-1889 KTW
N: KHi 15 feet
P: KHi
10304

Institutions

NEW ENGLAND EMIGRANT AID COMPANY,
Boston
Minutes of Trustees, 1854-1855 KHi
N: KHi 10 feet
P: KHi
10305

NORTHWEST COLONY AND RUSSELL, Kan.,
TOWNSITE COMPANY
Records, 1871-1874 KRu
N: KHi 10 feet
P: KHi
10306

SAC AND FOX CONFEDERATION
Petition to Governor Geary of Kansas for
removal of Agent Burton A. James, as
pre-requisite for treaty with U.S., Feb. 16,
1852, 1 p. KU
N: KU
10307

WISCONSIN COLONY, Russell Co., Kan.
Records, 1871-1874 KRu
N: KHi 10 feet
P: KHi
10308

NEBRASKA

NEBRASKA, see also BEADLE, ERASTUS, 6452, under NEW YORK, Personal Papers

Census

U.S. CENSUS. EIGHTH, 1860
    Population schedules, Nebraska   DNA
    N: DNA 1 reel   10309
    P: USIGS

U.S. CENSUS. NINTH, 1870
    Population schedules, Nebraska   DNA
    N: DNA 2 reels   10310

U.S. CENSUS. TENTH, 1880
    Population schedules, Nebraska   DNA
    N: DNA 15 reels   10311

Government Records

ATKINSON, FORT, Neb.
    Records, 1819-1827 (typescript)   NbHi
    N: NbHi 2 reels   10312

U.S. DEPT. OF STATE
    Territorial papers: Nebraska, 1854-1867   DNA
    N: DNA 1 reel [M-228]   10313
    P: WyU

State Records

CENTRAL NEBRASKA PUBLIC POWER AND
    IRRIGATION DISTRICT
    Project files, 1929-1944   DNA
    N: NbHi 25 reels 16 mm   10314

NEBRASKA. SECRETARY OF STATE
    Motor vehicles register, 1905-1907   Ibid.
    N: NbHi 1 reel   10315

County Records

HARLAN Co., Neb.
    Records   NbOr
    N: NbHi 1 reel   10316

SARPY Co., Neb.
    Documents and maps, 1856-1897   Sarpy
    County Historical Society
    N: NbHi 8 feet   10317

City Records

COLUMBUS, Neb.
    Town records, 1856-1885   Ibid.
    N: NbHi 1 reel   10318

LINCOLN, Neb.   FIRE DEPARTMENT
    Record of fires, 1867-1934   Ibid.
    N: NbHi 1 reel   10319

SEWARD, Neb.
    Ordinances, 1870-1887; proceedings of the
    Town Council, 1870-1877   priv.
    N: NbHi 1 reel   10320

Church Records

AMERICAN HOME MISSIONARY SOCIETY
    Letters and reports re: Nebraska, 1872-1899
    Ibid.
    N: NbHi 1 reel   10321

BAPTISTS. NEBRASKA. STATE CONVENTION
    Records and papers, ca. 1880-1956   Ibid.
    N: NbHi 3 reels   10322

CAMPBELL, Neb.   ZION LUTHERAN CHURCH

History: 50th anniversary, 60th anniversary
    1876-1936   priv.
    N: NbHi 3 feet   10323

CHURCH OF JESUS CHRIST OF LATTER-DAY
    SAINTS. NEBRASKA
    Ward records: Winter Quarters, 1846-1847
    USIC
    N: USIGS 1 reel   10324

CORDOVA, Neb.   ST. JOHN'S EVANGELICAL
    LUTHERAN CHURCH
    Records, 1889-1954   priv.
    N: NbHi 1 reel   10325

NEWMAN GROVE, Neb.   ZION LUTHERAN
    CHURCH
    Records and history, 1880-1949   priv.
    N: NbHi 1 reel   10326

PHILLIPS, Neb.   MONROE EVANGELICAL
    FREE CHURCH
    Records and history, 1887-1956   priv.
    N: NbHi 27 feet   10327

POLK, Neb.   BAPTIST CHURCH
    Church history, 1884-1950   priv.
    N: NbHi 1 foot   10328

POLK, Neb.   FIRST METHODIST CHURCH
    Records and history, 1878-1954   priv.
    N: NbHi 1 reel   10329

POLK, Neb.   SWEDE PLAIN METHODIST
    CHURCH
    Records and history, 1876-1955   priv.
    N: NbHi 1 reel   10330

PRESBYTERIAN CHURCH IN THE U.S.A.
    BOARD OF FOREIGN MISSIONS
    Letters and reports from Nebraska, 1846-1868
    PPPrHi
    N: NbHi 1 reel   10331

PRESBYTERIAN CHURCH IN THE U.S.A.
    PRESBYTERIES. NEBRASKA CITY
    Minutes, 1872-1946   PPPrHi
    N: NbHi 3 reels   10332

PRESBYTERIAN CHURCH IN THE U.S.A.
    SYNODS. NEBRASKA
    Minutes, 1874-1888   NbHi
    N: NbHi 1 reel   10333

SARONVILLE, Neb.   SARON EVANGELICAL
    LUTHERAN CHURCH
    Constitution and minutes, 1872-1932; early
    history of church and community   priv.
    N: NbHi 1 reel   10334

WAKEFIELD, Neb.   SALEM LUTHERAN CHURCH
    Church register, 1882-1956   priv.
    N: NbHi 1 reel   10335

WEST POINT, Neb.   EVANGELICAL CHURCH
    Records, 1871-1926   priv.
    N: NbHi 1 reel   10336

Personal Papers

AVERY, NELLIE (LEECH), 1879-
    Stories of the Avery family   priv.
    N: NbHi 1 reel   10337

DOUGHERTY, JOHN, 1791-1860
    Papers, 1823-1863   MoSHi
    N: NbHi 1 reel   10338

HILL, CHARLES, of Adams Co., Neb.
    Diaries, 1878 and 1888   priv.
    N: NbHi 1 reel   10339

HOAGLAND, HENRY V.
    Letters, etc., 1860-1918   NbHi
    N: NbHi 1 reel   10340

NIELSON, ALFRED JULIUS
    Papers, 1902, 1948   priv.
    N: NbHi 1 foot   10341

PAXSON, Dr. JOSEPH A.
    Diary while physician to the Winnebago
    Indians, 1869-1870   WHi
    N: NbHi 1 reel   P: NbHi   10342

PETERSEN, ERICK JOHN, of Inavale, Neb.,
    1857-1927
    Letters and papers, 1881-1927   priv.
    N: NbHi 6 feet   10343

REYNOLDS, EDGAR
    Diaries, 1852, 1857, 1864-1865   NbHi
    N: NbHi 20 feet   10344

RICKER, ELI S.
    Ricker interviews, tablets 1-30   NbHi
    N: NbHi 3 reels   10345

SMITH, W. EARLE
    Pioneer people of the prairies, 1954   priv.
    N: NbHi 1 reel   10346

College Records

NYSTED PEOPLE'S COLLEGE
    Scrapbook and photograph album   priv.
    N: NbHi 1 reel   10347

Institutions

LINCOLN, Neb.   CHAMBER OF COMMERCE
    Graphs of Lincoln business activity, 1916-1929
    original destroyed
    N: NbHi 1 reel   10348

SOUTH DAKOTA

Census

U.S. CENSUS. NINTH, 1870
    Population schedules, Dakota   DNA
    N: DNA 1 reel   10349

U.S. CENSUS. TENTH, 1880
    Population schedules, Dakota   DNA
    N: DNA 5 reels   10350

Government Records

RANDALL, FORT, S.D.
    Post returns, 1856-1892   DNA
    N: SdU 1 reel*   10351

U.S. DEPT. OF JUSTICE
    Selected records and letters re: Dakota
    Territory, 1871-1884   DNA
    N: SdU 1 reel*   10352

U.S. DEPT. OF THE INTERIOR
    Records and letters re: Dakota Territory:
    Proceedings re: Aberdeen, Dec. 15, 1887;
    correspondence re: removal of capital from
    Yankton to Bismarck   DNA
    N: SdU 1 reel*   10353

Territorial Records

DAKOTA (Ter.). SURVEYOR GENERAL
    Original survey maps, South Dakota   SdHi
    N: SdHi 4 reels*   10354
    P: SdU

Personal Papers

COOK, JOSEPH WITHERSPOON, 1836-1902
    Diaries and letters, 1868-1869, 1875-1885   MnU
    N: SdU 2 reels*   10355

DUGAS, CHARLES
    Letters, 1864, 3 items   SdHi
    DCO: MnHi   10356

GRIMSTEAD, CARL M.
    Memoirs of Dakota Territory, 1870-1887,
    602 p.   priv.
    N: WHi 1 reel   10357

MONTANA

Census

U.S. CENSUS. NINTH, 1870
 Population schedules, Montana DNA
 N: DNA 1 reel   10358
 P: USIGS

U.S. CENSUS. TENTH, 1880
 Agriculture schedules, Montana NcD
 N: NcD 1/4 reel   10359
 P: NNC

U.S. CENSUS. TENTH, 1880
 Population schedules, Montana DNA
 N: DNA 1 reel   10360

Government Records

U.S. DEPT. OF STATE
 Territorial papers: Montana, 1864-1872 DNA
 N: DNA 2 reels [T-254]   10361

U.S. DEPT. OF THE INTERIOR
 Territorial papers: Montana, 1867-1889 DNA
 N: DNA 2 reels [M-192]   10362
 P: WyU

State Records

MONTANA. STATE COLLEGE. AGRICULTURAL
 EXTENSION SERVICE
 Annual narrative and statistical reports from
 state offices and county agents, 1914-1944
 DNA
 N: MtBC 64 reels*   10363

Personal Papers

DUNIWAY, CLYDE AUGUSTUS
 Papers re: the University of Montana, 1908-
 1912 priv.
 N: Or-Ar 3 reels 16 mm.   10364

OWEN, JOHN
 Journal at Fort Owen, Mont., Sept. 1, 1865-
 Jan. 31, 1871 priv.
 DCO: NN   10365

WYOMING

Census

U.S. CENSUS. NINTH, 1870
 Population schedules, Wyoming DNA
 N: DNA 1 reel   10366
 P: USIGS

U.S. CENSUS. TENTH, 1880
 Agriculture schedules, Wyoming NcD
 N: NcD 1/4 reel   10367
 P: NNC

U.S. CENSUS. TENTH, 1880
 Population schedules, Wyoming DNA
 N: DNA 1 reel   10368

Government Records

BRIDGER, FORT
 Post records, 1858-1890 DNA
 N: CU-B 3 reels   10369

RUSSELL, FORT D.A.
 Medical history of Post, 1867-1910, 4 v. Ibid.
 N: WyHi   10370

U.S. ADJUTANT-GENERAL'S OFFICE
 Papers on the "Johnson County War," 1892
 DNA
 N: WyU 1 reel   10371

U.S. DEPT. OF JUSTICE
 Papers on the " Johnson County War," 1892
 DNA
 N: WyU 1 reel   10372

U.S. DEPT. OF STATE
 Territorial papers: Wyoming, 1868-1873 DNA
 N: DNA 1 reel [M-85]   10373
 P: WyU

U.S. DEPT. OF THE INTERIOR
 Records relating to the Yellowstone National
 Park, 1872-1886 DNA
 N: DNA 6 reels [M-62]   10374

U.S. DEPT. OF THE INTERIOR
 Territorial papers: Wyoming, 1878-1890 DNA
 N: DNA 6 reels [M-204]   10375
 P: WyU

U.S. POST OFFICE, Gillette, Wyo.
 Account and record books of postmasters,
 1896-1933, 8 items priv.
 N: WyHi   10376

State Records

WYOMING. BOARD OF CONTROL
 Orders on water rights, 1891-1958, 13 v. Ibid.
 N: WyHi   10377

WYOMING. COMMISSIONER OF PUBLIC LANDS
 General correspondence, 1890-1950, 50 cubic
 feet; miscellaneous land records, 1890-1940,
 6 3/5 cubic feet Ibid. [dest.]
 N: WyHi   10378

WYOMING. GOVERNOR
 Correspondence, 1878-1918, 30 cubic feet
 WyHi
 N: WyHi   10379

WYOMING. LIVE STOCK AND SANITARY BOARD
 Records, including brands, 1899- WyHi Ibid.
 [dest.]
 N: WyHi   10380

WYOMING. SECRETARY OF STATE
 Correspondence on notaries, corporations,
 inquiries, 1880-1910, 10 cubic feet [dest.]
 N: WyHi   10381

WYOMING. STATE ENGINEER
 General correspondence, 1880-1903; letter
 press books, 1888-1910; proofs of
 appropriations of water, 1891- ; water permits,
 1891-1958, 170 v. Ibid.
 N: WyHi   10382

Church Records

CHURCH OF JESUS CHRIST OF LATTER-DAY
 SAINTS. WYOMING
 Branch records: Elkol, Grovont, Oakley,
 Reliance, South Park, Turnerville, Wilson,
 Winton USlC
 N: USIGS 8 reels   10383

CHURCH OF JESUS CHRIST OF LATTER-DAY
 SAINTS. WYOMING
 Stake records: Big Horn USlC
 N: USIGS 14 reels   10384

CHURCH OF JESUS CHRIST OF LATTER-DAY
 SAINTS . WYOMING
 Ward records: Afton, Almy, Auburn, Bedford,
 Cheyenne, Cumberland, Diamondville, Diamond-
 ville-Kemmerer, Etna, Evanston, Fairview,
 Freedom, Green River, Grover, Hilliard, Jack-
 son, Laramie, Lyman, McKinnon, Millburne,
 Mountain View, Osmond, Rock Springs, Smoot,
 Spring Valley, Superior, Thayne USlC
 N: USIGS 44 reels   10385

Personal Papers

BISHOP, ARTEMAS
 Journal, 1823-1825, 37 p. priv.
 N: WyHi   10386

BISHOP, L.C.
 Notebooks and scrapbooks, 8 items priv.
 N: WyHi   10387

BISHOP, SERENO EDWARDS
 Journal, 1839-1840, 32 p. priv.
 N: WyHi   10388

CROSBY, JESSIE W., Jr., of Cowley, Wyo.
 Journals, 1844-1914 priv.
 N: UPB 1 reel   10389
 P: UPB

JENKINS, J. F.
 Autobiography, 102 p. priv.
 N: WyHi 1 reel   10390

MILLER, LESLIE A., Gov. Wyo.
 Autobiographical sketch and public career,
 332 p. priv.
 N: WyHi   10391

NICKERSON, H.G.
 Scrapbook of South Pass area WyHi
 N: WyHi   10392

RIDINGS, PETER JOSEPH
 Diary, Apr., 1859 - Oct., 1860, 31 p. priv.
 N: WyHi   10393

Business Papers

CHENEY, E.F., blacksmith
 Accounts, 1883, 161 p. priv.
 N: WyHi   10394

FUNSTON, JOHN, of Esterbrook, Wyo.
 Journal and account book, 1895-1907,
 394 p. priv.
 N: WyHi   10395

MOORE (J. K.) STORE, Lander, Wyo.
 Ledgers priv.
 N: WyHi 1 reel   10396

Collections

CONVERSE, JAMES W., collector
 Manuscripts, 1800-1895 MH
 N: WyU 1 reel   10397

DAUGHTERS OF THE AMERICAN REVOLUTION.
 WYOMING CHAPTER
 Scrapbooks, 5 items priv.
 N: WyHi 5 reels   10398

FREUND, F.W., collector
 Material re: Freund Brothers rifles,
 1873-1929 priv.
 N: WyHi   10399

MASSIE, HAROLD, collector
 Historical collection priv.
 N: WyHi   10400

WRIGHT, EDWARD, collector
 Historical collection priv.
 N: WyHi   10401

WYOMING HISTORICAL SOCIETY
 Diaries, 1880-1884 priv.
 N: WyHi   10402

Institutions

BEAR CREEK AND GOSHEN HOLE STOCK
 ASSOCIATION, LaGrange, Wyo.
 Minutes, 1895-1908, 36 p. priv.
 N: WyHi   10403

CHEYENNE CLUB, Cheyenne, Wyo.
 Papers, 1880-1951 priv.
 N: WyHi   10404

SIBLEY VALLEY HORSE AND CATTLE
GROWERS ASSOCIATION
Record book, 1902-1918, 180 p.   priv.
N: WyHi   10405

WYOMING FEDERATION OF WOMEN'S CLUBS
Minutes, 1904-1957, 1500 p.   WyHi
N: WyHi   10406

COLORADO

Bibliography

U.S. WORKS PROGRESS ADMINISTRATION.
COLORADO
Inventories of county archives and church
records
N: CoHi 4 reels 1 16 mm.   10407

Census

COLORADO. STATE CENSUS
Agriculture, manufactures, mortality, and
population schedules, 1885   DNA
N: DNA 8 reels [M-158]   10408

COLORADO. STATE CENSUS
Schedules, 1885   County Court Houses
N: CoHi 7 reels   10409

U.S. CENSUS. NINTH, 1870
Agriculture, recapitulation, manufacturing, and
social statistics, Colorado NcD
N: CoHi 1 reel*   10410

U.S. CENSUS. NINTH, 1870
Population schedules, Colorado DNA
N: DNA 1 reel   10411
P: USlGS

U.S. CENSUS. TENTH, 1880
Agriculture, defectives, Colorado NcD
N: CoHi 2 reels*   10412

U.S. CENSUS. TENTH, 1880
Population schedules, Colorado DNA
N: DNA 7 reels   10413

Government Records

U.S. DEPT. OF STATE
Territorial correspondence; Colorado, 1861-
1875 CoHi
N: CoHi 15 reels   10414
P: CoHi

U.S. DEPT. OF STATE
Territorial papers: Colorado, 1859-1874 DNA
N: DNA 1 reel [M-3]   10415
P: CoHi

U.S. FEDERAL CIVIL WORKS ADMINISTRATION
Officials of Denver and Colorado, alphabetical
and chronological indexes, 1858-1933
N: CoHi 2 reels   10416

U.S. OFFICE OF INDIAN AFFAIRS
Records relating to Ute Indians, 1849-1914
DNA
N: CoU   10417

U. S. PRISON INDUSTRIES REORGANIZATION
ADMINISTRATION
Report re: Colorado, 1940 Ibid.
N: CoHi 1 reel   10418

U.S. WORKS PROGRESS ADMINISTRATION.
COLORADO
Report on disposition of unpublished materials
of Writers' Program, 1943
N: CoHi 1 reel   10419

Territorial Records

COLORADO (Ter.). GOVERNOR
Executive proceedings, July-Nov., 1861,

48 items CoHi
N: CoHi 1 reel   10420

COLORADO (Ter.). SUPREME COURT
Territorial book of entry, 1861-1868 CoHi
N: CoHi 1 reel   10421

State Records

COLORADO. ADJUTANT GENERAL'S OFFICE
Civil, Spanish American, and World War I
records, 1861-1930 Ibid.
N: CoHi 8 reels   10422

COLORADO. BOARD OF MEDICAL EXAMINERS
Minutes, 1881-1954 Ibid.
N: CoHi 2 reels   10423

COLORADO. NATIONAL GUARD
Papers re: Ute uprising, 1887-1889 Ibid.
N: CoHi 1 reel   10424

COLORADO. SECRETARY OF STATE
Cattle industry records, 1879-1891 Ibid.
N: CoHi   10425

COLORADO. SECRETARY OF STATE
Incorporation documents - Domestic, 1863-
1916
N: CoHi 1 16mm. reel   10426

COLORADO. STOCK INSPECTION COMMIS-
SIONER
Colorado brands, 1885; brand records, 1915-
1924; report of stock killed by railroads, 1912
N: CoHi 1 reel   10427

County Records

CUSTER Co., Col.
Death records, 1888-1916
N: CoHi 1 reel   10428

LAKE Co., Col.
Militia enrollment, 1879; Leadville plat book,
1895 C.H. Leadville
N: CoHi 1 reel   10429

LARIMER Co., Col.
Proceedings, 1864-1875; brands, 1868-1885;
estray book, 1870-1905; marriage book, 1865-
1896; lode book, 1880-1881; deeds, 1862-1863;
court records, 1864-1871 C.H. Fort Collins
N: CoHi 2 reels   10430

PUEBLO Co., Col.
County court dockets, 1866-1877 C.H. Pueblo
N: CoHi 2 reels 16 mm.   10431

City Records

DENVER, Col.
Plat books, 1868-1933 Ibid.
N: CoHi   10432

DENVER, Col.
Records of annexed towns: Argo, 1883-1903;
Barnum, 1894-1908; Harman, 1886-1895;
Valverde, 1890-1903; Globeville, 1891-1903;
Highlands, 1875-1896; Montclair, 1888-1903;
North Denver and Berkley, 1892-1903; South
Denver, 1886-1894; Westwood, 1845-1847
CoHi
N: CoHi   10433

Church Records

CHURCH OF JESUS CHRIST OF LATTER-DAY
SAINTS. COLORADO
Ward and branch records: Alamosa, Allison,
Cortez, Denver, Durango, Eastdale, Englewood,
Fort Collins, Kline, Manassa, Mancos, Morgan,
Pueblo, Redmesa, Richfield, Romeo, Sanford
USlC
N: USlGS 20 reels   10434

DENVER, Col. ST. JAMES METHODIST
EPISCOPAL CHURCH
Church records Ibid.
N: CoHi 1 reel   10435

Personal Papers

ARGO, J.J., locomotive engineer
Topography down Bear River
N: CoHi 1 reel   10436

BARCLAY, ALEXANDER, 1810-1855
Papers and letters, 1823-1856 priv.
N: CoHi 1 reel   10437

BELL, WILLIAM ABRAHAM, 1841-1926
Papers, 1867-1921 priv.
N: CoHi 4 reels   10438

BENTON, CHARLES S.
Papers, 1853-1873 WHi
N: CoU 1 reel   10439

BLACKMORE, WILLIAM
Papers re: cattle industry NmHi
N: CoHi 3 reels   10440
P: CoHi NNC

BROMWELL, HENRY PELHAM HOLMES, 1823-
1903
Papers, 1869-1909 DLC
N: CoU 532 frames   10441

BYERS, WILLIAM NEWTON, 1831-1903
History of Colorado; newspaper press of
Colorado; the Sandy Creek affair CU-B
N: CoU   10442

CHIVINGTON, Col. J.M.
The First Colorado regiment, 1884, ms.
CU-B
N: CU-B 1 reel   10443
P: CStbS

EICHOLTZ, L.H., engineer
Diaries, 1867-1869 priv.
N: CoHi 1 reel   10444

EVANS, JOHN, 1814-1897
Papers   CoHi
N: CoHi 16 reels   10445
P: CoDU IEN

FREWEN, MORETON, 1853-1924
Papers: Western range cattle industry study...
Western Americana in Europe, v.d.   v.p.
N: CoHi 41 reels   10446
P: NNC

JACKSON, WILLIAM HENRY, 1843-1942
Diaries, 1866-1867, 1873-1874 priv.
N: priv.   1 reel*   10447
P: CU-B CoHi

JOHNSON, (ROLF ?), 1856-
Diaries, 1875-1880 priv.
N: CoHi 1 reel   10448

LAWRENCE, JOHN, 1835-1908,
of Saguache Co., Col.
Diaries, 1867-1907 priv.
N: CoU 1 reel   10449

PACKER, ALFRED, defendant
Court record of first trial, Hinsdale Co.
District Court   Colorado Supreme Court
N: CoHi 1 reel   10450
P: CoHi

PALMER, WILLIAM JACKSON, 1836-1909
Papers, 1853-1919 priv.
N: CoHi 24 reels*   10451
P: PHarH

PERKINS, CHARLES ELLIOTT, 1840-1907
Letter books and letters, 1862-1907 priv.
N: CoHi 23 reels   10452

THOMSON, JAMES, 1834-1882
Diary of residence in Colorado, 1872 priv.
N: CoU   10453

Business Papers

DENVER AND RIO GRANDE R.R.
Calendar of Archives, 1858-1946 Ibid.
N: CoHi 5 reels   10454
P: CoHi

DENVER AND RIO GRANDE R.R.
Locomotive record book, 1880 Ibid.
N: CoHi 1 reel   10455

DENVER AND RIO GRANDE R.R.
Minutes, 1886-1890 Ibid.
N: CoHi 1 reel   10456

DENVER AND RIO GRANDE R.R.
Original directors, 1871-1886 Ibid.
N: CoHi 1 reel 16 mm.   10457

DUPUY, LOUIS, collector
Hotel registers: Hotel de Paris, Brown Palace,
Barton House, 1875-1944 priv.
N: CoHi 6 reels   10458
P: CoHi

FRANCISCO, Col. JOHN M.
Business papers, 1851-1870 priv.
N: CoHi 1 reel   10459
P: CoHi

GREAT BRITAIN. GENERAL REGISTER OFFICE
(Bush House)
Records of companies organized to do business
in Colorado, 1867-1914 Ibid.
N: CoHi 47 reels   10460

JACKSON, W. S.
Correspondence re: Denver and Rio Grande
R.R., 1885-1886
N: CoHi 1 reel   10461

RIDGWAY, (ARTHUR?)
Diary re: Moffat R.R., 1904-1905
N: CoHi 1 reel   10462

RIDGWAY, ARTHUR
History of the Denver and Rio Grande R.R.,
1921
N: CoHi 1 reel   10463

SCOTLAND. GENERAL REGISTER HOUSE
Records of companies organized to do business
in Colorado, 1878-1904 Ibid.
N: CoHi 2 reels   10464

UNION PACIFIC R.R.
Historical data re: John D. Perry KHi
N: CoHi 1 reel   10465

Collections

COLORADO. STATE HISTORICAL SOCIETY
Records, 1887-1949 CoHi
N: CoHi 11 reels 2 16 mm.   10466

Institutions

COLORADO. AGRICULTURAL AND MECHANICAL
COLLEGE, Fort Collins
Reports and proceedings of the various groups
which preceded and evolved into the Great
Plains Agricultural Council CoGA
N: NNC 3 reels   10467

DENVER, Col. RIVERSIDE CEMETERY
Burials, 1876-1952 Ibid.
N: USIGS 1 reel   10468

NEW MEXICO

Census

U.S. CENSUS. SEVENTH, 1850
Population schedules, New Mexico DNA
N: DNA 1 reel   10469
P: USIGS

U.S. CENSUS. EIGHTH, 1860
Population schedules, New Mexico DNA
N: DNA 1 reel   10470
P: USIGS

U.S. CENSUS. NINTH, 1870
Population schedules, New Mexico DNA
N: DNA 1 reel   10471

U.S. CENSUS. TENTH, 1880
Population schedules, New Mexico DNA
N: DNA 1 reel   10472

Government Records

U.S. ADJUTANT-GENERAL'S OFFICE
Albuquerque, N.M., Post returns, 1846-1867
DNA
N: DNA 1 reel   10473

U.S. ADJUTANT-GENERAL'S OFFICE
Index to compiled service records of Volunteer
Union soldiers from the Territory of New Mexico
DNA
N: DNA 4 reels 16 mm. [M-242]   10474

U.S. BUREAU OF LAND MANAGEMENT
Papers re: New Mexico land grants Ibid.
N: NmU 66 reels
P: AzU CSmH CU-B   10475

U.S. COURT OF CLAIMS
Private land claims: Santa Fé, New Mexico
Territory. Trial of James Addison Reavis:
Exhibits AAA and BBB, Royal Patent, also
wills, codicils, and certified copy of posses-
sion given to Don Miguel de Peralta de la Cor-
doba; Justice of the Peace Record Book,
Apache Co., 1883-1886 Ibid.
N: Az-Ar 1 reel   10476

U.S. GENERAL LAND OFFICE
Records of Arizona and New Mexico Private
Land Claims DNA
N: CU-B 2 reels   10477

U.S. DEPT. OF STATE
Territorial papers: New Mexico, 1851-1872
DNA
N: DNA 4 reels [T-17]   10478

U.S. DEPT. OF THE INTERIOR
Records of the New Mexico Superintendency of
Indian Affairs, 1849-1873 DNA
N: DNA 30 rolls [T-21]   10479

U.S. WAR DEPT.
Records of U.S. Army Commands and of the
Adjutant General's Office re: Camp Ojo
Caliente, N.M., 1877-1882 DNA
N: DNA 1 reel [T-258]   10480

State Records

NEW MEXICO. ADJUTANT GENERAL
Muster rolls, 1883-1886, 13 items Ibid.
DCO: NmSM   10481

NEW MEXICO. ADJUTANT GENERAL
Papers re: outlawry in Rio Arriba County,
1881-1882, 65 items NmSM
DCO: NmSM   10482

NEW MEXICO. ADJUTANT GENERAL
Records, 1862-1898 Ibid.
N: Ibid. 5 reels   10483
P: NmSM

NEW MEXICO. HISTORICAL SOCIETY
Militia file, selections re: Civil War and
Indian Campaigns, 1854-1884, 27 items
NmSM
DCO: NmSM   10484

Local Records

LA PAZ, N.M. RECORDER
Claims and deeds, book 1, Oct., 1862-March,
1863, 169 claims Ibid.
N: Az-Ar   10485

Church Records

CHURCH OF JESUS CHRIST OF LATTER-DAY
SAINTS. NEW MEXICO
Ward and branch records: Animas, Aztec,
Bloomfield, Bluewater, Columbus, Farmington,

Gila, Hachita, Jewett, Kirtland, Las Cruces,
Lordsburg, Luna, Ramah, Virden USlC
N: USIGS 16 reels   10486

SANTA BARBARA MISSION, Cal.
Papers re: New Mexico, 1712-1811 (circular
letters, mission census of 1811), 6 items Ibid.
DCO: NmSM   10487

SANTA FE (Archdiocese)
Documents re: martyrdom of the Franciscans,
1692-1696; vital records, 1694-1846, 16 items
Ibid.
DCO: NmSM   10488

Personal Papers

ALVAREZ, MANUEL
Correspondence and papers, 1833-1862 NmHi
N: CU-B 4 reels   10489

ALVAREZ, MANUEL
Papers, including those of Donaciano Vigil
NmSM
N: NmU 4 reels   10490
P: NmSM

BENT, CHARLES, 1797-1847
Correspondence, 1839-1846 priv.
N: NmU 1 reel   10491
P: NmSM

CARLETON, JAMES HENRY, 1814-1873
Letters to Bigelow Bros. and Kennard, 1850-
1857 priv.
N: NmU 1 reel   10492

CHAVEZ, FELIPE, merchant and banker
Papers, 1861-1892, 23 items NmSM
DCO: NmSM   10493

EVANS, JOAN
Diary, July-Sept., 1853 priv.
N: NmU 1 reel   10494

GWYNN, JOHN, attorney
Papers re: Albert H. Pfeiffer, 36 items
NmSM
DCO: NmSM   10495

HAGERMAN, HERBERT J., 1871-1935
Papers priv.
N: NmU 1 reel   10496

PEREA FAMILY, of New Mexico
Papers, 1614-1897, 171 ff. priv.
DCO: NmSM   10497

VILLEGUTIERRE Y SOTOMAYOR, JUAN DE
Historia de la Conquista, Perdida y Res-
tauración de el Reyno y Provincia de la
Nueba Mexico SpBN
N: DLC 224 feet   10498
P: NmSM
PP: DLC

Collections

GARDESKY, MARTIN, collector
Spanish language documents re: New Mexico,
1612-1764, 27 items NmSM
DCO: NmSM   10499

NEW MEXICO. HISTORICAL SOCIETY
New Mexico Archives collection, 1600-1825,
1755 ff. MxAGN priv.
DCO: NmSM   10500

RITCH, WILLIAM GILLET, 1830-1904,
collector
Ritch papers concerning the history of New
Mexico, ca. 1539-1885 CSmH
N: NmU 10 reels   10501

ARIZONA

Census

ARIZONA (Ter.)
Census records, 1864, 1866, 1867, 1876, 1882
Ibid.
N: Az-Ar 4 reels   10502

U.S. CENSUS. NINTH, 1870
Population schedules, Arizona   DNA
N: DNA 1 reel   10503
P: USIGS

U.S. CENSUS. TENTH, 1880
Population schedules, Arizona   DNA
N: DNA 2 reels   10504

Government Records

BOWIE, FORT, Ariz.
Records, 1862-1894   DNA
N: DNA 5 reels   10505
P: AzU

U.S. ARMY. 6th INFANTRY
Unit returns, Jan.-May, 1859   DNA
DCO: AzFM*   10506

U.S. BUREAU OF LAND MANAGEMENT.
PHOENIX LAND OFFICE
Documents re: Peralta grant   Ibid.
N: AzU 1 reel   10507

U.S. DEPT. OF STATE
Territory of Arizona election returns,
1864-1866   Ibid.
N: Az-Ar 1 reel   10508

U.S. GENERAL LAND OFFICE
Records. Arizona private land claim docket
18; Peralta land grant claims   DNA
N: AzU 1 reel   10509

U.S. GENERAL LAND OFFICE. ARIZONA
AND NEW MEXICO DISTRICTS
Records, 1856-1888; letters received, 1856-
1888 Federal Records Center, Annex,
Wilmington, Cal.
N: CLU 7 reels   10510
P: AzU CU-B

U.S. WAR DEPT.
Correspondence on Mohave Indian attack on
emigrant train, autumn, 1859   DNA
DCO: AzFM*   10511

Territorial Records

ARIZONA (Ter.)
Prison records, 1875-1918   Ibid.
N: Az-Ar 6 reels   10512

ARIZONA (Ter.). DISTRICT COURT. SECOND
DISTRICT (Gila Co.)
Territory of Arizona v. Kid, Hale, Say-es,
and Pash-ten-tah. Indictment, Oct. 25, 1889,
19p. Ibid.
N: Az-Ar   10513

Church Records

CHURCH OF JESUS CHRIST OF LATTER-DAY
SAINTS. ARIZONA
Ward and branch records: Alpine, Artesia,
Ashurst, Avondale, Binghampton, Bisbee,
Buckeye, Byce, Chandler, Clay Springs,
Central, Clifton, Coolidge, Douglas, Duncan,
Eager, Eden, Elfrida, Flagstaff, Franklin,
Fredonia, Gilbert, Glendale, Globe, Graham,
Greer, Hayden, Heber, Holbrook, Joseph
City, Kingman, Lakeside, Lebanon, Lehi,
Linden, Littlefield, Mathews, McNary, Mesa,
Misimi, Moccasin, Morenci, Mount Trumbull,
Nephi, Nutrioso, Papago, Phoenix, Pima,

Pine, Pinedale, Pomerene, Ray, Safford, St.
David, St. John's, Scottsdale, Showlow, Shum-
way, Snowflake, Solomonsville, Taylor, Tempe,
Thacher, Tuba City, Tucson, Vernon, Winslow,
Woodruff, York USlC
N: USIGS 103 reels   10514

Personal Papers

ASHURST, HENRY FOUNTAIN, 1874-1937
Correspondence, 1919-1940; diary, 1910-1937,
1164 p. DLC
N: AzU*   10515

COLEMAN, CLAUDE C., M.D.
Papers, correspondence, material re: doctors
of the Gadsden Purchase   priv.
N: Az-Ar 1 reel   10516

DORR, L. L.
Letter to Dr. Geo. P. Hanawalt, Nov. 24, 1869,
2p. priv.
N: Az-Ar   10517

DOUGLASS, ANDREW E., and DAVIS, H.
FAUREST
Southwestern photographic ring sequence,
1939 AzU [Tree Laboratory]
N: AzU 32 feet   10518
P: AzFM

FISH, JOSEPH, 1840-1926
Fish manuscript (Arizona history), 1906
4 v., 762 p. priv.
N: Az-Ar 1 reel   10519
P: UPB

FLOYD, WILLIAM
Diary, Fort Smith, Ark., to Colorado River,
1858-1859 DNA
N: AzFM 25 feet*   10520

GREER, GILBERT DUNLAP, 1860-1895
Journal and sketches, 1879-1895, 219p. priv.
N: Az-Ar   10521

HOFFMAN, Major J.
Letters sent by Department of the Pacific
re: Colorado River Expedition, Jan.-May,
1859 DNA
N: AzFM 8 feet*   10522

JAEGER, LOUIS J.F.
Diary and records, 1854-1892
N: AzU*   10523

JENNEY, WILLIAM LeBARON, 1832-1907
Papers, 1885-1926, and Civil War scrapbook
priv.
N: ICU 725 frames   10524
P: AzFM

LORING, GEORGE
Diary, letters, 1876 AzTP
N: CSmH 50 feet*   10525
P: AzFM

McGEE, W. J., 1853-1912
Note books and itinerary, Papago and Seriland
expeditions, 1894-1895 DLC
N: AzU 2 reels   10526

McGEHEE, MICAJAH
Extract from diary, 1848 priv.
DCO: DLC   10527

UDALL, DAVID K., defendant
Transcript of testimony on indictment for
perjury, U.S. vs. Udall, Aug. 3-5, 1885
N: Az-Ar   10528

UTAH

Census

U.S. CENSUS. SEVENTH, 1850
Population schedules, Utah   DNA
N: DNA 1 reel   10529
P: USIGS

U.S. CENSUS. EIGHTH, 1860
Population schedules, Utah   DNA
N: DNA 1 reel   10530
P: USIGS

U.S. CENSUS. NINTH, 1870
Population schedules, Utah   DNA
N: DNA 1 reel   10531
P: USIGS

U.S. CENSUS. TENTH, 1880
Population schedules, Utah   DNA
N: DNA 16 reels   10532

Government Records

FLOYD, CAMP, Utah
Account book, 1858-1859, 383 p. priv.
N: UPB   10533

U.S. ADJUTANT - GENERAL'S OFFICE
Payrolls and miscellaneous papers re: Utah
rolls, 1953 DNA
N: UPB   10534

U.S. DEPT. OF STATE
Territorial papers: Utah, 1853-1873 DNA
N: DNA 2 reels [M-12]   10535
P: UHi

U.S. NATIONAL GUARD BUREAU
Annual returns of militia, Territory of Utah,
1851-1853 DNA
N: UPB   10536

U.S. RELOCATION CENTER, Topaz, Utah
Records, 1943 Ibid.
N: CU 1 reel   10537

U.S. RELOCATION CENTER, Topaz, Utah
Topaz clinical records book, 1943-1944,
152 p. Ibid.
N: UPB   10538

U.S. WAR DEPT. ORDNANCE DEPT.
Ledger re: arming and equipping the militia,
1851-1868, 1877-1884 R.G.156 DNA
N: UPB   10539

State Records

UTAH
Brand book, 1849-1874
N: CoHi   10540

County Records

DAVIS Co., Utah
Marriage licenses, 1888-1941 C.H. Farming-
ton
N: USIGS 12 reels   10541

MILLARD Co., Utah
Court minute books, 1852-1866 USlC
N: USIGS 1 reel   10542

City Records

FILLMORE, Utah
City docket, 1882- , 2 v. Ibid.;
(transcript) UPB
N: UPB 1 reel   10543

MANTI, Utah. CITY COUNCIL
Minutes, 1851-1870, 80 p. USlC
N: Ibid.   10544
P: UPB

MILFORD, Utah
School register, n.d., 11p. USlC
N: USIGS 1 reel   10545

OGDEN, Utah
Poll tax register, 1886-1918 Ibid.
N: USIGS 4 reels   10546

ORDERVILLE, Utah
Histories of early pioneers, n.d. (typescript)
USlC
N: USIGS 1 reel   10547

PROVO, Utah
Book of remembrance, pedigree charts, and family group sheets   USIC
N: USIGS 1 reel   10548

PROVO, Utah
Early history and records, 1849-1875   USIC
N: USIGS 1 reel   10549

ST. GEORGE, Utah
Miscellaneous material   USIC
N: UPB 1 reel   10550
P: UPB

SALT LAKE, Utah
Vital records, 1848-1950   Vital Statistics Office
N: USIGS 106 reels   10551

SANDY, Utah
Cemetery records, 1883-1952, 59 p.   Ibid.
N: USIGS 1 reel   10552

VERNAL CITY, Utah
Sexton's record, 1879-1953 (typescript)   USIC
N: USIGS 1 reel   10553

Church Records

BEAR RIVER CITY, Box Elder Co., Utah
Sextons' records of interments, ca. 1868-1956   USIC
N: USIGS 1 reel   10554

CHURCH OF JESUS CHRIST OF LATTER-DAY SAINTS
Missionary records, 1860-1950   USIC
N: USIGS 5 reels   10555

CHURCH OF JESUS CHRIST OF LATTER-DAY SAINTS
Nauvoo and Utah sealing record, 1846-1857   USIC
N: USIGS 1 reel   10556

CHURCH OF JESUS CHRIST OF LATTER-DAY SAINTS. CHURCH HISTORIAN'S OFFICE, Salt Lake City
The Book of Pioneers re: those who arrived in the Valley of the Great Salt Lake, 1847; pioneers' biographies (typescript)   Ibid.
N: USIGS 2 reels   10557

CHURCH OF JESUS CHRIST OF LATTER-DAY SAINTS. CHURCH HISTORIAN'S OFFICE, Salt Lake City
Persons killed and wounded in Indian raids in Utah, 1850-1868; missionary records, 1860-1868, 36 p.   USIC
N: USIGS   10558

CHURCH OF JESUS CHRIST OF LATTER-DAY SAINTS. ENDOWMENT HOUSE
Sealing record, 1851-1889; baptisms for the dead, 1857-1876; endowments for the living, 1851-1854   USIC
N: USIGS 21 reels   10559

CHURCH OF JESUS CHRIST OF LATTER-DAY SAINTS. LIVERPOOL OFFICE
L.D.S. emigrants from the British Isles and other European countries to Utah, 1849-1924   USIC
N: USIC 6 reels   10560
P: USIGS

CHURCH OF JESUS CHRIST OF LATTER-DAY SAINTS. LOGAN TEMPLE
Sealings of dead couples, 1884-1901; living sealings, 1884-1900; sealings of children to parents, 1884-1902; baptisms for the dead, 1884-1900   USIC
N: USIGS 31 reels   10561

CHURCH OF JESUS CHRIST OF LATTER-DAY SAINTS. MANTI TEMPLE
Sealings of dead couples, 1888-1905; sealings of children to parents and adoptions, 1888-1903; baptisms for the dead, 1888-1900; endowments for the dead, 1908-1911
N: USIGS 26 reels   10562

CHURCH OF JESUS CHRIST OF LATTER-DAY SAINTS. NAUVOO TEMPLE
Baptisms for the dead, 1840-1844   USIC
N: USIGS 1 reel   10563

CHURCH OF JESUS CHRIST OF LATTER-DAY SAINTS. NETHERLANDS MISSION
Records of emigrants sailing from Rotterdam via Liverpool, Eng., to Utah, 1904-1914   USIC
N: USIC 1 reel   10564
P: USIGS

CHURCH OF JESUS CHRIST OF LATTER-DAY SAINTS. QUORUM OF THE SEVENTY
Record of first Seventy Elders, 1835, 1836; record of members, 1844-1900   USIC
N: USIGS   10565

CHURCH OF JESUS CHRIST OF LATTER-DAY SAINTS. QUORUM OF THE SEVENTY
Records, n. d.   Ibid.
N: USIGS 1 reel   10566

CHURCH OF JESUS CHRIST OF LATTER-DAY SAINTS. ST. GEORGE TEMPLE
Sealings of dead couples, 1877-1908; living sealings, 1877-1903; adoptions and sealings of children to parents, 1889-; baptisms of the dead, 1877-1903   USIC
N: USIGS 40 reels   10567

CHURCH OF JESUS CHRIST OF LATTER-DAY SAINTS . SALT LAKE TEMPLE
Sealings (living and dead) of children to parents, 1893-1943; sealings of dead couples, 1893-1941; baptisms for the dead, 1893-1941   USIC
N: USIGS 420 reels   10568

CHURCH OF JESUS CHRIST OF LATTER-DAY SAINTS. SCANDINAVIAN MISSION
Records of emigrants from Denmark, Norway, and Sweden to Utah, 1854-1896, 1901-1920   USIC
N: USIC 1 reel   10569
P: USIGS

CHURCH OF JESUS CHRIST OF LATTER-DAY SAINTS. UTAH
Branch records: American Fork, Arsenal, Birdseye, Bonanza, Branch for the Deaf, Burmeister, Callao, Campus, Cedar Creek, Columbia, Deep Creek, Deseret, Diamond, Divident, Dragerton, Evans, Fruitland, Garrison, Gordon Creek, Greenwood, Grover, Heber, Iosepa, Lockerby, Manti, Mexican, Moorland, Ophir, Rains, Rolapp, Sahara, Stadium Village, Standardsville, Stoddard, Terrace, Tod Park, Topaz, West Tintic, West Warren, Wymount   USIC
N: USIGS 29 reels   10570

CHURCH OF JESUS CHRIST OF LATTER-DAY SAINTS. UTAH
Stake records: Alpine, Bear River, Beaver, Ben Lomond, Benson, Bonneville, North Box Elder, Smithfield, South Bear River   USIC
N: USIGS 196 reels   10571

CHURCH OF JESUS CHRIST OF LATTER-DAY SAINTS. UTAH
Ward records: Abraham, Airport, Alton, Altonah, Annabella, Antimony, Arbor, Arcadia, Argyle, Ashley, Aurora, Avon, Axtell, Ballard, Beacon, Belvedere, Benjamin, Benmore, Bennet, Bennison, Benson, Big Cottonwood, Bingham, Blanding, Bluebell, Bluff, Bluffdale, Boneta, Bonnerville, Boulder, Bountiful, Bridgeland, Brigham, Brighton, Brooklyn, Browning, Bryan, Burrville, Burton, Butler, Caineville, Cannon, Cannonville, Capitol Hill, Carbonville, Castle Dale, Castlegate, Cedar, Cedar City, Cedarfield, Cedarview, Center, Centerville, Central, Central Park, Charleston, Chester, Circleville, Clarion, Clawson, Clear Creek, Clearfield, Cleveland, Clinton, Clover, Cluff, Coalville, Colonial Hills, College, Columbia, Copperton, Cottonwood, Crescent, Croyden, Cummings, Daniel, Davis, Delta, Deseret, Draper, Duchesne, Duncan, East Bountiful, East Midvale, East Mill Creek, East Porterville, Echo, Eden, Edgehill, Edgemont, Edison, Elberta, Eldredge, Elkhorn, Elmo, Elsinore, Emerson, Emery, Emmigration, Enoch, Ensign, Enterprise, Ephraim, Erda, Escalante, Eureka, Evergreen, Fairmount, Fairview, Farmington, Far West, Fayette, Ferron, Filmore, Flowell, Forest Dale, Fountain Green, Freedom, Fremont, Garden View, Garfield, Geneva, Genola, Glendale, Granger, Grant, Grantsville, Grass Creek, Grayson, Greenriver, Grouse Creek, Grove, Gunlock, Gunnison, Hamilton, Hanksville, Hanna, Harrisville, Harvard, Hatch, Haven,

Hawthorne, Hayden, Heber, Hebron, Helper, Henefer, Henrieville, Herriman, Hiawatha, Highland, Highland Park, Hillcrest, Hill Crest, Hinkley, Holden, Holladay, Huntsville, Hurricane, Hyde Park, Hyrum, Imperium, Indianola, Ioka, Ivins, Jefferson, Jensen, Johnson, Jordan Park, Joseph, Juab, Junction, Kamas, Kanab, Kannara, Kannesville, Kanosh, Kaysville, Kenilworth, Kingston, Knightsville, Koosharem, Lake Point, Lake Shore, Lake View, Lamond View, Lapoint, Lark, La Sal, Laurelcrest, La Verkin, Lawrence, Layton, Leamington, Leeds, Le Grand, Lehi, Leland, Leota, Levan, Liberty, Lincoln, Loa, Logan, Lorraine, Lyman, Lynndyl, Maeser, Magna, Mammoth, Manavu, Manila, Manti, Manuta, Mapleton, Marlborough, Marrion, Marriot, Marysville, Mayfield, McCormick, McKay, McKinley, Meadow, Mendon, Mercur, Middleton, Midvale, Midway, Milburn, Mill Creek, Miller, Millville, Milton, Moab, Moffat, Molen, Mona, Monroe, Monticello, Montwell, Morgan, Moroni, Moulton, Mount Carmel, Mount Emmons, Mount Fort, Mount Ogden, Mount Olympus, Mount Pleasant, Mount Sterling, Mount View, Mountain Dell, Mountain Green, Mountain Home, Mountainville, Murray, Myton, Naples, Neola, Nephi, New Castle, New Harmony, Nibley, Nibley Park, North Escalante, North Logan, North Morgan, North Point, Oak City, Oak Hills, Oakville, Oasis, Ogden, Olympus, Orangeville, Orderville, Palmyra, Palmyra (Old), Panguitch, Paradise, Paragonah, Park, Park Avenue, Park City, Parley's, Parley's Park, Parowan, Payson, Peca, Perry, Peterson, Pine Valley, Pinto, Pioneer, Plain City, Pleasant Green, Pleasant Valley, Pleasant View, Poplar Grove, Portage, Porterville, Price, Princeton, Providence, Provo, Randlett, Randolph, Redmond, Richards, Richfield, Richville, Riverdale, Rivergrove, River Heights, Riverside, Riverton, Riverview, Rochester, Rockport, Rockville, Roosevelt, Rosecrest, Rosslyn Heights, Roy, St. George, St. John, Salem, Salina, Sandy, Santa Clara, Sataquin, Scipio, Scofield, Sevier, Sharon, Sigurd, Silver City, Slaterville, Slide, Smith, Soldier Summit, South Cottonwood, South Escalante, Southgate, South Jordan, South Weber, Spanish Fork, Spencer, Spring City, Springdale, Spring Glenn, Spring Lake, Spring View, Springville, Sterling, Stockton, Storrs, Stratford, Strawberry, Sugar House, Sugarville, Summit, Sunset, Sunnyside, Sutherland, Syracuse, Tabiona, Talmadge Taylor, Taylorsville, Teasdale, Thistle, Thurber, Timpanogas, Tooele, Toquerville, Torrey, Tridell, Tropic, Uintah, Union, University, Upalco, Upton, Utahn, Valley Center, Valley View, Venice, Vermont, Vernal, Vermillion, Vernon, Veyo, Victor, Vinyard, Virgin, Wales, Wallsburg, Wandamere, Wanship, Warren, Wasatch, Washakie, Washington, Waterloo, Webster, Wellington, Wells, Wellsville, Wendover, West Ensign, West Jordan, West Point, West Porterville, West Weber, Whiterocks, Whittier, Widstsaoe, Wilford, Willard, Wilson, Winder, Woodland, Woodruff, Woods Cross, Young, and 1st through 29th, 31st, 32nd, 34th, 67th, 80th Wards   USIC
N: USIGS 931 reels   10572

PRESBYTERIAN CHURCH IN THE U.S.A. SYNODS. UTAH
Minutes, 1900-1911   Ibid.
N: PPPrHi 1 reel   10573

PROVO, Utah. CHURCH OF JESUS CHRIST OF LATTER-DAY SAINTS
Business meetings, bishops and lesser priesthood, 1868-1875, 184 p.   Ibid.
N: USIGS   10574
P: UPB

REORGANIZED CHURCH OF JESUS CHRIST OF LATTER-DAY SAINTS. PROTESTING GROUP
Protest movement records, 1925-1927   Independence, Mo.
N: UPB   10575
P: UPB

SPAULDING, SOLOMON
The Solomon Spaulding manuscript re: Book of Mormon   OO
DCO: ?   10576
N: UPB
P: UPB

SPRINGVILLE, Utah. CHURCH OF JESUS
CHRIST OF LATTER-DAY SAINTS
Ward historical book, 1851-1875 Ibid.
N: ?
P: UPB   10577

Personal Papers

BEAN, GEORGE WASHINGTON, b. 1831
Papers   priv.
N: UPB 1 reel   10578
P: UPB

BIERBOWER, V.
Speech as Assistant U.S. District Attorney in
U.S. vs. Lorenzo Snow (polygamy case), 11 p.
MH
N: UPB   10579
P: UPB

BINGHAM, ERASTUS
Account book (while bishop), 1834-1852, and
other papers USlC
N: UPB 1 reel   10580
P: UPB

BLACKBURN, ELIAS H.
Journals and letters, 1849-1907 UHi
N: UHi 2 reels   10581
P: UHi

BOULTER, GRACE (FOUTZ)
Typescript re: Bishop Jacob Foutz, Sr., and
the Haun's Mill Massacre, n.d., 32 p.   priv.
N: UPB   10582

BROCKBANK, ISAAC, 1837-1927
Autobiography, 82 p. priv.
N: UPB   10583
P: UPB

CALL, ANSON, 1810-1890
Life and record, 1839- ca. 1872 priv.
N: priv. 1 reel   10584
P: UHi

CARD, CHARLES O., 1839-1906
Journal, memoranda books, 1871-1872, 1877-
1883 ULCHi
N: ULCHi   10585
P: UHi

CARPENTER, J. HATTEN, b. 1861
Journal, 1883-1885, 141 p.   priv.
N: UPB 1 reel   10586
P: UPB

CLAYTON, WILLIAM, 1814-1879
Letter books, 1860-1885 (continued by Nephi
Clayton after 1879): 1860-1869 CtY; 1869-
1885 UHi
N: CtY 1 reel (1860-1869) UHi 1 reel (1869-
    1885)   10587
P: UHi 2 reels

CLUFF, HARVEY HARRIS, 1836-1916
Autobiography, 2 v. priv.
N: UPB 1 reel   10588
P: UPB

CLYMAN, JAMES S., 1792-1881
Journals, 1844-1846 C SmH
N: CSmH 5 feet   10589
P: UHi

COWDERY, OLIVER
Letters, 1833-1838, 1846, 96 p. CSmH
N: CSmH   10590
P: UPB

CUMMING, ALFRED, Gov. Utah, 1802-1873
Papers re: governorship of Utah, 1857-1860 NcD
N: UPB 1 reel   10591
P: UHi UPB

DELLENBAUGH, FREDERICK S., 1853-1936
Journal, 1871-1873 NN
N: NN 10 feet   10592
P: UHi

EGAN, HOWARD, 1815-1878
Diary, Apr.-Sept., 1847 CtY
N: CtY 1 reel*   10593
P: UHi

HANSEN, PETER
Journal, 1865-1872 UHi
N: UHi 1 reel   P: UHi   10594

HASKELL FAMILY
Letters, 1845-1854 priv.
N: ? 1 reel   10595
P: UHi

HATCH, LORENZO HILL, 1826-1910
Journal, 1855-1885 priv.
N: UPB 1 reel   10596
P: UPB

HINCKLEY, IRA NATHANIEL, 1824-1910
Diary and other papers, 110 p. priv.
N: UPB   10597

HOVEY, M.R., Secretary, Logan Chamber of
Commerce
Early history of Cache Co., Utah, 195 p.   USlC
N: USlC 1 reel   10598
P: USlGS

IVINS, ANTHONY W., 1852-1934
Diary I, 1875-1882 priv.
N: priv. 1 reel   10599
P: UHi

JAMES, JOHN, 1864-1954
Diary, 1889-1891 UHi
N: UHi 1 reel   10600
P: UHi

JONES, A. WILL
Diary, 1903-1953, 2 v. priv.
N: UPB 1 reel   10601
P: UPB

JONES, ALBERT, 1839-1925
Autobiography and diary, 1881-1924, 282 p.
priv.
N: UPB 1 reel   10602
P: UPB

JONES, JOHN PIDDING, b. 1819
Biography priv.
N: UPB   10603
P: UPB

JONES, KUMAN
Historical notes re: early pioneer settlements
San Juan Co., Utah, from 1878 (typescript)
USlC
N: USlGS 1 reel   10604

JONES, MARGARET
Relief Society's book (Johnson Springs),
1882-1890 priv.
N: UPB 1 reel   10605
P: UPB

JONES, STEPHEN V.
Diary, Jan.-Feb., 1872 NN
N: NN 1 reel*   10606
P: UHi

LARPENTEUR, CHARLES, 1803?-1872
Journal, 1834-1872, 3 v.   MnHi
N: MnHi 1 reel   10607
P: UHi

LEE, JOHN DOYLE, 1812-1877
Journal, Mar., 1842-Aug., 1843 [unk.]
N: ? 1 reel   10608
P: UHi

LEE, JOHN DOYLE, 1812-1877, defendant
Trials for Mountain Meadows Massacre in
Utah Territorial Court Ibid.
N: UPB 4 reels   10609
P: UPB

LEGLER, HENRY E., 1861-1917
Papers re: James Jesse Strang, ca. 1840-
ca. 1904 WHi
N: WHi 1 reel*   10610
P: UHi

LUNT, HENRY
Journal and account books   priv.
N: UPB   10611

LYMAN, ELIZA M. PARTRIDGE (SMITH),
1820-1885
Diary, 1846-1885; autobiography, 1820-
1885 UPB
N: UPB 1 reel*   10612
P: UHi

LYMAN, FRANCIS MARION, b. 1863
Diaries, 1884-1915, 9 v. priv.
N: UPB   P: UPB   10613

McALLISTER, JOHN D. T., of St. George, Utah
Journals, 1876-1885 priv.
N: UPB 1 reel   10614
P: UPB

McNEIL, THOMAS
Diary, 1872-1877, 2v. priv.
N: UPB 1 reel   10615
P: UPB

MITCHELL, HEZEKIAL, 1810-1872
Journal, 1845-1848 ULCHi
N: ULCHi 1 reel   10616
P: UHi

NEWCOMB, SILAS
Journal, July 8-16, 1850 priv.
N: UHi 1 reel   10617
P: UHi

PARKINSON, WILLIAM C.
Journal, 1879-1882, 4 v. priv.
N: UPB 1 reel   10618
P: UPB

PHELPS, JOHN WALCOTT
Diary, Jan. 2-Mar. 11, 1858 NN
N: NN 1 reel   10619
P: UHi

PRATT, ORVILLE C., 1819-1891
Diary, ca. 1844- CtY
N: CtY 1 reel*   10620
P: UHi

RUSSELL, OSBORNE, 1814-1892
Journal, 1834-1843 CtY
N: CtY 1 reel*   10621
P: UHi

SAVAGE, LEVI MATHERS, 1851-1935
Diary, 2 v. priv.
N: UPB   10622
P: UPB

SHIRES, WILLIAM
Diary, 1862-1866 priv.
N: UHi 1 reel   10623
P: UHi

SMITH, E. WILLARD
Journal, 1839   CoHi
N: CoHi 1 reel   10624
P: UHi

SMITH, ELIAS, 1804-1888
Journals, 1836-1888 CSmH
N: CSmH 2 reels   10625
P: UHi

SMOOT, ABRAHAM OWEN, b. 1815
Scrapbook re: Provo priv.
N: UPB 1 reel   10626
P: UPB

SMOOT, MARGARET S.
Experiences of a Mormon wife, Provo, 1880,
9 p. CU
N: UPB   10627

SNOW, ELIZA ROXCY, 1804-1887
Diary, 1846-1849 priv.
N: UHi 1 reel   10628
P: UHi

STEWART, EUNICE
Diary (Provo), 1855-1858 priv.
N: UPB   10629
P: UPB

STOUT, HOSEA, 1810-1889
Autobiography, 1845-1861 UHi
N: UHi 1 reel   10630
P: UHi

SVENDSEN, KNUD
Journal, 1857-1900 priv.
N: priv. 1 reel   10631
P: UHi

TALBOT, THEODORE, d. 1862
Diaries, 1843-1852 DLC
N: DLC 1 reel*   10632
P: UHi

THATCHER, MOSES, b. 1842
Journals, 1866-1881 priv.
N: UHi 1 reel   10633
P: UHi

TUTTLE, NEWTON, 1825-1907

Journal: account book, Sept. 7, 1848-Apr. 3,
1854; diary, 1852-1860 UHi
N: UHi 1 reel
P: UHi   10634

WADDOUPS, THOMAS ANSON, 1876-
Biographical notes   priv.
N: UPB 1 reel
P: UPB   10635

WALKER, WILLIAM HOLMES, Elder, L.D.S.
Church
Life...and association with Joseph Smith, the
Prophet, 87 p. priv.
N: UPB
P: UPB   10636

WHITE, JOHN S., 1818-1907
Biography, 10 p. priv.
N: UPB
P: UPB   10637

WILSON, JAMES THOMAS, of Provo, Utah,
b. 1828
Autobiography, 130 p. priv.
N: UPB
P: UPB   10638

WOODRUFF, WILFORD, 1807-1898
Letters to Atkins Family, 1885-1894 priv.
N: UHi 1 reel
P: UHi   10639

YOUNG, ALFRED DOUGLAS, b. 1808
Journal, autobiographical material, 1808-1842
ULCHi
N: ULCHi 1 reel
P: UHi   10640

Business Papers

KIMBALL, HEBER CHASE, 1801-1868
Estate books, 1869   priv.
N: UPB   10641

Collections

BEADLE, J. H., collector
Scrapbook of Salt Lake Daily Reporter, Oct.,
1868-Aug.,1869 priv.
N: DLC 1 reel   10642

BRIGHAM YOUNG UNIVERSITY
Biographies of Southern Utah Pioneers UPB
N: UPB   10643
P: UPB

CACHE VALLEY HISTORICAL ASSOCIATION
Utah Manuscript Collection ULCHi
N: ULCHi 29 reels
P: UHi   10644

O'NEIL, HUGH F.
Collection of Utah documents, reports, etc.,
1851-1939 CU-B
N: CU-B 4 reels   10645

Institutions

SALT LAKE CITY, Utah. MT. OLIVET
CEMETERY
Cemetery and masonic burial records, 1872-
1956 USlC
N: USlGS 1 reel   10646

SALT LAKE CITY CEMETERY, Utah
Sextons'records, 1847-1950
N: USlGS 14 reels   10647

UTE INDIAN TRIBE
Census, 1944; land divisions; vital records,
early to 1946 Ibid.
N: USlGS 9 reels   10648

NEVADA

Census

U.S. CENSUS. NINTH, 1870
Population schedules, Nevada DNA
N: DNA 1 reel
P: USlGS   10649

U.S. CENSUS. TENTH, 1880
Agriculture schedules, Nevada NcD
N: NcD 1/4 reel   10650

U.S. CENSUS. TENTH, 1880
Population schedule, Nevada DNA
N: DNA 2 reels   10651

Government Records

U.S. DEPT. OF STATE
Territorial papers: Nevada, 1861-1864 DNA
N: DNA 1 reel [M-13]   10652

U.S. SURVEYOR GENERAL FOR NEVADA
Letter book, July, 1861 - Dec., 1869 [unk.]
N: ? 1 reel   10653
P: NvU*

Territorial Records

JEFFERSON TERRITORY. LAWS, STATUTES,
Etc.
Miners' laws of Nevada, 1860-1861
N: CoHi 1 reel   10654

Church Records

CHURCH OF JESUS CHRIST OF LATTER-DAY
SAINTS. NEVADA
Ward and branch records: Alamo, Boulder City,
Bunkerville, Caliente, Carlin, Carson City,
Elko, Ely, Fallon, Hawthorne, Henderson,
Las Vegas, Logandale, Lund, McGill, Mes-
quite, Metropolis, Montello, Overton, Panaca,
Pioche, Preston, Reno, Ruby Valley, Ruth,
St. Thomas, Sparks, Wells, Winnemucca USlC
N: USlGS 33 reels   10655

Business Papers

ROSS-BURKE FUNERAL HOME, Reno, Nev.
Funeral records, 1879, 1888-1891, 1900-
1953, 18 v. Ibid.
N: USlGS 3 reels   10656

PACIFIC COAST

Bancroft Interviews

The following are interviews written down between
1878 and 1883 by Hubert Howe Bancroft and kept in
manuscript at the Bancroft Library. The inter-
viewee is given as the author. The title of the interview includes the dates, when known, of the events to
which it refers. The entry ends with the date and
place of the interview, and the number of pages in
the manuscript, when known.

ANDERSON, ALEXANDER CAULFIELD
History of the Northwest Coast. 1878, Victoria,
B.C., 285 p. CU-B
N: WaU 1 reel
P: WaU   10657

APPLEGATE, JESSE
Views of Oregon history. 1878, Yoncalla, Ore.,
80 p. CU-B
N: WaU 1 reel   10658

BAGLEY, V. I.
San Juan and other sketches. 1884, Colorado,
19 p. CU-B
N: WaU
P: WaU   10659

BALLOU, WILLIAM T.
Adventures. 1878, Seattle CU-B
N: WaU 1 reel
P: WaU   10660

BANCROFT, A.L.
Diary of journey to Oregon. 1862, San
Francisco, 89 p. CU-B
N: WaU 1 reel   P: WaU   10661

BANCROFT, HUBERT HOWE, collector
British Columbia sketches. 1878, Victoria, B.C.
CU-B
N: WaU 1 reel
P: WaU   10662

BARNES, GEORGE A.
Oregon and California in 1849. 1878, Olympia,
Wash., 30 p. CU-B
N: WaU 1 reel
P: WaU   10663

BELL, WILLIAM ABRAHAM
Settlement of Seattle. 1878, 26 p. CU-B
N: WaU   10664
P: WaU

BOND, N.T.
Early history of Colorado, Montana,and Idaho.
1884, Denver, 86 p. CU-B
N: WaU   10665
P: WaU

BRADSHAW, CHARLES MINER
History of Jefferson and Clallam Counties,
Washington Ter. n.d., n.p., 235 p. CU-B
N: WaU   10666
P: WaU

BRISTOL, SHERLOCK
Idaho nomenclature. 1879, 12 p. CU-B
N: WaU   10667

BRISTOW, E.L.
Encounters with Indians, highwaymen,and
outlaws. 1878, Salem, Ore., 16 p. CU-B
N: WaU   10668

BROWN, JAMES HENRY
Autobiography, miscellanies, settlement of
Willamette Valley. n.d., n.p. CU-B
N: WaU   10669
P: WaU

BUTLER, J.S.
Life and times in Idaho. 1883, n.p., 16 p.
CU-B
N: WaU 1 reel   10670

COOPER, JAMES, b. 1821
Maritime matters on the Northwest Coast and
affairs of the Hudson's Bay Company. 1878,
Victoria, B.C. CU-B
N: WaU 1 reel   10671
P: WaU

DEADY, MATTHEW PAUL
History of Oregon after 1845. n.d., Portland,
80 p. CU-B
N: WaU   10672
P: WaU

DEADY, MATTHEW, PAUL, et al.
Wallamet [Willamette], scrapbook of letters on
spelling. 1874, Portland, Ore. CU-B
N: WaU 1 reel   10673
P: WaU

DE COMOS, AMOR
The Governments of Vancouver Island and
British Columbia. 1878, San Francisco CU-B
N: WaU 1 reel   10674
P: WaU

DENNY, A.A.
The Snoqualmie iron mountain. 1878, Seattle
CU-B
N: WaU 3 frames   10675
P: WaU

EASTWICK, PHILLIP G.
Coal mines on Puget Sound. 1878, Seattle,
W.T., 4 p. CU-B
N: WaU 1 reel   10676
P: WaU

ELDRIDGE, EDWARD
Sketch of Washington Territory. 1880,
Whatcom, Wash. CU-B
N: WaU 1 reel   10677
P: WaU

ELLICOTT, EUGENE
Puget Sound nomenclature and general descrip-
tion. 1878, Olympia, Wash. CU-B
N: WaU 1 reel   10678

FERY, JULES
    Gold searcher. 1879, Victoria, B.C., 3 p.
    CU-B
    N: CU-B
    P: WaU   10679

GIBBS, ADDISON CRANDELL
    Notes on the history of Oregon. n.d., n.p.
    CU-B
    N: WaU 1 reel   10680
    P: WaU

GILBERT, JOHN J.
    Logging and railroad building on Puget Sound.
    1878, Olympia, W.T., 13 p. CU-B
    N: WaU   10681
    P: WaU

GROVER, LAFAYETTE
    Notable things in a public life in Oregon.
    1878, San Francisco CU-B
    N: WaU 111 frames   10682
    P: WaU

HOFEN, LEO
    History of Idaho County. 1879, n.p., 1-9 p.
    CU-B
    N: WaU   10683

KNAPP, HENRY M.
    Statement of events in Idaho. 1879, n.p., 18 p.
    CU-B
    N: WaU   10684

LEWIS, PHILIP H.
    Coal discoveries in Washington Territory.
    1878, n.p., 19 p. CU-B
    N: WaU   10685
    P: WaU

McKAY, JOSEPH WILLIAM
    Recollections of a chief trader in the Hudson's
    Bay Company. 1878, Fort Simpson CU-B
    N: WaU 1 reel   10686
    P: WaU

MAIZE, HENRY B.
    Early events in Idaho. 1883, n.p., 12 p.
    CU-B
    N: WaU   10687
    P: WaU

NICHOLS, ROWENA
    Notes on Indian affairs in Oregon. 1879, n.p.,
    30 p.; Scenes from the Rogue River War. n.d.,
    n.p., 2 p. CU-B
    N: WaU   10688
    P: WaU

PARKER, JOHN GOLDSBURY
    Puget Sound. 1878, n.p., 17 p. CU-B
    N: WaU   10689
    P: WaU

PETTYGROVE, FRANCIS W., 1812-1887
    Oregon in 1843. 1878, Port Townsend,
    Washington CU-B
    N: CU-B WaU 1 reel   10690
    P: OrHi WaU

PLUMMER, ALFRED A.
    Reminiscences. 1878, n.p. CU-B
    N: WaU   10691
    P: WaU

RABBESON, A.B.
    Growth of towns, Olympia, Tumwater,
    Portland, and San Francisco. 1878, Olympia,
    Wash. CU-B
    N: WaU 1 reel   10692
    P: WaU

ROBERTS, GEORGE B.
    Recollections, 1878-1882. n.d., Cathlamet,
    W.T., 107 p. CU-B
    N: WaU   10693
    P: WaU

RODER, HENRY
    Bellingham Bay and the San Juan difficulty.
    1878, Port Townsend, Wash. CU-B
    N: WaU 1 reel   10694
    P: WaU

SAYWARD, W.T.
    Statement. n.d., San Francisco, 36 p. CU-B
    N: WaU   10695

SHOUP, GEORGE LAIRD
    Idaho ter. 1883, n.p., 16 p. CU-B
    N: WaU   10696

STARR, F. R.
    Idaho. 1879, n.p., 11 p. CU-B
    N: WaU   10697

STEELE, ALDEN HATCH
    With the rifle regiment. 1878, Olympia, W.T.,
    8 p. CU-B
    N: WaU   10698
    P: WaU

STRONG, WILLIAM
    History of Oregon. 1878, Portland, 84 p.
    CU-B
    N: WaU   10699
    P: WaU

SWAN, JAMES GILCHRIST
    Papers re: Port Townsend. 1878, n.p. CU-B
    N: WaU   10700

SWAN, JOHN M.
    Colonizations around Puget Sound.
    1878, Olympia, 8 p. CU-B
    N: WaU   10701
    P: WaU

SYLVESTER, EDMUND
    Founding of Olympia. 1878, Olympia, W.T.
    CU-B
    N: WaU 1 reel   10702
    P: WaU

TODD, JOHN, b. 1793
    History of New Caledonia and the Northwest
    Coast. 1879, Victoria, B.C. CU-B
    N: WaU 1 reel   10703
    P: WaU

TOLMIE, WILLIAM FRASER
    Journal [kept at] Nusqually House, Puget Sound,
    1833, 105 p.; memoirs. 1878, n.p., 61 p.
    N: WaU   10704
    P: WaU

WEED, C.E.
    Queen Charlotte Island expeditions. 1878,
    Olympia, Wash. CU-B
    N: WaU 1 reel   10705
    P: WaU

YESLER, H. L.
    Settlement of Washington Territory.
    1878, Seattle CU-B
    N: WaU 1 reel   10706
    P: WaU

Collections

BRITISH MUSEUM
    Material re: Spanish, English, and Russian
    discoveries on the Pacific Northwest Coast
    UKLBM
    N: WaPS 1 reel   10707

GREAT BRITAIN. FOREIGN OFFICE
    Correspondence and documents in manuscript
    re: San Juan boundary dispute, 1846-1869, 10 v.
    UKLPRO
    N: OrU 4 reels   10708

HENRY E. HUNTINGTON LIBRARY AND ART
    GALLERY, San Marino, Calif.
    Documents re: "el Puerto de Nutca," 1789-
    1793 CSmH
    N: CU-B 1 reel*   10709

MEXICO. ARCHIVO GENERAL DE LA NACIÓN
    Material re: California and Nootka Sound,
    including ships' logs, 1661-1801 MxAGN
    DCO: DLC 10924 sheets   10710

Ships' Logs

With ships' logs are included journals, diaries,
and other records of voyages. Logs, which are
the official records of vessels, are listed under
the vessels' names. Journals, which are personal

documents, even though they are sometimes
called supplementary logs, are listed under the
names of their authors.

BAKER, JOSEPH
    Journal kept on H. M. S. Discovery, Dec., 1790-
    July, 1795 UKLPRO
    N: WaU 1 reel   10711

BALLARD, VOLANT VASTION
    Journal kept on H. M. S. Discovery, 1791-1795,
    227 p. UKLPRO
    N: WaU 1 reel   10712

BROWNE, JOHN AISLEY
    Journal kept on H. M. S. Discovery, Jan., 1791-
    Mar., 1795, 92 p. UKLPRO
    N: WaU   10713

CALIFORNIA. UNIVERSITY. BANCROFT
    LIBRARY
    Diaries of voyages to California, 1849-1852
    v. p.
    N: CU-B 1 reel*   10714

CALIFORNIA. UNIVERSITY. BANCROFT
    LIBRARY
    Logbooks, etc., of vessels which touched
    California ports, 1824-1854 v. p.
    N: CU-B 1 reel*   10715

CHRISTIANSON, C. H.
    Journal, New York to San Francisco, on Bark
    Linda, Mar. 24-Sep. 26, 1849, 84 p. C
    DCO: C*   10716

COLLINS, SILAS MORTIMER
    Journal kept on a Cape Horn voyage, on the
    ship Magnolia, Jan. 25-Aug. 28, 1849, 23 p.
    C
    DCO: C*   10717

COLNETT, JAMES
    Journal kept on H. M. S. Argonaut, Apr., 1789-
    Nov., 1791 UKLPRO
    N: WaU   10718

COLVOCORESSES, Lt. GEORGE M., 1816-1872
    Journal of explorations under Wilkes
    Coe Collection CtY
    N: CtY   10719

DOBSON, T. J.
    Journal kept on H. M. S. Discovery, 1794-1795
    UKLPRO
    N: WaU 1 reel   10720

EWING (Survey schooner)
    Deck log, 1848-1850 DNA
    N: WaU 1 reel   10721

GEORGE WASHINGTON (Ship)
    Log, New York to San Francisco, 1849, 6 p. C
    DC: C*   10722

GILBERT, GEORGE
    Journal kept on H. M. S. Discovery, 1776-
    1780, 325 p. UKLBM
    N: HiU   10723

INGRAHAM, JOSEPH, 1762-1800
    Journal kept on the brigantine Hope from
    Boston to the Northwest coast, 1790-1796 DLC
    DCO: InU 241 p.   10724
    N: HiU 1 reel

MARTÍNEZ, ESTEVAN JOSÉ, fl. 1780-1790
    Diary of voyage, 1789 (translation) CU-B
    N: ?   10725
    P: WaU

MARTÍNEZ, ESTEVAN JOSÉ, fl. 1780-1790
    Journal of his voyage to Nootka Sound, 1789
    [Spanish], 318 p. CaOOA
    N: CaOOA   10726

MEARES, JOHN
    Memorial re: seizure by the Spaniards of his
    vessel Iphigenia, 1790, 31 p. DLC
    N: AU   10727

MENZIES, ARCHIBALD
    Journal, 1790-1794, 653 p. UKLBM
    N: WaU   10728
    P: WaU

MENZIES, ARCHIBALD
Letters from Pacific Coast, 1793-1795,
4 items UKLBM
DCO: C-S   10729

NUESTRA SA. DEL ROSARIO alias LA
PRINCESA (Frigate)
Inventario, Expedición del Nuca, 1792
MxAGN
N: WaU 1 reel   10730

ORCHARD, H. M.
Journal kept on H. M. S. Discovery, Dec.,1792-
Nov.,1794 UKLBM
N: WaU 1 reel   10731

PANAMA (Ship)
Agreement of conduct, 1849, 1 l. C
Ph: C*   10732

PORTSMOUTH (U. S. Sloop of War)
Logbooks, 1845-1847 DNA
N: CU-B 1 reel   10733

PUGET, PETER
Journal kept on H. M. S. Discovery, Aug., 1791-
July, 1792 UKLPRO
N: WaU 1 reel   10734

ROBERTS, EDWARD
Journal kept on H. M. S. Discovery, 1791-1795
UKLPRO
N: WaU 1 reel   10735

SAWYER, ASAPH
Diary, journey from Maine to California by
Isthmus of Panama, Apr. 10 (in Panama)-
May 3, 1852, 1 v. priv.
DCO: NN   10736

STEWART, JOHN
Journal kept on H. M. S. Discovery, Jan., 1791-
July, 1795 UKLPRO
N: WaU 1 reel   10737

SYKES, JOHN
Journal kept on H. M. S. Discovery, 1790-1795
UKLPRO
N: WaU 1 reel   10738

TAYLOR, AUGUSTUS F., d. 1889
Diary, voyage to California, 1849 (typescript)
C
DC: C*   10739

U. S. HYDROGRAPHIC OFFICE
Records of the U. S. Exploring Expedition
under the command of Lieutenant Charles
Wilkes, 1836-1842 DNA
N: DNA 27 reels [M-75]   10740
P: CaBVaU Or-Ar PPiU

U. S. NAVY DEPT.
Records relating to the U. S. Exploring
Expedition to the North Pacific, 1854-1856,
Lt. John Rodgers commanding DNA
N: DNA 2 reels [M-88]   10741
P: WaU

VALK, JAMES S.
Diary, 1836-1879, from Hanover, Germany,
to San Francisco priv.
DCO: NN 70 ll.   10742

WHIDBY, JOSEPH
Journal kept on H. M. S. Discovery, Jan. 1-
May 20, 1790 UKLBM
N: WaU 1 reel   10743
P: WaU

WOOD, ALPHONSO, 1810-1881
Journal, voyage to California, Oct., 1865-
Aug.,1866, 1 v. NhD
N: CU 1 reel   10744

CALIFORNIA

Bibliography

YALE UNIVERSITY. LIBRARY
[Bibliography of] the William Robertson Coe
collection of Western Americana, 1943, 110 p.
(typescript) CtY
N: CSmH   10745

Census

U.S. CENSUS. SEVENTH, 1850
Population schedules, California DNA
N: DNA 4 reels   10746
P: C USIGS

U.S. CENSUS. EIGHTH, 1860
Population schedules, California DNA
N: DNA 4 reels   10747
P: C USIGS

U.S. CENSUS. NINTH, 1870
Population schedules, California DNA
N: DNA 6 reels   10748
P: C USIGS

U.S. CENSUS. TENTH, 1880
Population schedules, California DNA
N: DNA 26 reels   10749
P: C

Government Records

MEXICO. ARCHIVO GENERAL DE LA NACIÓN
Correspondencia de los Virreyes, diary and
letters re: first expedition to California, 1774
MxAGN
DCO: DLC 46 sheets   10750

U.S. ADJUTANT-GENERAL'S OFFICE
Letters sent by the Military Governors and
the Secretary of State of California, 1847-1848
DNA
N: DNA 1 reel [M-182]   10751
P: MoI-HSt

U.S. ADJUTANT-GENERAL'S OFFICE
Sonoma, Cal., Post returns, Apr., 1847-
May, 1848, May, 1849-Dec., 1851 DNA
N: DNA 1 reel   10752

U. S. ARMY
Modoc War correspondence and documents,
1865-1873 DNA San Francisco Presidio
N: U. S. National Park Service, San Francisco
7 reels   10753
P: CU-B

U.S. CIRCUIT COURT (9th circuit)
Minutes for the Southern District of California,
1863-1866 DNA
N: DNA 1 reel 16 mm.   10754

U.S. CIRCUIT COURT (9th circuit)
Minutes, judgment and decree books,and rule
books for the District of California, 1855-1894
DNA
N: DNA 18 reels 16 mm.   10755

U.S. CIRCUIT COURT (9th circuit)
Minutes, judgment and decree records, and
rule books for the Northern District of California, 1859-1911 (with gaps) DNA
N: DNA 19 reels 16 mm.   10756

U.S. CONGRESS. HOUSE OF REPRESENTATIVES
Papers re: Mrs. Anne Glidden, 1858 DNA
N: DNA 1 reel   10757
P: CLO

U.S. DISTRICT COURT. CALIFORNIA
Minutes, 1867-1892; bankruptcy orders for
sale, 1870-1894 DNA
N: DNA 7 reels 16 mm.   10758

U.S. DISTRICT COURT. CALIFORNIA
(Northern district)
Minutes, judgment and decree records, and
order books, 1851-1950 (with gaps) DNA
N: DNA 101 reels 16 mm.   10759

U.S. DISTRICT COURT. CALIFORNIA
(Southern district)
Minutes, 1851-1866; decree records, 1855-
1865 DNA
N: DNA 3 reels 16 mm.   10760

U.S. FOREST SERVICE
Reports re: California forests, 1903-1907
(typescript) C
N: C 1 reel   10761

U.S. GENERAL LAND OFFICE
Grant to Julian Estrada of a tract of land
called "Santa Rosa," San Luis Obispo Co.,
Calif., May 3, 1859 Ibid.
DCO: CSbC   10762

U.S. SURVEYOR GENERAL
Report on surveys of Henry Hancock, 1858
DNA
N: DNA 1 reel   10763
P: CLO

State Records

CALIFORNIA. BOARD OF EDUCATION
Minutes, 1866-1911
N: ? 2 reels   10764
P: C

CALIFORNIA. UNIVERSITY. BUREAU OF
PUBLIC ADMINISTRATION
Reports for legislature, 1947 (typescript) C
N: C 1 reel   10765

County Records

KERN Co., Cal. GRAND JURY
Reports, 1895 CSmH
N: CSmH (filmstrip)   10766
P: CLO

MONTEREY Co., Cal. ARCHIVES
Documents of Spanish and Mexican periods
of administration, 1780-1849 C.H. Salinas
N: CU-B 16 reels   10767

Church Records

CHURCH OF JESUS CHRIST OF LATTER-DAY
SAINTS. CALIFORNIA
Ward and branch records: Adams, Alameda,
Alhambra, Arlington, Auburn, Baldwin Park,
Bell Gardens, Berkeley Stake, Beverly Hills,
Burbank, Burlingame, Chico, Colton,
Compton, Corning, Downey, El Monte,
El Segundo, Fontana, Glendale, Grass Valley,
Gridley, Hawthorne, Haywood, Hollywood,
Huntington, Inglewood, Iona, La Mesa,
Lomita, Long Beach, Los Angeles, North
Sacramento, Oakdale, Oakland, Ocean Park,
Ontario, Oroville, Palo Alto, Pasadena,
Placerville, Pomona, Portola, Redlands,
Redondo Beach, Redwood, Resada, Riverside,
Roseville, Sacramento, San Bernardino,
San Diego, San Francisco, San Gabriel,
San Jose, San Leandro, San Mateo,
San Rafael, Santa Monica, Santa Rosa,
South Gate, South Pasadena, Stockton,
Susanville, Sutter, Temple City, Torrance,
Tracy, Turlock, Van Nuys, Victorville,
Westwood, Whittier, Wilmar, Wilmington,
Wood, Woodland, Yuba City, Yucaipa USlC
N: USlGS 155 reels   10768

JESUITS. CALIFORNIA MISSION
El Atlante de las Californias, representado en
la Compañía de Jesús, missionero y conquistador
apostólica de las naciones de Californias, n. p.,
n.d. priv.
N: CSfU   10769

OUR LADY, QUEEN OF THE ANGELS, OLD
MISSION PLAZA, Los Angeles, Cal.
Vital records, 1826-1919 Ibid.
N: USlGS 9 reels   10770

SACRAMENTO, Cal. CONGREGATION B'NAI
ISRAEL
Minutes, 1906, 8 p. C
DCO: C*   10771

SAN GABRIEL MISSION (Catholic), San Gabriel,
Cal.
Records, 1771-1855, 1868-1908 [in Spanish]
Ibid.
N: USlGS 5 reels   10772

SAN JOSÉ de COMONDÚ MISSION, Cal.
Records, 1769-1826 Ibid.
N: CSfU   10773

Personal Papers

ARGÜELLO, JOSÉ DARÍO, 1753-1827
Provincia de Californias, 1798, 1 l.
Ph: C*   10774

BEALE, EDWARD FITZGERALD, 1822-1893
Papers, 1848-1892 CSt DLC DNA MH
N: CSt DLC DNA MH 8 reels, 4 filmstrips
P: CLO   10775

BIDWELL, JOHN, 1819-1900
California: An immigrant's recollections,
1841-1848 CU-B
N: CU-B 1 reel   10776

BIGLER, HENRY WILLIAM, 1815-1900
Diary of a Mormon in California, 1872 CU-B
N: CU-B 1 reel   10777

BREEN, PATRICK, 1805-1868
Diary, 1846-1847   CU-B
N: CU-B 1 reel   10778

BREWER, WILLIAM HENRY
Field work journal, 1860-1861, 188 p.
CU Geology Dept.
N: CU 1 reel
P: CU   10779

BULLARD, WILLIAM
Family letters, 1852-1863, 37 items C
DCO: C*   10780

CAMPBELL, ROBERT
Correspondence and papers, 1804-1879 priv.
N: priv. *
P: CU-B 1 reel   10781

CASTRO, MANUEL DE JESUS, b. 1821
Documentos para la historia de California,
1821-1850 CU-B
N: CU-B 1 reel   10782

DAVIS, WILLIAM HEATH, 1822-1909
Correspondence, 1849-1898 C
N: priv. 2 reels
P: CU-B   10783

DELAPP, JOHN
Letters, 1852-1853, 11 items C
DCO: C*   10784

DURAN, NARCISO, 1776-1846
Writings CU-B
N: CU-B 1 reel   10785

FORBES, JAMES ALEXANDER, 1804-1881
Letterbook, 1850-1879, 650 p. priv.
Ph: C*   10786

FRÉMONT, Mrs. JESSIE BENTON, d. 1902
Letters re: Cahuenga treaty of 1847,
written in 1890, 5 p. C
DCO: C*   10787

GILLESPIE, ARCHIBALD H., 1813-1873
Correspondence, 1845-1860, ca. 900 items
CLU
N: CLU 1 reel   10788

GWINN, WILLIAM McKENDREE, 1805-1885
Memoirs re: U.S., Mexico, California,
1850-1861 CU
DCO: DLC 1 v.   10789

HENEY, FRANCIS JOSEPH, 1859-1937
Correspondence and papers, 1903-1937 CU-B
N: CU-B 1 reel   10790

HENEY, FRANCIS JOSEPH, 1859-1937
Correspondence with Theodore Roosevelt, 1906-
1918 CtY
N: CU-B 1 reel*   10791

HEUSKEN, HENRI C.J., 1832-1861
Diary, 1855-1861, 384 p. CLU
N: CLU 1 reel   10792

HOLTZMANN, ROBERT

Selected correspondence, n.d.   priv.
N: CSt-H 1 reel   10793

HOPKINS, MARK, 1813-1878
Correspondence and papers, 1861-1878 CSt
N: CU-B 6 reels *   10794
P: CU-B

HUSE, CHARLES ENOCH
Diary, 1850-1852, 1853-1859, 2 v.   priv.
N: CStbS 1 reel   10795
PP: CStbS

JAMES, EDWIN, 1797-1861
Diary and journal notes, 1820-1827 NNC
N: CU-B 1 reel *   10796

JORDAN, Dr. DAVID, 1803-1857
Diary, 1849, 169 l. C
N: DCO: C *   10797

LEE, JESSE MATLOCK, Capt., b. 1843
Report re: Fort Bidwell, Calif., Dec., 1890
DNA
N: ICU   10798

LITTLE, JOHN T.
Letters, 1849-1885, 9 items C
DCO: C*   10799

LOW, FREDERICK F., b. 1828
Political affairs in California, 1883, 77 p.   C
N: CU 1 reel   10800
P: C

McCLEAVE, WILLIAM, 1823-1904
Papers, memoirs as officer of 1st Cavalry,
California volunteers, 1862-1904 CU-B
N: CU-B 1 reel   10801
P: CStbS

McDIARMID, FINLEY
Letters to his wife, 1850-1851 priv.
N: CU-B 1 reel   10802

MONTGOMERY, JOHN BERRIEN, 1794-1873
Letterbooks, 1844-1848 DNA
N: DNA 4 reels   10803
P: CU-B

NENTVIG, JUAN
Letters, 1764-1767, 9 items priv.
N: CSfU   10804

OTIS, ESTHER SOPHIA (Mrs. EMMANUEL)
Memorandum Book, 1863-1864 priv.
N: CSmH   10805

OWEN, ISAAC, 1809-1866
Correspondence, 1830-1868 CU-B CBPac
N: CU-B 2 reels   10806
PP: CBPac

PREUSS, GEORGE CARL LUDWIG, 1803-1854
Diaries, 1842-1849 DLC
N: CU-B 1 reel   10807
P: UHi

REID, WILLIAM THOMAS, 1843-1922
Letters, 1875-1896, 502 p. priv.
N: CU   10808

ROLLINS, JAMES SIDNEY, 1812-1888
Letters, 1862-1881, 95 items DLC
N: CSt   10809

SERRA, JUNÍPERO, fray, 1713-1784
Diary, California mission fathers, 1769-1777
OkTG
N: OkTG 2 reels   10810

SERRA, JUNÍPERO, fray, 1713-1784
History of Carmel Mission (translation),1784
MxAGN
N: CSbC 1 reel   10811

SHELDON, Rev. HENRY B.
Letters, 1851-1858, 45 items C
DCO: C*   10812

SMYTH, SAMUEL S.
Letters and journals, 1862-1864, 28 letters,
2 journals CStbS
N: CStbS 1 reel   10813
PP: CStbS 153 p.

SUTTER, JOHN AUGUSTUS, Jr., 1803-1880
Papers, 1849-1916, 49 items C
DCO: C*   10814

SUTTER, JOHN AUGUSTUS, Jr., 1803-1880
Personal reminiscences CU-B
N: CU-B 1 reel   10815

SUTTER, JOHN AUGUSTUS, Jr., 1803-1880
Reminiscences, 1876, 198 p. C
N: CU photo   10816
P: CU*

WATSON, ROBERT S.
San Francisco in 1849: "Stray leaves by a
pioneer," 146 p. priv.
DCO: C*   10817

WELDON, S.R.
Diary, 1871 priv.
N: CSmH 60 frames   10818

WHEELWRIGHT, WILLIAM, 1789-1873
Diary, 1872-1873   Wheelwright Scientific
School
N: CU-B 1 reel*   10819
P: CU-B

Business Papers

CROWE, EARLE E.
Tejon ranch documents, 1871 Title Insurance
and Trust
N: Ibid 1 reel   10820
P: CLO

FRANCE. ARCHIVES NATIONALES
Selections re: commerce and industry in
California, 1829-1874 FrAN
N: CU-B 2 reels   10821
P: CU-B

HOUGHTON MIFFLIN COMPANY
Correspondence with Mary Austin, 1904-1929
Ibid.
N: CU-B 1 reel   10822

MOUNTAIN VIEW HOUSE, Mariposa Co., Calif.
Register, 1870-1878, 213 p. Ibid.
DCO: C*   10823

TEAGUE, C.C., Southern California rancher
Business papers, 1901-1950 CU-B
N: CLU 22 reels 16 mm.   10824

Collections

DUNLAP, BOUTWELL, 1877-1930
California collection, 35 p. C
DCO: C*   10825

FARQUHAR, FRANCIS PELOUBET, b. 1887
Collection re: Clarence King priv.
N: CU-B 1 reel   10826

MEXICO. BIBLIOTECA NACIONAL, Mexico
Legajo series: documents for the history
of the Californias, 1596, 1699-1775, 1784;
documents for the history of New Mexico
and the Southwest, 1605-1818 MxBN
DCO: DLC 10239 sheets   10827

NEW YORK GENEALOGICAL AND BIOGRAPHICAL
SOCIETY
Vital records of Sacramento, San Francisco,
and Stockton, 1750-1924 (transcript) NNNG
N: USIGS 1 reel   10828

U. S. LIBRARY OF CONGRESS
Mormon diaries, journals, and life sketches
DLC
N: CU-B 13 reels   10829

Institutions

MARYSVILLE PIONEER SOCIETY
Register, 1869, 19 pp. C
DC: C*   10830

OREGON

Bibliography

FEDERAL WRITERS' PROJECT. OREGON
Dictionary of Oregon history   Or
N: OrHi 16 feet 16 mm.   10831

HISTORICAL RECORDS SURVEY. OREGON
Oregon subject file; Mation Co., Ore., file;
Secretary of State's inventory of records Ibid.
N: Or-Ar 2 reels 1 16 mm.   10832

LIBRARY ASSOCIATION OF PORTLAND, Oregon
Serials published in Oregon, 1854-1929 OrP
N: OrHi 28 frames   10833

OREGON. HISTORICAL SOCIETY
Index to vital statistics notices in the Oregon
press, 1846-1881   Card file OrHi
N: OrHi 7 reels   10834

OREGON. STATE LIBRARY
Index to Provisional Government Land Records,
1845-1849 Or-Ar
N: Or-Ar 100 feet 16 mm.   10835

Census

U.S. CENSUS. SEVENTH, 1850
Population schedules, Oregon DNA
N: DNA 1 reel   10836
P: OrHi USIGS

U.S. CENSUS. EIGHTH, 1860
Population schedules, Oregon DNA
N: DNA 1 reel   10837
P: OrHi USIGS

U.S. CENSUS. NINTH, 1870
Population schedules, Oregon DNA
N: DNA 4 reels   10838
P: OrHi

U.S. CENSUS. TENTH, 1880
Population schedules, Oregon   DNA
N: DNA 5 reels   10839
P: OrHi

U.S. CENSUS. TENTH, 1880
Schedule 2, production of agriculture for Oregon
Or
N: ? 2166 frames, 3 reels   10840
P: Or-Ar

U.S. CENSUS. ELEVENTH, 1890
Veterans' schedules, Oregon   DNA
N: DNA 1 reel   10841
P: OrHi

Government Records

UMATILLA INDIAN AGENCY, Ore.
Letters sent, 1860-1880 priv.
N: ? 20 feet   10842
P: Or-Ar

U.S. ADJUTANT - GENERAL'S OFFICE
Post records: Fort Hoskins, 1856-1865;
Fort Yamhill, 1856-1866 DNA
N: Or-Ar 1 reel   10843

U.S. ARMY. ENGINEERS. PORTLAND OFFICE
Civil files: letters, requisitions, and operations,
1878-1928 Ibid.
N: OrHi 410 reels   10844

U.S. BUREAU OF CUSTOMS
Papers, Astoria Customs House, 1848-1868
DNA
N: OrHi 6 reels   10845

U.S. DEPT. OF JUSTICE
Records relating to the Appointment of Federal
Judges, Attorneys, and Marshals for the Terri-
tory and State of Oregon, 1853-1903 DNA
N: DNA 3 reels [M-224]   10846
P: Or-Ar

U.S. FOREST SERVICE
Hearings re: establishment of Three Sisters'
Wilderness Area, Mt. Washington and Diamond
Peak Wild Areas, at Eugene, Ore., Feb. 16
and 17, 1955 Ibid.
N: Or-Ar 551 frames, 16 mm. [Loan micro-
film #73]   10847

U.S. GENERAL LAND OFFICE
Abstracts of Oregon Donation Land Claims,
1852-1903 DNA
N: DNA 6 reels [M-145]   10848
P: Or-Ar OrHi

U.S. GENERAL LAND OFFICE
Oregon City donation certificates for Willamette
Valley Methodist Mission and Northwest Com-
pany post DNA
N: Or-Ar   10849

U.S. OFFICE OF INDIAN AFFAIRS
Records of the Oregon Superintendency of
Indian Affairs, 1848-1873 DNA
N: DNA 29 reels [M-2]   10850
P: Or-Ar

VANCOUVER, FORT, Ore.
Records, 1857-1866 DNA
N: OrHi 63 feet   10851

YAMHILL, FORT, Ore.
Records, 1858-1860; letters sent, Sept., 1865-
June, 1866 CtY
N: Or-Ar 255 frames   10852

Territorial Records

OREGON. PROVISIONAL AND TERRITORIAL
GOVERNMENTS
Papers, 1841-1859 DS
N: OrHi 28 reels   10853
P: Or-Ar

OREGON. PROVISIONAL AND TERRITORIAL
GOVERNMENTS
Papers, 1841-1859 (indexed) OrHi
N: OrHi 26 reels 16 mm.   10854

OREGON (Provisional Government). ADJUTANT
GENERAL'S OFFICE
Cayuse War documents, 1847-1850 Oregon
Adjutant General's Office
N: Or-Ar 2 reels   10855

OREGON (Ter.). ADJUTANT GENERAL
Yakima and Rogue River wars, muster rolls,
August, 1852-June, 1856; unregistered corres-
pondence, 1851-1859 Ibid.
N: Or-Ar 2 reels   10856

OREGON (Ter.). SECRETARY
Land claims record, 1845-1849;
pre-emption land claims, 1860-1862 OrHi
N: Or-Ar   10857

OREGON (Ter.). SECRETARY
Territorial assessment rolls, 1851-1859;
county censuses, 1858, 1859 Ibid.
N: Or-Ar [Loan microfilm # 11]   10858

State Records

OREGON. GOVERNOR
Record of letters, June, 1859-May, 1878 Or-Ar
N: Or-Ar 281 frames [Loan microfilm #30]
                                          10859

OREGON. SECRETARY OF STATE. NOTARIAL
DIVISION
Wagon roads: maps, patents, and reports,
1873-1900 Or-Ar
N: Or-Ar 75 feet   10860

County Records

CLACKAMAS Co., Ore.
District court record, 1845-1848; land record,
1850-1853; stock mark and brand record, 1852-
1900; files relating to the citizenship of John
McLoughlin, 1849-1851 priv.
N: Or-Ar 280 frames   10861

GRANT Co., Ore. SOUTH FORK PRECINCT
Justice of the Peace daybook, 1883-1906,
283 p. priv.
N: Or-Ar 154 frames   10862

MARION Co., Ore.
Register of electors, 1914; enumeration of
inhabitants and industrial products, 1895;
enumeration of inhabitants and military enrollment, 1905 Or-Ar
N: Or-Ar 4 reels
[Loan Microfilms, #26, 27, 28]   10863

POLK Co., Ore.
Court records, 1846-1866; marriages, 1849-
1866; brands, 1849-1890 C.H. Dallas
N: Or-Ar 6 reels   10864

WASCO Co., Ore.
County Commissioners journal, 1854-1864;
court records, 1855-1864; marriages, 1856-
1865; muster roll, 1856; military list,
1872; brands, 1856-1892; estrays, 1860-1911
C.H. The Dalles
N: Or-Ar 1265 frames   10865

WASCO Co., Ore.
Probate records, 1859-1897; registers of
election, 1900, 1914; census, 1875; tax rolls,
1861-1865 C.H. The Dalles
N: Or-Ar 1355 frames   10866
[Loan microfilms #47-52]

WASHINGTON Co., Ore.
Court records, 1837-1893 C.H. Hillsboro
N: Or-Ar 3 reels 16 mm   10867

City Records

JEFFERSON, Ore.
City council minutes, 1870-1891, 1900-1918,
2 v. OrHi
N: Or-Ar 1 reel [Loan microfilm #14] 10868

JEFFERSON, Ore.
Record of ordinances, 1874-1919, 1 v. OrHi
N: Or-Ar 1 reel [Loan microfilm #15] 10869

PORTLAND, Ore.
Common council records, 1851-1876; ordinan-
ces, 1854-1868; births, 1864-1905 Ibid.
N: Or-Ar 3 reels   10870

Church Records

CHURCH OF JESUS CHRIST OF LATTER-DAY
SAINTS. OREGON
Ward and branch records, Nyssa Stake; ward
records, Alicel, Baker, Cove, Eugene, Hood
River, Imbler, La Grande, Mount Glen, Nibley,
Pendleton, Pine Grove, Portland, Salem, St.
Helens, Union, and Vanport City USlC
N: USlGS 33 reels   10871

CUMBERLAND PRESBYTERIAN CHURCH.
SYNODS. OREGON
Minutes: Oregon Presbytery, 1851-1902;
Oregon Synod, 1875-1906; Portland Presbytery,
1895-1906, 5 v. Ibid.
N: Or-Ar 711 frames [Loan microfilm #84]
                                          10872

METHODIST CHURCH (United States). CIRCUITS.
MONROE, Ore.
Records, 1858-1906 Ibid.
N: Or-Ar 283 frames [Loan microfilm #77]
                                          10873

MINNVILLE, Ore. FIRST BAPTIST CHURCH
Minutes, 1867-1951 Ibid.
N: OrHi 1 reel   10874

OAK RIDGE, Ore. PRESBYTERIAN CHURCH
    Minutes, 1878-1928 Ibid.
    N: Or-Ar 49 frames [Loan microfilm #82]
                                              10875

PLEASANT GROVE, Ore. PRESBYTERIAN
    CHURCH
    Records, 1856-1910 Ibid.
    N: Or-Ar 198 frames [Loan microfilm #52]
                                              10876

PORTLAND, Ore. BETH ISRAEL CONGREGATION
    Golden book, 1889 Ibid.
    N: OrHi 30 frames   10877

PRESBYTERIAN CHURCH IN THE U.S.A.
    MISSIONS. WIELETPOO [WAIILATPU]
    MISSION, Ore.
    Records, Aug., 1838 PPPrHi
    N: PPPrHi   10878

PRESBYTERIAN CHURCH IN THE U.S.A.
    PRESBYTERIES. OREGON(Ter.)
    Records, Oregon, Aug., 1838 PPPrHi
    N: PPPrHi 1 reel   10879

PRESBYTERIAN CHURCH IN THE U.S.A.
    PRESBYTERIES. OREGON
    Minutes, 1851-1890; Treasurer's reports,
    1877-1890 CSaT
    N: Or-Ar 778 frames [Loan microfilm #73]
                                              10880

PRESBYTERIAN CHURCH IN THE U.S.A.
    PRESBYTERIES. WILLAMETTE, Ore.
    Minutes, 1890-1925; Treasurer's reports,
    1890-1895 CSaT
    N: Or-Ar 745 frames [Loan microfilm #71]
    P: Or-Ar   10881

PRIMITIVE BAPTISTS. OREGON. SILOAM
    ASSOCIATION
    Minutes, 1851-1928 Elon College
    N: OrHi 1 reel   10882

SHEDD, Ore. METHODIST EPISCOPAL CHURCH
    Records, 1855-1952 Ibid.
    N: Or-Ar 2 reels   10883

WILLAMETTE STATION, Ore. METHODIST
    CHURCH
    Mission Record Book, 1834-1839 Board of
    Missions, Methodist Church
    N: Or-Ar 5 feet   10884

Personal Papers

BAEHERT, MICHAEL, et al., complainants
    In the matter of the dissolution of the Aurora,
    Ore., and Bethel, Mo., communities, 1881-
    1883 U.S. District Court, Oregon
    N: Or-Ar 1 reel   10885

BARKER, BURT BROWN
    Files re: Dr. John McLoughlin House in
    Oregon City priv.
    N: OrHi 28 feet   10886

BENNETT, ALEXANDER
    Correspondence, 1855-1910; diaries and papers,
    n.d. priv.
    N: Or-Ar 1081 frames 16 mm.   10887

BENSELL, ROYAL A.
    Diary, 1862-1864
    N: OrU   10888

BURBANK, AUGUST RIPLEY, b. 1817
    Journal, 1848-1880 DLC
    N: CU-B WaU 1 reel   10889

BURRES, JOHN LEWIS
    Reminiscences, 1904 priv.
    N: OrHi 20 feet   10890

CAMP, ELISHA
    Selected letters, 1852-1857 NIC
    N: OrHi 15 frames   10891

CHADWICK, STEPHEN JAMES, b. 1863
    Memoirs OrHi
    N: Or-Ar [Loan microfilm # 3.]   10892

CLEMENT, J.W.
    Letters, 1849-1864, 1 v. OrU
    N: OrU   10893

COE, NATHANIEL, 1788-1868
    Diary, Hood River, 1852-1874 priv.
    N: OrHi 40 feet   10894

CONDIT, Rev. PHILIP
    Journal, 1854 priv.
    N: Or-Ar 36 frames [Loan microfilm #51]
                                              10895

COX, JAMES W.
    Memoirs priv.
    N: Or-Ar 63 frames 16 mm.   10896
    [Loan microfilm # 17]

CUMMINS, HENRY, b. 1840
    Diaries, journal, notebook, 1857-1863, 1 v.
    CtY
    N: OrU   10897

CUMMINS, HENRY, b. 1840
    Letters OrU
    N: CtY   10898

DOWELL, BENJAMIN FRANKLIN, 1826-1897.
    Correspondence and papers, 1855-1886, 7v.
    N: CU-B   10899
    P: WaU

EBBERT, GEORGE WOOD, 1810-1890
    A trapper's life in the Rocky Mountains and
    Oregon, 1829-1839, 1878, 1 v. CU-B
    N: CU-B 46 frames   10900
    P: OrHi

ELD, HENRY, Jr.
    Journal and drawings, Oregon, California,
    and Pacific Islands, 1839-1841, 50 items
    CtY
    N: Or-Ar 40 feet*   10901

EVANS, JOHN, 1812-1861
    Diary, in Oregon and Washington Territories,
    July, 1854-Aug., 1856, 66 p. DSI
    N: OrPL 69 frames   10902
    P: Or-Ar

EVANS, JOHN, 1812-1861
    Journal of geological expedition in Oregon and
    Washington, 1854-1860 DSI
    Transcript, 68 p. priv.
    N: OrHi of transcript   10903

EVANS, JOHN, 1812-1861
    Selected letters to General Land Office, 1851-
    1861 DNA
    N: ? 1 reel   10904
    P: OrHi

FORD, NATHANIEL
    Papers, 1847-1848 (typescripts) priv.
    N: Or-Ar 15 frames   10905

FRENCH, PETE
    Excerpts from court transcript, Oregon vs.
    Oliver C.H. Burns; (transcript) priv.
    N: OrHi 8 frames transcript   10906

GIBBS, GEORGE
    Vocabularies of the Indian Languages DSI
    N: Or-Ar 20 feet   10907

HARKNESS, McDONOUGH
    Papers priv.
    N: OrHi 1 reel, two strips   10908

HASKIN, HARLEY THEODORE
    Papers, 1851-1897 priv.
    N: Or-Ar 62 frames [Loan microfilm #76]

HEMBREE, ABSALOM JEFFERSON, 1813-1856
    Donation land claim patent, Yamhill Co., Ore.
    1858 OrHi
    N: OrHi 30 frames   10910

HENDRICKS, ROBERT J.
    Papers re: Aurora community priv.
    N: Or-Ar [Loan microfilm #2]   10911

HYLAND, BENJAMIN, of Lancaster, Ore.
    Family and business records, 1853-1904 priv.
    N: Or-Ar 310 frames [Loan microfilm #100]
                                              10912

JOHNSON, Rev. NEILL
    Autobiography; diary (excerpts) priv.
    N: Or-Ar [Loan microfilms # 5, 96]   10913

LEE, DANIEL, 1806-1895
    Papers, 1833-1889 priv.
    N: OrHi 30 feet   10914

LEE, JASON
    Diary, 1834-1838 OrHi
    N: OrHi 10 feet   10915

LEONARD, MARY, defendant
    Documents in Oregon vs. Mary Leonard
    C.H. The Dalles (Wasco Co.)
    N: OrHi 33 frames   10916

LESLIE-JUDSON FAMILY
    Papers, 1829-1890, including papers of David
    Leslie, 1842-1868, Lewis Judson, 1829-1878,
    and miscellaneous items, 1843-1881 priv.
    N: Or-Ar 1764 frames 16 mm [Loan micro-
    film #26]   10917

LOUGHARY, Mrs. H.A.
    Journal, 1873-1876; papers re: Oregon, 1864-
    1890 priv.
    N: Or-Ar 1049 frames 16 mm. [Loan micro-
    film #98]   10918

McKAY, WILLIAM
    Papers re: Oregon history and Indian Wars,
    1846-1900 priv.
    N: ? 60 feet   10919
    P: Or-Ar

McKAY, WILLIAM CAMERON
    Papers, 1839-1892
    N: OrU   10920

McLOUGHLIN, JOHN, 1784-1857
    Letters written at Fort Vancouver, 1829-1832
    priv.
    N: ? 30 feet   10921
    P: OrHi

McLOUGHLIN, JOHN, 1784-1857
    Papers, 1806-1837, 3 items CaQMM priv.
    DCO: MnHi   10922

McLOUGHLIN, JOHN, 1784-1857
    Private papers, 1825-1856 CU-B
    N: WaU 1 reel   10923

MITCHELL, JOHN HIPPLE
    Letters, 1880-1904, 1 v. priv.
    N: Or-Ar   10924

MOWRY, SYLVESTER
    Letters,1853-1855 priv.
    N: OrHi 40 frames   10925

PALMER, JOEL
    Letters on his dismissal as Superintendent of
    Indian Affairs; papers, 1853-1856, 1 v. priv.
    N: OrU   10926

PAMBURN, PIERRE
    Papers, Fort Walla Walla, Oregon OrPe
    N: OrHi 18 feet   10927

PIERCE, HENRY AUGUSTUS
    Autobiographical papers, 1880, 287 p.
    CU-B
    N: WaU   10928
    P: WaU

PIERCE, HENRY HUBBARD
    Exploration from Fort Colville to Puget Sound,
    1882 DNA
    N: DNA ? 20 feet   10929
    P: OrHi

PORTER, LANGDON, pioneer
    Letters written from Marysville and Deer
    Creek, Ore, 1852-1854 priv.
    N: Or-Ar 80 frames 16 mm.   10930

PORTER, WILLIAM
    Diary, 1861-1871 OrHi
    N: Or-Ar 5 feet   10931

PRATT, ORVILLE C.,1819-1891
    Letters, 1850-1890 OrHi
    N: OrHi 20 feet   10932

ROOP, CHRISTIAN YOUNG
Journey, Indiana to Oregon and return,
1877-1878   priv.
N: Or-Ar 111 frames 16 mm.   10933

ST. JOHN, JAMES
Journal, May-Aug., 1841 OrHi
N: OrHi 1 reel   10934
P: UHi

SCHOLFIELD, SOCRATES
Journal of the Klamath exploring expedition,
1850; papers re: Umpqua River and Southern
Oregon, 1850-1856 priv.
N: Or-Ar 108 frames [Loan microfilm #45]
                                      10935

SMITH, WILLIAM BAN
Family papers, 1850-1919 priv.
N: Or-Ar 66 frames 16 mm.   10936

STAMBOUGH, BERT H.
Papers relating to American flag, assertedly
the first flown in Orange Co., Calif., and in
Ore. Or-Hi
N: Or-Ar 15 feet [Loan microfilm #7]
                                      10937

TELAKITE et al., defendants
Trial for Whitman Massacre in Clackamas
County court, March - May, 1848; U.S. District
Court, Nov., 1847 - May, 1850 C.H. Oregon
City Ibid.
N: Or-Ar 2 reels   10938

TWOGOOD, JAMES H.
Papers re: Southern Oregon Indian War and
Idaho gold rush, 1851-1908 priv.
N: Or-Ar 94 frames 16 mm.   10939

VANZANT, HENRY C.
Papers, 1838-1886, 195 items priv.
N: OrU   10940

VICTOR, FRANCES AURETTA (FULLER) B.
Letters, 1866-1902 OrHi
N: OrU   10941

WALKER, ELKANAH, 1805-1877
Elkanah Walker-Marcus Whitman papers,
1837-1872 CtY
N: WaPS 2 reels   10942

WHITE, ELLEN M.
Diaries, Salem, Ore., 1891-1900, 1902-1909,
1912, 1914-1917 priv.
N: Or-Ar 2266 frames 16 mm. [Loan microfilm #8]   10943

WILBUR, JAMES H.
Journal, Sept. 27, 1846-Jan. 25, 1848 priv.
N: Or-Ar 140 frames 16 mm. [Loan microfilm
#47]   10944

WILL, CLARK M.
Letters, 1877-1925 priv.
N: Or-Ar 45 frames [Loan microfilm #31]
                                      10945

Business Papers

A Baker, Ore., mortician's records, 1900-
1950   priv.
N: USlGS 3 reels   10946

BIRDSEYE, DAVID NELSON
Account book, 1852-1871 priv.
N: OrU   10947

CORBETT FAILING Co.
Records, 1851-1857 CStoC
N: OrU   10948

COX (THOMAS and WILLIAM) AND COMPANY,
Salem, Ore.
Day book and ledger, 1847-1860; accounts,
1867, 1873 priv.
N: Or-Ar 269 frames [Loan microfilm #23]
OrHi 30 feet   10949

CRAWFORD, MEDORUM
Account book, 1845 CStoC
N: OrU   10950

CRAWFORD, MEDORUM
Cash accounts, 1841-1849; ledger of accounts,

1848, 1850-1858 priv.
N: Or-Ar 44 frames [Loan microfilm #43]
                                      10951

FRENCH, PETER, of Steen's Mountain, Ore.
Account book, 1877-1879 priv.
N: OrU   10952

GUTHRIE, DAVID M.
Farm diary, 1890, Dallas, Ore. (with accounts)
priv.
N: Or-Ar 231 frames 16 mm. [Loan microfilm
#28]   10953

HART, H.B.
Accounts, 1853-1876, for sales of meat and
the breeding of a stallion, Red Buck priv.
N: Or-Ar 65 frames 16mm. [Loan microfilm
#15]   10954

HUDSON'S BAY COMPANY, 1670-
Documents re: Columbia District, 1844-
1866, 92 p. UKENRH
N: OrU   10955

OLD SHERARS HOTEL, Sherars Bridge, Ore.
Account book, 1875-1877 Hood River Museum
N: OrHi 10 feet   10956

OREGON HISTORICAL SOCIETY
Lumber resources of Klamath Co., Oregon,
1840-1910   OrHi
N: OrHi 40 feet   10957

SAILORS' UNION OF THE PACIFIC
Minutes, San Francisco headquarters, 1910
Ibid.
N: OrHi 70 feet   10958

SETTLEMIER (J.H.)NURSERIES
Correspondence, 1885-1903 priv.
N: Or-Ar 1345 frames   10959

TODD-MAYS BRIDGE (later SHERARS BRIDGE),
Ore.
Account book, 1862-1873 priv.
N: OrHi 12 feet   10960

WACHSMITH, LOUIS
Oyster industry scrapbook priv.
N: OrHi 10 feet   10961

Collections

BARRY, J. NEILSON, compiler
Material on Oregon history, 1811-1940 priv.
N: Or-Ar 7649 frames 16 mm. [Loan micro-
films # 27, 39, 44, 56, 57, 101] 10962

BEAN, ELLEN S., compiler
Eight biographical sketches of Union Stake
Church leaders (Oregon), 1 v. priv.
N: UPB   10963

Institutions

AURORA COLONY, Aurora, Ore.
Constitution (typescript) Or
DCO: Or-Ar   10964

AURORA COMMUNITY, see BAEHERT, MICHAEL,
10885, and HENDRICKS, ROBERT J., 10911,
under OREGON, Personal Papers

BURYING GROUND ASSOCIATION OF SCHOOL
DISTRICT #2, Champoeg, Ore.
Records, 1874-1954 Ibid.
N: Or-Ar 255 frames   10965

DAUGHTERS OF UNION VETERANS OF THE
CIVIL WAR. OREGON DEPT. BARBARA
FRITCHIE TENT NO. 2
Statements of eligibility Ibid.
N: Or-Ar 2 reels 16 mm.   10966

FREEMASONS. OREGON GRAND LODGE
Petitions to form lodges, and other documents,
1852-1859 Ibid.
N: Or-Ar 49 frames 16 mm. [Loan microfilm
#19]   10967

FREEMASONS. PORTLAND, Ore.
Royal Arch Chapter No. 3, Minutes, 1859-1949
priv.
N: priv. 105 feet   10968
P: OrHi

OREGON CITY, Ore. McLOUGHLIN FIRE EN-
GINE COMPANY NO. 1
Minutes, July,1858-June,1865 priv.
N: Or-Ar 95 frames [Loan microfilm #74]
                                      10969

OREGON CITY LYCEUM
Constitution, by-laws, journal, Nov.,1860-
Mar.,1862 Ibid.
N: Or-Ar 62 frames 16 mm.   10970

OREGON PIONEER ASSOCIATION
Transactions, 1873-1886 Or
N: Or-Ar 668 frames 16 mm.   10971
P: Or-Ar

SALEM, Ore. TIGER ENGINE COMPANY NO. 2
Records, 1869-1890 Ibid.
N: Or-Ar 535 frames [Loan microfilm # 58]
                                      10972

UMATILLA INDIAN RESERVATION. COUNCIL
Minutes, 1928-1934, 1 v. Ibid.
N: OrU   10973

School Records

LINN Co., Ore. SCHOOL DISTRICT No. 8
Accounts, [census] reports, minutes, 1864-
1873 priv.
N: Or-Ar 57 frames 16 mm.   10974

MARION Co., Ore. SUPERINTENDENT OF
SCHOOLS
Accounts, 1854-1872 Ibid.
N: Or-Ar 61 frames   10975

PORTLAND ACADEMY. TRUSTEES
Minutes, 1854-1888 OrHi
N: OrHi 15 feet   10976

STEVENS, MARY (FROST), b. 1855
Registers of schools kept by her, in Clackamas
Co., Oregon, 1872-1888 priv.
N: OrHi 24 frames   10977

IDAHO

Census

U.S. CENSUS. NINTH, 1870
Population schedules, Idaho DNA
N: DNA 1 reel   10978
P: USlGS

U.S. CENSUS. TENTH, 1880
Population schedules, Idaho DNA
N: DNA 1 reel   10979

Government Records

U.S. DEPT. OF THE INTERIOR
Territorial papers: Idaho, 1864-1890 DNA
N: DNA 3 reels [M-191]   10980
P: WaU

U.S. OFFICE OF INDIAN AFFAIRS
Documents re: Special case no. 99: Utah and
Northern Railway and Oregon Short Line Rail-
way right of way through Fort Hall Indian Reser-
vation, 1881-1892 DNA
N: DNA 50 feet   10981
P: IdPI

County Records

BANNOCK Co., Idaho
Land grants, patents, deeds, miscellaneous

records, 1880-1948 C.H. Pocatello
N: Ibid. 35 reels   10982
P: USlGS

Church Records

CHURCH OF JESUS CHRIST OF LATTER-DAY
SAINTS. IDAHO
Stake records: American Falls, Bannock,
Bear Lake, Bingham, Blackfoot, Blaine,
Boise, Burley, East Rigby, Franklin, Idaho,
Idaho Falls, Lost River, Malad, Minidoka,
Montpelier, Nampa, North Idaho, Oneida,
Pocatello, Portneuf, Raft River, Rigby,
Shelley, South Idaho Falls, Twin Falls,
Weiser, Yellowstone USlC
N: USlGS 188 reels   10983

CHURCH OF JESUS CHRIST OF LATTER-DAY
SAINTS. IDAHO
Ward and branch records: Alton, Arbon,
Archer, Ashton, Athol, Basin, Bates, Black
Pine, Bonner's Ferry, Burley, Burton, Butte,
Cache, Cambridge, Canyon Creek, Cedron,
Chapin, Chester, Churchill, Clawson,
Clementsville, Coeur D'Alene, Conda, Darby,
Davisville, Downey, Driggs, Eagle, Egin,
Egin Bench, Fairview, Farnum, Fayette,
Heman, Herbert, Hibbard, Holbrook, Indepen-
dence, Indian Valley, Juniper, Kellogg-Wallace,
Kelly-Topance, Kilgore, Kuna, Lava, Lava
Hot Springs, Lewiston, Linrose, Lyman,
Mapleton, Marion, Marysville, Mountainview,
Mount Sherman, Moscow, Newdale, Oakley,
Olive, Ora, Palisade, Parker, Plano, Pratt,
Preston, Rexburg, Richvale, Robin, Rowland,
St. Anthony, Salem, Sandpoint, Sublett, Sugar
City, Summit, Teton, Tetonia, Thornton,
Toponce, Topaz, Twin Groves, Valview,
Victor, Warm River, Weston, Whitney,
Wilford, Woodrow, Young USlC
N: USlGS 188 reels   10984

PRESTON, Idaho
Sexton's record, 1892-1953 Ibid.
N: USlGS 1 reel   10985

Personal Papers

COGHANOUR, DAVID
Boise basin, 1883, 3 p. CU-B
N: WaU   10986
P: WaU

HUMPHRYS, HUMPHRY M., farmer
Diary, Jan., 1895-Dec., 1896, July, 1899-July,
1901 priv.
N: IdHi 1 reel   10987
P: IdHi

Business Papers

FORT HALL, Idaho
Account books [Ledgers 1 and 2, Journal],
1834-1837 OrHi
N: OrHi 1 reel   10988
P: UHi

Collections

CHAPMAN, B.R., collector
Nez Percé war documents, 1877-1881 v.p.
DCO: priv.
N: OrHi 15 frames   10989

IDAHO HISTORICAL SOCIETY
Nez Percé war material, 1877-1881 IdHi
N: OrHi 53 frames   10990

WASHINGTON

Census

U.S. CENSUS. EIGHTH, 1860
Population schedules, Washington DNA
N: DNA 1 reel   10991
P: USlGS WaU

U.S. CENSUS. NINTH, 1870
Population schedules, Washington DNA
N: DNA 1 reel   10992
P: WaU

U.S. CENSUS. TENTH, 1880
Population schedules, Washington DNA
N: DNA 3 reels   10993
P: WaU

Government Records

COLVILLE, FORT
Post Orders, no. 87-114, Nov. 22, 1881 - Sept.
20, 1882 priv.
N: Or-Ar 2 reels   10994

U.S. ADJUTANT-GENERAL'S OFFICE
Monthly post returns DNA
N: DNA 1 reel   10995

U.S. CONGRESS. HOUSE
Territorial papers of the United States "House
file": Oregon and Washington territories DNA
N: WaU 1 reel   10996

U.S. CONGRESS. HOUSE. COMMITTEE ON
INTERSTATE AND FOREIGN COMMERCE
Transcript of proceedings of subcommittee
on interference of free flow of commerce
through the port of Seattle, 1953 Ibid.
N: WaU   10997

U.S. DEPT. OF JUSTICE
Records relating to the appointment of Federal
Judges and United States Attorneys and
Marshals for the Territory and State of Wash-
ington, 1853-1902 DNA
N: DNA 17 reels [M-198]   10998
P: WaU

U.S. DEPT. OF STATE
Appointment papers, Elwood Evans, 1861-1867
DNA
N: WaU 1 reel   10999

U.S. DEPT. OF STATE
Territorial papers: Washington, 1854-1872
DNA
N: DNA 2 reels [M-26]   11000

U.S. DEPT. OF STATE
Territorial papers: Washington, 1854-1872
DNA
N: DNA 2 reels [M-26]   11000
P: WaU

U.S. DEPT. OF THE INTERIOR
Territorial papers: Washington, 1854-1902
DNA
N: DNA 4 reels [M-189]   11001
P: WaU

U.S. GENERAL LAND OFFICE
Abstracts of Washington Donation land claims,
1855-1902 DNA
N: DNA 1 reel [M-203]   11002
P: WaU

U.S. INTERSTATE COMMERCE COMMISSION
Merchants' union of Spokane Falls vs. Northern
Pacific R.R. Co. DNA
N: WaU 1 reel   11003

U.S. NATIONAL RESOURCES PLANNING BOARD
Records, 1949 DNA
N: WaU   11004

U.S. OFFICE OF INDIAN AFFAIRS
Records of the Washington Superintendency of
Indian Affairs, 1853-1874 DNA
N: DNA 26 reels [M-5]   11005
P: WaU

U.S. POST OFFICE DEPT.
Records of appointment of postmasters,
Washington Territory, 1854-1875 DNA
N: WaU   11006

UNITED STATES SHIPPING BOARD. EMERGENCY
FLEET CORPORATION
Proceedings, labor conference, Seattle,
July 18, 1918 DNA
N: WaU 1 reel   11007

U.S. TREASURY DEPT.
"Nominations" letters from the collector of
customs at Port Townsend, Washington, 1865-
1910 DNA
N: DNA 14 reels [M-188]   11008
P: WaU 10 reels

Territorial Records

WASHINGTON (Ter.). INFANTRY
Muster in and muster out rolls, Oct. 19, 1861 -
Jan. 29, 1866 U.S. Dept. of War
DCO: InU 182 p.   11009

Local Records

KING Co., Wash. NEWCASTLE PRECINCT
Justice of the peace records, 1885-1921
N: priv. 1 reel   11010
P: WaU

SEATTLE. BOARD OF PUBLIC HEALTH
Fluoridation paper, 1949-1952 Ibid.
N: WHi 1 reel   11011

Church Records

BUREAU OF CATHOLIC INDIAN MISSIONS,
Washington, D.C.
Letters re: early Catholic activities
among the Nez Percés, 27 items Ibid.
N: WaPS 1 reel   11012

CHURCH HISTORICAL SOCIETY, Philadelphia
Letters of early bishops (Episcopal) of the
Pacific Northwest, 1861-1894 Ibid.
N: WaU 1 reel   11013

Personal Papers

ATKINSON, GEORGE HENRY
Papers, 1841-1887 CSmH
N: WaU   11014

COLMAN, CLARA
Journal, 1886-1890, 1893-1895 priv.
N: ? 2 reels   11015
P: WaU

CROWNINSHIELD, CLARA
Journal, May, 1835-June, 1836 MH
N: WaU   11016

EVANS, ELWOOD
Correspondence and papers, 1843-1894 CtY
N: WaU 2 reels   11017
P: Or-Ar

EVANS, ELWOOD
Scrapbook entitled "Campaign of Major-General
John E. Wool, U.S. Army, against the people and
the authorities of Oregon and Washington, 1855-
1856" CtY
N: OrHi 48 frames   11018

HENRY, ANSON G.
Appointment papers, as Surveyor General of
Washington Territory DNA
N: OrHi 15 feet   11019

HUSSEY, WARREN, 1836-1920
Diaries, notebooks, and miscellaneous papers,
1880-1920 priv.
N: CU-B 1 reel 11020

KAUTZ, AUGUST VALENTINE
Daily journal, 1857-1861 DLC
N: WaU 1 reel 11021

McCLELLAN, GEORGE BRINTON, 1826-1885
Diary, May 20-Dec. 15, 1853 DLC
N: WaU 1 reel 11022

PARKE, JOHN GRUBB
Letter to Col. J.J. Abert, Camp Simiakmoo,
Nov. 30, 1858 priv.
N: WaU 11023

PIERCE, ELIAS DAVIDSON, 1824-1897
Reminiscences, 1895 priv.
N: priv. 1 reel 11024
P: WaPS

SCHWELLENBACH, LEWIS BAXTER, 1894-1948
Correspondence and speeches, 1934-1948 priv.
N: WaU 1 reel 11025

SIEG, LEE PAUL, b.1879
Papers, 1934-1946, 536 p. priv.
N: WaU 11026

SMITH, JACKSON, AND SUBLETTE, Indian
traders
Depredations committed by Indians, 1826-
1829 KHi
N: WaPS 1 reel 11027

Business Papers

FORT NISQUALLY, Wash.
Journal of occurrences at Nisqually House,
Hudson's Bay Company Post, 1833-1859 CSmH
DCO: InU 1428 p. 11028

HUDSON'S BAY COMPANY, 1670-
Journal at Fort Langley, 1827-1829 CU-B
N: WaU 1 reel 11029
P: WaU

ALASKA

Government Records

RUSSIA (Empire). GOSUDARSTVENNYI
ARKHIV (State Archives)
Papers re: Russians in Alaska, 1732-1796 Ibid.
DCO: WaU 21 v. 11030
N: CU-B 2 reels

RUSSIA (Empire). GOSUDARSTVENNYI
ARKHIV (State Archives)
Selections: material on Kamchatka expeditions,
1732-1743, 1749; material on Russo-American
relations, 1781-1784 Ibid.
DCO: DLC 800 sheets 11031

RUSSIA (Empire). MINISTERSTVO INOSTRAN-
NYKH DEL (Ministry of Foreign Affairs)
Papers re: Alaska, 1783-1796, 1867; re: the
U.S., 1813-1863 Ibid.
DCO: DLC 1292 sheets 11032

RUSSIA (Empire). MORSKOE MINISTERSTVO
(Ministry of the Marine)
Logs of St. Peter and St. Paul and supplement-
ary material on Bering expedition, 1741-1744
Ibid.
DCO: DLC 413 sheets 11033

RUSSIA (1923- U.S.S.R.). MINISTERSTVO
INOSTRANNYKH DEL (Ministry of Foreign
Affairs)
Papers from the Russian Archives relating to
the cession of Alaska, 1856-1867 (transcript)
DNA
N: DNA 1 reel [T-273] 11034

U. S. COAST GUARD
Selected documents pertaining to Western

Union Telegraph Expedition, 1865-1867 DNN
N: CU-B 1 reel 11035

Personal Papers

ADAMS, GEORGE RUSSELL
First American exploring expedition to
Russian America, 1865-1867 priv.
N: WaU Cu-B 1 reel 11036
P: WaU

BUCKLEY, CHARLES S.
Journal, Russo-American telegraph expedition,
1865-1867, 291 p. OrP
N: OrP 146 frames 11037
P: CU OrHi
DCO: OrP 146 ll.

VENIAMINOV, IVAN EVSEEVICH, 1797-1879
Diary, 1821-1837 AkHi
N: DLC 1 reel 11038

Business Papers

ROSSIĬSKO-AMERIKANSKAĬA KOMPANIĬA
(Russian American Company), 1799-1867
Korrespondentsiia, 1820-1866 DLC
N: CU-B 85 reels 11039

ROSSIĬSKO-AMERIKANSKAĬA KOMPANIĬA
(Russian American Company), 1799-1867
Records, 1802-1867 DNA
N: DNA 77 reels 11040
P: AkHi AkU CaBVaU FU

Institutions

AKADEMIĬA NAUK, S.S.S.R. (formerly
IMPERIAL ACADEMY OF SCIENCES)
Tchitrev's nautical journal, Sept., 1840-Jan.,
1843; Stellar's list of plants and seeds gathered
on Bering's voyage, 1741-1742; description of
Russo-American Company, ca. 1830; descrip-
tion of St. George Island, 1833 Ibid.
DCO: DLC 647 sheets 11041

RUSSIAN-AMERICAN TELEGRAPH EXPEDITION
Letters from members, 1865-1867 OrHi
N: OrP 1 reel 11042

HAWAII

Government Records

FRANCE. MINISTÈRE DES AFFAIRES
ÉTRANGÈRES
Correspondance politique, Îles Sandwich,
1846-1862, v. 5-10 Ibid.
N: HiU 1 reel 11043

FRANCE. MINISTÈRE DES AFFAIRES
ÉTRANGÈRES
Mémoires et documents, Îles Sandwich, 1819-
1870, 15 v. FrAN
N: CU-B* 11044
P: CU-B

GREAT BRITAIN. CABINET
Correspondence re: Sandwich Islands, 1824-
1843, 400 p. HiU
N: HiU 11045

GREAT BRITAIN. FOREIGN OFFICE.
Sandwich Islands correspondence,
1824-1825 UKLPRO
DCO: HiU 78 p. 11046

HAWAII. ARCHIVES
Hawaiian genealogies [written in Hawaiian],
25 v. Hi-Ar
N: USIGS 1 reel 11047

HAWAIIAN ISLANDS. SOVEREIGNS, Etc.
Accounts, 1850-1899 CU-B
N: CU-B 1 reel 11048

U. S. DEPT. OF THE INTERIOR. DIVISION OF
TERRITORIES AND ISLAND POSSESSIONS
Filipino immigration to Hawaii,
1906-1946 DNA
N: HiU 1 reel 11049

Territorial Records

HAWAII (Ter.). GOVERNOR
Correspondence with Division of Territories
and Island Possessions re: Japanese immigration, 1907-1908 DNA
N: HiU 1 reel 11050

Church Records

CHURCH OF JESUS CHRIST OF LATTER-DAY
SAINTS. HAWAII
District, branch, and ward records: East Maui,
Honolulu, Kahana Kahana, Kailua, Kaneohe,
Laie, Nanakuli, Pearl City, Wahiawa USIC
N: USIGS 15 reels 11051

CHURCH OF JESUS CHRIST OF LATTER-DAY
SAINTS. HAWAII
Records of Hawaiian and Central Pacific
missions, 1907-1951 USIC
N: USIGS 23 reels 11052

CHURCH OF JESUS CHRIST OF LATTER-DAY
SAINTS. HAWAIIAN MISSION
Membership record book, ca. 1850-1889 Ibid.
N: USIGS 1 reel 11053

CHURCH OF JESUS CHRIST OF LATTER-DAY
SAINTS. HAWAIIAN MISSION
Records, 1850-1951 USIC
N: USIGS 24 reels 11054

CHURCH OF JESUS CHRIST OF LATTER-DAY
SAINTS. HAWAIIAN TEMPLE
Sealings of dead couples, 1919-1941; sealings
of children to parents and adoptions, 1919-1941;
living sealings, 1919-1941; sealings of the dead,
1919-1941; living endowments, 1919-1941; dead
endowments, 1919-1941 Ibid.
N: USIGS 4 reels 11055

Personal Papers

ALLEN, ELISHA HUNT, 1804-1883 *Lib. of Congress*
Papers, 1850-1883 DLC
N: HiU 4 reels 11056

COOK, JAMES, 1728-1779
Letter to Capt. William Hammond Hull, Jan. 3,
1772 [unk.]
DCO: Hi-Ar 2 p. 11057

FRANKLIN, JANE (GRIFFIN), Lady, 1792-1875
Journal.. copies of letters and articles re:
visit to Sandwich Islands, 1861, 1862, 1865,
3 v. UKC
N: HiU 11058

FRANKLIN, JANE (GRIFFIN), Lady, 1792-1875
Journals, 1861-1865 UKCSR
N: HiU 1 reel 11059

GRESHAM, WALTER QUINTIN, 1832-1895
Papers re: Hawaii, Nov., 1893-Apr., 1895,
34 items DLC
N: HiU 11060

KAMEHAMEHA IV, King of Hawaii, 1834-1863
(ALEXANDER LIHOLIHO)
Private journal, 1849 HiHi; (typescript)
181 p. HiU
N: HiU typescript 11061

LOOMIS, ELISHA, 1799-1836
Journal, 1824-1826, 148 p.
N: HiU 11062

QUIMPER, MANUEL, fl. 1791
Diary re: Hawaii, 1791, 58 p. MxAGN
Typescript Hi-Ar
N: HiU of typescript 11063

RAE, JOHN, 1796-1872
  Selected manuscripts, 1855, 232 p. HiU
  N: HiU   11064

STODDARD, CHARLES WILLIAM, 1843-1909
  Diaries, Aug. 3, 1882 - Nov. 6, 1883,
  9 v. HiU
  N: HiU 1 reel   11065

WILLIS, ALBERT S., 1843-1897
  Letter to Secretary of State Walter Q. Gresham,
  Dec. 9, 1893, 20 p. Cleveland Papers, DLC
  N: HiU   11066

Collections

HAWAII. UNIVERSITY. GREGG M. SINCLAIR
LIBRARY
  Letters and manuscripts re: Hawaii,
  1825-1931 HiU
  N: HiU 1 reel   11067

MANN, HORACE, collector
  Journals, notes, maps, clippings re: Hawaii,
  1864-1868 MiU-C
  N: HiU 1 reel   11068

Institutions

ROSSIĬSKO-AMERIKANSKAIA KOMPANIIA
  (Russian American Company), 1799-1867
  Papers re: Hawaii, 1816-1818; typescript
  translations CU-B
  N: HiU 2 reels   11069

THRUM, THOMAS G., editor
  Our Visitant (hand-written semi-monthly maga-
  zine), v. 1, nos. 1-4, July 3-Aug. 24, 1867
  N: HiU 1 reel   11070

Ships' Logs

With ships' logs are included journals, diaries,
and other records of voyages. Logs, which are
the official records of vessels, are listed under
the names of vessels. Journals, which are
personal documents, even though they are sometimes called supplementary logs, are listed
under the names of their authors.

ANDERSON, WILLIAM, ?1748-1778
  Journal kept on H. M. S. Resolution at Hawaiian
  Islands, Jan. 18-Feb. 2, 1778, 4 p. UKLPRO
  N: DCO: Hi-Ar   11071

BAYLY, WILLIAM, 1737-1810
  Journal kept on H. M. S. Discovery at Sandwich
  Islands, Jan. 18 - Feb. 3, 1778, Nov. 26? - Feb.
  28, 1779, 19 p. UKLPRO
  DCO: Hi-Ar   11072

BURNEY, JAMES, 1750-1821, lieutenant R.N.
  Journal while with Capt. James Cook,
  Jan. 18-Feb. 2, 1778, Nov. 25, 1778- Mar.
  30, 1779, 14 p. UKLBM
  DCO: Hi-Ar   11073

CLERKE, CHARLES, 1741-1779
  Journal kept on H. M. S. Discovery among the
  Sandwich Islands, Jan. 18-Feb. 2, 1778,
  Jan. 5-Feb. 14, 1779, 20 p. UKLPRO
  DCO: Hi-Ar   11074

CLERKE, CHARLES, 1741-1779
  Journal kept on H. M. S. Resolution, Feb. 14-
  Mar. 16, 1779, 34 p. UKLPRO
  DCO: Hi-Ar   11075

COOK, JAMES, 1728-1779
  Journals re: discovery of the Sandwich Islands,
  Jan. 18 - Feb. 2, 1778; return to Sandwich
  Islands, Nov. 26, 1778 - Jan. 6, 1779; supple-
  mentary logs, Series II, v. 112-113 UKLPRO
  DCO: Hi-Ar   11076

DISCOVERY (H. M. Sloop)
  Log, Jan. 18-Feb. 2, 1778, Nov. 25, 1778-
  Mar. 16, 1779, 46 p. UKLPRO
  DCO: Hi-Ar   11077

EDGAR, THOMAS
  Journal kept on H. M. S. Discovery, Jan. 2-
  June 6, 1778, 20 p. UKLBM
  DCO: Hi-Ar   11078

GOLOVNIN, VASILII MIKHAILOVICH, 1776-1832
  Tour around world on Sloop of War Kamchatka,
  1817-1819 (translation) HiU
  N: HiU 1 reel   11079

GORE, JOHN, 1730-1790
  Journal kept on H. M. S. Resolution at Sandwich
  Islands, Jan. 18-Feb. 2, 1778, 12 p. UKLPRO
  DCO: Hi-Ar   11080

HALCYON (Brig)
  Log of proceedings at the Sandwich Islands,
  Nov. 8-15, 1792, 4 p. [unk.]
  DCO: Hi-Ar   11081

HARVEY, WILLIAM
  Journal kept on H. M. S. Discovery at the
  Sandwich Islands, Jan. 18-Feb. 2, 1778,
  Nov. 26, 1778-Feb. 15, 1779; on H. M. S.
  Resolution, Feb. 15-Mar. 21, 1779, 32 p.
  UKLPRO
  DCO: Hi-Ar   11082

JEFFERSON (Ship)
  Log of proceedings at "Owyhee," "To i yah bay,"
  and "Karakakooa bay," Mar.,1793, Sept.-Oct.,
  1794, 9 p. [unk.]
  DCO: Hi-Ar   11083

KING GEORGE (Ship)
  Log, visits to Hawaiian Islands, Oct., 1786-
  Oct., 1787 UKLBM
  DCO: HiU 25 p.   11084

KING, JAMES, 1750-1784
  Journal kept on H. M. S. Resolution at Sandwich
  Islands, Jan. 18-Feb. 2, 1778, Nov. 25, 1778-
  Mar. 15, 1779, 52 p. UKLPRO
  DCO: Hi-Ar   11085

LAW, J., surgeon
  Journal re: Capt. Cook's return to Hawaii
  and death, Jan. 16 - Mar. 14, 1779, 14 p.
  UKBM
  DCO: Hi-Ar   11086

LOUDOUN (Ship)
  Log of proceedings at the Hawaiian Islands,
  May 19-26, 1787, 2 p. [unk.]
  DCO: Hi-Ar   11087

PUGET, PETER, d. 1882
  Journal of Hawaiian visit, March,1792;
  journal kept on H. M. S. Chatham at
  Hawaiian Islands, Jan., 1794 - Sept., 1795
  UKLBM
  DCO: HiU 26 p.   11088

RESOLUTION (H. M. Sloop)
  Log, Feb. 10, 1776-Nov. 29, 1779, 225 p.
  UKLPRO
  DCO: Hi-Ar   11089

RICKMAN, J.
  Journal kept on H. M. S. Discovery at Sandwich
  Islands, Jan. 16-29, 1778, Nov. 23, 1778 - Mar.
  17, 1779, 14 p. UKLPRO
  DCO: Hi-Ar   11090

SAMWELL, DAVID, 1751-1798, surgeon
  Account of voyage of H. M. S. Discovery,
  Feb., 1776 - Nov., 1779 UKLBM
  N: HiU 1 reel   11091

WILLIAMSON, JOHN
  Journal kept on H. M. S. Resolution at Hawaiian
  Islands, Jan. 15-Feb. 2, 1778, 3 p. UKLPRO
  DCO: Hi-Ar   11092

TUNIS

Personal Papers

AL-DUSTURI, 'ABD AL-RAHIM AL-SHAFI'I
  Istikhdam ahl al-dhimmah wa tahrim istikhda-
  muhum, 13 ff. TsTZ
  N: MH   11093

AL-KUTAMI, ABU BAKR
  Irshad al-hayara ila tahrim istikhdam al-Yahud
  wal-Nasara, 54 p.
  N: ?   11094
  P: MH

AL-MAGHILI, ABU'ABDALLAH MUHAMMAD
  Risalah lil-shaykh al-Maghili, 19 ff. TsTZ
  N: ?   11095
  P: MH

AL-NABULSI, OTHMAN IBN IBRAHIM
  Tajrid sayf al-himma listikhraj mafi dhimmat
  al-himmah, 1285 A.H. [1869], 189 p. TsTZ
  N: MH   11096

SUDAN

Personal Papers

DENISON, FREDERICK C., 1846-1896
  Diary, Nile Expedition, Sept., 1884 - Apr., 1885,
  190 p. CaOT
  N: CaOOA 15 feet   11097

WEST AFRICA

Government Records

BRITISH WEST AFRICA. NATIONAL CONGRESS
  Petition for reconstruction of legislative
  councils Colonial Office, London
  N: CSt-H 1 reel   11098

GREAT BRITAIN. COLONIAL OFFICE. C.O. 383
  Act registers, West Coast of Africa and St.
  Helena, 1782-1892, 93 v. UKLPRO
  N: DLC 18 reels   11099

UNION OF SOUTH AFRICA

Church Records

CHURCH OF JESUS CHRIST OF LATTER-DAY
SAINTS. SOUTH AFRICA
  Record of members and annual genealogical
  report, South Africa Mission, early to 1951
  USIC
  N: USIGS 4 reels   11100

Personal Papers

HOLE, HUGH MARSHALL, 1865-
  Papers re: South Africa, 1885-1928 UKLPRO
  N: CtY 1 reel   11101

SCOTT, JOHN, 1844-1922
  Notes from my notebook (9th Kaffir War, Zulu
  War, Cape Town Highlanders), 80 p. SaCU
  N: NN   11102

South African War

HARE, W. A.
  South African War diary, 1899-1901 priv.
  N: CaOOA 25 feet   11103

HILL, J. KENNEDY
  South African War Diary, 1899-1900,
  2nd Special Service Battalion, Royal Canadian
  Regiment priv.
  N: CaOOA 5 feet   11104

TURNER, Sir RICHARD ERNEST WILLIAM, 1871-
  South African War diary, 1900-1901 priv.
  N: CaOOA 10 feet   11105

AUSTRALIA

Church Records

CHURCH OF JESUS CHRIST OF LATTER-DAY
SAINTS. AUSTRALIA
Annual reports, 1907-1951; records,
Adelaide, Brisbane, Harrow, Melbourne,
Morphett Vale, Nambour, Norwood, Perth,
Queensland,and Sydney Branches, New South
Wales, Queensland, and South Australia
Districts USIC
N: USlGS 6 reels   11106

LONDON MISSIONARY SOCIETY
Correspondence, reports, and records re:
South Africa and Australia, 1794-1903 Ibid.
N: CLU 186 reels   11107

SOCIETY FOR THE PROPAGATION OF THE
GOSPEL IN FOREIGN PARTS
Australian papers, 1788-1900 Ibid.
N: DLC 33 reels   11108

TASMANIA

Church Records

CHURCH OF JESUS CHRIST OF LATTER-DAY
SAINTS. TASMANIA
Records: Hobart and Launceston Branches,
Tasmania District, 1894-1952 USIC
N: USlC 1 reel   11109

NEW ZEALAND

Church Records

CHURCH OF JESUS CHRIST OF LATTER-DAY
SAINTS. AUSTRALIAN AND NEW ZEALAND
MISSIONS
Journals of John Peter Beck, 1888-1892,and
Ezra Foss Richards, 1885-1888, 1896-1897
priv.
N: UPB 2 reels
P: UPB   11110

CHURCH OF JESUS CHRIST OF LATTER-DAY
SAINTS. NEW ZEALAND
Records, 1907-1951 USIC
N: USlGS 8 reels   11111

Collections

FIVE MAORI HIGH CHIEFS
Te Tahuhu (the main trunk of the Maori race):
compilation of the stories of the creation of the
earth and the traditional genealogies of the Maori
[in Maori] USlC
N: USlGS 1 reel   11112

PACIFIC ISLANDS

Bibliography

LONDON MISSIONARY SOCIETY
Catalogue of South Seas journals and letters,
1796-1906 AuC
N: AuCNL 1 reel
P: HiU   11113

Government Records

GREAT BRITAIN. FOREIGN OFFICE F. O. 58
Consular Despatches from the Pacific Islands,
1838-1902, 339 v. UKLPRO
N: CU-B
P: CU-B   11114

U.S. NATIONAL ARCHIVES
Recorded visits to the Bonin Islands by U.S.
naval vessels, 1836-1831 DNA
N: CU 1 reel   11115

Church Records

CHURCH OF JESUS CHRIST OF LATTER-DAY
SAINTS. SAMOA
List of missionaries, 1886-1947; records of
members USlC
N: USlGS 10 reels   11116

CHURCH OF JESUS CHRIST OF LATTER-DAY
SAINTS. TAHITIAN MISSION
Record of members, early to 1948 USlC
N: USlGS 4 reels   11117

CHURCH OF JESUS CHRIST OF LATTER-DAY
SAINTS. TONGAN MISSION
Vital records, 1867-1931; record of members,
1911-1952 USIC
N: USlGS 4 reels   11118

CHURCH OF JESUS CHRIST OF LATTER-DAY
SAINTS. TUAMOTU ARCHIPELAGO
Records USlC
N: USlGS 1 reel   11119

LONDON MISSIONARY SOCIETY
Records re: the South Seas, 1796-1906 Ibid.
N: AuCNL 117 reels*
P: HiU   11120

HANSEN, C. J.
Journal, account book (Tahitian Mission,
L.D.S. Church), 1899-1902, 2 v. priv.
N: UPB   11121

STEWART, RAY E.
Samoan mission journal, 1898-1900, 586 p.
priv.
N: UPB
P: UPB   11122

Personal Papers

BISHOP, FRANCIS T.
Narrative of a voyage in the North and South
Pacific Oceans, 1832-1835, 93 p. HiU
N: HiU   11123

Collections

SOUTH PACIFIC COMMISSION
Historical manuscripts Ibid.
N: AuCNL 78 reels
P: HiU   11124

GUAM

Government Records

U.S. NAVY DEPT.
Annual reports of the Governors of Guam,
1901-1941 DNA
N: DNA 3 reels [M-181]   11125

MICRONESIA

Church Records

AMERICAN BOARD OF COMMISSIONERS FOR
FOREIGN MISSIONS
Letters and papers of the A.B.C.F.M.
Mission to Micronesia, 1852-1929 MH
N: HiU 25 reels *   11126

AMERICAN BOARD OF COMMISSIONERS FOR
FOREIGN MISSIONS
Mission to Micronesia [Letters and papers,
v. 236], v.d. MH
N: HiU 7 reels   11127

Business Papers

U.S. COMMERCIAL COMPANY
Economic survey of Micronesia, 1946, 16 v.
DLC
N: DLC 5 reels
P: CU MWC   11128

INTERNATIONAL

Institutions

INTERNATIONAL LABOR OFFICE
Minutes of the governing body, Sessions 1-52,
Nov., 1919-Apr., 1931 Ibid.
N: NNC 9 reels   11129

INTERNATIONAL MILITARY TRIBUNAL FOR
THE FAR EAST
Chamber proceedings, 1946-1948, 1 v. Ibid.
N: OrU   11130

INTERNATIONAL WORKINGMEN'S ASSOCIATION
Minute book, 1866-1869; list of members,
1865-1870 Bishopsgate Foundation, London
N: DLC 1 reel*   11131

THE INTERNATIONAL (FIRST). 5th Congress,
1872
Protokoll, 118 p. priv.
N: WU   11132

INTERNATIONAL WORKINGMEN'S ASSOCIATION
Papers, 1871-1876 WHi
N: WHi 2 reels   11133

SUPREME COMMANDER FOR THE ALLIED
POWERS
Documents re: dissolution of Japanese
ultra-nationalistic societies, 1946-1948, 1 v.
Ibid.
N: CU 1 reel   11134

WORLD CENTER FOR WOMEN'S ARCHIVES
Papers re: distinguished women, 1779-1921
Ibid.
DCO: DLC 1 box   11135

WORLD FEDERATION OF TRADE UNIONS
Reports and minutes of Executive Bureau and
Executive Committee, 1945-1949 DCIO
N: NIC-I 1 reel   11136

WORLD TRADE UNION CONGRESS, 1st, Paris,
1945
Agenda, declarations,and reports, 1945 DCIO
N: NIC-I 1 reel   11137

INDEX